PHILIP'S

CW00392020

STREET ATLAS Glasgow and West Central Scotland

www.philips-maps.co.uk
First published in 1995 by Philip's,
a division of Octopus Publishing Group Ltd
www.octopusbooks.co.uk
Carmelite House
50 Victoria Embankment
London EC4Y 0DZ
www.hachette.co.uk

Fourth colour edition 2009
Second impression with revisions 2015
GLWDB

978-1-84907-387-5 (spiral)

Speed camera data provided by **PocketGPSWorld.com Ltd**

Printed in China

Contents

Key to map symbols

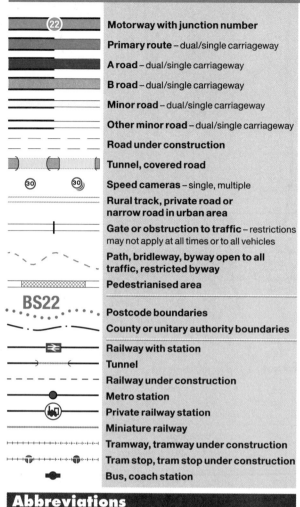

Motorway with junction number
Primary route – dual/single carriageway
A road – dual/single carriageway
B road – dual/single carriageway
Minor road – dual/single carriageway
Other minor road – dual/single carriageway
Road under construction
Tunnel, covered road
Speed cameras – single, multiple
Rural track, private road or narrow road in urban area
Gate or obstruction to traffic – restrictions may not apply at all times or to all vehicles
Path, bridleway, byway open to all traffic, restricted byway
Pedestrianised area

BS22 **Postcode boundaries**
County or unitary authority boundaries

Railway with station
Tunnel
Railway under construction
Metro station
Private railway station
Miniature railway
Tramway, tramway under construction
Tram stop, tram stop under construction
Bus, coach station

Ambulance station
Coastguard station
Fire station
Police station

Accident and Emergency entrance to hospital
Hospital

Place of worship
Information centre – open all year
Shopping centre, parking
Park and Ride, Post Office
Camping site, caravan site
Golf course, picnic site
ROMAN FORT **Non-Roman antiquity, Roman antiquity**

Univ **Important buildings, schools, colleges, universities and hospitals**
Woods, built-up area

River Medway **Water name**
River, weir
Stream
Canal, lock, tunnel
Water
Tidal water

58 87 246 **Adjoining page indicators and overlap bands** – the colour of the arrow and band indicates the scale of the adjoining or overlapping page (see scales below)

The dark grey border on the inside edge of some pages indicates that the mapping does not continue onto the adjacent page

The small numbers around the edges of the maps identify the 1-kilometre National Grid lines

Abbreviations

Acad	**Academy**	Meml	**Memorial**
Allot Gdns	**Allotments**	Mon	**Monument**
Cemy	**Cemetery**	Mus	**Museum**
C Ctr	**Civic centre**	Obsy	**Observatory**
CH	**Club house**	Pal	**Royal palace**
Coll	**College**	PH	**Public house**
Crem	**Crematorium**	Recn Gd	**Recreation ground**
Ent	**Enterprise**	Resr	**Reservoir**
Ex H	**Exhibition hall**	Ret Pk	**Retail park**
Ind Est	**Industrial Estate**	Sch	**School**
IRB Sta	**Inshore rescue boat station**	Sh Ctr	**Shopping centre**
Inst	**Institute**	TH	**Town hall / house**
Ct	**Law court**	Trad Est	**Trading estate**
L Ctr	**Leisure centre**	Univ	**University**
LC	**Level crossing**	W Twr	**Water tower**
Liby	**Library**	Wks	**Works**
Mkt	**Market**	YH	**Youth hostel**

Enlarged maps only

Railway or bus station building
Place of interest
Parkland

The map scale on the pages numbered in blue is 3½ inches to 1 mile
5.52 cm to 1 km • 1:18 103

0 – ¼ mile – ½ mile – ¾ mile – **1 mile**
0 – 250m – 500m – 750m – **1km**

The map scale on the pages numbered in red is 7 inches to 1 mile
11.04 cm to 1 km • 1:9 051

0 – 220yds – 440yds – 660yds – **½ mile**
0 – 125m – 250m – 375m – **500m**

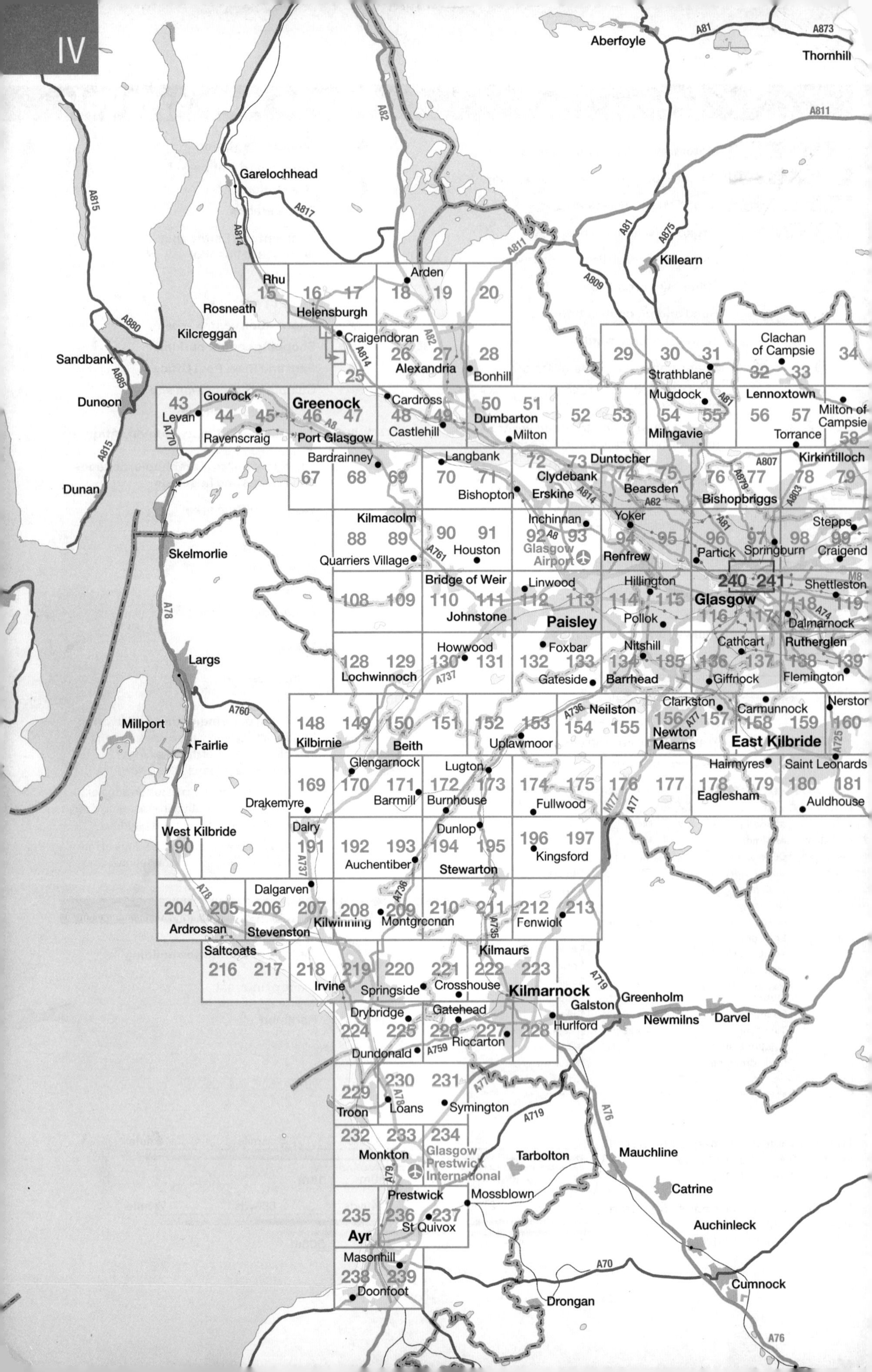

Aberfoyle
A81
A873
Thornhill
A811
A82
A815
Garelochhead
A817
A814
A81
A875
Killearn
A811
A809
Rhu
15
16
17
Arden
18
19
20
Rosneath
Helensburgh
A880
Kilcreggan
Craigendoran
A82
A814
26
27
28
Alexandria
Bonhill
29
30
31
Strathblane
Clachan of Campsie
32
33
34
Sandbank
A885
25
Dunoon
43
Levan
A770
Gourock
44
45
Ravenscraig
Greenock
46
47
A8
Port Glasgow
Cardross
48
49
Castlehill
50
51
Dumbarton
Milton
52
53
Mugdock
54
55
Milngavie
A81
Lennoxtown
56
57
Milton of Campsie
Torrance
58
A815
Dunan
Bardrainney
67
68
69
Langbank
70
71
Bishopton
72
73
Duntocher
Clydebank
Erskine
A814
74
75
Bearsden
A82
76
77
A879
A807
Bishopbriggs
Kirkintilloch
78
79
A803
Kilmacolm
88
89
Quarriers Village
A761
90
91
Houston
Inchinnan
92
A8
93
Glasgow Airport
Yoker
94
95
Renfrew
A81
96
97
Partick
Springburn
98
99
Stepps
Craigend
Skelmorlie
A78
108
109
Bridge of Weir
110
111
Johnstone
Linwood
112
113
Paisley
Hillington
114
115
Pollok
Glasgow
240
241
116
117
118
119
A74
Shettleston
M8
Dalmarnock
Largs
128
129
Lochwinnoch
Howwood
130
131
A737
132
133
Foxbar
Gateside
Nitshill
134
135
Barrhead
136
137
Cathcart
Giffnock
Rutherglen
138
139
Flemington
A760
Millport
148
149
Kilbirnie
150
151
Beith
152
153
Uplawmoor
A736
Neilston
154
155
Clarkston
156
157
A77
Newton Mearns
Carmunnock
158
159
East Kilbride
Nerston
160
A725
Fairlie
Glengarnock
169
170
171
Barrmill
Lugton
172
173
Burnhouse
174
175
Fullwood
176
177
M77
A77
Hairmyres
178
179
Eaglesham
Saint Leonards
180
181
Auldhouse
Drakemyre
West Kilbride
190
Dalry
191
A737
192
193
Auchentiber
Dunlop
194
195
Stewarton
196
197
Kingsford
A78
Dalgarven
204
205
Ardrossan
206
207
Stevenston
Kilwinning
A736
208
209
Montgreenan
210
211
A735
212
213
Fenwick
Saltcoats
216
217
218
Irvine
219
220
Springside
221
Crosshouse
Kilmaurs
222
223
Kilmarnock
A719
Galston
Greenholm
Newmilns
Darvel
Drybridge
224
225
Dundonald
Gatehead
226
227
Riccarton
A759
228
Hurlford
229
Troon
230
A78
Loans
231
Symington
A77
A719
A76
232
233
Monkton
234
Glasgow Prestwick International
A79
Tarbolton
Mauchline
Catrine
Prestwick
Mossblown
235
Ayr
236
237
St Quivox
Auchinleck
Masonhill
238
239
Doonfoot
A70
Drongan
Cumnock
A76

Key to map pages

123 Map pages at 3½ inches to 1 mile

241 Map pages at 7 inches to 1 mile

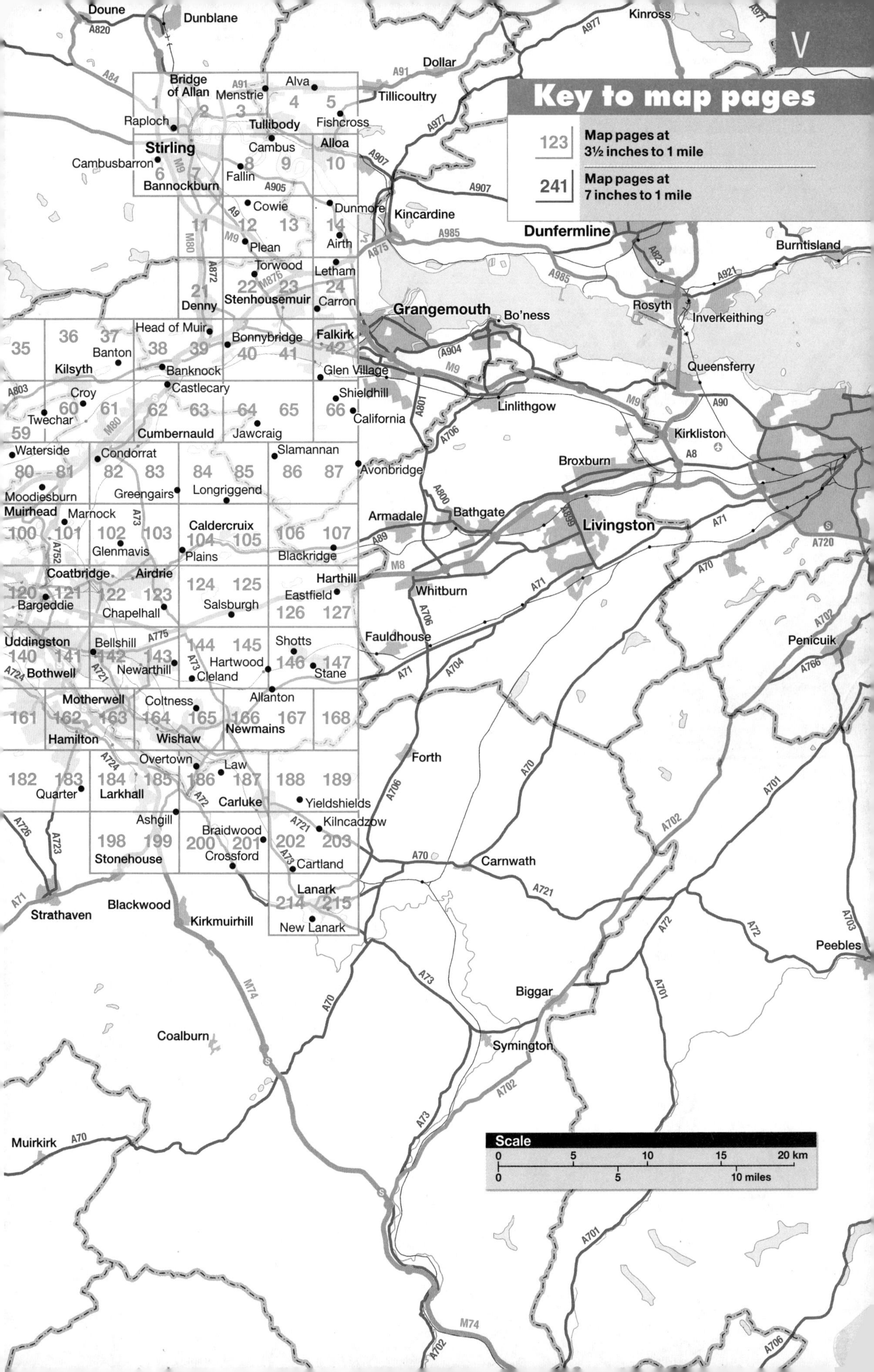

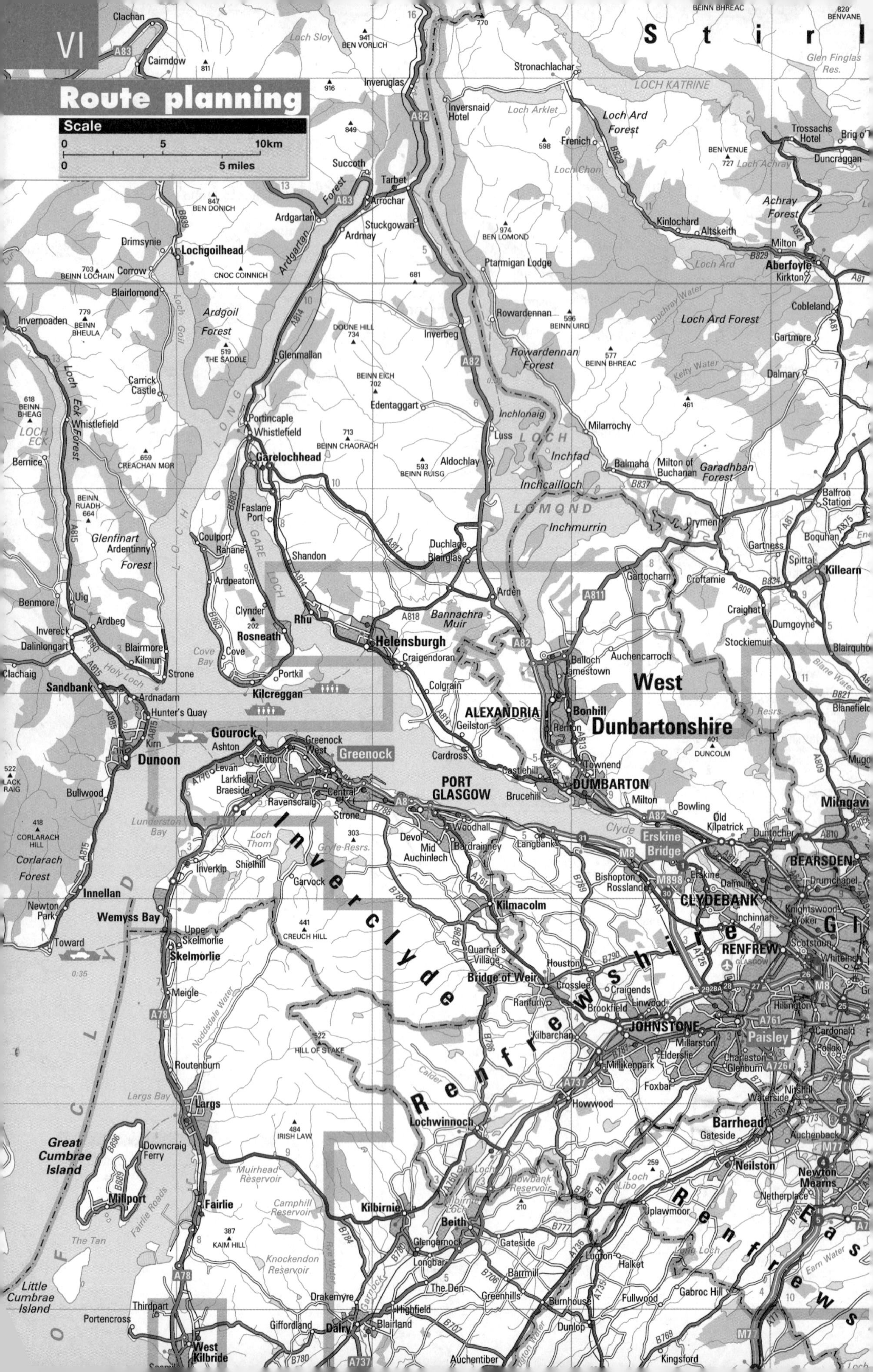
VI
Route planning
Scale
0
5
10km
0
5 miles
Stirl
Clachan
Cairndow
Loch Sloy
BEN VORLICH
Inveruglas
Stronachlachar
LOCH KATRINE
Glen Finglas Res.
BENVANE
BEINN BHREAC
Inversnaid Hotel
Loch Arklet
Loch Ard Forest
Frenich
Loch Chon
Trossachs Hotel
Brig o' T
BEN VENUE
Loch Achray
Duncraggan
Succoth
Tarbet
Arrochar
Ardgartan
Ardgartan Forest
Stuckgowan
Ardmay
BEN DONICH
BEN LOMOND
Kinlochard
Altskeith
Achray Forest
Milton
Aberfoyle
Kirkton
Loch Ard
Drimsynie
Lochgoilhead
BEINN LOCHAIN
Corrow
CNOC COINNICH
Ptarmigan Lodge
Blairlomond
Ardgoil Forest
Loch Goil
Rowardennan
BEINN UIRD
Cobleland
Loch Ard Forest
Duchray Water
Invernoaden
BEINN BHEULA
DOUNE HILL
Inverbeg
Gartmore
THE SADDLE
Glenmallan
Rowardennan Forest
BEINN BHREAC
Kelty Water
Dalmary
Carrick Castle
BEINN EICH
Loch Eck
Forest
BEINN BHEAG
LOCH ECK
Whistlefield
Edentaggart
Inchlonaig
Portincaple
Whistlefield
Luss
LOCH
Milarrochy
BEINN CHAORACH
Bernice
CREACHAN MOR
Garelochhead
BEINN RUISG
Aldochlay
Inchfad
Balmaha
Milton of Buchanan
Garadhban Forest
Inchcailloch
LOMOND
Balfron Station
BEINN RUADH
Faslane Port
Inchmurrin
Drymen
Glenfinart Ardentinny Forest
Coulport
Rahane
GARE LOCH
Shandon
Duchlage
Blairglas
Gartness
Boquhan
Spittal
Killearn
Gartocharn
Croftamie
Ardpeaton
Benmore
Uig
Arden
Craighat
Clynder
Rosneath
Rhu
Helensburgh
Bannachra Muir
Dumgoyne
Ardbeg
Invereck
Dalinlongart
Blairmore
Kilmun
Cove Bay
Cove
Strone
Craigendoran
Balloch
Jamestown
Auchencarroch
Stockiemuir
Blairquho
Holy Loch
Clachaig
Sandbank
Portkil
Kilcreggan
Colgrain
West
Blane Water
Ardnadam
Hunter's Quay
ALEXANDRIA
Geilston
Bonhill
Renton
Dunbartonshire
Blanefield
Gourock
Ashton
Greenock West
Greenock
Kirn
Dunoon
Cardross
Townend
DUNCOLM
Mugd
LACK RAIG
Levan
Midton
Larkfield
Braeside
Central
Ravenscraig
Strone
PORT GLASGOW
Castlehill
Brucehill
DUMBARTON
Milton
Bowling
Old Kilpatrick
Milngavi
Bullwood
Lunderston Bay
Inverclyde
Loch Thom
Gryfe Resrs.
Devol
Mid Auchinlech
Woodhall
Bardrainney
Langbank
Clyde
Erskine Bridge
Duntocher
BEARSDEN
CORLARACH HILL
Corlarach Forest
Inverkip
Shielhill
Garvock
Kilmacolm
Bishopton
Rossland
Erskine
Dalmuir
Drumchapel
Innellan
Newton Park
Wemyss Bay
CLYDEBANK
Knightswood
Yoker
Inchinnan
Upper Skelmorlie
Toward
Skelmorlie
CREUCH HILL
Quarrier's Village
Houston
RENFREW
Scotstoun
Whiteinch
Bridge of Weir
Crosslee
Craigends
Linwood
GLASGOW
Meigle
Noddsdale Water
Ranfurly
Brookfield
Renfrewshire
Hillington
HILL OF STAKE
Kilbarchan
JOHNSTONE
Paisley
Cardonald
Millarston
Elderslie
Charleston
Glenburn
Pollok
Routenburn
Calder
Milliken Park
Foxbar
Nitshill
Largs Bay
Largs
Howwood
Waterside
Renfrew
Lochwinnoch
Barrhead
Gateside
Auchenback
Great Cumbrae Island
Downcraig Ferry
IRISH LAW
Neilston
Newton Mearns
Muirhead Reservoir
Barr Loch
Rowbank Reservoir
Loch Libo
Millport
Fairlie
Fairlie Roads
Camphill Reservoir
Kilbirnie
Kilbirnie Loch
Beith
Uplawmoor
Netherplace
Renfrews
Eas
The Tan
KAIM HILL
Glengarnock
Gateside
Lugton
Halket
Knockendon Reservoir
Longbar
Barrmill
Long Loch
Earn Water
Rye Water
Little Cumbrae Island
The Den
Greenhills
Burnhouse
Fullwood
Gabroc Hill
Thirdpart
Drakemyre
Highfield
Portencross
Giffordland
Dalry
Blairland
Dunlop
West Kilbride
Auchentiber
Kingsford
A83
A82
A814
A817
A818
A815
A880
A885
A770
A78
A8
M8
M898
A761
A737
A760
A736
A735
A726
A811
A809
A81
A821
A875
A77
M77
B829
B837
B839
B828
B833
B834
B821
B788
B786
B789
B790
B787
B775
B776
B777
B706
B707
B769
B780
B784
B896
B899

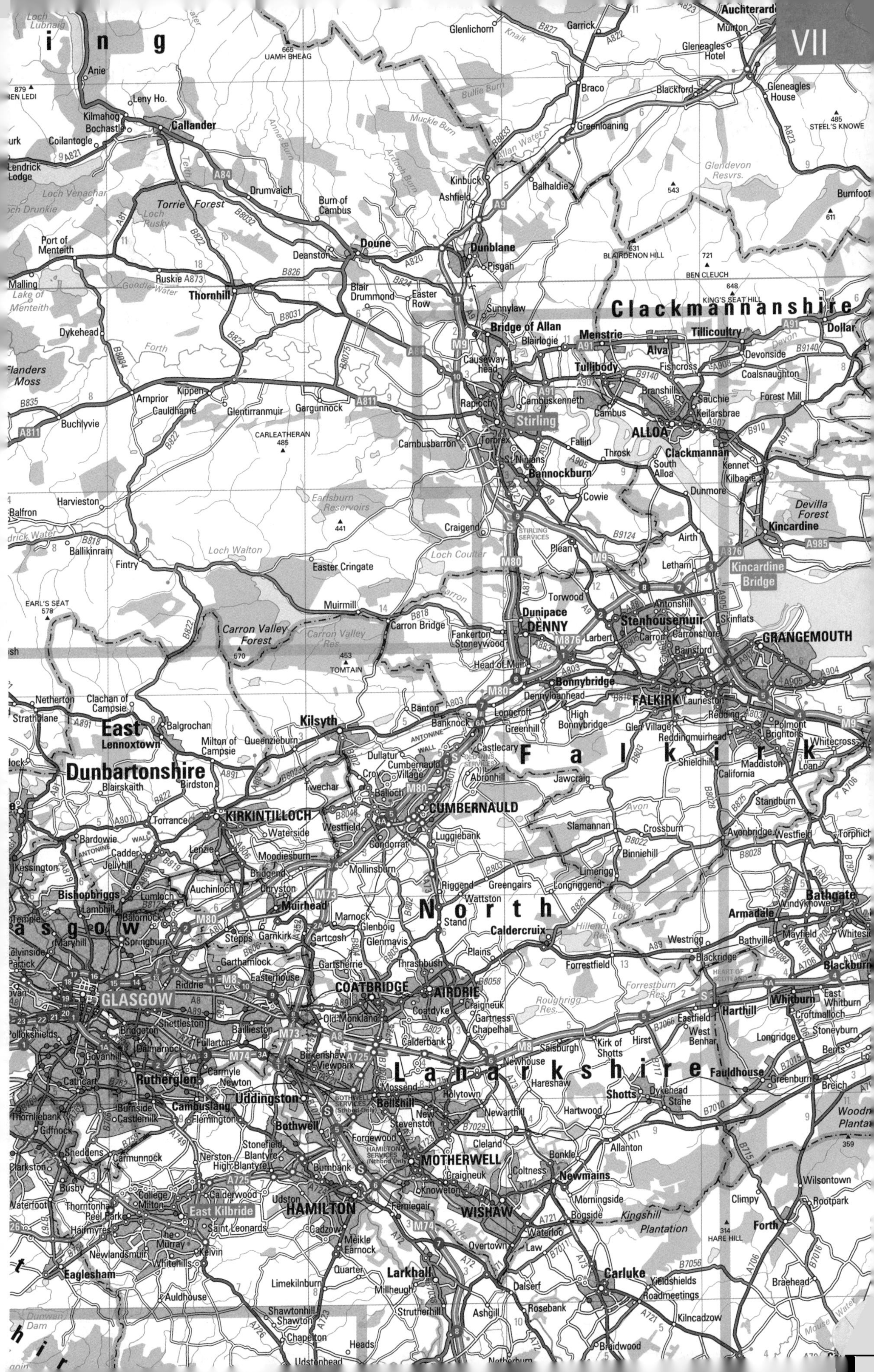
Stirling
Clackmannanshire
East Dunbartonshire
Falkirk
North Lanarkshire
GLASGOW
Loch Lubnaig
UAMH BHEAG
Glenlichorn
Garrick
Auchterarder
Muirton
Gleneagles Hotel
Gleneagles House
STEEL'S KNOWE
Anie
BEN LEDI
Leny Ho.
Kilmahog
Bochastle
Callander
Coilantogle
Lendrick Lodge
Loch Venachar
Loch Drunkie
Torrie Forest
Loch Rusky
Drumvaich
Burn of Cambus
Braco
Blackford
Greenloaning
Allan Water
Glendevon Resvrs.
Kinbuck
Ashfield
Balhaldie
Burnfoot
Port of Menteith
Deanston
Doune
Dunblane
Pisgah
BLAIRDENON HILL
BEN CLEUCH
KING'S SEAT HILL
Malling
Lake of Menteith
Ruskie
Thornhill
Goodie Water
Blair Drummond
Easter Row
Sunnylaw
Bridge of Allan
Blairlogie
Menstrie
Alva
Tillicoultry
Dollar
Devonside
Coalsnaughton
Forest Mill
Dykehead
Forth
Flanders Moss
Kippen
Arnprior
Cauldhame
Glentirranmuir
Gargunnock
Causewayhead
Raploch
Cambuskenneth
Tullibody
Fishcross
Branshill
Sauchie
Keilarsbrae
Cambus
ALLOA
Buchlyvie
CARLEATHERAN
Cambusbarron
Torbrex
St. Ninians
Bannockburn
Fallin
Throsk
Clackmannan
South Alloa
Kennet
Kilbagie
Dunmore
Devilla Forest
Kincardine
Balfron
Harvieston
Earlsburn Reservoirs
Cowie
Craigend
STIRLING SERVICES
Plean
Airth
Ballikinrain
Fintry
Loch Walton
Easter Cringate
Loch Coulter
Letham
Kincardine Bridge
EARL'S SEAT
Torwood
Antonshill
Muirmill
Carron Bridge
Dunipace
DENNY
Stenhousemuir
Skinflats
Carron Valley Forest
Carron Valley Res.
TOMTAIN
Fankerton
Stoneywood
Larbert
Carron
Carronshore
Bainsford
GRANGEMOUTH
Head of Muir
Bonnybridge
Dennyloanhead
FALKIRK
Laurieston
Netherton
Clachan of Campsie
Strathblane
Balgrochan
Lennoxtown
Kilsyth
Banton
Banknock
Longcroft
Greenhill
High Bonnybridge
Glen Village
Reddingmuirhead
Redding
Polmont
Brightons
Whitecross
Milton of Campsie
Queenzieburn
ANTONINE WALL
Castlecary
Dullatur
Cumbernauld Village
Croy
Shieldhill
Maddiston
California
Blairskaith
Birdston
Twechar
Balloch
Abronhill
Jawcraig
Loan
KIRKINTILLOCH
Torrance
Westfield
CUMBERNAULD
Slamannan
Avon
Standburn
Bardowie
Cadder
Waterside
Condorrat
Luggiebank
Crossburn
Avonbridge
Torphich
Kessington
Jellyhill
Lenzie
Moodiesburn
Binniehill
Bishopbriggs
Lambhill
Lumloch
Auchinloch
Bridgend
Chryston
Mollinsburn
Riggend
Greengairs
Limerigg
Longriggend
Bathgate
Balornock
Muirhead
Wattston
Armadale
Windyknowe
Springburn
Maryhill
Stepps
Garnkirk
Marnock
Glenboig
Gartcosh
Glenmavis
Stand
Caldercruix
Hillend Res.
Westrigg
Bathville
Mayfield
Whitburn
Kelvinside
Partick
Garthamlock
Gartsherrie
Thrashbush
Plains
Forrestfield
Blackridge
Blackburn
Riddrie
Easterhouse
COATBRIDGE
AIRDRIE
Forrestburn Res.
HEART OF SCOTLAND
Harthill
Roughrigg Res.
Craigneuk
Gartness
Chapelhall
Shettleston
Baillieston
Old Monkland
Coatdyke
Eastfield
West Benhar
East Whitburn
Croftmalloch
Pollokshields
Bridgeton
Dalmarnock
Fullarton
Calderbank
Salsburgh
Kirk of Shotts
Hirst
Longridge
Stoneyburn
Govanhill
Birkenshaw
Viewpark
Newhouse
Bents
Cathcart
Rutherglen
Carmyle
Newton
Mossend
Holytown
Hareshaw
Fauldhouse
Greenburn
Breich
Uddingston
BOTHWELL SERVICES
Bellshill
Shotts
Dykehead
Stane
Thornliebank
Giffnock
Burnside
Castlemilk
Cambuslang
Flemington
New Stevenston
Newarthill
Hartwood
Woodmuir Plantation
Bothwell
Forgewood
Cleland
Allanton
Sheddens
Carmunnock
Stonefield
Blantyre
HAMILTON SERVICES
Clarkston
Nerston
High Blantyre
Burnbank
MOTHERWELL
Craigneuk
Bonkle
Coltness
Newmains
Wilsontown
Busby
College Milton
Calderwood
Knowetop
Climpy
Rootpark
Waterfoot
Thorntonhall
Peel Park
East Kilbride
Udston
HAMILTON
Ferniegair
WISHAW
Morningside
Bogside
Kingshill Plantation
Forth
Hairmyres
Saint Leonards
Gadzow
The Murray
Kelvin
Clyde
Waterloo
HARE HILL
Newlandsmuir
Whitehills
Meikle Earnock
Overtown
Law
Eaglesham
Quarter
Larkhall
Carluke
Yieldshields
Braehead
Limekilnburn
Millheugh
Dalserf
Roadmeetings
Auldhouse
Shawtonhill
Shawton
Strutherhill
Ashgill
Rosebank
Kilncadzow
Dunwan Dam
Chapelton
Heads
Udstonhead
Netherburn
Braidwood
Mouse Water

VIII
GLASGOW
Brucehill
Milton
Bowling
Old Kilpatrick
Duntocher
Milngavie
BEARSDEN
Erskine Bridge
Erskine
Dalmuir
Drumchapel
CLYDEBANK
Knightswood
Yoker
Inchinnan
Scotstoun
RENFREW
Whiteinch
GLASGOW
Hillington
Cardonald
Paisley
Pollok
Ravenscraig
Strone
Lunderston Bay
Loch Thom
Gryfe Resrs.
Woodhall
Devol
Mid Auchinlech
Bardrainney
Langbank
Bishopton
Rossland
Corlarach Forest
Innellan
Newton Park
Wemyss Bay
Toward
Inverkip
Shielhill
Garvock
Upper Skelmorlie
Skelmorlie
CREUCH HILL
Kilmacolm
Quarrier's Village
Bridge of Weir
Houston
Crosslee
Craigends
Ranfurly
Linwood
Brookfield
JOHNSTONE
Kilbarchan
Millarston
Elderslie
Millikenpark
Charleston
Glenburn
Foxbar
Nitshill
Waterside
Meigle
Noddsdale Water
HILL OF STAKE
Routenburn
Largs Bay
Largs
Calder
Lochwinnoch
Howwood
Barrhead
Gateside
Auchenback
Great Cumbrae Island
Downcraig Ferry
Millport
IRISH LAW
Muirhead Reservoir
Camphill Reservoir
Fairlie
Fairlie Roads
Kilbirnie
Barr Loch
Kilbirnie Loch
Rowbank Reservoir
Beith
Loch Libo
Uplawmoor
Neilston
Newton Mearns
Netherplace
The Tan
KAIM HILL
Glengarnock
Longbar
Gateside
Lugton
Halket
Long Loch
Earn Water
Little Cumbrae Island
Knockendon Reservoir
Rye Water
The Den
Barrmill
Greenhills
Burnhouse
Fullwood
Gabroc Hill
Thirdpart
Portencross
Drakemyre
Highfield
Blairland
Giffordland
Dalry
Dunlop
West Kilbride
Seamill
Auchentiber
Kingsford
Stewarton
Laighmuir
Flow Moss
Dalgarven
Kilwinning
Torranyard
Annick Water
Waterside
Fenwick
Laigh Fenwick
Chapelhill
Dykesmains
Benslie
Cunninghamhead
Kilmaurs
Ardrossan
Stevenston
Saltcoats
BRODICK
CAMPBELTOWN
(MAY-SEPT)
Girdle Toll
Perceton
Onthank
Moscow
Wallace Muir
Irvine
Springside
Knockentiber
Knockinlaw
Fullarton
Dreghorn
Crosshouse
Kilmarnock
Grange
Crookedholm
Hurlford
Galston
Newmilns
Irvine Bay
Drybridge
Gatehead
Riccarton
Earlston
Shortlees
Dundonald
Crossroads
Sornhill
Barassie
North Bay
Muirhead
Craigie
Bogend
Loans
Symington
Troon
South Bay
Hansel Village
Millburn
Cessnock Water
Auchmillan
Mossgiel
LARNE
(March-Oct)
Monkton
GLASGOW PRESTWICK
Tarbolton
Mauchline
Catrine
Prestwick
Failford
Haugh
St Quivox
Mossblown
Woodfield
Crosshill
Stair
Newton on Ayr
Wallacetown
Annbank
Whitletts
Ayr
Trabboch
Ochiltree
Seafield
Belston
Coylton
Coalhall
Masonhill
Belmont
Hillhead
Drongan
Joppa
Doonfoot
Alloway
Laigh Glengall
Fisherton
Dunure
Martnaham Loch
Barbieston
Sinclairston
Skares
Hayhill
Littlemill
Culroy
Minishant
Hollybush
Dalrymple
Rankinston
Water of Coyle
Culzean Bay
Polnessan
KILMEIN HILL
Whitefaulds
Maybole
Patna
Burnfoot
Maidenhead Bay
Kirkmichael
Waterside
BENBEOCH
Inverclyde
Renfrewshire
East Renfrewshire
North Ayrshire
FIRTH OF CLYDE

KIRKINTILLOCH
CUMBERNAULD
Balloch
Torrance
Bardowie
Waterside
Westfield
Condorrat
Luggiebank
Slamannan
Avon
Crossburn
Avonbridge
Stand
Binniehill
Cadder
Jellyhill
Lenzie
Moodiesburn
Kessington
Mollinsburn
Limerigg
Longriggend
Bridgend
Chryston
Riggend
Greengairs
Bishopbriggs
Lumloch
Auchinloch
Wattston
Lambhill
Balornock
Muirhead
Marnock
North
Bathgate
Windyknowe
Armadale
Glasgow
Maryhill
Springburn
Stepps
Garnkirk
Gartcosh
Glenboig
Stand
Caldercruix
Hillend Res.
Glenmavis
Westrigg
Mayfield
Whitesid
Partick
Garthamlock
Plains
Bathville
Thrashbush
Gartsherrie
Forrestfield
Blackridge
Riddrie
Easterhouse
HEART OF SCOTLAND
Blackburn
COATBRIDGE
AIRDRIE
Forrestburn Res.
GLASGOW
Craigneuk
Roughrigg Res.
Whitburn
East Whitburn
Old Monkland
Coatdyke
Gartness
Harthill
Croftmalloch
Pollokshields
Shettleston
Baillieston
Chapelhall
Eastfield
West Benhar
Bridgeton
Stoneyburn
Dalmarnock
Calderbank
Salsburgh
Kirk of Shotts
Hirst
Longridge
Govanhill
Fullarton
Birkenshaw
Viewpark
Newhouse
Bents
Carmyle
Newton
Cathcart
Rutherglen
Mossend
Lanarkshire
Fauldhouse
Greenburn
Breich
Uddingston
Holytown
Hareshaw
Shotts
Dykehead
Stane
Woodm Plantati
Burnside
Castlemilk
Cambuslang
Bellshill
BOTHWELL SERVICES
New Stevenston
Newarthill
Thornliebank
Flemington
Hartwood
Giffnock
Bothwell
Forgewood
Cleland
Allanton
Sheddens
Carmunnock
Stonefield
Blantyre
HAMILTON SERVICES
MOTHERWELL
359
Clarkston
Nerston
High Blantyre
Burnbank
Bonkle
Craigneuk
Coltness
Newmains
Busby
College Milton
Calderwood
Knowetop
Wilsontown
Waterfoot
Thorntonhall
Peel Park
East Kilbride
Udston
HAMILTON
Ferniegair
WISHAW
Morningside
Clydesdale
Climpy
Rootpark
Hairmyres
The Murray
Saint Leonards
Cadzow
Bogside
Kingshill Plantation
Meikle Earnock
Waterloo
314 HARE HILL
Forth
Newlandsmuir
Whitehills
Kelvin
Overtown
Law
Eaglesham
Quarter
Larkhall
Carluke
Limekilnburn
Millheugh
Dalserf
Yieldshields
Braehead
Auldhouse
Roadmeetings
Dunwan Dam
Shawtonhill
Shawton
Strutherhill
Ashgill
Rosebank
Kilncadzow
Chapelton
Heads
Braidwood
Udstonhead
Glassford
Stonehouse
Netherburn
Carnduff
Cartland
Carstairs
West End
Carnwath
376 CORSE HILL
Crossford
Strathaven
Hazelbank
Nemphlar
Draffan
Carstairs Junction
Ravenstruther
Auchenheath
Sandford
Blackwood
Kirkfieldbank
Lanark
Pettinain
Whitelaw
Kirkmuirhill
New Lanark
Libberto
Calder Water
Caldermill
Avon Water
Boghead
Dillarburn
Hyndford Bridge
340
South
Stobieside
Gilmourton
329
Lesmahagow
Hawksland
Brocketsbrae
Covington
Drumclog
Kype Water
Glen Water
316
New Trows
Auchlochan
Sandilands
Harleyholm
Thank
Darvel
Rough Moss
Logan Water
Douglas Water
Lanarkshire
MILL RIG 335
457
Rigside
Coalburn
Glengavel Reservoir
522 NUTBERRY HILL
Braehead
Happendon
HAPPENDON (CAIRN LODGE) SERVICES
Uddington
569 TINTO
River Wethan
406
Garf Water
Wiston
434 WEDDER HILL
Douglas West
Newton
466 MIDDLEFIELD LAW
510 DUNGAVEL HILL
Glenbuck
465 HARESHAW HILL
Douglas
Netherwood
Glespin
Roberton
Smallburn
Muirkirk
392 AUCHENSAUGH HILL
Sorn
Kames
East
ABINGTON SERVICES
Glentaggart
Abington
593 CAIRN TABLE
Crawfordjohn
569 TEWSGILL HILL
Camps Water
Cronberry
Back Rogerton
Auchinleck
Lugar
497 WARDLAW HILL
DRAKE LAW 483
Duneaton Water
Holmhead
Logan
Kirkton
Crawford
Cumnock
Netherthird
Dalblair
Glenmuir Water
478 MOUNT STUART
Craigens
494 RAKE LAW
553 WELLGRAIN DOD
Elvanfoot
yrshire
Fingland
509 KIRKLAND HILL
Elvan Water
Pathhead
Kirkland
Leadhills
Mansfield
Nith
Watermeetings
Connel Park
Bankglen
New Cumnock
Kirkconnel
485 CONRIG HILL
Wanlockhead
Crawick Water
732 GREEN LOWTHER
Kelloholm
Burnside
THE KNIPE 575
Crawick
Dalleagles
Sanquhar
725 LOWTHER HILL
Afton Water
Kello Water
M8
M73
M74
M80
A71
A70
A73
A76
A725
A721
A706
B743
B7078
B797
B740
B7040

Major administrative and Postcode boundaries

County and unitary authority boundaries
Postcode boundaries
Area covered by this atlas
Scale
0 5 10 15km
0 5 10 miles
NN
NS
Stirling
Argyll and Bute
G84
Helensburgh
G83
Alexandria
G82
Gourock
PA19
Greenock
PA16
PA15
Port Glasgow
West Dunbartonshire
Dumbarton
G60
G81
PA14
PA7
Clydebank
PA8
Inverclyde
G63
Strathblane
G62
Milngavie
East Dunbartonshire
G66
G61
G64
G15
G23
Kirkintilloch
G65
Kilsyth
G68
Cumbernauld
G67
Moodiesburn
G69
Muirhead
Bridge of Allan
FK11
FK12
Alva
FK9
Clackmannanshire
FK8
FK10
Alloa
Stirling
Bannockburn
FK7
Airth
FK2
FK6
Denny
FK5
Stenhousemuir
FK3
Banknock
FK4
Falkirk
FK1
Slamannan
North Lanarkshire
EH48
West Lothia
Kilmacolm
PA13
PA6
Houston
PA4
Renfrew
PA11
Bridge of Weir
Renfrewshire
PA3
PA1
PA10
Johnstone
Paisley
PA5
PA2
PA12
PA9
Lochwinnoch
Barrhead
City of Glasgow
G33
G34
G69
G32
Airdrie
ML5
Coatbridge
ML6
ML7
G71
ML4
ML1
Shotts
G72
Cleland
Motherwell
G76
G74
Hamilton
Wishaw
ML2
Neilston
G78
East Renfrewshire
East Kilbride
Eaglesham
G77
G76
G75
ML3
KA25
Kilbirnie
Beith
KA14
KA15
KA24
Larkhall
Carluke
ML9
ML8
KA23
West Kilbride
Dalry
KA21
KA22
North Ayrshire
KA13
Dunlop
Stewarton
KA3
ML10
Stonehouse
Crossford
ML11
Lanark
South Lanarkshire
Ardrossan
Saltcoats
Stevenston
KA20
KA12
Irvine
KA11
Kilmarnock
KA1
East Ayrshire
KA2
Dundonald
KA10
Symington
Troon
KA1
KA9
South Ayrshire
Prestwick
KA8
KA6
Ayr
KA7
KA6
NS
G13
G22
Kelvinside
Milton
Balornock
Scotstoun
G20
G12
G21
G14
G11
G4
G3
Glasgow
G51
G2
Ibrox
G1
G31
G52
Gorbals
Dalmarnock
G41
Mosspark
Crossmyloof
G5
G40
G53
Govanhill
G42
Priesthill
G43
Rutherglen
Newlands
G44
G73
Cathcart
Giffnock
G46
G45
Cathkin

2

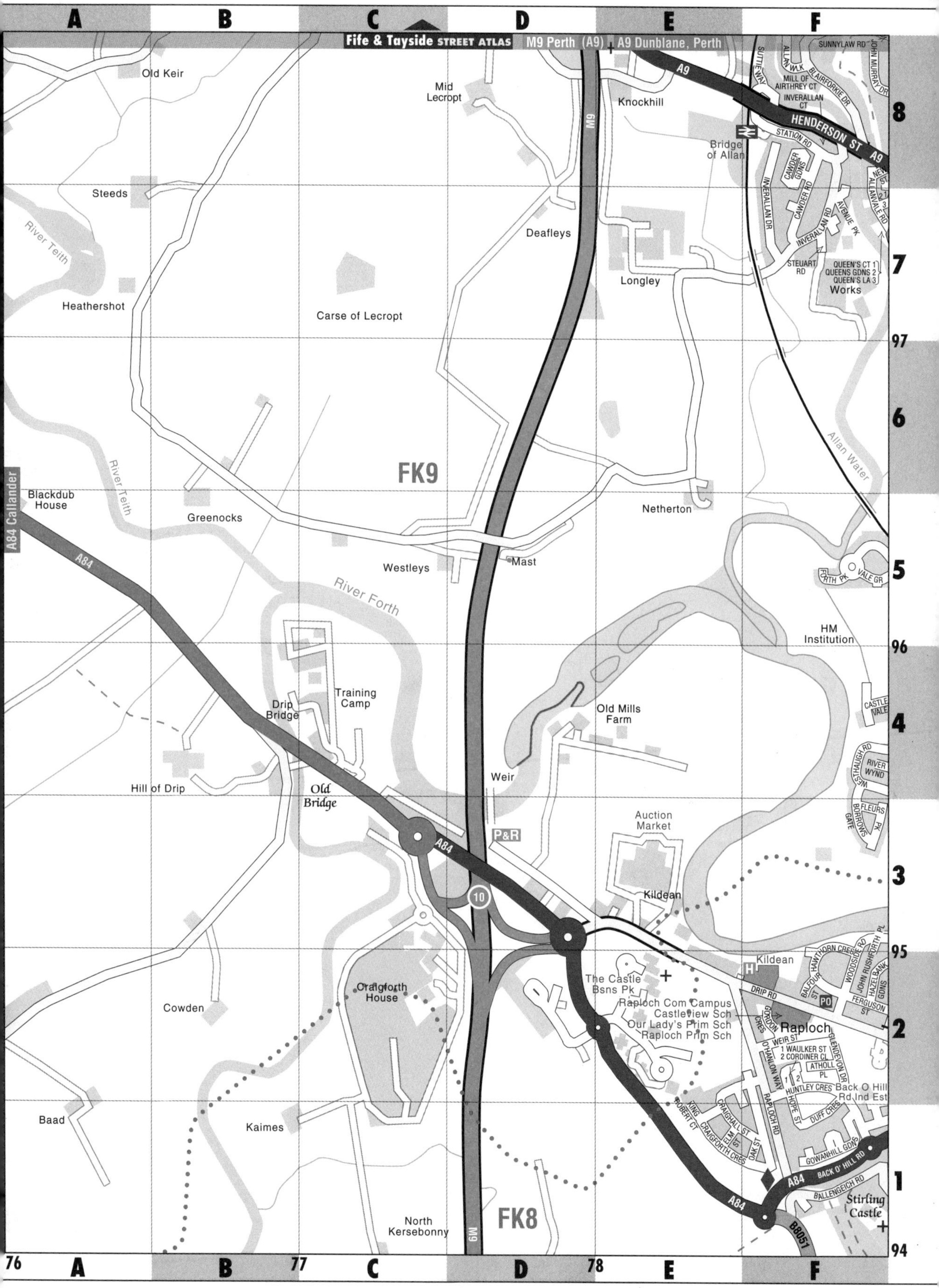

Fife & Tayside STREET ATLAS
M9 Perth (A9)
A9 Dunblane, Perth
A B C D E F
8 7 97 6 5 96 4 3 95 2 1 94
76 77 78
Old Keir
Mid Lecropt
Knockhill
Bridge of Allan
SUNNYLAW RD
JOHN MURRAY DR
SUTTIE WAY
ALLAN WLK
BLAIRFORKIE DR
MILL OF AIRTHREY CT
INVERALLAN CT
HENDERSON ST
STATION RD
CAWDER GDNS
CAWDER RD
INVERALLAN DR
INVERALLAN RD
AVENUE PK
ALLANVALE RD
STEUART RD
QUEEN'S CT 1
QUEENS GDNS 2
QUEEN'S LA 3
Works
Steeds
River Teith
Heathershot
Deafleys
Longley
Carse of Lecropt
Allan Water
FK9
Blackdub House
A84 Callander
A84
Greenocks
Netherton
Westleys
Mast
River Forth
FORTH PK
VALE GR
HM Institution
Training Camp
Drip Bridge
Old Mills Farm
CASTLE VALE
WESTHAUGH RD
RIVER WYND
FLEURS PK
BORROWS GATE
Hill of Drip
Old Bridge
Weir
P&R
Auction Market
10
Kildean
Craigforth House
The Castle Bsns Pk
Raploch Com Campus
Castleview Sch
Our Lady's Prim Sch
Raploch Prim Sch
DRIP RD
HAWTHORN CRES
WOODSIDE RD
JOHN RUSHFORTH PL
HAZELBANK GDNS
BALFOUR ST
FERGUSON ST
PO
Raploch
GORDON CRES
WEIR ST
O'HANLON WAY
1 WAULKER ST
2 CORDINER CL
ATHOLL PL
GLENDEVON DR
HUNTLEY CRES
Back O Hill Rd Ind Est
HOPE ST
DUFF CRES
RAPLOCH RD
KING ROBERT CT
CRAIGHALL ST
ELM ST
OAK ST
CRAIGFORTH CRES
GOWANHILL GDNS
BACK O' HILL RD
BALLENGEICH RD
Stirling Castle
B8051
Cowden
Baad
Kaimes
North Kersebonny
FK8
M9

6

2

1

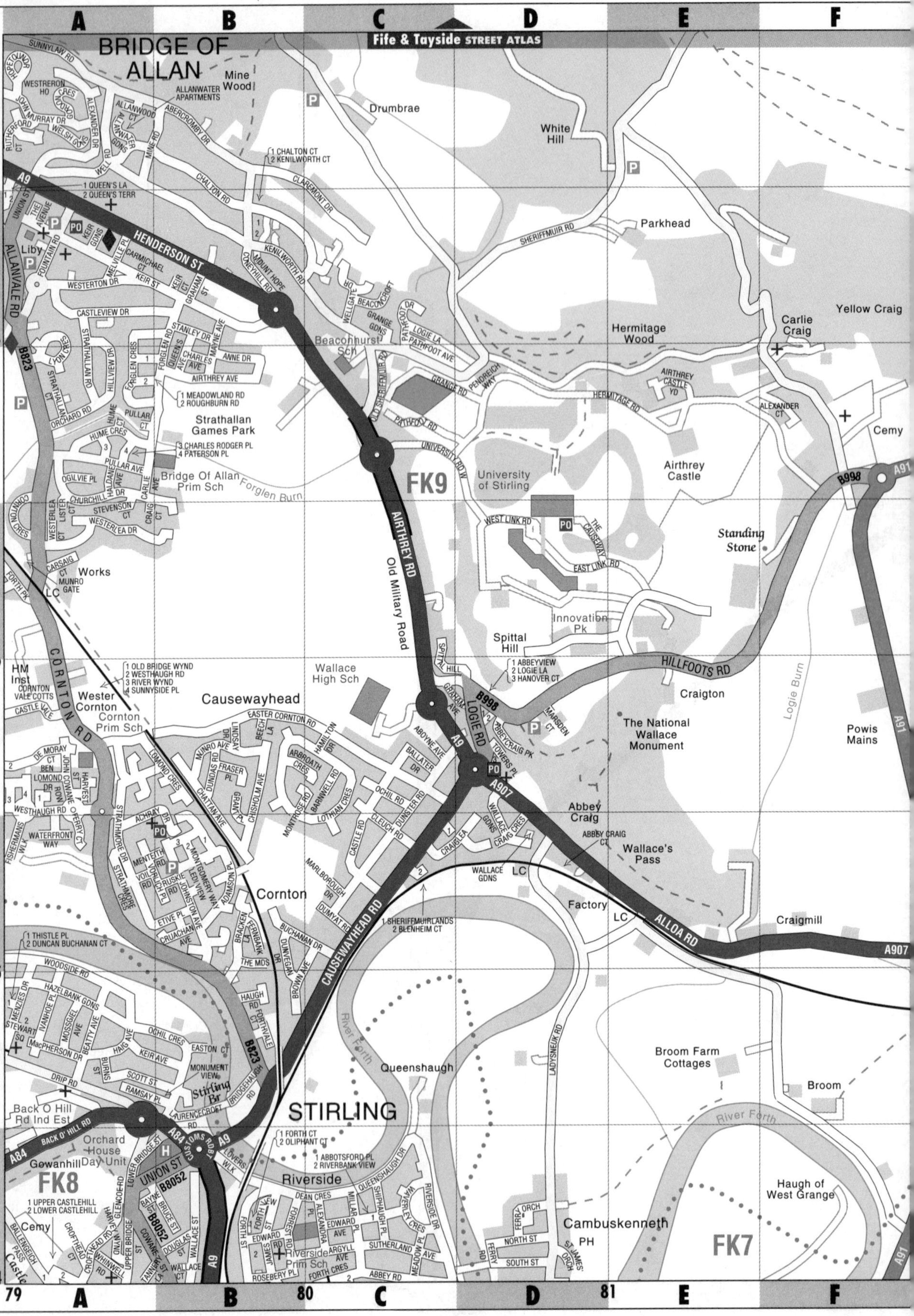
Fife & Tayside STREET ATLAS
A
B
C
D
E
F
8
7
97
6
5
96
4
3
95
2
1
94
79
80
81
BRIDGE OF ALLAN
Mine Wood
ALLANWATER APARTMENTS
Drumbrae
White Hill
Parkhead
SHERIFFMUIR RD
1 CHALTON CT
2 KENILWORTH CT
1 QUEEN'S LA
2 QUEEN'S TERR
HENDERSON ST
A9
Liby
ALLANVALE RD
B823
Beaconhurst Sch
Hermitage Wood
Carlie Craig
Yellow Craig
AIRTHREY CASTLE YD
HERMITAGE RD
ALEXANDER CT
Cemy
1 MEADOWLAND RD
2 ROUGHBURN RD
Strathallan Games Park
3 CHARLES RODGER PL
4 PATERSON PL
Bridge Of Allan Prim Sch
Forglen Burn
FK9
University of Stirling
Airthrey Castle
B998
A91
Standing Stone
AIRTHREY RD
Old Military Road
WEST LINK RD
EAST LINK RD
THE CAUSEWAY
Innovation Pk
Spittal Hill
Works
MUNRO GATE
LC
HM Inst
CORNTON VALE COTTS
1 OLD BRIDGE WYND
2 WESTHAUGH RD
3 RIVER WYND
4 SUNNYSIDE PL
Wester Cornton
Cornton Prim Sch
CORNTON RD
Causewayhead
Wallace High Sch
1 ABBEYVIEW
2 LOGIE LA
3 HANOVER CT
HILLFOOTS RD
Craigton
The National Wallace Monument
Logie Burn
Powis Mains
LOGIE RD
A907
Abbey Craig
ABBEY CRAIG CT
Wallace's Pass
WALLACE GDNS
Factory
ALLOA RD
Craigmill
Cornton
CAUSEWAYHEAD RD
1 SHERIFFMUIRLANDS
2 BLENHEIM CT
1 THISTLE PL
2 DUNCAN BUCHANAN CT
River Forth
Queenshaugh
LADYSNEUK RD
Broom Farm Cottages
Broom
MONUMENT VIEW
Stirling Br
Back O Hill Rd Ind Est
BACK O' HILL RD
A84
STIRLING
1 FORTH CT
2 OLIPHANT CT
1 ABBOTSFORD PL
2 RIVERBANK VIEW
Orchard House Day Unit
Gowanhill
FK8
Riverside
UNION ST
B8052
1 UPPER CASTLEHILL
2 LOWER CASTLEHILL
Cemy
Riverside Prim Sch
Cambuskenneth
PH
Haugh of West Grange
FK7
NORTH ST
SOUTH ST
ABBEY RD

1

7

4

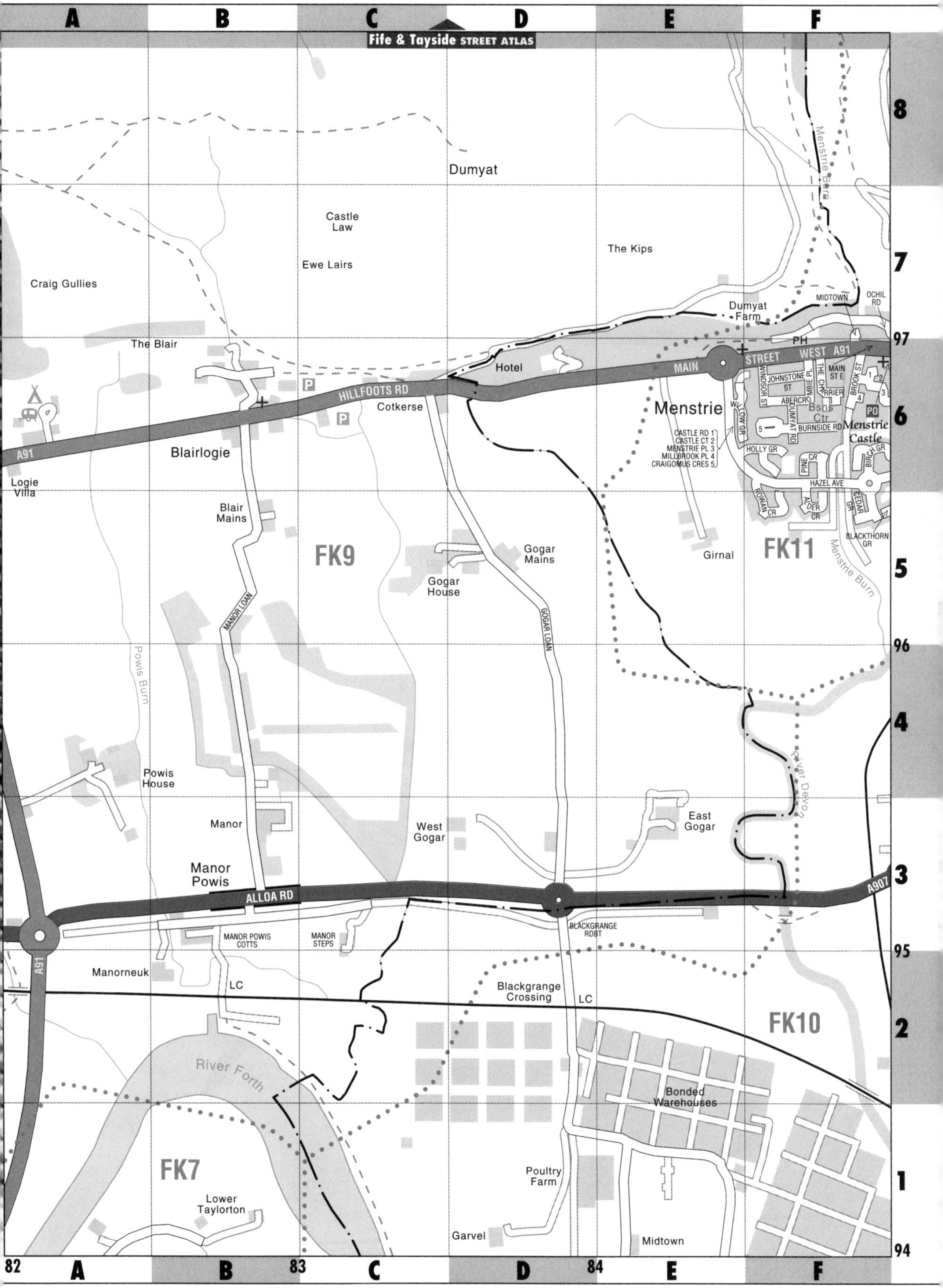
A
B
C
D
E
F
Fife & Tayside STREET ATLAS
8
7
6
5
4
3
2
1
97
96
95
94
82
83
84
Dumyat
Castle Law
Ewe Lairs
The Kips
Craig Gullies
The Blair
Dumyat Farm
MIDTOWN
OCHIL RD
PH
Hotel
MAIN STREET WEST A91
HILLFOOTS RD
Cotkerse
A91
Blairlogie
Logie Villa
Menstrie
JOHNSTONE ST
ABERCR
WINDSOR ST
DUMYAT RD
THE CARRIER
MAIN ST E
BROOK ST
Bsns Ctr
BURNSIDE RD
PO
Menstrie Castle
CASTLE RD 1
CASTLE CT 2
MENSTRIE PL 3
MILLBROOK PL 4
CRAIGOMUS CRES 5
HOLLY GR
PINE CR
BIRCH GR
HAZEL AVE
ROWAN CR
ALDER CR
CEDAR GR
BLACKTHORN GR
Menstrie Burn
Blair Mains
FK9
Gogar Mains
Gogar House
Girnal
FK11
MANOR LOAN
GOGAR LOAN
Powis Burn
River Devon
Powis House
Manor
West Gogar
East Gogar
Manor Powis
ALLOA RD
A907
MANOR POWIS COTTS
MANOR STEPS
BLACKGRANGE RDBT
Manorneuk
LC
Blackgrange Crossing
LC
FK10
A91
River Forth
Bonded Warehouses
FK7
Lower Taylorton
Poultry Farm
Garvel
Midtown

8

4

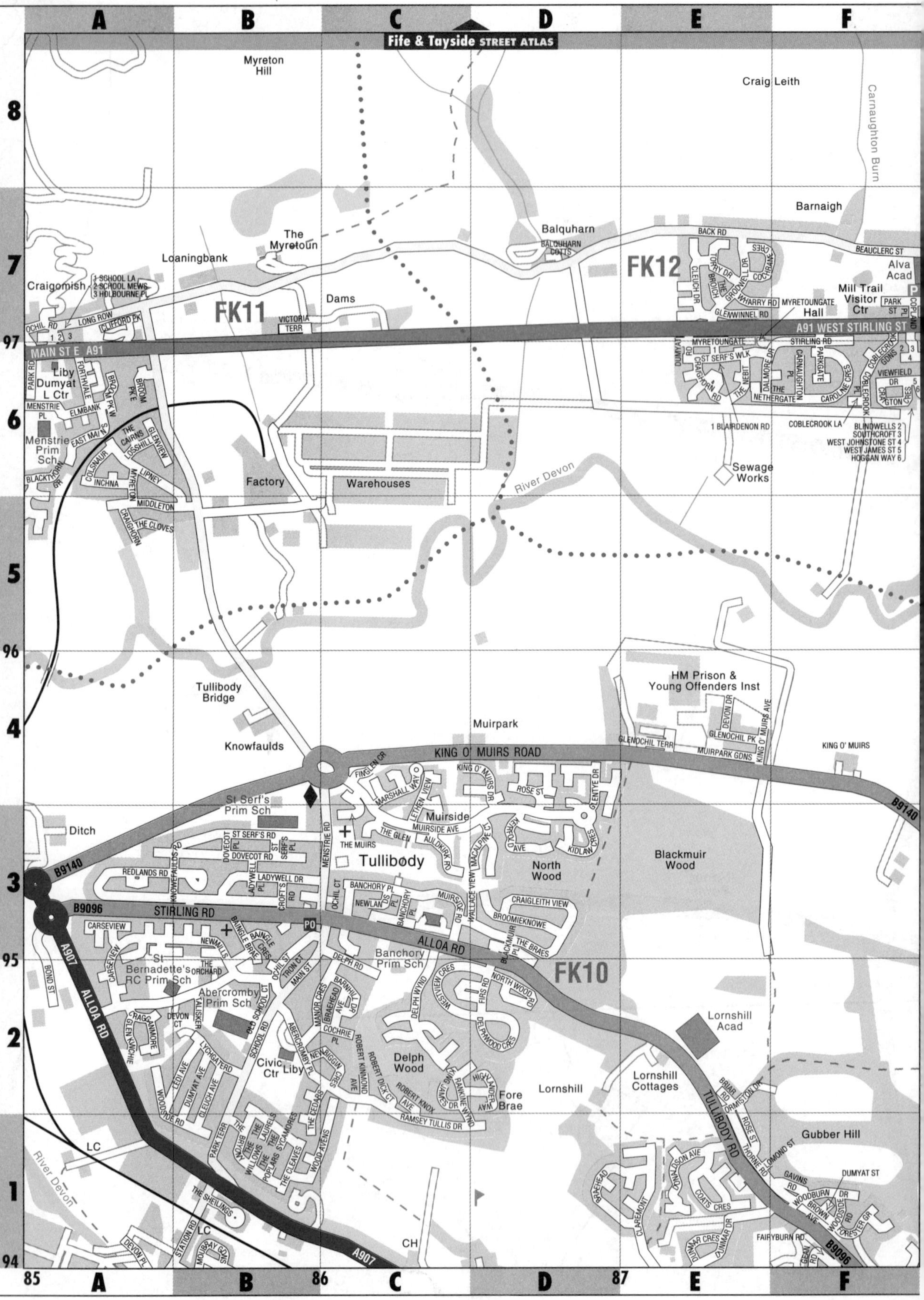
A
B
C
D
E
F
8
7
97
6
5
96
4
3
95
2
1
94
85
86
87
Myreton Hill
Craig Leith
Carnaughton Burn
Barnaigh
The Myretoun
Balquharn
BALQUHARN COTTS
BACK RD
BEAUCLERC ST
Loaningbank
Craigomish
1 SCHOOL LA
2 SCHOOL MEWS
3 HOLBOURNE PL
FK11
FK12
Dams
VICTORIA TERR
LONG ROW
CLIFFORD PK
OCHIL RD
MAIN ST E A91
A91 WEST STIRLING ST
Alva Acad
Mill Trail Visitor Ctr
Myretoungate Hall
MYRETOUNGATE
TORRY DR
BROICH
THE GROOVE
CLEUCH DR
GREENWELL DR
COCHRANE CRES
WHARRY RD
GLENWINNEL RD
STIRLING RD
ST SERF'S WLK
DUMYAT RD
CRAIGHORN RD
THE NEBIT
DALMORE DR
THE NETHERGATE
CARNAUGHTON
PARKGATE
CAROLINE CRES
COBLECROOK LA
COBLECROOK GDNS
VIEWFIELD DR
CRAIGTON CRES
1 BLAIRDENON RD
BLINDWELLS 2
SOUTHCROFT 3
WEST JOHNSTONE ST 4
WEST JAMES ST 5
HOGGAN WAY 6
PARK ST
COPLAND PL
Liby Dumyat L Ctr
PARK RD
FORTHVALE
BROOM PK W
BROOM PKE
MENSTRIE PL
ELMBANK
Menstrie Prim Sch
EAST MAIN ST
THE CAIRNS
GLENVIEW
LOSSHILL
COLSNAUR
INCHNA
MYRETON
LIPNEY
MIDDLETON
CRAIGHORN
THE CLOVES
BLACKTHORN GR
Factory
Warehouses
River Devon
Sewage Works
Tullibody Bridge
Knowfaulds
Muirpark
HM Prison & Young Offenders Inst
DEVON DR
GLENOCHIL PK
GLENOCHIL TERR
MUIRPARK GDNS
KING O' MUIRS AVE
KING O' MUIRS
KING O' MUIRS ROAD
B9140
St Serf's Prim Sch
Ditch
FINGLEN CR
MARSHALL WAY
LETHEN VIEW
KING O' MUIRS DR
ROSE ST
GLENTYE DR
Muirside
MUIRSIDE AVE
THE GLEN
AULDKIRK RD
MACALPINE CT
KERRCOLD AVE
KIDLAW CRES
THE MUIRS
Tullibody
North Wood
Blackmuir Wood
ST SERF'S RD
DOVECOT PL
DOVECOT RD
ST SERF'S PL
REDLANDS RD
KNOWEFAULDS RD
LADYWELL PL
LADYWELL DR
CROFT'S RD
MENSTRIE RD
OCHIL CT
BANCHORY PL
NEWLANDS PL
BANCHORY PL
MUIRSIDE RD
WALLACE VIEW
CRAIGLEITH VIEW
BROOMIEKNOWE
BLACKMUIR PL
THE BRAES
B9096
STIRLING RD
CARSEVIEW
NEWMILLS
BAINGLE BRAE
BAINGLE CRES
OCHIL ST
TRON CT
MAIN ST
PO
ALLOA RD
Banchory Prim Sch
DELPH RD
FK10
St Bernadette's RC Prim Sch
THE ORCHARD
BOND ST
A907
ALLOA RD
Abercromby Prim Sch
OLD SCHOOL CT
TALISKER
DEVON CT
CRAIGANMORE
GLEN KANCHIE
MANOR CRES
BRAEHEAD AVE
BARNHILL DR
COCHRIE PL
DELPH WYND
WESTVIEW CRES
FIRS RD
NORTH WOOD RD
DELPHWOOD CRES
Lornshill Acad
Delph Wood
SCHOOL RD
ABERCROMBY PL
Civic Ctr
Liby
LYCHGATE RD
LEDI AVE
DUMYAT AVE
CLEUCH AVE
WOODSIDE RD
ROBERT KINMOND AVE
ROBERT DICK CT
ROBERT KNOX AVE
KING JAMES IV DR
RANKINE WYND
HIGHLANDER WAY
Fore Brae
Lornshill
Lornshill Cottages
RAMSEY TULLIS DR
NEWBIGGIN CRES
THE CEDARS
PARK TERR
THE BIRCHES
THE WILLOWS
THE LAURELS
THE POPLARS
THE SYCAMORES
THE CLEAVES
WOOD AVENS
LC
River Devon
THE SHEILINGS
STATION RD
MOUBRAY GDNS
DEVON PL
CH
A907
TULLIBODY RD
BRIAR RD
ORMISTON DR
ROSE ST
THORNE RD
OSMOND ST
Gubber Hill
DUMYAT ST
GAVINS RD
WOODBURN DR
BROWN AVE
WOODSIDE RD
CRESTER GR
FAIRYBURN RD
GEAN RD
B9096
BRAEHEAD
CLAREMONT
DONALDSON AVE
COATS CRES
DUNMAR CRES
DUNMAR DR

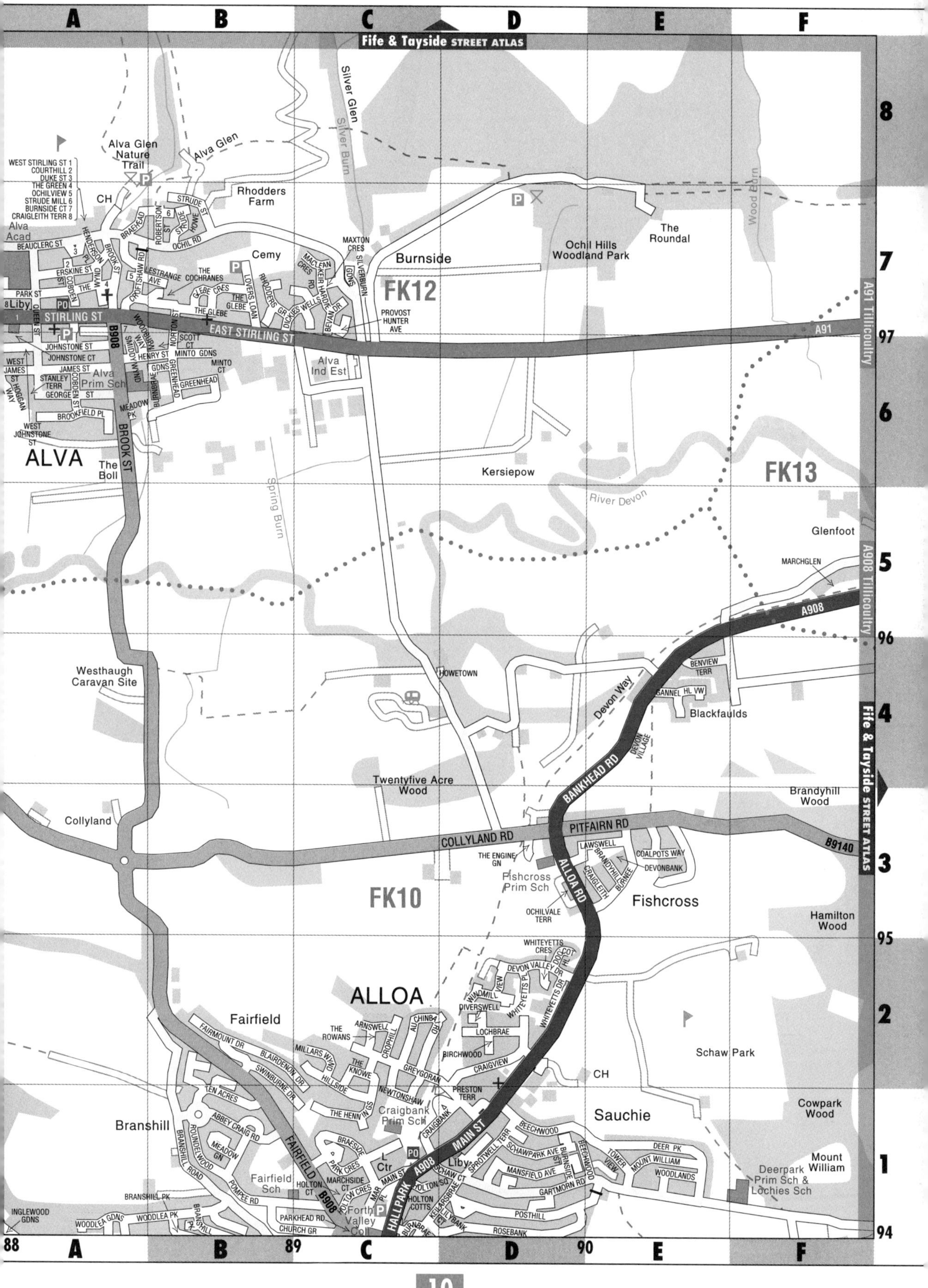
A
B
C
D
E
F
Fife & Tayside STREET ATLAS
8
7
97
6
5
96
4
3
95
2
1
94
88
89
90
Alva Glen Nature Trail
Alva Glen
Silver Glen
Silver Burn
WEST STIRLING ST 1
COURTHILL 2
DUKE ST 3
THE GREEN 4
OCHILVIEW 5
STRUDE MILL 6
BURNSIDE CT 7
CRAIGLEITH TERR 8
Rhodders Farm
The Roundal
Ochil Hills Woodland Park
Wood Burn
Alva Acad
Cemy
Burnside
FK12
MAXTON CRES
SILVERBURN
PROVOST HUNTER AVE
STIRLING ST
EAST STIRLING ST
A91
A91 Tillicoultry
Alva Ind Est
Alva Prim Sch
ALVA
The Boll
BROOK ST
B908
Kersiepow
FK13
River Devon
Spring Burn
Glenfoot
MARCHGLEN
A908
A908 Tillicoultry
Westhaugh Caravan Site
HOWETOWN
Devon Way
BENVIEW TERR
GANNEL HL VW
Blackfaulds
Fife & Tayside STREET ATLAS
Twentyfive Acre Wood
BANKHEAD RD
DEVON VILLAGE
Brandyhill Wood
Collyland
COLLYLAND RD
PITFAIRN RD
B9140
THE ENGINE GN
Fishcross Prim Sch
LAWSWELL
COALPOTS WAY
DEVONBANK
ALLOA RD
FK10
Fishcross
OCHILVALE TERR
Hamilton Wood
WHITEYETTS CRES
DOOCOT HL
DEVON VALLEY DR
WHITEYETTS DR
ALLOA
Fairfield
Schaw Park
CH
Sauchie
Cowpark Wood
Branshill
Fairfield Sch
Craigbank Prim Sch
MAIN ST
HALLPARK
Forth Valley Coll
Deerpark Prim Sch & Lochies Sch
Mount William
BEECHWOOD
DEER PK
MOUNT WILLIAM
WOODLANDS
GARTMORN RD
POSTHILL
ROSEBANK
INGLEWOOD GDNS
WOODLEA GDNS
WOODLEA PK
BRANSHILL PK
PARKHEAD RD
CHURCH GR

1

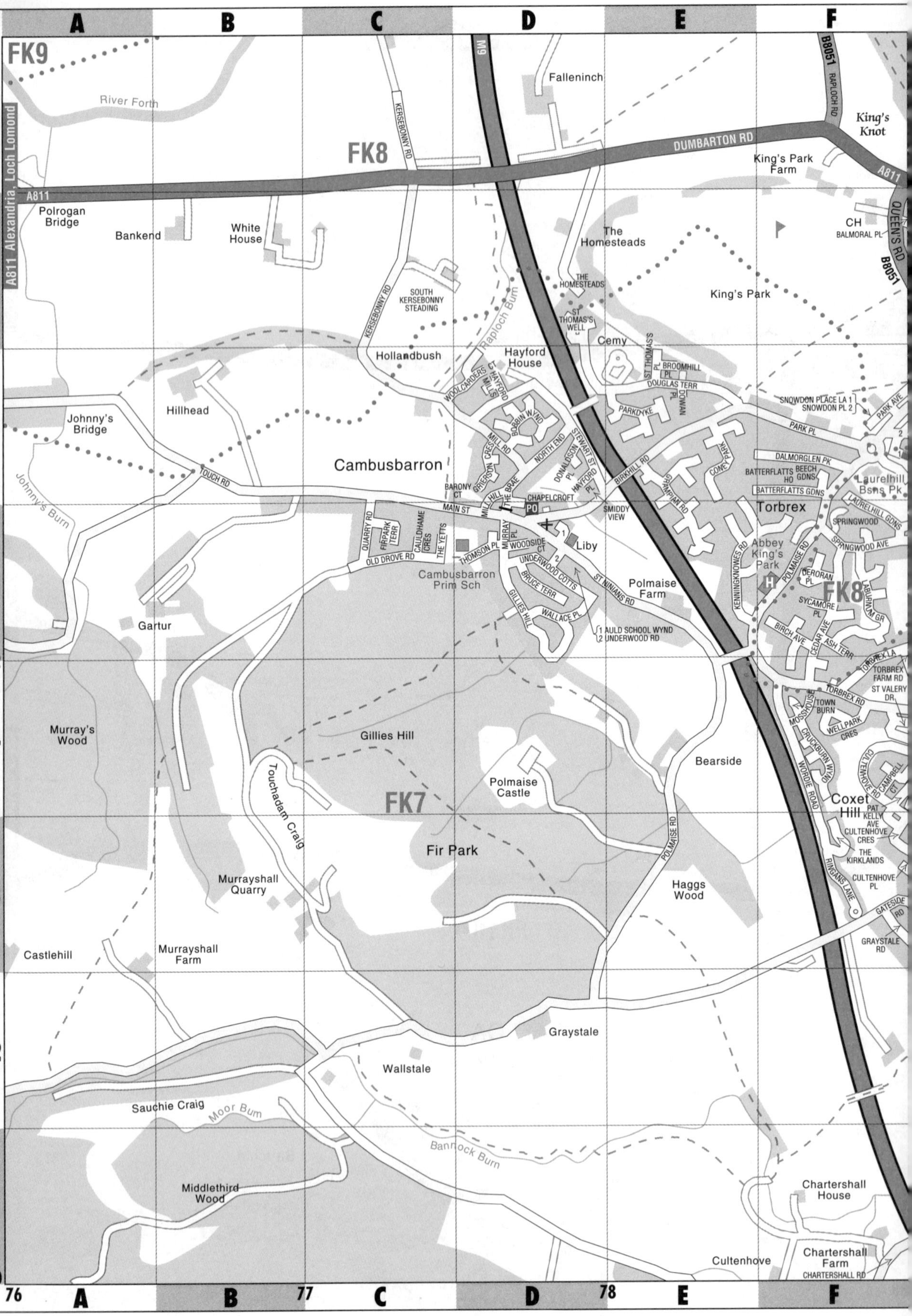
A
B
C
D
E
F
FK9
FK8
FK7
River Forth
A811 Alexandria, Loch Lomond
A811
Polrogan Bridge
Bankend
White House
KERSEBONNY RD
DUMBARTON RD
M9
Falleninch
B8051
RAPLOCH RD
King's Knot
King's Park Farm
QUEEN'S RD
CH
BALMORAL PL
The Homesteads
THE HOMESTEADS
King's Park
SOUTH KERSEBONNY STEADING
ST THOMAS'S WELL
Raploch Burn
Cemy
Hollandbush
Hayford House
ST THOMAS'S PL
BROOMHILL PL
DOUGLAS TERR
DOWAN PL
SNOWDON PLACE LA 1
SNOWDON PL 2
PARK AVE
PARK PL
PARKDYKE
WOOLCARDERS CT
MILLS
HAYFORD
BOBBIN WYND
MILL RD
NORTH END
STEWART ST
DONALDSON PL
Hillhead
Johnny's Bridge
Johnny's Burn
TOUCH RD
Cambusbarron
GRIERSON CRES
MILL HILL
THE BRAE
BARONY CT
MAIN ST
CHAPELCROFT
PO
HAYFORD PL
BIRKHILL RD
SMIDDY VIEW
GRAMPIAN RD
CONEY PARK
DALMORGLEN PK
BATTERFLATTS HO
BEECH GDNS
BATTERFLATTS GDNS
Laurelhill Bsns Pk
LAURELHILL GDNS
Torbrex
SPRINGWOOD
SPRINGWOOD AVE
QUARRY RD
FIRPARK TERR
CAULDHAME CRES
THE YETTS
THOMSON PL
MURRAY PL
WOODSIDE CT
Liby
OLD DROVE RD
UNDERWOOD COTTS
BRUCE TERR
Cambusbarron Prim Sch
GILLIES HILL
WALLACE PL
ST NINIANS RD
Polmaise Farm
1 AULD SCHOOL WYND
2 UNDERWOOD RD
KENNINGKNOWES RD
Abbey King's Park
POLMAISE RD
DERORAN PL
SYCAMORE PL
LABURNUM GR
BIRCH AVE
CEDAR AVE
ASH TERR
TORBREX LA
TORBREX FARM RD
ST VALERY DR
TORBREX RD
TOWN BURN
MOSSHOUSE
WELLPARK CRES
CRUICKBURN WYND
CULTENHOVE RD
CAMPBELL CT
Gartur
Murray's Wood
Gillies Hill
Touchadam Craig
Polmaise Castle
Bearside
WORDIE ROAD
Coxet Hill
PAT KELLY AVE
CULTENHOVE CRES
THE KIRKLANDS
CULTENHOVE PL
RINGANS LANE
Fir Park
POLMAISE RD
Haggs Wood
Murrayshall Quarry
GATESIDE RD
GRAYSTALE RD
Castlehill
Murrayshall Farm
Graystale
Wallstale
Sauchie Craig
Moor Burn
Bannock Burn
Middlethird Wood
Chartershall House
Cultenhove
Chartershall Farm
CHARTERSHALL RD
76
77
78
8
7
93
6
5
92
4
3
91
2
1
90

A8
1 ESPLANADE
2 UPPER CASTLEHILL
3 KINGSTABLES LA
4 CASTLE WYND
5 ST MARY'S WYND
6 BANK ST

B7
1 CORN EXCHANGE RD
2 BACK WLK
3 THE CRAWFORD SH ARC
4 THISTLE CHAMBERS
5 ORCHARDCROFT
6 CASTLEGAIT
7 BASTION WYND
8 THE MARCHES
9 CAMERONIAN ST
10 ALLAN PARK HO

B8
1 WALLACE ST
2 COWANE ST
3 VIEWFIELD PL
4 VIEWFIELD ST
5 SEAFORTH PL
6 MAXWELL PL
7 STATION RD

2
8

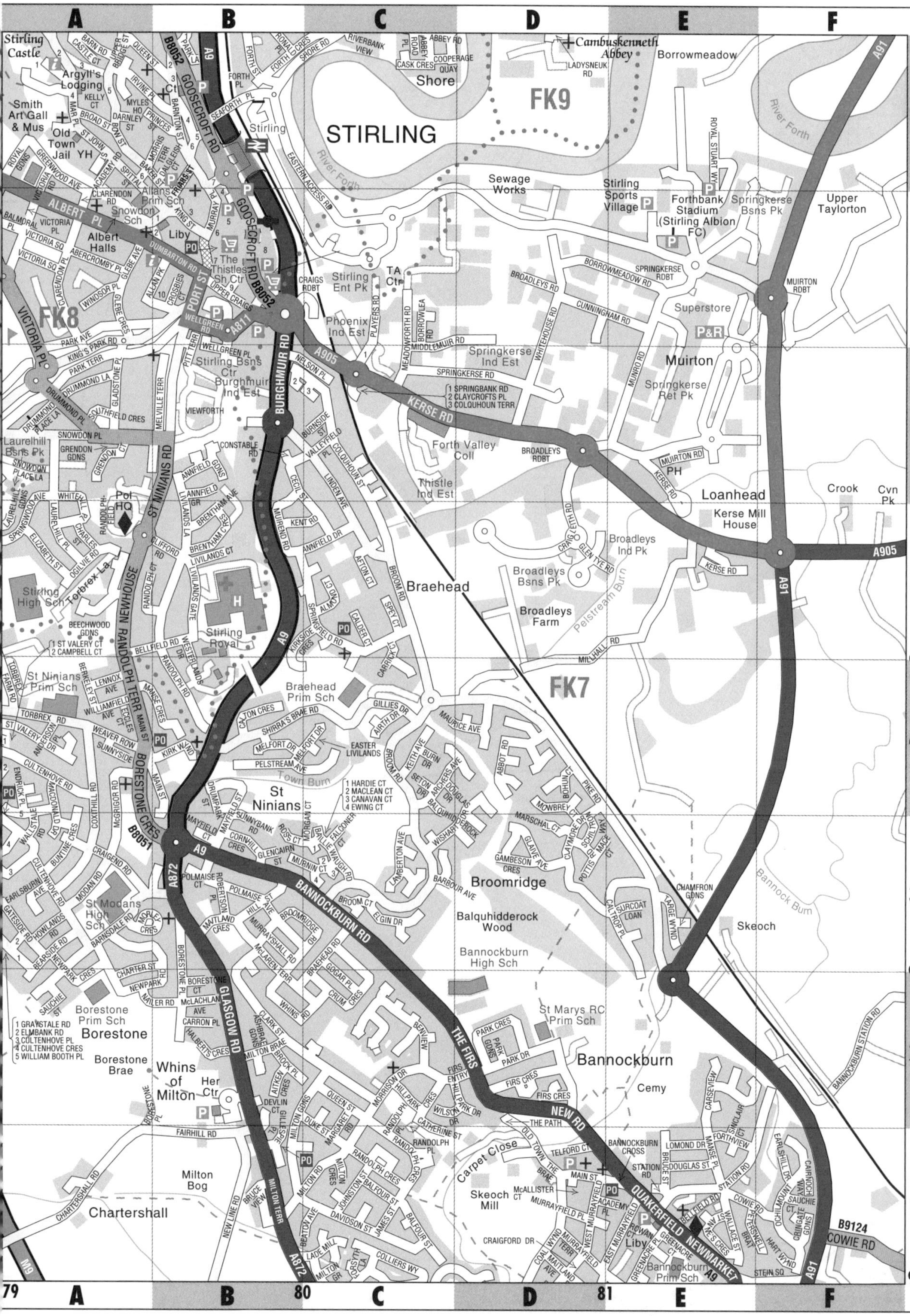

11
8

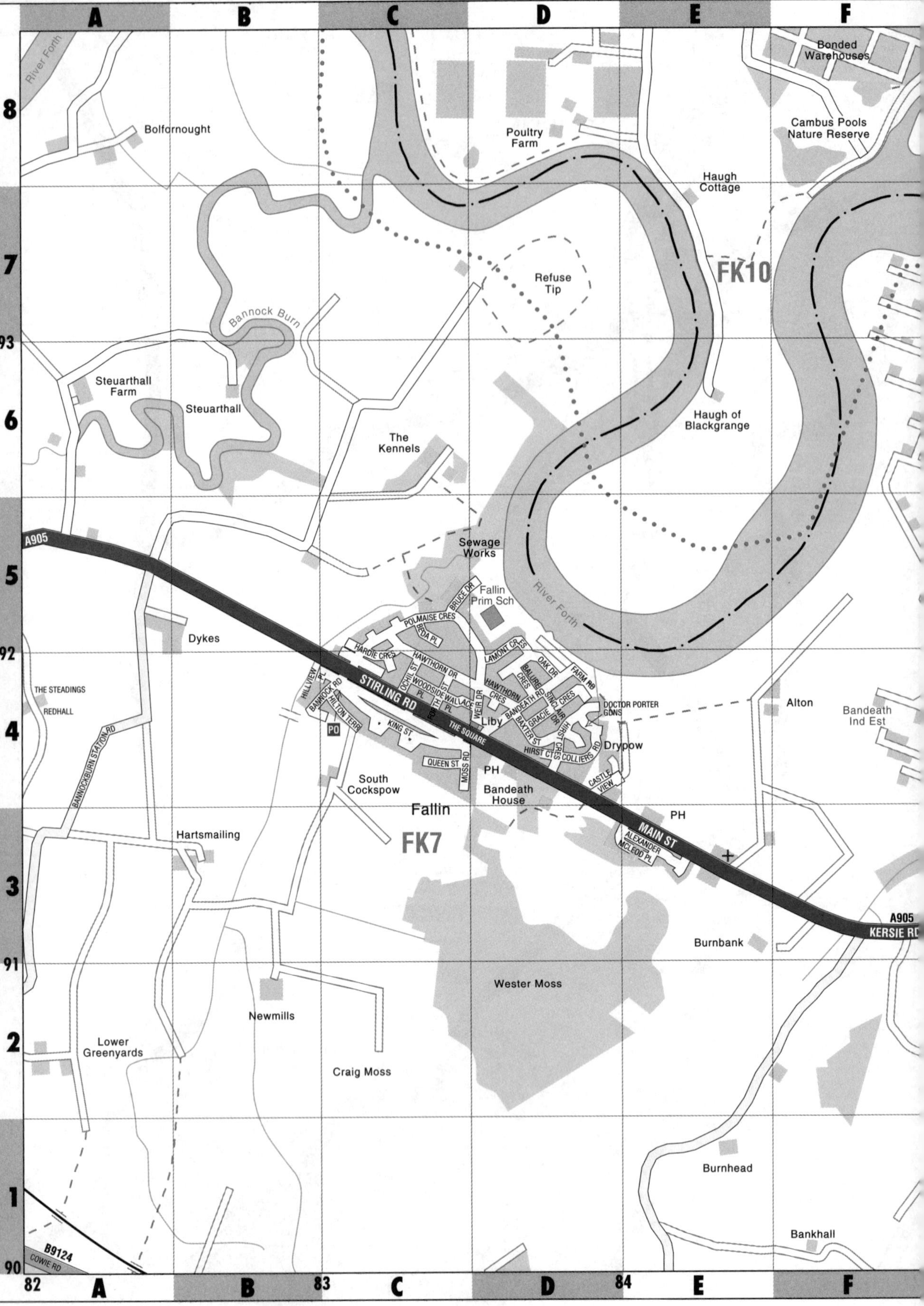
A
B
C
D
E
F
8
7
93
6
5
92
4
3
91
2
1
90
82
83
84
River Forth
Bolfornought
Poultry Farm
Bonded Warehouses
Cambus Pools Nature Reserve
Haugh Cottage
FK10
Refuse Tip
Bannock Burn
Steuarthall Farm
Steuarthall
Haugh of Blackgrange
The Kennels
Sewage Works
A905
Fallin Prim Sch
River Forth
Dykes
POLMAISE CRES
BRUCE DR
BEDA PL
HARDIE CRES
HAWTHORN DR
LAMONT CRES
OAK DR
FARM RD
BALURE CRES
THE STEADINGS
REDHALL
HILLVIEW PL
BANNOCK RD
HILTON TERR
OCHIL ST
WOODSIDE PL
WALLACE PL
STIRLING RD
FORTH ST
WEIR DR
HAWTHORN CRES
BANDEATH RD
GRACIE DR
SINCLAIR CRES
DOCTOR PORTER GDNS
Alton
Bandeath Ind Est
PO
KING ST
THE SQUARE
Liby
BAXTER ST
HIRST CRES
Drypow
BANNOCKBURN STATION RD
QUEEN ST
MOSS RD
HIRST CT
COLLIERS RD
PH
South Cockspow
Bandeath House
CASTLE VIEW
Fallin
PH
Hartsmailing
FK7
MAIN ST
ALEXANDER MCLEOD PL
A905
KERSIE RD
Burnbank
Wester Moss
Newmills
Lower Greenyards
Craig Moss
Burnhead
Bankhall
B9124
COWIE RD

4
10

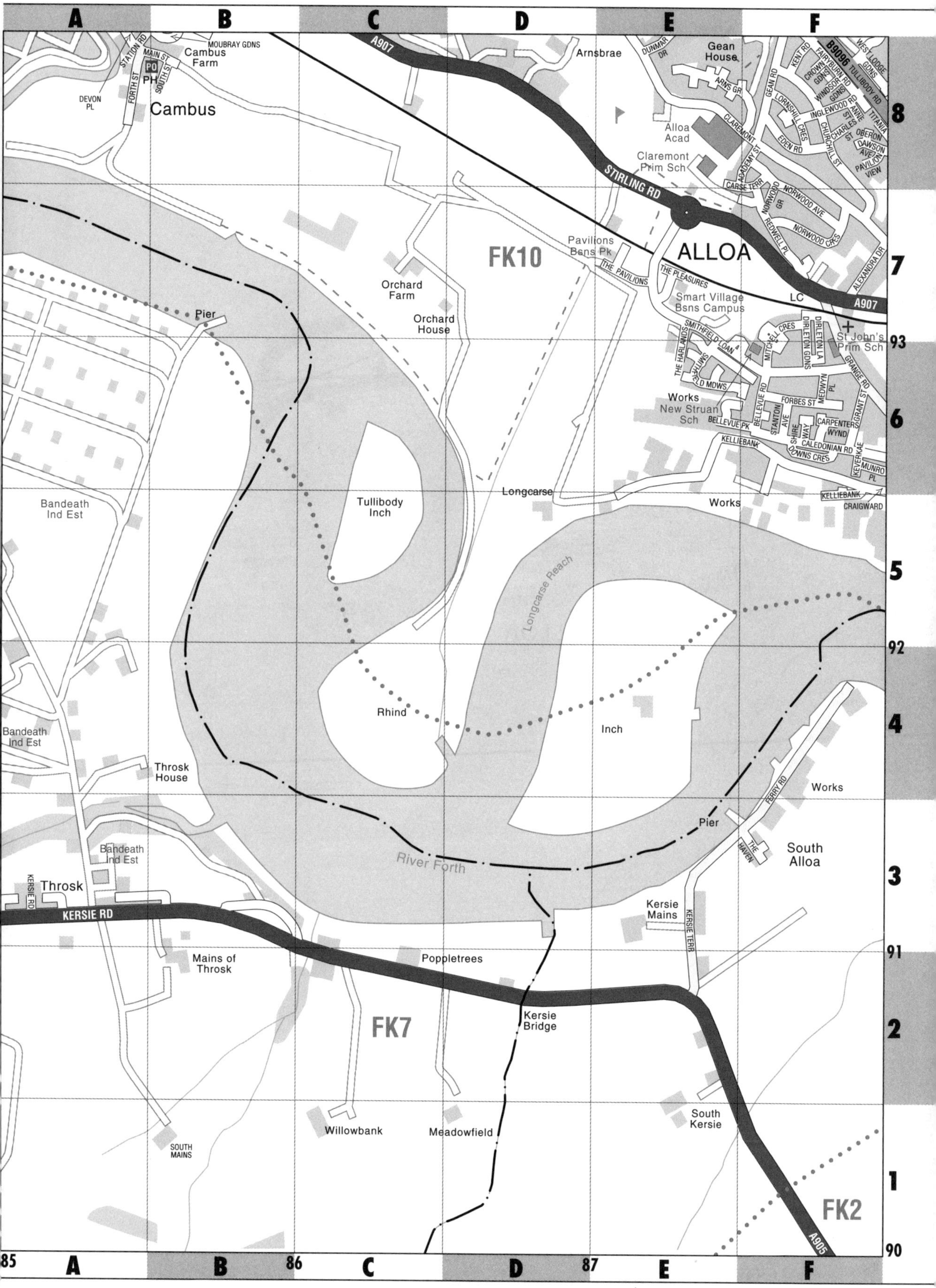
A
B
C
D
E
F
Cambus Farm
MOUBRAY GDNS
STATION RD
MAIN ST
SOUTH ST
FORTH ST
PO
PH
DEVON PL
Cambus
A907
Arnsbrae
DUNMAR DR
Gean House
ARNS GR
Alloa Acad
CLAREMONT
Claremont Prim Sch
STIRLING RD
ACADEMY ST
CARSE TERR
NORWOOD GR
NORWOOD AVE
NORWOOD CRES
REDWELL PL
GEAN RD
KENT RD
LORNSHILL CRES
EDEN RD
CHURCHILL ST
B9096
TULLIBODY RD
WEST LODGE GDNS
FAIRBURN RD
CROWN GDNS
WINDSOR GDNS
INGLEWOOD RD
ST ANNE
ST CHARLES
OBERON
DAWSON AVE
PAVILION VIEW
TITANIA
ALEXANDRA DR
Pavilions Bsns Pk
THE PAVILIONS
FK10
ALLOA
THE PLEASURES
Smart Village Bsns Campus
LC
A907
Orchard Farm
Orchard House
Pier
SMITHFIELD LOAN
THE HARLANDS
MITCHELL CRES
DIRLETON GDNS
DIRLETON LA
St John's Prim Sch
GRANGE RD
LD MDWS
Works
New Struan Sch
BELLEVUE RD
BELLEVUE PK
FORBES ST
MEDWYN PL
STANTON AVE
SHIRE WAY
CARPENTERS WYND
GRANT ST
CALEDONIAN RD
DOWNS CRES
KELLIEBANK
KEVERKAE
MUNRO PL
Tullibody Inch
Longcarse
Works
KELLIEBANK
CRAIGWARD
Bandeath Ind Est
Longcarse Reach
Rhind
Inch
Bandeath Ind Est
Throsk House
FERRY RD
Works
Pier
THE HAVEN
South Alloa
Bandeath Ind Est
River Forth
Throsk
KERSIE RD
KERSIE RD
Kersie Mains
KERSIE TERR
Mains of Throsk
Poppletrees
FK7
Kersie Bridge
Willowbank
Meadowfield
South Kersie
SOUTH MAINS
FK2
A905
8
7
93
6
5
92
4
3
91
2
1
90
85
86
87

13
10

B6
1 BURGH MEWS
2 MERCAT WYND
3 STRIPEHEAD
4 UNION ST
5 BREWHOUSE CT
6 WEST VENNEL
7 CANDLERIGGS CT
8 THE CROSS
9 TOWNHEAD APARTMENTS
10 MAPLE CT
11 OLD BRIDGE ST
12 JUNCTION PL
13 BRIDGE TERR

9

B7
1 Sunnyside Prim Sch

5

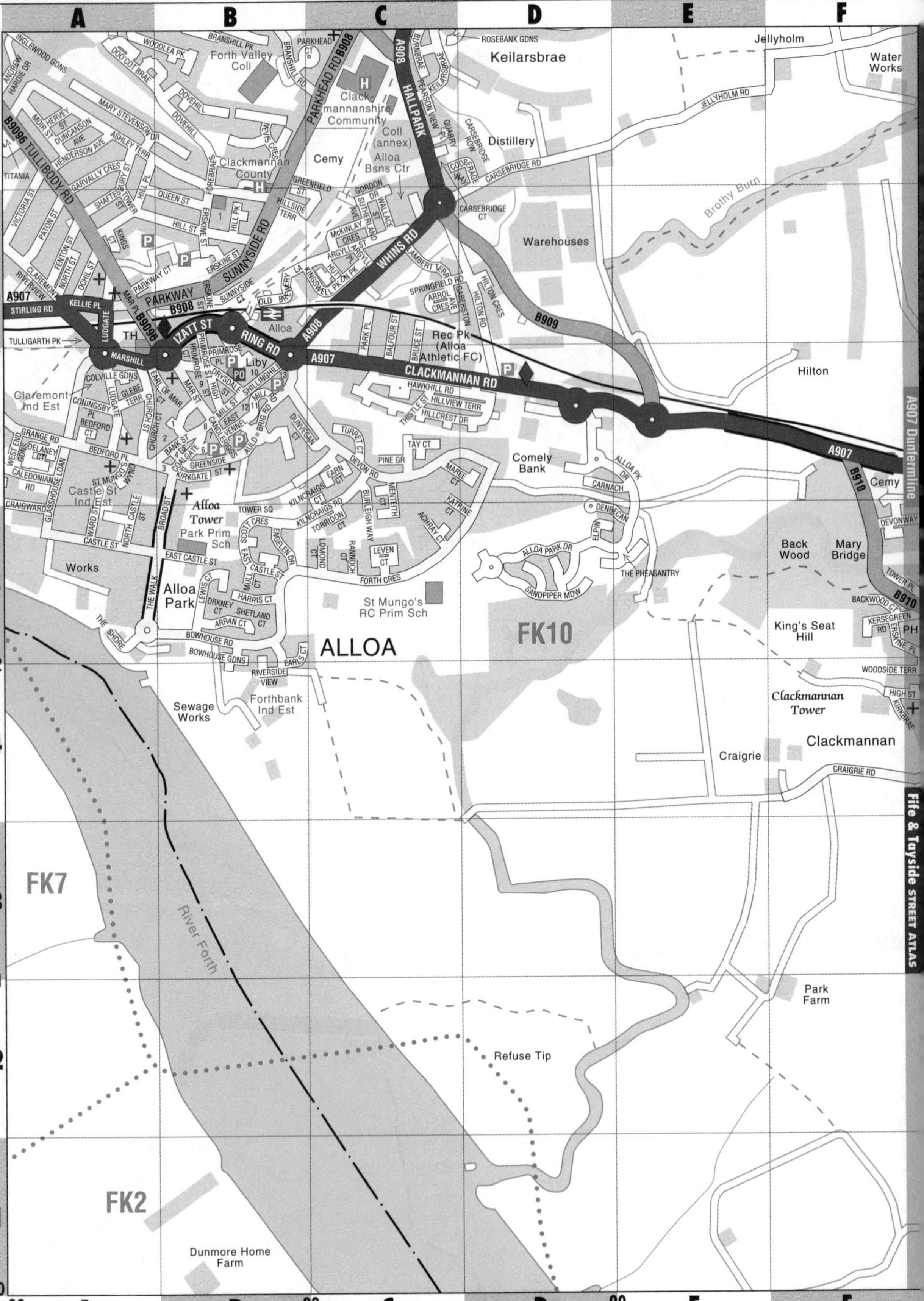

9

14

7
12

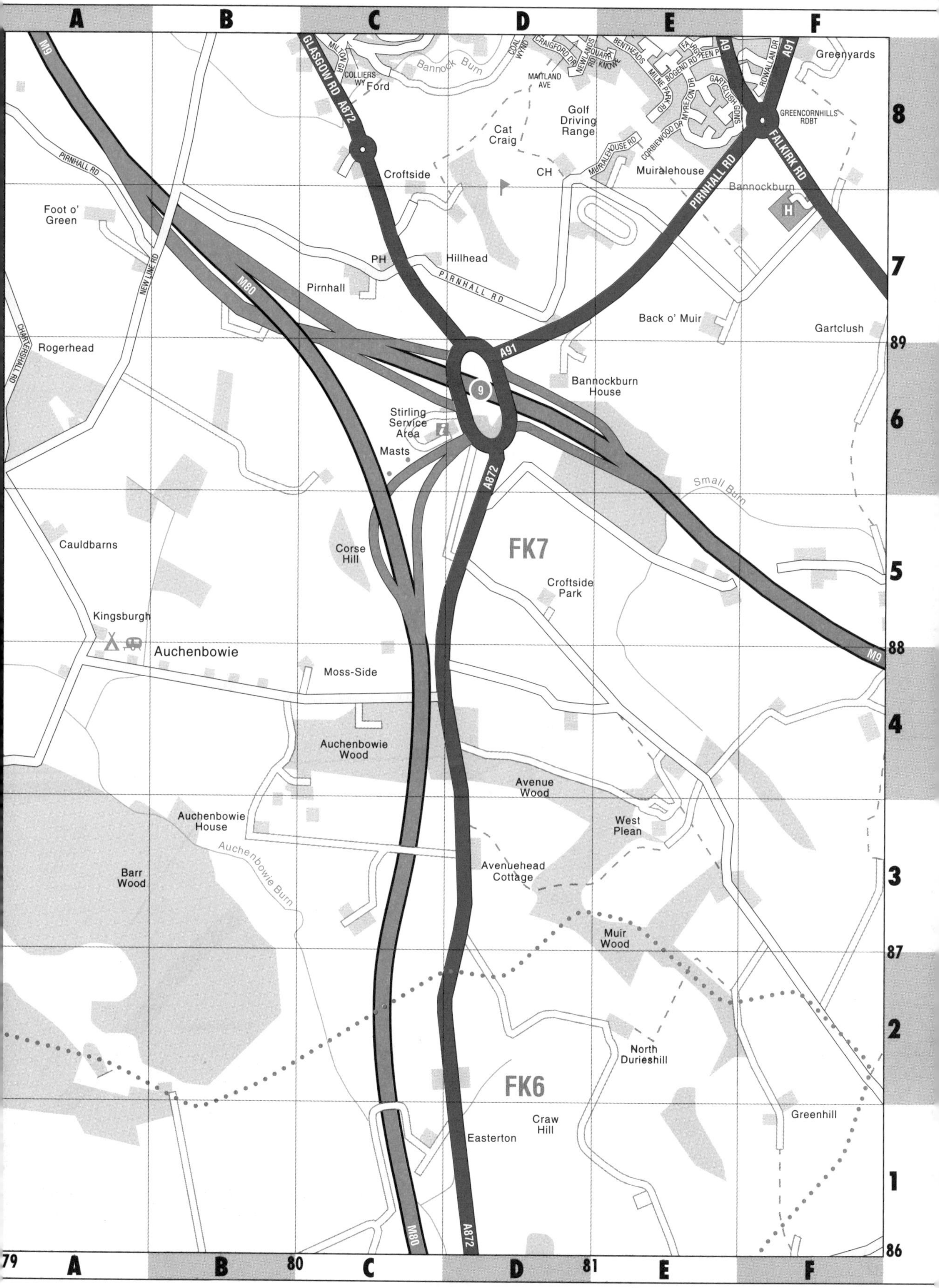
A
B
C
D
E
F
M9
GLASGOW RD
A872
Bannock Burn
COLLIERS WY
Ford
COAL WYND
CRAIGFORD DR
NEWLANDS RD
SQUARE KNOWE
BENTHEADS
MILNE PARK RD
BOGEND RD
MYRETON DR
GARTCLUSH GDNS
A9
ROWALLAN DR
A91
Greenyards
MAITLAND AVE
Golf Driving Range
Cat Craig
GREENCORNHILLS RDBT
FALKIRK RD
CORBIEWOOD DR
MURALEHOUSE RD
Muiralehouse
PIRNHALL RD
Croftside
CH
Bannockburn
Foot o' Green
NEW LINE RD
PH
Hillhead
Pirnhall
M80
Back o' Muir
Gartclush
CHARTERSHALL RD
Rogerhead
Bannockburn House
Stirling Service Area
Masts
Small Burn
Cauldbarns
Corse Hill
FK7
Croftside Park
Kingsburgh
Auchenbowie
Moss-Side
Auchenbowie Wood
Avenue Wood
West Plean
Auchenbowie House
Auchenbowie Burn
Barr Wood
Avenuehead Cottage
Muir Wood
North Durieshill
FK6
Craw Hill
Easterton
Greenhill
8
7
89
6
5
88
4
3
87
2
1
86
79
80
81

21
12

11
8

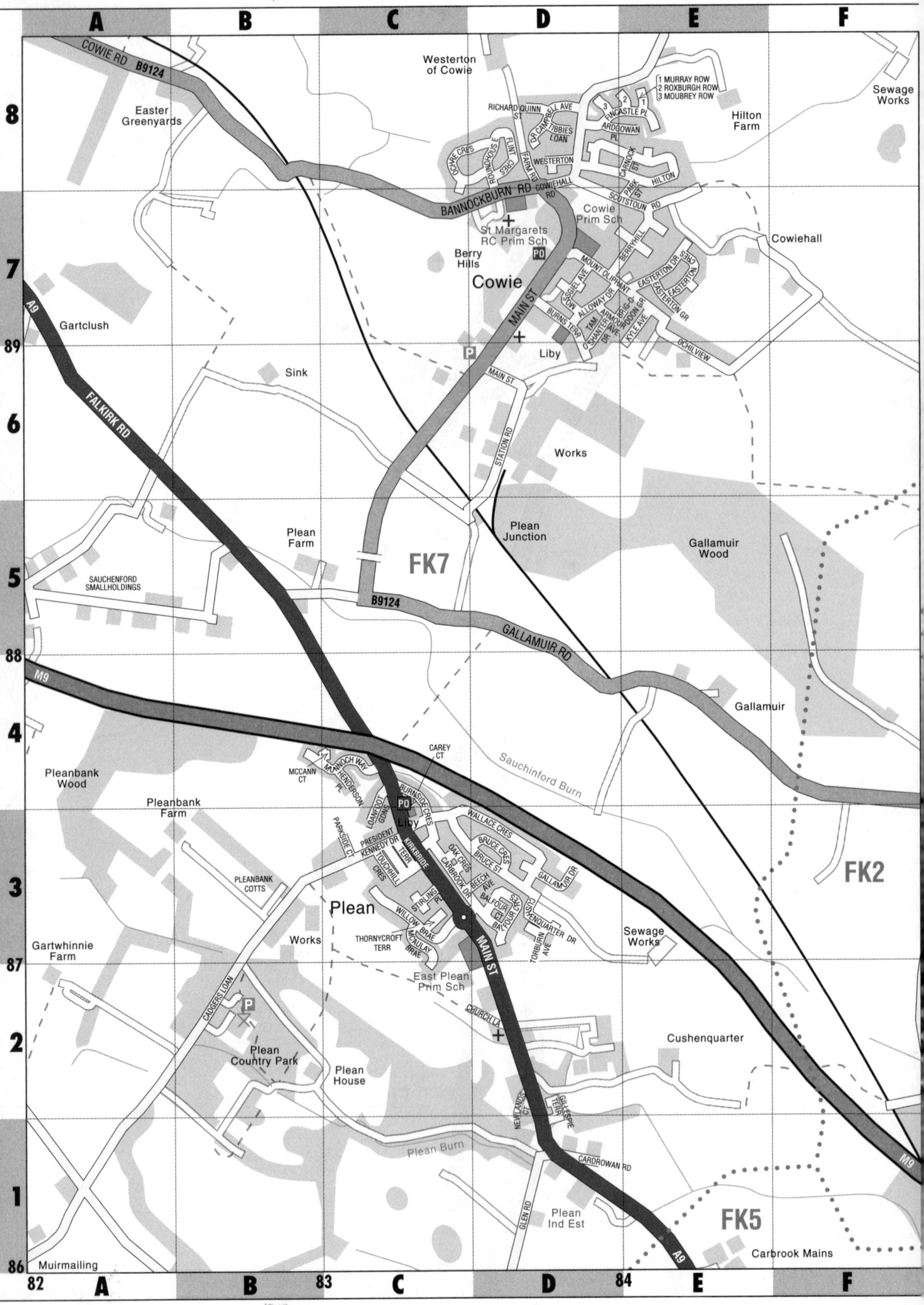
A
B
C
D
E
F
8
7
89
6
5
88
4
3
87
2
1
86
82
83
84
COWIE RD
B9124
Easter Greenyards
Westerton of Cowie
1 MURRAY ROW
2 ROXBURGH ROW
3 MOUBREY ROW
Sewage Works
Hilton Farm
RICHARD QUINN ST
DR CAMPBELL AVE
FINCASTLE PL
ARDGOWAN PL
TIBBIES LOAN
OCHRE CRES
ROUNDHOUSE
FLINT CRES
FARM RD
WESTERTON
CARNOCK ST
HILTON
PARK ST
COWIEHALL RD
BANNOCKBURN RD
SCOTSTOUN RD
Cowie Prim Sch
St Margarets RC Prim Sch
Berry Hills
Cowie
Cowiehall
BERRYHILL
MOUNT OLIPHANT
EASTERTON DR
EASTERTON CRES
EASTERTON GR
ALLOWAY DR
BURNS TERR
MAIN ST
TAM O SHANTER DR
ARMOUR AVE
BRIG-O-DOON GR
KYLE AVE
OCHILVIEW
Gartclush
Sink
Liby
MAIN ST
A9
FALKIRK RD
STATION RD
Works
Plean Junction
Plean Farm
FK7
Gallamuir Wood
SAUCHENFORD SMALLHOLDINGS
B9124
GALLAMUIR RD
Gallamuir
M9
Pleanbank Wood
Pleanbank Farm
CAREY CT
MCCANN CT
HENDERSON PL
Sauchinford Burn
BURNSIDE CRES
LOANFOOT GDNS
Liby
WALLACE CRES
PARKSIDE CT
PRESIDENT KENNEDY DR
KIRKBRIDE TERR
BRUCE CRES
BRUCE ST
OAK CRES
CARBROOK DR
BEECH AVE
GALLAMUIR DR
FK2
PLEANBANK COTTS
TOUCHHILL CRES
STIRLING PL
BALFOUR CT
BALFOUR CRES
Plean
WILLOW BRAE
CUSHENQUARTER DR
Works
THORNYCROFT TERR
MCAULAY BRAE
MAIN ST
TORBURN AVE
Sewage Works
Gartwhinnie Farm
East Plean Prim Sch
CADGERS LOAN
CHURCH LA
Cushenquarter
Plean Country Park
Plean House
NEWLANDS CT
GILLESPIE TERR
Plean Burn
CARDROWAN RD
M9
GLEN RD
Plean Ind Est
FK5
A9
Carbrook Mains
Muirmailing

11
22

9
14

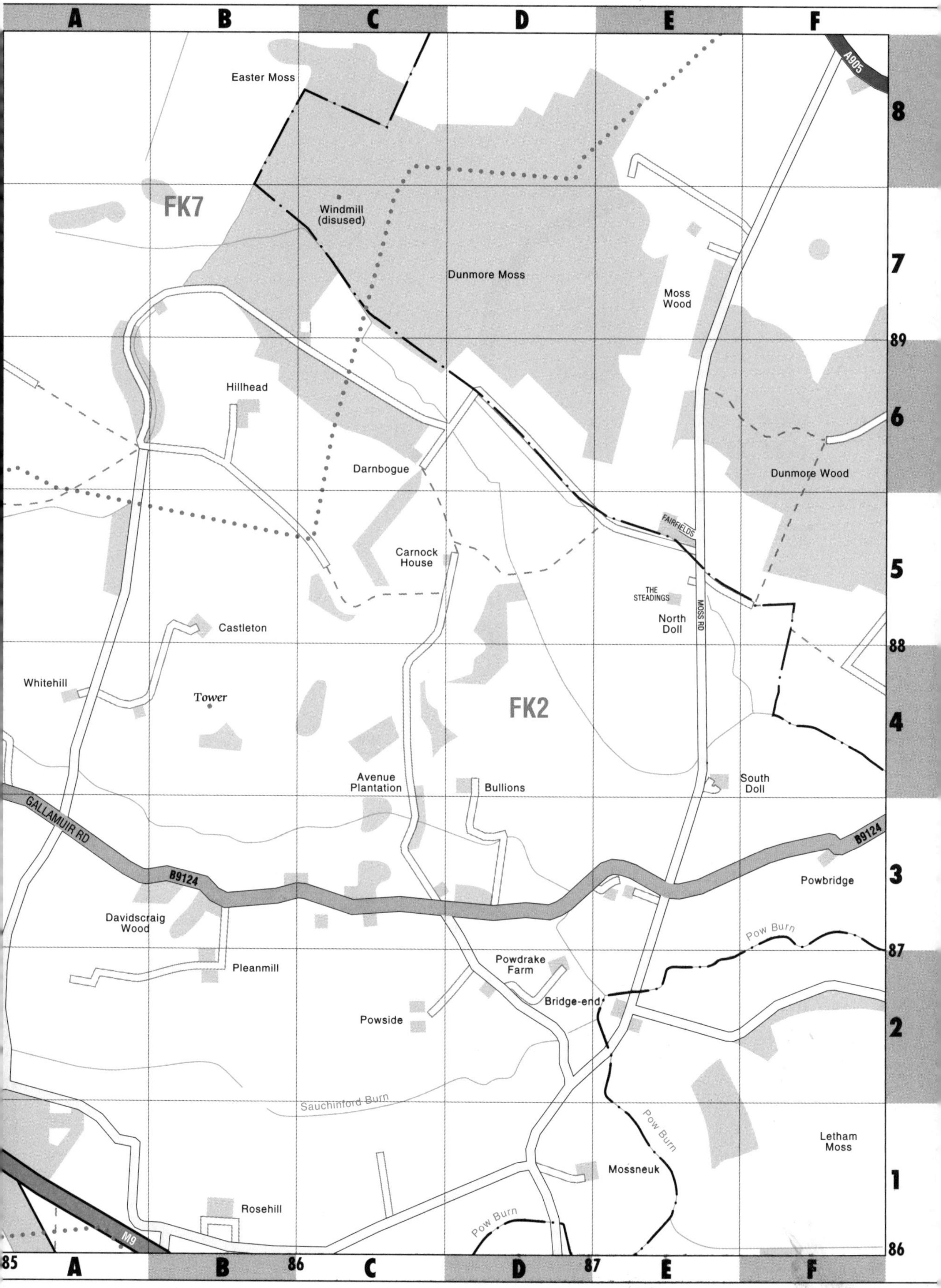
A
B
C
D
E
F
8
7
89
6
5
88
4
3
87
2
1
86
85
86
87
A905
Easter Moss
FK7
Windmill
(disused)
Dunmore Moss
Moss
Wood
Hillhead
Darnbogue
Dunmore Wood
FAIRFIELDS
Carnock
House
THE
STEADINGS
North
Doll
MOSS RD
Castleton
Whitehill
Tower
FK2
Avenue
Plantation
Bullions
South
Doll
GALLAMUIR RD
B9124
B9124
Powbridge
Davidscraig
Wood
Pow Burn
Pleanmill
Powdrake
Farm
Bridge-end
Powside
Sauchinford Burn
Pow Burn
Letham
Moss
Mossneuk
Rosehill
Pow Burn
M9

23
14

13
10

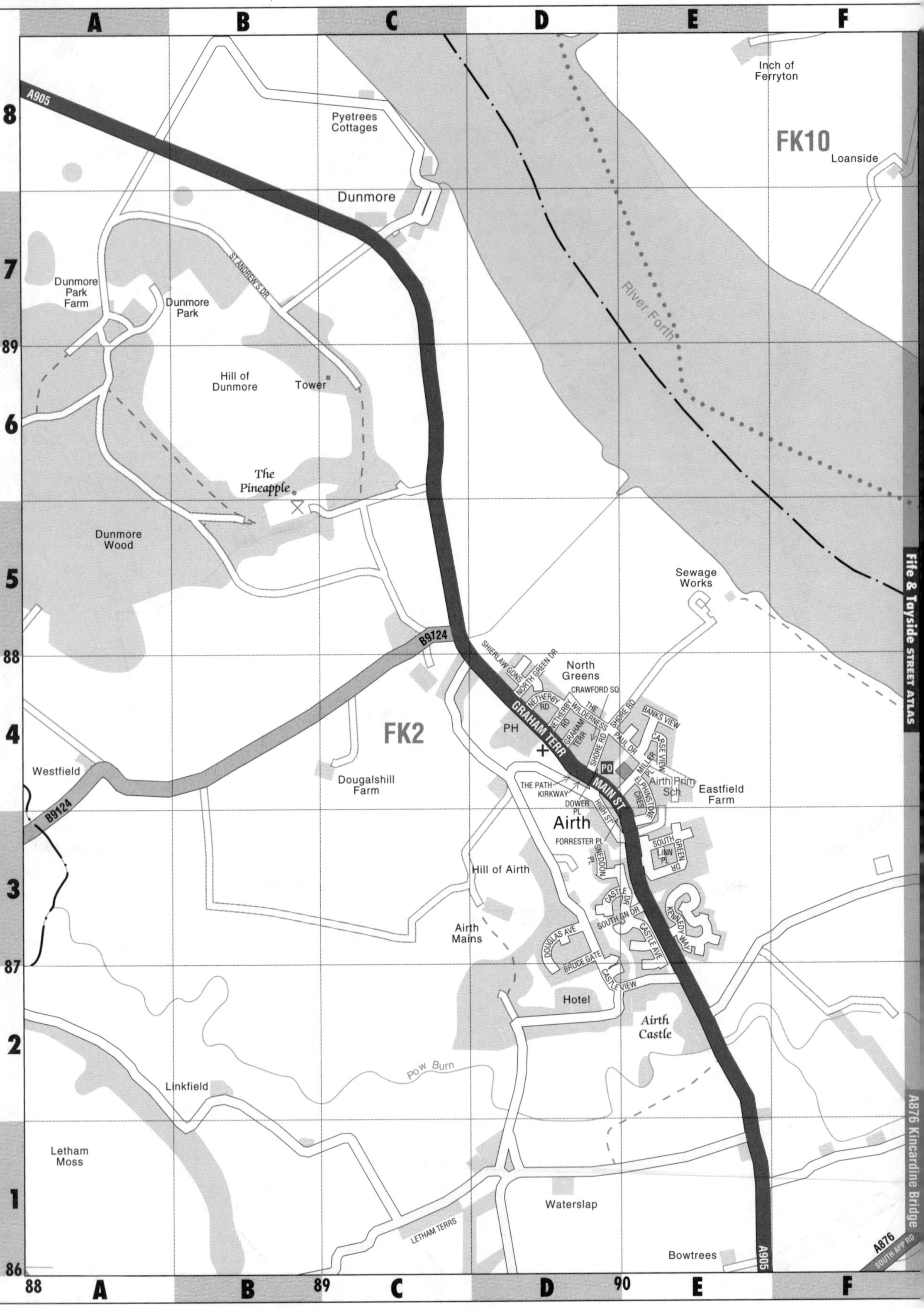
A
B
C
D
E
F
8
7
89
6
5
88
4
3
87
2
1
86
88
89
90
A905
Pyetrees Cottages
Dunmore
Inch of Ferryton
FK10
Loanside
ST ANDREW'S DR
Dunmore Park Farm
Dunmore Park
Hill of Dunmore
Tower
River Forth
The Pineapple
Dunmore Wood
Sewage Works
B9124
SHIERLAW GDNS
NORTH GREEN DR
North Greens
CRAWFORD SQ
NETHERBY RD
THE WILDERNESS
SHORE RD
BANKS VIEW
GRAHAM TERR
PAUL DR
CARSE VIEW
MILLER PL
PH
FK2
PO
MAIN ST
Airth Prim Sch
Eastfield Farm
Westfield
Dougalshill Farm
THE PATH
KIRKWAY
DOWER PL
HIGH ST
ELPHINSTONE CRES
Airth
FORRESTER PL
SOUTH LINN PL
SOUTH GREEN DR
SNEDDON PL
Hill of Airth
CASTLE DR
SOUTH GN DR
KENNEDY WAY
Airth Mains
DOUGLAS AVE
CASTLE AVE
BRUCE GATE
CASTLE VIEW
Hotel
Airth Castle
Pow Burn
Linkfield
Letham Moss
Waterslap
LETHAM TERRS
Bowtrees
A876
SOUTH APP RD
Fife & Tayside STREET ATLAS
A876 Kincardine Bridge

13
24

16

A
B
C
D
E
F
8
7
85
6
5
84
4
3
83
2
1
82
25
26
27
A814 Garelochhead
A814
ARDGARE
QUEENS POINT
Croy
Blairvadach
BROOMFIELD GDNS
Aldownick Glen
Resrs
Letrualt Farm
G84
ALEXANDER PL
AROS RD
JUPITER PL
BEECH GR
SMUGGLER'S WAY
ARDEN HILL
ARDENCONNEL MEWS
EDEN GR
ARDENCONNEL HO
Rhu
QUARRY KNOWE
LINESIDE WLK
STATION RD
Torr
EMPRESS RD
ARDENCONNEL WAY
CUMBERLAND RD
UPPER HALL RD
HALL RD
CUMBERLAND TERR
SCHOOL RD
Liby
INCHGOWER GR
GLEBEFIELD RD
STATION RD
TORR CRES
LAGGARY RD
1 BRAEHEAD PL
2 CALDWELL PL
Pier
Yacht Club
Rhu Prim Sch
CHURCH RD
PO
ARDWELL PL
MANSE BRAE
BARGE CT
MANSE PL
GUTHRIE PL
LAGGARY PK
SPY'S LA
GLENARN RD
UPPER TORWOODHILL RD
GLENORAN RD
CHURCH PL 1
BRAEHOUSE 2
RHU-ELLEN CT 3
WATERSEDGE CT 4
Gare Loch
ROWMORE QUAYS
PIER RD
WOODSTONE CT
ARTARMAN RD
ARMADALE RD
TORWOODHILL RD
TORWOODHILL PL
TORWOODHILL
Tor Wood
Rhu Bay
GARELOCH RD
B833
Stroul Bay
Jetty
Limekiln Point
Works
Rosneath Prim Sch
COURT HILL
Clachan Burn
HOWIE CRES
CLACHAN RD
MAIN RD
ST MODAN'S WAY
FERRY RD
GARE RD
1 NAVY WAY
2 PRINCESS WAY
Rosneath
THE CLACHAN
PO
CEDAR VIEW
A-MHOID
TOM-THE LOCHANS
ARGYLL RD
CAMSAIL RD
ROSNEATH RD
Marina
IRB Sta
RHU RD HIGHER
A814
RHU RD LOWER
DALMORE CRES 1
CUMBERLAND AVE 2
KIDSTON DR 3
Cairndhu Point
P
Broom Plantation
Clachan Glen
Clachan Burn
G84
Clachan Farm
Pier
Rosneath Bay
Castle Point
Castle Bay
Hill of Camsail Plantation
Camsail Wood
Camsail Bay
Creag na Goibhre
Crane Rock
Dark Wood
Rosneath Castle Caravan Pk
B833

16

15

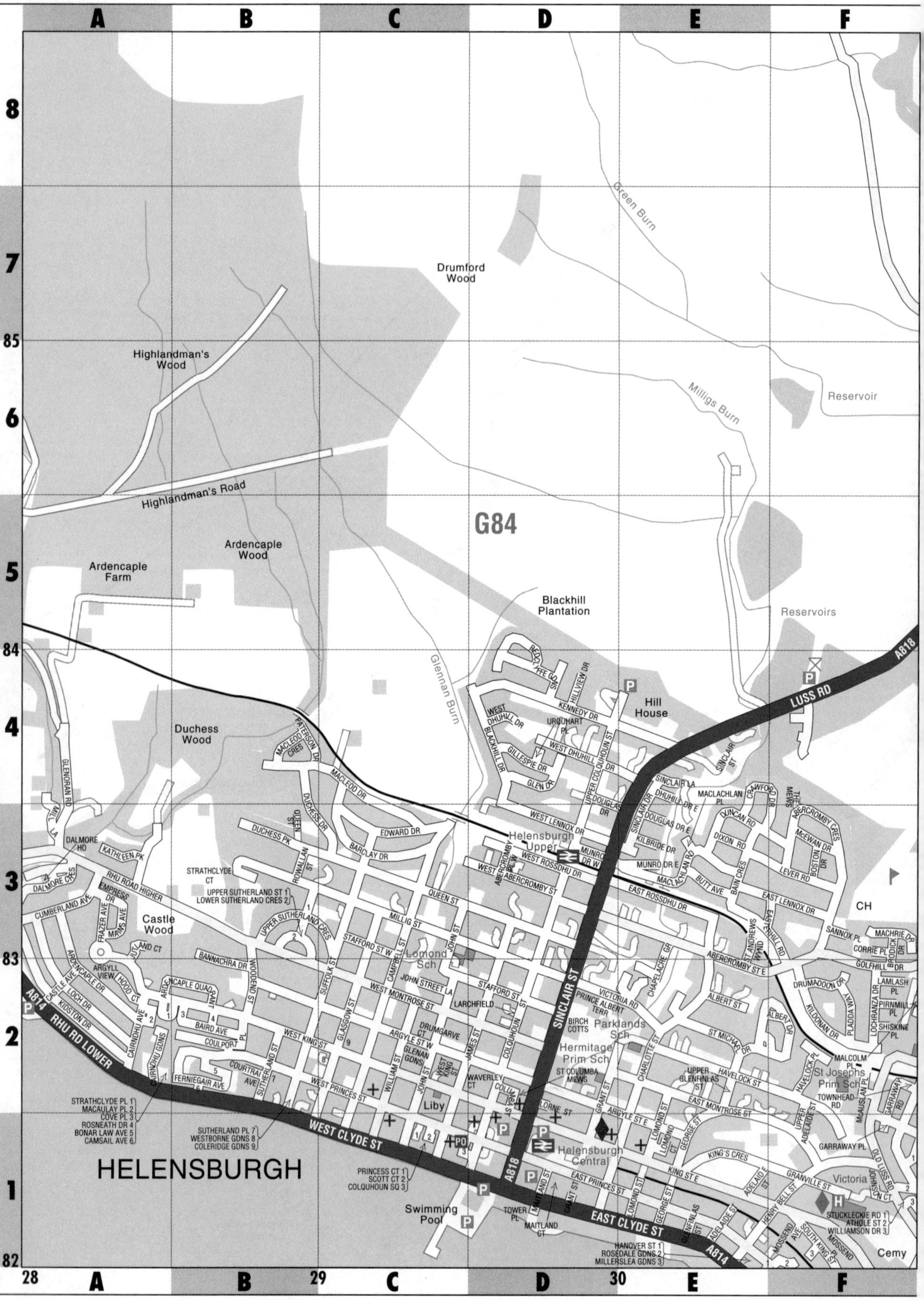

A
B
C
D
E
F
8
7
85
6
5
84
4
3
83
2
1
82
28
29
30
Drumford Wood
Green Burn
Highlandman's Wood
Millígs Burn
Reservoir
Highlandman's Road
G84
Ardencaple Wood
Ardencaple Farm
Blackhill Plantation
Reservoirs
Glennan Burn
Hill House
Duchess Wood
LUSS RD
A818
Helensburgh Upper
Castle Wood
Lomond Sch
Parklands Sch
Hermitage Prim Sch
St Josephs Prim Sch
CH
Liby
Helensburgh Central
Victoria
Swimming Pool
Cemy
HELENSBURGH
RHU RD LOWER
A814
WEST CLYDE ST
EAST CLYDE ST
SINCLAIR ST
RHU ROAD HIGHER
STRATHCLYDE PL 1
MACAULAY PL 2
COVE PL 3
ROSNEATH DR 4
BONAR LAW AVE 5
CAMSAIL AVE 6
SUTHERLAND PL 7
WESTBORNE GDNS 8
COLERIDGE GDNS 9
PRINCESS CT 1
SCOTT CT 2
COLQUHOUN SQ 3
HANOVER ST 1
ROSEDALE GDNS 2
MILLERSLEA GDNS 3
STUCKLECKIE RD 1
ATHOLE ST 2
WILLIAMSON DR 3
UPPER SUTHERLAND ST 1
LOWER SUTHERLAND CRES 2

18

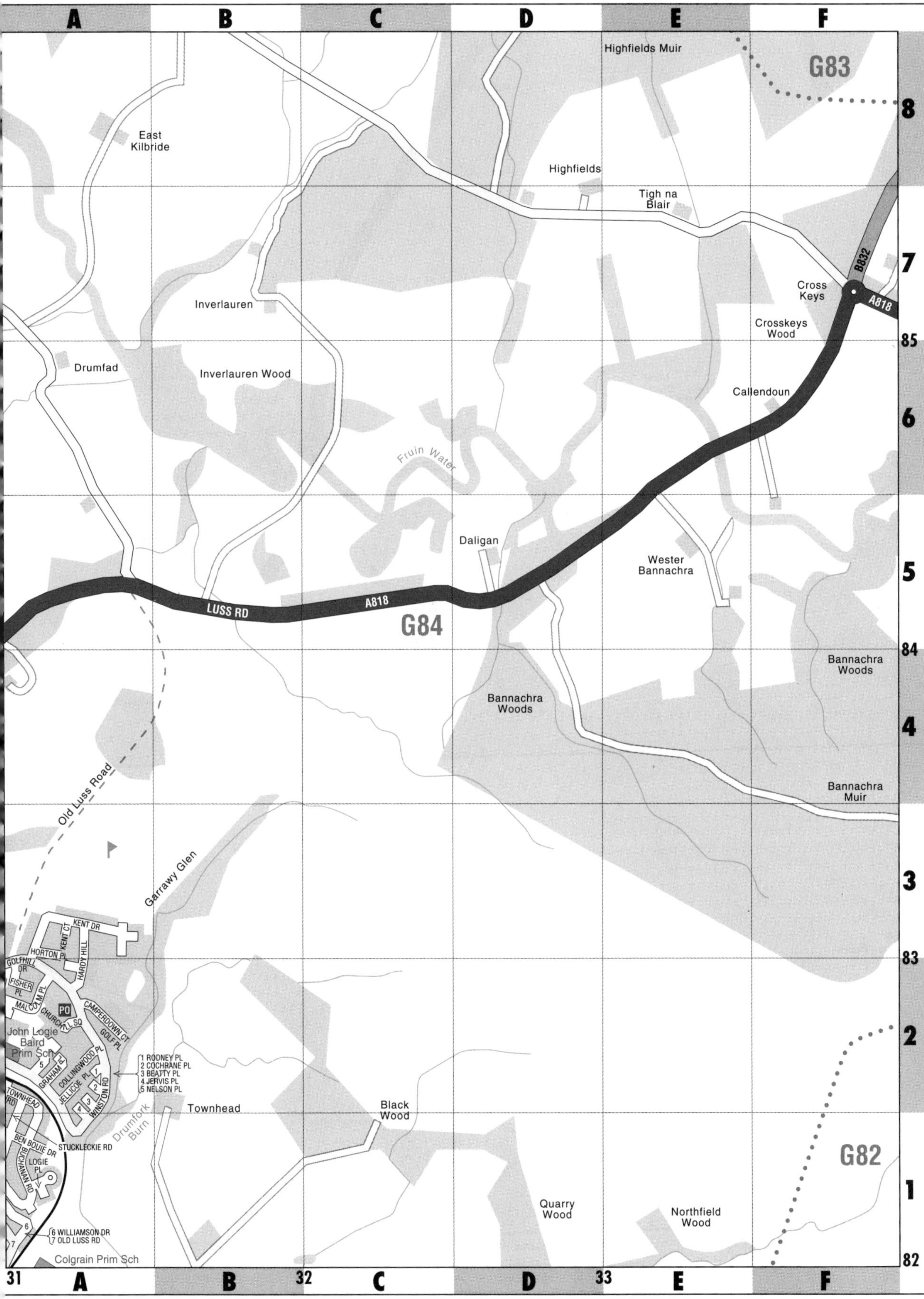
A
B
C
D
E
F
Highfields Muir
G83
8
East Kilbride
Highfields
Tigh na Blair
B832
7
Cross Keys
A818
Inverlauren
Crosskeys Wood
85
Drumfad
Inverlauren Wood
Callendoun
6
Fruin Water
Daligan
Wester Bannachra
5
LUSS RD
A818
G84
84
Bannachra Woods
Bannachra Woods
4
Bannachra Muir
Old Luss Road
Garrawy Glen
3
KENT DR
KENT CT
HORTON PL
HARDY HILL
GOLFHILL DR
FISHER PL
MALCOLM PL
83
PO
CHURCHILL SQ
CAMPERDOWN CT
GOLF PL
John Logie Baird Prim Sch
2
GRAHAM PL
COLLINGWOOD PL
JELLICOE PL
WINSTON RD
1 RODNEY PL
2 COCHRANE PL
3 BEATTY PL
4 JERVIS PL
5 NELSON PL
TOWNHEAD RD
Townhead
Drumfork Burn
Black Wood
BEN BOUIE DR
STUCKLECKIE RD
BUCHANAN RD
LOGIE PL
G82
1
Quarry Wood
Northfield Wood
6 WILLIAMSON DR
7 OLD LUSS RD
Colgrain Prim Sch
82
31
32
33

25
18

17

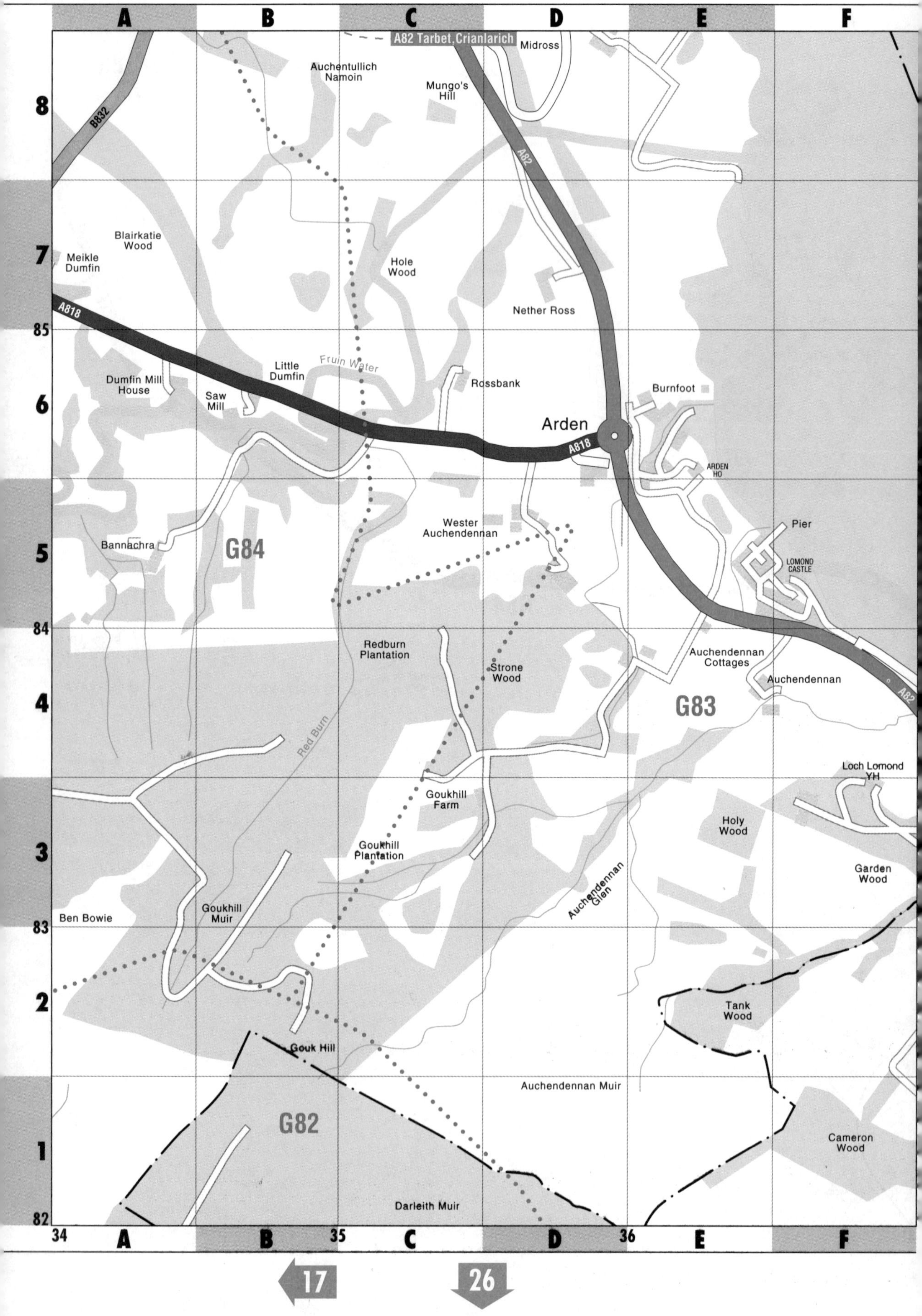
A
B
C
D
E
F
8
7
85
6
5
84
4
3
83
2
1
82
34
35
36
A82 Tarbet, Crianlarich
Midross
Auchentullich
Namoin
Mungo's
Hill
B832
A82
Blairkatie
Wood
Meikle
Dumfin
Hole
Wood
A818
Nether Ross
Little
Dumfin
Fruin Water
Dumfin Mill
House
Saw
Mill
Rossbank
Burnfoot
Arden
A818
ARDEN
HO
Wester
Auchendennan
Pier
Bannachra
G84
LOMOND
CASTLE
Redburn
Plantation
Strone
Wood
Auchendennan
Cottages
Auchendennan
G83
A82
Red Burn
Loch Lomond
YH
Goukhill
Farm
Holy
Wood
Goukhill
Plantation
Garden
Wood
Auchendennan
Glen
Goukhill
Muir
Ben Bowie
Tank
Wood
Gouk Hill
Auchendennan Muir
G82
Cameron
Wood
Darleith Muir

17

26

20

A B C D E F
Knockour Wood
Lorn
Knockour
Knockour Hill
Black Roundel
Boturich Castle
Meikle Boturich
Loch Lomond
Whinny Hill
Loch Lomond & The Trossachs National Park
Ledrishmore Wood
G83
Burn of Balloch
Over Balloch
Horsehouse Wood
Duck Bay
Stable Wood
Cameron Bay
Hotel
Balloch Castle
Cameron House Farm
Balloch Castle Country Park
Ledrishbeg
Balloch Pier
INCHFAD RD
INCHCONNACHAN AVE
TORRINCH DR
LEDRISH AVE
MOLLANBOWIE RD
CREINCH DR
INCHMURRIN CRES
INCHLONAIG DR
1 MCLEAN CRES
2 HARAN RD
3 SHANDON CRES
4 SHANDON BRAE
5 DUMBAIN RD
6 HALDANE TERR
OLD LUSS RD
Moss o' Balloch Plantations
Sea Life Loch Lomond
Loch Lomond Shores
River Leven
LORN DR
ENDRICK DR
Balloch
BOTURICH DR
PARK AVE
MOSSBURN AVE
BEN LOMOND WAY
PIER RD
CASTLE AVE
LAWRENCE DR
DRYMEN RD
A811
MAIN ST
LOMOND RD
McKENZIE DR
GALLACHER CRES
BALLOCH RD
INCHCRUIN
CLAIRINSH
A82
8 7 85 6 5 84 4 3 83 2 1 82
37 38 39

27

20

19

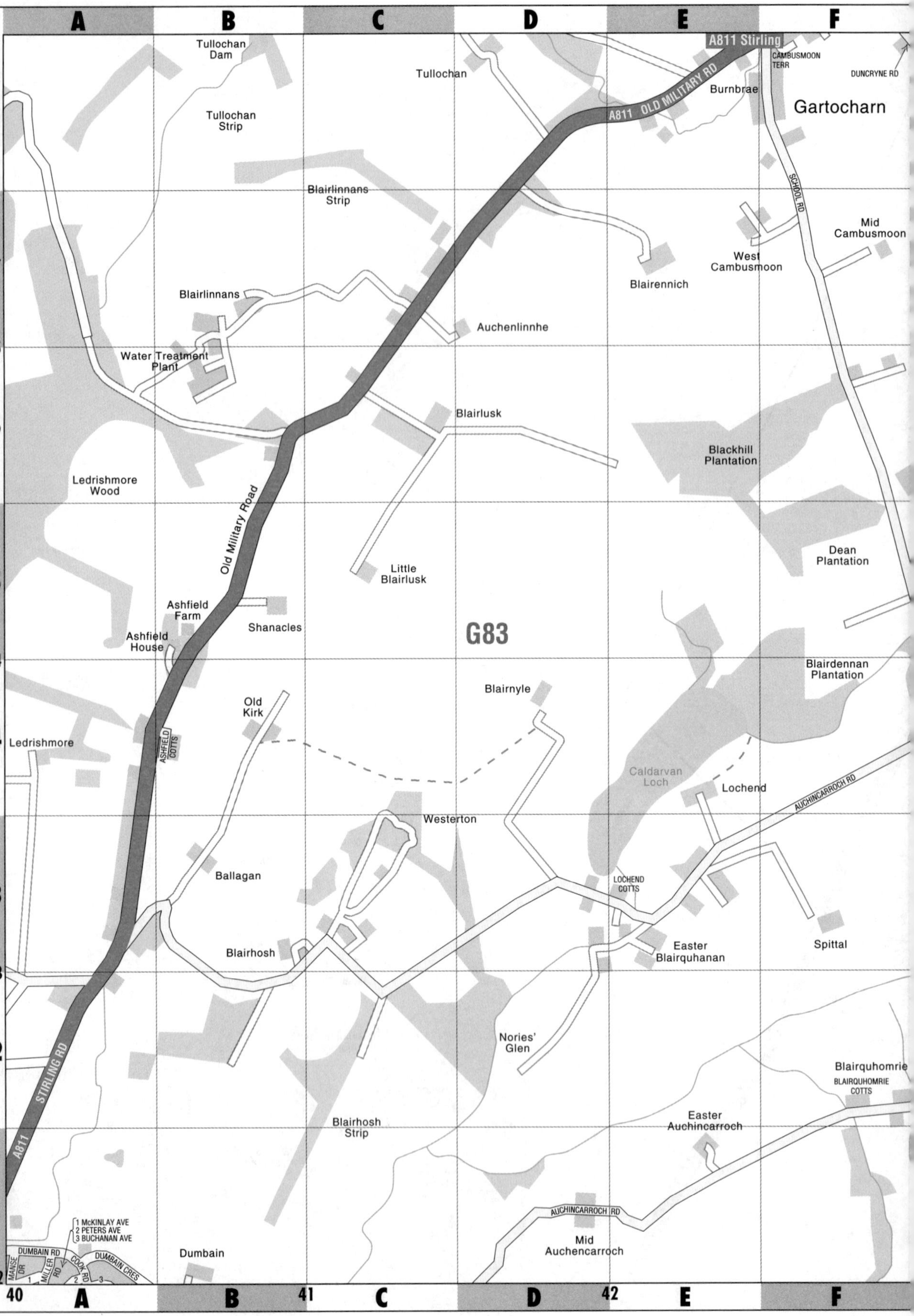
A
B
C
D
E
F
8
7
85
6
5
84
4
3
83
2
1
82
40
41
42
A811 Stirling
A811 OLD MILITARY RD
CAMBUSMOON TERR
DUNCRYNE RD
Tullochan Dam
Tullochan
Tullochan Strip
Burnbrae
Gartocharn
SCHOOL RD
Blairlinnans Strip
Mid Cambusmoon
West Cambusmoon
Blairennich
Blairlinnans
Auchenlinnhe
Water Treatment Plant
Blairlusk
Blackhill Plantation
Ledrishmore Wood
Old Military Road
Dean Plantation
Little Blairlusk
Ashfield Farm
Shanacles
G83
Ashfield House
Blairdennan Plantation
Blairnyle
Old Kirk
ASHFIELD COTTS
Ledrishmore
Caldarvan Loch
Lochend
AUCHINCARROCH RD
Westerton
Ballagan
LOCHEND COTTS
Easter Blairquhanan
Spittal
Blairhosh
Nories' Glen
STIRLING RD
A811
Blairquhomrie
BLAIRQUHOMRIE COTTS
Easter Auchincarroch
Blairhosh Strip
AUCHINCARROCH RD
1 McKINLAY AVE
2 PETERS AVE
3 BUCHANAN AVE
DUMBAIN RD
MANSE DR
MILLER RD
COOK RD
DUMBAIN CRES
Dumbain
Mid Auchencarroch

19

28

11
22

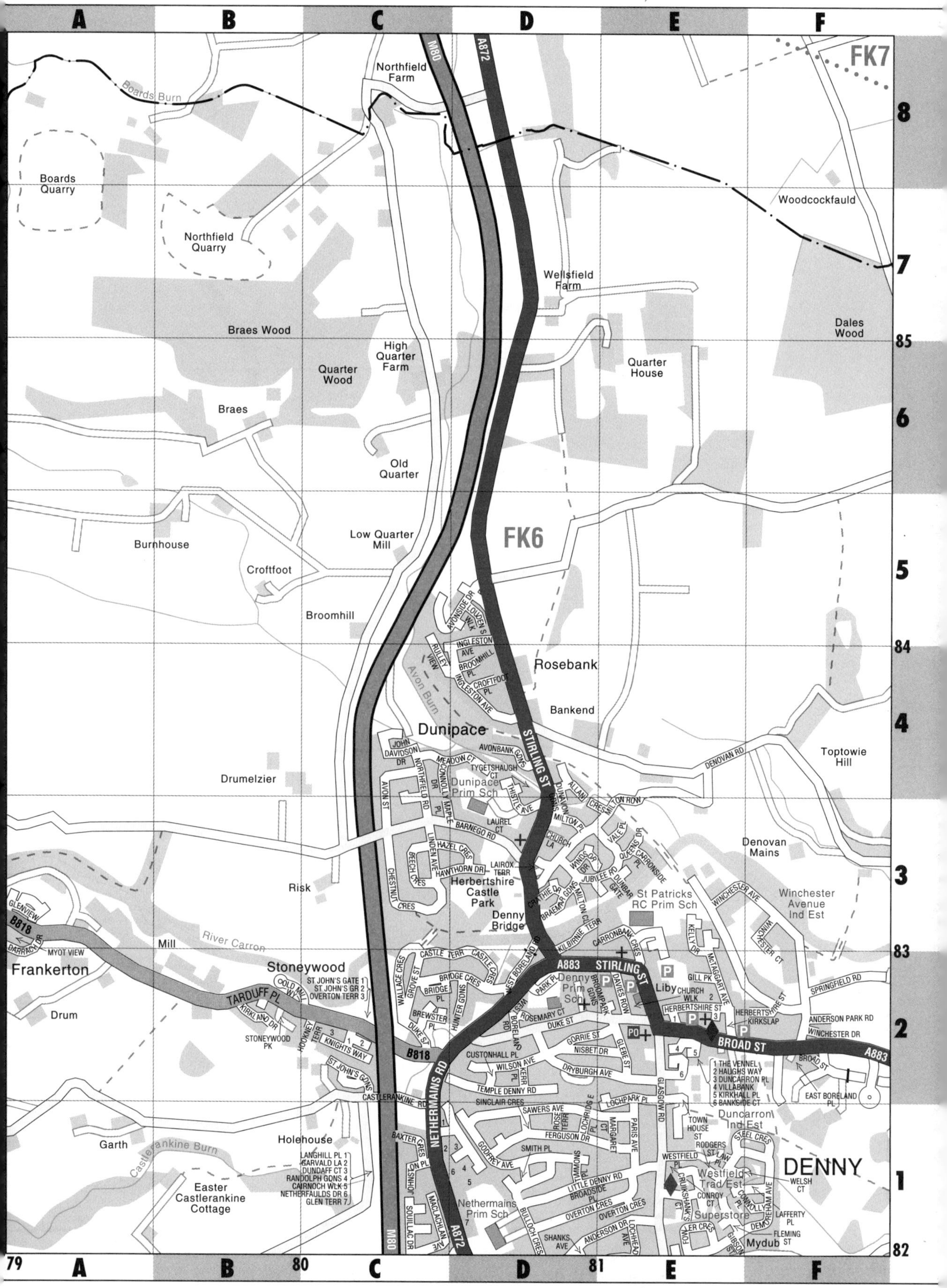
A
B
C
D
E
F
FK7
8
7
85
6
5
84
4
3
83
2
1
82
79
80
81
M80
A872
Northfield Farm
Boards Burn
Boards Quarry
Northfield Quarry
Woodcockfauld
Wellsfield Farm
Dales Wood
Braes Wood
High Quarter Farm
Quarter Wood
Quarter House
Braes
Old Quarter
FK6
Low Quarter Mill
Burnhouse
Croftfoot
Broomhill
Rosebank
Avon Burn
Bankend
Dunipace
Toptowie Hill
Drumelzier
Dunipace Prim Sch
Denovan Mains
Risk
Herbertshire Castle Park
St Patricks RC Prim Sch
Winchester Avenue Ind Est
Denny Bridge
Mill
River Carron
Frankerton
Stoneywood
Drum
Garth
Castlerankine Burn
Holehouse
Easter Castlerankine Cottage
Denny Prim Sch
Liby
Town House
Duncarron Ind Est
DENNY
Westfield Trad Est
Superstore
Mydub
Nethermains Prim Sch
STIRLING ST
A883
BROAD ST
B818
NETHERMAINS RD
DENOVAN RD
MILTON ROW
SPRINGFIELD RD
ANDERSON PARK RD
WINCHESTER DR
EAST BORELAND PL
WELSH CT
LAFFERTY PL
FLEMING ST
1 THE VENNEL
2 HAUGHS WAY
3 DUNCARRON PL
4 VILLABANK
5 KIRKHALL PL
6 BANKSIDE CT
ST JOHN'S GATE 1
ST JOHN'S GR 2
OVERTON TERR 3
LANGHILL PL 1
GARVALD LA 2
DUNDAFF CT 3
RANDOLPH GDNS 4
CAIRNOCH WLK 5
NETHERFAULDS DR 6
GLEN TERR 7
TARDUFF PL
MYOT VIEW
GLENVIEW
DARRACH DR
KIRKLAND DR
STONEYWOOD PK
KNIGHTS WAY
CASTLERANKINE RD
SINCLAIR CRES
TEMPLE DENNY RD
DUKE ST
ROSEMARY CT
GORRIE ST
NISBET DR
DRYBURGH AVE
WILSON AVE
CUSTONHALL PL
GLASGOW RD
LOCHPARK PL
FERGUSON DR
SMITH PL
GODFREY AVE
LITTLE DENNY RD
BROADSIDE PL
OVERTON CRES
ANDERSON DR
SHANKS AVE
BULLOCH CRES
BAXTER CRES
AVONSIDE DR
INGLESTON AVE
BROOMHILL PL
CROFTFOOT PL
ROLLEY VIEW
JOHN DAVIDSON DR
MEADOW CT
NORTHFIELD RD
AVONBANK GDNS
TYGETSHAUGH CT
AVON ST
BARNEGO RD
LAUREL CT
HAZEL CRES
LINDEN AVE
BEECH CRES
HAWTHORN DR
LAIROX TERR
CHESTNUT CRES
CASTLE TERR
CASTLE CRES
WALLACE CRES
GROVE ST
BRIDGE CRES
BRIDGE PL
BREWSTER PL
HUNTER GDNS
WEST BORELAND RD
PARK PL
KILBIRNIE TERR
CARRONBANK CRES
GILL PK
CHURCH WLK
HERBERTSHIRE ST
HERBERTSHIRE KIRKSLAP
McTAGGART AVE
KELLY DR
WINCHESTER AVE
WESTFIELD PL
STEEL CRES
RODGERS ST
CONROY CT
DEMOREHAM AVE
FOWLER CRES
GIBSON ST

39
22

21
12

A
B
C
D
E
F
8
7
85
6
5
84
4
3
83
2
1
82
83
84
FK7
Glenside
Tor Burn
GLEN RD
A9
Hollings
BOGEND RD
Langlands
GLEN RD
CASTLE CRES
NEWINGTON LA
FORRESTER GAIT
The Rocks
Tappoch
Torwood
Whinnie Muir
Torwood Sch
Tor Wood
Torwood Castle
FK5
Torwoodhead
STIRLING RD
CH
Doghillock
Tod Hill
Pamphellgoat Wood
M876
A9
STIRLING RD
2
M876
Baxter Wood
Denovan
FK6
DENOVAN RD
OLD DENNY RD
Oakbank Wood
Forth Valley Royal
H
Sewage Works
Big Wood
Kirkland
River Carron
P
A883
Evergreen Trailer Court
PH
Works
Househill Farm
Larbert House
Cemy
Headswood House
DENNY RD
M876
A883
B905

21
40

A
B
C
D
E
F
8
7
85
6
5
84
4
3
83
2
1
82
86
87
M9
Pow Burn
Bogend
BOGEND RD
Blairs
FK2
Kersebrock
Drum of Kinnaird
HILL OF KINNAIRD
8
North Inches
M876
Titlandhill
HAMILTON RD
Glenbervie House
Shiels Farm
Kinnaird Prim Sch
Bellsdyke
H
ANTONSHILL RDBT
A88
B902
B905
FK5
North Broomage
Hotel
Glenbervie Bsns Pk
Central Park Bsns Pk
CENTRAL BVD
CENTRAL PARKAVE
STIRLING RD
NORTH BROOMAGE RDBT
BELLSDYKE RDBT
INCHES RDBT
SOUTER WAY
ROBERT KAY PL
McCAMBRIDGE PL
TRYST PK
OCHIL VIEW CT
INCH GARVIE TERR
INCH COLM AVE
ROWANTREE WLK
LAWRENCE CT
MACDONALD CT
BURNS AVE
FULMAR CT
FINLAYSON PL
BRYSON PL
DUMYAT RISE
GALBRAITH CRES
McCARTNEY RD
McCORMACK PL
STANCE PL
DROVER PL
CLARINDA PL
ARMOUR MEWS
ALLOWAY WYND
Cemy
Antonshill
Stenhousemuir
Ochilview Pk (Stenhousemuir FC & East Stirlingshire FC)
Stenhousemuir Prim Sch
ADAM GROSSERT CT
TRYST RD
KING ST
MAIN ST
Larbert
Larbert Village Prim Sch
Works
Liby
Crownest Park
Carron Hill
Carrongrange Sch
Larbert High Sch
Carron Dams
Works
South Broomage
River Carron
FK2
Lochside House
LADYWELL CT
STIRLING RD
DENNY RD
A9
THE BUNGALOWS
ASHCROFT HO
ORCHARDSON RD 1
GRAWHALL PL 2
CURSITER CT 3
EARDLEY PL 4
RAEBURN RD 5
HENRYSON CRES 6
SIR JOHN GRAHAM CT 1
RUSSELL HILL CT 2
SIR WILLIAM WALLACE CT
CHARLOTTE HILL CT
GRAHAM AVE
TAPPOCH PL
OLD BELLSDYKE RD
BURNHEAD RD
MURRHALL RD
QUEEN'S DR
BALFOUR CRES
ALLANBANK RD
ELIZABETH AVE
LORNE RD
ROBERT HARDIE CT
WAVERLEY RD
JAMES ST
WAVERLEY TERR
McLACHLAN ST
CARRONVIEW
MUIR ST
VALEVIEW
PARK AVE
BRAEVIEW
LAMOND VIEW
SOUTH VIEW
CEDAR GR
HILLARY RD
LADESIDE CRES
CARRONGRANGE AVE
CARRONGRANGE RD
CARRONGRANGE GDNS
MUIRFIELD RD
GOSHEN PL
HALLAM RD
KINGS CT
PO
P
CH
GLADSTONE RD
STEPS ST
CHURCH ST
JOHNSTON AVE
STENHOUSE RD
LODGE DR
CASTLE DR
ADAM CRES
HOLLY AVE
BRUCE DR
CENTRAL DR
CHRISTIE TERR
SUTTON PARK CRES
WESTMINSTER PL
HOLYROOD PL
EDWARD AVE
BLENHEIM PL
FRANCHI DR
LOCHMABEN DR
STRATHMIGLO PL
ALLOA RD
DUNBAR AVE
NEIDPATH DR
FORBES CRES
PINE WLK
LIME GR
HAWTHORNE PL
OAK DR
ACORN CRES
ELM GR
TAYLOR'S RD
BROOMHILL AVE
DOBBIE AVE
BROOMSIDE PL
WEST DR
EAST DR
GODFREY CRES
CARRONVALE RD
SOUTH BROOMAGE AVE
BROOMAGE BANK
PRETORIA RD
VICTORIA RD
ST GEORGE'S CT
DUNDARROCH ST
FALKIRK RD
ST DAVID'S CT
UNION RD
GUTHRIE CRES
TORWOOD AVE
CAMPBELL DR
AITCHISON DR
FORTH AVE
CLYDE CRES
FALCON DR
TORLEA PL
ELLIOT PL

23
14

A
B
C
D
E
F
8
7
85
6
5
84
4
3
83
2
1
82
88
89
90
Letham
Lochs of Airth
LETHAM COTTS
Letham Farm
North Langdyke
A905
SOUTH APPROACH RD
M876
3
Southfield
North Bellsdyke
M9
7
Kinnaird House
M876
South Bellsdyke
BRACKENLEES RD
A905
A88
BELLSDYKE RD
Muirdyke Burn
A88
Bensfield
FK2
Howkerse
Kirkton
B905
B902
BARRA PL
BOXBURGH PL
WEIDPATH DR
CHATHES AVE
Carronshore Prim Sch
BRACKENLEES RD
Roughlands
Bothkennar Prim Sch
Dutch Inn (PH)
Skinflats
Westertown
Carronshore
AUCHENTYRE PL
BOTHKENNAR RD
WESTERTON TERR
NORTH MAIN ST
NEW CARRON RD
POTTER PL
ZETLAND PL
CORONATION PL
NEWTON AV
EDWARD P
BINNIE P
CAMPIE TERR
Backrow Farm
FRIENDSHIP GDNS
CASTLE AVE
MAIN ST
PO
THE AVENUE
Carron House
CARRONSHORE RD
WATERS END
THE MEADOWS
Carron Prim Sch
CHURCH ST
WADDELL ST
Carrongrove Bsns Pk
A905
Yonderhaugh
STENHOUSE RD
CARRON RDBT
Carron
River Carron
MONTGOMERY WELL
MONTGOMERY CRES
MONTGOMERY PL
FALKIRK
ADAMS LOAN
Langlees
BUCHAN AVE
STEVENSON CT
CROCKETT PL
LOMOND DR
MORAR DR
STRIVEN DR
DUNVEGAN DR
SEAFORTH RD
TORRIDON AVE
Sewage Works
DAVID'S LOAN
ABBOTS RD
FK3
M9
B902

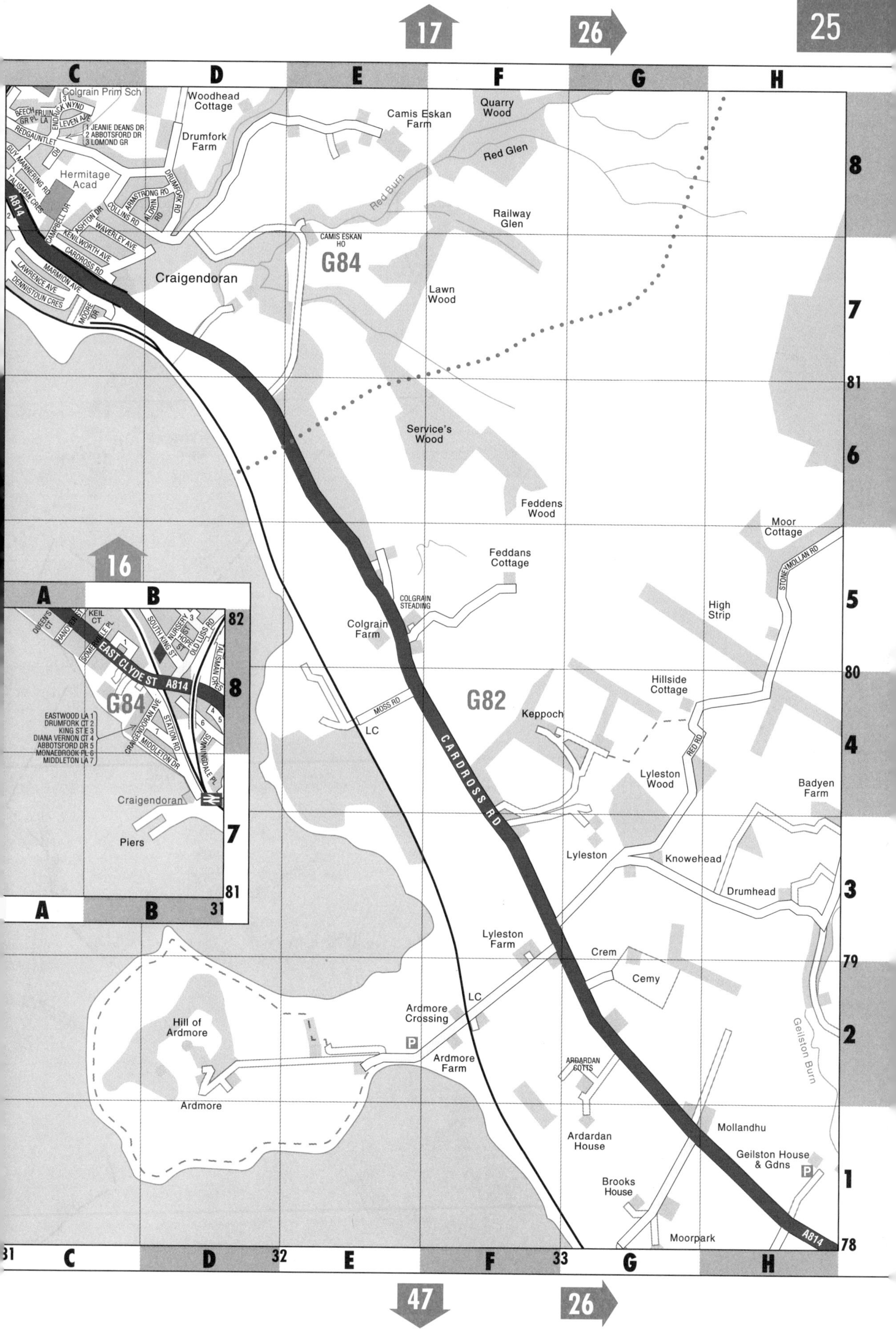
17
26
C D E F G H
Colgrain Prim Sch
Woodhead Cottage
Drumfork Farm
Camis Eskan Farm
Quarry Wood
Red Glen
Red Burn
Railway Glen
Hermitage Acad
CAMIS ESKAN HO
G84
Craigendoran
Lawn Wood
Service's Wood
Feddens Wood
Feddans Cottage
Moor Cottage
STONEYMOLLAN RD
COLGRAIN STEADING
Colgrain Farm
High Strip
MOSS RD
LC
CARDROSS RD
G82
Keppoch
Hillside Cottage
RED RD
Lyleston Wood
Badyen Farm
Lyleston
Knowehead
Drumhead
Lyleston Farm
Crem
Cemy
Ardmore Crossing
Ardmore Farm
Hill of Ardmore
Ardmore
ARDARDAN COTTS
Ardardan House
Geilston Burn
Mollandhu
Geilston House & Gdns
Brooks House
Moorpark
A814
1 JEANIE DEANS DR
2 ABBOTSFORD DR
3 LOMOND GR
BEECH GR
FRUIN PL
LA
ENDRICK WYND
LEVEN AVE
REDGAUNTLET RD
GUY MANNERING RD
TALISMAN CRES
ARMSTRONG RD
ALDRIN RD
DRUMFORK RD
COLLINS RD
ASHTON DR
CAMPBELL DR
KENILWORTH AVE
WAVERLEY AVE
CARDROSS RD
MARMION AVE
LAWRENCE AVE
DENNISTOUN CRES
MOORE DR
8 7 6 5 4 3 2 1
81 80 79 78
16
A B
QUEEN'S CT
HANOVER ST
KEIL CT
SOMERVILLE PL
SOUTH KING ST
NURSERY ST
HOPE ST
OLD LUSS RD
TALISMAN CRES
EAST CLYDE ST
A814
G84
CRAIGENDORAN AVE
STATION RD
SUNNINGDALE PL
MIDDLETON DR
EASTWOOD LA 1
DRUMFORK CT 2
KING ST E 3
DIANA VERNON CT 4
ABBOTSFORD DR 5
MONAEBROOK PL 6
MIDDLETON LA 7
Craigendoran
Piers
82 8 7 81
A B 31
31 C D 32 E F 33 G H
47
26

25
18

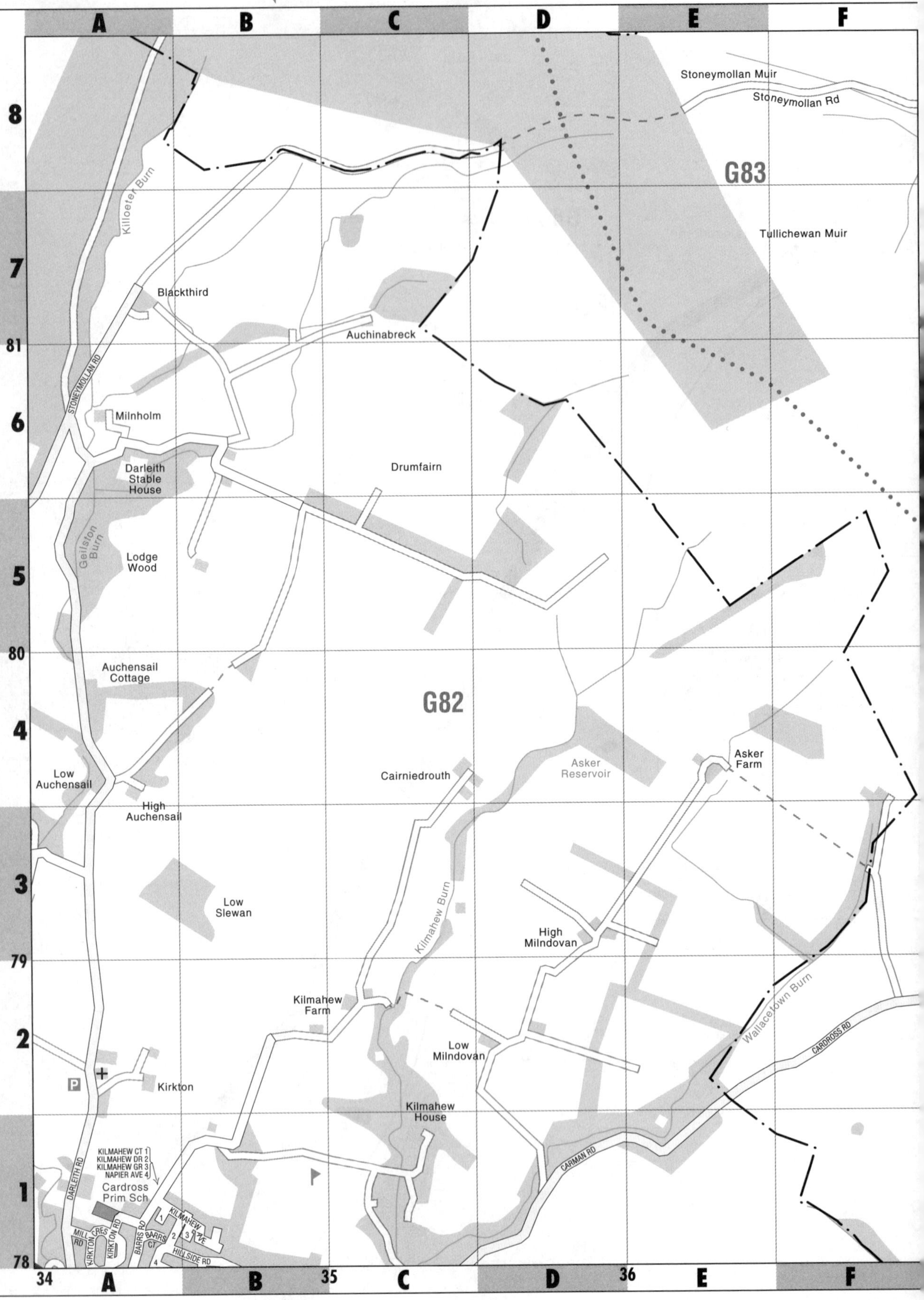
A
B
C
D
E
F
8
7
81
6
5
80
4
3
79
2
1
78
34
35
36
Stoneymollan Muir
Stoneymollan Rd
G83
Tullichewan Muir
Killoeter Burn
Blackthird
Auchinabreck
STONEYMOLLAN RD
Milnholm
Darleith Stable House
Drumfairn
Geilston Burn
Lodge Wood
Auchensail Cottage
G82
Asker Reservoir
Asker Farm
Low Auchensail
Cairniedrouth
High Auchensail
Low Slewan
Kilmahew Burn
High Milndovan
Kilmahew Farm
Wallacetown Burn
CARDROSS RD
Low Milndovan
Kirkton
Kilmahew House
CARMAN RD
KILMAHEW CT 1
KILMAHEW DR 2
KILMAHEW GR 3
NAPIER AVE 4
Cardross Prim Sch
DARLEITH RD
MILL RD
KIRKTON CRES
KIRKTON RD
BARRS RD
BARRS CT
KILMAHEW AVE
HILLSIDE RD

25
48

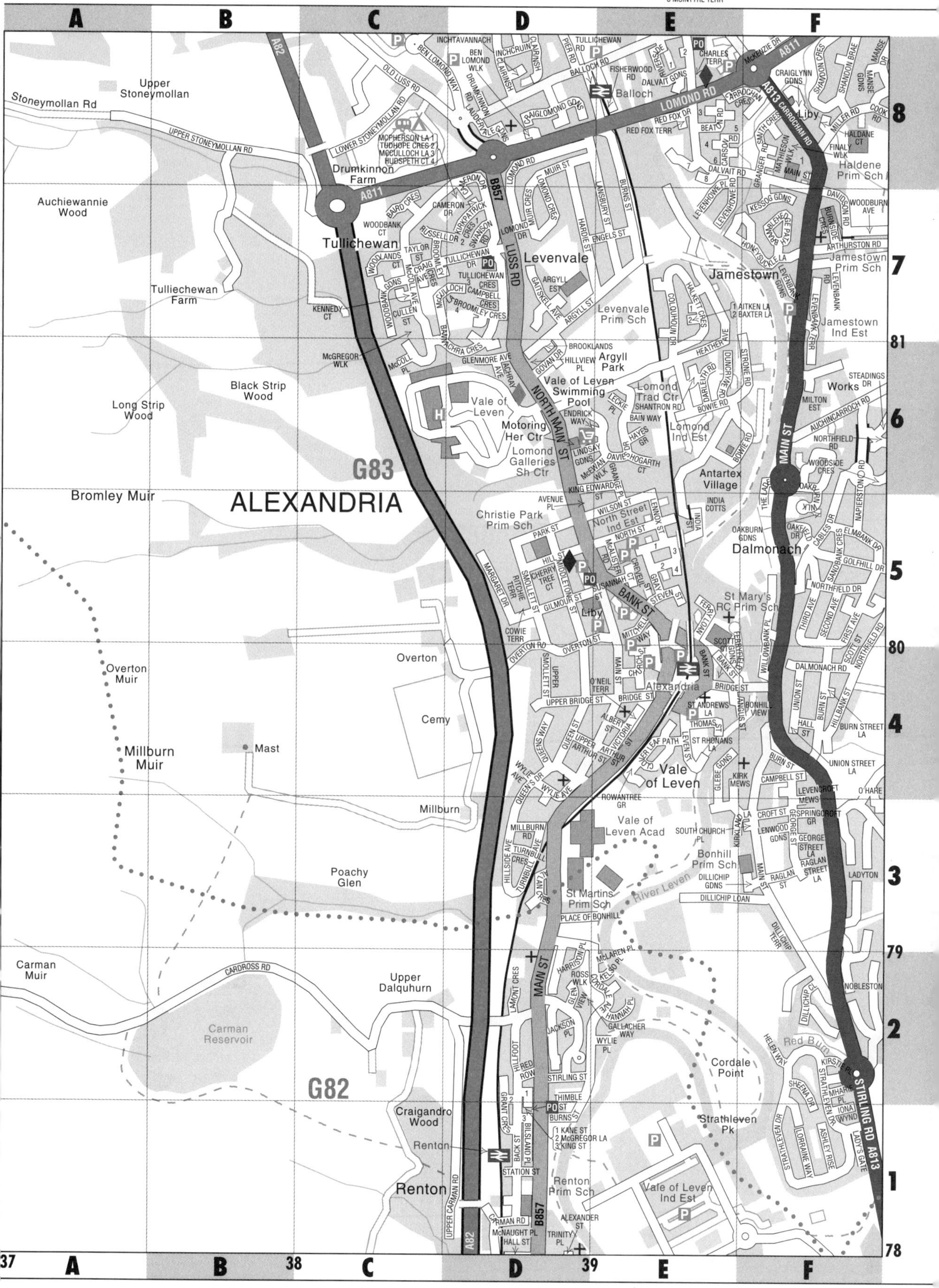
A
B
C
D
E
F
8
7
81
6
5
80
4
3
79
2
1
78
37
38
39
ALEXANDRIA
G83
G82
A82
A811
A813
B857
Upper Stoneymollan
Stoneymollan Rd
UPPER STONEYMOLLAN RD
LOWER STONEYMOLLAN RD
Drumkinnon Farm
Auchiewannie Wood
Tullichewan
Tulliechewan Farm
Black Strip Wood
Long Strip Wood
Bromley Muir
Overton Muir
Millburn Muir
Mast
Overton
Cemy
Millburn
Poachy Glen
Carman Muir
CARDROSS RD
Carman Reservoir
Upper Dalquhurn
Craigandro Wood
Renton
Balloch
LOMOND RD
LUSS RD
NORTH MAIN ST
BANK ST
MAIN ST
Levenvale
Levenvale Prim Sch
Argyll Park
Vale of Leven Swimming Pool
Vale of Leven
Motoring Her Ctr
Lomond Galleries Sh Ctr
Lomond Trad Ctr
Lomond Ind Est
Antartex Village
Christie Park Prim Sch
North Street Ind Est
Alexandria
Liby
Vale of Leven
Vale of Leven Acad
St Martins Prim Sch
Bonhill Prim Sch
River Leven
Cordale Point
Strathleven Pk
Vale of Leven Ind Est
Renton Prim Sch
Jamestown
Jamestown Prim Sch
Jamestown Ind Est
Haldene Prim Sch
Works
Dalmonach
St Mary's RC Prim Sch
Red Burn
STIRLING RD
1 KANE ST
2 McGREGOR LA
3 KING ST
McPHERSON LA 1
TUDHOPE CRES 2
McCULLOCH LA 3
HUDSPETH CT 4

27
20

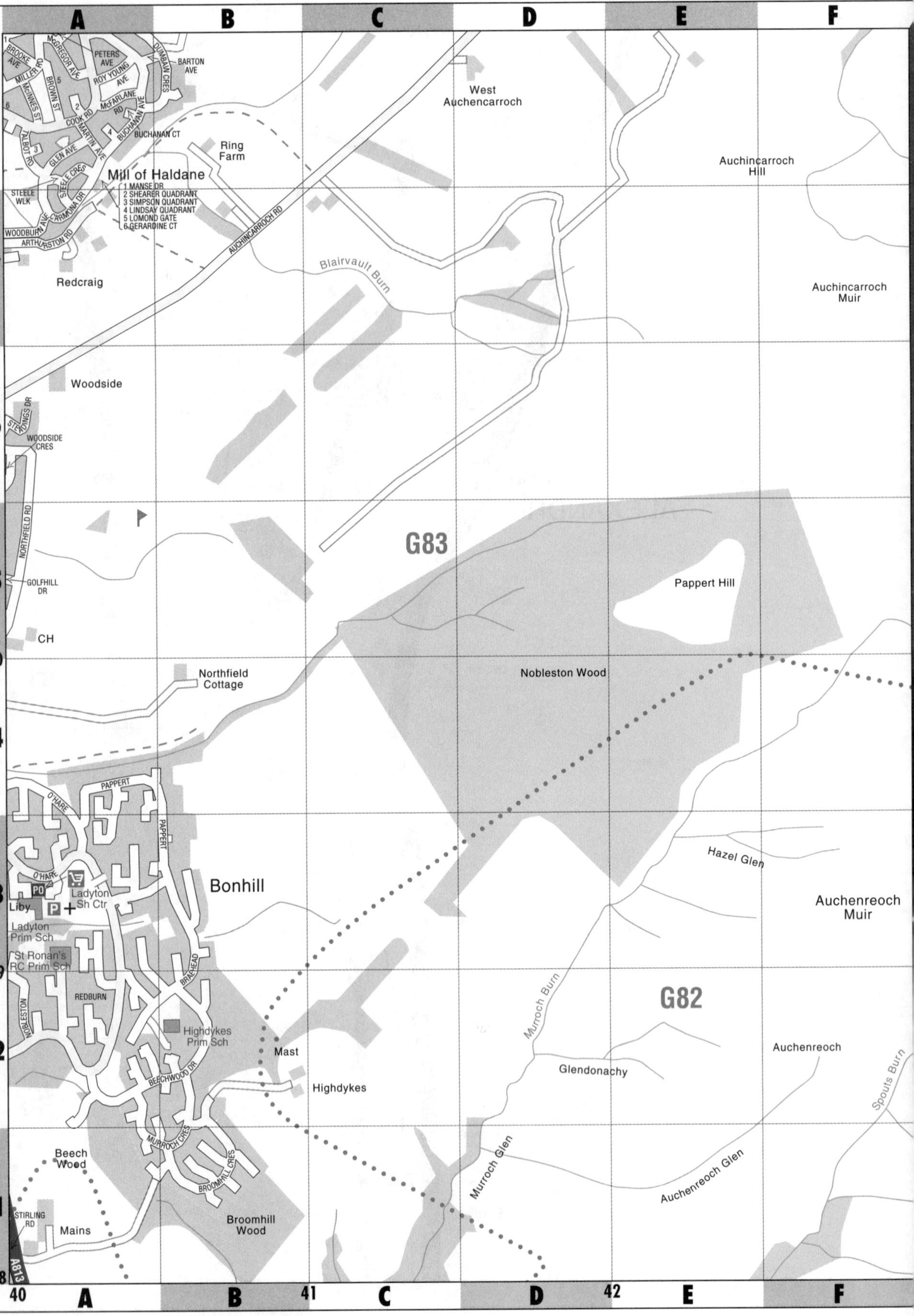
A
B
C
D
E
F
8
7
81
6
5
80
4
3
79
2
1
78
40
41
42
BROOKE AVE
MILLER RD
McGREGOR AVE
PETERS AVE
ROY YOUNG AVE
DUMBAIN CRES
BARTON AVE
McINNES ST
BROWN ST
COOK RD
McFARLANE RD
BUCHANAN AVE
MARTIN AVE
TALBOT RD
GLEN AVE
BUCHANAN CT
STEELE CRES
STEELE WLK
CARMONA DR
WOODBURN AVE
ARTHURSTON RD
Mill of Haldane
1 MANSE DR
2 SHEARER QUADRANT
3 SIMPSON QUADRANT
4 LINDSAY QUADRANT
5 LOMOND GATE
6 GERARDINE CT
Ring Farm
AUCHINCARROCH RD
West Auchencarroch
Auchincarroch Hill
Auchincarroch Muir
Blairvault Burn
Redcraig
Woodside
STEADINGS DR
WOODSIDE CRES
NORTHFIELD RD
GOLFHILL DR
CH
G83
Pappert Hill
Nobleston Wood
Northfield Cottage
PAPPERT
O'HARE
Bonhill
PO
Ladyton Sh Ctr
Liby
Ladyton Prim Sch
St Ronan's RC Prim Sch
BRAEHEAD
REDBURN
NOBLESTON
Highdykes Prim Sch
BEECHWOOD DR
Mast
Highdykes
Hazel Glen
Auchenreoch Muir
G82
Murroch Burn
Glendonachy
Auchenreoch
Spouts Burn
MURROCH CRES
BROOMHILL CRES
Beech Wood
STIRLING RD
Mains
A813
Broomhill Wood
Murroch Glen
Auchenreoch Glen

27
50

A
B
C
D
E
F
A809 Drymen
A809
Auchineden Burn
Quinloch
Quinloch Wood
Quinloch Muir
8
Catythirsty Well
7
81
P
Mast
The Whangie
Queen's View
6
Auchineden Hill
5
Auchengillan
Auchineden
G63
80
Low Auchengillan
A809
Stables
4
Lecher Burn
Works
Auchineden Farm
3
South Lodge
79
2
Audmurroch Burn
Greenan Glen
1
Kilmannan Resr
G62
78
49
A
B
50
C
D
51
E
F

29

A81 Killearn (A875)
A81
Blairquhosh Cottage
West Highland Way
Park Hill
Parkhill Wood
Craigbrock Wood
Dumgoyach Bridge
Cantywheery
Dumgoyach Farm
South Wood
Dumgoyach
Duntreath Castle
Craigbrock
Spittal Glen
The Ha
Strath Blane
Southbrae Wood
Middle Ballewan
Blane Water
West Highland Way
G63
East Arlehaven
Sewage Works
Arlehaven
A81
South Brae
Ardoch
Craigmore Cottage
Cuilt
A809
Craigmore Farm
Alreoch
Blair's Hill
B821
STATION RD
Craigmore
Braehead
BALLACHALAIRY YETT
CUILTS RD
B821
Easter Carbeth Farm
Carbeth Guthrie House
Carbeth Loch
Cuilt Brae
Red Brae Road
Boards
Carbeth Inn (PH)
Carbeth House
Carbeth Hill
Aulmurroch Farm
Garvel Bridge
West Highland Way
Allander Water
Carbeth Wood
Loch Wood
G62
Carglas Plantation
Craigallian Loch
A809
P
A B C D E F
8 7 6 5 4 3 2 1
81 80 79 78
52 53 54

29

54

32

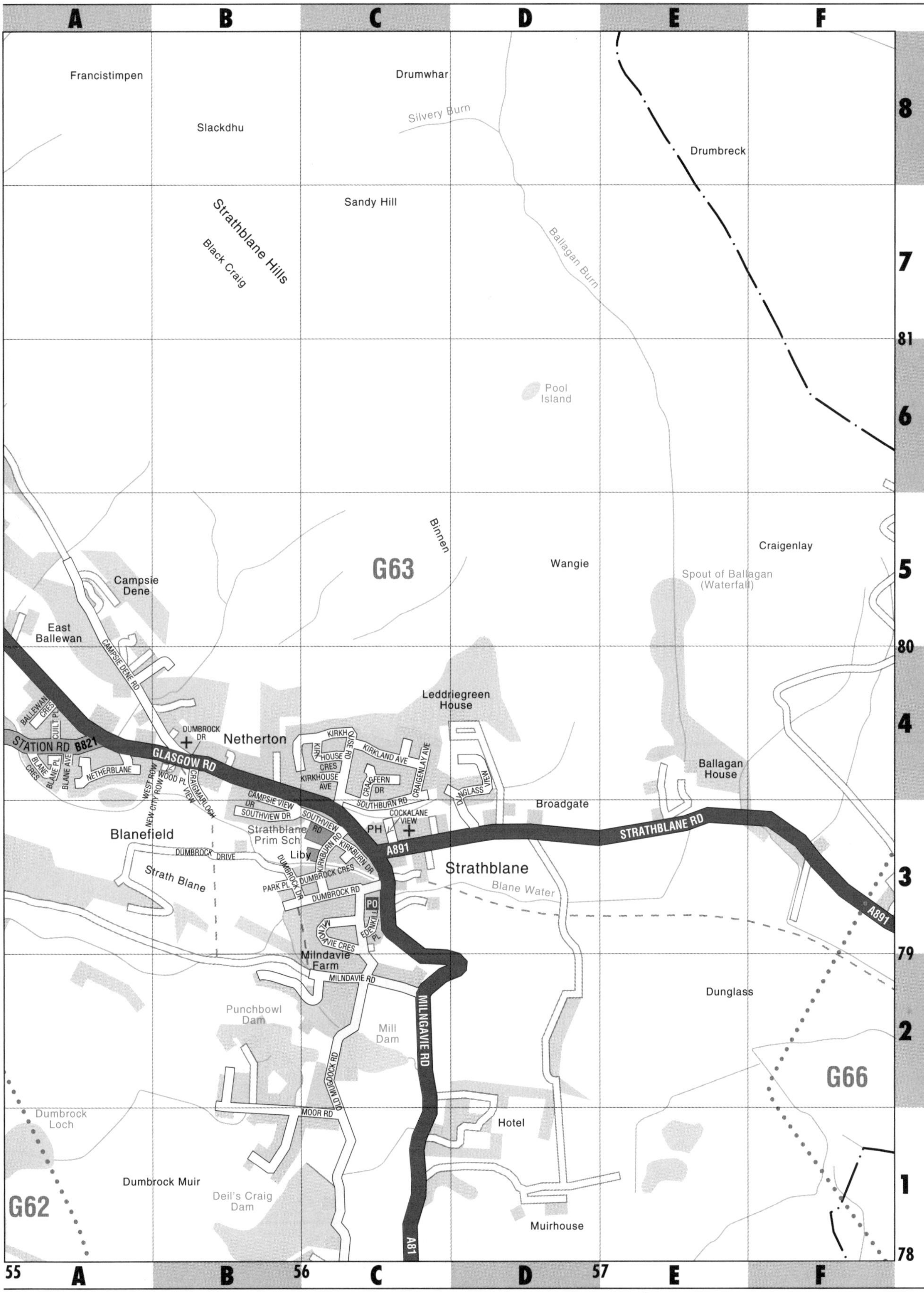
A
B
C
D
E
F
8
7
81
6
5
80
4
3
79
2
1
78
55
56
57
Francistimpen
Drumwhar
Silvery Burn
Slackdhu
Drumbreck
Sandy Hill
Strathblane Hills
Black Craig
Ballagan Burn
Pool Island
Binnen
G63
Wangie
Craigenlay
Spout of Ballagan (Waterfall)
Campsie Dene
East Ballewan
CAMPSIE DENE RD
Leddriegreen House
BALLEWAN CRES
CUILT PL
STATION RD
B821
DUMBROCK DR
Netherton
GLASGOW RD
KIRKHOUSE RD
KIRKHOUSE CRES
KIRKLAND AVE
CRAIGENLAY AVE
KIRKHOUSE AVE
CRAIGFERN DR
BLANE CRES
BLANE PL
BLANE AVE
NETHERBLANE
WOOD PL
WEST ROW
NEW CITY ROW
CRAIGMARLOCH VIEW
Ballagan House
DUNGLASS VIEW
SOUTHBURN RD
Broadgate
CAMPSIE VIEW DR
SOUTHVIEW DR
SOUTHVIEW RD
COCKALANE VIEW
Blanefield
Strathblane Prim Sch
PH
A891
STRATHBLANE RD
DUMBROCK DRIVE
Liby
KIRKBURN RD
KIRKBURN DR
Strathblane
Strath Blane
DUMBROCK CRES
Blane Water
PARK PL
DUMBROCK DR
DUMBROCK RD
PO
EDENKILL PL
MILNDAVIE CRES
Milndavie Farm
MILNDAVIE RD
Dunglass
Punchbowl Dam
MILNGAVIE RD
Mill Dam
G66
OLD MUGDOCK RD
Dumbrock Loch
MOOR RD
Hotel
Dumbrock Muir
G62
Deil's Craig Dam
Muirhouse
A81

55

32

31

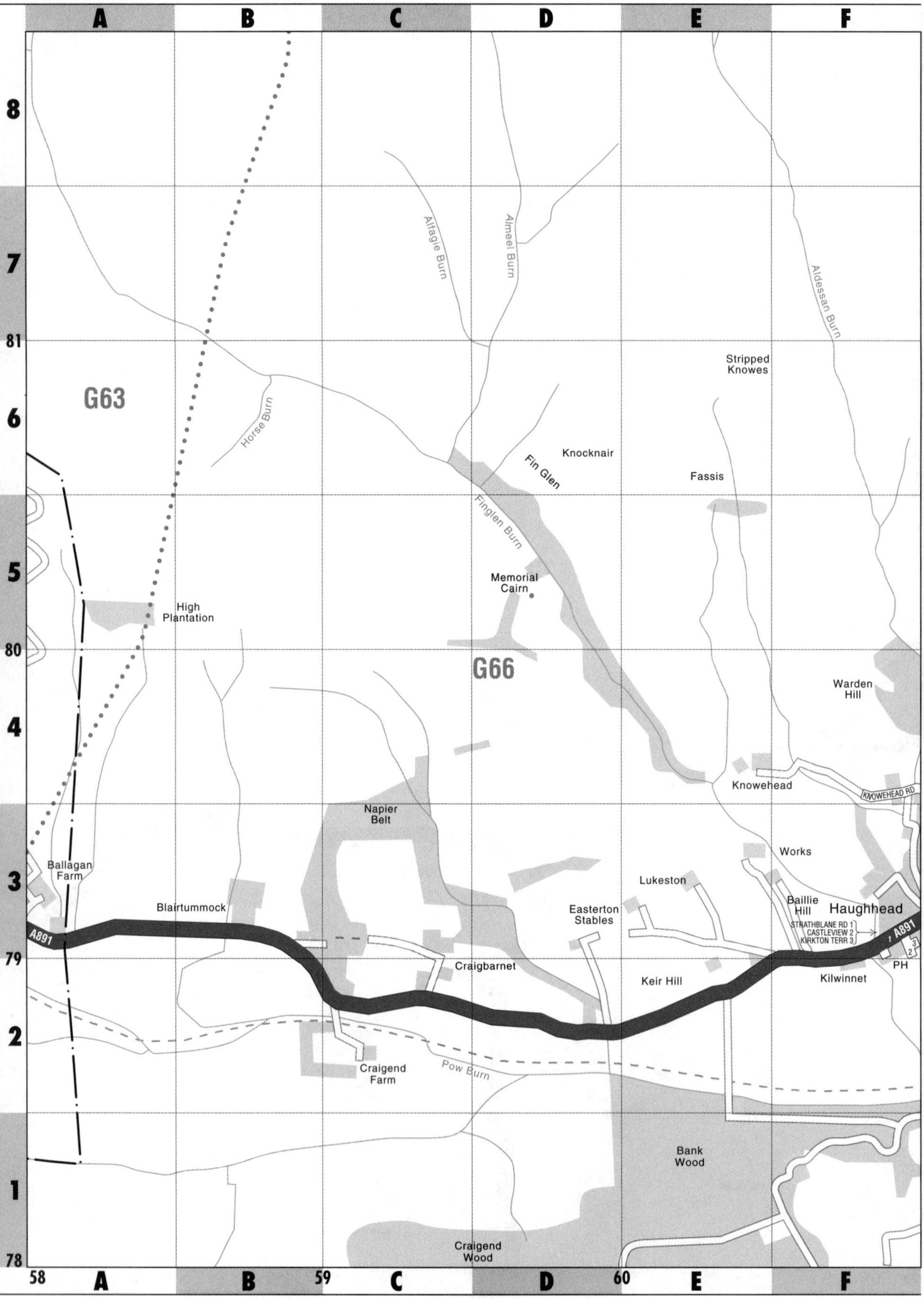
A
B
C
D
E
F
8
7
81
6
5
80
4
3
79
2
1
78
58
59
60
G63
G66
Alfagie Burn
Almeel Burn
Aldessan Burn
Stripped Knowes
Horse Burn
Knocknair
Fin Glen
Fassis
Finglen Burn
Memorial Cairn
High Plantation
Warden Hill
Knowehead
KNOWEHEAD RD
Napier Belt
Works
Ballagan Farm
Lukeston
Baillie Hill
Haughhead
Blairtummock
Easterton Stables
STRATHBLANE RD 1
CASTLEVIEW 2
KIRKTON TERR 3
A891
Craigbarnet
Keir Hill
Kilwinnet
PH
Craigend Farm
Pow Burn
Bank Wood
Craigend Wood

31

56

34

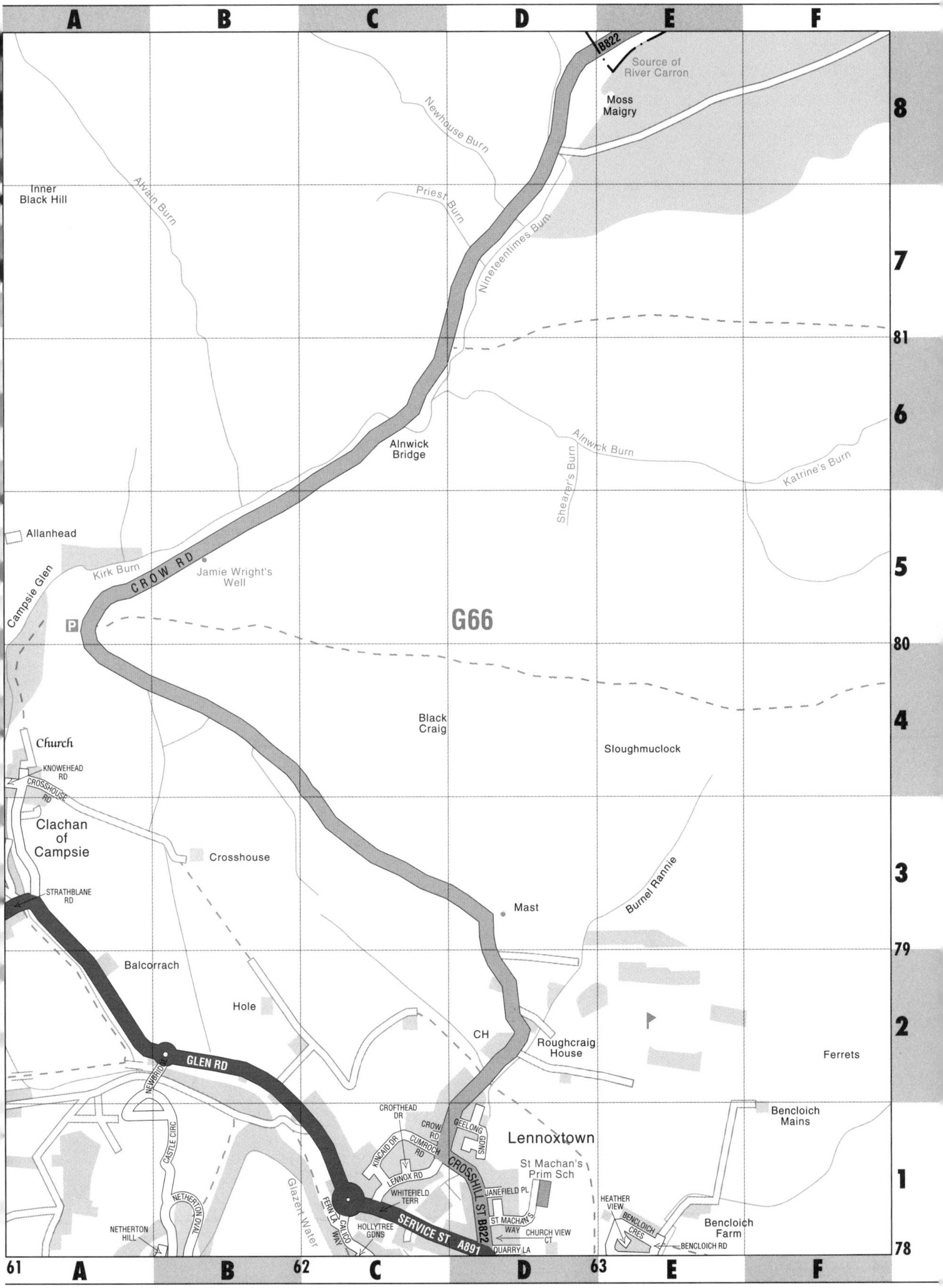
A
B
C
D
E
F
8
7
81
6
5
80
4
3
79
2
1
78
61
62
63
B822
Source of
River Carron
Moss
Maigry
Newhouse Burn
Inner
Black Hill
Alvain Burn
Priest Burn
Nineteentimes Burn
Alnwick
Bridge
Alnwick Burn
Shearer's Burn
Katrine's Burn
Allanhead
Campsie Glen
Kirk Burn
CROW RD
Jamie Wright's
Well
P
G66
Black
Craig
Sloughmuclock
Church
KNOWEHEAD
RD
CROSSHOUSE
RD
Clachan
of
Campsie
Crosshouse
Burnel Rannie
STRATHBLANE
RD
Mast
Balcorrach
Hole
CH
Roughcraig
House
Ferrets
GLEN RD
NEWBRIDGE
CASTLE CIRC
NETHERTON OVAL
NETHERTON
HILL
Glazert Water
FERN LA
CALICO
WAY
CROFTHEAD
DR
CROW
RD
KINCAID DR
CUMROCH
RD
LENNOX RD
WHITEFIELD
TERR
HOLLYTREE
GDNS
SERVICE ST
A891
GEELONG
GDNS
CROSSHILL ST B822
JANEFIELD PL
ST MACHAN'S
WAY
CHURCH VIEW
CT
QUARRY LA
Lennoxtown
St Machan's
Prim Sch
HEATHER
VIEW
BENCLOICH
CRES
BENCLOICH RD
Bencloich
Mains
Bencloich
Farm

57

34

33

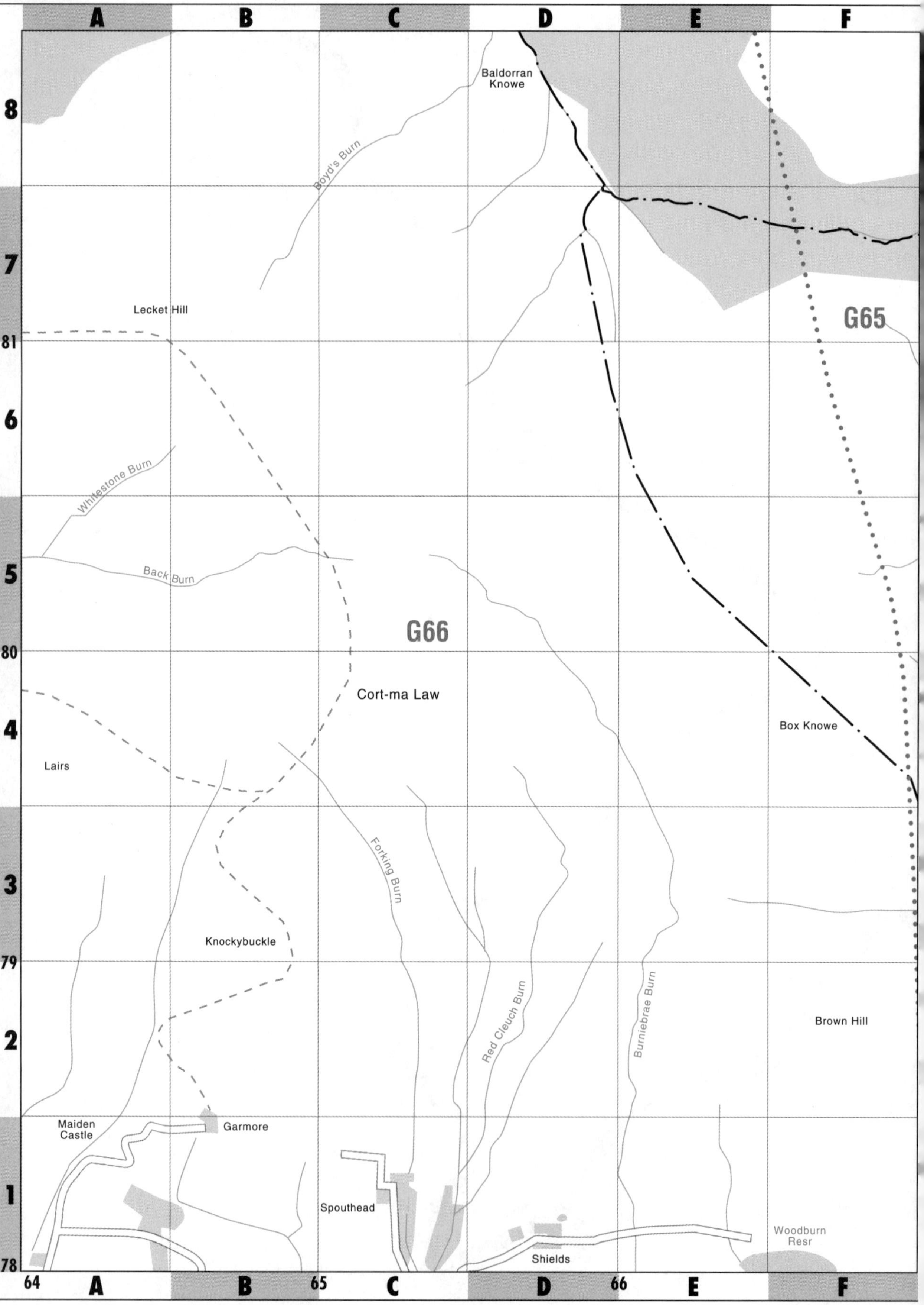
A
B
C
D
E
F
8
7
81
6
5
80
4
3
79
2
78
64
65
66
Baldorran Knowe
Boyd's Burn
Lecket Hill
G65
Whitestone Burn
Back Burn
G66
Cort-ma Law
Box Knowe
Lairs
Forking Burn
Knockybuckle
Red Cleuch Burn
Burniebrae Burn
Brown Hill
Maiden Castle
Garmore
Spouthead
Shields
Woodburn Resr

33
58

36

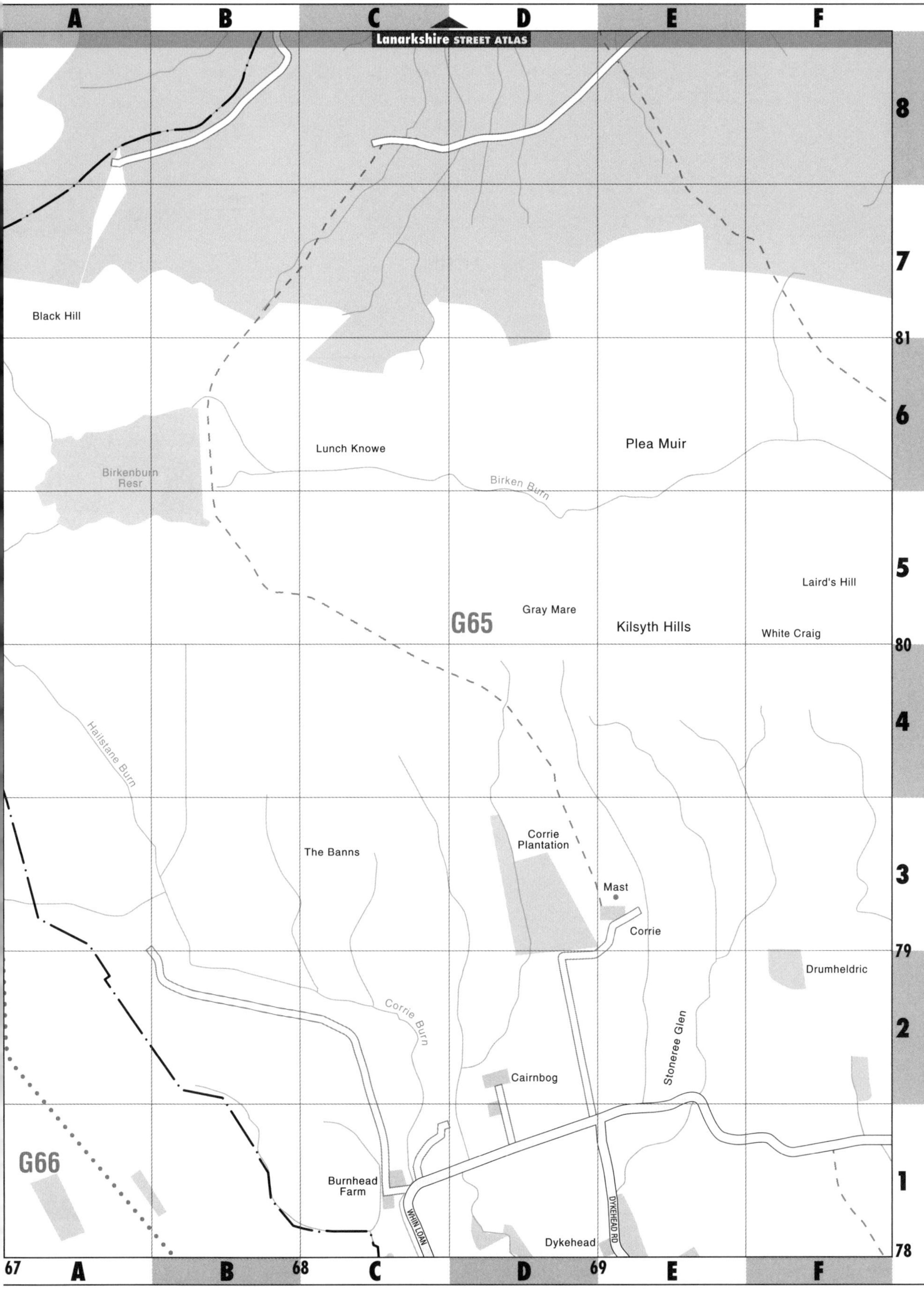
A B C D E F
Lanarkshire STREET ATLAS
8
7
81
6
5
80
4
3
79
2
1
78
67 68 69
Black Hill
Lunch Knowe
Plea Muir
Birkenburn Resr
Birken Burn
G65
Gray Mare
Kilsyth Hills
Laird's Hill
White Craig
Hailstane Burn
The Banns
Corrie Plantation
Mast
Corrie
Drumheldric
Corrie Burn
Stoneree Glen
Cairnbog
G66
Burnhead Farm
WHIN LOAN
DYKEHEAD RD
Dykehead

59
36

35

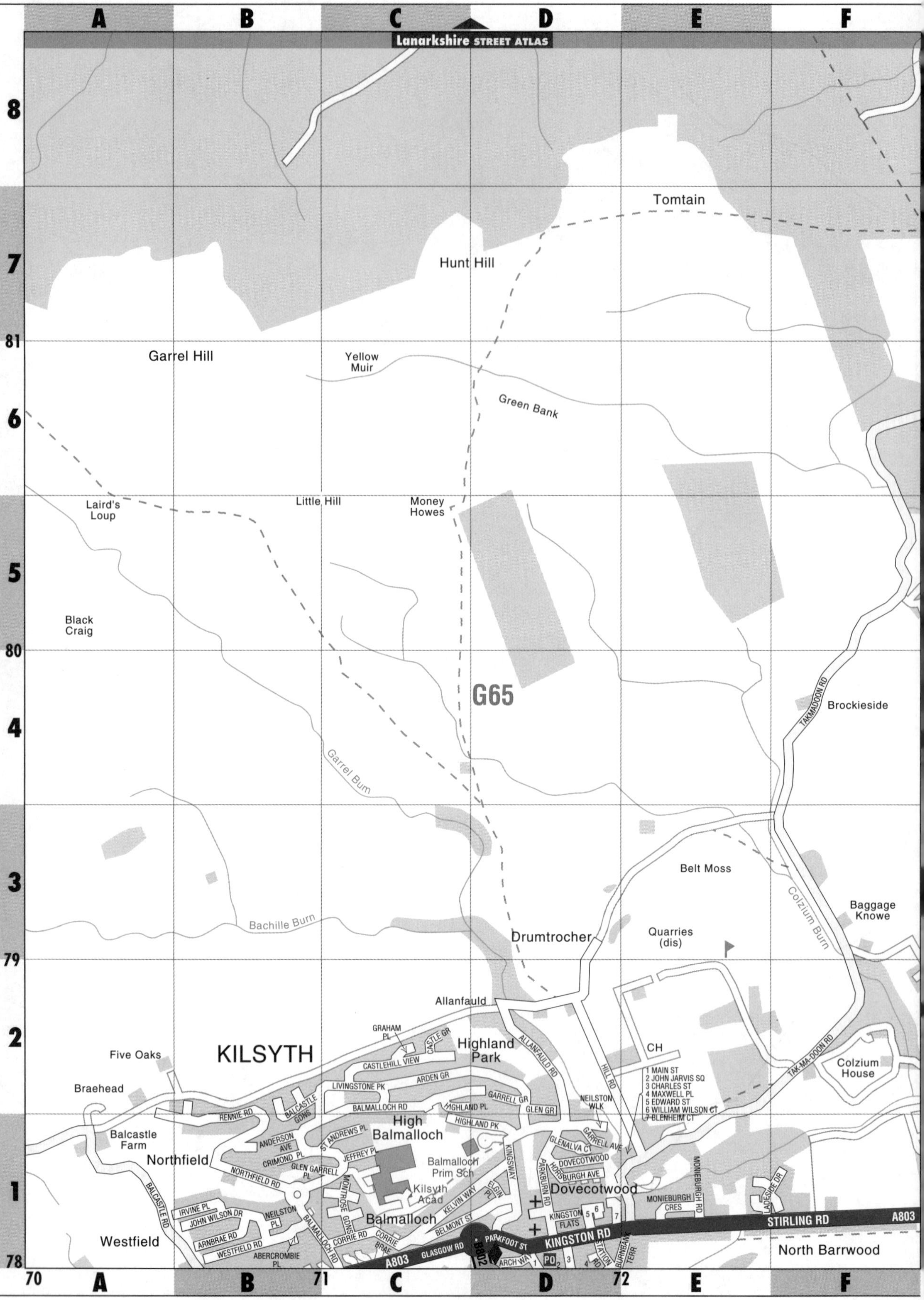
Lanarkshire STREET ATLAS
A
B
C
D
E
F
8
7
81
6
5
80
4
3
79
2
1
78
70
71
72
Tomtain
Hunt Hill
Garrel Hill
Yellow Muir
Green Bank
Laird's Loup
Little Hill
Money Howes
Black Craig
G65
Brockieside
TAKMADOON RD
Garrel Burn
Belt Moss
Colzium Burn
Baggage Knowe
Bachille Burn
Drumtrocher
Quarries (dis)
Allanfauld
KILSYTH
Highland Park
GRAHAM PL
CASTLE GR
CASTLEHILL VIEW
ARDEN GR
ALLANFAULD RD
HILL RD
CH
TAK-MA-DOON RD
Colzium House
Five Oaks
Braehead
LIVINGSTONE PK
GARRELL GR
GLEN GR
NEILSTON WLK
1 MAIN ST
2 JOHN JARVIS SQ
3 CHARLES ST
4 MAXWELL PL
5 EDWARD ST
6 WILLIAM WILSON CT
7 BLENHEIM CT
RENNIE RD
BALCASTLE GDNS
BALMALLOCH RD
HIGHLAND PL
HIGHLAND PK
High Balmalloch
Balcastle Farm
ANDERSON AVE
ST ANDREWS PL
GARRELL AVE
GLENALVA CT
Northfield
CRIMOND PL
JEFFREY PL
DOVECOTWOOD
HORSBURGH AVE
GLEN GARRELL PL
Balmalloch Prim Sch
KINGSWAY
PARKBURN RD
MONIEBURGH RD
LADESIDE DR
NORTHFIELD RD
Kilsyth Acad
Dovecotwood
BALCASTLE RD
IRVINE PL
JOHN WILSON DR
NEILSTON PL
MONTROSE GDNS
KELVIN WAY
ELGIN PL
MONIEBURGH CRES
KINGSTON FLATS
Balmalloch
BELMONT ST
STIRLING RD
A803
ARNBRAE RD
WESTFIELD RD
BALMALLOCH RD
CORRIE RD
CORRIE BRAE
PARKFOOT ST
KINGSTON RD
STATION RD
BURNBANK TERR
Westfield
ABERCROMBIE PL
GLASGOW RD
B802
ARCH WAY
PO
North Barrwood

35
60

38

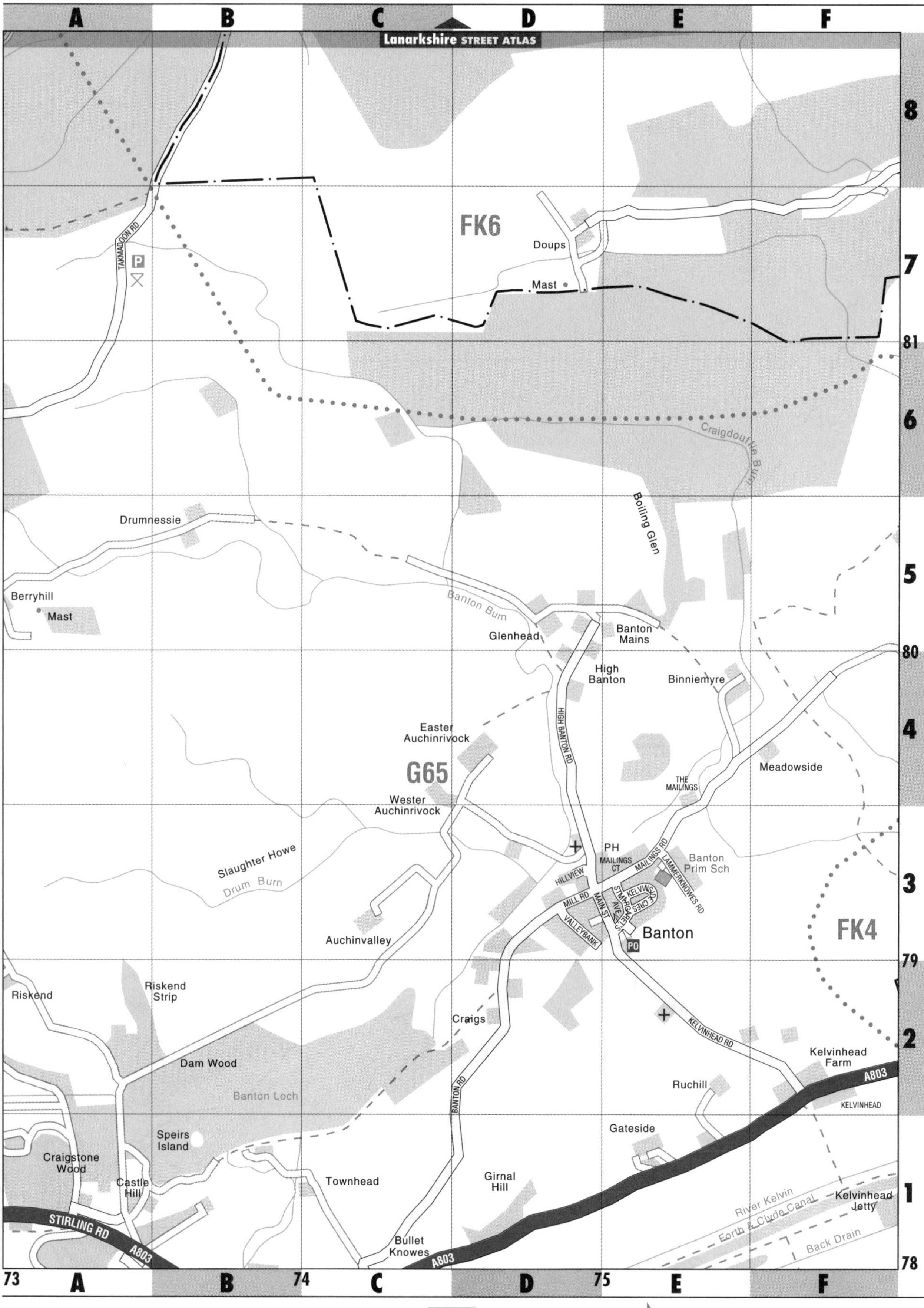
Lanarkshire STREET ATLAS
A
B
C
D
E
F
8
7
81
6
5
80
4
3
79
2
1
78
73
74
75
FK6
Doups
Mast
TAKMADOON RD
Craigdouffie Burn
Boiling Glen
Drumnessie
Berryhill
Mast
Banton Burn
Glenhead
Banton Mains
High Banton
Binniemyre
HIGH BANTON RD
Easter Auchinrivock
G65
Meadowside
THE MAILINGS
Wester Auchinrivock
PH
MAILINGS CT
MAILINGS RD
Banton Prim Sch
HILLVIEW
LAMMERKNOWES RD
Slaughter Howe
Drum Burn
MILL RD
MAIN ST
VALLEYBANK
Banton
PO
FK4
Auchinvalley
Riskend
Riskend Strip
Craigs
KELVINHEAD RD
Dam Wood
Kelvinhead Farm
A803
Banton Loch
Ruchill
KELVINHEAD
BANTON RD
Spiers Island
Gateside
Craigstone Wood
Castle Hill
Townhead
Girnal Hill
River Kelvin
Forth & Clyde Canal
Kelvinhead Jetty
STIRLING RD
A803
Bullet Knowes
A803
Back Drain

61
38

37

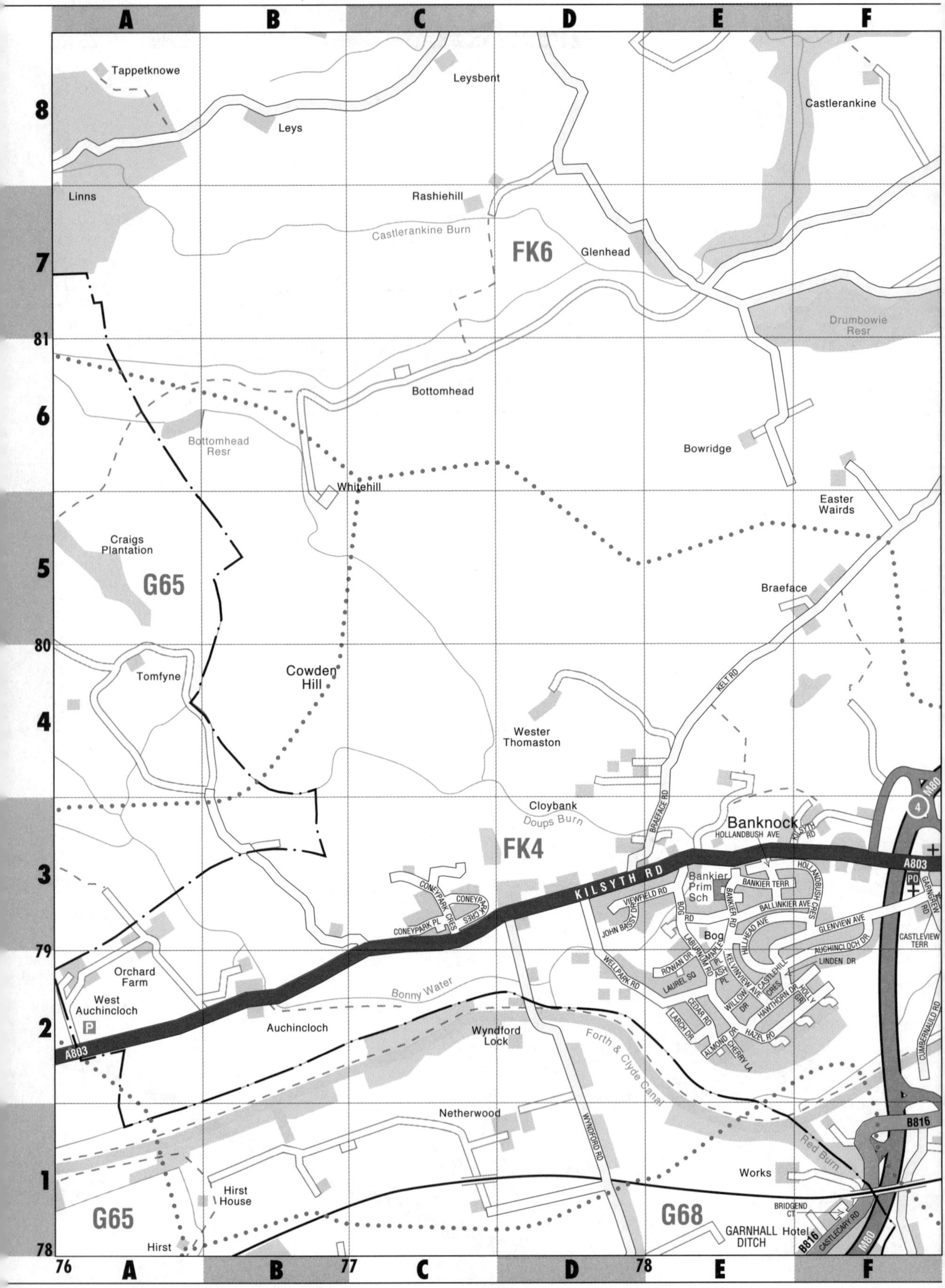

A
B
C
D
E
F
8
7
81
6
5
80
4
3
79
2
1
78
76
77
78
Tappetknowe
Leysbent
Castlerankine
Leys
Linns
Rashiehill
Castlerankine Burn
FK6
Glenhead
Drumbowie Resr
Bottomhead
Bottomhead Resr
Bowridge
Whitehill
Easter Wairds
Craigs Plantation
G65
Braeface
Tomfyne
Cowden Hill
KELT RD
Wester Thomaston
BRAEFACE RD
Cloybank
Doups Burn
Banknock
HOLLANDBUSH AVE
KILSYTH RD
FK4
M80
4
A803
PO
KILSYTH RD
Bankier Prim Sch
BANKIER TERR
HOLLANDBUSH CRES
GARNGREW RD
CONEYPARK CRES
CONEYPARK CRES
CONEYPARK PL
VIEWFIELD RD
BOG RD
BANKIER RD
BALLINKIER AVE
GLENVIEW AVE
JOHN BASSY DR
Bog
LABURNUM RD
HILLHEAD AVE
AUCHINCLOCH DR
CASTLEVIEW TERR
LINDEN DR
ROWAN DR
MAPLE PL
ASH PL
KELVINVIEW AVE
CASTLEHILL CRES
WELLPARK RD
LAUREL SQ
WILLOW DR
HAWTHORN DR
HOLLY GR
CEDAR RD
LARCH DR
ALMOND DR
CHERRY LA
HAZEL RD
CUMBERNAULD RD
Orchard Farm
West Auchincloch
P
Bonny Water
A803
Auchincloch
Wyndford Lock
Forth & Clyde Canal
Netherwood
WYNDFORD RD
B816
Red Burn
Works
Hirst House
G65
G68
BRIDGEND CT
GARNHALL DITCH
Hotel
B816
CASTLECARY RD
M80
Hirst

37

62

21
40

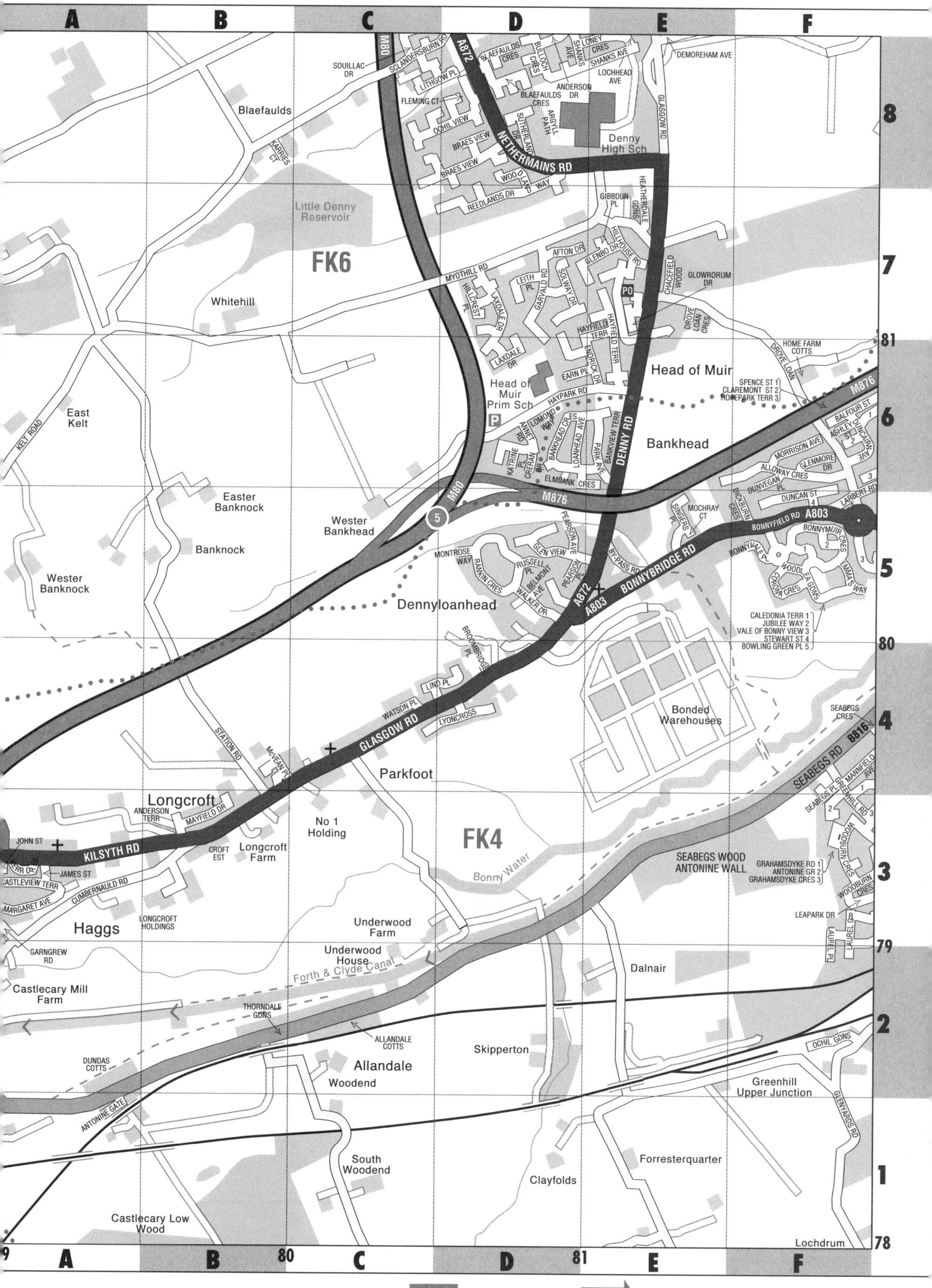
A
B
C
D
E
F
8
7
81
6
5
80
4
3
79
2
1
78
80
81
FK6
FK4
M80
A872
M876
A803
B816
SOUILLAC DR
SCLANDERSBURN RD
LITHGOW PL
FLEMING CT
OCHIL VIEW
BRAES VIEW
BLAEFAULDS CRES
BULLOCH CRES
SHANKS AVE
LONEY CRES
ANDERSON DR
LOCHHEAD AVE
DEMOREHAM AVE
GLASGOW RD
SUTHERLAND DR
ARGYLL PATH
NETHERMAINS RD
Denny High Sch
WOODLAND WAY
REEDLANDS DR
Blaefaulds
KARRIES CT
Little Denny Reservoir
GIBBDUN PL
HEATHERDALE GDNS
HILLHOUSE RD
AFTON DR
GLENBO DR
SOLWAY DR
GARVALD RD
LEITH PL
MYOTHILL RD
HILLCREST PL
LAXDALE DR
CHACEFIELD WOOD
GLOWRORUM DR
DROVE LOAN CRES
PO
HAYFIELD TERR
ENDRICK DR
EARN PL
Whitehill
HOME FARM COTTS
DROVE LOAN
Head of Muir
SPENCE ST 1
CLAREMONT ST 2
HOPEPARK TERR 3
Head of Muir Prim Sch
HAYPARK RD
LOMOND WAY
BANKHEAD CRES
LOANHEAD AVE
PARK AVE
BANKVIEW TERR
DENNY RD
ANNET RD
CRERAN DR
KATRINE PL
ELMBANK CRES
Bankhead
BALFOUR ST
ASHLEY ST
DUNCAIRN AVE
MORRISON AVE
GLENMORE DR
ALLOWAY CRES
DUNVEGAN PL
DUNCAN ST
LARBERT RD
KELT ROAD
East Kelt
Easter Banknock
Wester Bankhead
MOCHRAY CT
SINGERS PL
DICKBURN CRES
BONNYFIELD RD
BONNYMUIR CRES
Banknock
MONTROSE WAY
GLEN VIEW
PEARSON AVE
RANKIN CRES
RUSSELL PL
BELMONT AVE
WALKER DR
PEARSON PL
BY-PASS RD
BONNYBRIDGE RD
BONNYVALE
WOODLEA GDNS
CORONA CRES
EMMA'S WAY
Wester Banknock
Dennyloanhead
CALEDONIA TERR 1
JUBILEE WAY 2
VALE OF BONNY VIEW 3
STEWART ST 4
BOWLING GREEN PL 5
BROOMBRIDGE PL
LIND PL
WATSON PL
LYONCROSS
Bonded Warehouses
SEABEGS CRES
SEABEGS RD
MANNFIELD AVE
STATION RD
McVEAN PL
GLASGOW RD
Parkfoot
SEABEGS PL
GREENHILL RD
Longcroft
ANDERSON TERR
MAYFIELD DR
No 1 Holding
WOODBURN CRES
JOHN ST
KILSYTH RD
CROFT EST
Longcroft Farm
Bonny Water
SEABEGS WOOD ANTONINE WALL
GRAHAMSDYKE RD 1
ANTONINE GR 2
GRAHAMSDYKE CRES 3
JAMES ST
CASTLEVIEW TERR
CUMBERNAULD RD
MARGARET AVE
Haggs
LONGCROFT HOLDINGS
Underwood Farm
LEAPARK DR
LAUREL PL
GARNGREW RD
Underwood House
Forth & Clyde Canal
Dalnair
Castlecary Mill Farm
THORNDALE GDNS
ALLANDALE COTTS
OCHIL GDNS
DUNDAS COTTS
Allandale
Skipperton
Woodend
Greenhill Upper Junction
GLENYARDS RD
ANTONINE GATE
South Woodend
Forresterquarter
Clayfolds
Castlecary Low Wood
Lochdrum

63
40

39
22

A
B
C
D
E
F
8
7
81
6
5
80
4
3
79
2
1
78
82
83
84
Cuthelton
FK6
Chacefield Wood
M876
A883
A8004
B905
Cemy
Nursery
Hills of Dunipace
FK5
River Carron
CHECKBAR RDBT
Bogton
A883
CH
NORWOOD CT
Sewage Works
Wester Carmuirs
Works
A80
WEST CARMUIRS LOAN
Bonny Water
Rowan Tree Burn
DOD AVE
FAIRWAYS PL
PRIMROSE ST
NORWOOD PL
DRUMMOND PL
FERGUSON GR
CHACEFIELD ST
ROSE ST
BALFOUR ST
URE CRES
WHEATLANDS AVE
SPENCE ST
SKENE ST
LARBERT RD
HIGHLAND DYKES CRES
HIGHLAND DYKES DR
ROBERTSON AVE
BONNYVIEW GDNS
COWAN ST
GREENFIELD ST
Bonnybridge Prim Sch
THORNTON GDNS
THORNTON AVE
GATESIDE AVE
HOPEPARK TERR
FAIRFIELD AVE
PEATHILL RD
MARGARET DR
WELLPARK TERR
FORD RD
DUNURE CRES
DUNURE ST
PEATHILL TERR
LADE RD
COWDEN HILL GDNS
ANDERSON ST
FALKIRK RD
H
Bonnybridge
Park
WELLSTOOD CT
PATERSON PL
PRINCESS ST
BARLEYHILL
Forth and Clyde Canal
A803
HIGH ST
MAIN ST
Bonnybridge
MOUNT BARTHOLOMEW
P
PO
Cowden Hill
Liby
BONNYMUIR PL
VALE OF BONNY VIEW
BRIDGE ST
HUNTER GR
BONNYSIDE RD
BONNYMILL PL
FOUNDRY RD
HARLEY GDNS
Bonnyside Farm
Chattan Ind Est
SEABEGS RD
Canal Bank Ind Est
MURNIN RD
Murnin Road Ind Est
Antonine Prim Sch
ANTONINE WALL
Rough Castle ROMAN FORT
B816
SEABEGS CRES
MANNFIELD AVE
Bonnybridge Ind Est
MOFFAT PL
ROMAN RD
ALLAN PL
BROOMHILL RD
St Josephs RC Prim Sch
FK4
PARK ST
WILSON PL
Works
GRAHAMSDYKE RD
ATRIUM WAY
ARDGAY TERR
Milnquarter
ARDGAY RD
GREENACRE PL
ARDGAY ST
WAVERLEY CRES
MILLAR PL
LOCHNVAR PL
CHURCH ST
REILLY RD
REILLY GDNS
B81
MILNQUARTER RD
LEAPARK DR
FOXDALE DR
FOXDALE PL
GREENHILL RD
LAUREL GR
1 GRAHAMSDYKE CRES
2 WOODBURN CRES
3 BANTON PL
4 LAURELBANK AVE
5 GREENACRE DR
6 FOXDALE CT
7 FOXDALE AVE
8 GREENHILL SQ
HILLVIEW RD
BONNYHILL RD
Works
BROOMSIDE RD
High Bonnybridge
Greenhill
GLENYARDS RD
Margreta
Bonnyhill Farm
Howierig
FK1
Greenrig
Drum Wood
Drum Farm

39
64

F8
1 CAULDHAME FARM RD
2 CAULDHAME ST
3 WESTPARK CRES
4 MUNGAL MILL CT
5 GOOSEDUBS PL
6 STEPHENS CFT
7 COTLAND DR
8 WESTPARK CT

A8
1 MULLOCH AVE
2 ANDERSON AVE
3 NEWCARRON CT
4 WILLIAMSON AVE
5 DUNDEE CT
6 JARVIE PL
7 JOHNSTON CT
8 GASCOIGNE CT
9 STEPHENS CFT

41
24

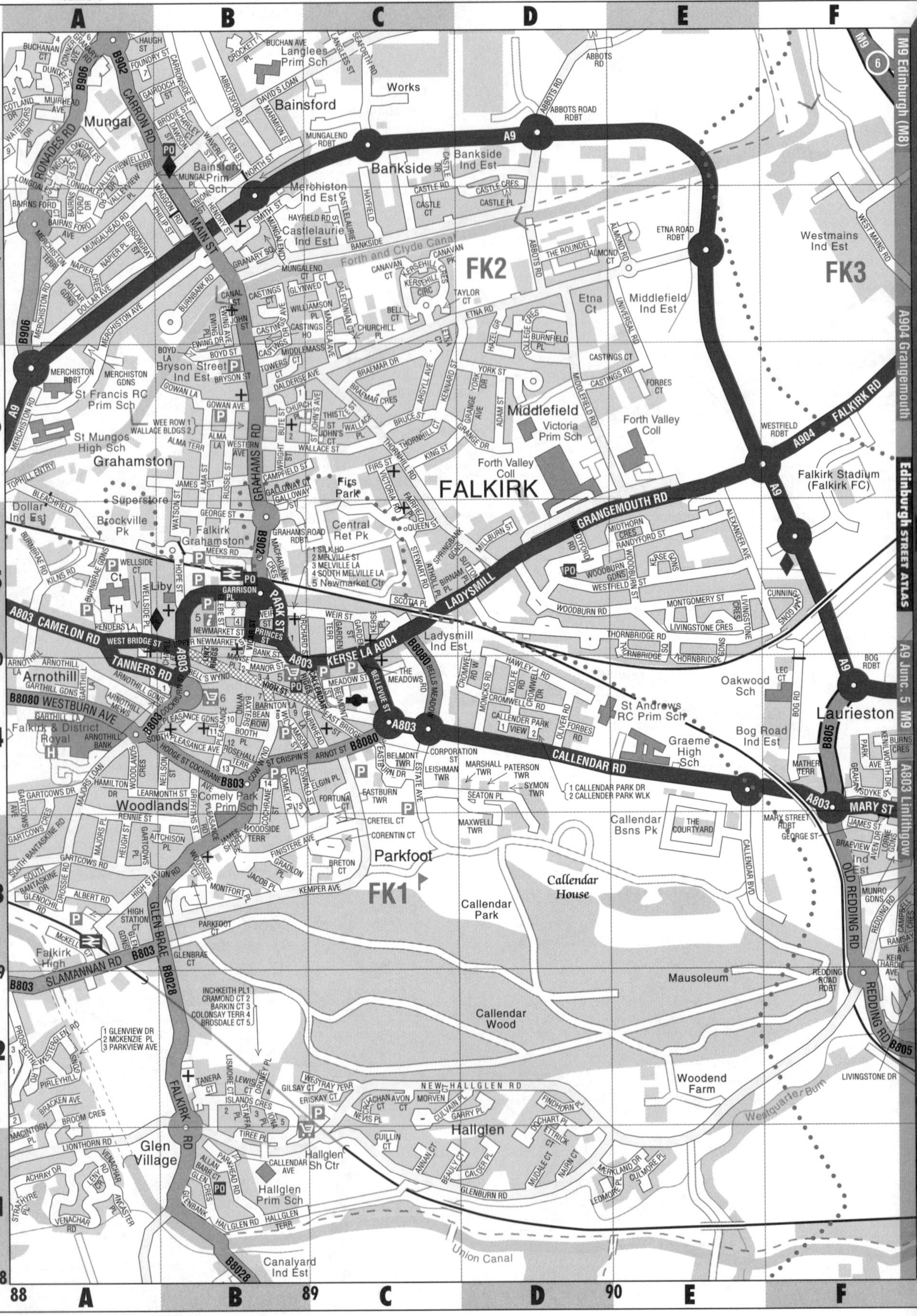

B4
1 BURNFOOT LA
2 KIRK WYND
3 TOLBOOTH ST
4 WOOER ST
5 Callendar Square Sh Ctr
6 Howgate Sh Ctr
7 KINGS CT
8 MISSION LA
9 MELROSE PL
10 ST ANDREWS PL
11 PLEASANCE SQ
12 PLEASANCE CT
13 ST MODANS CT
14 COMELY PARK TERR
15 COMELY PK GDNS

41
66

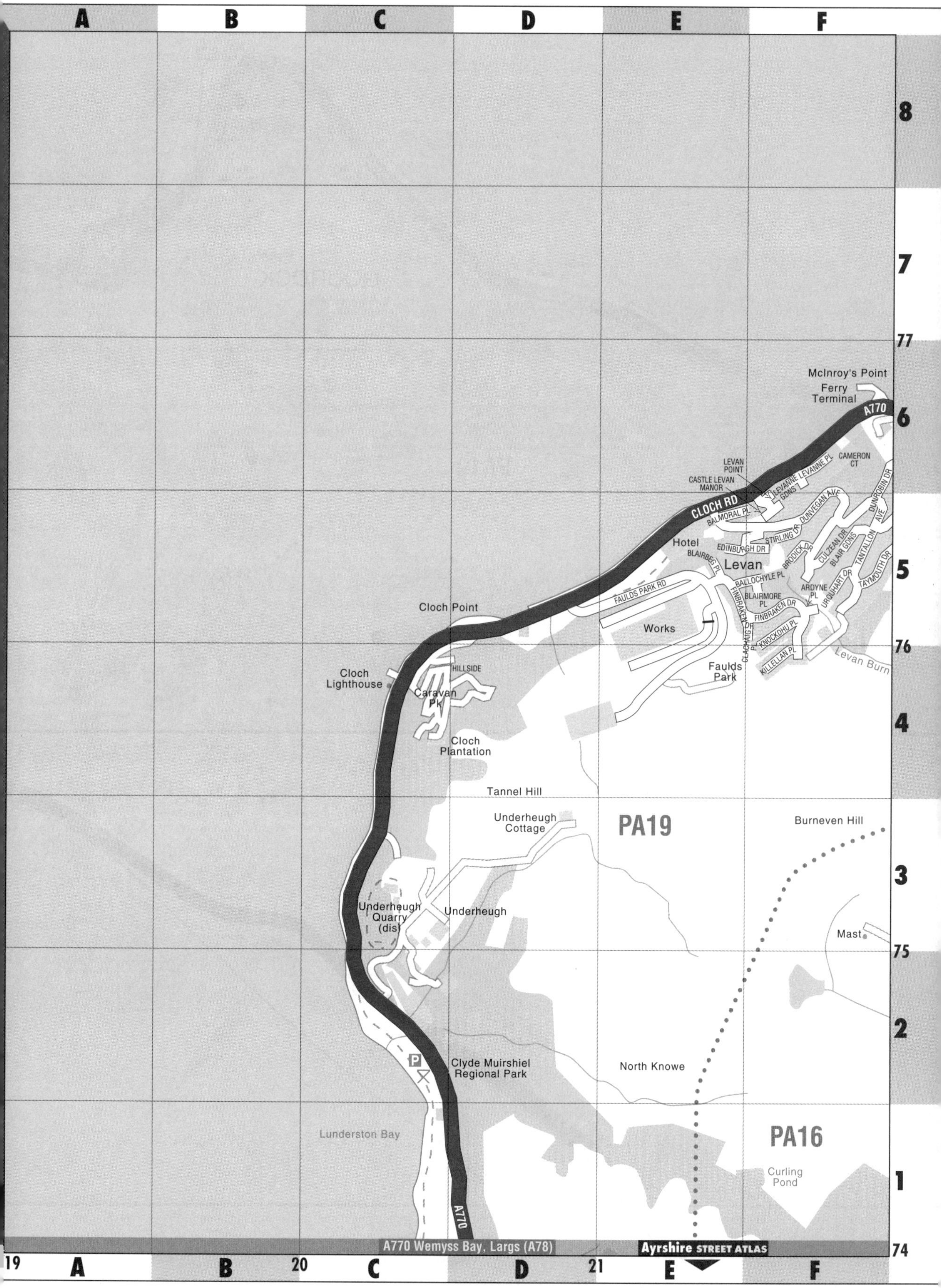
A
B
C
D
E
F
8
7
77
6
5
76
4
3
75
2
1
74
19
20
21
McInroy's Point
Ferry
Terminal
A770
CAMERON
CT
LEVAN
POINT
CASTLE LEVAN
MANOR
LEVANNE
GDNS
LEVANNE PL
CLOCH RD
BALMORAL PL
DUNVEGAN AVE
DUNROBIN DR
AVE
STIRLING DR
Hotel
EDINBURGH DR
BLAIRBEG PL
Levan
BRODICK DR
CULZEAN DR
BLAIR GDNS
TANTALLON
TAYMOUTH DR
FAULDS PARK RD
BALLOCHYLE PL
BLAIRMORE
PL
ARDYNE
PL
URQUHART DR
FINBRAKEN DR
FINBRAKEN DR
CLACHAIG PL
KNOCKDHU PL
KILLELLAN PL
Levan Burn
Cloch Point
Works
Faulds
Park
Cloch
Lighthouse
HILLSIDE
Caravan
Pk
Cloch
Plantation
Tannel Hill
Underheugh
Cottage
PA19
Burneven Hill
Underheugh
Quarry
(dis)
Underheugh
Mast
Clyde Muirshiel
Regional Park
North Knowe
Lunderston Bay
PA16
Curling
Pond
A770
A770 Wemyss Bay, Largs (A78)
Ayrshire STREET ATLAS

44

43

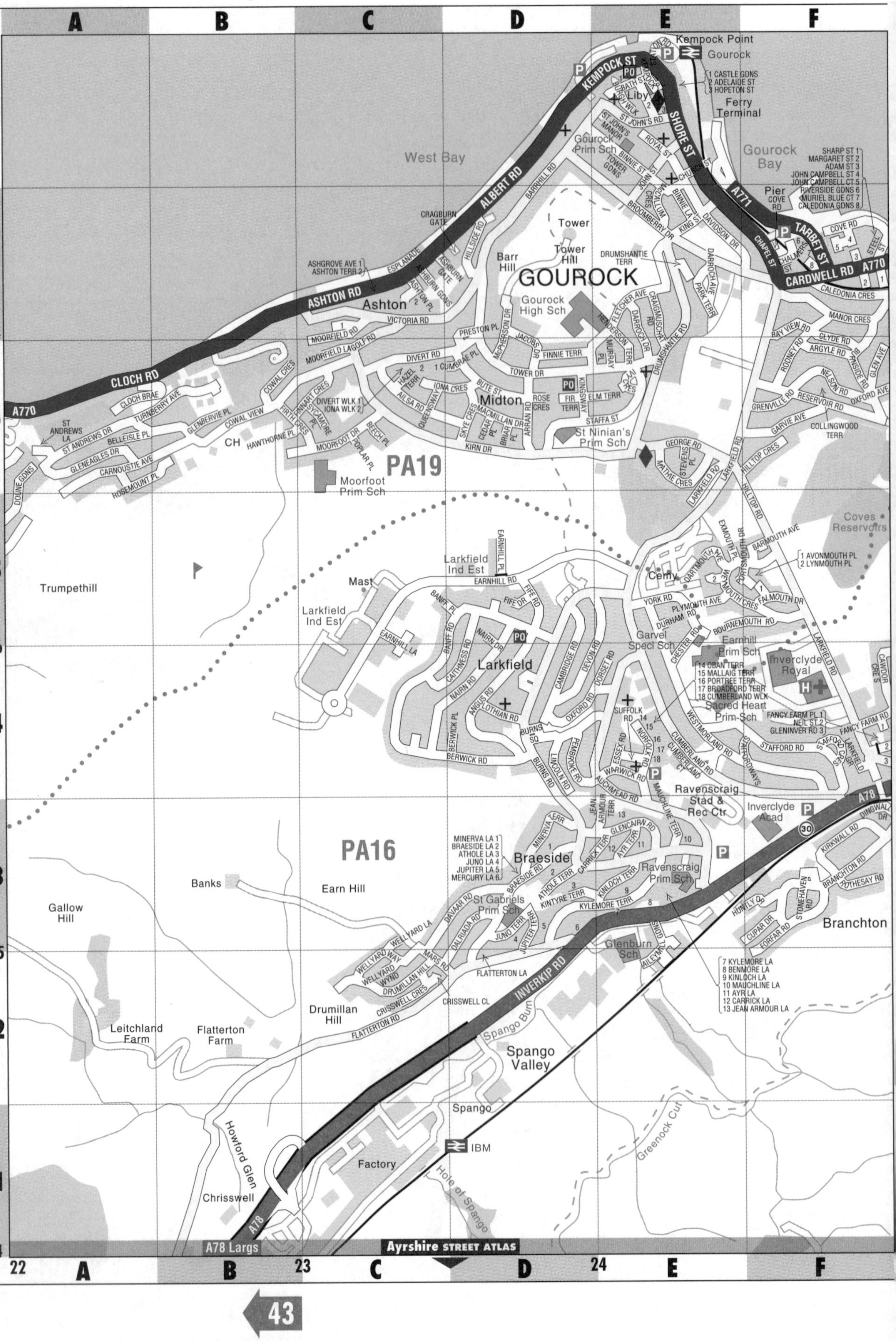
A
B
C
D
E
F
8
7
77
6
5
76
4
3
75
2
1
74
22
23
24
Kempock Point
Gourock
KEMPOCK ST
1 CASTLE GDNS
2 ADELAIDE ST
3 HOPETON ST
Ferry Terminal
Liby
ST JOHN'S RD
SHORE ST
Gourock Prim Sch
West Bay
Gourock Bay
SHARP ST 1
MARGARET ST 2
ADAM ST 3
JOHN CAMPBELL ST 4
JOHN CAMPBELL CT 5
RIVERSIDE GDNS 6
MURIEL BLUE CT 7
CALEDONIA GDNS 8
Pier
COVE RD
ALBERT RD
CRAGBURN GATE
BARRHILL RD
BINNIE ST
ROYAL ST
CHURCH ST
A771
TARBET ST
CHAPEL ST
CARDWELL RD
A770
KING ST
DAVIDSON DR
BROOMBERRY DR
Tower
Tower Hill
Barr Hill
GOUROCK
DRUMSHANTIE TERR
ASHGROVE AVE 1
ASHTON TERR 2
ESPLANADE
ASHTON RD
Ashton
Gourock High Sch
CALEDONIA CRES
MANOR CRES
BAY VIEW RD
CLYDE RD
ARGYLE RD
VICTORIA RD
MOORFIELD RD
PRESTON PL
MOORFIELD LA
GOLF RD
DIVERT RD
CUMBRAE PL
FINNIE TERR
TOWER DR
RODNEY RD
RESERVOIR RD
OXFORD AVE
GRENVILLE RD
GARVIE AVE
COLLINGWOOD TERR
CLOCH RD
CLOCH BRAE
TURNBERRY AVE
IONA CRES
Midton
ROSE CRES
FIR TERR
ELM TERR
STAFFA ST
DIVERT WLK 1
IONA WLK 2
A770
ST ANDREWS LA
ST ANDREWS DR
BELLEISLE PL
GLENBERVIE PL
COWAL VIEW
CH
HAWTHORNE PL
MOORFOOT DR
KIRN DR
St Ninian's Prim Sch
GEORGE RD
HILLTOP CRES
GLENEAGLES DR
CARNOUSTIE AVE
ROSEMOUNT PL
DOUNE GDNS
PA19
Moorfoot Prim Sch
Coves Reservoirs
EARNHILL PL
BARMOUTH AVE
1 AVONMOUTH PL
2 LYNMOUTH PL
Larkfield Ind Est
Cemy
Trumpethill
Mast
EARNHILL RD
YORK RD
PLYMOUTH AVE
FALMOUTH DR
Larkfield Ind Est
DURHAM RD
BOURNEMOUTH RD
Garvel Spec Sch
Earnhill Prim Sch
Inverclyde Royal
EARNHILL LA
Larkfield
14 OBAN TERR
15 MALLAIG TERR
16 PORTREE TERR
17 BROADFORD TERR
18 CUMBERLAND WLK
Sacred Heart Prim Sch
FANCY FARM PL 1
NEIL ST 2
GLENINVER RD 3
FANCY FARM RD
STAFFORD RD
BERWICK RD
Ravenscraig Stad & Rec Ctr
Inverclyde Acad
A78
MINERVA LA 1
BRAESIDE LA 2
ATHOLE LA 3
JUNO LA 4
JUPITER LA 5
MERCURY LA 6
Braeside
PA16
Ravenscraig Prim Sch
Banks
Earn Hill
Gallow Hill
St Gabriels Prim Sch
KYLEMORE TERR
Branchton
Glenburn Sch
FLATTERTON LA
7 KYLEMORE LA
8 BENMORE LA
9 KINLOCH LA
10 MAUCHLINE LA
11 AYR LA
12 CARRICK LA
13 JEAN ARMOUR LA
CRISSWELL CL
Drumillan Hill
FLATTERTON RD
INVERKIP RD
Leitchland Farm
Flatterton Farm
Spango Burn
Spango Valley
Spango
Howford Glen
IBM
Greenock Cut
Factory
Hole of Spango
Chrisswell
A78
A78 Largs
Ayrshire STREET ATLAS

43

46

F5
1 WEST BLACKHALL ST
2 WESTBURN BLDGS
3 Oak Mall Sh Ctr
4 CHARLES PL
5 HIGHLAND MARY PL
6 HAMILTON GATE
7 THE OAK MALL
8 HAMILTON WAY
9 CLYDE SQ
10 CATHCART SQ
11 KILBLAIN ST
12 KILBLAIN CT
13 SIR MICHAEL CT

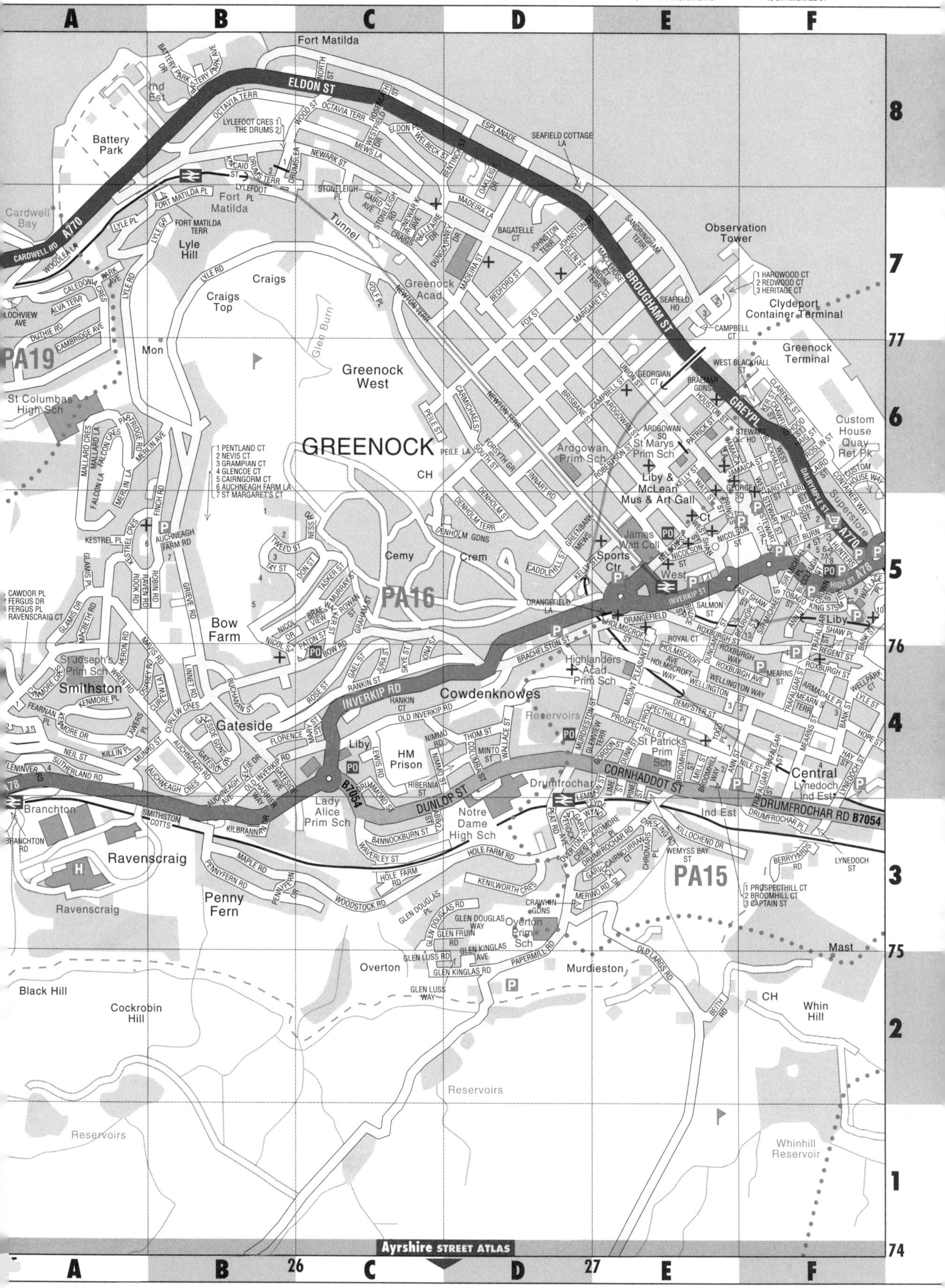

46

F4
1 REGENT CT
2 WHINHILL CT
3 ARMADALE CT
4 DEMPSTER CT

45

Firth of Clyde
GREENOCK
Custom House Quay Ret Pk
Waterfront Leisure Complex
1 WILLIAM ST
2 CROSS SHORE ST
3 EAST BREAST
4 BRYMNER ST
5 NEW DOCK LA
6 OPEN SHORE
7 CATHCART BLDGS
8 STATION AVE
James Watt Coll
Custom House Mus
East India Harbour
Victoria Harbour
1 EAST BLACKHALL ST
2 ST ANDREW ST
3 EMPRESS CT
4 EAST STEWART ST
5 ST ANDREW SQ
Garvel Point
Superstore
Greenock Central
Motel
Dock
Piers
Pier
Great Harbour
Works
Cartsdyke
Bridgend
Cappielow Ind Est
Cappielow Park (Greenock Morton FC)
Ladyburn
Strathclyde Bsns Ctr
Lynedoch Ind Est
Ind Est
St Laurence's Prim Sch
Whinhill
Kings Oak Prim Sch
Bogston
Gibshill
Lady Octavia Park
Rec Ctr
PA15
Strone
PA16
Works
Auchmountain Glen
St Kenneth's Prim Sch
Cemy
Knocknairs Hill
PA14
Craigieknowe Burn
MACGOWAN WAY 1
MACGREGOR RD 2
ALPINE GR 3
THOMAS MUIR LA 1
LILYBANK RD 2
FARQUHAR RD 3
BROADSTONE AVE 4
A8
B788
B7054
RUE END ST
MAIN ST
EAST HAMILTON ST
PORT GLASGOW RD
GREENOCK RD
INGLESTON ST
BAKER ST
KILMACOLM RD
AUCHMOUNTAIN RD
DALRYMPLE ST
JAMES WATT WAY
DRUMFROCHAR RD
KILMUN RD
RIVERSIDE RD
A B C D E F
8 7 77 6 5 76 4 3 75 2 1 74
28 29 30

A4
1 VIRGINIA ST
2 STATION AVE
3 WELLPARK BLDGS
4 LYNEDOCH CT
5 ANTIGUA CT
6 DELLINGBURN ST

B3
1 TREVIOT PL
2 DUNS PL
3 ETTRICK PL
4 JEDBURGH CT
5 KELSO CT
6 LANGHOLM CT
7 MELROSE CT
8 PEEBLES CT
9 SELKIRK CT
10 HAWICK CT
11 FINNESTON LA
12 FINNESTON WAY

45
67

25
48

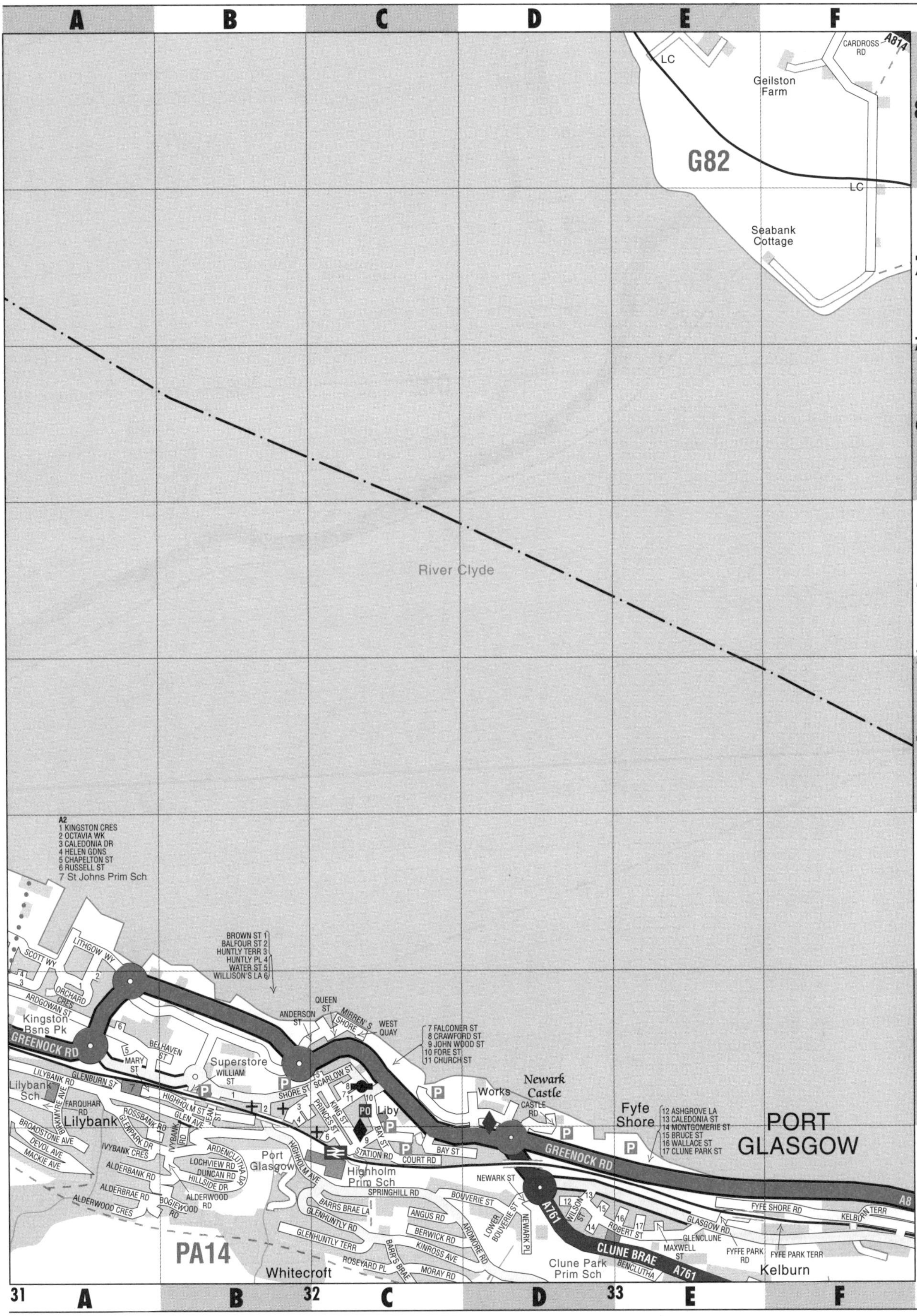
A
B
C
D
E
F
8
7
77
6
5
76
4
3
75
2
1
74
31
32
33
LC
CARDROSS RD
A814
Geilston Farm
G82
LC
Seabank Cottage
River Clyde
A2
1 KINGSTON CRES
2 OCTAVIA WK
3 CALEDONIA DR
4 HELEN GDNS
5 CHAPELTON ST
6 RUSSELL ST
7 St Johns Prim Sch
BROWN ST 1
BALFOUR ST 2
HUNTLY TERR 3
HUNTLY PL 4
WATER ST 5
WILLISON'S LA 6
7 FALCONER ST
8 CRAWFORD ST
9 JOHN WOOD ST
10 FORE ST
11 CHURCH ST
12 ASHGROVE LA
13 CALEDONIA ST
14 MONTGOMERIE ST
15 BRUCE ST
16 WALLACE ST
17 CLUNE PARK ST
SCOTT WY
LITHGOW WY
ORCHARD CRES
ARDGOWAN ST
Kingston Bsns Pk
GREENOCK RD
BELHAVEN ST
MARY ST
Superstore
WILLIAM ST
QUEEN ST
ANDERSON ST
MIRREN'S SHORE
WEST QUAY
SHORE ST
SCARLOW ST
KING ST
PRINCES ST
Liby
BAY ST
STATION RD
COURT RD
Works
Newark Castle
CASTLE RD
Fyfe Shore
PORT GLASGOW
Lilybank Sch
LILYBANK RD
GLENBURN ST
FARQUHAR RD
BRAKMYRE AVE
Lilybank
ROSSBANK RD
GLENPARK DR
HIGHHOLM ST
GLEN AVE
JEAN ST
IVYBANK RD
BROADSTONE AVE
DEVOL AVE
MACKIE AVE
IVYBANK CRES
ALDERBANK RD
ALDERBRAE RD
ALDERWOOD CRES
LOCHVIEW RD
DUNCAN RD
HILLSIDE DR
ARDENCLUTHA DR
ALDERWOOD RD
BOGIEWOOD RD
Port Glasgow
HIGHHOLM AVE
Highholm Prim Sch
SPRINGHILL RD
BARRS BRAE LA
GLENHUNTLY RD
GLENHUNTLY TERR
ROSEYARD PL
BARR'S BRAE
ANGUS RD
BERWICK RD
KINROSS AVE
MORAY RD
ARDMORE RD
BOUVERIE ST
LOWER BOUVERIE ST
NEWARK ST
NEWARK PL
A761
WILSON ST
ROBERT ST
CLUNE BRAE
BENCLUTHA
Clune Park Prim Sch
MAXWELL ST
GLENCLUNE
GLASGOW RD
FYFE SHORE RD
FYFFE PARK RD
FYFFE PARK TERR
KELBURN TERR
Kelburn
A8
PA14
Whitecroft

68
48

47
26

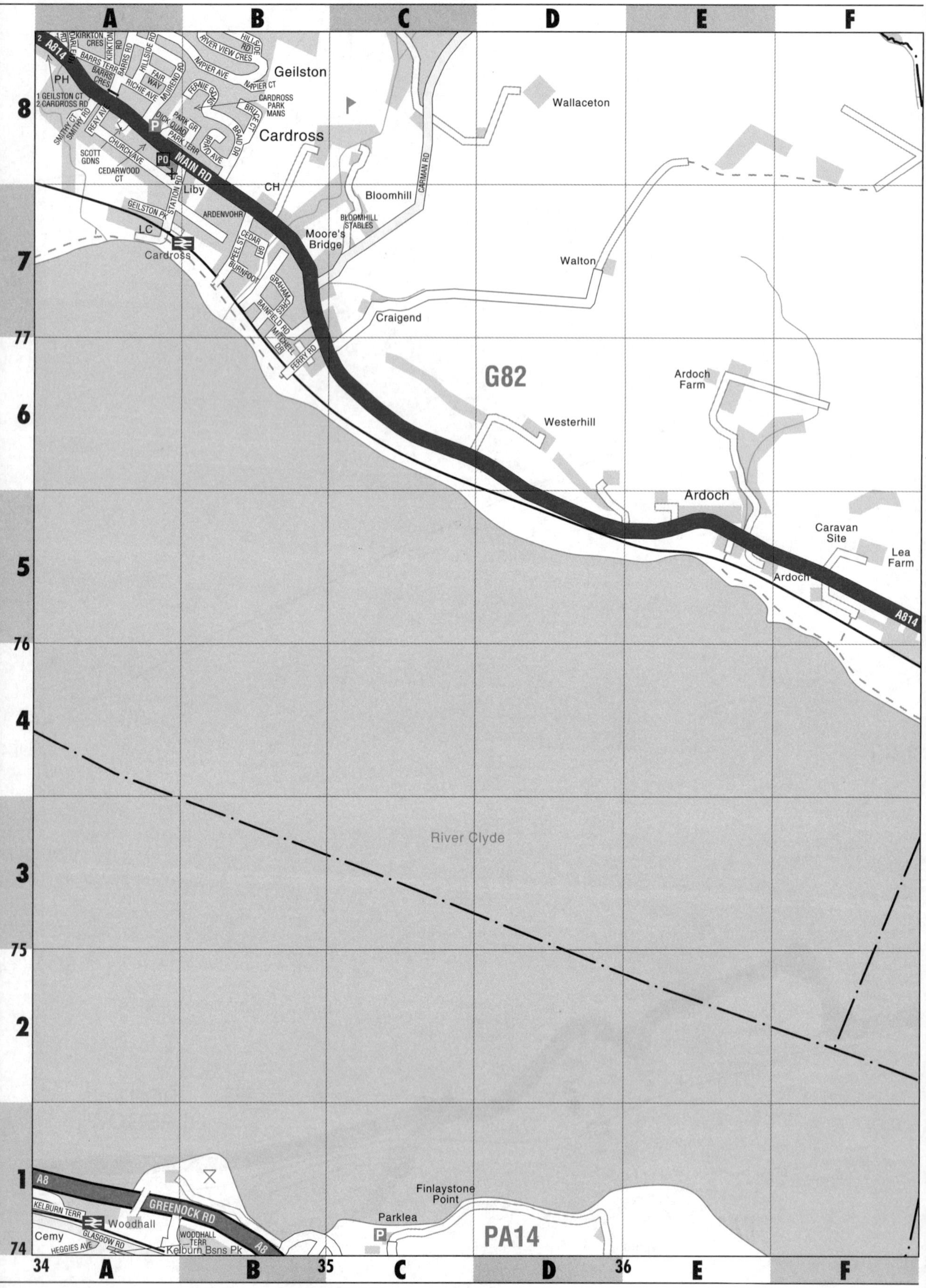
A
B
C
D
E
F
8
7
77
6
5
76
4
3
75
2
1
74
34
35
36
A814
KIRKTON CRES
KIRKTON RD
DARLEITH RD
BARRS TERR
BARRS CRES
BARRS RD
HILLSIDE RD
HILLSIDE RD
RIVER VIEW CRES
NAPIER AVE
NAPIER CT
Geilston
FAIR WAY
MUIREND RD
RICHIE AVE
FERNIE GDNS
CARDROSS PARK MANS
BRUCE CT
PH
1 GEILSTON CT
2 CARDROSS RD
SMITHY CT
SMITHY RD
REAY AVE
P
DICK QUAD
PARK GR
PARK TERR
BRAID DR
BRAID AVE
Cardross
SCOTT GDNS
CHURCH AVE
PO
MAIN RD
CEDARWOOD CT
Liby
CH
STATION RD
GEILSTON PK
ARDENVOHR
Bloomhill
BLOOMHILL STABLES
CARMAN RD
Wallaceton
LC
Cardross
Moore's Bridge
CEDAR GR
PEEL ST
BURNFOOT
GRAHAM CRES
BAINFIELD RD
MITCHELL DR
FERRY RD
Craigend
Walton
G82
Ardoch Farm
Westerhill
Ardoch
Caravan Site
Lea Farm
Ardoch
A814
River Clyde
A8
GREENOCK RD
KELBURN TERR
Woodhall
Cemy
GLASGOW RD
HEGGIES AVE
WOODHALL TERR
Kelburn Bsns Pk
A8
Finlaystone Point
Parklea
P
PA14

47
69

27
50

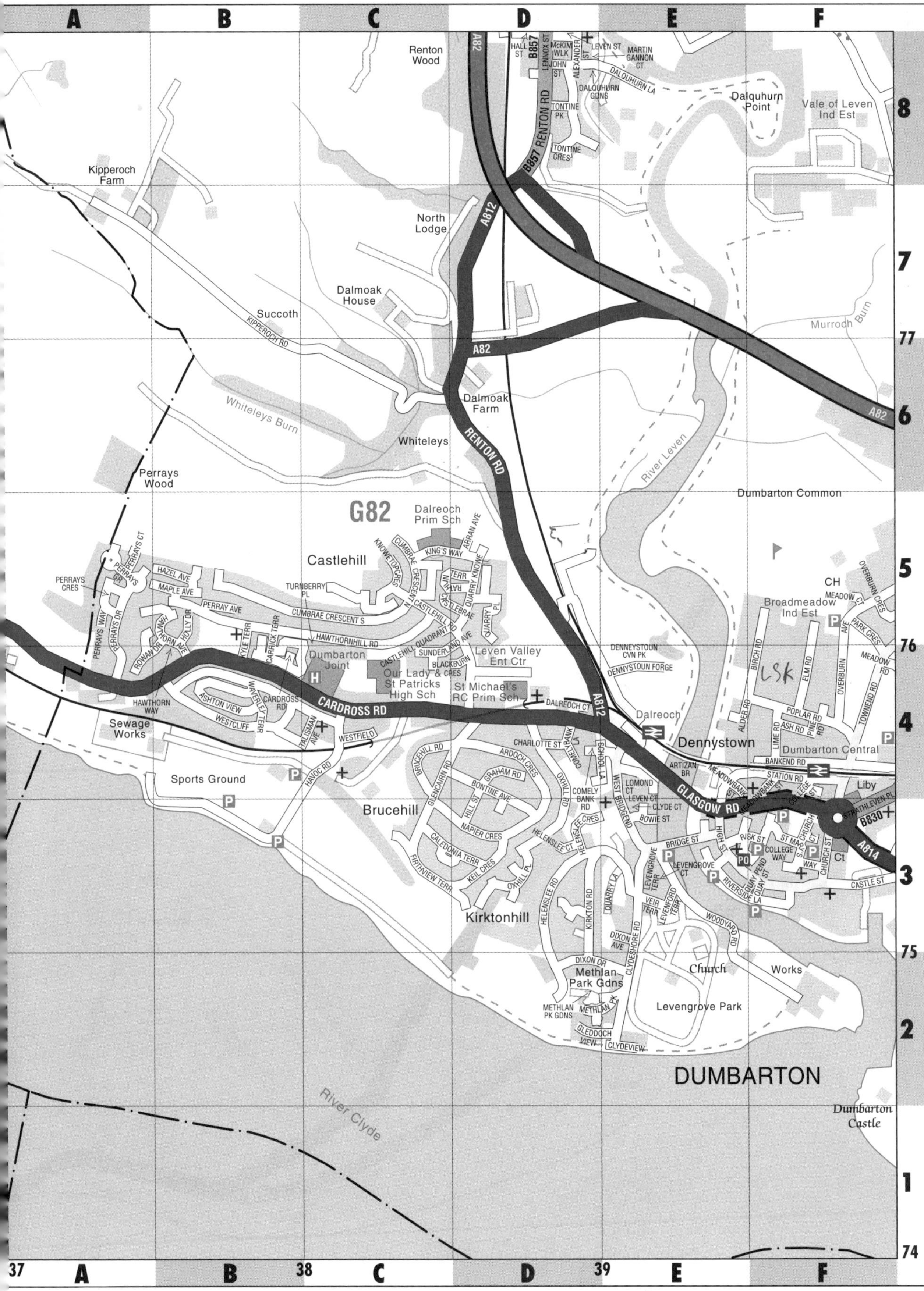
A
B
C
D
E
F
Renton Wood
Kipperoch Farm
Dalquhurn Point
Vale of Leven Ind Est
North Lodge
Dalmoak House
Succoth
KIPPEROCH RD
A82
A812
B857 RENTON RD
HALL ST
McKIM WLK
LENNOX ST
JOHN ST
ALEXANDER ST
LEVEN ST
MARTIN GANNON CT
DALQUHURN LA
DALQUHURN GDNS
TONTINE PK
TONTINE CRES
Murroch Burn
Dalmoak Farm
Whiteleys Burn
Whiteleys
RENTON RD
Perrays Wood
River Leven
Dumbarton Common
G82
Dalreoch Prim Sch
Castlehill
KING'S WAY
ARRAN AVE
CUMBRAE CRESCENT N
KNOWETOP CRES
QUARRY KNOWE
CASTLEHILL RD
QUARRY PL
CASTLEBRAE
TURNBERRY PL
CUMBRAE CRESCENT S
HAWTHORNHILL RD
CASTLEHILL QUADRANT
SUNDERLAND AVE
BLACKBURN CRES
PERRAYS CT
PERRAYS CRES
PERRAYS GR
PERRAYS WAY
PERRAYS DR
HAZEL AVE
MAPLE AVE
PERRAY AVE
HOLLY DR
ROWAN DR
KYLE TERR
CARRICK TERR
Dumbarton Joint
Our Lady & St Patricks High Sch
Leven Valley Ent Ctr
St Michael's RC Prim Sch
DALREOCH CT
HAWTHORN WAY
ASHTON VIEW
WAVERLEY TERR
CARDROSS RD
WESTCLIFF
TALISMAN AVE
WESTFIELD
Sewage Works
Sports Ground
HAVOC RD
Brucehill
BRUCEHILL RD
GLENCAIRN RD
HILL ST
GRAHAM RD
BONTINE AVE
ARDOCH CRES
NAPIER CRES
CALEDONIA TERR
KEIL CRES
FIRTHVIEW TERR
OXHILL RD
OXHILL PL
CHARLOTTE ST
COMELY BANK
COMELY BANK RD
SCHOOL LA
WEST BRIDGEND
HELENSLEE CT
HELENSLEE CRES
HELENSLEE RD
Kirktonhill
KIRKTON RD
QUARRY LA
DIXON AVE
DIXON DR
CLYDESHORE RD
Methlan Park Gdns
METHLAN PK GDNS
METHLAN PK
GLEDDOCH VIEW
CLYDEVIEW
DENNEYSTOUN CVN PK
DENNYSTOUN FORGE
Dalreoch
Dennystown
ARTIZAN BR
MEADOWBANK
GLASGOW RD
LOMOND CT
LEVEN CT
CLYDE CT
BOWIE ST
BRIDGE ST
LEVENGROVE TERR
LEVENGROVE CT
VEIR TERR
LEVENFORD TERR
WOODYARD RD
HIGH ST
RISK ST
QUAY PEND
QUAY ST
RIVERSIDE LA
COLLEGE WAY
ST MARY'S WAY
CHURCH CT
CHURCH ST
CASTLE ST
STRATHLEVEN PL
B830
A814
Church
Works
Levengrove Park
Broadmeadow Ind Est
CH
MEADOW CT
OVERBURN CRES
PARK CRES
MEADOW RD
BIRCH RD
ELM RD
OVERBURN AVE
TOWNEND RD
ALDER RD
LIME RD
ASH RD
PINE RD
POPLAR RD
Dumbarton Central
BANKEND RD
STATION RD
Liby
Ct
DUMBARTON
Dumbarton Castle
River Clyde
8
7
77
6
5
76
4
3
75
2
1
74
37
38
39

70
50

49
28

A
B
C
D
E
F
8
7
77
6
5
76
4
3
75
2
1
74
40
41
42
A813
STIRLING RD
Murroch Burn
G83
Murroch
Square Wood
Black Wood
Barr Wood
Maryland
Garshake Burn
Overtoun Burn
KINGLAS HO 1
FRUIN HO 2
ENDRICK HO 3
TAY PL
DOUGLAS HO
ALLAN CRES
Bellsmyre
St Peter's RC Prim Sch
BELLSMYRE AVE
VALEVIEW TERR
LANGLANDS TERR
MERKINS AVE
LOANINGHEAD DR
BARWOOD HILL
HOWATSHAWS RD
MURROCH AVE
LONG CRAGS VIEW
MARYLAND RD
MUIR RD
BRACKENHURST ST
GLENSIDE RD
AUCHENREOCH AVE
AITKENBAR DR
STONEYFLATT AVE
Lomondgate
A82
CARMAN VIEW
LOMOND DR
ST ANDREW'S BRAE
AITKENBAR CIRC
BRAESIDE DR
BROOMHILL DR
STONEYFLATT RD
WHITEFORD AVE
PENNIECROFT AVE
Aitkenbar Prim Sch
Water Works
Garshake
Garshake Reservoir
GOOSEHOLM CRES
GOOSEHOLM RD
BARLOAN PL
GLEBE PK
STONEYFLATT CT
ST ANDREW'S CRES
MANSEWOOD DR
WHITEFORD CRES
1 WHITEFORD GDNS
2 STONEYFLATT GDNS
OVERBURN AVE
STRATHCLYDE RD
DOVEHOLM
B830
BARLOAN CRES
DUMBUCK RD
PINEWOOD CT
WHITEFORD PL
Cemy
GARSHAKE AVE
GARSHAKE TERR
HILLFOOT AVE
GARSHAKE RD
MACPHIE RD
Spardie Linn
Overtoun Estate
OVERBURN CRES
TOWNEND RD
CHAPELTON AVE
CHAPELTON GDNS
BONHILL RD
COLQUHOUN RD
GIBSON AVE
DOVEHOLM AVE
KILPATRICK VIEW
Townend
ALLAN PL
ALEXANDER ST
GIBSON ST
OVERWOOD GR
McLEOD RD
McGREGOR DR
CAMPBELL TERR
CAMPBELL AVE
POWDFAULD TERR
MEADOW RD
WILLIAMSON AVE
SCAPESLAND TERR
ROUND RIDING RD
NETHERBOG RD
MILLER CT
OVERWOOD DR
BROWN AVE
DUMBARTON
Tom's Seat
HAMILTON ST
LATTA ST
NETHERBOG AVE
BOGHEAD RD
MILLER ST
STUART RD
FRASER AVE
Gruggies Burn
Barwood Hill
HARTFIELD GDNS
Silverton
Dumbarton Acad
BOGHEAD AVE
DUMBUIE AVE
WHITE AVE
CROSSLET AVE
ARGYLL PL
ARGYLL AVE
ERLAND AVE
DUMBUCK RD
MURRAY PL
CAMPBELL DR
Barnhill
PAPPERT
HARTFIELD CT
BROOMFAULD GDNS
MILLBURN RD
MILLBURN AVE
CROSSLET CT
Crosslet
G82
1 BANKEND RD
2 STRATHLEVEN PL
Superstores
St Patrick's RC Prim Sch
CROSSLET RD
CROSSLET PL
DOUGLAS RD
LENNOX CRES
LENNOX RD
ALCLUTHA AVE
DUNBRITTON RD
STROWAN'S WELL RD
Loch Bowie
Middleton
A814
Dumbarton East
PARK ST
SMOLLETT RD
STROWAN'S RD
GLENPATH
BARNHILL RD
HUNTER'S AVE
CASTLE ST
LEVEN ST
LENNOX ST
PARK AVE
SILVERTON AVE
OVERTOUN AVE
GREENHEAD RD
GEILS QUADRANT
HIGH MAINS AVE
FOURTH AVE
Northwood
Denny Tank (Mus)
Knoxland Prim Sch
WALLACE ST
VICTORIA ST
BRUCE ST
BUCHANAN ST
GREENHEAD GDNS
GREENHEAD AVE
GEILS AVE
SECOND AVE
THIRD AVE
Dumbowie
Superstores
DENNY CRES
CASTLEGREEN LA
CASTLEGREEN CRES
EASTFIELD CRES
DUMBUCK GDNS
DUMBUCK CRES
FIRST AVE
MILTON BRAE
Milton House
DENNY RD
KNOXLAND SQ
PIONEER PK
CASTLEGREEN ST
Strathclyde Homes Stad (Dumbarton FC)
KNOXLAND ST 1
BURNSIDE PL 2
BURNSIDE ST 3
EASTFIELD PL 4
CASTLEGREEN GDNS
CATRIONA PL
MARY FISHER CRES
BERENICE PL
OTAGO PL
CUTTY SARK PL
OAKTREE GDNS
CASTLE RD
Works
Hotel
MILTON CT
MILTON HILL
Milton
HILL VIEW
WHYTE CNR
PH
Dumbuck
LENNOX RD
COLQUHOUN RD
CRANNOG CT
CRANNOG RD
DUMBARTON RD
MILLERSLEA
River Clyde

A4
1 Braehead
Prim Sch

49
71

52

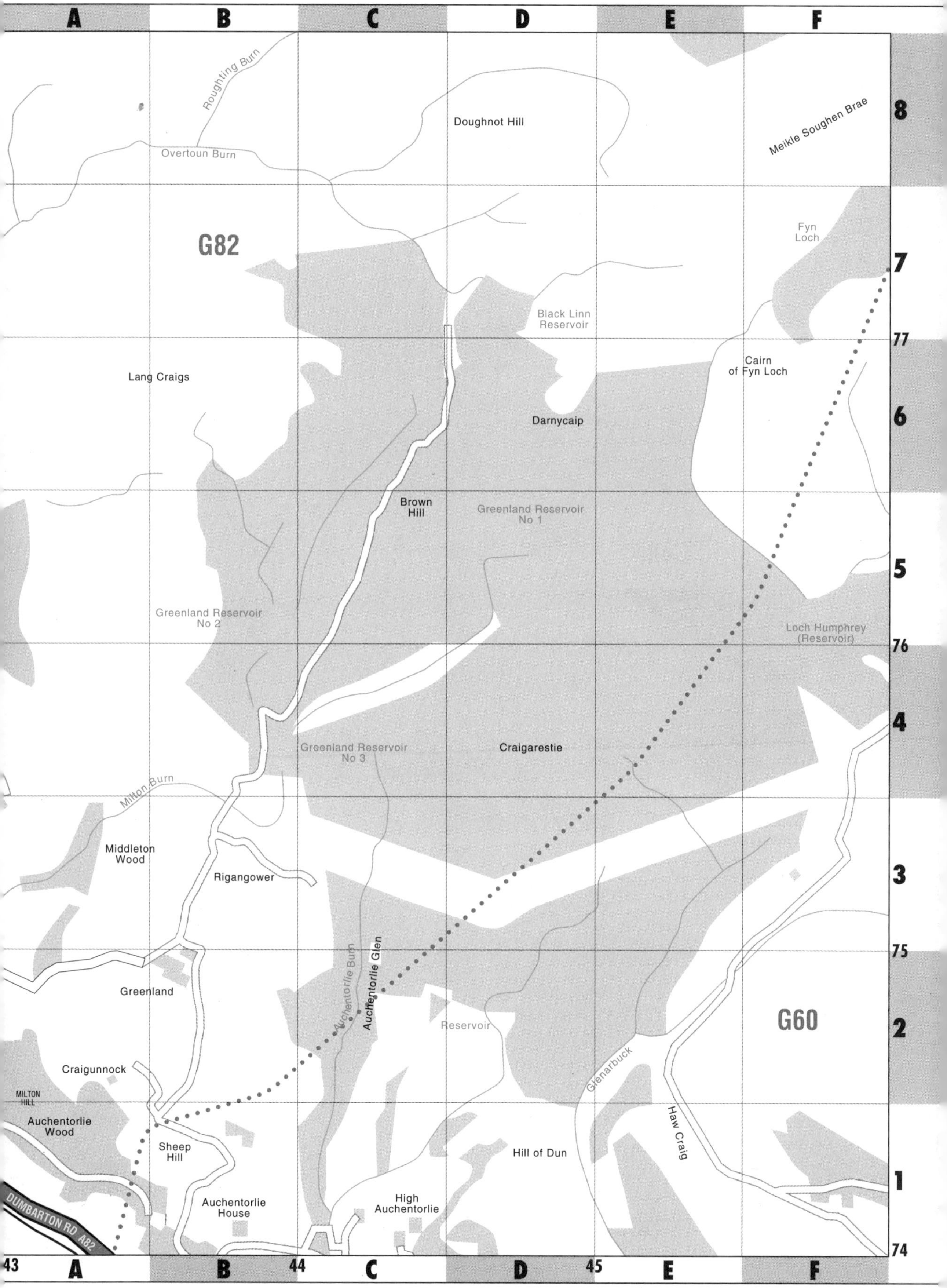
A
B
C
D
E
F
8
7
77
6
5
76
4
3
75
2
1
74
Roughting Burn
Overtoun Burn
Doughnot Hill
Meikle Soughen Brae
G82
Fyn
Loch
Black Linn
Reservoir
Lang Craigs
Cairn
of Fyn Loch
Darnycaip
Brown
Hill
Greenland Reservoir
No 1
Greenland Reservoir
No 2
Loch Humphrey
(Reservoir)
Greenland Reservoir
No 3
Craigarestie
Milton Burn
Middleton
Wood
Rigangower
Auchentorlie Burn
Auchentorlie Glen
Greenland
Reservoir
G60
Craigunnock
Glenarbuck
MILTON
HILL
Auchentorlie
Wood
Haw Craig
Sheep
Hill
Hill of Dun
DUMBARTON RD A82
Auchentorlie
House
High
Auchentorlie
43
44
45

72
52

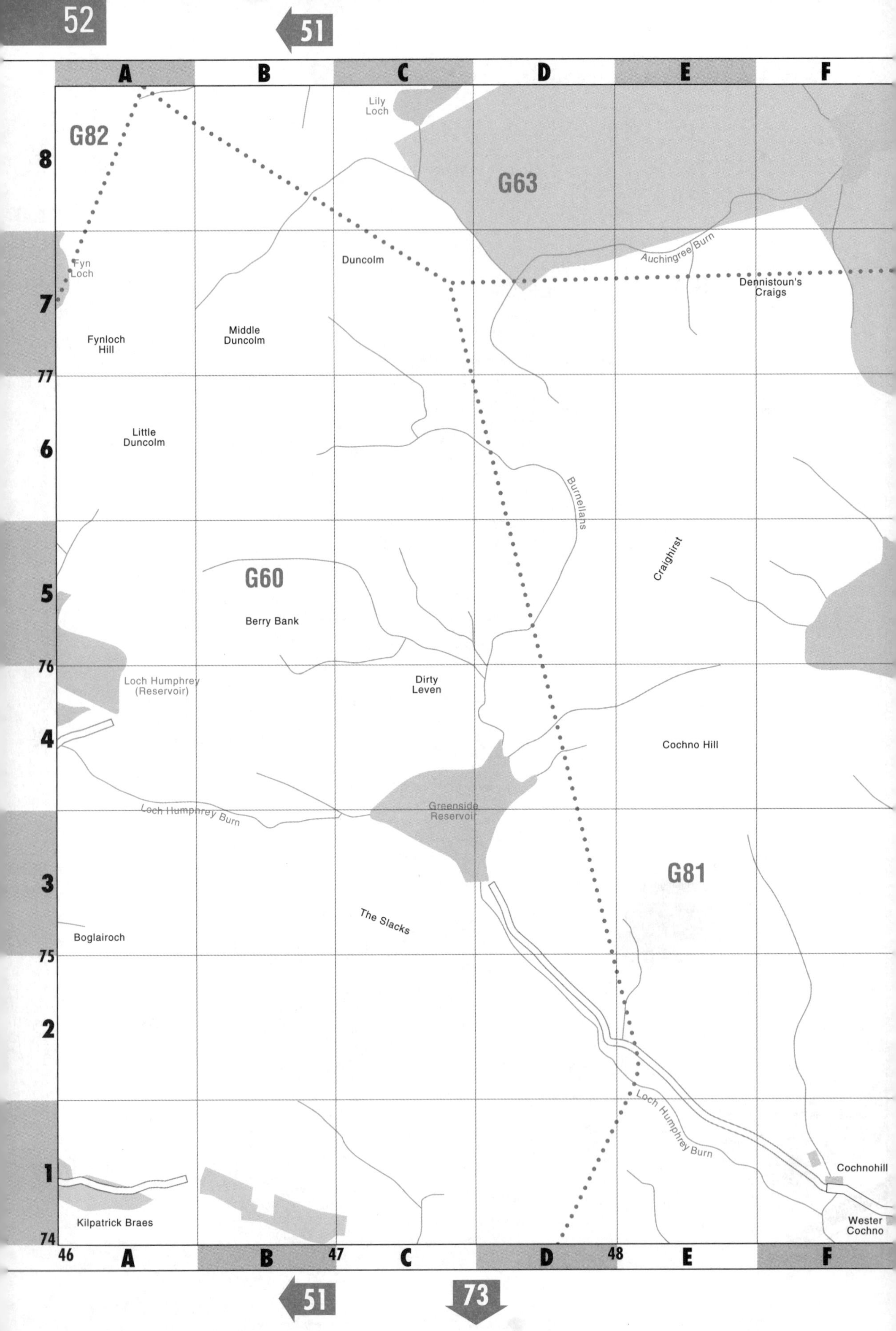
51
A
B
C
D
E
F
Lily Loch
G82
8
G63
Fyn Loch
Duncolm
Auchingree Burn
Dennistoun's Craigs
7
Fynloch Hill
Middle Duncolm
77
Little Duncolm
6
Burnellans
Craighirst
G60
5
Berry Bank
76
Loch Humphrey (Reservoir)
Dirty Leven
4
Cochno Hill
Loch Humphrey Burn
Greenside Reservoir
3
G81
The Slacks
Boglairoch
75
2
Loch Humphrey Burn
1
Cochnohill
Kilpatrick Braes
Wester Cochno
74
46
47
48
A
B
C
D
E
F
51
73

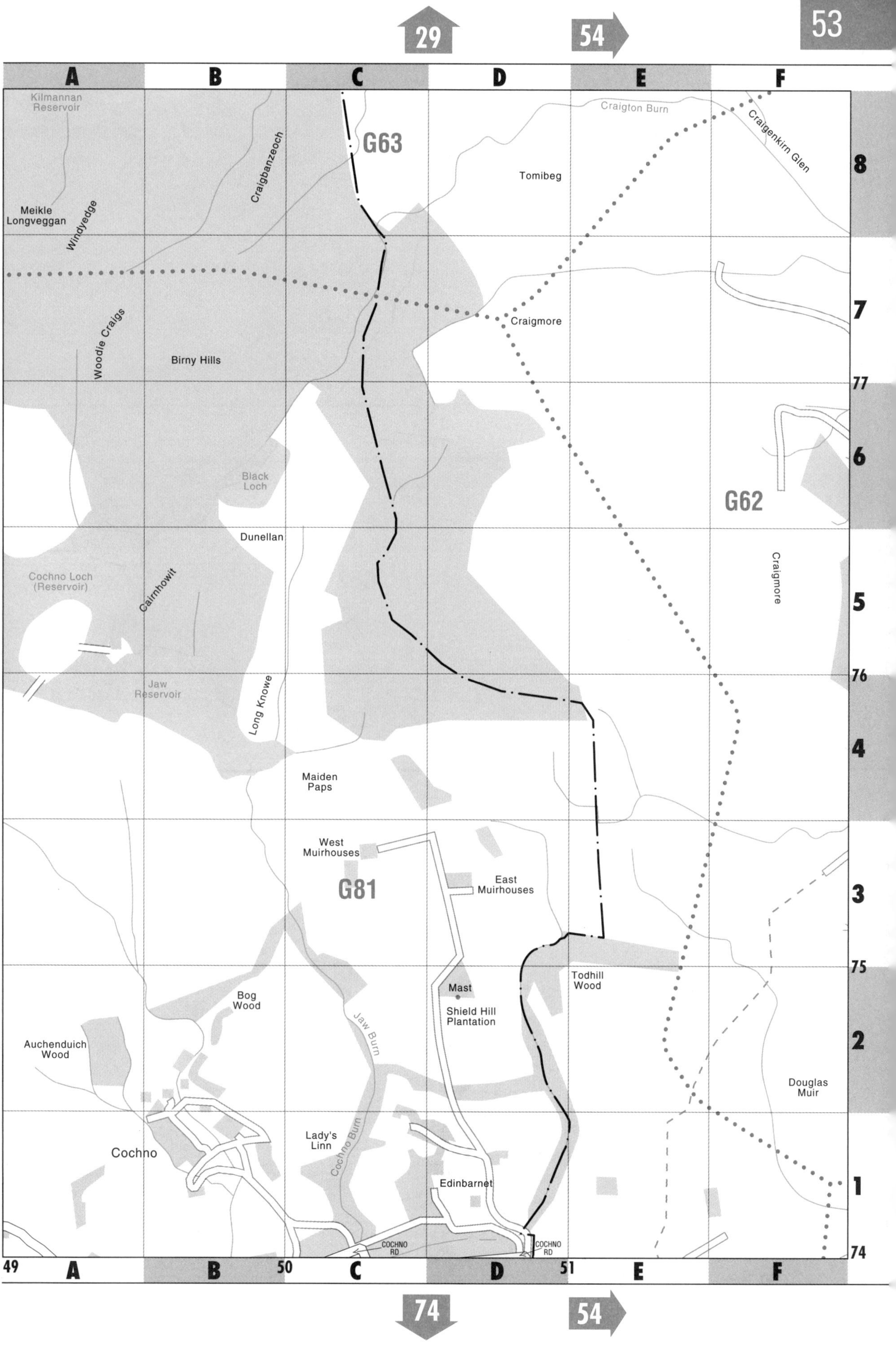
29
54
A
B
C
D
E
F
Kilmannan Reservoir
G63
Craigton Burn
Craigenkirn Glen
8
Craigbanzeoch
Tomibeg
Meikle Longveggan
Windyedge
7
Craigmore
Woodie Craigs
Birny Hills
77
6
Black Loch
G62
Dunellan
Craigmore
Cochno Loch (Reservoir)
Cairnhowit
5
76
Jaw Reservoir
Long Knowe
4
Maiden Paps
West Muirhouses
East Muirhouses
G81
3
75
Todhill Wood
Mast
Bog Wood
Shield Hill Plantation
Jaw Burn
Auchenduich Wood
2
Douglas Muir
Lady's Linn
Cochno
Cochno Burn
Edinbarnet
1
COCHNO RD
COCHNO RD
74
49
50
51
74
54

53
30

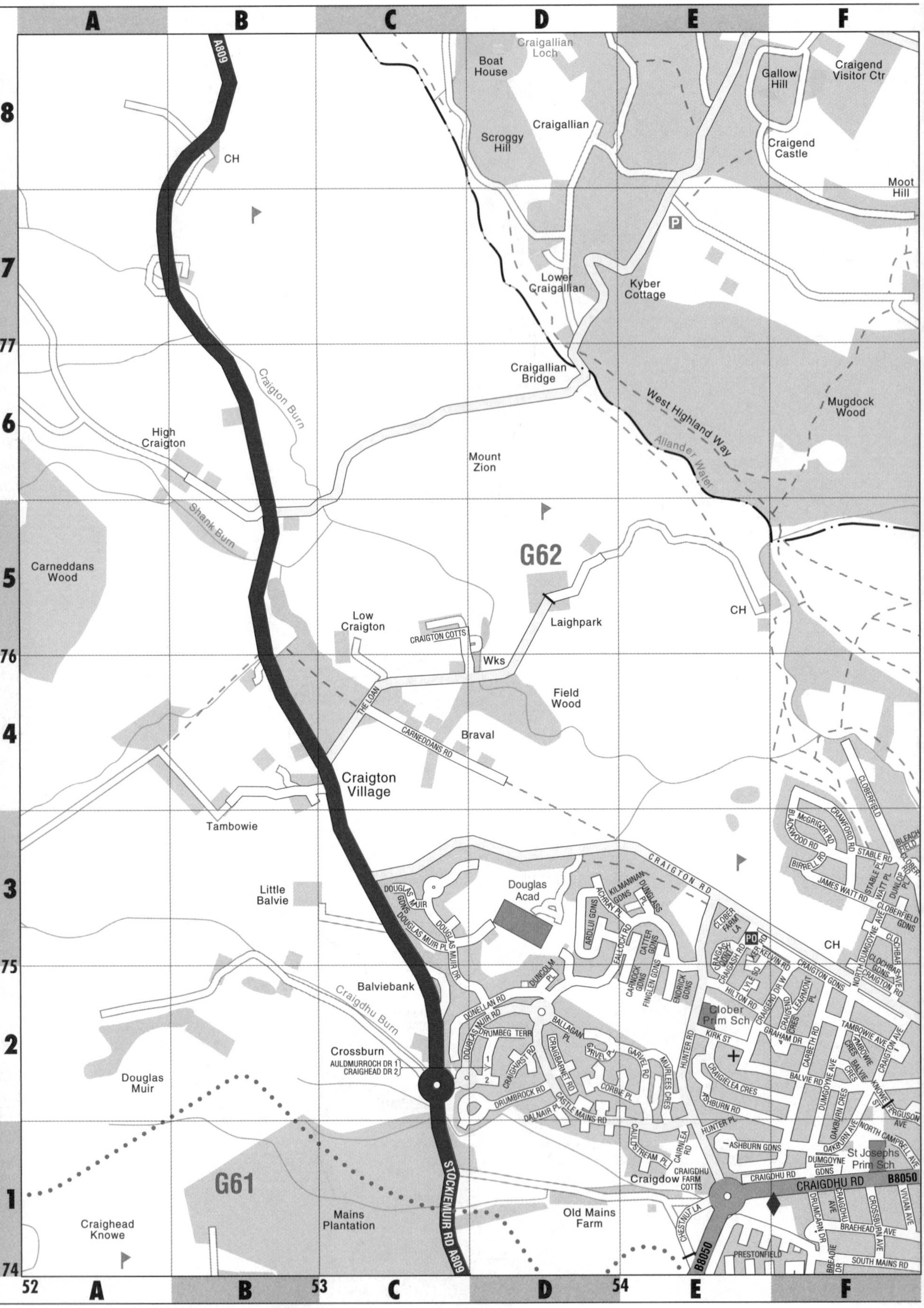
A
B
C
D
E
F
8
7
77
6
5
76
4
3
75
2
1
74
52
53
54
A809
Craigallian Loch
Boat House
Gallow Hill
Craigend Visitor Ctr
Craigallian
Scroggy Hill
CH
Craigend Castle
Moot Hill
P
Lower Craigallian
Kyber Cottage
Craigallian Bridge
Craigton Burn
West Highland Way
Mugdock Wood
High Craigton
Allander Water
Mount Zion
Shank Burn
G62
Carneddans Wood
CH
Low Craigton
Laighpark
CRAIGTON COTTS
Wks
Field Wood
THE LOAN
Braval
CARNEDDANS RD
Craigton Village
Tambowie
CLOBERFIELD
McGRIGOR RD
CRAWFORD RD
BLACKWOOD RD
STABLE RD
BIRRELL RD
JAMES WATT RD
STABLE PL
WATT PL
DUNLOP PL
CLOBERFIELD GDNS
BLEACH FIELD
CLOBER RD
CRAIGTON RD
Little Balvie
DOUGLAS MUIR GDNS
Douglas Acad
KILMANNAN GDNS
ACHRAY PL
DUNGLASS PL
DOUGLAS MUIR PL
ARDLUI GDNS
FALLOCH RD
CATTER GDNS
CLOBER FARM LA
PO
CH
NORTH DUMGOYNE AVE
CLOCHBAR AVE
CLOCHBAR GDNS
CRAIGTON RD
DOUGLAS MUIR DR
DUNCOLM PL
CARNOCK GDNS
FINGLEN GDNS
ENDRICK GDNS
KELVIN RD
CRAIGASH RD
LYLE SQ
HILTON RD
CRAIGTON GDNS
LEARMONT PL
Balviebank
DUNELLAN RD
Clober Prim Sch
CRAIGEND DR W
Craigdhu Burn
DOUGLAS MUIR RD
DRUMBEG TERR
BALLAGAN PL
KIRK ST
GRAHAM DR
CARBETH RD
TAMBOWIE AVE
TAMBOWIE CRES
CRAIGTON AVE
Crossburn
AULDMURROCH DR 1
CRAIGHEAD DR 2
CRAIGHIRST RD
CRAIGBARNET RD
GARVEL PL
GARVEL RD
MUIRLEES CRES
HUNTER RD
CRAIGIELEA CRES
BALVIE RD
DUMGOYNE AVE
BALVIE CRES
KNOWE ST
Douglas Muir
CORBIE PL
ASHBURN RD
DUMBURN CRES
FERGUSON AVE
DRUMBROCK RD
DALNAIR PL
CASTLE MAINS RD
HUNTER PL
OAKBURN CRES
OAKBURN AVE
NORTH CAMPBELL AVE
CAULDSTREAM PL
CAIRNLEA RD
ASHBURN GDNS
DUMGOYNE GDNS
St Josephs Prim Sch
STOCKIEMUIR RD A809
G61
Craigdow
CRAIGDHU FARM COTTS
CRAIGDHU RD
CRAIGDHU RD
B8050
Mains Plantation
Old Mains Farm
CHESTNUT LA
DRUMCAIRN DR
CRAIGDHU AVE
CROSSBURN AVE
VIVIAN AVE
BRAEHEAD AVE
Craighead Knowe
B8050
PRESTONFIELD
BREADIE DR
SOUTH MAINS RD

53
75

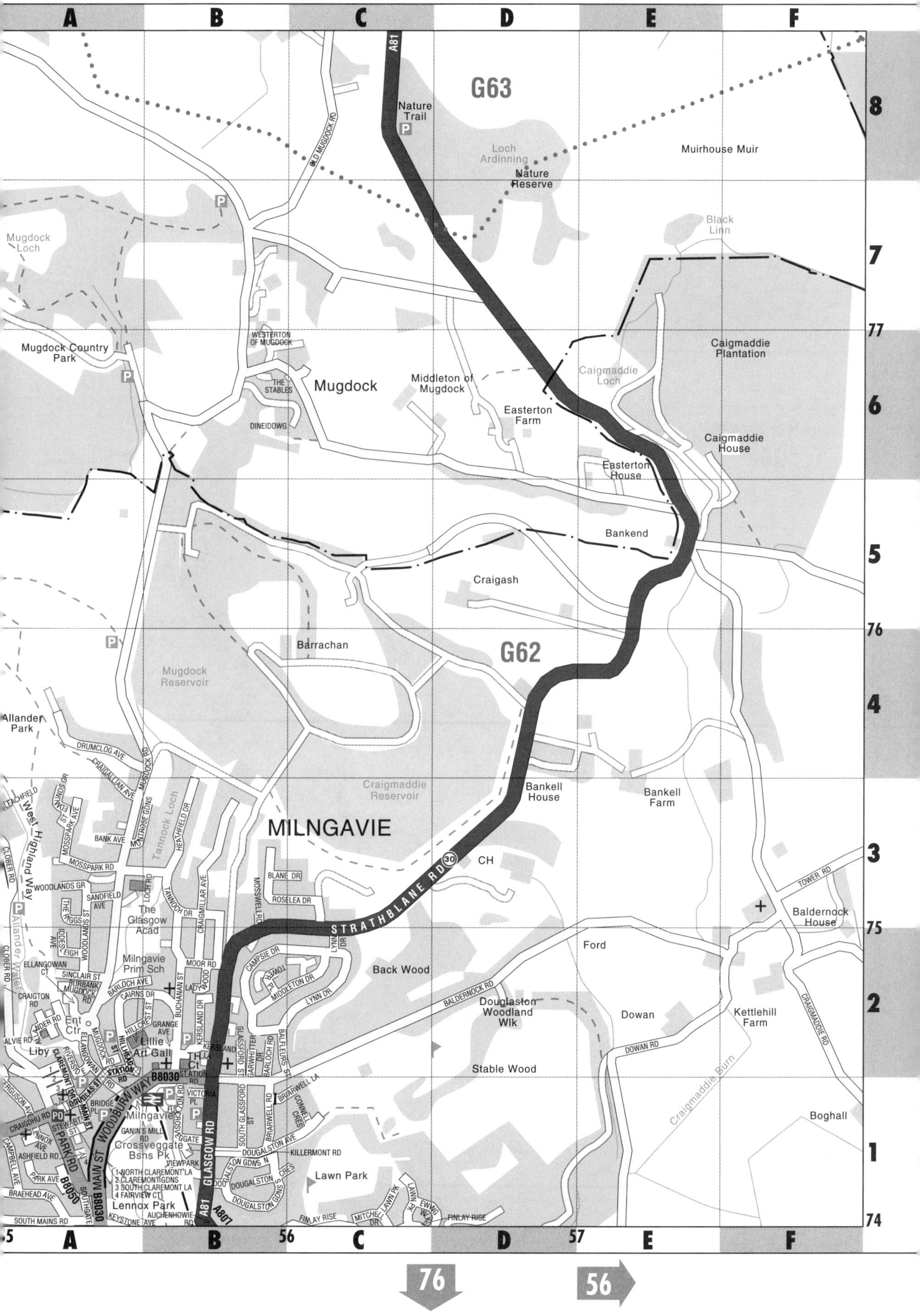
31
56
A
B
C
D
E
F
8
7
77
6
5
76
4
3
75
2
1
74
G63
G62
Nature Trail
Loch Ardinning
Nature Reserve
Muirhouse Muir
Black Linn
Mugdock Loch
Mugdock Country Park
Westerton of Mugdock
The Stables
Mugdock
Dineiddwg
Middleton of Mugdock
Easterton Farm
Caigmaddie Loch
Caigmaddie Plantation
Caigmaddie House
Easterton House
Bankend
Craigash
Barrachan
Mugdock Reservoir
Allander Park
Craigmaddie Reservoir
Bankell House
Bankell Farm
MILNGAVIE
Tannock Loch
West Highland Way
Allander Water
STRATHBLANE RD
CH
Baldernock House
Tower Rd
Ford
Back Wood
Douglaston Woodland Wlk
Dowan
Kettlehill Farm
Stable Wood
Craigmaddie Burn
Boghall
Lawn Park
The Glasgow Acad
Milngavie Prim Sch
Lillie Art Gall
Ent Ctr
Liby
Milngavie
Crossveggate Bsns Pk
Lennox Park
1 North Claremont La
2 Claremont Gdns
3 South Claremont La
4 Fairview Ct
Glasgow Rd
A81
A807
B8030
B8050
Main St
Woodburn Way
Station Rd
Baldernock Rd
Dowan Rd
Craigmaddie Rd
Killermont Rd
Douglaston Ave
Finlay Rise
Keystone Ave
South Mains Rd
Braehead Ave
Park Ave
Campbell Ave
Ashfield Rd
Craigdhu Rd
Stewart St
Park Rd
Southgate
Old Mugdock Rd
Mugdock Rd
Drumclog Ave
Craigallian Ave
Montrose Gdns
Heathfield Dr
Mosspark Ave
Mosspark Rd
Bank Ave
Woodlands Gr
Sandfield Ave
Woodlands St
Loch Rd
Tannoch Dr
Craigmillar Ave
Moor Rd
Blane Dr
Roselea Dr
Mosswell Rd
Campsie Dr
Tower Pl
Middleton Dr
Lynn Dr
Kersland Dr
Buchanan St
Barloch Ave
Cairns Dr
Grange Ave
Hillcrest St
Glassford St
Garwhitter Dr
Barloch Rd
Balfleurs St
Briarwell La
Briarwell Rd
South Glassford St
Connell Cres
Douglaston Gdns N
Douglaston Gdns S
Douglaston Cres
Ellangowan Ct
Sinclair St
Burbank
Craigton Rd
Clober Rd
Station Rd
Victoria Pl
Gavin's Mill Rd
Viewpark
Auchenhowie Rd
Mitchell Dr
Lawn Pk
Ewing Wlk
56
57
76
56

55
32

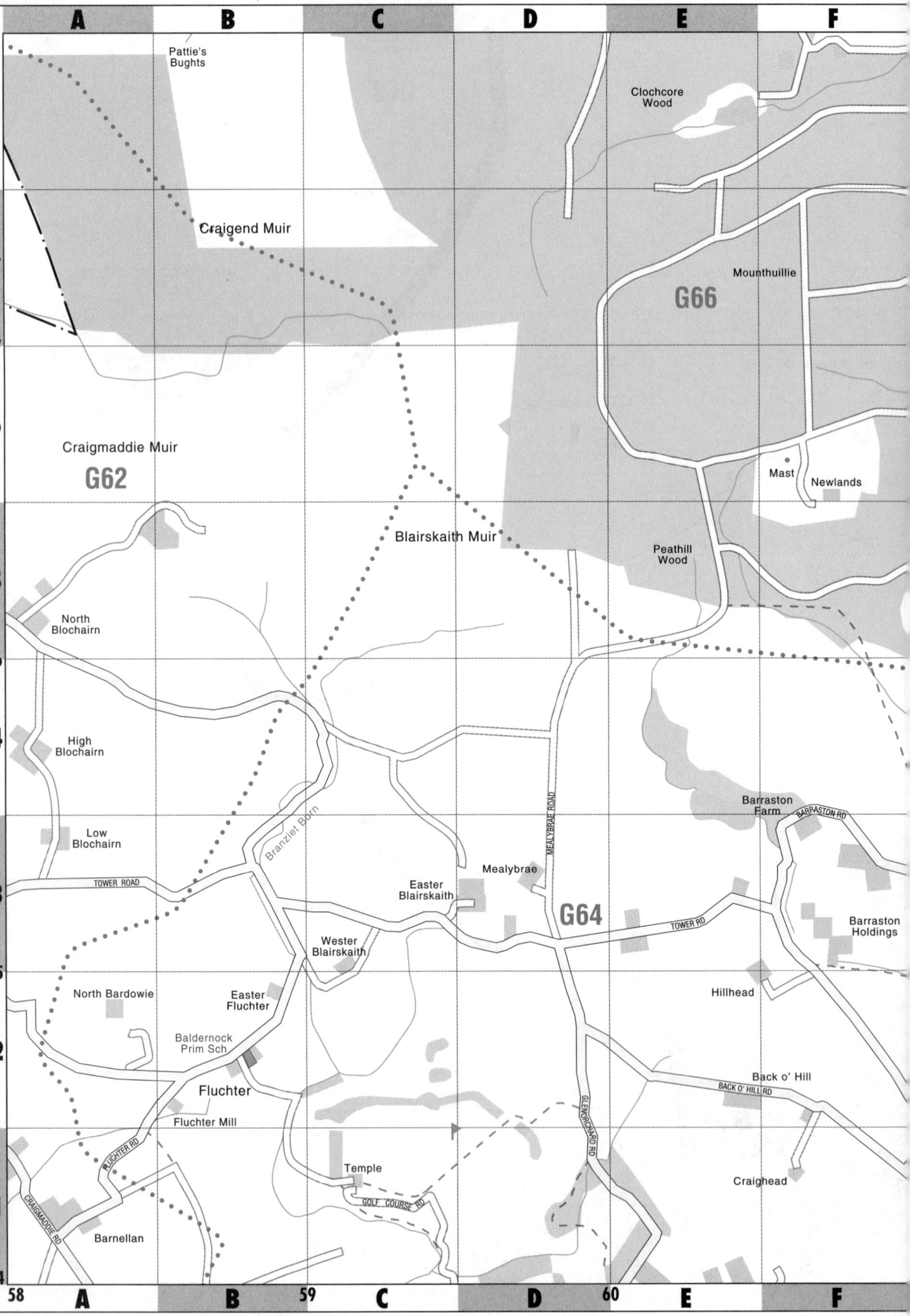
A
B
C
D
E
F
8
7
77
6
5
76
4
3
75
2
1
74
58
59
60
Pattie's Bughts
Clochcore Wood
Craigend Muir
Mounthuillie
G66
Craigmaddie Muir
G62
Mast
Newlands
Blairskaith Muir
Peathill Wood
North Blochairn
High Blochairn
Barraston Farm
BARRASTON RD
MEALYBRAE ROAD
Low Blochairn
Branziet Burn
Mealybrae
TOWER ROAD
Easter Blairskaith
G64
TOWER RD
Barraston Holdings
Wester Blairskaith
North Bardowie
Easter Fluchter
Hillhead
Baldernock Prim Sch
Back o' Hill
BACK O' HILL RD
Fluchter
Fluchter Mill
GLENORCHARD RD
FLUCHTER RD
Temple
Craighead
GOLF COURSE RD
CRAIGMADDIE RD
Barnellan

55
77

33 58

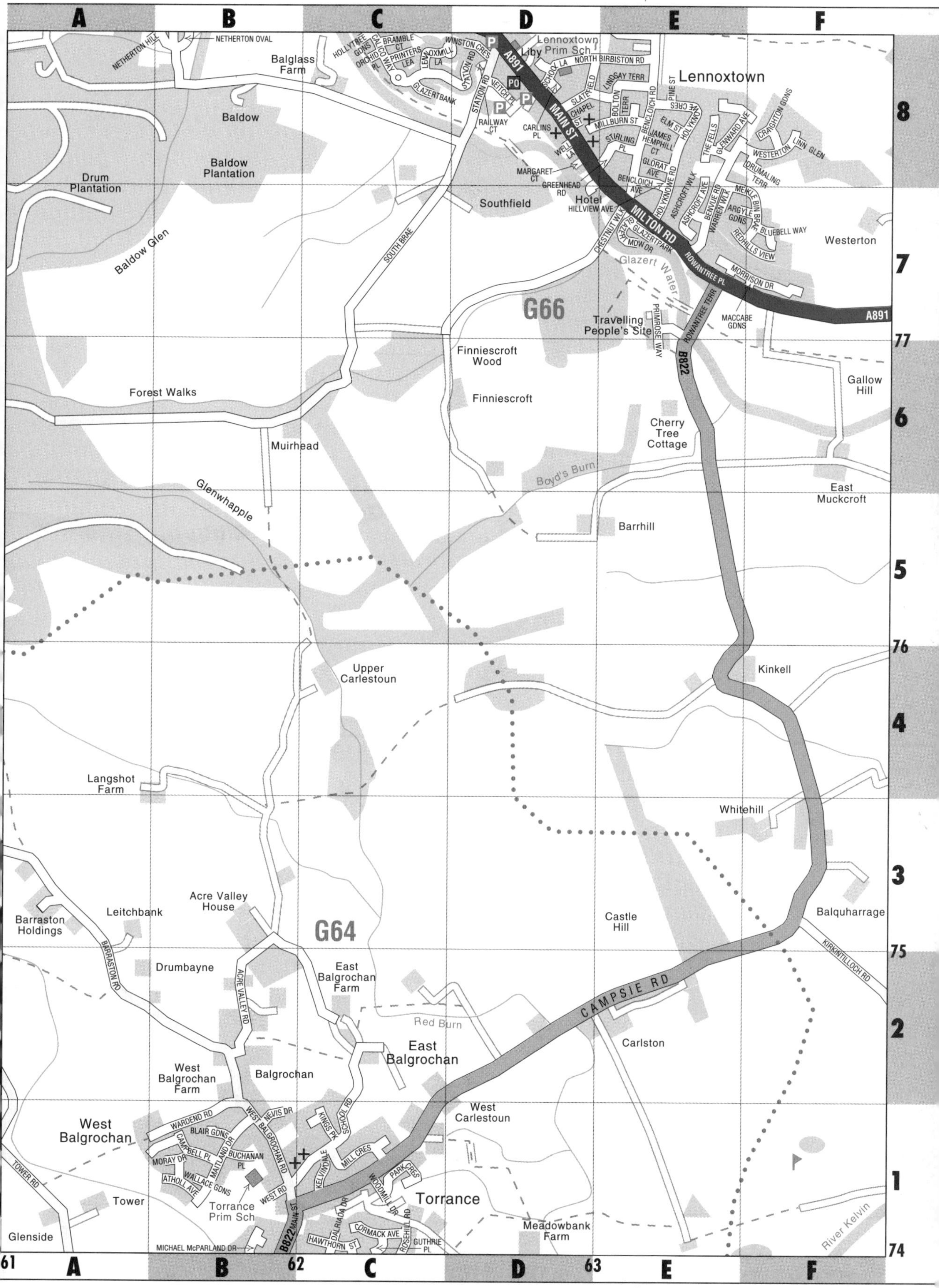

A B C D E F
8 7 6 5 4 3 2 1
77 76 75 74
61 62 63
Lennoxtown
Lennoxtown Prim Sch
Liby
Balglass Farm
Baldow
Baldow Plantation
Drum Plantation
Baldow Glen
Southfield
Hotel
Westerton
Glazert Water
G66
Travelling People's Site
Finniescroft Wood
Finniescroft
Forest Walks
Muirhead
Cherry Tree Cottage
Gallow Hill
Boyd's Burn
East Muckcroft
Glenwhapple
Barrhill
Upper Carlestoun
Kinkell
Langshot Farm
Whitehill
Acre Valley House
Leitchbank
Barraston Holdings
Castle Hill
Balquharrage
G64
Drumbayne
East Balgrochan Farm
Red Burn
East Balgrochan
Carlston
Balgrochan
West Balgrochan Farm
West Balgrochan
West Carlestoun
Torrance
Torrance Prim Sch
Tower
Glenside
Meadowbank Farm
River Kelvin
A891
B822
MAIN ST
MILTON RD
ROWANTREE PL
ROWANTREE TERR
CAMPSIE RD
SOUTH BRAE
NETHERTON OVAL
NETHERTON HILL
STATION RD
RAILWAY CT
CARLINS PL
MARGARET CT
GREENHEAD RD
HILLVIEW AVE
CHESTNUT WALK
GLAZERTPARK
MDW DR
PRIMROSE WAY
MACCABE GDNS
MORRISON DR
KIRKINTILLOCH RD
BARRASTON RD
ACRE VALLEY RD
WARDEND RD
BLAIR GDNS
CAMPBELL PL
MORAY DR
MAITLAND DR
BUCHANAN PL
WALLACE GDNS
ATHOLL AVE
WEST BALGROCHAN RD
NEVIS DR
WEST RD
KELVINDALE
KINGS PK
SCHOOL RD
MILL CRES
PARK CRES
WOODMILL DR
DALRIADA DR
CORMACK AVE
HAWTHORN ST
ROSEHILL RD
GUTHRIE PL
MICHAEL McPARLAND DR
TOWER RD
NORTH BIRBISTON RD
LINDSAY TERR
SLATEFIELD
BOLTON TERR
BENCLOICH RD
PINE ST
ELM ST
MILLBURN ST
STIRLING PL
JAMES HEMPHILL CT
GLORAT AVE
BENCLOICH AVE
HOLYKNOWE RD
HOLYKNOWE CRES
ASHCROFT WALK
ASHCROFT AVE
BENVUE RD
WARREN WALK
ARGYLE GDNS
MEIKLE BIN BRAE
BLUEBELL WAY
REDHILLS VIEW
THE FELLS
GLENWARD AVE
CRAIGHTON GDNS
WESTERTON
LINN GLEN
DRUMALING TERR
SCHOOL LA
CHAPEL ST
WELL LA
VEITCH PL
WINSTON CRES
HOLLYTREE GDNS
CALICO WAY
ORCHID PL
BRAMBLE CT
PRINTERS LEA
LENA LA
OXMILL LA
GLAZERTBANK
PO
P

57
34

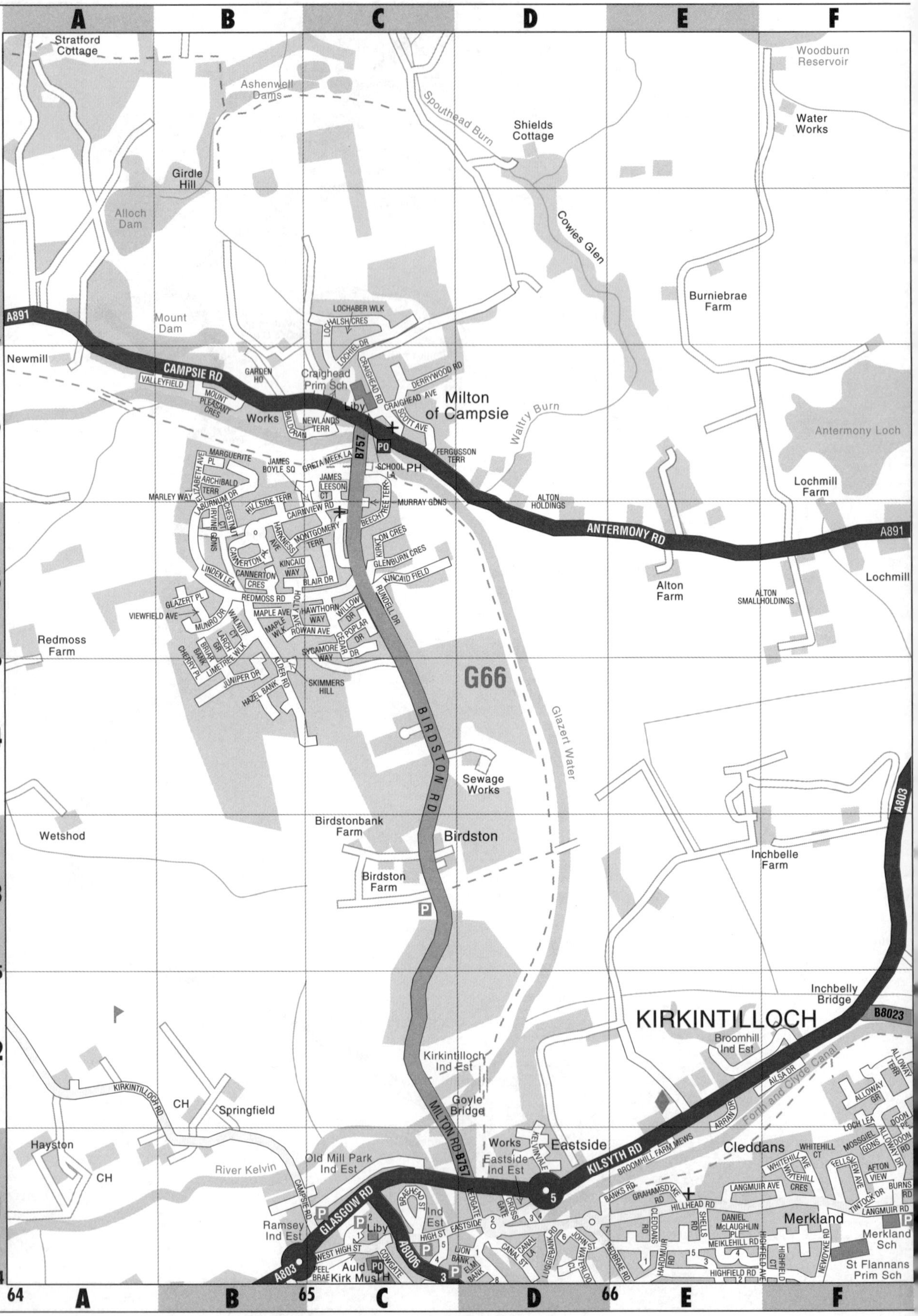
A
B
C
D
E
F
8
7
77
6
5
76
4
3
75
2
1
74
64
65
66
Stratford Cottage
Ashenwell Dams
Southead Burn
Shields Cottage
Woodburn Reservoir
Water Works
Girdle Hill
Alloch Dam
Cowies Glen
Burniebrae Farm
Mount Dam
A891
LOCHABER WLK
LOCHALSH CRES
LOCHIEL DR
Newmill
CAMPSIE RD
VALLEYFIELD
MOUNT PLEASANT CRES
GARDEN HO
Craighead Prim Sch
CRAIGHEAD RD
DERRYWOOD RD
CRAIGHEAD AVE
Milton of Campsie
Waltry Burn
Antermony Loch
Works
BALDORAN
NEWLANDS TERR
Liby
SCOTT AVE
PO
B757
FERGUSSON TERR
MARGUERITE PL
JAMES BOYLE SQ
GRETA MEEK LA
SCHOOL LA
PH
ELIZABETH AVE
ARCHIBALD TERR
JAMES LEESON CT
Lochmill Farm
MARLEY WAY
LABURNUM DR
HILLSIDE TERR
MURRAY GDNS
ALTON HOLDINGS
IRVINE GDNS
CHESTNUT CT
CAIRNVIEW RD
BEECH TREE TERR
ANTERMONY RD
A891
HARKNESS AVE
MONTGOMERY TERR
CANNERTON PK
KIRKTON CRES
GLENBURN CRES
KINCAID WAY
Lochmill
LINDEN LEA
CANNERTON CRES
BLAIR DR
KINCAID FIELD
REDMOSS RD
Alton Farm
ALTON SMALLHOLDINGS
GLAZERT PL
MAPLE AVE
HOLLY AVE
HAWTHORN WAY
WILLOW DR
RUNDELL DR
VIEWFIELD AVE
MUNRO DR
WALNUT CT
LARCH GR
MAPLE WLK
ROWAN AVE
POPLAR DR
CEDAR DR
Redmoss Farm
CHERRY PL
BIRCH BANK
LIMETREE WLK
SYCAMORE WAY
JUNIPER DR
ALDER RD
SKIMMERS HILL
HAZEL BANK
G66
BIRDSTON RD
Glazert Water
Sewage Works
A803
Wetshod
Birdstonbank Farm
Birdston
Inchbelle Farm
Birdston Farm
P
Inchbelly Bridge
KIRKINTILLOCH
B8023
Broomhill Ind Est
ALLOWAY TERR
Kirkintilloch Ind Est
AILSA DR
Forth and Clyde Canal
ALLOWAY GR
KIRKINTILLOCH RD
CH
Goyle Bridge
Springfield
ARRAN DR
MILTON RD
B757
DOON
LOCH LEA
Hayston
Works
KELVINVALE
Eastside
KILSYTH RD
BROOMHILL FARM MEWS
Cleddans
WHITEHILL CT
MOSSGIEL GDNS
ALLOWAY DR
Old Mill Park Ind Est
Eastside Ind Est
WHITEHILL AVE
WHITEHILL CRES
FELLS VIEW AVE
AFTON VIEW
River Kelvin
CH
5
BANKS RD
GRAHAMSDYKE RD
LANGMUIR AVE
TINTOCK DR
BURNS RD
CAMPSIE RD
GLASGOW RD
BRAEHEAD ST
Ind Est
EDGATE
CROSS
GATE
HILLHEAD RD
DANIEL McLAUGHLIN PL
Merkland
LANGMUIR RD
Ramsey Ind Est
Liby
HIGH ST
EASTSIDE
CLEDDANS RD
SHELLS RD
MEIKLEHILL RD
HIGHFIELD AVE
HIGHFIELD CT
NEWDYKE RD
Merkland Sch
WEST HIGH ST
A8006
LION BANK
ELM BANK
CANAL ST
CANAL LA
LUGGIEBANK RD
JOHN ST
WATERLOO
REDBRAE RD
HARDMUIR RD
HIGHFIELD RD
St Flannans Prim Sch
A803
PEEL BRAE
Auld Kirk Mus
COWGATE
PO
H

57
79

C1
1 KELVIN CT
2 SALFORD PL
3 ROCHDALE PL
4 BROADCROFT
5 BROADCROFT RD

D1
1 PETER D.STIRLING RD
2 HILLHEAD RDBT
3 HOPKIN'S BRAE
4 BROOMHILL CT
5 EASTSIDE RDBT
6 WATERLOO GDNS
7 REDBRAE PL
8 GLENVIEW

E1
1 HARDMUIR GDNS
2 HIGHFIELD GR
3 HIGHFIELD CRES
4 MEIKLEHILL AVE
5 FERNLEA RD

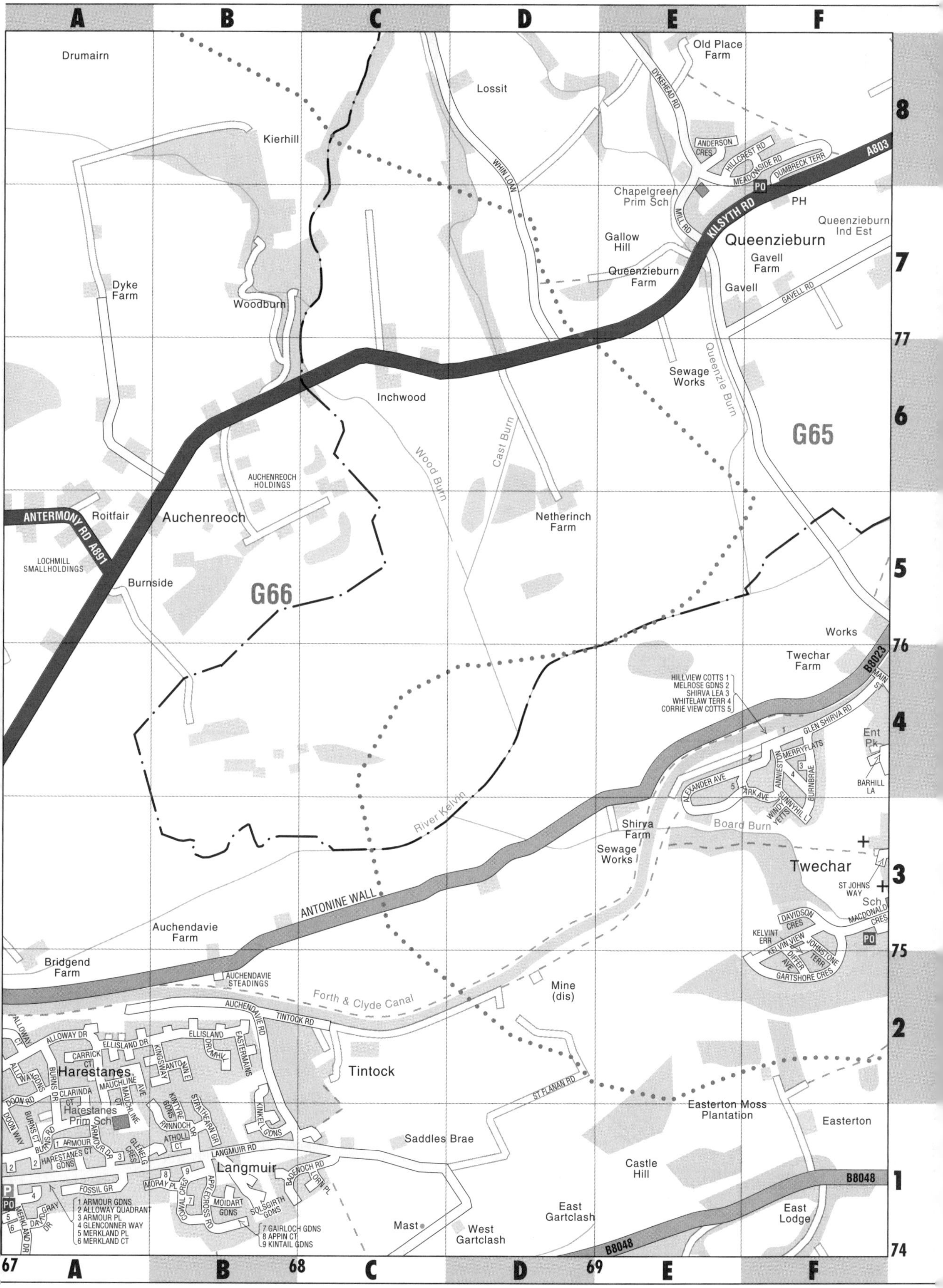
35
60
A B C D E F
Drumairn
Lossit
Old Place Farm
Kierhill
Chapelgreen Prim Sch
PH
Queenzieburn Ind Est
Gallow Hill
Queenzieburn
Gavell Farm
Gavell
Queenzieburn Farm
Dyke Farm
Woodburn
Sewage Works
Inchwood
G65
AUCHENREOCH HOLDINGS
Roitfair
Auchenreoch
Netherinch Farm
LOCHMILL SMALLHOLDINGS
Burnside
G66
Works
Twechar Farm
HILLVIEW COTTS 1
MELROSE GDNS 2
SHIRVA LEA 3
WHITELAW TERR 4
CORRIE VIEW COTTS 5
Ent Pk
BARHILL LA
Shirva Farm
Sewage Works
Twechar
ST JOHNS WAY
Sch
Auchendavie Farm
Bridgend Farm
AUCHENDAVIE STEADINGS
Mine (dis)
Forth & Clyde Canal
Harestanes
Harestanes Prim Sch
Tintock
Easterton Moss Plantation
Easterton
Saddles Brae
Castle Hill
Langmuir
East Gartclash
East Lodge
Mast
West Gartclash
1 ARMOUR GDNS
2 ALLOWAY QUADRANT
3 ARMOUR PL
4 GLENCONNER WAY
5 MERKLAND PL
6 MERKLAND CT
7 GAIRLOCH GDNS
8 APPIN CT
9 KINTAIL GDNS
A803
KILSYTH RD
ANTERMONY RD A891
ANTONINE WALL
B8023
B8048
River Kelvin
Wood Burn
Cast Burn
Queenzie Burn
Board Burn
67 68 69
74 75 76 77
80
60

59
36

D8
1 CHARLES ST
2 EAST BURNSIDE ST
3 KING ST LA
4 KING ST
5 MARKET PL
6 MARKET SQ
7 MARKET CL
8 CHURCH LA
9 FINDLAY ST
10 WESTPORT ST
11 WILLIAM ST
12 PARKER PL
13 KEIR HARDIE DR
14 ARRAN VIEW
15 MARKET CT
16 LENNOX CT
17 BACKBRAE ST

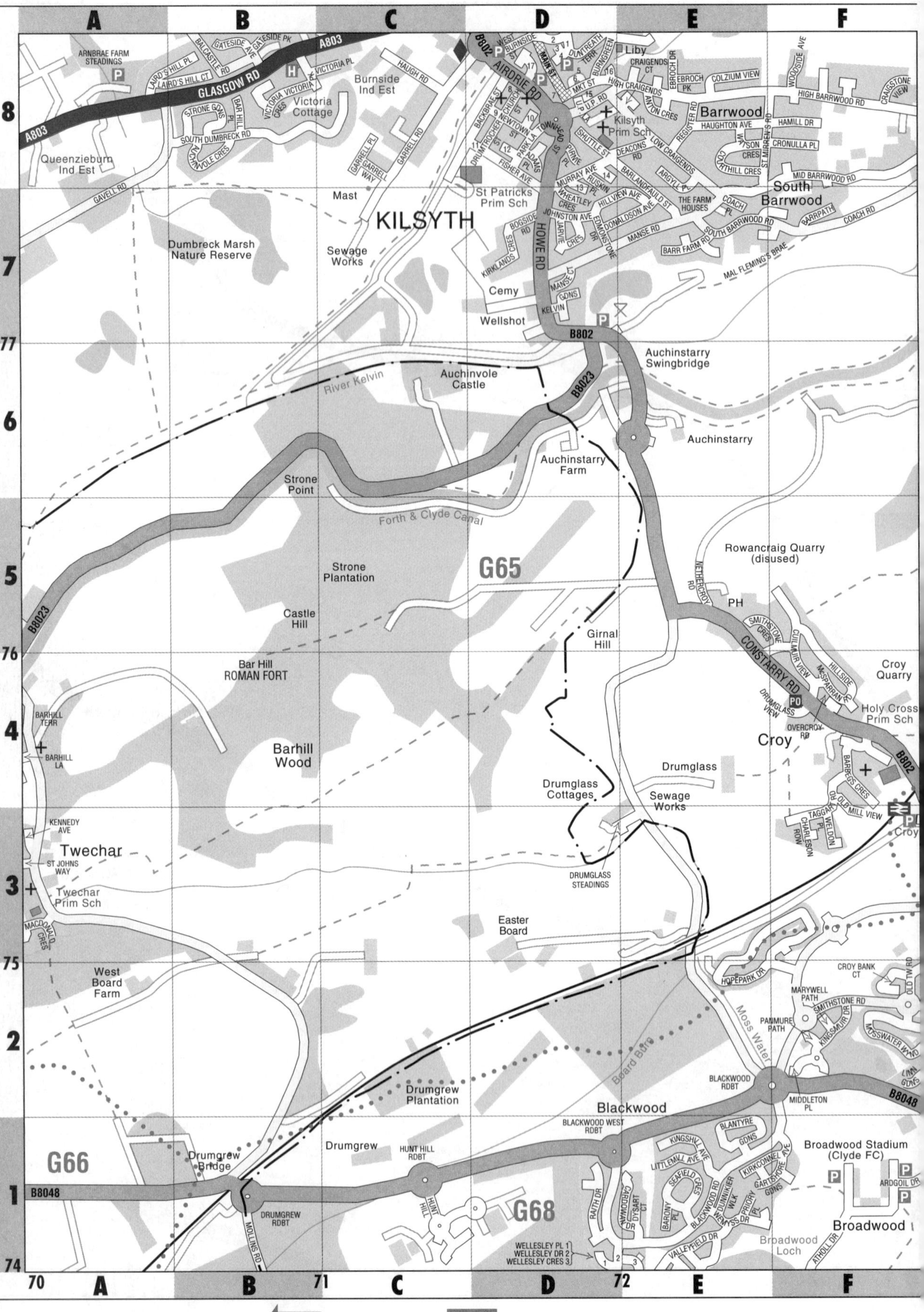
A
B
C
D
E
F
8
7
77
6
5
76
4
3
75
2
1
74
70
71
72
A803
GLASGOW RD
ARNBRAE FARM STEADINGS
LAIRD'S HILL PL
LAIRD'S HILL CT
BALCASTLE RD
GATESIDE AVE
GATESIDE PK
VICTORIA PL
VICTORIA PK
VICTORIA CRES
Victoria Cottage
STRONE GDNS
BAR HILL PL
SOUTH DUMBRECK RD
AUCHINVOLE CRES
Queenzieburn Ind Est
GAVELL RD
Burnside Ind Est
HAUGH RD
GARRELL RD
GARRELL PL
GARRELL WAY
Mast
KILSYTH
Sewage Works
Dumbreck Marsh Nature Reserve
B802
AIRDRIE RD
WEST BURNSIDE
MAIN ST
BACKBRAE ST
CHURCH ST
NEWTOWN ST
DRUMTROCHER ST
PARK LA
ADAMS PL
FISHER AVE
TOWNHEAD ST
MKT ST
DUNTREATH TERR
BURNGREEN
Liby
CRAIGENDS CT
HIGH CRAIGENDS
U.P. RD
ANTON CRES
EBROCH DR
EBROCH PK
COLZIUM VIEW
WOODSIDE AVE
CRAIGSTONE VIEW
HIGH BARRWOOD RD
Barrwood
REGISTER RD
HAUGHTON AVE
HAMILL DR
CRONULLA PL
WATSON CRES
COURTHILL CRES
ST MIRREN'S RD
Kilsyth Prim Sch
SHUTTLE ST
DEACONS RD
LOW CRAIGENDS
PIRNIE PL
MURRAY AVE
RUSKIN PL
WHEATLEY CRES
HILLVIEW AVE
BARLANDFAULD ST
ARGYLL PL
MID BARRWOOD RD
South Barrwood
THE FARM HOUSES
COACH PL
COACH RD
BARRPATH
SOUTH BARRWOOD RD
St Patricks Prim Sch
HOWE RD
BOGSIDE RD
JOHNSTON AVE
JARVIE CRES
EDMONSTONE DR
DONALDSON AVE
MANSE RD
BARR FARM RD
MAL FLEMING'S BRAE
KIRKLANDS CRES
Cemy
MANSE CT
GDNS
KELVIN
Wellshot
B802
Auchinstarry Swingbridge
Auchinvole Castle
River Kelvin
B8023
Auchinstarry
Auchinstarry Farm
Strone Point
Forth & Clyde Canal
Rowancraig Quarry (disused)
NETHERCROY RD
G65
Strone Plantation
Castle Hill
PH
SMITHSTONE CRES
CUILMUIR VIEW
CONSTARRY RD
HILLSIDE
McSPARRAN RD
Girnal Hill
Croy Quarry
Bar Hill ROMAN FORT
DRUMGLASS VIEW
PO
OVERCROY RD
Holy Cross Prim Sch
BARHILL TERR
BARHILL LA
Barhill Wood
Croy
B802
Drumglass
Drumglass Cottages
Sewage Works
BARRBLUES CRES
OLD MILL VIEW
TAGGART PL
CHARLESON ROW
WELDON PL
Croy
KENNEDY AVE
Twechar
ST JOHNS WAY
Twechar Prim Sch
DRUMGLASS STEADINGS
MACDONALD CRES
Easter Board
West Board Farm
HOPEPARK DR
CROY BANK CT
OLD TWR RD
MARYWELL PATH
SMITHSTONE RD
PANMURE PATH
KINGSMUIR DR
MOSSWATER WYND
Moss Water
Board Burn
BLACKWOOD RDBT
MIDDLETON PL
B8048
Drumgrew Plantation
Blackwood
BLACKWOOD WEST RDBT
BLANTYRE GDNS
KINGSHILL AVE
LITTLEMILL AVE
SEAFIELD CRES
GARTSHORE AVE
KIRKCONNEL AVE
Broadwood Stadium (Clyde FC)
ARDGOIL DR
G66
Drumgrew Bridge
Drumgrew
HUNT HILL RDBT
B8048
DRUMGREW RDBT
MOLLINS RD
HUNT HILL
G68
RAITH DR
CARDOWAN DR
DYSART CT
BARONY PL
BLACKWOOD RD
DUNNIKIER WLK
WEMYSS DR
PRIORY PL
GDNS
Broadwood
WELLESLEY PL 1
WELLESLEY DR 2
WELLESLEY CRES 3
VALLEYFIELD DR
Broadwood Loch
ATHOLL DR

59
81

37
62

82
62

F1
1 CLYDE WLK
2 CLYDE SQ
3 CLYDE WAY
4 AVON WLK
5 FORTH WLK
6 LEVEN WAY
7 ANNAN WAY
8 SPEY WLK
9 ETTRICK WAY
10 TAY WLK
11 Antonine Sh Ctr

61
38

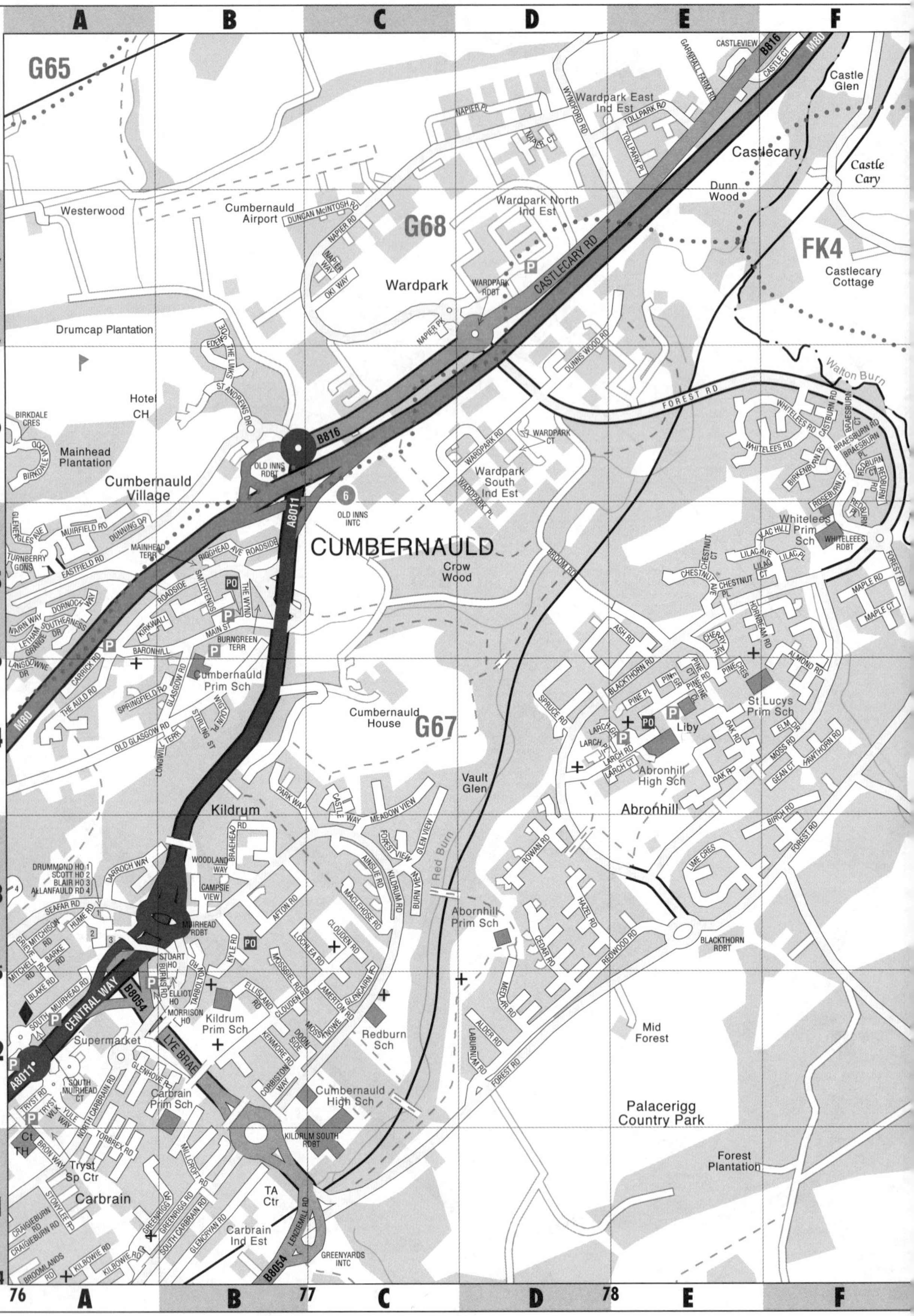
A
B
C
D
E
F
8
7
77
6
5
76
4
3
75
2
1
74
76
77
78
G65
G68
G67
FK4
CUMBERNAULD
Westerwood
Cumbernauld Airport
Drumcap Plantation
Wardpark
Wardpark East Ind Est
Wardpark North Ind Est
Wardpark South Ind Est
Castlecary
Castle Cary
Castle Glen
Dunn Wood
Castlecary Cottage
Walton Burn
Hotel CH
Mainhead Plantation
Cumbernauld Village
OLD INNS RDBT
OLD INNS INTC
Crow Wood
Cumbernauld Prim Sch
Cumbernauld House
Vault Glen
Kildrum
Kildrum Prim Sch
Redburn Sch
Abornhill Prim Sch
Red Burn
Abronhill
Abronhill High Sch
St Lucys Prim Sch
Whitelees Prim Sch
WHITELEES RDBT
Liby
Mid Forest
Palacerigg Country Park
Forest Plantation
BLACKTHORN RDBT
Supermarket
Carbrain Prim Sch
Cumbernauld High Sch
KILDRUM SOUTH RDBT
MUIRHEAD RDBT
Tryst Sp Ctr
Carbrain
Ct TH
TA Ctr
Carbrain Ind Est
GREENYARDS INTC
WARDPARK RDBT
M80
B816
A8011
B8054
CENTRAL WAY
LYE BRAE
CASTLECARY RD
FOREST RD
BROOM RD
NAPIER RD
NAPIER PL
NAPIER CT
NAPIER WAY
NAPIER PK
OKI WAY
DUNCAN McINTOSH RD
WYNDFORD RD
TOLLPARK RD
TOLLPARK PL
GARNHALL FARM RD
CASTLEVIEW
CASTLE CT
DUNNS WOOD RD
WARDPARK RD
WARDPARK CT
WARDPARK PL
EDEN
THE LINKS
ST ANDREWS DR
BIRKDALE CRES
BIRKDALE WOOD
GLENEAGLES AVE
MUIRFIELD RD
DUNNING DR
TURNBERRY GDNS
EASTFIELD RD
MAINHEAD TERR
RIGGHEAD AVE
ROADSIDE
SMITHYENDS
THE WYND
KIRKWALL
MAIN ST
BURNGREEN TERR
BARONHILL
NAIRN WAY
DORNOCH WAY
LETHAM DR
SOUTHERNESS DR
GRANGE DR
LANSDOWNE DR
CARRICK RD
THE AULD RD
SPRINGFIELD RD
GLASGOW RD
WIGTOUN PL
STIRLING ST
OLD GLASGOW RD
LONGWILL TERR
PARK WAY
CASTLE WAY
MEADOW VIEW
FOREST VIEW
GLEN VIEW
BURN VIEW
KILDRUM RD
AINSLIE RD
MACLEHOSE RD
BRAEHEAD RD
WOODLAND WAY
CAMPSIE VIEW
AFTON RD
DARROCH WAY
DRUMMOND HO 1
SCOTT HO 2
BLAIR HO 3
ALLANFAULD RD 4
SEAFAR RD
HUME RD
MITCHISON RD
GRIERSON
BARKE RD
MITCHELL RD
BLAKE RD
MUIRHEAD RD
SOUTH MUIRHEAD RD
STUART HO
BURNS HO
ELLIOT HO
MORRISON HO
TARBOLTON RD
KYLE RD
ELLISLAND RD
CLOUDEN RD
LOCHLEA RD
MOSSGIEL RD
LAMERTON RD
GLENCAIRN RD
MOSSGIEL
DOON SIDE
KENMORE RD
CORBISTON WAY
GLENHOVE RD
SOUTH MUIRHEAD CT
NORTH CARBRAIN RD
TRYST RD
TRYST WLK
YULE WAY
TORBREX RD
BRON WAY
MILLCROFT RD
GREENRIGG RD
SOUTH CARBRAIN RD
GLENCRYAN RD
LENZIEMILL RD
STONYLEE RD
CRAIGIEBURN RD
KILBOWIE RD
BROOMLANDS RD
ROWAN RD
HAZEL RD
CEDAR RD
REDWOOD RD
MEDLAR RD
ALDER RD
LABURNUM RD
SPRUCE RD
ASH RD
BLACKTHORN RD
PINE PL
PINE CT
PINE RD
PINE CRES
PINE GR
CHERRY AVE
LARCH RD
LARCH GR
LARCH PL
LARCH CT
OAK RD
ELM DR
MOSS RD
GEAN CT
HAWTHORN RD
ALMOND RD
HORNBEAM RD
CHESTNUT CT
CHESTNUT AVE
CHESTNUT PL
LILAC AVE
LILAC HILL
LILAC CT
LILAC PL
MAPLE RD
MAPLE CT
BIRCH RD
LIME CRES
WHITELEES RD
WHITELEES CT
CASTBURN RD
BRAESBURN RD
BRAESBURN CT
BRAESBURN PL
BIRKENBURN RD
ROSEBURN CT
REDBURN CT
REDBURN RD
PO
P

61
83

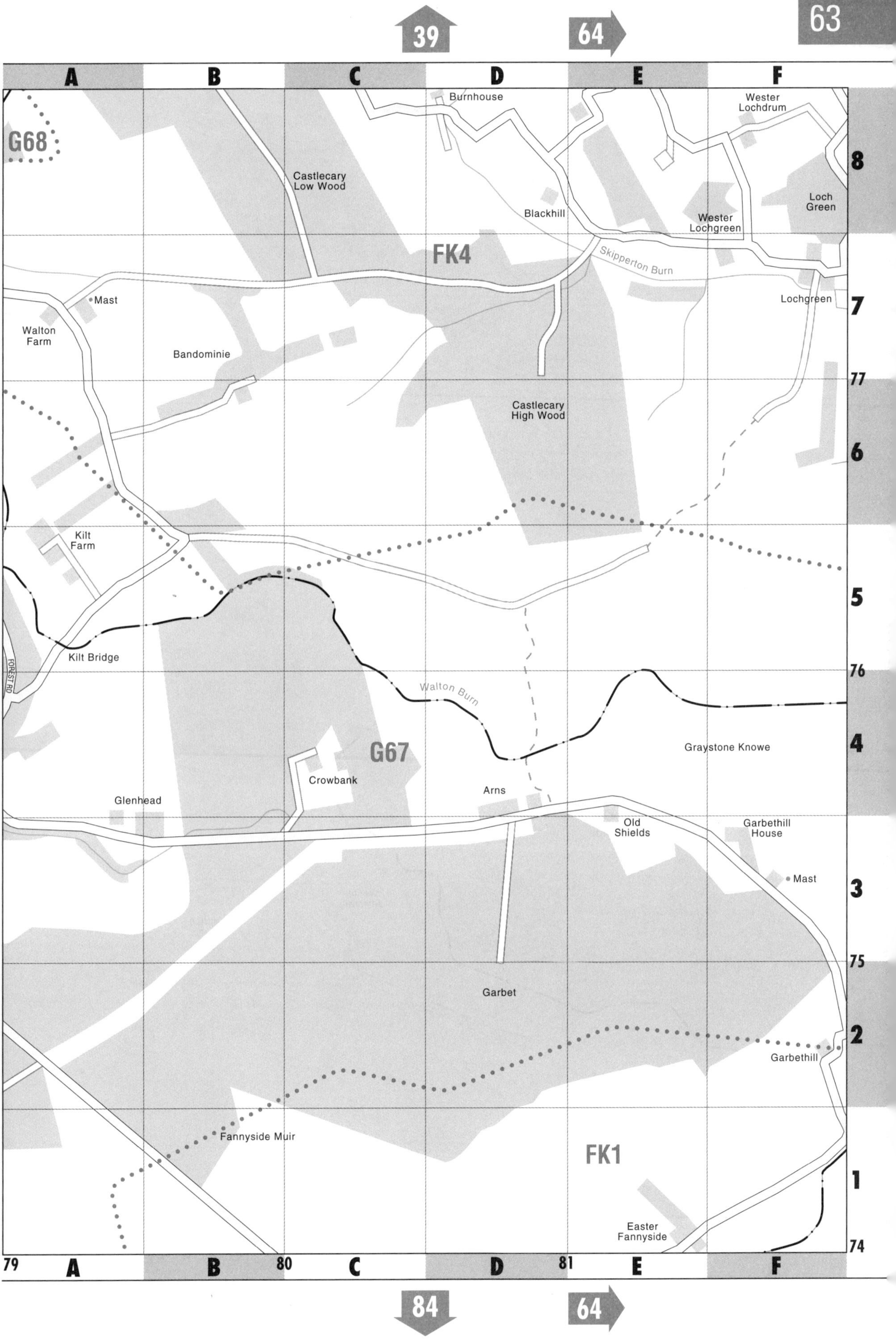
39
64
A
B
C
D
E
F
G68
Burnhouse
Wester Lochdrum
Castlecary Low Wood
Blackhill
Wester Lochgreen
Loch Green
FK4
Skipperton Burn
Mast
Walton Farm
Bandominie
Lochgreen
Castlecary High Wood
Kilt Farm
Kilt Bridge
FOREST RD
Walton Burn
G67
Crowbank
Glenhead
Arns
Graystone Knowe
Old Shields
Garbethill House
Mast
Garbet
Garbethill
Fannyside Muir
FK1
Easter Fannyside
8
7
77
6
5
76
4
3
75
2
1
74
79
80
81
84
64

63
40

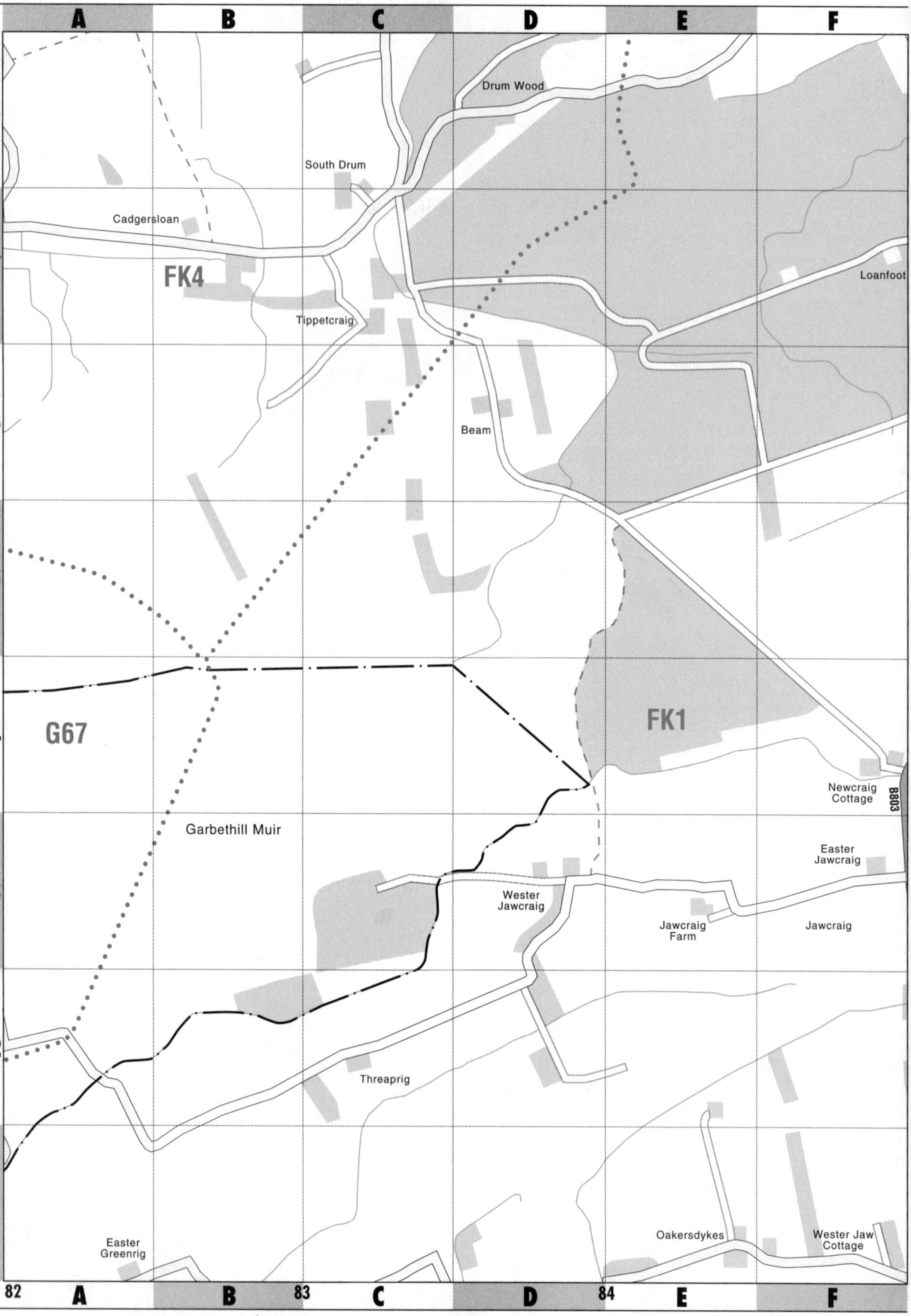
A
B
C
D
E
F
8
7
77
6
5
76
4
3
75
2
1
74
82
83
84
Drum Wood
South Drum
Cadgersloan
FK4
Tippetcraig
Loanfoot
Beam
G67
FK1
Newcraig
Cottage
B803
Garbethill Muir
Easter
Jawcraig
Wester
Jawcraig
Jawcraig
Farm
Jawcraig
Threaprig
Easter
Greenrig
Oakersdykes
Wester Jaw
Cottage

63
85

41
66

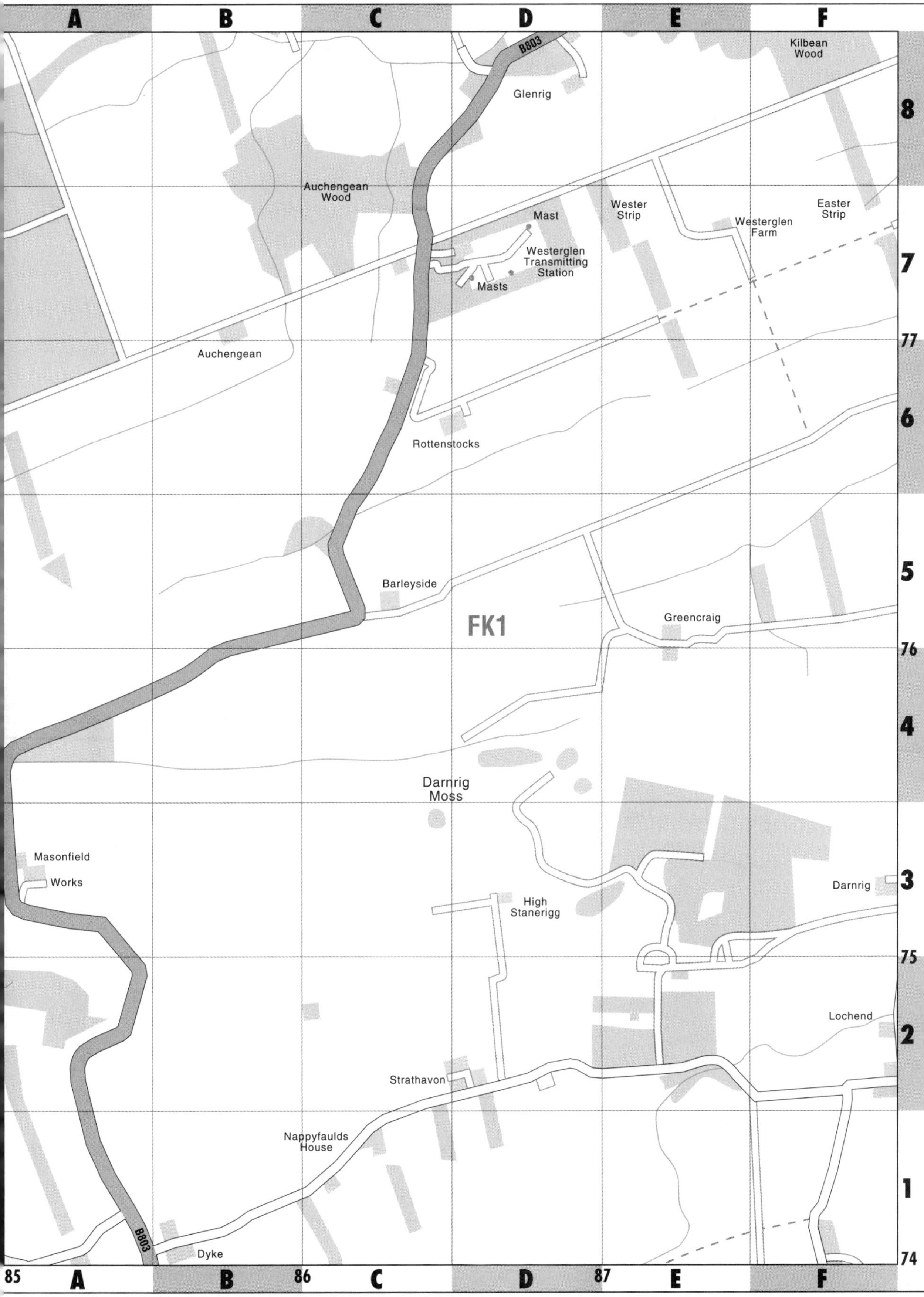
A
B
C
D
E
F
B803
Kilbean Wood
Glenrig
8
Auchengean Wood
Mast
Wester Strip
Westerglen Farm
Easter Strip
Westerglen Transmitting Station
Masts
7
77
Auchengean
6
Rottenstocks
5
Barleyside
FK1
Greencraig
76
4
Darnrig Moss
Masonfield
Works
3
High Stanerigg
Darnrig
75
Lochend
2
Strathavon
Nappyfaulds House
1
Dyke
B803
74
85
86
87

86
66

65
42

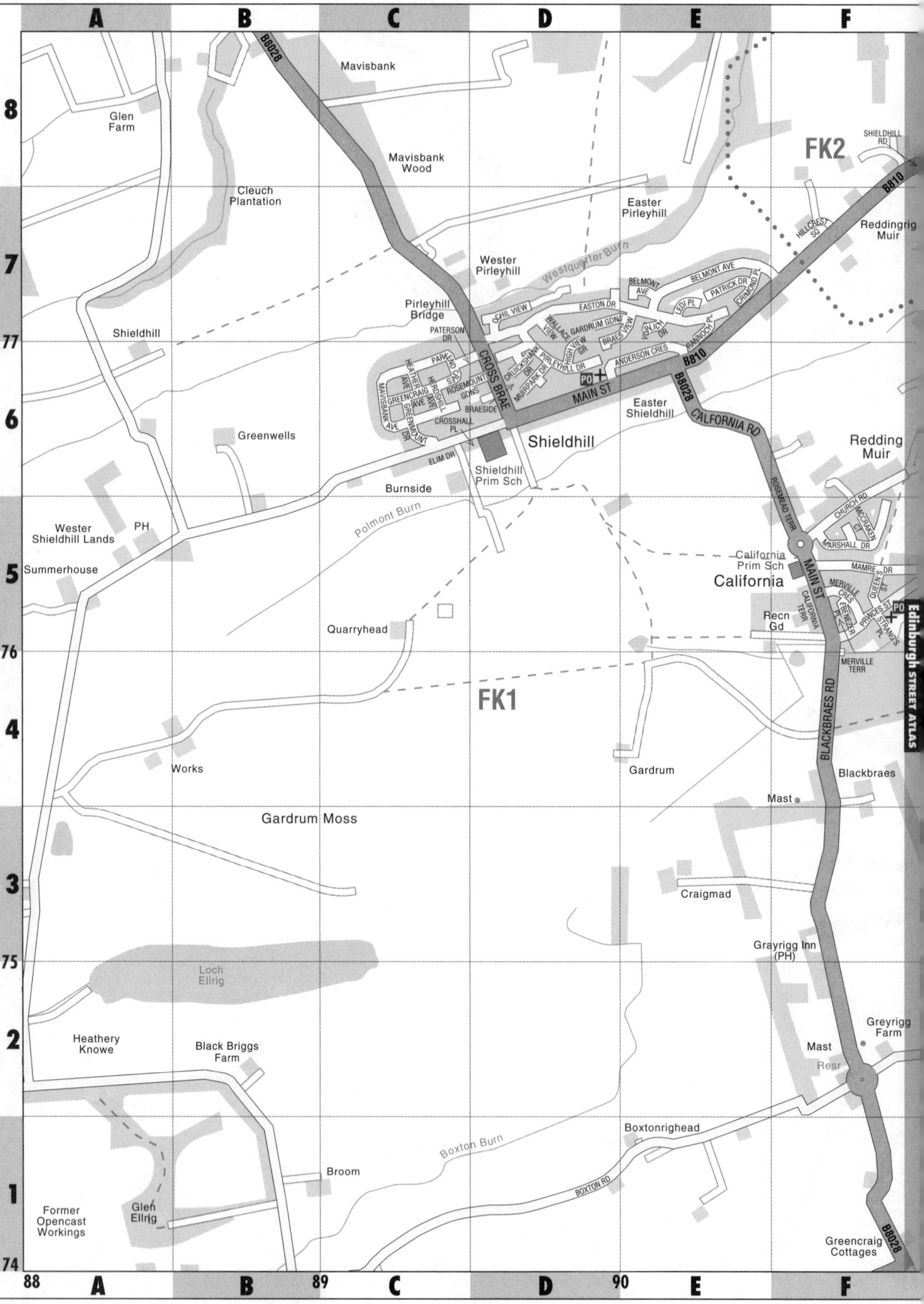
A
B
C
D
E
F
8
7
77
6
5
76
4
3
75
2
1
74
88
89
90
B8028
Mavisbank
Glen
Farm
Mavisbank
Wood
Cleuch
Plantation
FK2
SHIELDHILL
RD
B810
Easter
Pirleyhill
Reddingrig
Muir
HILLCREST
SQ
Wester
Pirleyhill
Westquarter Burn
BELMONT
AVE
BELMONT AVE
PATRICK DR
CRIMOND PL
LEDI PL
Pirleyhill
Bridge
OCHIL VIEW
EASTON DR
WALLACE
VIEW
GARDRUM GDNS
BRAES VIEW
VORLICH
DR
RANNOCH PL
Shieldhill
PATERSON
DR
HIGH VIEW
GR
ANDERSON CRES
PIRLEYHILL DR
CROSS BRAE
CRUICKSHANK
DR
MUIRPARK DR
HEATHER
AVE
HEROSHILL
AVE
ROSEMOUNT
GDNS
GREENCRAIG
AVE
MAVISBANK
AVE
GREENMOUNT
DR
BRAESIDE
CROSSHALL
PL
PO
MAIN ST
B8028
Easter
Shieldhill
CALIFORNIA RD
Greenwells
Shieldhill
ELIM DR
Shieldhill
Prim Sch
Burnside
Redding
Muir
ROSEMEAD TERR
CHURCH RD
McCRAKEN
CT
Wester
Shieldhill Lands
PH
Polmont Burn
MARSHALL DR
California
Prim Sch
MAMRE DR
Summerhouse
MAIN ST
California
MERVILLE
CRES
QUEENS
ST
EBENEZER
PL
PRINCES ST
Recn
Gd
CALIFORNIA
TERR
PO
STRANGS
PL
Quarryhead
MERVILLE
TERR
FK1
BLACKBRAES RD
Works
Gardrum
Blackbraes
Mast
Gardrum Moss
Craigmad
Grayrigg Inn
(PH)
Loch
Ellrig
Greyrigg
Farm
Heathery
Knowe
Black Briggs
Farm
Mast
Resr
Boxtonrighead
Boxton Burn
Broom
BOXTON RD
Former
Opencast
Workings
Glen
Ellrig
Greencraig
Cottages
B8028
Edinburgh STREET ATLAS

65
87

46
68

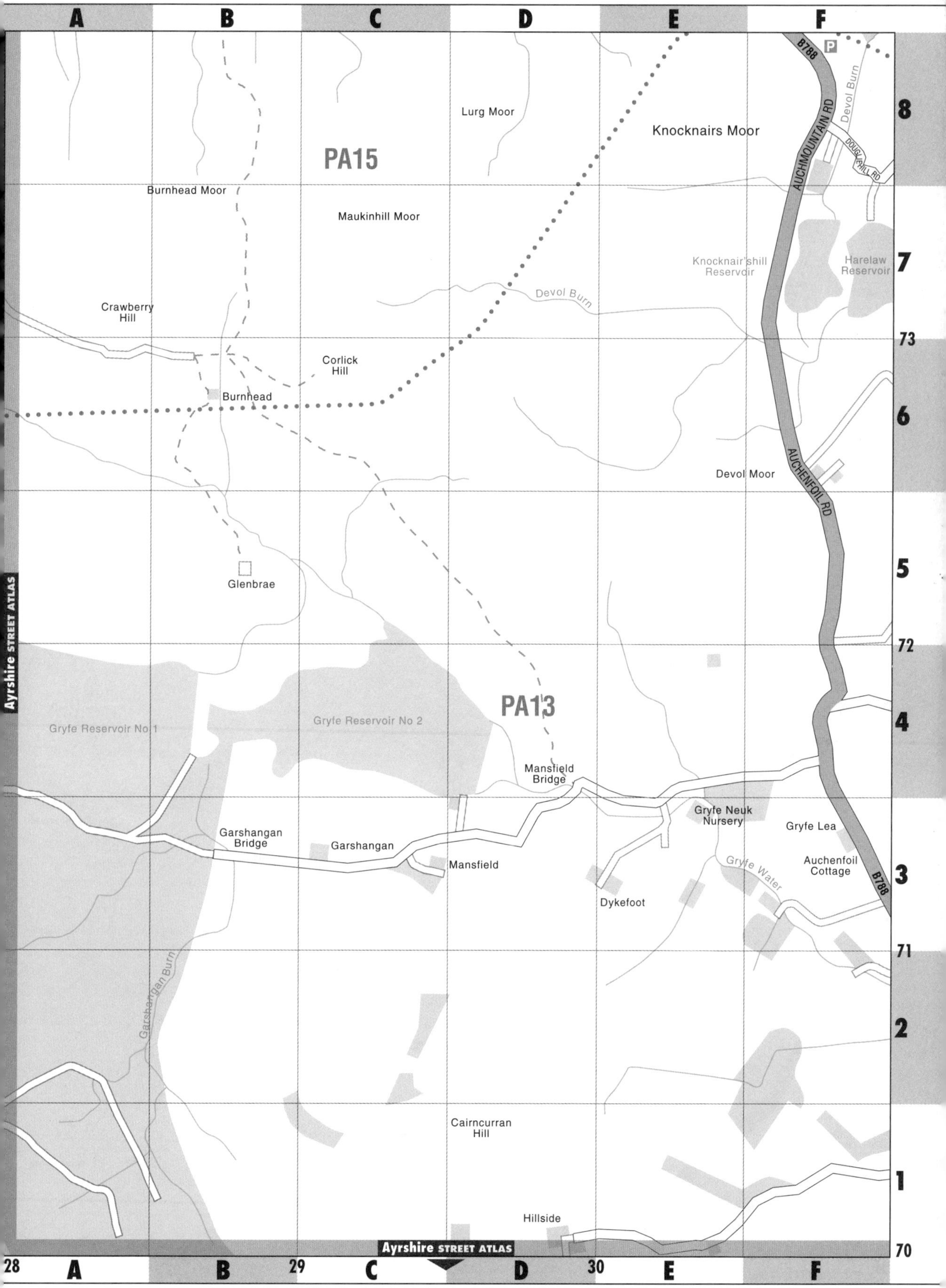
A
B
C
D
E
F
8
7
73
6
5
72
4
3
71
2
1
70
28
29
30
PA15
PA13
Lurg Moor
Knocknairs Moor
B788
P
Devol Burn
AUCHMOUNTAIN RD
DOUGLIEHILL RD
Burnhead Moor
Maukinhill Moor
Knocknair'shill Reservoir
Harelaw Reservoir
Crawberry Hill
Devol Burn
Corlick Hill
Burnhead
Devol Moor
AUCHENFOIL RD
Glenbrae
Gryfe Reservoir No 1
Gryfe Reservoir No 2
Mansfield Bridge
Gryfe Neuk Nursery
Gryfe Lea
Garshangan Bridge
Garshangan
Mansfield
Auchenfoil Cottage
Gryfe Water
B788
Dykefoot
Garshangan Burn
Cairncurran Hill
Hillside
Ayrshire STREET ATLAS

68

67
47

F8
1 St Michaels Prim Sch
2 Newark Prim Sch

A
B
C
D
E
F
8
7
73
6
5
72
4
3
71
2
1
70
31
32
33
West Dougliehill
Dougliehill Reservoir
East Dougliehill
DOUGLIEHILL RD
DOUGLIEHILL TERR
DOUGLIEHILL PL
BARR'S BRAE
MORAY RD
Devol Ind Est
Ind Est
Harelaw Reservoir
Devol Moor
Harelaw
PA14
CH
Devol
Mid Auchinleck
PORT GLASGOW
High Auchenleck
Boglestone
Port Glasgow Ind Est
St Francis Prim Sch
Bardrainney
PH
Cemy
CLUNE BRAE
A761
KILMACOLM RD
DEVOL RD
Cunston
CROSSHILL RD
West Kilbride
AUCHENBOTHIE RD
MILLPORT RD
Auchentiber
Auchentiber Bridge
Pennytersal
Priestside Farm
PA13
High Mathernock
Mathernock Bridge
Auchenfoyle
B788
Gryfe Water
Gryfeside
Horsecraigs
Cauldside
Blacksholm Bridge
Strathgryfe
Faulds

67
88

48 70

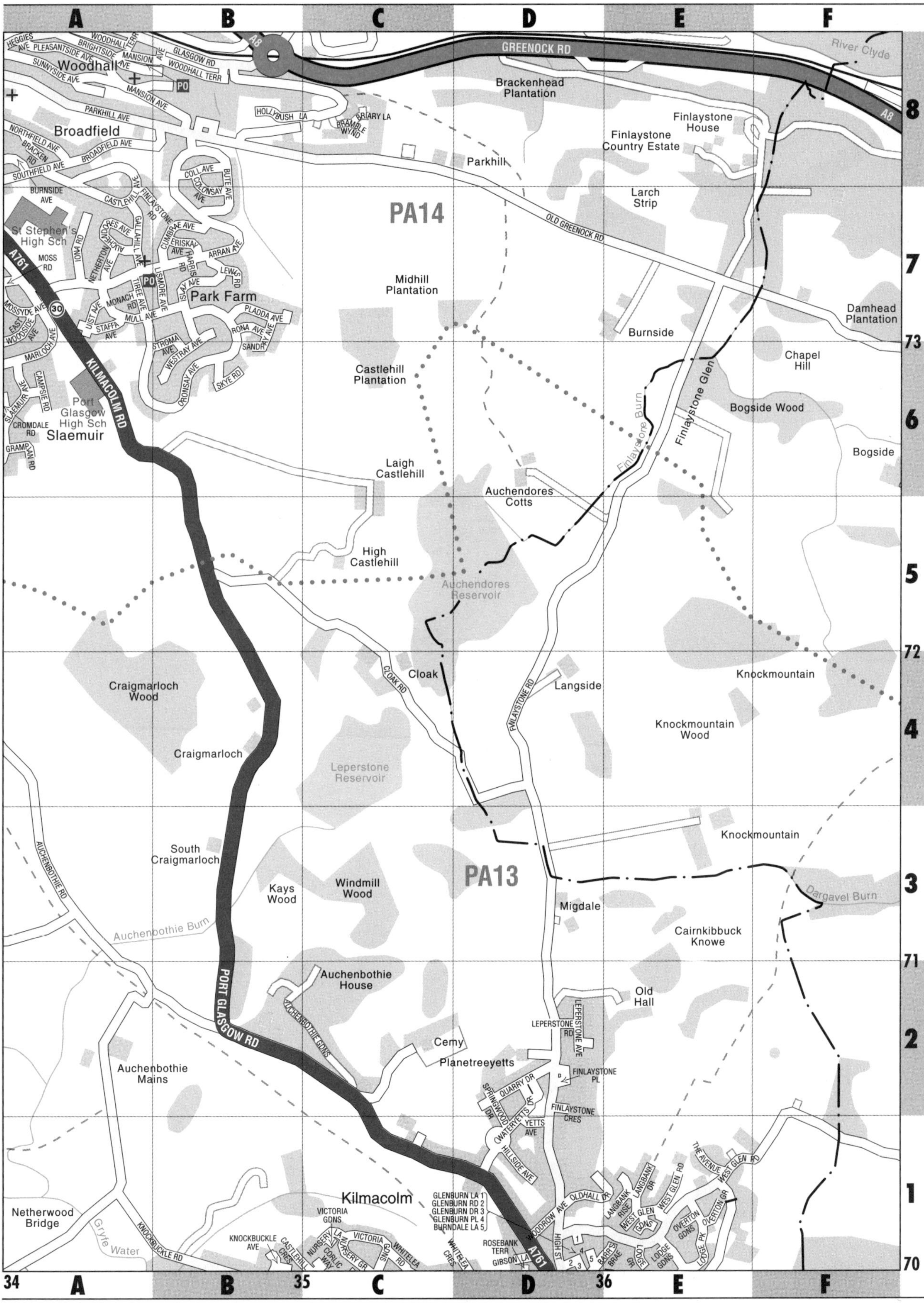
A B C D E F
8 7 73 6 5 72 4 3 71 2 1 70
34 35 36
GREENOCK RD
A8
River Clyde
Woodhall
Broadfield
Brackenhead Plantation
Finlaystone House
Finlaystone Country Estate
Parkhill
Larch Strip
PA14
OLD GREENOCK RD
St Stephen's High Sch
Park Farm
Midhill Plantation
Damhead Plantation
Burnside
Chapel Hill
Castlehill Plantation
Bogside Wood
Bogside
Port Glasgow High Sch
Slaemuir
KILMACOLM RD
A761
Laigh Castlehill
Auchendores Cotts
Finlaystone Burn
Finlaystone Glen
High Castlehill
Auchendores Reservoir
Cloak
CLOAK RD
Langside
Knockmountain
Craigmarloch Wood
Craigmarloch
Knockmountain Wood
FINLAYSTONE RD
Leperstone Reservoir
Knockmountain
South Craigmarloch
PA13
Kays Wood
Windmill Wood
Migdale
Dargavel Burn
Cairnkibbuck Knowe
Auchenbothie Burn
AUCHENBOTHIE RD
Auchenbothie House
Old Hall
PORT GLASGOW RD
Cemy
Planetreeyetts
Auchenbothie Mains
Kilmacolm
Netherwood Bridge
Gryfe Water
KNOCKBUCKLE RD
GLENBURN LA 1
GLENBURN RD 2
GLENBURN DR 3
GLENBURN PL 4
BURNDALE LA 5

89 70

69
49

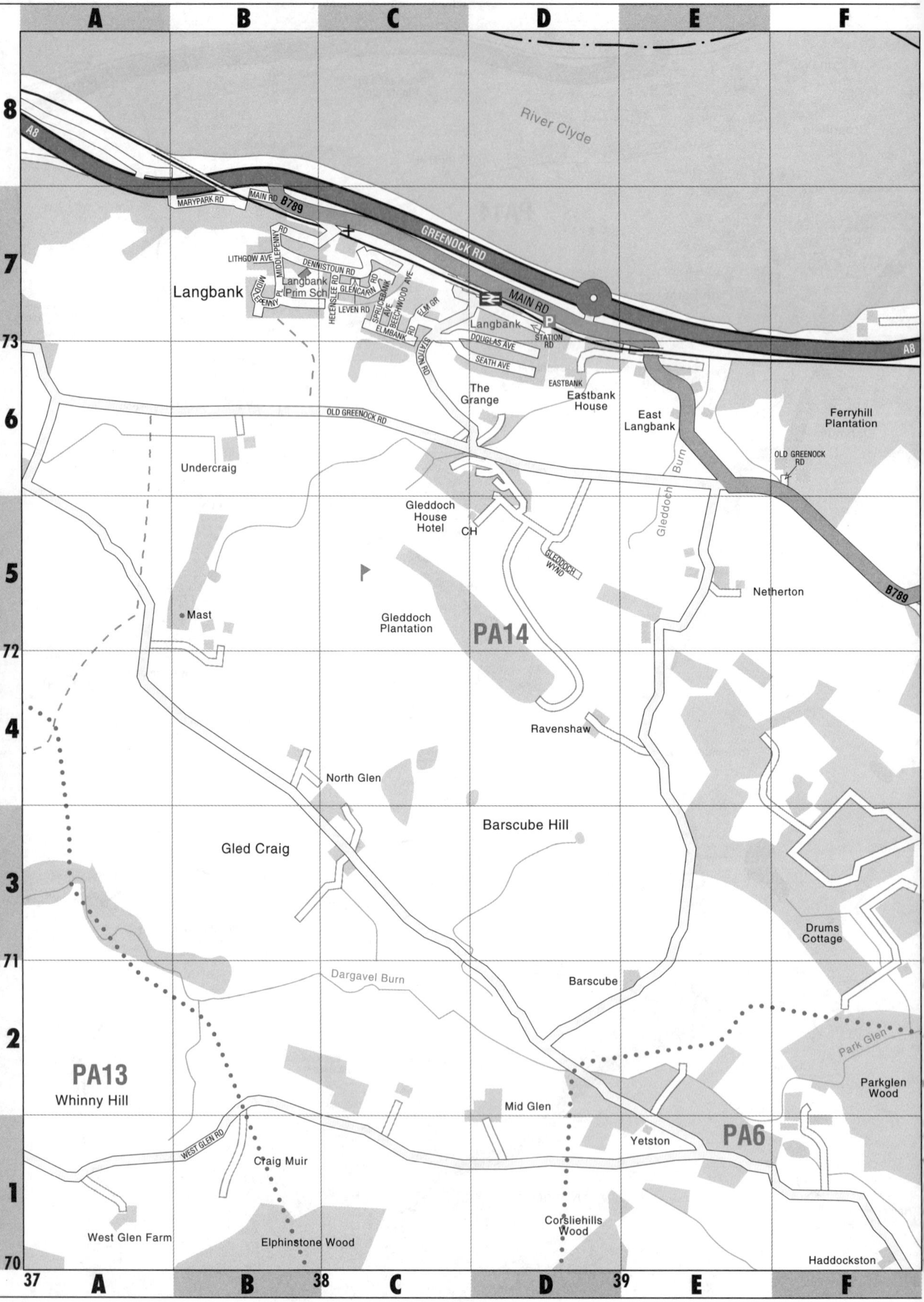
A
B
C
D
E
F
8
7
73
6
5
72
4
3
71
2
1
70
37
38
39
River Clyde
A8
MARYPARK RD
MAIN RD
B789
GREENOCK RD
MAIN RD
LITHGOW AVE
MIDDLEPENNY RD
DENNISTOUN RD
Langbank
Langbank Prim Sch
GLENCAIRN RD
MIDDLEPENNY PL
HELENSLEE RD
LEVEN RD
SPRUCEBANK AVE
BEECHWOOD AVE
ELMBANK RD
ELM GR
STATION RD
Langbank
DOUGLAS AVE
SEATH AVE
EASTBANK
The Grange
Eastbank House
East Langbank
Ferryhill Plantation
OLD GREENOCK RD
OLD GREENOCK RD
Undercraig
Gleddoch Burn
Gleddoch House Hotel
CH
GLEDDOCH WYND
Netherton
B789
Mast
Gleddoch Plantation
PA14
Ravenshaw
North Glen
Barscube Hill
Gled Craig
Drums Cottage
Dargavel Burn
Barscube
Park Glen
Parkglen Wood
PA13
Whinny Hill
Mid Glen
WEST GLEN RD
Yetston
PA6
Craig Muir
Corsliehills Wood
West Glen Farm
Elphinstone Wood
Haddockston

69
90

A
B
C
D
E
F
G82
Milton Island
8
River Clyde
7
Inner Clyde
Nature Reserve
Longhaugh
Point
73
M8
31
Fornet Cottage
A8
Ferryhill
Plantation
6
Convent
High
Hatton
Laigh
Hatton
Lodge
Cora
Campus
GREENOCK RD
OLD GREENOCK RD
5
M8
B789
Lodge
PA14
Slateford
CHESTNUT AVE
72
Whitemoss Dam
Bishopton Tunnels
KINGSWOOD RD
LYLE CRES
PA7
4
Drums
Castlehill
Cottage
Whitemoss
Ingliston
House
Mast
NEWTON RD 1
CROSSGATES 2
WEST PORTON PL 3
WRAISLAND CRES 4
A8
Cemy
HAMILTON CRES
INGLISTON DR
3
Barbeg Hill
Easter Newton
Ingliston
71
Barmore Hill
Formakin
Paddockcraig
Gatehead
2
Formakin
Estate
P
Parkglen Wood
Nether Mill
West
Glenshinnoch
Meiklefield
BAROCHAN RD
1
Dargavel Burn
PA6
B789
REILLY RD
70
40
A
B
41
C
D
42
E
F

71
51

A
B
C
D
E
F
8
7
73
6
5
72
4
3
71
2
1
70
43
44
45
Bowling
G60
G82
A82
A814
LITTLEMILL CT
GREAT WESTERN RD
MANSE RD
SCOTT AVE
DUMBARTON RD
Glenarbuck House
Gavinburn
Pier
Piers
Mon
LITTLEMILL LA
CLYDE VIEW CT
Bowling
Frisky Wharf
Bowling Harbour
Jetty
River Clyde
Forth & Clyde Canal
Liby
ROMAN CRES
Gavinburn Prim Sch
PORTPATRICK RD
Longhaugh Point
Dove Cottage
Big Wood
Hotel
Erskine Park
Freeland House
Erskine Home Farm
The Erskine Home
Conyston Plantation
CH
M8
GARDEN VETERAN'S COTTS
A898
CHESTNUT AVE
Mon
Ritchieston
GOLF RD
Kirkton Cottages
PRINCES PK
Boden Boo Plantation
1 WRAISLAND CRES
2 CROSSGATES
West Porton
FERRY RD
PA7
NURSERY AVE
B815
A726
SHILTON LA
Laighpark
1 SEMPLE AVE
2 BURNS AVE
3 LANG AVE
NORTH PORTON RD
North Porton
BLANTYRE DR
LYLE CRES
DUNSMORE RD
ANDERSON RD
CAIRNS RD
GLEN RD
CAMPBELL AVE
BUCHANAN AVE
FRASER AVE
GORDON AVE
CAMERON AVE
STUART RD
BRUCE RD
A8
PORTON PL
Liby
NEWTON RD
WALLACE AVE
LESLIE AVE
LENNOX AVE
QUEENS DR
MAR AVE
SHAW AVE
LAIGHPARK AVE
Toll
Bargarran
DARROCH DR
Bishopton Prim Sch
THE GROVE
PH
CHARTWELL RD
Kingston
DRUMCROSS RD
Drumcross
BAIRD DR
DOUGLAS CRES
MAXWELL DR
HAMILTON DR
BRIDGEND
ROSSLAND GDNS
ROSSLAND CRES
BRISBANE RD
FLEMING RD
RENSHAW RD
LAMONT AVE
HAY AVE
CHISHOLM AVE
M898
Bishopton
ROSSLAND VIEW
HOLMPARK
CHURCHILL DR
MAXWELL RD
DARGAVEL AVE
KINGSTON RD
CAMPHILL GDNS
KINGSTON GR
DOUGLAS RD
DEVON DR
ETIVE DR
CARRON DR
OLD GREENOCK RD
BARGARRAN RD
AYTOUN DR
SEMPILL AVE
ALLISON AVE
SHAW CT
Bargarran Prim Sch
CASTLE CRES
GREENOCK RD
Wester Rossland
CAWDOR CRES
MORAR CRES
YARROW CRES
HOLMS CRES
St John Bosco Prim Sch
ALMOND DR
CARRICK RD
LEVIOT DR
ETTRICK DR
CRAIGHEAD RD
POPLAR CRES
GLEDSTANE RD
MORAL DR
Craigend Hill
PA8
Bishopton
POPLAR AVE
STATION RD
Craigton Burn
SACHELCOURT AVE
PO
Sewage Works
P&R
Rossland
Craigton
LADYMUIR CIRC
GLENMOSS AVE
LITTLESTON GDNS
LOCHY PL
LINBURN RD
LACHLAN CRES
LAXFORD RD
RYATT LINN
LEVEN PL
LEATHEN PL
LOYAL AVE
QUEENSIDE CRES
Linburn
LUBNAIG RD
West Craigend
LINNHE PL
LOMOND DR
MILLFIELD HILL
MILLFIELD PL
MILLFIELD VIEW
Bolerno
DARGAVEL RD
Linburn
MILLFIELD MDWS
MILLFIELD LA
MILLFIELD WYND
DARGAVEL RD
30

71
92

52
74

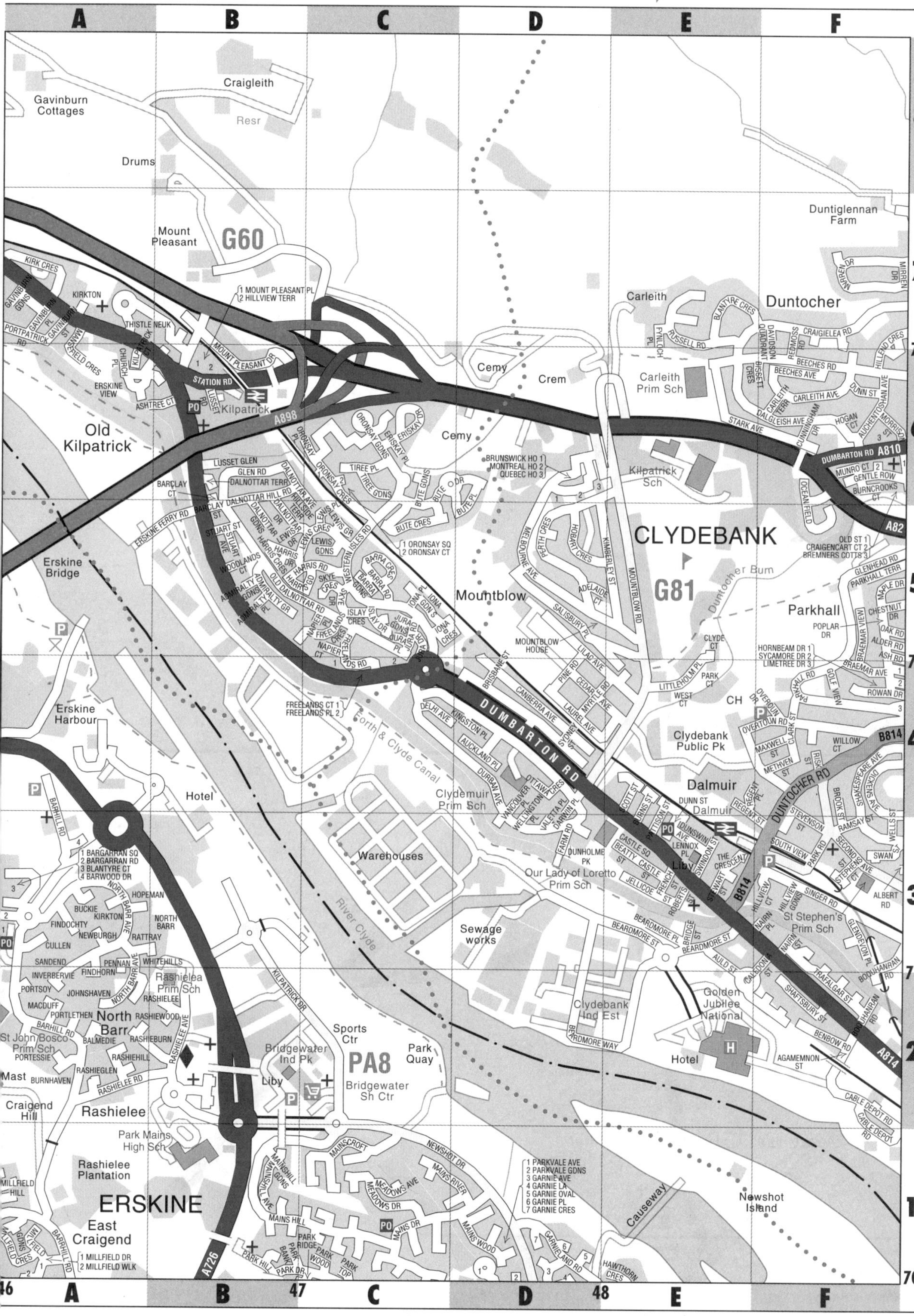
A
B
C
D
E
F
8
7
73
6
5
72
4
3
71
2
1
70
46
47
48
Craigleith
Resr
Gavinburn Cottages
Drums
Mount Pleasant
G60
Duntiglennan Farm
Carleith
Duntocher
Carleith Prim Sch
Cemy
Crem
Old Kilpatrick
Kilpatrick
STATION RD
A898
1 MOUNT PLEASANT PL
2 HILLVIEW TERR
KIRK CRES
KIRKTON
THISTLE NEUK
ASHTREE CT
ERSKINE VIEW
CHURCH PL
ORONSAY CRES
ORONSAY GDNS
ERISKAY PL
TIREE PL
TIREE GDNS
BUTE GDNS
BUTE DR
BUTE CRES
BUTE PL
1 ORONSAY SQ
2 ORONSAY CT
LUSSET GLEN
GLEN RD
DALNOTTAR TERR
BARCLAY CT
DALNOTTAR HILL RD
ERSKINE FERRY RD
STUART AVE
WOODLANDS CT
ADMIRALTY GDNS
ADMIRALTY GR
ADMIRALTY PL
OLD DALNOTTAR RD
HARRIS RD
SKYE CRES
LEWIS GDNS
WESTERN ISLES RD
BARRA CRES
BARRA RD
ISLAY CRES
ISLAY DR
IONA PL
IONA GDNS
IONA CRES
JURA GDNS
DURA PL
JURA DR
NAPIER CT
FREELANDS CRES
FREELANDS CT 1
FREELANDS PL 2
BRUNSWICK HO 1
MONTREAL HO 2
QUEBEC HO 3
MELBOURNE AVE
PERTH CRES
HOBART CRES
KIMBERLEY ST
MOUNTBLOW RD
ADELAIDE CT
SALISBURY PL
Kilpatrick Sch
CLYDEBANK
G81
Duntocher Burn
Mountblow
MOUNTBLOW HOUSE
LILAC AVE
PINE RD
CEDAR RD
MYRTLE RD
LAUREL AVE
CANBERRA AVE
BRISBANE ST
SYDNEY ST
Erskine Bridge
Erskine Harbour
Hotel
DUMBARTON RD
DELHI AVE
KINGSTON PL
AUCKLAND PL
DURBAN AVE
OTTAWA CRES
VANCOUVER PL
WELLINGTON PL
VALETTA PL
DARWIN PL
FARM RD
Forth & Clyde Canal
Clydemuir Prim Sch
Warehouses
River Clyde
DUNHOLME PK
Our Lady of Loretto Prim Sch
Sewage works
Clydebank Ind Est
BEARDMORE WAY
BEARDMORE ST
BEARDMORE PL
Golden Jubilee National
Hotel
Causeway
Newshot Island
CLYDE CT
LITTLEHOLM PL
PARK CT
WEST CT
CH
Clydebank Public Pk
Dalmuir
DUNN ST
SCOTT ST
BURNS ST
PATTISON ST
DUNSWINN AVE
LENNOX PL
SWINDON ST
CASTLE SQ
BEATTY ST
CASTLE ST
JELLICOE ST
FRENCH ST
ROBERTS ST
STEWART ST
THE CRESCENT
Liby
BRIDGE ST
AULD ST
CALEDONIA ST
SHAFTSBURY ST
TRAFALGAR ST
BENBOW RD
AGAMEMNON ST
CABLE DEPOT RD
B814
DUNTOCHER RD
A814
BROOK ST
SHAKESPEARE AVE
DICKENS AVE
RAMSAY ST
WELLS ST
SWAN ST
SECOND AVE
ST STEPHENS AVE
ALBERT RD
SINGER RD
HILLVIEW CT
HILLVIEW GDNS
NAIRN ST
NAIRN PL
St Stephen's Prim Sch
GLENDEVON PL
BOQUHANRAN RD
SOUTH VIEW
PARK RD
STEVENSON ST
METHVEN ST
MAXWELL ST
CLARK ST
OVERTOUN RD
OVERTOUN DR
WILLOW CT
Parkhall
POPLAR DR
HORNBEAM DR 1
SYCAMORE DR 2
LIMETREE DR 3
BRAEMAR VIEW
BRAEMAR AVE
CHESTNUT DR
OAK RD
ALDER RD
ASH RD
ROWAN DR
GOLF VIEW
PARKHALL RD
GLENHEAD RD
PARKHALL TERR
MAPLE DR
OLD ST 1
CRAIGENCART CT 2
BREMNERS COTTS 3
DUMBARTON RD A810
MUNRO CT
GENTLE ROW
BURNCROOKS CT
OCEANFIELD
A82
FYNLOCH PL
RUSSELL RD
BLANTYRE CRES
DAVIDSON QUADRANT
REDMOSS RD
CRAIGIELEA RD
BISSETT CRES
BEECHES RD
BEECHES AVE
CARLEITH TERR
CARLEITH AVE
DALGLEISH AVE
STARK AVE
CUNNINGHAM DR
DUNN ST
HOGAN CT
AUCHENTOSHAN AVE
MORRISON
HILLEND CRES
NAYRNE DR
MIRREN DR
1 BARGARRAN SQ
2 BARGARRAN RD
3 BLANTYRE CT
4 BARWOOD DR
BARHILL RD
HOPEMAN
NORTH BARR AVE
BUCKIE
KIRKTON
FINDOCHTY
NEWBURGH
CULLEN
NORTH BARR
RATTRAY
SANDEND
PENNAN
WHITEHILLS
INVERBERVIE
FINDHORN
PORTSOY
JOHNSHAVEN
MACDUFF
PORTLETHEN
Rashielea Prim Sch
RASHIELEE
North Barr
RASHIEWOOD
BARHILL RD
BALMEDIE
RASHIEBURN
RASHIELEE AVE
St John Bosco Prim Sch
PORTESSIE
RASHIEHILL
RASHIEGLEN
RASHIELEE RD
Mast
BURNHAVEN
Craigend Hill
Rashielee
Park Mains High Sch
Rashielee Plantation
MILLFIELD HILL
ERSKINE
East Craigend
1 MILLFIELD DR
2 MILLFIELD WLK
A726
KILPATRICK DR
Bridgewater Ind Pk
Liby
Sports Ctr
PA8
Park Quay
Bridgewater Sh Ctr
MAINSCROFT
NEWSHOT DR
MAINS RIVER
MAINSHILL GDNS
MAINSHILL AVE
MEADOWS AVE
MEADOWS DR
MAINS HILL
MAINS DR
PARK RIDGE
PARK BANK
PARK WOOD
PARK TOP
PARK HILL
PARK DR
MAINS WOOD
1 PARKVALE AVE
2 PARKVALE GDNS
3 GARNIE AVE
4 GARNIE LA
5 GARNIE OVAL
6 GARNIE PL
7 GARNIE CRES
GARNIELAND RD
HAWTHORN CRES
PO
P

93
74

73
53

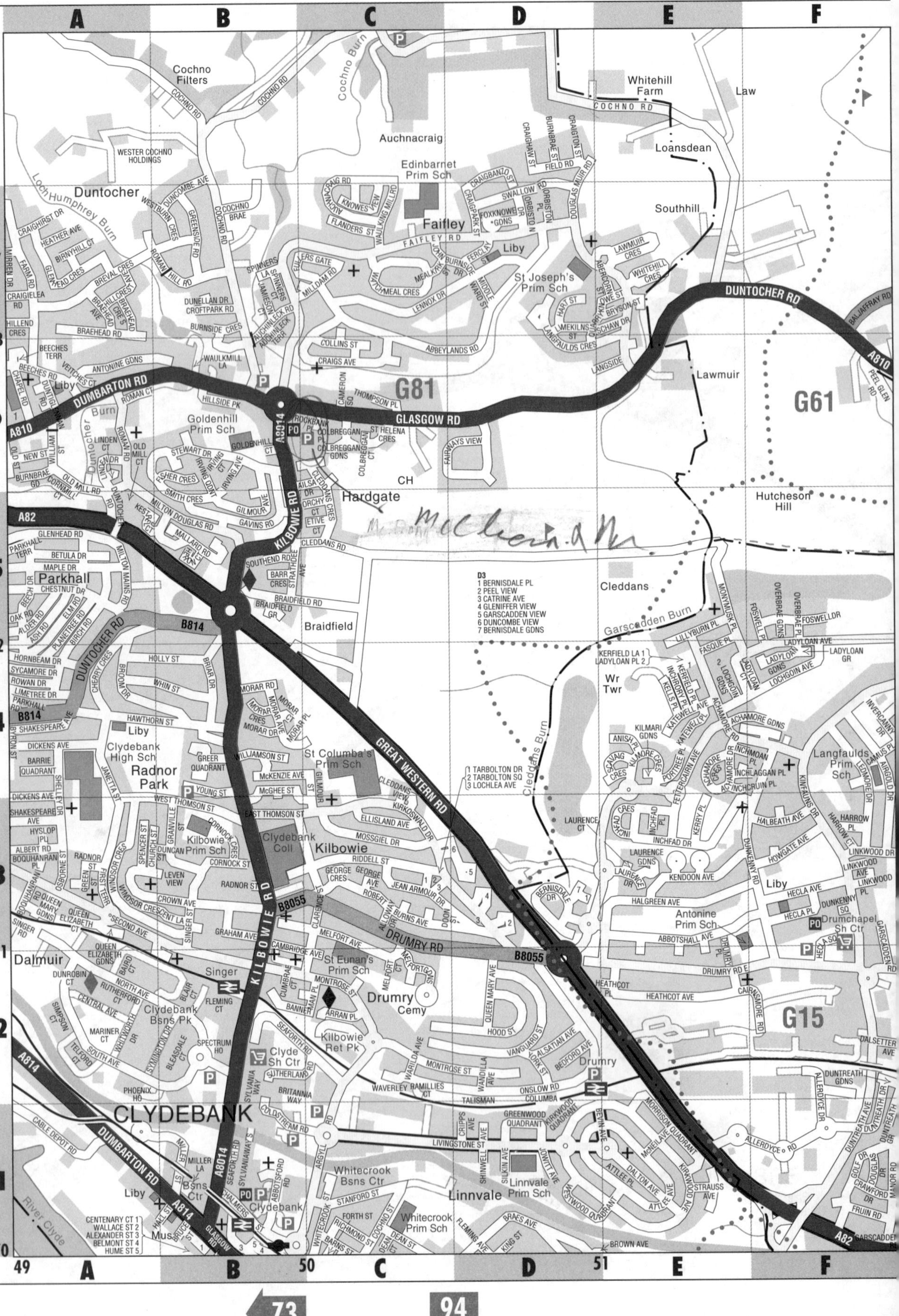
A
B
C
D
E
F
8
7
73
6
5
72
4
3
71
2
1
70
49
50
51
Cochno Filters
COCHNO RD
WESTER COCHNO HOLDINGS
Cochno Burn
Auchnacraig
Whitehill Farm
Law
Loansdean
Southhill
Duntocher
Loch Humphrey Burn
Edinbarnet Prim Sch
Faifley
FAIFLEY RD
Liby
St Joseph's Prim Sch
DUNTOCHER RD
BALJAFFRAY RD
A810
G81
G61
Lawmuir
DUMBARTON RD
GLASGOW RD
A8014
Goldenhill Prim Sch
Hardgate
CH
Hutcheson Hill
A82
KILBOWIE RD
CLEDDANS RD
Parkhall
Cleddans
Garscadden Burn
Braidfield
B814
D3
1 BERNISDALE PL
2 PEEL VIEW
3 CATRINE AVE
4 GLENIFFER VIEW
5 GARSCADDEN VIEW
6 DUNCOMBE VIEW
7 BERNISDALE GDNS
Wr Twr
GREAT WESTERN RD
Clydebank High Sch
Radnor Park
St Columba's Prim Sch
Cleddans Burn
Langfaulds Prim Sch
1 TARBOLTON DR
2 TARBOLTON SQ
3 LOCHLEA AVE
Kilbowie Prim Sch
Clydebank Coll
Kilbowie
B8055
DRUMRY RD
Antonine Prim Sch
Drumchapel Sh Ctr
Dalmuir
Singer
St Eunan's Prim Sch
Drumry Cemy
Clydebank Bsns Pk
Kilbowie Ret Pk
G15
A814
Clyde Sh Ctr
Drumry
CLYDEBANK
Whitecrook Bsns Ctr
Linnvale
Linnvale Prim Sch
Whitecrook Prim Sch
Bsns Ctr
Clydebank
Mus
River Clyde
CENTENARY CT 1
WALLACE ST 2
ALEXANDER ST 3
BELMONT ST 4
HUME ST 5

73
94

54
76

E5
1 DOUGLAS PL
2 KIRK LA
3 JEDWORTH CT
4 THE LOANING

95
76

B3
1 KINCLAVEN PL
2 KINCLAVEN GDNS
3 MERRYTON GDNS
4 LINKWOOD GR
5 SOUTHDEEN GR

F3
1 PINEWOOD
2 CANNIESBURN TOLL
3 KILLERMONT RD
4 SECOND AVE 5
5 MACFARLANE RD
6 CARRICKARDEN RD
7 BEECHWOOD LA
8 DRYMEN RD

75
55

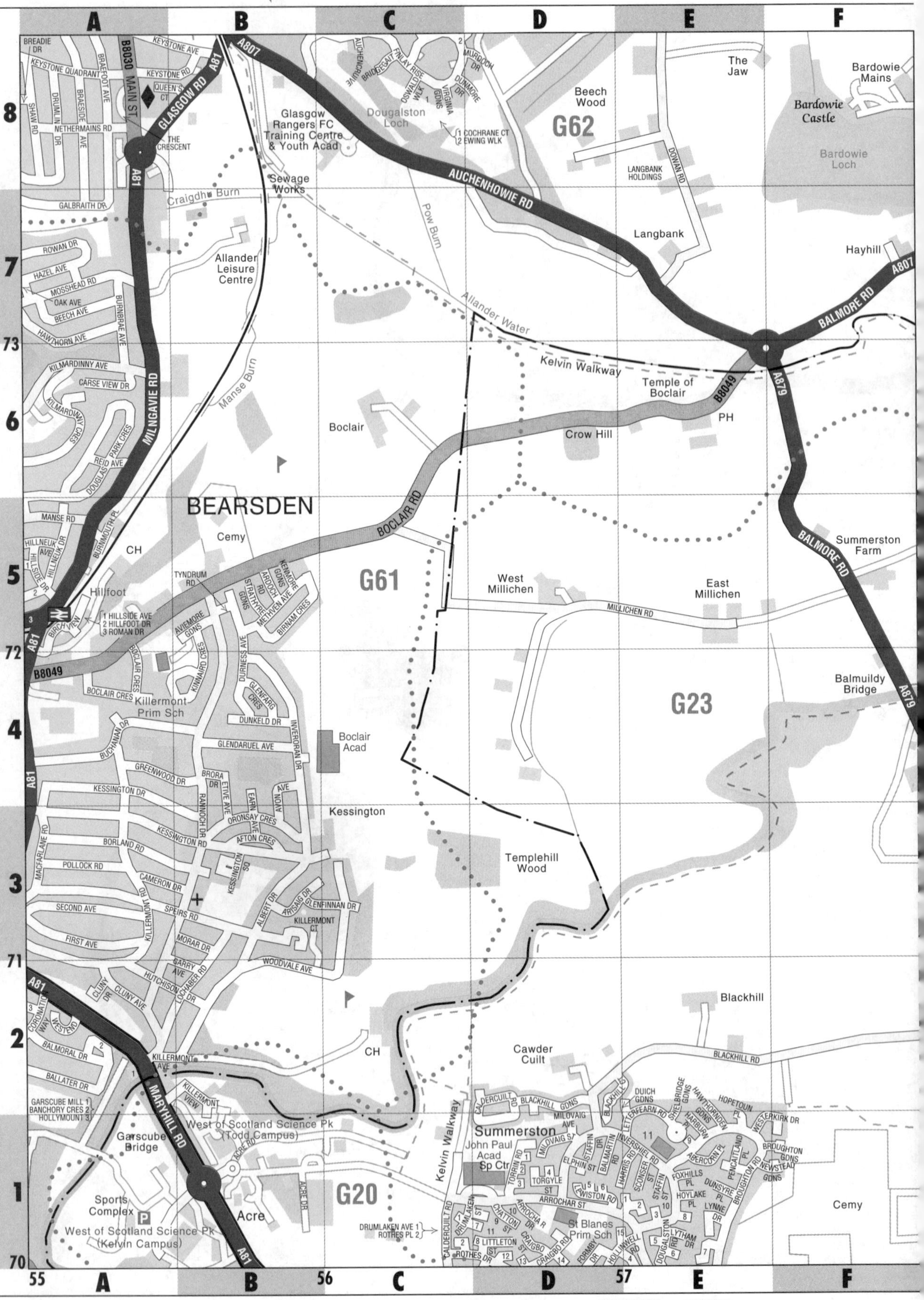

D1
1 CARNOCH ST
2 ARDESSIE ST
3 GEARY ST
4 CARBOST ST
5 LEWISTON DR
6 LEWISTON PL
7 DRUMLAKEN CT
8 LITTLETON DR
9 DRUMLAKEN PL
10 ARROCHAR PATH
11 DRUMLAKEN PATH
12 MULLARDOCH ST
13 CRAIGBO DR
14 CRAIGBO AVE
15 GLENBERVIE PL

E1
1 FORRES ST
2 TOLSTA ST
3 GALLAN AVE
4 LINDRICK DR
5 WENTWORTH DR
6 MUIRFIELD CRES
7 CROSSFORD DR
8 CROSSPOINT DR
9 NEWCASTLETON DR
10 STAFFIN PATH
11 Caldercuilt Prim Sch

75
96

Braeside
CRAIGMADDIE RD
NEW BRANZIET COTTS
Branziet Bridge
Whitefauld
CH
Collalis
GOLF COURSE RD
GLEN ORCHARD RD
CROFT RD
Balmore
Works
BALMORE RD
A807
Branziet Farm
Laverockhill
Bardowie
ROBINSFIELD
STATION RD
ALLANDER AVE
PATERSON'S LA
OLD BALMORE RD
Bogside
South Bardowie
G62
Branziet Burn
Balmore Haughs
Allander Water
River Kelvin
Cawder House (CH)
BUCHLEY COTTS
Buchley
BALMUILDY RD
G64
Kelvin Walkway
Wilderness Plantation
Depot
Easter Balmuidy
Factory
Farm Bridge
Mavis Valley Road
Jellyhill
Wester Balmuidy Farm
Leisuredrome
Refuse Tip
Forth & Clyde Canal
Balmuildy Prim Sch
Mast
Works
G23
Bishopbriggs
Bishopbriggs Burn
BALMORE RD
BLACKHILL RD
Parkholm Farm
LOCHFAULD RD
Lochfauld Farm
Turnbull High Sch
ST ANDREW'S AVE
BISHOP GDNS
CH
St Marys Sch Kenmure
Kenmure St Mary's Secure Unit
NOVAR GDNS
ELDON GDNS
BEAUFORT GDNS
KENMURE AVE
KENMURE GDNS
G22
Cemy
A879
Possil Loch (Bird Sanctuary)
CASTLEBAY DR
Laigh Kenmure
CLOVERGATE
HEATHERBRAE
GORSEWOOD
A803
KIRKINTILLOCH RD
CROSS CT
KENMURE DR
KENMURE LA
BRACKENBRAE AVE
GLENBURN GDNS
THE ROWANS
DALHOUSIE GDNS
CARROUR GDNS
MORAR CRES
MARCHMONT GDNS
LOMOND DR
HILTON RD
ATHOLL GDNS
GLENEAGLES GDNS
HILTON TERR
DARNLEY CRES
MARCHFIELD
WESTFIELDS
MIDCROFT
PARKLEA
NORFOLK CRES
STIRLING GDNS
STIRLING DR
FASKALLY AVE
MUIRTON DR
SOUTHESK GDNS
SOUTHESK AVE
BROADLEYS AVE
TOFTHILL AVE
TOFTHILL GDNS
KEIR DR
ST MARY'S RD
BARDRILL DR
DUNCRUB DR
POLLOK DR
BRACKENBRAE RD
CROWHILL RD
A B C D E F
8 7 73 6 5 72 4 3 71 2 1 70
58 59 60

77
57

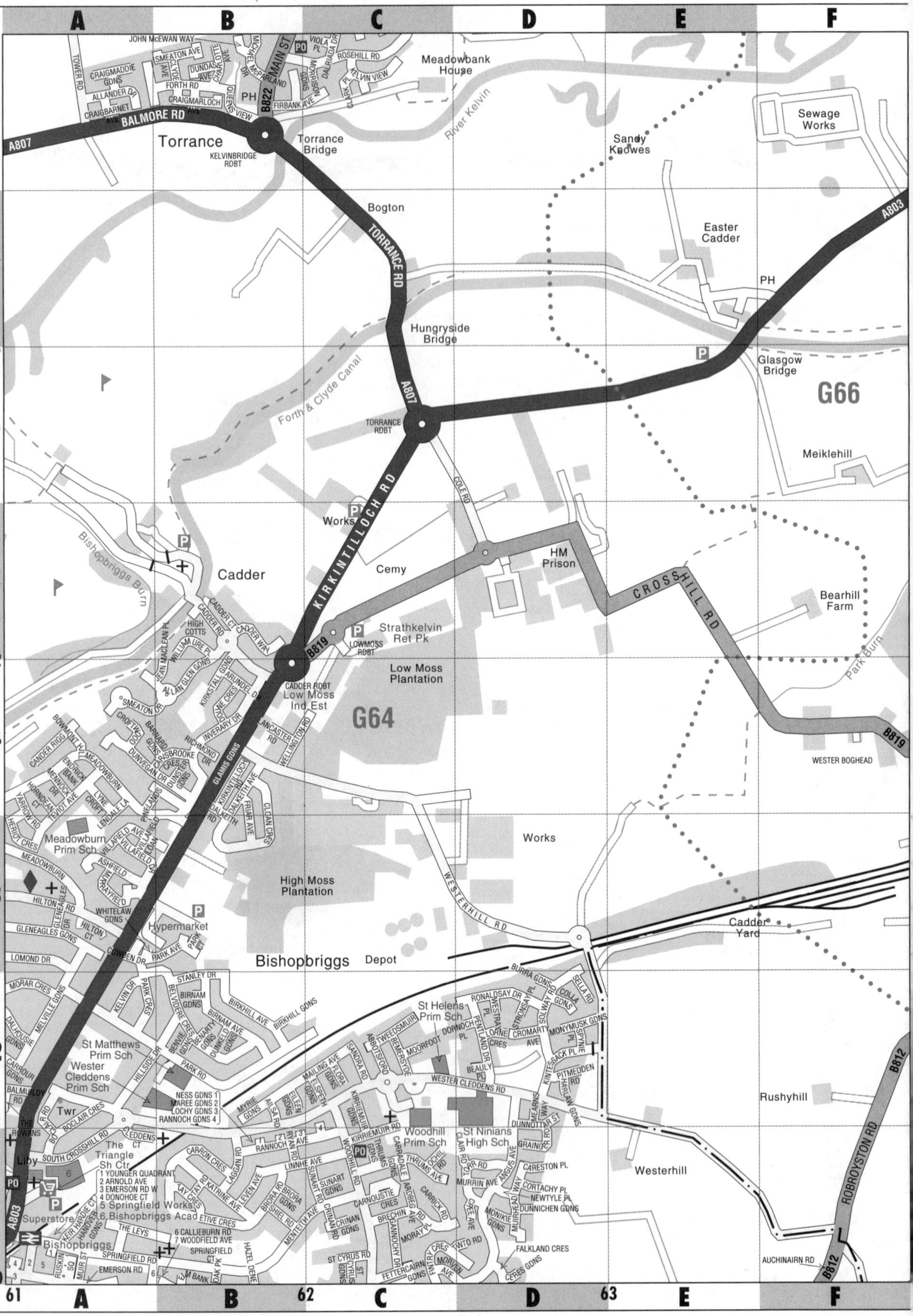
A
B
C
D
E
F
8
7
73
6
5
72
4
3
71
2
1
70
61
62
63
JOHN McEWAN WAY
CRAIGMADDIE GDNS
ALLANDER DR
CRAIGBARNET AVE
TOWER RD
SMEATON AVE
CLYDE AVE
DUNDAS AVE
CHARLOTTE AVE
FORTH RD
CRAIGMARLOCH AVE
QUEENS VIEW
MICHAEL McPARLAND DR
B822 MAIN ST
PH
PO
VIOLA PL
MORRISON GDNS
DALRIADA DR
ROSEHILL RD
KELVIN VIEW
CLARK PL
FIRBANK AVE
BALMORE RD
A807
Torrance
KELVINBRIDGE RDBT
Torrance Bridge
Meadowbank House
River Kelvin
Sandy Knowes
Sewage Works
Bogton
TORRANCE RD
Easter Cadder
PH
A803
Hungryside Bridge
Forth & Clyde Canal
P
Glasgow Bridge
G66
TORRANCE RDBT
A807
Meiklehill
KIRKINTILLOCH RD
COLE RD
P
Works
Bishopbriggs Burn
P
Cadder
Cemy
HM Prison
CROSSHILL RD
Bearhill Farm
Strathkelvin Ret Pk
P
LOWMOSS RDBT
B819
Park Burn
Low Moss Plantation
CADDER RDBT
Low Moss Ind Est
G64
WESTER BOGHEAD
B819
CADDER RD
CADDER CT
CADDER WAY
HIGH COTTS
JEAN MACLEAN PL
WILLIAM URE PL
ALAN GLEN GDNS
KIRKSTALL GDNS
ARUNDEL DR
SMEATON DR
CROFTFOOT DR
BARNARD GDNS
RICHMOND DR
INVERARY DR
LANCASTER RD
WELLINGTON RD
GLAMIS GDNS
DUNVEGAN DR
DUNSTER GDNS
KIRKINTILLOCH RD
DALKEITH AVE
FRIAR AVE
CLOAN CRES
BOWMONT HILL
CANDER RIGG
MEADOWBURN
HORNDEAN CT
YARROW RD
HERIOT CRES
TEVIOT AVE
LENDALE LA
PINELANDS
VILLAFIELD AVE
VILLAFIELD LOAN
Meadowburn Prim Sch
ASHFIELD
Works
High Moss Plantation
WESTERHILL RD
MEADOWBURN
HILTON RD
GLENEAGLES DR
GLENEAGLES GDNS
HILTON CT
WHITELAW GDNS
Hypermarket
P
PARK AVE
COWDEN DR
LOMOND DR
Bishopbriggs
Depot
Cadder Yard
MORAR CRES
MELVILLE GDNS
KELVIN DR
PARK CRES
STANLEY DR
BIRNAM GDNS
BIRKHILL AVE
BIRKHILL GDNS
BURRA GDNS
SELLA RD
COLLA GDNS
RONALDSAY DR
WESTRAY CIRC
STRONSAY PL
SOLWAY RD
MONYMUSK GDNS
SPYNIE PL
St Helens Prim Sch
DALHOUSIE GDNS
St Matthews Prim Sch
Wester Cleddens Prim Sch
CARROUR GDNS
BALMUILDY RD
Twr
BOCLAIR CRES
HILLSIDE DR
PARK RD
NESS GDNS 1
MAREE GDNS 2
LOCHY GDNS 3
RANNOCH GDNS 4
MYRIE GDNS
AILSA RD
ELSPETH GDNS
FLORA GDNS
MAILING AVE
SANDRA RD
ABBOTSFORD
TWEEDSMUIR
BEMERSYDE
MOORFOOT
DORNOCH PL
PENTLAND DR
LORNE CRES
CROMARTY AVE
BEAULY PL
KINTESSACK PL
PITMEDDEN RD
HARLAW GDNS
WESTER CLEDDENS RD
Rushyhill
B812
THE ROWANS
The Triangle Sh Ctr
SOUTH CROSSHILL RD
CLEDDENS CT
Liby
PO
1 YOUNGER QUADRANT
2 ARNOLD AVE
3 EMERSON RD W
4 DONOHOE CT
5 Springfield Works
6 Bishopbriggs Acad
CARRON CRES
LAGGAN RD
RANNOCH AVE
RYAN RD
KIRRIEMUIR RD
Woodhill Prim Sch
St Ninians High Sch
DUNNOTTAR ST
GRAINGER RD
MEARNS WAY
ROWAN ST
Westerhill
ROBROYSTON RD
LINNHE AVE
SUNART RD
SUNART GDNS
WOODHILL RD
THRUMS GDNS
CARRADALE GDNS
THRUMS AVE
OCHIL RD
CLAIR RD
TORR RD
MURRIN AVE
ANGUS AVE
CARESTON PL
CORTACHY PL
NEWTYLE PL
DUNNICHEN GDNS
A803
Superstore
P
KEIR HARDIE CT
HANOVER GDNS
TAY CRES
KATRINE AVE
LEVEN AVE
BRORA RD
BRORA GDNS
SHIEL RD
MENTEITH AVE
CRINAN RD
CRINAN GDNS
CARNOUSTIE CRES
ARDBEG AVE
CARRICK RD
CREE AVE
MONIKIE GDNS
MUIRHEAD WAY
Bishopbriggs
THE LEYS
ETIVE CRES
6 CALLIEBURN RD
7 WOODFIELD AVE
SPRINGFIELD CT
BRECHIN RD
BANNOCHY DR
MORAY PL
FINTRY CRES
MORVEN AVE
ONTO RD
FALKLAND CRES
CERES GDNS
AUCHINAIRN RD
B812
RUSKIN SQ
MUIR ST
SPRINGFIELD RD
EMERSON RD
ELM BANK
OAK PK
HAZEL DENE
ST CYRUS RD
ST CYRUS GDNS
FETTERCAIRN GDNS

77
98

C8
1 YORK PL
2 Regent Sh Ctr
3 BROADCROFT
4 ROCHDALE PL
5 Lairdsland Prim Sch

58

D8
1 GLENVIEW
2 PETER D.STIRLING RD
3 GLENBURN CT
4 STRATHALLAN GDNS
5 BROOMFIELD WLK
6 BELMONT CT

80

D7
1 MUIRHEAD ST
2 DONALDSON PL
3 DALRYMPLE CT
4 ST ANDREWS CT
5 GLENCAIRN ST
6 DROMORE ST
7 CRAIGMOUNT ST

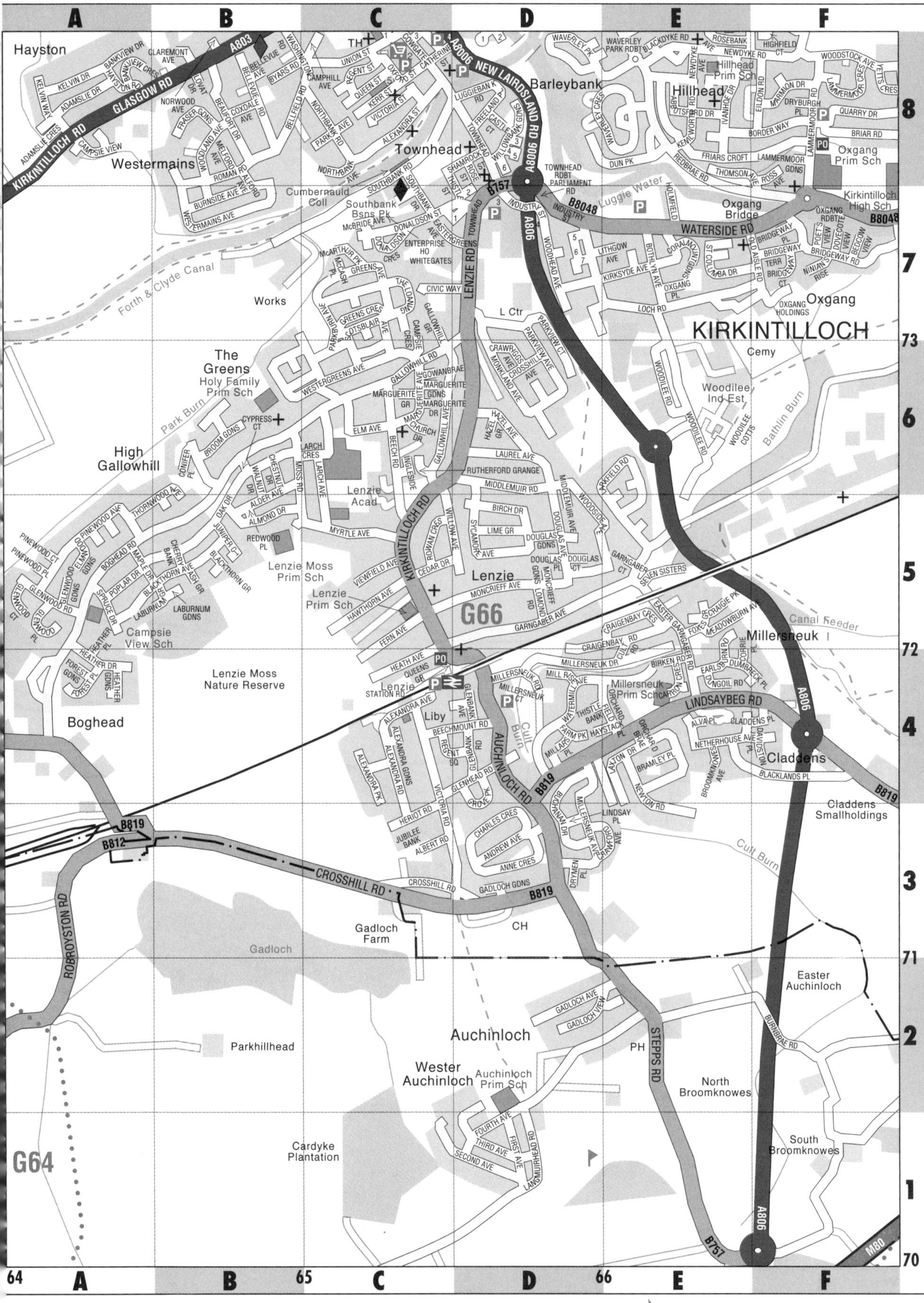

99
80

79
59

A
B
C
D
E
F
8
7
73
6
5
72
4
3
71
2
1
70
67
68
69
1 WOODSTOCK AVE
2 BRAES O' YETTS
3 QUARRY DR
Rosebank
Braes of Yetts
B8048
Black Burn
KIRKINTILLOCH RD
Gartconner Prim Sch
St Agathas Prim Sch
WATERSIDE RD
Kirkintilloch High Sch
KIRKINTILLOCH
Wester Gartshore
Heronryhill Plantation
BRIDGEND COTTS
Duntiblae
Waterside
G66
Drumbreck
BACK O DYKES RD 1
CRAIG CRES 2
LONG ROW 3
MUIRHEAD COTTS 4
BERRYKNOWE 5
PIT RD
Luggie Water
Twr
Fauldhead
Drumshanty
CALFMUIR RD
CHRYSTON RD
Wester Bedcow
Easter Bedcow
MUCKCROFT RD
VIEWFIELD
M80
CLADDENS HOLDINGS
Bothlin Burn
B819
Burnbrae Farm
G69
AUCHENGEICH RD
Sewage Works
Netherhouses
Works
GARTFERRY RD
BURNBRAE RD
Davidston
Glenmanor Prim Sch
Bridgend
Blacklands
Hill of Chryston
Liby
PO
Moodiesburn
Garnkirk Burn
Peathill
Lindsaybeg House
1 HERMISTON GDNS
2 MINTLAW WY
3 MONKTON BRAE
4 COLINTON GDNS
5 HERMISTON GDNS
6 BALLAYNE DR
Lanrigg
GLENARTNEY RD
PH
DORNOCH PL
CROMARTY PL
GRAYSTON MANOR
Bedlay Castle
A80
CUMBERNAULD RD
30
Hotel
Cemy
AVENUEHEAD RD
Drumsack
HEATHFIELD AVE 11
NETHERHILL RD 12
DUNELLAN GR 13
BEECHGROVE 14
DEEPDENE RD 15
ASHGROVE 16
EARLSCOURT 17
AUCHENGLEN DR 3
MEADOWHEAD AVE 4
FERNLEIGH PL 5
ARDOCH WAY 6
ARNPRIOR GDNS 7
MARNOCH WAY 8
BURNBRAE AVE 9
LANGHOLM CT 10
GLENAPP PL 1
WHITHORN CRES 2
BLAIRDENAN AVE

79
100

60
82

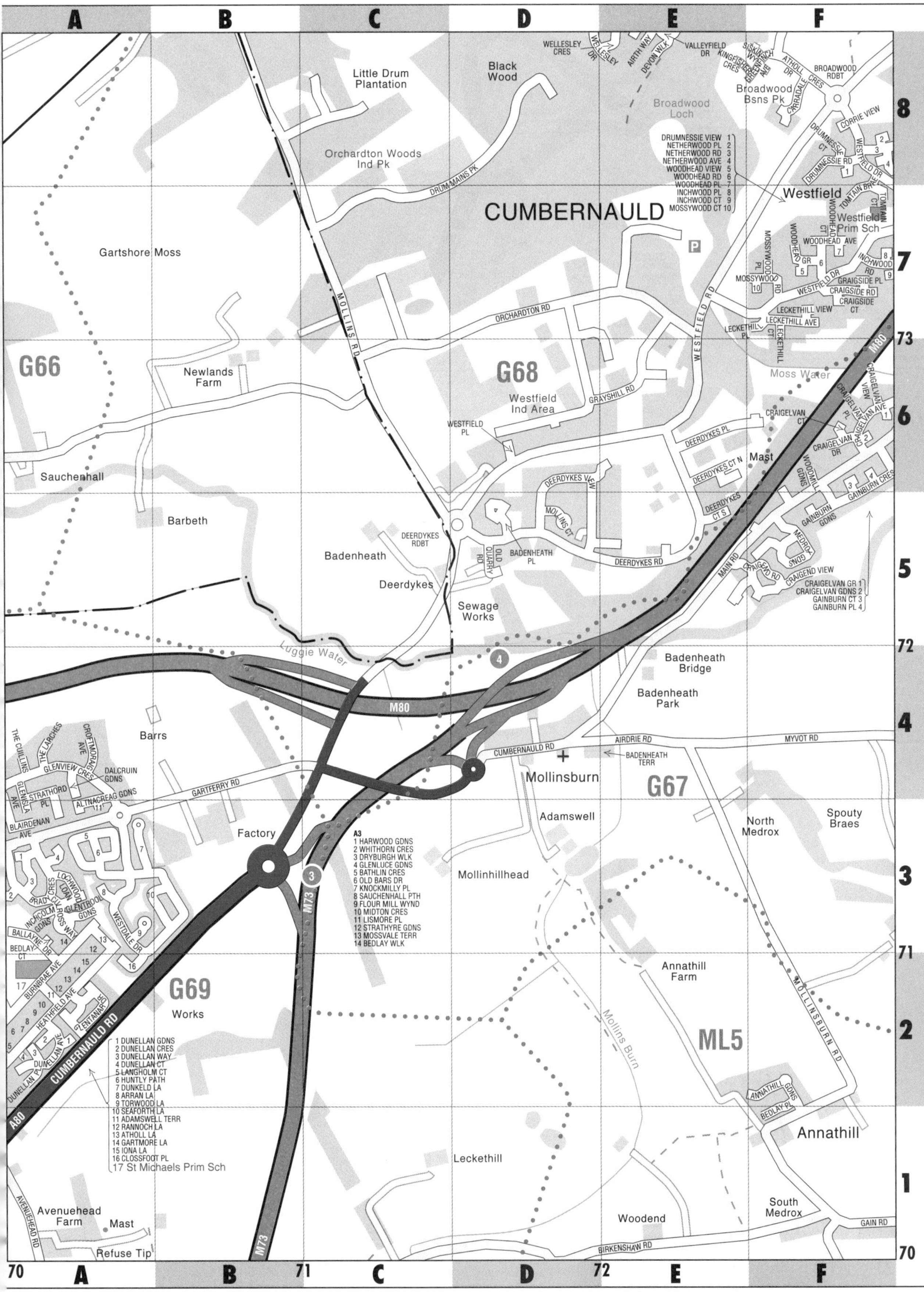
A
B
C
D
E
F
8
7
73
6
5
72
4
3
71
2
1
70
71
72
CUMBERNAULD
G66
G68
G67
G69
ML5
Little Drum Plantation
Black Wood
Orchardton Woods Ind Pk
Broadwood Loch
Broadwood Bsns Pk
Westfield
Westfield Prim Sch
Gartshore Moss
Newlands Farm
Westfield Ind Area
Sauchenhall
Barbeth
Badenheath
Deerdykes
Sewage Works
Mast
Moss Water
Luggie Water
Badenheath Bridge
Badenheath Park
Barrs
Mollinsburn
Adamswell
Factory
Mollinhillhead
North Medrox
Spouty Braes
Annathill Farm
Works
Mollins Burn
Annathill
Leckethill
Woodend
South Medrox
Avenuehead Farm
Mast
Refuse Tip
M80
M73
A80
WELLESLEY CRES
WELLESLEY DR
AIRTH WAY
DEVON WLK
VALLEYFIELD DR
SISKIN WYND
KINGFISHER CRES
GREENFINCH AVE
ATHOLL CRES
ATHOLL DR
BROADWOOD RDBT
CARRADALE CRES
CORRIE VIEW
DRUMNESSIE CT
DRUMNESSIE RD
WESTFIELD DR
TOMTAIN BRAE
TOMTAIN CT
WOODHEAD CT
WOODHEAD AVE
WOODHEAD GR
INCHWOOD RD
GRAIGSIDE PL
CRAIGSIDE RD
CRAIGSIDE CT
MOSSYWOOD PL
MOSSYWOOD RD
LECKETHILL VIEW
LECKETHILL AVE
LECKETHILL PL
LECKETHILL CT
DRUM MAINS PK
MOLLINS RD
ORCHARDTON RD
WESTFIELD RD
GRAYSHILL RD
WESTFIELD PL
DEERDYKES PL
DEERDYKES CT N
DEERDYKES CT S
DEERDYKES VIEW
MOLLINS CT
DEERDYKES RDBT
QUARRY RD
OLD QUARRY RD
BADENHEATH PL
DEERDYKES RD
CRAIGELVAN CT
CRAIGELVAN VIEW
CRAIGELVAN PL
CRAIGELVAN AVE
CRAIGELVAN DR
CRAIGELVAN CT
WOODMILL GDNS
GAINBURN CRES
GAINBURN GDNS
MEDROX GDNS
MAIN RD
CRAIGELVAN GDNS
CRAIGEND VIEW
DRUMNESSIE VIEW 1
NETHERWOOD PL 2
NETHERWOOD RD 3
NETHERWOOD AVE 4
WOODHEAD VIEW 5
WOODHEAD RD 6
WOODHEAD PL 7
INCHWOOD PL 8
INCHWOOD CT 9
MOSSYWOOD CT 10
CRAIGELVAN GR 1
CRAIGELVAN GDNS 2
GAINBURN CT 3
GAINBURN PL 4
AIRDRIE RD
MYVOT RD
CUMBERNAULD RD
BADENHEATH TERR
THE CUILLINS
THE LARCHES
CROFTMORAIG AVE
GLENVIEW CRES
DALCRUIN GDNS
GLENISLA AVE
STRATHORD PL
ALTNACREAG GDNS
GARTFERRY RD
BLAIRDENAN AVE
LOCHWOOD LOAN
BRAIDCRAFT CRES
INCHCOLM GDNS
GLENTROOL GDNS
ROSS WAY
WESTDALE DR
BALLAYNE DR
BEDLAY CT
BURNBRAE AVE
HEATHFIELD AVE
LENTANAR DR
DUNELLAN AVE
DUNELLAN PL
CUMBERNAULD RD
A3
1 HARWOOD GDNS
2 WHITHORN CRES
3 DRYBURGH WLK
4 GLENLUCE GDNS
5 BATHLIN CRES
6 OLD BARS DR
7 KNOCKMILLY PL
8 SAUCHENHALL PTH
9 FLOUR MILL WYND
10 MIDTON CRES
11 LISMORE PL
12 STRATHYRE GDNS
13 MOSSVALE TERR
14 BEDLAY WLK
1 DUNELLAN GDNS
2 DUNELLAN CRES
3 DUNELLAN WAY
4 DUNELLAN CT
5 LANGHOLM CT
6 HUNTLY PATH
7 DUNKELD LA
8 ARRAN LA
9 TORWOOD LA
10 SEAFORTH LA
11 ADAMSWELL TERR
12 RANNOCH LA
13 ATHOLL LA
14 GARTMORE LA
15 IONA LA
16 CLOSSFOOT PL
17 St Michaels Prim Sch
MOLLINSBURN RD
ANNATHILL GDNS
BEDLAY PL
GAIN RD
BIRKENSHAW RD
AVENUEHEAD RD

101
82

81
61

F8
1 St Margaret of Scotland Prim Sch

81
102

62
84

A
B
C
D
E
F
8
7
73
6
5
72
4
3
71
2
1
70
76
77
78
GLENCRYAN RD
B8054
KILBOWIE RD
BROOMLANDS RD
GREENFAULDS CRES
WALLBRAE RD
SANDYKNOWES RD
SOUTH CARBRAIN RD
Cumbernauld
GREENFAULDS RD
St Margaret of Scotland Prim Sch
KELVIN RD N
KELVIN RD
LENZIEMILL RD
Ind Est
Lenziemill
TELFORD PL
TELFORD RD
JANE'S BRAE
Glencryan Plantation
Glencryan Burn
Greenside
Palacerigg Country Park
Visitor Ctr
Palacerigg Cottage
West Waterhead
CH
East Waterhead
G67
Sandyknowes
Tannoch
BROOMLEE RD
BLAIRLINN RD
STIRLING RD
BLAIRLINN VW
Blairlinn Ind Est
TOWER RD
GREENS RD
BELSTANE RD
Luggiebank
Luggie Water
Acrecroft Farm
Easter Blairlinn Cottages
Glenhove
Wester Glentore
Craigelvan
Pedderland
Coathill
Greens
MILLCROFT RD
HULKS RD
SPAIRDRUM RD
Muirhead
Muirhead Glen
Boglea
Loanhead
Auldshields Bridge
Staylee Glen
Staylee
ML6
BRACKENKNOWE RD
BLACKBOG RD
Blacktongue Farm
Cameron Burn
Whinrigg Farm
B8039
B803
BLACKTONGUE FARM RD
RANKIN CRES
ELM PK GR
HILLVIEW
PO
COALBURN ST
ANNANDALE
LAUREL GR
CAMERON RD
Cameron
Greengairs Prim Sch
Cameron Glen
GREENGAIRS RD
Greengairs
OLD BIGGAR RD
DRUMGRAY GDNS
Cullochrig Plantation
Drumgray Farm
MILL RD
DRUMGRAY LA
BRACKENHIRST RD
Berryhill Cottage
Riggend
MEIKLE DRUMGRAY RD
HILLRIGG
A73

103
84

83
63

A
B
C
D
E
F
8
7
73
6
5
72
4
3
71
2
1
70
79
80
81
Palacerigg Country Park
G67
Herd's Hill
Fannyside Lochs
Fannyside Lodge
Fannyside Mill
Garbethill Burn
Jawhills
River Avon
Thieves Hill
Scar Hill
West Fannyside
FK1
Toddle Knowe
Bog Bridge
Luggie Water
Avon Water
Black Hill
Blackhill
Torbrex
HULKS RD
Bogside
Netherton of Glentore
B803
P
Easter Glentore Farm
Shielhill Burn
Langdales
ML6
DERVAIG GDNS
LUCKENHILL DR
AVON AVE
SCAMADALE RD
Easter Glentore
Upperton Farm
THE CRESCENT
GREENGAIRS RD
Meadowfield
B803
PH
Greendykeside
Avalon
BRIDGE ST
83
104

64
86

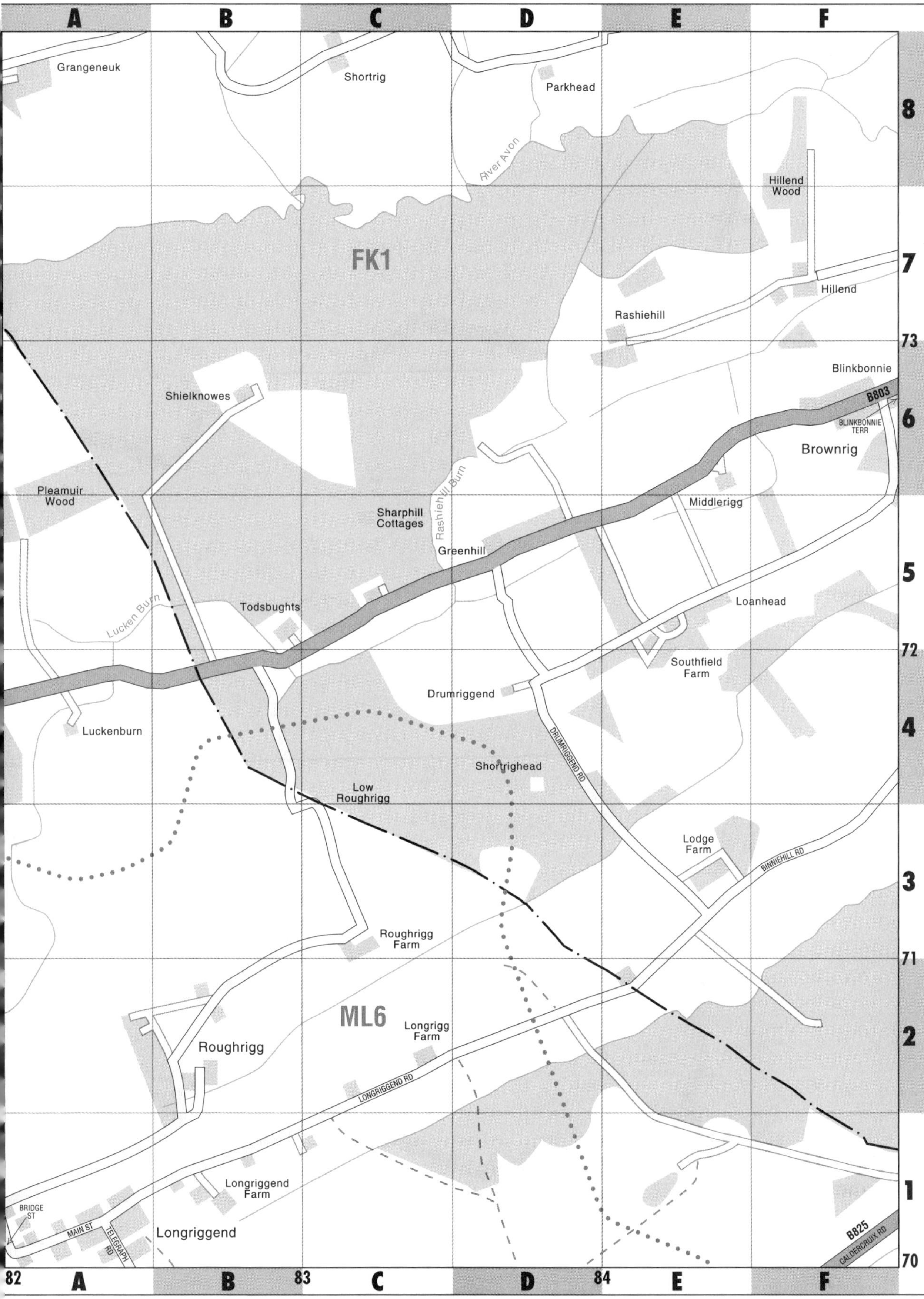
A
B
C
D
E
F
Grangeneuk
Shortrig
Parkhead
River Avon
Hillend Wood
FK1
Hillend
Rashiehill
Blinkbonnie
B803
BLINKBONNIE TERR
Shielknowes
Brownrig
Pleamuir Wood
Middlerigg
Sharphill Cottages
Rashiehill Burn
Greenhill
Lucken Burn
Todsbughts
Loanhead
Southfield Farm
Drumriggend
Luckenburn
DRUMRIGGEND RD
Shortrighead
Low Roughrigg
Lodge Farm
BINNIEHILL RD
Roughrigg Farm
ML6
Longrigg Farm
Roughrigg
LONGRIGGEND RD
Longriggend Farm
BRIDGE ST
MAIN ST
TELEGRAPH RD
Longriggend
B825
CALDERCRUIX RD
8
7
73
6
5
72
4
3
71
2
1
70
82
83
84

105
86

85
65

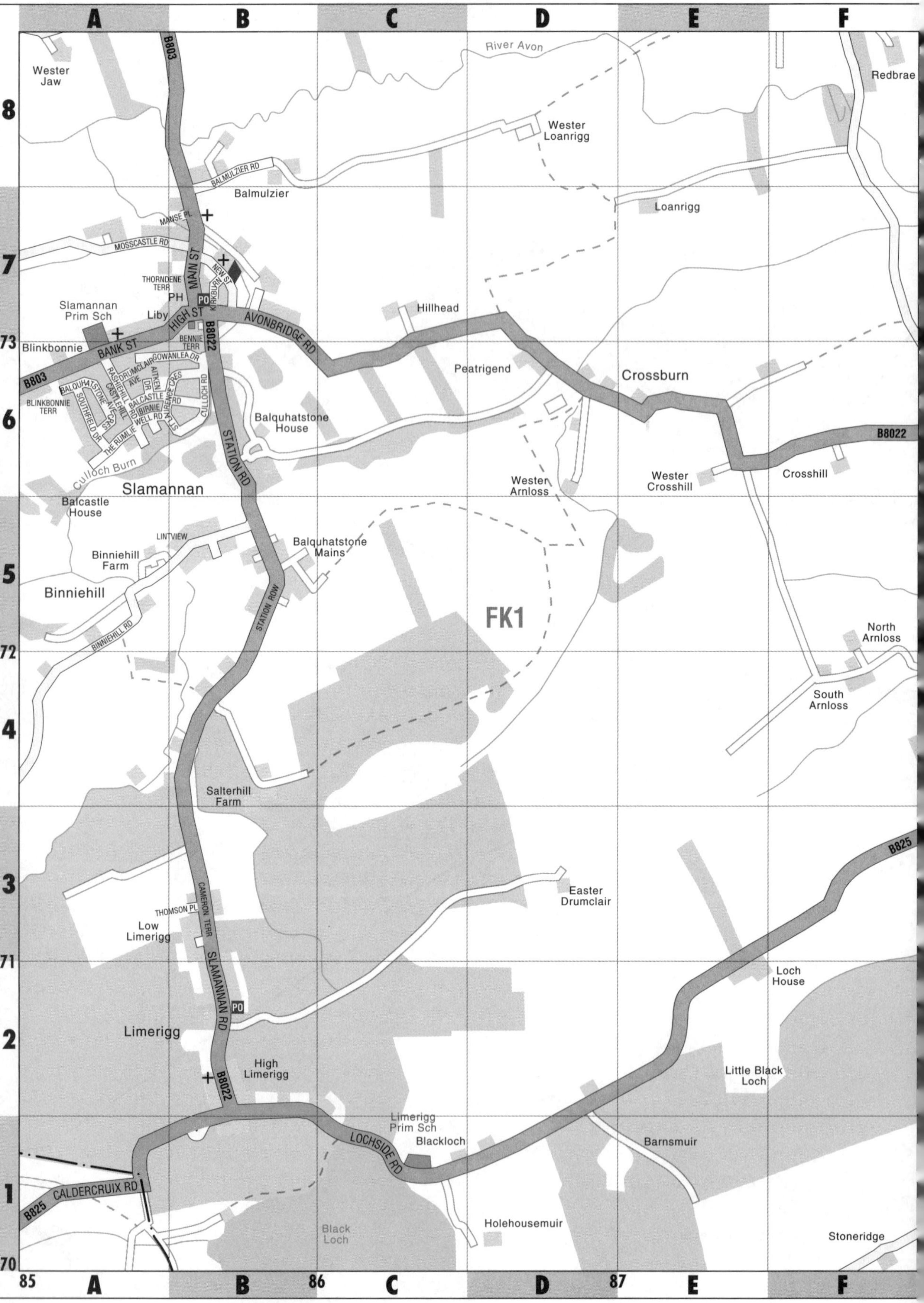
River Avon
Wester Jaw
Redbrae
Wester Loanrigg
BALMULZIER RD
Balmulzier
Loanrigg
MANSE PL
MOSSCASTLE RD
MAIN ST
NEW ST
THORNDENE TERR
PH
PO
KIRKBURN
Slamannan Prim Sch
Liby
HIGH ST
AVONBRIDGE RD
Hillhead
Blinkbonnie
BANK ST
B8022
BENNIE TERR
GOWANLEA DR
DRUMCLAIR AVE
Peatrigend
Crossburn
B803
BALQUHATSTONE
RASHIEHILL RD
CASTLEHILL AVE
AITKEN DR
LAURENCE CRES
CULLOCH RD
BLINKBONNIE TERR
SOUTHFIELD DR
BALCASTLE RD
BIRNIE
WELL RD
THE RUMLIE
Balquhatstone House
STATION RD
B8022
Crosshill
Culloch Burn
Slamannan
Wester Arnloss
Wester Crosshill
Balcastle House
LINTVIEW
Balquhatstone Mains
Binniehill Farm
Binniehill
STATION ROW
FK1
North Arnloss
BINNIEHILL RD
South Arnloss
Salterhill Farm
B825
Easter Drumclair
THOMSON PL
CAMERON TERR
Low Limerigg
SLAMANNAN RD
Loch House
PO
Limerigg
High Limerigg
B8022
Little Black Loch
Limerigg Prim Sch
LOCHSIDE RD
Blackloch
Barnsmuir
CALDERCRUIX RD
B825
Black Loch
Holehousemuir
Stoneridge
A B C D E F
8 7 6 5 4 3 2 1
73 72 71 70
85 86 87

66
A B C D E F
Lower Boxton
BOXTON RD
Boagstown
Hareburn
B8028
North Bankhead
Balmitchell
Windy-yett
Avonview
Manse
Whinny Knowes
South Bankhead
River Avon
Bogo
Avonbridge
The Neucks
Avonvale
Summerhouse
AVONPARK
SLAMANNAN RD
B825
Avonbridge Prim Sch
B8022
Babbithill
Crossroads
Craigend
Bulliondale House
Edinburgh STREET ATLAS
FK1
Dykehead
Redhall
Wester Holehouse
North East Holehouse
Holehouse
Lin Mill Burn
Elrigside Wood
South Holehouse
Easter Greenhill
Linhouse Farm
East Plantation
Wester Greenhill
Drumtassie Burn
Barns
North Rhodens Plantation
8 7 73 6 5 72 4 3 71 2 1 70
88 89 90
107

68

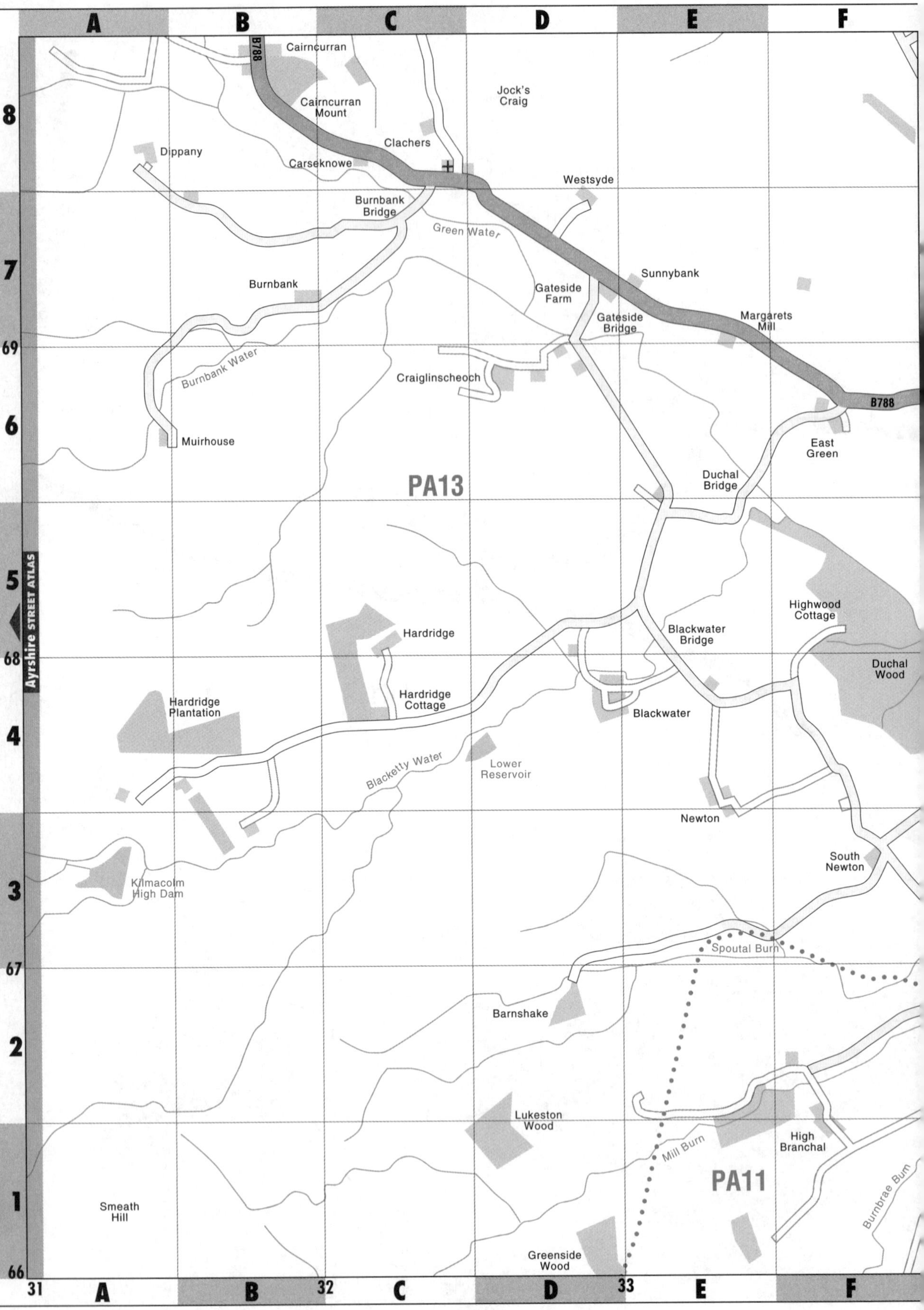
A B C D E F
8 7 6 5 4 3 2 1
69 68 67 66
31 32 33
B788
Cairncurran
Cairncurran Mount
Jock's Craig
Dippany
Clachers
Carseknowe
Westsyde
Burnbank Bridge
Green Water
Burnbank
Sunnybank
Gateside Farm
Gateside Bridge
Margarets Mill
Burnbank Water
Craiglinscheoch
Muirhouse
East Green
Duchal Bridge
PA13
Highwood Cottage
Hardridge
Blackwater Bridge
Duchal Wood
Hardridge Plantation
Hardridge Cottage
Blackwater
Lower Reservoir
Blacketty Water
Newton
South Newton
Kilmacolm High Dam
Spoutal Burn
Barnshake
Lukeston Wood
High Branchal
Mill Burn
PA11
Burnbrae Burn
Smeath Hill
Greenside Wood
Ayrshire STREET ATLAS

108

69
90

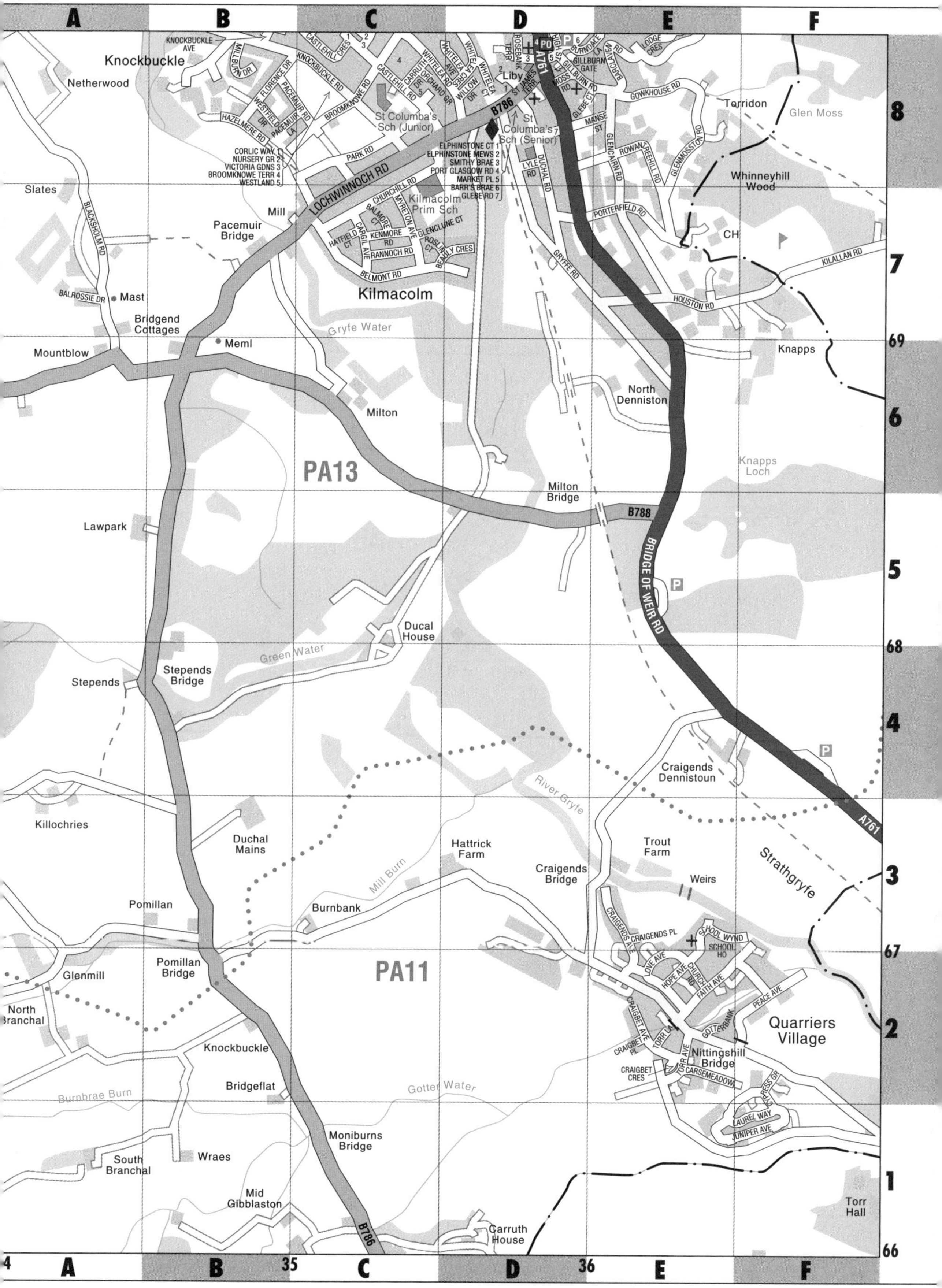
A
B
C
D
E
F
Knockbuckle
Netherwood
KNOCKBUCKLE AVE
MILLBURN DR
FLORENCE DR
WESTFIELD DR
PACEMUIR RD
PACEMUIR LA
HAZELMERE RD
KNOCKBUCKLE RD
CASTLEHILL CRES
CASTLEHILL RD
BROOMKNOWE RD
CARRUTH DR
WHITELEA RD
WHITELEA AVE
WHITELEA CRES
WHITELEA CT
ORCHARD GR
WILLOW DR
ROSEBANK TERR
ST JAMES TERR
Liby
PO
A761
HIGH ST
BURNSIDE LA
GILLBURN GATE
GILLBURN RD
MOSS RD
GLEBE CT
BARCLAVEN RD
LODGE CRES
GOWKHOUSE RD
Torridon
Glen Moss
St Columba's Sch (Junior)
St Columba's Sch (Senior)
B786
CORLIC WAY 1
NURSERY GR 2
VICTORIA GDNS 3
BROOMKNOWE TERR 4
WESTLAND 5
PARK RD
ELPHINSTONE CT 1
ELPHINSTONE MEWS 2
SMITHY BRAE 3
PORT GLASGOW RD 4
MARKET PL 5
BARR'S BRAE 6
GLEBE RD 7
LYLE RD
DUCHAL RD
MANSE ST
GLENCAIRN RD
ROWAN
REEHILL RD
GLENMOSSTON RD
Whinneyhill Wood
8
Slates
LOCHWINNOCH RD
CHURCHILL RD
BALMORE CT
MYRETON AVE
Kilmacolm Prim Sch
Mill
Pacemuir Bridge
BLACKSHOLM RD
HATFIELD CT
CARGIL AVE
KENMORE RD
GLENCLUNE CT
ROSLIN CT
BEATTY CRES
RANNOCH RD
BELMONT RD
PORTERFIELD RD
CH
GRYFFE RD
KILALLAN RD
7
BALROSSIE DR
Mast
Kilmacolm
HOUSTON RD
Bridgend Cottages
Gryfe Water
Mountblow
Meml
69
Knapps
North Denniston
Milton
6
PA13
Knapps Loch
Lawpark
Milton Bridge
B788
BRIDGE OF WEIR RD
5
P
Ducal House
68
Green Water
Stepends
Stepends Bridge
4
P
Craigends Dennistoun
River Gryfe
Killochries
A761
Duchal Mains
Hattrick Farm
Trout Farm
Craigends Bridge
Strathgryfe
Weirs
3
Mill Burn
Pomillan
Burnbank
CRAIGENDS AVE
CRAIGENDS PL
SCHOOL WYND
SCHOOL HO
67
PA11
Pomillan Bridge
Glenmill
LOVE AVE
HOPE AVE
CHURCH RD
FAITH AVE
PEACE AVE
North Branchal
CRAIGBET AVE
TORR LA
GOTTERBANK
Quarriers Village
2
Knockbuckle
CRAIGBET PL
TORR AVE
Nittingshill Bridge
CRAIGBET CRES
CARSEMEADOW
CYPRESS GR
Bridgeflat
Burnbrae Burn
Gotter Water
LAUREL WAY
JUNIPER AVE
Moniburns Bridge
South Branchal
Wraes
1
Torr Hall
Mid Gibblaston
Carruth House
B786
66
4
A
B
35
C
D
36
E
F

109
90

89
70

A
B
C
D
E
F
8
7
69
6
5
68
4
3
67
2
1
66
37
38
39
PA14
Elphinstone Wood
Corsliehills Wood
Lawfield Dam
Corsliehills Cottage
CORSLIEHILL RD
Kirkton Wood
High Lawfield
Shovelboard
Hogs Burn
Kilallan
Wraes
PA13
Kirkton Farm
Wraes Wood
PA6
KILALLAN RD
North Barlogan Wood
Houston Burn
Mashington Wood
Peter's Burn
Wellees Farm
Barfillan Cottage
Ennelly Wood
Barfillan
Ennelly
Barlogan Wood
Barlogan Farm
Waterlea
BRIDGE OF WEIR RD
A761
PA11
WARLOCK RD
Bothenrickfield Wood
Scart Wood
Botherickfield
Scart
Houstonfield Dam
West Yonderton
East Yonderton
KILMACOLM RD
Law Hill
Girthill
River Gryfe
Gryffe Wraes
B790
GRYFFE CASTLE
Bridge of Weir Prim Sch
CASTLE RD
Fodston
HOUSTON RD
BEECH AVE
PARK RD
SOUTHVIEW
FREELAND DR
WARLOCK DR
Threeply
THISTLEBANK 1
GLENGOWAN RD 2
STRATHGRYFFE CRES
GRYFFE AVE
KILALLAN AVE
WOODSIDE AVE
ELM RD
LOCH RD
Houstonhead Dam

89
110

71
92

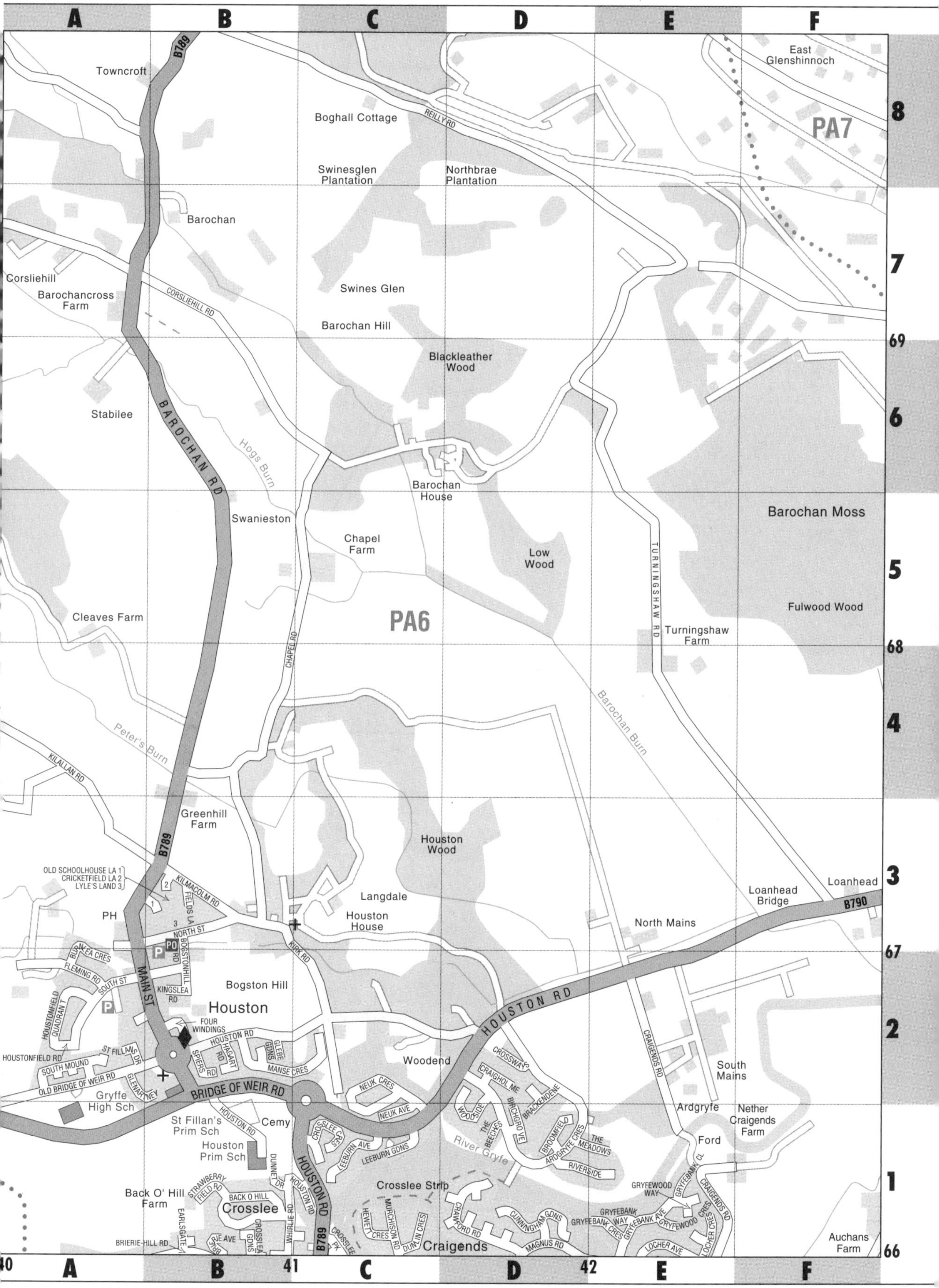
A
B
C
D
E
F
8
7
69
6
5
68
4
3
67
2
1
66
40
41
42
B789
Towncroft
Boghall Cottage
REILLY RD
East Glenshinnoch
PA7
Swinesglen Plantation
Northbrae Plantation
Barochan
Corsliehill
Barochancross Farm
CORSLIEHILL RD
Swines Glen
Barochan Hill
Blackleather Wood
Stabilee
BAROCHAN RD
Hogs Burn
Barochan House
Swanieston
Chapel Farm
Low Wood
TURNINGSHAW RD
Barochan Moss
Cleaves Farm
PA6
CHAPEL RD
Fulwood Wood
Turningshaw Farm
Barochan Burn
Peter's Burn
KILALLAN RD
Greenhill Farm
Houston Wood
OLD SCHOOLHOUSE LA 1
CRICKETFIELD LA 2
LYLE'S LAND 3
KILMACOLM RD
FIELDS LA
Langdale
Houston House
Loanhead Bridge
Loanhead
B790
North Mains
PH
NORTH ST
PO
BORSTONHILL RD
KIRK RD
BURNLEA CRES
FLEMING RD
SOUTH ST
KINGSLEA RD
MAIN ST
Bogston Hill
Houston
HOUSTON RD
HOUSTONFIELD QUADRANT
FOUR WINDINGS
HOUSTON RD
GLEBE GDNS
HASGART RD
SPIERS RD
MANSE CRES
CRAIGENDS RD
South Mains
HOUSTONFIELD RD
ST FILLAN'S DR
SOUTH MOUND
OLD BRIDGE OF WEIR RD
GLENBARNEY
Woodend
CROSSWAYS
CRAIGHOLME
BRACKENDENE
BIRCHGROVE
THE BEECHES
WOODSIDE
BRIDGE OF WEIR RD
NEUK CRES
NEUK AVE
Gryffe High Sch
St Fillan's Prim Sch
Cemy
Houston Prim Sch
CROSSLEE CRES
LEEBURN AVE
LEEBURN GDNS
River Gryfe
BROOMFIELD
ARDGRYFE CRES
THE MEADOWS
RIVERSIDE
Ardgryfe
Nether Craigends Farm
Ford
GRYFEBANK CL
Back O' Hill Farm
STRAWBERRY FIELD RD
BACK O HILL
DUNNET DR
Crosslee Strip
GRYFEWOOD WAY
CRAIGENDS RD
Crosslee
EARLSGATE
CROSSLEA GDNS
WHIRLIE RD
HOUSTON RD
HEWETT CRES
MURCHISON RD
DUNLIN CRES
CRAWFORD RD
CUNNINGHAM GDNS
GRYFEBANK WAY
GRYFEBANK CRES
GRYFEBANK AVE
GRYFEWOOD CRES
LOCHER CRES
BRIERIE-HILL RD
CROSSLEE PK
Craigends
MAGNUS RD
LOCHER AVE
Auchans Farm

111
92

91
72

A B C D E F
8 7 69 6 5 68 4 3 67 2 1 66
43 44 45
A8
DARGAVEL RD
Barrangary
Craigmuir
PA8
OLD GREENOCK RD
Southbar
Linburn Plantation
Southbar House
GREENOCK RD
Dargavel House
PA7
Dargavel Burn
Nether Southbar
North Commonside
A8
Barochan Moss
PA4
Lin Burn
Fulwood Moss
East Fulwood
B790
PA6
Dargavel Burn
HOUSTON RD
Barnhill
Netherfield
B790
River Gryfe
Fulwood Mains
SELVIELAND FARM COTTS
Wester Fulwood
Birkenhead Farm
PA3
MOSS RD
AUCHANS RD
Knowes
Locher Water
Blackstoun Mains
Black Cart Water
Linwoodmoss Wood
Moss Cottage
Blackstoun
Auchans

91
112

73
94

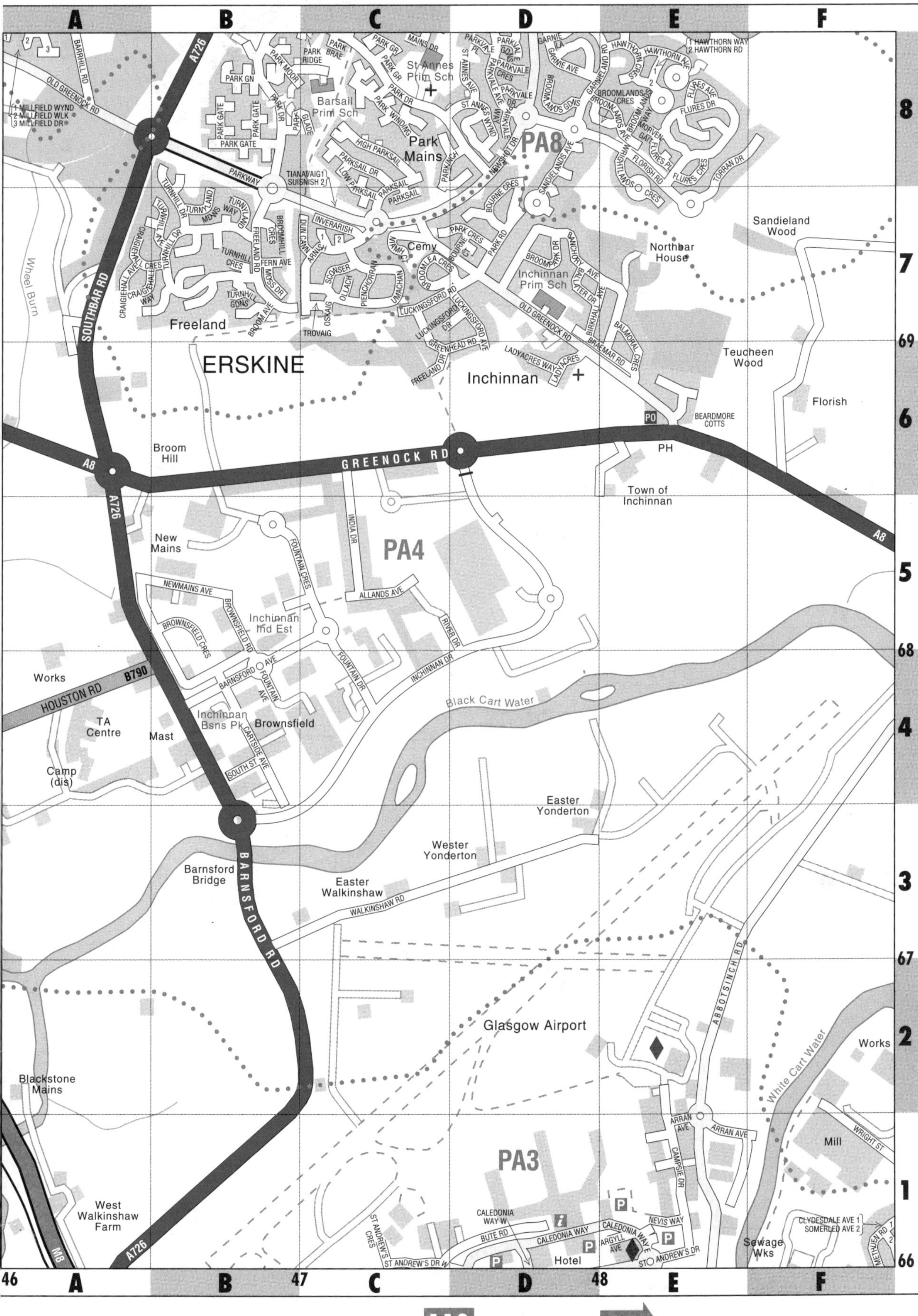
A
B
C
D
E
F
8
7
69
6
5
68
4
3
67
2
1
66
46
47
48
ERSKINE
Freeland
Park Mains
PA8
PA4
PA3
Inchinnan
Broom Hill
New Mains
Inchinnan Ind Est
Inchinnan Bsns Pk
Brownsfield
Works
TA Centre
Mast
Camp (dis)
Barnsford Bridge
Easter Walkinshaw
Wester Yonderton
Easter Yonderton
Glasgow Airport
Blackstone Mains
West Walkinshaw Farm
Town of Inchinnan
Sandieland Wood
Northbar House
Teucheen Wood
Florish
BEARDMORE COTTS
PH
Cemy
Barsail Prim Sch
St Annes Prim Sch
Inchinnan Prim Sch
Works
Mill
Sewage Wks
Hotel
GREENOCK RD
A8
A726
B790
SOUTHBAR RD
BARNSFORD RD
HOUSTON RD
OLD GREENOCK RD
WALKINSHAW RD
ABBOTSINCH RD
INCHINNAN RD
FOUNTAIN CRES
FOUNTAIN DR
INDIA DR
ALLANDS AVE
RIVER DR
NEWMAINS AVE
BROWNSFIELD CRES
BROWNSFIELD RD
BARNSFORD AVE
FOUNTAIN AVE
CARTSIDE AVE
SOUTH ST
Black Cart Water
White Cart Water
Wheel Burn
LADYACRES WAY
LADYACRES
ARRAN AVE
CAMPSIE DR
NEVIS WAY
CALEDONIA WAY
CALEDONIA WAY W
CALEDONIA WAY E
BUTE RD
ARGYLL AVE
ST ANDREW'S DR
ST ANDREW'S DR W
ST ANDREW'S CRES
WRIGHT ST
CLYDESDALE AVE 1
SOMERLED AVE 2
METHUEN RD
1 HAWTHORN WAY
2 HAWTHORN RD
1 MILLFIELD WYND
2 MILLFIELD WLK
3 MILLFIELD DR
BARRHILL RD
PARK GN
PARK GATE
PARK RIDGE
PARK BRAE
PARK MOOR
PARK DR
PARK GR
PARK WINDING
PARKWAY
HIGH PARKSAIL
PARKSAIL DR
LOW PARKSAIL
PARKSAIL
TIANAVAIG 1
SUISNISH 2
INVERARISH
TURNHILL DR
TURNHILL CRES
TURNHILL GDNS
TURNLAW MDWS
TURNYLAND WAY
CRAIGIEHALL CRES
CRAIGIEHALL AVE
CRAIGIEHALL WAY
BROOMHILL CRES
FREELAND RD
FERN AVE
MOSS DR
BROOM AVE
OSKAIG
TROVAIG
OLLACH
PIENCHORRAN
UNACHAN
BROOMLEA CRES
BOURNE CT
BOURNE CRES
PARK CRES
PARK RD
LUCKINGSFORD RD
LUCKINGSFORD DR
LUCKINGSFORD AVE
GREENHEAD RD
FREELAND DR
BROOMPARK DR
BANCHORY AVE
BALLATER DR
BIRKHALL AVE
BALMORAL CRES
BRAEMAR RD
MAINS DR
PARKVALE PL
PARKVALE CRES
PARKVALE DR
PARKVALE AVE
PARKVALE WAY
ST ANNES AVE
ST ANNES WYND
NEWSHOT DR
SANDIELANDS AVE
GARNIE LA
GARNIE AVE
GARNIELAND RD
BROOMLANDS GDNS
BROOMLANDS CRES
BROOMLANDS AVE
BROOMLANDS WAY
WRIGHTLANDS CRES
MORVEN GAIT
FLURES PL
FLURES CRES
FLURES AVE
FLURES DR
FLORISH RD
TORRAN DR
HAWTHORN CRES
HAWTHORN AVE
M8
PO

113
94

93
74

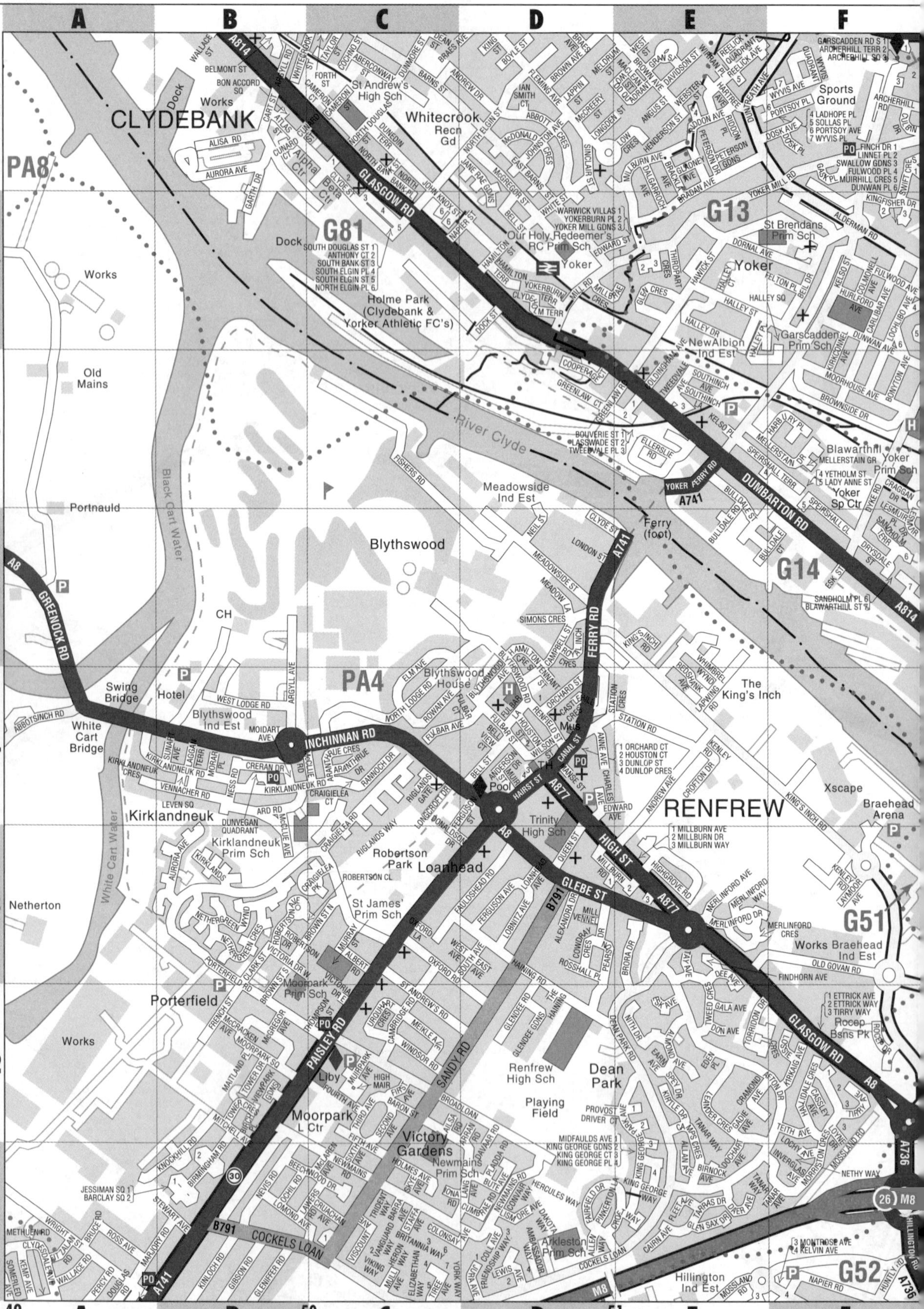

C1
1 CLAIRINSH GDNS
2 HERALD WAY
3 ARGOSY WAY
4 LANCASTER WAY
5 WELLINGTON WAY
6 ANSON WAY
7 HALIFAX WAY

D1
1 STIRLING WAY
2 LYSANDER WAY
3 CARAVELLE WAY
4 HAMPDEN WAY

93
114

D6
1 DUTHIE PARK PL
2 DUTHIE PARK GDNS
3 PRIORWOOD GDNS
4 BRANKLYN CL
5 BRANKLYN PL
6 BRANKLYN CT
7 PRIORWOOD CT

D8
1 ROTHERWOOD PL

E5
1 SELBORNE PL
2 WOODEND LA
3 SOUTHBRAE LA
4 BORDEN RD

75

F5
1 FERN COTTS
2 ALBANY COTTS
3 AIGAS COTTS
4 Anniesland Coll

96

F7
1 TEMPLE LOCKS CT
2 TEMPLE LOCKS PL
3 WALDO ST
4 STRATHCONA DR

F8
1 NETHERTON FARM LA
2 OLD FARM RD

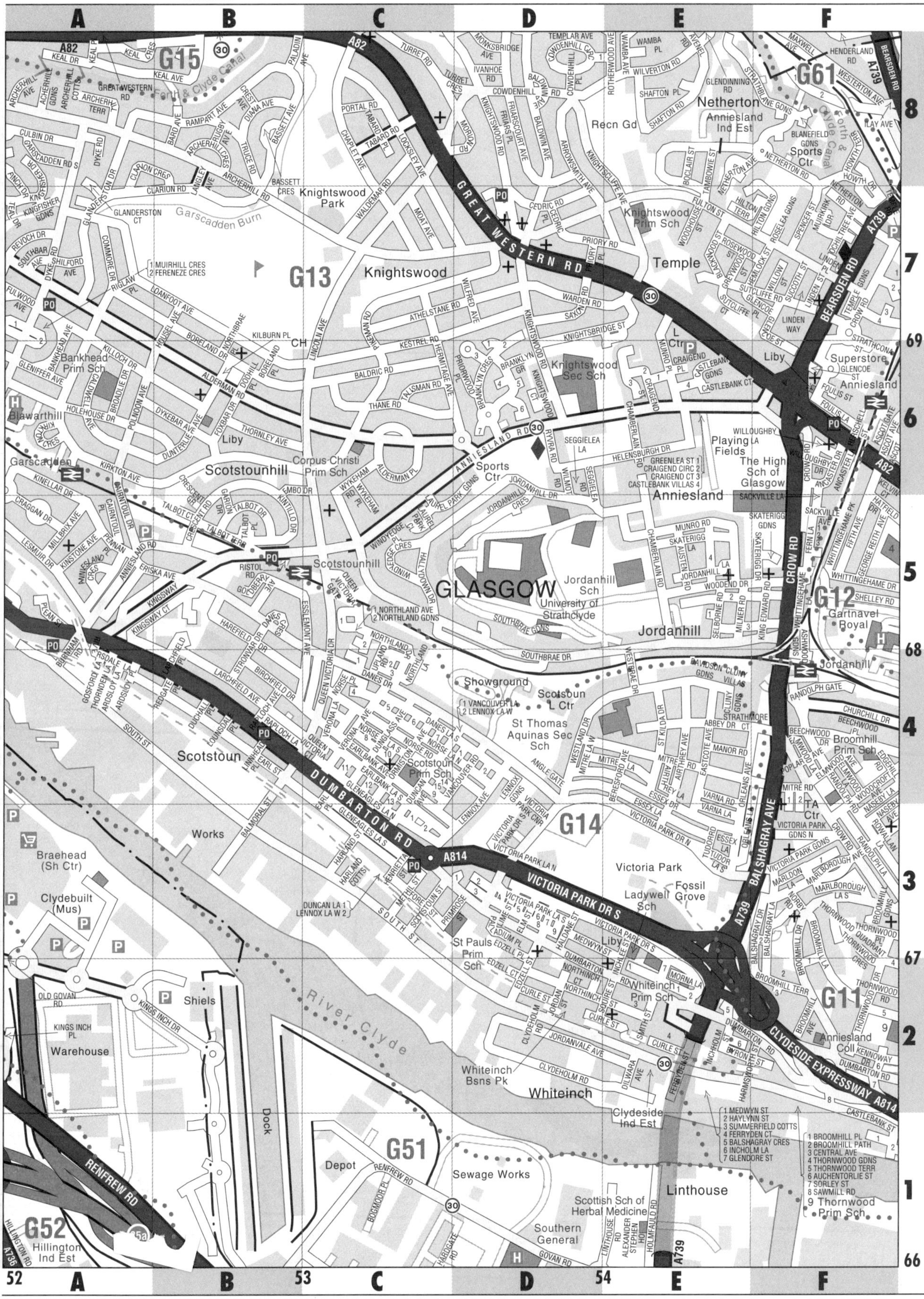

C4
1 DANES AVE
2 UPLAND LA
3 DANES LA N
4 VERONA GDNS
5 DUNGLASS LA N
6 ORMISTON LA N
7 DUNCAN LA N
8 DUNGLASS LA
9 EARLBANK LA N
10 ORMISTON LA
11 DUNGLASS LA S
12 ORMISTON LA S
13 DUNCAN LA S
14 NORSE LA S
15 VANCOUVER LA

115

D3
1 PRIMROSE CT
2 BOWLING GREEN LA
3 BOWLING GREEN RD
4 LIME LA
5 ELM LA W
6 ELM LA E
7 VICTORIA PARK ST
8 WESTLAND DRIVE LA
9 HALDANE LA

96

F1
1 GLASGOW HARBOUR TERR
2 CASTLEBANK PL

F3
1 MARLBOROUGH LA N
2 BALSHAGRAY PL

F4
1 MITRE GATE
2 MITRE CT

A3
1 MONKSCROFT AVE
2 KIRKMICHAEL GDNS
3 KIRKMICHAEL AVE
4 THORNWOOD DR
5 BLAIRATHOLL GDNS
6 TIBBERMORE RD

B3
1 KINGSBOROUGH GATE
2 TURNBERRY AVE
3 HILLSIDE GARDENS LA
4 QUEENSBOROUGH GDNS
5 PRINCES GARDENS LA
6 NORTH GARDNER ST

95

B4
1 DEVONSHIRE GDNS
2 DEVONSHIRE GDNS LA
3 WESTBOURNE TERR LA S

C5
1 THORNBRIDGE AVE
2 BELLSHAUGH PL

76

D5
1 GARRIOCH CRES
2 GARRIOCH QUADRANT
3 WYNDFORD PL
4 DUNBEITH PL
5 LATHERTON DR
6 INVERSHIN DR
7 KIRKHILL PL
8 GARRIOCH GATE

For full street detail of the highlighted area see page 240.

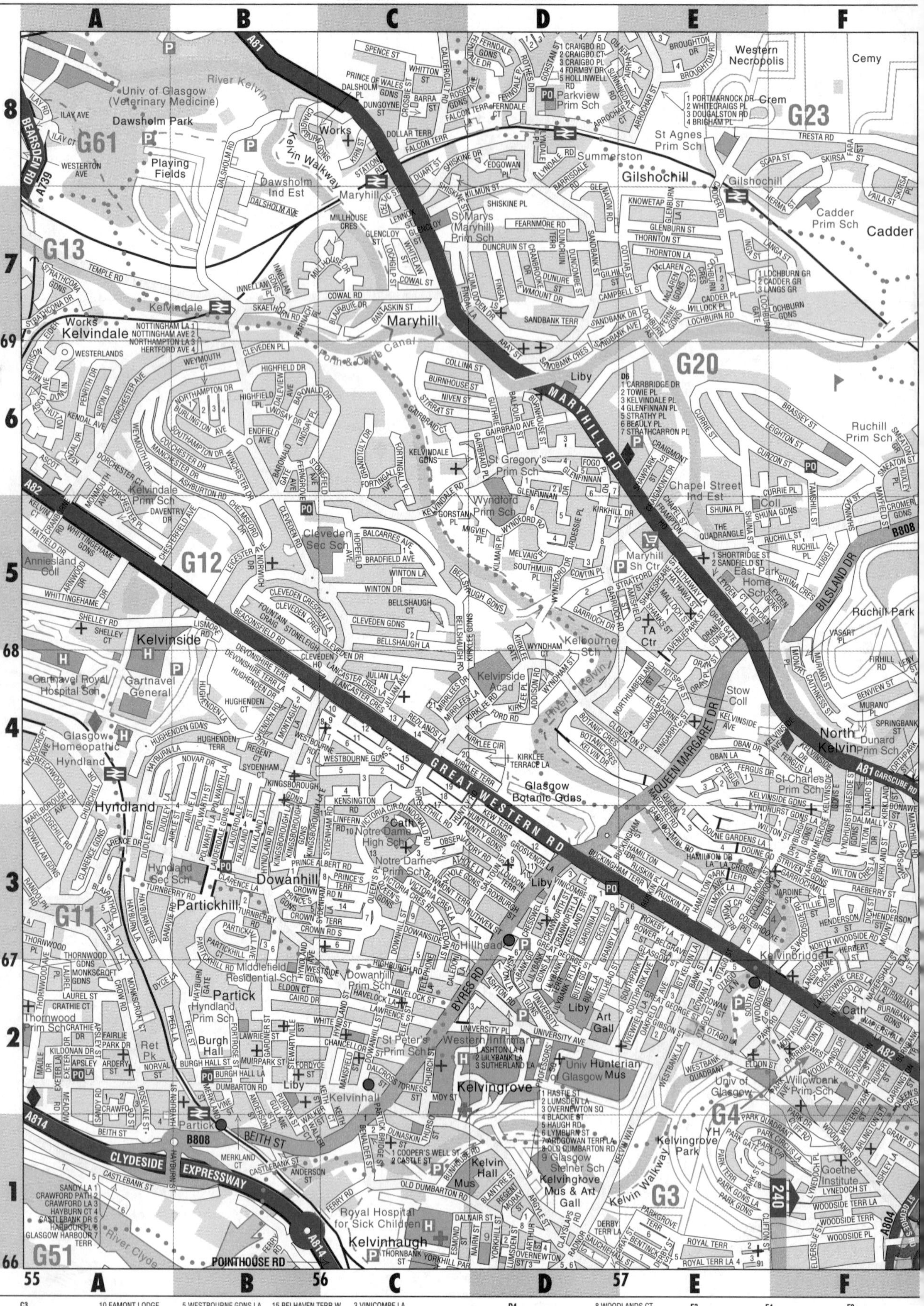

55 A B 56 C D 57 E F

C3
1 DOWANSIDE LA
2 MARCHMONT TERR
3 BOWMONT GDNS
4 VICTORIA CRES PL
5 BEAUMONT GATE
6 FOREMOUNT TERR LA
7 CROWN CIR
8 PRINCE'S PL
9 QUEENS GATE LA
10 EAMONT LODGE
11 HYNDLAND CT
12 ROSSLYN CT
13 ROSEBERRY HO
14 CROWN GDNS

C4
1 KENSINGTON GATE
2 KENSINGTON GATE LA
3 LORRAINE RD
4 LORRAINE GDNS
5 WESTBOURNE GDNS LA
6 WESTBOURNE GDNS N
7 WESTBOURNE GDNS W
8 WESTBOURNE TERR LA N
9 LANCASTER TERR LA
10 LANCASTER TERR
11 GREAT WESTERN TERR LA
12 GREAT WESTERN TERR
13 REDLANDS TERR
14 LOWTHER TERR
15 BELHAVEN TERR W
16 BELHAVEN TERR W LA
17 ROSSLYN TERR
18 BELHAVEN TERR LA
19 BELHAVEN TERR
20 KIRKLEE TERR RD
21 REDLANDS RD

D3
1 KERSLAND LA
2 SANDRINGHAM LA
3 VINICOMBE LA
4 BURGH LA
5 CRESSWELL ST
6 GREAT GEORGE LA
7 RUTHVEN LA
8 Hillhead Prim Sch
9 GROSVENOR CRES
10 OBSERVATORY LA
11 GROSVENOR CRES
12 GROSVENOR TERR

116

D4
1 KIRKLEE QUADRANT

E1
1 PARK TERR LA
2 LA BELLE PL
3 LA BELLE ALLEE
4 N CLAREMONT ST
5 KELVINGROVE ST
6 PARKGROVE TERR LA
7 CRAIGMADDIE TERR LA
8 WOODLANDS CT
9 CLIFTON HO

E2
1 Hillhead High Sch
2 OAKFIELD LA
3 ETON LA
4 BOTHWELL LA
5 CALEDONIAN CRES
6 WEST PRINCE'S ST
7 WESTBANK CT

E3
1 LOTHIAN GDNS
2 KELVINSIDE TERR W
3 KELVINSIDE TERR S
4 DOUNE QUADRANT
5 ALFRED LA
6 ALFRED TERR
7 OAKFIELD AVE
8 GRANBY HO
9 COLEBROOKE ST

E4
1 CLOUSTON CT
2 OBAN CT
3 QUEEN MARGARET CT
4 KELVINSIDE GDNS LA

F2
1 WILLOWBANK CRES
2 HOLYROOD QUADRANT
3 NAPIERSHALL PL
4 SEAMORE ST

F3
1 JEDBURGH GDNS
2 YARROW GDNS LA
3 GARRIOCHMILL WAY
4 The Glasgow Acad

A7
1 BALMORE RD
2 STRACHUR GDNS
3 ERRADALE PL
4 STRACHUR PL
5 STRACHUR GR

77

E7
1 COLSTON PL
2 EVERARD PL
3 BISHOPSGATE PL

98

F7
1 MILTON DR
2 NEWBOLD AVE
3 SOUTHVIEW CT
4 STRATHKELVIN AVE

F8
1 FORRESTER CT
2 MUIRPARK TERR
3 HUNTERSHILL RD
4 FULMAR CT
5 RAVENS CT
6 HILLCROFT TERR

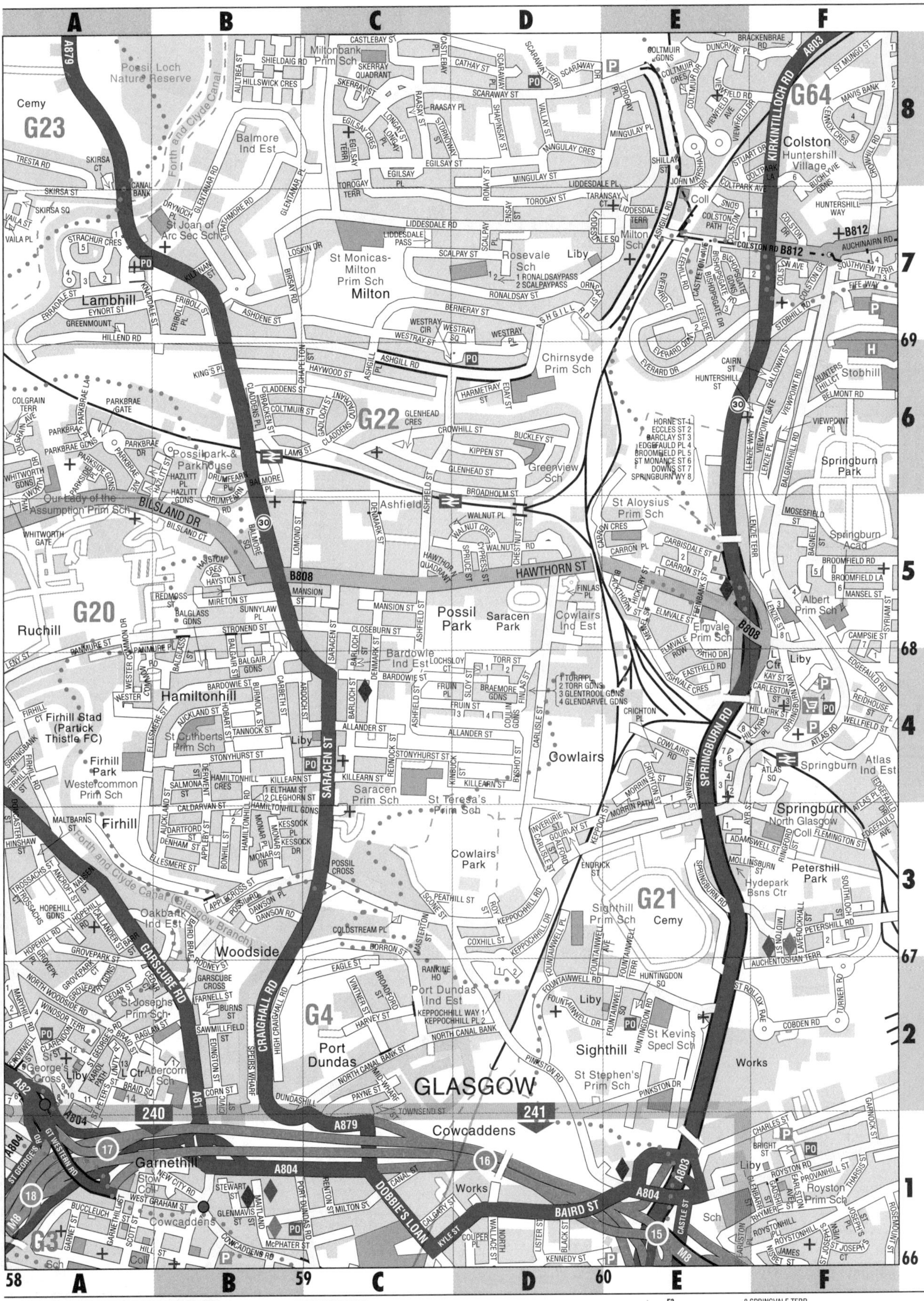

For full street detail of the highlighted area see pages 240 and 241.

A2
1 SEAMORE ST
2 BURNBANK PL
3 BURNBANK TERR
4 WINDSOR ST
5 CROMWELL LA
6 MELROSE ST
7 QUEEN'S CRES
8 ST GEORGE'S PL
9 CLARENDON PL
10 ST GEORGE'S CROSS
11 GLADSTONE ST
12 GLENFARG ST
13 ST PETER'S PATH
14 Oakgrove Prim Sch

B2
1 MANRESA PL

117

98

E3
1 VALLEYFIELD ST

E4
1 GOURLAY ST
2 PALERMO ST
3 SPRINGBURN WAY
4 VULCAN ST
5 COWLAIRS RD
6 ANGUS ST
7 KEMP ST
8 SPRINGVALE TERR

F3
1 SOUTHLOCH GDNS
2 AUCHINLOCH ST

F4
1 SYRIAM PL
2 CROFTBANK ST
3 HILLKIRK STREET LA
4 Springburn Sh Ctr

97
78

D8
1 WALLACE PL
2 WALLACE GATE
3 WALLACE DR
4 GREENACRES RDBT
5 MILLAR PL

97
118

79
100

B2
1 Avenue End Prim Sch
2 Croftcroighn Sch

119
100

99
C8
1 FLEMINGTON WY
2 MONKTON BRAE
3 CLIFFVALE RD
80

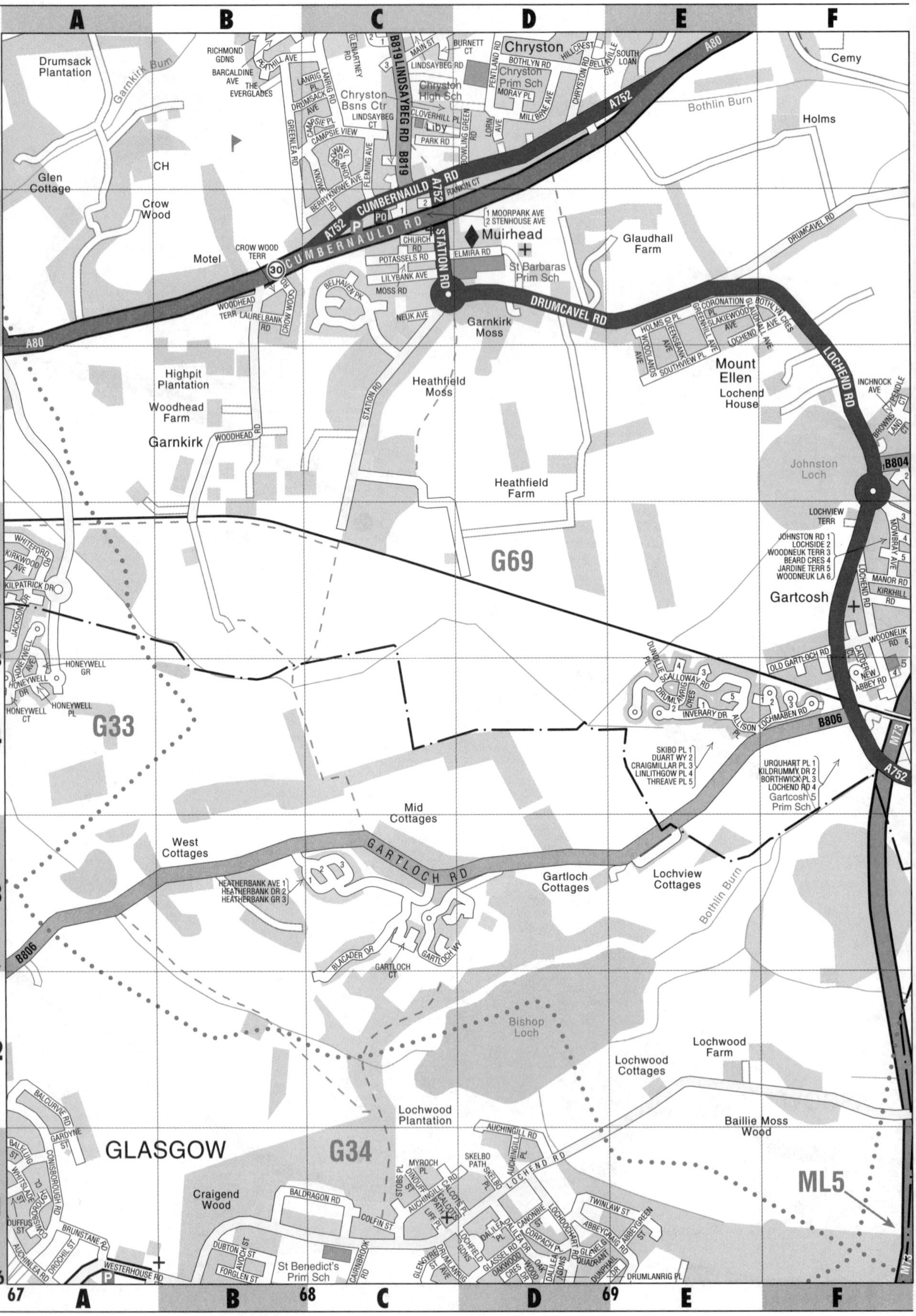
A B C D E F
8 7 6 5 4 3 2 1
69 68 67 66
Drumsack Plantation
Garnkirk Burn
Glen Cottage
CH
Crow Wood
Motel
Chryston
Chryston Prim Sch
Chryston High Sch
Chryston Bsns Ctr
Liby
Muirhead
St Barbaras Prim Sch
Cemy
Holms
Bothlin Burn
Glaudhall Farm
CUMBERNAULD RD
STATION RD
DRUMCAVEL RD
LOCHEND RD
A80
A752
B819
1 MOORPARK AVE
2 STENHOUSE AVE
Garnkirk Moss
Highpit Plantation
Woodhead Farm
Garnkirk
Heathfield Moss
Heathfield Farm
Mount Ellen
Lochend House
Johnston Loch
B804
G69
Gartcosh
JOHNSTON RD 1
LOCHSIDE 2
WOODNEUK TERR 3
BEARD CRES 4
JARDINE TERR 5
WOODNEUK LA 6
G33
SKIBO PL 1
DUART WY 2
CRAIGMILLAR PL 3
LINLITHGOW PL 4
THREAVE PL 5
URQUHART PL 1
KILDRUMMY DR 2
BORTHWICK PL 3
LOCHEND RD 4
Gartcosh Prim Sch
M73
B806
Mid Cottages
West Cottages
GARTLOCH RD
HEATHERBANK AVE 1
HEATHERBANK DR 2
HEATHERBANK GR 3
Gartloch Cottages
Lochview Cottages
Bishop Loch
Lochwood Cottages
Lochwood Farm
Lochwood Plantation
Baillie Moss Wood
GLASGOW
G34
Craigend Wood
ML5
St Benedict's Prim Sch
67 68 69

81
102

121
102

101
82

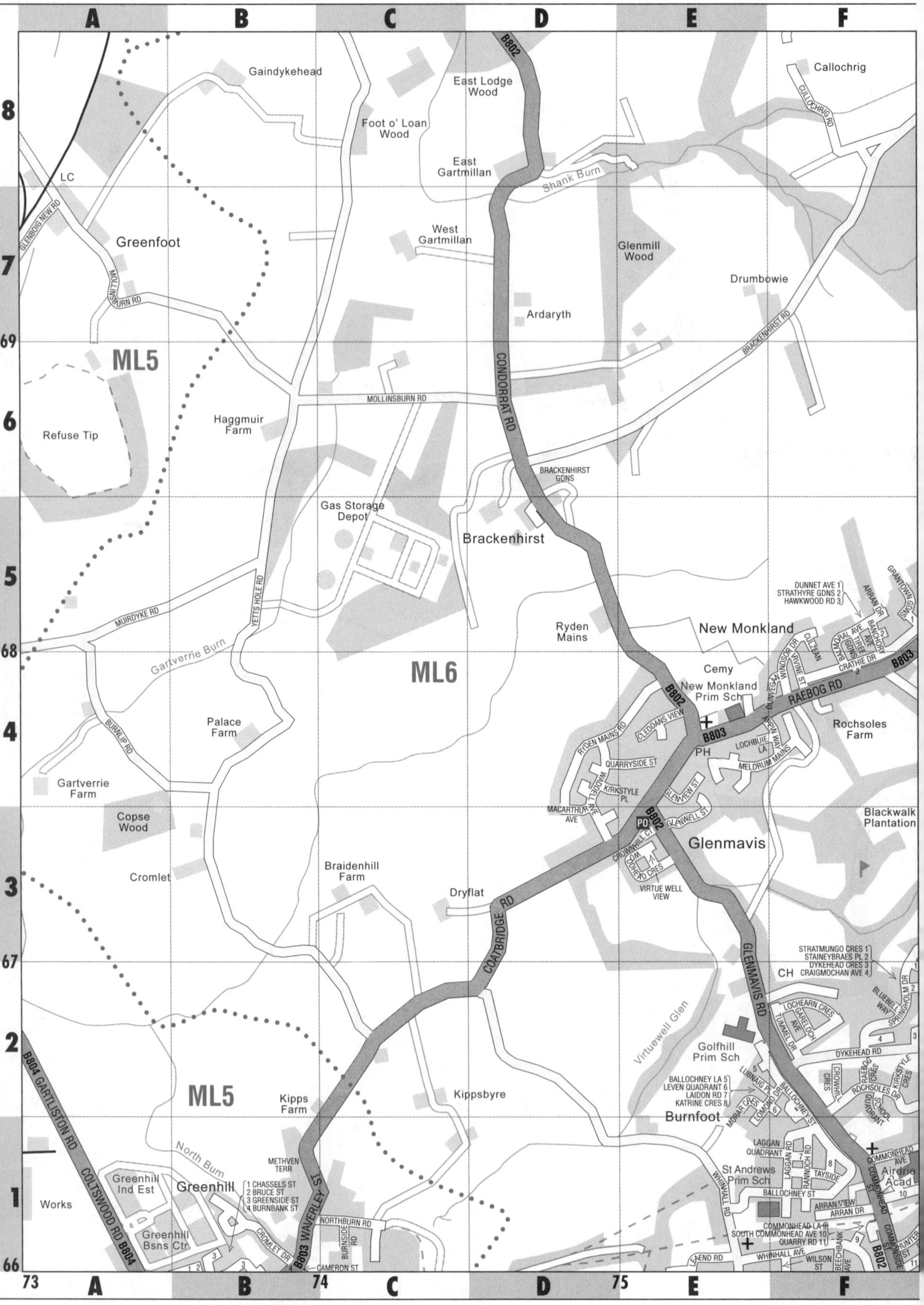
A
B
C
D
E
F
8
7
69
6
5
68
4
3
67
2
1
66
73
74
75
B802
Gaindykehead
East Lodge
Wood
Callochrig
CULLOCHRIG RD
Foot o' Loan
Wood
East
Gartmillan
Shank Burn
LC
GLENBOIG NEW RD
Greenfoot
West
Gartmillan
Glenmill
Wood
Drumbowie
MOLLINSBURN RD
Ardaryth
BRACKENHIRST RD
69
ML5
CONDORRAT RD
MOLLINSBURN RD
Refuse Tip
Haggmuir
Farm
BRACKENHIRST
GDNS
Gas Storage
Depot
Brackenhirst
DUNNET AVE 1
STRATHYRE GDNS 2
HAWKWOOD RD 3
GRANTOWN GDNS
ARRAN DR
MUIRDYKE RD
YETTS HOLE RD
Ryden
Mains
New Monkland
CULZEAN
WINDSOR DR
IRVINE ST
BALMORAL AVE
TIREE GDNS
BANCHORY AVE
CRATHIE DR
B803
Gartverrie Burn
ML6
Cemy
New Monkland
Prim Sch
DUNVEGAN
RAEBOG RD
B802
Palace
Farm
BURNLIP RD
RYDEN MAINS RD
CLEDDANS VIEW
B803
PH
LOCHBUIE LA
ARRAN WAY
Rochsoles
Farm
QUARRYSIDE ST
MELDRUM MAINS
Gartverrie
Farm
WADDELL AVE
KIRKSTYLE PL
GLENVIEW ST
Copse
Wood
MACARTHUR AVE
PO
B802
GLENWELL ST
Glenmavis
Blackwalk
Plantation
CROWNHILL CT
WOODHEAD CRES
VIRTUE WELL
VIEW
Cromlet
Braidenhill
Farm
Dryflat
COATBRIDGE RD
GLENMAVIS RD
STRATMUNGO CRES 1
STAINEYBRAES PL 2
DYKEHEAD CRES 3
CH
CRAIGMOCHAN AVE 4
SPRINGHOLM DR
BLUEBELL WAY
LOCHEARN CRES
GARELOCH AVE
TUMMEL DR
Virtuewell Glen
Golfhill
Prim Sch
DYKEHEAD RD
B804 GARTLISTON RD
ML5
Kipps
Farm
Kippsbyre
BALLOCHNEY LA 5
LEVEN QUADRANT 6
LAIDON RD 7
KATRINE CRES 8
LUBNAIG PL
LOMOND DR
MORAR CRES
BALLOCHNEY ST
CROWHILL CRES
RAEBOG CRES
ROCHSOLES DR
SCHOOL QUADRANT
KIRKSTYLE CRES
Burnfoot
North Burn
METHVEN
TERR
LAGGAN
QUADRANT
COMMONHEAD AVE
Airdrie
Acad
Greenhill
Ind Est
Greenhill
1 CHASSELS ST
2 BRUCE ST
3 GREENSIDE ST
4 BURNBANK ST
B803 WAVERLEY ST
St Andrews
Prim Sch
WHINHALL RD
LAGGAN RD
RANNOCH RD
TAYSIDE
COMMONHEAD ST
Works
COLTSWOOD RD B804
BALLOCHNEY ST
ARRAN VIEW
ARRAN DR
NORTHBURN RD
Greenhill
Bsns Ctr
CROMLET DR
BURNSIDE RD
COMMONHEAD LA 9
SOUTH COMMONHEAD AVE 10
QUARRY RD 11
LAWEND RD
WHINHALL AVE
WILSON ST
BEECHBANK AVE
COMMONSIDE ST
HUNTER ST
B802
CAMERON ST

83
104

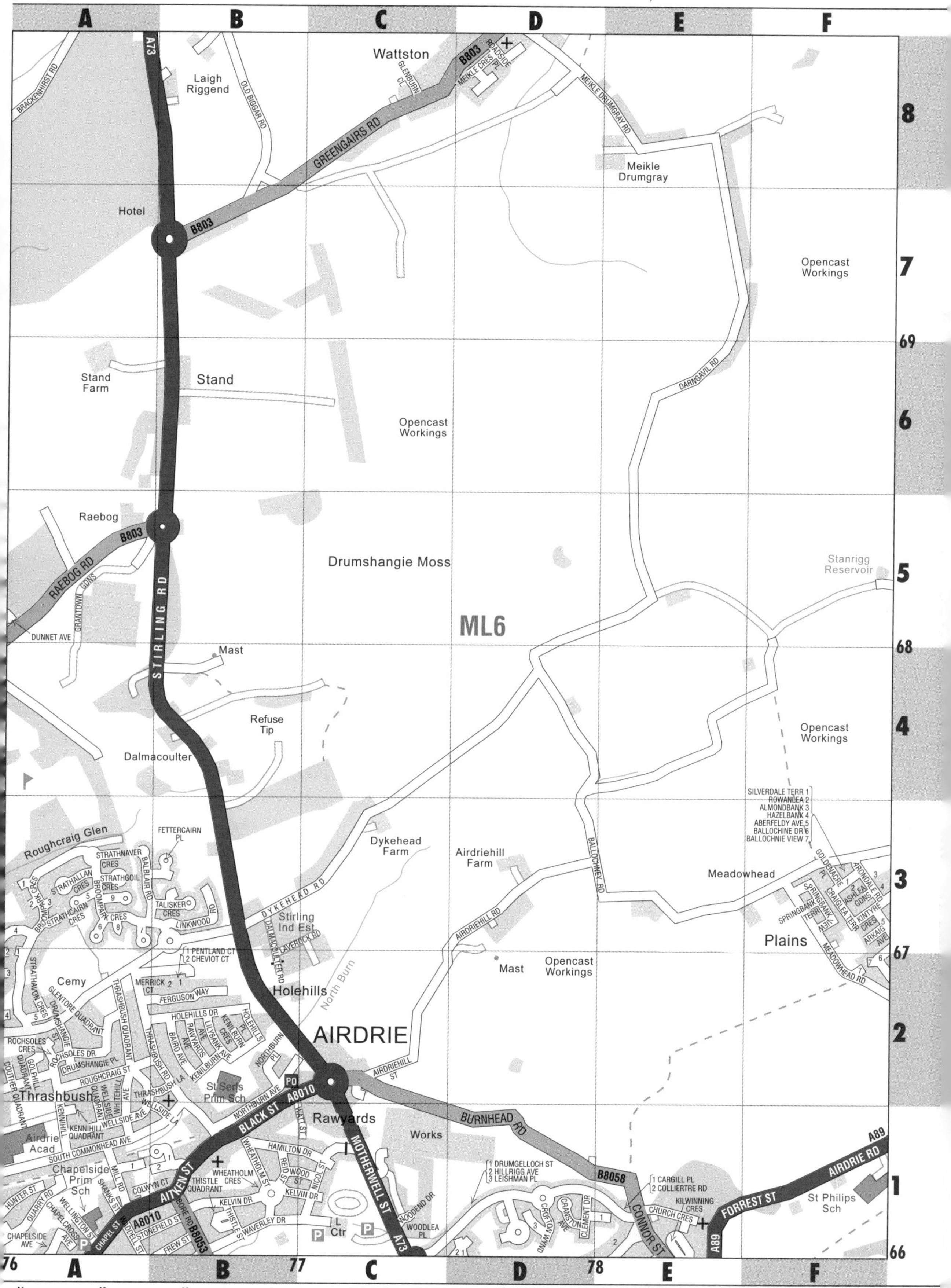

A1
1 COTTONMILL CT

A2
1 STRATHMORE CRES
2 STRATHMUNGO CRES
3 STAINEYBRAES PL
4 DYKEHEAD CRES
5 STRATHPEFFER CRES

A3
1 STRATHSPEY CRES
2 STRATHBLANE CRES
3 STRATHTUMMEL CRES
4 SPRINGHOLM DR
5 ARDBEG CRES
6 LOCHSIDE CRES
7 TOBERMORY GDNS
8 SPEYBURN PL
9 ARDMORE CRES

B1
1 BRAMBLE GDNS
2 THORNLEA GDNS

123
104

103
84

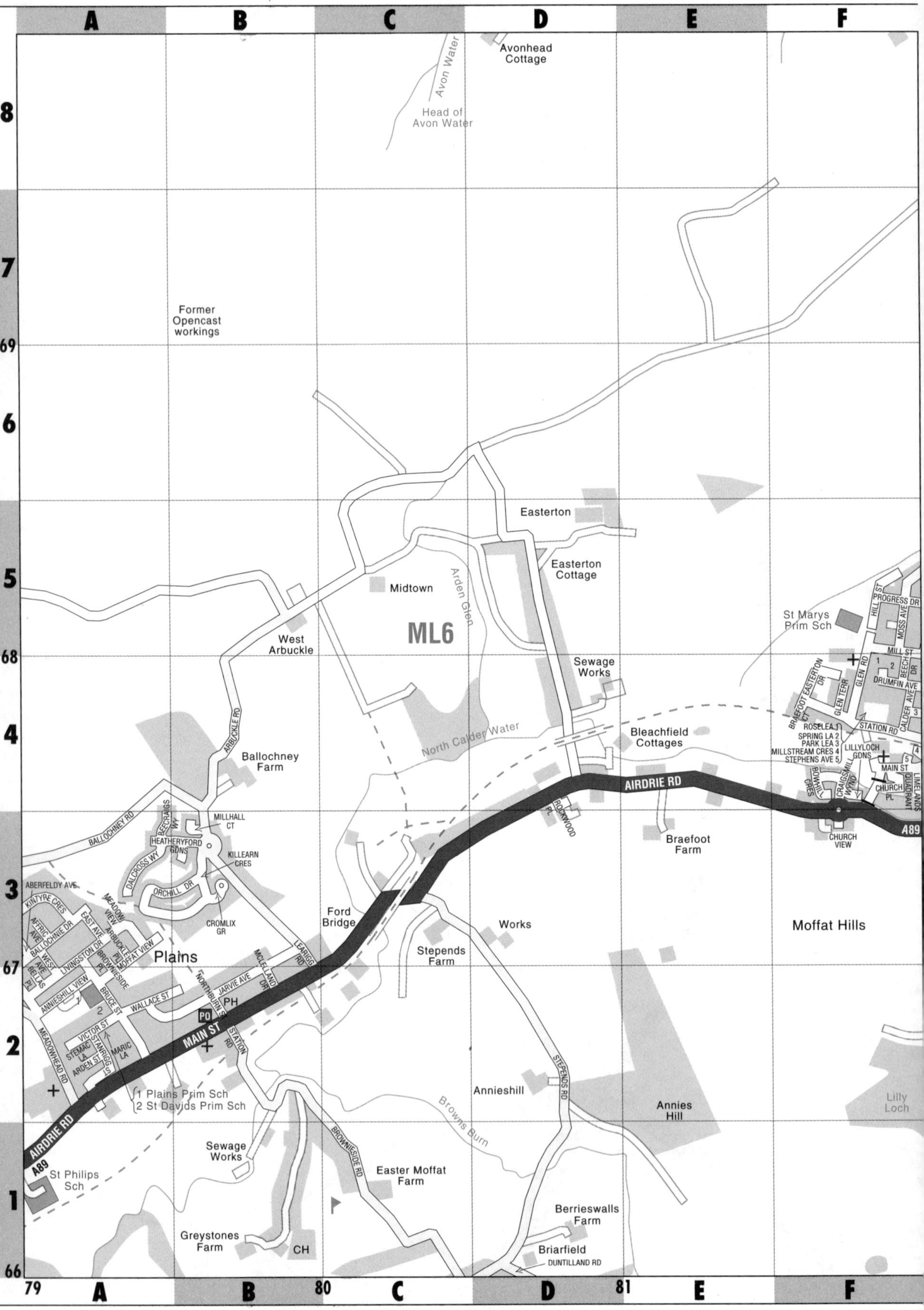
A
B
C
D
E
F
8
7
69
6
5
68
4
3
67
2
1
66
79
80
81
Avon Water
Avonhead Cottage
Head of Avon Water
Former Opencast workings
Easterton
Easterton Cottage
Midtown
Arden Glen
ML6
West Arbuckle
Sewage Works
St Marys Prim Sch
HILL ST
PROGRESS DR
MOSS AVE
MILL ST
BEECH DR
GLEN RD
DRUMFIN AVE
EASTERTON DR
BRAEFOOT CT
GLEN TERR
CALDER AVE
STATION RD
ROSELEA 1
SPRING LA 2
PARK LEA 3
MILLSTREAM CRES 4
STEPHENS AVE 5
LILLYLOCH GDNS
MAIN ST
CHURCH PL
LIMELANDS QUADRANT
BOWHILL CRES
CRAIGSMILL WYND
CHURCH VIEW
A89
Bleachfield Cottages
North Calder Water
ARBUCKLE RD
Ballochney Farm
AIRDRIE RD
ROCKWOOD PL
Braefoot Farm
BALLOCHNEY RD
BEECRAIGS WY
MILLHALL CT
HEATHERYFORD GDNS
KILLEARN CRES
DALCROSS WY
ORCHILL DR
CROMLIX GR
ABERFELDY AVE
KINTYRE CRES
AFFRIC AVE
BALLOCHNIE DR
EAST AVE
MEADOW VIEW
ARBUCKLE PL
MOFFAT VIEW
BROWNIESIDE PL
LIVINGSTON DR
WEST AVE
ANNIESHILL VIEW
BRUCE ST
WALLACE ST
Plains
NORTHBURN ST
JARVIE AVE
MCLELLAND DR
LEARIGG RD
Ford Bridge
Stepends Farm
Works
Moffat Hills
PO
PH
MAIN ST
STATION RD
MEADOWHEAD RD
VICTOR ST
STEMAC LA
STANRIGG ST
ARDEN ST
MARIC LA
1 Plains Prim Sch
2 St Davids Prim Sch
Annieshill
STEPENDS RD
Browns Burn
Annies Hill
Lilly Loch
Sewage Works
St Philips Sch
BROWNIESIDE RD
Easter Moffat Farm
Berrieswalls Farm
Greystones Farm
CH
Briarfield
DUNTILLAND RD

103
124

85
106

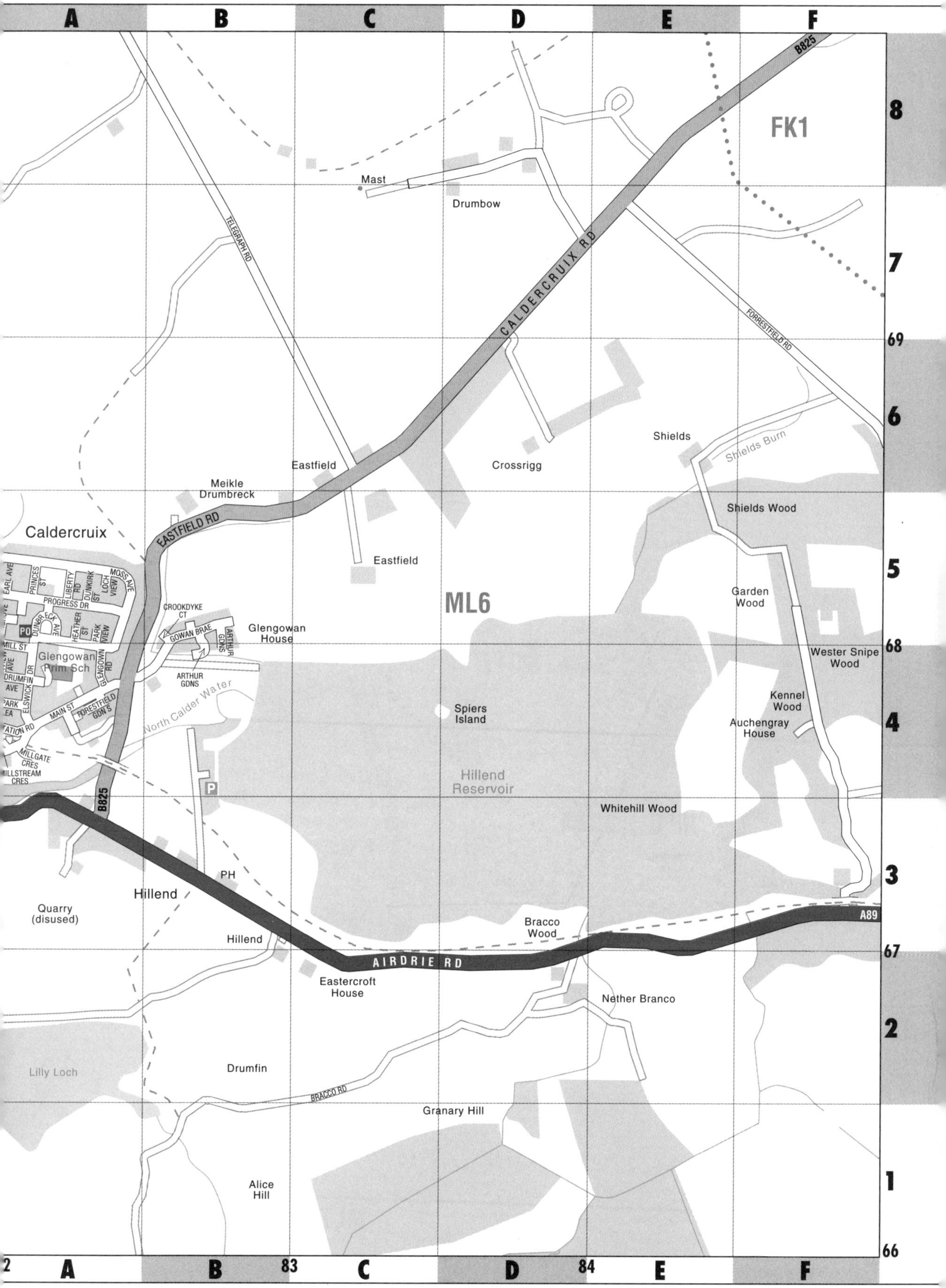

125
106

105
86

A
B
C
D
E
F
8
7
69
6
5
68
4
3
67
2
1
66
85
86
87
Lochend
Black Loch
Lochstank
Hillhead
FK1
Easter
Whin
Wester
Whin
Whiteside
North Calder Water
Drumtassie Burn
Stooprigg
Wood
FORRESTFIELD RD
Easter
Snipe
Wood
Wester
Snipe
Wood
Snipe
Quarry
(dis)
Westfield
Drumbeg
West Drumbey
Wood
Bedlormie
EH48
ML6
Woodside
Woodside
Bridge
Forrestfield
Moss
WOODSIDE RD
Forrestfield
Raiziehill
Wood
East Fardrum
Wood
Bedlormie
Wood
Langside
Wood
Wind
Pump
A89
AIRDRIE RD
Raiziehill
Entryfoot
Garrieston
Bedlormie
Toll
Crawberry
Hill
The Kaims
Cairneyhill
Quarry
FORREST RD
Forrest
ML7

A
B
C
D
E
F
8
7
69
6
5
68
4
3
67
2
1
66
Burnhead Moss
Burnhead
Drum Park Plantation
Croft Plantation
Wester Burnhead Wood
Drumtassie Burn
Opencast Workings
Heights
Tawnycraw Hill
West Rhodens Plantation
FK1
Drumelzie
East Backmuir Wood
Blawhorn Moss
Reservoir (covered)
Eastcraigs Hill
Edinburgh STREET ATLAS
Crowns Hill
Blawhorn Wood
EH48
Craigs
1 CRAIGHILL VIEW
2 BLACKHILL RD
3 SUNNYDALE RD
A89 Bathgate
Barn Wood
Westcraigs Hill
GREENHILL RD
SUNNYDALE DR
PARK RD
CRAIG ST
A89
Heatherhouse Wood
Wester Redburn
Easter Redburn
Blackridge
Blackridge Prim Sch
FARQUHAR SQ
Blackridge Community Mus
FLEMING PL
PARKVILLE CT
Westrigg
Bedlormie House
LANGSIDE DR
WOODHILL RD
BLAIRHILL VW
DRUMMOND PL
HEIGHTS RD
HILLSIDE DR
HILLSIDE PL
Liby
CRAIGINN TERR
PH
MAIN ST
PO
MACLEAN TERR
B718
QUARRY COTTS
BEDLORMIE DR
REDBURN RD
OGILFACE CRES
WESTCRAIGS PK
LOUBURN
CRAIGLEA CT
FRESHMAN CT
WESTCRAIGS RD
CRAIGINN CT
ALLISON GDNS
Mosshouse
Standhill Farm
STATION RD
HARTHILL RD
WHITELAW ST
Torrance Farm
Bogend Farm
ML7
B718
88
89
90

88

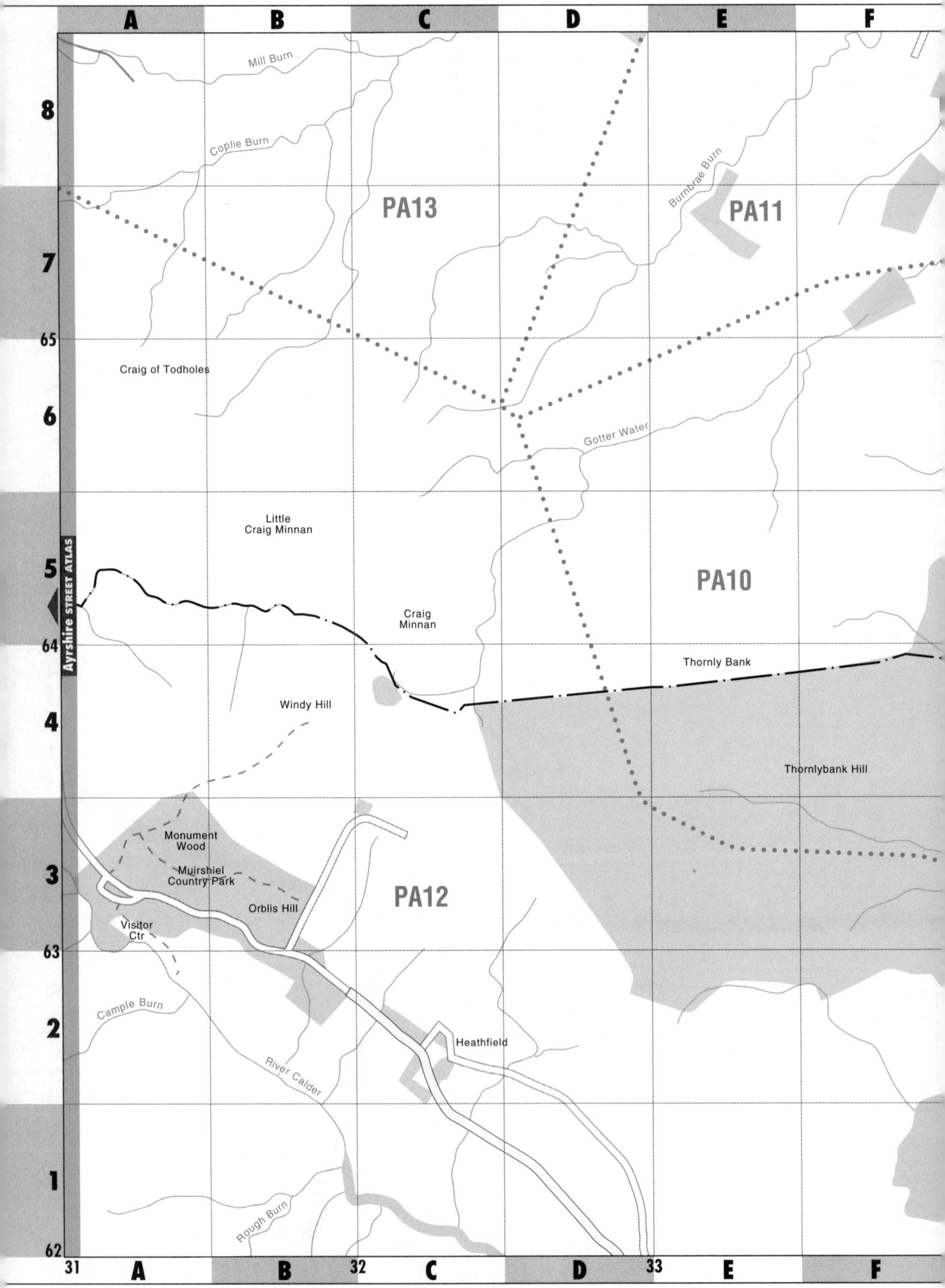
A
B
C
D
E
F
8
7
65
6
5
64
4
3
63
2
1
62
31
32
33
Mill Burn
Coplie Burn
PA13
Burnbrae Burn
PA11
Craig of Todholes
Gotter Water
Little
Craig Minnan
PA10
Craig
Minnan
Thornly Bank
Windy Hill
Thornlybank Hill
Monument
Wood
Muirshiel
Country Park
Orblis Hill
PA12
Visitor
Ctr
Cample Burn
Heathfield
River Calder
Rough Burn
Ayrshire STREET ATLAS

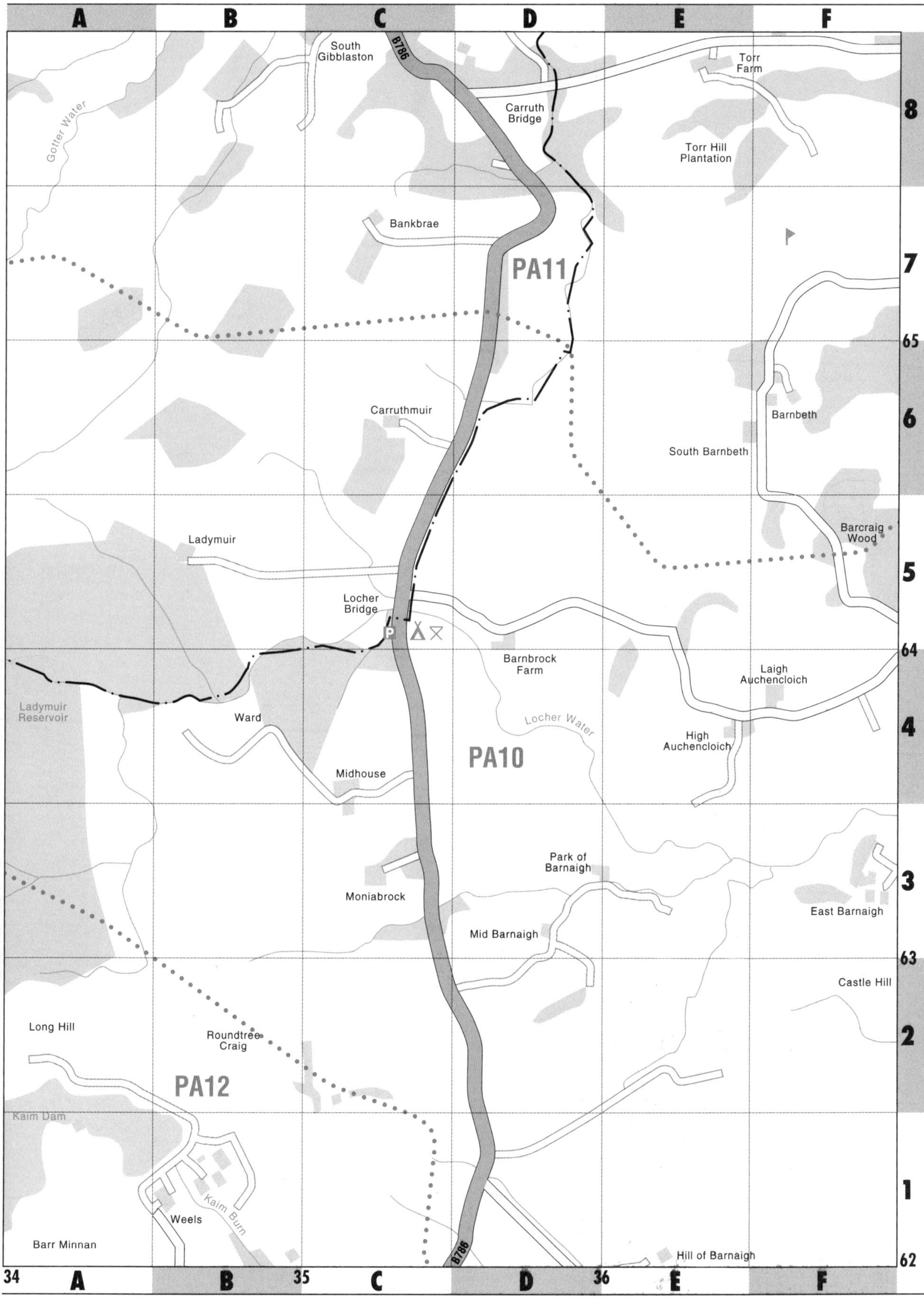
A
B
C
D
E
F
8
7
65
6
5
64
4
3
63
2
1
62
34
35
36
B786
South Gibblaston
Carruth Bridge
Torr Farm
Gotter Water
Torr Hill Plantation
Bankbrae
PA11
Carruthmuir
Barnbeth
South Barnbeth
Ladymuir
Barcraig Wood
Locher Bridge
P
Barnbrock Farm
Laigh Auchencloich
Ladymuir Reservoir
Ward
Locher Water
High Auchencloich
PA10
Midhouse
Park of Barnaigh
Moniabrock
East Barnaigh
Mid Barnaigh
Castle Hill
Long Hill
Roundtree Craig
PA12
Kaim Dam
Kaim Burn
Weels
Barr Minnan
Hill of Barnaigh

109
90

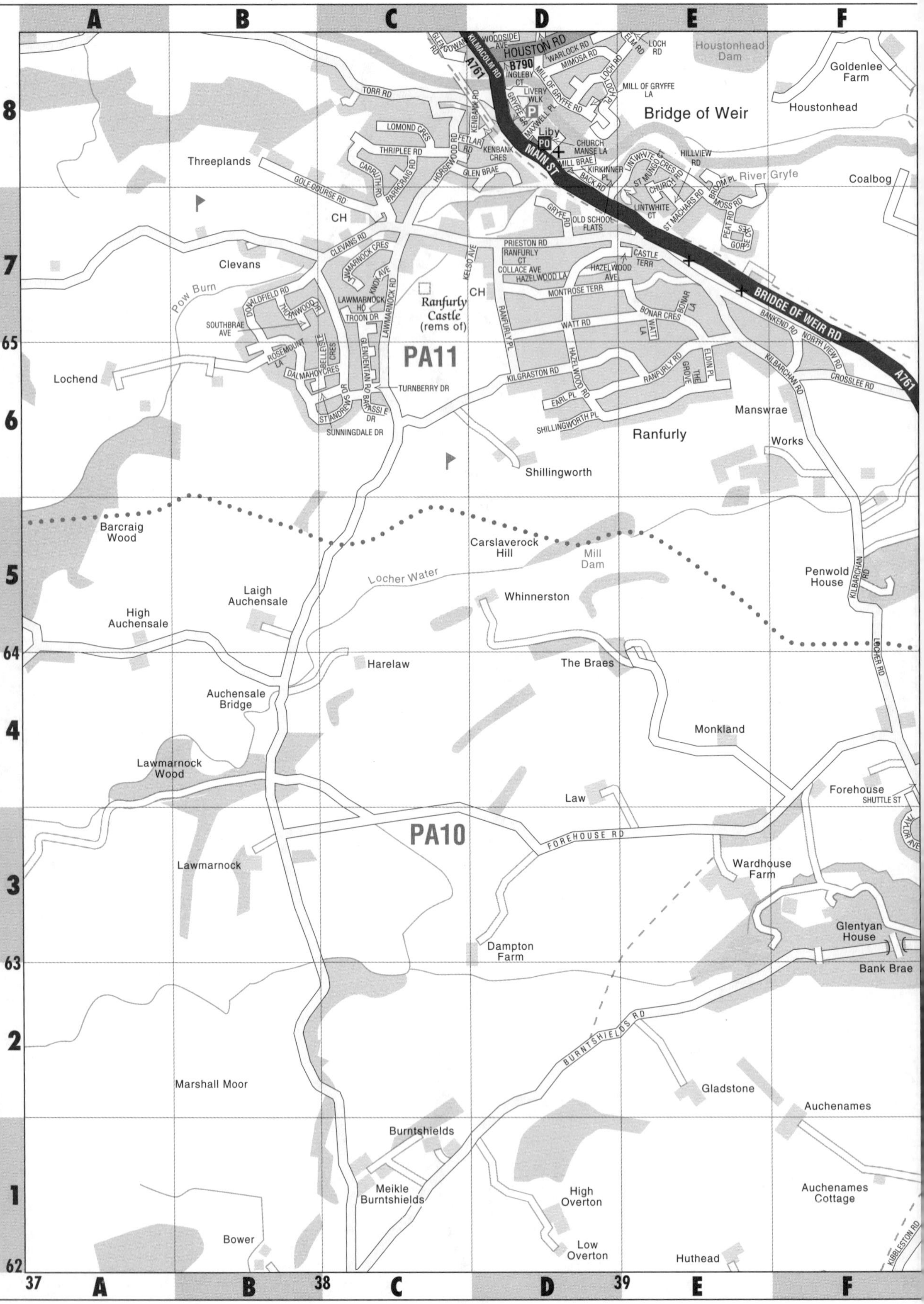
A
B
C
D
E
F
8
7
65
6
5
64
4
3
63
2
1
62
37
38
39
Bridge of Weir
Houstonhead Dam
Goldenlee Farm
Houstonhead
Coalbog
River Gryfe
Threeplands
Clevans
Pow Burn
Lochend
Ranfurly Castle (rems of)
PA11
Ranfurly
Manswrae
Works
Shillingworth
Barcraig Wood
Carslaverock Hill
Mill Dam
Locher Water
Penwold House
Laigh Auchensale
High Auchensale
Whinnerston
Harelaw
The Braes
Auchensale Bridge
Monkland
Lawmarnock Wood
Law
Forehouse
SHUTTLE ST
PA10
FOREHOUSE RD
Lawmarnock
Wardhouse Farm
Glentyan House
Dampton Farm
Bank Brae
BURNTSHIELDS RD
Marshall Moor
Gladstone
Auchenames
Burntshields
Meikle Burntshields
High Overton
Low Overton
Auchenames Cottage
Bower
Huthead
KIBBLESTON RD
HOUSTON RD
KILMACOLM RD
A761
B790
WOODSIDE AVE
GLENGOWAN RD
WARLOCK RD
MIMOSA RD
ELM RD
LOCH RD
MILL OF GRYFFE LA
MILL OF GRYFFE RD
TORR RD
INGLEBY CT
LIVERY WLK
GRYFFE GR
MAXWELL PL
KENBANK RD
KENBANK CRES
LOMOND CRES
THRIPLEE RD
CARRUTH RD
BARRCRAIG RD
HORSEWOOD RD
FETLAR RD
GLEN BRAE
Liby
PO
MAIN ST
CHURCH
MANSE LA
MILL BRAE
KIRKINNER PL
BACK RD
LINTWHITE CT
ST MUNGO CRES
CHURCH RD
LINTWHITE CT
ST MACHARS RD
HILLVIEW RD
BROOM PL
MOSS RD
PEAT RD
GORSE CT
GOLF COURSE RD
CH
CLEVANS RD
LAWMARNOCK CRES
KNOX AVE
GRYFFE RD
OLD SCHOOL FLATS
PRIESTON RD
RANFURLY CT
COLLACE AVE
HAZELWOOD LA
HAZELWOOD AVE
CASTLE TERR
KELSO AVE
MONTROSE TERR
BONAR CRES
BONAR LA
WATT LA
WATT RD
BRIDGE OF WEIR RD
BANKEND RD
NORTH VIEW RD
KILBARCHAN RD
CROSSLEE RD
LAWMARNOCK RD
LAWMARNOCK HO
TROON DR
SOUTHBRAE AVE
ROSEMOUNT LA
DALMAHOY CRES
BELLEISLE CRES
GLENDENTAN RD
ST ANDREWS DR
BARASSIE DR
TURNBERRY DR
SUNNINGDALE DR
RANFURLY PL
KILGRASTON RD
HAZELWOOD RD
EARL PL
SHILLINGWORTH PL
RANFURLY RD
THE GROVE
ELDIN PL
LOCHER RD
KILBARCHAN RD

109
130

91
112

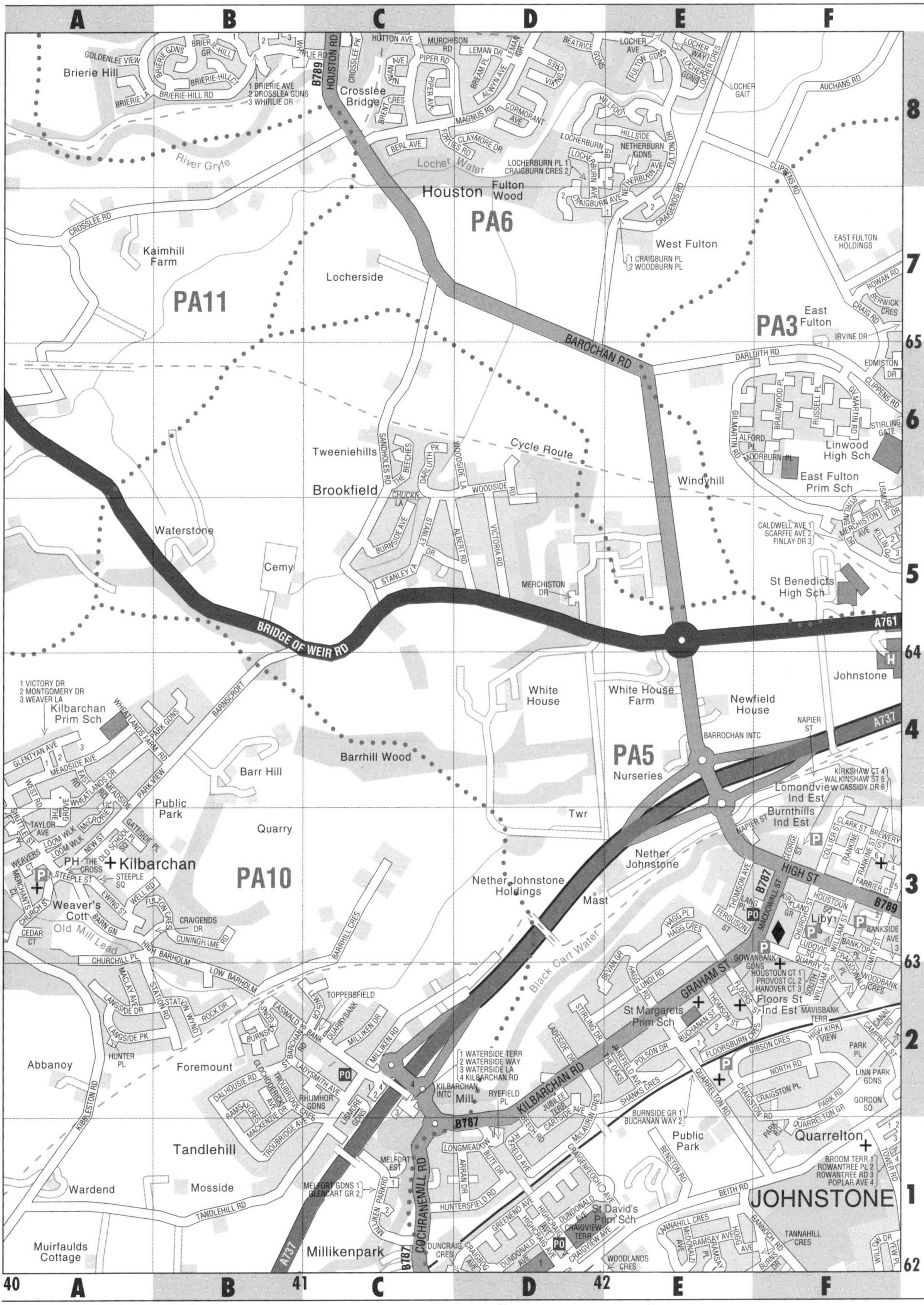
A
B
C
D
E
F
8
7
65
6
5
64
4
3
63
2
1
62
40
41
42
Brierie Hill
Crosslee Bridge
River Gryfe
Locher Water
Houston
Fulton Wood
PA6
West Fulton
Kaimhill Farm
Locherside
PA11
PA3
East Fulton
East Fulton Holdings
BAROCHAN RD
Cycle Route
Tweeniehills
Brookfield
Windyhill
Linwood High Sch
East Fulton Prim Sch
Waterstone
Cemy
St Benedicts High Sch
BRIDGE OF WEIR RD
A761
Johnstone
White House
White House Farm
Newfield House
Kilbarchan Prim Sch
Barrhill Wood
Barr Hill
PA5
Nurseries
A737
Lomondview Ind Est
Burnthills Ind Est
Public Park
Quarry
Twr
Nether Johnstone
Kilbarchan
PA10
Nether Johnstone Holdings
Mast
Weaver's Cott
Old Mill Lead
Black Cart Water
HIGH ST
B789
B787
GRAHAM ST
St Margarets Prim Sch
Floors St Ind Est
Abbanoy
Foremount
Mill
KILBARCHAN RD
Tandlehill
Public Park
Quarrelton
Wardend
Mosside
St David's Prim Sch
JOHNSTONE
Muirfaulds Cottage
Millikenpark
COCHRANEMILL RD

131
112
D1
1 Cochrane Castle Prim Sch

111
92

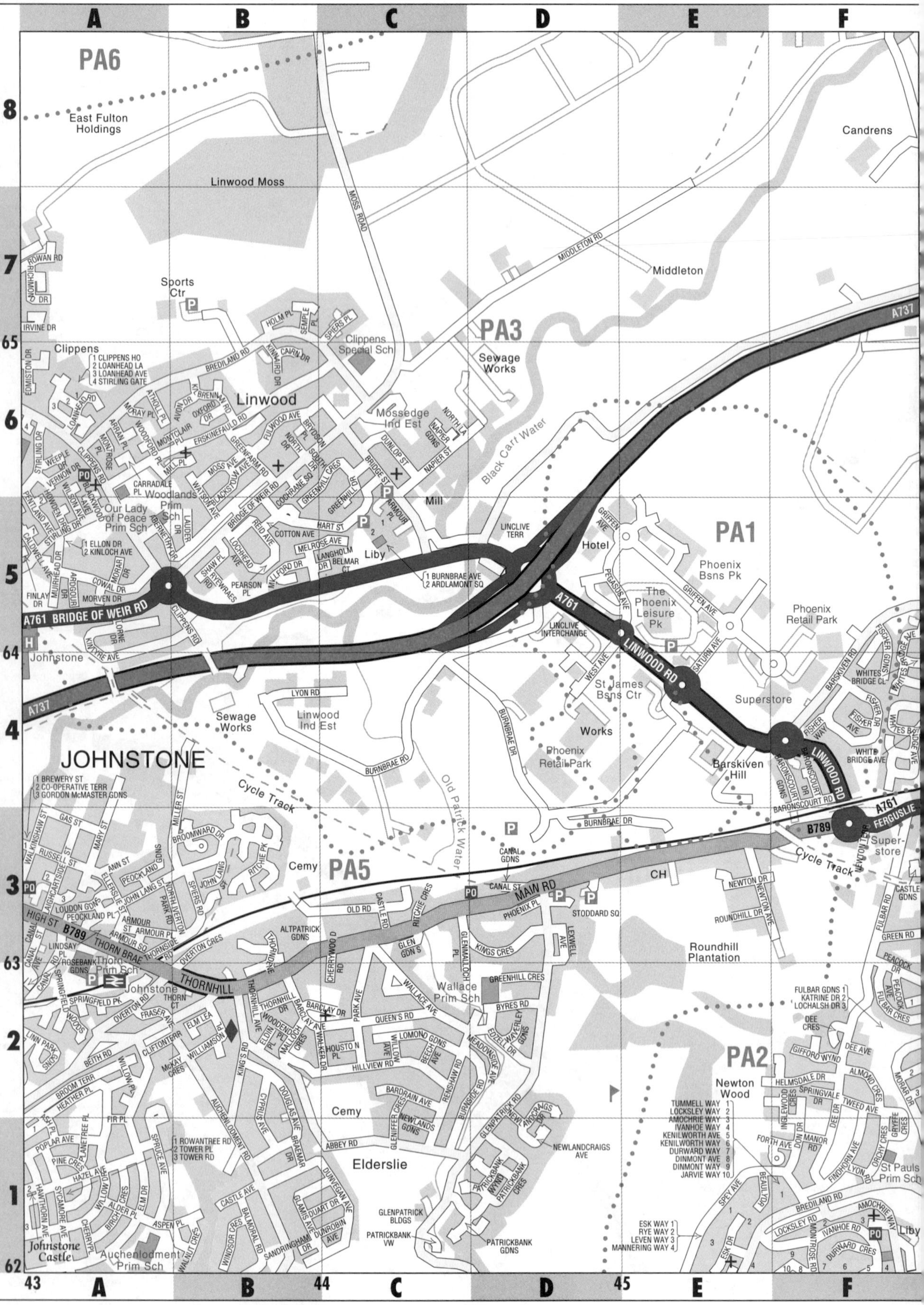

111
132

E5
1 MONCRIEFF ST
2 STONEY BRAE
3 BACK SNEDDON ST
4 MAXWELL ST
5 MEETINGHOUSE LA
6 COUNTY SQ
7 COUNTY PL
8 CENTRAL WAY

93

D8
1 ABBOTSBURN WAY
2 BROOMDYKE WAY
3 CONVAL WAY
4 MALVERN WAY
5 WENDUR WAY

114

F5
1 BRICK LA
2 WALLNEUK
3 EAST BUCHANAN MEWS

133

D1
1 KILPATRICK CRES
2 LAMMERMUIR DR

E1
1 BRAIDS CT
2 CHEVIOT RD

114

E4
1 JOHNSTON ST
2 ST GEORGE'S GATE
3 BROWNS LA
4 CAUSEYSIDE ST

113
94

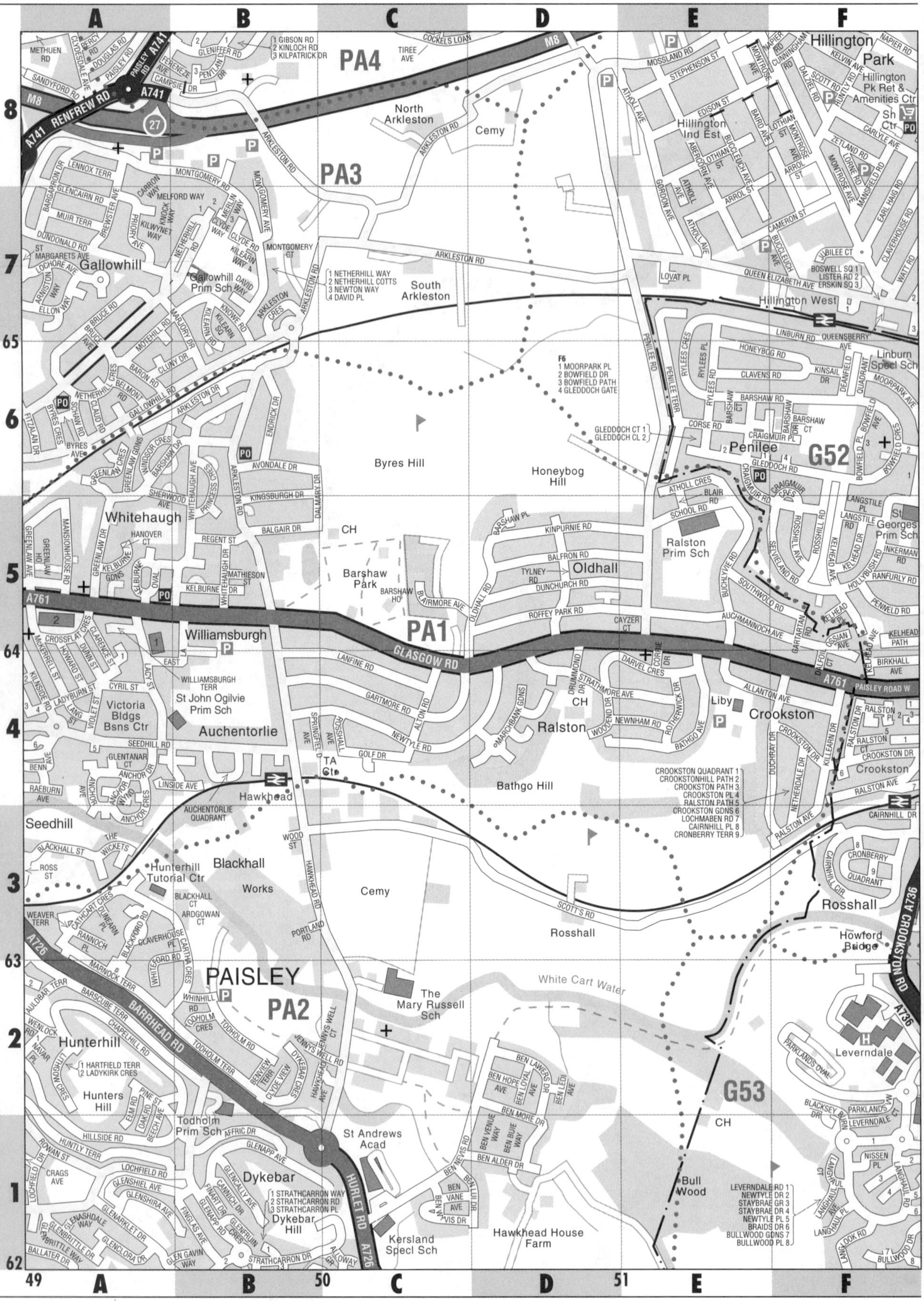

A4
1 CLARENCE DR
2 DIXON ST
3 BANK ST
4 UNSTED PL
5 RALSTON ST
6 MILLSTREAM CT

A5
1 Williamsburgh Prim Sch
2 Paisley Grammar Sch

113
134

A
B
C
D
E
F
8
7
65
6
5
64
4
3
63
2
1
62
52
53
54
Shieldhall
Southern General
North Cardonald
Colquhoun Pk
Hillington Ind Est
Hillington East
Cardonald Pk Works
G51
Govan High Sch
West Drumoyne
Drumoyne Prim Sch
Elder Park
Elder Park Prim Sch
St Constantine's Prim Sch
Greenfield Prim Sch
Elderpark Workspace
Ind Est
Hillington Prim Sch
Hillington
Cardonald
Cardonald Crem
Tinto Park
Drumoyne
Superstore
Works
Craigton Ind Est
Cemy
Craigton
GLASGOW
Lourdes Prim Sch
Palace of Art
Bellahouston L Ctr
Bellahouston Park
Lourdes Sec Sch
Our Lady of the Rosary Prim Sch
Cardonald Prim Sch
South Cardonald
Rosshall Academy
Crookston Wood
Mosspark
G52
Cardonald Coll
Mosspark Prim Sch
Rosshall (private)
Rosshall Park
Howford Specl Sch
Crookston Wood
Lochar Park
Nethercraigs Sp Complex
Corkerhill
Crookston Castle
Crookston Castle Prim Sch
G53
Pollok
St Monicas Prim Sch
St Marnocks Prim Sch
Corker Hill
G41
Pollok Country Park
G43
HILLINGTON RD
SHIELDHALL RD
PAISLEY RD W
CROOKSTON RD
SANDWOOD RD
BERRYKNOWES RD
MEIKLEWOOD RD
EDMISTON DR
M8
M77
A8
A736
A739
A761
Levern Water
White Cart Water

A8
1 HARMONY ROW
2 WARDROP ST
3 GARMOUTH CT
4 GARMOUTH GDNS
D5
1 CLIFFORD PL

2 LANGSHOT ST
3 PLANTATION PARK GDNS
E5
1 MILNPARK GDNS
2 LAMBHILL QUADRANT
3 SEAWARD ST

115

E6
1 EAGLESHAM CT
2 EAGLESHAM PL
3 MIDDLESEX GDNS

96

E8
1 CLIFTON PL
2 FITZROY PL
3 WESTMINSTER TERR
4 DERBY TERRACE LA
5 CORUNNA ST
6 Stobcross Bsns Pk
7 HOULDSWORTH LA
8 Clydeway Ind Est
9 FINNIESTON SQ
10 MINERVA CT
11 SANFORD PL

For full street detail of the highlighted area see page 240.

A B C D E F

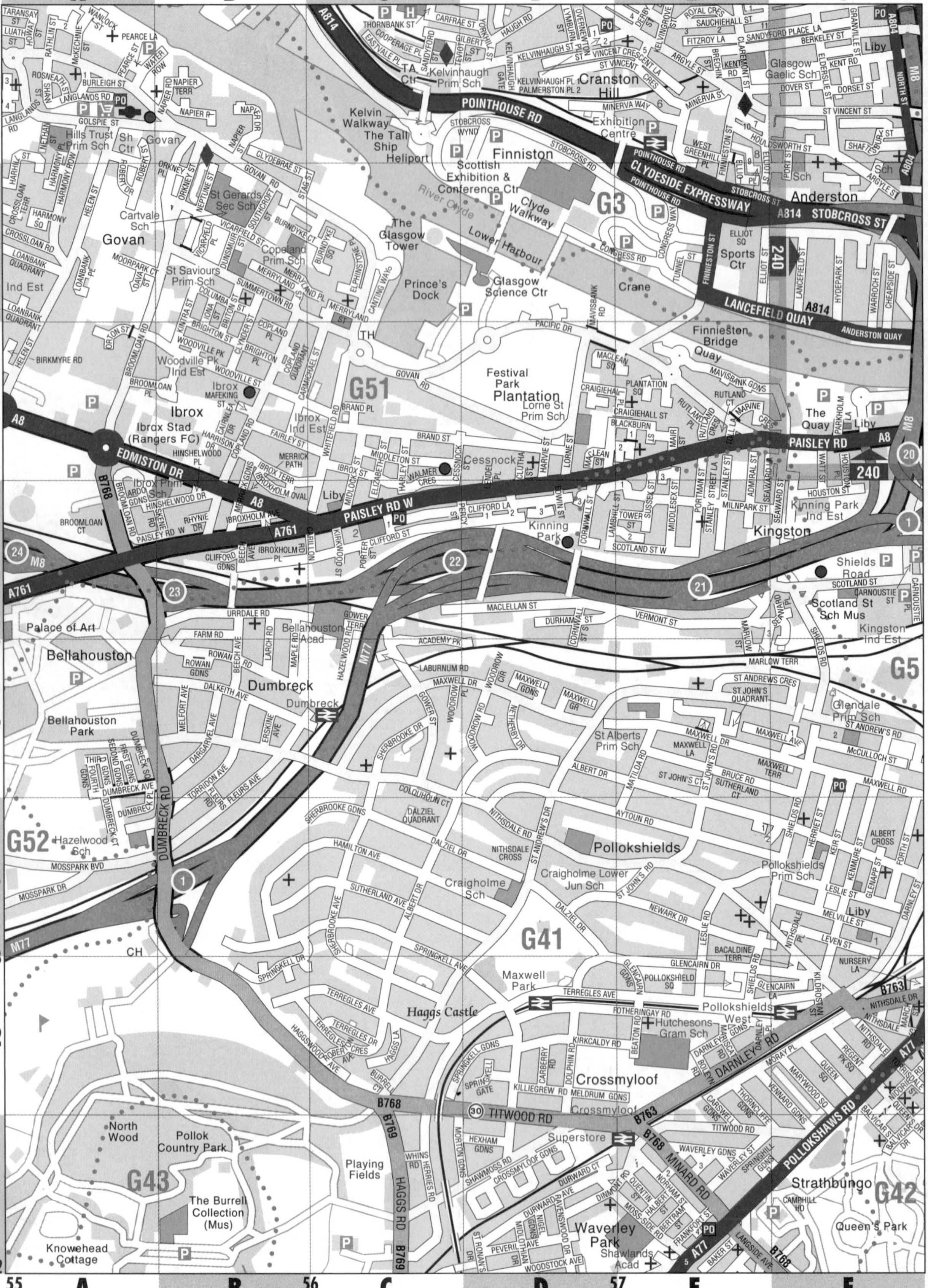

A B C D E F

55 56 57

115

C5
1 NORTH GOWER ST
2 Bellahouston Prim Sch

136

E1
1 DINMONT PL
2 LOCHSIDE ST
3 WESTCLYFFE ST
4 ABBOT ST
5 SHAWLANDS CROSS
E3
1 KNOWEHEAD TERR
2 KNOWEHEAD GDNS

F2
1 NIDDRIE SQ
2 BARBRECK RD
F4
1 MAXWELL OVAL
2 LINCLUDEN PATH
3 ST ANDREWS CL

F3
1 Pollokshields Prim Sch Annexe

For full street detail of the highlighted area see pages 240 and 241.

A5
1 KINNING ST
2 LAIDLAW ST
3 PATERSON ST
B5
1 LANGBANK ST
2 KILBARCHAN ST
3 COBURG ST
4 HERBERTSON ST
5 S PORTLAND ST
6 BEDFORD LA
7 STIRLINGFAULD PL

97

F5
1FORBESDR
2 REDAN ST
3 OLYMPIA ST
4 Bridgeton Bsns Ctr
F6
1 ABERCROMBY SQ

118

2 MILLROAD GDNS
E5
1 ABERCROMBY ST
2 GRAIGNESTOCK PL
3 MONTEITH PL
F7
1 McINTOSH CT
2 CARDROSS CT
3 SETON TERR
4 OAKLEY TERR
5 CLAYTON TERR
6 BROOMPARK ST
7 WESTERCRAIGS CT
8 BROOMPARK CIR

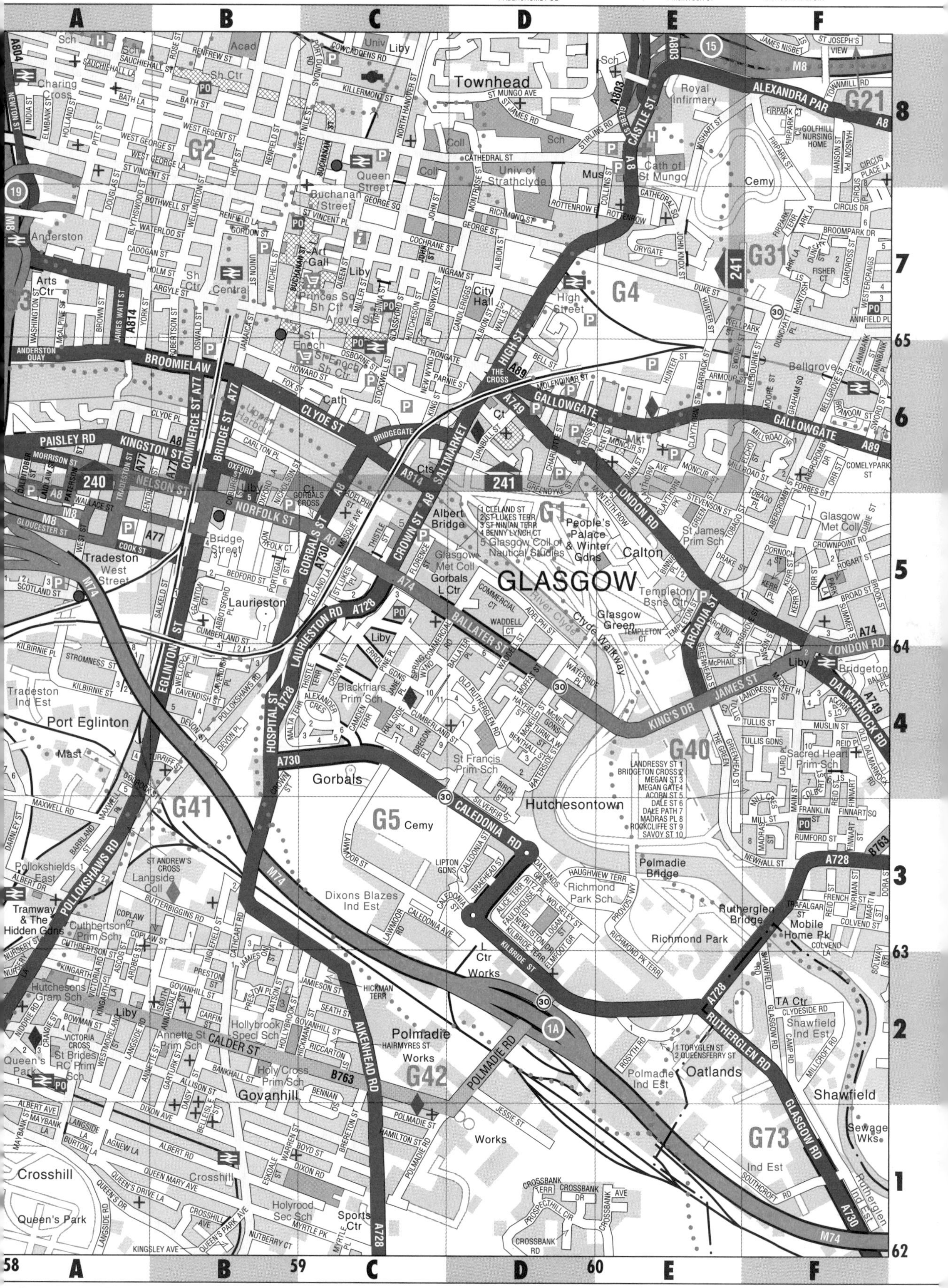

58 A B 59 C D 60 E F

A2
1 TORRISDALE ST
2 PRINCE EDWARD ST
3 ALLISON PL
4 CHAPMAN ST
A3
1 MUIRHOUSE ST
2 BUTTERFIELD PL
A4
1 FALFIELD ST
2 FRANCIS ST
3 RITCHIE ST
4 LAUDER ST
5 CARDWELL ST
6 ST ANDREW'S RD
7 McCULLOCH ST
8 MAUCHLINE ST
B2
1 JAMIESON CT
2 HOLLYBROOK PL
3 Victoria Prim Sch
B3
1 ANNANDALE ST
2 LARKFIELD ST
3 ROBSON GR
4 MORGAN MEWS
B4
1 SURREY LA
2 SALISBURY ST
3 SURREY ST
4 ABBOTSFORD PL
5 CAVENDISH CT
C4
1 SANDIEFIELD RD
2 SOUTHSIDE CRES
3 HANDEL PL
4 KIDSTON TERR
5 KIDSTON PL
6 NABURN GATE
7 GILMOUR PL
8 HUTCHINSON TOWN CT
9 CUMBERLAND PL
10 QUEEN ELIZABETH GDNS
11 QUEEN ELIZABETH SQ

137

D4
1 SANDYFAULDS ST
2 SNOWDON PL
3 SNOWDON ST
4 ST FRANCIS RIGG
5 ST VALENTINE TERR
6 MATHIESON TERR

118

A8
1 ALEXANDRA GATE
2 Alexandra Parade Prim Sch

117
98

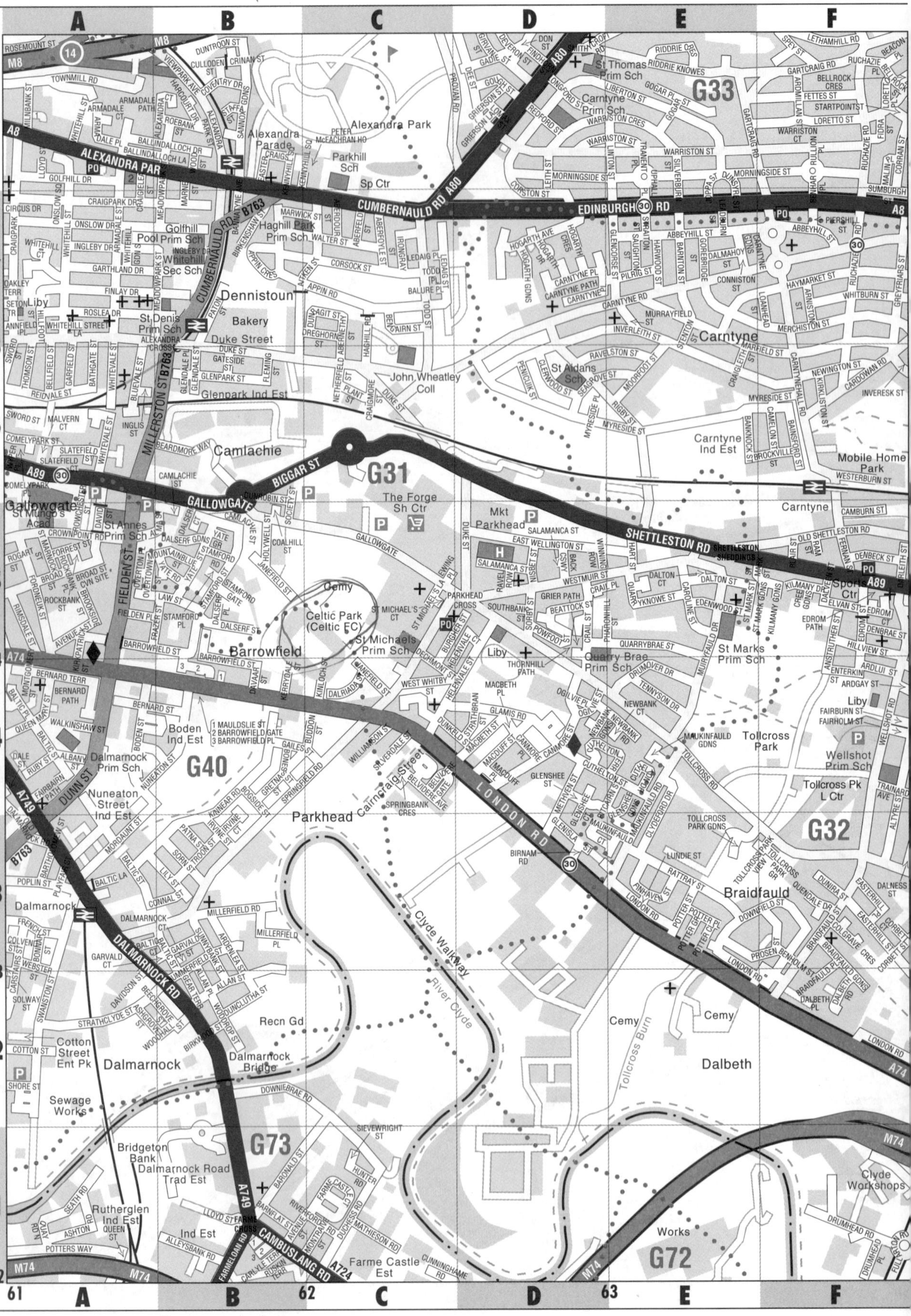

B1
1 SMITH TERR
2 MILLAR TERR
3 WILLIE ROSS LA

117
138

99
120

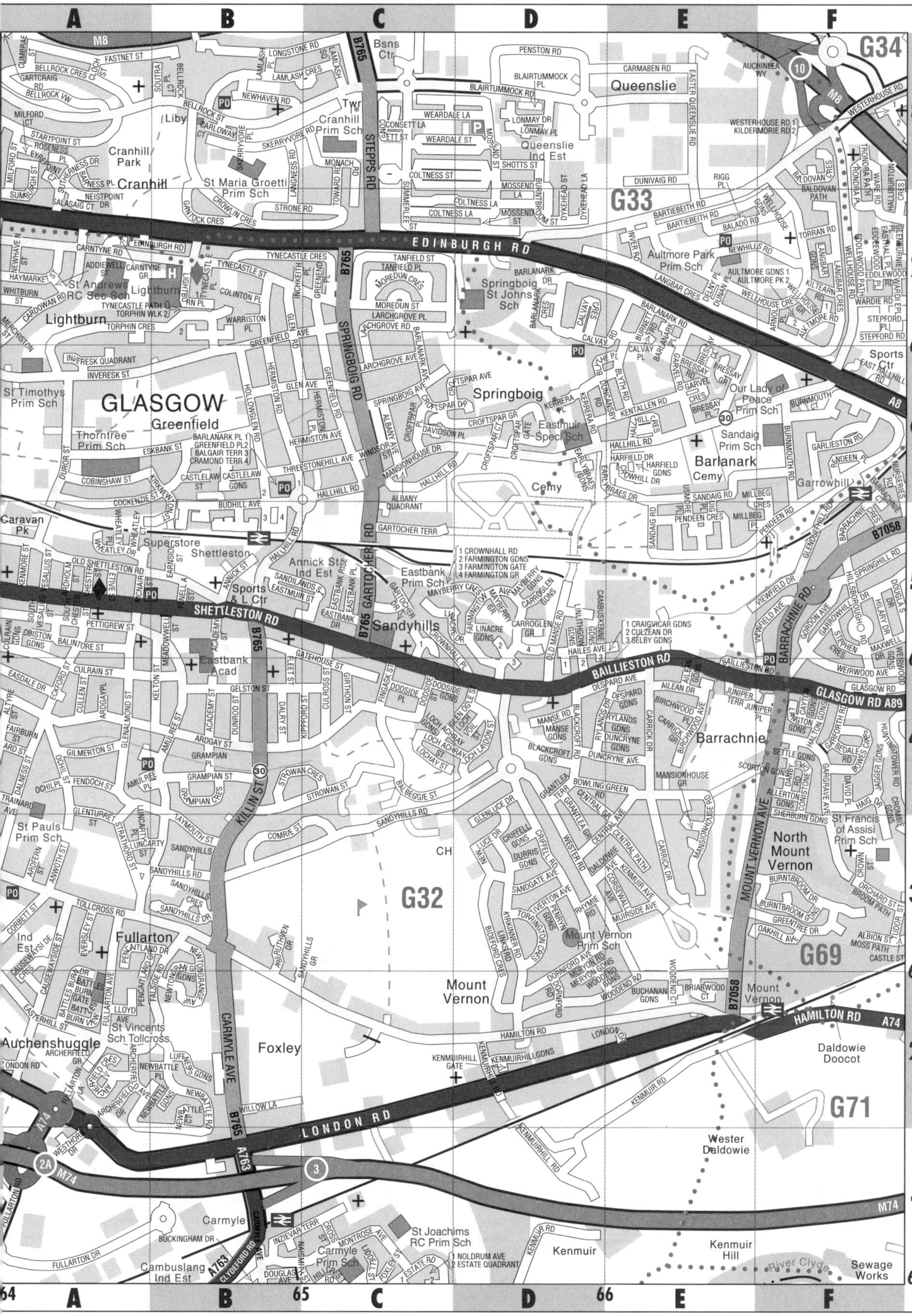

139
120

A6
1 SPRINGHILL FARM PL
2 SPRINGHILL FARM WAY
3 SPRINGHILL FARM GR
4 BARRACHNIE PL

A5
1 BANNERCROSS GDNS
2 BANNERCROSS AVE
3 THORNBRIDGE GDNS

B6
1 MICKLEHOUSE PL
2 MICKLEHOUSE OVAL
3 MICKLEHOUSE WYND
4 BARONY CT
5 BARONY WYND
6 QUEENSBY AVE

B5
1 THORNBRIDGE AVE
2 HATHERSAGE GDNS

101
122

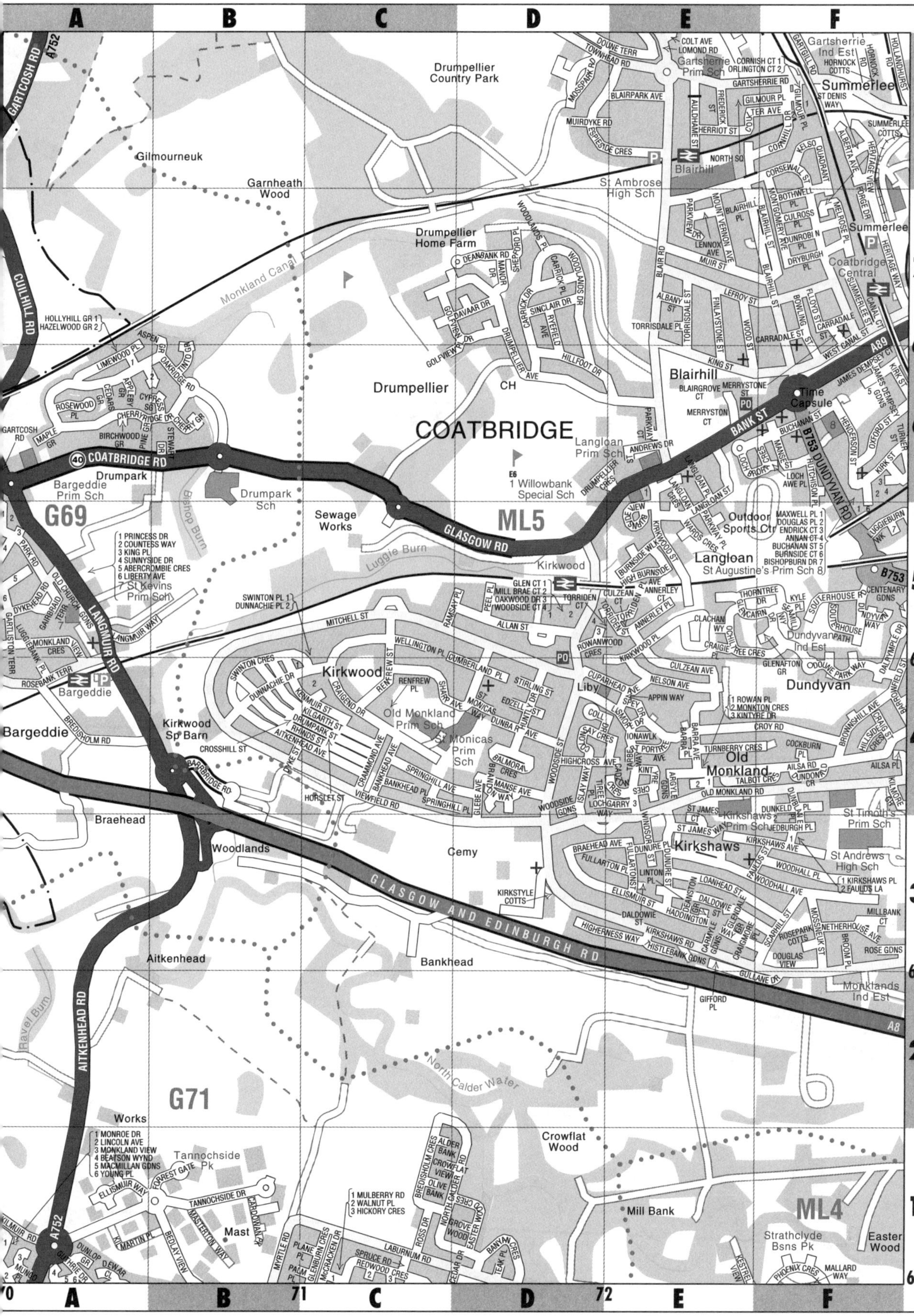

141
122

A8
1 COLTSWOOD CT
2 RONALD ST
3 RED BRIDGE CT
4 LINCOLN CT
5 CALEDONIAN GATE

121
102

F8
1 NORTH BRIDGE ST
2 WELLWYND GDNS
3 WILLOWPARK CT
4 AITCHISON CT

121
142

A8
1 ANDERSON LA
2 AULD'S BRAE
3 PARKHEAD LA
4 OLD CROSS
5 ANDERSON ST

B7
1 GARTLEA GDNS
2 SOUTH NIMMO ST
3 ALBERT CRES

C7
1 KINGSTON AVE
2 COLSTON PL
3 COLSTON ROW
4 COLSTON TERR

E7
1 FINLAYSON QUADRANT
2 WESTER MOFFAT CRES
3 MOORPARK AVE
4 CRAIGNURE CRES

103
124

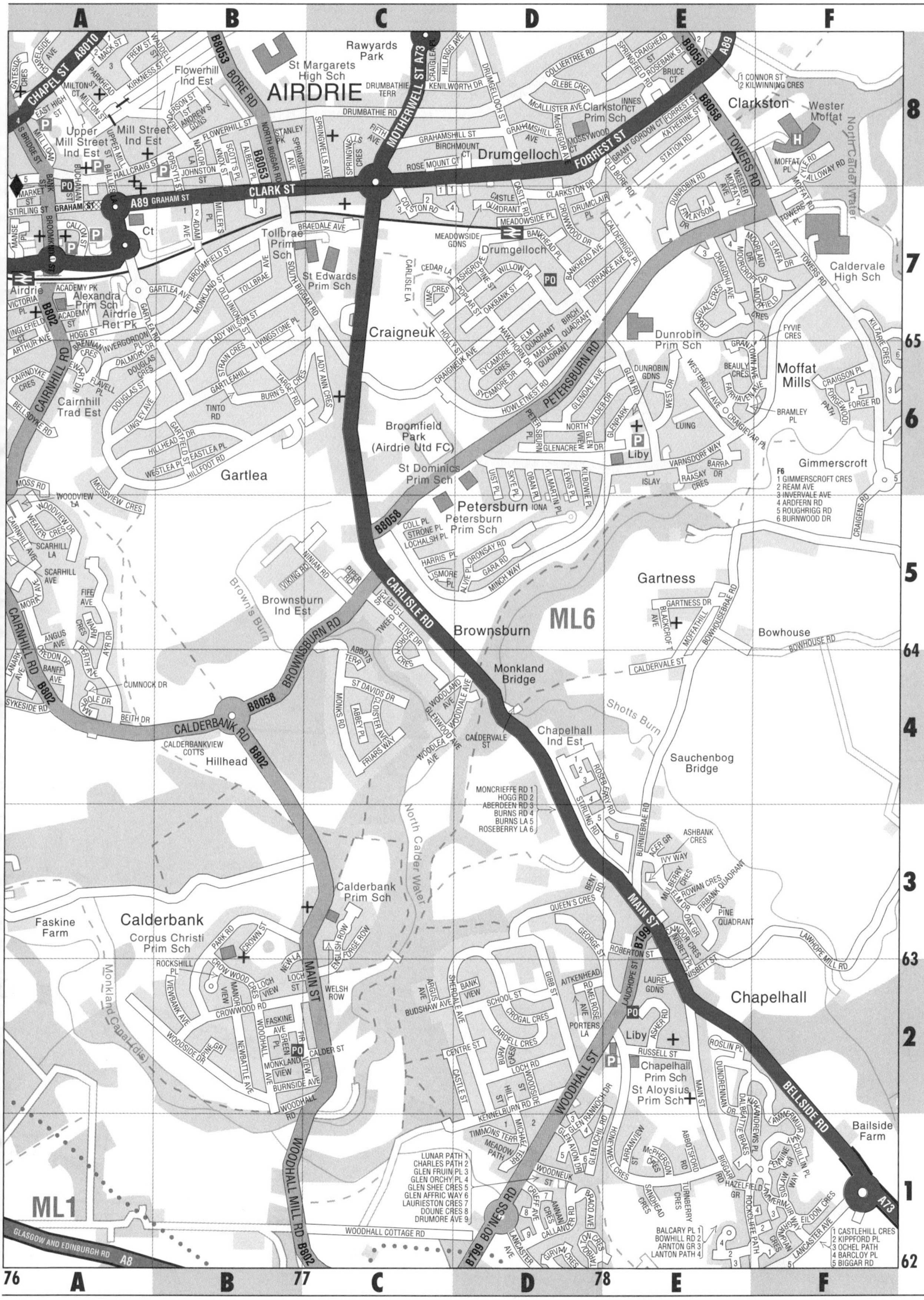

143
124

123
104

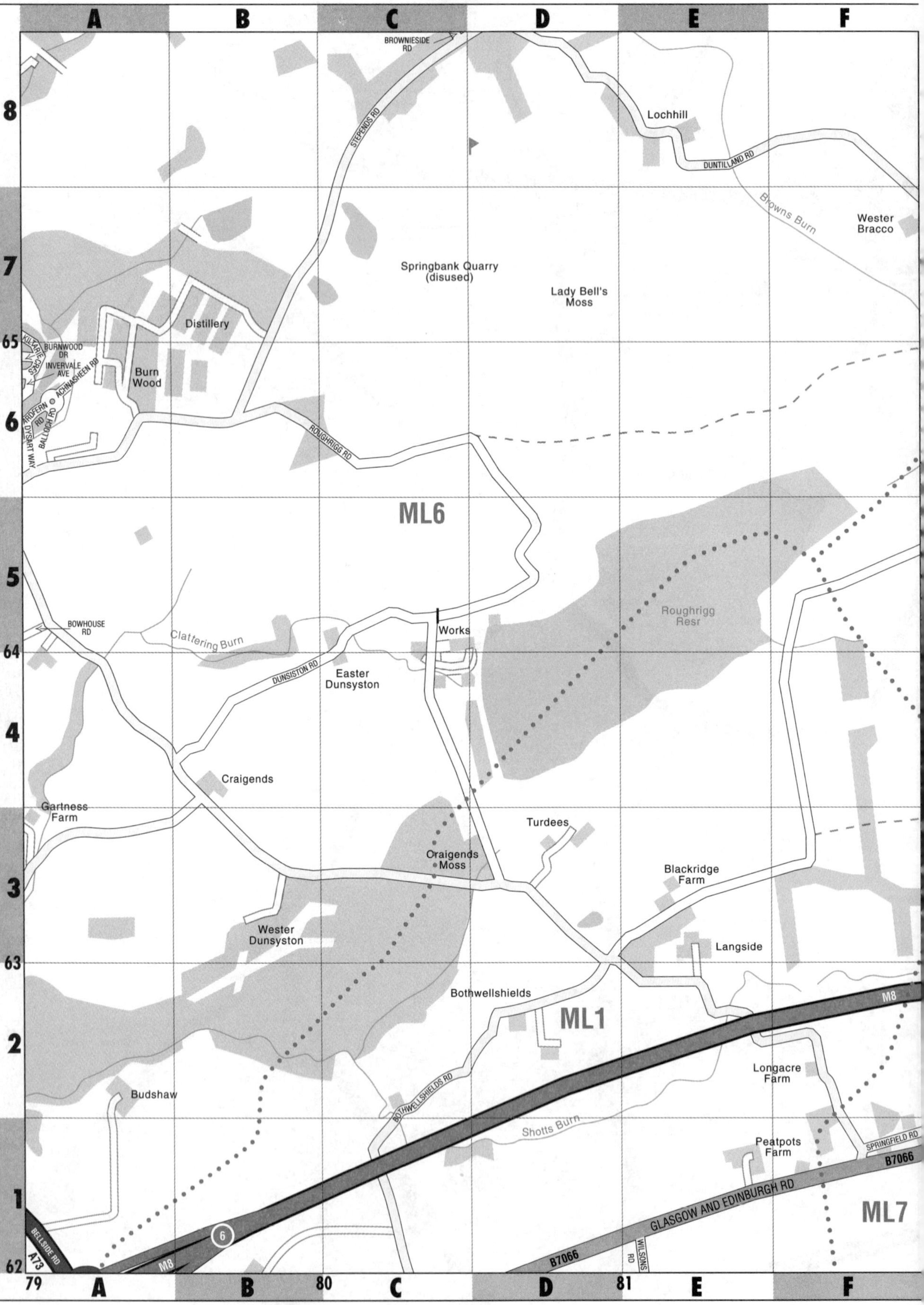

123
144

105
126

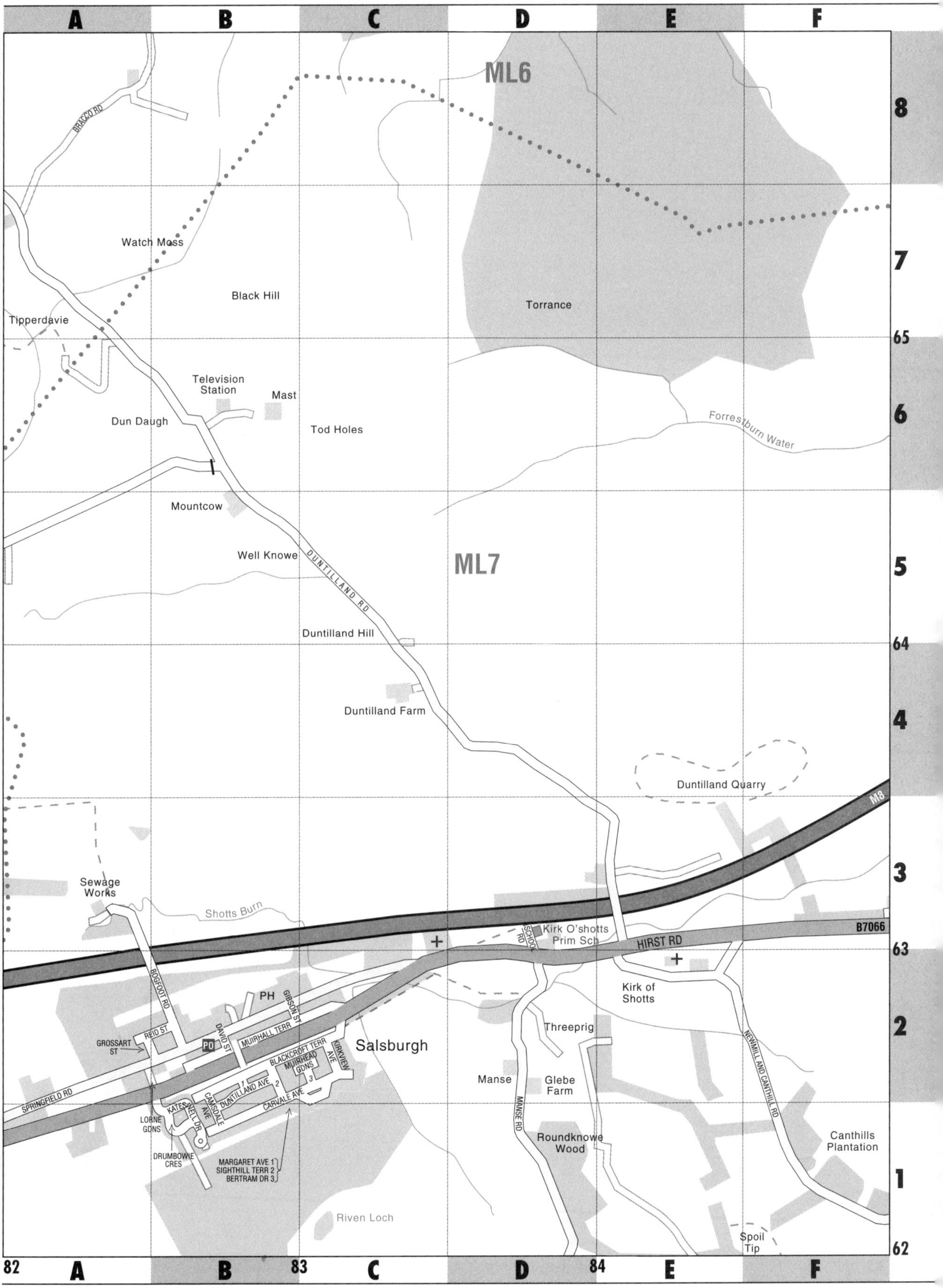
A
B
C
D
E
F
ML6
BRACCO RD
8
Watch Moss
Black Hill
Torrance
7
Tipperdavie
65
Television
Station
Mast
Dun Daugh
Tod Holes
Forrestburn Water
6
Mountcow
Well Knowe
DUNTILLAND RD
ML7
5
Duntilland Hill
64
Duntilland Farm
4
Duntilland Quarry
M8
3
Sewage
Works
Shotts Burn
B7066
SCHOOL RD
Kirk O'shotts
Prim Sch
HIRST RD
63
BOGFOOT RD
GIBSON ST
PH
Kirk of
Shotts
2
REID ST
GROSSART
ST
DAVID ST
MUIRHALL TERR
PO
BLACKCROFT TERR
MUIRHEAD
GDNS
KIRKVIEW
AVE
Salsburgh
Threeprig
NEWMILL AND CANTHILL RD
SPRINGFIELD RD
DUNTILLAND AVE
CARVALE AVE
CAMSDALE AVE
KATESANELL DR
Manse
Glebe
Farm
MANSE RD
LORNE
GDNS
DRUMBOWIE
CRES
MARGARET AVE 1
SIGHTHILL TERR 2
BERTRAM DR 3
Roundknowe
Wood
Canthills
Plantation
1
Riven Loch
Spoil
Tip
62
82
A
B
83
C
D
84
E
F

145
126

125
106

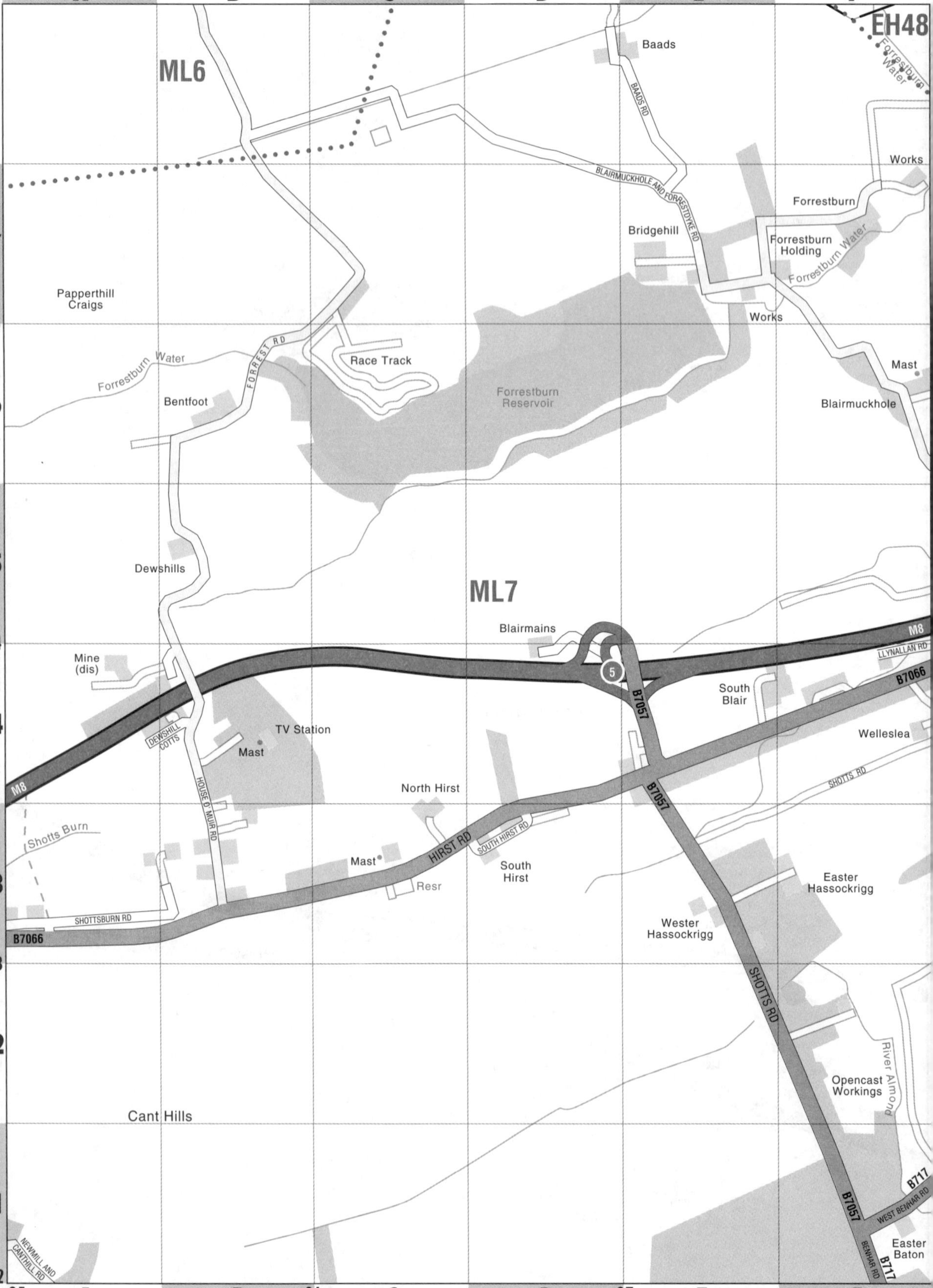
A
B
C
D
E
F
8
7
65
6
5
64
4
3
63
2
1
62
85
86
87
ML6
EH48
ML7
Baads
BAADS RD
Forrestburn Water
Works
BLAIRMUCKHOLE AND FORRESTDYKE RD
Forrestburn
Bridgehill
Forrestburn Holding
Works
Papperthill Craigs
FORREST RD
Race Track
Forrestburn Reservoir
Mast
Blairmuckhole
Bentfoot
Dewshills
Blairmains
M8
LLYNALLAN RD
Mine (dis)
5
B7057
South Blair
B7066
TV Station
Mast
DEWSHILL COTTS
Welleslea
HOUSE O' MUIR RD
North Hirst
SHOTTS RD
Shotts Burn
HIRST RD
SOUTH HIRST RD
Mast
South Hirst
Resr
Easter Hassockrigg
SHOTTSBURN RD
Wester Hassockrigg
SHOTTS RD
River Almond
Opencast Workings
Cant Hills
B717
WEST BENHAR RD
Easter Baton
BENHAR RD
NEWMILL AND CANTHILL RD

125
146

107

EH48
Blairhill Quarry
Loan Farm
Hill Farm
Blairmuckhill Farm
Netherton Farm
Knowehead
Mast
M8
Harthill Service Area
Sewage Works
Greenrigg Prim Sch
WESTCRAIGS RD
Service Area
Treesbank Farm
Harthill Ind Est
Mossburn Ind Est
WEST MAIN ST
EAST MAIN ST B7066
B718
B717
CHURCH ST
Alexander Peden Prim Sch
Harthill
How Burn
HIRST RD
Tam's Loup Quarry
Eastfield
Paxtane
ML7
West Benhar
WEST BENHAR RD
Works
River Almond
Active Workings
Spoil Heap
Mon
Brownhill Farm
Forestburn Water
M8 Edinburgh (A71)
Edinburgh STREET ATLAS

147

108

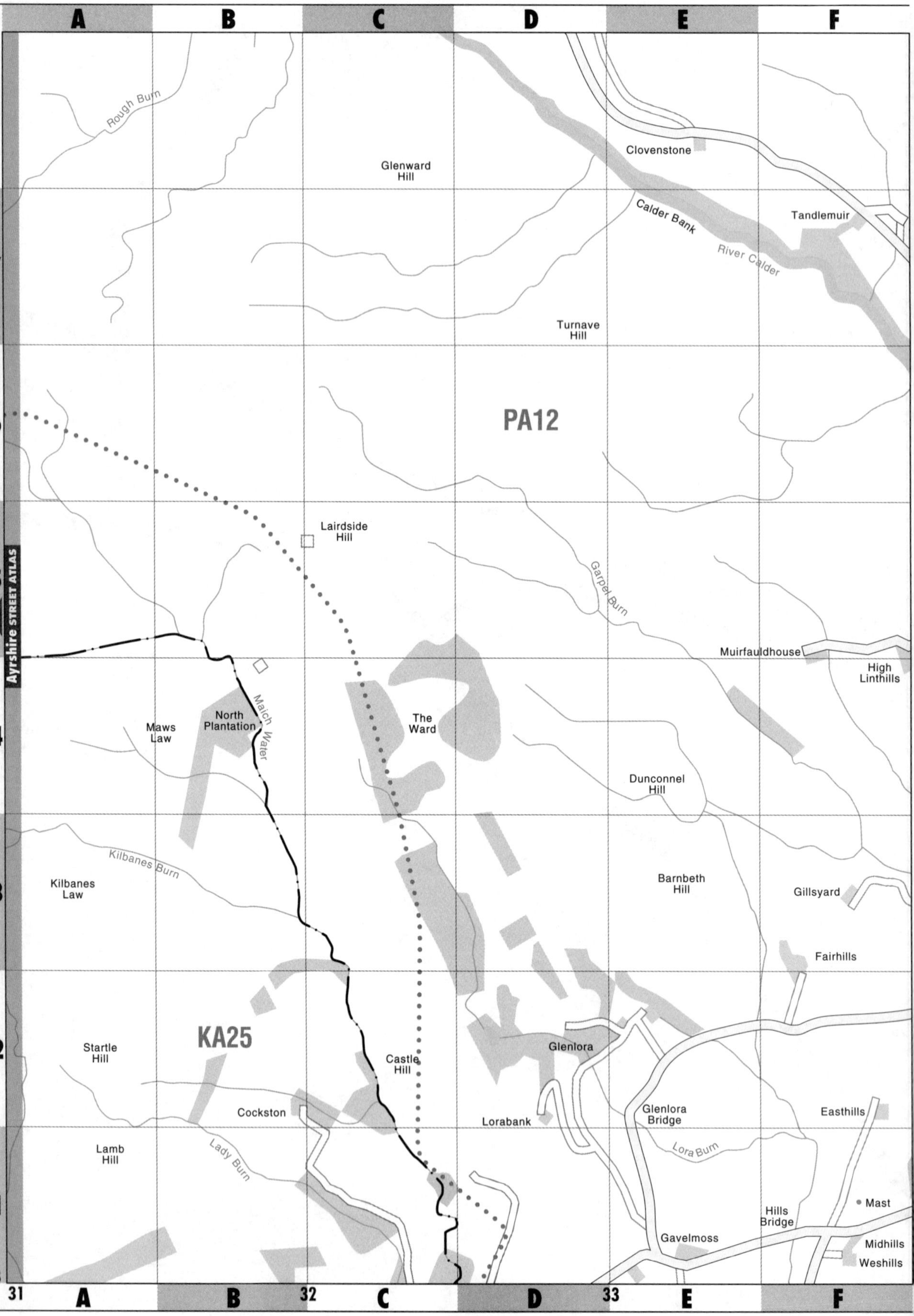

A
B
C
D
E
F
8
7
61
6
5
60
4
3
59
2
1
58
31
32
33
Rough Burn
Glenward Hill
Clovenstone
Calder Bank
River Calder
Tandlemuir
Turnave Hill
PA12
Lairdside Hill
Garpel Burn
Muirfauldhouse
High Linthills
Maws Law
North Plantation
Maich Water
The Ward
Dunconnel Hill
Kilbanes Burn
Kilbanes Law
Barnbeth Hill
Gillsyard
Fairhills
KA25
Startle Hill
Castle Hill
Glenlora
Cockston
Lorabank
Glenlora Bridge
Easthills
Lamb Hill
Lady Burn
Lora Burn
Mast
Hills Bridge
Gavelmoss
Midhills
Weshills
Ayrshire STREET ATLAS

149

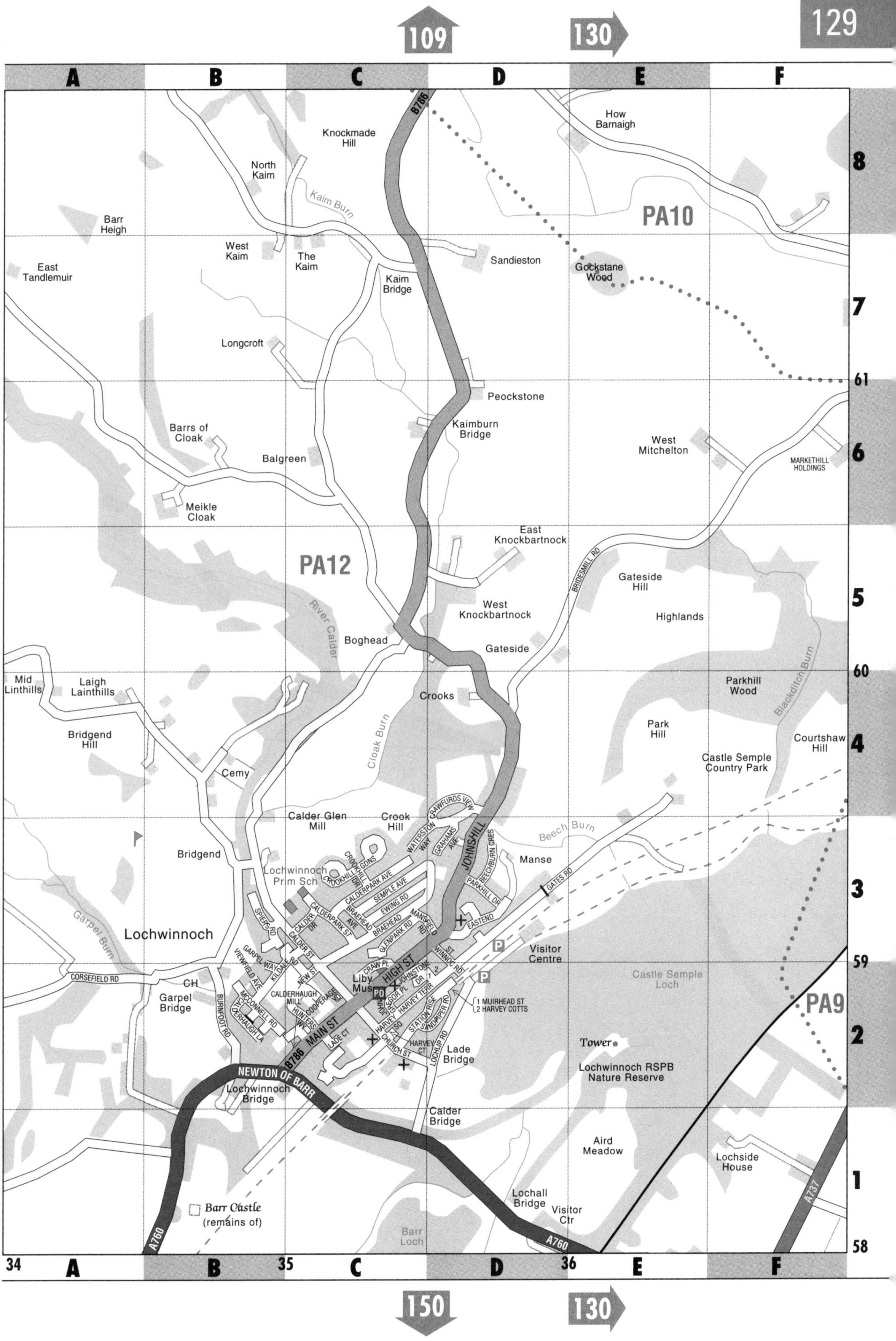
109
130
A
B
C
D
E
F
8
7
61
6
5
60
4
3
59
2
1
58
34
35
36
Knockmade Hill
North Kaim
Kaim Burn
Barr Heigh
How Barnaigh
PA10
West Kaim
The Kaim
East Tandlemuir
Sandieston
Gockstane Wood
Kaim Bridge
Longcroft
Peockstone
Kaimburn Bridge
Barrs of Cloak
West Mitchelton
MARKETHILL HOLDINGS
Balgreen
Meikle Cloak
East Knockbartnock
PA12
BRIDESMILL RD
Gateside Hill
West Knockbartnock
River Calder
Highlands
Boghead
Gateside
Mid Linthills
Laigh Lainthills
Parkhill Wood
Blackditch Burn
Crooks
Park Hill
Bridgend Hill
Cloak Burn
Courtshaw Hill
Castle Semple Country Park
Cemy
Calder Glen Mill
Crook Hill
CRAWFURDS VIEW
WATERSTON WAY
GRAHAMS AVE
JOHNSHILL
BEECHBURN CRES
Beech Burn
Bridgend
Manse
Lochwinnoch Prim Sch
CROOKHILL GDNS
CROOKHILL DR
CALDERPARK AVE
SEMPLE AVE
EWING RD
PARKHILL DR
GATES RD
Garpel Burn
SPIERS RD
CALDER DR
CALDERPARK ST
BRAEHEAD AVE
BRAEHEAD
MANSFIELD RD
EASTEND
Lochwinnoch
CALDER ST
GLENPARK RD
ST WINNOC RD
Visitor Centre
GARPEL WAY
VIEWFIELD AVE
KILDALE RD
CRAW PL
HIGH ST
JOHNSTONE DR
CORSEFIELD RD
CH
NEW ST
Liby Mus
Castle Semple Loch
Garpel Bridge
BURNFOOT RD
MCCONNELL RD
CALDERHAUGH LA
CALDERHAUGH MILL
COOPERAGE CT
HUNTERS WY
PO
GREGOR PL
HARVEY TERR
STATION RISE
SANDPIPER RD
1 MUIRHEAD ST
2 HARVEY COTTS
PA9
MAIN ST
LADE CT
HARVEY SQ
CHURCH ST
HARVEY CT
LOCHLIP RD
Lade Bridge
Tower
B786
NEWTON OF BARR
Lochwinnoch RSPB Nature Reserve
Lochwinnoch Bridge
Calder Bridge
Aird Meadow
Lochside House
A737
Barr Castle (remains of)
Lochall Bridge
Visitor Ctr
Barr Loch
A760
150
130

129
110

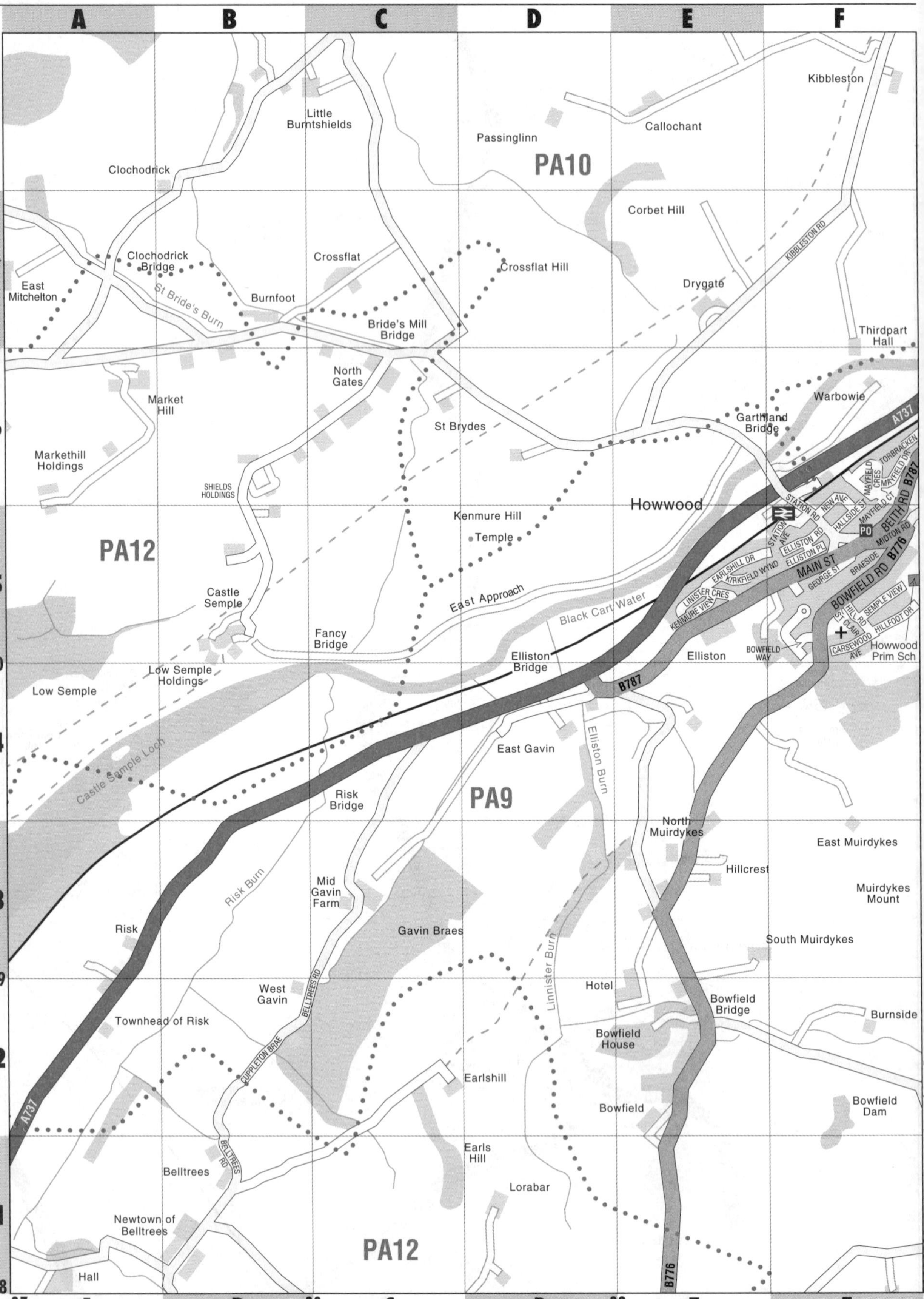

129
151

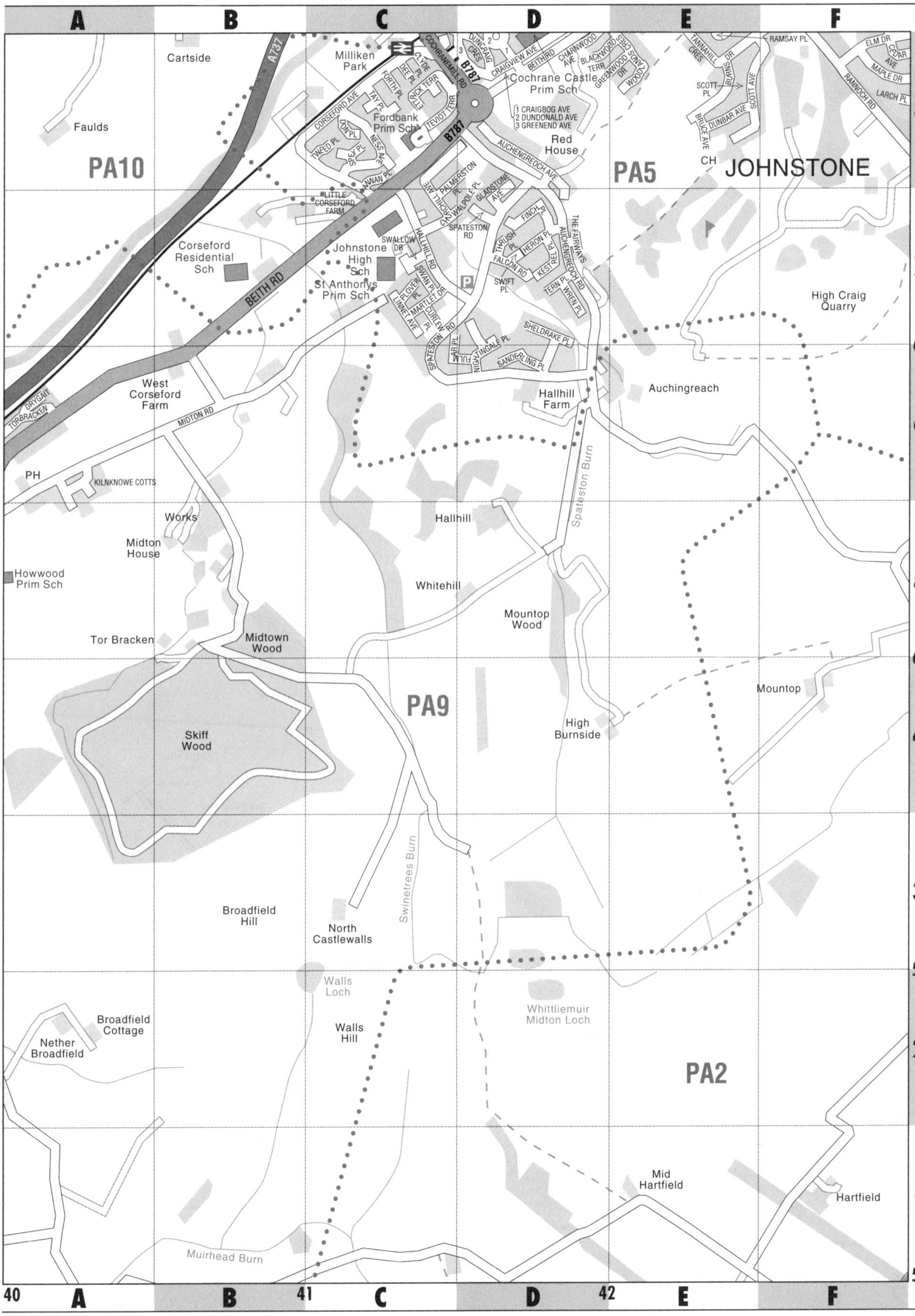
A
B
C
D
E
F
Cartside
Milliken Park
Faulds
PA10
A737
B787
COCHRANEMILL RD
CORSEFORD AVE
TWEED PL
DON PL
SPEY PL
NESS AVE
ANNAN PL
FORTH PL
TAY PL
DEE PL
CLYDE PL
ETTRICK TERR
TEVIOT TERR
Fordbank Prim Sch
DUNCRAIG CRES
CRAIGVIEW AVE
BEITH RD
CHARNWOOD AVE
BLACKWOOD TERR
GREENWOOD DR
WOODLANDS CRES
Cochrane Castle Prim Sch
1 CRAIGBOG AVE
2 DUNDONALD AVE
3 GREENEND AVE
Red House
AUCHENGREOCH AVE
PA5
TANNAHILL CRES
BURNS DR
RAMSAY PL
SCOTT PL
SCOTT AVE
DUNBAR AVE
BRUCE AVE
ELM DR
CEDAR AVE
MAPLE DR
LARCH PL
RANNOCH RD
CH
JOHNSTONE
LITTLE CORSEFORD FARM
PALMERSTON PL
GLADSTONE AVE
WALPOLE PL
CHURCHILL AVE
SPATESTON RD
FINCH PL
THRUSH PL
HERON PL
FALCON RD
KESTREL PL
SWIFT PL
TERN PL
WREN PL
AUCHENGREOCH RD
THE FAIRWAYS
Corseford Residential Sch
BEITH RD
Johnstone High Sch
SWALLOW DR
HALLHILL RD
St Anthony's Prim Sch
SWAN PL
PLOVER PL
MARTLET DR
LINNET AVE
CURLEW PL
SPATESTON RD
FULMAR PL
NIGHTINGALE PL
SANDERLING PL
SHELDRAKE PL
P
High Craig Quarry
DRYGAIT
TORBRACKEN
West Corseford Farm
MIDTON RD
Hallhill Farm
Auchingreach
PH
KILNKNOWE COTTS
Spateston Burn
Works
Hallhill
Midton House
Howwood Prim Sch
Whitehill
Mountop Wood
Tor Bracken
Midtown Wood
Mountop
PA9
Skiff Wood
High Burnside
Broadfield Hill
North Castlewalls
Swinetrees Burn
Walls Loch
Whittliemuir Midton Loch
Broadfield Cottage
Nether Broadfield
Walls Hill
PA2
Mid Hartfield
Hartfield
Muirhead Burn
8
7
61
6
5
60
4
3
59
2
1
58
40
41
42

131
112

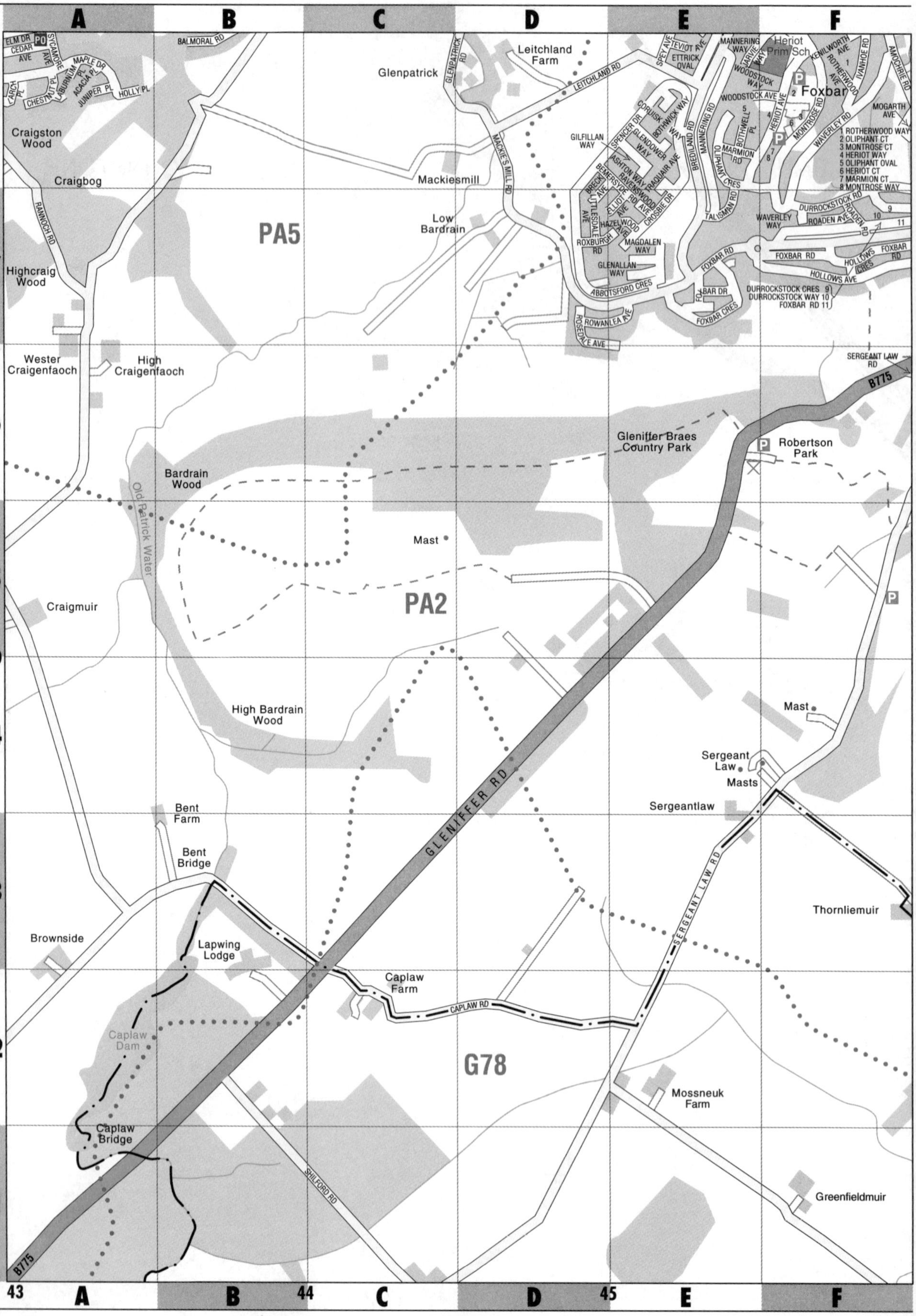

131
153

113
134

A B C D E F

8

Gleniffer High Sch
MOGARTH AVE
SELKIRK AVE
STANELY AVE
STANELY CRES
STANELY GR
STANELY AVE
B775
Stanely Reservoir
AMOCHRIE DR
AMOCHRIE RD
AMOCHRIE GLEN
DURROCKSTOCK RD
GLENIFFER CT
STRAVAIG PATH
STRAVAIG WLK
FOXBAR RD
HOLLOWS AVE
CASTLEVIEW AVE
CASTLEVIEW DR
1 DURROCKSTOCK CRES
2 HOLLOWS CRES
3 CASTLEVIEW PL
STANELY GRANGE
GLENIFFER RD
Works
GRANTS PL
GRANTS AVE
GRANTS CRES
DONALDSWOOD RD
DONALDSWOOD PK
MOSSNEUK DR
Glenburn
NEWARK DR
NETHERCRAIGS DR
CRAIGBAR DR
ROCKWELL AVE
LANGCRAIGS CT
BURNFOOT CRES
LINN CRES
HARELAW CRES
FERENEZE DR
GLENBURN ROAD
BRAEVIEW DR
BRAEVIEW GDNS
BRAEVIEW RD
BRAEVIEW WAY
REDHURST LA
REDHURST CRES
REDHURST WAY
LIMECRAIGS AVE
LIMECRAIGS RD
LIMECRAIGS CRES
LIMEVIEW CRES
LIMEVIEW AVE
LIMEVIEW RD
LIMEVIEW WAY
NETHERCRAIGS RD
HOLLYBUSH AVE
CARSEGREEN AVE
WARDHOUSE RD
Langcraigs Prim Sch
BRAEHEAD RD
BROWNSIDE AVE
BRAEHEAD RD
DENEWOOD AVE
St Peter's Prim Sch
Liby
PO
HIGHFIELD AVE
HIGHFIELD CRES
LINNWELL CRES
GLENBURN CRES
GREENBANK DR
KNOCKSIDE AVE
GLENBURN RD
BARDRAIN RD
KILPATRICK CRES
PARK RD
LOMOND CRES
GRAMPIAN AVE
MOORFOOT AVE
MOORFOOT PATH
Bushes Prim Sch
OCHIL DR
CAMPSIE DR
MORVEN AVE
PENTLAND CRES
LAMMERMUIR DR
CRUACHAN AVE
CAIRNGORM CRES
CRESTLEA AVE
LAPSLEY AVE
LEABANK AVE
LAMMERMUIR CT
POTTERHILL AVE
ARTHUR RD
WOODLAND AVE
SOUTHFIELD AVE
FAIRWAY AVE
FINTRY AVE
SKYE CRES
BUTE CRES
TIREE AVE
COLONSAY RD
RAASAY DR
AILSA DR
ISLAY CRES
JURA RD
SANDA WY
TOWARD WY
IONA DR
STAFFA DR
MULL AVE
LISMORE DR
ARRAN DR
CUMBRAE RD
MAY RD
DAVAAR DR
GLENBURN RD
NEILSTON RD
B774
STONEFIELD PK
THORNLY PARK RD
THORNLY PARK DR
THORNLY PARK AVE
BARCRAIGS DR
STEWART RD
SOUTH AVE
STONEY BRAE
CARS
BRAEFOOT
TODBURN DR
30

7

THORNLY PARK RESIDENCE
CAPLETHILL RD

61

B774
PAISLEY
Gleniffer Braes Country Park
CRAIGIELINN AVE
CAPLAN RD
BRAEMOUNT AVE
HILLCREST AVE
CRAIGENDON OVAL
CRAIGENDON RD
CRAIGENDON TERR
CRAIGMOUNT AVE
LANGCRAIGS DR
LANGCRAIGS TERR
GLENFIELD AVE
GLENFIELD RD
GLENFIELD CRES
GLENFIELD GDNS
GLENFIELD GR
GLENFIELD GRANGE
GLENBURN RD
Thornley Dam
SERGEANT LAW RD
Braemount
P
PA2
PROCESSION RD
Nature Trail
P
Glen Park
P

6

Brownside
Gleniffer Burn
CH

5

Brownside Braes
Glenburn Reservoir

60

Harelaw Burn
Knockindon Burn

4

Reservoir
Harelaw Reservoir
Masts
Mast

3

Thornliemuir
Fereneze Hills
Mast

59

HILLSIDE RD
G78
Woodneuk

2

Killoch Hill
GATESIDE GDNS
Capellie Farm
Reservoir
Capellie Cottage
Gateside
GATESIDE RD
WRAES VIEW

1

Killoch Water
FERENEZE RD
A736
LOCHLIBO RD
Killoch
DONNIES BRAE 1
NEILSTON RD 2

58

46 A B 47 C D 48 E F

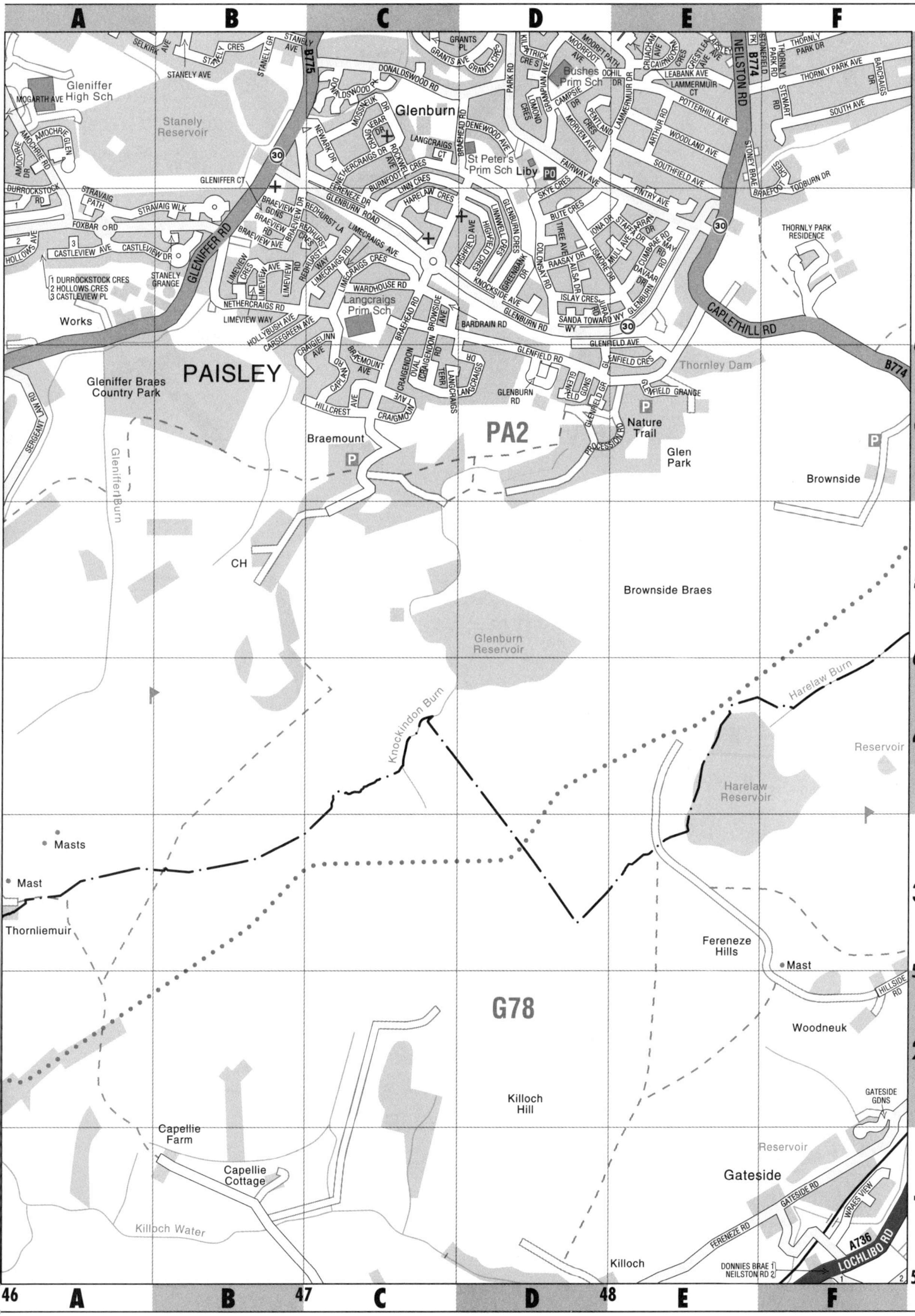

154
134

133
114

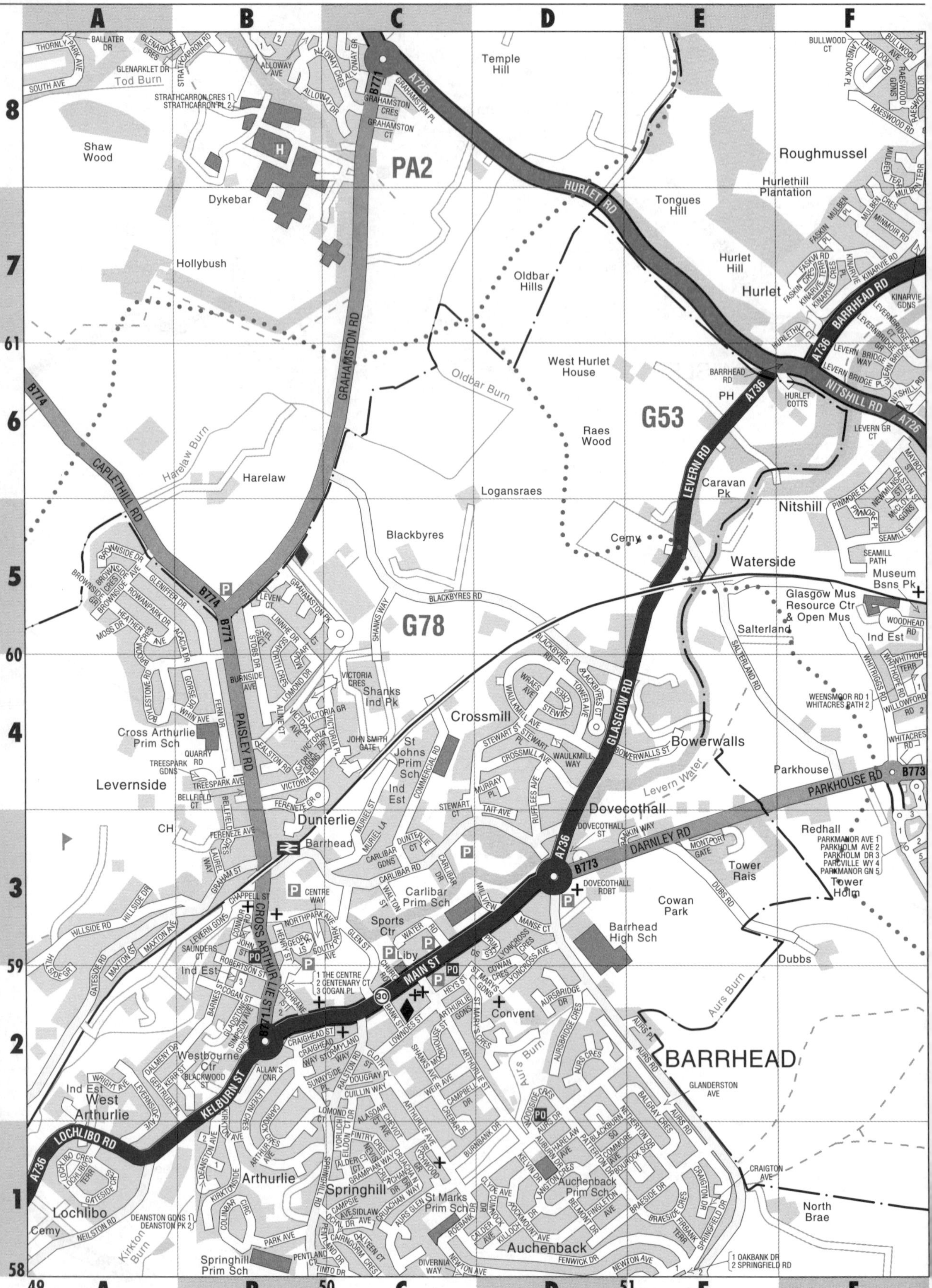

133
155

A8
1 SANQUHAR GDNS
2 SANQUHAR PL
3 RAESWOOD PL
4 POLQUHAP CT
5 POLQUHAP PL
6 POLQUHAP GDNS
7 CATRINE GDNS
8 CATRINE CT
9 DALMELLINGTON DR
10 LITTLEMILL GDNS
11 BALLOCHMYLE CRES
12 BALLOCHMYLE PL
13 MARLACH PL
14 BALLOCHMYLE DR
15 BARGANY PL

115
136

156
136

135

C7
1 JOHNSHAVEN ST
2 BENGAL PL

116

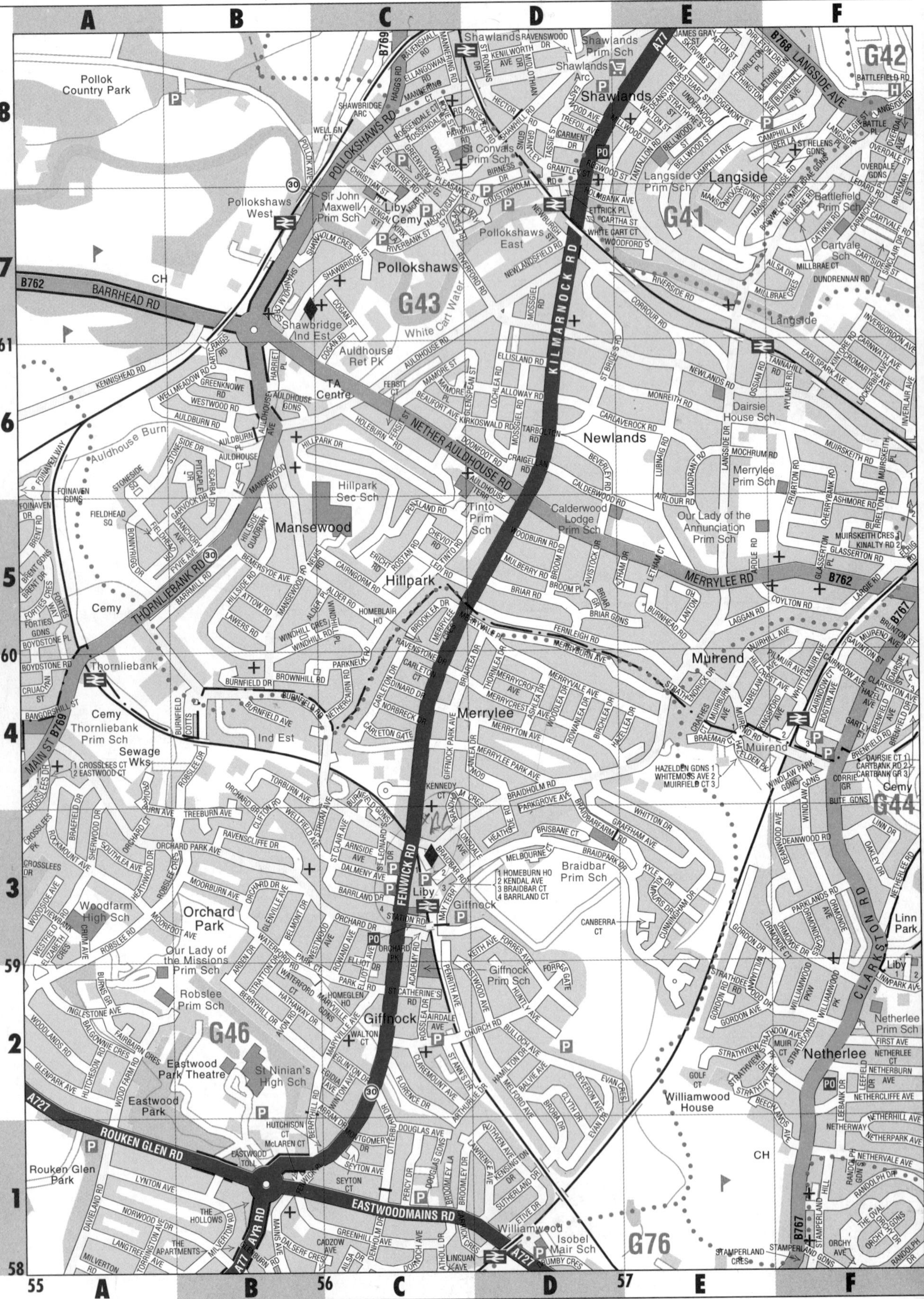

F2
1 RIVERSIDE CT
2 LINNPARK CT
3 MACLAREN PL

135

157

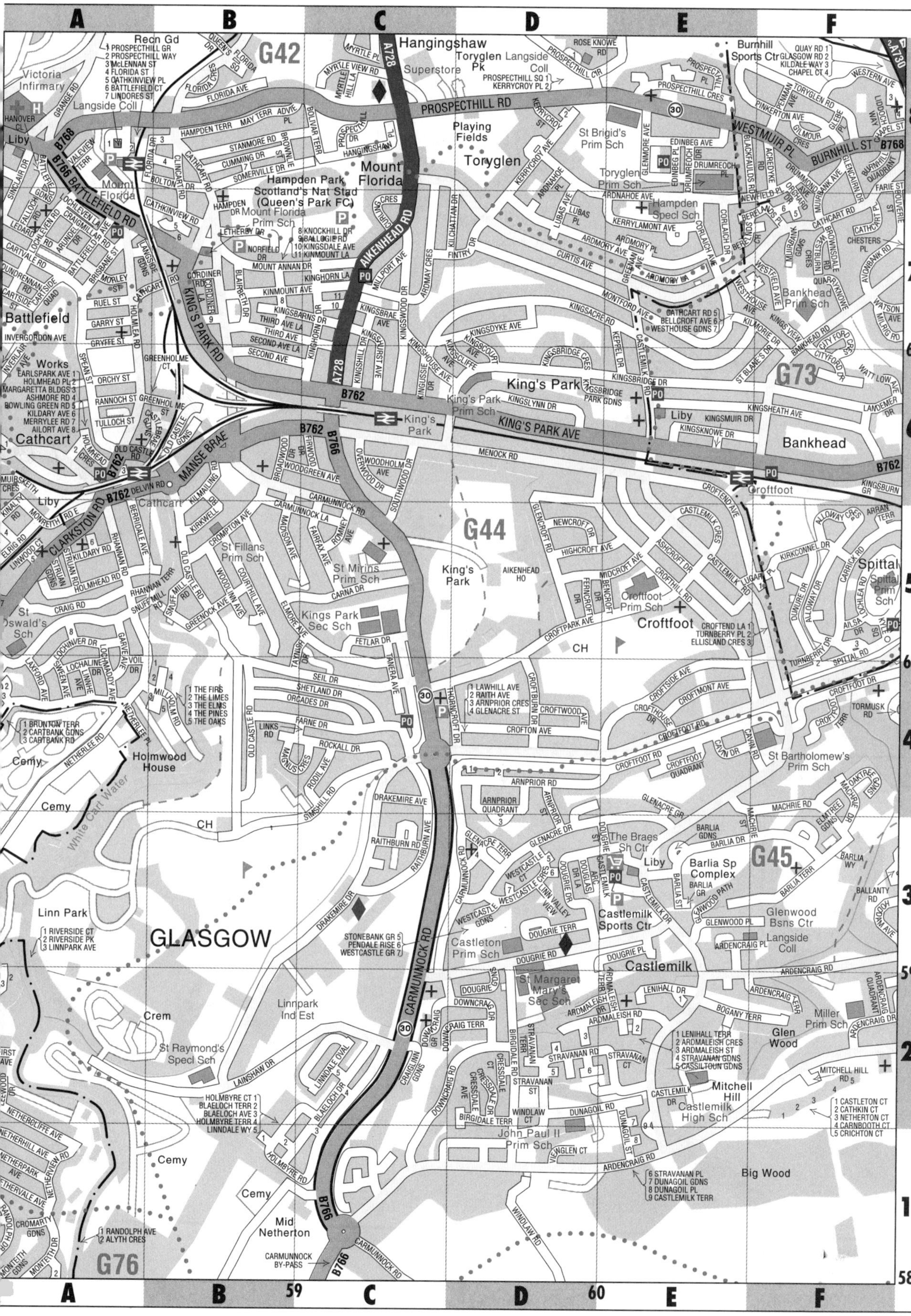
A
B
C
D
E
F
G42
G44
G45
G73
G76
GLASGOW
Hangingshaw
Toryglen Pk
Langside Coll
Superstore
Victoria Infirmary
Recn Gd
Langside Coll
Mount Florida
Hampden Park Scotland's Nat Stad (Queen's Park FC)
Mount Florida Prim Sch
Playing Fields
Toryglen
St Brigid's Prim Sch
Toryglen Prim Sch
Hampden Specl Sch
Burnhill Sports Ctr
Bankhead Prim Sch
Bankhead
Battlefield
Works
Cathcart
Liby
King's Park
King's Park Prim Sch
King's Park
KING'S PARK AVE
PROSPECTHILL RD
WESTMUIR PL
BURNHILL ST
BATTLEFIELD RD
KING'S PARK RD
MANSE BRAE
CLARKSTON RD
AIKENHEAD RD
CARMUNNOCK RD
MENOCK RD
Croftfoot
Croftfoot Prim Sch
AIKENHEAD HO
St Fillans Prim Sch
St Mirins Prim Sch
Kings Park Sec Sch
St Oswald's Sch
Spittal
Spittal Prim Sch
Holmwood House
Cemy
White Cart Water
Linn Park
Crem
St Raymond's Specl Sch
Linnpark Ind Est
St Bartholomew's Prim Sch
The Braes Sh Ctr
Barlia Sp Complex
Glenwood Bsns Ctr
Langside Coll
Castlemilk Sports Ctr
Castleton Prim Sch
Castlemilk
St Margaret Mary's Sec Sch
Miller Prim Sch
Glen Wood
Mitchell Hill
Castlemilk High Sch
John Paul II Prim Sch
Big Wood
Mid Netherton
CARMUNNOCK BY-PASS
A728
A730
B762
B766
B768
8
7
61
6
5
60
4
3
59
2
1
58
59
60

A7
1 MACDONALD ST
2 BALVAIRD CRES
3 CHESTERS PL

A8
1 WESTERN AVE
2 CHAPEL ST
3 GREENBANK ST
4 VICTORIA PL
5 KING STREET LA

137

B7
1 St Columbkilles Prim Sch
2 Stonelaw High Sch

118

B8
1 CHURCH PL
2 GALLOWFLAT ST
3 WARDLAW DR
4 Rutherglen High Sch

E6
1 SILVERBANKS RD
2 SILVERBANKS GAIT
3 SILVERBANKS CT

F6
1 BRIDGE ST
2 LIBRARY GDNS
3 ARDOCH GDNS
4 CENTRAL GR
5 SIR THOMAS LIPTON WY

D3
1 TULLOCHARD PL
2 LYBSTER CRES
3 GLENALMOND RD

D4
1 WARRISTON WAY
2 STRATHMORE GDNS
3 APPIN TERR
4 BREADALBANE GDNS
5 STRATHCONA PL

E3
1 ISLAY AVE
2 BOWMORE GDNS

137
159

119
D6
1 NORTHBANK ST
2 FINDLAY TERR
3 DALZIEL GAIT
4 DALZIEL PTH
5 DALZIEL GR
140

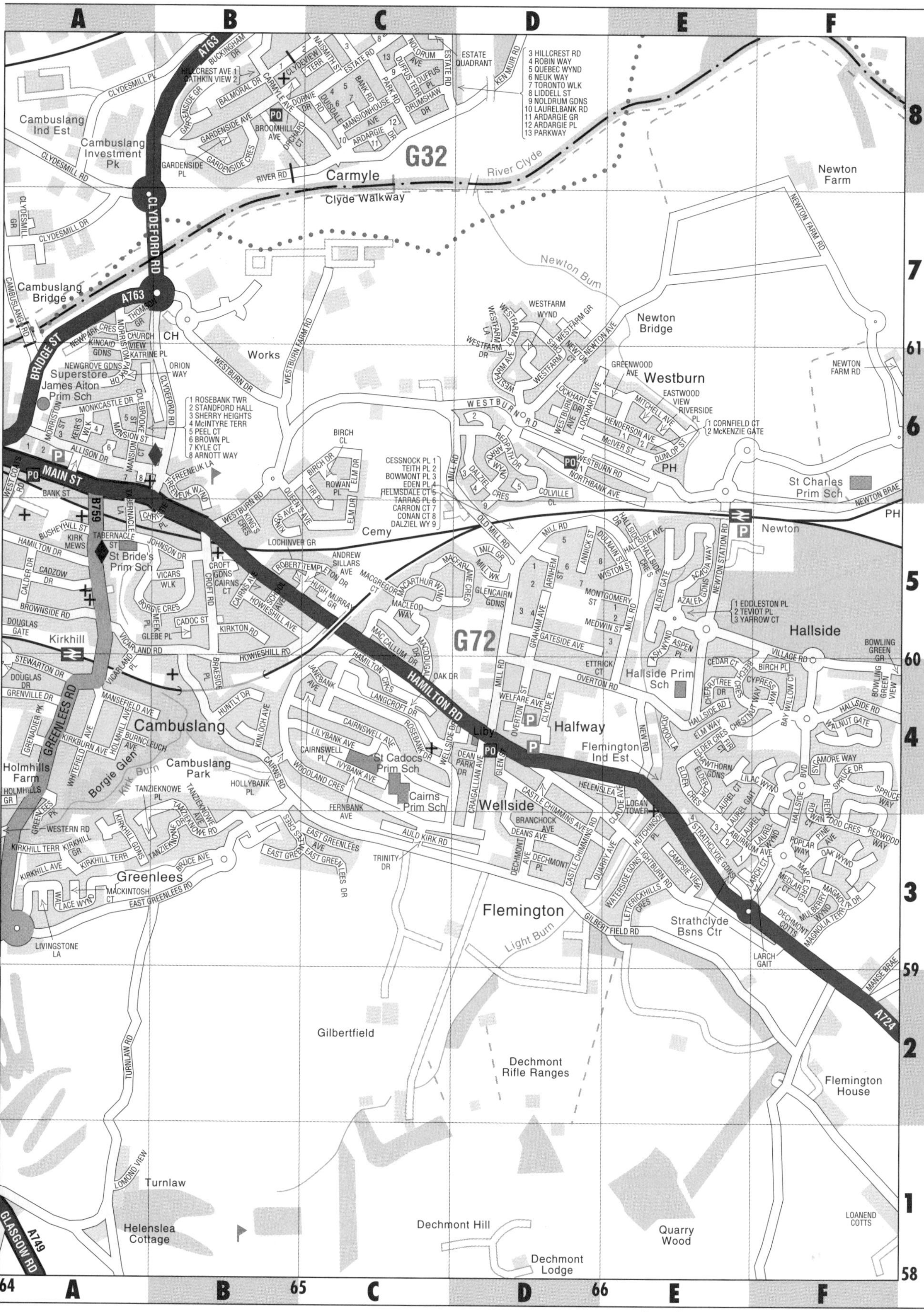

160
140
E3
1 LARCH CL
2 LARCH PL
3 LARCH SQ
4 BARONY GR

139
120

A
B
C
D
E
F
8
7
61
6
5
60
4
3
59
2
1
58
67
68
69
Sewage Works
Chuckle Hill
Crem
Maryville
M74
M73
A74
B7001
GREYFRIARS RD
THE CUILLINS
KENMAR GDNS
BOWMORE GDNS
MILTON GDNS
Calderbraes
WATLING ST
OLD EDINBURGH RD
KIRKWOOD RD
LAUREL GDNS
GARTMORE GDNS
TALBOT TERR
CALDERBRAES AVE
MOSSGIEL GDNS
DALVEEN DR
GLENCROFT AVE
HILLFOOT GDNS
MILLGATE AVE
MILLGATE
Powburn
DUNVEGAN
LUCY BRAE
ROSELEA RD
GLENACRE CRES
B758
A74
A721
NEW EDINBURGH RD
A752
HOLMBRAE RD
WOODHEAD CRES
LYNNHURST
ALPINE GR
Haughhead Bridge
OLD GLASGOW RD
Honeyhill Plantation
East Haughhead
Clyde Walkway
GREENHOLM AVE 1
ALDERSIDE GDNS 2
CLYDENEUK DR
BURNPARK AVE
POWBURN CRES
CLYDEFORD DR
Kylepark
KYLEPARK DR
KYLEPARK CRES
PRIORY DR
HUME DR
CRANFORD CRES
SHEEPBURN RD
BELMONT AVE
BROOKLANDS AVE
GLASGOW RD
B7071
ROSEFIELD GDNS
HOLMWOOD AVE
HOLMWOOD GDNS
OLD MILL RD
OLD MILL LA
M74
BELLEISLE AVE
KYLEPARK AVE
GIRDONS WAY
CRESWELL TERR
Slag Heap
Viaduct
Uddingston Gram Sch
Uddingston
CALEY BRAE
NEWTON FARM RD
REDLAWOOD PL
REDLAWOOD RD
NEWTON BRAE
Newton
Mast
Works
Clyde Walkway
Chy
River Clyde
MEADOWBANK LA 1
CROWFLATS RD 2
STRATHCLYDE PATH
FERRY RD
CASTLE PL
MURRAY PATH
GENERALS GATE
KNOWEHEAD GDNS
JAMIESON GDNS
GARDENSIDE AVE
GARDENSIDE ST
EASTER MEWS
COBBLERIGG WAY
OLD GLASGOW RD
MAIN ST
STATION RD
Gardenside
CHURCH ST
WELLBANK
KIRK PL
PORTERS WELL
CASTLECROFT GDNS
POYNTER CT
LOANCROFT GDNS
LOANCROFT GATE
BLANTYRE FARM RD
WESTBURN RD
Redlees Bridge
Townfoot Farm
Hallside Newhouse Farm
CALDER RD
Bothwell Castle Park
Uddingston
Blantyreferme
GATE
VISCOUNT GATE
KNIGHTS GATE
MARQUIS GATE
CASTLE GATE
THANES GATE
LAIRDS GATE
MORAY GATE
SPRINGFIELD GDNS
B756
BELLSHILL RD
LINDAMS
Liby
SPRINGFIELD AVE
DOUGLAS GDNS
BRIGHTSIDE AVE
SUNNYSIDE
G71
G72
BOWLING GN GR
HALLSIDE RD
VALENCE TWR 1
HAMILTON TWR 2
DOUGLAS TWR 3
REGENTS GATE
BARONS GATE
DUKES GATE
LADY JANE GATE
PRINCES GATE
BOTHWELL RD
CH
HORNAL RD
WOODLANDS GDNS
Calderglen
CALDERGLEN AVE
Rotten Calder
Spittal Burn
COUNTESS GATE
EARLS GATE
CASTLE AVE
Bothwell Castle
UDDINGSTON RD 1
WOODLANDS TERR 2
WOODLANDS CRES 3
B7071
MANSE BRAE
Spoil Heap
Craigknowe
JURA DR
KIRKWALL AVE
TARBERT AVE
SUNNINGDALE WYND
TURNBERRY WYND
KILLERMONT MDWS
MOUNT MDWS
CARNOUSTIE CT 1
BIRKDALE CT 2
Spittal Burn
BALMORAL GDNS
MONTROSE GDNS
LAUDER GDNS
NAIRN AVE
BULLER CRES
Priory Plantation
LYTHAM MDWS
MUIRFIELD MDWS
ROYAL GDNS
GLENEAGLES PK
HOYLAKE PK
GAILES PK
BARASSIE CT
ARRAN WAY
A724
HAMILTON RD
DALCRAIG CRES
DALWHINNIE AVE
LINNHE PL
BULLER CL
DOWNFIELD GDNS
Bothwell Prim Sch
Spittal Farm
Priory Bridge
SANQUHAR GDNS
LOCHALSH PL
KYLEAKEN TERR
GORDON TERR
MOSSGIEL
NORTHWAY
MILLANDS AVE
BELLAIRS PL
CARLOWRIE AVE
ZAMBESI DR
LINTLAW
HILLVIEW DR
DEVONDALE AVE
Works
Coatshill
David Livingstone Meml Prim Sch
David Livingstone Ctr
BLANTYRE MILL RD
Recr Gd
ANNFIELD GDNS 1
DECHMONT GDNS 2
BURNS GDNS 3
GLASGOW RD
B758
STRATHMORE AVE
MORVEN AVE
LIME GR
GLENVIEW
CRAIGTON PL
LIVINGSTONE CRES
DALY GDNS
NESS GDNS
WINNING CT
BEECROFT PL
ANDERSON GDNS
Clyde Walkway
Sewage Works
CLYDE AVE
GRIEVE CROFT
Caldergrove House
CALLAGHAN WYND
MORAG AVE
SOUTH VIEW
COATSHILL AVE
ROSELEA PL
KILBURN GR
ABIEGAIL PL
HOLMSWOOD AVE
MOFFAT PL
THORNHILL AVE
NESS DR
VIEWFIELD AVE
STATION RD
CASTLE DR
ROSEBANK AVE
Bardykes
HERBERTSON GR
BARDYKES RD
CYPRESS
CEDAR PL
POPLAR
LOUDHOWE TERR
MELROSE PL
BERKELEY DR
HEATHCLIFFE AVE
CRAWFORD CRES
MYRTLE ST
COWAN AVE
WILSON AVE
FARM RD
MANUS RD
DUDLEY
A724
B758
WALLACE PL
BRUCE TERR
VILLAGE TERR
GDNS

121
142

A8
1 YOUNG PL
2 WALKER PATH
3 CHRIGHTON GN
4 MUIRHEAD GATE
5 PRENTICE LA
6 HADDOW GR
7 CAMPSIE VIEW
8 OCHIL VIEW
9 KILPATRICK WAY
10 RUSSELL GDNS
11 BAILLE WYND
12 KIRKWOOD RD

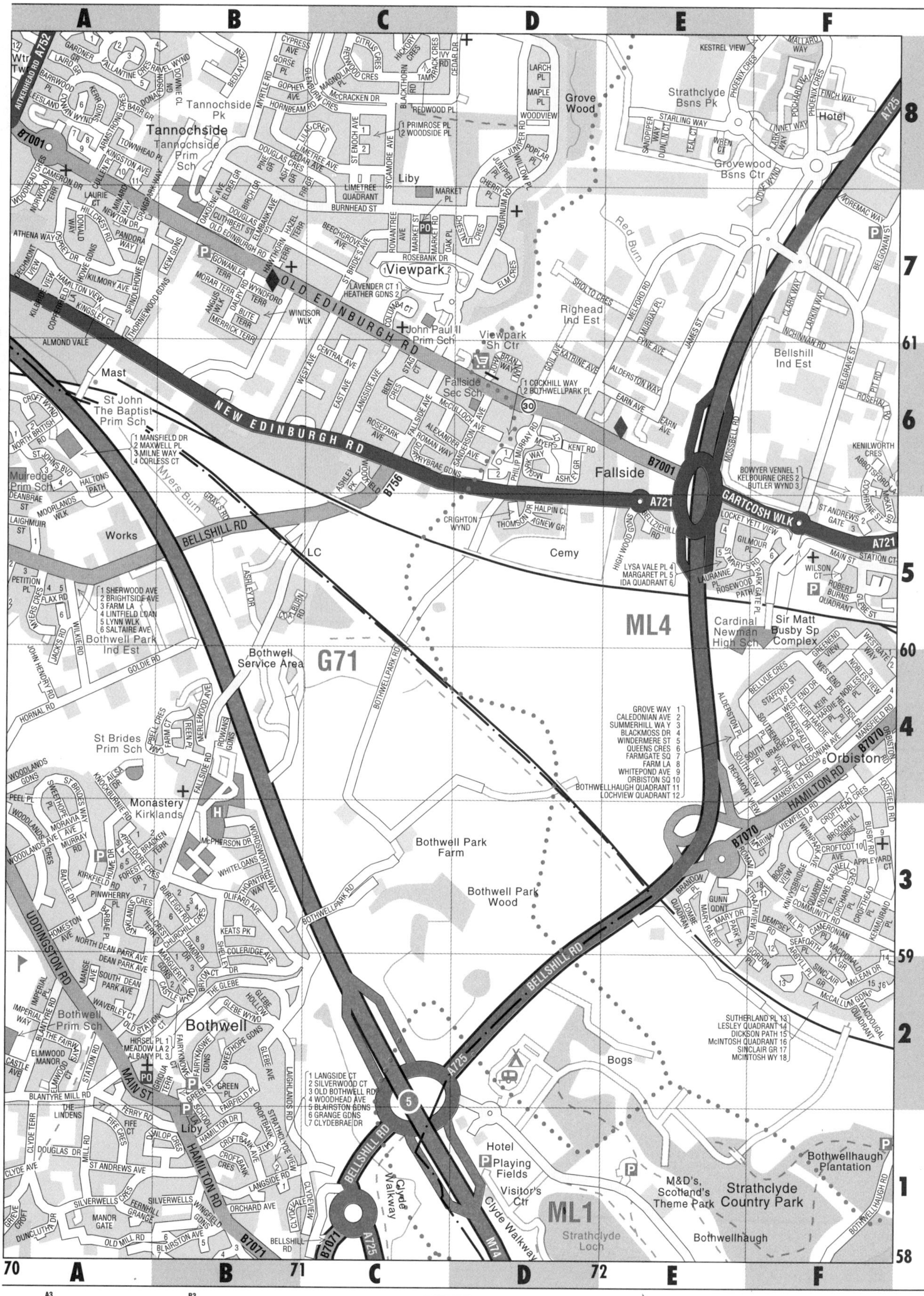

A3
1 KELVIN WAY
2 APPIN WAY
3 LIVINGSTONE LA
4 BELSTANE PL
5 KATRINE WAY
6 RANNOCH WAY
7 CARRICK WAY

B3
1 MORVEN WAY
2 TANTALLON RD
3 ROSEBANK LA
4 THORNHILL LA
5 ALDERSIDE PL
6 BARNSWOOD PL
7 MALLARD LA
8 NEWFIELD LA
9 HOZIER PL

162
142

141
122

141
163

123
144

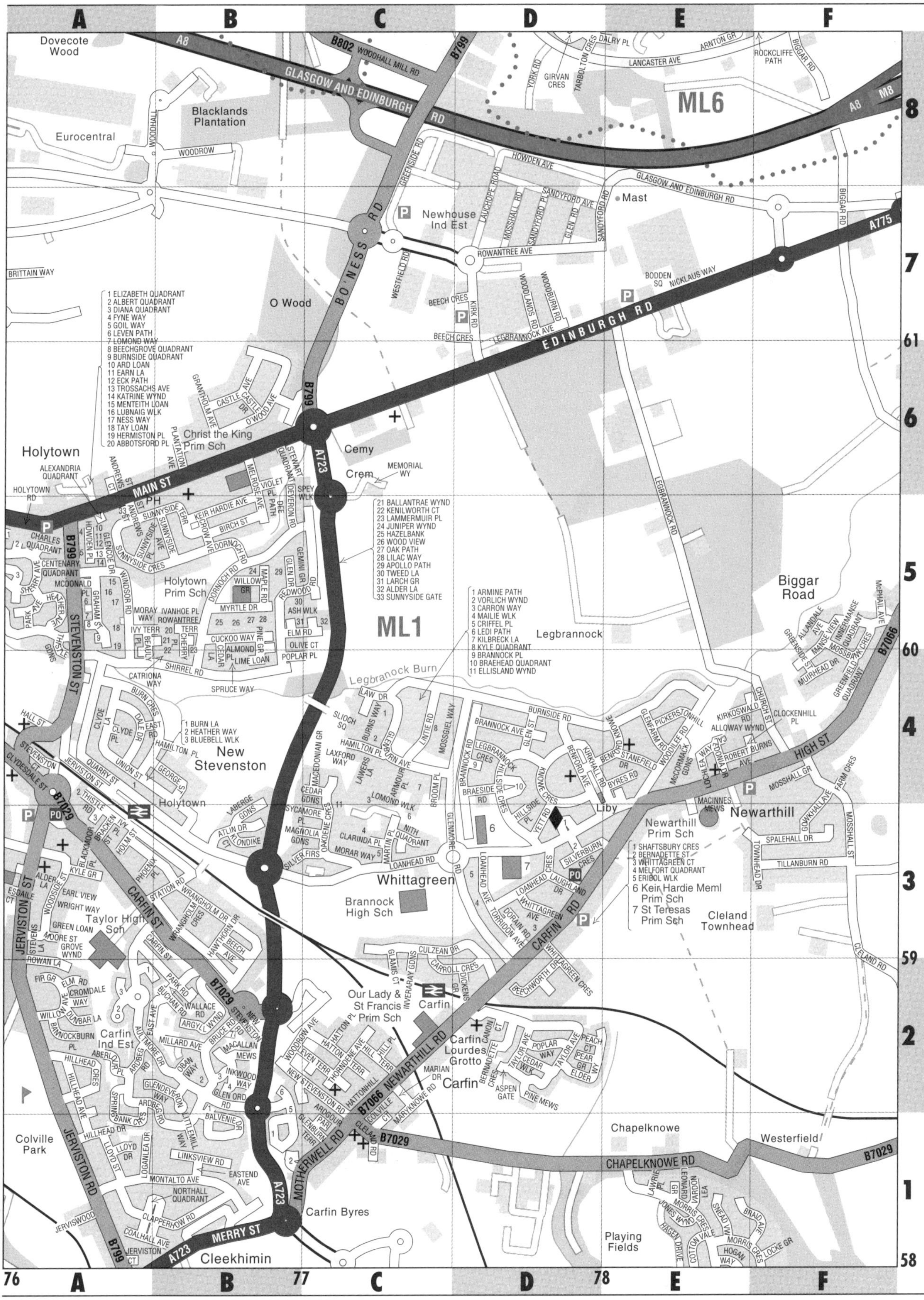

A2
1 DALMORE CRES
2 INCHGOWER PL
3 GLENGOYNE DR

B1
1 DERBY WYND
2 BYRESKNOWE LA

B2
1 LONGMORN PL
2 LOCHRANZA CT
3 STRATHISLA WAY
4 BLAIRATHOL WYND
5 ST MUNGOS CRES
6 THE LAURELS
7 MONTROSE CT

164
144

143
124

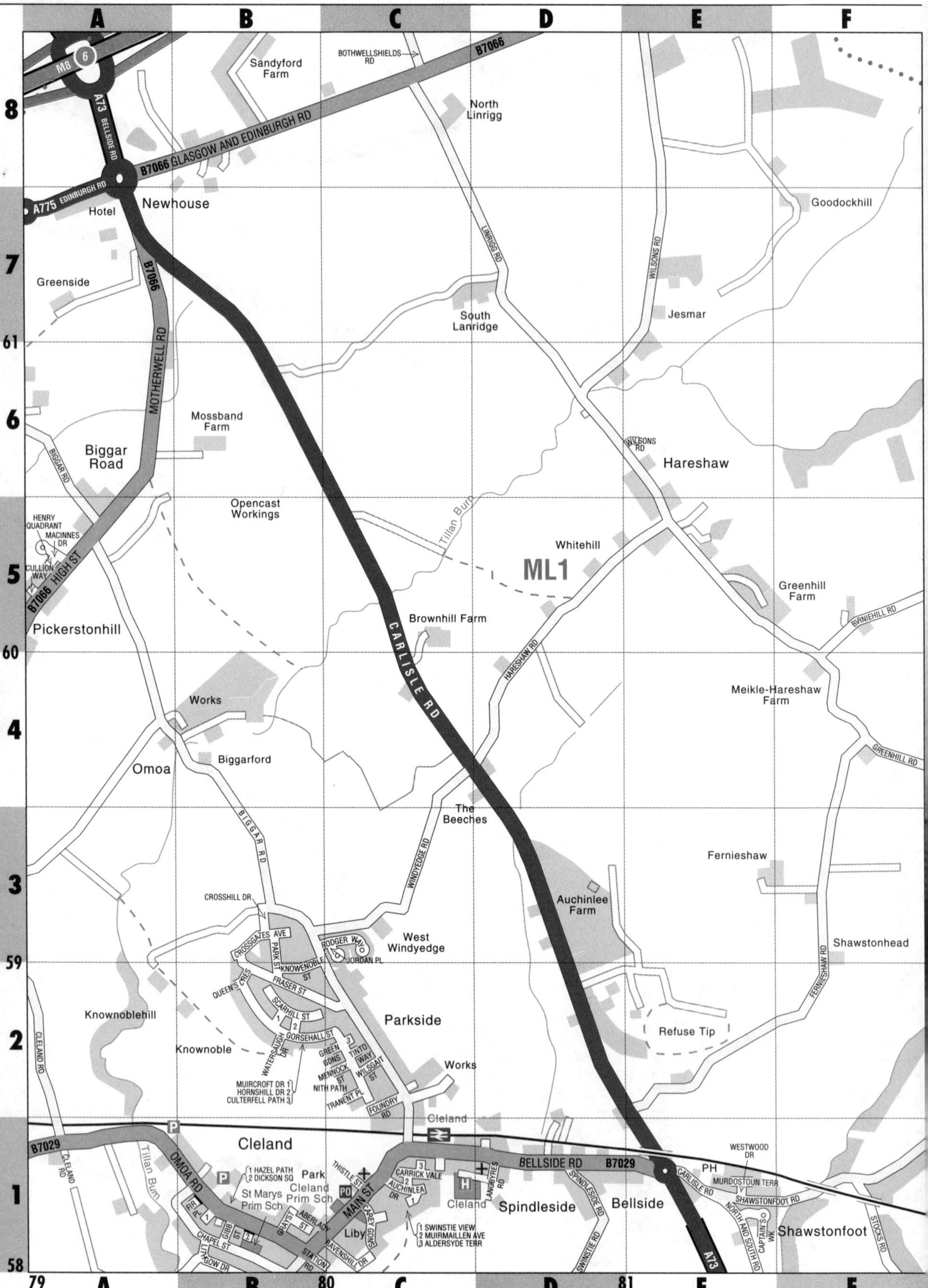

143
165

125
146
A
B
C
D
E
F
Spoil Tip
Well Hill
8
MANSE RD
Westfield
Fortissat View
Roughdike
Mains
Jersay
7
Law's Castle
Tillan Burn
61
6
MUIREDGE AND JERSY RD
ML7
Pell Hill
BIRNIEHILL RD
Pellhill Wood
Muirhouse
5
Mine (dis)
Heatherhead Plantation
Hareshaw Moss
60
ML1
4
GREENHILL RD
Mast
3
Home Farm
HOME FARM RD
ASHGROVE
Hartwood
NEWMILL GDNS
CANTHILL GDNS
59
HARTWOOD GDNS
Penty
MUIREDGE AND JERSY RD
HARTWOOD RD
2
Hill of Murdostoun
Penty Wood
FOULBURN RD
BOWHOUSEBOG RD
Newmill Cottage
SHAWSTONFOOT RD
Big Wood
Newmill Wood
1
ML2
Muiredge Wood
MURDOSTOUN RD
MILL RD
ALLANTON RD
58
82
83
84
166
146

145
126

145
167

127

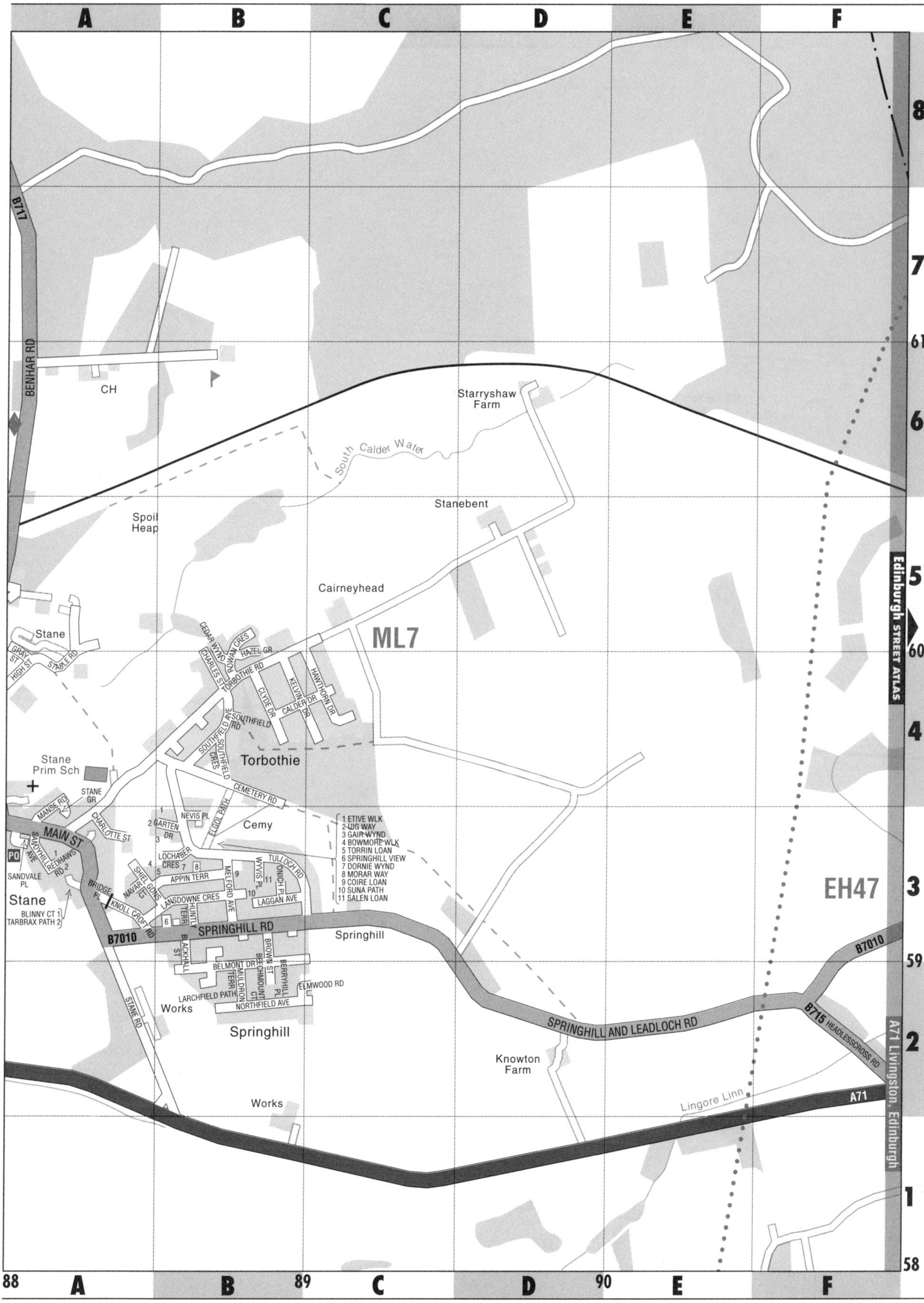
A B C D E F
8
7
61
6
5
60
4
3
59
2
1
58
88 89 90
B717
BENHAR RD
CH
Starryshaw Farm
South Calder Water
Stanebent
Spoil Heap
Cairneyhead
ML7
Edinburgh STREET ATLAS
Stane
GRAY ST
HIGH ST
STABLE RD
CEDAR WYND
ROWAN CRES
HAZEL GR
CHARLES ST
TORBOTHIE RD
CLYDE DR
KELVIN DR
CALDER DR
HAWTHORN DR
SOUTHFIELD AVE
SOUTHFIELD RD
SOUTHFIELD CRES
Torbothie
Stane Prim Sch
STANE GR
MANSE RD
CEMETERY RD
ELGOL PATH
NEVIS PL
GARTEN DR
Cemy
CHARLOTTE ST
MAIN ST
PO
SANDYHILL AVE
REDHAWS RD
SANDVALE PL
Stane
BLINNY CT 1
TARBRAX PATH 2
LOCHABER CRES
SHIEL GDNS
NAVAR CT
APPIN TERR
MELFORD AVE
WYVIS PL
ONICH PL
TULLOCH RD
LANSDOWNE CRES
LAGGAN AVE
HUNTLY TERR
BRIDGE PL
KNOLL CROFT RD
1 ETIVE WLK
2 UIG WAY
3 GAIR WYND
4 BOWMORE WLK
5 TORRIN LOAN
6 SPRINGHILL VIEW
7 DORNIE WYND
8 MORAR WAY
9 COIRE LOAN
10 SUNA PATH
11 SALEN LOAN
EH47
B7010
SPRINGHILL RD
Springhill
BLACKHALL ST
BROWN ST
BERRYHILL PL
BELMONT DR
BEECHMOUNT CT
MULDRON TERR
ELMWOOD RD
LARCHFIELD PATH
NORTHFIELD AVE
Works
Springhill
STANE RD
SPRINGHILL AND LEADLOCH RD
B7010
B715 HEADLESSCROSS RD
A71 Livingston, Edinburgh
Knowton Farm
Lingore Linn
A71
Works

168

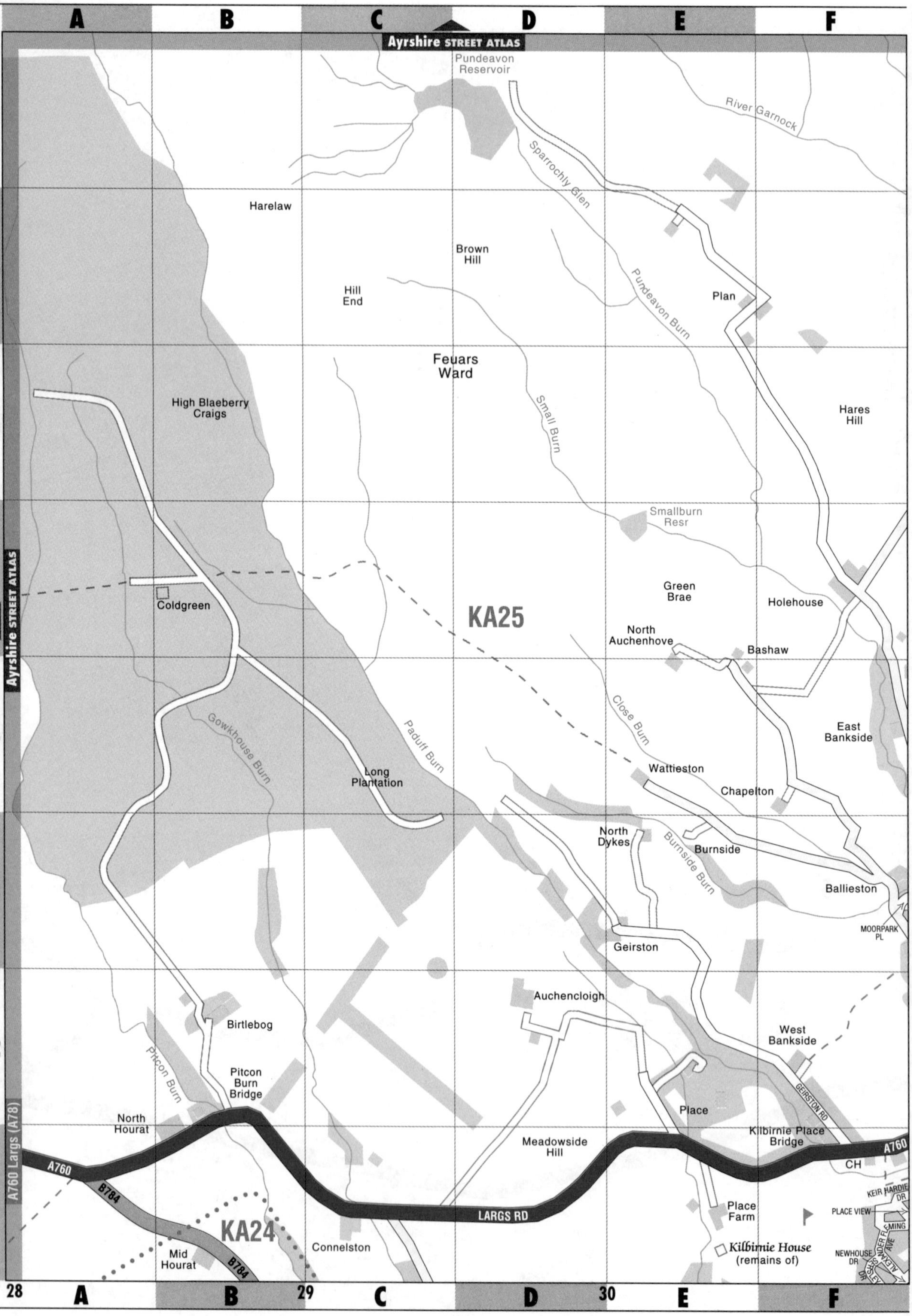
A
B
C
D
E
F
Ayrshire STREET ATLAS
Pundeavon Reservoir
River Garnock
Sparrochly Glen
Harelaw
Brown Hill
Hill End
Plan
Pundeavon Burn
8
7
57
6
5
56
4
3
55
2
1
54
Feuars Ward
High Blaeberry Craigs
Small Burn
Hares Hill
Smallburn Resr
Green Brae
Holehouse
Coldgreen
KA25
North Auchenhove
Bashaw
Ayrshire STREET ATLAS
East Bankside
Gowkhouse Burn
Paduff Burn
Close Burn
Long Plantation
Wattieston
Chapelton
North Dykes
Burnside Burn
Burnside
Ballieston
MOORPARK PL
Geirston
Auchencloigh
Birtlebog
West Bankside
Pitcon Burn
Pitcon Burn Bridge
GEIRSTON RD
North Hourat
Place
Kilbirnie Place Bridge
Meadowside Hill
A760 Largs (A78)
A760
A760
B784
CH
LARGS RD
KEIR HARDIE DR
PLACE VIEW
Place Farm
KA24
Kilbirnie House (remains of)
Mid Hourat
Connelston
B784
NEWHOUSE DR
28
29
30
A
B
C
D
E
F

169

128
150

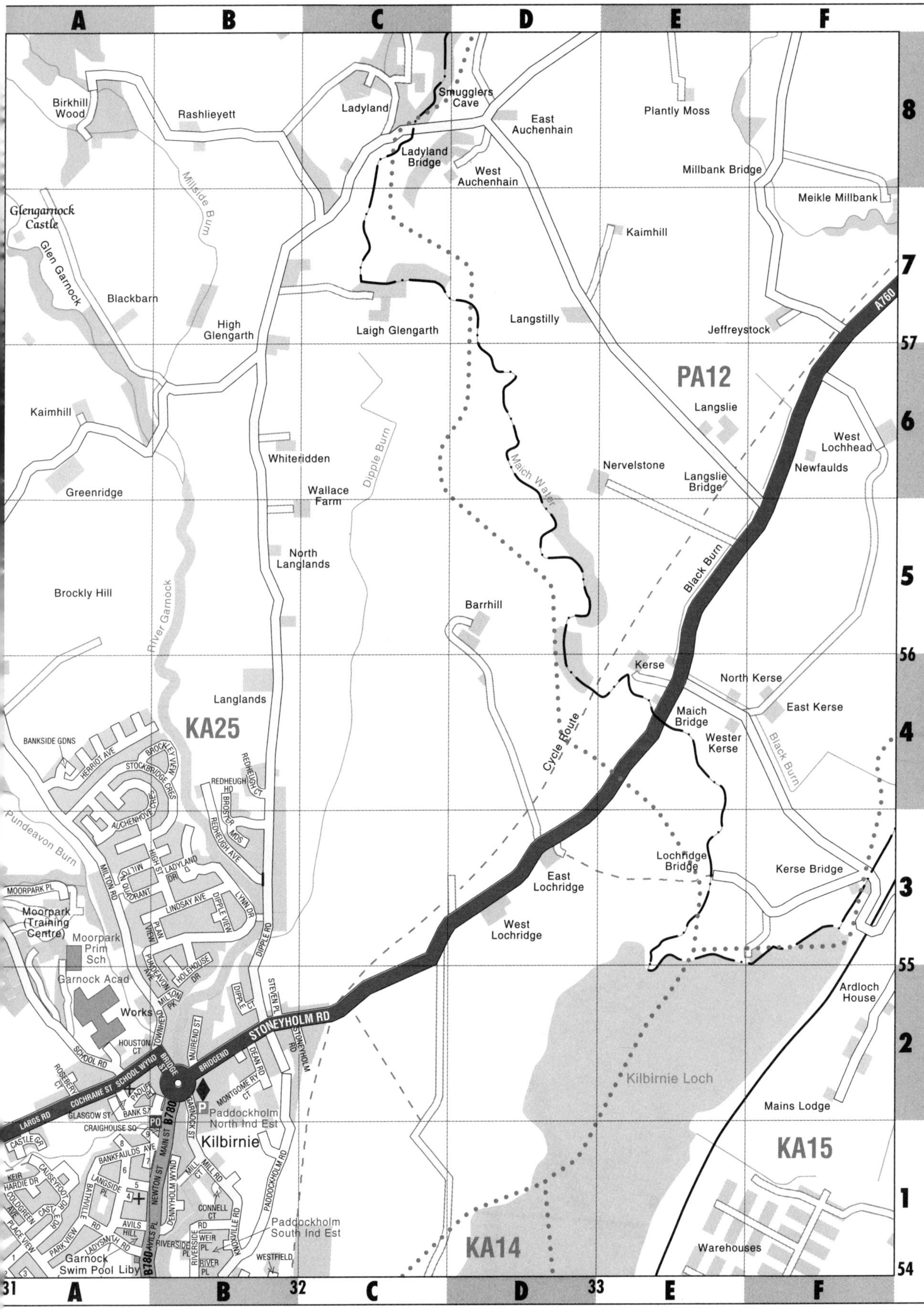
A
B
C
D
E
F
8
7
57
6
5
56
4
3
55
2
1
54
31
32
33
Birkhill Wood
Rashlieyett
Ladyland
Smugglers Cave
East Auchenhain
Plantly Moss
Ladyland Bridge
West Auchenhain
Millbank Bridge
Meikle Millbank
Glengarnock Castle
Glen Garnock
Millside Burn
Kaimhill
Blackbarn
High Glengarth
Laigh Glengarth
Langstilly
Jeffreystock
A760
PA12
Langslie
Kaimhill
Dipple Burn
Whiteridden
Maich Water
Nervelstone
Langslie Bridge
West Lochhead
Newfaulds
Greenridge
Wallace Farm
North Langlands
Black Burn
Brockly Hill
Barrhill
River Garnock
Kerse
North Kerse
Langlands
KA25
Maich Bridge
East Kerse
Wester Kerse
Cycle Route
Black Burn
BANKSIDE GDNS
HERRIOT AVE
STOCKBRIDGE CRES
BROCKLEY VIEW
REDHEUGH HO
REDHEUGH CT
BROSTER MDS
REDHEUGH AVE
AUCHENHOVE CRES
Pundeavon Burn
MILTON RD
HIGH ST
LADYLAND DR
Lochridge Bridge
East Lochridge
Kerse Bridge
MOORPARK PL
Moorpark (Training Centre)
QUADRANT
LINDSAY AVE
LYNN DR
DIPPLE VIEW
Moorpark Prim Sch
PLAN VIEW
PUNDEAVON AVE
HOLEHOUSE DR
West Lochridge
Garnock Acad
MILTON PK
DIPPLE CT
DIPPLE RD
STEVEN PL
Ardloch House
Works
TOWNHEAD
MUIREND ST
STONEYHOLM RD
SCHOOL RD
HOUSTON CT
BRIDGE ST
BRIDGEND
DEAN RD
STONEYHOLM RD
ROSEBERY CT
SCHOOL WYND
COCHRANE ST
PADUFF
MONTGOMERY CT
Kilbirnie Loch
LARGS RD
GLASGOW ST
BANK ST
B780
P
Paddockholm North Ind Est
Mains Lodge
CRAIGHOUSE SQ
PO
GARNOCK ST
Kilbirnie
CASTLE GR
BANKFAULDS AVE
KA15
KEIR HARDIE DR
CAUSEYFOOT DR
LANGSIDE PL
NEWTON ST
MAIN ST
DENNYHOLM WYND
MILL CT
MILL RD
PADDOCKHOLM RD
COLDGREEN AVE
CASTLE DR
BATHVILLE RD
CONNELL CT
AVILS HILL
AVILS PL
Paddockholm South Ind Est
PLACE VIEW
PARK VIEW
LADYSMITH RD
RIVERSIDE PL
RIVERSIDE RD
WEIR PL
KNOXVILLE RD
KA14
Warehouses
Garnock Swim Pool Liby
RIVER PL
WESTFIELD

A1
1 NEWHOUSE DR
2 BROWNHILL DR
3 LADESIDE CT
4 GARNOCK CT
5 WALKER ST
6 PARKHOUSE DR
7 BANKFAULDS CT
8 MONTGOMERIESTON PL
9 MONTGOMERIESTON ST

170
150

149
129

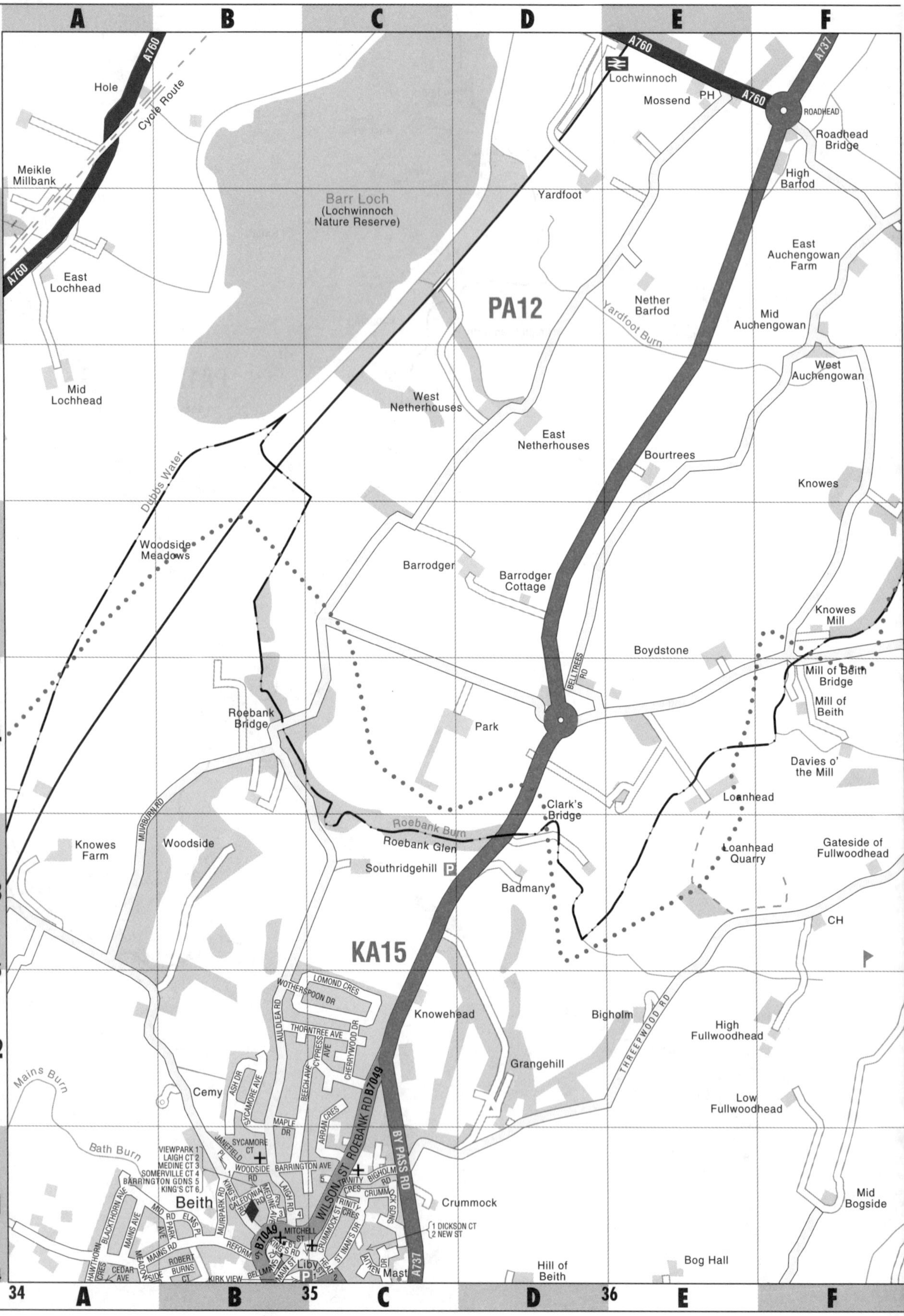

149
171

130
152

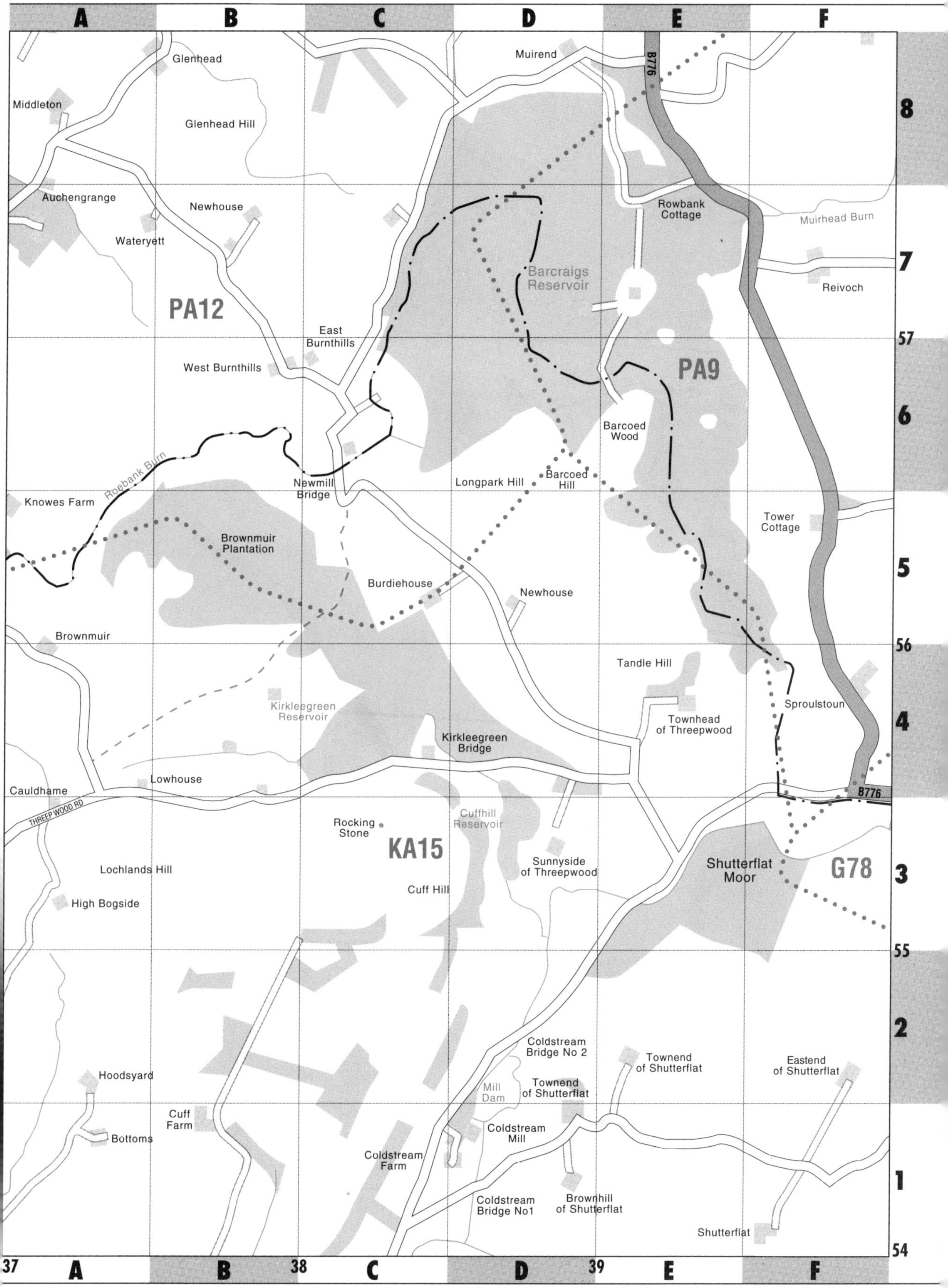

172
152

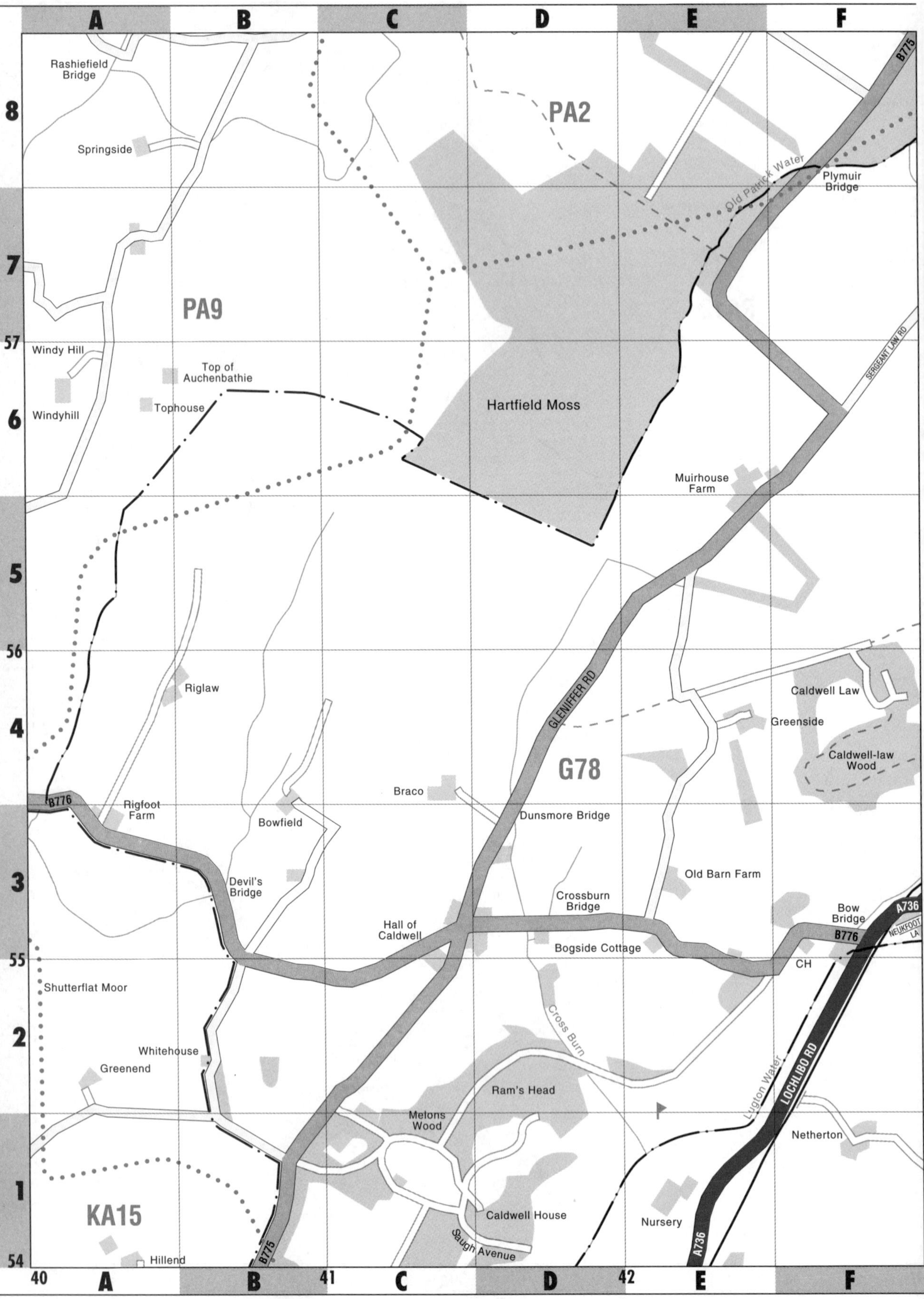
151
131
A
B
C
D
E
F
8
7
57
6
5
56
4
3
55
2
1
54
40
41
42
Rashiefield Bridge
Springside
PA2
B775
Old Patrick Water
Plymuir Bridge
PA9
Windy Hill
Top of Auchenbathie
Windyhill
Tophouse
Hartfield Moss
SERGEANT LAW RD
Muirhouse Farm
GLENIFFER RD
Riglaw
Caldwell Law
Greenside
Caldwell-law Wood
G78
B776
Rigfoot Farm
Bowfield
Braco
Dunsmore Bridge
Devil's Bridge
Old Barn Farm
Crossburn Bridge
Hall of Caldwell
Bow Bridge
A736
NEUKFOOT LA
Bogside Cottage
CH
Shutterflat Moor
Cross Burn
Whitehouse
Greenend
Ram's Head
Lugton Water
LOCHLIBO RD
Melons Wood
Netherton
KA15
Caldwell House
Nursery
Saugh Avenue
Hillend

151
173

132
154

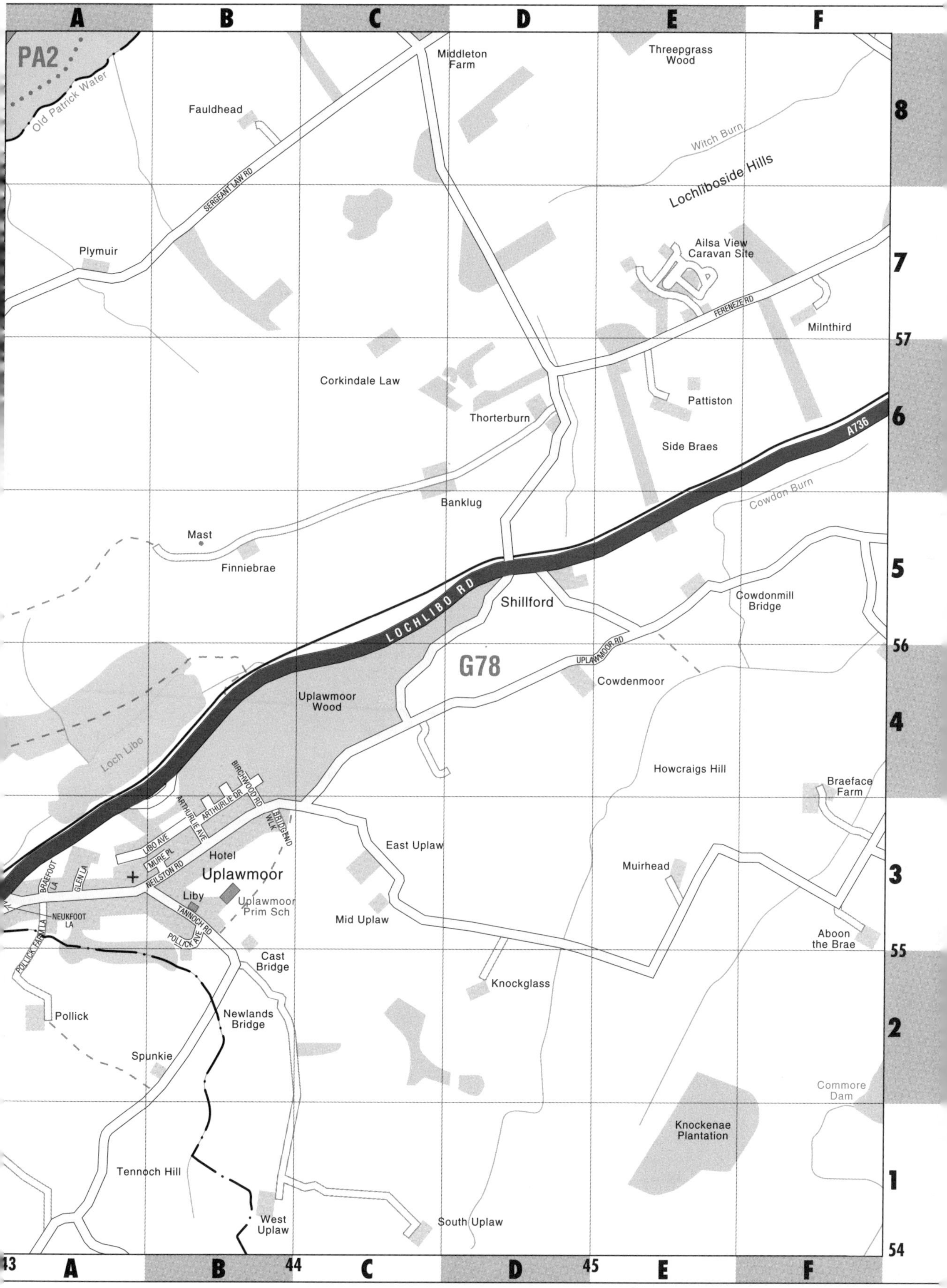

174
154

153
133

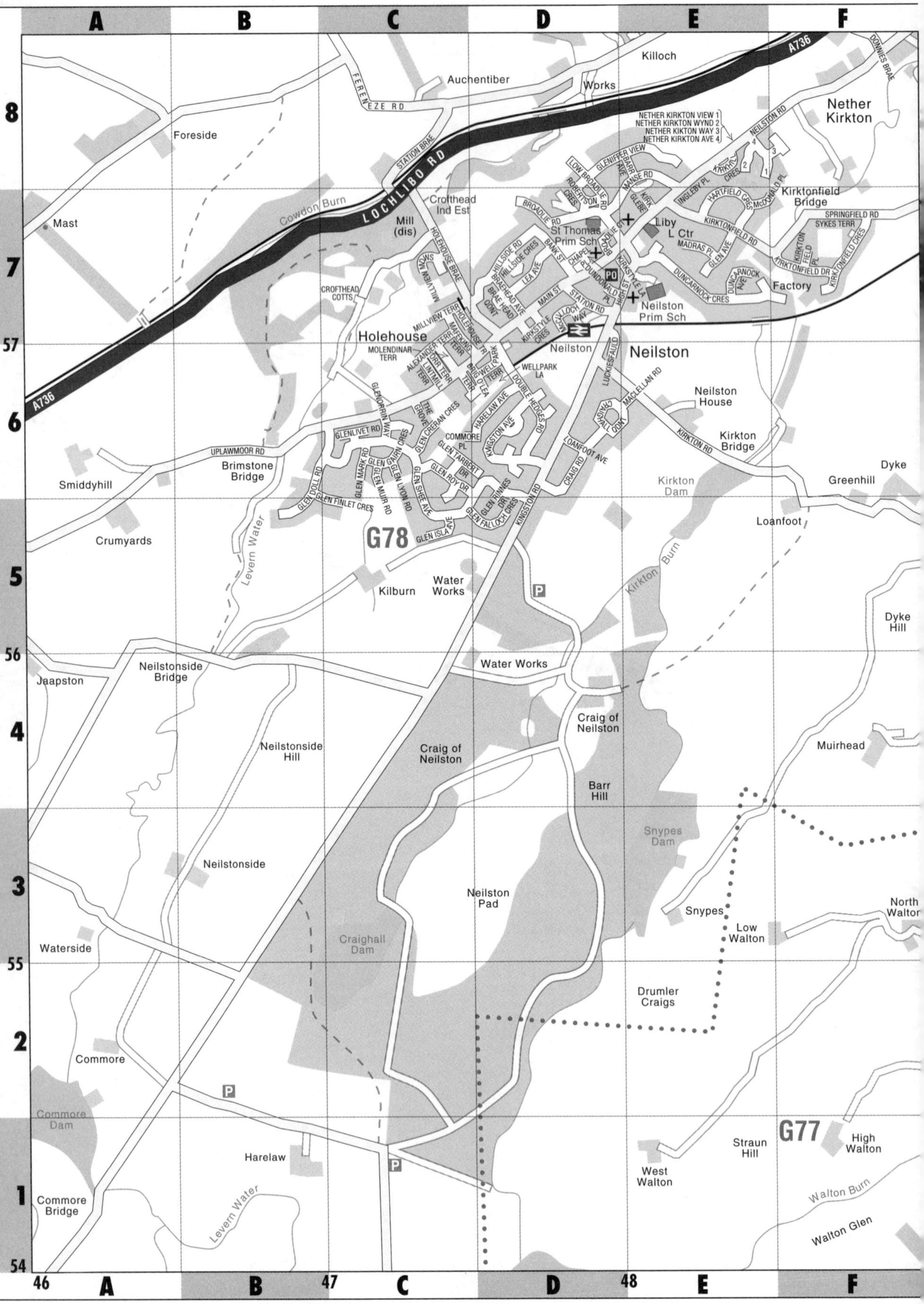

153
175

134
156

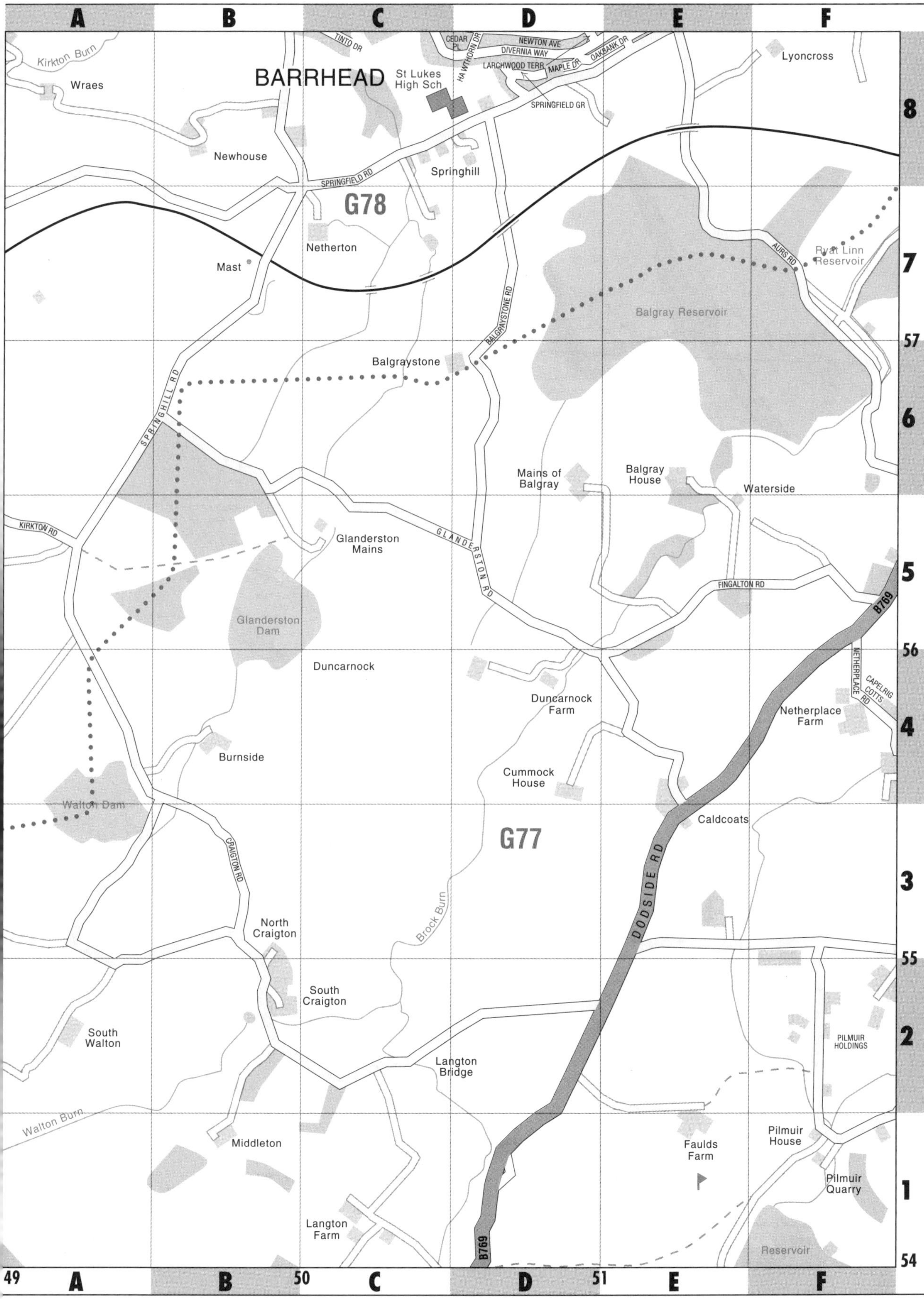

176
156

155
135

G78
Waulkmill Glen Resr
Walden
Patterton
Tower
Rouken Glen Park
G46
CAPELRIG DR
BARCAPEL AVE
Barcapel Holm Farm
Eastwood High Sch
Auldhouse Burn
Ryat
Ryat Linn Resr
Craigend
Greenlaw
STEWARTON RD
M77
B769
B7087
Crookfur Prim Sch
CROOKFUR RDBT
Capelrig Burn
Crookfur
Broom Burn
NETHERTON RD
THE BEECHES
A77
Todhill
West Lodge
Mast
B769
WESTCROSS RDBT
St Cadocs Prim Sch
Broom
Parklands Country Club
G77
Newton Mearns
The Avenue Sh Ctr
Liby
AYR RD
Works
Lofts
Malletsheugh
Mearns Prim Sch
MALLETSHEUGH RDBT
Mearns
Cemy
White Hill
PH
Pilmuir Holdings
Faside House
Maidenhill Farm
Humbie House
Westfield
East Titwood
Earn Water
A726
TITWOOD RD
MEARNS RD
HAZELDEN RD
52
53
54
54
55
56
57
A
B
C
D
E
F
1
2
3
4
5
6
7
8

136
158

178
158

157
137

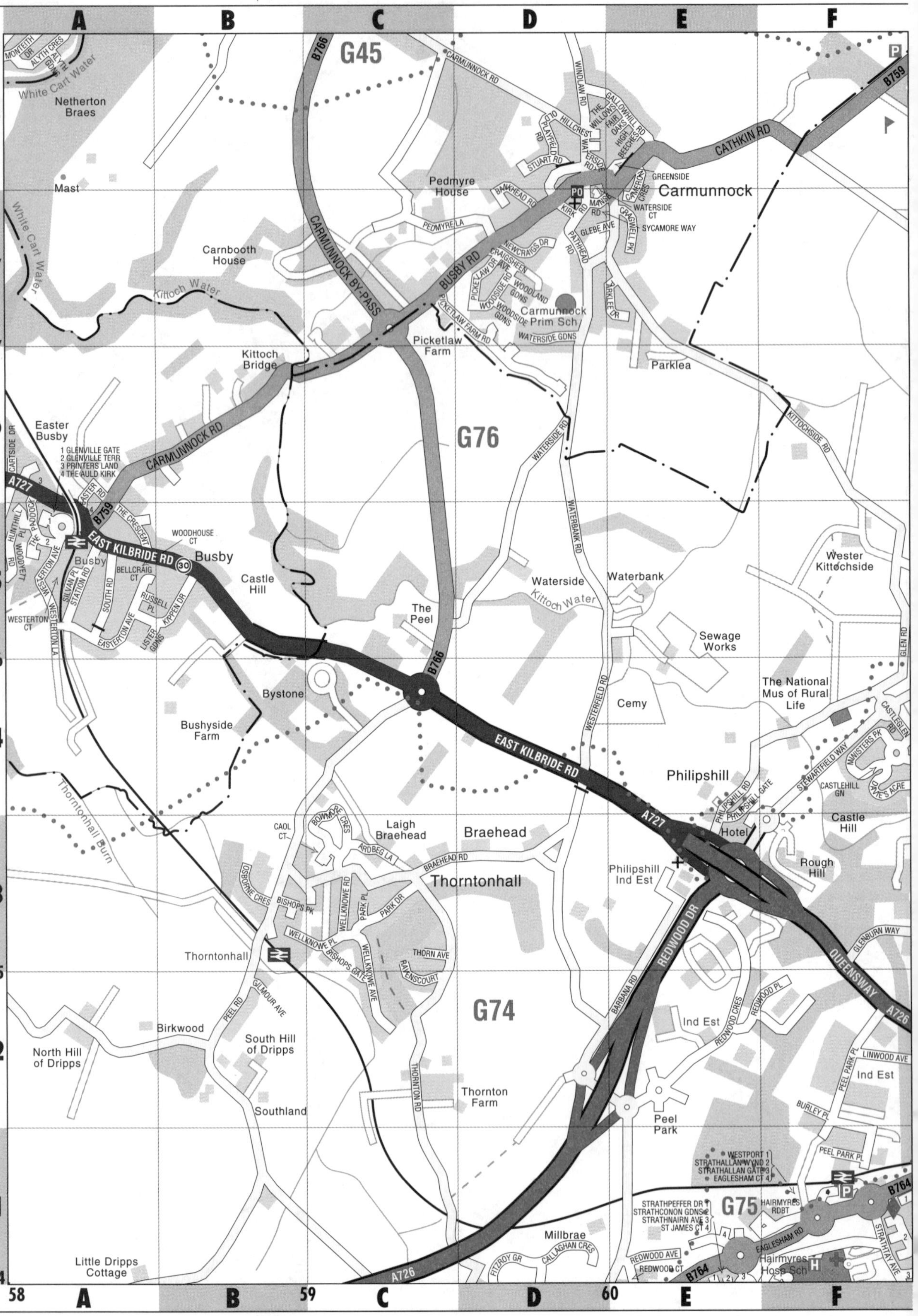

157
179

138
160

A
B
C
D
E
F
8
7
57
6
5
56
4
3
55
2
1
54
61
62
63
CATHKIN RD
South Cathkin Farm
SOUTH CATHKIN COTTS
G73
G72
Muir Farm
Works
G76
Bellcraig
Highflat Farm
Mast
CAIRNMUIR RD
NERSTON RD
East Rogerton Lodge Farm
Rogerton
West Rogerton
Kingsgate Ret Pk
MAINS RD
Kittochside
High Mains
Lee's Burn
EAST KILBRIDE
Mains Castle
Law Knowe
Laigh Mains
KITTOCHSIDE RD
Eastend
Dykehead Farm
East Kittochside Farm
WELLS QUARRY RD
MARKETHILL RD
CARMUNNOCK RD
James Hamilton Heritage Park
STEWARTFIELD WAY
LAW PL
Ind Est
MACARTHUR CRES 1
BURNET ROSE CT 2
BURNET ROSE PL 3
MACARTHUR CT 4
WENSLEYDALE 5
WINTERGREEN DR 6
KILDRUMMY PL 7
SANDALWOOD CT 8
STEWARTFIELD GDNS 9
G74
Stewartfield
Nerston
LAW RDBT
Mast
Cemy
MAVOR RDBT
MAVOR AVE
B783
MARKETHILL RDBT
LADYKIRK WAY
EAST MAINS RD
PH
Ind Est
HAWBANK RD
College Milton
Kittoch Water
STEWARTFIELD CRES
CAIRNRYAN
HAWBANK RDBT
ROSENHEATH GATE
1 DOONFOOT CT
2 DALMELLINGTON CT
St Kenneths Prim Sch
East Mains
1 GLENBURN CT
2 GLENBURN WAY
Ind Est
WEST MAINS RD
Kirktonhole Prim Sch
LADYBANK CT
KIRKTON GATE
East Kilbride
B761
MILTON RD
LINWOOD AVE
The Tennant Complex
Ind Est
NEIDPATH E 3
NEIDPATH W 4
PRIESTKNOWE RDBT
B764
EAGLESHAM RD
West Mains
5 ST LAWRENCE PK
6 RAYMOND PL
7 LE FROY GDNS
Civic Centre
THE CENTRE RDBT
QUEENSWAY
East Milton Prim Sch
Duncanrig Sec Sch
G75
VANCOUVER CT 1
SUDBURY CRES 2
A726
RIGHEAD RDBT
East Kilbride Sh Ctr
1 CORNWALL WAY
2 OLYMPIA WAY

A1
1 NASSAU PL
2 MONTEGO GN
3 TRINIDAD GN
4 DOMINICA GN
5 BARBADOS GN
6 BAHAMAS WAY
7 WATLING PL
8 AUCKLAND PK
9 HAVELOCK PK
10 STRATHALLAN WYND
11 STRATHALLAN GATE
12 STRATHALLAN AVE

180
160

F2
1 WEAVERS CT
2 LADYBANK PL
3 MONTGOMERY PL
4 MONTGOMERY ST
5 KITTOCH PL
6 ELIZABETH CT
7 WELLBECK HO
8 ST BRYDE ST

159
139

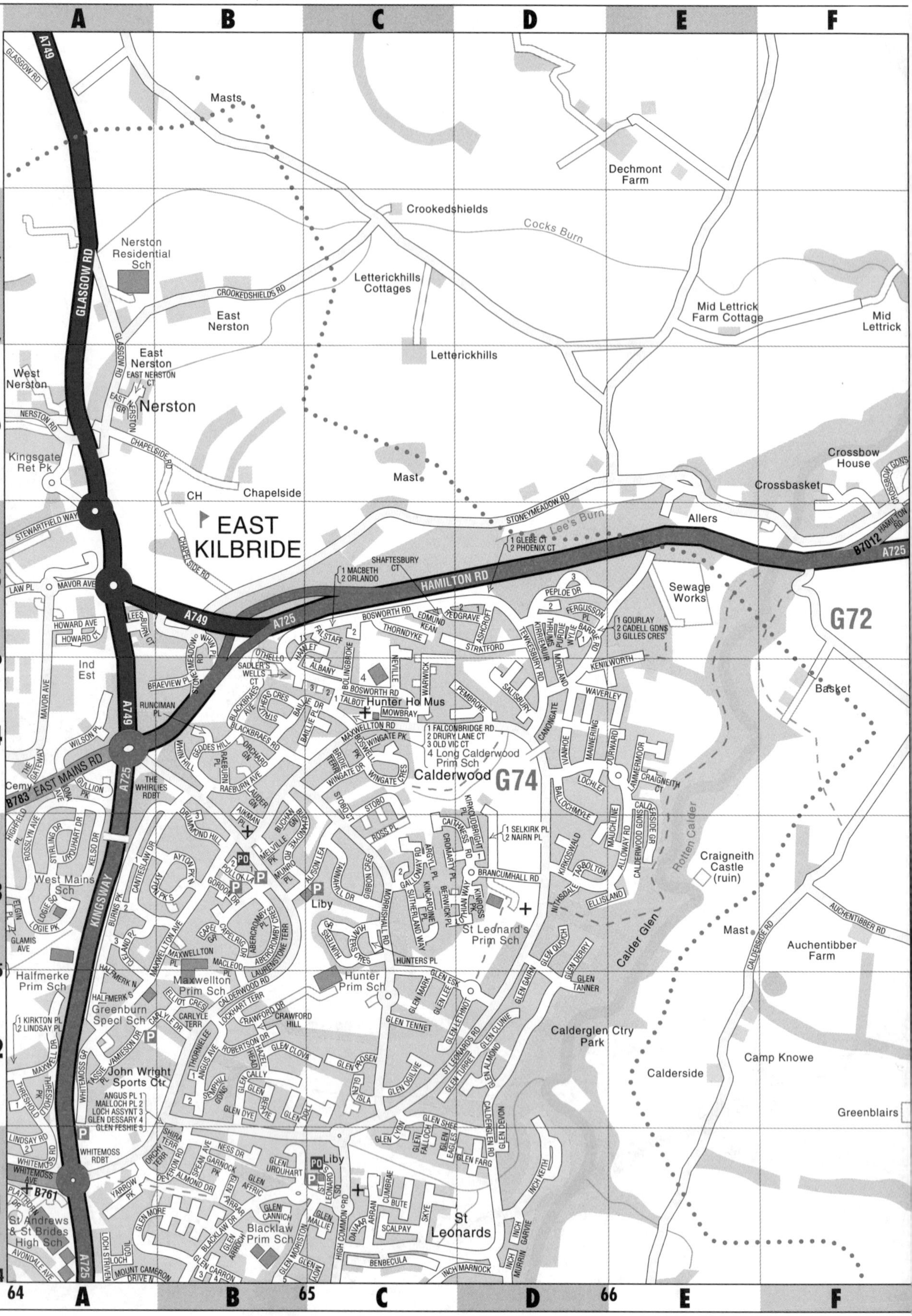

A3
1 SCOTT HILL
2 ETTRICK HILL
3 RAMSAY HILL

B3
1 CALDERWOOD SQ
2 POLLOK PL
3 DRUMMOND PL

159
181

C6
1 CAERLAVEROCK PL
2 SANDALE PATH
3 MALVAIG LA

D7
1 DRYBURGH WAY
2 ALLENDALE PATH
3 BARNETT PATH
4 CAUSEYSTANES
5 ROXBURGH PL
6 GREENBANK
7 LIBERTY PATH
8 LOCHABER PATH
9 MADISON PATH
10 TOURNAI PATH

140

162

E7
1 ELM CT
2 HERBERTSON ST
3 NORDIC GDNS
4 ALPINE WLK
5 ALPINE PATH
6 NORDIC GR
7 ANFORD LA

182

D3
1 DALBEATTIE DR
2 THORN AVE
3 GLAMIS CRES
4 GLAMIS LA
5 BLACKCRAIG BRAE
6 KIRKMAIDEN WY

162

E3
1 TOWNHILL TERR
2 GLAMIS GAIT

A5
1 GLADSTONE CT
2 LIMETREE CT
3 GEORGE STEWART GDNS
4 WILSON CT
5 GEORGE CT
6 BURNBANK GDNS
7 GEORGES CL
8 Glenlee Prim Sch
9 Hamilton Sch for the Deaf
10 St Cuthberts Prim Sch

161

A6
1 PARKWOOD LEA
2 PARKWOOD TERR
3 JAMES MURDIE GDNS
4 ALBERT LA

141

B5
1 COPPERWOOD CT
2 COPPERWOOD WYND
3 COPPERWOOD CRES

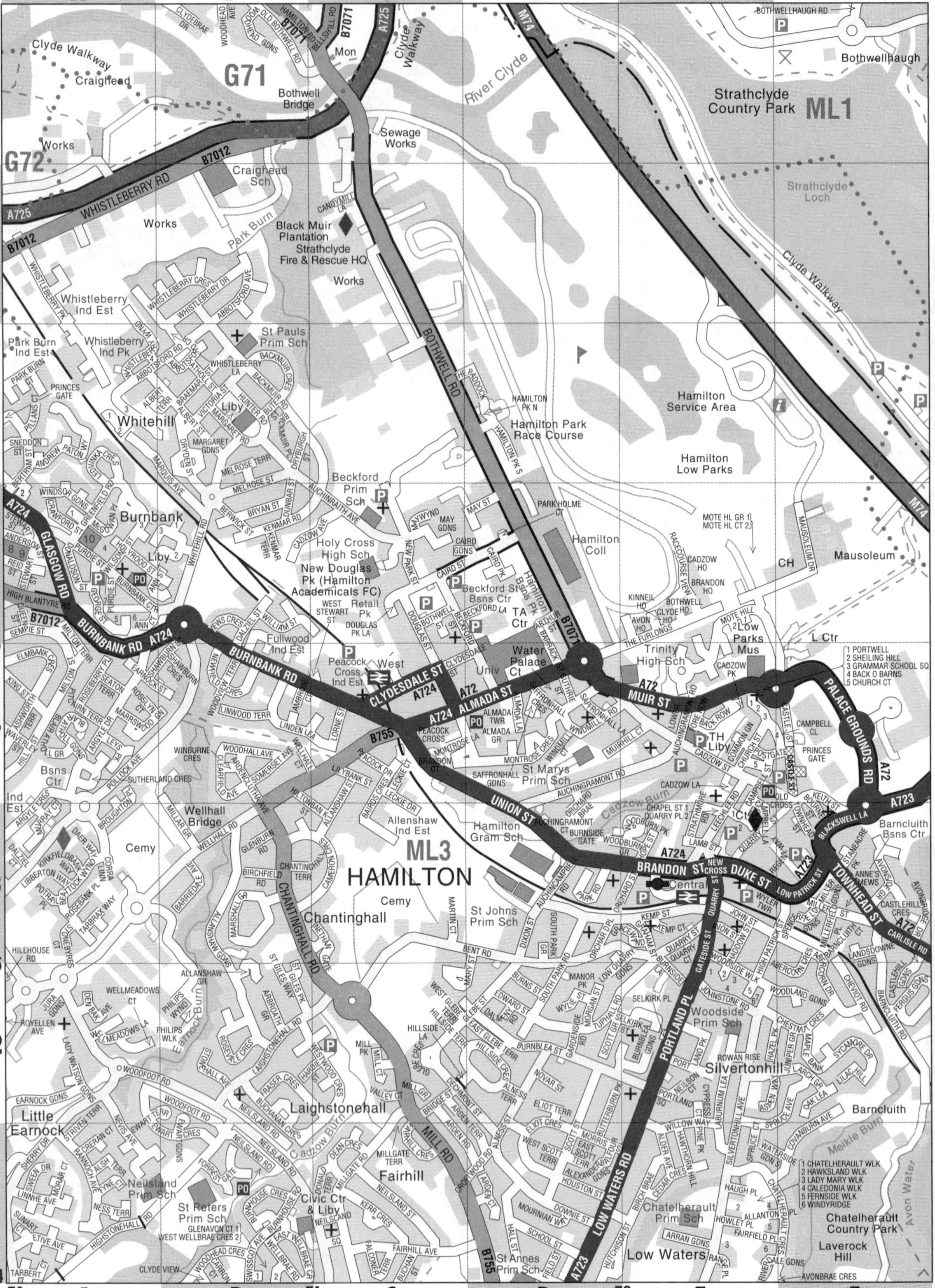

161

183

E2
1 BROWN ST
2 CENTENARY GDNS
3 WEAVERS CT
4 WOODSIDE CT
5 WOODSIDE AVE
6 CARLTON CT
7 HILTON CT

C8
1 MARIUS CRES
2 SENATE PL
3 MARCUS WY
4 TARQUIN PL

142

D8
1 LANTANA GR
2 Braidhurst Ind Est
3 FINDLAY CT
4 CERES PL
5 Muir St Prim Sch

164

E5
1 OAKFIELD TWR
2 ALBION TWR
3 McCLURG CT
4 ELVAN TWR
5 KERR GRIEVE CT
6 CALDER TWR
7 AVON TWR
8 CLYDE TWR

E6
1 BRANDON ARC
2 OAKFIELD DR
3 WATSONVILLE PK
4 WATSON ST

F5
1 GLENCAIRN TWR
2 CAIRN CT
3 MACDONALD ST
4 CIVIC SQ
5 BLAIR PATH
6 ELLIS WAY

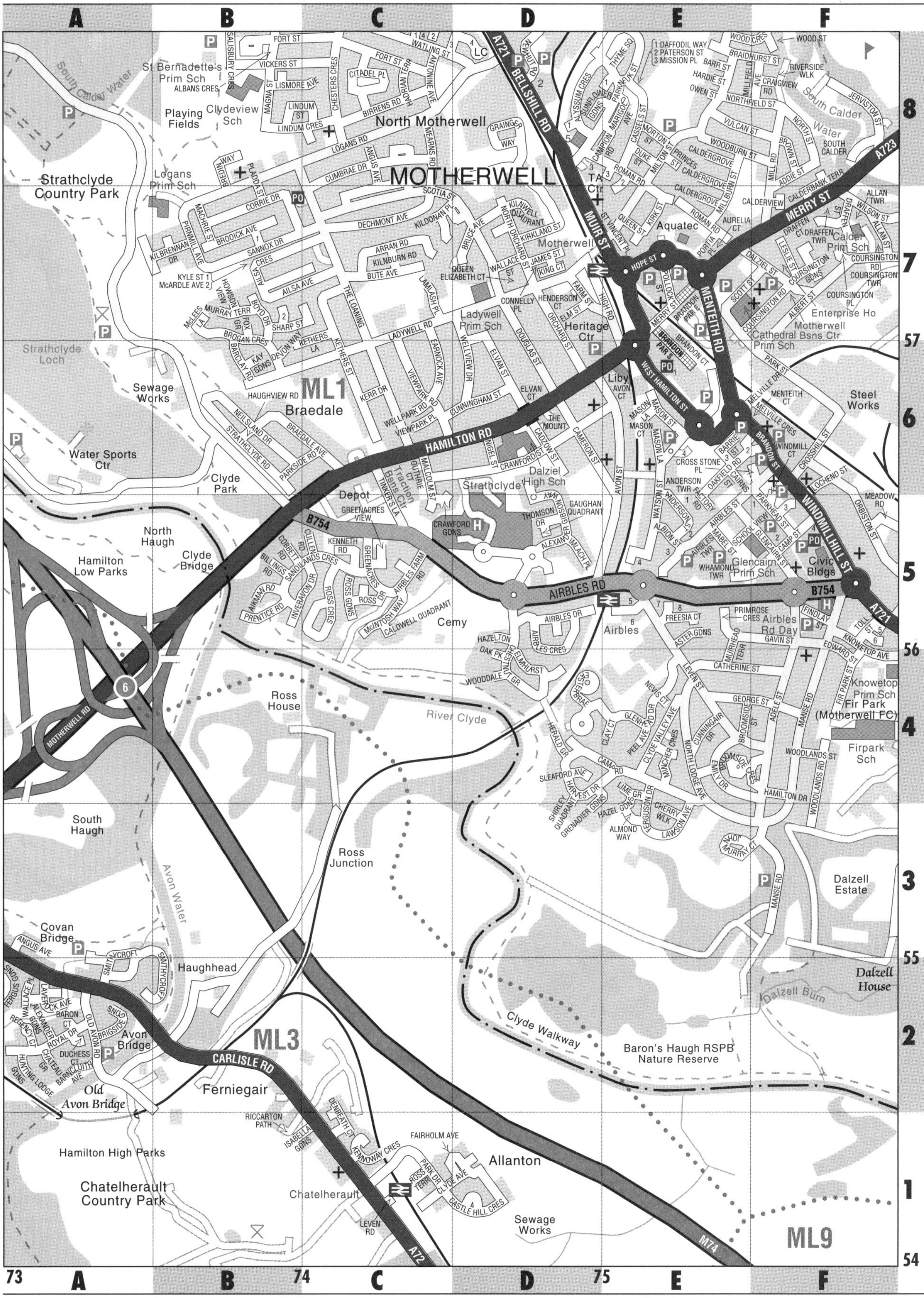

184
164

163
143

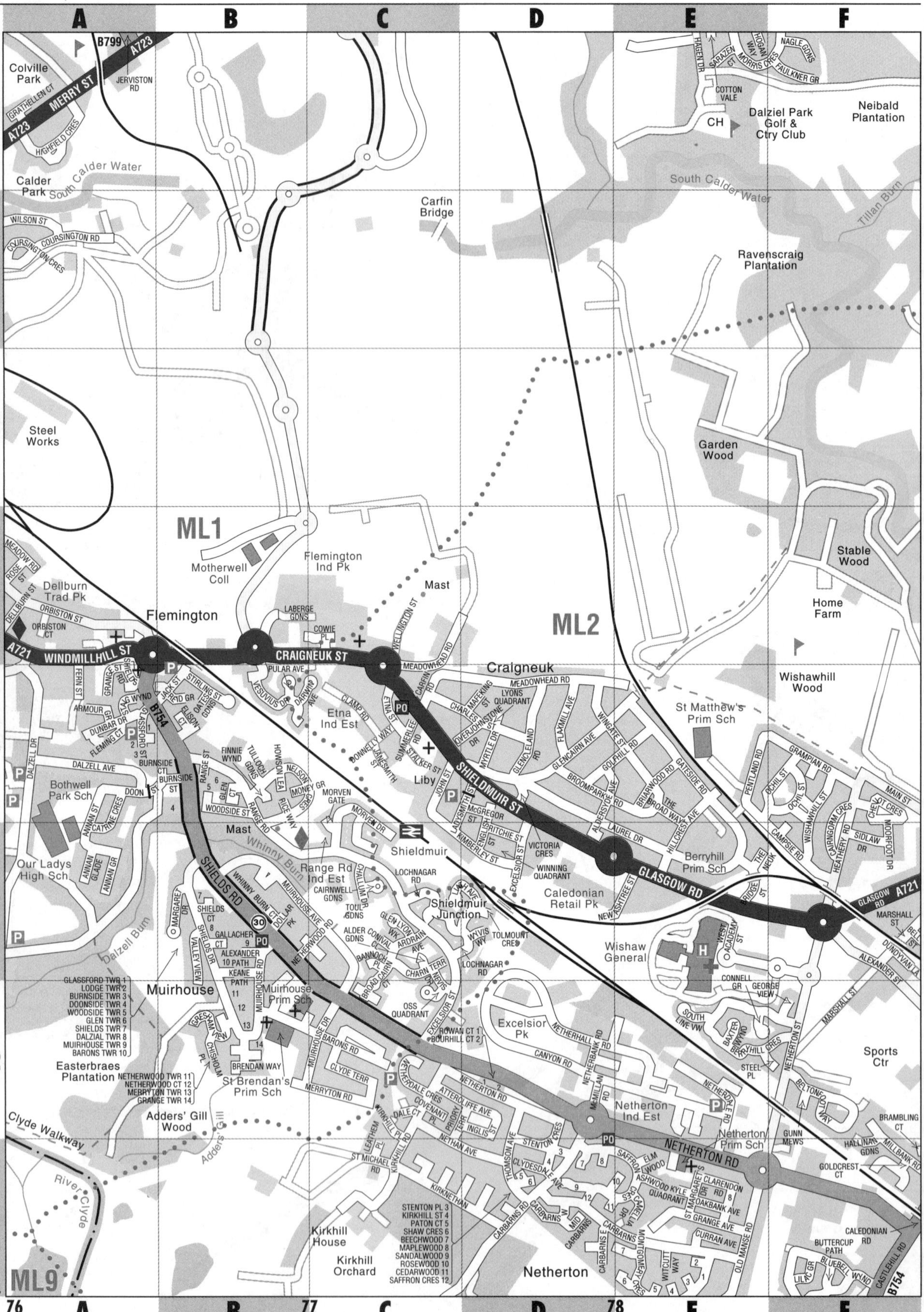

163
185

E1
1 MONTGOMERY CRES
2 ISLAY QUADRANT
3 JURA QUADRANT
4 GIGHA QUADRANT
5 SCARBA QUADRANT
6 PARK QUADRANT
7 STUART QUADRANT
8 ROSEHALL TERR

144
166

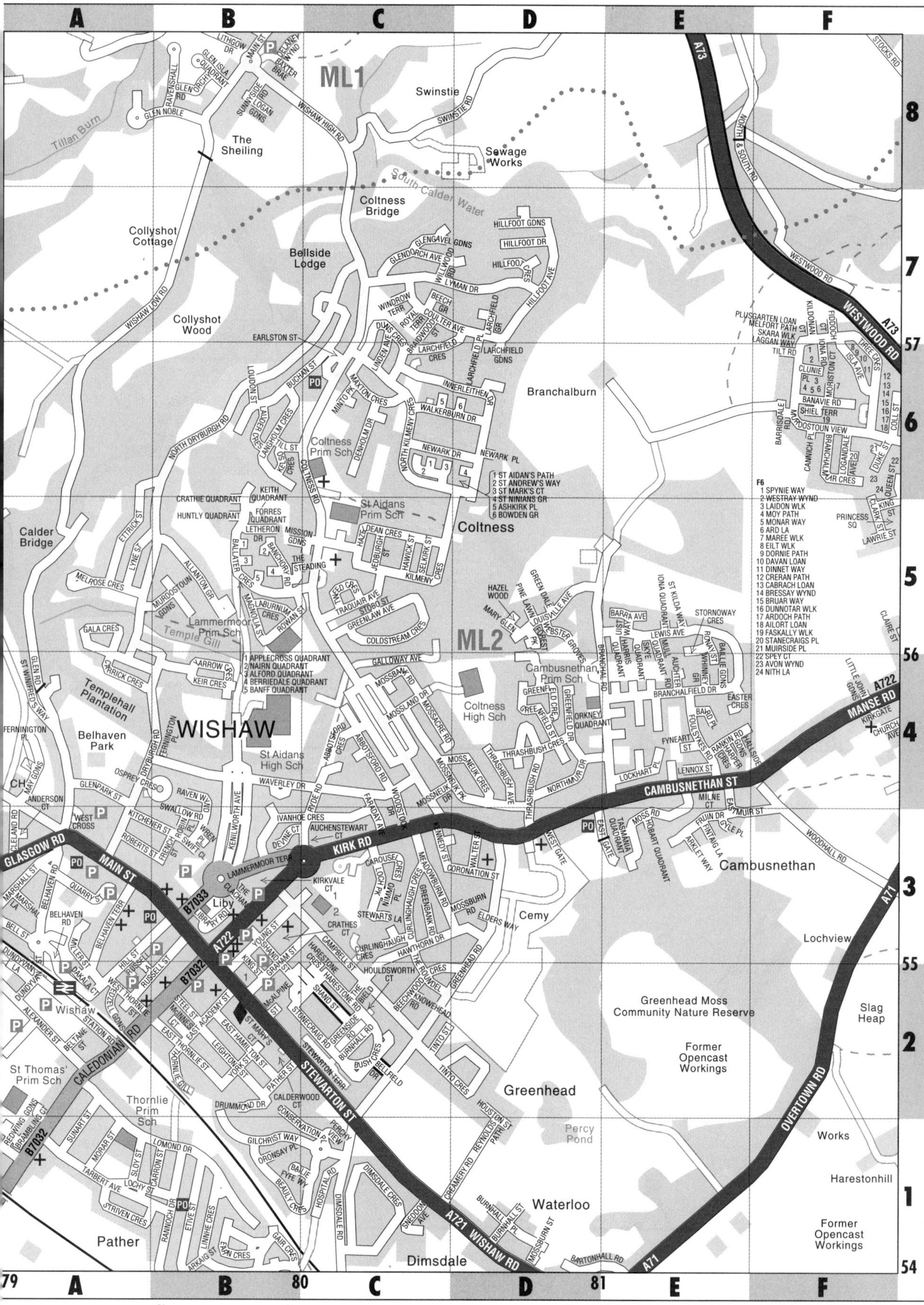

B2
1 Wishaw Bsns Ctr

C3
1 St Ignatius' RC Prim Sch
2 Wishaw Acad Prim Sch

186
166

165
145

A
B
C
D
E
F
8
7
57
6
5
56
4
3
55
2
1
54
82
83
84
ML1
Mill
STOCKS RD
Mill
Murdostoun Castle
Easterhouse
MURDOSTOUN RD
Brucefield
ALLANTON RD
MILL RD
SUMMERHILL PL
A71
WOOD VIEW
CALDER RD
NEWARK GATE
COLTNESS AVE
MILL RD
AUCHTERBURN RD
ALLANBANK ST
Crosshill
WOOD END CVN SITE
WILSON RD
ML7
ALLANTON RD
Kennel Knowe Wood
South Calder Water
Murdostoun Bridge
UNDERWOOD DR
MURRAY CRES
DEVINE GR
McGARRISON RD
McMAHON DR
1 AITKEN CL
2 ROBERT WYND
3 DARRAGH GN
4 McCAROLE WY
CALDER AVE
KILMICHAEL AVE
BELL VW
East Crindledyke
BOLEYN CT
BONDS DR
WOODSIDE CRES
FIRTREE RD
FIRTREE PL
ALCATH RD
Bonkle
CHURCH RD
CAIRNEY PL
BROWNHILL VIEW
MEADOWFIELD PL
A73
CASTLE VIEW
MURDOSTOUN VIEW
PRINCE PL
CLYDE WLK
KING ST
EASTWOOD DR
NORTHWOOD DR
ABERNETHYN RD
BAILLIESMUIR PL
MUIRHOUSE AVE
LYNNWOOD PL
HAWTHORN AVE
Crindledyke
Mast
SHARNOTHSHIELD SMALL HOLDINGS
Calkers Wood
TAY LA
WEST PL
STEWART CRES
WESTWOOD RD
CRINDLEDYKE CRES
BONKLE RD
BONKLE GDNS
BRAEDALE PL
MAVISBANK ST
AUCHTER AVE
BRAEDALE CRES
Gallow Hill
YOUNG PL
GODDARD PL
BROWN WLK
St Brigid's Prim Sch
PARK DR
DOUGAN DR
McSHANE CT
KILDARE PL
CATHBURN HOLDINGS
CATHBURN RD
MILL RD
Newmains
NEWTON DR
TOLL PARK CRES
CLAIRE ST
PO
A722 MANSE RD
Liby
A71
WALKERS CT
Mast
HOPE ST
PARKVIEW CRES
CHURCH AVE
SCHOOL RD
Mast
1 MANSE MEWS
2 BROWN ST
Newmains Prim Sch
Works
VICTORIA ST
MAIN ST
ML2
Morningside Farm
Morningside Prim Sch
SCHOOL RD
Torbush
MORNINGSIDE RD
Woodside Farm
Watstonfoot
OVERTOWN RD
A71
Works
DALGLEISH PL
STEIN PL
SHANKLY DR
WOODHALL RD
MAIN ST
Opencast Workings
Morningside
Watstonmids
Slag Heap
Chapel
CHAPEL RD
Holmhill
Harestonhill
Watstonheads
Herdshill
ML8
Bogside Farm
ML8
A73

165
187

146
168
A
B
C
D
E
F
COLTNESS AVE
PO
ALLANTON RD A71
Allanton Prim Sch
PH
SCHOOL LA
Coal Burn
REDMIRE CRES
DAR PL
MEID
HARTFIELD TERR
KINGSHILL RD
HOULDSWORTH CRES
SPRINGHEAD RD
KIRK PATH
Allanton
WILSON RD
HAWTHORN PL
8
Opencast Workings
Hartfield
ML7
Netherhall
7
57
6
Newark Plantation
5
Upper Daviesdykes
DURA RD
56
Kirkhall
Lower Daviesdykes
4
Lodge Hill
Winterhill
Dura
Mountpleasant
Brow Farm
Sunnyside
ML2
3
Auchterhead
55
Summerside
Kingshill
Auchter Water
2
1
ML8
54
85
86
87
188
168

167
147

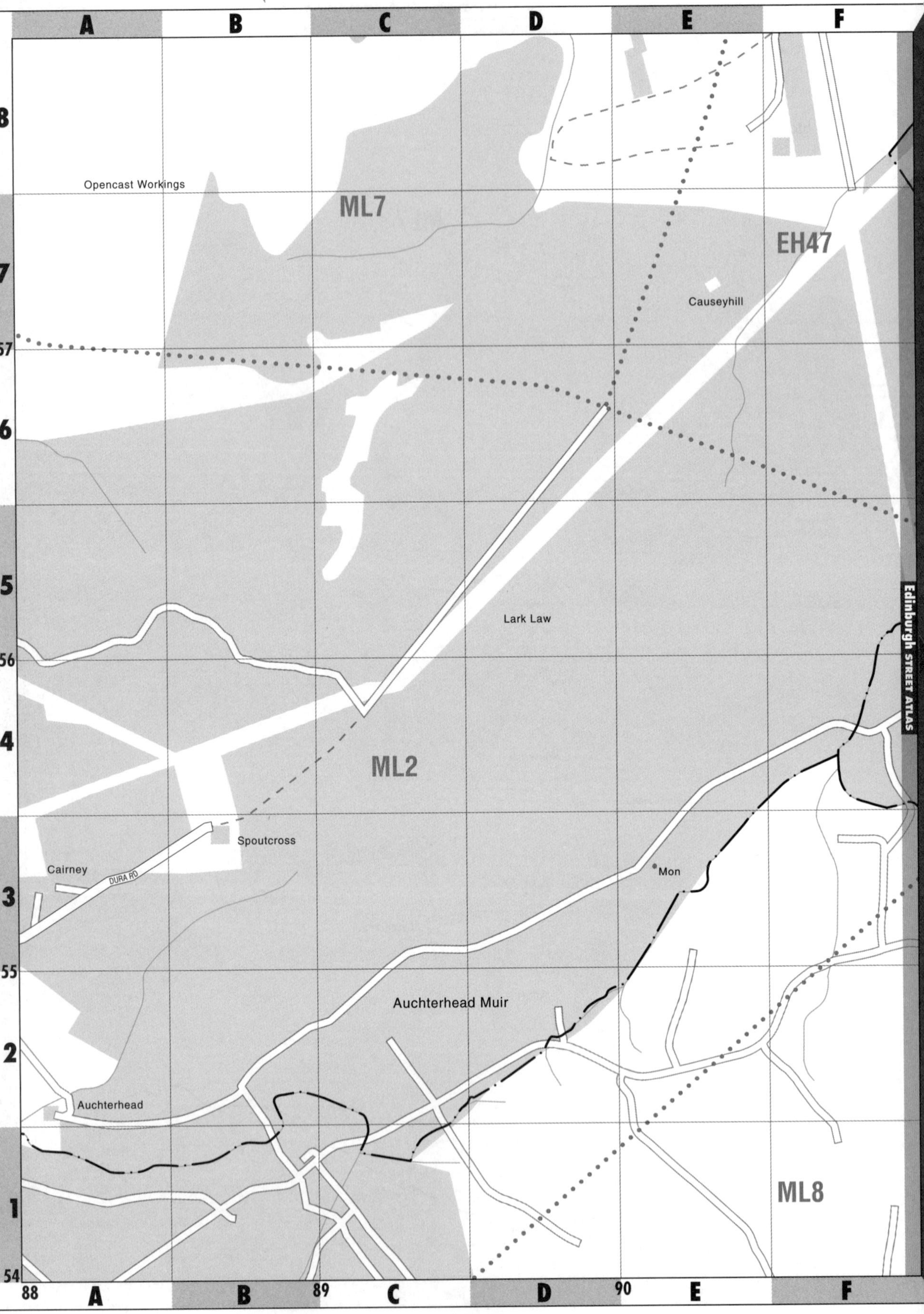
A
B
C
D
E
F
8
7
57
6
5
56
4
3
55
2
1
54
88
89
90
Opencast Workings
ML7
EH47
Causeyhill
Lark Law
ML2
Spoutcross
Cairney
DURA RD
Mon
Auchterhead Muir
Auchterhead
ML8

167
189

148
170

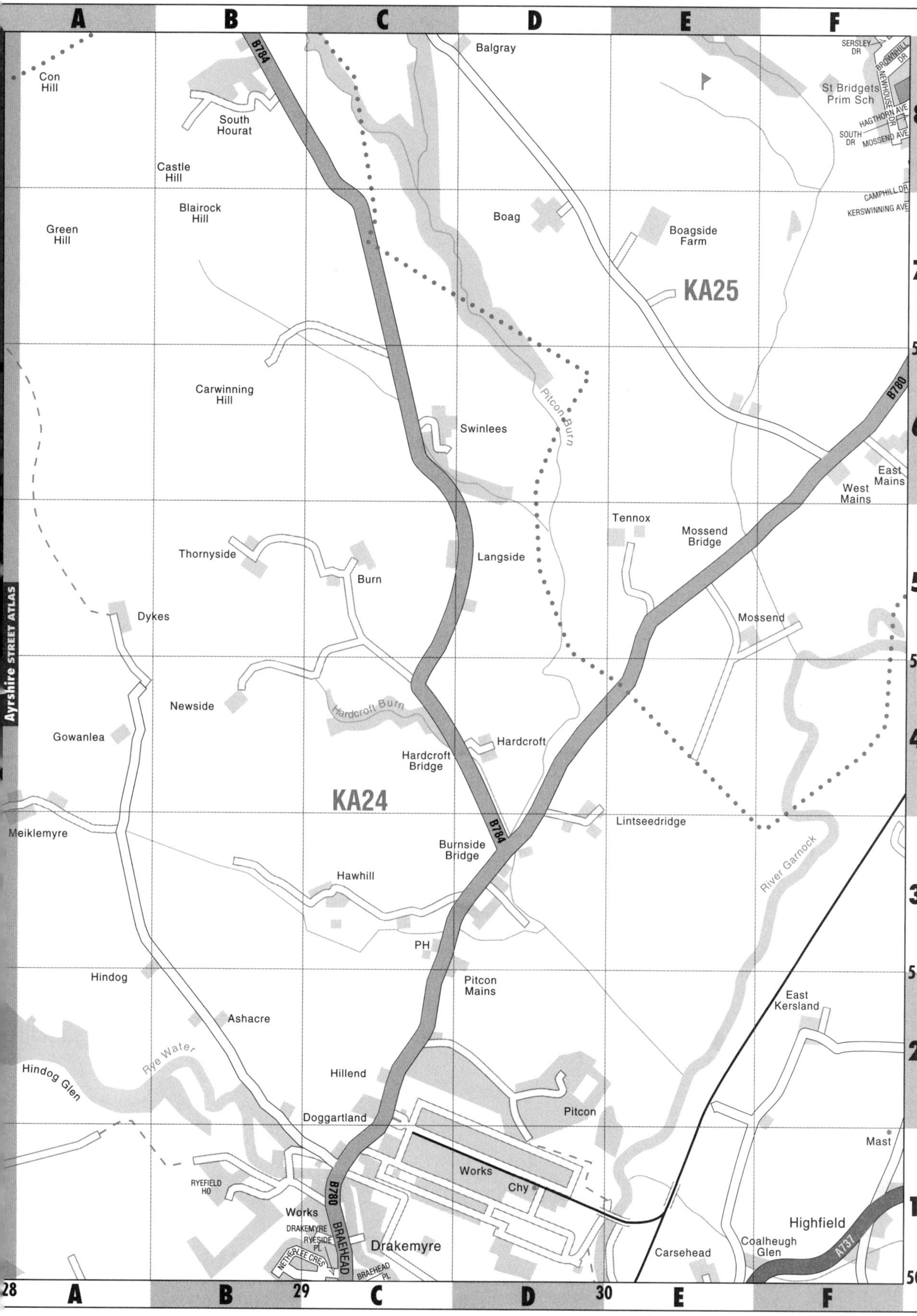

191
170

169
149

169
192

150
172

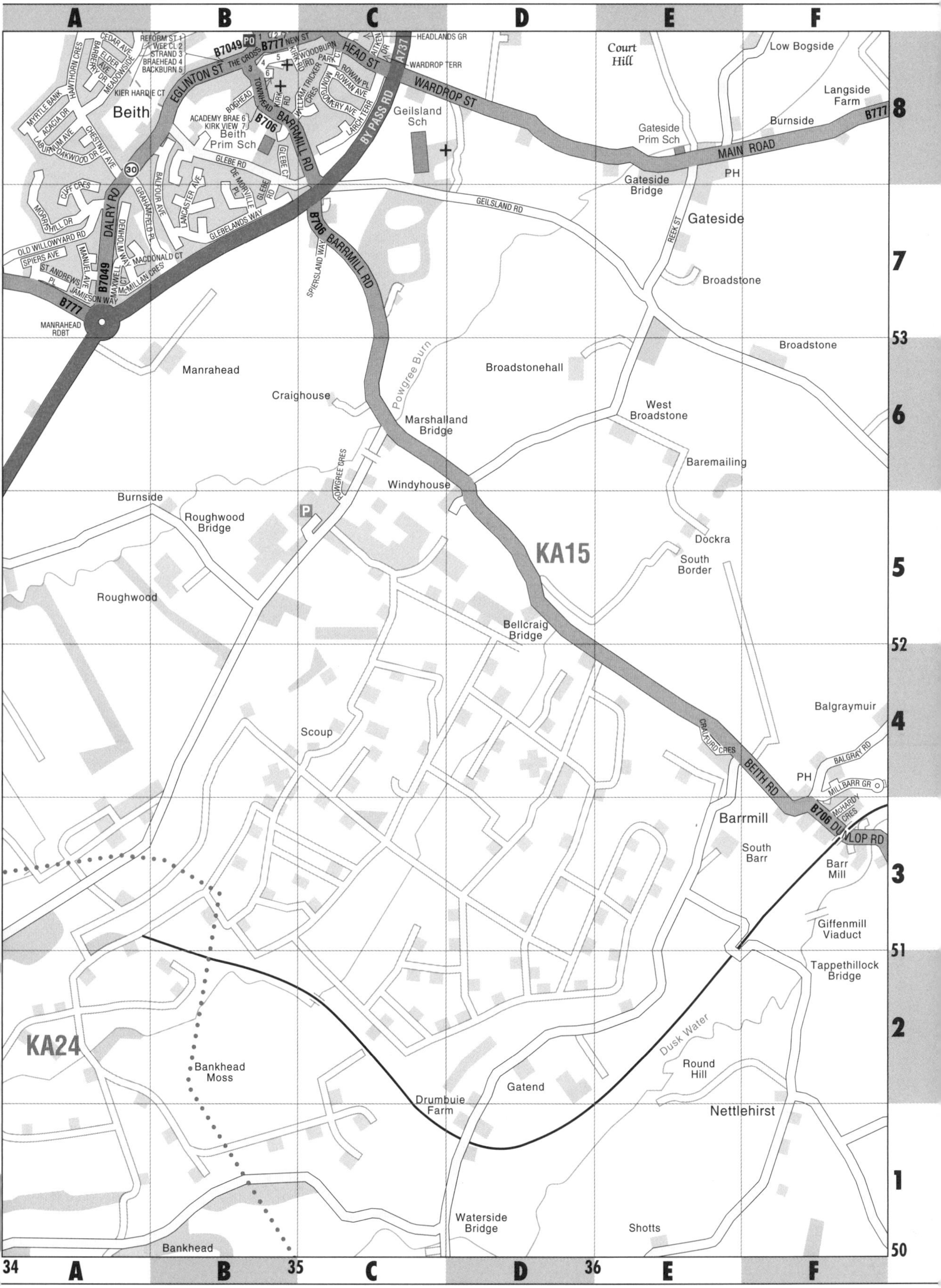

193
172

171
151

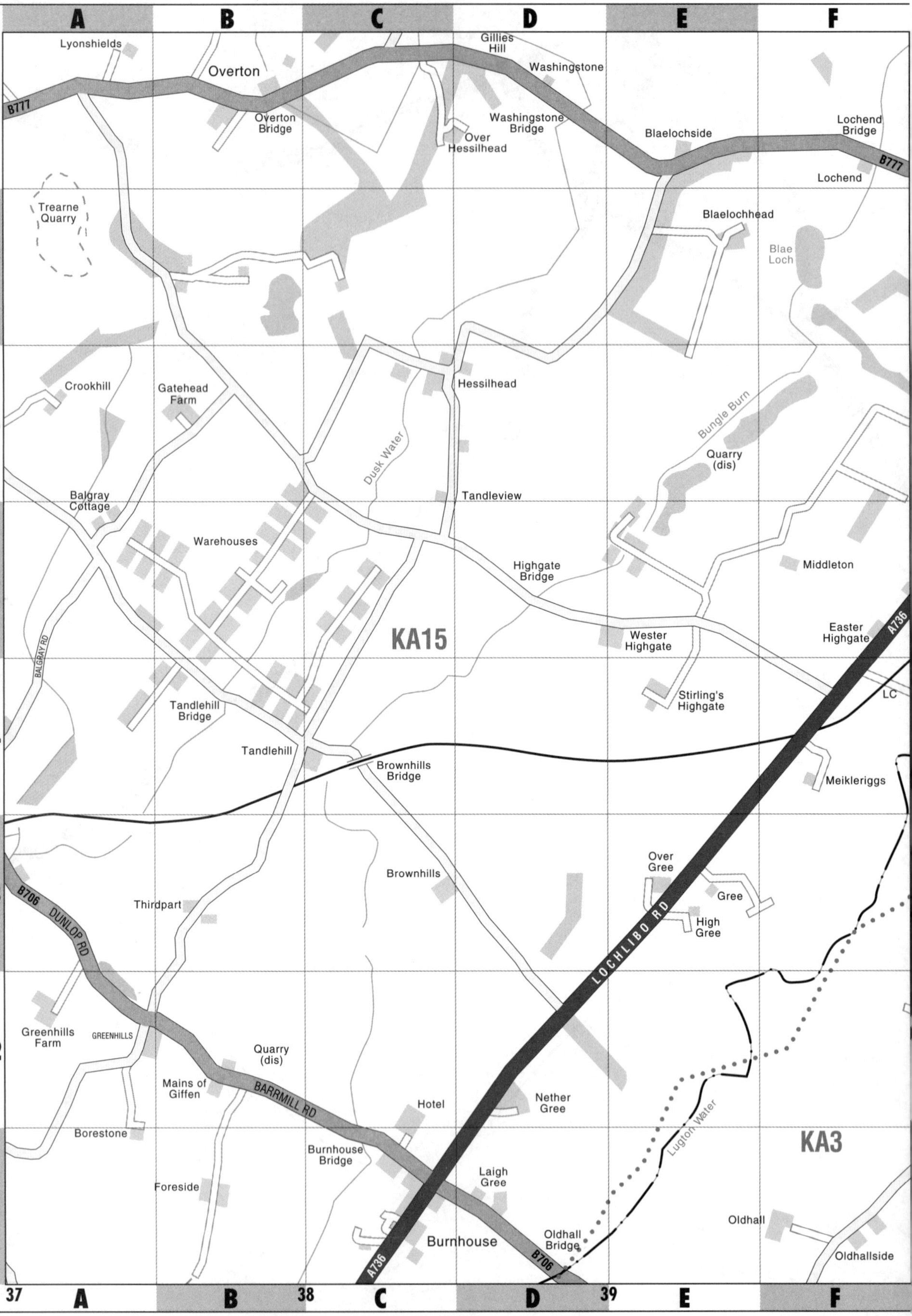
A
B
C
D
E
F
8
7
53
6
5
52
4
3
51
2
1
50
37
38
39
Lyonshields
Overton
Overton Bridge
Gillies Hill
Washingstone
Washingstone Bridge
Over Hessilhead
Blaelochside
Lochend Bridge
Lochend
B777
Trearne Quarry
Blaelochhead
Blae Loch
Crookhill
Gatehead Farm
Hessilhead
Bungle Burn
Dusk Water
Quarry (dis)
Tandleview
Balgray Cottage
Warehouses
Highgate Bridge
Middleton
KA15
Wester Highgate
Easter Highgate
A736
BALGRAY RD
LC
Stirling's Highgate
Tandlehill Bridge
Tandlehill
Brownhills Bridge
Meikleriggs
Brownhills
Over Gree
Gree
High Gree
B706
DUNLOP RD
Thirdpart
LOCHLIBO RD
Greenhills Farm
GREENHILLS
Quarry (dis)
Mains of Giffen
BARRMILL RD
Hotel
Nether Gree
Lugton Water
Borestone
Burnhouse Bridge
KA3
Laigh Gree
Foreside
Oldhall
Oldhall Bridge
Burnhouse
Oldhallside

171
194

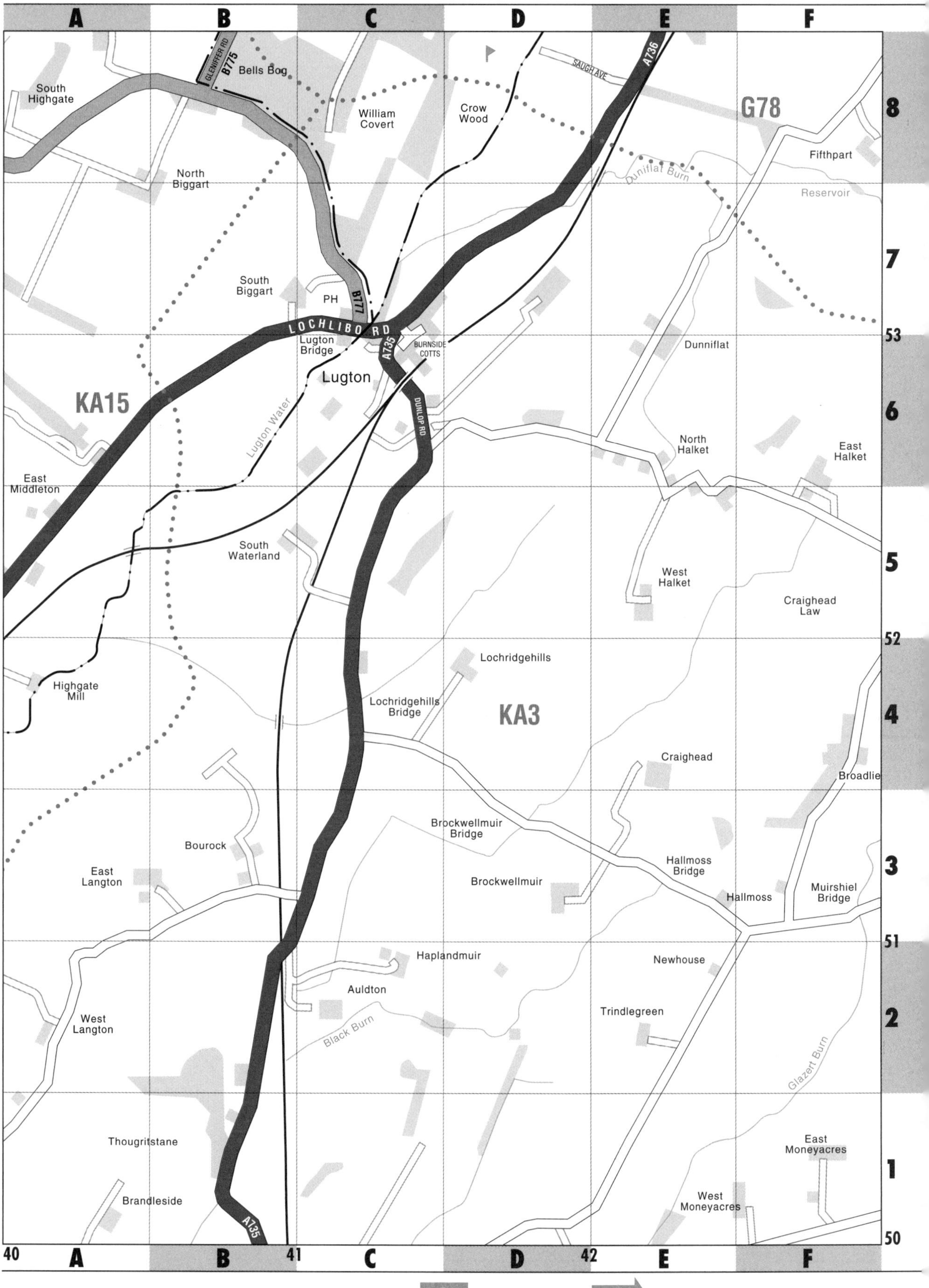
A
B
C
D
E
F
South Highgate
GLENIFFER RD
B775
Bells Bog
William Covert
Crow Wood
SAUGH AVE
A736
G78
8
Fifthpart
North Biggart
Duniflat Burn
Reservoir
7
South Biggart
PH
B777
LOCHLIBO RD
Lugton Bridge
A735
BURNSIDE COTTS
53
Dunniflat
Lugton
KA15
Lugton Water
DUNLOP RD
6
North Halket
East Halket
East Middleton
South Waterland
5
West Halket
Craighead Law
52
Lochridgehills
Highgate Mill
Lochridgehills Bridge
KA3
4
Craighead
Broadlie
Brockwellmuir Bridge
Bourock
Hallmoss Bridge
3
East Langton
Brockwellmuir
Hallmoss
Muirshiel Bridge
51
Haplandmuir
Newhouse
Auldton
Trindlegreen
West Langton
2
Black Burn
Glazert Burn
East Moneyacres
Thougritstane
1
Brandleside
West Moneyacres
A735
50
40
41
42

173
153

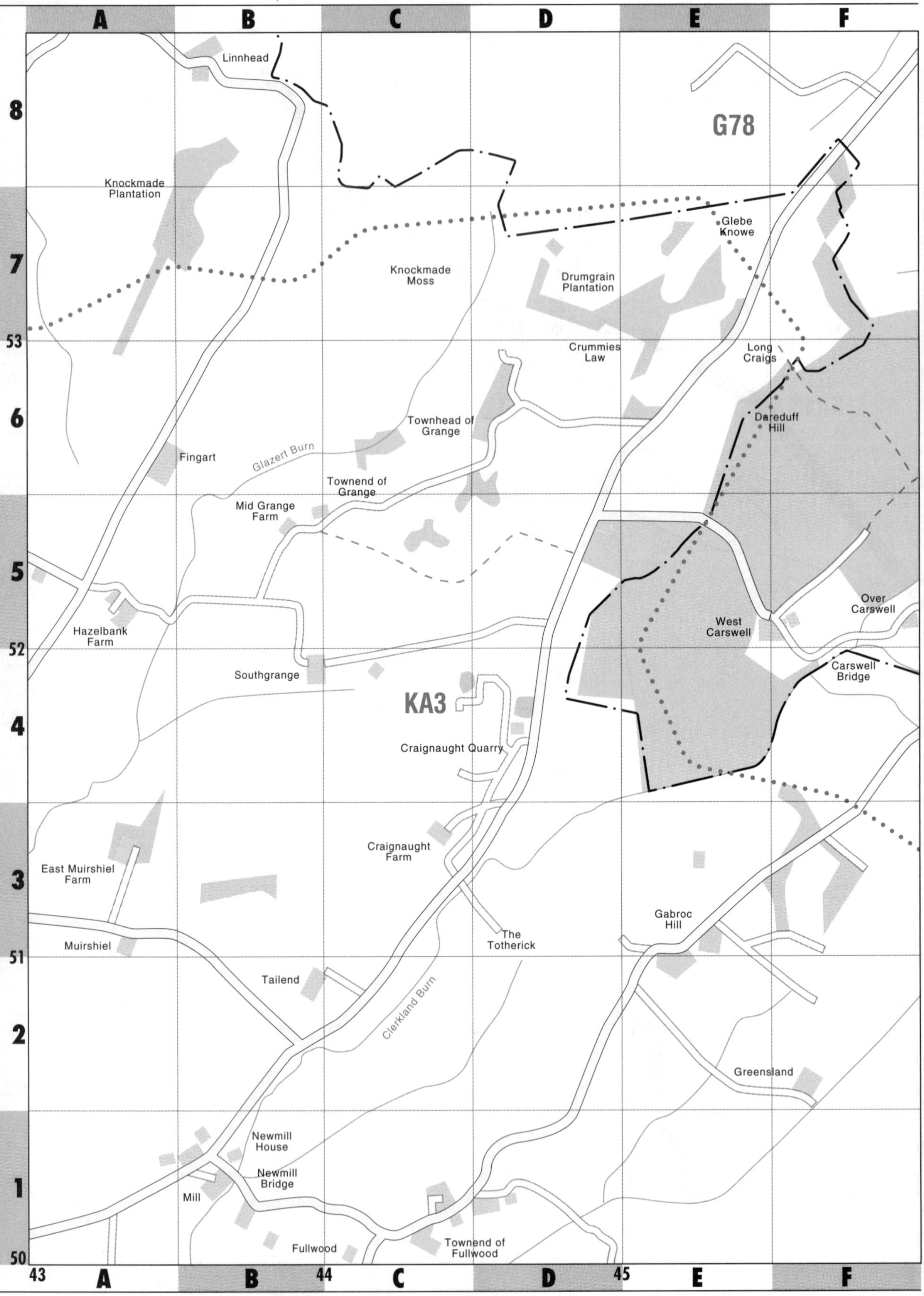
A
B
C
D
E
F
8
7
53
6
5
52
4
3
51
2
1
50
43
44
45
G78
KA3
Linnhead
Knockmade Plantation
Knockmade Moss
Drumgrain Plantation
Glebe Knowe
Crummies Law
Long Craigs
Townhead of Grange
Dareduff Hill
Fingart
Glazert Burn
Townend of Grange
Mid Grange Farm
Over Carswell
West Carswell
Hazelbank Farm
Carswell Bridge
Southgrange
Craignaught Quarry
Craignaught Farm
East Muirshiel Farm
Gabroc Hill
The Totherick
Muirshiel
Tailend
Clerkland Burn
Greensland
Newmill House
Newmill Bridge
Mill
Fullwood
Townend of Fullwood

173
196

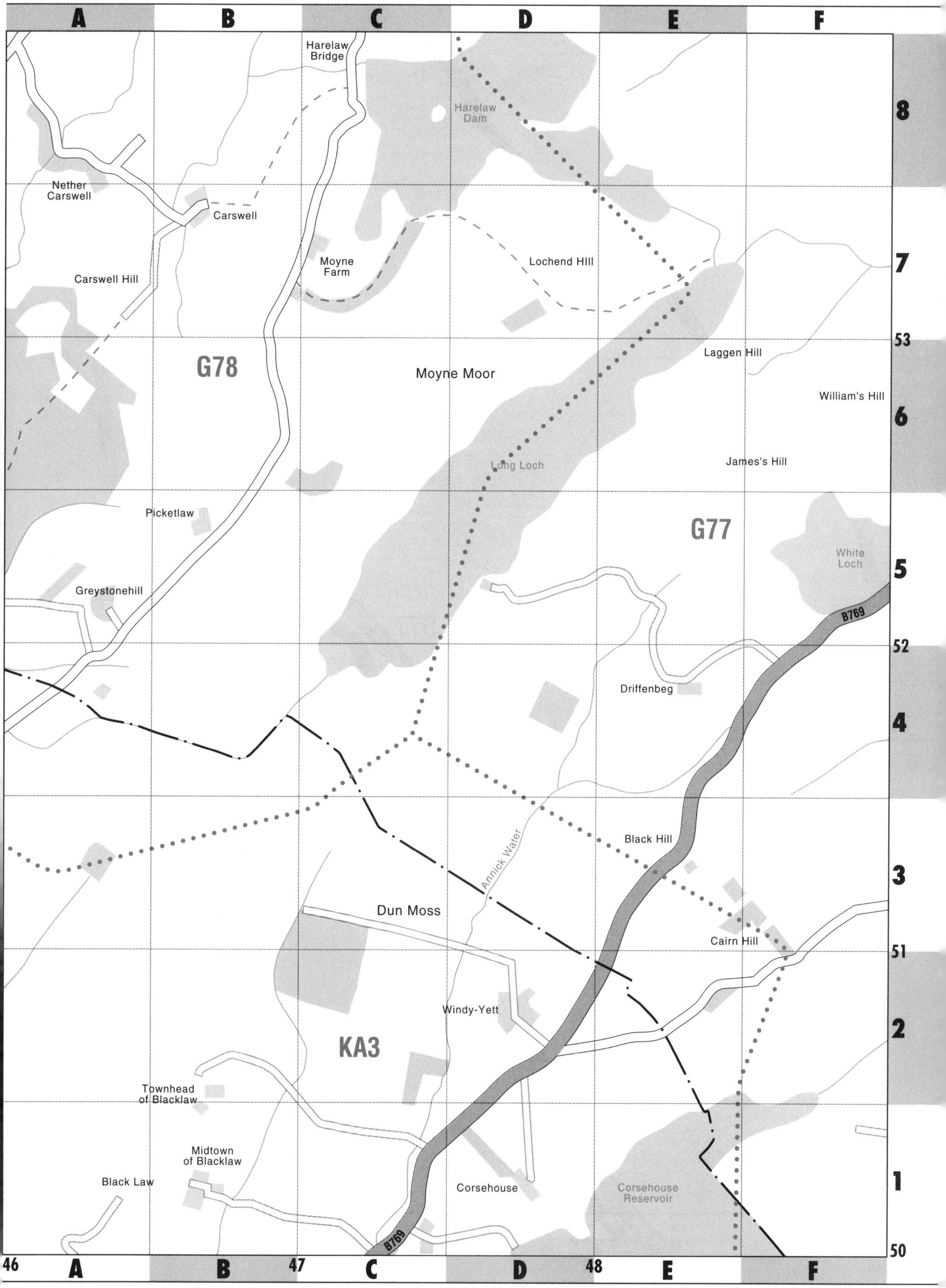
A
B
C
D
E
F
Harelaw Bridge
Harelaw Dam
8
Nether Carswell
Carswell
Moyne Farm
Lochend HIll
Carswell Hill
7
53
G78
Moyne Moor
Laggen Hill
William's Hill
6
Long Loch
James's Hill
Picketlaw
G77
White Loch
5
Greystonehill
B769
52
Driffenbeg
4
Black Hill
Annick Water
3
Dun Moss
Cairn Hill
51
Windy-Yett
2
KA3
Townhead of Blacklaw
Midtown of Blacklaw
Black Law
Corsehouse
Corsehouse Reservoir
1
B769
50
46
A
B
47
C
D
48
E
F

175
155

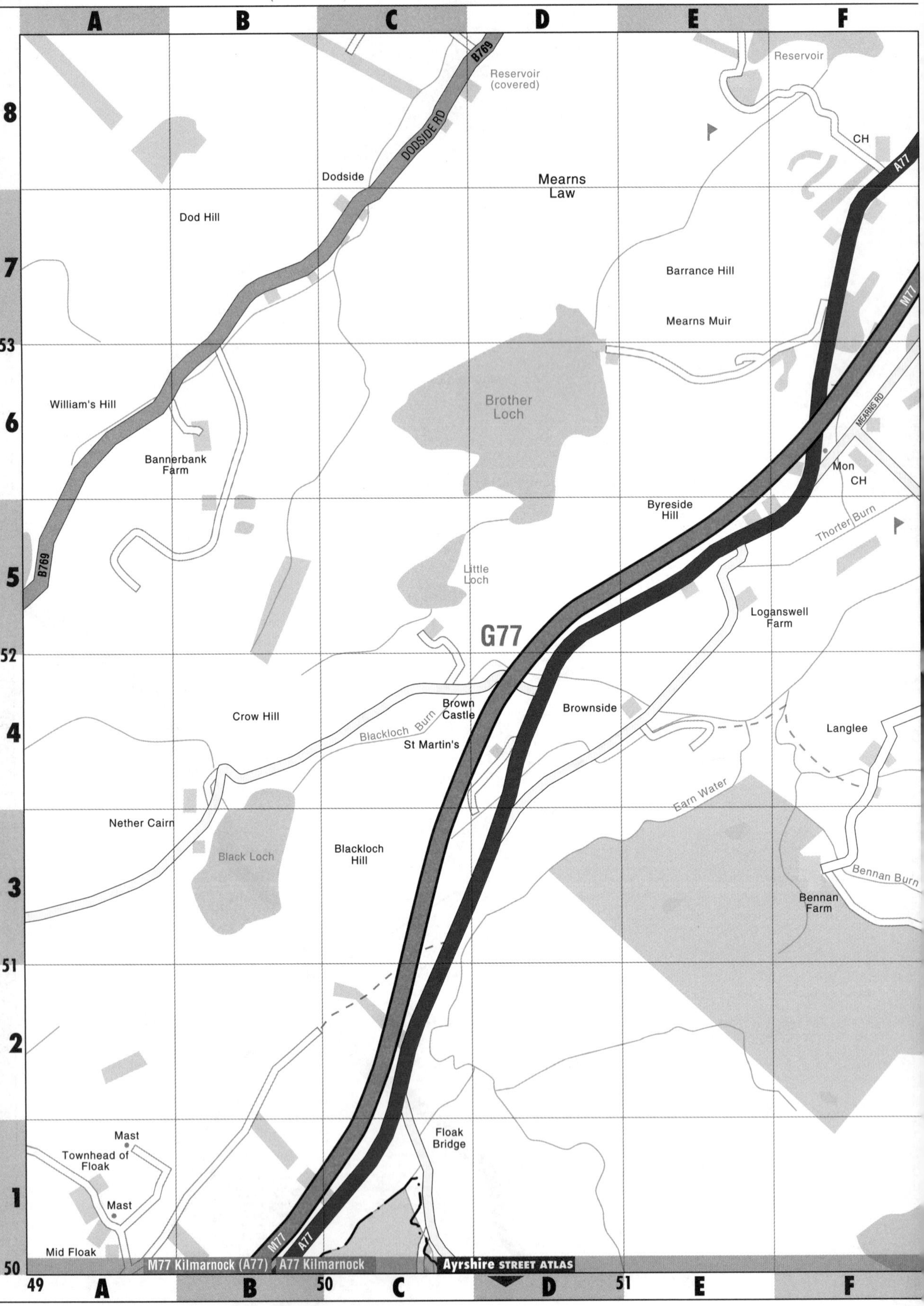
A
B
C
D
E
F
8
7
53
6
5
52
4
3
51
2
1
50
49
50
51
B769
DODSIDE RD
Reservoir
(covered)
Reservoir
CH
A77
Dodside
Mearns
Law
Dod Hill
Barrance Hill
Mearns Muir
M77
William's Hill
Brother
Loch
MEARNS RD
Bannerbank
Farm
Mon
CH
Byreside
Hill
Thorter Burn
Little
Loch
Loganswell
Farm
G77
Brown
Castle
Brownside
Crow Hill
Blackloch Burn
St Martin's
Langlee
Earn Water
Nether Cairn
Black Loch
Blackloch
Hill
Bennan Burn
Bennan
Farm
Mast
Townhead of
Floak
Floak
Bridge
Mast
Mid Floak
M77 Kilmarnock (A77)
A77 Kilmarnock
Ayrshire STREET ATLAS

175

156
178

A
B
C
D
E
F
A77
M77
A726
Nursery
Crook
Hazeldean
House
HAZELDEN RD
MEARNS RD
TITWOOD RD
West
Titwood
8
Harelea
Hill
Mast
Star and
Garter
Hazeldenhill
Hazelden
Mains
7
G77
Broadlees
Earn Water
Fauldside Hill
53
Blackhouse
Farm
6
Bonnyton
Moor
Thorter Burn
Long
Wood
BONNYTON MOOR RD
North
Moorhouse
Muirshield
Bridge
5
KIRKTON MOOR RD
52
East
Moorhouse
4
Boshee Hill
G76
3
Water
Works
South
Moorhouse
51
Lochcraig Reservoir
Bennan Burn
2
Rieve Hill
Melowther
1
Bennan Loch
Ballageich Hill
Ayrshire STREET ATLAS
50
52
53
54

178

177
157

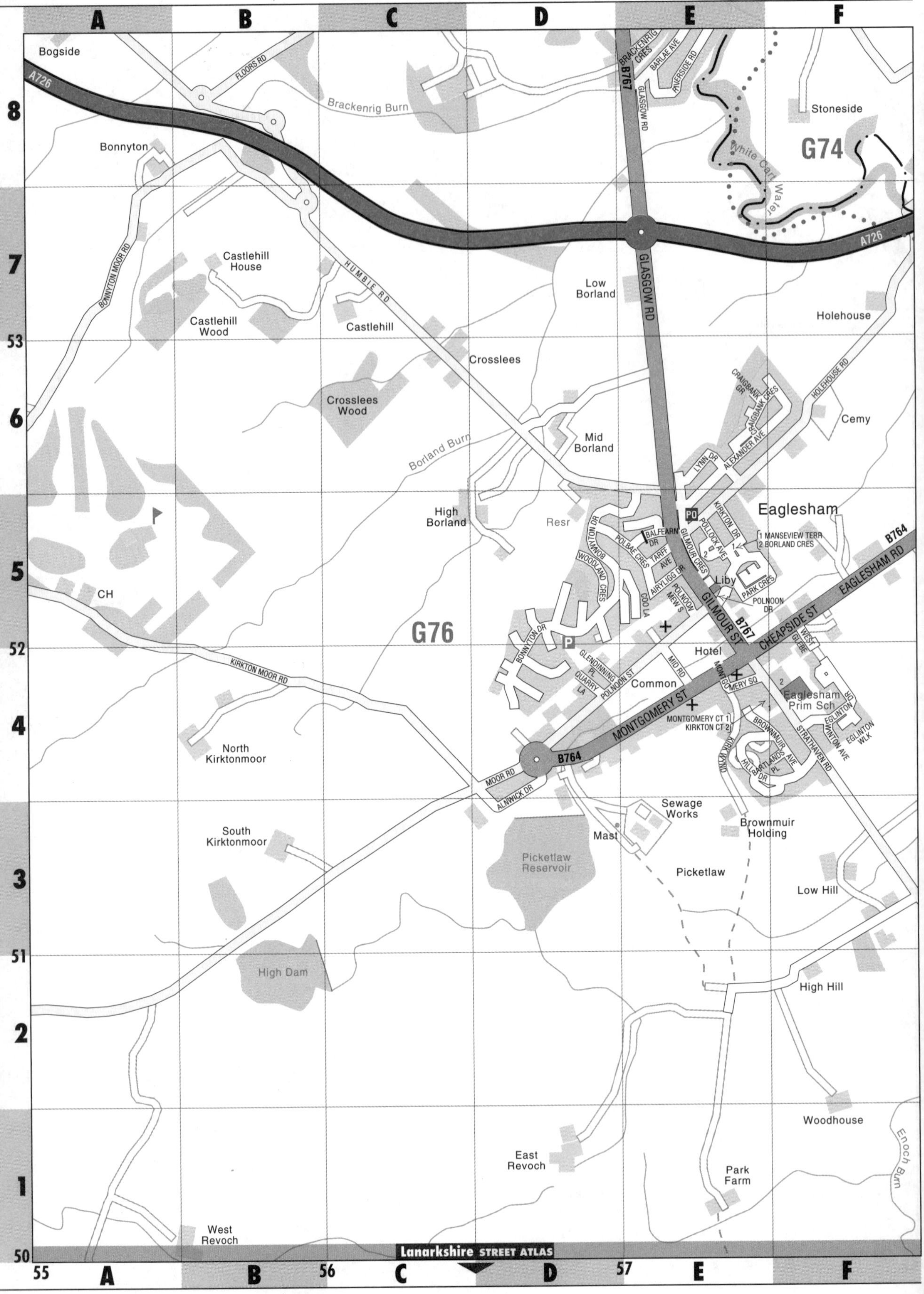
A
B
C
D
E
F
8
7
53
6
5
52
4
3
51
2
1
50
55
56
57
Bogside
A726
FLOORS RD
Brackenrig Burn
BRACKENRIG CRES
BARLAE AVE
RIVERSIDE RD
B767
GLASGOW RD
Stoneside
G74
White Cart Water
Bonnyton
A726
BONNYTON MOOR RD
Castlehill House
HUMBIE RD
Castlehill Wood
Castlehill
Low Borland
GLASGOW RD
Holehouse
Crosslees
Crosslees Wood
CRAIGBANK GR
CRAIGBANK CRES
HOLEHOUSE RD
Cemy
ALEXANDER AVE
LYNN DR
Mid Borland
Borland Burn
High Borland
Resr
PO
Eaglesham
KIRKTON DR
POLLOCK AVE
BALFEARN DR
GILMOUR CRES
1 MANSEVIEW TERR
2 BORLAND CRES
B764
EAGLESHAM RD
BONNYTON DR
WOODLAND CRES
POLBAE CRES
TARFF AVE
AIRYLIGG DR
COO LA
POLNOON MEWS
Liby
PARK CRES
POLNOON DR
GILMOUR ST
B767
CHEAPSIDE ST
CH
G76
BONNYTON DR
P
Hotel
GLEBE
WEST
KIRKTON MOOR RD
GLENDINNING PL
QUARRY LA
POLNOON ST
MID RD
Common
MONTGOMERY SQ
Eaglesham Prim Sch
EGLINTON
EGLINTON WLK
WINTON AVE
MONTGOMERY ST
MONTGOMERY CT 1
KIRKTON CT 2
BROWNMUIR AVE
STRATHAVEN RD
North Kirktonmoor
B764
MOOR RD
ALNWICK DR
KIRK WYND
HILL DR
BARTLANDS PL
Sewage Works
Mast
Brownmuir Holding
South Kirktonmoor
Picketlaw Reservoir
Picketlaw
Low Hill
High Dam
High Hill
Woodhouse
East Revoch
Enoch Burn
Park Farm
West Revoch
Lanarkshire STREET ATLAS

177

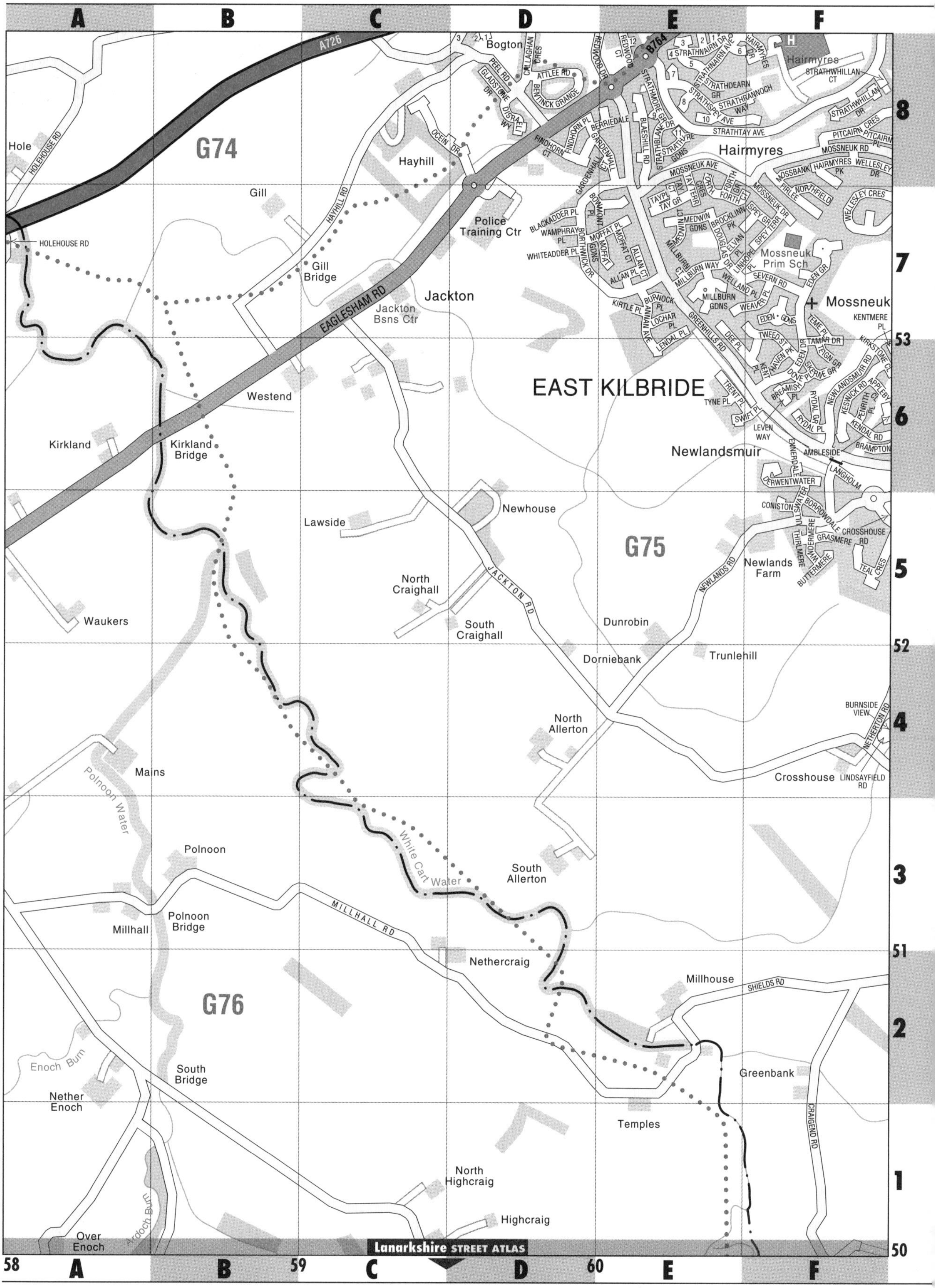
A
B
C
D
E
F
8
7
53
6
5
52
4
3
51
2
1
50
58
59
60
A726
B764
G74
G75
G76
Hole
HOLEHOUSE RD
Gill
Hayhill
HAYHILL RD
Gill Bridge
Police Training Ctr
Jackton
Jackton Bsns Ctr
EAGLESHAM RD
Westend
Kirkland
Kirkland Bridge
Lawside
Newhouse
North Craighall
South Craighall
JACKTON RD
Waukers
Bogton
PEEL RD
GLADSTONE DR
DISRAELI WAY
ATTLEE RD
BENTINCK GRANGE
CALLAGHAN CRES
OCEIN DR
REDWOOD DR
REDWOOD CT
FINDHORN CT
FINDHORN PL
BERRIEDALE
GARDENHALL
BLAESHILL RD
STRATHMORE GR
STRATHBLANE GDNS
STRATHYRE GDNS
STRATHDEARN GR
STRATHRANNOCH WAY
STRATHSPEY AVE
STRATHTAY AVE
STRATHNAIRN DR
STRATHNAIRN AVE
HAIRMYRES DR
Hairmyres
STRATHWHILLAN CT
STRATHWHILLAN DR
PITCAIRN CRES
PITCAIRN PL
MOSSNEUK RD
MOSSNEUK AVE
MOSSNEUK DR
HAIRMYRES PK
WELLESLEY DR
WELLESLEY CRES
MOSSBANK
NORTHFIELD
PIRLEE
TAY PL
TAY GR
TAY CT
TAY TERR
FORTH CRES
FORTH PL
FORTH GR
SPEY GR
SPEY TERR
MEDWIN GDNS
MEDWIN CT
BROCKLINN PK
DOUGLAS DR
ELVAN PL
LINHOPE PL
BLACKADDER PL
WAMPHRAY PL
WHITEADDER PL
BONMONT PL
BORTHWICK DR
MOFFAT GDNS
MOFFAT PL
MOFFAT CT
ALLAN CT
ALLAN PL
MILLBURN WAY
MILLBURN CT
MILLBURN GDNS
WELLAND PL
SEVERN RD
WEAVER PL
EDEN GR
EDEN GDNS
Mossneuk Prim Sch
Mossneuk
KENTMERE PL
KIRTLE PL
BURNOCK PL
ANNAN AVE
LOCHAR PL
LENDAL PL
GREENHILLS RD
DEE PL
TWEED ST
TEME PL
TAMAR DR
KIRKSTONE CL
TEIGN GR
SKERNE GR
EDEN DR
HAVEN PK
KENT PL
DOVE PL
BREAMISH PL
RYDAL GR
RYDAL PL
NEWLANDSMUIR RD
KESWICK RD
APPLEBY CL
PENRITH PL
KENDAL RD
BRAMPTON
EAST KILBRIDE
TRENT PL
TYNE PL
SWIFT PL
LEVEN WAY
Newlandsmuir
AMBLESIDE
ENNERDALE
LANGHOLM
DERWENTWATER
CONISTON
BORROWDALE
CROSSHOUSE RD
RYDAL MT
WASTWATER
GRASMERE
THIRLMERE
WINDERMERE
BUTTERMERE
TEAL CRES
NEWLANDS RD
Newlands Farm
Dunrobin
Dorniebank
Trunlehill
North Allerton
BURNSIDE VIEW
NETHERTON RD
Crosshouse
LINDSAYFIELD RD
Mains
Polnoon Water
Polnoon
White Cart Water
South Allerton
Millhall
Polnoon Bridge
MILLHALL RD
Nethercraig
Millhouse
SHIELDS RD
Enoch Burn
Greenbank
Nether Enoch
South Bridge
Temples
CRAIGEND RD
North Highcraig
Highcraig
Ardoch Burn
Over Enoch

179

C7
1 COOLGARDIE PL
2 COOLGARDIE GN

C8
1 ALBERTA CRES
2 BARKLY TERR
3 BUNBURY TERR
4 LETHBRIDGE PL
5 MELBOURNE GN
6 SYDNEY PL

D8
1 CALGARY PL
2 ALBERTA PL
3 STEPHENSON PL
4 STEPHENSON SQ

159

E7
1 CULLEN LA
2 THE MURRAY SQ
3 HEATHER GR
4 STRATHCONA LA

F7
1 SOMERVILLE TERR
2 SOMERVILLE LA
3 SHEILDHILL

F8
1 East Kilbride Shop Ctr
2 DENHOLM GN
3 SINCLAIR PK
4 MUIRHOUSE LA
5 HENRY BELL GN
6 FREELAND LA
7 TELFORD TERR
8 SYMINGTON SQ
9 TODHILLS

179

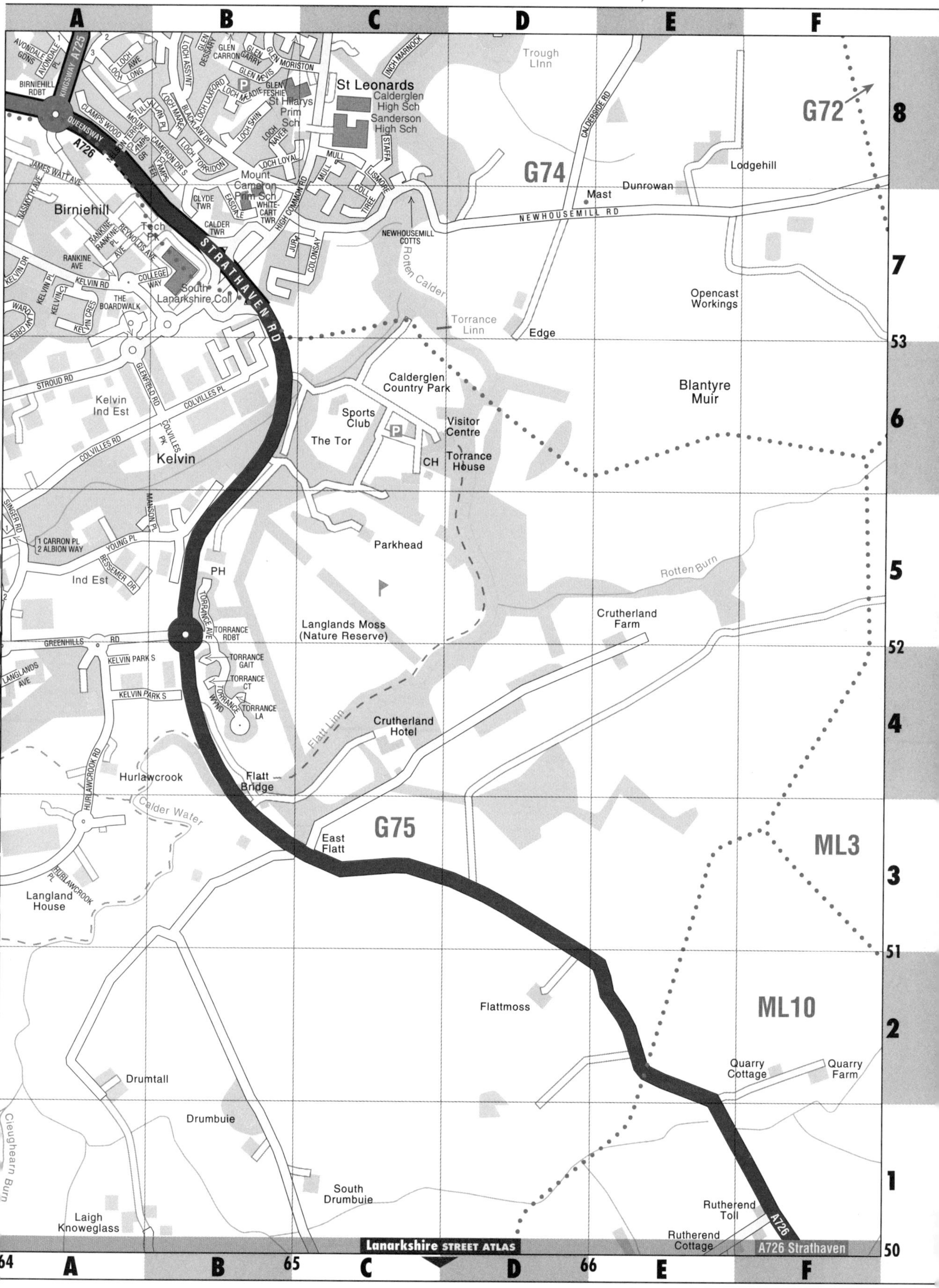
St Leonards
Calderglen High Sch
Sanderson High Sch
St Hilarys Prim Sch
Mount Cameron Prim Sch
Birniehill
Kelvin
Kelvin Ind Est
Ind Est
South Lanarkshire Coll
Tech Pk
STRATHAVEN RD
QUEENSWAY
A726
A725
KINGSWAY
BIRNIEHILL RDBT
NEWHOUSEMILL RD
NEWHOUSEMILL COTTS
CALDERSIDE RD
G74
G72
G75
ML3
ML10
Trough Linn
Lodgehill
Dunrowan
Mast
Rotten Calder
Torrance Linn
Edge
Opencast Workings
Blantyre Muir
Calderglen Country Park
Sports Club
The Tor
Visitor Centre
Torrance House
CH
PH
Parkhead
Rotten Burn
Langlands Moss (Nature Reserve)
Crutherland Farm
Crutherland Hotel
Flatt Linn
Flatt Bridge
Hurlawcrook
Calder Water
East Flatt
Langland House
Flattmoss
Quarry Cottage
Quarry Farm
Drumtall
Drumbuie
South Drumbuie
Laigh Knoweglass
Rutherend Toll
Rutherend Cottage
Cleughearn Burn
A726 Strathaven
GREENHILLS RD
TORRANCE RDBT
TORRANCE AVE
KELVIN PARK S
LANGLANDS AVE
HURLAWCROOK RD
HURLAWCROOK PL
1 CARRON PL
2 ALBION WAY
YOUNG PL
BESSEMER DR
COLVILLES RD
COLVILLES PL
STROUD RD
KELVIN RD
RANKINE AVE
JAMES WATT AVE
NASMYTH AVE
A B C D E F
1 2 3 4 5 6 7 8
64 65 66
50 51 52 53

181
161

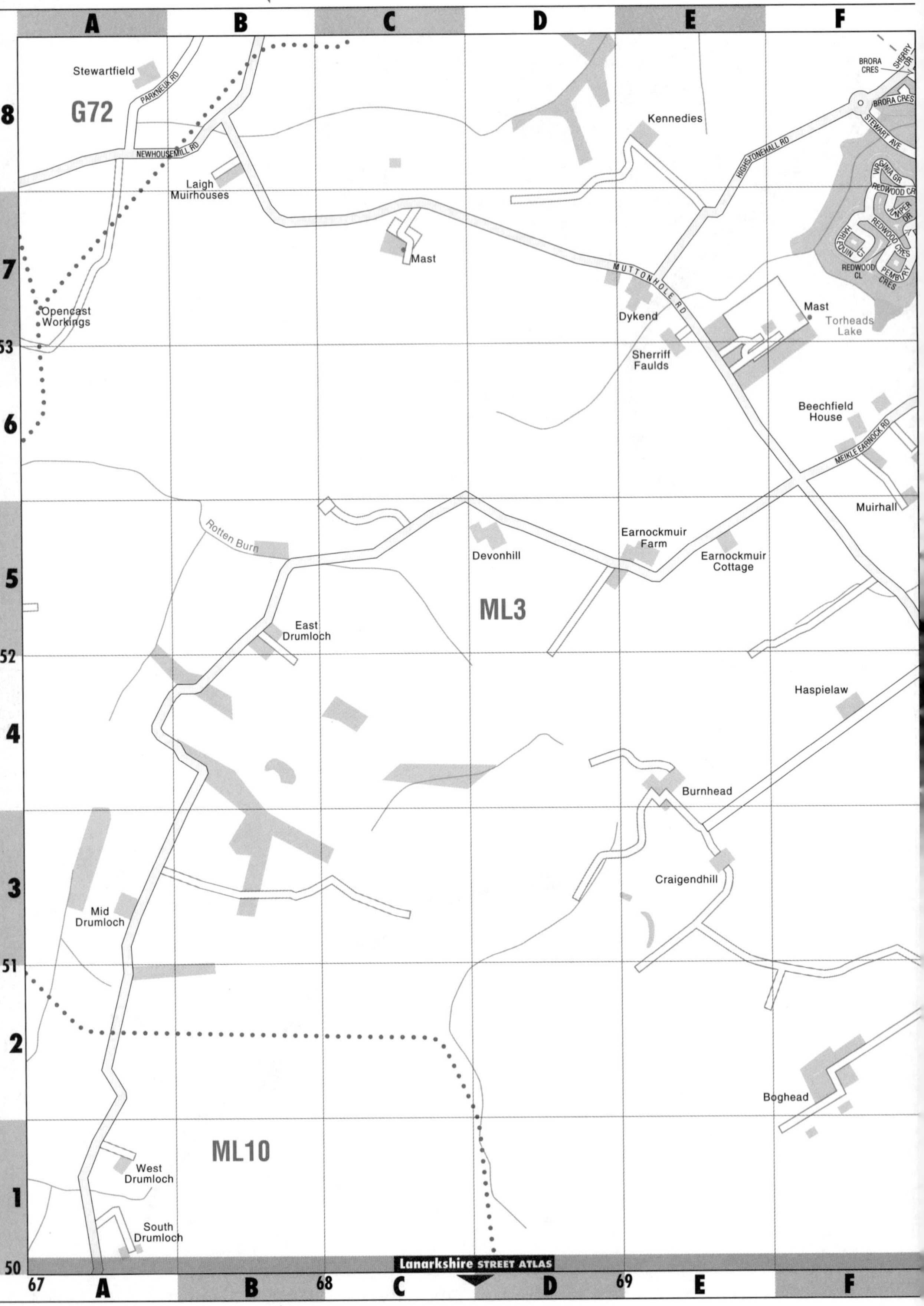
A
B
C
D
E
F
8
7
53
6
5
52
4
3
51
2
1
50
67
68
69
G72
ML3
ML10
Stewartfield
PARKNEUK RD
NEWHOUSEMILL RD
Laigh Muirhouses
Opencast Workings
Mast
MUTTONHOLE RD
Kennedies
HIGHSTONEHALL RD
BRORA CRES
SHERRY DR
BRORA CRES
STEWART AVE
VIRGINIA GR
REDWOOD CR
JUNIPER DR
REDWOOD CRES
HARLEQUIN CT
REDWOOD CL
PEMBURY CRES
Dykend
Mast
Torheads Lake
Sherriff Faulds
Beechfield House
MEIKLE EARNOCK RD
Muirhall
Rotten Burn
Devonhill
Earnockmuir Farm
Earnockmuir Cottage
East Drumloch
Haspielaw
Burnhead
Craigendhill
Mid Drumloch
Boghead
West Drumloch
South Drumloch

181

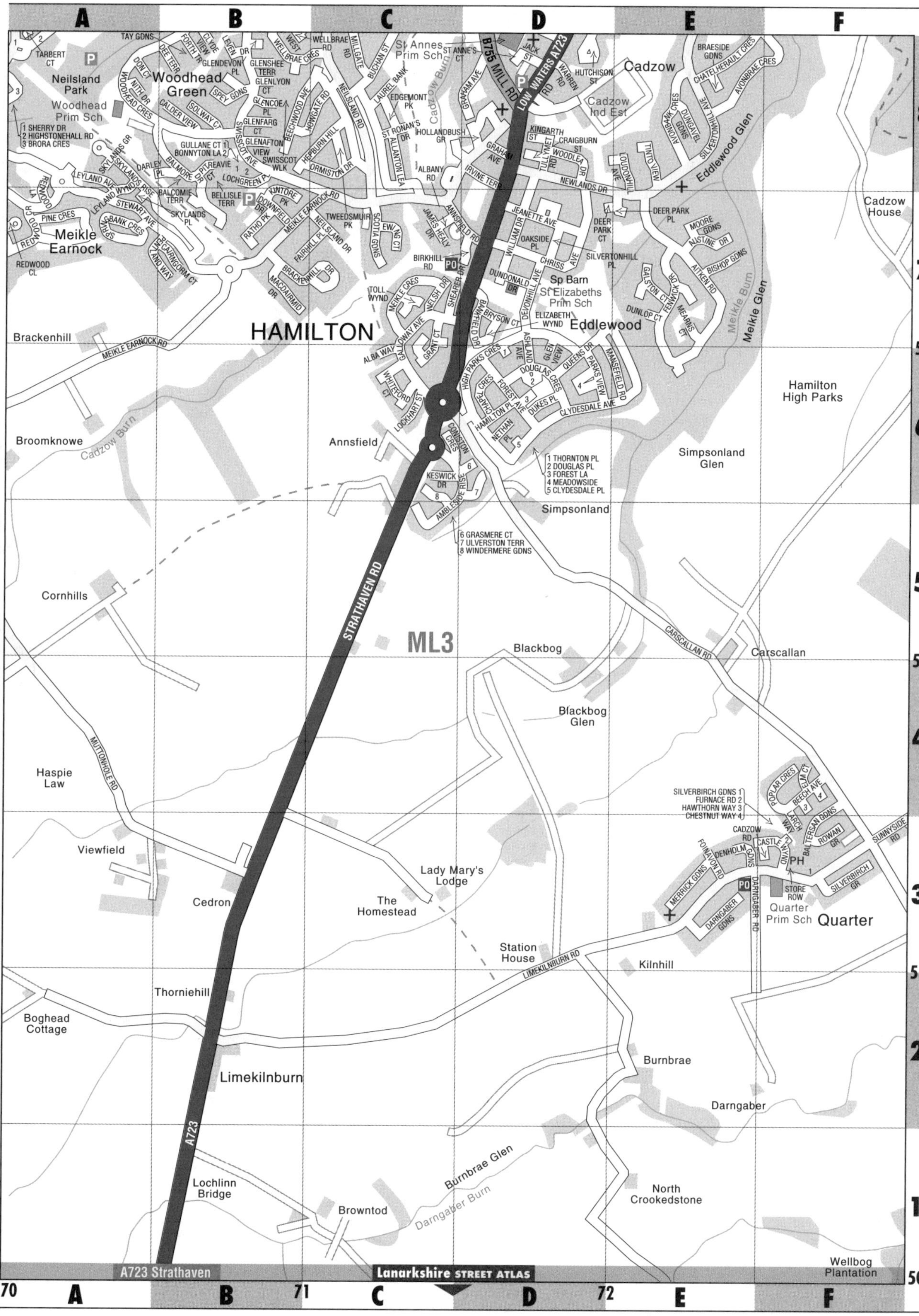
HAMILTON
ML3
Neilsland Park
Woodhead Green
Woodhead Prim Sch
Meikle Earnock
Cadzow
Cadzow Ind Est
St Annes Prim Sch
Sp Barn
St Elizabeths Prim Sch
Eddlewood
Eddlewood Glen
Meikle Glen
Meikle Burn
Cadzow Burn
Cadzow House
Brackenhill
Broomknowe
Annsfield
Simpsonland
Simpsonland Glen
Hamilton High Parks
Cornhills
Blackbog
Blackbog Glen
Carscallan
Haspie Law
Viewfield
Cedron
Lady Mary's Lodge
The Homestead
Station House
Kilnhill
Quarter
Quarter Prim Sch
Thorniehill
Boghead Cottage
Limekilnburn
Burnbrae
Darngaber
Lochlinn Bridge
Browntod
Burnbrae Glen
Darngaber Burn
North Crookedstone
Wellbog Plantation
STRATHAVEN RD
A723
B755 MILL RD
LOW WATERS A723
MEIKLE EARNOCK RD
CARSCALLAN RD
LIMEKILNBURN RD
MUTTONHOLE RD
1 SHERRY DR
2 HIGHSTONEHALL RD
3 BRORA CRES
1 THORNTON PL
2 DOUGLAS PL
3 FOREST LA
4 MEADOWSIDE
5 CLYDESDALE PL
6 GRASMERE CT
7 ULVERSTON TERR
8 WINDERMERE GDNS
SILVERBIRCH GDNS 1
FURNACE RD 2
HAWTHORN WAY 3
CHESTNUT WAY 4
A B C D E F
8 7 6 5 4 3 2 1
53 52 51 50
70 71 72
A723 Strathaven

183
163

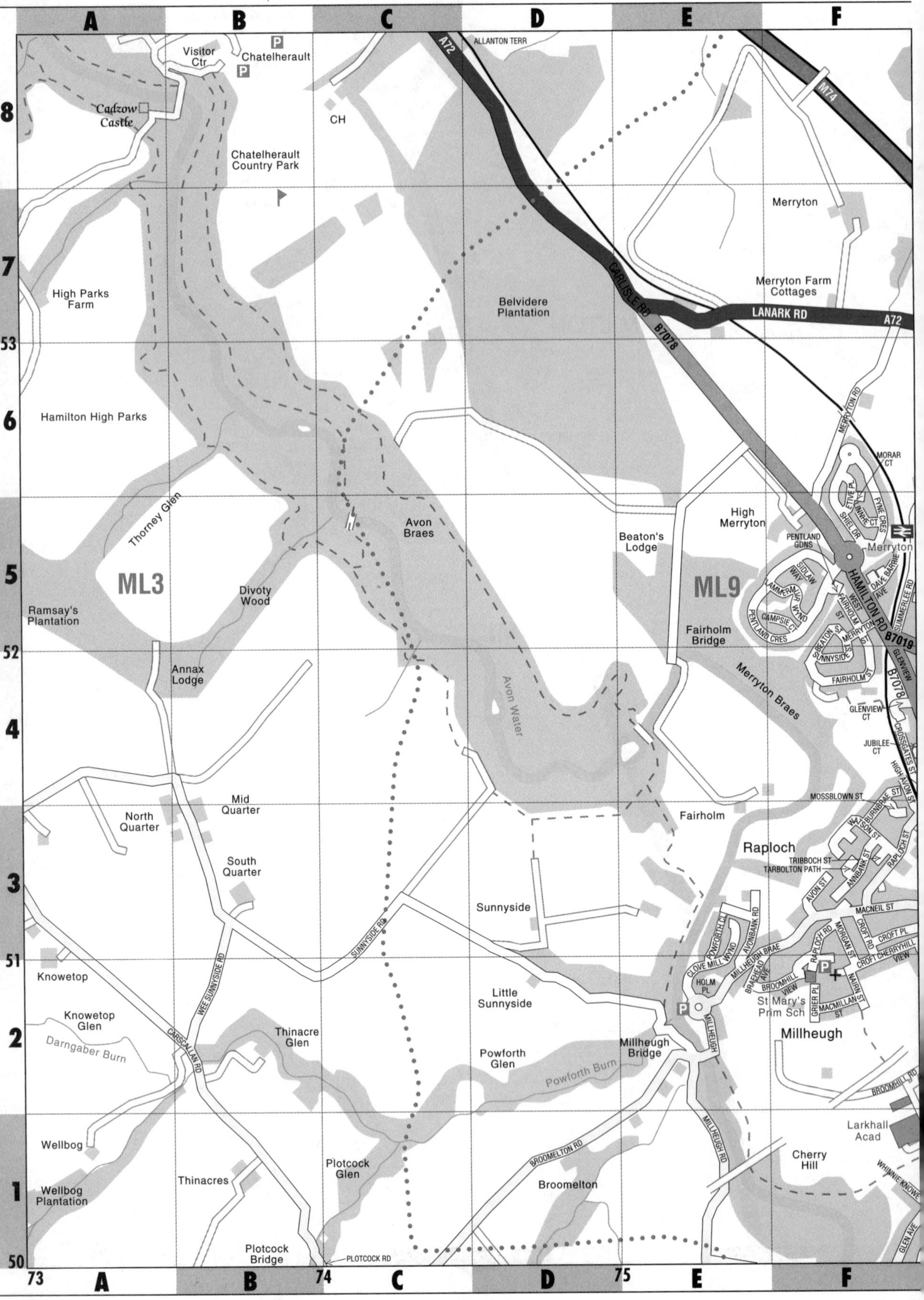
A
B
C
D
E
F
8
7
53
6
5
52
4
3
51
2
1
50
73
74
75
Visitor Ctr
Chatelherault
Cadzow Castle
CH
Chatelherault Country Park
ALLANTON TERR
A72
M74
Merryton
Merryton Farm Cottages
High Parks Farm
Belvidere Plantation
CARLISLE RD
B7078
LANARK RD
A72
Hamilton High Parks
MERRYTON RD
MORAR CT
ETIVE PL
FYNE CRES
INNHOE CT
SHIEL DR
High Merryton
Beaton's Lodge
PENTLAND GDNS
Merryton
Thorney Glen
Avon Braes
ML3
ML9
SIDLAW WAY
LAMMERMUIR WYND
CAMPSIE CT
PENTLAND CRES
FAIRHOLM ST
WEST
HAMILTON RD
DALE BARRIE AVE
SUMMERLEE RD
Ramsay's Plantation
Divoty Wood
Fairholm Bridge
BEATON ST
MERRYTON ST
SUNNYSIDE ST
FAIRHOLM ST
B7019
GLENVIEW
B7078
Annax Lodge
Avon Water
Merryton Braes
GLENVIEW CT
CROSSGATES ST
JUBILEE CT
HIGH AVON ST
MOSSBLOWN ST
BURNBRAE ST
WATSON ST
Mid Quarter
North Quarter
Fairholm
Raploch
RAPLOCH ST
TRIBBOCH ST
TARBOLTON PATH
ANNBANK ST
South Quarter
AVON ST
MACNEIL ST
Sunnyside
POWFORTH CL
AVONBANK RD
SUNNYSIDE RD
CLOVE MILL WYND
MILLHEUGH BRAE
RAPLOCH RD
MORGAN ST
CROFT RD
CROFT PL
CROFT CHERRYHILL VIEW
WEE SUNNYSIDE RD
Knowetop
HOLM PL
BRAEHEAD AVE
BROOMHILL VIEW
GRIER PL
MACMILLAN ST
NAIRN ST
Little Sunnyside
St Mary's Prim Sch
Knowetop Glen
MILLHEUGH
Millheugh
Darngaber Burn
CARSCALLAN RD
Thinacre Glen
Powforth Glen
Millheugh Bridge
Powforth Burn
BROOMHILL RD
Larkhall Acad
Wellbog
MILLHEUGH RD
BROOMELTON RD
Plotcock Glen
Cherry Hill
Thinacres
Broomelton
WHINNIE KNOWE
Wellbog Plantation
GLEN AVE
Plotcock Bridge
PLOTCOCK RD

A
B
C
D
E
F
Randalls Orchard
Carbarns Orchard
Sewage Works
Carbarns Rd
Lower Carbarns
Carbarnswood
Carbarns Wood
ML2
Hall Gill
North Lodge
Castlehill
Castlehill Rd
B754
Allershaw Rd
ALLERSHAW TWR 1
BIRKSHAW TWR 2
CAPLAW TWR 3
LINGHOPE PL 4
BLUEBELL WYND 5
Cala Sona Ct
Old Manse Rd
Montgomery Cres
Tammy's Burn
River Clyde
Upper Carbarns
Cambusnethan House
Highmainshead Wood
Highlees
Prince's Lodge
Whittrick Burn
Lanark Rd
Skelly Gill
Nursery
Tilework Cottage
Sewage Works
Cemy
East Station Ind Est
Meadowhill
Skellyton Wood
Skellyton
1 SUMMERLEE RD
2 BEECHWOOD
3 WILLOWBANK
Hamilton St
Drygate St
Larkhall
ML9
Burnside Pl
Burnhead
Millburn Glen
Milburn Cottage
A72
A71
Cornsilloch Brae
Mill Burn
Cornsilloch
Ayr Rd
CH
Millburn
Glengowan Prim Sch
Charing Cross
Machanhill Prim Sch
Union St
Church St
Machan Rd
B7078
Machan
Burnhead Rd
B7019
Shawsburn
Shawsgate
M74
Nurseries
Ashgillhead Rd
Ashgillhead
CRAIGBURN CT 1
MILLBURN GATE 2
RORISON PL 3
Stewart Gill
Works
Shawsrigg
Shaws Rd
Tinto View Rd
Sp Barn
Hareleeshill
Ind Est
Duneaton Wynd
5 CLEM ATTLEE GDNS
6 EAST MACHAN ST
7 GREENLOAN VIEW
8 REDHOLME
9 BRAESIDE WAY
8
7
53
6
5
52
4
3
51
2
1
50
77
78

A1
1 Robert Smillie Meml Prim Sch

B4
1 GLENORAN LA
2 EASTWOOD WAY
3 GLENBURN WYND
4 PORTLAND WYND
5 SIGHTHILL LOAN
6 PARKNOOK WAY
7 LOMOND WLK
8 HOZIER LOAN
9 CRAIGIE LA
10 GEORGE WAY
11 ALBANY WYND
12 CRAIGMORE WYND
13 BURNS LOAN
14 BANK WAY
15 BRAESIDE LA

C2
1 LOANING
2 LOVAT PATH
3 BALMORAL PATH
4 LOCHLEA LOAN
5 CATRINE ST
6 GILLBANK LA
7 CARRICK ST
8 WINDSOR PATH
9 WOODBURN TERR
10 MAXWELL PATH
11 HAWTHORN GDNS

C1
1 MOSSGIEL LA
2 BERTRAM ST
3 HAZELDENE LA
4 ROSEMOUNT LA
5 LAUREL LA
6 BRACKEN WAY
7 LAMMER WYND
8 CAMERONIAN WAY
9 GLEN FRUIN DR
10 ST ANDREWS PATH
11 LAWRIE WAY
12 KATRIONA PATH
13 CAMERON PATH
14 TRINITY WAY
15 BLAIR ATHOLL DR
16 ALBA WAY
17 ARRAN PATH
18 DALSERF PATH
19 BANNOCKBURN DR
20 LOCHNAGAR WAY
21 FLEMING WAY
22 BRUCE'S LOAN
23 Hareleeshill Prim Sch

185
165

A
B
C
D
E
F
Gowkthrapple
Castlehill Prim Sch
Garrion Bsns Pk
LINNHE CRES
ETIVE CRES
RANNOCH DR
NESS ST
HOSPITAL RD
DIMSDALE RD
Pather Farm
Waterloo
WELLINGTON PL
A721
A71
PO
OVERTOWN RD
WISHAW RD
Gillhead
A721
ALLERSHAW RD
BIRKSHAW PL
BIRKSHAW BRAE
LINGHOPE PL
STANHOPE PL
SMITH AVE
WOODGREEN CT
HEATHFIELD
B754
30
Clyde Valley High Sch
Overtown Prim Sch
1 SMITHVIEW
2 GLIDDEN CT
3 GILFILLAN PL
4 McNEIL PL
PRIORY GATE
JENNIE LEE DR
BAILIE FYFE WAY
KENNEDY GDNS
TONER GDNS
McINNES PL
CASTLEHILL RD
LASHLEY GR
HOD DR
COWAN WYND
BENTFOOT RD
YERSHAW ST
GILL RD
DOUGLAS ST
HUTCHINSON ST
JACOB'S LADDER WAY
LAW VIEW
GILL RD
BROOKLYN PL
TROWS RD
ORCHARD ST
BELMONT ST
GREENKNOWE ST
PO
B754
MAIN ST
GARRION ST
GILLBURN ST
OVERDALE PL
GOURLAY DR
ROSEBANK RD
1 RHU QUADRANT
2 BRUCE LOAN
3 COVENANTERS WAY
Wemysshill
ML2
Overtown
P
Garrion Burn
ASHFIELD
ASH GR 1
HAZEL GR 2
HAWTHORN GR 3
CEDAR GDNS 4
MAULDSLIE DR 5
WOODLANDSAVE 6
BEECH GR
SHAWFIELD CRES
GREENKNOWE DR
MUIR
LAWMUIR RD
Law
P
STATION RD
B7011
PO
STRATH
PEFFER
BLUEKNOWES RD
LAWHILL RD
CARMICHAEL WAY
CARMICHAEL ST
ANSTRUTHER CT
ANSTRUTHER ST
McMILLAN WAY
BRAEFOOT CT
BRAEFOOT CRES
WESTEND CT
SHAWGILL CT
MURRAY RD
WEIR PL 1
SWAN WAY 2
GRIFFITHS WAY 3
Shawgill
A71
Horsleyhead
Blairs Orchard
Trotterbank
Birks
HORSLEY BRAE
BROWNLEE RD
ML8
STRAVENHOUSE RD
Garrionhaugh Farm
B7011
Cardies Bridge
BIRKS RD
LARNARK RD
Nursery
A71 CORNSILLOCH BRAE
Stravenhouse Farm
River Clyde
Garrion Farm
Brownlee House
Bensilloch Nurseries
The Beeches
Garrion Tower
Garrion Bridge
A72
Clyde Walkway
MAULDSLIE RD
QUARRY RD
Castlehill Nursery
Dalserf
KIRK RD
Stewart Gill
Mauldslie Mains
MILLBURN RD
ML9
East Lodge
Millburn House
Works
Mauldslie Stables
MANSE BRAE
Mauldslie Bridge
Mauldslie House
Auldton
A72
Jock's Gill Wood
Nurseries
8
7
53
6
5
52
4
3
51
2
1
50
79
80
81

A
B
C
D
E
F
8
7
53
6
5
52
4
3
51
2
1
50
82
83
84
ML2
ML8
A721
WISHAW RD
HYNDSHAW RD
A73
Bogside
Lanniemuirs
Twelve Acre Plantation
Mid Hyndshaw
Hyndshaw
Law Hospital (dis)
Wildmanbridge
B7011
Works
Gillhead
WILDMAN RD
Wildman Bridge
STATION PL
MUIRHEAD DR
WALLACE WYND
STATION ROW
Nursery
BELL GR
Mast
ASHFIELD RD
MAULDSLIE DR
WOODLANDS CRES
DOBBIES AVE
KIRK LA
GALBRAITH CRES
STATION RD
TEMPLE CT
BUCHANAN DR
ST ANDREWS DR
SCOTT DR
PATTERSON DR
BOURTREE CRES
BRACKENHILL RD
Brackenhill
STRATH CARRON
STRATH DEARN
STRATH HALLADALE
STRATH NAIRN
STRATH ELGIN
1 STRATH PEFFER
2 STRATH NAVER
3 WISHART LA
4 CRAIG PL
5 SPIERS GATE
WATERLANDS RD
Waterlands
Garrion Burn
Bowridge Bridge
Bowridge Burn
Belstane Place
Castlehill Bridge
Castlehill Farm
Castlehill
CASTLEHILL RD
Law Prim Sch
BLACKHILL VIEW
WEIR PL
MANSE CT
CASTLEHILL CRES
HYNDSHAW VIEW
1 WATERLANDS PL
2 SWAN WAY
3 MURRAY RD
4 GRIFFITHS WAY
5 KINGSHILL VIEW
6 OLD SCHOOL PL
STRAVENHOUSE RD
Law Hill
East Law
Hillview
QUARRY RD
Law of Mauldslie
LAWHILL RD
WHITESHAW RD
AIRDRIE RD
HEATHER ROW
Castlehill Ind Est
KINTYRE WYND 1
KILMARTIN LA 2
DUNARD CT 3
PEACOCK LOAN 4
CAIRNBAN CT 5
KENMORE WAY 6
BARRS LA 7
KILMORY GDNS 8
BELSTANE PK 9
GLENDERMOTT CT 10
STONEFIELD GDNS 11
REDHOUSE LA 12
HONEYBANK CRES
BELSTANE GATE
CRAIGNETHAN RD
CRATHIE CT
NIMMO PL
WEIGHHOUSE RD
Carluke
GASWORKS RD
NEWBARNS ST
SANDY RD
WINDSOR QUADRANT
HOZIER ST
MARKET RD
GLAMIS AVE
CHAPEL ST
MILLER ST
CARNWATH RD
A721
STEWART ST
KIRKTON ST
WESTERHOUSE CT
MAULDSLIE RD
CH
Hallcraig
Mauldslie Cottage
Jock's Gill
Jock's Burn
Kirkton Prim Sch
St Athanasius' Prim Sch
Carluke
STATION RD
Liby
UNITAS CRES
A73

F2
1 STEWART PL
2 MARKET RD
3 Rankin Gate Ctr
4 GREENBANK TERR
5 High Mill Prim Sch
6 Victoria Park Sch

187
167

187
202

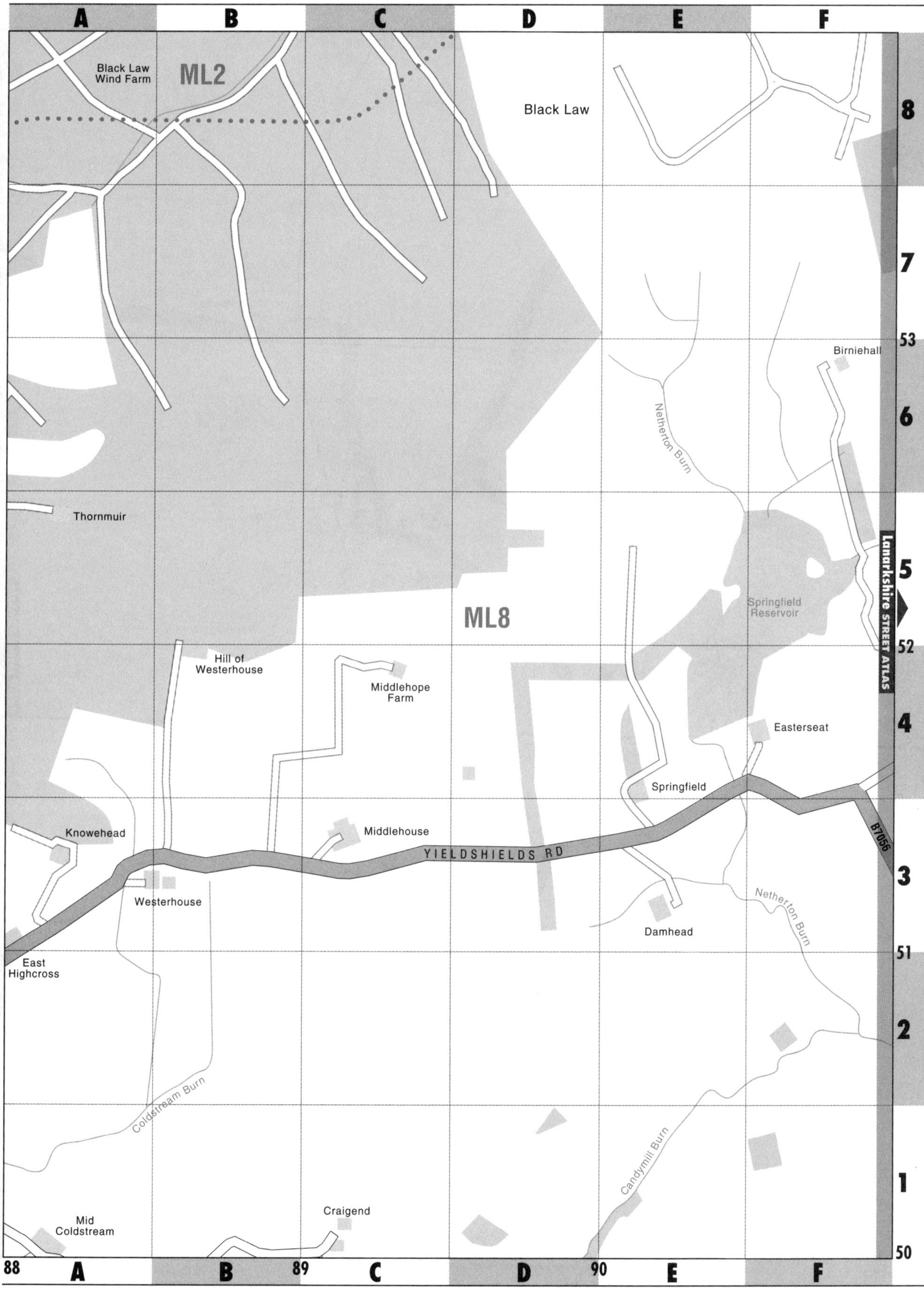
A
B
C
D
E
F
Black Law Wind Farm
ML2
Black Law
8
7
53
Birniehall
Netherton Burn
6
Thornmuir
5
Springfield Reservoir
ML8
Lanarkshire STREET ATLAS
52
Hill of Westerhouse
Middlehope Farm
Easterseat
4
Springfield
Knowehead
Middlehouse
YIELDSHIELDS RD
B7056
3
Westerhouse
Damhead
Netherton Burn
East Highcross
51
2
Coldstream Burn
Candymill Burn
1
Mid Coldstream
Craigend
50
88
89
90

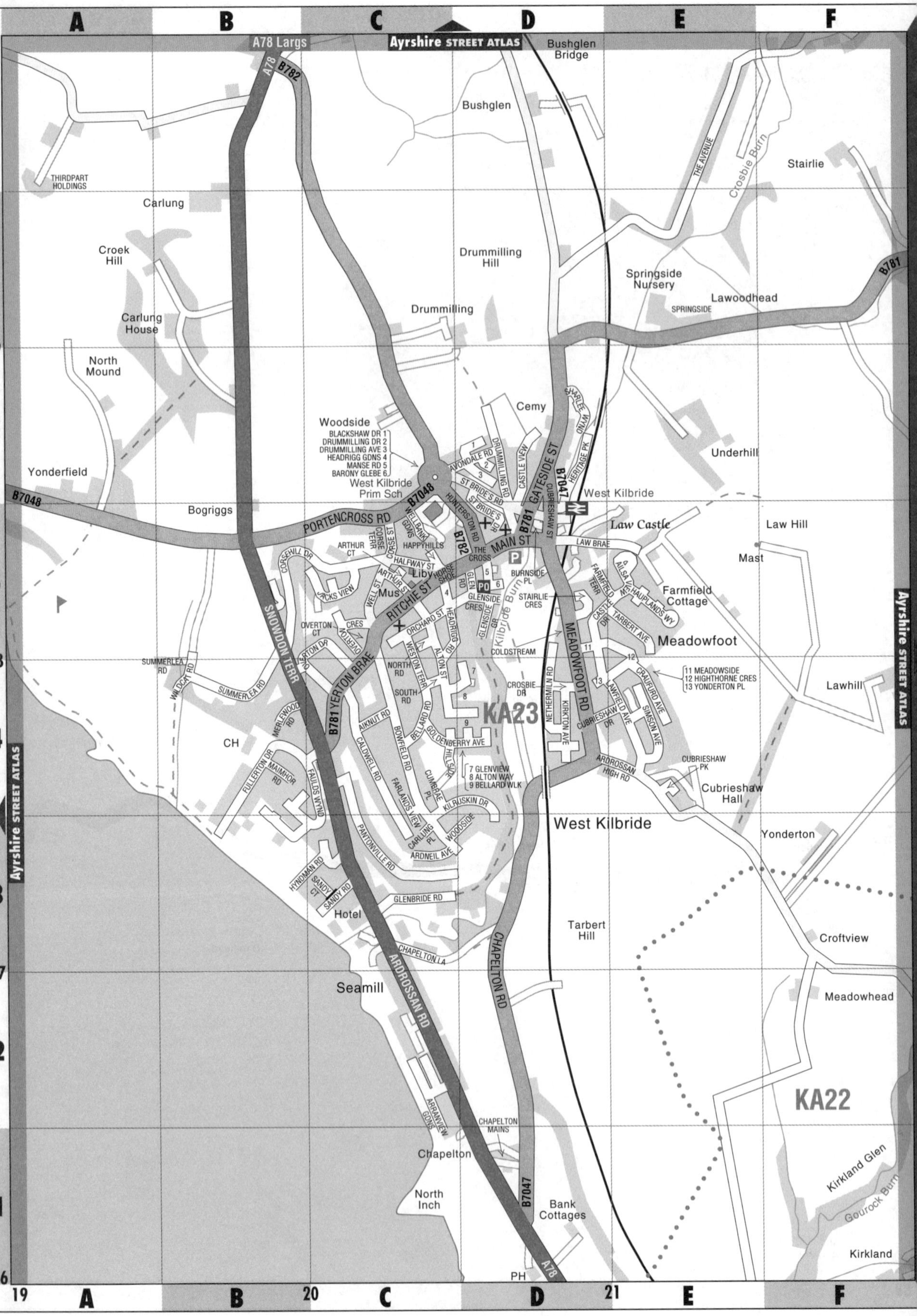
A
B
C
D
E
F
A78 Largs
Ayrshire STREET ATLAS
Bushglen Bridge
Bushglen
8
7
6
5
4
3
2
1
49
48
47
46
19
20
21
THIRDPART HOLDINGS
Carlung
Croek Hill
Carlung House
North Mound
Yonderfield
Bogriggs
Drummilling Hill
Drummilling
Springside Nursery
SPRINGSIDE
Lawoodhead
Stairlie
Crosbie Burn
THE AVENUE
B781
Cemy
Woodside
BLACKSHAW DR 1
DRUMMILLING DR 2
DRUMMILLING AVE 3
HEADRIGG GDNS 4
MANSE RD 5
BARONY GLEBE 6
West Kilbride Prim Sch
B7048
PORTENCROSS RD
AVONDALE RD
DRUMMILLING RD
CASTLE VIEW
ST BRIDE'S RD
ST BRIDE'S DR
HUNTERSTON RD
GATESIDE ST
B7047
CUBRIESHAW ST
HERITAGE PK
OWYN
SHARLEE
West Kilbride
Law Castle
LAW BRAE
Law Hill
Mast
Underhill
WELLBANK GDNS
CORSE TERR
ARTHUR CT
HAPPYHILLS
HALFWAY ST
ARTHUR ST
HORSE SHOE
THE CROSS
MAIN ST
B782
Liby
Mus
PO
GLEN RD
BURNSIDE PL
STAIRLIE CRES
GLENSIDE CRES
GLENSIDE GR
Kilbride Burn
FARMFIELD TERR
ALSA VW
HAUPLANDS WY
Farmfield Cottage
TARBERT AVE
CASTLE DR
Meadowfoot
CORSEHILL DR
JACKS VIEW
WELL ST
RITCHIE ST
OVERTON CT
OVERTON CRES
OVERTON DR
ORCHARD ST
WESTON TERR
HEADRIGG RD
ALTON ST
NORTH RD
SOUTH RD
COLDSTREAM
MEADOWFOOT RD
CROSBIE DR
11 MEADOWSIDE
12 HIGHTHORNE CRES
13 YONDERTON PL
CRAUFURD AVE
LAWFIELD AVE
SIMSON AVE
CUBRIESHAW DR
KIRKTON AVE
NETHERMILN RD
KA23
Lawhill
SUMMERLEA RD
WILDCAT RD
SUMMERLEA RD
SNOWDON TERR
B781 YERTON BRAE
MERLEWOOD RD
AIKNUT RD
BOWFIELD RD
BELLARD RD
GOLDENBERRY AVE
HILLSIDE
7 GLENVIEW
8 ALTON WAY
9 BELLARD WLK
CALDWELL RD
CUMBRAE PL
FARLANDS VIEW
KILRUSKIN DR
CARLING PL
WOODSIDE
ARDNEIL AVE
PANTONVILLE RD
ARDROSSAN HIGH RD
CUBRIESHAW PK
Cubrieshaw Hall
CH
FULLERTON DR
MAIMHOR RD
FAULDS WYND
West Kilbride
Yonderton
HYNDMAN RD
SANDY CT
SANDY RD
GLENBRIDGE RD
Hotel
CHAPELTON LA
Tarbert Hill
Croftview
Seamill
ARDROSSAN RD
CHAPELTON RD
Meadowhead
ARRANVIEW GDNS
CHAPELTON MAINS
KA22
Chapelton
North Inch
B7047
Bank Cottages
Kirkland Glen
Gourock Burn
Kirkland
PH
A78

B7
1 CARSWELL CT
2 ARCHIBALD DR

169
192

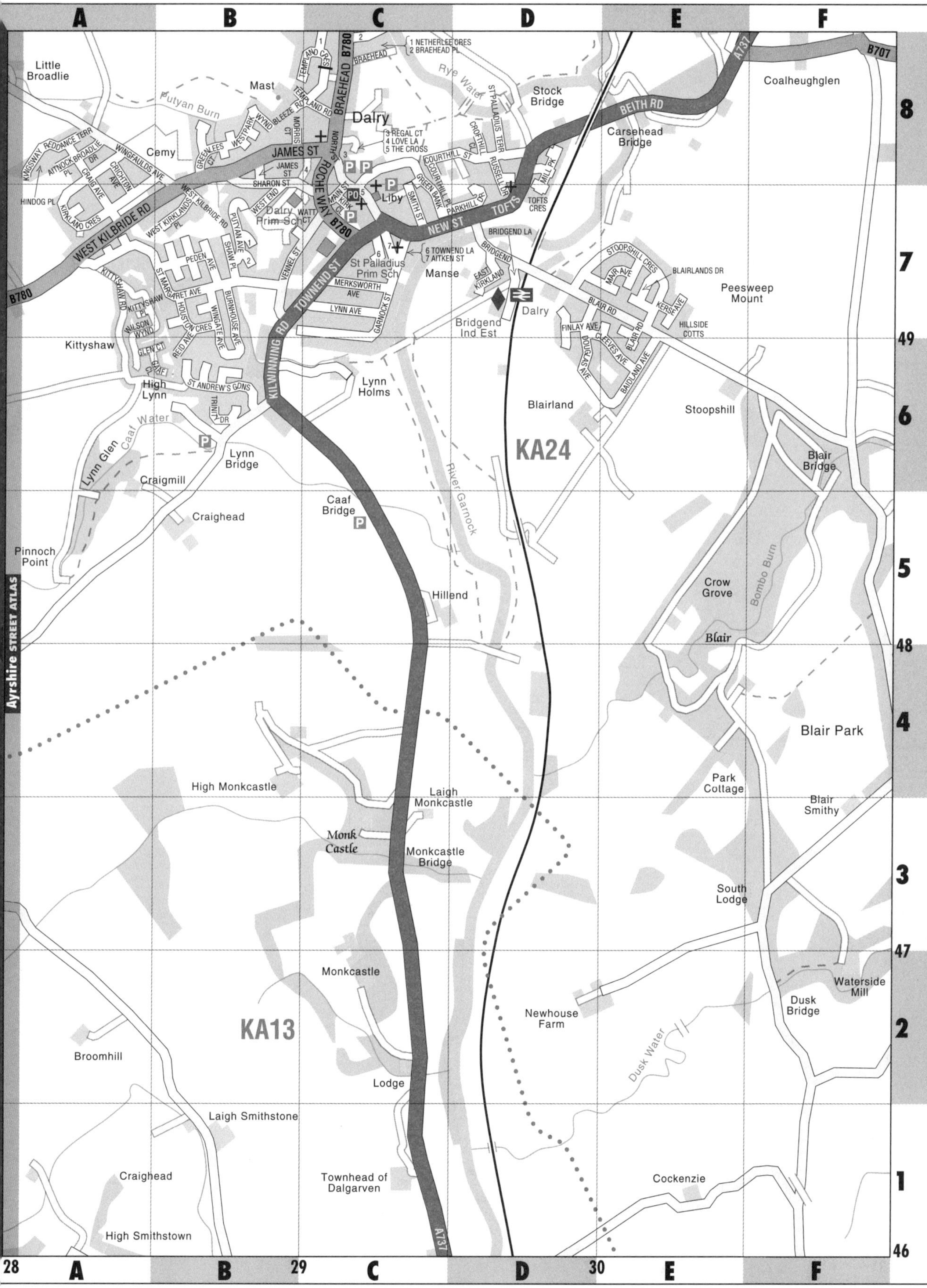

207
192

191
170

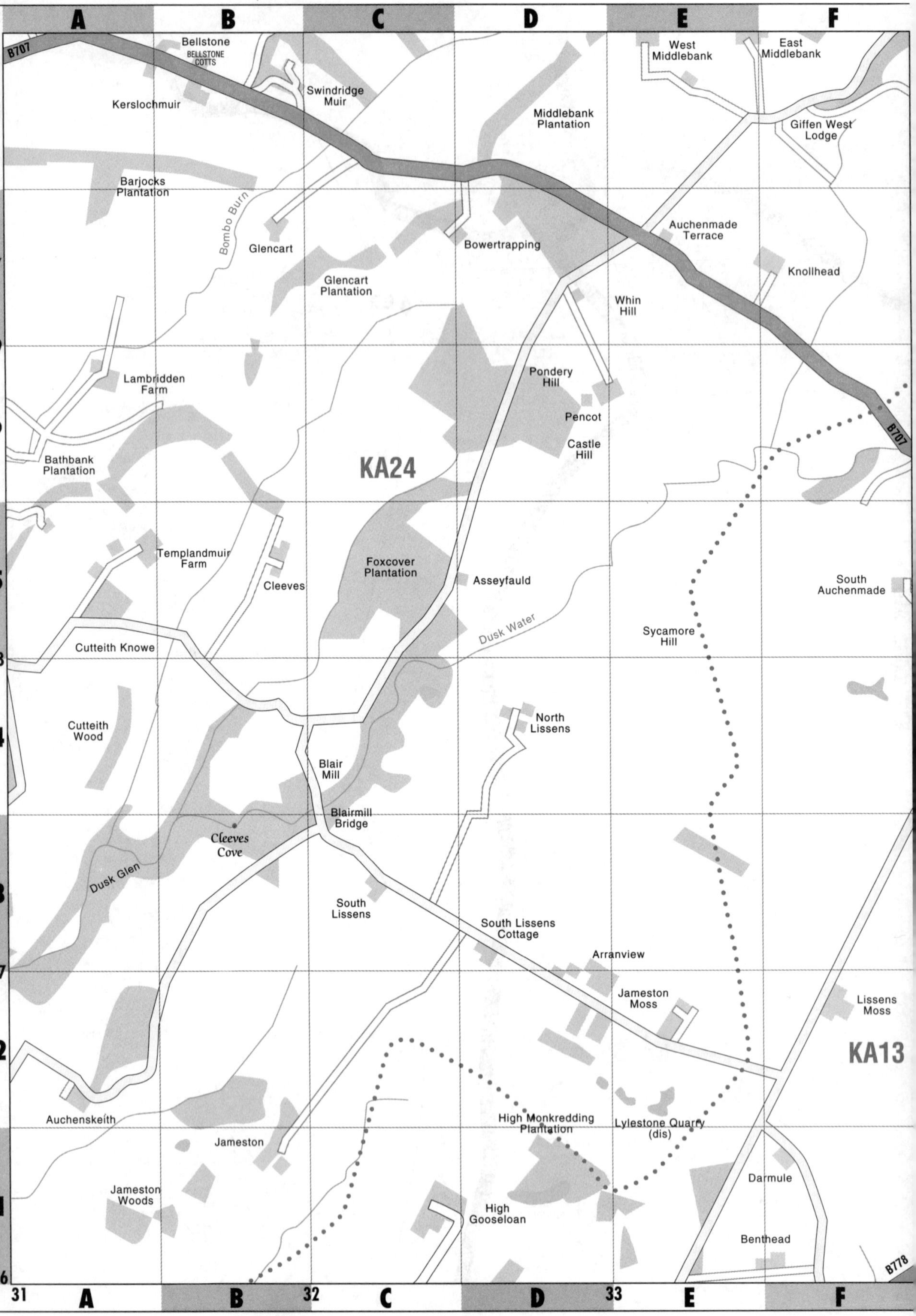

191
208

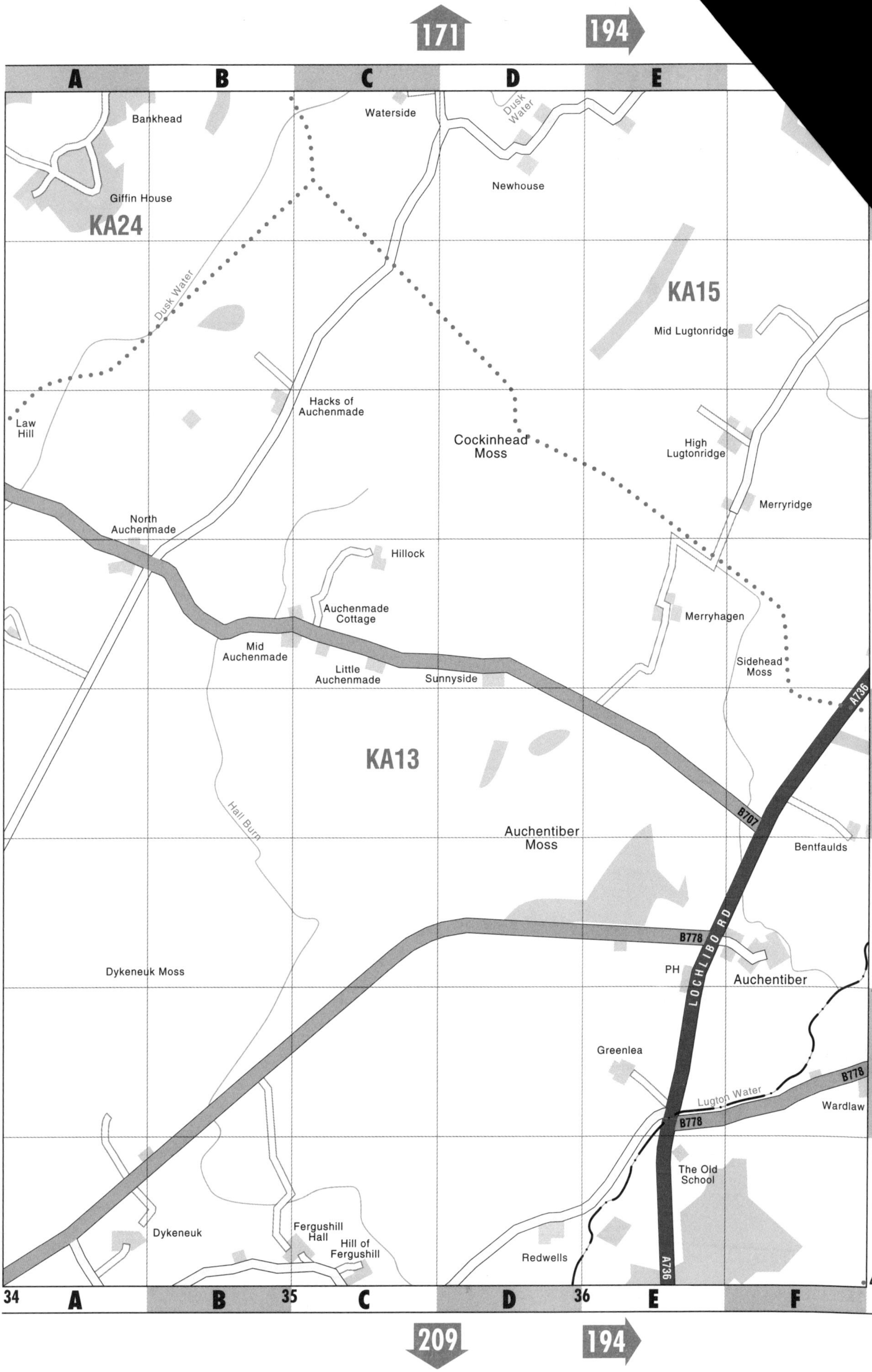
171
194
A
B
C
D
E
Bankhead
Waterside
Dusk Water
Newhouse
Giffin House
KA24
Dusk Water
KA15
Mid Lugtonridge
7
49
Law Hill
Hacks of Auchenmade
Cockinhead Moss
High Lugtonridge
6
Merryridge
North Auchenmade
Hillock
Auchenmade Cottage
Merryhagen
5
Mid Auchenmade
Little Auchenmade
Sunnyside
Sidehead Moss
48
A736
KA13
4
Hall Burn
B707
Auchentiber Moss
Bentfaulds
3
B778
LOCHLIBO RD
PH
Auchentiber
Dykeneuk Moss
47
Greenlea
2
B778
Lugton Water
Wardlaw
B778
The Old School
1
Fergushill Hall
Dykeneuk
Hill of Fergushill
Redwells
A736
46
34
A
B
35
C
D
36
E
F
209
194

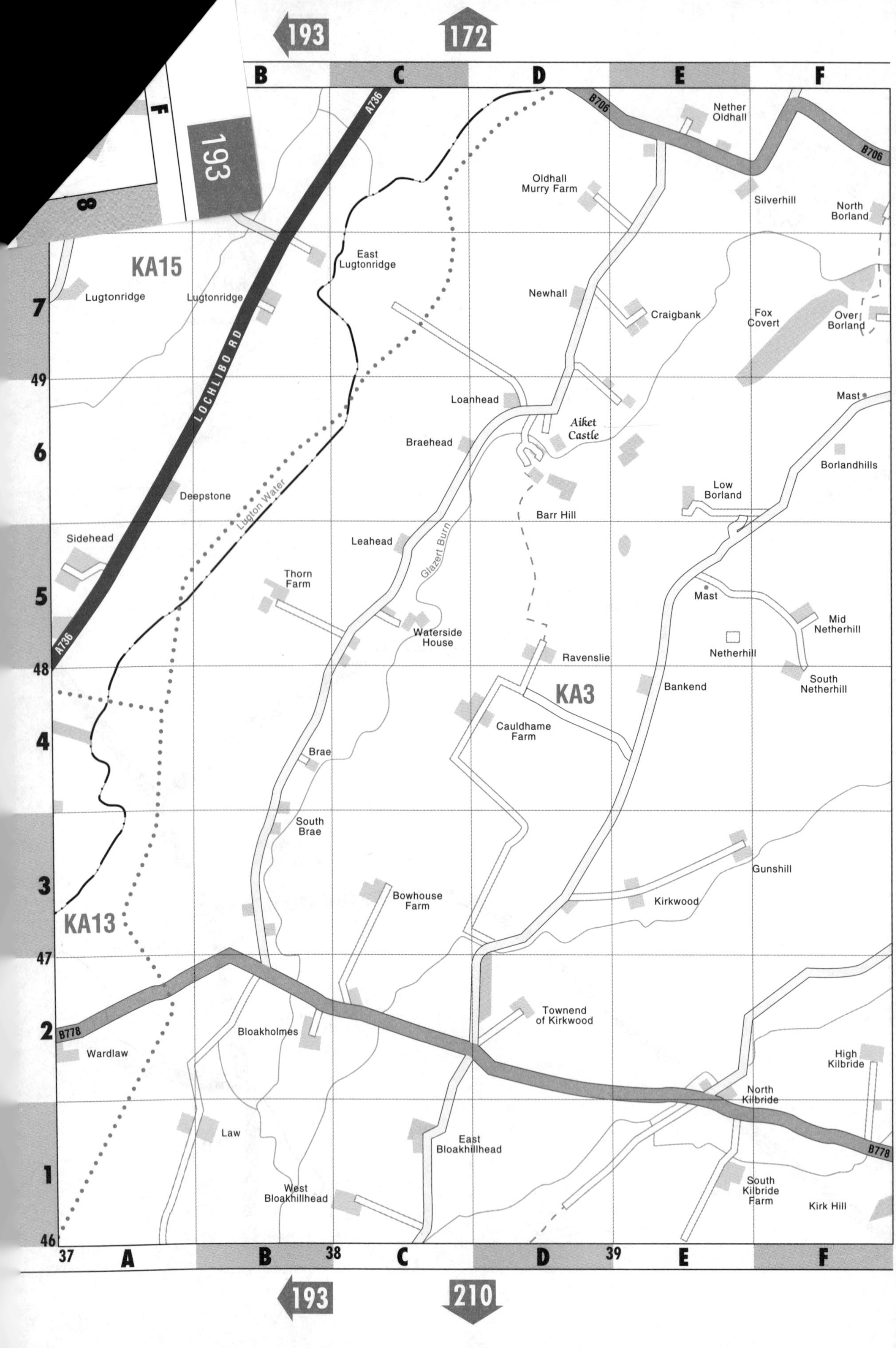
193
172
B
C
D
E
F
193
F
8
KA15
Lugtonridge
Lugtonridge
East Lugtonridge
A736
LOCHLIBO RD
B706
Nether Oldhall
Oldhall Murry Farm
Silverhill
North Borland
Newhall
Craigbank
Fox Covert
Over Borland
7
49
Loanhead
Mast
Aiket Castle
Braehead
6
Borlandhills
Low Borland
Deepstone
Lugton Water
Barr Hill
Sidehead
Leahead
Glazert Burn
Thorn Farm
5
Mast
Mid Netherhill
Waterside House
Netherhill
48
Ravenslie
South Netherhill
KA3
Bankend
Cauldhame Farm
4
Brae
South Brae
Gunshill
3
Bowhouse Farm
Kirkwood
KA13
47
Townend of Kirkwood
2
B778
Bloakholmes
Wardlaw
High Kilbride
North Kilbride
Law
East Bloakhillhead
B778
1
South Kilbride Farm
West Bloakhillhead
Kirk Hill
46
37
A
B
38
C
D
39
E
F
193
210

173
196

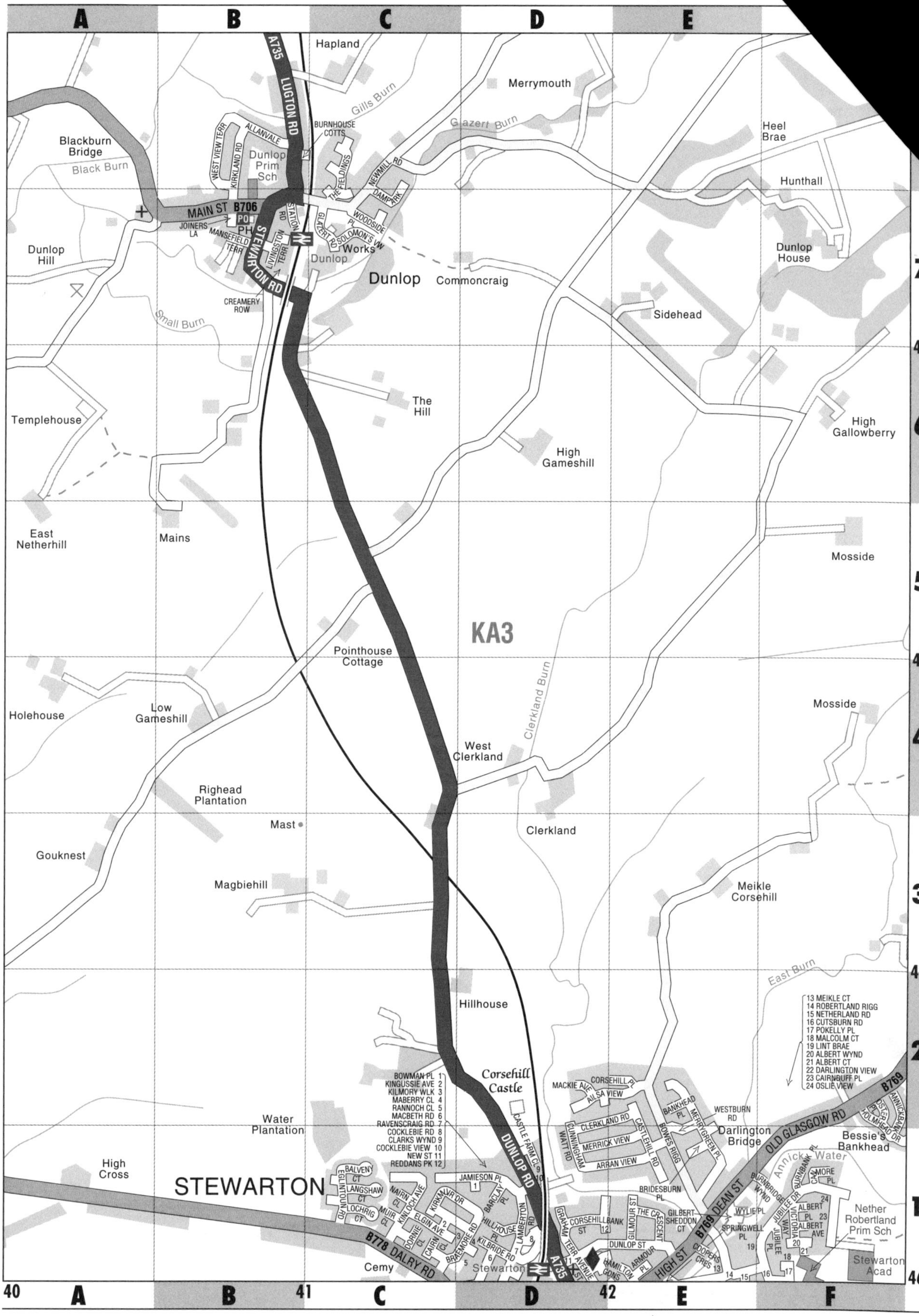
A
B
C
D
E
A735
LUGTON RD
Hapland
Merrymouth
Gills Burn
Glazert Burn
Heel Brae
Hunthall
Blackburn Bridge
Black Burn
WEST VIEW TERR
ALLANVALE
KIRKLAND RD
Dunlop Prim Sch
BURNHOUSE COTTS
THE FIELDINGS
NEWMILL RD
DAMPARK
MAIN ST
B706
PO
PH
JOINERS LA
MANSEFIELD TERR
STEWARTON RD
LIVINGSTON TERR
STATION RD
GLAZERT RD
WOODSIDE PL
SOLOMON'S VW
Works
Dunlop
Dunlop Hill
Dunlop House
Commoncraig
CREAMERY ROW
Small Burn
Sidehead
7
49
Templehouse
The Hill
High Gameshill
High Gallowberry
6
East Netherhill
Mains
Mosside
5
KA3
Pointhouse Cottage
48
Holehouse
Low Gameshill
Clerkland Burn
Mosside
4
West Clerkland
Righead Plantation
Mast
Clerkland
Gouknest
Magbiehill
Meikle Corsehill
3
47
East Burn
Hillhouse
13 MEIKLE CT
14 ROBERTLAND RIGG
15 NETHERLAND RD
16 CUTSBURN RD
17 POKELLY PL
18 MALCOLM CT
19 LINT BRAE
20 ALBERT WYND
21 ALBERT CT
22 DARLINGTON VIEW
23 CAIRNDUFF PL
24 OSLIE VIEW
2
BOWMAN PL 1
KINGUSSIE AVE 2
KILMORY WLK 3
MABERRY CL 4
RANNOCH CL 5
MACBETH RD 6
RAVENSCRAIG RD 7
COCKLEBIE RD 8
CLARKS WYND 9
COCKLEBIE VIEW 10
NEW ST 11
REDDANS PK 12
Corsehill Castle
MACKIE AVE
CORSEHILL PL
AILSA VIEW
BANKHEAD PL
MERRYGREEN PL
WESTBURN RD
Darlington Bridge
OLD GLASGOW RD
B769
Bessie's Bankhead
Water Plantation
CASTLE FARM CL
DUNLOP RD
CLERKLAND RD
CUNNINGHAM
WATT RD
MERRICK VIEW
ARRAN VIEW
CASTLEHILL RD
BOWES RIGG
BRIDESBURN PL
Annick Water
High Cross
STEWARTON
BALVENY CT
EGLINTOUN RD
LANGSHAW CT
LOCHRIG CT
NAIRN CL
MUIR CL
KINLOCH AVE
DORNIE CL
ELGIN AVE
CAIRN CL
KIRKHILL
JAMIESON PL
BARCLAY PL
HILLHOUSE PL
KILBRIDE RD
BRAEMORE RD
LAMBERTON RD
GRAHAM TERR
AVENUE
CORSEHILLBANK ST
GILMOUR ST
THE CRESCENT
GILBERT SHEDDON CT
DEAN ST
WYLIE PL
SPRINGWELL PL
JUBILEE DR
VICTORIA WAY
ALBERT PL
ALBERT AVE
DUNLOP ST
HAMILTON GDNS
ARMOUR PL
HIGH ST
COOPERS CRES
Nether Robertland Prim Sch
Stewarton Acad
1
B778 DALRY RD
Cemy
Stewarton
A735
46
40
41
42
F

211
196

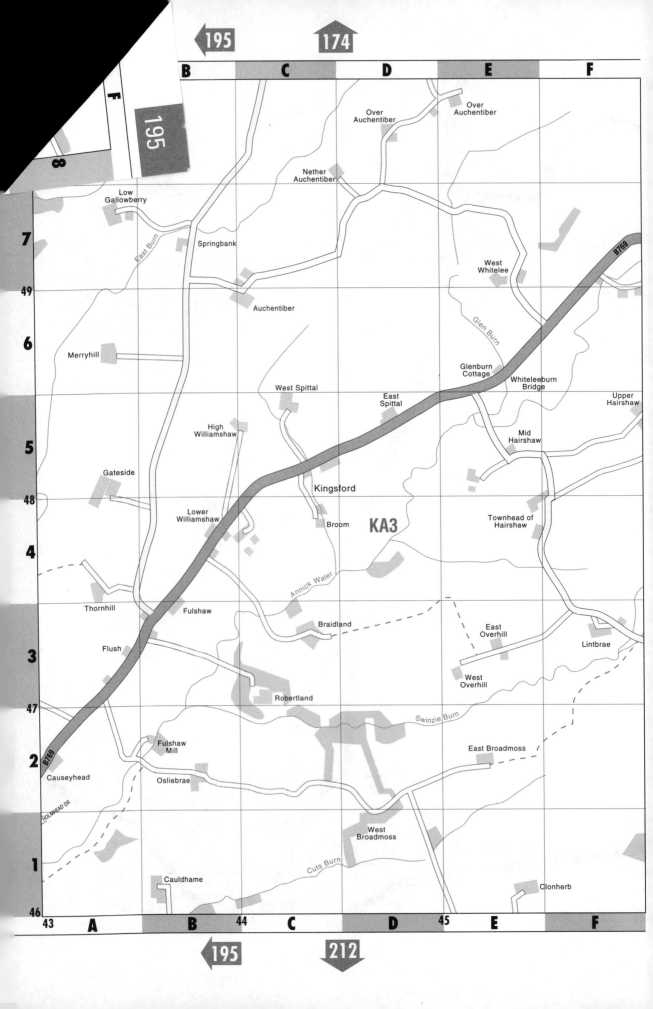

195
174

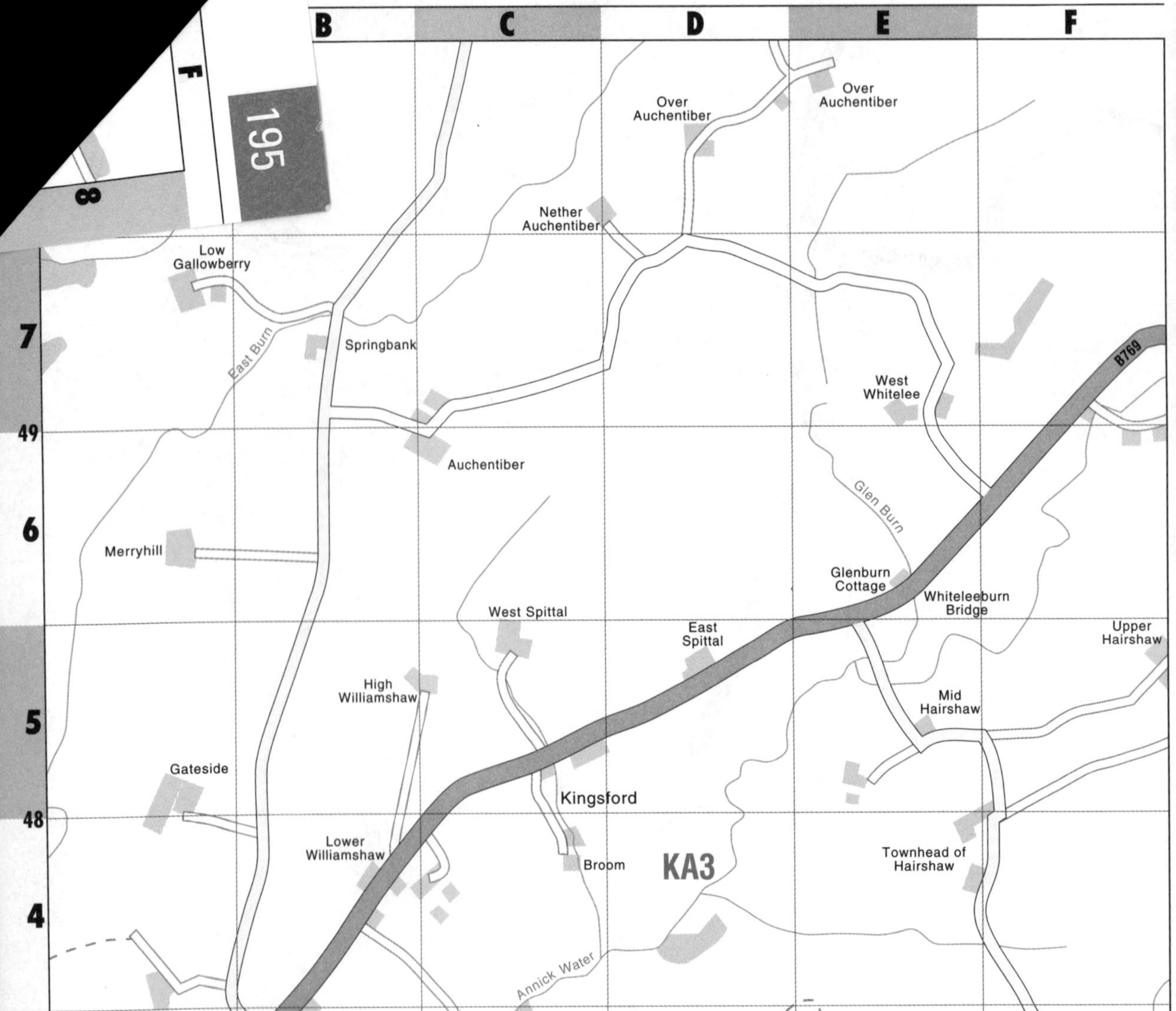
B
C
D
E
F
195
F
8
Over Auchentiber
Over Auchentiber
Nether Auchentiber
Low Gallowberry
7
Springbank
East Burn
B769
West Whitelee
49
Auchentiber
Glen Burn
6
Merryhill
Glenburn Cottage
Whiteleeburn Bridge
West Spittal
East Spittal
Upper Hairshaw
High Williamshaw
Mid Hairshaw
5
Gateside
Kingsford
48
Lower Williamshaw
Broom
KA3
Townhead of Hairshaw
4
Annick Water
Thornhill
Fulshaw
Braidland
East Overhill
Flush
Lintbrae
3
West Overhill
Robertland
47
Swinzie Burn
Fulshaw Mill
East Broadmoss
2
B769
Causeyhead
Osliebrae
HOLMHEAD DR
West Broadmoss
1
Cuts Burn
Cauldhame
Clonherb
46
43
A
B
44
C
D
45
E
F

195
212

175

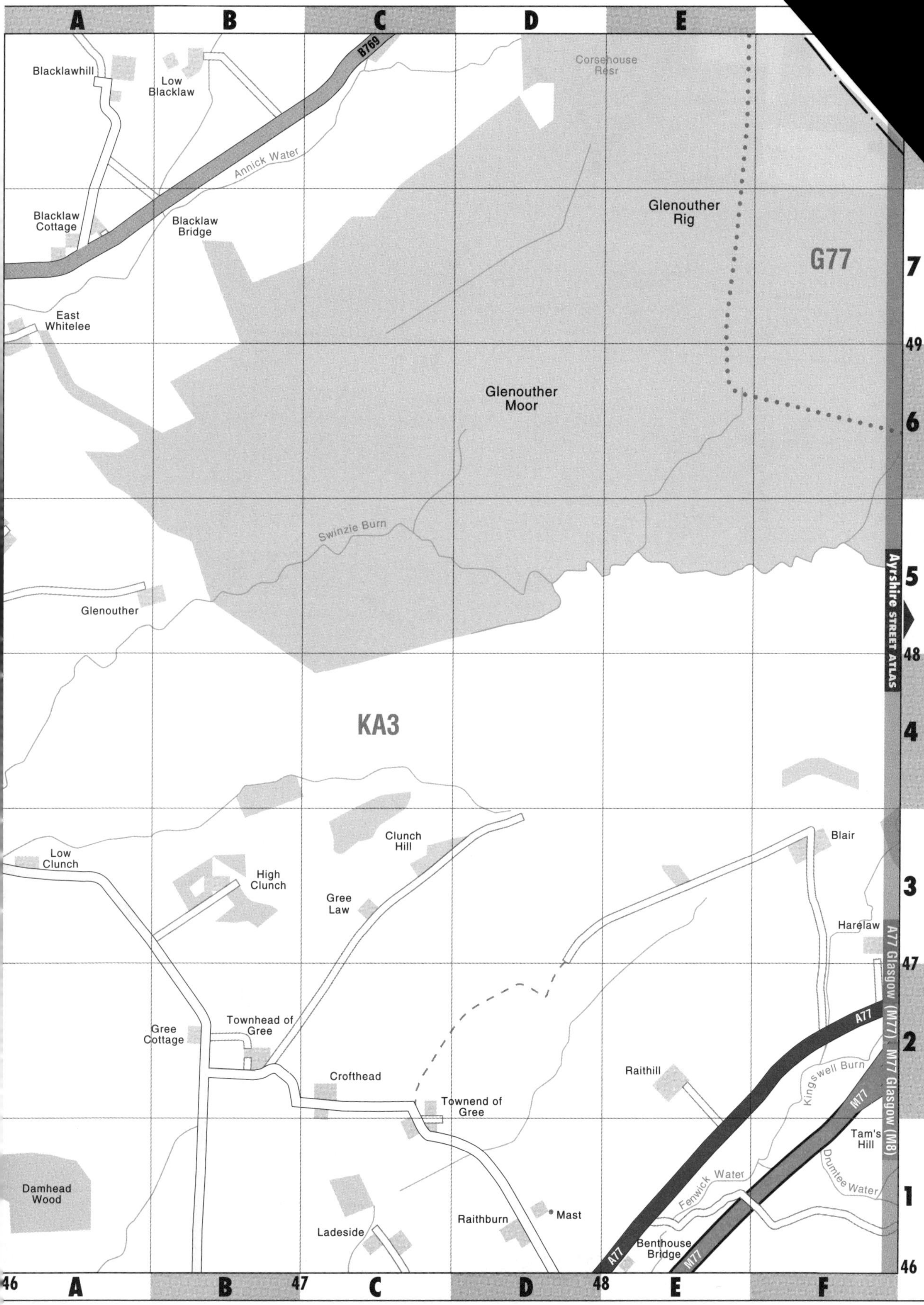
A
B
C
D
E
F
B769
Blacklawhill
Low Blacklaw
Corsehouse Resr
Annick Water
Blacklaw Cottage
Blacklaw Bridge
Glenouther Rig
G77
7
East Whitelee
49
Glenouther Moor
6
Swinzie Burn
5
Ayrshire STREET ATLAS
Glenouther
48
KA3
4
Low Clunch
High Clunch
Clunch Hill
Gree Law
Blair
3
Harelaw
A77 Glasgow (M77), M77 Glasgow (M8)
47
A77
2
Gree Cottage
Townhead of Gree
Crofthead
Townend of Gree
Raithill
Kingswell Burn
M77
Tam's Hill
Drumtee Water
Fenwick Water
Damhead Wood
1
Mast
Raithburn
Ladeside
Benthouse Bridge
46
47
48

213

184

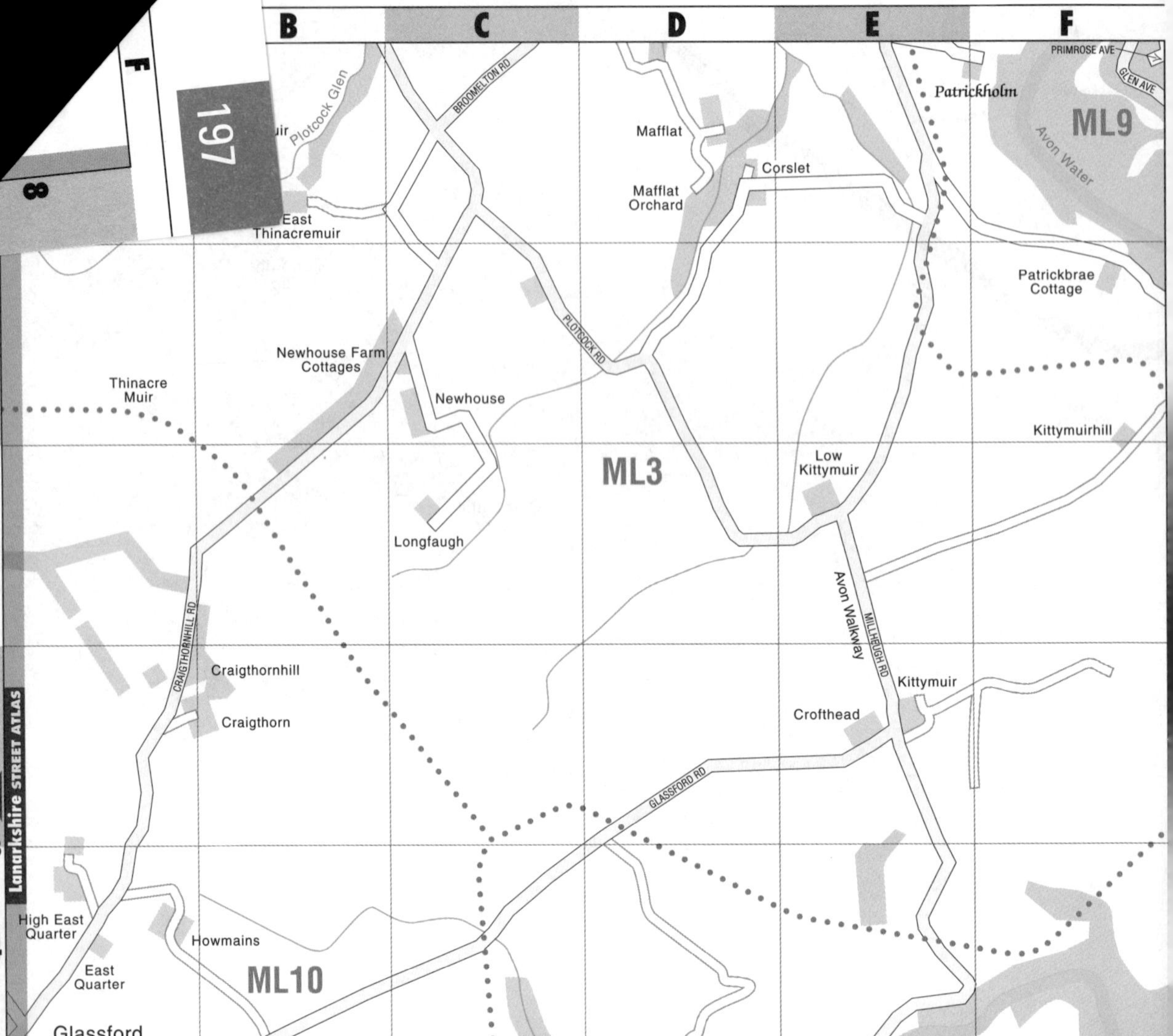
B C D E F
197
8
F
Plotcock Glen
East Thinacremuir
BROOMELTON RD
Mafflat
Mafflat Orchard
Corslet
Patrickholm
PRIMROSE AVE
GLEN AVE
ML9
Avon Water
Patrickbrae Cottage
7
Newhouse Farm Cottages
Thinacre Muir
PLOTCOCK RD
Newhouse
Kittymuirhill
49
ML3
Low Kittymuir
Longfaugh
6
Avon Walkway
MILLHAUGH RD
CRAIGTHORNHILL RD
Craigthornhill
Craigthorn
Kittymuir
Crofthead
5
Lanarkshire STREET ATLAS
GLASSFORD RD
48
High East Quarter
Howmains
4
East Quarter
ML10
Glassford
Linthaugh Bridge
Burnside
HUNTERLEES RD
Holm
Linthaugh
Hunterlees
Alexander Hamilton Memorial Park
3
Knowehead
Priest's Burn
Avon Water
A71
Cemy
ML9
Loch Park Ind Est
47
Cemy
Manse
Whitehill Cottage
Tapped Hill
Cemy
Liby
PO
Stonehouse
Whitehill
2
MANSE RD
East Mains
MUIRBURN RD
White Hill
Thorndale
Braehead
Stonehouse Prim Sch
Avonholm
East Mains Holdings
SANDYVALE
1
North Lodge
West Mains
PEBBLE DR
Homeleigh
Stonehouse
Bankhead
STRATHAVEN RD
RHYMEBANK
MURRAYSIDE
WHINRIGGS
SPINNINGDALE
1 TRONGATE
2 THE CROSS
1 DAVIDSON GDNS
2 WEAVERS WAY
3 PATRICKHOLM AVE
4 LINTHAUGH GDNS
Lanarkshire STREET ATLAS
A71 Kilmarnock
46
73 A B 74 C D 75 E F

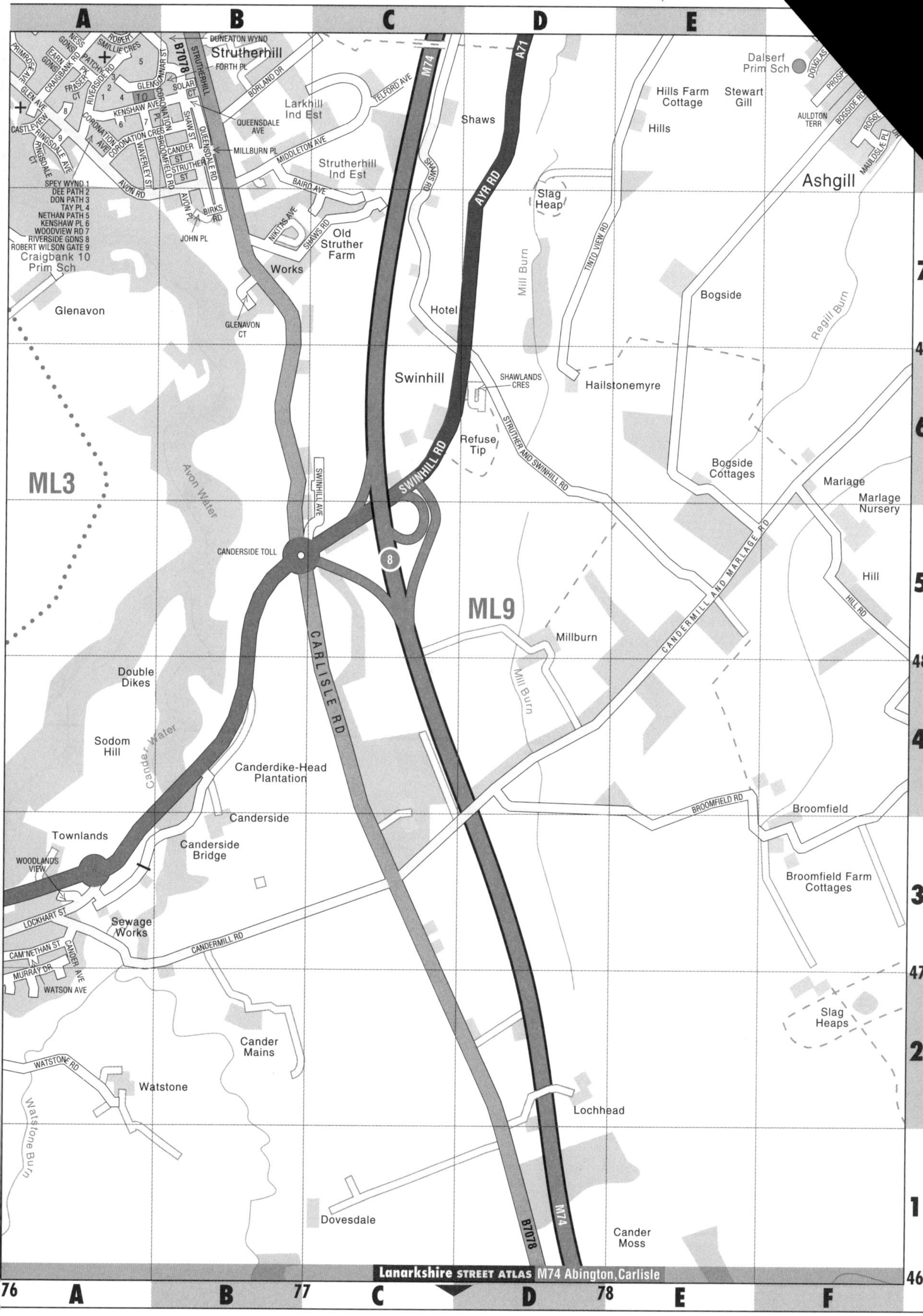
A
B
C
D
E
F
Strutherhill
DUNEATON WYND
FORTH PL
B7078
STRUTHERHILL
BORLAND DR
Larkhill Ind Est
TELFORD AVE
M74
A71
Shaws
Hills Farm Cottage
Stewart Gill
Hills
Dalserf Prim Sch
AULDTON TERR
BOGSIDE RD
MAULDSLIE PL
Ashgill
QUEENSDALE AVE
MILLBURN PL
MIDDLETON AVE
Strutherhill Ind Est
BAIRD AVE
SHAWS RD
AYR RD
Slag Heap
TINTO VIEW RD
SPEY WYND 1
DEE PATH 2
DON PATH 3
TAY PL 4
NETHAN PATH 5
KENSHAW PL 6
WOODVIEW RD 7
RIVERSIDE GDNS 8
ROBERT WILSON GATE 9
Craigbank 10 Prim Sch
ROBERT SMILLIE CRES
CRAIGBANK RD
KENSHAW AVE
CORONATION AVE
CORONATION CRES
CASTLEVIEW
RINGSDALE AVE
WAVERLEY ST
BROOMFIELD RD
CANDER ST
STRUTHER ST
SHAW ST
QUEENSDALE RD
AVON RD
AVON PL
BIRKS RD
JOHN PL
NIKITAS AVE
Old Struther Farm
Works
Mill Burn
Glenavon
GLENAVON CT
Hotel
Bogside
Regill Burn
Swinhill
SHAWLANDS CRES
Hailstonemyre
Refuse Tip
STRUTHER AND SWINHILL RD
Bogside Cottages
Marlage
Marlage Nursery
ML3
Avon Water
SWINHILL AVE
SWINHILL RD
CANDERSIDE TOLL
8
ML9
CANDERMILL AND MARLAGE RD
Hill
HILL RD
Millburn
Double Dikes
CARLISLE RD
Sodom Hill
Cander Water
Canderdike-Head Plantation
Canderside
BROOMFIELD RD
Broomfield
Townlands
WOODLANDS VIEW
Canderside Bridge
Broomfield Farm Cottages
LOCKHART ST
Sewage Works
CANDERMILL RD
CAM'NETHAN ST
CANDER RIGG
MURRAY DR
WATSON AVE
Cander Mains
Slag Heaps
WATSTONE RD
Watstone
Lochhead
Watstone Burn
Dovesdale
B7078
M74
Cander Moss
Lanarkshire STREET ATLAS M74 Abington, Carlisle
7
49
6
5
48
4
3
47
2
1
46
76
77
78

199
186

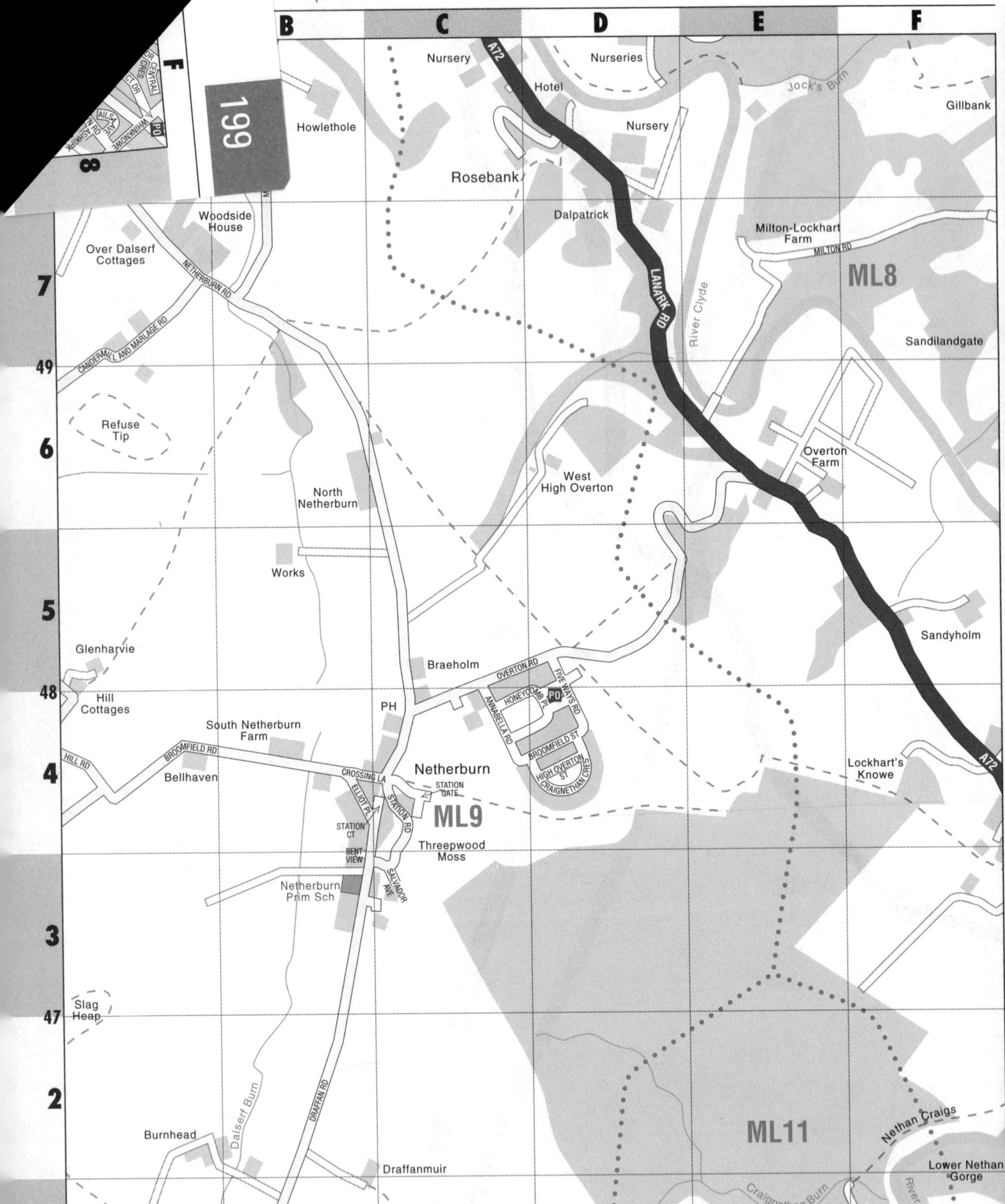
B
C
D
E
F
A72
Nursery
Nurseries
Hotel
Jock's Burn
Gillbank
Howlethole
Nursery
Rosebank
199
Woodside House
Dalpatrick
Milton-Lockhart Farm
MILTON RD
Over Dalserf Cottages
NETHERBURN RD
LANARK RD
ML8
River Clyde
7
CANDERMILL AND MARLAGE RD
Sandilandgate
49
Refuse Tip
6
Overton Farm
West High Overton
North Netherburn
Works
5
Sandyholm
Glenharvie
Braeholm
OVERTON RD
FIVE WAYS RD
HONEYCOMB PL
PO
48
Hill Cottages
PH
ANNABELLA RD
South Netherburn Farm
BROOMFIELD ST
BROOMFIELD RD
HILL RD
Bellhaven
Netherburn
HIGH OVERTON ST
CRAIGNETHAN CRES
Lockhart's Knowe
A72
4
CROSSING LA
ELLIOT PL
STATION GATE
STATION RD
ML9
STATION CT
BENT VIEW
Threepwood Moss
Netherburn Prim Sch
SALVADOR AVE
3
Slag Heap
47
2
Dalserf Burn
DRAFFAN RD
ML11
Nethan Craigs
Burnhead
Draffanmuir
Lower Nethan Gorge
Craignethan Burn
River Nethan
P
Craignethan Castle
1
CORRA MILL RD
46
Lanarkshire STREET ATLAS
79
A
B
80
C
D
81
E
F

199

A
B
C
D
E
F
Under Shieldhill
UNITAS CRES
GLENBURN TERR
SHIELDHILL RD
BENTY'S LA
A73
OLD LANARK RD
AIRAN GDNS
SPRINGFIELD CRES
VIOLET GDNS
UNITAS CRES 1
MILTON CRES 2
COLUMBINE WAY
PRIMROSE WAY
WISTERIA LA
LAVENDER LA
JASMINE WAY
ST LUKE'S AVE
LOCH PARK AVE
HYACINTH WAY
LARKSPUR
JONQUIL WAY
CARTLAND AVE
MARIGOLD WAY
BLUEBELL WAY
ISLAY GDNS
8
RAES RD
STATION RD
Miltonhead (Birthplace of General Roy)
Miltonhead Farm
MILTON RD
South Hillhead
Wellriggs
7
Meadowhead
Townhead Burn
49
Townhead
Mast
Oldhill
LANARK RD
6
Twr
Waygateshawhead
BUSHELHEAD RD
Waygateshaw House
Maregill Burn
Bushelhead
Harestanes Ind Est
B7056
5
ML8
Braidwood House
LOCHKNOWE ST
LOAN FOOT GDNS
Gills
HARESTANES RD
MONKS LA
LOCH AVE
BEANSHIELDS RD
48
Orchard Knowe
Braidwood Prim Sch
Threepwood
MID-LOAN ST
1 HALL BAR GDNS
2 OSWALD GDNS
Poplarglen
Braidwood
4
BRAIDWOOD RD
Clyde Walkway
Yett Holm
WOODHALL RD
WOODHEADS ROAD
Linnside
HOLMWOOD GN
Orchard House
Swinsy Hill
Woodhall
3
Hallbar Tower
AUCHENGLEN RD
HOLMWOOD PK
River Clyde
Millwood
Nethanfoot
HOLM CT
47
NETHAN GLEN
1 JAMES WILSON PL
2 NETHANFOOT BRIG RD
DARK BRIG RD
HOLM RD
Hamper Hill
LANARK RD
Lodge
NETHAN VIEW
River Nethan
BRIG RD
HOLM CREST
Mashock Burn
Derwent Wood
2
PO
Birkhill
BLAIR RD
PH
MASHOCK PATH
CARFIN DR
BIRKHILL RD
B7056
Valley International Pk
Auchenglen
Crossford
PL
FORREST
GRAHAM RD
DEWAR WLK
TAIT WLK
CROSSCLYDE VIEW
NEMPHLAR MOOR RD
Auchenglen Hill
1
Bird of Prey Ctr
Aaronshill Wood
A72
Blair Cottage
Burned Wood
Carfin
ML11
46
A72 Lanark
2
A
B
83
C
D
84
E
F

B8
1 CAMERON RD
2 BRAEHEAD LOAN
3 CHARLES CRES
4 GLEN MS

201
188

A B C D E F
8 7 49 6 5 48 4 3 47 2 1 46
85 86 87

201
214

189

East Coldstream
Callagreen
Craighead Farm
Candymill Burn
Gowanside
Hill Rigg
Mast
ML8
Mast
KILNCADZOW RD
Greenbank Farm
Back Burn
Hill of Kilncadzow
Westtown
Midtown
Kilncadzow
CARNWATH RD
CRAIGENHILL RD
Hole
Muirhead
Drums
A721
Collielaw Cottage
Collielaw
Tinto View
Birkenhead
Fullwood
MOOR RD
WHITELEES RD
Fulwood Burn
Wellhead
ML11
Camp Wood
Cleghorn
Lanarkshire STREET ATLAS
A721 Carstairs
A B C D E F
8 7 6 5 4 3 2 1
49 48 47 46
88 89 90

215

190

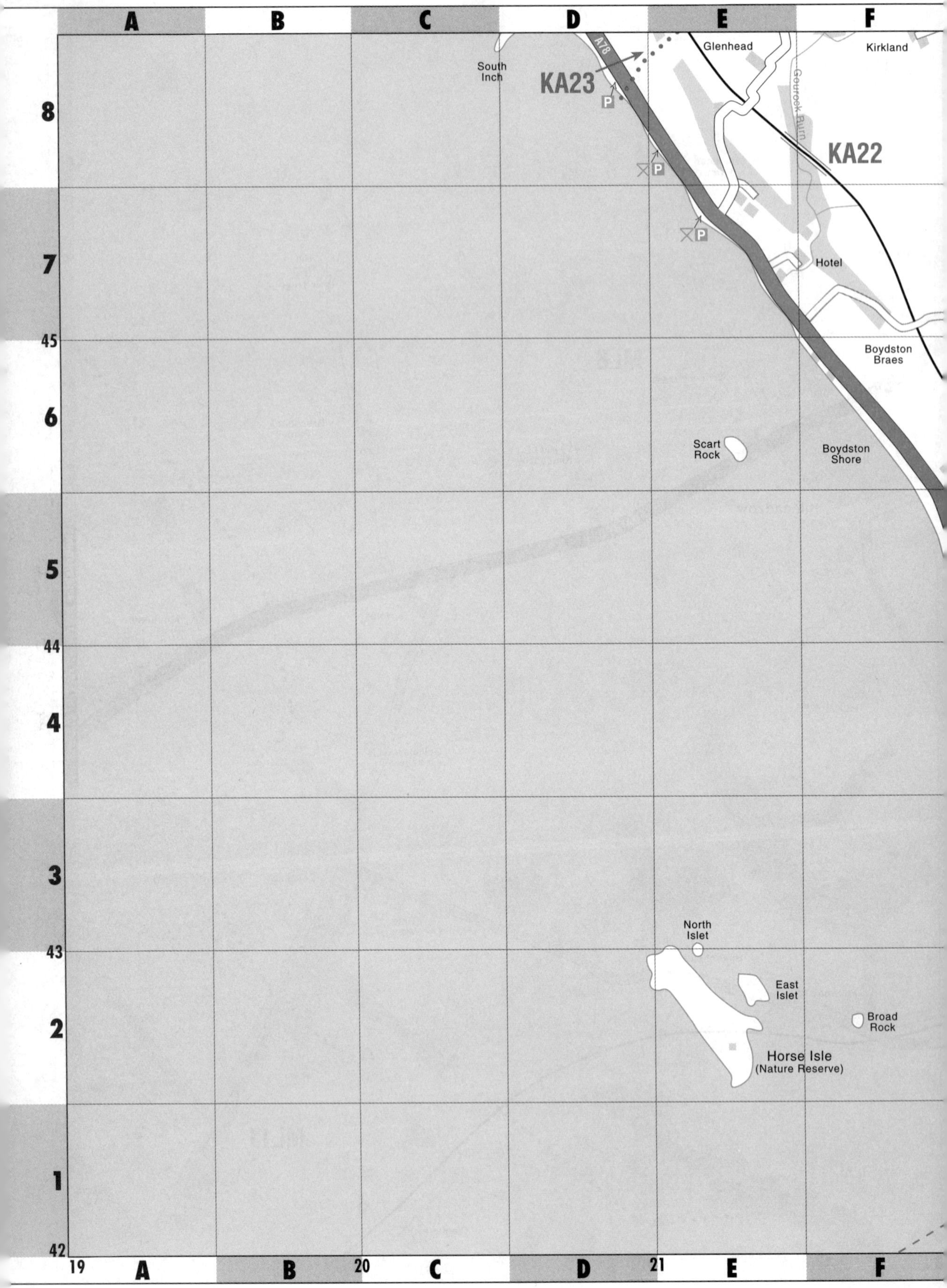
A
B
C
D
E
F
8
7
45
6
5
44
4
3
43
2
1
42
19
20
21
South Inch
A78
KA23
Glenhead
Kirkland
Gourock Burn
KA22
Hotel
Boydston Braes
Scart Rock
Boydston Shore
North Islet
East Islet
Broad Rock
Horse Isle
(Nature Reserve)

206

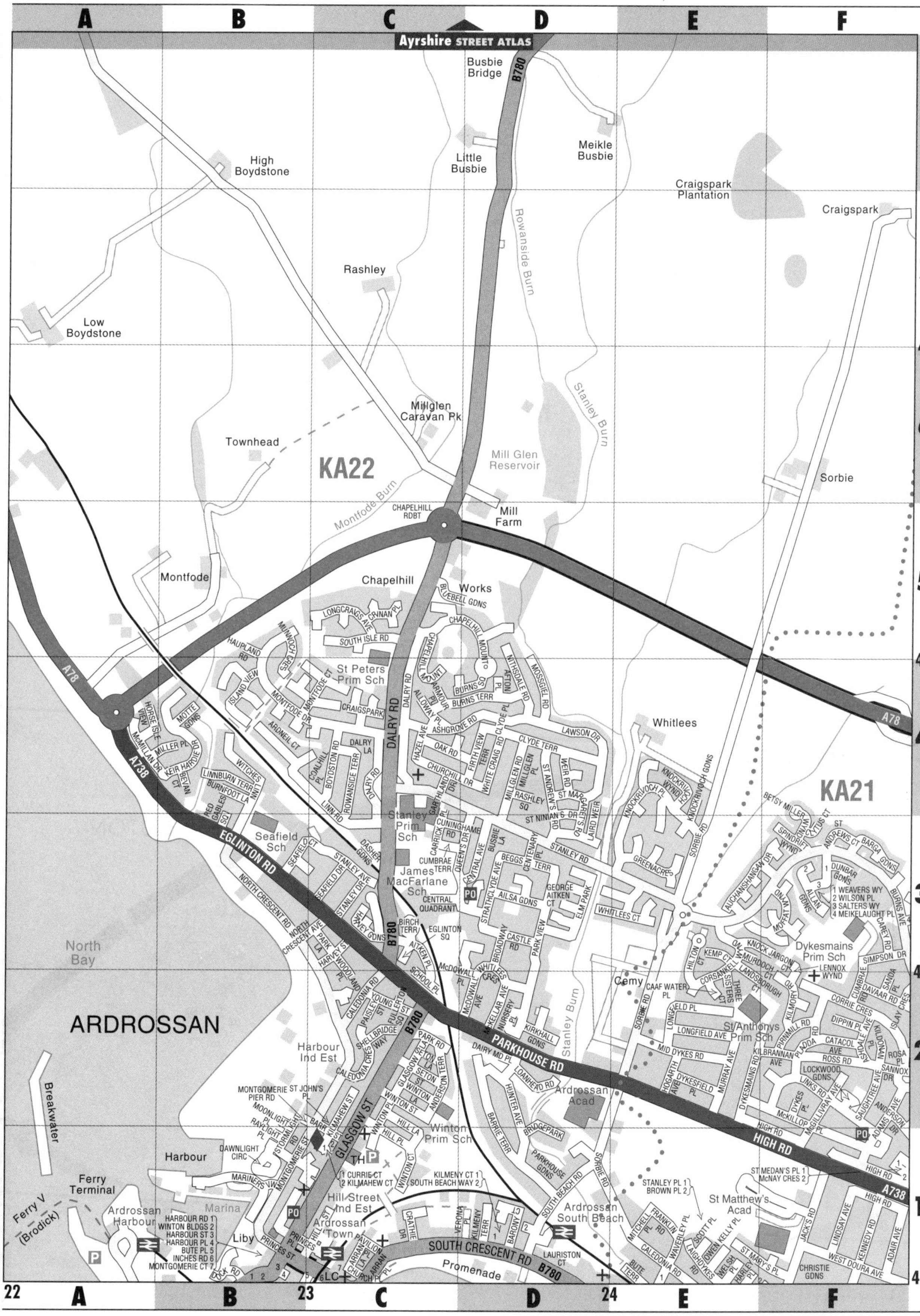

Ayrshire STREET ATLAS
A
B
C
D
E
F
8
7
45
6
5
44
4
3
43
2
1
42
22
23
24
Busbie Bridge
B780
High Boydstone
Little Busbie
Meikle Busbie
Craigspark Plantation
Craigspark
Rowanside Burn
Rashley
Low Boydstone
Stanley Burn
Millglen Caravan Pk
Mill Glen Reservoir
Townhead
KA22
Sorbie
Montfode Burn
CHAPELHILL RDBT
Mill Farm
Montfode
Chapelhill
Works
A78
A738
St Peters Prim Sch
Whitlees
KA21
DALRY RD
Seafield Sch
Stanley Prim Sch
James MacFarlane Sch
EGLINTON RD
North Bay
Dykesmains Prim Sch
Cemy
ARDROSSAN
St Anthonys Prim Sch
Harbour Ind Est
PARKHOUSE RD
Breakwater
Ardrossan Acad
HIGH RD
Winton Prim Sch
Harbour
Ferry Terminal
Hill Street Ind Est
Ardrossan Town
St Matthew's Acad
Marina
Ardrossan Harbour
Ferry V (Brodick)
Ardrossan South Beach
SOUTH CRESCENT RD
Promenade
Liby
GLASGOW ST
HARBOUR RD 1
WINTON BLDGS 2
HARBOUR ST 3
HARBOUR PL 4
BUTE PL 5
INCHES RD 6
MONTGOMERIE CT 7
1 CURRIE CT
2 KILMAHEW CT
KILMENY CT 1
SOUTH BEACH WAY 2
STANLEY PL 1
BROWN PL 2
ST MEDAN'S PL 1
McNAY CRES 2
1 WEAVERS WY
2 WILSON PL
3 SALTERS WY
4 MEIKELAUGHT PL

216

206

205

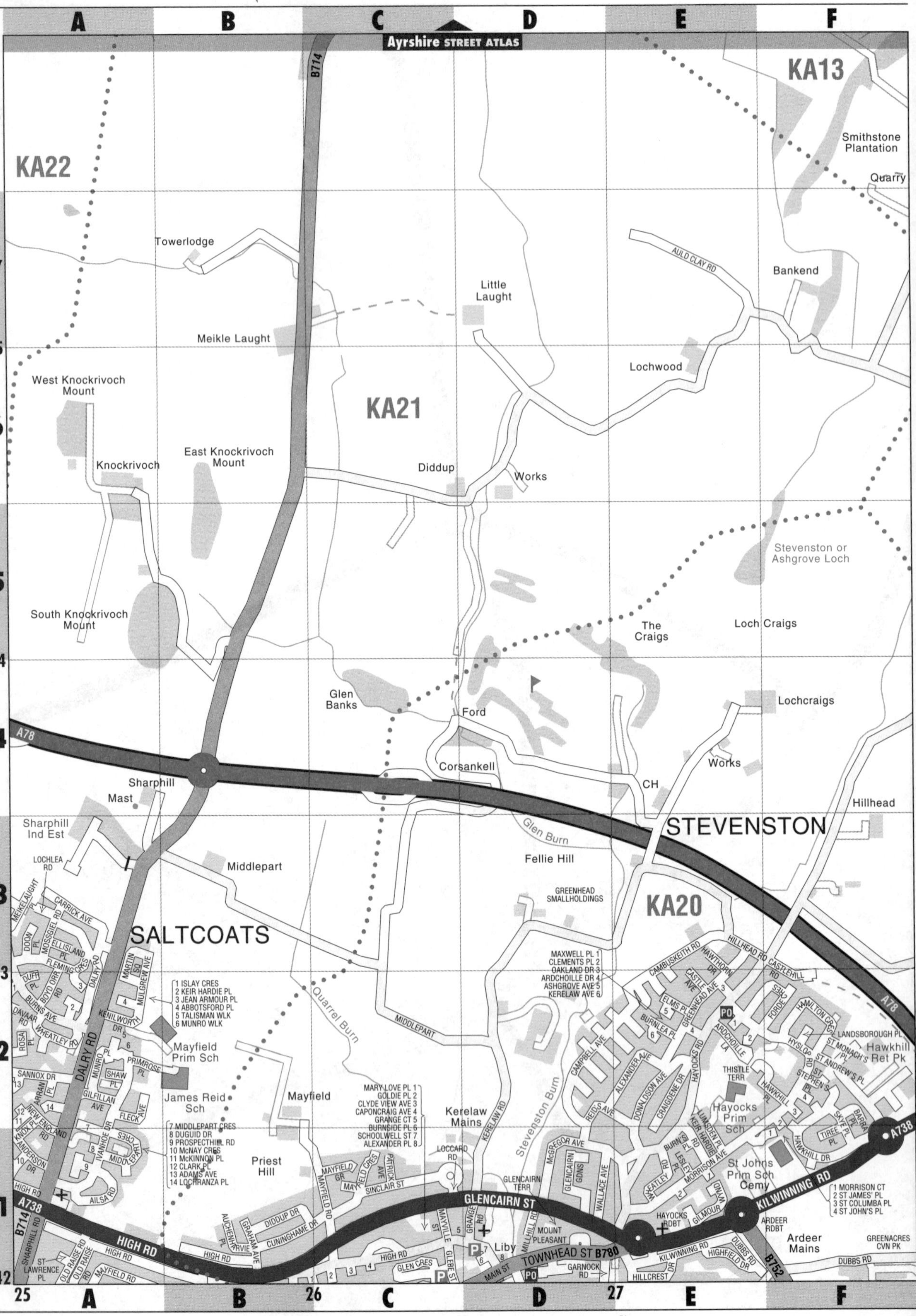

Ayrshire STREET ATLAS
A
B
C
D
E
F
8
7
45
6
5
44
4
3
43
2
1
42
25
26
27
KA22
KA13
KA21
KA20
B714
Smithstone Plantation
Quarry
Towerlodge
AULD CLAY RD
Bankend
Little Laught
Meikle Laught
Lochwood
West Knockrivoch Mount
Knockrivoch
East Knockrivoch Mount
Diddup
Works
Stevenston or Ashgrove Loch
South Knockrivoch Mount
The Craigs
Loch Craigs
Glen Banks
Ford
Lochcraigs
A78
Corsankell
Works
Sharphill
CH
Mast
Hillhead
Sharphill Ind Est
Glen Burn
STEVENSTON
LOCHLEA RD
Middlepart
Fellie Hill
MEIKLAUGHT
CARRICK AVE
GREENHEAD SMALLHOLDINGS
MOSSGIEL RD
DOON PL
ELLISLAND PL
SALTCOATS
FLEMING CRES
DALRY RD
MARTIN SQ
MULGREW AVE
DUFF PL
BOYD ORR RD
BURNS AVE
DAVAAR RD
WHEATLEY RD
ROSA PL
KENILWORTH DR
1 ISLAY CRES
2 KEIR HARDIE PL
3 JEAN ARMOUR PL
4 ABBOTSFORD PL
5 TALISMAN WLK
6 MUNRO WLK
Mayfield Prim Sch
Quarrel Burn
MIDDLEPART
MAXWELL PL 1
CLEMENTS PL 2
OAKLAND DR 3
ARDCHOILLE DR 4
ASHGROVE AVE 5
KERELAW AVE 6
CAMBUSKEITH RD
HAWTHORN DR
HILLHEAD RD
CASTLEHILL RD
CASTLE AVE
GREENHEAD AVE
ELMS PL
BURNLEA PL
FORDE CRES
HAMILTON CRES
LANDSBOROUGH PL
Hawkhill Ret Pk
HYSLOP RD
ST MONACH'S PL
ST ANDREW'S PL
ST STEPHEN'S PL
ARDCHOILLE LA
SANNOX DR
ARRAN PL
MUNRO PL
SHAW PL
PRIMROSE PL
GILFILLAN AVE
FLECK AVE
NEW ENGLAND RD
KNOX PL
ANDERSON DR
IVANHOE DR
MIDDLEPART CRES
AILSA RD
James Reid Sch
Mayfield
MARY LOVE PL 1
GOLDIE PL 2
CLYDE VIEW AVE 3
CAPONCRAIG AVE 4
GRANGE CT 5
BURNSIDE PL 6
SCHOOLWELL ST 7
ALEXANDER PL 8
Kerelaw Mains
KERELAW RD
Stevenston Burn
CAMPBELL AVE
ALEXANDER AVE
DONALDSON AVE
CRAIGDENE DR
HAYOCKS RD
THISTLE TERR
Hayocks Prim Sch
HAWKHILL PL
SKYE PL
BARRA PL
TIREE PL
HAWKHILL DR
A738
REID'S AVE
McGREGOR AVE
7 MIDDLEPART CRES
8 DUGUID DR
9 PROSPECTHILL RD
10 McNAY CRES
11 McKINNON PL
12 CLARK PL
13 ADAMS AVE
14 LOCHRANZA PL
Priest Hill
LOCCARD RD
MAYFIELD GR
MAYFIELD CRES
PATRICK AVE
SINCLAIR ST
MAYFIELD RD
GLENCAIRN TERR
GLENCAIRN GDNS
WALLACE AVE
LUMSDEN PL
KEIR HARDIE RD
BURNS PL
LESLEY PL
WHEATLEY RD
MORRISON AVE
St Johns Prim Sch
Cemy
KILWINNING RD
1 MORRISON CT
2 ST JAMES' PL
3 ST COLUMBA PL
4 ST JOHN'S PL
HIGH RD
A738
GLENCAIRN ST
HAYOCKS RDBT
GILMOUR
DIDDUP DR
CUNINGHAME DR
GRAHAM AVE
AUCHENHARVIE PL
MAYVILLE ST
GRANGE RD
MILLHILL RD
MOUNT PLEASANT
ARDEER RDBT
Ardeer Mains
GREENACRES CVN PK
Liby
TOWNHEAD ST B780
KILWINNING RD
HIGHFIELD DR
DUBBS RD
B752
DUBBS RD
SHARPHILL RD
B714
ST LAWRENCE PL
OLD RAISE RD
OLD RAISE RD
MAYFIELD RD
HIGH RD
HIGH RD
HIGH RD
GLEN CRES
GLEBE ST
MAIN ST
GARNOCK RD
HILLCREST

205

217

E1
1 MOSSGIEL PL
2 LOCHLIE PL

191
208

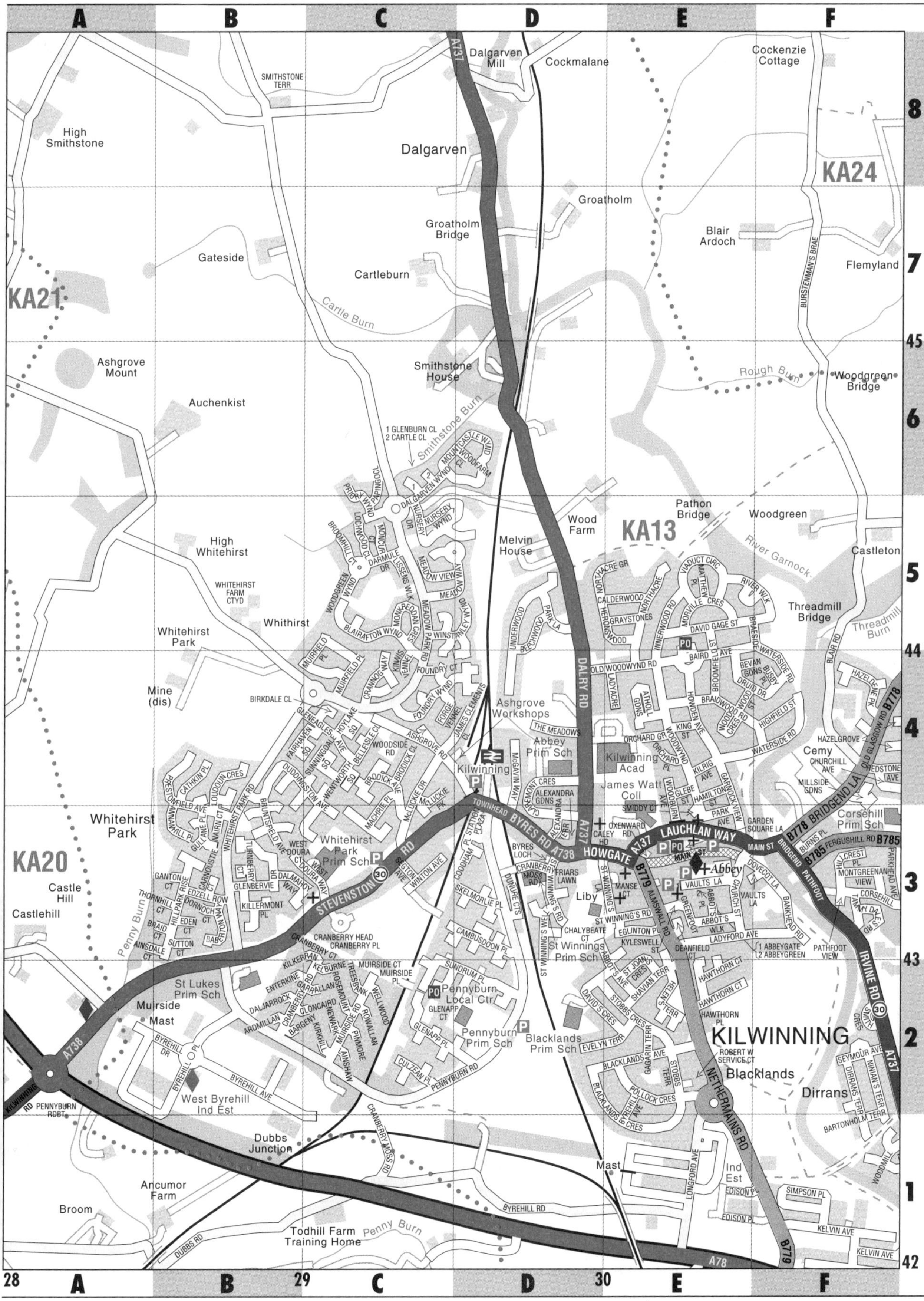

218
208

207
192

A B C D E F
8 7 6 5 4 3 2 1
45 44 43 42
31 32 33
KA24
Barneyhill Plantation
Laigh Gooseloan
Lylestone Farm
B778
Clonbeith Castle (remains of)
Rough Burn
Monkredding House
LYLESTONE TERR
Lylestone Cottage
CVN SITE
Sevenacres Wood
Monkreddan Kennels
Outer Ardoch
Threadmill Burn
Hullerhill
Ardoch
Crofthead
Sevenacres Mains
Bannoch Burn
Sevenacres Mill
KA13
Burrowland
Bannoch
High Moncur
Redston
Bannoch Bridge
Corsehillmuir Wood
HAZELGROVE
Nursery
Corsehill Prim Sch
Mid Moncur
Windyhall
REDSTONE AVE
CHURCHHILL AVE
BANNOCH GDNS
BANNOCH PL
BANNOCH RD
McGAVIN AVE
KEIR HARDIE CRES
FIVE ROADS
Broomhill
North Fergushill
Lugton Water
B785 FERGUSHILL RD
MONTGOMERIE TERR
LOVE ST
QUEEN'S PL
QUEEN ST
MONCUR RD
HUNTER PL
CORSEHILL PL
WEIRSTON RD
KILWINNING
South Fergushill
PARKHEAD AVE
Eglinton Kennels
Benslie
BENSLIE ROW
Benslie Fauld
Benslie Wood
BANNOCH RD
Eglinton Country Park
Chapelholms Wood
Weirston
North Millburn
A737
Ladyha' Park
KA12
B785
WOODMILL
IRVINE RD
Eglinton Castle (remains of)
Kilwinning Gates
1 KELVIN AVE
2 WATERCUT RD
KA11
Auchenwinsey
Factory
Millburn Lodge

207
219

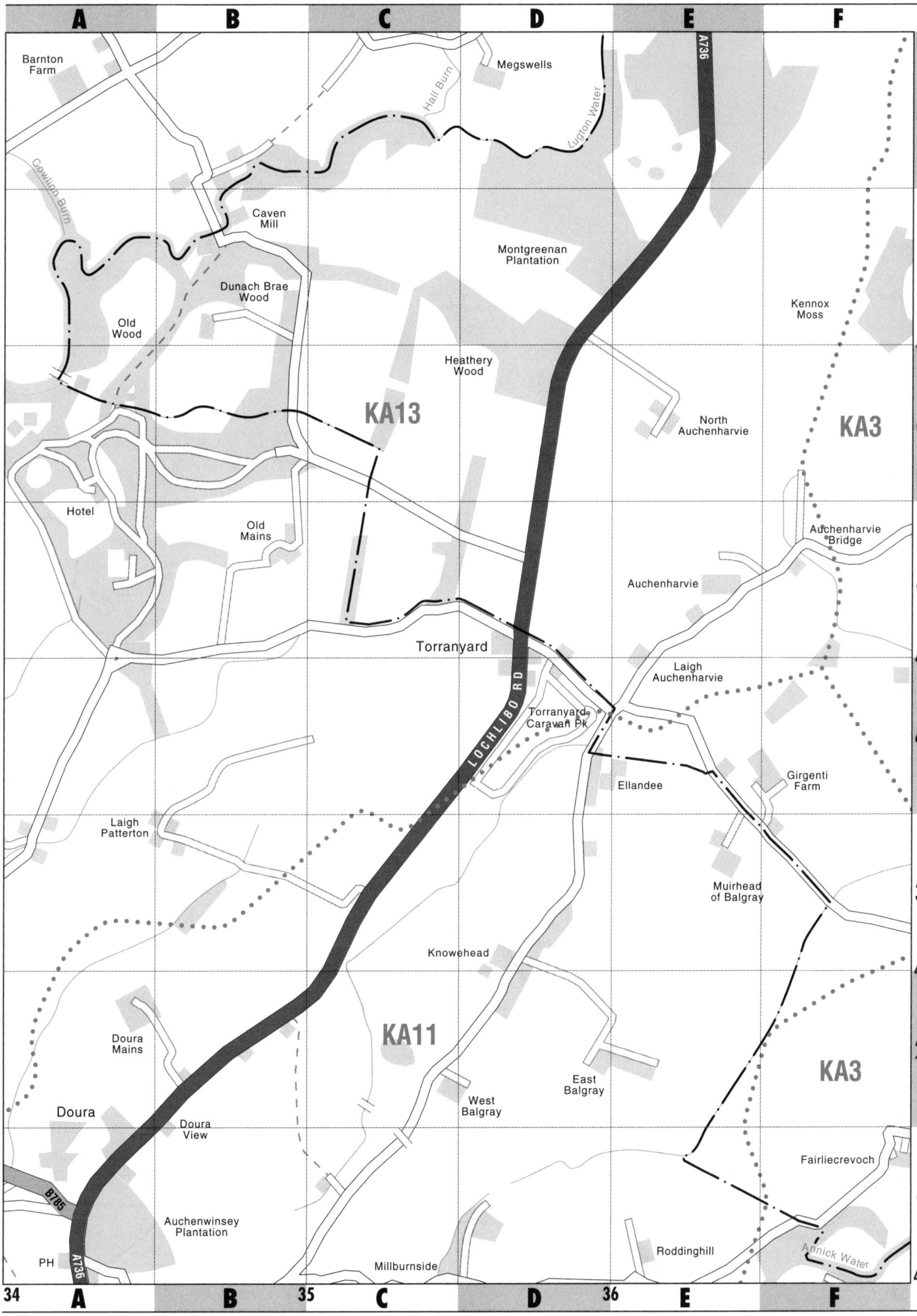
A
B
C
D
E
F
8
7
6
5
4
3
2
1
45
44
43
42
34
35
36
Barnton Farm
Megswells
Hall Burn
Lugton Water
A736
Cowlinn Burn
Caven Mill
Montgreenan Plantation
Dunach Brae Wood
Old Wood
Kennox Moss
Heathery Wood
KA13
North Auchenharvie
KA3
Hotel
Old Mains
Auchenharvie Bridge
Auchenharvie
Torranyard
Laigh Auchenharvie
LOCHLIBO RD
Torranyard Caravan Pk
Ellandee
Girgenti Farm
Laigh Patterton
Muirhead of Balgray
Knowehead
KA11
Doura Mains
East Balgray
West Balgray
Doura
Doura View
Fairliecrevoch
B785
Auchenwinsey Plantation
Roddinghill
Annick Water
PH
Millburnside

209
194

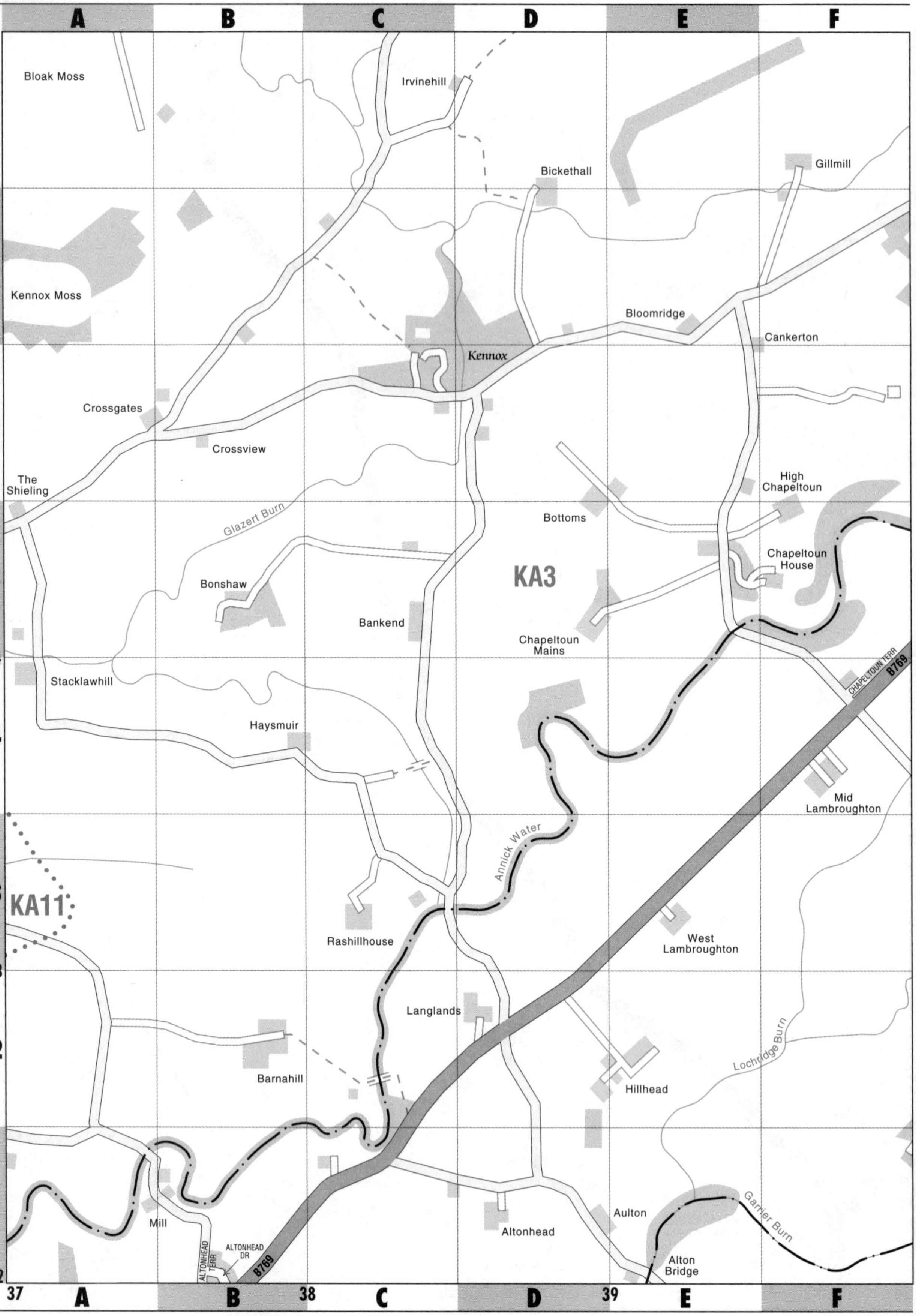

209
221

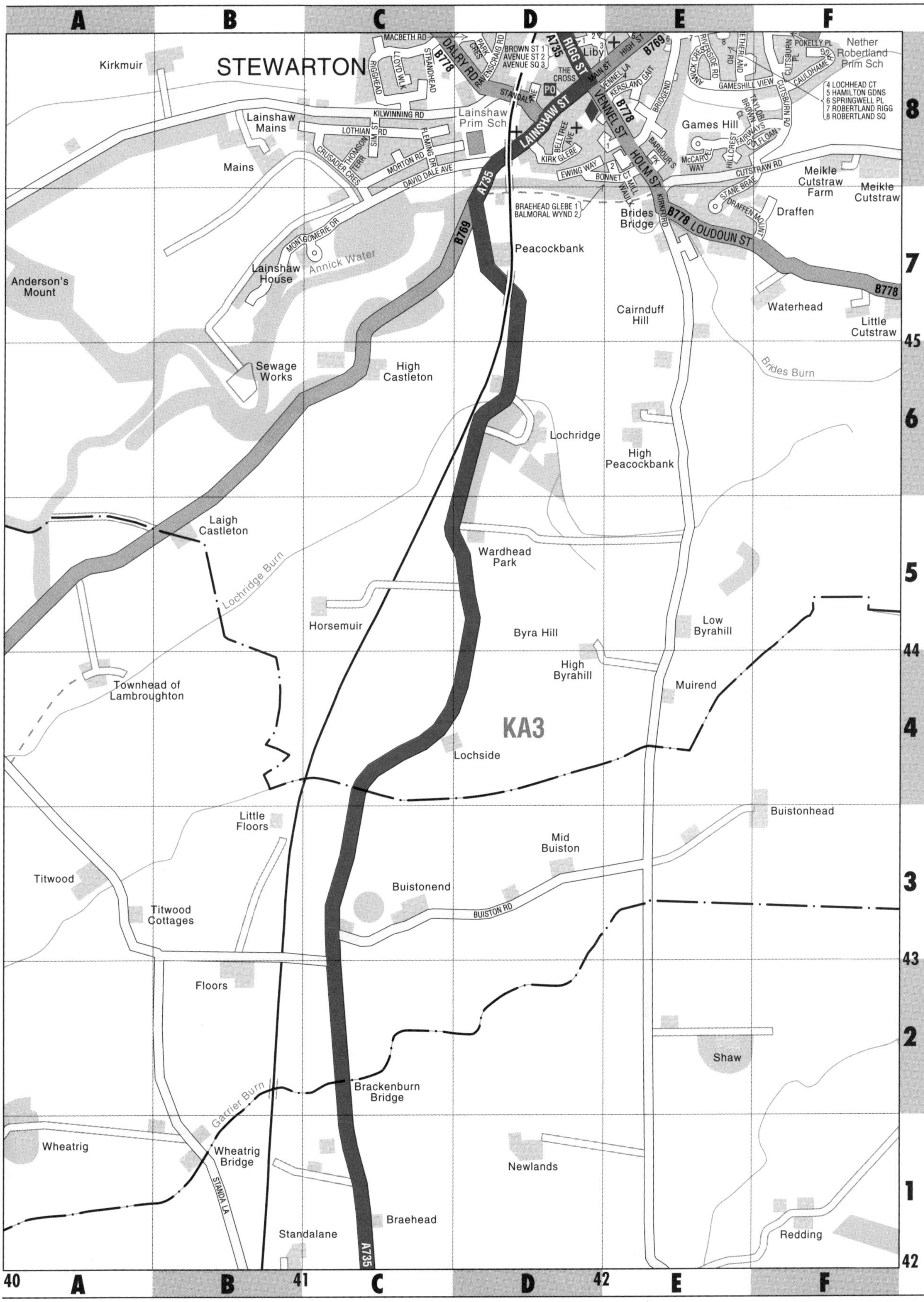
A
B
C
D
E
F
STEWARTON
Kirkmuir
Lainshaw Mains
Mains
Lainshaw Prim Sch
MACBETH RD
LLOYD WLK
RIGGHEAD
STRANDHEAD
DALRY RD
B778
PARK CRES
RAVENSCRAIG RD
BROWN ST 1
AVENUE ST 2
AVENUE SQ 3
A735
RIGG ST
THE CROSS
Liby
HIGH ST
B769
MAIN ST
VENNEL LA
KERSLAND GAIT
VENNEL ST
STANDALANE
PO
LAINSHAW ST
KILWINNING RD
LOTHIAN RD
SIMS ST
FLEMING DR
THOMSON TERR
CRUSADER CRES
MORTON RD
DAVID DALE AVE
BELLTREE AVE
KIRK GLEBE
EWING WAY
BONNET CT
MILL WALK
HOLM ST
BARBOUR'S PK
KIRKFORD
BRIDGEND
ANNICK CRES
RIVERSIDE RD
RD
NETHERLAND
CUTSBURN PL
POKELLY PL
Nether Robertland Prim Sch
CAULDHAME
GAMESHILL VIEW
CUTSBURN RD
TAYLOR BROWN CL
FAIRWAYS
FLOAN
HILLCREST
McCARDEL WAY
Games Hill
4 LOCHHEAD CT
5 HAMILTON GDNS
6 SPRINGWELL PL
7 ROBERTLAND RIGG
8 ROBERTLAND SQ
CUTSTRAW RD
STANE BRAE
DRAFFEN MOUNT
Meikle Cutstraw Farm
Meikle Cutstraw
Draffen
BRAEHEAD GLEBE 1
BALMORAL WYND 2
Brides Bridge
B778
LOUDOUN ST
MONTGOMERIE DR
Lainshaw House
Annick Water
Anderson's Mount
Peacockbank
Cairnduff Hill
Waterhead
Little Cutstraw
Brides Burn
Sewage Works
High Castleton
Lochridge
High Peacockbank
Laigh Castleton
Lochridge Burn
Wardhead Park
Horsemuir
Byra Hill
Low Byrahill
High Byrahill
Muirend
Townhead of Lambroughton
KA3
Lochside
Little Floors
Mid Buiston
Buistonhead
Titwood
Buistonend
BUISTON RD
Titwood Cottages
Floors
Shaw
Garrier Burn
Brackenburn Bridge
Wheatrig
Wheatrig Bridge
STANDA LA
Newlands
Braehead
Standalane
Redding
8
7
45
6
5
44
4
3
43
2
1
42
40
41
42

211
196

211
223

A
B
C
D
E
F
Damhead
Laighmuir
Glassock Bridge
North Glassock
South Glassock
Mast
A77
M77
A719
Pokelly Hill
Rigghill
Gardrum Mill
Gardrum Mill Burn
High Gardrum
Gardrum
Midton
Townend
Warnockland
Water Works
Amlaird
Shelgo Burn
KA3
Fenwick Water
Glaister Bridge
RYSLAND DR
BLACKFAULDS DR
BLACKFAULDS GDNS
SKERNIELAND RD
Cemy
Skernieland
STEWARTON RD
Fenwick Prim Sch
Hall
PH
PO
B7061
Fenwick
REELSHAUGH RD
KIRKTON RD
GLEBE TERR
Kirkton Bridge
KIRKTON PL
POLES RD
DUNLOP ST
MURCHLAND AVE
BRAEHEAD RD
MAUNSHEUGH RD
RAITH RD
AUCHANS PL
GLENCRAIG TERR
HOLM CRES
MAIN RD
BOWLING GREEN RD
Wyllieland
Wyllielandhill
McKNIGHT AVE
FENWICK RD
WEST VIEW
Waterside
Waterside Bridge
MILL WYND
Arness
Hareshaw
Hareshaw Mill
Hareshawmuir Water
Bruntland
Bruntland Bridge
Craufurdland Water
Laigh Fenwick
KILMAURS RD
WATERSLAP
BROOKFIELD GR
Fenwick Bridge
Midland
Midland Craft Ctr
Dalsraith Bridge
Horsehill
Pockinan Bridge
Aikenhead
Dalsraith
Darwhilling
8
7
45
6
5
44
4
3
43
2
1
42
46
47
48

202

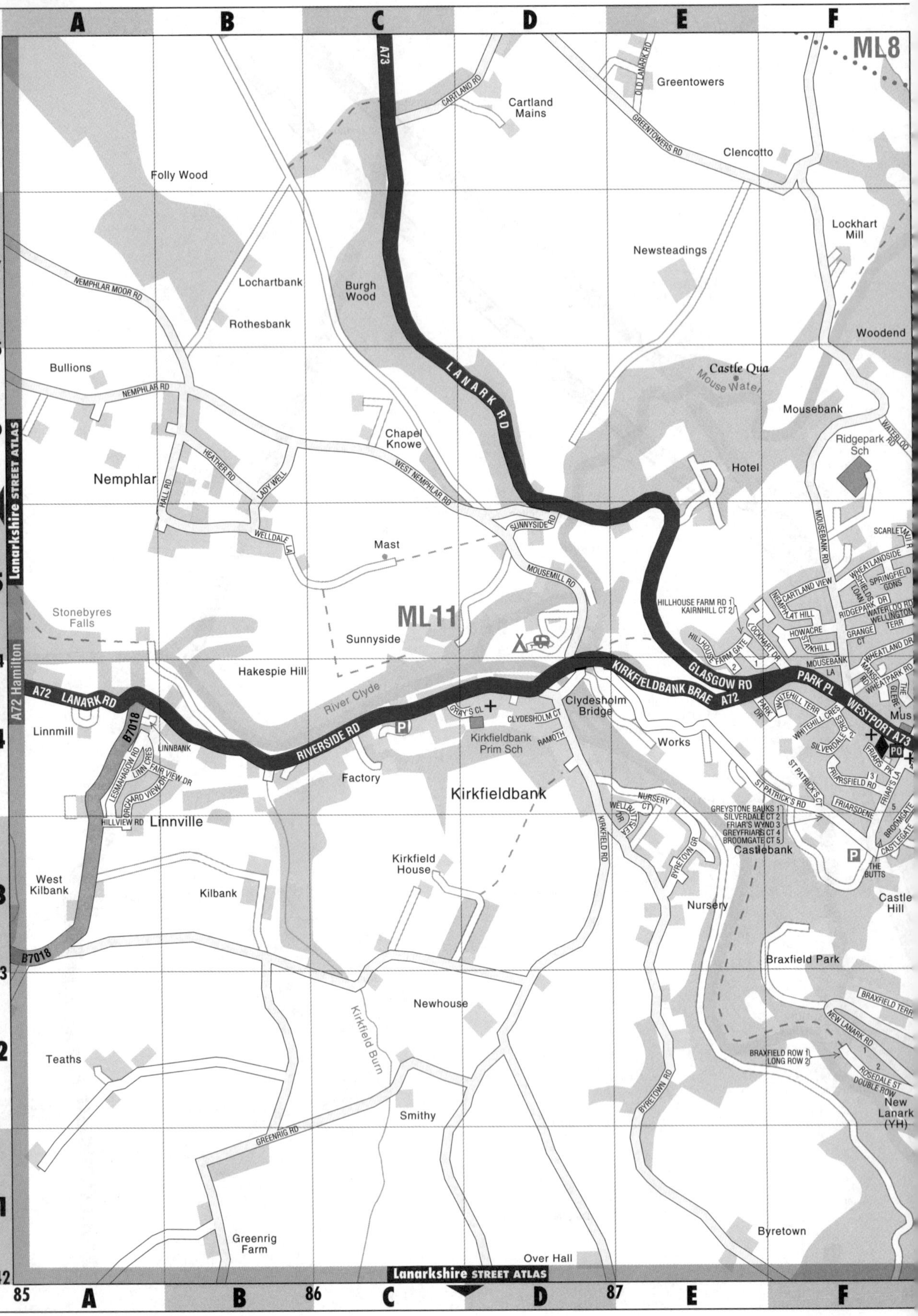
A
B
C
D
E
F
ML8
8
7
45
6
5
44
4
3
43
2
1
42
85
86
87
A73
CARTLAND RD
Cartland
Mains
OLD LANARK RD
Greentowers
GREENTOWERS RD
Clencotto
Folly Wood
Lockhart
Mill
Newsteadings
NEMPHLAR MOOR RD
Lochartbank
Burgh
Wood
Rothesbank
Woodend
Bullions
NEMPHLAR RD
LANARK RD
Castle Qua
Mouse Water
Mousebank
WATERLOO RD
Ridgepark
Sch
Chapel
Knowe
Hotel
Lanarkshire STREET ATLAS
HEATHER RD
LADY WELL
WEST NEMPHLAR RD
Nemphlar
HALL RD
SUNNYSIDE RD
MOUSEBANK RD
SCARLET MUIR
WELLDALE LA
Mast
MOUSEMILL RD
CARTLAND VIEW
WHEATLANDSIDE
SPRINGFIELD GDNS
HILLHOUSE FARM RD 1
KAIRNHILL CT 2
RIDGEPARK DR
WATERLOO RD
WELLINGTON TERR
ML11
Stonebyres
Falls
Sunnyside
HOWACRE
GRANGE CT
LOCKHART DR
STAKHILL
WHEATLAND DR
Hakespie Hill
HILLHOUSE FARM GATE
MOUSEBANK LA
WHEATPARK RD
A72 Hamilton
A72
LANARK RD
River Clyde
KIRKFIELDBANK BRAE
GLASGOW RD
A72
PARK PL
WESTPORT A73
Clydesholm
Bridge
GRAY'S CL
CLYDESHOLM CT
B7018
Linnmill
RIVERSIDE RD
Kirkfieldbank
Prim Sch
RAMOTH
Works
WHITEHILL TERR
WHITEHILL CRES
SILVERDALE
FRIARS PK
LINNBANK
LINN CRES
LESMAHAGOW RD
FAIR VIEW DR
ORCHARD VIEW DR
Factory
Kirkfieldbank
ST PATRICK'S CT
ST PATRICK'S RD
FRIARSFIELD RD
FRIARSDENE
FRIARS LA
HILLVIEW RD
Linnville
NURSERY CT
WELLBUT DR
KIRKFIELD RD
GREYSTONE BAUKS 1
SILVERDALE CT 2
FRIAR'S WYND 3
GREYFRIARS CT 4
BROOMGATE CT 5
BROOMGATE
CASTLEGATE
Castlebank
BYRETOWN GR
West
Kilbank
Kirkfield
House
THE BUTTS
Kilbank
Castle
Hill
Nursery
B7018
Braxfield Park
BRAXFIELD TERR
Newhouse
Kirkfield Burn
NEW LANARK RD
Teaths
BRAXFIELD ROW 1
LONG ROW 2
ROSEDALE ST
DOUBLE ROW
New
Lanark
(YH)
BYRETOWN RD
Smithy
GREENRIG RD
Greenrig
Farm
Byretown
Over Hall
Lanarkshire STREET ATLAS

203

ML8
Fulwood Burn
Mouse Water
Jerviswood
Nursery
Nursery
Works
LC
Mill House
A706 STANMORE RD
A706 Livingston (A71)
THORNLEA PL
HAGHOLM RD
SILVERMUIR AVE
ROMAN CT
JERVISWOOD DR
Cleghorn
Richland
Jerviswood Mains
THE PADDOCK
Northfaulds
STANMORE GDNS
STANMORE RD
Stanmore House Sch
BELLEFIELD CRES
BELLEFIELD WY
1 WHEATLANDSIDE
2 WELLINGTON TERR
3 WHEATLAND DR
ST TEILING 4
LEECHFORD 5
WATERLOO RD
BELLEFIELD RD
CLEGHORN RD
HARDACRES
WATERLOO DR
CHAPLAND RD
ST NINIAN'S
LIMPETLAW
WELLWOOD AVE
ST NICHOLAS RD
ST KENTIGERNS RD
FORREST
LAVEROCKHALL
THE MARCHES
RUSSELL RD
LYTHGOW WAY
MAINS CT
WESTCOTT PL
BELL'S WYND
MARR'S WYND
POTTERS WYND
GILROY CL
STANMORE CRES
Stanmore Home Farm
Caldwellside Farm
A743 Carstairs
A743
MELVINHALL RD
CLEGHORN DR
RHYBER AVE
Lanark Prim Sch
Gallow Hill
BRAEDALE RD
CLEGHORN AVE
STANMORE AVE
STUART DR
CLYDE CRES
THE RODDING
1 RENWICK PL
2 DENNISTON PL
3 LINDSAY LOAN
4 WHITE'S NEUK
Lanark Ind Est
NORTH FAULDS RD
YOUNG RD
Caldwellside Ind Est
WEST FAULDS RD
EAST FAULDS RD
ST LEONARD ST
CAMERONIAN CT
BRAIDFUTE
WALLACE WAY
QUARRYKNOWE
Ind Est
BIRKS PL
KILDARE DR
ML11
CARMICHAEL CT
JERVISWOOD RD
A706
GALLOWHILL RD
SMIDDY CT
DOVECOT LA
NORTH VENNEL
HOPE ST
Ct
Liby
HIGH ST
A743
WELLHEAD CT
WOODSTOCK RD
KENILWORTH RD
HIGHBURGH AVE
ST LEONARD'S
HOSPITALAND DR
WAVERLEY CRES
WOODSTOCK AVE
ABBOTSFORD TR
SMYLLUM RD
HONEYMAN CRES
ARMADALE RD
Robert Owen Mem Prim Sch
Smyllum Park
KINGSMYRE
BATTISMAINS
FORSYTH CT
GREENLADY WLK
EAST HO
SMYLLUM HO
1 HIGHBURGH CT
2 WOODSTOCK DR
THOMAS TAYLOR AVE
B7017
BANNATYNE ST
ST VINCENT PL
Lanark
Works
St Marys Prim Sch
ST MARYS CT
LANARK
Lanarkshire STREET ATLAS
WELLGATE
A73
SOUTH VENNEL
BENDIGO PL
GUSCHET
LADYACRE RD
PORTLAND PL
OLD MKT RD
WELLGATEHEAD A73
DELVES CT
DELVES PK
DELVES RD
WEAVERS WLK
ST MUNGO'S
Swimming Pool
Castlegate Pk
ALBANY DR
BRIERYBANK AVE
KIRKLANDS RD
BONNINGTON AVE
Lanark Gram Sch
BIDDERS GAIT
WHITELEES RD
CROSSLAW GDNS
CH
Lockhart
HOME ST
NEWLANDS ST
Cemy
WOODBURN GAIT
WILLOW PL
WOODLANDS AVE
ROWAN VW
WOODBURN CT
WOODSIDE LA
CROSSLAW AVE
COUNTY DR
WOODLANDS AVE
WOODLANDS DR
LAKE AVE
Lanark Loch
Lanark Moor
WELL RD
BRAXFIELD RD
BANKHEAD TERR
Kingson's Knowe
THE BEECHES
C3
1 BEECHWOOD CT
2 BEECHWOOD GATE
3 AUCTIONEERS WY
4 GAVEL LA
5 MUIR GLEN
6 GAVEL GR
HYNDFORD RD
PH
Cemy
Playing Fields
New Lanark Prim Sch
NEW LANARK RD
BRAXFIELD TERR
Bankhead
NEW BLDGS
NURSERY BLDGS
CAITHNESS ROW
New Lanark World Heritage Site
Visitor Ctr
NEW LANARK RD
ACORN RD
Langloch
A73 Abington (A702), Biggar (A72)
Nature Trail
River Clyde
Bonnington Mains
Lanarkshire STREET ATLAS
A B C D E F
8 7 45 6 5 44 4 3 43 2 1 42
89 90

A4
1 GLEBE DR
2 WALLACE CT
3 BONNET RD
4 WHEATPARK RD
5 GREYSTONE BAULKS
6 GREENSIDE CL
7 GREENSIDE LA
8 AITKEN PL
9 BLOOMGATE
10 SHIRLEY'S CL
11 DUNCAN'S CL
12 CROSS KEY'S CL
13 RITCHIE'S CL
14 HUNTER'S CL
15 BULL'S CL
16 McKENZIES CL
17 MARKET END
18 MARKET CT
19 HYNDFORD PL
20 BERNARD'S WYND
21 BERNARD'S CT
22 THOMSON'S CL
23 GLEBE CT

205

A
B
C
D
E
F
8
7
6
5
4
3
2
1
41
40
39
38
22
23
24
Eagle Rock
LC
HARBOUR RD
B780
KA22
INCHES RD
PRINCES ST
BUTE PL
BATH SQ
BATH ST
BATH VILLAS
South Beach
Promenade
South Bay
KA22
BURN RD
SALTCOATS
ARDROSSAN RD
MONTGOMERIE RD
MONTGOMERIE CRES
KERRS LA
STANLEY RD
ARTHURLIE PL
CALEDONIA RD
Caledonia Prim Sch
CAMPBELL AVE
LAMBIE CT
DONALDSON AVE
JACK'S RD
ARGYLE PL
ARGYLE RD
CHRISTIE GDNS
KENNEDY
BERCHEM PL
BORDER AVE
BORDER PL
B714
BRAEHEAD LA
SHARPHILL RD
KA21
Liby
GLEBE PL
GLEBE ST
SPRINGVALE ST
WELLPARK RD
RAISE ST
FACTORY PL
RENNIE PL
MANSE ST
SPRINGVALE PL
UNION ST
BARNETT CRES
WINTON ST
PARK RD
HAMILTON ST
MELBOURNE TERR
MELBOURNE RD
WESTFIELD CT
EGLINTON PL
EGLINTON ST
Mus
PO
KIRKGATE
VERNON ST
GLENCAIRN ST
Pol HQ
B780
KYLESHILL
Saltcoats
TH
CHAPELWELL ST
DOCKHEAD ST
DOCKHEAD PL
COUNTESS ST
HILL ST
SEAVIEW RD
WINTON CIR
EGLINTON CT
SIDNEY ST
WINDMILL ST
BRAES RD
West Shore
L Ctr
Harbour
HARBOUR POINT
HARBOUR ST
SOUTH CRESCENT RD 1
BUTE TERR 2
STANLEY PL 3
GALLOWAY PL 4
LAIGHDYKES RD 5
HARLEY PL 6
BROWN PL 7
TAYLOR PL 8
O'CONNOR CT 9
BARNETT CT 10
WELLPARK LA 11
VICTORIA RD 12
BRAEHEAD PL 13
GLADSTONE RD 14
PARKEND RD 15
NINEYARD ST 16
FINDLAY'S BRAE 17
ERSKINE PL 18
BRADSHAW ST 19
QUAY ST 20
GREEN ST 21
SPRINGVALE CT 22
Rennie Bsns Units 23
ST CUTHBERTS CT 24

206
218

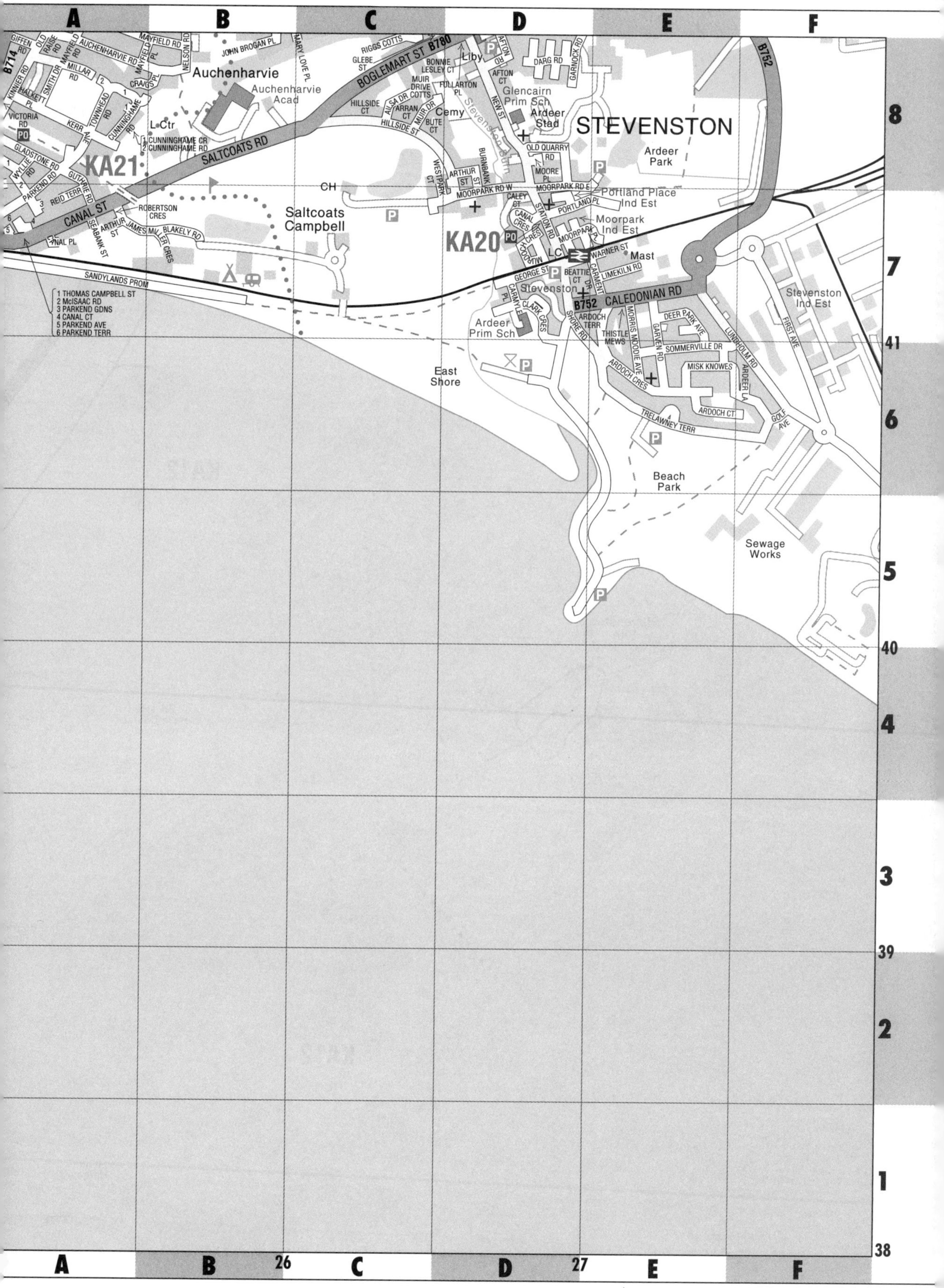
A
B
C
D
E
F
STEVENSTON
Auchenharvie
Auchenharvie Acad
Saltcoats Campbell
KA21
KA20
SALTCOATS RD
BOGLEMART ST B780
CANAL ST
B714
B752
CALEDONIAN RD
SANDYLANDS PROM
1 THOMAS CAMPBELL ST
2 McISAAC RD
3 PARKEND GDNS
4 CANAL CT
5 PARKEND AVE
6 PARKEND TERR
GIFFEN RD
OLD RAISE RD
MAYFIELD RD
AUCHENHARVIE RD
MILLAR RD
SMITH DR
KINNIER RD
HALKETT PL
VICTORIA RD
KERR AVE
TOWNHEAD RD
CUNNINGHAME RD
CRAIGS
L Ctr
1 CUNNINGHAME CR
2 CUNNINGHAME RD
GLADSTONE RD
WYLLIE RD
PARKEND RD
GUTHRIE RD
REID TERR
ROBERTSON CRES
SEABANK ST
ARTHUR ST
JAMES MILLER CRES
BLAKELY RD
CANAL PL
JOHN BROGAN PL
NELSON RD
MARY LOVE PL
RIGGS COTTS
GLEBE ST
BONNIE LESLEY CT
Liby
MUIR DRIVE COTTS
FULLARTON PL
HILLSIDE CT
AILSA DR
ARRAN CT
MUIR DR
BUTE CT
Cemy
HILLSIDE ST
AFTON RD
AFTON CT
NEW ST
DARG RD
GARNOCK RD
Glencairn Prim Sch
Ardeer Stad
Stevenston Burn
OLD QUARRY RD
MOORE PL
Ardeer Park
CH
WESTPARK CT
ARTHUR ST
BURNBANK
MOORPARK RD W
MOORPARK RD E
Portland Place Ind Est
CALEY CT
CANAL CRES
STATION RD
PORTLAND PL
Moorpark Ind Est
MOORPARK RD
PO
LC
WARNER ST
Mast
BEATTIE CT
CARMENT DR
LIMEKILN RD
GEORGE ST
Stevenston
CARMYLE PL
CLARK CRES
Ardeer Prim Sch
SHORE RD
ARDOCH TERR
THISTLE MEWS
MORRIS MOODIE AVE
GARVEN RD
DEER PARK AVE
SOMMERVILLE DR
MISK KNOWES
LUNDHOLM RD
ARDEER LA
ARDOCH CRES
ARDOCH CT
TRELAWNEY TERR
GOLF AVE
FIRST AVE
Stevenston Ind Est
East Shore
Beach Park
Sewage Works
8
7
6
5
4
3
2
1
41
40
39
38
26
27

217
207

A
B
C
D
E
F
8
7
41
6
5
40
4
3
39
2
1
38
28
29
30
DUBBS RD
Penny Burn
A78
B779
Nethermains
Bridge
WATERCUT RD
Garnock Floods
Nature Reserve
KA13
Refuse
Tip
STOBBS
TERR
Stevenston
Site
KA20
MISK ROAD
GARNOCK RD
WEST RD
POWER PLANT
RD
POWER PLANT RD
NORTH RING RD
CENTRAL AVE
SOLVENTS
RD
River Garnock
KA12
Works
ACIDS RD
WORKSHOP
RD
BURMA ROAD
Stevenston
Site
SOUTH RING ROUND
WORKSHOP
RD
NEW HILL RD
PROPULSIVES RD
CH
Bogside
Bogside
Race Course
(disused)
Crooky's
Point
WHARF RD
Bogsid
Flats
KA12
Irvine
Harbour
River Irvi
HARBOUR ST
PH
BEACH DR
Magnum
L Ctr

217

208
220

A
B
C
D
E
F
8
7
41
6
5
40
4
3
39
2
1
38
32
33
Eglinton Country Park Visitor Ctr
Belvidere Hill
Old Wood
KA13
Eglinton Country Park
Draught Burn
WATERCUT RD
IRVINE RD
KILWINNING RD
A737
B7080
EGLINTON INTC
LONG DR
Red Burn
Dykehead
Works
FIRST ST
EAST RD
REDBURN RDBT
Redburn Caravan Pk
Hotel
REDBURN GATE
FAIRWAYS
Redburn Ind Est
WEST RD
The Circle
F6
1 AUCHENHARVIE PL
2 LOCHWOOD PL
A736
CAIRNMOUNT RD
Ayrshire Central
Morven Lodge
MORAR PL
MAREE PL
LOMOND PL
RANNOCH PL
SHIEL PL
LEVEN PL
CARRON PL
DUNVEGAN PL
ETIVE PL
TRINE PL
KIDSNEUK GDNS
KIDSNEUK
CH
CASTLEPARK CRES
CASTLEPARK RD
Castlepark Prim Sch
HILL INTC
REGALIA WY
ARCHERS CT
ARCHERS AVE
KA11
EARLSWOOD WY
EARLSWOOD AVE
PAVILION GDNS
ROSEBANK GDNS
DALMORE WAY
DALMORE PL
ABERLOUR PL
ABERLOUR RD
LITTLESTANE RD
HIGHFIELD PL
SMITHSTONE WAY
LADYBURN CT
COLEBURN CT
SPEYBURN PL
ARDBEG CT
DALWHINNIE CT
LANEFINE TERR
GATESIDE
CRAIGMARK PL
KERSLAND FOOT
SANDY RD
B779
Irvine Royal Acad
RAVENSCROFT
RACECOURSE PL
DOURA PL
DICKSON DR
PO
BILBY TERR
ST BRIDE'S PL
FREW TERR
STEPS RD
BROWN WLK
DICK TERR
PATERSON CRES
NEIL AVE
Red Burn
Cemy
Stanecastle
ALFORD PL
STANECASTLE DR
BERESFORD GR
CRAVEN GR
GLENLYON GR
CHESTNUT GDNS
WILLOW GDNS
CYPRESS GDNS
CHERRY GDNS
BRAEFOOT
BRAESIDE
BRAEHEAD
GIRDLE TOLL
LOCHLIBO RD
NEWCASTLE GATE
SOURLIE TERR
DOURA AVE
BENSLIE
BARONY CT
CASTLE KEEP GDNS
KILLOCH WAY
Towns Moor
NORMAN CRES
CARRICK DR
FLEMING TERR
CARMICHAEL PL
SEATON TERR
BEATON TERR
LIVINGSTONE TERR
ANDERSON DR
BRUCE TERR
MARTIN AVE
PATERSON AVE
JERMOND DR
SMITHSTONE AVE
BURNS CRES
JAMES CRES
WINTON PL
QUEEN RD
ASHGROVE
IRVINE MAINS CRES
OAKLANDS AVE
ELMBANK TERR
GREEN AVE
KILWINNING RD
THE VINES
BARR CRES
OLD CALEY RD
WALLACE RD
HIGHET GDNS
ALEXANDER PL
MEADOW AVE
VINEBURGH AVE
DUNTONKNOLL
CALDON RD
DALE CRES
CEDAR RD
STEWART DR
EASTWOOD AVE
DONALDSON DR
ROWAN TERR
Haysholm Sch
MACKINNON TERR
BANK ST
BANK CT
BANK PL
A736
MANSON RD
STANECASTLE INTC
B769
MIDDLETON RD
B7080
FENCEDYKE WAY
FENCEDYKE CL
Weir
IRVINE
VINEBURGH CT
John Galt Prim Sch
TOLLERTON DR
MAPLE TERR
HENDERSON CRES
RANKEN DR
McDONALD DR
MOSSGIEL DR
RANKEN CRES
WOODLANDS AVE
CLAYTON AVE
GEORGE AVE
QUARRY RD
WILSON AVE
CROCUS GR
HEATHFIELD HO
MARRESS RD
BURNS ST
A736
MCCLURE GDNS
KA12
Woodlands Prim Sch
St Marks Prim Sch
CROMPTON WAY
CORSERINE BANK
LONG DR
Burns Mus & Club
EGLINTON GDNS
THORNHOUSE CT
SHAWHOLM GDNS
East Rd Ret Pk
BANK ST
MUIR DR
GALT AVE
DALRYMPLE DR
DALRYMPLE CT
CLARK DR
HOWAT CRES
BERRY DR
MACARA DR
ST INAN AVE
TOWERLANDS RD
ARKWRIGHT WAY
TOWERLANDS INTC
CHEVIOT HEAD
WATERSIDE
ANNFIELD GDNS
ARRANVIEW CT
CASTLE ST
SEAGATE
WEST RD
Liby
EAST RD
CARTERS PL
BALLOT RD
COTTON ROW
QUEENS CT
SLOAN PL
THORNHOUSE AVE
PO
ALLAN SQ
MILL CRES
North Newmoor Ind Est
ARKWRIGHT WAY
LEWIS WYND 1
LEWIS CRES 2
BROOMLANDS BUSWAY
CRAMOND WAY
Works
BOYLE ST
COCHRANE ST
CHURCH ST
MARRESS RDBT
LOW GREEN RD
WEST CT
CHAPEL LA
HIGH ST
TH & Ct
BRIDGEGATE
HILL ST
KIRKGATE
GLASGOW VENNEL
KILNWLK
B7081
SLOAN AVE
DUNCAN DR
WATSON TERR
BEECH AVE
MILL RD
SILLARS MDW
ADAMS WLK
ROSEHOLM AVE
ANNICK VW
SLATE MILL GDNS
River Irvine
FULLARTON
Vennel Mus
TOWNHEAD
Glebe Prim Sch
GILBERTFIELD PL
MALCOLM GDNS
KERR DR
KERR PL
ST KILDA BANK
VICTORIA RDBT
BELFAST QUAY
FRIARS CROFT
NEW ST
AFTON CT
ANNICK CT
DOON CT
GARNOCK CT
Cemy
BROOMLANDS DR
TARRYHOLME DR
WARRIX AVE
GREENFIELD DR
Annick Water
South Newmoor Ind Est
WHITTLE PL
Scottish Maritime Mus
Rivergate Sh Ctr
MONTGOMERY PL 1
LINTHOUSE VENNEL 2
MONTGOMERY ST
FULLARTON RDBT
Irvine
FULLARTON ST
KIRK VENNEL
BRADBURY GLEBE
HAWTHORN DR
GOLFFIELDS RD
Loudoun-Montgomery Prim Sch
ANNICK RDBT
ANNICK RD
Hotel
MACADAM PL
TELFORD PL
SOUTH NEWMOOR AVE
HARBOUR ST
GOTTRIES RD
BIMSON PL
BIMSON ROW
HARBOUR RD
Scottish Maritime Mus
RIVERWAY
Riverway Ret Pk
VICTORIA
MCKINLAY CRES
SANDERSON AVE
CARTERS RIGG
LOUDOUN RIGG
LUGTON CT
SCHOOL LA
MERRYVALE RD
GREENBANK CT
GREENBANK RD
WHYTE AVE
McGIBNEY DR
MILGARHOLM AVE
LOACH AVE
GULLILAND PL
A78
B7081
CORSEHILL MOUNT RD
NEWMOOR INTC
MACKINTOSH PL
PETER ST
PORTLAND RDBT
BEACH DR
Fullarton
Works
SCOTT RD
MERRYVALE RDBT
AYR RD
A737
A71
RUBIE CRES
LAMONT DR
MILGARHOLM RDBT
LYLE GDNS
WARRIX INTC
PORTLAND RD
PORTLAND PL

219
209

219
225

210
222

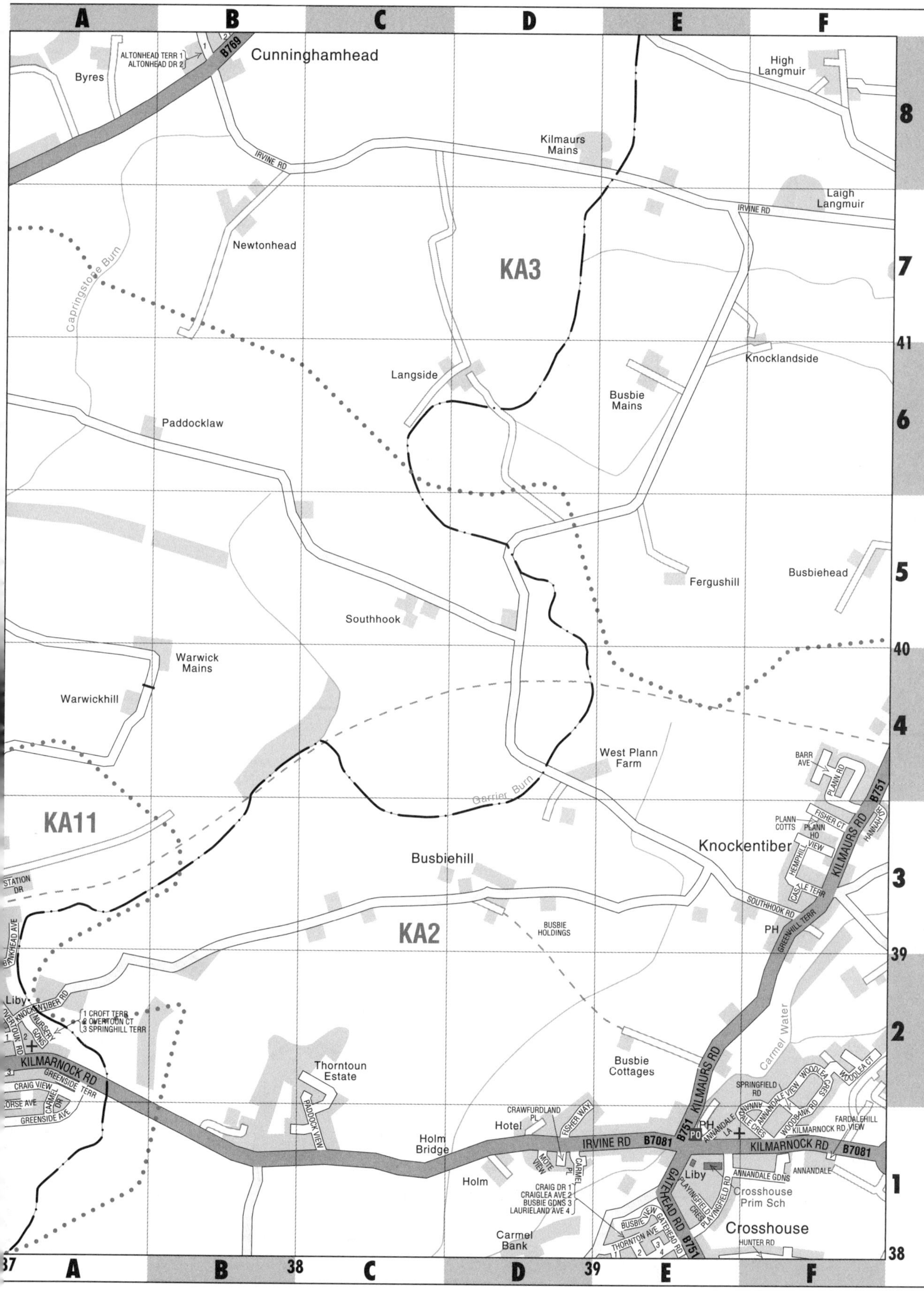
A
B
C
D
E
F
8
7
41
6
5
40
4
3
39
2
1
38
37
38
39
Cunninghamhead
Byres
ALTONHEAD TERR 1
ALTONHEAD DR 2
B769
High Langmuir
Kilmaurs Mains
IRVINE RD
Laigh Langmuir
Newtonhead
Capringstone Burn
KA3
Knocklandside
Langside
Busbie Mains
Paddocklaw
Fergushill
Busbiehead
Southhook
Warwick Mains
Warwickhill
West Plann Farm
BARR AVE
PLANN RD
B751
Garrier Burn
KA11
PLANN COTTS
FISHER CT
PLANN HO
HANNAH ST
KILMAURS RD
HEMPHILL VIEW
Knockentiber
Busbiehill
STATION DR
CASTLE TERR
SOUTHHOOK RD
KA2
BUSBIE HOLDINGS
PH
GREENHILL TERR
Liby
KNOCKENTIBER RD
1 CROFT TERR
2 OVERTOUN CT
3 SPRINGHILL TERR
OVERTOUN RD
NURSERY GDNS
Carmel Water
KILMARNOCK RD
GREENSIDE TERR
CRAIG VIEW
GORSE AVE
CARMEL DR
GREENSIDE AVE
Thorntoun Estate
PADDOCK VIEW
Busbie Cottages
WOODLEA CRES
WOODLEA CT
SPRINGFIELD RD
ANNANDALE VIEW
CRAWFURDLAND PL
FISHER WAY
Hotel
PH
ANNANDALE CRES
WOODBANK RD
FARDALEHILL VIEW
KILMARNOCK RD
Holm Bridge
IRVINE RD
B7081
PO
ANNANDALE LA
B7081
MOTE VIEW
CARMEL PL
ANNANDALE GDNS
ANNANDALE
Holm
CRAIG DR 1
CRAIGLEA AVE 2
BUSBIE GDNS 3
LAURIELAND AVE 4
GATEHEAD RD
PLAYINGFIELD CRES
PLAYINGFIELD RD
Crosshouse Prim Sch
Carmel Bank
BUSBIE VIEW
THORNTON AVE
GATEHEAD RD
Crosshouse
HUNTER RD

226
222

221 211

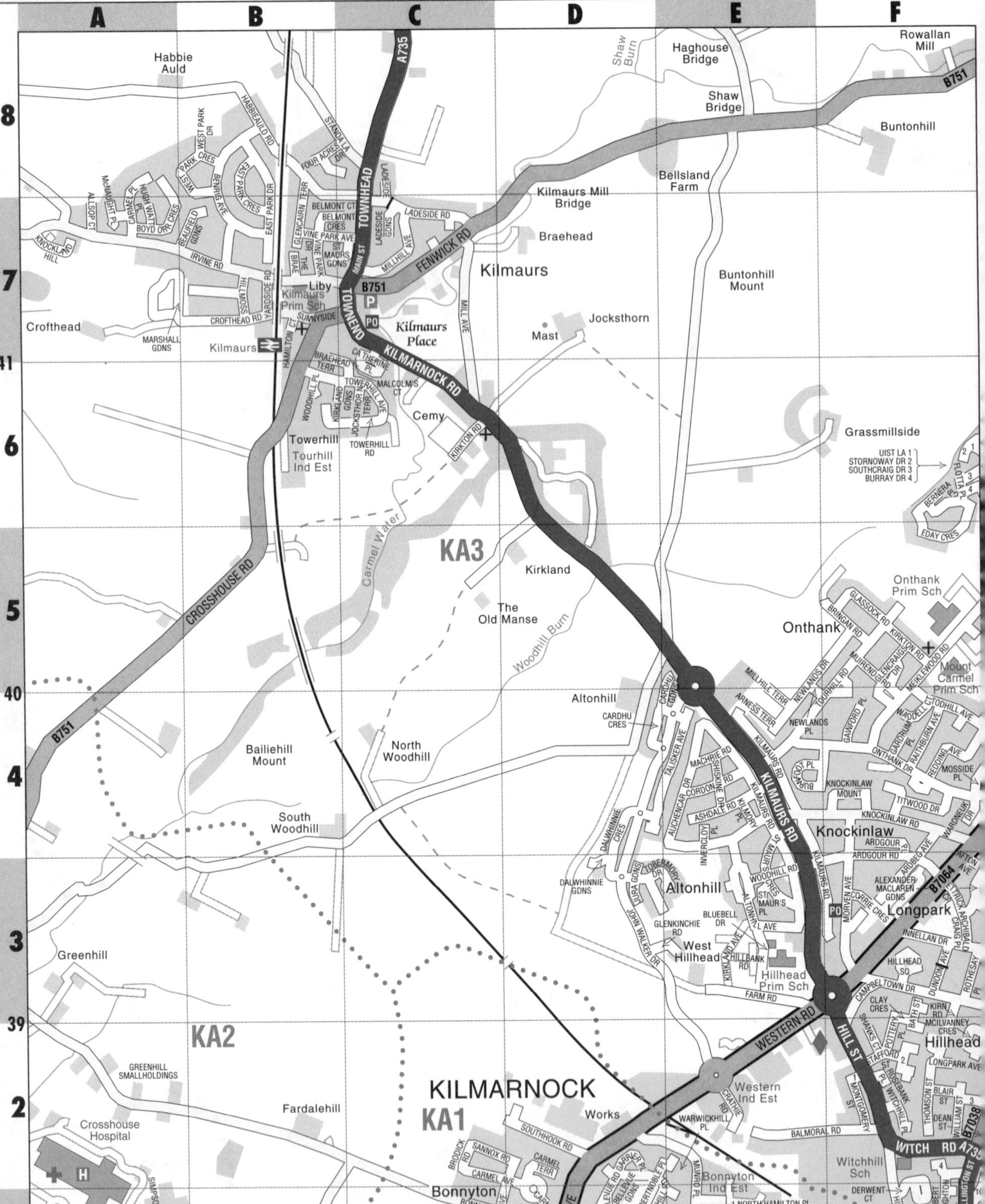

221 227

F1
1 UNION ST
2 HIGH CHURCH LA
3 SQUARE OF ALES
4 THE FOREGATE
5 JAMES SHAW LA
6 FOREGATE SQ
7 WEST GEORGE ST
8 LANGLANDS BRAE
9 JOHN DICKIE ST
10 FULTON'S LA
11 DEAN CT

F2
1 MONTGOMERY PL
2 HILLPARK DR
3 ORCHARD ST
4 WELLINGTON PL

212

A
B
C
D
E
F
8
7
6
5
4
3
2
1
41
40
39
38
43
44
45
B751
A77
B7038
Meikle
Mosside
Moss
Wood
Tannahill
Dalmusternock
Little
Mosside
Meiklewood
Bsns Ctr
Meiklewood
Craufurdland
Loch
North Craig
Resr
Loch
Plantation
Wardknowe
Plantation
Northcraig
LAURISTON WAY 7
LOCHMABEN WYND 8
DUNDONALD CT 9
PRIESTLAND CL 10
NEWMILNS GDN 11
LUGAR WYND 12
KINGSFORD PL 13
HOLLYBUSH PL 14
PORTING CROSS PL 15
1 UIST LA
2 BURRAY DR
Fenwick Water
1 AUCHENTIBER PL
2 TARBOLTON PL
3 BOYDSTON WAY
4 CROSSHILL WYND
5 DALGARVEN MEWS
6 WALLACETOWN AVE
Rushybog
Plantation
Borland
Craufurdland
Castle
SOUTHCRAIG
HOLDINGS
Broombrae
Greenhead
Plantation
Borland
Bridge
Craufurdland Water
KA3
GLASGOW RD
Hotel
Mast
Bringan
Ford
WARDLAW RD
Assloss
Assloss
House
B7064
WESTERN RD
East
Wardlaw
Assloss
Bridge
ASSLOSS RD
Dean Castle
Country Park
Hillhouse
Dean
Castle
Visitor
Ctr
B7038
BEANSBURN
B7082
GRASSYARDS
INTC
Silverwood
Prim Sch
Whinpark
1 FRASER WLK
2 DUNDAS WLK
3 DONALDSON RD
4 FINLAYSON DR
5 LINDSAY GDNS
1 THOMAS BAIRD GDNS
2 JOHN BURTT PL
3 JOHN KENNEDY PL
4 JAMES JOHNSTON PL
Ford
Beansburn
GRASSYARDS RD
Kilmarnock Water
Townholm
St Josephs
Acad
New Farm
Loch
Silverwood
Newhouse
URQUHART
RD
DEAN ST
Kilmarnock Coll
of Sporting Excellence
St Andrews
Prim Sch
STRAWBERRYBANK RD
DEAN LA
Mon
Cemy
James
Hamilton
Acad
New Farm
Prim Sch
MACALLISTER PL 1
MACINNES PL 2
MACINTOSH PL 3
MACDOUGALL DR 4
MACMILLAN DR 5
MACMILLAN PL 6
MACEWAN PL 7
Ralstonhill
HIGH ST A735
1 MORRIS LA
2 SOULIS ST
3 FULTON'S LA
4 BOYD CT
Burns
Mon
8 MACPHERSON WLK
9 MACPHERSON GDNS
10 MACDONALD GDNS
11 MACNICHOL GDNS
12 MACANDREW PL
13 MACDONALD PL
14 MILTON AVE
15 MILTON RD
16 MACBETH WLK
Templetonburn
Kilmarnock
Coll
KAY PARK TERR
MILTON RD
River Irvine
Ayrshire STREET ATLAS

228

219

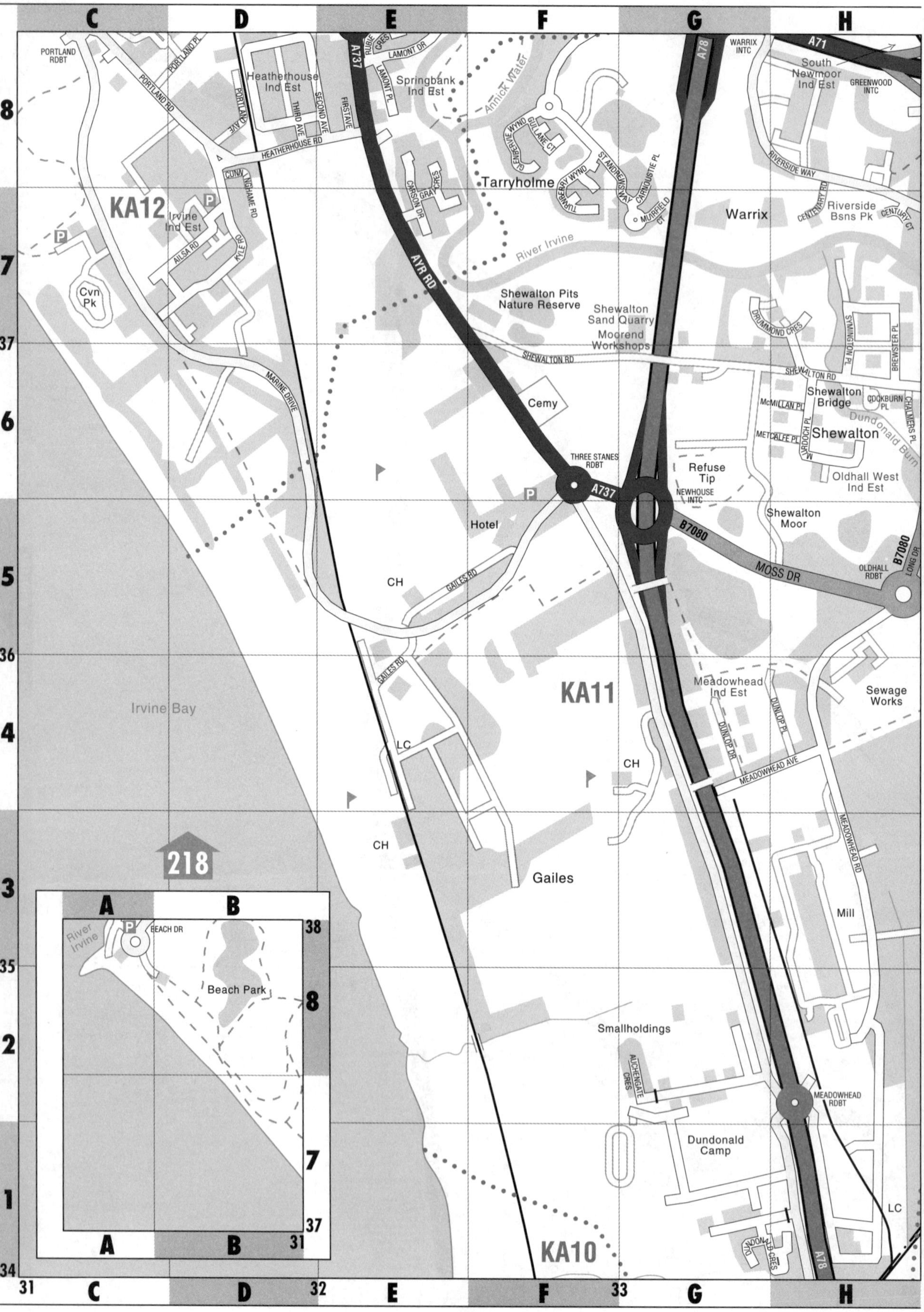

C
D
E
F
G
H
8
7
37
6
5
36
4
3
35
2
1
34
31
32
33
PORTLAND RDBT
PORTLAND PL
PORTLAND RD
PORTLAND AVE
Heatherhouse Ind Est
THIRD AVE
SECOND AVE
FIRSTAVE
HEATHERHOUSE RD
CUNNINGHAME RD
KA12
Irvine Ind Est
AILSA RD
KYLE RD
Cvn Pk
A737
RUBIE CRES
LAMONT DR
LAMONT PL
Springbank Ind Est
Annick Water
GLENBERVIE WYND
GULLANE CT
TURNBERRY WYND
ST ANDREWS WAY
CARNOUSTIE PL
MUIRFIELD CT
CARSON DR
GRAY CRES
Tarryholme
River Irvine
AYR RD
Shewalton Pits Nature Reserve
Shewalton Sand Quarry
Moorend Workshops
SHEWALTON RD
Cemy
MARINE DRIVE
THREE STANES RDBT
A737
Hotel
GAILES RD
CH
A78
WARRIX INTC
A71
South Newmoor Ind Est
GREENWOOD INTC
RIVERSIDE WAY
CENTENARY RD
Riverside Bsns Pk
CENTURY CT
Warrix
DRUMMOND CRES
SYMINGTON PL
BREWSTER PL
SHEWALTON RD
Shewalton Bridge
COCKBURN PL
CHALMERS PL
McMILLAN PL
METCALFE PL
MURDOCH PL
Shewalton
Dundonald Burn
Refuse Tip
NEWHOUSE INTC
Oldhall West Ind Est
Shewalton Moor
B7080
MOSS DR
OLDHALL RDBT
LONG DR
Irvine Bay
KA11
Meadowhead Ind Est
DUNLOP PL
DUNLOP DR
MEADOWHEAD AVE
Sewage Works
LC
MEADOWHEAD RD
Gailes
Mill
Smallholdings
AUCHENGATE CRES
MEADOWHEAD RDBT
Dundonald Camp
DUNDONALD CRES
KA10
River Irvine
BEACH DR
Beach Park
A
B
38
8
7
37
31

218

229

220
226

A
B
C
D
E
F
8
7
37
6
5
36
4
3
35
2
1
34
35
36
GREENWOOD INTC
CORSEHILL MOUNT RD
CAMPBELL PL
DUNOP CRES
TOWNFOOT
B7081
TA Ctr
KENNEDY PK
COLL GDNS
MONACH GDNS
STAFFA CT
RONALDSAY CT
TIREE CT
SKYE CT
LISMORE WAY
IONA PL
ISLAY CT
JURA CT
STROMA CT
ISMORE DR
CUMBRAE CT
THE GLEBE
GLEBE AVE
ERISKAY CT
MAID MORVILLE AVE
MANUEL TERR
HARRIS CT
HARRIS TERR
MANUEL CT
DUNDONALD RD
FORD AVE
McLEAN DR
SHARPE AVE
CORSEHILL PK
B730
A71
Crem
CORSEHILL MOUNT RDBT
Garrier Burn
Carmel Water
GREENWOOD GATE
MONTGOMERYFIELD
B7080
STEADMAN PL
RIVERSIDE RDBT
Riverside Bsns Pk
RIVERSIDE WAY
Holmsford Bridge
River Irvine
LONG DR
KA11
Holms
Holm's Bridge
SHEWALTON RDBT
P
Works
SHEWALTON DR
GRIERS WLK
MOSS
SHEWALTON
DREGHORN RD
Pipeline
SHEWALTON RD
Works
Drybridge
MAIN ST
STATION ROW
Girtridge Mount
Girtridge
Pipeline
Ploughland
Olympic Bsns Pk
Nature Reserve
Dundonald Burn
Ploughland Mount
PLOUGHLAND HOLDINGS
KA2
Palmer Mount
Shewalton Moss
Refuse Tip
A759
CASTLEVIEW
L Ctr
Dundonald Prim Sch
Guilliland
AUCHANS DR
COCHRANE DR
CASTLE DR
NEWFIELD DR
NEWFIELD PL
GUILLILAND AVE
COCHRANE AVE
AUCHANS AVE
FULLARTON AVE
STUART PL
KILNFORD DR
OLD AUCHANS VIEW
KILNFORD CRES
OATS PL
WILSON PL
THORN VIEW
PARK
VERNON PL
DRYBRIDGE RD
SCHOOL WYND
WINEHOUSE YETT
Liby
KILMARNOCK RD
B750
Old Auchans
Auchans
Dundonald Castle
Beech Wood
Parkthorn
PO
Dundonald
WALLACE AVE
BRUCE AVE
RICHMOND TERR
WARLY DR
MERKLAND PK
BEATON
EARL MOUNT 1
EARL CRES 2
MERKLAND PL 3
GLENFOOT GDNS
PH
LAURIESTON CT
EARL RISE
LOCHSIDE CT
TARBOLTON RD
KA10
Hillhouse Quarry
Old Bank
Dundonald Burn
A759
34

230
226

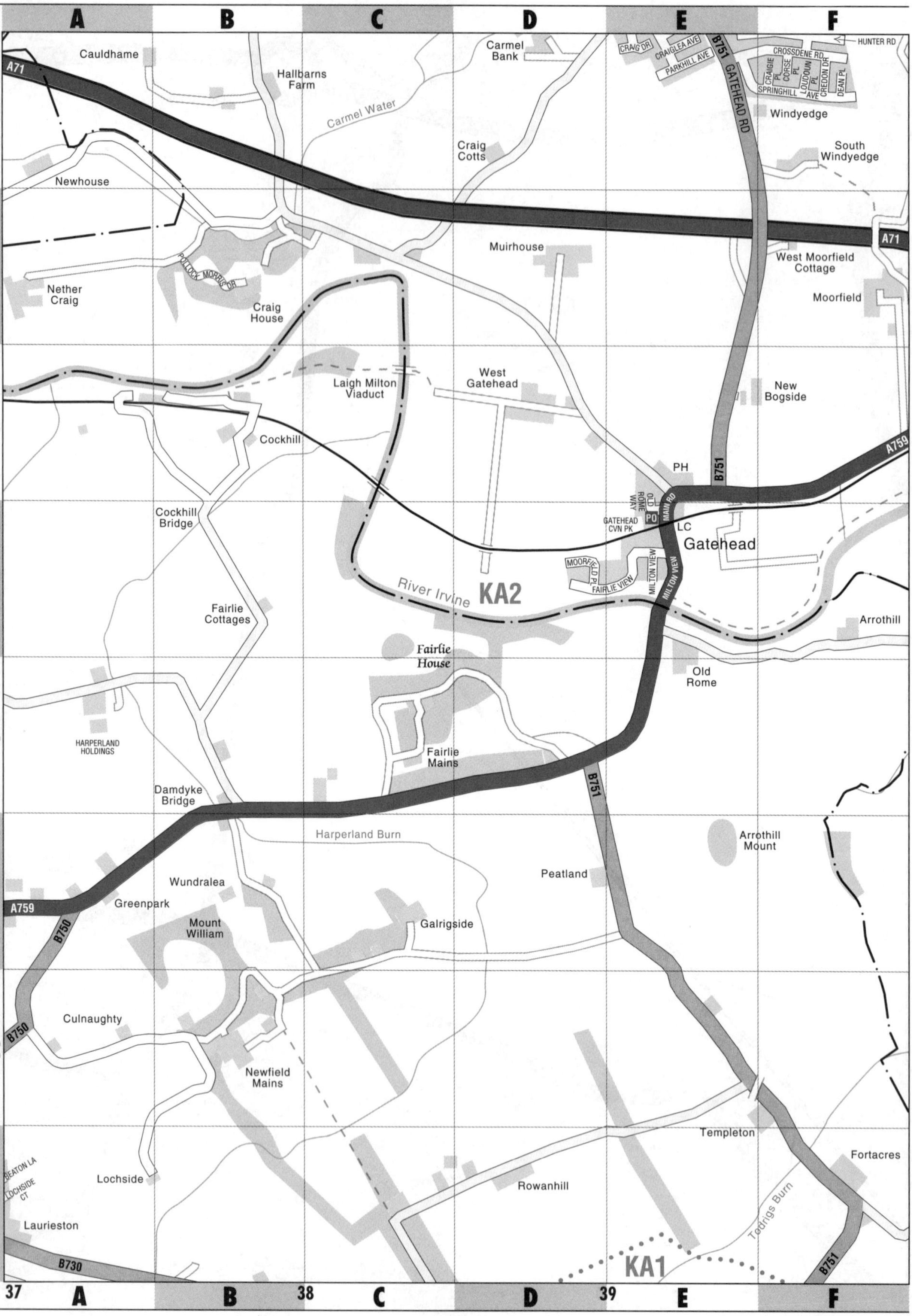
A
B
C
D
E
F
8
7
37
6
5
36
4
3
35
2
1
34
37
38
39
A71
Cauldhame
Hallbarns
Farm
Carmel
Bank
CRAIG DR
CRAIGLEA AVE
PARKHILL AVE
B751
GATEHEAD RD
HUNTER RD
CROSSDENE RD
CRAIGIE PL
CORSE PL
LOUDOUN PL
CREDON DR
DEAN PL
SPRINGHILL AVE
Windyedge
South
Windyedge
Carmel Water
Craig
Cotts
Newhouse
Muirhouse
West Moorfield
Cottage
Moorfield
POLLOCK MORRIS DR
Nether
Craig
Craig
House
West
Gatehead
Laigh Milton
Viaduct
New
Bogside
Cockhill
PH
A759
OLD ROME WAY
MAIN RD
PO
GATEHEAD
CVN PK
LC
Gatehead
Cockhill
Bridge
MOORFIELD PL
FAIRLIE VIEW
MILTON VIEW
River Irvine
KA2
Fairlie
Cottages
Arrothill
Fairlie
House
Old
Rome
HARPERLAND
HOLDINGS
Fairlie
Mains
Damdyke
Bridge
Harperland Burn
Arrothill
Mount
Wundralea
Peatland
A759
Greenpark
B750
Mount
William
Galrigside
Culnaughty
Newfield
Mains
Templeton
BEATON LA
LOCHSIDE CT
Lochside
Rowanhill
Fortacres
Todrigs Burn
Laurieston
KA1
B730

E8
1 SOUTH HAMILTON CT
2 EAST WOODSTOCK CT
3 WEST WOODSTOCK CT
F8
1 BANK PL
2 COLLEGE WYND

F8
3 LOW CHURCH LA
4 CHEAPSIDE ST
5 Burns Prec
6 GREEN ST
7 SANDBED LA
8 WATER LA

222

F8
9 BRIDGE LA
10 ST MARNOCK PL
11 QUEEN ST
12 BRAESIDE ST
13 KIRKTONHOLM ST
14 GALLION WLK

228

15 Kilmarnock Acad
F7
1 KIRKTONHOLM PL
2 ST ANDREW'S WLK
3 RICHARDLAND RD
4 BREWERY RD

5 EAST NETHERTON ST

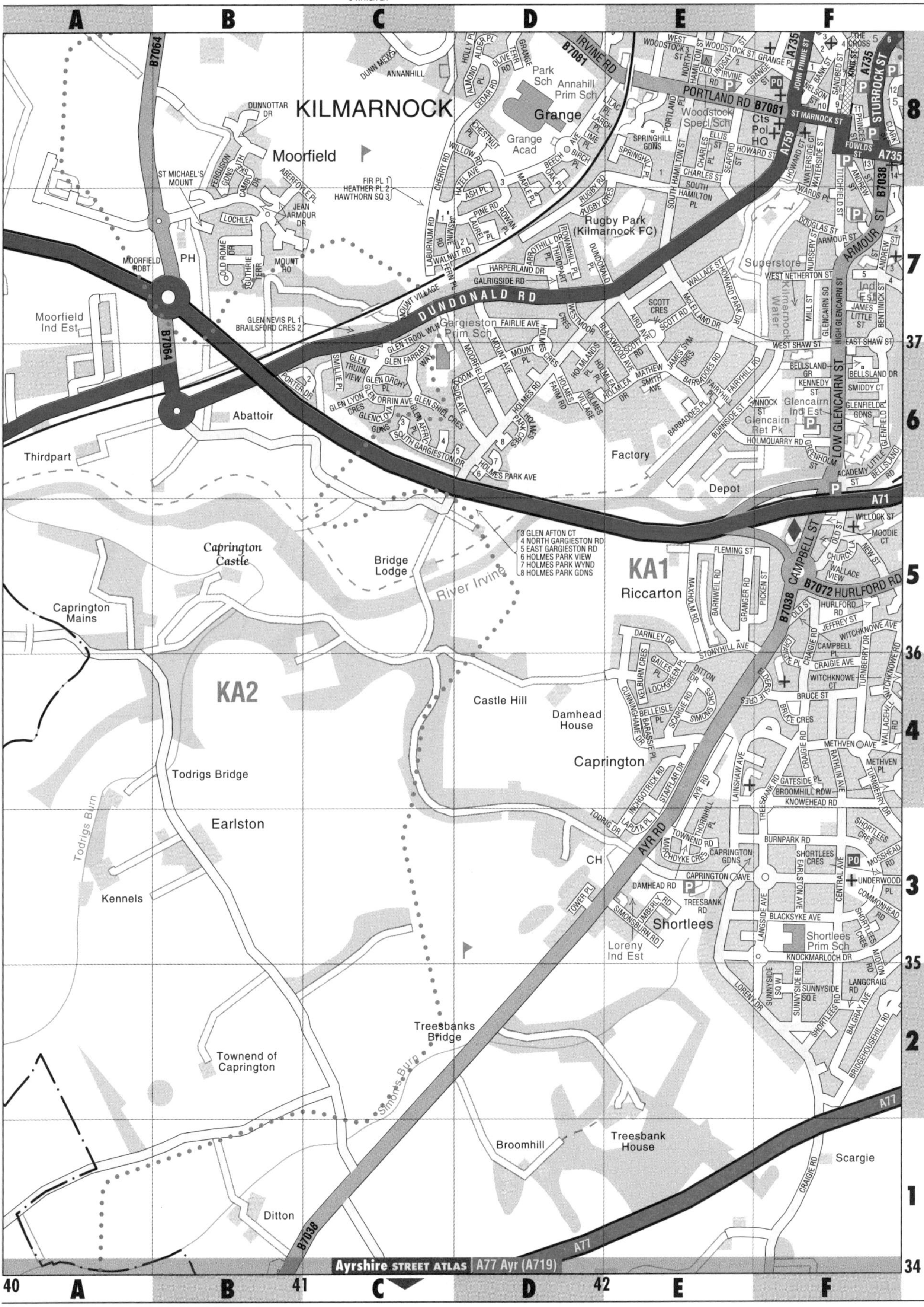

228

A8
1 ACADAEMY APARTMENTS
2 GLEBE CT
3 MITCHELL CT
4 Loanhead Prim Sch

227
223

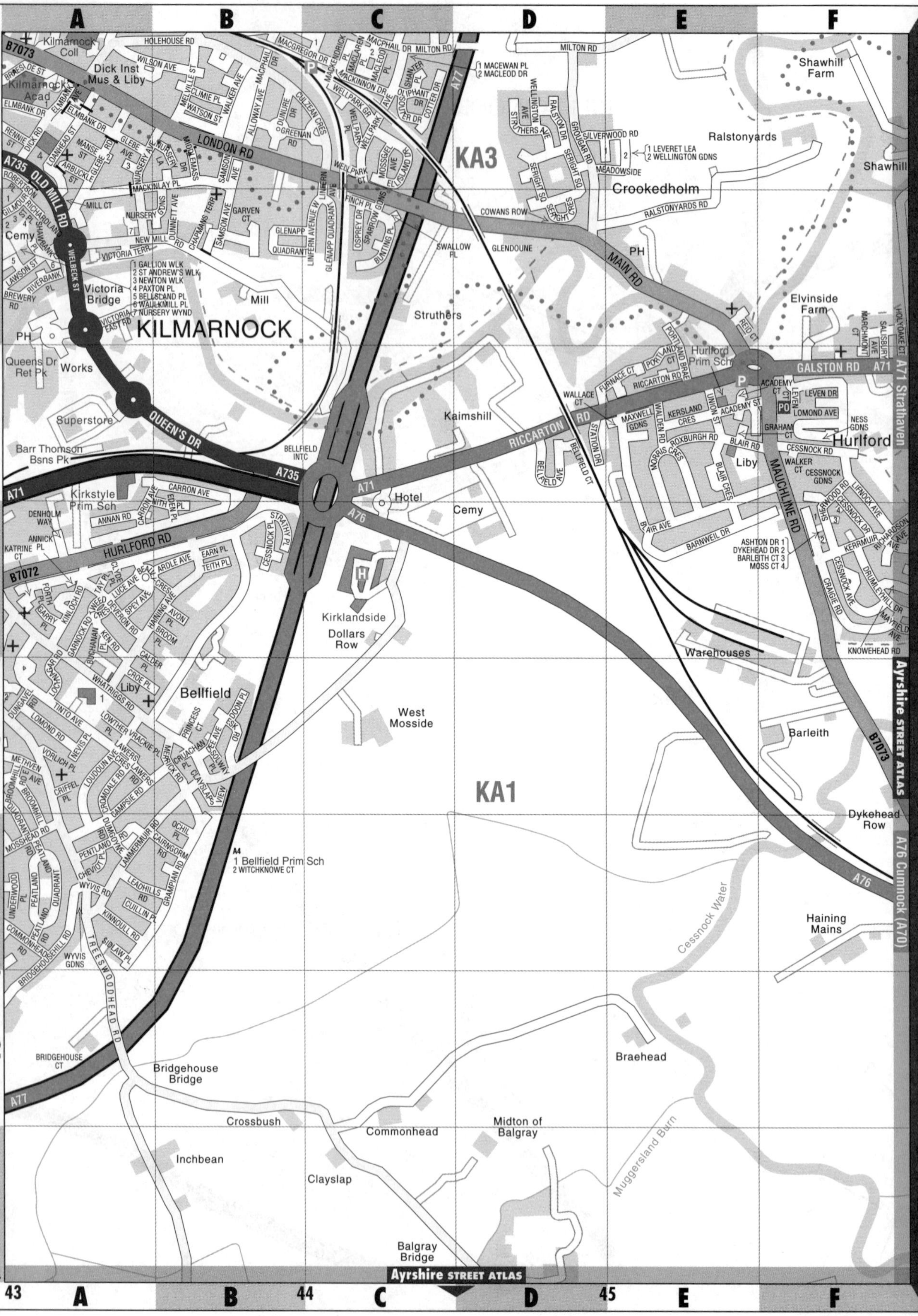

227

224
230
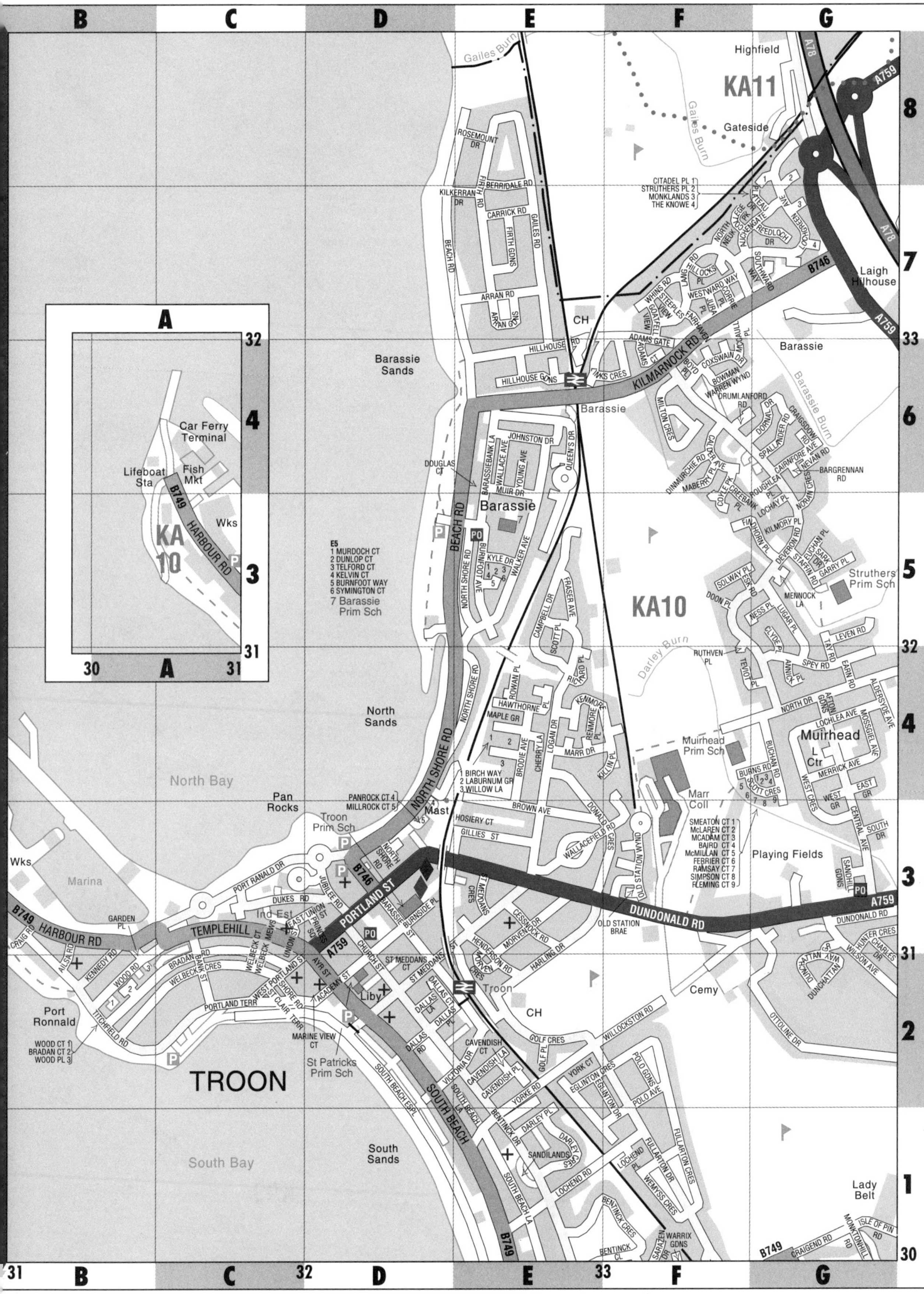
B
C
D
E
F
G
8
7
33
6
5
32
4
3
31
2
1
30
31
32
33
Highfield
KA11
Gateside
Gailes Burn
A78
A759
Laigh Hilhouse
CITADEL PL 1
STRUTHERS PL 2
MONKLANDS 3
THE KNOWE 4
ROSEMOUNT DR
KILKERRAN DR
BERRIDALE RD
CARRICK RD
FIRTH RD
FIRTH GDNS
GAILES RD
BEACH RD
ARRAN RD
ARRAN GDNS
HILLHOUSE RD
HILLHOUSE GDNS
CH
B746
KILMARNOCK RD
Barassie
Barassie Sands
Barassie Burn
LINKS CRES
ADAMS GATE
MILTON CRES
COXSWAIN DR
BOWMAN
WARREN WYND
DRUMLANFORD RD
CRAIGSDOW RD
BARGRENNAN RD
JOHNSTON DR
WALLACE AVE
YOUNG AVE
MUIR DR
QUEEN'S DR
BARASSIEBANK LA
DOUGLAS CT
KYLE DR
WALKER AVE
BURNFOOT AVE
NORTH SHORE RD
PO
P
E5
1 MURDOCH CT
2 DUNLOP CT
3 TELFORD CT
4 KELVIN CT
5 BURNFOOT WAY
6 SYMINGTON CT
7 Barassie Prim Sch
A
Car Ferry Terminal
Lifeboat Sta
Fish Mkt
Wks
B749
HARBOUR RD
KA 10
30
KA10
Struthers Prim Sch
Darley Burn
RUTHVEN PL
FRASER AVE
CAMPBELL DR
SCOTT PL
RICHARD PL
KENMORE
HAWTHORNE PL
ROWAN PL
MAPLE GR
BRODIE AVE
CHERRY LA
LOGAN DR
MARR DR
KILLIN PL
North Sands
North Bay
Pan Rocks
1 BIRCH WAY
2 LABURNUM GR
3 WILLOW LA
PANROCK CT 4
MILLROCK CT 5
Mast
Troon Prim Sch
BROWN AVE
HOSIERY CT
GILLIES ST
DONALD CRES
WALLACEFIELD RD
Muirhead Prim Sch
Marr Coll
Muirhead
L Ctr
NORTH DR
LOCHLEA AVE
MERRICK AVE
MOSSGIEL AVE
ALDERSYDE AVE
WEST GR
EAST GR
CENTRAL AVE
SOUTH DR
WEST CRES
BURNS RD
SCOTT CRES
BUCHAN RD
SMEATON CT 1
McLAREN CT 2
MCADAM CT 3
BAIRD CT 4
McMILLAN CT 5
FEBRIER CT 6
RAMSAY CT 7
SIMPSON CT 8
FLEMING CT 9
Playing Fields
SANDHILL GDNS
Wks
Marina
PORT RANALD DR
JUBILEE RD
PORTLAND ST
A759
DUKES RD
Ind Est
GARDEN PL
HARBOUR RD
TEMPLEHILL
CRAIG RD
KENNEDY RD
WOOD RD
BRADAN RD
WELBECK CRES
PORTLAND TERR
ST CLAIR TERR
AYR ST
ACADEMY ST
CHURCH ST
BARASSIE ST
BURNSIDE PL
ST MEDDANS CT
ST MEDDANS
DUNDONALD RD
OLD STATION BRAE
OLD STATION WAY
CESSNOCK DR
MORVEN DR
HARLING DR
HENDERSON RD
Troon
Liby
DALLAS RD
Port Ronnald
WOOD CT 1
BRADAN CT 2
WOOD PL 3
TITCHFIELD RD
MARINE VIEW CT
St Patricks Prim Sch
TROON
SOUTH BEACH ESPL
SOUTH BEACH
Cemy
WILLOCKSTON RD
GOLF CRES
CAVENDISH CT
VICTORIA DR
YORKE RD
YORK CT
EGLINTON CRES
EGLINTON DR
POLO GDNS
POLO AVE
FULLARTON CRES
FULLARTON DR
WEMYSS CRES
LOCHEND RD
DARLEY PL
DARLEY CRES
SANDILANDS
BENTINCK DR
BENTINCK CRES
BENTINCK CL
WARRIX GDNS
SOUTH BEACH LA
South Sands
South Bay
OTTOLINE DR
DUNCHATTAN
WILSON AVE
CHARLES DR
HUNTER CRES
Lady Belt
B749
CRAIGEND RD
MONKTONHILL RD
ISLE OF PIN RD
232
230

229
225

A
B
C
D
E
F
8
7
6
5
4
3
2
1
33
32
31
30
34
35
36
A759
A78
B746
Hillhouse Quarry
Hillhouse
Chapel Hill
Merkland Loch
Dundonald Burn
Hallyards Quarry
Hallyards
Highlees
Highlees Mount
Works
Aught Wood
Collenan
COLLENAN SMALLHOLDINGS
Wardlaw Hill
Harpercroft
Mast
KA2
Works
Clevance
Langholm
KA10
Highgrove House
WARDLAW CRES 1
CRUMMIEHOLM GDNS 2
CROSSBURN DR 3
CROSSBURN TERR 4
CROSSBURN LA 5
HALL LA 6
Beattock Burn
Clevance Cottage
Corraith
SEAVIEW TERR
COLLENAN AVE
STABLE WYND
MAIN ST
PH
FULLARTON PL
PO
Loans
CRAIKSLAND RD
CRAIKSLAND PL
KYLE CRES
COLLINS DR
TROON RD
BEECHWOOD PADDOCK
Crossburn
Craiksland
Wester Croft
DUNDONALD RD
HUNTER CRES
CHARLES GDNS
ELMS DR
KA1
High Wexford
Darley Burn
Southside
Rumbling Burn
WILSON AVE
OTTOLINE DR
LADY MARGARET DR
BALCOMIE CRES
Southside Cottages
Wexford Cottage
KERRIX RD
Darley Plantation
WILSON AVE
ISLE OF PIN RD
FULLARTON CTYD
KA9
Lady Belt
Crosbie House
Fairlees
Crookside

229
233

226

A
B
C
D
E
F
8
7
33
6
5
32
4
3
31
2
1
30
37
38
39
B730
B751
Broomhill
Crooks
Slough Burn
Whitehill
Muirmill
Mast
Todrigs Burn
Brownlee
Dankeith
Craigs
Dankeith
L Pk
High
Coodham
Cemy
KA2
Coodham
Lake
A77 Kilmarnock
STABLE
HOUSES
Coodham
A77
Dyke
Catcraig
Plantation
Fairfield
Nursery
Holehouse
KA1
Bogend
Rumbling Burn
Knockendale
MUIRHOUSE RD
Burnbrae
TARBOLTON RD
Symington
Mount
Whitelees
LOMOND VIEW
DANKEITH RD
BREWLANDS DR
MOUNT AVE
DANKEITH DR
Mill
Townend
TOWNEND TERR
PO
BREWLANDS DR
DOON PL
1 MERRICK PL
2 LOUDOUN PL
3 BREWLANDS RD
Works
Townend
House
BREWLANDS CRES
Liby
Craigowan
TOWNEND RD
MAIN ST
BREWLANDS RD
Symington
Prim Sch
South
Townend
TOWNEND BRAE
TOWNEND PL
Symington
PARK CT
Helentongate
SYMINGTON RD N
PH
THE GLEBE
Craigrethill
Trynlaw
Burnbank
SYMINGTON RD S
KILMARNOCK RD
KERRIX RD
Stockbridge
Auld
Helenton
Jeanfield
Low
Wexford
Danepark
Helenton
Hill
Pow Burn
Helenton
Mains
Hansel
Village
Broad Tongue
Wood
Ayrshire STREET ATLAS

234

229

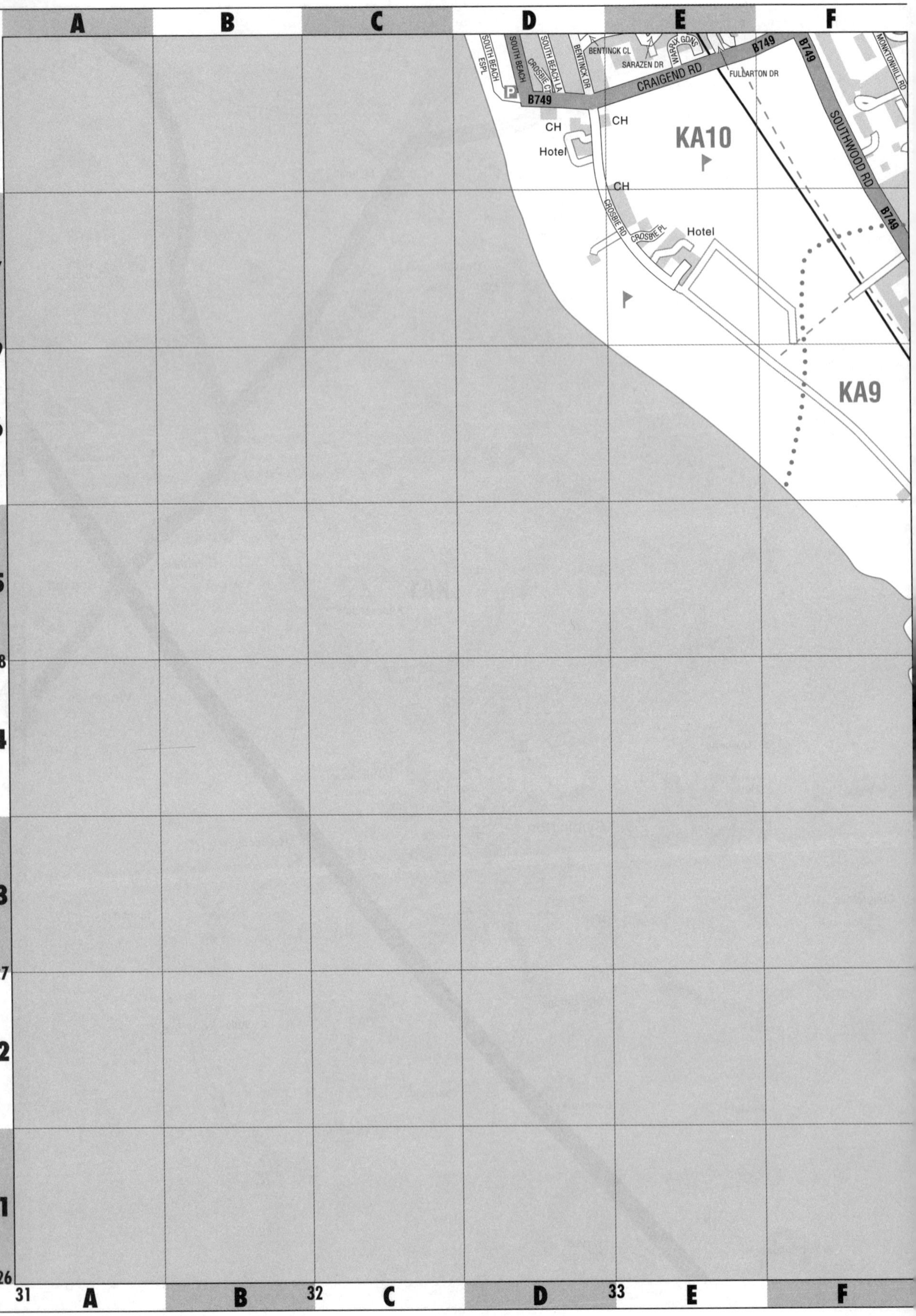
A
B
C
D
E
F
SOUTH BEACH ESPL
SOUTH BEACH
CROSBIE CT
SOUTH BEACH LA
BENTINCK DR
BENTINCK CL
SARAZEN DR
WARRIX GDNS
B749
CRAIGEND RD
FULLARTON DR
MONKTONHILL RD
SOUTHWOOD RD
P
CH
CH
Hotel
CH
KA10
CROSBIE RD
CROSBIE PL
Hotel
KA9
8
7
29
6
5
28
4
3
27
2
1
26
31
32
33

235

230
234
A
B
C
D
E
F
ISLE OF PIN RD
Lawhill Cottages
KA10
Mount William
Lochgreen House
Frognal
South Wood
Kersland
Hillhouse
Hobsland
Rumbling Burn
KERRIX RD
Blackside Wood
Brocket
Crookside Bridge
Monktonhill
SOUTHWOOD RD
MONKTONHILL RD
Monktonhead
High Monktonhill
MONKTONHILL RDBT
Crow Wood
Nethermuir
A78
DUTCH HOUSE RDBT
A77
A79
B749
The White House
Monktonhead Farm
Sandhill
Dow's Burn
KILMARNOCK RD
Motel
Monkton Services
Townhead Bridge
Mon
KA9
B739
DOW AVE
Ind Pk
Windmill
Hotel
St Andrew's House
STATION RD
DOW RD
Monkton
Monkton Prim Sch
MAIN ST
QUEEN'S DR
CHARLES AVE
FIRHILL DR
CORONATION ST
GREENKNOWE PK
BAIRD RD
BAIRD PL
BURNSIDE RD
WHITESIDE GDNS
WHITESIDE PK
WHITESIDE PL
TARBOLTON RD
Whiteside
FINDHORN RD
Factory
ROBERTSON RD
Terminal Buildings
1 MOFFAT RD
2 MORRISON RD
Prestwick International Airport
McNEE RD
MONKTON RD
ELVIS ST
WELSH RD
HUDSON PL
MILLER SQ
YOUNGER DR
McINTYRE AVE
Orangefield Ind Est
Pow Burn
Glasgow Prestwick International Airport
4 HAMILTON WAY
5 THE CRESCENT
6 TEMPLERIGG CT
POWMILL RD
POWMILL GDNS
MACRAE DR
TOWANS CT
SHAWFARM GDNS
MACINTYRE RD
CAPPER VIEW
SEAGATE
MONKTON CT
ESPLANADE
TEMPLERIGG ST
KIRK ST
BURNSIDE GDNS
BERELANDS GDNS 1
HILLSIDE CRES 2
BOYDFIELD AVE 3
Newdykes Court
SHAWFARM PL
PRESTWICK
Cemy
REGENT PK 1
MONTGOMERIE RD 2
ALLANVALE RD 3
Prestwick Town
CH
STATION DR
MANSEWELL RD
THE RIGGS
OSWALD DR
Prestwick Acad
ALEXANDRA CT
ALEXANDRA AVE
FARM RD
SHAWFARM CT
ORANGEFIELD DR
NEWDYKES RD
SHAW RD
SKYE RD
Shaw Farm Ind Est
MONUMENT CRES
THE CROSS
MEIKLEWOOD AVE
MERRICK AVE
WEIR AVE
McNEILL AVE
ALVORD AVE
SHAWFARM RD
LINKS RD
ARDAYRE RD
SEABANK RD
QUEENS TERR
MIDTON RD
STATION RD
MAIN ST
SAUNTERNE RD
CROFTHEAD RD
CAERLAVEROCK RD
MORRIS RD
BERELANDS RD
BOYDFIELD AVE
MANSON AVE
SHAW RD
BLACKFORD CRES
LANGCROFT AVE
GLENBURN RD
MARSMOUNT RD
Mon
8
7
29
6
5
28
4
3
27
2
1
26
35
36
236
234

233 231

A B C D E F
8
7
29
6
5
28
4
3
27
2
1
26
37 A B 38 C D 39 E F
A77
KILMARNOCK RD
Langlands
Pow Bridge
Rose Cottage
KA1
Underwood Mains
Baillieston
Baillieston Glen
Lodge
Underwood
Rosemount
Underwood Burn
Underwood Glen
Low Wardneuk
Adamton Mains
High Wardneuk
North Bogside
Pow Burn
Woodside
KA9
Adamton House
ADAMTON EST
Mid Foulton
B739
TARBOLTON RD
Newlands
Foulton
Brieryside
Old Newlands
Bogside House
Meikle Foulton
Tarshaw
KA5
Raith Burn Bridge
Raith Burn
Ladykirk
Raith
Raith Hill
A719
Shawhill Farm
SANDYFORD RD
Glasgow Prestwick International Airport
Fox Covert
Springbank Cottage
Ladykirk Burn
Ladykirk Bridge
Ayrshire STREET ATLAS

233 237

232
236

A
B
C
D
E
F
8
7
25
6
5
24
4
3
23
2
1
22
31
32
33
F2
1 TAYLOR CT
2 SALTFIELD LA
3 HALLS VENNAL
4 Green Street La Bsns Pk
PROMENADE
SALTPANS RD
LIMEKILN RD
SHORE RD
ELMBANK ST
WEIR RD
GLEBE RD
GLEBE CRES
WAGGON RD
North Breakwater
KA8
Dock
GRIFFIN DOCK RD
YORK ST LA
TAYLOR ST
GREEN STREET LA
YORK STREET LA
BACK PEEBLES ST
PEEBLES ST
NEW RD
WEAVER ST
Ayr Harbour
OSWALD LA
YORK ST
South Pier
SPUR RD
GREEN ST
CROWN SQ
DAMSIDE
CROWN SQ
CHURCHILL TWR
YORK PL
CROWN ST
PO
E1
1 BRUCE CRES
2 QUEEN'S TERR LA
3 MARLBOROUGH CT
4 BUCHAN CT
5 TRANCHARD CT
6 ROWALLAN CT
7 DONNINI CT
8 INKERMAN CT
River Ayr
SOUTH BEACH RD
SOUTH HARBOUR ST
NORTH HARBOUR ST
GREEN ST LA
BACK MAIN ST
MAIN ST
A719
A79
KING ST
ESPLANADE
Citadel L Ctr
Liby
GARDEN ST
JOHN ST
A713
AYR
SEABANK RD
MONTGOMERIE TERR
B748
Ayr Academy
NEW BRIDGE ST
RIVER ST
KA7
ARRAN TERR
EGLINTON PL
EGLINTON TERR
TH
CROMWELL RD
AILSA PL
CITADEL PL
FORT ST
HIGH ST
OLD BRIDGE ST
RIVER TERR
Auld Brig
Ct

238
236

F1
1 ALLISON ST
2 GARDEN CT
3 GEORGE ST
4 STRATHAYR PL
5 SANDGATE
6 ST JOHN ST
7 CATHCART ST
8 ACADEMY ST
9 BOAT VENNAL
10 North Harbour Ind Est

235
233

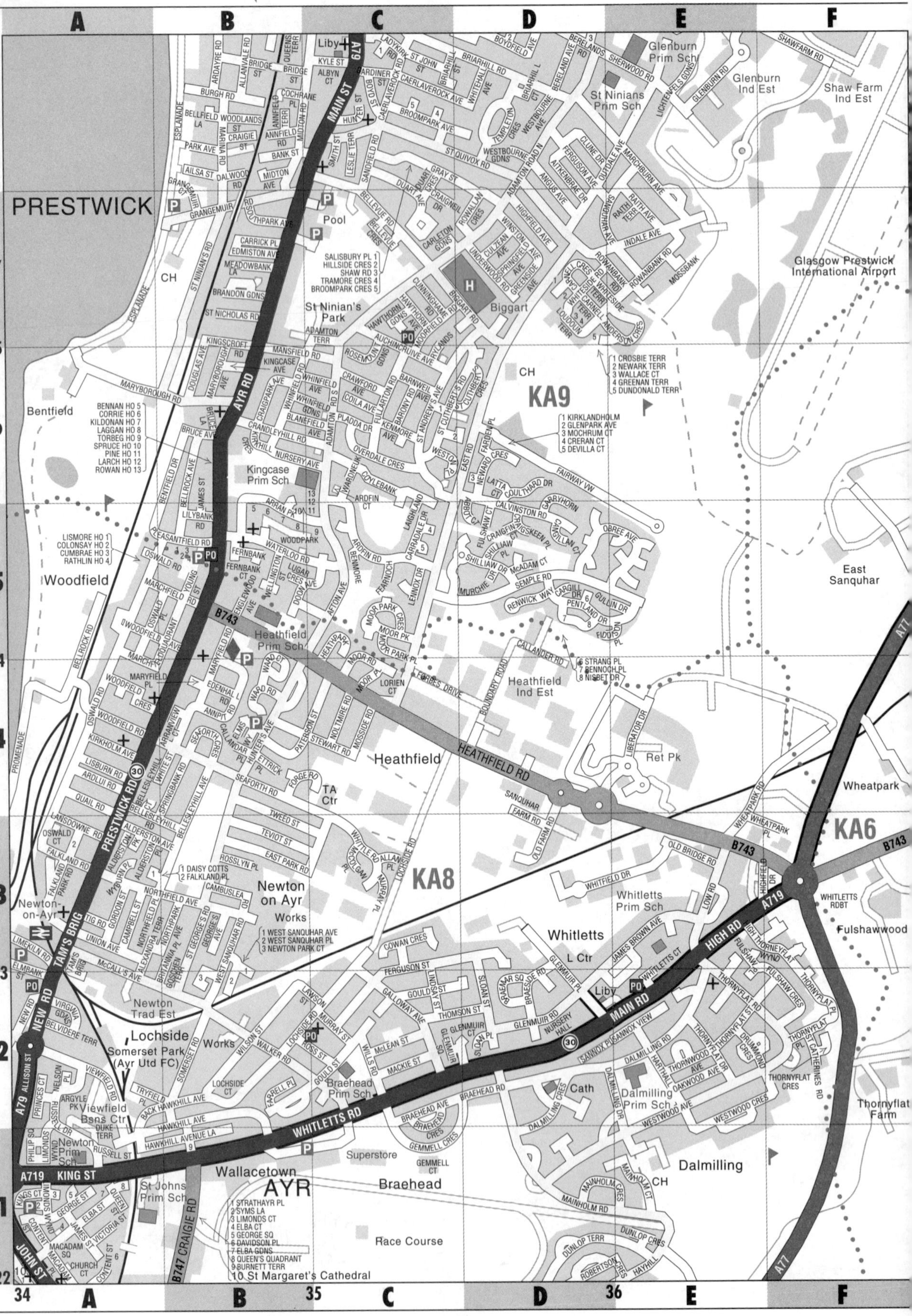
A
B
C
D
E
F
8
7
25
6
5
24
4
3
23
2
1
22
34
35
36
PRESTWICK
Woodfield
Bentfield
Heathfield
Newton on Ayr
Whitletts
Dalmilling
Wallacetown
AYR
Braehead
Lochside
Somerset Park (Ayr Utd FC)
Glasgow Prestwick International Airport
Glenburn Ind Est
Shaw Farm Ind Est
East Sanquhar
Wheatpark
Fulshawwood
Thornyflat Farm
Race Course
Heathfield Ind Est
Newton Trad Est
Viewfield Bsns Ctr
St Ninian's Park
Biggart
Kingcase Prim Sch
Heathfield Prim Sch
Whitletts Prim Sch
Braehead Prim Sch
Dalmilling Prim Sch
St Johns Prim Sch
Glenburn Prim Sch
St Ninians Prim Sch
Newton Prim Sch
Ret Pk
TA Ctr
Superstore
Pool
KA9
KA8
KA6
A79
A719
A77
B743
B747
MAIN ST
AYR RD
PRESTWICK RD
HEATHFIELD RD
WHITLETTS RD
KING ST
MAIN RD
HIGH RD
CRAIGIE RD
NEW RD
TAM'S BRIG
WHITLETTS RDBT
1 STRATHAYR PL
2 SYMS LA
3 LIMONDS CT
4 ELBA CT
5 GEORGE SQ
6 DAVIDSON PL
7 ELBA GDNS
8 QUEEN'S QUADRANT
9 BURNETT TERR
10 St Margaret's Cathedral

234

Ayrshire STREET ATLAS

235

AYR
QUEEN'S TERRACE LA 1
CROMWELL RD 2
AILSA PL 3
BRUCE CRES 4
DOUGLAS LA 5
DOUGLAS ST 6
HOPE ST 7
LORNE ARC 8
BLACKFRIARS WLK 9
HOMEBRIAR HO 10
ARRAN MALL 11
KILLOCH PL 13
BURNS STATUE SQ 14
SMITH ST 15
PARKHOUSE ST 16
BURNS STATUE ARC 17
Low Green
ESPLANADE
ALLOWAY PL
A70 MILLER RD
RACECOURSE RD
Wellington Sch
Grammar Prim Sch
Kyle Ctr
CARRICK RD
Seafield
Playing Fields
RACECOURSE VIEW
DOONFOOT RD
KA7
Cunning Park
Belleisle Bridge
Slaphouse
Slaphouse Burn
Slaphouse Bridge
Belleisle
Hotel
CH
Belleisle Park
MONUMENT RD
Rozelle Park
Rozelle House MacLaurin Galleries
Burns Cottage & Mus
Longhill Point
Greenan
Doonfoot Prim Sch
Burton Smithy
High Greenan
DUNURE RD
Doonfoot
Mill
River Doon
Doonbank Farm
MOUNTCHARLES
Alloway
Alloway Prim Sch
Burns Mon
Liby
Tam O'Shanter Experience
A719
B7024
A719 Turnberry, Girvan (A77)
Ayrshire STREET ATLAS

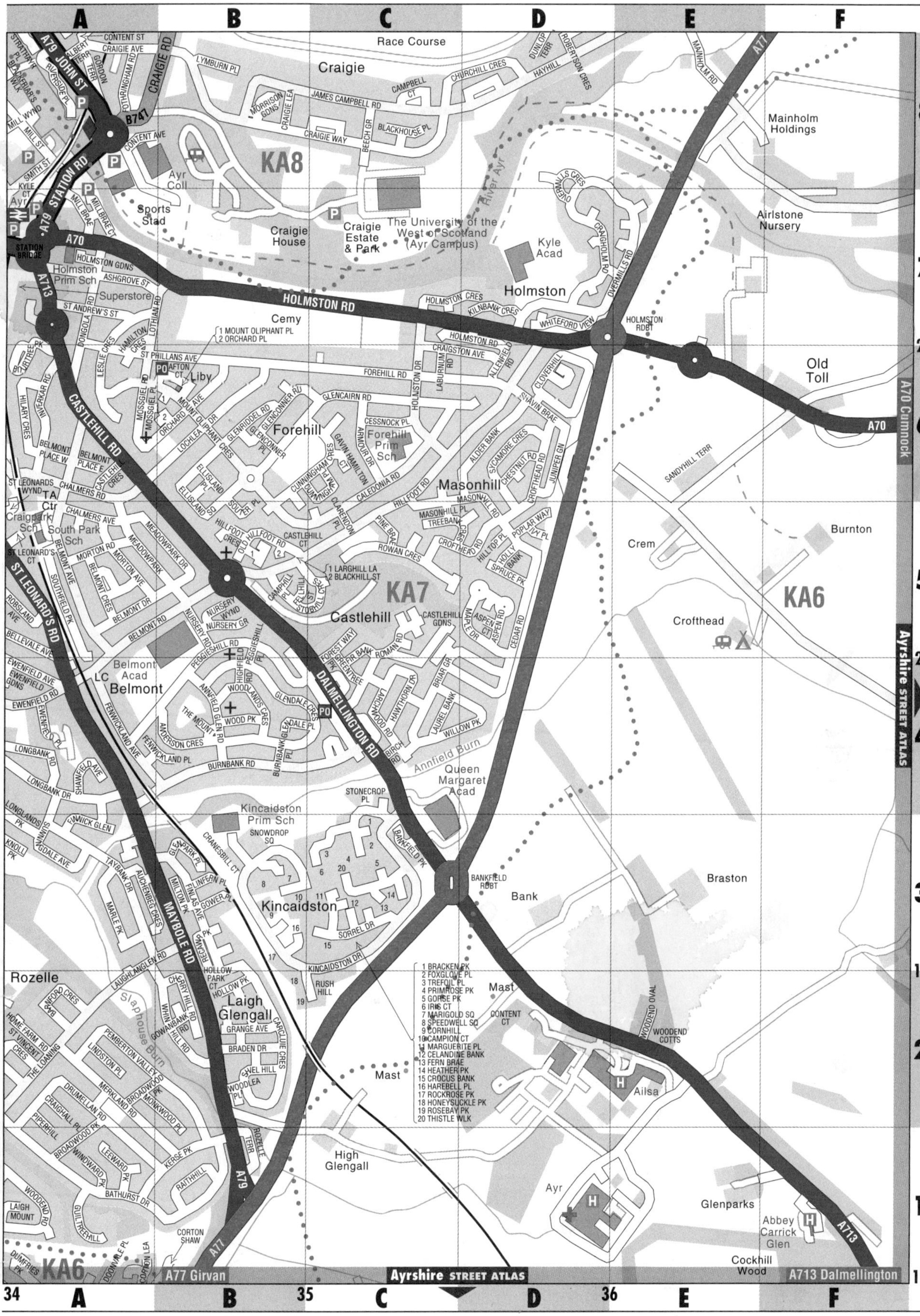
A
B
C
D
E
F
8
7
21
6
5
20
4
3
19
2
1
18
34
35
36
Race Course
Craigie
KA8
Mainholm Holdings
Airlstone Nursery
Ayr Coll
Sports Stad
Craigie House
Craigie Estate & Park
The University of the West of Scotland (Ayr Campus)
River Ayr
Kyle Acad
Holmston
HOLMSTON RD
HOLMSTON RDBT
Old Toll
A70 Cumnock
Holmston Prim Sch
Superstore
Cemy
1 MOUNT OLIPHANT PL
2 ORCHARD PL
Liby
Forehill
Forehill Prim Sch
Masonhill
Crem
Burnton
KA6
Crofthead
KA7
Castlehill
1 LARGHILL LA
2 BLACKHILL ST
TA Ctr
Craigpark Sch
South Park Sch
Belmont Acad
Belmont
LC
Annfield Burn
Queen Margaret Acad
Kincaidston Prim Sch
Kincaidston
BANKFIELD RDBT
Bank
Braston
Mast
Rozelle
Slaphouse Burn
Laigh Glengall
1 BRACKEN PK
2 FOXGLOVE PL
3 TREFOIL PL
4 PRIMROSE PK
5 GORSE PK
6 IRIS CT
7 MARIGOLD SQ
8 SPEEDWELL SQ
9 CORNHILL
10 CAMPION CT
11 MARGUERITE PL
12 CELANDINE BANK
13 FERN BRAE
14 HEATHER PK
15 CROCUS BANK
16 HAREBELL PL
17 ROCKROSE PK
18 HONEYSUCKLE PK
19 ROSEBAY PK
20 THISTLE WLK
CONTENT CT
WOODEND COTTS
Ailsa
High Glengall
Ayr
Glenparks
Abbey Carrick Glen
Cockhill Wood
CORTON SHAW
KA6
A77 Girvan
Ayrshire STREET ATLAS
A713 Dalmellington
A79
A77
A70
A713
B747
JOHN ST
STATION RD
CRAIGIE RD
CASTLEHILL RD
DALMELLINGTON RD
ST LEONARD'S RD
MAYBOLE RD
STATION BRIDGE

96 96 97

1 The Works C3
2 Raymond ct
Chan Loong
1 Mont Drive

Scale: 7 inches to 1 mile
0 110 yards 220 yards
0 125 m 250 m

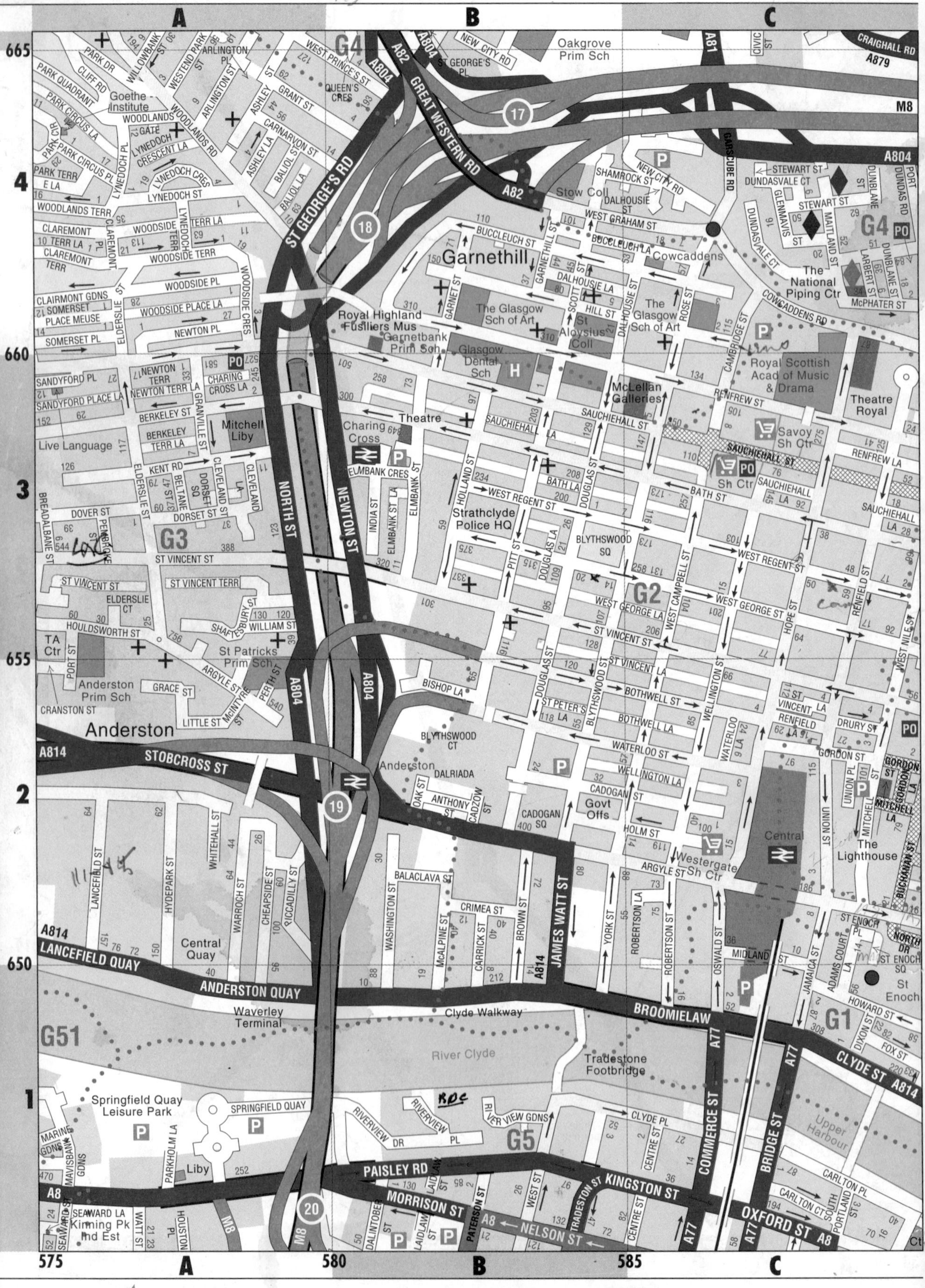

116 116 117

Map of C2. Bottom
× SCOTISH FREADAY
B3

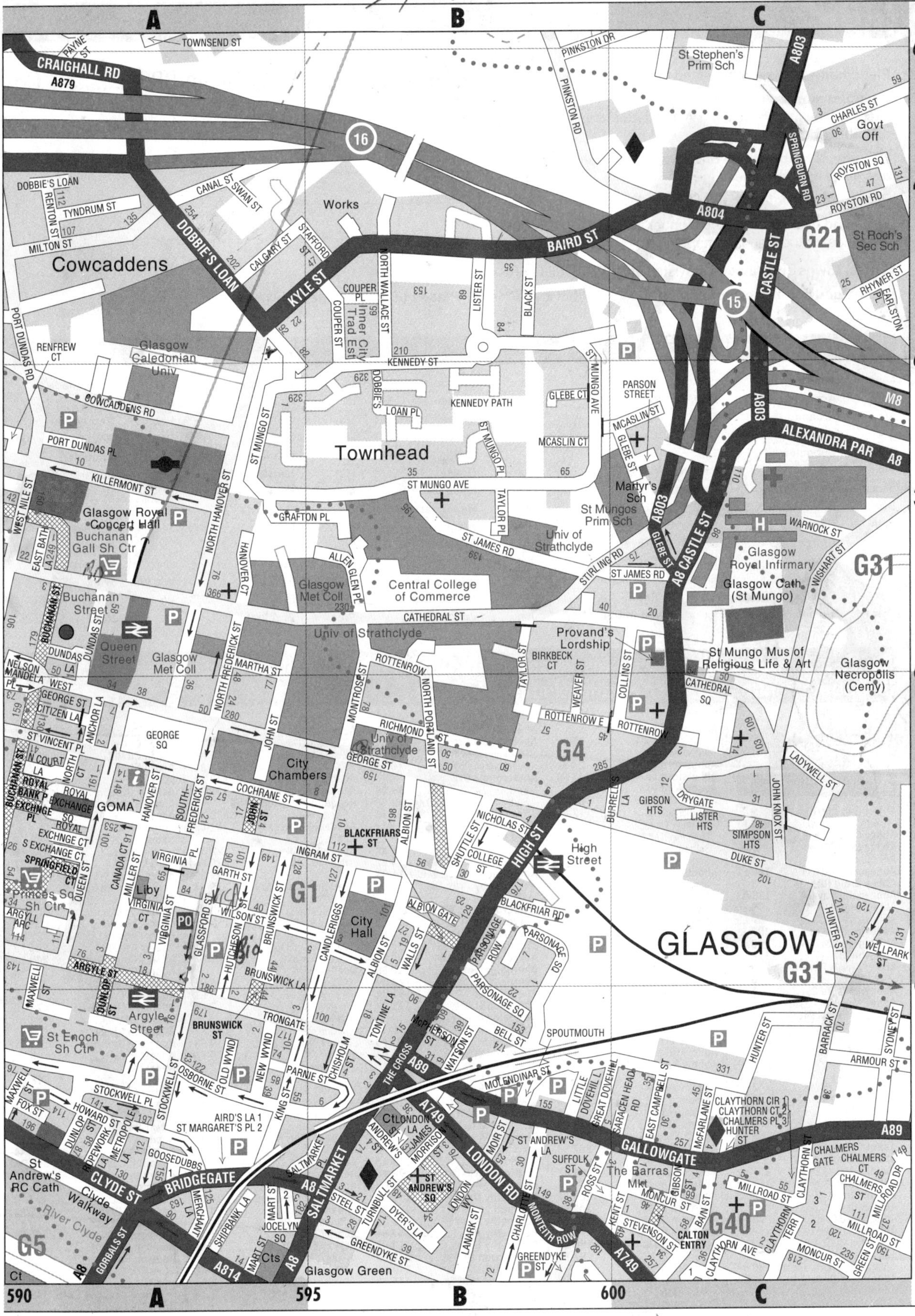
A
B
C
665
660
655
650
4
3
2
1
590
595
600
TOWNSEND ST
PAYNE ST
CRAIGHALL RD
A879
16
PINKSTON DR
PINKSTON RD
St Stephen's Prim Sch
A803
59
CHARLES ST
Govt Off
SPRINGBURN RD
ROYSTON SQ
ROYSTON RD
DOBBIE'S LOAN
RENTON ST
TYNDRUM ST
CANAL ST
SWAN ST
Works
MILTON ST
Cowcaddens
DOBBIE'S LOAN
CALGARY ST
STAFFORD ST
KYLE ST
BAIRD ST
A804
G21
St Roch's Sec Sch
CASTLE ST
RHYMER ST
EARLSTON PL
15
COUPER PL
COUPER ST
NORTH WALLACE ST
Inner City Trad Est
LISTER ST
BLACK ST
PORT DUNDAS RD
RENFREW CT
Glasgow Caledonian Univ
KENNEDY ST
KENNEDY PATH
DOBBIE'S LOAN PL
GLEBE CT
ST MUNGO AVE
PARSON STREET
MCASLIN ST
MCASLIN CT
GLEBE ST
M8
ALEXANDRA PAR
A8
COWCADDENS RD
PORT DUNDAS PL
KILLERMONT ST
ST MUNGO ST
Townhead
ST MUNGO PL
ST MUNGO AVE
TAYLOR PL
Martyr's Sch
St Mungos Prim Sch
WEST NILE ST
Glasgow Royal Concert Hall
NORTH HANOVER ST
GRAFTON PL
ST JAMES RD
Univ of Strathclyde
WARNOCK ST
EAST BATH LA
Buchanan Gall Sh Ctr
ALLEN GLEN PL
STIRLING RD
ST JAMES RD
A8 CASTLE ST
Glasgow Royal Infirmary
WISHART ST
G31
Buchanan Street
HANOVER CT
Glasgow Met Coll
Central College of Commerce
Glasgow Cath (St Mungo)
BUCHANAN ST
CATHEDRAL ST
Univ of Strathclyde
Provand's Lordship
DUNDAS ST
Queen Street
Glasgow Met Coll
NORTH FREDERICK ST
BIRKBECK CT
St Mungo Mus of Religious Life & Art
NELSON MANDELA PL
DUNDAS LA
WEST GEORGE ST
MARTHA ST
MONTROSE ST
ROTTENROW
NORTH PORTLAND ST
TAYLOR ST
WEAVER ST
COLLINS ST
CATHEDRAL SQ
Glasgow Necropolis (Cemy)
CITIZEN LA
ANCHOR LA
GEORGE SQ
JOHN ST
ROTTENROW E
ROTTENROW
ST VINCENT PL
RICHMOND ST
Univ of Strathclyde
G4
LADYWELL ST
City Chambers
GEORGE ST
NORTH CT
ROYAL BANK PL
ROYAL EXCHANGE SQ
GOMA
HANOVER ST
SOUTH FREDERICK ST
COCHRANE ST
JOHN ST
BURRELL'S LA
GIBSON HTS
DRYGATE
LISTER HTS
SIMPSON HTS
JOHN KNOX ST
EXCHANGE PL
ROYAL EXCHANGE CT
S EXCHANGE CT
SPRINGFIELD CT
QUEEN ST
CANADA CT
MILLER ST
VIRGINIA PL
GARTH ST
BLACKFRIARS ST
ALBION ST
NICHOLAS ST
SHUTTLE ST
COLLEGE ST
High Street
INGRAM ST
HIGH ST
DUKE ST
Princes Sq Sh Ctr
Liby
VIRGINIA ST
VIRGINIA CT
G1
City Hall
ALBION GATE
BLACKFRIAR RD
ARGYLE ARC
GLASSFORD ST
WILSON ST
BRUNSWICK ST
CANDLERIGGS
ALBION ST
WALLS ST
PARSONAGE ROW
PARSONAGE SQ
HUNTER ST
WELLPARK ST
GLASGOW
ARGYLE ST
HUTCHESON ST
BRUNSWICK LA
G31
MAXWELL ST
DUNLOP ST
Argyle Street
BRUNSWICK ST
TRONGATE
TONTINE LA
McPHERSON ST
WATSON ST
BELL ST
SPOUTMOUTH
BARRACK ST
SYDNEY ST
St Enoch Sh Ctr
OLD WYND
NEW WYND
CHISHOLM ST
ARMOUR ST
OSBORNE ST
PARNIE ST
THE CROSS
A89
MOLENDINAR ST
LITTLE DOVEHILL
GREAT DOVEHILL
SARACEN HEAD RD
EAST CAMPBELL ST
MAXWELL ST
FOX ST
HOWARD ST
STOCKWELL PL
STOCKWELL ST
KING ST
A749
MOIR ST
McFARLANE ST
CLAYTHORN CIR 1
CLAYTHORN CT 2
CHALMERS PL 3
HUNTER ST
A89
AIRD'S LA 1
ST MARGARET'S PL 2
LONDON LA
ST ANDREW'S LA
GALLOWGATE
CHALMERS GATE
CHALMERS CT
DUNLOP ST
ROPEWORK LA
METROPOLE LA
GOOSEDUBBS
SALTMARKET PL
MORRISON ST
LONDON RD
SUFFOLK ST
The Barras Mkt
GIBSON ST
CLAYTHORN ST
CHALMERS ST
MILLROAD DR
St Andrew's RC Cath
CLYDE ST
BRIDGEGATE
MERCHANT LA
A8
SALTMARKET
ST ANDREW'S SQ
ROSS ST
MONCUR ST
BAIN ST
MILLROAD ST
Clyde Walkway
River Clyde
GORBALS ST
SHIPBANK LA
MART ST
JOCELYN SQ
STEEL ST
TURNBULL ST
DYER'S LA
LONDON WY
CHARLOTTE ST
MONTEITH ROW
KENT ST
STEVENSON ST
CALTON ENTRY
G40
CLAYTHORN AVE
CLAYTHORN TERR
MONCUR ST
MILLROAD ST
GREEN ST
G5
A814
Cts
A8
Glasgow Green
GREENDYKE ST
LANARK ST
GREENDYKE ST
A749

Index

Place name May be abbreviated on the map → **Church Rd** [6] Beckenham BR2.........**53** C6

Location number Present when a number indicates the place's position in a crowded area of mapping

Locality, town or village Shown when more than one place has the same name

Postcode district District for the indexed place

Page and grid square Page number and grid reference for the standard mapping

Cities, towns and villages are listed in CAPITAL LETTERS

Public and commercial buildings are highlighted in **magenta** **Places of interest** are highlighted in **blue** with a star★

Abbreviations used in the index

Acad	**Academy**	Comm	**Common**	Gd	**Ground**	L	**Leisure**	Prom	**Promenade**
App	**Approach**	Cott	**Cottage**	Gdn	**Garden**	La	**Lane**	Rd	**Road**
Arc	**Arcade**	Cres	**Crescent**	Gn	**Green**	Liby	**Library**	Recn	**Recreation**
Ave	**Avenue**	Cswy	**Causeway**	Gr	**Grove**	Mdw	**Meadow**	Ret	**Retail**
Bglw	**Bungalow**	Ct	**Court**	H	**Hall**	Meml	**Memorial**	Sh	**Shopping**
Bldg	**Building**	Ctr	**Centre**	Ho	**House**	Mkt	**Market**	Sq	**Square**
Bsns, Bus	**Business**	Ctry	**Country**	Hospl	**Hospital**	Mus	**Museum**	St	**Street**
Bvd	**Boulevard**	Cty	**County**	HQ	**Headquarters**	Orch	**Orchard**	Sta	**Station**
Cath	**Cathedral**	Dr	**Drive**	Hts	**Heights**	Pal	**Palace**	Terr	**Terrace**
Cir	**Circus**	Dro	**Drove**	Ind	**Industrial**	Par	**Parade**	TH	**Town Hall**
Cl	**Close**	Ed	**Education**	Inst	**Institute**	Pas	**Passage**	Univ	**University**
Cnr	**Corner**	Emb	**Embankment**	Int	**International**	Pk	**Park**	Wk, Wlk	**Walk**
Coll	**College**	Est	**Estate**	Intc	**Interchange**	Pl	**Place**	Wr	**Water**
Com	**Community**	Ex	**Exhibition**	Junc	**Junction**	Prec	**Precinct**	Yd	**Yard**

Index of towns, villages, streets, hospitals, industrial estates, railway stations, schools, shopping centres, universities and places of interest

Abb–Ade

A

Abbey Carrick Glen Hospl KA6 .... 239 F1
Abbey Cl PA1 .... 113 F4
Abbey Craig Ct FK9 .... 2 D3
Abbeycraig Pk FK9 .... 2 D4
Abbeycraig Rd G34 .... 100 E1
Abbey Craig Rd FK10 .... 5 B1
Abbeydale Way G73 .... 138 C3
Abbey Dr G14 .... 95 E4
Abbeygate KA13 .... 207 E3
Abbeygreen KA13 .... 207 E3
Abbeygreen St G34 .... 100 E1
Abbeyhill St G32 .... 118 E7
Abbey King's Park Hospl FK7 .... 6 F5
Abbeylands Rd G81 .... 74 D6
Abbey Mill FK8 .... 7 C8
Abbeymill Bsns Ctr PA1 .... 113 F4
Abbey Pl ML6 .... 123 C4
Abbey Prim Sch KA13 .... 207 D4
Abbey Rd
Elderslie PA5 .... 112 C1
Stirling FK8 .... 2 C1
Abbey Road Pl FK8 .... 7 C8
Abbeyview FK9 .... 2 D4
Abbey Wlk
Coatbridge G69 .... 120 F5
Larkhall ML9 .... 185 B4
Abbot Ct KA9 .... 236 D5
Abbot Rd FK7 .... 7 D4
Abbot's Ave KA13 .... 207 E2
Abbotsburn Way [1] PA3 .... 113 D8
Abbots Cres KA7 .... 238 B2
Abbots Ct G68 .... 61 D7
Abbotsford G64 .... 78 C2
Abbotsford Ave
Hamilton ML3 .... 162 B7
Larkhall ML9 .... 185 A1
Rutherglen G73 .... 138 B7
Abbotsford Brae G74 .... 159 E3
Abbotsford Cres
Hamilton ML3 .... 162 B6
Paisley PA2 .... 132 E7
Shotts ML7 .... 146 F5
Wishaw ML2 .... 165 C4
Abbotsford Ct G67 .... 82 F7
Abbotsford Dr
Helensburgh G84 .... 25 B8
Kirkintilloch G66 .... 79 E8
Abbotsford Gdns FK2 .... 24 B1
Abbotsford La ML4 .... 141 F6
Abbotsford Pl
Cumbernauld G67 .... 82 F7
[4] Glasgow G5 .... 117 B4
Glasgow, Laurieston G5 .... 117 B5
Motherwell ML1 .... 143 B5
Saltcoats KA21 .... 206 A2
Stirling FK8 .... 2 C1
Abbotsford Rd
Bearsden G61 .... 75 C6
Chapelhall ML6 .... 123 E1
Clydebank G81 .... 74 B1
Cumbernauld G67 .... 82 F7
Hamilton ML3 .... 162 B6
Wishaw ML2 .... 165 C4
Abbotsford St FK2 .... 42 B8
Abbotsford Terr ML11 .... 215 C4
Abbotshall Ave G15 .... 74 E3
Abbotsinch Rd
Paisley PA3 .... 113 E8
Renfrew PA3 .... 93 E2
Abbots Moss Dr FK1 .... 41 F1
Abbot's Pl KA13 .... 207 E3
Abbots Rd FK2 .... 42 D7
Abbots Road Rdbt FK2 .... 42 D8
Abbot St
[4] Glasgow G41 .... 116 E1
Greenock PA16 .... 45 C3
Paisley PA3 .... 113 F6
Abbots Terr ML6 .... 123 C4
Abbots Way KA7 .... 238 C3
Abbot's Wlk KA13 .... 207 E3
Abbott Cres G81 .... 94 D8
Aberconway St G81 .... 94 C8
Abercorn Ave G52 .... 114 E8
Abercorn Cres ML3 .... 162 F2
Abercorn Dr ML3 .... 162 F2
Abercorn Ind Est PA3 .... 113 F6
Abercorn Pl G23 .... 76 E1
Abercorn Rd G77 .... 156 C6
Abercorn Sch G4 .... 97 B2
Abercorn St
Clydebank G81 .... 74 E7
Paisley PA3 .... 113 F6
Abercrombie Cres G69 .... 120 F5
Abercrombie Dr G61 .... 75 B8
Abercrombie Pl
Kilsyth G65 .... 36 B1
Menstrie FK11 .... 3 F6
Abercrombie St FK1 .... 41 E6
Abercromby Cres
East Kilbride G74 .... 160 B3
Helensburgh G84 .... 16 F3
Abercromby Dr
Ayr KA7 .... 238 D4
Bridge of Allan FK9 .... 2 B8
Glasgow G40 .... 117 F6
Abercromby Pl
East Kilbride G74 .... 160 B3
Stirling FK8 .... 7 A7
Tullibody FK10 .... 4 B2
Abercromby Place W G84 .... 16 D3
Abercromby Prim Sch FK10 .... 4 B2
Abercromby Sq [1] G40 .... 117 F6
Abercromby St [1] G40 .... 117 E5
Abercromby Street E G84 .... 16 E2
Aberdalgie Gdns G34 .... 120 B8
Aberdalgie Path G34 .... 120 B8
Aberdalgie Rd G34 .... 120 B8
Aberdeen Rd ML6 .... 123 D4
Aberdour Ct G72 .... 161 D2
Aberdour St G31 .... 118 C7
Aberfeldy Ave
Hamilton G72 .... 161 D3
Plains ML6 .... 103 F3
Aberfeldy St G31 .... 118 C7
Aberfeldy Terr KA11 .... 220 A6
Aberfoyle Pl KA1 .... 227 B8
Aberfoyle Rd PA15 .... 46 B2
Aberfoyle St G31 .... 118 C7
Aberlady Rd G51 .... 115 E6
Aberlady St ML1 .... 144 B1
Aberlour Pl
Irvine KA11 .... 219 F6
Motherwell ML1 .... 143 A2
Aberlour Rd KA11 .... 219 F6
Abernethy Ave G72 .... 161 D3
Abernethy Dr PA3 .... 112 A5
Abernethyn Rd ML2 .... 166 B6
Abernethy Pk G74 .... 159 D2
Abernethy Pl G77 .... 157 B4
Abernethy St G31 .... 118 C7
Aberuthven Dr G32 .... 119 B3
Abiegail Pl G72 .... 140 D1
Aboukir St G51 .... 115 E8
Aboyne Ave FK9 .... 2 C4
Aboyne Dr PA2 .... 113 F1
Aboyne St G51 .... 115 F6
ABRONHILL 62 E4
Abronhill High Sch G67 .... 62 E4
Abronhill Prim Sch G67 .... 62 D3
Acacia Dr
Barrhead G78 .... 134 B5
Beith KA15 .... 171 A8
Paisley PA2 .... 113 B1
Acacia Pl PA5 .... 132 A8
Acacia Way G72 .... 139 E5
Academy Apartments [1] KA1 .... 228 A8
Academy Brae KA15 .... 171 B8
Academy Ct
Coatbridge ML5 .... 122 A7
Hurlford KA1 .... 228 E6
Irvine KA12 .... 219 B3
Academy Gdns KA12 .... 219 B4
Academy Pk
Airdrie ML6 .... 123 A7
Glasgow G51 .... 116 C4
Academy Pl
Bannockburn FK7 .... 7 E1
Coatbridge ML5 .... 122 A7
Academy Rd
Glasgow G46 .... 136 C2
Irvine KA12 .... 219 B3
Stirling FK8 .... 7 A8
Academy St
Airdrie ML6 .... 123 A7
Alloa FK10 .... 9 F8
[8] Ayr KA7 .... 235 F1
Coatbridge ML5 .... 122 A7
Glasgow G32 .... 119 B4
Hurlford KA1 .... 228 E6
Kilmarnock KA1 .... 227 F6
Larkhall ML9 .... 185 A3
Troon KA10 .... 229 D2
Academy Terr ML4 .... 142 B5
Acer Cres PA2 .... 113 B1
Acer Gr ML6 .... 123 E3
Achamore Cres G15 .... 74 E4
Achamore Dr G15 .... 74 E4
Achamore Gdns G15 .... 74 E4
Achamore Rd G15 .... 74 E4
Achnasheen Rd ML6 .... 124 A6
Achray Ave G83 .... 27 D6
Achray Ct FK10 .... 10 C5
Achray Dr
Falkirk FK1 .... 42 A1
Paisley PA2 .... 113 A1
Stirling FK9 .... 2 A4
Achray Pl
Coatbridge ML5 .... 101 D1
Milngavie G62 .... 54 D3
Achray Rd G67 .... 82 C6
Acids Rd KA20 .... 218 B5
Acorn Cres FK5 .... 23 D1
Acorn Ct G40 .... 117 F4
Acorn Rd ML11 .... 215 E1
Acorn St G40 .... 117 F4
ACRE 76 B1
Acre Dr G20 .... 76 B1
Acredyke Cres G21 .... 98 C7
Acredyke Pl G21 .... 98 C6
Acredyke Rd
Glasgow G21 .... 98 C7
Rutherglen G73 .... 137 F8
Acre Rd G20 .... 76 B1
Acres The ML9 .... 185 B2
Acre Valley Rd G64 .... 57 B2
Adair Ave KA21 .... 205 F1
Adam Ave ML6 .... 123 B7
Adam Cres FK5 .... 23 F2
Adam Grossert Ct FK5 .... 23 D3
Adams Ave KA21 .... 205 F2
Adams Court La G1 .... 240 C1
Adams Ct KA10 .... 229 F6
Adams Gate KA10 .... 229 F6
Adamslie Cres G66 .... 79 A8
Adamslie Dr G66 .... 79 A8
Adams Loan FK2 .... 24 A1
Adamson Pl FK9 .... 2 B3
Adamson St ML4 .... 142 D5
Adams Pl G65 .... 60 D8
Adam St
Falkirk FK2 .... 42 D6
Gourock PA19 .... 44 F7
Greenock PA15 .... 46 B3
Adamswell St G21 .... 97 F3
Adamswell Terr G69 .... 81 A2
Adams Wlk KA12 .... 219 E2
Adamton Est KA9 .... 234 A4
Adamton Road N KA9 .... 236 D8
Adamton Road S KA9 .... 236 C6
Adamton Terr KA9 .... 236 C7
Addie St ML1 .... 163 F8
Addiewell Pl ML5 .... 122 A4
Addiewell St G32 .... 119 A7
Addison Gr G46 .... 135 F4
Addison Pl G46 .... 135 F4
Addison Rd
Glasgow, Carnwadric G46 .... 135 E4
Glasgow, Dowanhill G12 .... 96 D4
Adelaide Ct G81 .... 73 D5
Adelaide Rd G75 .... 180 C7
Adelaide St
Gourock PA19 .... 44 E8
Helensburgh G84 .... 16 E1

Adele St ML1 163 F4
Adelphi St
Glasgow G5 117 C5
Glasgow G5 117 D5
Admiral St G41 116 E5
Admiralty Gdns G60 73 B5
Admiralty Gr G60 73 B5
Admiralty Pl G60 73 B5
Advie Pl G42 137 B8
Affric Ave ML6 104 A3
Affric Dr
Falkirk FK2 24 C1
Paisley PA2 114 B1
Affric Loan ML7 146 E6
Afton Ave
Kilmarnock KA3 222 F3
Prestwick KA9 236 C5
Afton Cres G61 76 B3
Afton Ct
Ayr KA7 239 B6
Irvine KA12 219 B2
Stevenston KA20 217 D8
Stirling FK7 7 C5
Afton Dr
Denny FK6 39 D7
Renfrew PA4 94 F2
Afton Gdns
Coatbridge ML5 122 D5
Hamilton G72 161 B6
Troon KA10 229 G4
Afton Pl KA22 205 D4
Afton Rd
Cumbernauld G67 62 B3
Stevenston KA20 217 D8
Afton St
Glasgow G41 136 E8
Larkhall ML9 185 C2
Afton View G66 58 F1
Agamemnon St G81 73 F2
Agate Terr ML4 142 A4
Agnew Ave ML5 122 D7
Agnew Gr ML4 141 D5
Agnew La G42 117 A1
Aidans Brae G76 157 E7
Aidrie L Ctr ML6 103 C1
Aigas Cotts 3 G13 95 F5
Aikenhead House G44 137 D5
Aikenhead Rd
Glasgow, Mount Florida
G44 137 C7
Glasgow, Polmadie G42 117 C2
Aikman Pl G74 160 B4
Aikman Rd ML1 163 B5
Aiknut Rd KA23 190 C4
Ailean Dr G32 119 E4
Ailean Gdns G32 119 E4
Aileymill Gdns PA16 44 E2
Aillort Pl G74 159 E3
Ailort Ave G44 137 A5
Ailort Loan 13 ML2 165 F6
Ailsa Ave
Ashgill ML9 199 F8
Motherwell ML1 163 D7
Ailsa Cres ML1 163 B7
Ailsa Ct ML3 161 D1
Ailsa Dr
Bothwell G71 141 A4
Clydebank G81 74 C6
Giffnock G46 136 C1
Glasgow G42 136 F7
Kirkintilloch G66 58 F2
Paisley PA2 133 D7
Rutherglen, Croftfoot G73 137 F5
Rutherglen G46 157 C8
Stevenston KA20 217 C8
Ailsa Gdns KA22 205 D3
Ailsa Hospl KA6 239 E2
Ailsa Pl
Ayr KA7 235 E1
Coatbridge ML5 121 F4
Kilmarnock KA3 223 B5
Ailsa Rd
Bishopbriggs G64 78 B2
Coatbridge ML5 121 F4
Gourock PA19 44 C6
Irvine KA12 224 D7
Renfrew PA4 94 C2
Saltcoats KA21 206 A1
Troon KA10 229 B3
Ailsa St KA9 236 B8
Ailsa Twr G72 138 E3
Ailsa View
Doonfoot KA7 238 B2
Stewarton KA3 195 E2
West Kilbride KA23 190 E5
Ailsa View Cvn Site G78 153 E7
Ailsa View Gdns KA7 238 B2
Ailsa View Pl KA7 238 C2
Ailsa View Wynd KA7 238 C2
Ainsdale Ct KA13 207 B3
Ainslie Ave G52 115 A8
Ainslie Rd
Cumbernauld G67 62 C3
Glasgow G52 115 A7
Glasgow G52 115 B7
Airbles Cres ML1 163 D5
Airbles Dr ML1 163 D5
Airbles Farm Rd ML1 163 C5
Airbles Rd ML1 163 D5
Airbles Road Day Hospl
ML1 163 F5
Airbles St ML1 163 E5
Airbles Sta ML1 163 E5
Airbles Twr ML1 163 E5
Airdale Ave G46 136 C2
Aird Ave KA1 227 E7
AIRDRIE 123 B8
Airdrie Acad ML6 103 A1
Airdriehill Rd ML6 103 D3
Airdriehill St ML6 103 C2
Airdrie Rd
Caldercruix ML6 105 C2
Carluke ML8 187 E4
Cumbernauld G67 82 A7
Cumbernauld G67 82 B6
Cumbernauld, Mollinsburn
G67 81 E4
Kilsyth G65 60 D8
Plains ML6 103 F1
Airdrie Ret Pk ML6 123 A7
Airdrie Sta ML6 123 A7
Aird's La G1 241 A1
Airgold Dr G15 74 F4
Airlie Ave G61 75 E7
Airlie Ct KA7 238 E6
Airlie Dr ML4 142 A6
Airlie Gdns G73 138 D4
Airlie La G12 96 B3
Airlie Rd G69 120 A3
Airlie St G12 96 B3
Airlink Ind Est PA3 113 E8
Airlour Rd G44 136 E5
AIRTH 14 D3
Airth Ct ML1 142 D1
Airth Dr
Glasgow G52 115 F3
Stirling FK7 7 C4
Airth La G52 115 F3
Airth Prim Sch FK2 14 E4
Airthrey Ave
Bridge of Allan FK9 2 B6
Glasgow G14 95 E4
Airthrey Castle Yd FK9 2 E6
Airthrey Dr FK5 23 F4
Airthrey La G14 95 E4
Airthrey Rd FK9 2 C5
Airth Way G68 81 E8
Airyligg Dr G76 178 E5
Aitchison Ct 4 ML6 122 F8
Aitchison Dr FK5 23 B3
Aitchison Pl FK1 42 B3
Aitchison St ML6 122 E7
Aitkenbar Circ G82 50 B6
Aitkenbar Dr G82 50 B6
Aitkenbar Prim Sch G82 50 C5
Aitkenbrae Dr KA9 236 D8
Aitken Cl ML2 166 A7
Aitken Cres FK7 7 B2
Aitken Dr
Beith KA15 150 C1
Slamannan FK1 86 A6
Aitken Gdns FK1 41 E6
Aitkenhead Ave ML5 121 B4
Aitkenhead Prim Sch
G71 120 F1
Aitkenhead Rd
Chapelhall ML6 123 D2
Uddingston G71 121 A2
Aitken La G83 27 E7
Aitken Pl
Ardrossan KA22 205 C3
8 Lanark ML11 215 A4
Aitken Rd
Falkirk FK1 41 D6
Hamilton ML3 183 E7
Aitken St
Airdrie ML6 103 B1
Dalry KA24 191 C7
Glasgow G31 118 C7
Aitken Terr FK1 41 D6
Aitnock Pl KA24 191 A8
Akarit Rd FK5 23 E2
Alasdair Ct G78 134 C2
Alba Gdns ML8 187 E3
Albans Cres ML1 163 B8
Albany G74 160 C4
Albany Ave G32 119 C6
Albany Cotts 2 G13 95 F5
Albany Dr
Lanark ML11 215 B3
Rutherglen G73 138 B6
Albany Pl G71 141 B2
Albany Quadrant G32 119 C6
Albany Rd ML3 183 C7
Albany St
Coatbridge ML5 121 E7
Glasgow G40 118 A4
Albany Terr G72 138 E3
Albany Way PA3 113 E8
Albany Wynd 11 ML9 185 B4
Alba Way
Hamilton ML3 183 C6
16 Larkhall ML9 185 C1
Alberta Ave
Coatbridge ML5 121 F8
East Kilbride G75 180 C8
Alberta Cres 1 G75 180 C8
Alberta Pk G75 180 D8
Alberta Pl 2 G75 180 D8
Albert Ave
Glasgow G42 117 A1
Stewarton KA3 195 F1
Albert Cres 3 ML6 123 B7
Albert Cross G41 116 F3
Albert Ct KA3 195 F1
Albert Dr
Bearsden G61 76 B3
Glasgow G41 116 D4
Helensburgh G84 16 F2
Larkhall ML9 185 B2
Rutherglen G73 138 B5
Albert Halls* FK8 7 A7
Albert La 4 ML3 162 A6
Albert Pk ML8 202 A6
Albert Pl
Airdrie ML6 123 B8
Albert Pl *continued*
Stewarton KA3 195 F1
Stirling FK8 7 A7
Albert Prim Sch G21 97 F5
Albert Quadrant ML1 143 A5
Albert Rd
Brookfield PA5 111 D5
Clydebank G81 74 A3
Falkirk FK1 42 A3
Glasgow G42 117 B1
Gourock PA19 44 D8
Harthill ML7 127 E5
Kirkintilloch G66 79 C3
Renfrew PA4 94 C3
Albert St
Alexandria G83 27 E4
Coatbridge ML5 122 A7
Hamilton ML3 162 B6
Helensburgh G84 16 E2
Motherwell ML1 163 F7
Albert Terr
Ayr KA8 239 A8
Hamilton ML3 162 A6
Albert Wynd KA3 195 F1
Albion Ct ML5 122 C6
Albion Gate
Glasgow G1 241 B2
Paisley PA3 113 D6
Albion St
Coatbridge ML5 122 C6
Glasgow G1 241 B2
Glasgow, North Mount Vernon
G69 119 F3
Motherwell ML1 163 E5
Paisley PA3 113 E6
Albion Twr 2 ML1 163 E5
Albion Way G75 180 F5
Albyn Ct KA9 236 C8
Alcaig Rd G52 115 E2
Alcath Rd ML2 166 B6
Alclutha Ave G82 50 B3
Alder Ave
Hamilton ML3 162 E1
Kirkintilloch G66 79 B5
Alder Bank
Ayr KA7 239 D6
Motherwell G71 121 C1
Alderbank Rd PA14 47 A1
Alderbrae Rd PA14 47 A1
Alder Cres
East Kilbride G75 180 C5
Menstrie FK11 3 F5
Alder Ct
Barrhead G78 134 C1
East Kilbride G75 180 C5
Alder Gate G72 139 E5
Alder Gdns ML1 164 C3
Alder Gn KA11 220 A4
Alder Gr ML5 122 B6
Alder La
Motherwell, Clydesdale
ML1 143 A3
Motherwell, Holytown ML1 143 C5
Alderman Pl G13 95 C6
Alderman Rd G13 95 B6
Alder Pl
East Kilbride G75 180 C5
Glasgow G43 136 C5
Johnstone PA5 112 A1
Kilmarnock KA1 227 D8
Alder Rd
Clydebank G81 74 A5
Cumbernauld G67 62 D2
Dumbarton G82 49 E4
Glasgow G43 136 C5
Milton of Campsie G66 58 B4
Alderside Gdns G71 140 E7
Alderside Pl 5 G71 141 B3
Alderstocks G75 180 E5
Alderston Ave KA8 236 A3
Alderston Pk KA8 236 A3
Alderston Pl
Ayr KA8 236 A3
Bellshill ML4 141 E4
Alderston Way ML4 141 E6
Aldersyde Ave
Troon KA10 229 G4
Wishaw ML2 164 D4
Aldersyde Pl G72 140 C1
Aldersyde Terr ML1 144 C1
Alderwood Cres PA14 47 A1
Alderwood Rd PA14 47 B1
Aldrin Rd G84 25 D8
Alexander Ave
Eaglesham G76 178 E6
Falkirk FK2 42 E5
Stevenston KA20 206 E2
Twechar G65 59 E4
Uddingston G71 141 C6
Alexander Balfour Gdns
ML3 162 D1
Alexander Cres G5 117 C4
Alexander Ct FK9 2 F6
Alexander Dr FK9 2 A8
Alexander Fleming Ave
KA25 148 F1
Alexander Gdns ML3 163 A2
Alexander Gibson Way
ML1 163 D5
Alexander MacLaren Gdns
KA3 222 F3
Alexander McLeod Pl FK7 8 E3
Alexander Path ML1 164 B3
Alexander Peden Prim Sch
ML7 127 E5
Alexander Pl
Irvine KA12 219 C4
Kirkintilloch G66 80 B7
Alexander Pl *continued*
Rhu G84 15 D6
Stevenston KA20 206 D1
Alexander Rd ML7 146 D6
Alexander St
Airdrie ML6 122 F7
1 Alexandria G83 27 E5
Clydebank G81 74 B1
Coatbridge ML5 122 B8
Dumbarton G81 50 A4
Renton G82 49 D8
Wishaw ML2 165 A2
Alexander Stephen Ho
G51 95 E1
Alexander Terr G78 154 C6
Alexandra Ave
Kirkintilloch G66 79 C4
Prestwick KA9 233 C1
Stepps G33 99 D6
Alexandra Cross G31 118 B7
Alexandra Ct
Glasgow G31 118 B8
Prestwick KA9 233 C1
Alexandra Dr
Alloa FK10 9 F7
Paisley PA2 113 B3
Renfrew PA4 94 D3
Alexandra Gate 1 G31 118 A8
Alexandra Gdns
Kilwinning KA13 207 D3
Kirkintilloch G66 79 C4
Alexandra Par G31 118 A8
Alexandra Parade Prim Sch
2 G31 118 A8
Alexandra Parade Sta
G31 118 B8
Alexandra Park St G31 118 B8
Alexandra Pk G66 79 C4
Alexandra Pl FK8 2 C1
Alexandra Prim Sch
ML6 123 A7
Alexandra Rd G66 79 C4
Alexandra St G66 79 C8
Alexandra Terr
Ayr KA8 236 A3
Kilwinning KA13 207 D3
ALEXANDRIA 27 B5
Alexandria Quadrant
ML1 143 A5
Alexandria Sta G83 27 E4
Alexandria Terr KA8 236 A3
Alford Ave
Hamilton G72 161 C3
Kirkintilloch G66 79 B8
Alford Pl
Irvine KA11 219 E5
Linwood PA3 111 E6
Alford Quadrant ML2 165 B5
Alford St G21 97 D3
Alfred La 5 G12 96 E3
Alfred Terr 6 G12 96 E3
Algie St G41 136 F8
Algoma Pl G75 180 B8
Alice Ave ML4 142 A4
Alice St PA2 113 E2
Alice Terr G5 117 D3
Aline Ct G78 134 B4
Alisa Rd G81 94 B8
Alison Lea G74 160 C3
Allan Ave
Carluke ML8 187 E3
Renfrew PA4 94 E1
Allanbank Rd FK5 23 C2
Allanbank St ML7 166 F8
Allan Barr Ct FK1 42 B1
Allan Cres
Alexandria G83 27 D3
Denny FK6 21 D3
Dumbarton G82 50 B6
Allan Ct G75 179 E7
ALLANDALE 39 C2
Allandale Ave ML1 143 F5
Allandale Cotts FK4 39 C2
Allander Ave G62 77 B7
Allander Dr G64 78 A8
Allander Gdns G64 77 F4
Allander L Ctr G61 76 B7
Allander Rd
Bearsden G61 75 D2
Milngavie G62 55 A2
Allander St
Glasgow G22 97 C4
Glasgow G22 97 D4
Allands Ave PA4 93 C5
Allanfauld Rd
Cumbernauld G67 61 F2
Kilsyth G65 36 D2
Allan Gdns KA21 205 F3
Allan Glen Gdns G64 78 B4
Allan Gr ML4 142 B6
Allan Park Ho 10 FK8 7 B7
Allan Pk FK8 7 A7
Allan Pl
Ayr KA8 236 C3
Dumbarton G82 50 A4
East Kilbride G75 179 E7
Glasgow G40 118 B2
Allan's Cnr G78 134 B2
Allanshaw Gdns ML3 162 B3
Allanshaw Gr ML3 162 B2
Allanshaw St ML3 162 C3
Allans Prim Sch FK8 7 A7
Allan Sq KA12 219 E2
Allan St
Coatbridge ML5 121 D5
Glasgow G40 118 B2
Motherwell ML1 163 F7
ALLANTON
Hamilton 163 D1
Wishaw 167 A8
Allanton Ave PA1 114 E4
Allanton Dr G52 115 C5
Allanton Gr ML2 165 B5
Allanton Lea ML3 183 C8
Allanton Pl ML3 162 E1
Allanton Prim Sch ML7 167 B8
Allanton Rd
Crosshill ML2, ML7 166 E7
Shotts ML7 146 D2
Allanton Terr ML3 184 D8
Allan Twr ML1 163 F7
Allanvale KA3 195 B8
Allanvale Rd
Bridge of Allan FK9 1 F7
Prestwick KA9 236 B8
Allanwater Apartments
FK9 2 A8
Allanwater Gdns FK9 2 A8
Allan Wlk FK9 1 F8
Allanwood Ct FK9 2 A8
Allbany Cres ML1 142 F5
Allendale G74 159 C3
Allendale Path 2 G72 161 D7
Allenfield Rd KA7 239 D6
Allen Glen Pl G1 241 B3
Allenshaw Ind Est ML3 162 C3
Allen Way PA4 94 D1
Allerdyce Dr G15 74 F1
Allerdyce Rd G15 74 F1
Allershaw Pl ML2 185 F8
Allershaw Rd ML2 185 F8
Allershaw Tower ML2 185 F8
Allerton Gdns G69 119 F4
Alleysbank Rd G73 118 B1
Allison Ave PA8 72 F2
Allison Dr G72 139 A6
Allison Gdns EH48 107 D2
Allison Hall PA1 114 B5
Allison Pl
Gartcosh G69 100 E4
3 Glasgow G42 117 A2
Newton Mearns G77 156 C4
Allison St
Ayr KA8 236 A2
Glasgow G42 117 B2
Allnach Pl G34 120 E8
ALLOA 10 C5
Alloa Acad FK10 9 E8
ALLOA PARK 10 B5
Alloa Park Dr FK10 10 E6
Alloa Rd
Fishcross FK10 5 D3
Menstrie FK9 3 B3
Stenhousemuir FK5 23 F4
Stirling FK9 2 E3
Tullibody FK10 4 A2
Tullibody FK10 4 C3
Alloa Sta FK10 10 B7
Alloa Tower* FK10 10 B5
Alloa Trad Ctr FK10 10 C7
ALLOWAY 238 E1
Alloway KA7 238 E1
Alloway Ave
Kilmarnock KA3 228 B8
Paisley PA2 134 B8
Alloway Cres
Bonnybridge FK4 39 F6
Paisley PA2 134 C8
Rutherglen G73 137 F5
Alloway Ct G66 59 A2
Alloway Dr
Clydebank G81 74 C3
Cowie FK7 12 D7
Kirkintilloch G66 59 A2
Newton Mearns G77 157 A4
Paisley PA2 134 B8
Rutherglen G73 137 F5
Alloway Gdns
Hamilton ML3 161 D2
Kirkintilloch G66 59 A2
Alloway Gr
Kirkintilloch G66 58 F2
Paisley PA2 114 C1
Alloway Pk KA7 238 E8
Alloway Pl
Ardrossan KA22 205 C4
Ayr KA7 238 E8
Alloway Place La KA7 238 E8
Alloway Prim Sch KA7 238 F1
Alloway Quadrant G66 59 A1
Alloway Rd
Airdrie ML6 123 F8
East Kilbride G74 160 E3
Glasgow G43 136 D6
Alloway St
Ayr KA7 238 F8
Larkhall ML9 185 C2
Alloway Terr G66 58 F2
Alloway Wynd
Motherwell ML1 143 E4
Stenhousemuir FK5 23 C4
All Saints Sec Sch G21 98 C5
Allsop Ct KA3 222 A7
Almada Gr ML3 162 D4
Almada La ML3 162 D4
Almada St ML3 162 D4
Almada Twr ML3 162 D4
Alma La FK2 42 B6
Alma St
Falkirk FK2 42 B6
Glasgow G31 118 B5
Alma Terr FK2 42 B6

Almond Ave PA4 94 E2
Almondbank ML6 103 F3
Almond Bank G61 75 C2
Almond Cres PA2 112 F2
Almond Ct
Falkirk FK2 42 E7
Stirling FK7 7 C5
Almond Dr
Banknock FK4 38 E2
Bishopton PA7 72 B2
East Kilbride G74 160 B1
Kirkintilloch G66 79 B5
Almond Pl
Coatbridge ML5 101 D1
Kilmarnock KA1 227 D8
Motherwell ML1 143 B5
Almond Rd
Bearsden G61 75 D2
Cumbernauld G67 62 F4
Falkirk FK2 42 E7
Stepps G33 99 C5
Almond St G33 98 D1
Almond Terr ML7 127 C5
Almond Vale G71 141 A7
Almond Way ML1 163 E3
Almswall Rd KA13 207 E3
Alness Cres G52 115 E3
Alness St ML3 162 D1
Alness Terr ML3 162 D2
Alnwick Dr G76 178 D4
Alpha Ctr G81 94 C8
Alpine Gr
Greenock PA15 46 E3
Uddingston G71 140 F7
Alpine Path [5] G72 161 E7
Alpine Wlk [4] G72 161 E7
Alsatian Ave G81 74 D2
Alsh Terr ML3 162 A1
Alston Ave ML5 122 B8
Alston Gdns G61 75 B8
Altnacreag Gdns G69 81 A3
Altonhead Dr KA3 210 B1
Altonhead Terr KA3 210 B1
ALTONHILL 222 E3
Altonhill Ave KA3 222 E3
Alton Holdings
Auchenreoch G66 58 F5
Milton of Campsie G66 58 D5
Alton Rd PA1 114 C4
Alton St KA23 190 C5
Alton Way KA23 190 D4
Altpatrick Gdns PA5 112 B3
Altry Pl KA7 238 B1
Altyre St G32 118 F4
ALVA 5 A6
Alva Acad FK12 5 A7
Alva Gate G52 115 E3
Alva Gdns
Bearsden G61 75 D8
Glasgow G52 115 E2
Alva Glen Nature Trail* FK12 5 A8
Alva Ind Est FK12 5 C6
Alva Pl G66 79 E4
Alva Prim Sch FK12 5 A6
Alva Terr PA19 45 A7
Alvie Pl ML6 123 D5
Alvord Ave KA9 233 D1
Alwyn Ave PA6 111 D8
Alwyn Ct G74 159 E3
Alwyn Dr G74 159 E3
Alyssum Cres ML1 163 D8
Alyth Cres G76 158 A8
Alyth Gdns
Clarkston G76 158 A8
Glasgow G52 115 E3
Ambassador Way PA4 94 D1
Amber Terr ML4 142 A4
Ambleside G75 180 A6
Ambleside Rise ML3 183 D6
Ambrose Ct ML3 162 B4
Amethyst Ave ML4 142 A4
Amisfield St G20 96 E5
Amlaird Rd KA3 223 A5
Amochrie Dr PA2 133 A8
Amochrie Glen PA2 133 A8
Amochrie Rd PA2 133 A8
Amochrie Way PA2 112 F1
Amulree Pl G32 119 A4
Amulree St G32 119 B4
Ancaster Dr G13 95 F6
Ancaster La G13 95 F6
Ancaster Pl FK1 42 A1
Anchor Ave PA1 114 A4
Anchor Cres PA1 114 A3
Anchor Dr PA1 114 A4
Anchor La G1 241 A2
Anchor Wynd PA1 114 A4
Ancroft St G20 97 A3
Andersen Ct G75 180 E6
Anderside G75 180 E5
Anderson Ave
[2] Falkirk FK2 42 A8
Kilsyth G65 36 B1
Anderson Cres
Ayr KA7 239 B4
Prestwick KA9 236 E7
Queenzieburn G65 59 E8
Shieldhill FK1 66 E6
Anderson Ct
Bellshill ML4 142 B5
Newton Mearns G77 156 C4
Wishaw ML2 165 A3
Anderson Dr
Denny FK6 21 E1
Anderson Dr *continued*
Falkirk FK2 24 B2
Irvine KA12 219 D5
Newton Mearns G77 156 C4
Renfrew PA4 94 D4
Saltcoats KA21 206 A1
Anderson Gdns G72 140 E1
Anderson La [1] ML6 123 A8
Anderson Park Rd FK6 21 F2
Anderson Pl
Kilmarnock KA3 223 D2
Stirling FK7 7 A4
Anderson Rd PA7 72 A4
Anderson St
[5] Airdrie ML6 123 A8
Bonnybridge FK4 40 B5
Glasgow G11 96 B1
Hamilton ML3 161 F5
Motherwell ML1 163 E5
Port Glasgow PA14 47 C2
Anderson Terr
Ardrossan KA22 205 C2
Longcroft FK4 39 B3
Anderson Twr ML1 163 E6
ANDERSTON 240 A2
Anderston Prim Sch G3 240 A2
Anderston Quay G3 240 A1
Anderston Sta G3 240 B2
Andrew Ave
Kirkintilloch G66 79 D3
Renfrew PA4 94 E3
Andrew Baxter Ave ML9 185 E1
Andrew Cres FK5 23 D4
Andrew Dr G81 94 D8
Andrew Hardie Dr FK10 10 A8
Andrew Paton Way ML3 162 A6
Andrew Pl ML8 187 E3
Andrew Sillars Ave G72 139 C5
Andrew St
East Kilbride G74 159 F1
Paisley PA3 113 E6
Anford Gdns G72 161 E7
Anford La [7] G72 161 E7
Anford Pl G72 161 E7
Anford Terr G72 161 E6
Angela Way G71 140 F6
Angle Gate G14 95 D4
Angle St ML9 198 F2
Angus Ave
Airdrie ML6 123 A5
Bishopbriggs G64 78 D1
East Kilbride G74 160 B2
Glasgow G52 115 C3
Hamilton ML3 163 A3
Motherwell ML1 163 C8
Prestwick KA9 236 D8
Angus Gdns G71 140 F8
Angus Oval G52 115 B4
Angus Pl
East Kilbride G74 160 B2
Glasgow G52 115 B4
Angus Rd
Carluke ML8 188 B1
Greenock PA16 44 D4
Port Glasgow PA14 47 C1
Angus St
Alexandria G83 27 F4
Clydebank G81 94 E8
[6] Glasgow G21 97 E4
Angus Wlk G71 141 B7
Anish Pl G15 74 E4
Annabella Rd ML9 200 C4
Annan Ave
East Kilbride G75 179 E7
Hamilton G72 161 D3
Annan Cres ML6 123 D1
Annan Ct
Coatbridge ML5 121 F6
Falkirk FK1 42 C1
Annandale
Crosshouse KA2 221 F1
Greengairs ML6 83 F2
Annandale Cres KA2 221 F1
Annandale Gdns KA2 221 F1
Annandale La KA2 221 E1
Annandale St [1] G42 117 B3
Annandale View KA2 221 F2
Annandale Way KA11 220 A5
Annan Dr
Bearsden G61 75 D3
Rutherglen G73 138 D7
Annan Glade ML1 164 A3
Annan Gr ML1 164 A3
Annanhill KA1 227 C8
Annanhill Ave KA1 222 C1
Annanhill Pl KA13 207 B3
Annanhill Prim Sch KA1 227 D8
Annan Pl PA5 131 C8
Annan Rd KA1 228 A5
Annan St ML1 164 A3
Annan Way [7] G67 61 F1
ANNATHILL 81 F1
Annathill Gdns ML5 81 F2
Annbank Pl G31 117 F6
Annbank St
Glasgow G31 117 F6
Larkhall ML9 184 F3
Ann Ct ML3 162 A5
Anne Ave PA4 94 D4
Anne Cres G66 79 D3
Anne Dr
Bridge of Allan FK9 2 B6
Stenhousemuir FK5 23 E4
Annerley Ct ML5 121 E5
Annerley Pl ML5 121 E5
Anne's Mews ML3 162 F3
Anne St FK10 9 F8
Annet Rd FK6 39 D6
Annette St G42 117 A2
Annette Street Prim Sch G42 117 B2
Annfield Dr FK7 7 C5
Annfield Gdns
Blantyre G72 140 C1
Irvine KA12 219 B3
Stirling FK8 7 B6
Annfield Glen Rd KA7 239 B4
Annfield Gr FK8 7 B6
Annfield Pl G31 117 F7
Annfield Rd KA9 236 B8
Annfield Terr KA9 236 B8
Annickbank KA3 195 F2
Annick Cres KA3 211 E8
Annick Ct KA12 219 C2
Annick Dr
Bearsden G61 75 C2
Irvine KA11 220 B1
Annick Pl
Kilmarnock KA1 228 A5
Troon KA10 229 G4
Annick Prim Sch [1] KA11 220 A5
Annick Rd
Irvine, Dreghorn KA11 220 B1
Irvine KA11, KA12 219 E1
Annick Rdbt KA12 219 E2
Annick St
Cambuslang G72 139 D5
Glasgow G32 119 B5
Annick Street Ind Est G32 119 C5
Annick View KA12 219 E2
ANNICK WATER 220 B3
Anniesdale Ave G33 99 D6
Annieshill View ML6 104 A2
ANNIESLAND 95 E6
Anniesland Coll (Balshagray Campus) G11 95 F2
Anniesland Coll (Hatfield Campus) G12 96 A5
Anniesland Coll (Milton Resource Ctr) G22 97 E7
Anniesland Coll (Ruchill Com Learning Ctr) G20 96 E5
Anniesland Cres G14 95 A5
Anniesland Ind Est G13 95 E8
Anniesland Rd
Glasgow, Anniesland G14 95 C5
Glasgow, Scotstounhill G14 95 A5
Anniesland Sta G13 95 F6
Annieston G65 59 F4
Anniversary Ave G75 180 C7
Annpit Rd KA8 236 B4
Annsfield Rd ML3 183 D7
Ann St
Greenock, Central PA15 45 E4
Greenock PA15 45 F5
Hamilton ML3 162 A5
Johnstone PA5 112 A3
Ansdell Ave G72 161 C8
Anson Ave FK1 41 E4
Anson St G40 117 F4
Anson Way [6] PA4 94 C1
Anstruther Ct ML8 186 F5
Anstruther St
Glasgow G32 118 F5
Law ML8 186 F5
Antermony Rd G66 58 E5
Anthony Ct G81 94 C8
Anthony St G2 240 B2
Antigua Ct [5] PA15 46 A4
Antigua St PA15 46 A4
Antigua Way G75 159 A1
Anton Cres G65 60 E8
Antonine G66 59 B2
Antonine Ave ML1 163 C8
Antonine Gate FK4 39 A1
Antonine Gdns
Clydebank G81 74 A6
Falkirk FK1 41 C5
Antonine Gr FK4 39 F3
Antonine Prim Sch
Bonnybridge FK4 40 A4
Clydebank G15 74 E3
Antonine Rd
Bearsden G61 75 B6
Dullatur G68 61 D6
Antonine Sh Ctr [11] G67 61 F1
Antonine St FK1 41 C5
Antonine Wall*
Bonnybridge FK4 40 D4
Kirkintilloch G66 59 C3
ANTONSHILL 23 E4
Antonshill Rdbt FK5 23 F5
Antrim La ML9 185 B4
Anwoth St G32 119 A3
Apartments The G46 136 B1
Apollo Path ML1 143 B5
Appin Cres G31 118 B7
Appin Ct G66 59 B1
Appin Rd G31 118 C7
Appin Terr
Hamilton ML3 161 E4
[3] Rutherglen G73 138 D4
Shotts ML7 147 B3
Appin Way
[2] Bothwell G71 141 A3
Coatbridge ML5 121 E4
Glenmavis ML6 102 F4
Appleby Cl G75 179 F6
Appleby Gr G69 121 A6
Appleby St G22 97 B3
Applecross Gdns G69 80 F3
Applecross Quadrant ML2 165 B5
Applecross Rd G66 59 B1
Applecross St G4, G22 97 B3
Appledore Cres G71 141 A3
Apple Way G75 180 F6
Appleyard Ct ML4 141 F3
Apsley La G11 96 A2
Apsley St G11 96 A2
Aqua Ave ML3 161 E2
Aqua Ct ML3 161 E2
Aquatech ML1 163 E7
Aquila Way ML8 187 D2
Araburn Dr G75 180 E5
Aranthrue Cres PA4 94 C4
Aranthrue Dr PA4 94 C4
Aray St G20 96 D6
Arbroath Ave G52 115 B4
Arbroath Cres FK9 2 B4
Arbroath Gr ML3 162 B2
Arbuckle Pl ML6 104 A3
Arbuckle Rd ML6 104 B4
Arbuckle St KA1 228 A8
Arbuthnot St FK1 41 E6
Arcadia Bsns Ctr G81 74 B1
Arcadia Pl G40 117 E5
Arcadia St
Bellshill ML4 142 A7
Glasgow G40 117 E5
Arcan Cres G15 75 B2
Archerfield Ave G32 119 A2
Archerfield Cres G32 119 A2
Archerfield Dr G32 119 A2
Archerfield Gr G32 119 A2
Archerhill Ave G13 95 A8
Archerhill Cotts G13 95 A8
Archerhill Cres G13 95 B8
Archerhill Gdns G13 95 A8
Archerhill Rd G13 95 B7
Archerhill Sq G13 94 F8
Archerhill Terr G13 95 A8
Archers Ave
Irvine KA11 219 E6
Stirling FK7 7 C4
Archers Ct KA11 219 E6
Archibald Craig Pl KA3 222 F3
Archibald Dr [2] KA24 191 B7
Archibald Kelly Ct G75 180 E7
Archibald Terr G66 58 B6
Archiebald Pl ML4 142 D4
Arch Way G65 36 D1
Arcon Ave KA6 237 F6
Ardardan Cotts G82 25 G2
Ardargie Dr G32 139 C8
Ardargie Gr G32 139 C8
Ardargie Pl G32 139 C8
Ardayre Rd KA9 236 B8
Ardbeg Ave
Bishopbriggs G64 78 C1
Kilmarnock KA3 222 F3
Rutherglen G73 138 E3
Ardbeg Cres [5] ML6 103 A3
Ardbeg Ct KA11 219 F6
Ardbeg La
Glasgow G42 117 A2
Greenock PA15 46 C2
Thorntonhall G74 158 C3
Ardbeg Rd
Greenock PA15 46 C2
Motherwell ML1 143 B2
Ardbeg St G42 117 A2
Ardchoille Dr KA20 206 E2
Ardchoille La KA20 206 E2
Ardconnel St G46 135 F4
Ardeer La KA20 217 F6
Ardeer Prim Sch KA20 217 D7
Ardeer Rdbt KA20 206 E1
ARDEN
Glasgow 135 E4
Helensburgh 18 D6
Arden Ave G46 135 E2
Ardencaple Dr G84 16 A2
Ardencaple Quadrant G84 16 B2
Ardenclutha Ave ML3 162 B4
Ardenclutha Dr PA14 47 B1
Ardenconnel Ho G84 15 D5
Ardenconnel Mews G84 15 D6
Ardenconnel Way G84 15 D5
Ardencraig Cres G45 137 C1
Ardencraig Dr G45 138 A2
Ardencraig Gdns G45 138 A2
Ardencraig Pl G45 137 E3
Ardencraig Quadrant G45 137 F2
Ardencraig Rd
Glasgow G45 137 E1
Glasgow G45 137 F3
Ardencraig St G45 138 A2
Ardencraig Terr G45 137 F2
Arden Ct
Airdrie ML6 122 D8
Hamilton ML3 162 D1
Arden Dr G46 136 B3
Arden Gr G65 36 C2
Arden Hill G84 15 D6
Arden Ho G83 18 E6
Ardenlea G71 140 F7
Ardenlea St G40 118 B3
Arden Pl G46 135 E2
Arden Rd
Greenock PA15 46 D1
Hamilton ML3 162 C1
Arden St ML6 104 A2
Arden Terr ML3 162 C2
Ardenvohr G82 48 B7
Ardery St G11 96 A2
Ardessie Pl G20 96 D5
Ardessie St [2] G23 76 D1
Ardfern Rd ML6 124 A6
Ardfern St G32 119 A3
Ardfin Ct KA9 236 C6
Ardfin Rd KA9 236 C5
Ardgare G84 15 A7
Ardgay Dr FK4 40 A3
Ardgay Pl G32 119 A4
Ardgay Rd FK4 40 A3
Ardgay St G32 119 B4
Ardgay Terr FK4 40 A4
Ardgay Way G73 138 B3
Ardgoil Dr G68 61 A1
Ardgour Ct G72 161 F6
Ardgour Dr PA3 112 A5
Ardgour Par ML1 143 C1
Ardgour Pl KA3 222 F4
Ardgour Rd KA3 222 F3
Ardgowan Ave PA2 113 F3
Ardgowan Ct PA2 114 B3
Ardgowan Dr G71 140 F7
Ardgowan Pl
Cowie FK7 12 D8
Shotts ML7 146 E6
Ardgowan Prim Sch PA16 45 D6
Ardgowan Sq PA16 45 E6
Ardgowan St
Greenock PA16 45 E6
Paisley PA2 113 F3
Port Glasgow PA14 47 A2
Ardgowan Terrace La G3 96 D1
Ardgryfe Cres PA6 91 D1
Ardholm St G32 119 A5
Ardhu Pl G15 75 A4
Ard La [6] ML2 165 F6
Ardlamont Sq PA3 112 C5
Ardlaw St G51 115 F6
Ardle Ave KA1 228 B5
Ardle Rd G43 136 E5
Ard Loan ML1 143 A5
Ardlui Gdns G62 54 D3
Ardlui Rd KA8 236 A4
Ardlui St G32 118 F4
Ardmaleish Cres G45 137 E2
Ardmaleish Dr G45 137 D2
Ardmaleish Rd G45 137 E2
Ardmaleish St G45 137 D2
Ardmaleish Terr G45 137 E2
Ardmay Cres G44 137 C7
Ardmillan KA13 207 B2
Ardmillan St G33 118 F8
Ardmore Cresent [9] ML6 103 A3
Ardmore Ct KA11 220 A6
Ardmore Pl PA15 45 E3
Ardmore Rd
Greenock PA15 46 C1
Port Glasgow PA14 68 D8
Ardmory Ave G42 137 D7
Ardmory La G42 137 E7
Ardmory Pl G42 137 E7
Ardnahoe Ave G42 137 E7
Ardnahoe Pl G42 137 D8
Ardneil Ave KA23 190 C3
Ardneil Ct KA22 205 B4
Ardneil Rd G51 115 F6
Ardnish St G51 115 F7
ARDOCH 48 E5
Ardoch Cres
Dumbarton G82 49 D4
Stevenston KA20 217 E6
Ardoch Ct KA20 217 E6
Ardoch Gdns [3] G72 138 F6
Ardoch Gr G72 138 F6
Ardoch Path [17] ML2 165 F6
Ardoch Rd G61 76 B5
Ardochrig G75 180 F5
Ardoch St G22 97 C4
Ardoch Terr KA20 217 E7
Ardoch Way G69 80 F2
Ardo Gdns G51 116 A5
Ardrain Ave ML1 164 C3
Ard Rd PA4 94 B4
ARDROSSAN 205 A2
Ardrossan Acad KA22 205 D2
Ardrossan Harbour Sta KA22 205 A1
Ardrossan High Rd KA23 190 E4
Ardrossan Rd
Saltcoats KA21 216 E8
West Kilbride KA23 190 C2
Ardrossan South Beach Sta KA22 205 D1
Ardrossan Town Sta KA22 205 C1
Ardshiel Rd G51 115 E7
Ardsloy La G14 95 A4
Ardsloy Pl G14 95 A4
Ard St G32 119 A4
Ardtoe Cres G33 99 E5
Ardtoe Pl G33 99 E5
Arduthie Rd G51 115 E7
Ardvreck Pl FK2 24 A3
Ardwell Pl G84 15 D4
Ardwell Rd G52 115 E3
Ardyne Pl PA19 43 F5
Argosy Way [3] PA4 94 C1
Argus Ave ML6 123 C2
Argyle Cres
Airdrie ML6 122 F5
Hamilton ML3 162 A3
Argyle Dr ML3 162 A4
Argyle Gdns
Coatbridge ML5 121 E4
Lennoxtown G66 57 E7
Argyle Pk KA8 236 A2
Argyle Pl KA21 216 F8
Argyle Rd
Gourock PA19 44 F6
Saltcoats KA21 216 F8
Argyle St
Glasgow, Anderston G3 240 A2

Argyle St *continued*
Glasgow, Cranston Hill G3. 116 E8
Glasgow G2 240 C2
Glasgow, Kelvingrove G3 96 D1
Greenock PA15 45 F6
Paisley PA1 113 D4
Stonehouse ML9 198 F2
Argyle Street E G84 16 E1
Argyle Street Sta G1 241 A1
Argyll Arc G2 241 A2
Argyll Ave
Dumbarton G82 50 C4
Falkirk FK2 42 C6
Renfrew, Kirklandneuk PA4 94 B4
Renfrew PA3 93 E1
Stirling FK8 2 C1
Argyll Ct ML7 127 F5
Argyll Est G83 27 D7
Argyll Gdns ML9 185 B3
Argyll Path FK6 39 D8
Argyll Pl
Alloa FK10 10 C7
Bellshill ML4 141 F2
Dumbarton G82 50 C4
East Kilbride G74 160 C3
Kilsyth G65 60 E8
Argyll Rd
Bearsden G61 75 E7
Clydebank G81 74 C1
Rosneath G84 15 B3
Argyll's Lodging★ FK8 7 A8
Argyll St
Alexandria G83 27 D7
Alloa FK10 10 C7
Argyll Street W G84 16 C2
Argyll View G84 16 A2
Argyll Wynd ML1 143 B2
Arisaig Dr
Bearsden G61 76 B3
Glasgow G52 115 E3
Arisaig Pl G52 115 E3
Arisdale Cres G77 156 E6
Arkaig Ave ML6 103 F3
Arkaig Pl G77 157 B4
Arkaig St ML2 165 B1
Ark La G31 117 F7
Arkleston Cres PA3 114 B7
Arkleston Dr PA1 114 B6
Arkleston Prim Sch PA4 94 D1
Arkleston Rd PA4, PA3 114 C8
Arkle Terr G72 138 F3
Arklet Rd G51 115 F7
Arklet Way ML2 165 E3
Arkwrights Way PA1 113 B3
Arkwright Way
Irvine KA11 219 F2
Irvine KA11 219 F3
Arlington Pl G3 240 A4
Arlington St G3 240 A4
Armadale Ct
Glasgow G31 118 A8
3 Greenock PA15 45 F4
Armadale Path G31 118 A8
Armadale Pl
Glasgow G31 118 A8
Greenock PA15 45 F4
Armadale Rd
Lanark ML11 215 C4
Rhu G84 15 F4
Armadale St G31 118 A7
Armine Path ML1 143 C4
Armour Ave
Airdrie ML6 122 E7
Cowie FK7 12 D7
Armour Ct
Hamilton G72 161 B6
Kirkintilloch G66 59 A1
Armour Dr
Ayr KA7 239 C6
Kirkintilloch G66 59 A1
Armour Gdns G66 59 A1
Armour Gr ML1 164 A4
Armour Mews FK5 23 B4
Armour Pl
Ardrossan KA22 205 C4
Johnstone PA5 112 A3
Kirkintilloch G66 59 A1
Linwood PA3 112 C5
Motherwell ML1 143 C4
Stewarton KA3 195 E1
Armour Sq PA5 112 A3
Armour St
Glasgow G4 241 C1
Johnstone PA5 112 A3
Kilmarnock KA1 227 F7
Armstrong Cres G71 141 A8
Armstrong Gr G75 180 D7
Armstrong Rd
Helensburgh G84 25 D8
Kilmarnock KA3 223 C2
Arnbrae Farm Steadings
G65 60 A8
Arnbrae Rd G65 36 B1
Arness Terr KA3 222 E4
Arngask Rd G51 115 E7
Arnhall Pl G52 115 E3
Arnhem St G72 139 D5
Arnholm Pl G52 115 E3
Arnisdale Pl G34 120 A8
Arnisdale Rd G34 120 A8
Arnisdale Way G73 138 B3
Arnish PA4 93 C7
Arniston St G32 118 F7
Arniston Way PA3 114 A7
Arnold Ave G64 78 A1
Arnol Pl G33 119 F7
ARNOTHILL 42 A4
Arnothill FK1 42 A4
Arnothill Bank FK1 42 A4
Arnothill Ct FK1 41 F5
Arnothill Gdns FK1 42 A4
Arnothill La FK1 41 F4
Arnothill Mews FK1 42 A4
Arnot St FK1 42 C4
Arnott Dr ML5 122 A4
Arnott Quadrant ML1 142 C1
Arnott Way G72 139 A6
Arnprior Cres G45 137 D3
Arnprior Gdns G69 80 F2
Arnprior Pl KA7 238 F2
Arnprior Quadrant G45 137 D4
Arnprior Rd G45 137 D4
Arnprior St G45 137 D4
Arns Gr FK10 9 E8
Arnside Ave G46 136 C3
Arnswell FK10 5 C2
Arnton Gr ML6 123 E1
Arnum Gdns ML8 187 F1
Arnum Pl ML8 187 F1
Arnwood Dr G12 96 A5
Arondale Rd ML6 103 F3
Aron Terr G72 138 F3
Aros Dr G52 115 E2
Aros La G52 115 D2
Aros Rd G84 15 D6
Arran G74 160 C1
Arran Ave
Coatbridge ML5 122 D4
Dumbarton G82 49 D5
Kilmarnock KA3 223 A4
Port Glasgow PA14 69 B7
Renfrew PA3 93 E1
Arran Cres KA15 150 C1
Arran Ct
Alloa FK10 10 B5
Stevenston KA20 217 C8
Arran Dr
Airdrie ML6 102 F1
Cumbernauld G67 82 D8
Glasgow G52 115 F3
Glasgow, Giffnock G46 136 C2
Glenmavis ML6 102 F5
Johnstone PA5 111 D1
Kirkintilloch G66 58 E2
Paisley PA2 133 E7
Arran Gdns
Carluke ML8 201 F8
Hamilton ML3 162 E1
Troon KA10 229 E7
Arran La
Ardrossan KA22 205 C1
Moodiesburn G69 81 A2
Arran Mall KA7 238 F8
Arran Path 17 ML9 185 C1
Arran Pk KA9 236 B6
Arran Pl
Ardrossan KA22 205 C1
Clydebank G81 74 C2
Coatbridge ML5 122 D4
Irvine KA12 219 B5
Linwood PA3 112 A6
Saltcoats KA21 206 A2
Arran Rd
Gourock PA19 44 D6
Motherwell ML1 163 C7
Renfrew PA4 94 D2
Troon KA10 229 E7
Arran Terr
Ayr KA7 235 E1
Falkirk FK1 41 C4
Rutherglen G73 137 F5
Arran Twr G72 138 E3
Arran View
Airdrie ML6 102 F1
14 Kilsyth G65 60 D8
Stewarton KA3 195 E1
Troon KA10 229 D3
Arranview Ct
Ayr KA8 236 B4
Irvine KA12 219 B3
Arranview Gdns KA23 190 C2
Arranview St ML6 123 E1
Arran Way G71 140 F2
Arrochar Ct G23 96 E8
Arrochar Dr G23 76 D1
Arrochar Path 10 G23 76 D1
Arrochar St G23 76 D1
Arrol Cres FK10 10 C7
Arrol Dr KA7 238 D5
Arrol Pk KA7 238 E5
Arrol Pl G40 118 B4
Arrol St
Glasgow G52 114 E7
Glasgow G52 114 F8
Arrol Wynd G72 139 D6
Arrothill Dr KA1 227 D7
Arrotshole Ct G74 159 B4
Arrotshole Rd G74 159 B3
Arrowsmith Ave G13 95 D8
Artarman Rd G84 15 E4
Artartex Village★ G83 27 E6
Arthur Ave
Airdrie ML6 123 A6
Barrhead G78 134 B1
Arthur Ct KA23 190 C5
Arthur Gdns ML6 105 B4
ARTHURLIE 134 B1
Arthurlie Ave
Barrhead G78 134 C1
Uplawmoor G78 153 B3
Arthurlie Dr
Glasgow G46 136 C2
Newton Mearns G77 156 D3
Uplawmoor G78 153 B3
Arthurlie Gdns G78 134 C2
Arthurlie Pl KA21 216 E8
Arthurlie St
Barrhead G78 134 C2
Glasgow G51 115 F6
Arthur Pl G76 157 E6
Arthur Rd PA2 133 E8
Arthur's Dr FK5 23 F2
Arthur St
Alexandria G83 27 E4
Ayr KA7 238 F8
Clarkston G76 157 E6
Glasgow G3 96 D1
Greenock PA15 46 B4
Hamilton ML3 162 D5
Paisley PA1 113 C5
Saltcoats KA21 217 A7
Stevenston KA20 217 D8
West Kilbride KA23 190 C5
Arthurston Rd
Alexandria G83 27 F7
Balloch G83 28 A7
Artizan Br G82 49 E3
Arundel Dr
Bishopbriggs G64 78 B4
Glasgow G42 137 A7
Ascaig Cres G52 115 E2
Ascog Rd G61 75 F2
Ascog St G42 117 A2
Ascot G12 96 A6
Ascot Ave G12 95 F6
Ascot Gate G12 95 F6
Ash Ave G75 180 C6
Ashbank Cres ML6 123 E3
Ashbrae Gdns FK7 7 B2
Ashburn Gate PA19 44 C7
Ashburn Gdns
Gourock PA19 44 C7
Milngavie G62 54 E1
Ashburn Loan ML9 185 B4
Ashburn Rd G62 54 E2
Ashburton Pk G75 180 A7
Ashburton Rd G12 96 B6
Ashby Cres G13 75 E1
Ashcraig Sch G33 99 B3
Ashcroft G74 160 D5
Ashcroft Ave G66 57 E7
Ashcroft Dr G44 137 E5
Ashcroft Ho FK5 23 B1
Ashcroft Wlk G66 57 E7
Ash Ct G75 180 C6
Ashdale Ave KA21 205 F2
Ashdale Dr G52 115 E3
Ashdale Rd KA3 222 E4
Ashdene St G22 97 B7
Ash Dr KA15 150 B2
Asher Rd ML6 123 E2
Ashfield G64 78 A3
Ashfield Rd
Clarkston G76 157 E6
Milngavie G62 55 A1
Ashfield St
Glasgow G22 97 C4
Glasgow G22 97 C5
Ashfield Sta G22 97 C5
ASHGILL 199 F8
Ashgillhead Rd ML9 185 E1
Ashgill Pl G22 97 C6
Ashgill Rd G22 97 D7
Ash Gr
Bishopbriggs G64 98 B8
Kirkintilloch G66 79 B5
Law ML8 186 F6
Stenhousemuir FK5 23 F2
Uddingston G71 141 B8
Ashgrove
Airdrie ML6 123 D7
Caldercruix ML6 105 A5
Coatbridge ML5 122 A4
Hartwood ML7 145 F3
Irvine KA12 219 C5
Moodiesburn G69 80 F1
Ashgrove Ave
Gourock PA19 44 C7
Stevenston KA20 206 E2
Ashgrove La PA14 47 D1
Ashgrove Rd
Ardrossan KA22 205 C4
Bellshill ML4 142 B7
Kilwinning KA13 207 C4
Ashgrove St
Ayr KA7 239 A7
Glasgow G40 118 A2
Ashgrove Workshops
KA13 207 D4
Ashiestiel Ct G67 82 E7
Ashiestiel Pl G67 82 E7
Ashiestiel Rd G67 82 E7
Ashkirk Dr
Ashgill ML9 199 F8
Glasgow G52 115 F3
Ashkirk Pl ML2 165 C6
Ash La ML9 198 D1
Ashland Ave ML3 183 D6
Ashlar Ave G68 61 D5
Ashlea Dr G46 136 D4
Ashlea Gdns ML6 103 F3
Ashley Dr G71 141 B5
Ashley Gr ML4 141 D6
Ashley La G3 240 A4
Ashley Pk G71 141 C6
Ashley Pl G72 161 C8
Ashley Rise G83 27 F1
Ashley St
Bonnybridge FK4 39 F6
Glasgow G3 240 A4
Ashley Terr FK10 10 A8
Ashmore Rd G44 136 F5
Ashpark Prim Sch G46 135 D4
Ash Pl
Banknock FK4 38 E2
East Kilbride G75 180 C6
Johnstone PA5 112 A1
Kilmarnock KA1 227 D7
Ash Rd
Clydebank G81 74 A5
Cumbernauld G67 62 E5
Dumbarton G82 49 F4
Glasgow G69 120 A4
Ash Terr FK8 6 F5
Ashton Dr
Helensburgh G84 25 C8
Hurlford KA1 228 F5
Ashton Gdns G69 101 A6
Ashton Gn G74 159 E2
Ashton La G12 96 D2
Ashton Lane N G12 96 D2
Ashton Pl PA19 44 C7
Ashton Rd
Glasgow, Dalmarnock
G73 118 A1
Glasgow, Kelvingrove G12 96 D2
Gourock PA19 44 C7
Ashton St ML1 142 D2
Ashton Terr PA19 44 C7
Ashton View G82 49 B4
Ashton Way PA2 132 E8
Ashtree Ct G60 73 B6
Ashtree Gr G77 156 C3
Ashtree Rd G43 136 C8
Ashvale Cres G21 97 E4
Ash Wlk
Motherwell ML1 143 B5
Rutherglen G73 138 C3
Ashwood ML2 164 E1
Ashwood Gdns G13 95 F5
Ashworth Terr ML3 162 A4
Ash Wynd G72 139 E5
Aspen Ct KA7 239 D5
Aspen Dr G21 98 A3
Aspen Gate ML1 143 D2
Aspen Gr G69 121 B6
Aspen Pl
Cambuslang G72 139 E5
Johnstone PA5 112 A1
Aspen Rd KA7 239 D5
Aspen Way ML3 162 E2
Asquith Pl ML4 142 D5
Assloss Rd KA3 223 C4
Aster Dr G45 138 A3
Aster Gdns
Glasgow G53 135 C3
Motherwell ML1 163 E5
Athelstane Dr G67 82 D7
Athelstane Rd G13 95 C7
Athena Way G71 141 A7
Athole Gdns G12 96 C3
Athole La
Glasgow G12 96 D3
Greenock PA16 44 D3
Athole St G84 16 F1
Athole Terr PA16 44 D3
Atholl Ave
Glasgow G52 114 E7
Torrance G64 57 B1
Atholl Cres PA1 114 E6
Atholl Ct
Hamilton G72 161 F6
Kirkintilloch G66 59 B1
Atholl Dr
Cumbernauld G68 81 F8
Giffnock G46 136 C1
Rutherglen G46 157 C8
Atholl Gdns
Bearsden G61 75 E7
Bishopbriggs G64 77 F3
Glasgow G46 135 F2
Kilwinning KA13 207 E4
Rutherglen G73 138 E4
Atholl La G69 81 A2
Atholl Pl
Coatbridge ML5 122 B3
Falkirk FK2 42 C5
Glasgow G46 135 F2
Linwood PA3 112 A6
Stirling FK8 1 F2
Atholl St ML3 162 B6
Atholl Terr G71 120 F1
Atlas Ind Est G21 97 F4
Atlas Pl G21 97 F4
Atlas Rd G21 97 F4
Atlas Sq G21 97 F4
Atlas St G81 94 B8
Atlin Dr ML1 143 B3
Atrium Way FK4 40 A3
Attercliffe Ave ML2 164 D2
Attlee Ave G81 74 E1
Attlee Pl G81 74 E1
Attlee Rd G75 179 D8
Attow Rd G43 136 B5
Auburn Dr G78 134 D1
Auchans Ave KA2 225 E2
Auchans Dr KA2 225 E2
Auchanshangan Dr KA21 205 E3
Auchans Pl KA3 213 B3
Auchans Rd PA6 92 A2
AUCHENBACK 134 D1
Auchenback Prim Sch
G78 134 D1
Auchenbeg Cres KA7 239 A3
Auchenbothie Cres G33 98 E5
Auchenbothie Gdns PA13 69 C2
Auchenbothie Pl G33 98 E5
Auchenbothie Rd PA14 68 F6
AUCHENBOWIE 11 B4
Auchencar Dr KA3 222 E4
Auchencrow St G34 120 D8
Auchencruive G62 76 C8
Auchendarroch St PA15 46 C3
Auchendavie Rd G66 59 B2
Auchendavie Steadings
G66 59 B2
Auchendoon Cres KA7 238 D4
Auchendores Ave PA14 69 A7
Auchenfoil La PA14 68 D8
Auchenfoil Rd
Knocknairs Moor PA13 67 F6
Port Glasgow PA14 68 D8
Auchengate KA10 229 G7
Auchengate Cres KA11 224 G2
Auchengeich Gdns G69 80 F2
Auchengeich Rd G69 80 D3
Auchengilloch G75 180 E5
Auchenglen Dr G69 80 E2
Auchenglen Rd ML8 201 F3
Auchengree Rd KA14 170 D6
Auchengreoch Ave PA5 131 D8
Auchengreoch Rd PA5 131 D7
AUCHENHARVIE 217 B8
Auchenharvie Acad
KA21 217 B8
Auchenharvie L Ctr
KA21 217 B8
Auchenharvie Pl
Irvine KA11 219 F6
Stevenston KA20 206 B1
Auchenharvie Rd KA21 217 A8
Auchenhove Cres KA25 149 A3
Auchenhowie Rd G62 76 D7
Auchenkilns Holdings
Cumbernauld, Balloch G68 61 C1
Cumbernauld, Condorrat
G67 82 D6
Auchenkilns Pk G68 61 C1
Auchenkilns Rd G67 82 D6
Auchenleck La PA14 68 E7
Auchenleck Rd PA14 68 E7
Auchenlodment Prim Sch
PA5 112 A1
Auchenlodment Rd PA5 112 B1
AUCHENREOCH 59 B5
Auchenreoch Ave G82 50 B6
Auchenreoch Holdings
G66 59 B6
AUCHENSHUGGLE 119 A2
Auchenstewart Ct ML2 165 C3
AUCHENTIBBER 161 A2
Auchentibber Ct G72 161 F6
Auchentibber Rd G72 161 A3
AUCHENTIBER 193 F3
Auchentiber Pl KA3 223 C6
AUCHENTORLIE 114 B4
Auchentorlie Quadrant
PA1 114 B4
Auchentorlie St G11 95 F2
Auchentoshan Ave G81 73 F6
Auchentoshan Terr G21 97 F2
Auchentrae Cres KA7 238 D5
Auchentyre Pl FK2 24 C3
AUCHINAIRN 98 A8
Auchinairn Gdns G64 98 D8
Auchinairn Prim Sch G64 98 B8
Auchinairn Rd G64 98 C7
Auchinairn Rdbt G64 98 E8
Auchinbaird FK10 5 C2
Auchinbee Farm Rd G68 61 B4
Auchinbee Way G68 61 B3
Auchincampbell Rd ML3 162 D3
Auchincarroch Rd
Alexandria G83 27 F6
Bonhill G83 28 B7
Gartocharn G83 20 F4
Auchincloch Dr FK4 38 F3
Auchincruive Ave KA9 236 C6
Auchineden Ct G61 75 C7
Auchingill Pl G34 100 D1
Auchingill Rd
Glasgow G34 100 C1
Glasgow G34 100 D1
Auchingramont Ct ML3 162 D3
Auchingramont Rd ML3 162 D4
Auchinlea Dr ML1 144 C1
Auchinlea Rd G34 99 F1
Auchinleck Ave G33 98 F6
Auchinleck Cres G33 98 E6
Auchinleck Dr G33 98 E6
Auchinleck Gdns G33 98 E6
Auchinleck Rd
Clydebank G81 74 B7
Glasgow G33 98 F7
Auchinleck Terr G81 74 B7
AUCHINLOCH 79 D2
Auchinloch Prim Sch G66 79 D2
Auchinloch Rd G66 79 D4
Auchinloch St 2 G21 97 F3
Auchinraith Ave ML3 162 C5
Auchinraith Ind Est G72 161 E7
Auchinraith Prim Sch
G72 161 D7
Auchinraith Rd G72 161 E6
Auchinraith Terr G72 161 F7
Auchinvole Cres G65 60 B8
Auchmannoch Ave PA1 114 E5
Auchmead Rd PA16 44 E4
Auchmountain Rd
Greenock, Bridgend PA15 46 C3
Greenock PA15, PA13 46 E1
Auchnacraig Rd G81 74 C7
Auchneagh Ave PA16 45 B4
Auchneagh Cres PA16 45 B4
Auchneagh Farm La PA16 45 A5
Auchneagh Farm Rd PA16 45 B5

Auchneagh Rd PA16 . . . . . 45 B4
Auchter Ave ML2 . . . . 166 C5
Auchterburn Rd ML7 . . . . 166 F8
Auchter Rd ML2 . . . . 165 E4
Auckland Pk 8 G75 . . . . . 159 A1
Auckland Pl G81 . . . . 73 D4
Auckland St
Glasgow G22 . . . . 97 B3
Glasgow G22 . . . . 97 B4
Auctioneers Way 3
ML11 . . . . 215 C3
Auldbar Rd G52 . . . . 115 F3
Auldbar Terr PA2 . . . . 114 A2
Auld Brig Rd FK10 . . . . 10 B6
Auldburn Pl G43 . . . . 136 B6
Auldburn Rd G43 . . . . 136 B6
Auld Clay Rd KA21 . . . . . . 206 E7
Auldearn Rd G21 . . . . 98 D7
Auldgirth Rd G52 . . . . 115 F3
Auldhame St ML5 . . . . 121 E8
AULDHOUSE 180 D1
Auldhouse Ave G43 . . . . . 136 B6
Auldhouse Ct G43 . . . . 136 B6
Auldhouse Gdns G43 . . . . 136 B6
Auldhouse Prim Sch
G75 . . . . 180 C1
Auldhouse Rd
East Kilbride G75 . . . . 180 C2
Glasgow G43 . . . . 136 C6
Auldhouse Ret Pk G43 . . 136 C6
Auldhouse Terr G43 . . . . . 136 D6
Auld Kirk Mus* G66 . . . . . 58 C1
Auldkirk Rd FK10 . . . . 4 C3
Auld Kirk Rd G72 . . . . 139 C3
Auld Kirk The G76 . . . . . . 158 A5
Auldlea Rd KA15 . . . . 150 B2
Auldmurroch Dr G62 . . . . . 54 D2
Auld Nicks View KA7 . . . . 238 E1
Auld Rd The G67 . . . . 62 A4
Auld's Brae 2 ML6 . . . . . 123 A8
Auld School Wynd FK7 . . . . 6 D5
Auld St G81 . . . . 73 E3
Auldton Terr ML9 . . . . 185 F1
Aultbea St G22 . . . . 97 B8
Aultmore Dr ML1 . . . . 143 B2
Aultmore Gdns G33 . . . . . 119 F7
Aultmore Park Prim Sch
G33 . . . . 119 E7
Aultmore Pk G33 . . . . 119 F7
Aultmore Rd G33 . . . . 119 F7
Aurelia Ct ML1 . . . . 163 E7
Aurora Ave
Clydebank G81 . . . . 94 B8
Renfrew PA4 . . . . 94 C1
Aursbridge Cres G78 . . . . 134 D2
Aursbridge Dr G78 . . . . . . 134 D2
Aurs Cres G78 . . . . 134 D2
Aurs Dr G78 . . . . 134 D2
Aurs Glen G78 . . . . 134 C1
Aurs Pl G78 . . . . 134 E2
Aurs Rd
Barrhead G78 . . . . 134 E2
Newton Mearns G77 . . . . . 155 F7
Austen Rd G13 . . . . 95 E5
Austine Dr ML3 . . . . 183 E7
Aven Dr FK2 . . . . 42 F3
Avenel Rd G13 . . . . 75 E1
Avenue End Gate G33 . . . . 99 B2
Avenue End Prim Sch 1
G33 . . . . 99 B2
Avenue End Rd G33 . . . . . . 99 B3
Avenuehead Rd
Moodiesburn G69 . . . . 81 A1
Muirhead G69 . . . . 101 A8
Avenuepark St G20 . . . . . . 96 E5
Avenue Pk FK9 . . . . 1 F7
Avenue Pl G83 . . . . 27 D5
Avenue Sh Ctr The G77 . . 156 D4
Avenue Sq KA3 . . . . 211 D8
Avenue St
Glasgow G40 . . . . 118 A5
Rutherglen G73 . . . . 118 B1
Stewarton KA3 . . . . 195 D1
Avenue The
Bridge of Allan FK9 . . . . 2 A7
Falkirk FK2 . . . . 24 D2
Kilmacolm PA13 . . . . 69 E1
West Kilbride KA23 . . . . . . 190 E8
Aviemore Gdns G61 . . . . . . 76 B5
Aviemore Rd G52 . . . . 115 E3
Avils Hill KA25 . . . . 149 A1
Avils Pl KA25 . . . . 149 B1
Avoch St G34 . . . . 100 B1
Avon Ave
Bearsden G61 . . . . 76 B4
Carluke ML8 . . . . 187 E2
Longriggend ML6 . . . . 84 D3
Avonbank Cres ML3 . . . . . 183 E8
Avonbank Gdns FK6 . . . . . . 21 D4
Avonbank Rd
Larkhall ML9 . . . . 184 E3
Rutherglen G73 . . . . 137 F7
Avonbrae Cres ML3 . . . . . 183 E8
AVONBRIDGE 87 F6
Avonbridge Dr ML3 . . . . . 162 F3
Avonbridge Prim Sch FK1 87 F5
Avonbridge Rd FK1 . . . . . . 86 B7
Avon Ct
Falkirk FK1 . . . . 42 C2
Irvine KA11 . . . . 220 A4
Motherwell ML1 . . . . 163 E6
Avondale Ave G74 . . . . . . 159 F1
Avondale Dr PA1 . . . . 114 B6
Avondale Gdns G74 . . . . . 181 A8
Avondale Pl G74 . . . . 181 A8
Avondale Rd KA23 . . . . . . 190 D6
Avondale St G33 . . . . 99 A1
Avon Dr
Bellshill ML4 . . . . 142 C4
Linwood PA3 . . . . 112 B6
Avonhead G75 . . . . 180 E5
Avonhead Ave G67 . . . . 82 C7
Avonhead Gdns G67 . . . . . . 82 C7
Avonhead Pl G67 . . . . 82 C7
Avonhead Rd G67 . . . . 82 C7
Avon Ho ML3 . . . . 162 E5
Avonmouth Pl PA19 . . . . . . 44 F5
Avonpark FK1 . . . . 87 F6
Avon Pl
Coatbridge ML5 . . . . 101 D1
Kilmarnock KA1 . . . . 228 B5
Larkhall ML9 . . . . 199 B7
Avon Rd
Bishopbriggs G64 . . . . 98 A8
Glasgow G46 . . . . 136 B2
Larkhall ML9 . . . . 199 A7
Avonside Dr FK6 . . . . 21 D5
Avonside Gr ML3 . . . . 162 F3
Avonspark St G21 . . . . 98 A3
Avon St
Denny FK6 . . . . 21 C4
Hamilton ML3 . . . . 162 E3
Larkhall ML9 . . . . 184 F3
Motherwell ML1 . . . . 163 E6
Avon Twr 7 ML1 . . . . 163 E5
Avon Wlk 4 G67 . . . . 61 F1
Avon Wynd 23 ML2 . . . . . . 165 F6
Aylmer Rd G43 . . . . 136 F6
AYR 238 D7
Ayr Acad KA7 . . . . 235 E1
Ayr Coll (Dam Park Campus)
KA8 . . . . 239 B8
Ayr Dr ML6 . . . . 123 A5
Ayr Hospl KA6 . . . . 239 D1
Ayr La PA16 . . . . 44 E3
Ayr Rd
Ashgill ML9 . . . . 185 E2
Giffnock G46 . . . . 136 B1
Irvine KA11, KA12 . . . . 224 E7
Kilmarnock KA1 . . . . 227 E3
Newton Mearns G77 . . . . . 156 B2
Newton Mearns G77 . . . . . 156 D4
Prestwick KA9 . . . . 236 B6
Rutherglen G77 . . . . 157 A7
Ayrshire Central Hospl
KA12 . . . . 219 B7
Ayr St
Glasgow G21 . . . . 97 E3
Troon KA10 . . . . 229 D2
Ayr Sta KA7 . . . . 239 A7
Ayr Terr PA16 . . . . 44 E3
Ayton Park N G74 . . . . . . 160 B3
Ayton Park S G74 . . . . . . 160 A3
Aytoun Dr PA8 . . . . 72 F3
Aytoun Rd G41 . . . . 116 E3
Azalea Gdns G72 . . . . 139 E5

B

Baads Rd ML7 . . . . 126 E8
Baberton Way KA13 . . . . . 207 B3
Babylon Ave ML4 . . . . 142 A3
Babylon Dr ML4 . . . . 142 A3
Babylon Pl ML4 . . . . 142 A3
Babylon Rd ML4 . . . . 142 A3
Backbrae St 17 G65 . . . . . . 60 D8
Backburn KA15 . . . . 171 B8
Back Cswy G31 . . . . 118 D5
Back Hawkhill Ave KA8 . . 236 B2
Back Main St KA8 . . . . 235 F1
Backmuir Cres ML3 . . . . . 162 B6
Backmuir Pl ML3 . . . . 162 B6
Backmuir Rd
Clydebank G15 . . . . 75 B4
Hamilton ML3 . . . . 162 B6
Back O Barns ML3 . . . . . . 162 E4
Back O Dykes Rd G66 . . . . . 80 B7
Back O Hill PA6 . . . . 91 B1
Back O' Hill Ind Est FK8 . . . 2 A2
Back O' Hill Rd
Fluchter G64 . . . . 56 E2
Stirling FK8 . . . . 1 F1
Back Peebles St KA8 . . . . 235 F2
Back Rd
Alva FK12 . . . . 4 E7
Bridge of Weir PA11 . . . . . 110 D8
Back Row ML3 . . . . 162 E4
Back Sneddon St PA3 . . . 113 E6
Back St G82 . . . . 27 D1
Back Wlk 2 FK8 . . . . 7 B7
Backwood Ct FK10 . . . . 10 F5
Badenheath Pl G68 . . . . . . 81 D5
Badenheath Terr G67 . . . . 81 E4
Badenoch Rd G66 . . . . 59 C1
Bagatelle Ct PA16 . . . . 45 D7
Bagnell St G21 . . . . 97 F5
Bahamas Way 6 G75 . . . 159 A1
Baidland Ave KA24 . . . . . . 191 E6
Bailie Dr G61 . . . . 75 D7
Bailie Fyfe Way
Overtown ML2 . . . . 186 B7
Wishaw ML2 . . . . 165 C1
Bailiehill Pl KA1 . . . . 222 D1
Baillie Ave ML7 . . . . 127 F5
Baillie Dr
Bothwell G71 . . . . 141 A3
East Kilbride G74 . . . . 160 C4
Baillie Gdns ML2 . . . . 165 E4
Baillie Pl G74 . . . . 160 C4
Baillies La ML6 . . . . 123 A8
Bailliesmuir Pl ML2 . . . . 166 A6
BAILLIESTON 120 A4
Baillieston Ave KA25 . . . . 170 A8
Baillieston Rd
Glasgow, Barrachnie
G32 . . . . 119 E4
Glasgow, Broomhouse
G71 . . . . 120 B2
Baillieston Sta G69 . . . . . 120 B3
Baillie Waugh Rd FK7 . . . . . 7 C3
Baillie Wynd 11 G71 . . . . 141 A8
Bain Cres G84 . . . . 16 E3
Bainfield Rd G82 . . . . 48 B7
Baingle Brae FK10 . . . . 4 B3
Baingle Cres FK10 . . . . 4 B3
BAINSFORD 42 B8
Bainsford Prim Sch FK2 . . 42 B8
Bainsford St G32 . . . . 118 F6
Bain St G40 . . . . 241 C1
Bain Way G83 . . . . 27 E6
Baird Ave
Airdrie ML6 . . . . 103 B2
Glasgow G52 . . . . 114 E8
Helensburgh G84 . . . . 16 B2
Kilwinning KA13 . . . . 207 E4
Larkhall ML9 . . . . 199 C8
Baird Brae G4 . . . . 97 B3
Baird Cres
Alexandria G83 . . . . 27 C7
Cumbernauld G67 . . . . 82 B7
Baird Ct
Clydebank G81 . . . . 74 A2
Troon KA10 . . . . 229 G4
Baird Dr
Bearsden G61 . . . . 75 D5
Erskine PA8 . . . . 72 F3
Baird Gdns G72 . . . . 161 E6
Baird Hill G75 . . . . 180 E8
Baird Memorial Prim Sch
G67 . . . . 82 C7
Baird Pl
Bellshill ML4 . . . . 142 A7
Kilmarnock KA3 . . . . 223 B2
Monkton KA9 . . . . 233 D4
Wishaw ML2 . . . . 165 E4
Baird Rd
Alloway KA7 . . . . 238 E2
Kilmarnock KA3 . . . . 223 B2
Monkton KA9 . . . . 233 D4
Bairds Cres ML3 . . . . 162 C3
Bairdsland View ML4 . . . . 142 B6
Baird St
Coatbridge ML5 . . . . 122 A7
Falkirk FK1 . . . . 41 D5
Glasgow G4 . . . . 241 B4
Baird Terr ML7 . . . . 127 C5
Bairns Ford Ave FK2 . . . . . 42 A7
Bairns Ford Ct FK2 . . . . . . 42 A7
Bairns Ford Dr FK2 . . . . . . 42 A7
Baker St
Glasgow G41 . . . . 116 E1
Greenock PA15 . . . . 46 A3
Stirling FK8 . . . . 7 A8
Bakewell Rd G69 . . . . 120 A5
Balaclava St G2, G3 . . . . . 240 B2
Balado Rd G33 . . . . 119 E7
Balbakie Rd ML7 . . . . 127 E5
Balbeggie St G32 . . . . 119 C4
Balbeg St G51 . . . . 115 E6
Balblair Rd
Airdrie ML6 . . . . 103 A3
Glasgow G52 . . . . 115 F2
Balcarres Ave G12 . . . . 96 C5
Balcary Pl ML6 . . . . 123 E1
Balcastle Gdns G65 . . . . . . 36 B2
Balcastle Rd
Kilsyth G65 . . . . 36 A1
Slamannan FK1 . . . . 86 A6
Balcomie Cres KA10 . . . . . 230 A2
Balcomie St G33 . . . . 99 A1
Balcomie Terr ML3 . . . . . . 183 B8
Balcurvie Rd G34 . . . . 100 A2
Baldernock Prim Sch G64 56 B2
Baldernock Rd G62 . . . . . . 55 D2
Baldinnie Rd G34 . . . . 120 B8
Baldoran Dr G66 . . . . 58 B6
Baldorran Cres G68 . . . . . . 61 B3
Baldovan Cres G33 . . . . . . 119 F8
Baldovan Path G33 . . . . . . 119 F7
Baldovie Rd G52 . . . . 115 C3
Baldragon Rd G34 . . . . . . 100 C1
Baldric Rd G13 . . . . 95 C6
Baldwin Ave G13 . . . . 95 D8
Balerno Dr G52 . . . . 115 E3
Baleshrae Cres KA3 . . . . . 223 A6
Balfearn Dr G76 . . . . 178 E5
Balfleurs St G62 . . . . 55 B2
Balfluig St G34 . . . . 99 F1
Balfour Ave KA15 . . . . 171 B7
Balfour Cres
Plean FK7 . . . . 12 D3
Stenhousemuir FK5 . . . . 23 C2
Balfour Ct
Kilmarnock KA3 . . . . 223 D3
Plean FK7 . . . . 12 D3
Balfour St
Alloa FK10 . . . . 10 C7
Bannockburn FK7 . . . . 7 C1
Bonnybridge FK4 . . . . 39 F6
Glasgow G20 . . . . 96 D6
Port Glasgow PA14 . . . . 47 B2
Stirling FK8 . . . . 1 F2
Balfour Terr G75 . . . . 180 F7
Balfour Wynd ML9 . . . . . . 185 B1
Balfron Cres ML3 . . . . 161 F3
Balfron Dr ML5 . . . . 122 C3
Balfron Pl ML5 . . . . 122 C4
Balfron Rd
Glasgow G51 . . . . 115 E7
Greenock PA15 . . . . 46 C1
Balfron Rd *continued*
Paisley PA1 . . . . 114 D5
Balgair Dr PA1 . . . . 114 B5
Balgair Pl G22 . . . . 97 B5
Balgair St G22 . . . . 97 B4
Balgair Terr G32 . . . . 119 B5
Balglass Gdns G22 . . . . 97 B4
Balglass St G22 . . . . 97 B4
Balgonie PA2 . . . . 113 B1
Balgonie Ave PA2 . . . . 113 B1
Balgonie Dr PA2 . . . . 113 C1
Balgonie Rd G52 . . . . 115 E4
Balgonie Woods PA2 . . . . 113 C1
Balgownie Cres G46 . . . . 136 A2
Balgray Ave
Kilbirnie KA25 . . . . 170 A8
Kilmarnock KA1 . . . . 227 F2
Balgraybank St G21 . . . . . . 98 A4
Balgray Cres G78 . . . . 134 E2
Balgrayhill Rd G21 . . . . 97 F6
Balgray Rd
Barrmill KA15 . . . . 172 A5
Glengarnock KA14 . . . . . . 170 B7
Newton Mearns G77 . . . . . 156 A5
Balgraystone Rd G78 . . . . 155 D7
Balgray Way KA11 . . . . . . 220 A6
Balintore St G32 . . . . 119 A5
Baliol La G3 . . . . 240 A4
Baliol St G3 . . . . 240 A4
Baljaffray Prim Sch G61 . . 75 C8
Baljaffray Rd G61 . . . . 75 B8
Baljaffrey Sh Ctr G61 . . . . 75 C8
Ballachalairy Yett G63 . . . 30 D4
Ballagan Pl G62 . . . . 54 D2
Ballaig Ave G61 . . . . 75 D5
Ballaig Cres G33 . . . . 99 C5
Ballantay Quadrant G45 . 138 A3
Ballantay Rd G45 . . . . 138 A3
Ballantay Terr G45 . . . . . . 138 A3
Ballantine Ave G52 . . . . . . 115 A7
Ballantine Dr KA7 . . . . 238 F6
Ballantrae G74 . . . . 159 D2
Ballantrae Cres G77 . . . . . 157 A4
Ballantrae Dr G77 . . . . 157 A4
Ballantrae Rd G72 . . . . 161 F6
Ballantrae Wynd ML1 . . . 143 B5
Ballantyne Drive La KA7 . 238 F6
Ballater Cres ML2 . . . . 165 B5
Ballater Dr
Bearsden G61 . . . . 76 A2
Inchinnan PA4 . . . . 93 D7
Paisley PA2 . . . . 114 A1
Stirling FK9 . . . . 2 C4
Ballater Pl G5 . . . . 117 D4
Ballater St G5 . . . . 117 D5
Ballater Way ML5 . . . . 101 C6
Ballayne Dr
Chryston G69 . . . . 80 C1
Moodiesburn G69 . . . . 81 A3
Ballengeich Pass FK8 . . . . . 2 A1
Ballengeich Rd FK8 . . . . 1 F1
Ballerup Terr G75 . . . . 180 E6
Ballewan Cres G63 . . . . 31 A4
Ballindalloch Dr G31 . . . . 118 B8
Ballindalloch La G31 . . . . 118 A8
Ballinkier Ave FK4 . . . . 38 E3
BALLOCH
Alexandria 19 E1
Cumbernauld 61 C2
Balloch Castle* G83 . . . . . . 19 D2
Balloch Castle Ctry Pk*
G83 . . . . 19 D2
Balloch Gdns G52 . . . . 115 F3
Balloch Holdings G68 . . . . 61 B1
Ballochmill Bsns Pk G73 138 D8
Ballochmill Rd G73 . . . . . 138 D8
Ballochmyle G74 . . . . 160 D4
Ballochmyle Cres 11
G53 . . . . 135 A8
Ballochmyle Dr 14 G53 . . 135 A8
Ballochmyle Gdns G53 . . 135 A8
Ballochmyle Pl 12 G53 . . 135 A8
Ballochney La ML6 . . . . . . 102 E2
Ballochney Rd
Plains ML6 . . . . 103 E3
Plains ML6 . . . . 104 A3
Ballochney St
Airdrie ML6 . . . . 102 F1
Airdrie ML6 . . . . 102 F2
Ballochnie Dr ML6 . . . . . . 104 A3
Ballochnie View ML6 . . . . 103 F2
Balloch Rd
Airdrie ML6 . . . . 124 A6
Balloch G83 . . . . 27 D8
Cumbernauld G68 . . . . 61 D2
Greenock PA15 . . . . 46 B1
Shotts ML7 . . . . 146 E6
Balloch Rdbt G68 . . . . 61 A2
Balloch Sta G83 . . . . 27 E8
Balloch View G67 . . . . 61 F2
Ballochyle Pl PA19 . . . . 43 F5
Ballogie Rd G44 . . . . 137 B7
Ballot Rd KA12 . . . . 219 C3
BALMALLOCH 36 C1
Balmalloch Prim Sch G65 36 C1
Balmalloch Rd G65 . . . . 36 B1
Balmartin Rd G23 . . . . 76 D1
Balmedie PA8 . . . . 73 A2
Balmeg Ave G46 . . . . 157 C8
Balmerino Pl G64 . . . . 98 D8
Balminnoch Pk KA7 . . . . . 238 D1
Balmoral Ave ML6 . . . . . . 102 F5
Balmoral Cres
Coatbridge ML5 . . . . 121 D4
Inchinnan PA4 . . . . 93 E6
Balmoral Dr
Bearsden G61 . . . . 76 A2
Bishopton PA7 . . . . 72 C2
Balmoral Dr *continued*
Cambuslang G72 . . . . 138 E6
Falkirk FK1 . . . . 41 E3
Glasgow G32 . . . . 139 B8
Balmoral Gdns
Blantyre G72 . . . . 140 C2
Uddingston G71 . . . . 120 F1
Balmoral Path 3 ML9 . . . 185 C2
Balmoral Pl
East Kilbride G74 . . . . 159 C1
Gourock PA19 . . . . 43 E5
Stenhousemuir FK5 . . . . 23 E4
Stirling FK8 . . . . 7 A7
Balmoral Rd
Elderslie PA5 . . . . 112 B1
Kilmarnock KA3 . . . . 222 E2
Balmoral St
Falkirk FK1 . . . . 41 E3
Glasgow G14 . . . . 95 B3
Balmoral Wynd KA3 . . . . . 211 E8
BALMORE 77 E8
Balmore Ct PA13 . . . . 89 C7
Balmore Dr ML3 . . . . 183 B8
Balmore Ind Est G22 . . . . . 97 B8
Balmore Pl G22 . . . . 97 B6
Balmore Rd
Balmore G62, G64 . . . . 77 C8
Bardowie G62, G64 . . . . 77 C8
1 Glasgow G22 . . . . 97 A7
Glasgow G22, G23 . . . . 77 A2
Greenock PA15 . . . . 46 C1
Balmore Sq G22 . . . . 97 B5
Balmuildy Prim Sch G64 . 77 F3
Balmuildy Rd G64 . . . . 77 D5
Balmulzier Rd FK1 . . . . 86 B8
BALORNOCK 98 C6
Balornock Prim Sch G21 . 98 A4
Balornock Rd G64 . . . . 98 A6
Balquharn Cotts FK12 . . . . . 4 D7
Balquhatstone Cres FK1 . . 86 A6
Balquhidderock FK7 . . . . . . 7 C4
Balrossie Dr PA13 . . . . 89 A7
Balruddery Pl G64 . . . . 98 D8
Balshagray Ave G11 . . . . . . 95 F3
Balshagray Cres G14 . . . . . 95 E2
Balshagray Dr G11 . . . . 95 F3
Balshagray La G11 . . . . 95 F3
Balshagray Pl 2 G11 . . . . . 95 F3
Balta Cres G72 . . . . 138 F3
Baltersan Gdns ML3 . . . . . 183 F3
Baltic Ct G40 . . . . 118 A3
Baltic La G40 . . . . 118 A3
Baltic Pl G40 . . . . 118 A4
Baltic St
Glasgow G40 . . . . 118 A3
Glasgow G40 . . . . 118 A4
Glasgow G40 . . . . 118 B3
Balure Cres FK7 . . . . 8 D4
Balure Pl G31 . . . . 118 C7
Balvaird Cres 2 G73 . . . . 138 A7
Balvaird Dr G73 . . . . 138 A7
Balvenie Dr ML1 . . . . 143 B1
Balvenie St ML5 . . . . 122 B3
Balveny Ave 3 G33 . . . . . . 99 D2
Balveny Ct KA3 . . . . 195 C1
Balveny Dr 2 G33 . . . . 99 D2
Balveny Pl 1 G33 . . . . 99 D2
Balveny St G33 . . . . 99 D2
Balvicar Dr G42 . . . . 116 F1
Balvicar St G42 . . . . 116 F1
Balvie Ave
Clydebank G15 . . . . 75 A1
Glasgow, Giffnock G46 . . . 136 D2
Balvie Cres G62 . . . . 54 F2
Balvie Rd G62 . . . . 54 F2
Banavie La G11 . . . . 96 A3
Banavie Rd ML2 . . . . 165 F6
Banchory Ave
Glasgow G43 . . . . 136 B5
Glenmavis ML6 . . . . 102 F5
Inchinnan PA4 . . . . 93 D7
Banchory Cres G61 . . . . . . 76 A2
Banchory Pl FK10 . . . . 4 C3
Banchory Prim Sch FK10 . . 4 C3
Banchory Rd ML2 . . . . 165 B5
Bandeath Ind Est FK7 . . . . . 9 A5
Bandeath Rd FK7 . . . . 8 D4
Baneberry Path G74 . . . . 159 D4
Banff Ave ML6 . . . . 123 A4
Banff Pl
East Kilbride G75 . . . . 180 C8
Greenock PA16 . . . . 44 D5
Banff Quadrant ML2 . . . . . 165 B5
Banff Rd PA16 . . . . 44 D5
Banff St G33 . . . . 99 B2
Bangorshill St
Glasgow G46 . . . . 135 F4
Thornliebank G46 . . . . 136 A4
Bank Ave G62 . . . . 55 A3
Bankbrae Ave G53 . . . . . . 135 A6
Bank Ct KA12 . . . . 219 E4
Bankend Pl KA3 . . . . 223 A5
Bankend Rd
Bridge of Weir PA11 . . . . . 110 E7
Dumbarton G82 . . . . 49 F4
Bankend St G33 . . . . 99 A1
Bankfaulds Ave KA25 . . . . 149 A1
Bankfaulds Ct 7 KA25 . . . 149 A1
Bankfield Dr ML3 . . . . 183 D7
Bankfield Pk KA7 . . . . 239 C3
Bankfield Rdbt KA7 . . . . . 239 D3
Bankfoot Dr G52 . . . . 115 B4
Bankfoot Pl G77 . . . . 157 B4
Bankfoot Rd
Glasgow G52 . . . . 115 B4
Paisley PA3 . . . . 113 B6
Bankglen Rd G15 . . . . 75 B4
Bankhall St G42 . . . . 117 B2

BANKHEAD
Denny 39 E6
Rutherglen 137 F6
Bankhead Ave
Airdrie ML6 123 D7
Bellshill ML4 142 B3
Coatbridge ML5 121 C4
Glasgow G13 95 A6
Springside KA11 221 A2
Bankhead Cres FK4 39 D6
Bankhead Dr G73 138 A7
Bankhead Pl
Airdrie ML6 123 D7
Coatbridge ML5 121 C4
Stewarton KA3 195 E2
Bankhead Prim Sch
Glasgow G13 95 A6
Rutherglen G73 137 F7
Bankhead Rd
Carmunnock G76 158 D7
Fishcross FK10 5 D3
Kilwinning KA13 207 F3
Kirkintilloch G66 80 B7
Rutherglen G73 137 F7
Bankhead Terr ML11 215 B2
Bankholm Pl G76 157 F5
Bankier Prim Sch FK4 38 E3
Bankier Rd FK4 38 E3
Bankier Terr FK4 38 E3
BANKNOCK 38 E3
Banknock St G32 118 E6
Bank Pk G75 180 D8
Bank Pl
Irvine KA12 219 E4
1 Kilmarnock KA1 227 F8
Shotts ML7 146 F4
Bank Rd
Glasgow G32 139 C8
Harthill ML7 127 E5
BANKSIDE 42 C8
Bankside FK2 42 C7
Bankside Ave PA5 111 F3
Bankside Ct FK6 21 E2
Bankside Gdns KA25 149 A4
Bankside Ind Est FK2 42 D8
Banks Rd G66 58 E1
Bank St
Airdrie ML6 123 A8
Alexandria G83 27 E5
Alloa FK10 10 B6
Barrhead G78 134 C2
Cambuslang G72 139 A6
Coatbridge ML5 121 E6
Falkirk FK1 42 B5
Glasgow G12 96 E2
Greenock PA15 45 F4
Greenock PA15 45 F5
Irvine KA12 219 D3
Irvine, Stanecastle KA12 219 E4
Kilbirnie KA25 149 A2
Kilmarnock KA1 227 F8
Neilston G78 154 D7
Paisley PA1 113 F5
Prestwick KA9 236 B8
Slamannan FK1 86 A6
6 Stirling FK8 7 A8
Troon KA10 229 C2
Banks View FK2 14 E4
Banktop Pl PA5 111 F3
Bank View ML6 123 D2
Bankview Cres G66 79 A8
Bankview Dr G66 79 A8
Bankview Terr FK4 39 E6
Bank Way 14 ML9 185 B4
Bannachra Cres G83 27 D6
Bannachra Dr G84 16 B2
Bannatyne Ave G31 118 B7
Bannatyne St ML11 215 B4
Bannercross Ave 2 G69 120 A5
Bannercross Dr G69 120 A5
Bannercross Gdns 1
G69 120 A5
Banner Dr G13 75 C1
Bannerman Dr
Bellshill ML4 142 D5
Kilmarnock KA3 223 D2
Bannerman High Sch
G69 120 A4
Bannerman Pl G81 74 B2
Banner Rd G13 75 D1
Bannoch Gdns KA13 208 A4
Bannoch Pl
Kilwinning KA13 208 A3
Motherwell ML1 164 C3
Bannoch Rd
Kilwinning KA13 208 A2
Kilwinning KA13 208 A3
BANNOCKBURN 7 E2
Bannockburn Cross FK7 7 E1
Bannockburn Dr 10 ML9 185 C1
Bannockburn Heritage Ctr★
FK7 7 B2
Bannockburn High Sch
FK7 7 D2
Bannockburn Hospl FK7 11 F7
Bannockburn Pl
Kilmarnock KA3 223 B3
Motherwell ML1 143 A2
Bannockburn Prim Sch
FK7 7 E1
Bannockburn Rd
Cowie FK7 12 C8
Stirling FK7 7 C3
Bannockburn St PA16 45 C3
Bannockburn Station Rd
Bannockburn FK7 7 F2
Fallin FK7 8 A4
Bannock Rd FK7 8 C4
BANTASKIN 41 F4
Bantaskine Dr FK1 41 F4
Bantaskine Gdns FK1 41 E3
Bantaskine Rd FK1 41 F4
Bantaskine St FK1 41 E3
Bantaskin Prim Sch FK1 41 E4
Bantaskin St G20 96 C7
BANTON 37 E3
Banton Pl
Bonnybridge FK4 40 A3
Glasgow G33 120 A7
Banton Prim Sch G65 37 E3
Banton Rd G65 37 D2
Banyan Cres G71 121 D1
BARASSIE 229 E5
Barassie G74 159 D3
Barassiebank La KA10 229 E6
Barassie Cres G68 61 F6
Barassie Ct G71 140 F2
Barassie Dr PA11 110 C6
Barassie Pl KA1 227 E4
Barassie Prim Sch 7
KA10 229 E5
Barassie St KA10 229 D3
Barassie Sta KA10 229 E6
Barbadoes Pl KA1 227 E6
Barbadoes Rd KA1 227 E6
Barbados Gn 5 G75 159 A1
Barbae Pl G71 141 A3
Barbana Rd G74 158 E2
Barbegs Cres G65 60 F4
Barberry Ave G53 135 B2
Barberry Cres G67 82 D6
Barberry Dr KA15 171 A8
Barberry Gdns G53 135 B2
Barberry Pl G53 135 C2
Barbeth Gdns G67 82 B6
Barbeth Pl
Cumbernauld G67 82 B6
Irvine KA11 220 A5
Barbeth Rd G67 82 B6
Barbeth Way G67 82 A6
Barbour Ave FK7 7 C3
Barbour's Pk KA3 211 E8
Barbreck Rd 2 G42 116 F2
Barcaldine Ave G69 80 B1
Barcaldine Terr G41 116 F2
Barcapel Ave G77 156 E8
Barcapel Flats G77 156 E7
Barclaven Rd PA13 89 E8
Barclay Ave PA5 112 B2
Barclay Ct G60 73 B6
Barclay Dr
Helensburgh G84 16 C3
Johnstone PA5 112 B2
Kilmarnock KA3 223 C2
Barclay Gdns KA11 220 D6
Barclay Pl KA3 195 D1
Barclay Rd ML1 163 B6
Barclay Sq PA4 94 B1
Barclay St
Glasgow G21 97 F5
Old Kilpatrick G60 73 B5
Barcloy Pl ML6 123 F1
Barcraigs Dr PA2 133 F8
Bard Ave G13 95 B8
BARDOWIE 77 B7
Bardowie Ind Est G22 97 C4
Bardowie St
Glasgow G22 97 B4
Glasgow G22 97 C4
Bardrain Ave PA5 112 C2
BARDRAINNEY 68 F6
Bardrainney Ave PA14 68 F7
Bardrain Rd PA2 133 C7
Bardrill Dr G64 77 E1
Bardykes Rd
Blantyre G72 140 C1
Hamilton G72 161 B8
Barefield St ML9 185 A4
Barfillan Dr G52 115 E5
Barga Gdns KA21 205 F3
Bargany Ct G53 115 A1
Bargany Pl
8 Glasgow G53 115 A1
Glasgow G53 115 B1
Bargany Rd G53 115 A1
Bargaran Rd G53 115 B3
BARGARRAN 72 F3
Bargarran Prim Sch PA8 72 F2
Bargarran Rd PA8 72 F3
Bargarran Sq PA8 73 A3
Bargarron Dr PA3 114 A8
Barge Ct G84 15 D5
BARGEDDIE 121 A4
Bargeddie Prim Sch
G69 121 A6
Bargeddie St G33 98 D2
Bargeddie Sta G69 121 A4
Bargeny KA13 207 B2
Bargrennan Rd KA10 229 G6
Barhill La G65 59 F4
Bar Hill Pl G65 60 B8
Barhill Rd PA8 73 A2
Bar Hill Roman Fort★
G65 60 B4
Barhill Terr G65 60 A4
Barholm Sq G33 99 D1
Barholm St G33 99 D1
Barke Rd G67 62 A3
Barkin Ct FK1 42 B2
Barkly Terr 2 G75 180 C8
Barlae Ave G76 178 E8
BARLANARK 119 E6
Barlanark Ave G32 119 C6
Barlanark Cres G33 119 D7
Barlanark Dr G33 119 D7
Barlanark Pl
Glasgow G33 119 E7
Glasgow, Greenfield G32 119 B6
Barlanark Rd G33 119 E7
Barlandfauld St G65 60 E7
Barleith Ct KA1 228 F5
BARLEYBANK 79 D8
Barleyhill FK4 40 B5
Barlia Dr G45 137 E3
Barlia Gdns G45 137 E3
Barlia Gr G45 137 E3
Barlia Sports Complex
G45 137 E3
Barlia St G45 137 E3
Barlia Terr G45 137 F3
Barlia Way G45 137 F3
Barloan Cres G82 50 A5
Barloan Pl G82 50 A5
Barloch Ave G62 55 A2
Barloch Rd G62 55 B2
Barloch St G22 97 C4
Barlogan Ave G52 115 E5
Barlogan Quadrant G52 115 E5
Barmore Ave ML8 202 A8
Barmouth Ave PA19 44 F5
BARMULLOCH 98 D4
Barmulloch Prim Sch
G21 98 C4
Barmulloch Rd G21 98 B4
Barnard Gdns G64 78 B4
Barnbeth Rd G53 115 B2
Barncluith Ave ML3 163 A2
Barncluith Bsns Ctr ML3 162 F3
Barncluith Ct ML3 162 F3
Barncluith Rd ML3 162 F2
Barnego Rd FK6 21 D3
Barness Pl G33 119 A8
Barnes St G78 134 B2
Barnett Cres KA21 216 F7
Barnett Ct KA21 216 F7
Barnett Path 3 G72 161 D7
Barnflat St G73 118 B1
Barnford Cres KA7 239 A2
Barn Gn PA10 111 A3
BARNHILL 161 B8
Barnhill Ct G77 156 D3
Barnhill Dr
Glasgow G21 98 A3
Hamilton ML3 161 D2
Newton Mearns G77 156 D2
Tullibody FK10 4 C2
Barnhill Rd G82 50 D3
Barnhill St PA15 46 C3
Barnhill Sta G21 98 A3
Barnkirk Ave G15 75 A3
Barn Rd FK8 7 A8
Barns Cres KA7 238 F8
Barnscroft PA5, PA10 111 B4
Barnsdale Rd FK7 7 A3
Barnsford Ave PA4 93 B4
Barnsford Rd
Inchinnan PA4 93 B3
Paisley PA3 113 B8
Barns Pk KA7 238 F8
Barns St
Ayr KA7 238 F8
Clydebank G81 94 C8
Barns Street La KA7 238 F8
Barns Terr KA7 238 F8
Barnswood Pl 6 G71 141 B3
Barnton La FK1 42 B4
Barnton St
Glasgow G32 118 E7
Stirling FK8 7 B8
Barnweil Ave KA9 236 C6
Barnweil Dr KA1 228 E5
Barnweil Rd KA1 227 E5
Barnwell Rd FK9 2 C4
Barnwell Terr G51 115 E7
Barochan Cres PA3 113 A4
Barochan Pl G53 115 B3
Barochan Rd
Bellshill ML4 142 D6
Brookfield PA3, PA6, PA10,
PA11 111 D6
Glasgow G53 115 B3
Houston PA6 91 B6
Barochan Way PA3 113 A4
Baronald Dr G12 96 B6
Baronald Gate G12 96 B6
Baronald St G73 118 B1
Baron Ct ML3 163 A2
Barone Dr G76 157 C8
Baronhall Dr G72 161 C8
Baronhill G67 62 B5
Baron Path G69 120 F5
Baron Rd PA3 114 A6
Baronscourt Dr PA1 112 F4
Baronscourt Gdns PA1 112 F4
Baronscourt Rd PA1 112 F4
Barons Gate G71 140 E4
Baron's Haugh RSPB Nature
Reserve★ ML1 163 E2
Barons Rd ML1 164 C2
Baron St PA4 94 C2
Barons Twr ML1 164 B3
Barony Ct
Ardrossan KA22 205 D1
Cambusbarron FK7 6 D6
4 Glasgow G69 120 B6
Irvine KA11 219 F5
Barony Dr G69 120 B5
Barony Gdns G69 120 B5
Barony Glebe KA23 190 D5
Barony Gr 4 G72 139 E3
Barony Pl G68 60 E1
Barony Rd KA9 236 C6
Barony Terr KA25 170 A8
Barony Wynd 5 G69 120 B6
Barra Ave
Coatbridge ML5 121 E4
Renfrew PA4 94 C1
Wishaw ML2 165 E5
BARRACHNIE 119 E4
Barrachnie Ave G69 120 A6
Barrachnie Cres G69 119 F5
Barrachnie Ct G69 119 F6
Barrachnie Dr G69 120 A5
Barrachnie Gr G69 120 A6
Barrachnie Pl 4 G69 120 A6
Barrachnie Rd G69 119 F5
Barrack St
Glasgow G4 241 C1
Hamilton ML3 162 D4
Barra Cres
Irvine KA11 220 C2
Old Kilpatrick G60 73 C5
Barra Dr ML6 123 E6
Barra Gdns G60 73 C5
Barra La KA11 220 C2
Barra Pl
Coatbridge ML5 121 E4
Irvine KA11 220 C2
Stenhousemuir FK5 24 A4
Stevenston KA20 206 F2
Barra Rd G60 73 C5
Barras Mkt The G4 241 C1
Barra St G20 96 C8
Barraston Holdings G64 57 A3
Barraston Rd
Fluchter G64 56 F4
Torrance G64 57 A2
Barr Ave
Crosshouse KA2 221 F4
Knockentiber KA2 221 F4
Neilston G78 154 E8
Barra Wynd KA11 220 C2
Barrbridge Rd ML5 121 B4
Barrcraig Rd PA11 110 C8
Barr Cres
Clydebank G81 74 B5
Irvine KA12 219 C4
Barr Farm Rd G65 60 E7
Barr Gr G71 141 A8
BARRHEAD 134 E2
Barrhead High Sch G78 134 D3
Barrhead Rd
Glasgow G43, G53 135 C7
Newton Mearns G77 156 B5
Paisley PA2 114 A2
Barrhead Sp Ctr G78 134 C3
Barrhead Sta G78 134 B3
Barrhill Cres PA10 111 C3
Barrhill Ct G66 80 A8
Barrhill Rd
Erskine PA8 73 A2
Gourock PA19 44 D8
Kirkintilloch G66 80 A8
Barriedale Ave ML3 162 B3
Barrie Quadrant G81 74 A4
Barrie Rd
East Kilbride G74 160 D5
Glasgow G52 115 A7
Stenhousemuir FK5 23 F3
Barrie St ML1 163 E6
Barrie Terr KA22 205 D1
Barrington Ave KA15 150 B1
Barrington Dr G4 96 F2
Barrington Gdns KA15 150 C1
Barrisdale Rd
Glasgow G20 96 D8
Wishaw ML2 165 F6
Barrisdale Way G73 138 B4
Barrland Ct G46 136 C3
Barrland Dr G46 136 C3
Barrland St G41 117 A3
BARRMILL 171 F3
Barrmill Rd
Beith KA15 171 C8
Burnhouse KA15 172 B2
Glasgow G43 136 B5
Barrochan Intc PA5 111 E4
BARROWFIELD
Coatbridge 122 A4
Glasgow 118 B5
Barrowfield Gate G40 118 B4
Barrowfield Pl G40 118 B4
Barrowfield St
Coatbridge ML5 121 F4
Glasgow G40 118 A5
Barrpath G65 60 F7
Barr Pl
Newton Mearns G77 156 C5
Paisley PA1 113 D4
Barr's Brae
Kilmacolm PA13 69 D1
Port Glasgow PA14 68 C8
Barrs Brae La PA14 47 C1
Barrs Cres G82 48 A8
Barrs Ct G82 26 A1
Barrs La ML8 187 F3
Barrs Rd G82 48 A8
Barr St
Ardrossan KA22 205 C1
Glasgow G20 97 A3
Motherwell ML1 163 E8
Barrs Terr G82 48 A8
Barr Terr G74 159 E2
Barr Thomson Bsns Pk
KA1 228 A6
BARRWOOD 60 E8
Barrwood Pl G71 141 A8
Barrwood St G33 98 E2
Barry Gdns G72 161 D6
Barsail Prim Sch PA8 93 C8
Barscube Ave PA14 68 E7
Barscube Terr PA2 114 A2
Barshaw Ct G52 114 E6
Barshaw Dr PA1 114 A6
Barshaw Ho PA1 114 C5
Barshaw Pl PA1 114 D5
Barshaw Rd G52 114 F6
Barskiven Rd PA1 112 F4
Barterholm Rd PA2 113 F2
Bartholomew St G40 118 A3
Bartiebeith Rd G33 119 E7
Bartie Gdns ML9 185 F1
Bartlands Pl G76 178 F4
Barton Ave G83 28 A8
Bartonhall Rd ML2 165 D1
Bartonholm Terr KA13 207 F1
Barty's Rd ML4 142 C5
Barwheys Dr KA6 237 F6
Barwood Dr PA8 73 A3
Barwood Hill G82 50 B6
Bassett Ave G13 95 B8
Bassett Cres G13 95 B8
Bastion Wynd 7 FK8 7 B7
Bathgate St G31 118 A6
Bathgo Ave PA1 114 E4
Bath La G2 240 B3
Bathlin Cres 5 G69 81 A3
Bath Pl KA7 238 E8
Bath Sq KA22 216 C8
Bath St
Glasgow G2 240 C3
Gourock PA19 44 E8
Kilmarnock KA3 222 F3
Bathurst Dr KA7 239 A1
Bath Villas KA22 216 C8
Bathville Rd KA25 149 A1
Baton Rd ML7 146 D6
Batson St G42 117 B2
Batterflatts Gdns FK7 6 F6
Batterflatts Ho FK7 6 F6
Battery Park Ave PA16 45 B8
Battery Park Dr PA16 45 B8
Battismains ML11 215 C4
BATTLEFIELD 137 A7
Battlefield Ave G42 137 A7
Battlefield Ct G42 137 B7
Battlefield Gdns G42 137 A8
Battlefield Prim Sch
G42 136 F7
Battlefield Rd G42 137 A7
Battle Pl G42 136 F8
Battles Burn Dr G32 119 A2
Battles Burn Gate G32 119 A2
Battles Burn View G32 119 A2
Bavelaw St G33 99 D2
Bawhirley Rd PA15 46 C3
Baxter Brae ML1 165 B8
Baxter Cres FK6 21 C1
Baxter La
Alexandria G83 27 E7
Lanark ML11 215 A4
Baxter St
Fallin FK7 8 D4
Greenock PA15 46 D3
Baxters Wynd FK1 42 B4
Baxter Wynd ML2 164 E2
Bayfield Ave G15 75 A3
Bayfield Terr G15 75 A3
Bayne St FK8 2 A1
Bay St PA14 47 C1
Bay View Rd PA19 44 F7
Bay Willow Ct G72 139 F4
Beach Dr KA12 218 F1
Beach Rd
Troon KA10 229 D7
Troon KA10 229 E5
Beaconcroft FK9 2 C7
Beaconhurst Sch FK9 2 C6
Beacon Pl G33 118 F8
Beaconsfield Rd G12 96 B5
Beagle Cres KA7 238 C3
Bean Row FK1 42 B4
BEANSBURN 223 A2
Beansburn KA3 223 A3
Beanshields Rd ML8 201 F4
Beard Cres G69 101 A5
Beardmore Cotts PA4 93 E6
Beardmore Pl G81 73 E3
Beardmore St G81 73 E3
Beardmore Way
Clydebank G81 73 D2
Glasgow G31 118 B6
Bearford Dr G52 115 B6
Bearhope St PA15 45 F5
BEARSDEN 75 E6
Bearsden Acad G61 75 D7
Bearsden Bath House★
G61 75 F5
Bearsden Prim Sch G61 75 E5
Bearsden Rd
Bearsden G61 95 F7
Bearsden G61 95 F8
Bearsden Sta G61 75 E4
Bearside Rd FK7 7 A3
Beaton Ave FK7 7 C1
Beaton La KA2 225 F1
Beaton Rd
Balloch G83 27 E8
Glasgow G41 116 E2
Beaton St ML9 184 F5
Beaton Terr KA12 219 C5
Beatrice Dr ML1 142 F5
Beatrice Gdns PA6 111 D8
Beatson Wynd G71 121 A1
Beattie Ct KA20 217 D7
Beattock St G31 118 D5

Beattock Wynd ML3 162 A3
Beatty Ave FK8 2 A2
Beatty Pl G84 17 A2
Beatty St G81 73 E3
Beauclerc St FK12 5 A7
Beaufield Gdns KA3 222 B7
Beaufort Ave G43 136 C6
Beaufort Dr
Falkirk FK2 24 A3
Kirkintilloch G66 79 B8
Beaufort Gdns G64 77 E1
Beauly Cres
Airdrie ML6 123 E6
Kilmacolm PA13 89 D7
Kilmarnock KA1 228 A5
Newton Mearns G77 157 B4
Wishaw ML2 165 B1
Beauly Ct FK1 42 C1
Beauly Dr PA2 112 E1
Beauly Pl
Bishopbriggs G64 78 D2
Chryston G69 80 D1
Coatbridge ML5 122 B3
East Kilbride G74 159 D2
6 Glasgow G20 96 D6
Motherwell ML1 143 A5
Beauly Rd G69 120 A3
Beaumont Dr FK2 24 B2
Beaumont Gate 5 G12 96 C3
Beckfield Cres G33 98 D7
Beckfield Dr G33 98 D7
Beckfield Gate G33 98 D7
Beckfield Gr G33 98 D7
Beckfield Wlk G33 98 D7
Beckford La ML3 162 D5
Beckford Prim Sch ML3 162 C5
Beckford St Bsns Ctr
ML3 162 D5
Beckford St ML3 162 D5
Bedale Rd G69 119 F4
Beda Pl FK7 8 C5
Bedcow View G66 79 F7
Bedford Ave G81 74 D2
Bedford Ct FK10 10 A6
Bedford La 6 G5 117 B5
Bedford Pl FK10 10 A6
Bedford St
Glasgow G5 117 B5
Greenock PA16 45 D7
Bedlay Ct G69 81 A3
Bedlay Pl ML5 81 F1
Bedlay View G71 141 B8
Bedlay Wlk 14 G69 81 A3
Bedlormie Dr EH48 107 C2
Beech Ave
Bearsden G61 76 A7
Beith KA15 150 B2
Bridge of Weir PA11 90 D1
Cambuslang G72 138 F6
Elderslie PA5 112 C2
Glasgow, Dumbreck G41 116 B4
Glasgow, Garrowhill G69 120 A5
Glasgow, Ibrox G41 116 B5
Irvine KA12 219 D2
Kilmarnock KA1 227 D8
Larkhall ML9 185 D2
Motherwell ML1 143 B3
Newton Mearns G77 156 E4
Paisley PA2 114 A1
Plean FK7 12 C3
Quarter ML3 183 F4
Rutherglen G73 138 C4
Beechbank Ave ML6 102 F1
Beechburn Cres PA12 129 D3
Beech Cres
Cambuslang G72 139 E4
Denny FK6 21 C3
Larbert FK5 41 C8
Motherwell ML1 143 D7
Newton Mearns G77 156 E4
Beech Dr
Caldercruix ML6 104 F4
Clydebank G81 74 A5
Beeches Ave G81 73 F6
Beeches Rd G81 73 F6
Beeches Terr G81 74 A6
Beeches The
Brookfield PA5 111 C6
3 Hamilton G72 161 C7
Houston PA6 91 D1
Lanark ML11 215 B2
Newton Mearns G77 156 F6
Beechfield Dr ML8 202 A8
Beechfield Rd KA15 170 F7
Beech Gdns
Glasgow G69 120 A5
Stirling FK7 6 F6
Beech Gr
Ayr KA8 239 C8
East Kilbride G75 180 B6
Gartcosh G69 101 A5
Law ML8 186 F6
Rhu G84 15 D6
Wishaw ML2 165 C7
Beechgrove G69 80 F2
Beechgrove Ave G71 141 C7
Beechgrove Pl G84 25 C8
Beechgrove Quadrant
ML1 143 A5
Beechgrove St G40 118 B2
Beech La FK9 2 B4
Beechlands Ave G44 136 F1
Beechlands Dr G76 157 C6
Beechmount Ct ML7 147 B2
Beechmount Rd G66 79 D4
Beech Pl
Bishopbriggs G64 98 B8
Gourock PA19 44 C6
Beech Rd
Bishopbriggs G64 98 B8
Johnstone PA5 111 D1
Kirkintilloch G66 79 C6
Beech Terr ML9 185 B1
Beechtree Terr G66 58 C6
Beechwood
Alloa FK10 5 E1
Kilwinning KA13 207 D5
Larkhall ML9 185 A5
Sauchie FK10 5 D1
Wishaw ML2 164 D1
Beechwood Ave
Clarkston G76 157 C6
Hamilton ML3 183 B8
Langbank PA14 70 C7
Rutherglen G73 138 C6
Beechwood Cres ML2 165 C2
Beechwood Ct
Bearsden G61 75 F3
Cumbernauld G67 82 F8
1 Lanark ML11 215 C3
Beechwood Dr
Bonhill G83 28 B2
Coatbridge ML5 122 D5
Glasgow G11 95 F4
Renfrew PA4 94 C1
Beechwood Gate 2
ML11 215 C3
Beechwood Gdns
Bellshill ML4 142 C4
Moodiesburn G69 80 F1
Stirling FK8 7 A5
Beechwood Gr G78 134 C1
Beechwood La 7 G61 75 F3
Beechwood Paddock
KA10 230 B4
Beechwood Pl
Bellshill ML4 142 C4
Glasgow G11 95 F4
Beechwood Rd G67 82 F8
Beechworth Dr ML1 143 D2
Beecraigs Way ML6 104 A3
Beecroft Pl G72 140 E1
Begg Ave FK1 41 E4
Beggs Terr KA22 205 D3
Beil Dr G13 94 F7
BEITH 150 B1
Beith Dr ML6 123 A4
Beith Prim Sch KA15 171 B8
Beith Rd
Barrmill KA15 171 F4
Dalry KA24 191 E8
Glengarnock KA14 170 C6
Greenock PA16 45 E2
Johnstone PA9, PA10, PA5 131 B7
Johnstone, Quarrelton
PA5 111 E1
Beith St G11 96 B1
Beith Way G72 161 D2
Belfast Quay KA12 219 A2
Belford Ct G77 156 D2
Belford Gr G77 156 D2
Belgowan St ML4 141 F7
Belgrave La G12 96 E3
Belgrave St ML4 141 F6
Belhaven Ct G77 156 D2
Belhaven Pk G69 100 C7
Belhaven Pl
Glenboig ML5 101 F6
Newton Mearns G77 156 D2
Belhaven Rd
Hamilton ML3 161 E3
Wishaw ML2 165 A3
Belhaven St PA14 47 B2
Belhaven Terr
20 Glasgow G12 96 C4
Wishaw ML2 165 A3
Belhaven Terrace La 19
G12 96 C4
Belhaven Terrace West La 17
G12 96 C4
Belhaven Terr W 18 G12 96 C4
BELLAHOUSTON 116 A4
Bellahouston Acad G41 116 C5
Bellahouston Dr G52 115 E3
Bellahouston L Ctr G52 115 F4
Bellahouston Pk* G41 115 F4
Bellahouston Prim Sch 2
G51 116 C5
Bellairs Pl G72 140 C1
Bellard Rd KA23 190 C4
Bellard Wlk KA23 190 D4
Bellas Pl ML6 104 A2
Bellaville Gr G69 100 D8
Bellcote Rd G68 61 D5
Bellcraig Ct G76 158 A5
Bell Cres KA12 219 D5
Bell Ct FK2 42 C7
Bell Dr G72 161 C4
Belleaire Dr PA16 45 C7
Bellefield Cres ML11 215 A6
Bellefield Rd ML11 215 A5
Bellefield Way ML11 215 A6
BELLEISLE 238 E3
Belleisle Ave G71 140 E7
Belleisle Cl KA13 207 C4
Belleisle Cotts KA7 238 D3
Belleisle Cres PA11 110 C6
Belleisle Ct G68 61 E4
Belleisle Dr G68 61 E4
Belleisle Gdns G68 61 E4
Belleisle Gr G68 61 E4
Belleisle Pk* KA7 238 E3
Belleisle Pl
Gourock PA19 44 A6
Kilmarnock KA1 227 E4
Belleisle St G42 117 B1
Bellesleyhill Ave KA8 236 B3
Bellesleyhill Ct KA8 236 A4
Bellesleyhill Rd KA8 236 A3
Bellevale Ave KA7 239 A5
Bellevale Quadrant KA7 238 F5
Bellevue Ave G66 79 B8
Bellevue Cotts KA7 238 F7
Bellevue Cres
Ayr KA7 238 F7
Prestwick KA9 236 C7
Bellevue Gdns KA1 222 D1
Bellevue La KA7 238 F7
Bellevue Pk FK10 9 E6
Bellevue Rd
Alloa FK10 9 F6
Ayr KA7 238 F7
Kilmarnock KA1 222 D1
Kirkintilloch G66 79 B8
Prestwick KA9 236 C7
Bellevue St
Ayr KA7 238 F7
Falkirk FK1 42 C4
BELLFIELD 228 B4
Bellfield Ave KA1 228 D6
Bellfield Cres G78 134 B3
Bellfield Ct
Barrhead G78 134 B4
Hurlford KA1 228 D6
Bellfield Dr ML2 165 C1
Bellfield Intc KA1 228 C6
Bellfield La KA9 236 B8
Bellfield Prim Sch 1
KA1 228 A4
Bellfield Rd
Bannockburn FK7 7 E1
Kirkintilloch G66 79 B8
Stirling FK8 7 B5
Bellfield St G31 118 A6
Bellflower Ave G53 135 C3
Bellflower Ct G74 159 C3
Bellflower Gdns G53 135 C3
Bellflower Gr G74 159 C4
Bellflower Pl G53 135 C3
Bell Gr ML8 187 B6
Bell Green E G75 180 F8
Bell Green W G75 180 E8
Bellgrove St G31 117 F6
Bellgrove Sta G31 117 F6
Bellisle Terr ML3 183 B8
Bellmans Cl KA15 150 B1
Bellrock Ave KA9 236 B6
Bellrock Cres G33 119 A8
Bellrock Ct G33 119 B8
Bellrock Rd KA8 236 A4
Bellrock St G33 119 B8
Bellrock View G33 119 A8
Bellscroft Ave G73 137 F7
Bellsdyke Hospl FK5 23 D5
Bellsdyke Pl FK5 23 A3
Bellsdyke Rd
Airdrie ML6 123 A6
Falkirk FK2 24 C6
Stenhousemuir FK5 23 D4
Bellsdyke Rdbt FK5 23 B3
Bellsfield Dr G72 161 E6
Bellshaugh Ct G12 96 C5
Bellshaugh Gdns G12 96 C5
Bellshaugh La G12 96 C5
Bellshaugh Pl 2 G12 96 C5
Bellshaugh Rd G12 96 C4
BELLSHILL 142 B4
Bellshill Acad ML4 142 B5
Bellshill Ind Est ML4 141 F6
Bellshill Rd
Bellshill G71, ML1, ML4 141 D2
Bothwell G71 141 B5
Motherwell ML1 142 C2
Bellshill Sta ML4 142 A5
BELLSIDE 144 E1
Bellside Rd
Chapelhall ML6 123 F2
Cleland ML1 144 D1
Motherwell ML1 144 A8
Bellsland Dr KA1 227 F6
Bellsland Gr KA1 227 F6
Bellsland Pl KA1 228 A7
Bellsmeadow Rd FK1 42 C4
BELLSMYRE 50 B6
Bellsmyre Ave G82 50 A6
Bell St
Airdrie ML6 122 F7
Bellshill ML4 142 B7
Clydebank G81 94 D7
Glasgow G1 241 B1
Greenock PA15 46 E2
Renfrew PA4 94 D4
Wishaw ML2 165 A3
Bellstone Cotts KA24 192 B8
Bells Wynd ML11 215 C5
Bell's Wynd
Falkirk FK1 42 B4
Lanark ML11 215 C5
Belltree Ave KA3 211 D8
Belltrees Cres PA3 113 A4
Belltrees Rd
Howwood PA9 130 C2
Lochwinnoch PA12 150 D4
Bell View ML2 166 A6
Bell View Ct PA4 94 D4
Bellvue Cres ML4 141 F4
Bellvue Way ML5 122 D4
Bellwood St G41 136 E8
Bellziehill Rd ML4 141 E5
Belmar Ct PA3 112 C5
BELMONT 239 A4
Belmont Acad KA7 239 B5
Belmont Ave
Ayr KA7 239 A5
Bonnybridge FK4 39 D5
Shieldhill FK1 66 E7
Uddingston G71 140 E7
Belmont Cres
Ayr KA7 239 A5
Glasgow G12 96 E3
Kilmaurs KA3 222 B7
Belmont Ct
Kilmaurs KA3 222 C7
6 Kirkintilloch G66 79 D8
Belmont Dr
Ayr KA7 239 A5
Barrhead G78 134 D1
East Kilbride G75 180 B8
Glasgow G46 136 B3
Rutherglen G73 138 B7
Shotts ML7 147 B2
Belmont House Sch G77 157 A6
Belmont La G12 96 E3
Belmont Place E KA7 239 A6
Belmont Place W KA7 239 A6
Belmont Rd
Ayr KA7 239 A5
Cambuslang G72 138 E3
Glasgow G21 97 F6
Kilmacolm PA13 89 C7
Paisley PA3 114 A6
Belmont St
Clydebank G81 94 B8
Coatbridge ML5 101 D1
Falkirk FK1 42 C4
Glasgow G12 96 E3
Kilsyth G65 36 C1
Overtown ML2 186 B6
Belmont Twr FK1 42 C4
Belses Dr G52 115 C5
Belses Gdns G52 115 C5
Belstane Gate ML8 188 A3
Belstane Mews ML8 188 A3
Belstane Pk ML8 187 F3
Belstane Pl 4 G71 141 A3
Belstane Rd
Carluke ML8 188 A3
Cumbernauld G67 82 F5
Belsyde Ave G15 75 B2
Beltane St
Glasgow G3 240 A3
Wishaw ML2 165 A2
Beltonfoot Way ML2 164 F2
Beltrees Ave G53 115 A2
Beltrees Cres G53 115 A2
Beltrees Rd G53 115 A1
Belvidere Ave G31 118 C4
Belvidere Cres
Bellshill ML4 142 B4
Bishopbriggs G64 78 B2
Belvidere Gate G31 118 C4
Belvidere Prim Sch ML4 142 A4
Belvidere Rd ML4 142 A4
Belvidere Terr KA8 236 A2
Belville Ave PA15 46 C3
Belville Dr PA15 46 B3
Belville St PA15 46 B3
Belvoir Pl G72 161 D8
Bemersyde G64 78 C2
Bemersyde Ave G43 136 B5
Bemersyde Pl ML9 185 A1
Bemersyde Rd PA2 132 E8
Ben Aigan Pl G53 135 C4
Ben Alder Dr PA2 114 D1
Benalder St G11 96 C1
Benarty Gdns G64 78 B2
Benbain Pl KA11 220 B6
Benbecula G74 160 C1
Benbecula Rd KA3 223 A5
Ben Bouie Dr G84 16 F1
Benbow Rd G81 73 F2
Ben Buie Way PA2 114 D1
Bencleuch Pl KA11 220 B3
Bencloich Ave G66 57 E8
Bencloich Cres G66 33 E1
Bencloich Rd G66 57 E8
Benclutha PA14 47 E1
Bencroft Dr G44 137 E5
Bendigo Pl ML11 215 A4
Ben Donich Pl G53 135 D4
Ben Edra Pl G53 135 D4
Benford Ave ML1 143 D4
Benford Knowe ML1 143 E4
Bengairn St G31 118 C7
Bengal Pl 2 G43 136 C7
Bengal St G43 136 C7
Ben Garrisdale Pl G53 135 D4
Ben Glas Pl G53 135 D4
Benhar Pl G33 118 F8
Benhar Rd ML7 147 A6
Benholm St G32 118 F3
Ben Hope Ave PA2 114 D2
Ben Laga Pl G53 135 D4
Ben Lawers Dr
Cumbernauld G68 61 B2
Paisley PA2 114 D2
Ben Ledi Ave PA2 114 D2
Ben Ledi Cres G68 61 B2
Ben Lomond Dr FK9 2 A4
Ben Lomond Wlk G83 19 D1
Ben Lomond Wlk G83 27 D8
Ben Loyal Ave PA2 114 D2
Ben Lui Dr PA2 114 D1
Ben Lui Pl
Cumbernauld G68 61 B2
Glasgow G53 135 D4
Ben MacDui Gdns G53 135 D4
Benmore KA9 236 C5
Ben More Dr
Cumbernauld G68 61 A2
Paisley PA2 114 D1
Benmore La PA16 44 E3
Benmore Terr G72 138 E3
Bennan Ho KA9 236 B5
Bennan Pl G75 180 C4
Bennan Sq G42 117 C2
Benn Ave PA1 114 A4
Ben Nevis Rd PA2 114 C1
Ben Nevis Way G68 61 B2
Bennie Terr FK1 86 B7
Bennoch Pl KA9 236 D5
Benny Lynch Ct G5 117 C5
Ben Oss Pl G53 135 C4
Benrig Ave KA3 222 B8
Bensley Ave KA11 219 F5
Bensley Rise KA11 219 F5
BENSLIE 208 F3
Benslie Row KA13 208 F2
Benson St ML5 122 A4
Benston Rd PA5 111 E1
Bent Cres G71 141 C6
Bentfield Ave KA7 238 E6
Bentfield Dr KA9 236 B6
Bentfoot Rd ML2 186 C7
Benthall St G5 117 D4
Bentheads FK7 11 E8
Bentinck Cres KA10 229 F1
Bentinck Dr KA10 229 E1
Bentinck Grange G75 179 D8
Bentinck St
Glasgow G3 96 E1
Greenock PA16 45 D8
Kilmarnock KA1 227 F7
Bent Rd
Chapelhall ML6 123 D3
Hamilton ML3 162 D3
Bents Rd G69 120 B5
Bent View ML9 200 B3
Benty's La ML8 201 F8
Ben Uird Pl G53 135 D4
Ben Vane Ave PA2 114 C1
Ben Venue Rd G68 61 A2
Ben Venue Way PA2 114 D1
Benvie Gdns G64 78 B2
Benview FK7 7 C2
Benview Ave PA14 68 F8
Benview Rd
Clarkston G76 157 E7
Port Glasgow PA14 68 F8
Benview St G20 96 F4
Benview Terr
Fishcross FK10 5 E4
Paisley PA2 114 B2
Ben Vorlich Dr G53 135 D4
Ben Vorlich Pl G53 135 D4
Benvue Rd G66 57 E7
Ben Wyvis Dr PA2 114 C1
Berchem Pl KA21 216 F8
Bereland Ave KA9 236 D8
Berelands Cres G73 137 E7
Berelands Gdns KA9 233 D1
Berelands Pl G73 137 F7
Berelands Rd KA9 233 D1
Berenice Pl G82 50 C2
Beresford Ave G14 95 E4
Beresford Ct KA7 238 F7
Beresford Gr KA11 219 E5
Beresford La KA7 238 F7
Beresford Terr KA7 238 F7
Berkeley St
Glasgow G3 240 A3
Stirling FK7 7 A4
Berkeley Terrace La G3 240 A3
Berkley Dr G72 140 D1
Berl Ave PA6 111 C8
Bernadette Cres ML1 143 D2
Bernadette St ML1 143 D3
Bernard Path G40 118 A4
Bernard's Ct 21 ML11 215 A4
Bernard St G40 118 A4
Bernard's Wynd 20 ML11 215 A4
Bernard Terr G40 118 A4
Bernera Pl KA3 222 F6
Berneray St G22 97 C7
Bernisdale Dr G15 74 D3
Bernisdale Gdns 7 G15 74 D3
Bernisdale Pl 1 G15 74 D3
Berridale Ave G44 137 A5
Berridale Rd KA10 229 E7
Berriedale G75 179 E8
Berriedale Ave G69 120 A4
Berriedale Cres G72 161 C3
Berriedale Path G72 161 C3
Berriedale Quadrant
ML2 165 B5
Berriedale Terr G72 161 C3
Berryburn Rd G21 98 C4
Berry Dr KA12 219 E3
Berryhill FK7 12 E7
Berryhill Ave KA11 220 B6
Berryhill Cres ML2 164 F2
Berryhill Dr G46 136 B2
Berryhill Pl ML7 147 B2
Berryhill Prim Sch ML2 164 E3
Berryhill Rd
Cumbernauld G67 61 E2
Glasgow G46 136 B2
Berryknowe G66 80 B7
Berryknowe Ave G69 100 C7
Berryknowes Ave G52 115 D5
Berryknowes La G52 115 C5
Berryknowes Rd G52 115 C5
Berryyards Rd PA15 45 F3
Bertram Dr ML7 125 C2
Bertram Pl ML7 146 D5

Brent Gdns
Glasgow G46 . . . . **135** F5
Thornliebank G46 . . . . **136** A5
Brentham Ave FK8 . . . . **7** B5
Brentham Cres FK8 . . . . **7** B5
Brent Rd
East Kilbride G74. . . . . **159** E3
Glasgow G46 . . . . **135** F5
Thornliebank G46 . . . . **136** A5
Brent Way G46 . . . . **135** F5
Brentwood Ave G53. . . . . **135** B4
Brentwood Dr G53 . . . . . . **135** B4
Brentwood Sq G53. . . . . . **135** B4
Brereton St G42 . . . . **117** C1
Breslin Terr ML7. . . . . **127** C5
Bressay G74 . . . . **159** E4
Bressay Cl G33 . . . . **119** E6
Bressay Gr
Cambuslang G72 . . . . **138** E3
Glasgow G33. . . . . **119** E6
Bressay Pl
Glasgow G33. . . . . **119** E6
Kilmarnock KA3 . . . . **223** B5
Bressay Rd G33. . . . . **119** E6
Bressay Wynd 14 ML2 . . . **165** F6
Breton Ct FK1 . . . . **42** C3
Breval Cres G81 . . . . **74** A7
Breval Ct G69. . . . . **120** C4
Brewery Rd 4 KA1. . . . . . **227** F7
Brewery St PA5 . . . . **111** F3
Brewhouse Ct 5 FK10 . . . **10** B6
Brewlands Cres KA1 . . . . **231** C4
Brewlands Dr KA1 . . . . . . **231** C4
Brewlands Rd KA1 . . . . . . **231** D4
Brewster Ave PA3. . . . . . . **114** A7
Brewster Pl
Denny FK6 . . . . **21** C2
Irvine KA11 . . . . **224** H6
Briar Bank G66 . . . . **58** B5
Briarbush Way 12 G72. . . **161** C7
Briarcroft Dr G33 . . . . **98** D7
Briarcroft Pl G33 . . . . **98** E6
Briarcroft Rd G33. . . . . **98** D6
Briar Dr G81. . . . . **74** B4
Briar Gdns G43 . . . . **136** D5
Briar Gr
Ayr KA7 . . . . **239** C4
Glasgow G43 . . . . **136** D5
Briarhill Ct KA9. . . . . **236** D8
Briarhill Rd KA9 . . . . **236** D8
Briarhill St KA9 . . . . **236** C8
Briarlea Dr G46. . . . . **136** C4
Briar Neuk G64 . . . . **98** B8
Briar Pl PA19 . . . . **44** D6
Briar Rd
Alloa FK10. . . . . **4** E2
Glasgow G43 . . . . **136** D5
Kirkintilloch G66 . . . . **79** F8
Briarwell La G62. . . . . **55** B1
Briarwell Rd G62. . . . . **55** B1
Briar Wlk G66 . . . . **80** A8
Briarwood Ct G32. . . . . . . **119** E2
Briarwood Rd ML2 . . . . . . **164** E4
Briary La PA14. . . . . **69** C8
Brick La 1 PA3. . . . . **113** F5
Bridesburn Pl KA3 . . . . . . **195** E1
Bridesmill Rd PA12 . . . . . **129** E5
Bridgeburn Dr G69. . . . . . . **80** F1
Bridge Cres FK6 . . . . **21** D2
Bridge End ML7. . . . . **146** C6
Bridgeford Ave ML4. . . . . **142** C7
Bridgegait G62 . . . . **76** C8
Bridgegate
Glasgow G1 . . . . **241** A1
Irvine KA12 . . . . **219** C2
Bridgehaugh Rd FK9 . . . . **2** B2
Bridgehouse Ct KA1. . . . . . **228** A2
Bridgehousehill Rd KA1 . **228** A3
Bridge La
9 Kilmarnock KA1 . . . . . . **227** F8
Paisley PA2 . . . . **113** B3
BRIDGEND
Greenock. **46** D4
Moodiesburn **80** E2
Bridgend
Bishopton PA7 . . . . **72** A3
Dalry KA24. . . . . **191** D7
Kilbirnie KA25 . . . . **149** B2
Kilwinning KA13. . . . . **207** F3
Stewarton KA3. . . . . **211** E8
Bridgend Ave PA14. . . . . . . **68** E8
Bridgend Cotts G66 . . . . . . **80** A7
Bridgend Cres G69. . . . . . . **80** E2
Bridgend Ct G68 . . . . **38** F1
Bridgend Ind Est KA24 . . **191** D7
Bridgend La
Dalry KA24. . . . . **191** D7
Kilwinning KA13. . . . . **207** F4
Bridgend Pl G69 . . . . **80** E2
Bridgend Rd PA15 . . . . **46** C2
Bridgend View ML8 . . . . . **187** F1
Bridgend Wlk G78 . . . . . . **153** B3
BRIDGE OF ALLAN **2** A8
Bridge of Allan Prim Sch
FK9. . . . . **2** B6
Bridge of Allan Sta FK9 . . . . **1** E8
BRIDGE OF WEIR **110** E8
Bridge of Weir Prim Sch
PA11. . . . . **90** D1
Bridge of Weir Rd
Bridge of Weir PA11 . . . . . **110** F7
Brookfield PA5, PA11. . . . . **111** C5
Houston PA6 . . . . **91** B2
Kilmacolm PA13. . . . . **89** E6
Linwood PA3 . . . . **112** B5
Bridgepark KA22. . . . . **205** D2
Bridge Pl
Denny FK6 . . . . **21** C2
Bridge Pl *continued*
Milngavie G62 . . . . **55** A1
Shotts ML7. . . . . **147** A3
Bridge Rd PA14. . . . . **68** E8
Bridge St
Alexandria G83 . . . . **27** E4
Bonnybridge FK4 . . . . **40** A5
Cambuslang G72 . . . . **139** A6
Clydebank G81. . . . . **73** E3
Dumbarton G82 . . . . **49** E3
Glasgow G5 . . . . **240** C1
Hamilton ML3 . . . . **162** C2
Kilbirnie KA25 . . . . **149** B2
Linwood PA3 . . . . **112** C6
Longriggend ML6. . . . . **84** F1
Paisley PA1 . . . . **113** F4
Prestwick KA9 . . . . **236** B8
Wishaw ML2 . . . . **164** E3
Bridge Street Underground
Sta G5 . . . . **117** B5
Bridge Terr 13 FK10. . . . . . **10** B6
Bridgeton Bsns Ctr 4
G40. . . . . **117** F5
Bridgeton Cross G40. . . . **117** F4
Bridgeton Sta G40 . . . . . . **117** F4
Bridgewater Ind Pk PA8. . **73** C2
Bridgewater Sh Ctr PA8 . . **73** C2
Bridgeway Ct G66. . . . . **79** F7
Bridgeway Pl G66. . . . . **79** F7
Bridgeway Rd G66 . . . . **79** F7
Bridgeway Terr G66. . . . . . **79** F7
Bridie Terr G74 . . . . **160** C4
Brierie Ave PA6. . . . . **91** B1
Brierie Gdns PA6 . . . . **111** B8
Brierie Hill Ct PA6 . . . . . . **111** B8
Brierie-Hill Gr PA6. . . . . . **111** B8
Brierie-Hill Rd PA6 . . . . . **111** B8
Brierie La PA6 . . . . **111** A8
Brierybank Ave ML11. . . . **215** A3
Briery Ct KA25 . . . . **170** A7
Brigbrae Ave ML4. . . . . . . **142** C3
Brigham Pl G23. . . . . **96** E8
Brighton Pl G51 . . . . **116** B6
Brighton St G51 . . . . **116** B6
Brightside Ave
Port Glasgow PA14 . . . . **69** A8
Uddingston G71. . . . . **140** F5
Bright St G21. . . . . **97** F1
Brig-O-Doon Gr FK7. . . . . . **12** E7
Brig O'lea Terr G78 . . . . . **154** D6
Brigside Gdns ML3. . . . . . **163** A2
Bringan Rd KA3. . . . . **222** F5
Brisbane Ct G46 . . . . **136** D3
Brisbane Rd PA7 . . . . **72** B3
Brisbane St
Clydebank G81. . . . . **73** D4
Glasgow G42 . . . . **137** A7
Greenock PA16 . . . . **45** D6
Brisbane Terr G75 . . . . . . **180** C7
Britannia Pl KA8 . . . . **236** B2
Britannia Way
Clydebank G81. . . . . **74** B2
Renfrew PA4 . . . . **94** C1
Briton St G51. . . . . **116** B7
Brittain Way ML1 . . . . **142** F7
Broad Cairn Ct ML1 . . . . . **164** C2
Broadcroft 4 G66 . . . . **58** C1
Broadcroft Rd 5 G66 . . . . **58** C1
BROADFIELD. **69** A8
Broadfield Ave PA14 . . . . . **69** A8
Broadford St G4 . . . . **97** C2
Broadford Terr PA16 . . . . . **44** E4
Broadholm St G22 . . . . **97** C6
Broadleys Ave G64. . . . . . . **77** F2
Broadleys Bsns Pk FK7. . . . **7** D5
Broadleys Ind Pk FK7 . . . . . **7** E5
Broadleys Rd FK7 . . . . **7** D7
Broadleys Rdbt FK7 . . . . **7** D6
Broadlie Ct G78. . . . . **154** D7
Broadlie Dr
Dalry KA24. . . . . **191** A8
Glasgow G13 . . . . **95** A6
Broadlie Rd G78 . . . . **154** D7
Broadloan PA4 . . . . **94** C2
Broadmeadow Ind Est
G82. **49** F5
Broadmoss Ave G77. . . . . **157** C4
Broad St Cvn Site G40. . . **118** A5
Broadside Pl FK6 . . . . **21** D1
Broad Sq G72. . . . . **161** D8
Broad St
Alloa FK10. . . . . **10** B5
Denny FK6 . . . . **21** F2
Glasgow G40 . . . . **118** A5
Stirling FK8 . . . . **7** A8
Broadstone Ave
Greenock PA14 . . . . **46** F2
Port Glasgow PA14 . . . . **47** A1
Broadway KA22 . . . . **205** D3
Broad Way The ML2. . . . . **164** E4
BROADWOOD **60** F1
Broadwood Bsns Pk G68 . **81** F8
Broadwood Dr G44. . . . . . **137** B6
Broadwood Pk KA7 . . . . . **239** A1
Broadwood Rdbt G68 . . . . **81** F8
Broadwood Stadium (Clyde
FC) G68. . . . . **60** F1
Brockburn Cres G53 . . . . **135** B8
Brockburn Pl G53. . . . . . . **115** A2
Brockburn Rd G53 . . . . . . **115** B1
Brockburn Terr G53. . . . . **135** C8
Brockley View KA25. . . . . **149** B4
Brocklinn Pk G75 . . . . **179** E7
Brock Oval G53 . . . . **135** C6
Brock Pl
Glasgow G53 . . . . **135** C7
Stirling FK7 . . . . **7** B2
Brock Rd G53. . . . . **135** C6
Brock Terr G53 . . . . **135** C6
Brockville St G32 . . . . **118** F6
Brodick Ave
Kilwinning KA13. . . . . **207** C4
Motherwell ML1. . . . . **163** B7
Brodick Cl KA13 . . . . **207** C4
Brodick Dr
East Kilbride G74. . . . . **159** D3
Gourock PA19 . . . . **43** F5
Helensburgh G84. . . . . **16** F3
Brodick Pl
Falkirk FK1. . . . . **41** C4
Newton Mearns G77 . . . . . **156** A4
Brodick Rd KA1. . . . . **222** C2
Brodick Sq G64 . . . . **98** C7
Brodick St G21 . . . . **98** A1
Brodie Ave KA10. . . . . **229** E4
Brodie Gdns G69. . . . . . . **120** C6
Brodie Gr G69 . . . . **120** C6
Brodie Park Ave PA2. . . . . **113** E2
Brodie Park Cres PA2 . . . **113** D2
Brodie Park Gdns PA2. . . **113** E2
Brodie Pl
East Kilbride G74. . . . . **159** D3
Kilmarnock KA3 . . . . **223** C2
Stonehouse ML9 . . . . **198** E1
Brodie Rd G21. . . . . **98** D7
Brodie St FK2. . . . . **42** B8
Brogan Cres ML1 . . . . **163** B7
Broich The FK12 . . . . **4** E7
Bronte Pl FK5. . . . . **24** A3
Bron Way G67 . . . . **62** A1
Brookbank Terr ML8 . . . . **188** A1
Brooke Ave G83 . . . . **28** A8
BROOKFIELD. **111** C6
Brookfield Ave G33 . . . . . . **98** D7
Brookfield Cnr G33 . . . . . . **98** D7
Brookfield Dr G33 . . . . **98** D7
Brookfield Gate G33 . . . . . **98** D8
Brookfield Gdns G33. . . . . **98** D7
Brookfield Gr KA3 . . . . . . **213** A2
Brookfield Pl
Alva FK12. . . . . **5** A6
Glasgow G33 . . . . **98** E7
Brookfield Rd
Glasgow G33 . . . . **98** D7
Port Glasgow PA14 . . . . **68** F8
Brooklands
Alexandria G83 . . . . **27** D6
East Kilbride G74. . . . . **159** A1
Brooklands Ave G71 . . . . **140** E7
Brooklea Dr G46. . . . . **136** C5
Brooklime Dr G74. . . . . . . **159** D4
Brooklime Gdns G74 . . . . **159** C4
Brooklyn Pl ML2 . . . . **186** B7
Brookside St G40 . . . . **118** A5
Brook St
Alva FK12. . . . . **5** A7
Clydebank G81. . . . . **73** F4
Glasgow G40 . . . . **117** F5
Menstrie FK11. . . . . **3** F6
BROOM **156** F5
Broomage Ave FK5. . . . . . . **23** B3
Broomage Bank FK5 . . . . . **23** C2
Broomage Cres FK5. . . . . . **23** B3
Broomage Dr FK5 . . . . **23** B3
Broomage Pk FK5. . . . . **23** C1
Broom Ave PA8 . . . . **93** B7
Broomberry Dr PA19 . . . . . **44** E7
Broomburn Dr G77. . . . . . **157** A4
Broom Cliff G77 . . . . **156** F3
Broom Cres
Barrhead G78 . . . . **134** A5
East Kilbride G75. . . . . **180** D5
Falkirk FK1. . . . . **42** A2
Broomcroft Rd G46 . . . . . **157** A6
Broom Ct FK7 . . . . **7** C3
Broom Dr
Clydebank G81. . . . . **74** A4
Larkhall ML9 . . . . **185** A5
Broomdyke Way 2 PA3 . **113** D8
Broomelton Rd ML3, ML9 **184** D1
Broomfauld Gdns G82. . . . **50** A3
Broomfield PA6. . . . . **91** D1
Broomfield Ave
Cambuslang G72 . . . . **138** D7
Newton Mearns G77 . . . . . **156** F3
Broomfield Ct G21 . . . . **98** C3
Broomfield Gdn KA7 . . . . **238** F6
Broomfield Gdns G84 . . . . **15** C7
Broomfield La G21. . . . . . . **97** F5
Broomfield Pl G21 . . . . **97** F5
Broomfield Rd
Ayr KA7 . . . . **238** F6
Glasgow G21. . . . . **98** B4
Larkhall ML9 . . . . **199** B8
Netherburn ML9 . . . . **199** E4
Rutherglen G46 . . . . **157** A6
Broomfield St
Airdrie ML6 . . . . **123** B7
Kilwinning KA13. . . . . **207** E4
Netherburn ML9 . . . . **200** D4
Broomfield Terr G71. . . . **120** F1
Broomfield Wlk 5 G66. . . . **79** D8
Broomgate ML11. . . . . **215** A4
Broomgate Ct ML11 . . . . . **214** F4
Broom Gdns G66. . . . . **79** B6
Broomhill Ave
Glasgow G32 . . . . **139** B8
Glasgow, Whiteinch G11 . . . **95** F2
Larbert FK5 . . . . **41** C8
Newton Mearns G77 . . . . . **156** F4
Broomhill Cres
Bellshill ML4 . . . . **141** F3
Bonhill G83 . . . . **28** B1
Erskine PA8 . . . . **93** B7
Broomhill Ct
Greenock PA15 . . . . **45** E4
Broomhill Ct *continued*
Kilwinning KA13. . . . . **207** C5
4 Kirkintilloch G66. . . . . . . **58** D1
Larkhall ML9 . . . . **185** A2
Broomhill Dr
Dumbarton G82 . . . . **50** B5
Glasgow G11 . . . . **95** F3
Rutherglen G73 . . . . **138** B5
Broomhill Farm Mews
G66 . . . . **58** E1
Broomhill Gate ML9. . . . . **185** A2
Broomhill Gdns
Glasgow G11 . . . . **95** F3
Newton Mearns G77 . . . . . **156** F4
Broomhill Ind Est G66. . . . . **58** E2
Broomhill La G11 . . . . **95** F3
Broomhill Path G11 . . . . . . **95** F2
Broomhill Pl
Denny FK6 . . . . **21** D4
Glasgow G11 . . . . **95** F2
Stirling FK7 . . . . **6** E6
Broomhill Prim Sch G11 . **95** F4
Broomhill Quadrant KA1 **228** A4
Broomhill Rd
Bonnybridge FK4 . . . . **40** B4
Larkhall ML9 . . . . **185** A2
Broomhill Road E KA1. . . **228** A4
Broomhill Road W KA1 . . **227** F4
Broomhill St
Greenock PA15 . . . . **45** E4
Harthill ML7. . . . . **127** C5
Broomhill Terr G11 . . . . . . **95** F2
Broomhill View ML9 . . . . . **184** F2
Broomhill Way PA15 . . . . . **45** E4
BROOMHOUSE **120** B2
Broomhouse Cres G71 . . **120** B3
Broomieknowe FK10 . . . . . . **4** D3
Broomieknowe Dr G73 . . **138** B6
Broomieknowe Gdns
G73 . . . . **138** B6
Broomieknowe Rd G73. . **138** B6
Broomielaw G1, G2. . . . . . **240** C1
Broomknoll St ML6 . . . . . **123** A7
Broomknowe G68. . . . . **61** D3
Broomknowe Rd PA13. . . . **89** C8
Broomknowes Ave G66. . . **79** E4
Broomknowes Rd G21. . . . **98** A4
Broomknowe Terr PA13 . . **89** C8
BROOMLANDS **220** A1
Broomlands Ave PA8. . . . . **93** E8
Broomlands Busway
KA11 . . . . **220** A2
Broomlands Cres PA8. . . . **93** E8
Broomlands Ct
Irvine KA11 . . . . **220** A2
Paisley PA1 . . . . **113** C4
Broomlands Dr KA12. . . . **219** D2
Broomlands Gdns PA8 . . . **93** D8
Broomlands La PA1. . . . . . **113** B4
Broomlands Pl KA12 . . . . **219** D2
Broomlands Prim Sch
KA11. . . . . **220** A2
Broomlands Rd
Cumbernauld G67 . . . . **83** A8
Irvine KA11 . . . . **220** B1
Broomlands St PA1 . . . . . **113** C4
Broomlands Way PA8 . . . . . **93** E8
Broomlea Cres PA4 . . . . . . **93** D7
Broomlee Rd G67. . . . . **82** F6
Broomley Cres G83 . . . . . . **27** D7
Broomley Dr G46 . . . . **136** C1
Broomley La G46 . . . . **136** C1
Broomloan Ct G51 . . . . . . **116** A5
Broomloan Pl G51 . . . . . . **116** B6
Broomloan Rd
Glasgow G51 . . . . **116** A5
Glasgow G51 . . . . **116** A6
Broompark Ave
Hamilton G72. . . . . **161** C6
Prestwick KA9. . . . . **236** C8
Broompark Cir 8 G31. . . **117** F7
Broompark Cres
Airdrie ML6 . . . . **103** A3
Prestwick KA9. . . . . **236** C8
Broompark Dr
Glasgow G31. . . . . **117** F7
Inchinnan PA4 . . . . **93** D7
Newton Mearns G77 . . . . . **157** A5
Broompark E FK11 . . . . **4** A6
Broompark Gdns FK6 . . . . . **21** E2
Broompark Rd
Hamilton G72. . . . . **161** C7
Wishaw ML2 . . . . **164** D4
Broompark St 6 G31 . . . **117** F7
Broompark W FK11 . . . . **4** A6
Broom Path G69 . . . . **119** F3
Broom Pl
Bridge of Weir PA11 . . . . . **110** E7
Coatbridge ML5. . . . . **121** F3
Glasgow G43. . . . . **136** D5
Kilmarnock KA1 . . . . **228** B5
Motherwell ML1. . . . . **143** C4
Broom Rd
Cumbernauld G67 . . . . **62** D5
Glasgow G43. . . . . **136** D5
Newton Mearns G77 . . . . . **157** A6
Rosneath G84 . . . . **15** B3
Stirling FK7 . . . . **7** C4
BROOMRIDGE. **7** D3
Broomridge Pl FK4. . . . . **39** D4
Broomridge Rd FK7 . . . . **7** B3
Broom Road E G77. . . . . . **157** B4
Broomside Cres ML1 . . . . **163** E4
Broomside Pl FK5. . . . . **23** C1
Broomside Rd FK4 . . . . **40** B3
Broomside St ML1 . . . . . . **163** E4
Broomstone Ave G77. . . . **156** F3
Broom Terr PA5 . . . . **112** A2
Broomton Rd G21. . . . . **98** C7
Broomvale Dr G77 . . . . . . **156** F5
Broomward Dr PA5 . . . . . **112** B3
Broom Wynd ML7 . . . . **146** E6
Brora Cres ML3 . . . . **182** F8
Brora Dr
Bearsden G61 . . . . **76** B4
Glasgow G46 . . . . **136** D2
Renfrew PA4 . . . . **94** E3
Brora Gdns G64. . . . . **78** B1
Brora Rd G64. . . . . **78** B1
Brora St G33 . . . . **98** D1
Brosdale Ct FK1 . . . . **42** B2
Broster Mdws KA25 . . . . . **149** B3
Brougham St PA16. . . . . . . **45** E7
Broughton G75 . . . . **180** E5
Broughton Dr G23 . . . . **96** E8
Broughton Gdns G23. . . . . **76** F1
Broughton Gn KA11 . . . . . **220** B6
Broughton Pl
Coatbridge ML5. . . . . **122** B3
Hamilton ML3 . . . . **162** A3
Broughton Rd G23 . . . . **76** E1
Broun Dr KA7. . . . . **238** E1
Brouster Hill G74 . . . . **159** E1
Brouster Pl G74. . . . . **159** E1
Brown Ave
Alloa FK10 . . . . **4** F1
Clydebank G81. . . . . **94** E8
Dumbarton G82. . . . . **50** C4
Stirling FK9 . . . . **2** B2
Troon KA10 . . . . **229** E3
Browncarrick Dr KA7. . . . **238** B1
Brown Ct G33. . . . . **99** E5
Brownhill Dr KA25 . . . . . . **169** F8
Brownhill Rd G43 . . . . **136** B4
Brownhill View ML2. . . . . **166** D6
Brownieknowe Pl FK2. . . . **41** F8
Brownieside Pl ML6. . . . . **104** A3
Brownieside Rd ML6 . . . . **104** C1
Brownlee Rd ML8 . . . . **186** D4
Brownlie St G42 . . . . **137** B8
Brownmuir Ave G76. . . . . **178** F4
Brown Pl
Cambuslang G72 . . . . **139** A6
Saltcoats KA21 . . . . **205** F1
Brown Rd G67 . . . . **61** F2
BROWNRIG **85** F6
BROWNSBURN **123** D5
Brownsburn Ind Est ML6 **123** B5
Brownsburn Rd ML6 . . . . **123** C5
Brownsdale Rd G73 . . . . . **137** F7
Brownsfield Cres PA4 . . . . **93** B5
Brownsfield Rd PA4. . . . . . **93** B5
Brownshill Ave ML5 . . . . . **121** F4
Brownside Ave
Barrhead G78 . . . . **134** A5
Cambuslang G72 . . . . **138** E5
Brownside Cres G78 . . . . **134** A5
Brownside Dr
Barrhead G78 . . . . **134** A5
Glasgow G13 . . . . **94** F6
Brownside Gr G78 . . . . . . **134** A5
Brownside Mews G72 . . . **138** E5
Brownside Rd G72, G73 . . **138** E5
Browns La 3 PA1. . . . . . . **113** E4
Brownsland Ct G69 . . . . . **100** F6
Brown St
Balloch G83 . . . . **28** A8
Carluke ML8. . . . . **187** F3
Coatbridge ML5. . . . . **122** A5
Falkirk FK1. . . . . **41** D5
Glasgow G2 . . . . **240** B2
Greenock PA15 . . . . **46** D3
1 Hamilton ML3. . . . . **162** E2
Larkhall ML9 . . . . **185** A4
Motherwell ML1. . . . . **163** F8
Paisley PA1 . . . . **113** D5
Port Glasgow PA14 . . . . **47** B2
Shotts ML7. . . . . **147** B3
Stewarton KA3. . . . . **211** D8
Wishaw ML2 . . . . **166** A4
Brown Street N PA4. . . . . . **94** C3
Brown Street S PA4 . . . . . . **94** B3
Brown Wlk
Irvine KA12 . . . . **219** D5
Wishaw ML2 . . . . **166** B5
Browside Ave PA2 . . . . . . **133** C7
Bruart Ave FK5 . . . . **23** F3
Bruar Way 15 ML2 . . . . . . **165** F6
Bruce Ave
Cambuslang G72 . . . . **139** B3
Dundonald KA2 . . . . **225** F1
Johnstone PA5. . . . . **131** E8
Motherwell ML1. . . . . **163** D7
Paisley PA3 . . . . **114** A7
Prestwick KA9. . . . . **236** B6
Bruce Cres
1 Ayr KA7 . . . . **235** E1
Falkirk FK2. . . . . **24** B3
Kilmarnock KA1 . . . . **227** F4
Plean FK7 . . . . **12** D3
Bruce Ct
Airdrie ML6 . . . . **123** E8
Cardross G82. . . . . **48** B8
Bruce Dr
Fallin FK7. . . . . **8** C5
Stenhousemuir FK5 . . . . **23** F3
Brucefield Pl G34 . . . . **120** D8
Bruce Gate FK2 . . . . **14** D2
BRUCEHILL **49** C3
Brucehill Rd G82. . . . . **49** C4
Bruce Ho G67. . . . . **61** F3
Bruce La KA9 . . . . **236** B6
Bruce Loan ML2 . . . . **186** C6

Bruce Pl G75 180 F7
Bruce Rd
- Bishopton PA7 72 B3
- Glasgow G41 116 E4
- Motherwell ML1 143 B2
- Paisley PA3 114 A7
- Renfrew PA4 94 A1

Bruce's Loan 22 ML9 185 C1
Bruce St
- Alloa FK10 10 C7
- Bannockburn FK7 7 E1
- Bellshill ML4 142 B5
- Clydebank G81 74 B1
- Coatbridge ML5 122 B8
- Dumbarton G82 50 A2
- Falkirk FK2 42 C6
- Greenock PA15 45 E5
- Kilmarnock KA1 227 F4
- Plains ML6 104 A2
- Plean FK7 12 D3
- Port Glasgow PA14 47 D1
- Stirling FK8 2 B1

Bruce Terr
- Blantyre G72 140 E1
- Cambusbarron FK7 6 D5
- East Kilbride G75 180 F7
- Irvine KA12 219 D5

Bruce View FK7 7 B1
Brunel Way G75 180 F8
Brunstane Rd G34 100 A1
Brunswick Ho G81 73 D6
Brunswick La G1 241 A2
Brunswick St G1 241 A2
Brunton St G44 137 A5
Brunton Terr G44 137 A4
Bruntsfield Ave
- Glasgow G53 135 B3
- Kilwinning KA13 207 B3

Bruntsfield Gdns G53 135 B3
Bryan St ML3 162 B5
Bryce Ave FK2 24 B2
Bryce Gdns ML9 185 A4
Bryce Knox Ct KA11 220 A6
Bryce Pl G75 180 D6
Brydson Pl PA3 112 B6
Brymner St PA15 46 A5
Bryon Ct G71 141 B2
Bryony The FK10 4 B1
Bryson Ct ML3 183 D7
Bryson Pl FK5 23 C5
Bryson St
- Clydebank G81 74 E7
- Falkirk FK2 42 B6

Bryson Street Ind Est FK2 42 B6
Buccleuch Ave
- Clarkston G76 157 D7
- Glasgow G52 114 E8
- Glasgow G52 114 F7

Buccleuch Ct G61 75 E7
Buccleuch Dr G61 75 E7
Buccleuch La G3 240 B4
Buccleuch St G3 240 B4
Buccleugh St PA15 45 F5
Buchanan Ave
- Balloch G83 28 A8
- Bishopton PA7 72 B4

Buchanan Bsns Pk G33 99 E6
Buchanan Cres
- Bishopbriggs G64 98 C7
- Hamilton ML3 162 B2

Buchanan Ct
- Balloch G83 28 A8
- Falkirk FK2 42 A8
- Stepps G33 99 F6

Buchanan Dr
- Bearsden G61 76 A4
- Bishopbriggs G64 98 C8
- Cambuslang G72 138 E6
- Carluke ML8 202 C8
- Kirkintilloch G66 79 D3
- Law ML8 187 A6
- Newton Mearns G77 156 E7
- Rutherglen G73 138 C6
- Stirling FK9 2 B3

Buchanan Galleries Sh Ctr G1 241 A3
Buchanan Gate G33 99 F6
Buchanan Gdns G32 119 E2
Buchanan Gr G69 120 B5
Buchanan Pl
- Kilmarnock KA1 228 A5
- Torrance G64 57 B1

Buchanan Rd G84 17 A1
Buchanan St
- Airdrie ML6 123 A7
- Coatbridge ML5 121 F6
- Dumbarton G82 50 B2
- Glasgow G1 240 C2
- Glasgow G1 241 A3
- Glasgow, Muirhead G69 120 B4
- Greenock PA16 45 B4
- Johnstone PA5 111 E2
- Milngavie G62 55 B2

Buchanan Street Underground Sta G1 241 A3
Buchanan Way PA5 111 E2
Buchan Ave FK2 24 B1
Buchan Ct 4 KA7 235 E1
Buchandyke Rd G74 160 B3
Buchan Gn G74 160 B3
Buchan Ho G67 61 F2
Buchan Rd
- Motherwell ML1 143 B2
- Troon KA10 229 G4

Buchan St
- Hamilton ML3 183 C8
- Wishaw ML2 165 B6

Buchan Terr G72 138 F3
Buchley Cotts G64 77 C5
Buchlyvie Gdns G64 97 F8
Buchlyvie Rd PA1 114 E5
Buchlyvie St G34 120 B7
Buckie PA8 73 A3
Buckie Wlk ML4 142 A6
Buckingham Ct ML3 161 E4
Buckingham Dr
- Glasgow G32 139 B8
- Rutherglen G73 138 D7

Buckingham St G12 96 D3
Buckingham Terr G12 96 D3
Bucklaw Gdns G52 115 C4
Bucklaw Pl G52 115 C4
Bucklaw Terr G52 115 C4
Buckley St G22 97 D6
Bucksburn Rd G21 98 C4
Buckthorne Pl G53 135 B3
Buddon St G31 118 C4
Budhill Ave G32 119 B5
Budshaw Ave ML6 123 C2
Buiston Rd KA3 211 D3
Bulldale Ct G14 94 F5
Bulldale Rd G14 94 E5
Bulldale St G14 94 E6
Buller Cl G72 140 D2
Buller Cres G72 140 C2
Bullionslaw Dr G73 138 D6
Bulloch Ave G46 136 D2
Bulloch Cres FK6 21 D1
Bull Rd G76 157 F6
Bull's Cl 15 ML11 215 A4
Bullwood Ave G53 134 F8
Bullwood Ct 6 G53 115 A1
Bullwood Dr G53 114 F1
Bullwood Gdns G53 114 F1
Bullwood Pl G53 114 F1
Bunbury Terr 3 G75 180 C8
Bunessan St G52 115 F5
Bungalows The FK5 23 B1
Bunhouse Rd G3 96 C1
Buntine Cres FK7 7 A3
Bunting Pl KA1 228 C7
Burbank G62 55 A2
Burder Pk FK2 24 A2
BURGH 138 B7
Burghead Dr G51 115 E8
Burghead Pl G51 115 E8
Burgher St G31 118 C5
Burgh Hall La G11 96 B2
Burgh Hall St G11 96 B2
Burgh La 4 G12 96 D3
Burgh Mews 1 FK10 10 B6
Burghmuir Ind Est FK8 7 B6
Burghmuir Rd FK7 7 B6
Burgh Prim Sch G73 138 A8
Burgh Rd KA9 236 B8
Burgh Wlk PA19 44 E8
Burleigh Rd G71 141 B3
Burleigh St
- Coatbridge ML5 122 B3
- Glasgow G51 116 A8

Burleigh Way FK10 10 C6
Burley Pl G74 158 F2
Burlington Ave G12 96 B6
Burma Rd KA20 218 A5
Burmola St G22 97 B4
Burnacre Gdns G71 140 E7
Burnawn Gdns G33 98 D7
Burnawn Gr G33 98 D7
Burnawn Pl G33 98 D7
BURNBANK 162 A5
Burnbank Braes ML8 187 F1
Burnbank Ctr ML3 162 A5
Burnbank Dr G78 134 D1
Burnbank Gdns
- Glasgow G20 96 F2
- 6 Hamilton ML3 162 A5

Burnbank La G20 96 F2
Burnbank Pl
- Ayr KA7 239 B4
- 2 Glasgow G20 97 A2
- Stewarton KA3 195 F1

Burnbank Quadrant ML6 122 F8
Burnbank Rd
- Ayr KA7 239 B4
- Falkirk FK2 42 B7
- Hamilton ML3 162 B4

Burnbank St
- Airdrie ML6 122 F8
- Coatbridge ML5 122 B8
- Stevenston KA20 217 D8

Burnbank Terr
- Glasgow G20 96 F2
- Kilsyth G65 36 D1
- Port Glasgow PA14 68 D8

Burnblea Gdns ML3 162 E2
Burnblea St ML3 162 D2
Burnbrae
- Alloa FK10 10 C8
- Clydebank G81 74 A6
- Sauchie FK10 5 C1
- Twechar G65 59 F4

Burnbrae Ave
- Bearsden G61 76 A7
- Linwood PA3 112 C5
- Moodiesburn G69 81 A2

Burnbrae Cres KA11 220 C5
Burnbrae Dr
- Linwood PA3 112 D4
- Perceton KA11 220 C5
- Rutherglen G73 138 D5

Burnbrae Gdns
- Alva FK12 5 B6

Burnbrae Gdns *continued*
- Falkirk FK1 42 A5
- Glasgow G53 135 D6

Burnbrae Pl G74 159 C2
Burnbrae Rd
- Falkirk FK1 42 A5
- Hamilton G72 161 C7
- Harthill ML7 127 F6
- Kirkintilloch, Auchinloch G66 79 F2
- Kirkintilloch G66 80 B2
- Kirkintilloch, Waterside G66 80 B7
- Linwood PA3 112 C4
- Shotts ML7 146 E3

Burnbrae St
- Clydebank G81 74 D8
- Glasgow G21 98 A4
- Larkhall ML9 184 F3

Burnbridge Wynd KA3 195 F1
Burncleuch Ave G72 139 A4
Burn Cres
- Chapelhall ML6 123 D2
- Motherwell ML1 143 B4

Burncrooks Ave
- Bearsden G61 75 D7
- East Kilbride G74 159 C2

Burncrooks Ct G81 73 F6
Burndale La PA13 89 D8
Burn Dr FK7 7 C4
Burndyke Ct G51 116 C7
Burndyke Sq G51 116 C7
Burnee FK10 5 E3
Burness Ave KA7 238 F2
Burnet Rose Ct G74 159 C4
Burnet Rose Gdns G74 159 C4
Burnet Rose Pl G74 159 C4
Burnett Ct G69 100 C8
Burnett Rd G33 119 E7
Burnett Terr KA8 236 B1
Burnfield Ave G46 136 B4
Burnfield Cotts G46 136 B4
Burnfield Dr G43 136 B4
Burnfield Gdns G46 136 C4
Burnfield Pl FK2 42 D7
Burnfield Rd G46 136 B4
BURNFOOT 102 E1
Burnfoot G82 48 B7
Burnfoot Ave KA10 229 E5
Burnfoot Cres
- Paisley PA2 133 C8
- Rutherglen G73 138 D5

Burnfoot Dr G52 115 B5
Burnfoot La
- Ardrossan KA22 205 B4
- 1 Falkirk FK1 42 B4

Burnfoot Pl KA3 222 E4
Burnfoot Rd
- Airdrie ML6 122 E8
- Lochwinnoch PA12 129 B2

Burnfoot Way 5 KA10 229 E5
Burngreen G65 60 D8
Burngreen Terr G67 62 B5
Burnhall Pl ML2 165 D1
Burnhall Rd ML2 165 C2
Burnhall St ML2 165 D1
Burnham Rd G14 95 A4
Burnhaven PA8 73 A2
BURNHEAD 185 C3
Burnhead La FK1 42 C4
Burnhead Rd
- Airdrie ML6 103 D1
- Cumbernauld G68 61 C2
- Glasgow G43 136 E5
- Larkhall ML9 185 C2
- Port Glasgow PA14 68 D8
- Stenhousemuir FK5 23 C3

Burnhead St
- Greenock PA15 46 B2
- Uddingston G71 141 C7

Burnhill Quadrant G73 137 F8
Burnhill Sp Ctr G73 137 F8
Burnhill St G73 137 F8
BURNHOUSE 172 C1
Burnhouse Ave
- Cumbernauld G68 61 B2
- Dalry KA24 191 B7

Burnhouse Brae G77 157 A3
Burnhouse Cotts KA3 195 B8
Burnhouse Cres ML3 162 B1
Burnhouse Rd
- East Kilbride G75 180 A1
- Hamilton ML3 162 B1

Burnhouse St
- Glasgow G20 96 C6
- Glasgow G20 96 D6

Burniebrae ML6 122 F8
Burniebrae Rd ML6 123 E3
Burn La ML1 143 A4
Burnlea Cres PA6 91 A3
Burnlea Pl KA20 206 E2
Burnlip Rd ML6 102 A4
Burnmouth Ct G33 119 F6
Burnmouth Pl G61 76 A5
Burnmouth Rd G33 119 F6
Burnock Pl G75 179 E7
Burnpark Ave G71 140 D7
Burnpark Rd KA1 227 F3
Burn Pl G72 138 E7
Burn Rd
- Carluke ML8 187 F3
- Saltcoats KA21 216 D8

Burns Ave
- Bishopton PA7 72 B3
- Kilmarnock KA3 223 A3
- Saltcoats KA21 205 F3
- Stenhousemuir FK5 23 C5

Burns Cottage & Mus★ KA7 238 E2

Burns Cres
- Harthill ML7 127 F6
- Irvine KA11 220 A5
- Kilmarnock KA3 223 B5
- Laurieston FK2 42 F4

Burn's Cres ML6 123 B6
Burns Ct G66 59 A1
Burns Dr
- Johnstone PA5 131 E8
- Kirkintilloch G66 59 A2

Burns Gdns G72 140 C1
Burns Gr G46 136 A2
BURNSIDE
- Alva 5 C7
- Rutherglen 138 D5

Burnside G61 75 C7
Burnside Ave
- Barrhead G78 134 B4
- Bellshill ML4 142 C4
- Brookfield PA5 111 C5
- Calderbank ML6 123 B2
- Kirkintilloch G66 79 B7
- Port Glasgow PA14 68 F8

Burnside Cotts KA3 173 C6
Burnside Cres
- Balloch G83 27 F7
- Clydebank G81 74 B7
- Hamilton G72 161 F6
- Plean FK7 12 C4
- Shotts ML7 146 D6

Burnside Ct
- Alva FK12 5 A7
- Bearsden G61 75 C7
- Coatbridge ML5 121 F5
- Falkirk, Camelon FK1 41 E5
- Motherwell ML1 164 B4
- Rutherglen G73 138 C5

Burnside Gate
- Hamilton ML3 162 D3
- Rutherglen G73 138 C5

Burnside Gdns
- Clarkston G76 157 D7
- Johnstone PA10 111 B2
- Prestwick KA9 233 C1

Burnside Gr PA5 111 E2
Burnside Ind Est G65 60 C8
Burnside La ML3 162 E2
Burnside Pl
- Dumbarton G82 50 B2
- Falkirk FK2 24 B3
- Irvine KA12 219 B4
- Larkhall ML9 185 B3
- Paisley PA3 113 A7
- Stevenston KA20 206 D1
- Troon KA10 229 D3
- West Kilbride KA23 190 D5

Burnside Prim Sch G73 138 B5
Burnside Quadrant ML1 143 A5
Burnside Rd
- Elderslie PA5 112 D2
- Glenmavis ML5 102 C1
- Gourock PA19 44 F6
- Menstrie FK11 3 F6
- Monkton KA9 233 D4
- Motherwell ML1 143 D4
- Rutherglen G46 157 B6
- Rutherglen, High Burnside G73 138 C4

Burnside St
- Alloa FK10 5 D1
- Dumbarton G82 50 B2
- Glengarnock KA14 170 B6
- Kilmarnock KA1 227 E6
- Motherwell ML1 164 B4
- Stirling FK7 7 C6

Burnside Sta G73 138 C5
Burnside Terr FK1 41 E5
Burnside Twr ML1 164 B3
Burnside View
- Coatbridge ML5 121 E5
- East Kilbride G75 180 A4

Burnside Wlk
- Bearsden G61 75 C7
- Coatbridge ML5 121 E5

Burns La ML6 123 D3
Burns Loan 13 ML9 185 B4
Burns Mon★
- Ayr KA7 238 E1
- Kilmarnock KA3 223 A1

Burns Path ML4 142 B7
Burns Pk G74 160 A3
Burns Pl
- Kilwinning KA13 207 F3
- Shotts ML7 146 A6

Burn's Pl KA20 206 E1
Burns Prec 5 KA1 227 F8
Burns Rd
- Chapelhall ML6 123 D4
- Cumbernauld G67 62 B2
- Greenock PA16 44 D4
- Kirkintilloch G66 59 A1
- Troon KA10 229 G4

Burns Sq
- Ardrossan KA22 205 D4
- Greenock PA16 44 D4

Burns St
- Alexandria G83 27 E7
- Clydebank G81 73 E4
- Glasgow G4 97 B2
- Hamilton ML3 162 D2
- Irvine KA12 219 B3
- Renton G82 27 D1
- Stirling FK8 2 A2

Burns Statue Arc KA7 238 F7
Burns Statue Sq KA7 238 F7
Burn St G83 27 F4
Burns Terr
- Ardrossan KA22 205 D4

Burns Terr *continued*
- Cowie FK7 12 D7

Burn Street La G83 27 F4
Burns Way
- Kilmarnock KA3 223 B5
- Motherwell ML1 143 C4

Burns' Wicket KA7 238 E1
Burns Wynd ML9 198 E1
Burntbroom Dr G69 119 F3
Burntbroom Gdns G69 119 F3
Burntbroom Rd G69 119 F2
Burntbroom St G33 119 D7
Burn Terr G72 138 E7
Burnthills Ind Est PA5 111 F3
Burntshields Rd PA10 110 D2
Burn View G67 62 C3
Burnwood Dr ML6 124 A6
Burra Gdns G64 78 D2
Burray Dr KA3 223 A6
Burrell Collection The (Mus)★ G43 116 B1
Burrell Ct G41 116 C2
Burrell's La G4 241 C2
Burrelton Rd G43 136 F5
Burstenman's Brae KA13, KA24 207 F7
Burte Ct ML4 142 A7
Burton La
- Carluke ML8 187 E2
- Glasgow G42 117 A1

Busbie Gdns KA2 221 E1
Busbiehead KA11 220 B5
Busbiehill Pl KA1 222 D1
Busbie Holdings KA2 221 D3
Busbie La KA22 205 D3
Busbie View KA2 221 E1
BUSBY 158 B5
Busby Pl KA13 207 F4
Busby Prim Sch G76 157 F6
Busby Rd
- Bellshill ML4 141 F3
- Carmunnock G76 158 C7
- Clarkston G76 157 E7

Busby Sta G76 158 A5
Bush Cres ML2 165 C2
Bushelhead Rd ML8 201 E6
Bushes Ave PA2 113 D1
Bushes Prim Sch PA2 133 D8
Busheyhill St G72 139 A5
Bute G74 160 C1
Bute Ave
- Motherwell ML1 163 C7
- Port Glasgow PA14 69 B8
- Renfrew PA4 94 D1

Bute Cres
- Bearsden G61 75 F2
- Old Kilpatrick G60 73 C5
- Paisley PA2 133 D7
- Shotts ML7 146 D6

Bute Ct
- Irvine KA11 220 C1
- Stevenston KA20 217 C8

Bute Dr
- Johnstone PA5 111 D1
- Old Kilpatrick G60 73 C6

Bute Gdns
- Glasgow G44 136 F4
- Glasgow, Kelvingrove G12 96 D2
- Old Kilpatrick G60 73 C6

Bute La G12 96 D2
Bute Pl
- Ardrossan KA22 205 C1
- Old Kilpatrick G60 73 D5

Bute Rd
- Kirkintilloch G66 80 B8
- Renfrew PA3 93 D1
- Rutherglen G73 138 D3

Bute St
- Coatbridge ML5 122 B4
- Falkirk FK2 42 B6
- Gourock PA19 44 D6
- Hamilton ML3 162 B6

Bute Terr
- Rutherglen G73 138 A5
- Saltcoats KA21 205 E1
- Uddingston G71 141 B7

Bute Twr G72 138 E3
Butler Wynd ML4 141 F5
Butt Ave G84 16 E3
Butterbiggins Rd G42 117 B3
Butterburnpark St ML3 162 D2
Buttercup Path ML2 164 F1
Butterfield Pl 2 G41 117 A3
Buttermere G75 179 F5
Buttsley Ct ML11 214 E4
Butts The ML11 214 F3
Byars Rd G66 79 B8
By Pass Rd KA15 150 C1
By-Pass Rd FK4 39 E5
Byramsmuir Rd ML1 142 E8
Byrebush Rd G53 115 C1
Byrehill Ave KA13 207 B2
Byrehill Dr KA13 207 B2
Byrehill Pl KA13 207 B2
Byrehill Rd KA13, KA20 207 D1
Byres Ave PA3 114 A6
Byres Cres PA3 114 A6
Byresknowe La 2 ML1 143 B1
Byres Loch KA13 207 D3
Byres Rd
- Elderslie PA5 112 D2
- Glasgow G12 96 C2
- Kilwinning KA13 207 D3
- Motherwell ML1 143 E4

Byrestone Ave G77 157 C4
Byretovn Gr ML11 214 E3
Byretown Rd ML11 214 E2
Byron Rd ML7 146 B6

Captain's Wlk ML1 144 E1

Charles St
Alloa FK10 ... 9 F8
Glasgow G21 ... 97 F1
Kilmarnock KA1 ... 227 E8
Kilsyth G65 ... 36 D1
Shotts ML7 ... 147 B4
Stirling FK8 ... 7 A5
Wishaw ML2 ... 164 D4
Charles Terr G83 ... 27 E8
Charlotte Ave G64 ... 78 B8
Charlotte Hill Ct FK5 ... 23 B3
Charlotte Path ML9 ... 185 A2
Charlotte Pl PA2 ... 113 E2
Charlotte St
Ayr KA7 ... 238 E8
Dumbarton G82 ... 49 D4
Glasgow G1 ... 241 B1
Helensburgh G84 ... 16 E2
Shotts ML7 ... 147 A3
Charnwood Ave PA5 ... 131 D8
Charrier The FK11 ... 3 F6
CHARTERSHALL ... 7 A1
Chartershall Rd
Bannockburn FK7 ... 11 A6
Stirling FK7 ... 7 A1
Charter St FK7 ... 7 A3
Chartwell Rd PA7 ... 72 B3
Chassels St ML5 ... 122 A8
Chateau Gr ML3 ... 163 A2
Chatelherault Ave G72 ... 138 E5
Chatelherault Country Pk* ML3 ... 184 B8
Chatelherault Cres ML3 ... 162 F1
Chatelherault Prim Sch ML3 ... 162 E1
Chatelherault Sta ML3 ... 163 C1
Chatelherault Wlk ML3 ... 162 E1
Chatham G75 ... 180 C7
Chattan Ave FK9 ... 2 B4
Chattan Ind Est FK4 ... 40 C4
Chatton St G23 ... 76 D1
Chatton Wlk ML5 ... 122 D3
Cheapside St
Eaglesham G76 ... 178 F5
Glasgow G3 ... 240 A2
4 Kilmarnock KA1 ... 227 F8
Checkbar Rdbt FK5 ... 40 C7
Chelmsford Dr G12 ... 96 B5
Cherry Ave G67 ... 62 E5
Cherry Bank G66 ... 79 B5
Cherrybank Rd G43 ... 136 F5
Cherrybank Wlk ML6 ... 122 D8
Cherry Cres G81 ... 74 A4
Cherry Gdns KA11 ... 219 E5
Cherry Gr G69 ... 121 B6
Cherry Hill Rd KA7 ... 239 B2
Cherryhill View ML9 ... 184 F3
Cherry La
Banknock FK4 ... 38 E2
Troon KA10 ... 229 E4
Cherry Pl
Bishopbriggs G64 ... 98 B8
Johnstone PA5 ... 112 A1
Milton of Campsie G66 ... 58 B4
Motherwell ML1 ... 143 B5
Uddingston G71 ... 141 D7
Cherry Rd KA1 ... 227 C8
Cherryridge Dr G69 ... 121 A6
Cherrytree Cres ML9 ... 185 A5
Cherry Tree Ct G83 ... 27 D5
Cherrytree Dr G72 ... 139 E4
Cherrytree Wynd G75 ... 180 F6
Cherry Wlk ML1 ... 163 E3
Cherrywood Dr KA15 ... 150 C2
Cherrywood Rd PA5 ... 112 C2
Chesterfield Ave G12 ... 96 B5
Chester Rd PA16 ... 44 E4
Chesters Cres ML1 ... 163 C8
Chesters Pl 3 G73 ... 138 A7
Chesters Rd G61 ... 75 D4
Chester St G32 ... 119 A5
Chestnut Ave
Beith KA15 ... 171 A8
Bishopton PA7 ... 71 F5
Cumbernauld G67 ... 62 E5
Chestnut Cres
Denny FK6 ... 21 C3
East Kilbride G75 ... 180 C6
Hamilton ML3 ... 162 F2
Uddingston G71 ... 141 D7
Chestnut Ct
Cumbernauld G67 ... 62 E5
Milton of Campsie G66 ... 58 B5
Chestnut Dr
Clydebank G81 ... 74 A5
Kirkintilloch G66 ... 79 B6
Chestnut Gdns KA11 ... 219 E5
Chestnut Gr
Carluke ML8 ... 187 F1
Glenboig G69 ... 101 C6
Hamilton G72 ... 161 C8
Larkhall ML9 ... 185 A5
Motherwell ML1 ... 163 D4
Stenhousemuir FK5 ... 23 F3
Chestnut La G62 ... 54 E1
Chestnut Pl
Cumbernauld G67 ... 62 E5
Johnstone PA5 ... 132 A8
Kilmarnock KA1 ... 227 D8
Chestnut Rd KA7 ... 239 D6
Chestnut St G22 ... 97 D5
Chestnut Way
Cambuslang G72 ... 139 E4
Quarter ML3 ... 183 F4
Chestnut Wlk G66 ... 57 E7
Cheviot Ave G78 ... 134 C1
Cheviot Cres
East Kilbride G75 ... 180 B4
Wishaw ML2 ... 164 F4
Cheviot Ct
Airdrie ML6 ... 103 B2
Coatbridge ML5 ... 122 C3
Irvine KA11 ... 220 A3
Cheviot Dr G77 ... 156 C3
Cheviot Gdns G61 ... 75 D7
Cheviot Head
Irvine, Bourtreehill KA11 ... 220 A3
Irvine KA11 ... 219 F3
Cheviot Pl KA1 ... 228 A3
Cheviot Rd
Glasgow G43 ... 136 C5
Hamilton ML3 ... 162 F2
Larkhall ML9 ... 185 C2
2 Paisley PA2 ... 113 E1
Cheviot St G72 ... 161 C7
Cheviot Way KA11 ... 220 A3
Chirmorie Cres G53 ... 115 A1
Chirmorie Pl G53 ... 115 A1
Chirnside Ct G72 ... 161 F5
Chirnside Pl G52 ... 115 B6
Chirnside Rd G52 ... 115 A6
Chirnsyde Prim Sch G22 ... 97 D6
Chisholm Ave
Bishopton PA7 ... 72 C3
Stirling FK9 ... 2 B4
Chisholm Dr G77 ... 156 E6
Chisholm Pl ML1 ... 164 B2
Chisholm St
Coatbridge ML5 ... 122 B8
Glasgow G1 ... 241 B1
Chrighton Gn 3 G71 ... 141 A8
Chriss Ave ML3 ... 183 D7
Christchurch Pl G75 ... 180 B7
Christian St G43 ... 136 C8
Christie Gdns KA21 ... 216 F8
Christie La PA3 ... 113 E5
Christie Park Prim Sch G83 ... 27 D5
Christie Pl G72 ... 139 B5
Christie St
Bellshill ML4 ... 142 D5
Paisley PA1 ... 113 F5
Christie Terr FK5 ... 23 E3
Christopher St G21 ... 98 A1
Christ the King Prim Sch ML1 ... 143 B6
Chromars Pl PA15 ... 45 E3
CHRYSTON ... 100 D8
Chryston Bsns Ctr G69 ... 100 C8
Chryston High Sch G69 ... 100 C8
Chryston Prim Sch G69 ... 100 D8
Chryston Rd
Chryston G69 ... 100 D8
Kirkintilloch G69, G66 ... 80 C5
Chuckie La PA5 ... 111 C6
Church Ave
Cardross G82 ... 48 A8
Rutherglen G73 ... 138 C5
Stepps G33 ... 99 D6
Wishaw ML2 ... 166 A4
Church Cres ML6 ... 103 E1
Church Ct
Alloa FK10 ... 10 A6
Ayr KA8 ... 236 A1
Dumbarton G82 ... 49 F3
Hamilton ML3 ... 162 E4
Church Dr G66 ... 79 C6
Church Gr FK10 ... 5 C1
Church Hill PA1 ... 113 E5
Churchhill Ave KA13 ... 208 A4
Churchill Ave
East Kilbride G74 ... 159 F1
Johnstone PA5 ... 131 C7
Churchill Cres
Ayr KA8 ... 239 D8
Bothwell G71 ... 141 B3
Churchill Dr
Ardrossan KA22 ... 205 D4
Bishopton PA7 ... 72 B3
Bridge of Allan FK9 ... 2 A6
Glasgow G11 ... 96 A4
Churchill Pl
Falkirk FK2 ... 42 C7
Kilbarchan PA10 ... 111 A3
Churchill Rd PA13 ... 89 C7
Churchill Sq G84 ... 17 A2
Churchill St FK10 ... 9 F8
Churchill Twr KA7 ... 235 E2
Church La
Carluke ML8 ... 187 F1
Coatbridge ML5 ... 122 A7
Denny FK6 ... 21 D3
Kilmarnock KA1 ... 227 F5
8 Kilsyth G65 ... 60 D8
Plean FK7 ... 12 D2
Church Manse La PA11 ... 110 D8
Church Pl
Ardrossan KA22 ... 205 C1
Caldercruix ML6 ... 104 F4
Falkirk FK2 ... 42 B6
Old Kilpatrick G60 ... 73 A6
Rhu G84 ... 15 D4
Rutherglen G73 ... 138 B8
Church Rd
Barrhead G78 ... 134 C2
Bridge of Weir PA11 ... 110 E8
California FK1 ... 66 F5
Clarkston G76 ... 157 F6
Glasgow G46 ... 136 D2
Muirhead G69 ... 100 C7
Quarriers Village PA11 ... 89 E2
Rhu G84 ... 15 D5
Church Rd *continued*
Wishaw ML2 ... 166 D6
Church St
Alexandria G83 ... 27 E4
Alloa FK10 ... 10 A6
Bonnybridge FK4 ... 40 C3
Clydebank G81 ... 74 A3
Coatbridge ML5 ... 122 A7
Dumbarton G82 ... 49 F3
Falkirk FK2 ... 24 C2
Glasgow, Kelvingrove G11 ... 96 C2
Glasgow, Muirhead G69 ... 120 C4
Gourock PA19 ... 44 E8
Hamilton, Blantyre G72 ... 161 E7
Hamilton ML3 ... 162 E4
Harthill ML7 ... 127 C5
Irvine KA12 ... 219 B2
Johnstone PA5 ... 111 F3
Kilbarchan PA10 ... 111 A3
Kilmarnock KA3 ... 222 F1
Kilsyth G65 ... 60 D8
Kilwinning KA13 ... 207 E3
Larkhall ML9 ... 185 A2
Lochwinnoch PA12 ... 129 C2
Motherwell ML1 ... 143 F4
Port Glasgow PA14 ... 47 C2
Stenhousemuir FK5 ... 23 E3
Troon KA10 ... 229 D2
Uddingston G71 ... 140 F5
Church View
Caldercruix ML6 ... 104 F3
Cambuslang G72 ... 139 A7
Coatbridge ML5 ... 122 A7
Church View Ct G66 ... 33 D1
Church View Gdns ML4 ... 142 A5
Church Wlk FK6 ... 21 E2
Churchyard Ct ML7 ... 146 E4
Circus Dr G31 ... 117 F7
Circus Pl G31 ... 117 F8
Circus Place La G31 ... 117 F8
Citadel L Ctr KA7 ... 235 E1
Citadel Pl
Ayr KA7 ... 235 E1
Motherwell ML1 ... 163 C8
Citadel Way KA10 ... 229 G8
Citizen La G1 ... 241 A2
Citrus Cres G71 ... 141 C8
Cityford Cres G73 ... 137 F7
Cityford Dr G73 ... 137 F6
Civic Sq 4 ML1 ... 163 F5
Civic St G4 ... 97 B2
Civic Way G66 ... 79 C7
Clachaig Pl PA19 ... 43 F5
Clachan Dr 4 G51 ... 115 E8
CLACHAN OF CAMPSIE ... 33 A3
Clachan Rd G84 ... 15 A3
Clachan The
Rosneath G84 ... 15 A3
Wishaw ML2 ... 165 B3
Clachan Way ML5 ... 121 E5
CLACKMANNAN ... 10 F4
Clackmannan County Hospl FK10 ... 10 B8
Clackmannan Rd FK10 ... 10 D6
Clackmannanshire Com Hospl FK10 ... 10 C8
Clackmannan Tower* FK10 ... 10 F4
CLADDENS ... 79 F4
Claddens Holdings G66 ... 80 A4
Claddens Pl
Glasgow G22 ... 97 B6
Kirkintilloch G66 ... 79 E4
Claddens Quadrant G22 ... 97 C6
Claddens St G22 ... 97 B6
Cladence Gr G75 ... 180 F5
Claire St ML2 ... 166 A5
Clairinsh G83 ... 27 D8
Clairinsh Gdns 1 PA4 ... 94 C1
Clairmont Gdns G3 ... 240 A4
Clair Rd G64 ... 78 D1
Clamp Rd ML2 ... 164 C4
Clamps Gr G74 ... 181 A8
Clamps Terr G74 ... 181 B8
Clamps Wood G74 ... 181 A8
Clanranald Pl FK1 ... 41 F1
Clanrye Dr ML5 ... 122 A4
Clapperhow Rd ML1 ... 143 B1
Claremont FK10 ... 9 F8
Claremont Ave G66 ... 79 B8
Claremont Cres KA13 ... 207 D4
Claremont Dr
Bridge of Allan FK9 ... 2 C7
Milngavie G62 ... 55 A2
Claremont Gdns G62 ... 55 A1
Claremont Ind Est FK10 ... 10 A6
Claremont Passage G3 ... 240 A4
Claremont Pl G3 ... 240 A4
Claremont Prim Sch FK10 ... 9 E8
Claremont St
Bonnybridge FK4 ... 39 F6
Glasgow G3 ... 116 E8
Claremont Terr G3 ... 240 A4
Claremont Terrace La G3 ... 240 A4
Claremount Ave G46 ... 136 C2
Claremount View ML5 ... 122 C3
Clarence Dr
Glasgow G12 ... 96 A3
1 Paisley PA1 ... 114 A4
Clarence Gdns G11 ... 96 A3
Clarence La G12 ... 96 B3
Clarence St
Clydebank G81 ... 74 C3
Greenock PA15 ... 45 F6
Paisley PA1 ... 114 A5
Clarendon Pl
Ayr KA7 ... 239 C5
Clarendon Pl *continued*
9 Glasgow G20 ... 97 A2
Stepps G33 ... 99 D5
Stirling FK8 ... 7 A7
Clarendon Rd
Stirling FK8 ... 7 A7
Wishaw ML2 ... 164 E1
Clarendon St G20 ... 97 A2
Clare St G21 ... 98 A2
Clarinda Ave FK1 ... 41 B5
Clarinda Ct G66 ... 59 A2
Clarinda Pl
Motherwell ML1 ... 143 C3
Stenhousemuir FK5 ... 23 C4
Clarion Cres G13 ... 95 A8
Clarion Rd G13 ... 95 B7
Clark Cres KA20 ... 217 D7
Clark Dr KA12 ... 219 E3
Clarke Ave KA7 ... 238 E6
Clarkin Ave G75 ... 180 A4
Clark Pl
Newton Mearns G77 ... 156 B4
Saltcoats KA21 ... 206 A2
Torrance G64 ... 78 C8
Clark St
Airdrie ML6 ... 123 B7
Clydebank G81 ... 73 F4
Johnstone PA5 ... 111 F3
Kilmarnock KA1 ... 227 F8
Paisley PA3 ... 113 C6
Renfrew PA4 ... 94 B3
Stirling FK7 ... 7 B2
Wishaw ML2 ... 165 F5
CLARKSTON
Airdrie ... 123 E8
Newton Mearns ... 157 E7
Clarkston Ave G44 ... 136 F4
Clarkston Dr ML6 ... 123 D7
Clarkston Prim Sch ML6 ... 123 D8
Clarkston Rd
Clarkston G76 ... 157 E8
Glasgow G44, G76 ... 136 F3
Clarkston Sta G76 ... 157 E7
Clark Way ML4 ... 141 F7
Clarkwell Rd ML3 ... 161 E3
Clarkwell Terr ML3 ... 161 F3
Clathic Ave G61 ... 76 A4
Claude Ave G72 ... 139 E4
Claude St ML9 ... 185 A3
Claud Rd PA3 ... 114 A6
Clavens Rd G52 ... 114 E6
Claverhouse Pl PA2 ... 114 B3
Claverhouse Rd G52 ... 114 F7
Clavering Street E PA1 ... 113 C5
Clavering Street W PA1 ... 113 C4
Clay Cres
Bellshill ML4 ... 142 C7
Kilmarnock KA3 ... 222 F2
Claycrofts Pl FK7 ... 7 B6
Clay Ct ML1 ... 163 E4
Clayhouse Rd G33 ... 99 E5
Claymore Dr
Houston PA6 ... 111 D8
Stirling FK7 ... 7 D3
Claypotts Pl G33 ... 99 A1
Claypotts Rd G33 ... 99 A1
Clay Rd ML4 ... 142 C7
Clayslaps Rd G3 ... 96 D1
Clayslaps View KA1 ... 228 B4
Claythorn Ave G40 ... 241 C1
Claythorn Cir G40 ... 241 C1
Claythorn Ct G40 ... 241 C1
Claythorn Pk G40 ... 117 E5
Claythorn St G40 ... 241 C1
Claythorn Terr G40 ... 241 C1
Clayton Ave KA12 ... 219 C4
Clayton Path ML4 ... 142 B7
Clayton Terr 5 G31 ... 117 F7
Clearfield Ave ML3 ... 162 B4
Cleaves The FK10 ... 4 B1
CLEDDANS ... 58 E1
Cleddans Cres G81 ... 74 C5
Cleddans Rd
Clydebank G81 ... 74 C5
Kirkintilloch G66 ... 58 E1
Cleddans View
Clydebank G81 ... 74 C4
Glenmavis ML6 ... 102 E4
Cleddens Ct
Airdrie ML6 ... 122 D8
Bishopbriggs G64 ... 78 A1
CLEEKHIMIN ... 143 B1
Cleeves Ave KA24 ... 191 E6
Cleeves Prim Sch G53 ... 135 A5
Cleeves Quadrant G53 ... 135 B5
Cleeves Rd G53 ... 135 A5
CLEGHORN ... 215 F7
Cleghorn Ave ML11 ... 215 B5
Cleghorn Dr ML11 ... 215 A5
Cleghorn Rd ML11 ... 215 A5
Cleghorn St G22 ... 97 B3
Cleish Ave G61 ... 75 C8
CLELAND ... 144 B1
Cleland Hospl ML1 ... 144 C1
Cleland La G5 ... 117 C5
Cleland Pl G74 ... 160 A3
Cleland Prim Sch ML1 ... 144 C1
Cleland Rd
Cleland ML1 ... 144 A2
Wishaw ML2 ... 165 A3
Cleland St G5 ... 117 C5
Cleland Sta ML1 ... 144 C1
Clelland Ave G64 ... 98 A8
Clem Attlee Gdns ML9 ... 185 B2
Clement Dr ML6 ... 103 D1
Clements Pl KA20 ... 206 E2
Clerkland Rd KA3 ... 195 D2
Clerwood St G32 ... 118 D6
Cleuch Ave FK10 ... 4 B2
Cleuch Dr FK12 ... 4 E7
Cleuch Gdns G76 ... 157 D8
Cleuch Rd FK9 ... 2 C3
Cleughearn Rd G75 ... 180 D1
Clevans Rd PA11 ... 110 C7
Cleveden Cres G12 ... 96 B5
Cleveden Crescent La G12 ... 96 B5
Cleveden Dr
Glasgow G12 ... 96 C4
Rutherglen G73 ... 138 C6
Cleveden Gdns G12 ... 96 C5
Cleveden Ho G12 ... 96 C4
Cleveden Pl G12 ... 96 B6
Cleveden Rd G12 ... 96 B5
Cleveden Sec Sch G12 ... 96 C5
Cleveland La G3 ... 240 A3
Cleveland St G3 ... 240 A3
Clifford Gdns G51 ... 116 B5
Clifford La G51 ... 116 D5
Clifford Pk FK11 ... 4 A7
Clifford Pl 1 G51 ... 116 D5
Clifford Rd FK8 ... 7 B5
Clifford St G51 ... 116 C5
Cliff Rd G3 ... 240 A4
Cliffvale Rd 3 G69 ... 100 C8
Clifton Ho 9 G3 ... 96 E1
Clifton Pl
Coatbridge ML5 ... 122 C6
1 Glasgow G3 ... 116 E8
Clifton Rd G46 ... 136 B3
Clifton St G3 ... 96 E1
Clifton Terr
Cambuslang G72 ... 138 E3
Johnstone PA5 ... 112 A2
CLIFTONVILLE ... 122 C7
Cliftonville Ct ML5 ... 122 C6
Climie Pl KA3 ... 228 B8
CLINCARTHILL ... 138 B7
Clincarthill Rd G73 ... 138 A7
Clincart Rd G42 ... 137 B8
Clippens Ho PA3 ... 112 A6
Clippens Rd
Houston PA3, PA6 ... 111 F8
Linwood PA3 ... 112 A6
Clippens Sch PA3 ... 112 C6
Clive St ML7 ... 146 E5
Cloak Rd PA13 ... 69 C4
Cloan Ave G15 ... 75 B2
Cloan Cres G64 ... 78 B3
Clober Farm La G62 ... 54 E3
Cloberfield G62 ... 54 F4
Cloberfield Gdns G62 ... 54 F3
Cloberhill Rd G13 ... 75 D1
Clober Prim Sch G62 ... 54 E2
Clober Rd G62 ... 55 A2
Clochbar Ave G62 ... 54 F3
Clochbar Gdns G62 ... 54 F2
Cloch Brae PA19 ... 44 A6
Clochoderick Ave PA10 ... 111 B2
Clochranhill Rd KA7 ... 238 F2
Cloch Rd PA19 ... 43 E5
Cloch St G33 ... 119 A8
Clockenhill Pl ML1 ... 143 E4
Cloister Ave ML6 ... 123 C4
Cloncaird KA13 ... 207 C2
Closeburn St G22 ... 97 C5
Clossfoot Pl G69 ... 81 A2
Cloth St G78 ... 134 C2
Clouden Rd G67 ... 62 B2
Cloudhowe Terr G72 ... 140 C1
Clouston Ct 1 G20 ... 96 E4
Clouston St G20 ... 96 E4
Clova Pl G71 ... 140 F6
Clova St G46 ... 135 F4
Clove Mill Wynd ML9 ... 184 E2
Cloverbank Gdns G21 ... 98 A1
Cloverbank St G21 ... 98 A1
Clovergate G64 ... 77 E1
Cloverhill KA7 ... 239 D6
Cloverhill Pl G69 ... 100 C8
Cloverhill Terr G74 ... 159 E1
Cloverhill View G74 ... 159 D1
Clover Leaf Path G83 ... 27 E4
Cloves The FK11 ... 4 A5
Cluanie Ave ML7 ... 146 E6
Clune Brae PA14 ... 47 E1
Clune Dr KA9 ... 236 D8
Clune Park Prim Sch PA14 ... 47 E1
Clune Park St PA14 ... 47 E1
Clunie Pl
Coatbridge ML5 ... 122 B3
Wishaw ML2 ... 165 F6
Clunie Rd G52 ... 115 E6
Cluny Ave G61 ... 76 A2
Cluny Dr
Bearsden G61 ... 76 A2
Newton Mearns G77 ... 156 B5
Paisley PA3 ... 114 A6
Stenhousemuir FK5 ... 23 F4
Cluny Gdns
Glasgow, Baillieston G69 ... 120 A4
Glasgow, Jordanhill G14 ... 95 E4
Cluny Villas G14 ... 95 E4
Clutha Pl G75 ... 180 A7
Clutha St G51 ... 116 D6
Clyde Ave
Barrhead G78 ... 134 D1
Bothwell G71 ... 140 F1
Hamilton ML3 ... 163 C1
Torrance G64 ... 78 B8
CLYDEBANK ... 74 B1
Clydebank Bsns Pk G81 ... 74 B2
Clydebank Coll G81 ... 74 B3
Clydebank High Sch G81 ... 74 A4

Clydebank Ind Est G81 . . . **73** D2
Clydebank Mus★ G81 . . . . **74** B1
Clydebank Sta G81. . . . . . . **74** B1
Clydebrae Dr G71 . . . . **162** B8
Clydebrae St G51 . . . . **116** B8
Clydebuilt (Mus)★ G51 . . . **95** A3
Clyde Cres
Lanark ML11 . . . . **215** B5
Larbert FK5 . . . . **23** B3
Clyde Ct
Carluke ML8. . . . . **187** E2
Clydebank G81. . . . . **73** E5
Coatbridge ML5 . . . . **122** C6
Dumbarton G82 . . . . **49** E3
Clyde Dr
Bellshill ML4 . . . . **142** D4
Shotts ML7. . . . . **147** B4
Clydeford Dr
Glasgow G32 . . . . **118** E3
Uddingston G71. . . . . **140** E7
Clydeford Rd G32, G72 . . . **139** A7
Clyde Ho ML3. . . . . **162** E5
Clydeholm Rd G14 . . . . **95** D2
Clydeholm Terr G81. . . . . . **94** D7
Clyde La ML1 . . . . **143** A4
Clydemuir Prim Sch G81 . **73** D4
Clyde Muirshiel Regional Pk★ PA19 . . . . **43** D2
Clydeneuk Dr G71 . . . . . . **140** D7
Clyde Pl
Ardrossan KA22. . . . . **205** D4
Cambuslang G72 . . . . **139** D4
Glasgow G5 . . . . **240** C1
Johnstone PA5. . . . . **131** C8
Kilmarnock KA1. . . . . **228** A5
Motherwell ML1. . . . . **143** A4
Troon KA10 . . . . **229** G5
Clyde Rd
Gourock PA19 . . . . **44** F6
Paisley PA3 . . . . **114** B7
CLYDESDALE **142** E4
Clydesdale Ave
Hamilton ML3 . . . . **183** D6
Paisley PA3 . . . . **94** A1
Wishaw ML2 . . . . **164** D1
Clydesdale Pl ML3 . . . . . . **183** D6
Clydesdale Rd ML4. . . . . . **142** D4
Clydesdale St
Hamilton ML3 . . . . **162** C4
Larkhall ML9 . . . . **185** A4
Motherwell ML1. . . . . **142** F4
Clyde Sh Ctr G81 . . . . **74** B2
Clydesholm Ct ML11 . . . . **214** D4
Clydeshore Rd G82. . . . . . . **49** E3
Clydeside Expressway
G3 . . . . **116** E7
Clydeside Ind Est G14. . . . **95** E1
Clydeside Rd G73 . . . . **117** F2
Clydesmill Dr G32. . . . . . . **139** A7
Clydesmill Gr G32. . . . . . . **139** A7
Clydesmill Pl G32 . . . . **139** A8
Clydesmill Rd G32 . . . . . . **139** A8
Clyde Sq
[2] Cumbernauld G67 . . . . . **61** F1
[9] Greenock PA15. . . . . **45** F5
Clyde St
Carluke ML8. . . . . **187** E2
Clydebank G81. . . . . **94** C8
Coatbridge ML5 . . . . **122** C7
Falkirk FK1. . . . . **41** E5
Glasgow G1 . . . . **241** A1
Renfrew PA4 . . . . **94** D5
Clyde Terr
Ardrossan KA22. . . . . **205** D4
Bothwell G71 . . . . **141** A1
Motherwell ML1. . . . . **164** C2
Clyde Twr
East Kilbride G74. . . . . **181** B7
[8] Motherwell ML1 . . . . . . **163** E5
Clydevale G71 . . . . **141** B1
Clyde Valley Ave ML1 . . . . **163** E4
Clyde Valley High Sch
ML2. . . . . **186** B7
Clydeview
Bothwell G71. . . . . **141** C1
Dumbarton G82 . . . . **49** E2
Clyde View
Ashgill ML9 . . . . **200** A8
Hamilton ML3 . . . . **162** B1
Paisley PA2 . . . . **114** B2
Clyde View Ave KA20. . . . **206** C1
Clyde View Ct G60 . . . . **72** C8
Clydeview Rd
Greenock PA15 . . . . **46** B2
Port Glasgow PA14 . . . . **68** E8
Clydeview Sch ML1 . . . . . **163** B8
Clydeview Sh Ctr G72 . . . **161** E7
Clydeview Terr G32 . . . . . **139** C8
Clyde Way
[3] Cumbernauld G67 . . . . . **61** F1
Paisley PA3 . . . . **114** B7
Clydeway Ind Est [8] G3 . **116** E8
Clyde Wlk
[1] Cumbernauld G67 . . . . . **61** F1
Wishaw ML2 . . . . **166** A6
Clyde Workshops G32. . . **118** F1
Clyde Wynd PA15 . . . . **45** E3
Clynder Rd PA15 . . . . **46** C2
Clynder St G51 . . . . **116** B6
Clyth Dr G46. . . . . **136** D2
Clytus Ct KA21. . . . . **205** F3
Coach Brae View KA11 . . **220** E2
Coach Cl G65 . . . . **61** A8
Coach Pl G65. . . . . **60** E7
Coach Rd G65 . . . . **60** F7
Coalburn Rd G71 . . . . **141** B5
Coalburn St ML6. . . . . **83** F2
Coalgate FK10 . . . . **10** B6
Coalhall Ave ML1 . . . . **143** A1
Coalhill Pl KA22. . . . . **205** C4
Coalhill St G31 . . . . **118** B5
Coalpots Way FK10. . . . . **5** E3
Coal Wynd FK7 . . . . **7** D1
Coatbank St ML5. . . . . **122** B6
Coatbank Way ML5 . . . . . **122** B6
COATBRIDGE **122** A6
Coatbridge Bsns Ctr
ML5. . . . . **122** C6
Coatbridge Central Sta
ML5. . . . . **121** F7
Coatbridge Coll ML5 . . . . **122** B7
Coatbridge High Sch
ML5. . . . . **122** B7
Coatbridge Outdoor Sp Ctr
ML5. . . . . **121** E5
Coatbridge Rd
Coatbridge G69 . . . . **121** A6
Gartcosh G69. . . . . **101** A3
Glasgow G69 . . . . **120** E5
Glenboig ML5. . . . . **101** F5
Glenmavis ML6 . . . . **102** D3
Coatbridge Sunnyside Sta
ML5. . . . . **122** A8
Coatbridge Workshops
ML5. . . . . **122** B6
COATDYKE **122** D6
Coatdyke Sta ML5. . . . . . . **122** D7
Coathill Hospl ML5. . . . . . **122** A4
Coathill St ML5 . . . . **122** B4
Coats Cres
Glasgow G69 . . . . **120** A5
Tullibody FK10 . . . . **4** E1
Coats Dr PA2 . . . . **113** B3
COATSHILL **140** D1
Coatshill Ave G72 . . . . **140** C1
Coats Pl KA2. . . . . **225** E2
Coats St ML5 . . . . **122** B6
Cobbett Rd ML1. . . . . **163** B5
Cobblebrae Cres FK2. . . . . **24** B1
Cobblerigg Way G71 . . . . . **140** E6
Cobbleton Rd ML1 . . . . . . **142** F2
Cobden St
Alva FK12. . . . . **5** A6
Alva FK12. . . . . **5** A7
Cobham St PA15 . . . . **46** E2
Cobington Pl G33. . . . . **99** B1
Cobinshaw St G32 . . . . . . **119** A6
Coblecrook Gdns FK12 . . . . . **4** F6
Coblecrook La FK12. . . . . **4** F6
Coblecrook Pl FK12 . . . . **4** F6
Coburg St [3] G5 . . . . **117** B5
COCHNO **53** B1
Cochno Brae G81 . . . . **74** B7
Cochno Rd
Clydebank, Duntocher G81 . **74** B8
Clydebank, Faifley G81 . . . . **74** E8
Cochno St G81. . . . . **74** C1
Cochrane Ave
Dundonald KA2 . . . . **225** F2
Falkirk FK1. . . . . **42** B4
Cochrane Castle Prim Sch [1]
PA5. . . . . **111** D1
Cochrane Cres FK12 . . . . **4** E7
Cochrane Ct G62. . . . . **76** C8
Cochrane Dr KA2 . . . . **225** E2
Cochranemill Rd PA5 . . . **111** C1
Cochrane Pl
Helensburgh G84. . . . . **17** A2
Prestwick KA9 . . . . **236** B8
Cochrane Sq PA3 . . . . **112** B6
Cochrane St
Barrhead G78 . . . . **134** B2
Bellshill ML4 . . . . **141** F5
Falkirk FK1. . . . . **42** B4
Glasgow G1 . . . . **241** A2
Irvine KA12 . . . . **219** B2
Kilbirnie KA25 . . . . **149** A2
Cochranes The FK12 . . . . **5** A7
Cochran St PA1. . . . . **113** F4
Cochrie Pl FK10. . . . . **4** C2
Cockalane View G63 . . . . . **31** C3
Cockburn Pl
Coatbridge ML5. . . . . **121** F4
Irvine KA11 . . . . **224** H6
Cockburn St FK1. . . . . **42** B4
Cockels Loan PA4. . . . . **94** D1
Cockenzie St G32 . . . . **119** A6
Cockhill Way ML4. . . . . . . **141** D6
Cocklebie Rd KA3. . . . . . . **195** D1
Cocklebie View KA3. . . . . **195** D1
Cockmuir St G21. . . . . **98** A4
Coddington Cres ML1 . . . **142** F7
Cogan Pl G78. . . . . **134** B2
Cogan Rd G43 . . . . **136** C6
Cogan St
Barrhead G78 . . . . **134** B2
Glasgow G43 . . . . **136** C7
Coila Ave KA9 . . . . **236** C6
Coire Loan ML7. . . . . **147** B3
Colbert St G40. . . . . **117** F4
Colbreggan Ct G81. . . . . . . **74** C6
Colbreggan Gdns G81. . . . **74** C6
Colbreggan Pl G81. . . . . . . **74** C6
Colchester Dr G12 . . . . **96** B6
Coldgreen Ave KA25 . . . . **149** A1
Coldingham Ave G14. . . . . . **94** E6
Coldstream KA23 . . . . **190** D5
Coldstream Cres ML2 . . . **165** C5
Coldstream Dr
Paisley PA2 . . . . **113** A1
Rutherglen G73 . . . . **138** D6
Coldstream Pl G21 . . . . **97** C3
Coldstream Rd G81 . . . . . . **74** B1
Coldstream St G72. . . . . . . **161** D7
Colebrooke Pl G12. . . . . . . **96** E3
Colebrooke St
Cambuslang G72 . . . . **139** A6
[9] Glasgow G12 . . . . **96** E3
Colebrooke Terr G12. . . . . **96** E3
Coleburn Ct KA11. . . . . . . **219** F6
Cole Rd G64 . . . . **78** D6
Coleridge G75 . . . . **180** A7
Coleridge Ave G71 . . . . . . **141** B3
Coleridge Gdns G84. . . . . . **16** C2
Colfin St G34 . . . . **100** C1
Colgrain Ave G20 . . . . **97** A6
Colgrain Prim Sch G84. . . **25** C8
Colgrain Steading G82 . . . **25** E5
Colgrain Terr G20. . . . . **97** A6
Colgrave Cres G32 . . . . . . **118** F3
Colinbar Circ G78. . . . . . . **134** B1
Colinslee Ave PA2 . . . . . . **113** F1
Colinslee Cres PA2. . . . . . **113** F1
Colinslee Dr PA2. . . . . **113** F1
Colinslie Rd G53. . . . . **135** D8
Colinton Gdns G69. . . . . . . **80** C1
Colinton Pl G32. . . . . **119** B7
Colintraive Ave G33. . . . . . **98** F4
Colintraive Cres G33 . . . . **98** E4
Coll G74. . . . . **181** C7
Collace Ave PA11 . . . . **110** D7
Colla Gdns G64 . . . . **78** D2
Coll Ave
Port Glasgow PA14 . . . . **69** B8
Renfrew PA4 . . . . **94** D1
Coll Dr ML5. . . . . **121** E4
College Cres FK2 . . . . **42** D7
College Gate G61 . . . . **75** C6
College La G1 . . . . **241** B2
COLLEGE MILTON **159** B3
College Pk KA10 . . . . **229** F7
College St
Dumbarton G82. . . . . **49** F4
Glasgow G1 . . . . **241** B2
College Way
Dumbarton G82. . . . . **49** F3
East Kilbride G75. . . . . **181** A7
College Wynd [2] KA1 . . . **227** F8
COLLENAN **230** A6
Collenan Ave KA10. . . . . . . **230** A4
Collenan Smallholdings
KA10 . . . . **230** B6
Collessie Dr G33. . . . . **99** C2
Coll Gdns KA11 . . . . **225** B8
Colliers Rd FK7 . . . . **8** D4
Collier St PA5 . . . . **111** F3
Colliers Way FK7. . . . . **7** C1
Colliertree Rd ML6. . . . . . **123** D8
Collina St G20 . . . . **96** C6
Collingwood Ct FK1 . . . . . . **41** E5
Collingwood Pl G84. . . . . . **17** A2
Collingwood Terr PA19. . . **44** F6
Collins Dr KA10 . . . . **230** A4
Collins Rd G84. . . . . **25** C8
Collins St
Clydebank G81. . . . . **74** C6
Glasgow G4 . . . . **241** C2
Coll Lea ML3. . . . . **161** F1
Coll Pl
Airdrie ML6 . . . . **123** C5
Glasgow G21 . . . . **98** B2
Collree Gdns G34 . . . . **120** C7
Coll St
Glasgow G21 . . . . **98** B2
Wishaw ML2 . . . . **165** F6
Collyland Rd FK10 . . . . **5** D3
Collylinn Rd G61. . . . . **75** E4
Colmonell Ave G13. . . . . . . **94** F7
Colonsay G74. . . . . **181** C7
Colonsay Ave
Port Glasgow PA14 . . . . **69** B7
Renfrew PA4 . . . . **94** C1
Colonsay Cres ML5. . . . . . **121** D4
Colonsay Dr G77. . . . . **156** B5
Colonsay Ho KA9 . . . . **236** B5
Colonsay Pl KA3 . . . . **223** B6
Colonsay Rd
[2] Glasgow G52 . . . . **115** E5
Paisley PA2 . . . . **133** D7
Colonsay Terr FK1 . . . . **42** B2
Colquhoun G82. . . . . **50** A4
Colquhoun Ave G52. . . . . **115** A7
Colquhoun Ct G41 . . . . . . **116** C3
Colquhoun Dr
Alexandria G83 . . . . **27** E7
Bearsden G61 . . . . **75** E5
Colquhoun Park Prim Sch
G61. **75** D3
Colquhoun Pk G52. . . . . . . **115** B7
Colquhoun Rd
Kilmarnock KA3 . . . . **223** C2
Milton G82. . . . . **50** F1
Colquhoun Sq G84. . . . . **16** C1
Colquhoun St
Dumbarton G82. . . . . **50** A4
Helensburgh G84. . . . . **16** D2
Stirling FK7 . . . . **7** C6
Colquhoun Terr FK7 . . . . . . **7** C6
Colsnaur FK11 . . . . **4** A6
Colson Pl ML4 . . . . **142** C3
COLSTON **97** F8
Colston Ave G64 . . . . **97** F7
Colston Dr G64 . . . . **97** F7
Colston Gdns G64. . . . . **97** E7
Colston Gr G64 . . . . **97** F7
Colston Path G64 . . . . **97** E7
Colston Pl
[2] Airdrie ML6 . . . . **123** C7
[1] Bishopbriggs G64. . . . . . **97** E7
Colston Rd
Airdrie ML6 . . . . **123** C7
Bishopbriggs G64 . . . . **97** F7
Colston Row [3] ML6 . . . . **123** C7
Colston Terr [4] ML6. . . . . **123** C7
Colt Ave ML5 . . . . **101** E1
Coltmuir Cres G64 . . . . **97** E8
Coltmuir Dr G64 . . . . **97** E8
Coltmuir Gdns G64. . . . . . . **97** E8
Coltmuir St G22 . . . . **97** B6
COLTNESS. **165** D5
Coltness Ave ML7 . . . . **166** F8
Coltness Dr ML4 . . . . **142** B4
Coltness High Sch ML2. . **165** D4
Coltness La G33 . . . . **119** D7
Coltness Prim Sch ML2. . **165** C6
Coltness Rd ML2 . . . . **165** C6
Coltness St G33. . . . . **119** C8
Coltpark Ave G64 . . . . **97** E7
Coltpark La G64 . . . . **97** F8
Colt Pl ML5. . . . . **122** A8
Coltsfoot Dr G53. . . . . **135** B3
Coltswood Ct [1] ML5. . . . **122** A8
Coltswood Rd ML5 . . . . . . **122** A8
Colt Terr ML5. . . . . **122** A8
Columba G81 . . . . **74** D2
Columba Cres ML1. . . . . . . **142** D2
Columba Ct G71 . . . . **141** C7
Columba Path G72 . . . . . . **161** C8
Columba St
Glasgow G51 . . . . **116** B7
Greenock PA16 . . . . **45** D4
Helensburgh G84. . . . . **16** D2
Columbia Pl G75 . . . . **180** B8
Columbia Way G75. . . . . . **180** B8
Columbine Way ML8 . . . . . **201** F8
Colvend Dr G73 . . . . **138** B3
Colvend La G40. . . . . **117** F3
Colvend St G40 . . . . **117** F3
Colville Cl G72. . . . . **139** D6
Colville Ct ML1 . . . . **143** C1
Colville Dr G73 . . . . **138** D6
Colville Gdns FK10. . . . . . . **10** A6
Colvilles Pk G75 . . . . **181** B6
Colvilles Pl G75. . . . . **181** B6
Colvilles Rd G75. . . . . **181** A6
Colwood Ave G53 . . . . **135** A3
Colwood Gdns G53. . . . . . **135** A3
Colwood Path G53 . . . . . . **135** A4
Colwood Pl G53 . . . . **135** A3
Colwood Sq G53 . . . . **135** A3
Colwyn Ct ML6. . . . . **103** A1
Colzium Ho★ G65. . . . . **36** F2
Colzium View G65 . . . . **60** E8
Combe Quadrant ML4 . . . **141** E3
Comedie Rd G33. . . . . **99** E4
Comely Bank ML3. . . . . **161** F3
Comelybank La G82. . . . . . **49** D4
Comelybank Rd G82 . . . . . **49** D4
Comely Park Gdns
[15] Falkirk FK1. . . . . **41** B4
[15] Falkirk FK1. . . . . **42** B4
Comelypark Pl G31 . . . . . **118** A6
Comely Park Prim Sch
FK1. **42** B4
Comelypark St G31 . . . . . **118** A6
Comely Park Terr [14] FK1 . **42** B4
Comely Pl FK1. . . . . **42** B4
Commerce St G5 . . . . **240** C1
Commercial Ct G5 . . . . **117** D5
Commercial Rd
Barrhead G78 . . . . **134** C4
Glasgow G5 . . . . **117** D5
Common Gn ML3 . . . . **162** E4
Commonhead Ave ML6 . . **102** F1
Commonhead La ML6 . . . **102** F1
Commonhead Rd
Glasgow G34, G69. . . . . . . **120** E8
Kilmarnock KA1 . . . . **228** A3
Commonhead St ML6 . . . **102** F1
Commonside St ML6 . . . . **102** F1
Commore Ave G78. . . . . . . **134** D1
Commore Dr G13 . . . . **95** A7
Commore Pl G78 . . . . **154** C6
Community Ave ML4 . . . . **142** A2
Community Pl ML4. . . . . . **142** B3
Community Rd ML4 . . . . . **142** A2
Comrie Cres ML3 . . . . **161** E3
Comrie Rd G33 . . . . **99** C5
Comrie St G32. . . . . **119** B3
Conan Ct G72. . . . . **139** D5
Cona St G46. . . . . **135** E4
Condor Glen ML1 . . . . **142** E7
CONDORRAT. **82** B7
Condorrat Intc G67 . . . . . . **82** C8
Condorrat Prim Sch G67 . **82** B7
Condorrat Rd
Cumbernauld G67, ML6. . . . **82** B3
Glenmavis ML6 . . . . **102** D6
Condorrat Ring Rd
Cumbernauld, Condorrat
G67. **82** A6
Cumbernauld, Dalshannon
G67. **82** C7
Coneyhill Rd FK9 . . . . **2** B7
Coneypark FK7 . . . . **6** E6
Coneypark Cres FK4 . . . . . **38** C3
Coneypark Pl FK4. . . . . **38** C3
Congress Rd G3 . . . . **116** D7
Congress Way G3. . . . . **116** E7
Conifer Pl G66. . . . . **79** B6
Coningsby Pl FK10. . . . . . . **10** A6
Conisborough Cl G34 . . . **100** A1
Conisborough Path G34. . . **99** F1
Conisborough Rd G34. . . **100** A1
Coniston G75. . . . . **179** F5
Coniston Cres ML3. . . . . . **183** C6
Coniston Dr ML4. . . . . **142** B3
Conistone Cres G69. . . . . **119** F4
Conival Cl ML1. . . . . **164** C3
Connal St G40 . . . . **118** B3
Connell Cres G62 . . . . **55** C1
Connell Ct KA25 . . . . **149** B1
Connell Gr ML2 . . . . **164** E2
Connelly Pl ML1 . . . . **163** D7
Conner Ave FK2. . . . . **42** A8
Conniston St G32 . . . . **118** E7
Connolly Dr FK6 . . . . **21** C4
Connolly Pl FK6. . . . . **21** F1
Connor Rd G78 . . . . **134** B3
Connor St ML6. . . . . **103** E1
Conon Ave G61 . . . . **75** D3
Conroy Ct FK6 . . . . **21** E1
Conservation Pl ML2 . . . . **165** C1
Consett La G33 . . . . **119** C8
Consett St G33 . . . . **119** C8
Constable Rd FK7. . . . . **7** B6
Constantine Way ML1 . . . **142** C1
Constarry Rd G65. . . . . **60** F4
Consul Way ML1 . . . . **142** C1
Container Way PA15 . . . . . **45** F5
Content Ave KA8. . . . . **239** A8
Content Ct KA6 . . . . **239** D2
Content St KA8 . . . . **239** A8
Contin Pl G20. . . . . **96** D5
Convair Way PA4 . . . . **94** D1
Conval Way [3] PA3. . . . . . **113** D8
Conway Ct FK1 . . . . **41** F4
Coodham Pl KA13. . . . . . . **207** D3
Cook Rd G83 . . . . **28** A8
Cook St G5 . . . . **117** A5
Coo La G76 . . . . **178** E5
Coolgardie Gn [2] G75 . . . **180** C7
Coolgardie Pl [1] G75. . . . **180** C7
Cooperage Ct G14 . . . . **94** D6
Cooperage Pl G3 . . . . **116** C8
Cooperage Quay FK8. . . . . . . **7** C8
Cooperage Way FK10 . . . . . **10** D8
Cooperage Yd PA12 . . . . . **129** C2
Co-Operative Terr PA5. . **112** A3
Cooper Ave ML8 . . . . **187** E3
Coopers Cres KA3. . . . . . . **195** E1
Cooper's Well St G11 . . . . . **96** C1
Copeland Prim Sch G51. **116** B7
Copenhagen Ave G75 . . . **180** E6
Copland Pl
Alva FK12. . . . . **4** F7
Glasgow G51 . . . . **116** B6
Copland Quadrant G51 . . **116** B6
Copland Rd G51 . . . . **116** B6
Coplaw Ct G42. . . . . **117** A3
Coplaw St G42. . . . . **117** A3
Copperfield La G71 . . . . . **141** A7
Copperwood Cres [3]
ML3 . . . . **162** B5
Copperwood Ct [1] ML3. . **162** B5
Copperwood Wynd [2]
ML3 . . . . **162** B5
Coralmount Gdns G66. . . . **79** E7
Coranbae Pl KA7. . . . . **238** B1
Corbett Ct G32. . . . . **118** F3
Corbett St G32. . . . . **119** A3
Corbie Pl G62 . . . . **54** D2
Corbiewood Dr FK7 . . . . . . **11** E8
Corbiston Way G67 . . . . . . **62** B2
Cordale Ave G82. . . . . **27** E2
Cordiner Cl FK8. . . . . **1** F2
Cordiner La G44 . . . . **137** D2
Cordiner St G44 . . . . **137** B7
Cordon Rd KA3 . . . . **222** E4
Corentin Ct FK1. . . . . **42** C3
CORKERHILL. **115** E2
Corkerhill Gdns G52 . . . . **115** E4
Corkerhill Pl G52 . . . . **115** E2
Corkerhill Rd G52. . . . . . . **115** D3
Corkerhill Sta G52 . . . . . . **115** D2
Corlaich Ave G42 . . . . **137** E7
Corlaich Dr G42 . . . . **137** E7
Corless Ct G71. . . . . **141** A6
Corlic St PA15 . . . . **46** B2
Corlic Way PA13 . . . . **69** C1
Cormack Ave G64. . . . . **57** C1
Cormorant Ave PA6 . . . . . **111** D8
Cornaig Rd G53. . . . . **135** B8
Cornalee Gdns G53 . . . . . **135** B8
Cornalee Pl G53 . . . . **135** B8
Cornalee Rd G53. . . . . **135** B8
Cornelian Terr ML4 . . . . . **142** A4
Cornelia St ML1. . . . . **142** B1
Corn Exchange Rd [1] FK8 . . **7** B7
Cornfield Ct G72. . . . . **139** E6
Cornhaddock St PA15 . . . . **45** E4
Cornhill KA7. . . . . **239** B3
Cornhill Cres FK7 . . . . **7** B3
Cornhill Dr ML5. . . . . **121** F8
Cornhill St G21 . . . . **98** A5
Cornish Ct ML5 . . . . **121** F8
Cornmill Ct G81 . . . . **74** A6
Cornock Cres G81 . . . . **74** B3
Cornock St G81. . . . . **74** B3
Cornsilloch Brae ML9 . . . **186** A3
Corn St G4 . . . . **97** B2
CORNTON **2** B3
Cornton Bsns Pk FK9 . . . . . . **2** B3
Cornton Cres FK9. . . . . **2** A5
Cornton Prim Sch FK9 . . . . **2** A4
Cornton Rd FK9. . . . . **2** A4
Cornton Vale Cotts FK9 . . . **2** A4
Cornwall Ave G73. . . . . . . **138** D5
Cornwall St
East Kilbride G74. . . . . **159** E1
Glasgow G41. . . . . **116** D5
Cornwall Street S G41. . . **116** D5
Cornwall Way G74 . . . . . . **159** F1
Corona Cres FK4. . . . . **39** F5
Coronation Ave ML9 . . . . **199** A8
Coronation Cres ML9. . . . **199** A8

Culrain St G32 119 A4
Culross Hill G74 159 D1
Culross Pl
Coatbridge ML5 121 F7
East Kilbride G74 159 D1
Culross St G32 119 C4
Culross Way G69 81 A3
Cultenhove Cres FK7 7 A3
Cultenhove Pl FK7 7 A3
Cultenhove Rd
Stirling, Coxet Hill FK7 7 A3
Stirling FK7 7 A4
Culterfell Path ML1 144 C2
Cult Rd G66 79 E4
Cults St G51 115 F6
Culvain Ave G61 75 B7
Culvain Pl FK1 42 C2
Culzean ML6 102 F5
Culzean Ave
Coatbridge ML5 121 E4
Prestwick KA9 236 D7
Culzean Cres
Glasgow G69 120 A4
Kilmarnock KA3 228 C8
Newton Mearns G77 157 A4
Culzean Ct ML5 121 E5
Culzean Dr
East Kilbride G74 159 D3
Glasgow G32 119 D4
Gourock PA19 43 F5
Motherwell ML1 143 C3
Culzean Pl
East Kilbride G74 159 D3
Kilwinning KA13 207 C2
Stenhousemuir FK5 23 F4
Culzean Rd KA7 238 D3
Cumberland Ave G84 16 A3
Cumberland Ct PA16 44 E4
Cumberland Pl
Coatbridge ML5 121 D4
9 Glasgow G5 117 C4
Cumberland Rd
Greenock PA16 44 E4
Rhu G84 15 D5
Cumberland St
Glasgow G5 117 B5
Glasgow G5 117 C4
Cumberland Terr G84 15 D5
Cumberland Wlk PA16 44 E4
CUMBERNAULD 62 C5
Cumbernauld Airport G68 62 B7
Cumbernauld Coll (Cumbernauld Campus)
G67 61 F1
Cumbernauld Coll (East Dunbartonshire Campus)
G66 79 C8
Cumbernauld High Sch
G67 62 C1
Cumbernauld Prim Sch
Cumbernauld, Carrickstone G68 61 D5
Cumbernauld, Kildrum G67 62 B4
Cumbernauld Rd
Chryston G69 100 C7
Cumbernauld G67 81 D4
Glasgow, Dennistoun G31 118 B7
Glasgow, Dennistoun G31, G33 118 C7
Glasgow, Riddrie G33 98 A2
Haggs FK4 39 A3
Moodiesburn G68, G69 81 B3
Muirhead G69 100 C7
Stepps G33 99 D5
Cumbernauld Sta G67 83 A8
CUMBERNAULD VILLAGE 62 A6
Cumbrae G74 160 C1
Cumbrae Ave PA14 69 B7
Cumbrae Cres ML5 122 E5
Cumbrae Crescent N G82 49 C5
Cumbrae Crescent S G82 49 C5
Cumbrae Ct
Clydebank G81 74 B2
Irvine KA11 225 C8
Cumbrae Dr
Falkirk FK1 41 C4
Kilmarnock KA3 223 B5
Motherwell ML1 163 C8
Cumbrae Ho KA9 236 B5
Cumbrae Pl
Coatbridge ML5 122 E4
Gourock PA19 44 D6
West Kilbride KA23 190 C4
Cumbrae Rd
Paisley PA2 133 E7
Renfrew PA4 94 D1
Saltcoats KA21 205 F2
Cumbrae St G33 119 A8
Cumbrae Terr KA22 205 C3
Cumlodden Dr G20 96 D7
Cumming Ave ML8 202 C8
Cumming Dr G42 137 B8
Cumnock Dr
Airdrie ML6 123 A4
Barrhead G78 134 D1
Hamilton ML3 161 D1
Cumnock Rd G33 98 E6
Cumroch Rd G66 33 C1
Cunard Ct G81 94 B8
Cunard St G81 94 B8
Cuninghame Dr KA20 206 B1
Cuninghame Rd
Ardrossan KA22 205 C3
Kilbarchan PA10 111 B3
Cunningair Dr ML1 163 E4
Cunningham Cres KA7 239 C6
Cunningham Dr
Duntocher G81 73 F6
Glasgow G46 136 E3
Harthill ML7 127 D5
Cunninghame Cres
KA21 217 A8
Cunninghame Dr KA1 227 E4
Cunninghame Rd
East Kilbride G74 159 E1
Irvine KA12 224 D8
Prestwick KA9 236 C7
Rutherglen G73 138 C8
Saltcoats KA21 217 A8
Cunningham Gdns
Falkirk FK2 42 F5
Houston PA6 91 D1
CUNNINGHAMHEAD 221 B8
Cunninghamhead Est Cvn Pk
KA3 220 F8
Cunningham Pl KA7 239 C6
Cunningham Rd
Glasgow G52 114 F8
Stenhousemuir FK5 24 A3
Stirling FK7 7 D7
Cunningham St ML1 163 D6
Cunningham Watt Rd
KA3 195 D1
Cunning Park Dr KA7 238 D3
Cupar Dr PA16 44 F3
Cuparhead Ave ML5 121 E4
Cuppleton Brae PA9, PA12 130 B2
Curfew Rd G13 75 D1
Curle St
Glasgow G14 95 D2
Glasgow G14 95 E2
Curlew Cres PA16 45 B4
Curlew Dr G75 180 A5
Curlew La PA16 45 B4
Curlew Pl PA5 131 C7
Curling Cres G44 137 C5
Curlinghaugh Cres ML2 165 C3
Curlingmire G75 180 E7
Curran Ave ML2 164 E1
Currie Ct KA22 205 C1
Currie Pl G20 96 F6
Currieside Ave ML7 146 E4
Currieside Pl ML7 146 D4
Currie St G20 96 E6
Cursiter Ct FK5 23 B2
Curtecan Pl KA7 238 F6
Curtis Ave G44 137 D7
Curzon St G20 96 F6
Cushenquarter Dr FK7 12 D3
Custom House Mus★
PA15 46 A5
Customhouse Pl PA15 46 A5
Custom House Quay Ret Pk
PA15 46 A6
Custom House Way PA15 46 A5
Customs Rdbt FK8 2 B1
Custonhall Pl FK6 21 D2
Cuthbert Pl KA3 223 A2
Cuthbertson Prim Sch
G42 117 A3
Cuthbertson St G42 117 A2
Cuthbert St G71 141 B7
Cuthelton Dr G31 118 E4
Cuthelton St G31 118 D4
Cuthelton Terr G31 118 D4
Cutsburn Pl KA3 211 F8
Cutsburn Rd KA3 211 F8
Cutstraw Rd KA3 211 F8
Cut The G71 140 F5
Cuttyfield Pl FK2 24 C3
Cutty Sark Pl G82 50 C2
Cypress Ave
Beith KA15 150 C2
Blantyre G72 140 C1
Uddingston G71 141 B8
Cypress Cres G75 180 C5
Cypress Ct
East Kilbride G75 180 C5
Hamilton ML3 162 E2
Kirkintilloch G66 79 B6
Cypress Gdns KA11 219 E5
Cypress Gr
Coatbridge G69 121 B6
Quarriers Village PA11 89 F2
Cypress Pl G75 180 C5
Cypress St G22 97 D5
Cypress Way G72 139 F4
Cyprus Ave PA5 112 B2
Cyril St PA1 114 A4

D

Daer Ave PA4 94 E1
Daer Way ML3 162 A3
Daffodil Way ML1 163 E8
Daintree Terr FK1 41 E5
Dairsie Ct G44 136 F4
Dairsie Gdns G64 98 D8
Dairsie House Sch G43 136 E6
Dairsie St G44 136 F4
Dairy Mead Pl KA22 205 D2
Daisybank KA14 170 C6
Daisy Cotts KA8 236 A3
Daisy St G42 117 B2
Dakala Ct ML2 165 A2
Dakota Way PA4 94 D1
Dalbeattie Braes ML6 123 E1
Dalbeattie Dr 1 G72 161 D3
DALBETH 118 E2
Dalbeth Pl G32 118 F2
Dalbeth Rd G32 118 F2
Dalblair Ct KA7 238 F8
Dalblair Rd KA7 238 F7
Dalby Gr ML5 101 F7
Dalcharn Pl G34 120 A8
Dalcraig Cres G72 140 C2
Dalcross St G11 96 C2
Dalcross Way ML6 104 A3
Dalcruin Gdns G69 81 A4
Dalderse Ave FK2 42 B6
Daldowie Ave G32 119 D3
Daldowie Doocot★ G69 119 F2
Daldowie Rd G71 120 A2
Daldowie St ML5 121 E3
Dale Ave G75 180 D6
Dale Cres KA12 219 D4
Dale Ct ML2 164 C2
Dale Dr ML1 143 A4
Dale Path G40 117 F4
Dalespark Rdbt KA2 222 A1
Dale St
Glasgow G40 117 F4
Glasgow G40 118 A4
Daleview Ave G12 96 B6
Daleview Dr G76 157 D6
Daleview Gr G76 157 D6
Dale Way G73 138 B4
Dalfoil Ct PA1 114 F4
Dalgain Ct KA11 220 A5
Dalgarroch Ave G81 94 E8
DALGARVEN 207 D8
Dalgarven Mews KA3 223 C6
Dalgarven Mill-Ayrshire Mus of Country Life & Costume★ KA13 207 D8
Dalgarven Wynd KA13 207 C6
Dalgleish Ave G81 73 F6
Dalgleish Ct FK8 7 B8
Dalgleish Pl ML2 166 B3
Dalhousie Gdns G64 78 A2
Dalhousie La G3 240 B4
Dalhousie Rd PA10 111 B2
Dalhousie St G3 240 C4
Dalilea Dr G34 100 D1
Dalilea Pl G34 100 D1
Dalintober St G5 240 B1
Daljarrock KA13 207 B2
Dalkeith Ave
Bishopbriggs G64 78 B4
Glasgow G41 116 B4
Dalkeith Rd G64 78 B4
Dallas Ct KA10 229 D2
Dallas La KA10 229 D2
Dallas Pl KA10 229 D2
Dallas Rd KA10 229 D2
Dalmacoulter Rd ML6 103 B3
Dalmahoy Cres PA11 110 C6
Dalmahoy St G32 118 E7
Dalmahoy Way KA13 207 B3
Dalmailing Ave KA11 220 B1
Dalmally St
Glasgow G20 96 F3
Greenock PA15 46 F2
DALMARNOCK 118 A2
Dalmarnock Ct G40 118 B3
Dalmarnock Prim Sch
G40 118 A4
Dalmarnock Rd G40 118 A3
Dalmarnock Road Trad Est
G73 118 B1
Dalmarnock Sta G40 118 A3
Dalmary Dr PA1 114 B5
Dalmellington Ct
East Kilbride G74 159 D2
Hamilton ML3 161 D1
Dalmellington Dr
East Kilbride G74 159 D2
9 Glasgow G53 135 A8
Dalmellington Rd
Ayr KA7 239 C4
Glasgow G53 115 A1
Dalmeny Ave G46 136 C3
Dalmeny Dr G78 134 A2
Dalmeny Rd ML3 162 D2
DALMILLING 236 E1
Dalmilling Cres KA8 236 D2
Dalmilling Dr KA8 236 E2
Dalmilling Prim Sch KA8 236 E2
Dalmilling Rd KA8 236 E2
Dalmoak Rd PA15 46 C1
DALMONACH 27 F5
Dalmonach Rd G83 27 F4
Dalmore Cres
Helensburgh G84 16 A3
1 Motherwell ML1 143 A2
Dalmore Dr
Airdrie ML6 123 A6
Alva FK12 4 E6
Dalmore Ho G84 16 A3
Dalmore Pl KA11 219 F6
Dalmore Way KA11 219 F6
Dalmorglen Pk FK7 6 F6
DALMUIR 73 E4
Dalmuir Sta G81 73 E3
Dalnair Pl G62 54 D2
Dalnair St G3 96 D1
Dalness St G32 119 A4
Dalnottar Ave G60 73 B6
Dalnottar Dr G60 73 B5
Dalnottar Gdns G60 73 B5
Dalnottar Hill Rd G60 73 B6
Dalnottar Terr G60 73 B6
Dalquhurn Gdns G82 49 D8
Dalquhurn La
Dumbarton G82 49 E8
Renton G82 49 E8
Dalreoch Ave G69 120 C6
Dalreoch Ct G82 49 D4
Dalreoch Path G69 120 C5
Dalreoch Prim Sch G82 49 C5
Dalreoch Sta G82 49 E4
Dalriada G2 240 B2
Dalriada Cres ML1 142 D1
Dalriada Dr G64 78 C8
Dalriada Rd PA16 44 D3
Dalriada St G40 118 C4
DALRY 191 C8
Dalry Gdns ML3 161 D2
Dalry La KA22 205 C4
Dalrymple Ct
Irvine KA12 219 E3
3 Kirkintilloch G66 79 D7
Dalrymple Dr
Coatbridge ML5 121 F5
East Kilbride G74 159 E3
Irvine KA12 219 E3
Newton Mearns G77 157 A4
Dalrymple Pl KA12 219 D3
Dalrymple St PA15 45 F6
Dalry Pl ML6 143 D8
Dalry Prim Sch KA24 191 B7
Dalry Rd
Ardrossan KA22 205 C4
Beith KA15 171 A7
Kilbirnie KA25 170 A7
Kilwinning KA13 207 D4
Saltcoats KA21 206 A2
Stewarton KA3 211 C8
Uddingston G71 141 B7
Dalry St G32 119 B4
Dalry Sta KA24 191 D7
DALSERF 186 C2
Dalserf Cres G46 136 B1
Dalserf Ct G31 118 B5
Dalserf Gdns G31 118 B5
Dalserf Path 18 ML9 185 C1
Dalserf Pl G31 118 B5
Dalserf Prim Sch ML9 199 F8
Dalserf St G31 118 B5
Dalsetter Ave G15 75 A2
Dalsetter Bsns Ctr G15 75 A2
Dalsetter Pl G15 75 A2
DALSHANNON 82 A6
Dalshannon Pl G67 82 A7
Dalshannon Rd G67 82 B7
Dalshannon View G67 82 B7
Dalshannon Way G67 82 A7
Dalsholm Ave G20 96 B7
Dalsholm Rd G20 96 B8
Dalskeith Ave PA3 113 A5
Dalskeith Cres PA3 113 A5
Dalskeith Rd PA3 113 A5
Dalswinton Path G34 120 D8
Dalswinton St G34 120 C8
Dalton Ave G81 74 E1
Dalton Ct G31 118 E5
Dalton Hill ML3 161 E2
Dalton Pk KA7 238 B2
Dalton St G31 118 E5
Dalvait Ct G83 27 F8
Dalvait Gdns G83 27 E8
Dalvait Rd 2 G83 27 E8
Dalveen Ct G78 134 C1
Dalveen Dr G71 140 F8
Dalveen Quadrant ML5 122 D5
Dalveen St G32 118 F5
Dalveen Way G73 138 C3
Dalwhinnie Ave G72 140 C2
Dalwhinnie Cres KA3 222 D4
Dalwhinnie Ct KA11 219 F6
Dalwhinnie Gdns KA3 222 D3
Dalwood Rd KA9 236 B8
Daly Gdns G72 140 E1
Dalzell Ave ML1 164 A4
Dalzell Dr ML1 164 A4
Dalzell Estate★ ML1 163 F3
Dalziel Cres G72 139 D6
Dalziel Ct ML3 162 A3
Dalziel Dr
Glasgow G41 116 C3
Glasgow G41 116 D3
Dalziel Gait 3 G72 139 D6
Dalziel Gr 5 G72 139 D6
Dalziel High Sch ML1 163 D6
Dalziel Path 4 G72 139 D6
Dalziel Quadrant G41 116 C3
Dalziel Rd G52 114 F8
Dalziel St
Hamilton ML3 162 B5
Motherwell ML1 163 F7
Dalziel Twr ML1 164 B3
Dalziel Way G72 139 D5
Damhead Rd KA1 227 E3
Dampark KA3 195 C7
Damshot Cres G53 115 D1
Damshot Rd G53 135 D8
Damside KA8 235 F2
Danby Rd G69 119 F4
Danes Ave 1 G14 95 C4
Danes Cres G14 95 B5
Danes Dr G14 95 C4
Danes Lane N 3 G14 95 C4
Danes Lane S G14 95 C4
Daniel McLaughlin Pl
G66 58 E1
Dankeith Dr KA1 231 C4
Dankeith Rd KA1 231 C4
Dargarvel Ave G41 116 B4
Dargavel Ave PA7 72 B3
Dargavel Rd
Bishopton PA7 72 D1
Erskine PA8 72 E1
Darg Rd KA20 217 D8
Dark Brig Rd ML8 201 B2
Darkwood Cres PA3 113 B6
Darkwood Ct PA3 113 B6
Darkwood Dr PA3 113 B6
Darleith Rd
Alexandria G83 27 E6
Cardross G82 26 A1
Darleith St G32 118 F5
Darley Cres KA10 229 E1
Darley Pl
Hamilton ML3 183 B8
Troon KA10 229 E1
Darley Rd G68 61 E5
Darlington View KA3 195 F1
Darluith Pk PA5 111 C6
Darluith Rd PA3 111 F6
Darmeid Pl ML7 167 B8
Darmule Dr KA13 207 C5
Darnaway Ave G33 99 D2
Darnaway Dr G33 99 D2
Darnaway St G33 99 D2
Darndaff Rd PA15 46 A2
Darngaber Gdns ML3 183 E3
Darngaber Rd ML3 183 E3
Darngavel Ct ML6 122 D8
Darngavil Rd ML6 103 E6
Darnick St G21 98 B2
Darnley Cres G64 77 F3
Darnley Dr KA1 227 E5
Darnley Gdns G41 116 E2
Darnley Ind Est G53 135 B5
Darnley Mains Rd G53 135 C3
Darnley Path G46 135 E5
Darnley Pl G41 116 E2
Darnley Prim Sch G53 135 C4
Darnley Rd
Barrhead G78 134 E3
Glasgow G41 116 E2
Darnley St
Glasgow G41 116 F3
Stirling FK8 7 A8
Darnshaw Cl KA11 220 C5
Darrach Dr FK6 21 A2
Darragh Gn ML2 166 A6
Darroch Ave PA19 44 E7
Darroch Dr
Erskine PA8 72 F3
Gourock PA19 44 E7
Darroch Way G67 62 A3
Dartford St G22 97 B3
Dartmouth Ave PA19 44 E5
Darvel Ave KA3 223 B6
Darvel Cres PA1 114 E4
Darvel Dr G77 157 A5
Darvel Gr G72 161 D2
Darwin Ave ML2 164 B4
Darwin Pl G81 73 D4
Darwin Rd G75 180 C8
Davaar G74 160 C1
Davaar Dr
Coatbridge ML5 121 D7
Kilmarnock KA3 223 B5
Motherwell ML1 142 C2
Paisley PA2 133 E7
Davaar Pl
Falkirk FK1 41 C4
Newton Mearns G77 156 C6
Davaar Rd
Greenock PA16 44 D3
Renfrew PA4 94 D2
Saltcoats KA21 205 F2
Davaar St G40 118 B4
Davan Loan 10 ML2 165 F6
Dava St G51 116 A7
Dave Barrie Ave ML9 184 F5
Daventry Dr G12 96 A5
Davey St PA16 45 C5
David Dale Ave KA3 211 C8
David Gage St KA13 207 E5
David Gray Dr G66 59 A1
David Livingstone Ctr★
G72 140 E2
David Livingstone Meml Prim Sch G72 140 D1
David Orr St KA1 222 E1
David Pl
Glasgow G69 119 F4
Paisley PA3 114 B7
David's Cres KA13 207 D2
David's Loan FK2 24 D1
Davidson Ave KA14 170 D6
Davidson Cres G65 59 F3
Davidson Dr PA19 44 E7
Davidson Gdns
Glasgow G14 95 E4
Stonehouse ML9 198 E1
Davidson La ML8 188 B1
Davidson Pl
Ayr KA8 236 A1
Glasgow G32 119 C6
Davidson Quadrant G81 73 F7
Davidson Rd G83 27 F7
Davidson St
Airdrie ML6 122 F8
Bannockburn FK7 7 C1
Clydebank G81 94 E8
Coatbridge ML5 122 B4
Glasgow G40 118 A2
David St
Coatbridge ML5 122 C7
Glasgow G40 118 A5
Salsburgh ML7 125 B2
Davidston Pl G66 79 F4
David Way PA3 114 B7
Davieland Rd G46 136 A1
Davie's Acre G74 158 F4
Davies Dr G83 27 E6
Davies Quadrant ML1 142 D2
Davies Row FK6 21 E2
Davington Dr ML3 161 D1
Daviot St 2 G51 115 D6
Dawnlight Circ KA22 205 B1

Dawsholm Ind Est G20 ... 96 B7
Dawson Ave
Alloa FK10 ... 9 F8
East Kilbride G75 ... 159 B1
Dawson Pl G4 ... 97 B3
Dawson Rd G4 ... 97 B3
Dawson St FK2 ... 42 B8
Deaconsbank Ave G46 ... 135 E1
Deaconsbank Cres G46 ... 135 D1
Deaconsbank Gdns G46 ... 135 E1
Deaconsbank Gr G46 ... 135 D1
Deaconsbank Pl G46 ... 135 D1
Deaconsbrook La G46 ... 135 D1
Deaconsbrook Rd G46 ... 135 D1
Deaconsgait Way G46 ... 135 D1
Deaconsgrange Rd G46 ... 135 D1
Deacons Rd G65 ... 60 E8
Deacons View G46 ... 135 D1
Dealston Rd G78 ... 134 B4
Deanbank Rd ML5 ... 121 D7
Deanbrae St G71 ... 140 F6
Dean Castle★ KA3 ... 223 B3
Dean Castle Ctry Pk★ KA3 ... 223 B4
Dean Cres
Chryston G69 ... 80 D1
Hamilton ML3 ... 162 C1
Stirling FK8 ... 2 C1
Dean Ct
Clydebank G81 ... 74 C1
11 Kilmarnock KA3 ... 222 F1
Deanfield Ct KA13 ... 207 E3
Deanfield Quadrant G52 ... 114 F6
Dean La KA3 ... 223 A1
DEAN PARK ... 94 D2
Dean Park Ave G71 ... 141 A2
Dean Park Dr G72 ... 139 D4
Dean Park Rd PA4 ... 94 E2
Dean Pl KA2 ... 226 F8
Dean Rd
Kilbirnie KA25 ... 149 B2
Kilmarnock KA3 ... 223 B3
Deans Ave G72 ... 139 D3
Deanside Rd G52 ... 115 A8
Dean St
Bellshill ML4 ... 142 B5
Clydebank G81 ... 74 C1
Kilmarnock KA3 ... 223 A2
Stewarton KA3 ... 195 E1
Deanston Ave G78 ... 134 B1
Deanston Dr G41 ... 136 E8
Deanstone Pl ML5 ... 122 D3
Deanstone Wlk ML5 ... 122 D2
Deanston Gdns G78 ... 134 B1
Deanston Gr ML5 ... 121 E3
Deanston Pk G78 ... 134 B1
Dean Terr KA3 ... 223 A3
Dean View KA3 ... 223 D4
Deanwood Ave G44 ... 136 F3
Deanwood Rd G44 ... 136 F3
Deas Rd ML7 ... 146 C5
Dechmont G75 ... 180 D5
Dechmont Ave
Cambuslang G72 ... 139 D3
Motherwell ML1 ... 163 C7
Dechmont Cotts G72 ... 139 F3
Dechmont Gdns
Blantyre G72 ... 140 C1
Uddingston G71 ... 120 E1
Dechmont Pl G72 ... 139 D3
Dechmont Rd G71 ... 120 E1
Dechmont St
Glasgow G31 ... 118 C4
Hamilton ML3 ... 162 C2
Dechmont View
Bellshill ML4 ... 141 F3
Uddingston G71 ... 141 A7
Dee Ave
Kilmarnock KA1 ... 228 B4
Paisley PA2 ... 112 F2
Renfrew PA4 ... 94 E3
Dee Cres PA2 ... 112 F2
Deedes St ML6 ... 122 D6
Dee Dr PA2 ... 112 F2
Dee Path
Larkhall ML9 ... 199 A8
Motherwell ML1 ... 143 B5
Deep Dale G74 ... 159 C3
Deepdene Rd
Bearsden G61 ... 75 D2
Moodiesburn G69 ... 80 F2
Dee Pl
East Kilbride G75 ... 179 E6
Johnstone PA5 ... 131 C8
Deerdykes Court N G68 ... 81 E6
Deerdykes Court S G68 ... 81 E5
Deerdykes Pl G68 ... 81 E6
Deerdykes Rd G67, G68 ... 81 E5
Deerdykes Rdbt G68 ... 81 C5
Deerdykes View G68 ... 81 D6
Deer Park FK10 ... 5 E1
Deer Park Ave KA20 ... 217 E7
Deer Park Ct ML3 ... 183 D7
Deer Park Pl ML3 ... 183 E7
Deerpark Prim Sch FK10 ... 5 F1
Deer Path ML7 ... 127 E5
Deeside Dr ML8 ... 188 A3
Deeside Pl ML5 ... 122 D4
Dee St
Coatbridge ML5 ... 101 D2
Glasgow G33 ... 118 D8
Shotts ML7 ... 146 D5
Dee Terr ML3 ... 183 B8
Delaney Ct FK10 ... 10 A6
Delaney Wynd ML1 ... 165 B8
Delfie Dr PA16 ... 45 B4
Delhi Ave G81 ... 73 C4
Dellburn St ML1 ... 164 A5
Dellburn Trad Pk ML1 ... 164 A5
Dellingburn St 6 PA15 ... 46 A4
Dell The
Bellshill ML4 ... 142 D3
Newton Mearns G77 ... 157 B5
Delny Pl G33 ... 119 E7
Delph Rd FK10 ... 4 C2
Delphwood Cres FK10 ... 4 D2
Delph Wynd FK10 ... 4 C2
Delves Ct ML11 ... 215 A4
Delves Pk ML11 ... 215 A4
Delves Rd ML11 ... 215 A3
Delvin Rd G44 ... 137 A6
De Moray Ct FK9 ... 2 A4
Demoreham Ave FK6 ... 21 F1
De Morville Pl KA15 ... 171 B7
Dempsey Rd ML4 ... 141 F3
Dempster Ct 4 PA15 ... 45 F4
Dempster St PA15 ... 45 E4
Den Bak Ave ML3 ... 162 A2
Denbeath Ct ML3 ... 163 C1
Denbecan FK10 ... 10 D5
Denbeck St G32 ... 118 F5
Denbrae St G32 ... 118 F5
Dene Wlk G64 ... 98 C8
Denewood Ave PA2 ... 133 D8
Denham St G22 ... 97 B3
Denholm Cres G75 ... 180 E8
Denholm Dr
Glasgow G46 ... 136 C1
Wishaw ML2 ... 165 C6
Denholm Gdns
Greenock PA16 ... 45 C5
Quarter ML3 ... 183 E3
Denholm Gn 2 G75 ... 180 F8
Denholm St PA16 ... 45 D5
Denholm Terr
Greenock PA16 ... 45 D5
Hamilton ML3 ... 161 E3
Denholm Way
Beith KA15 ... 171 A7
Kilmarnock KA1 ... 228 A5
Den La ML7 ... 146 D6
Denmark St
Glasgow G22 ... 97 C4
Glasgow G22 ... 97 C5
Denmilne Gdns G34 ... 120 C7
Denmilne Path G34 ... 120 C7
Denmilne Rd G34 ... 120 D7
Denmilne St G34 ... 120 C7
Denneystoun Cvn Pk G82 ... 49 E4
Denniston Pl ML11 ... 215 C5
DENNISTOUN ... 118 B7
Dennistoun Cres G84 ... 25 C7
Dennistoun Rd PA14 ... 70 C7
Dennistoun St ML4 ... 142 B5
DENNY ... 21 F1
Denny Cres G82 ... 50 A2
Denny High Sch FK6 ... 39 E8
Dennyholm Wynd KA25 ... 149 B1
DENNYLOANHEAD ... 39 D5
Denny Prim Sch FK6 ... 21 D2
Denny Rd
Denny FK4 ... 39 E6
Dumbarton G82 ... 50 A2
Larbert FK5 ... 23 A1
Dennystoun Forge G82 ... 49 E4
DENNYSTOWN ... 49 E4
Denny Tank (Mus)★ G82 ... 50 A3
Denovan Rd FK6 ... 21 E4
Dentdale G74 ... 159 C3
Den The KA24 ... 170 D3
Deramore Ave G46 ... 157 A7
Derby St G3 ... 96 E1
Derby Terrace La 4 G3 ... 116 E8
Derby Wynd 1 ML1 ... 143 B1
Deroran Pl FK8 ... 6 F5
Derrywood Rd G66 ... 58 C6
Dervaig Gdns ML6 ... 84 D3
Derwent Ave FK1 ... 41 F4
Derwent Ct KA3 ... 222 F1
Derwent Dr ML5 ... 101 D2
Derwent St G22 ... 97 B4
Derwentwater G75 ... 179 F6
Despard Ave G32 ... 119 E4
Despard Gdns G32 ... 119 E4
Deveron Ave G46 ... 136 D2
Deveron Cres ML3 ... 161 E4
Deveron Rd
Bearsden G61 ... 75 D2
East Kilbride G74 ... 160 B1
Kilmarnock KA1 ... 228 A5
Motherwell ML1 ... 143 B5
Troon KA10 ... 229 G5
Deveron St
Coatbridge ML5 ... 101 D1
Glasgow G33 ... 98 D1
Devilla Ct KA9 ... 236 C5
Devine Ct ML2 ... 165 B3
Devine Gr ML2 ... 166 A7
Devlin Ct
Hamilton G72 ... 161 E7
Stirling FK7 ... 7 B2
Devlin Gr G72 ... 161 E7
DEVOL ... 68 D7
Devol Ave PA14 ... 47 A1
Devol Cres G53 ... 135 B8
Devol Ind Est PA14 ... 68 D8
Devol Rd PA14 ... 68 C6
Devonbank FK10 ... 5 E3
Devon Ct FK10 ... 4 B2
Devondale Ave G72 ... 140 D1
Devon Dr
Bishopton PA7 ... 72 C3
Tullibody FK10 ... 4 E4
Devon Gdns
Bishopbriggs G64 ... 77 F3
Carluke ML8 ... 187 E2
Devonhill Ave ML3 ... 183 D7
Devon Pl
Cambus FK10 ... 4 A1
Glasgow G41 ... 117 B4
Devonport Pk G75 ... 180 A7
Devon Rd
Alloa FK10 ... 10 C6
Greenock PA16 ... 44 D4
Devonshire Gardens La 2 G12 ... 96 B4
Devonshire Gdns 1 G12 ... 96 B4
Devonshire Terr G12 ... 96 B4
Devonshire Terrace La G12 ... 96 B4
Devon St G5 ... 117 B4
Devon Valley Dr FK10 ... 5 D2
Devonview Pl ML6 ... 122 F6
Devonview St ML6 ... 122 F6
Devon Village FK10 ... 5 E4
Devonway FK10 ... 10 F5
Devon Way ML1 ... 163 B6
Devon Wlk G68 ... 81 E8
De Walden Dr KA3 ... 223 B5
De Walden Terr KA3 ... 223 A1
Dewar Cl G71 ... 121 A1
Dewar Dr G15 ... 75 A3
Dewar Gate G15 ... 75 A3
Dewar Wlk ML8 ... 201 B1
Dewshill Cotts ML7 ... 126 B4
Dhuhill Drive E G84 ... 16 E4
Diamond Cotts KA6 ... 237 B4
Diamond St ML4 ... 142 A4
Diana Ave G13 ... 95 B8
Diana Quadrant ML1 ... 143 A5
Diana Vernon Ct G84 ... 25 B8
Dickburn Cres FK4 ... 39 F5
Dick Cres KA12 ... 219 D5
Dick Ct ML9 ... 198 E2
Dickens Ave G81 ... 74 A4
Dickens Gr ML1 ... 143 D2
Dickies Wells FK12 ... 5 C7
Dick Institute Mus★ KA1 ... 228 A8
Dick Quad G82 ... 48 A8
Dick Rd KA1 ... 228 A8
Dickson Ct KA15 ... 150 C1
Dickson Dr KA12 ... 219 C5
Dickson Path ML4 ... 141 F2
Dickson Sq ML1 ... 144 B1
Dickson St ML9 ... 185 C1
Dicks Pk G75 ... 180 D8
Dick St G20 ... 96 F3
Dick Terr KA12 ... 219 D5
Diddup Dr KA20 ... 206 B1
Differ Ave G65 ... 59 F2
Dillichip Cl G83 ... 27 F2
Dillichip Gdns G83 ... 27 F3
Dillichip Loan G83 ... 27 E3
Dillichip Terr G83 ... 27 F3
Dilwara Ave G14 ... 95 E2
Dimity St PA5 ... 111 F3
DIMSDALE ... 165 C1
Dimsdale Cres ML2 ... 165 C1
Dimsdale Rd ML2 ... 165 C1
Dinard Dr G46 ... 136 C4
Dinart St G33 ... 98 D1
Dinduff St G34 ... 100 C1
Dineiddwg G62 ... 55 B6
Dingwall Dr PA16 ... 44 F3
Dinmont Ave PA2 ... 112 F1
Dinmont Cres ML1 ... 142 D2
Dinmont Pl 1 G41 ... 116 E1
Dinmont Rd G41 ... 116 D1
Dinmont Way PA2 ... 112 F1
Dinmurchie Rd KA10 ... 229 F6
Dinnet Way 11 ML2 ... 165 F6
Dinwiddie St G21 ... 98 C2
Dinyra Pl ML5 ... 101 C6
Dippin Pl KA21 ... 205 F2
Dipple Ct KA25 ... 149 B2
Dipple Pl G15 ... 75 B2
Dipple Rd KA25 ... 149 B3
Dipple View KA25 ... 149 B3
Dirleton Dr
Glasgow G41 ... 136 F8
Paisley PA2 ... 113 A1
Dirleton Gate G61 ... 75 D2
Dirleton Gdns FK10 ... 9 F7
Dirleton La FK10 ... 9 F6
Dirleton Pl G41 ... 136 E8
DIRRANS ... 207 F2
Dirrans Terr KA13 ... 207 F2
Disraeli Way G75 ... 179 D8
Ditton Dr KA1 ... 227 E4
Divernia Way G78 ... 155 D8
Diverswell FK10 ... 5 D2
Divert Rd PA19 ... 44 C6
Divert Wlk PA19 ... 44 C6
Dixon Ave
Dumbarton G82 ... 49 E3
Glasgow G42 ... 117 B1
Dixon Dr G82 ... 49 D2
Dixon Pl G74 ... 159 B3
Dixon Rd
Glasgow G42 ... 117 C1
Helensburgh G84 ... 16 E3
Dixons Blazes Ind Est G42, G5 ... 117 C3
Dixon St
Coatbridge ML5 ... 122 B4
Glasgow G1 ... 240 C1
Hamilton ML3 ... 162 D3
Paisley PA1 ... 113 F4
Dobbie Ave
Larbert FK5 ... 41 C8
Stenhousemuir FK5 ... 23 C1
Dobbies Ct ML8 ... 187 A6
Dobbie's Loan G4 ... 241 A4
Dobbie's Loan Pl G4 ... 241 B3
Dochart Ave PA4 ... 94 E1
Dochart Dr ML5 ... 101 D2
Dochart Pl FK1 ... 42 D2
Dochart St G33 ... 98 E2
Dock Breast PA15 ... 46 A5
Dockhead Pl KA21 ... 216 F7
Dockhead St KA21 ... 216 F7
Dock Rd KA22 ... 205 B1
Dock St
Clydebank G81 ... 94 D7
Falkirk FK2 ... 24 C2
Dodhill Pl G13 ... 95 B6
Dodside Gdns G32 ... 119 C4
Dodside Pl G32 ... 119 C4
Dodside Rd G77 ... 155 E3
Dodside St G32 ... 119 C4
Dolan St G69 ... 120 B5
Dollar Ave FK2 ... 42 A7
Dollar Gdns FK2 ... 42 A7
Dollar Ind Est FK1, FK2 ... 42 A5
Dollar Pk ML1 ... 164 B3
Dollar Terr G20 ... 96 C8
Dolphin Rd G41 ... 116 D2
Dominica Gn 4 G75 ... 159 A1
Donald Cres KA10 ... 229 E3
Donal Dewar L Ctr G15 ... 75 A3
Donaldfield Rd PA11 ... 110 B7
Donaldson Ave
Alloa FK10 ... 4 E1
Kilsyth G65 ... 60 E7
Saltcoats KA21 ... 216 F8
Stevenston KA20 ... 206 E2
Donaldson Cres G66 ... 79 C7
Donaldson Dr
Irvine KA12 ... 219 D4
Kilmarnock KA3 ... 223 D3
Renfrew PA4 ... 94 D3
Donaldson Gn G71 ... 141 B8
Donaldson Pl
Cambusbarron FK7 ... 6 D6
2 Kirkintilloch G66 ... 79 D7
Donaldson Rd
Kilmarnock KA3 ... 223 D3
Larkhall ML9 ... 185 C1
Donaldson St
Hamilton ML3 ... 162 A5
Kirkintilloch G66 ... 79 C7
Donaldswood Pk PA2 ... 133 C8
Donaldswood Rd PA2 ... 133 C8
Donald Terr ML3 ... 162 C1
Donald Way G71 ... 141 A7
Don Ave PA4 ... 94 E2
Doncaster St G20 ... 97 A3
Don Ct ML3 ... 183 A8
Don Dr PA2 ... 112 F1
Dongola Rd KA7 ... 239 A7
Donnelly Way ML2 ... 164 C4
Donnies Brae G78 ... 154 F8
Donnini Ct 7 KA7 ... 235 E1
Donohoe Ct G64 ... 78 A1
Don Path ML9 ... 199 A8
Don Pl PA5 ... 131 C8
Don St
Glasgow G33 ... 98 D1
Greenock PA16 ... 45 C5
Doo'cot Brae FK10 ... 10 A8
Doo'cot Hill FK10 ... 5 D2
Doon Ave KA9 ... 236 B5
Doon Cres G61 ... 75 D3
Doon Ct KA12 ... 219 C2
DOONFOOT ... 238 C2
Doonfoot Ct G74 ... 159 D2
Doonfoot Gdns G74 ... 159 D2
Doonfoot Prim Sch KA7 ... 238 B3
Doonfoot Rd
Ayr KA7 ... 238 E4
Glasgow G43 ... 136 D6
Doonholm Pk KA6 ... 238 F1
Doonholm Pl KA7 ... 238 F1
Doonholm Rd KA7 ... 238 F1
Doon Pl
Kilmarnock KA1 ... 228 B4
Kirkintilloch G66 ... 58 F2
Saltcoats KA21 ... 206 A3
Symington KA1 ... 231 D4
Troon KA10 ... 229 F5
Doon Rd G66 ... 59 A2
Doon Side G67 ... 62 B2
Doonside Twr ML1 ... 164 B3
Doon St
Clydebank G81 ... 74 D3
Larkhall ML9 ... 185 C2
Motherwell ML1 ... 164 A4
Doonvale Pl KA7 ... 239 A1
Doonview Gdns KA7 ... 238 D2
Doonview Wynd KA7 ... 238 C2
Doon Way G66 ... 59 A1
Dorain Rd ML1 ... 143 D3
Dora St G40 ... 117 F3
Dorchester Ave G12 ... 96 A6
Dorchester Ct G12 ... 96 A6
Dorchester Pl G12 ... 96 A5
Dorian Dr G76 ... 157 C8
Dorlin Rd G33 ... 99 F5
Dormanside Ct G53 ... 115 B3
Dormanside Gate G53 ... 115 B3
Dormanside Gr G53 ... 115 B3
Dormanside Pl G53 ... 115 C2
Dormanside Rd G53 ... 115 C3
Dornal Ave G13 ... 94 E7
Dornal Dr KA10 ... 229 G6
Dornford Ave G32 ... 119 D3
Dornford Rd G32 ... 119 D2
Dornie Cl KA3 ... 195 C1
Dornie Ct G46 ... 135 E3
Dornie Dr G32 ... 139 B8
Dornie Path 9 ML2 ... 165 F6
Dornie Wynd ML7 ... 147 B3
Dornoch Ave G46 ... 136 C1
Dornoch Ct
Bellshill ML4 ... 142 A5
Kilwinning KA13 ... 207 B3
Dornoch Dr G72 ... 161 D4
Dornoch Pk KA7 ... 238 E6
Dornoch Pl
Bishopbriggs G64 ... 78 D2
Chryston G69 ... 80 D1
East Kilbride G74 ... 159 C2
Dornoch Rd
Bearsden G61 ... 75 D2
Motherwell ML1 ... 143 B5
Dornoch St G40 ... 117 F5
Dornoch Way
Airdrie ML6 ... 122 F5
Cumbernauld G68 ... 62 A5
Hamilton G72 ... 161 D4
Dorrator Ct FK1 ... 41 E5
Dorrator Rd FK1 ... 41 E6
Dorset Rd PA16 ... 44 E4
Dorset Sq G3 ... 240 A3
Dorset St G3 ... 240 A3
Dosk Ave G13 ... 94 F8
Dosk Pl G13 ... 94 F8
Double Hedges Rd G78 ... 154 D6
Double Row ML11 ... 214 F2
Dougalston Ave G62 ... 55 B1
Dougalston Cres G62 ... 55 B1
Dougalston Gardens N G62 ... 55 B1
Dougalston Gardens S G62 ... 55 B1
Dougalston Rd G23 ... 76 E1
Dougan Dr ML2 ... 166 B5
Douglas Acad G62 ... 54 D3
Douglas Ave
Airth FK2 ... 14 D3
Dalry KA24 ... 191 D6
Elderslie PA5 ... 112 B2
Glasgow, Carmyle G32 ... 119 B1
Glasgow G46 ... 136 C1
Kirkintilloch G66 ... 79 D5
Langbank PA14 ... 70 D7
Prestwick KA9 ... 236 B6
Rutherglen G73 ... 138 C5
Douglas Cres
Airdrie ML6 ... 123 A6
Erskine PA8 ... 72 F3
Hamilton ML3 ... 183 D6
Uddingston G71 ... 141 B8
Douglas Ct
Kirkintilloch G66 ... 79 D5
Troon KA10 ... 229 E6
Douglasdale G74 ... 159 D2
Douglas Dr
Ashgill ML9 ... 199 F8
Bellshill ML4 ... 142 D4
Bothwell G71 ... 141 A1
Cambuslang G72 ... 138 F5
Clydebank G15 ... 74 F1
East Kilbride G75 ... 179 E7
Glasgow G69 ... 119 F5
Helensburgh G84 ... 16 D4
Newton Mearns G77 ... 156 E6
Stirling FK7 ... 7 C4
Douglas Drive E G84 ... 16 E3
Douglas Drive La G45 ... 137 D3
Douglas Gate G72 ... 138 F5
Douglas Gdns
Bearsden G61 ... 75 F4
Glasgow G46 ... 136 C1
Kirkintilloch G66 ... 79 D5
Uddingston G71 ... 140 F5
Douglas Ho G82 ... 50 B7
Douglas La
Ayr KA7 ... 238 F8
Glasgow G2 ... 240 B3
Douglas Muir Dr G62 ... 54 C3
Douglas Muir Gdns G62 ... 54 C3
Douglas Muir Pl G62 ... 54 C3
Douglas Muir Rd
Clydebank G81 ... 74 D7
Milngavie G62 ... 54 D2
Douglas Park Cres G61 ... 76 A6
Douglas Park La ML3 ... 162 C5
Douglas Pl
1 Bearsden G61 ... 75 E5
Coatbridge ML5 ... 121 F6
Hamilton ML3 ... 183 D6
Kirkintilloch G66 ... 79 D5
Stenhousemuir FK5 ... 23 F4
Douglas Rd
Dumbarton G82 ... 50 B3
Paisley PA4 ... 114 A8
Douglas St
Airdrie ML6 ... 123 A6
Ayr KA7 ... 238 F8
Bannockburn FK7 ... 7 E1
Carluke ML8 ... 187 E2
Glasgow G2 ... 240 B3
Hamilton, High Blantyre G72 ... 161 C6
Hamilton ML3 ... 162 C5
Kilmarnock KA1 ... 227 F7
Larkhall ML9 ... 185 A4
Milngavie G62 ... 55 A1
Motherwell ML1 ... 163 D6
Overtown ML2 ... 186 D7
Paisley PA1 ... 113 C5
Stirling FK8 ... 2 B1
Uddingston G71 ... 141 B7
Douglas Terr FK7 ... 6 E6

Douglaston Woodland Wlk★
G62 55 D2
Douglas Twr G71 140 D4
Douglas View ML5 121 F3
Dougliehill Pl PA14 68 C8
Dougliehill Rd
Knocknairs Moor PA13 67 F8
Port Glasgow PA14 68 B8
Dougliehill Terr PA14 68 C8
Dougray Pl G78 134 C2
Dougrie Dr G45 137 D3
Dougrie Gdns G45 137 D2
Dougrie Pl G45 137 E3
Dougrie Rd G45 137 D3
Dougrie St G45 137 E3
Dougrie Terr G45 137 D3
Doune Cres
Bishopbriggs G64 78 B4
Chapelhall ML6 123 D1
Newton Mearns G77 156 F5
Stenhousemuir FK5 24 A4
Doune Gardens La G20 96 E3
Doune Gdns
Glasgow G20 96 E3
Gourock PA19 44 A6
Doune Park Way ML5 121 F4
Doune Quadrant 4 G20 96 E3
Doune Terr ML5 121 E8
Doura Dr KA11 219 F5
Doura Pl KA12 219 C5
Dovecot G43 136 C8
Dovecote View G66 79 F7
DOVECOTHALL 134 D3
Dovecothall Rdbt G78 134 D3
Dovecothall St G78 134 D3
Dovecot La
Kilwinning KA13 207 F3
Lanark ML11 215 A4
Dovecot Pl FK10 4 B3
Dovecot Rd FK10 4 B3
DOVECOTWOOD 36 D1
Dovecotwood G65 36 D1
Dovehill FK10 10 B8
Doveholm G82 50 A5
Doveholm Ave G82 50 B5
Dove Pl G75 179 F6
Dover St
Coatbridge ML5 101 D2
Glasgow G3 240 A3
Dove St G53 135 A5
Dove Wynd ML4 141 F8
Dowanfield Rd G67 61 E1
DOWANHILL 96 C3
Dowanhill Prim Sch G11 96 C2
Dowanhill St G12 96 C2
Dowan Pl FK7 6 E6
Dowan Rd
Glasgow G62 76 E8
Milngavie G62 55 E2
Dowanside La 1 G12 96 C3
Dowanside Rd G12 96 C3
Dow Ave KA9 233 C5
Dower Pl FK2 14 D4
Downcraig Dr G45 137 D2
Downcraig Gr G45 137 C2
Downcraig Rd G45 137 C2
Downcraig Terr G45 137 D2
Downfield Dr ML3 183 B7
Downfield Gdns G71 140 F2
Downfield St G32 118 E3
Downhill St G12 96 C3
Downiebrae Rd G73 118 B2
Downie Cl G71 141 B8
Downie St ML3 162 D1
Downs Cres FK10 9 F6
Downs St G21 97 F5
Dow Rd KA9 233 C4
Dowrie Cres G53 115 B1
Draffan Rd ML9 200 B2
Draffen Ct ML1 163 F7
Draffen Mount KA3 211 F7
Draffen St ML1 163 F7
Draffen Twr ML1 163 F7
Drakemire Ave G45 137 C4
Drakemire Dr G45 137 C3
DRAKEMYRE 169 C1
Drakemyre KA24 169 C1
Drake St G40 117 E5
Dr Campbell Ave FK7 12 D8
DREGHORN 220 D1
Dreghorn Prim Sch
KA11 220 D1
Dreghorn Rd KA11 225 D6
Dreghorn St G31 118 C7
Dresling Rd PA15 45 E3
Drimnin Rd G33 99 F5
Drip Rd FK9 1 F2
Drive Rd G51 115 E8
Drochil St G34 100 A1
Dromore St 6 G66 79 D7
Drossie Rd FK1 42 A3
Drove Hill G68 61 B3
Drove Loan FK6 39 F6
Drove Loan Cres FK6 39 E7
Drover Pl FK5 23 C4
Dr Porter Gdns FK7 8 D4
Druid Dr KA13 207 E4
Drumadoon Dr G84 16 F2
Drumaling Terr G66 57 F8
Drumbathie Rd ML6 123 C8
Drumbathie Terr ML6 123 C8
Drumbeg Dr G53 135 A6
Drumbeg Path G72 161 C3
Drumbeg Pl G53 135 A6
Drumbeg Terr G62 54 D2
Drumbottie Rd G21 98 A5
Drumbowie Cres ML7 125 B1
Drumbowie View G68 61 C3
Drumbrock Rd G62 54 D2
Drumby Cres G76 157 D8
Drumby Dr G76 157 D8
Drumcarn Dr G62 54 F1
Drumcavel Rd
Mount Ellen G69 100 F7
Muirhead G69 100 D7
DRUMCHAPEL 75 A3
Drumchapel Gdns G15 75 A2
Drumchapel High Sch
G15 75 A4
Drumchapel Hospl G15 75 B2
Drumchapel Pl G15 75 B2
Drumchapel Pool G15 74 F2
Drumchapel Rd G15 75 B2
Drumchapel Sh Ctr G15 74 F3
Drumchapel Sta G15 75 A1
Drumclair Ave FK1 86 A6
Drumclair Pl ML6 123 D7
Drumclog Ave G62 55 A4
Drumclog Gdns G33 98 F6
Drumclog Pl KA3 223 B3
Drumcross Pl G53 115 C1
Drumcross Rd
Erskine PA7 72 D3
Glasgow G53 115 C1
Drumduff G75 180 D5
Drumellan Rd KA7 239 A2
Drumelzier Ct KA11 220 A4
Drumfearn Pl G20 /G22 97 B6
Drumfearn Rd G20 /G22 97 B6
Drumfin Ave ML6 105 A4
Drumfork Ct G84 25 B8
Drumfork Rd G84 25 D8
Drumfrochar Rd
Greenock PA15 45 E3
Greenock PA15 45 F3
Drumfrochar Sta PA15 45 D4
Drumgarve Ct G84 16 C2
DRUMGELLOCH 123 D8
Drumgelloch St ML6 123 D8
Drumgelloch Sta ML6 123 D7
Drumglass Steadings G65 60 E3
Drumglass View G65 60 F4
Drumgray Gdns ML6 83 D1
Drumgray La ML6 83 D1
Drumgrew Rdbt G68 60 B1
Drumhead Pl G32 118 F1
Drumhead Rd G32 118 F1
Drumhill G66 59 B2
Drumilaw Cres G73 138 A5
Drumilaw Rd G73 138 A5
Drumilaw Way G73 138 A5
Drumillan Hill PA16 44 C2
Drumkinnon Rd G83 27 D8
Drumlaken Ave G23 76 C1
Drumlaken Ct 7 G23 76 D1
Drumlaken Path 11 G23 76 D1
Drumlaken Pl 9 G23 76 D1
Drumlaken St G23 76 C1
Drumlanford Rd KA10 229 F6
Drumlanrig Ave G34 120 D8
Drumlanrig Cres G69 100 E4
Drumlanrig Pl
Glasgow G34 100 D1
Stenhousemuir FK5 23 F4
Drumley Ave KA6 237 F6
Drumleyhill Dr KA1 228 F5
Drumlin Dr G62 75 F8
Drumloch Gdns G75 180 E5
Drumlochy Rd G33 99 B1
Drum Mains Pk G68 81 D8
Drummilling Ave KA23 190 D6
Drummilling Dr KA23 190 D6
Drummilling Rd KA23 190 D6
Drummond Ave G73 137 F8
Drummond Cres
Ayr KA8 236 E2
Irvine KA11 224 H7
Drummond Dr
Paisley PA1 114 D4
Wishaw ML2 165 B2
Drummond Hill G74 160 B3
Drummond Ho G67 62 A3
Drummond La FK8 7 A6
Drummond Pl
Blackridge EH48 107 C3
Bonnybridge FK4 40 A7
3 East Kilbride G74 160 B3
Falkirk FK1 41 F2
Kilmarnock KA3 223 D2
Stirling FK8 7 A6
Drummond Place La FK8 7 A6
Drummond St PA16 45 C4
Drummond Way G77 156 A5
Drummore Ave ML5 122 D3
Drummore Rd G15 75 B4
Drummore Sch G15 75 C4
Drummuir Foot KA11 220 B5
Drumnessie Ct G68 81 F8
Drumnessie Rd G68 81 F8
Drumnessie View G68 81 F8
Drumore Ave ML6 123 D1
Drumover Dr G31 118 E4
DRUMOYNE 115 E6
Drumoyne Ave G51 115 E7
Drumoyne Cir G51 115 E6
Drumoyne Dr G51 115 E6
Drumoyne Pl G51 115 E6
Drumoyne Prim Sch G51 115 E6
Drumoyne Quadrant
G51 115 E6
Drumoyne Rd
Glasgow, Drumoyne G51 115 E6
Drumoyne Rd *continued*
Glasgow, West Drumoyne
G51 115 E7
Drumoyne Sq G51 115 E7
Drumpark Sch G69 121 B6
Drumpark St
Coatbridge ML5 121 C4
Glasgow G46 135 F4
Stirling FK7 7 B3
DRUMPELLIER 121 C6
Drumpellier Ave
Coatbridge ML5 121 D6
Cumbernauld G67 82 C7
Glasgow G69 120 B3
Drumpellier Country Pk★
ML5 101 C1
Drumpellier Cres ML5 121 D6
Drumpellier Ct G67 82 C7
Drumpellier Gdns G67 82 C7
Drumpellier Gr G67 82 C7
Drumpellier Pl
Cumbernauld G67 82 C7
Glasgow G69 120 B4
Drumpellier Rd G69 120 A4
Drumpellier St G33 98 D2
Drumreoch Dr G42 137 E8
Drumreoch Pl G42 137 E8
Drumriggend Rd FK1 85 D4
DRUMRY 74 C2
Drumry Pl G15 74 E2
Drumry Rd G81 74 C3
Drumry Road E G15 74 E2
Drumry Sta G81 74 D2
Drumsack Ave G69 100 C8
Drumsargard Rd G73 138 D5
Drums Ave PA3 113 C6
Drums Cres PA3 113 C5
Drumshangie Pl ML6 103 A2
Drumshangie St ML6 103 A2
Drumshantie Rd PA19 44 E6
Drumshantie Terr PA19 44 E7
Drumshaw Dr G32 139 C8
Drumslea PA16 45 C8
Drums Rd G53 115 A3
Drums Terr PA16 45 B8
Drums The PA16 45 B8
DRUMTROCHER 36 D3
Drumtrocher St G65 60 D8
Drumvale Dr G69 80 E2
Drury Lane Ct G74 160 C4
Drury St G2 240 C2
Dryad St G46 135 E5
DRYBRIDGE 225 D6
Drybridge Rd KA2 225 E2
Dryburgh Ave
Denny FK6 21 D2
Paisley PA2 113 A1
Rutherglen G73 138 B7
Dryburgh Gdns G20 96 F3
Dryburgh Hill G74 159 D1
Dryburgh La G74 159 D1
Dryburgh Pl
Coatbridge ML5 121 F7
Kirkintilloch G66 79 F8
Dryburgh Rd
Bearsden G61 75 C6
Wishaw ML2 165 B4
Dryburgh St ML3 162 B6
Dryburgh Way 1 G72 161 D7
Dryburgh Wlk 3 G69 81 A3
Dryburn Ave G52 115 B5
Dryden St ML3 162 B6
Drygait PA9 131 A6
Drygate G4 241 C2
Drygate St ML9 185 B4
Drygrange Rd G33 99 C2
Drymen Pl G66 79 D3
Drymen Rd
Balloch G83 19 F1
Bearsden G61 75 E5
8 Bearsden G61 75 F3
Drymen St G52 115 E5
Drymen Wynd G61 75 F3
Drynoch Pl G22 97 B7
Drysdale St
Alloa FK10 10 B6
Glasgow G14 94 F5
Duart Ave KA9 236 C8
Duart Cres KA9 236 C8
Duart Dr
East Kilbride G74 159 D3
Elderslie PA5 112 C1
Newton Mearns G77 157 A5
Duart St G20 96 C8
Duart Way G69 100 E4
Dubbs Rd
Kilwinning KA20 207 B1
Port Glasgow PA14 68 E7
Port Glasgow PA14 68 F7
Stevenston KA20 206 E1
Stevenston KA20 206 F1
Dubs Rd G78 134 E3
Dubton St G34 100 B1
Duchall Pl G14 95 B4
Duchal Rd PA13 89 D8
Duchal St PA14 68 D8
Duchess Ct ML3 163 A2
Duchess Dr G84 16 B3
Duchess Pk G84 16 B3
Duchess Pl G73 138 C8
Duchess Rd G73 118 C1
Duchess Way G69 120 F5
Duchray Dr PA1 114 F4
Duchray La G33 98 D1
Duchray St G33 98 D1
Duddingston Ave KA13 207 B4
Dudley Dr
Coatbridge ML5 101 C2
Dudley Dr *continued*
Glasgow G12 96 A3
Dudley La G12 96 A3
Duff Cres FK8 1 F1
Duff Pl
Kilmarnock KA3 223 C3
Saltcoats KA21 206 A2
Duff St PA15 46 A5
Duffus Pl G32 139 C8
Duffus St G34 100 A1
Duffus Terr G32 139 C8
Duguid Dr KA21 206 A1
Duich Gdns G23 76 E1
Duisdale Rd G32 139 C8
Dukes Ct G72 138 E7
Duke's Ct ML9 185 A4
Dukes Gate G71 140 E4
Dukes Pl ML3 183 D6
Dukes Rd
Coatbridge G69 120 F5
Troon KA10 229 C3
Duke's Rd G72, G73 138 D6
Duke St
Alva FK12 5 A7
Bannockburn FK7 7 C1
Denny FK6 21 C2
Glasgow, Barrowfield G31 118 D5
Glasgow, Dennistoun G31 118 B6
Glasgow G4 241 C2
Hamilton ML3 162 E3
Larkhall ML9 185 A4
Motherwell ML1 163 E8
Paisley PA2 113 E2
Wishaw ML2 165 F6
Duke Street Sta G31 118 B7
Duke Terr KA8 236 A1
DULLATUR 61 D6
Dullatur Rd G68 61 D6
Dullatur Rdbt G68 61 F5
Dulnain St G72 139 E5
Dulsie Rd G21 98 C6
Dumbain Cres G83 28 B8
Dumbain Rd G83 20 A1
DUMBARTON 49 E2
Dumbarton Acad G82 50 A4
Dumbarton Castle★ G82 49 F2
Dumbarton Central Sta
G82 49 F4
Dumbarton East Sta G82 50 B3
Dumbarton Joint Hospl
G82 49 C4
Dumbarton Rd
Bowling G60 72 D8
Cambusbarron FK8 6 E8
Clydebank, Duntocher G81 74 A6
Clydebank G60, G81 73 D4
Glasgow G11 95 F2
Glasgow G14 94 E6
Glasgow, Partick G11 96 B2
Milton G82 50 F1
Stirling FK8 7 B7
DUMBRECK 116 B4
Dumbreck Ave G41 116 A4
Dumbreck Ct G41 116 A3
Dumbreck Marsh Nature
Reserve★ G65 60 B7
Dumbreck Pl
Glasgow G41 116 A3
Kirkintilloch G66 79 E4
Dumbreck Rd G41 116 B3
Dumbreck Sq G41 116 A4
Dumbreck Sta G41 116 C4
Dumbreck Terr G65 59 F8
Dumbrock Cres G63 31 C3
Dumbrock Dr G63 31 B3
Dumbrock Rd
Milngavie G62 54 D2
Strathblane G63 31 C3
DUMBUCK 50 E1
Dumbuck Cres G82 50 C2
Dumbuck Gdns G82 50 B2
Dumbuck Rd
Dumbarton G82 50 B4
Dumbarton G82 50 B5
Dumbuie Ave G82 50 B3
Dumfries Cres ML6 122 F5
Dumfries Pk KA6 239 A1
Dumgoyne Ave G62 54 F2
Dumgoyne Dr G61 75 D7
Dumgoyne Gdns G62 54 F1
Dumgoyne Pl G76 157 C7
Dumgoyne Rd KA1 228 A3
Dumyat Ave FK10 4 B2
Dumyat Dr FK1 41 E3
Dumyat Rd
Alva FK12 4 E6
Menstrie FK11 3 F6
Stirling FK9 2 C3
Dumyat Rise FK5 23 C5
Dumyat St FK10 4 F1
Dunagoil Gdns G45 137 E2
Dunagoil Pl G45 137 E1
Dunagoil Rd G45 137 D2
Dunagoil St G45 137 E1
Dunalastair Dr G33 99 B5
Dunan Pl G33 119 E7
Dunard Ct ML8 187 F3
Dunard Prim Sch G20 96 F4
Dunard Rd G73 138 B7
Dunard St G20 96 F4
Dunard Way PA3 113 D7
Dunaskin St G11 96 C1
Dunavon Gdns FK6 21 D4
Dunavon Pl ML5 122 D4
Dunbar Ave
Coatbridge ML5 121 D4
Johnstone PA5 131 E8
Rutherglen G73 138 C7
Dunbar Ave *continued*
Stenhousemuir FK5 23 F4
Dunbar Dr
Kilmarnock KA3 223 C2
Motherwell ML1 164 A4
Dunbar Gate FK6 21 E3
Dunbar Gdns KA21 205 F3
Dunbar Hill G74 159 C1
Dunbar La ML1 143 A2
Dunbar Pl G74 159 C1
Dunbar Rd PA2 113 A1
Dunbar St ML3 162 B5
Dunbeath Ave G77 156 F5
Dunbeath Gr G72 161 C3
Dunbeith Pl 4 G20 96 D5
DUNBETH 122 B7
Dunbeth Ave ML5 122 B7
Dunbeth Ct ML5 122 B7
Dunbeth Rd ML5 122 B7
Dunblane Dr G74 159 F2
Dunblane Pl
Coatbridge ML5 121 F4
East Kilbride G74 159 F2
Dunblane St G4 240 C4
Dunbrach Rd G68 61 C2
Dunbreck Ave ML6 105 A5
Dunbritton Rd G82 50 C3
Duncairn Ave FK4 39 F6
Duncan Ave
Falkirk FK2 24 B3
Glasgow G14 95 C4
Duncan Buchanan Ct FK8 2 A2
Duncan Ct
Kilmarnock KA3 223 D4
Motherwell ML1 142 D1
Duncan Dr KA12 219 D2
Duncan Graham St ML9 185 B4
Duncan La G14 95 C3
Duncan Lane N 7 G14 95 C4
Duncan Lane S 13 G14 95 C4
Duncan McIntosh Rd G68 62 C7
Dun Cann PA4 93 C7
Duncan Rd
Helensburgh G84 16 E3
Port Glasgow PA14 47 B1
Duncanrig Sec Sch G75 159 B1
Duncansby Dr G72 161 C3
Duncansby Rd G33 119 D6
Duncan's Cl 11 ML11 215 A4
Duncanson Ave FK10 10 A8
Duncan St
Bonnybridge FK4 39 F5
Clydebank G81 74 B3
Greenock PA15 45 E5
Duncarnock Ave G78 154 E7
Duncarnock Cres G78 154 E7
Duncarron Ind Est FK6 21 F1
Duncarron Pl FK6 21 E2
Dunchattan Gr KA10 229 G2
Dunchattan Pl G31 117 F7
Dunchattan St G31 117 F7
Dunchattan Way KA10 229 G2
Dunchurch Rd PA1 114 D5
Dunclutha Dr G71 141 A1
Dunclutha St G40 118 B2
Duncolm Pl G62 54 D2
Duncombe Ave G81 74 B7
Duncombe St G20 96 D7
Duncombe View 6 G81 74 D3
Duncraig Cres PA5 131 D8
Duncrub Dr G64 77 E1
Duncruin St G20 96 D7
Duncruin Terr G20 96 D7
Duncryne Ave G32 119 E4
Duncryne Gdns G32 119 E4
Duncryne Pl G64 97 E8
Duncryne Rd
Alexandria G83 27 E6
Gartocharn G83 20 F8
Dundaff Ct FK6 21 D1
Dundaff Hill G68 61 C2
Dundarroch St FK5 23 B1
Dundas Ave G64 78 B8
Dundas Cotts FK4 39 A2
Dundas Ct G74 159 E2
Dundashill G4 97 B2
Dundas La G1 241 A3
Dundas Pl G74 159 E2
Dundas Rd FK9 2 B4
Dundas St G1 241 A3
Dundasvale Ct
Glasgow G2 240 C4
Glasgow G4 240 C4
Dundas Wlk KA3 223 D3
Dundee Ct 5 FK2 42 A8
Dundee Dr G52 115 B3
Dundee Path G52 115 C3
Dundee Pl FK2 42 A8
DUNDONALD 225 E1
Dundonald Ave PA5 111 D1
Dundonald Castle★ KA2 225 E2
Dundonald Cres
Coatbridge ML5 121 F4
Irvine KA11 224 H1
Newton Mearns G77 157 A4
Dundonald Ct KA3 223 B6
Dundonald Dr ML3 183 D7
Dundonald Pl
Kilmarnock KA1 227 D7
Neilston G78 154 D7
Dundonald Prim Sch
KA2 225 F2
Dundonald Rd
Glasgow G12 96 C3
Irvine KA11 225 C8
Kilmarnock KA1, KA2 227 D7
Paisley PA3 114 A7
Troon KA10 229 F3

Dundonald St G72 161 C8
Dundonald Terr KA9 236 D7
Dundrennan Dr ML6 123 E2
Dundrennan Rd G42 136 F7
DUNDYVAN 121 F4
Dundyvan Gate ML5 122 A5
Dundyvan Gdns ML5 122 A5
Dundyvan Ind Est ML5 121 F5
Dundyvan La ML2 165 A2
Dundyvan Rd ML5 121 F5
Dundyvan St ML2 165 A2
Dundyvan Way ML5 121 F5
Dunearn Pl PA2 114 A3
Dunearn St G4 96 F2
Duneaton Wynd ML9 185 B1
Dunedin Ct G75 180 A8
Dunedin Dr G75 180 A8
Dunedin Rd ML9 185 B1
Dunedin Terr G81 94 C8
Dunellan Ave G69 81 A2
Dunellan Cres G69 81 A2
Dunellan Ct G69 81 A2
Dunellan Dr G81 74 B7
Dunellan Gdns G69 81 A2
Dunellan Gr G69 80 F2
Dunellan Pl G69 81 A2
Dunellan Rd G62 54 D2
Dunellan St G52 115 E5
Dunellan Way G69 81 A2
Dungavel Gdns ML3 183 E8
Dungavel La ML8 188 B1
Dungavel Rd KA1 228 A4
Dungeonhill Rd G34 120 D8
Dunglass Ave
East Kilbride G74 159 F3
Glasgow G14 95 C4
Dunglass La [8] G14 95 C4
Dunglass Lane N [5] G14 95 C4
Dunglass Lane S [11] G14 95 C4
Dunglass Pl
Milngavie G62 54 E3
Newton Mearns G77 156 A5
Dunglass Rd PA7 72 C2
Dunglass Sq G74 159 F3
Dunglass View G63 31 D4
Dungoil Ave G68 61 B3
Dungoil Rd G66 79 E4
Dungourney Dr PA16 45 D7
Dungoyne St G20 96 C8
Dunholme Pk G81 73 D3
DUNIPACE 21 D4
Dunipace Prim Sch FK6 21 D3
Dunira St G32 118 F3
Dunivaig Rd G33 119 E8
Dunkeld Ave G73 138 B7
Dunkeld Dr G61 76 B4
Dunkeld Gdns G64 78 B2
Dunkeld La G69 81 A2
Dunkeld Pl
Coatbridge ML5 121 F4
Falkirk FK2 24 C1
Hamilton ML3 161 E3
Newton Mearns G77 157 B4
Dunkeld St G31 118 C4
Dunkenny Rd G15 74 F3
Dunkenny Sq G15 74 F3
Dunkirk St ML6 105 A5
Dunlin
East Kilbride G74 159 E4
Glasgow G12 96 A6
Dunlin Cres PA6 91 C1
Dunlin Ct ML4 141 E8
Dunlin Way ML5 122 E2
DUNLOP 195 C7
Dunlop Cres
Ayr KA8 236 E1
Bothwell G71 141 B1
Irvine KA11 220 B1
Renfrew PA4 94 D4
Dunlop Ct
Hamilton ML3 183 E7
[2] Troon KA10 229 E5
Dunlop Dr KA11 224 G4
Dunlop Gr G71 121 A1
Dunlop Pl
Ashgill ML9 200 A8
Irvine KA11 224 H4
Milngavie G62 54 F3
Dunlop Prim Sch KA3 195 B8
Dunlop Rd
Barrmill KA15 172 A3
Lugton KA3 173 C6
Stewarton KA3 195 D1
Dunlop St
Cambuslang G72 139 E6
Fenwick KA3 213 A3
Glasgow G2 241 A1
Greenock PA16 45 D3
Kilmarnock KA1 222 F1
Linwood PA3 112 C6
Renfrew PA4 94 D4
Stewarton KA3 195 E1
Dunlop Sta KA3 195 B7
Dunlop Terr KA8 236 D1
Dunlop Twr G75 180 E8
Dunmar Cres FK10 4 E1
Dunmar Dr FK10 4 E1
DUNMORE 14 C7
Dunmore Dr G62 76 D8
Dunmore St G81 94 C8
Dunnachie Dr ML5 121 B4
Dunnachie Pl ML5 121 C4
Dunnet Ave ML6 102 F5
Dunnet Ct G72 161 D4
Dunnet Dr PA6 91 B1
Dunnett Ave KA1 228 B7
Dunnichen Gdns G64 78 D1
Dunnikier Wlk G68 60 E1
Dunning Dr G68 62 A5
Dunning Pl FK2 24 C1
Dunn Mews KA1 227 C8
Dunnock Pl ML5 122 E3
Dunnotar Wlk [16] ML2 165 F6
Dunnottar Cres G74 159 D3
Dunnottar Ct G74 159 C3
Dunnottar Dr
Kilmarnock KA1 227 B8
Stenhousemuir FK5 23 F4
Dunnottar St
Bishopbriggs G64 78 D2
Glasgow G33 99 B2
Dunn St
Clydebank G81 73 E3
Duntocher G81 73 F6
Glasgow G40 118 A4
Greenock PA15 45 E4
Paisley PA1 114 A4
Dunns Wood Rd G67 62 D6
Dunn Terr ML7 127 F6
Dunollie Gdns KA3 223 B6
Dunollie Pl G69 100 E4
Dunolly Dr G77 156 F5
Dunolly St G21 98 A1
Dunoon Ave KA3 222 F3
Dunottar Ave ML5 122 B2
Dunottar Pl ML5 122 B3
Dunphail Dr G34 100 D1
Dunphail Rd G34 120 D8
Dun Pk G66 79 E8
Dunragit St G31 118 C7
Dunrobin Ave
Elderslie PA5 112 C1
Stenhousemuir FK5 23 F5
Dunrobin Cres G74 159 D3
Dunrobin Ct
Clydebank G81 74 A2
East Kilbride G74 159 D3
Dunrobin Dr
East Kilbride G74 159 D3
Gourock PA19 43 F6
Dunrobin Gdns ML6 123 E6
Dunrobin Pl ML5 121 F7
Dunrobin Prim Sch ML6 123 E7
Dunrobin Rd ML6 123 E7
Dunrobin St G31 118 B6
Dunrod Hill G74 159 F3
Dunrod St G32 119 B4
Dunscore Brae ML3 161 E2
Duns Cres ML2 165 C7
Dunside Dr G53 135 A6
Dunsiston Rd ML6 124 B4
Dunskaith Pl G34 120 D7
Dunskaith St G34 120 D7
Dunskey Rd KA3 223 B6
Dunsmore Rd PA7 72 A4
Dunsmuir St G51 116 B7
Duns Path ML5 122 D3
Duns Pl [2] PA15 46 B3
Dunster Gdns G64 78 B4
Dunster Rd FK9 2 C3
Dunswin Ave G81 73 E3
Dunsyre Pl G23 76 E1
Dunsyre St G33 118 E8
Duntarvie Ave G34 120 C8
Duntarvie Cl G34 120 C8
Duntarvie Cres G34 120 C8
Duntarvie Dr G34 120 B8
Duntarvie Gdns G34 120 C8
Duntarvie Gr G34 120 C8
Duntarvie Pl G34 120 B8
Duntarvie Rd G34 120 B8
DUNTERLIE 134 C3
Dunterlie Ave G13 95 B6
Dunterlie Ct G78 134 C3
DUNTIBLAE 80 A7
Duntiblae G66 80 A7
Duntiblae Rd G66 80 A7
Duntiglennan Rd G81 74 A6
Duntilland Ave ML7 125 B2
Duntilland Rd
Airdrie ML6 124 E8
Salsburgh ML7 125 C5
DUNTOCHER 74 A7
Duntocher Rd
Bearsden G61 75 B6
Clydebank G81 74 A4
Clydebank, Parkhall G81 74 A5
Duntonknoll KA12 219 C4
Duntreath Ave
Clydebank G15 74 F1
Glasgow G13 94 E8
Duntreath Dr G15 74 F1
Duntreath Gdns G15 74 F2
Duntreath Gr G15 74 F1
Duntreath Terr G65 60 D8
Duntroon Pl ML4 142 B3
Duntroon St G31 118 B8
Dunure Cres FK4 40 A5
Dunure Cts KA13 207 D3
Dunure Dr
Hamilton ML3 161 D2
Kilmarnock KA3 228 B8
Newton Mearns G77 157 A5
Rutherglen G73 137 F5
Dunure Pl
Coatbridge ML5 121 E3
Kilmarnock KA3 223 B6
Newton Mearns G77 157 A4
Dunure Rd KA7 238 B2
Dunure St
Bonnybridge FK4 40 A5
Coatbridge ML5 121 E3
Glasgow G20 96 D7
Dunvegan ML6 102 F4
Dunvegan Ave
Coatbridge ML5 101 D1
Dunvegan Ave *continued*
Elderslie PA5 112 C1
Gourock PA19 43 F5
Stenhousemuir FK5 23 F4
Dunvegan Ct FK10 10 B6
Dunvegan Dr
Bishopbriggs G64 78 A4
Falkirk FK2 24 C1
Newton Mearns G77 157 A5
Stirling FK9 2 B3
Dunvegan Pl
Bonnybridge FK4 39 F6
East Kilbride G74 159 D3
Irvine KA12 219 D6
Uddingston G71 140 D8
Dunvegan Quadrant PA4 94 B4
Dunwan Ave G13 94 F7
Dunwan Pl G13 94 F7
Dura Rd ML2, ML7 167 C5
Durban Ave
Clydebank G81 73 D4
East Kilbride G75 180 B4
Durham Rd PA16 44 E5
Durham St G41 116 D5
Durisdeer Dr ML3 161 E1
Durness Ave G61 76 B4
Duror St G32 119 A6
Durris Gdns G32 119 D3
Durrockstock Cres PA2 132 F7
Durrockstock Rd PA2 132 F7
Durrockstock Way PA2 132 F7
Durward G74 160 E4
Durward Ave G41 116 D1
Durward Cres PA2 112 F1
Durward Ct
Glasgow G41 116 D1
Motherwell ML1 142 D1
Durward Way PA2 112 F1
Dutch House Rdbt KA9 233 F6
Duthie Park Gdns [2] G13 95 D6
Duthie Park Pl [1] G13 95 D6
Duthie Rd PA19 45 A7
Duthil St G51 115 D6
Dyce Ave ML6 122 E4
Dyce La G11 96 A2
Dyer's La G1 241 B1
Dyfrig St
Hamilton G72 161 C8
Shotts ML7 146 E5
DYKEBAR 114 B1
Dykebar Ave G13 95 B6
Dykebar Cres PA2 114 B2
Dykebar Hospl PA2 134 B8
DYKEHEAD 146 D5
Dykehead Cres ML6 102 F2
Dykehead Dr KA1 228 F5
Dykehead La G33 119 D7
Dykehead Prim Sch ML7 146 E5
Dykehead Rd
Airdrie ML6 103 B3
Coatbridge G69 121 A5
Cumbernauld G68 61 D3
Dullatur G68 61 C6
Queenzieburn G65 59 E8
Dykehead Sq ML3 161 F2
Dykehead St G33 119 D7
Dykemuir Pl G21 98 B4
Dykemuir Quadrant G21 98 A4
Dykemuir St G21 98 A4
Dykeneuk Rd PA14 68 D7
Dyke Rd G13, G14 95 A7
Dykesfield Pl KA21 205 E2
Dykesmains Prim Sch
KA21 205 F3
Dykesmains Rd KA21 205 E2
Dykes Pl KA21 205 F2
Dyke St
Coatbridge ML5 121 B4
Glasgow G69 120 C5
Dykes The KA25 170 A8
Dysart Ct G68 60 E1
Dysart Dr G72 161 D3
Dysart Way ML6 124 A6

E

Eagle Cres G61 75 B5
EAGLESHAM 178 F5
Eaglesham Ct
East Kilbride G74, G75 158 F1
[1] Glasgow G51 116 E6
Eaglesham Path ML5 101 C6
Eaglesham Pl [2] G51 116 E6
Eaglesham Prim Sch
G76 178 F4
Eaglesham Rd
Clarkston G76 157 E5
East Kilbride G75 179 C7
Newton Mearns G77 156 D3
Eagle St G4 97 C2
Eamont Lodge [10] G12 96 C3
Eardley Pl FK5 23 B2
Earl Ave ML6 105 A5
Earlbank Ave G14 95 C4
Earlbank Lane N [9] G14 95 C4
Earlbank Lane S G14 95 C4
Earl Cres KA2 225 F1
Earl Dr KA2 225 F2
Earl Haig Rd G52 114 F7
Earl Mount KA2 225 F2
Earl of Mar Ct FK10 10 B6
Earl Pl
Bridge of Weir PA11 110 D6
Glasgow G14 95 C4
Earl Rise KA2 225 F1
Earlsburn Ave FK7 7 A3
Earlsburn Rd G66 79 E4
Earlscourt G69 80 F1
Earls Ct FK10 10 B5
Earlsgate PA6 91 B1
Earl's Gate G71 140 E3
Earl's Hill G68 61 B3
Earlshill Dr
Bannockburn FK7 7 F1
Howwood PA9 130 E5
Earlspark Ave G43 136 F6
Earl St G14 95 B4
EARLSTON 227 B3
Earlston Ave KA1 227 F3
Earlston Cres ML5 122 D3
Earlston Pl G21 241 C4
Earlston St ML2 165 C6
Earls Way KA7 238 C2
Earlswood Ave KA11 219 E6
Earlswood View KA11 219 E6
Earlswood Way KA11 219 E6
Earlswood Wynd KA12 219 E6
Earl View ML1 143 A3
Earlybraes Dr G33 119 E6
Earlybraes Gdns G33 119 D6
Earn Ave
Bearsden G61 76 B3
Bellshill ML4 141 E6
Renfrew PA4 94 E2
Earncraig Gn KA11 220 A3
Earn Cres ML2 165 B1
Earn Ct FK10 10 C6
Earn Gdns ML9 199 A8
Earnhill La PA16 44 C5
Earnhill Pl PA16 44 D5
Earnhill Prim Sch PA16 44 E4
Earnhill Rd PA16 44 D5
Earn La ML1 143 A5
EARNOCK 161 E1
Earnock Ave ML1 163 C6
Earnock Gdns ML3 162 A2
Earnock Rd ML3 161 E2
Earnock St
Glasgow G33 98 D4
Hamilton ML3 162 A4
Earn Pl
Denny FK6 39 D6
Kilmarnock KA1 228 B5
Earn Rd
Newton Mearns G77 156 D7
Troon KA10 229 G4
Earnside St G32 119 B5
Earn St G33 98 E1
Earn Terr ML7 146 E6
Easdale G74 181 B7
Easdale Dr G32 119 A4
Easdale Path
Coatbridge ML5 122 D4
Glenboig ML5 101 C6
Easdale Pl G77 156 B5
Easdale Rise ML3 161 E3
Eason Dr ML8 187 D2
East Academy St ML2 165 B2
East Ave
Carluke ML8 187 D2
Hamilton G72 161 E5
Motherwell ML1 143 A2
Plains ML6 104 A3
Renfrew PA4 94 D3
Uddingston G71 141 C6
EAST BALGROCHAN 57 C2
Eastbank PA14 70 D6
Eastbank Acad G32 119 B4
Eastbank Dr G32 119 C5
Eastbank Pl G32 119 C5
Eastbank Prim Sch G32 119 C5
Eastbank Rise G32 119 C5
East Barmoss Ave PA14 68 F7
East Barns St G81 94 D7
East Bath La G1 241 A3
East Blackhall St PA15 46 B4
East Boreland Pl FK6 21 D3
East Bowhouse Head
KA11 220 B5
East Bowhouse Way
KA11 220 B5
East Breast PA15 46 A5
East Bridge St FK1 42 C4
East Broomlands KA11 220 B2
East Buchanan Mews [3]
PA1 113 F5
East Buchanan St PA1 113 F5
Eastburn Cres G21 98 B6
Eastburn Dr FK1 42 C4
Eastburn Pl G21 98 B6
Eastburn Rd G21 98 B6
East Burnside St [2] G65 60 D8
Eastburn Twr FK1 42 C4
East Campbell St G1 241 C1
East Castle St FK10 10 B5
East Clyde St G84 16 E1
Eastcote Ave G14 95 E4
EAST CRAIGEND 73 A1
East Crawford St PA15 46 C3
Eastcroft G73 138 B8
Eastcroft St FK5 23 B1
Eastcroft Terr G21 98 A4
East Dean St ML4 142 B5
East Dr FK5 23 C1
Eastend PA12 129 D3
Eastend Ave ML1 143 B1
Easterbrae ML1 163 D4
Easter Carmuirs Prim Sch
FK1 41 B6
Easter Cornton Rd FK9 2 B4
Easter Craigs G31 118 B8
Easter Cres ML2 165 E4
Easter Garngaber Rd G66 79 E5
Eastergreens Ave G66 79 C7
Easterhill Pl G32 118 F3
Easterhill Rd G84 16 F3
Easterhill St G32 119 A2
EASTERHOUSE 120 B8
Easterhouse Pl G34 120 C8
Easterhouse Quadrant
G34 120 C7
Easterhouse Rd G69 120 C7
Easterhouse Sp Ctr G34 99 F1
Easterhouse Sta G69 120 C6
Easter Livilands FK7 7 C4
Eastermains G66 59 B2
Easter Mews G71 140 E5
Eastern Access Rd FK8 7 B8
Eastern Cres KA25 170 A7
Easter Queenslie Rd
G33 119 E8
Easter Rd
Clarkston G76 158 A6
Shotts ML7 146 D5
Easterton Ave G76 158 A5
Easterton Cres FK7 12 E7
Easterton Dr
Caldercruix ML6 104 F4
Cowie FK7 12 E7
Easterton Gr FK7 12 E7
Easterton Stables* G66 32 D3
Easter Wood Cres G71 121 D1
Easterwood Pl ML5 122 A6
East Faulds Rd ML11 215 E5
EASTFIELD
Cumbernauld 61 E3
Harthill 127 C4
Rutherglen 138 D7
Eastfield Ave G72 138 E6
Eastfield Cres G82 50 B2
Eastfield Pl G82 50 B2
Eastfield Prim Sch G68 61 B1
Eastfield Rd
Caldercruix ML6 105 B5
Carluke ML8 202 A8
Cumbernauld, Carrickstone
G68 61 D4
Cumbernauld, Cumbernauld
Village G68 62 A5
Glasgow G21 97 E4
Eastfield Terr ML4 142 D4
East Fulton Holdings
PA3 111 F7
East Fulton Prim Sch
PA3 111 F6
East Gargieston Ave
KA1 227 D6
Eastgate G69 101 A5
East Gate
Glenboig ML5 101 D7
Wishaw ML2 165 D3
East George St ML5 122 B8
East Glebe Terr ML3 162 D2
East Gr KA10 229 G4
East Greenlees Ave G72 139 C3
East Greenlees Cres G72 139 B3
East Greenlees Dr G72 139 C3
East Greenlees Gr G72 138 F3
East Greenlees Rd G72 139 B3
East Hallhill Rd
Baillieston G69 119 F6
Glasgow G33 119 F6
Easthall Pl G33 119 F7
East Hamilton St
Greenock PA15 46 D4
Wishaw ML2 165 B2
East High St ML6 123 A8
East Ho ML11 215 C4
East India Breast PA15 46 A4
EAST KILBRIDE 159 C5
East Kilbride Rd
Carmunnock G74, G76 158 D4
Clarkston G76 157 F6
Rutherglen G73 138 E4
East Kilbride Sh Ctr G74 159 E1
East Kilbride Sta G74 159 E2
East Kirkland KA24 191 D7
East La PA1 114 B4
Eastlea Pl ML6 123 B6
East Lennox Dr G84 16 F3
East Link Rd FK9 2 D5
East Machan St ML9 185 B1
EAST MAINS 159 F2
East Mains FK11 4 A6
East Mains Rd G74 159 E3
East Main St ML7 127 F5
East Milton Gr G75 159 B1
East Milton Prim Sch
G75 159 C1
East Montrose St G84 16 E2
Eastmuir Specl Sch G33 119 D6
Eastmuir St
Glasgow G32 119 B5
Wishaw ML2 165 E3
East Murrayfield FK7 7 E1
East Nerston Ct G74 160 A6
East Nerston Gr G74 160 A6
East Netherton St [5]
KA1 227 F7
Easton Ct FK8 2 B2
Easton Dr FK1 66 D7
Easton Pl ML5 122 B5
East Park Cres KA3 222 B7
East Park Dr KA3 222 B7
East Park Rd KA8 236 B3
East Plean Prim Sch FK7 12 C3
East Princes St G84 16 D1
East Rd
Irvine KA12 219 B8
Irvine KA12 219 C2

Etive Dr *continued*
Glasgow G46 136 D1
Etive Pl
Cumbernauld G67 82 C6
Irvine KA12 219 D5
Larkhall ML9 184 F5
Stirling FK9 2 B3
Etive St
Glasgow G32 119 A5
Wishaw ML2 165 B1
Etive Wlk ML7 147 B3
Etna Ct FK2 42 D7
Etna Ind Est ML2 164 C4
Etna Rd FK2 42 D7
Etna Road Rdbt FK2 42 E7
Etna St ML2 164 C4
Eton La 3 G12 96 E2
Etterick Wynd 9 G72 161 C7
Ettrick Ave
Hattonrig ML4 142 A7
Renfrew PA4 94 F2
Ettrick Cres
Kilmarnock KA3 222 F3
Rutherglen G73 138 C7
Ettrick Ct
Cambuslang G72 139 D4
Coatbridge ML5 122 C3
Falkirk FK1 42 D1
Ettrick Dr
Bearsden G61 75 C7
Bishopton PA7 72 C2
Ettrick Hill 2 G74 160 A3
Ettrick Oval PA2 132 E8
Ettrick Pl
Ayr KA8 236 B4
Glasgow G43 136 D7
3 Greenock PA15 46 B3
Ettrick Sq G67 61 F2
Ettrick St ML2 165 A5
Ettrick Terr PA5 131 C8
Ettrick Way
9 Cumbernauld G67 61 F1
Renfrew PA4 94 F2
Ettrick Wlk G67 61 F2
Euchan Pl KA10 229 G5
Eurocentral ML4 142 F8
Eurocentral Rail Terminal
ML1 142 D7
Evan Cres G46 136 D2
Evan Dr G46 136 D2
Evans St FK5 23 C3
Evanton Dr G46 135 E3
Evanton Pl G46 135 E3
Evelyn Terr KA13 207 E2
Everard Ct G21 97 E7
Everard Dr G21 97 E6
Everard Pl 2 G21 97 E7
Everard Quadrant G21 97 E7
Everglades The G69 100 B8
Evergreen Trailer Ct FK6 22 A2
Eversley St G32 119 A3
Everton Rd G53 115 C2
Ewart Cres ML3 162 B1
Ewart Dr ML6 123 A6
Ewart Gdns ML3 162 B1
Ewart Terr ML3 162 A2
Ewenfield Ave KA7 239 A4
Ewenfield Gdns KA7 239 A4
Ewenfield Pk KA7 238 F4
Ewenfield Pl KA7 239 A4
Ewenfield Rd KA7 239 A4
Ewing Ave FK2 42 B7
Ewing Ct
Hamilton ML3 183 C7
Stirling FK7 7 C3
Ewing Dr FK2 42 B7
Ewing Pl
Falkirk FK2 42 B7
Glasgow G31 118 C5
Ewing Rd PA12 129 C3
Ewing St
Kilbarchan PA10 111 A3
Rutherglen G73 138 A7
Ewing Way KA3 211 D8
Ewing Wlk G62 55 C1
Excelsior Pk ML2 164 D2
Excelsior St ML1 164 C2
Exchange Pl G1 241 A2
Exeter Dr G11 96 A2
Exeter La G11 96 A2
Exeter St ML5 122 A5
Exhibition Centre Sta
G3 116 E8
Exmouth Pl PA19 44 E5
Eynort St G22 97 A7
Eyrepoint Ct G33 119 A8

F

Factory Pl KA21 216 F8
Factory Rd ML1 163 E5
Fagan Ct G72 140 E1
FAIFLEY 74 C7
Faifley Rd G81 74 C7
Failford Pl KA3 223 B4
Fairbairn Cres G46 136 A2
Fairbairn Path G40 118 A4
Fairburn St G32 118 F4
Fairfax Ave G44 137 C5
FAIRFIELD 5 B2
Fairfield FK10 5 C1
Fairfield Ave FK4 40 A6
Fairfield Ct G76 157 E5
Fairfield Dr
Clarkston G76 157 E5
Renfrew PA4 94 D1
Fairfield Gdns G51 115 F8
Fairfield Pk KA7 238 E7
Fairfield Pl
Bothwell G71 141 B2
East Kilbride G74 159 C2
Falkirk FK2 42 C5
Glasgow G51 115 F8
Hamilton ML3 162 E1
Fairfield Rd
Ayr KA7 238 E7
Sauchie FK10 5 C1
Fairfields FK2 13 E5
Fairfield Sch FK10 5 B1
Fairfield St G51 115 F8
Fairford Dr G67 82 D7
Fairgreen Pl FK7 11 E8
Fairhaven KA10 229 F7
Fairhaven Ave ML6 123 E6
Fairhaven Rd G23 96 E8
Fairhaven Sq KA13 207 B4
FAIRHILL 162 C1
Fairhill Ave ML3 162 C1
Fairhill Cres ML3 162 C1
Fairhill Pl ML3 183 C7
Fairhill Rd FK7 7 B1
Fairholm Ave ML3 163 D1
Fairholm St
Glasgow G32 118 F4
Larkhall ML9 184 F4
Fair Isle Pl KA3 223 A6
Fairley Dr FK5 23 A3
Fairley St G51 116 B6
Fairlie G74 159 D3
Fairlie Ave KA1 227 D7
Fairlie Dr
Falkirk FK1 41 D5
Irvine KA11 220 B6
Fairlie Gdns FK1 41 D5
Fairlie Park Dr G11 96 A2
Fairlie St FK1 41 C5
Fairlie View KA2 226 E5
Fairmount Dr FK10 5 B2
Fair Oaks G76 158 E8
Fairrie St PA15 46 D3
Fairview Ct G62 55 A1
Fair View Dr ML11 214 A4
Fairway G61 75 C5
Fair Way G82 48 A8
Fairway Ave PA2 133 D8
Fairways
Irvine KA12 219 A7
Larkhall ML9 185 C3
Stewarton KA3 211 E8
Fairways Pl FK4 40 B7
Fairways The
Bothwell G71 141 A2
Johnstone PA5 131 D7
Fairways View G81 74 D6
Fairway View KA9 236 D6
Fairweather Pl G77 156 C3
Fairyburn Rd FK10 9 F8
Fairyhill Pl KA1 227 E6
Fairyhill Rd KA1 227 E6
Fairyknowe Ct G71 141 B2
Fairyknowe Gdns G71 141 B2
Faith Ave PA11 89 E2
Falconbridge Rd G74 160 C4
Falcon Cres
Greenock PA16 45 A6
Paisley PA3 113 B6
Falcon Dr FK5 23 B3
Falconer Ct FK7 7 C3
Falconer St PA14 47 C2
Falconer Terr ML3 162 C1
Falcon La PA16 45 A5
Falcon Rd PA5 131 D7
Falcon Terr G20 96 C8
Falcon Terrace La G20 96 C8
Falfield St 1 G5 117 A4
FALKIRK 42 D6
Falkirk & District Royal Infmy
FK1 42 A4
Falkirk Grahamston Sta
FK1 42 B5
Falkirk High Sch FK1 41 E4
Falkirk High Sta FK1 42 A3
Falkirk Rd
Bannockburn FK7 11 F8
Bonnybridge FK4 40 C6
Cowie FK7 12 A6
Falkirk FK2, FK3 42 F6
Falkirk, Glen Village FK1 42 B1
Larbert FK5 23 B1
Falkirk Stadium (Falkirk FC)
FK2 42 F6
Falkirk Wheel* FK1 41 A5
Falkland Ave G77 157 A5
Falkland Cres G64 98 D8
Falkland Dr G74 159 D1
Falkland La G12 96 B3
Falkland Park Rd KA8 236 A3
Falkland Pk G74 159 D1
Falkland Pl
Ayr KA8 236 A3
Coatbridge ML5 122 B3
East Kilbride G74 159 D1
Stenhousemuir FK5 23 E4
Falkland Rd KA8 236 A3
Falkland St G12 96 B3
FALLIN 8 C3
Fallin Prim Sch FK7 8 D5
Falloch Pl ML2 165 F6
Falloch Rd
Bearsden G61 75 C2
Glasgow G42 137 A7
Milngavie G62 54 E3
FALLSIDE 141 D6
Fallside Ave G71 141 C6
Fallside Rd G71 141 B4
Fallside Sec Sch G71 141 D6
Falmouth Dr PA19 44 F5
Falside Ave PA2 113 E1
Falside Rd
Glasgow G32 119 B2
Paisley PA2 113 E1
Falstaff G74 160 C5
Fancy Farm Pl PA16 44 F4
Fancy Farm Rd PA16 45 A4
Faraday Ave ML2 165 C3
Faraday Ret Pk ML5 122 A6
Faransay Pl KA3 223 A5
Fara St G23 96 F8
Fardalehill View KA2 221 F1
Farden Pl KA9 236 D6
Farie St G73 137 F8
Farlands View KA23 190 C4
Farm Cres ML1 143 F4
Farm Ct G71 141 B4
Farme Castle Ct G73 118 C1
Farme Castle Est G73 118 C1
Farme Cross G73 118 B1
Farmeloan Rd G73 138 B8
Farmfield Terr KA23 190 D5
Farmgate Sq ML4 141 F4
Farm Houses The G65 60 E7
Farmington Ave G32 119 D5
Farmington Gate G32 119 D4
Farmington Gdns G32 119 D5
Farmington Gr G32 119 D5
Farm La ML4 141 F3
Farm Pk G66 79 D4
Farm Rd
Blantyre G72 140 D1
Clydebank, Duntocher G81 74 A7
Clydebank G81 73 D3
Cowie FK7 12 D8
Fallin FK7 8 D4
Glasgow G41 116 B5
Hamilton ML3 161 F4
Kilmarnock KA3 222 E3
Port Glasgow PA14 68 E7
Prestwick KA9 233 D1
Farm St
Falkirk FK2 24 A1
Motherwell ML1 163 D7
Farm Terr ML3 161 F4
Farndale G74 159 C3
Farne Dr G44 137 C4
Farnell St G4 97 B2
Farquhar Rd
Greenock PA14 46 F2
Port Glasgow PA14 47 A2
Farquharson Way FK1 41 F1
Farquhar Sq EH48 107 C3
Farrell Pl KA8 236 B2
Farrier Ct PA5 111 F3
Faskally Ave G64 77 E3
Faskally Wlk 13 ML2 165 F6
Faskin Cres G53 134 F7
Faskine Ave
Airdrie ML6 122 F6
Calderbank ML6 123 B2
Faskine Cres ML6 122 F6
Faskin Pl G53 134 F7
Faskin Rd G53 134 F7
Fasque Pl G15 74 E4
Fastnet St G33 119 A8
FAULDHEAD 80 B6
Fauldhouse St G5 117 D3
Faulds G69 120 C5
Faulds Gdns G69 120 C5
Fauldshead Rd PA4 94 D3
Faulds La ML5 121 F3
Fauldspark Cres G69 120 C6
Faulds Park Rd PA19 43 E5
Faulds St ML5 121 F3
Fauldswood Cres PA2 113 B2
Fauldswood Dr PA2 113 B2
Faulds Wynd KA23 190 C4
Faulkner Gr ML1 164 F8
Fearnach Pl G20 96 B7
Fearnan Pl PA16 45 A4
Fearnmore Rd G20 96 D7
Fearnoch KA9 236 C5
Fellhill St KA7 239 B5
Fells The G66 57 E8
Fellsview Ave G66 58 F1
Felton Pl G13 94 F7
Fencedyke Cl KA11 219 F4
Fencedyke Prim Sch
KA11 220 A3
Fencedyke Way KA11 220 A4
Fendoch St G32 119 A4
Fenella St G32 119 B5
Fennsbank Ave G73 138 D3
Fenton St FK10 10 A7
FENWICK 213 B4
Fenwick Cl KA3 223 C6
Fenwick Dr
Barrhead G78 134 D1
Hamilton ML3 183 E7
Fenwickland Ave KA7 239 A4
Fenwickland Pl KA7 239 B4
Fenwick Pl G46 136 B1
Fenwick Prim Sch KA3 213 A4
Fenwick Rd
Glasgow G46 136 C3
Kilmaurs KA3 222 C7
Waterside KA3 213 E4
Ferclay St G81 74 D7
Fereneze Ave
Barrhead G78 134 B3
Clarkston G76 157 C8
Paisley PA4 114 A8
Fereneze Cres
Glasgow G13 95 A7
Hamilton ML3 161 F3
Fereneze Dr PA2 133 C7
Fereneze Gr G78 134 B4
Fereneze Rd G78 154 C8
Fergus Ave PA3 113 A5
Fergus Ct G20 96 E4
Fergus Dr
Glasgow G20 96 E4
Greenock PA16 45 A4
Paisley PA3 113 A5
Fergus Gdns ML3 162 F2
Fergushill Rd KA13 208 A3
Fergus La G20 96 F4
Ferguslie PA1 113 B4
FERGUSLIE PARK 113 A5
Ferguslie Park Ave PA3 113 A5
Ferguslie Park Cres PA3 113 A4
Ferguslie Wlk PA1 113 B4
Ferguson Ave
Milngavie G62 55 A1
Prestwick KA9 236 D8
Renfrew PA4 94 D3
Ferguson Dr
Denny FK6 21 D1
Motherwell ML1 163 E3
Stenhousemuir FK2 24 A5
Ferguson Gdns KA1 227 B8
Ferguson Gr FK4 40 B6
Ferguson St
Ayr KA8 236 C3
Johnstone PA5 111 E3
Renfrew PA4 94 D3
Stirling FK8 1 F2
Ferguson Way ML6 103 B2
Fergus Pl PA16 45 A4
Fergus Rd PA16 45 A4
Fergusson Pl G74 160 D5
Fergusson Rd G67 61 F2
Fergusson Terr G66 58 C5
Ferguston Rd G61 75 F3
Fernan St G32 118 F5
Fern Ave
Bishopbriggs G64 98 B8
Erskine PA8 93 B7
Kirkintilloch G66 79 C5
Fernbank
Prestwick KA9 236 B5
Stirling FK9 2 B3
Fernbank Ave G72 139 C4
Fernbank Ct KA9 236 B5
Fernbank St G22 97 E5
Fern Brae KA7 239 C3
Fernbrae Ave G73 138 C3
Fernbrae Way G73 138 B3
Fern Cotts 1 G13 95 F5
Ferncroft Dr G44 137 D5
Ferndale ML9 185 A1
Ferndale Ct G23 96 D8
Ferndale Dr G23 96 D8
Ferndale Gdns G23 96 D8
Ferndale Pl G23 96 D8
Fern Dr G78 134 B4
Ferness Oval G21 98 C7
Ferness Pl G21 98 C7
Ferness Rd G21 98 C6
Fern Gr G69 101 A6
Ferngrove Ave G12 96 B6
FERNHILL 138 B3
Fernhill Grange G71 141 A1
Fernhill Rd G73 138 B3
Fernhill Sch G73 138 C3
FERNIEGAIR 163 B2
Ferniegair Ave G84 16 B2
Fernie Gdns
Cardross G82 48 B8
Glasgow G20 96 E7
Fernieshaw Rd ML1 144 F2
Fernington Pl ML2 165 B4
Ferninigton Pl ML2 165 A4
Fern La
Glasgow G13 95 F5
Lennoxtown G66 33 C1
Fernlea G61 75 E3
Fern Lea Gr FK2 24 C3
Fernlea Rd 5 G66 58 E1
Fernleigh Pl G69 80 F2
Fernleigh Rd G43 136 D5
Fern Pl KA1 227 C7
Fernside Wlk ML3 162 E1
Fernslea Ave G72 161 C8
Fern St ML1 164 A4
Ferrier Ct KA10 229 F4
Ferry Ct FK9 2 A3
Ferryden Ct G14 95 E2
Ferryden St G14 95 E2
Ferryfield Gdns G83 27 F4
Ferry Loan G83 27 E5
Ferry Orch FK9 2 D1
Ferry Rd
Bishopton PA7 72 B4
Bothwell G71 141 A1
Cardross G82 48 B6
Glasgow G3 96 B1
Glasgow G3 96 C1
Renfrew PA4 94 D5
Rosneath G84 15 B3
South Alloa FK7 9 F4
Stirling FK9 2 D1
Uddingston G71 140 E6
Fersit Ct G43 136 C6
Fersit St G43 136 C6
Fetlar Ct G72 138 F3
Fetlar Dr
Glasgow G44 137 C5
Kilmarnock KA3 223 A6
Fetlar Rd PA11 110 D8
Fettercairn Ave G15 74 E4
Fettercairn Gdns G64 78 C1
Fettercairn Pl ML6 103 B3
Fettes St G33 118 F8
Fiddison Pl KA9 236 E5
Fiddoch Ct ML2 165 F7
Fidra St G33 118 F8
Fielden Pl G40 118 A5
Fielden St G40 118 A5
Field Gr G76 157 F5
Fieldhead Dr G43 136 A5
Fieldhead Sq G43 136 A5
Fieldings The KA3 195 C8
Field Rd
Clarkston G76 157 F5
Clydebank G81 74 D8
Larkhall ML9 185 B2
Fields La PA6 91 B3
Field St ML3 162 D1
Fife Ave
Airdrie ML6 123 A5
Glasgow G52 115 B4
Fife Cres G71 141 A1
Fife Ct G71 141 A1
Fife Dr
Greenock PA16 44 D5
Motherwell ML1 142 D2
Fife Rd PA16 44 D5
Fife Way
Bishopbriggs G64 98 D8
Glasgow G64 97 F7
Fifth Ave
Airdrie ML6 123 C8
Glasgow G12 95 F5
Millerston G33 99 B5
Renfrew PA4 94 C1
Fifth Rd G72 161 E5
Fifty Pitches Pl G51 115 C7
Fifty Pitches Rd G52 115 B7
Fifty Pitches Way G51 115 B7
Finaly Wlk G83 27 F8
Finart Dr PA2 114 B1
Finaven Gdns G61 75 B8
Finbraken Dr PA19 43 E5
Fincastle Pl FK7 12 E8
Finch Dr G13 95 A8
Finch Gr ML5 122 E3
Finch Pl
Johnstone PA5 131 D7
Kilmarnock KA1 228 C7
Finch Rd PA16 45 B5
Finch Way ML4 141 F8
Findhorn PA8 73 A2
Findhorn Ave
Paisley PA2 112 F1
Renfrew PA4 94 E3
Findhorn Ct G75 179 D8
Findhorn Pl
East Kilbride G75 179 D8
Falkirk FK1 42 D2
Troon KA10 229 G5
Findhorn Rd KA9 233 F4
Findhorn St G33 118 D8
Findlay Ct 3 ML1 163 D8
Findlay's Brae KA21 216 F7
Findlay St
9 Kilsyth G65 60 D8
Motherwell ML1 163 F5
Findlay Terr 2 G72 139 D6
Findochty PA8 73 A3
Findochty Pl G33 99 E2
Findochty St G33 99 E2
Fingal La G20 96 C7
Fingal St G20 96 D7
Fingalton Rd G77 155 E5
Fingask St G32 119 C4
Finglas Ave PA2 114 B1
Finglen Cres FK10 4 C4
Finglen Gdns G62 54 E2
Finglen Pl G53 135 B5
Fingleton Ave G78 134 D1
Finhaven St G32 118 E3
Finistere Ave FK1 42 B3
Finlarig Ct FK5 23 F4
Finlarig St G34 120 C7
Finlas Ave KA7 239 B3
Finlas Pl G22 97 D5
Finlas St G22 97 D4
Finlay Ave KA24 191 D7
Finlay Dr
Glasgow G31 118 A7
Linwood PA3 111 F5
Finlay Rise G62 76 C8
Finlayson Dr
Airdrie ML6 123 E7
Kilmarnock KA3 223 D3
Finlayson Pl FK5 23 C5
Finlayson Quadrant 1
ML6 123 E7
Finlaystone Country Estate*
PA14 69 E8
Finlaystone Cres PA13 69 D2
Finlaystone Pl PA13 69 D2
Finlaystone Rd
Kilmacolm PA13 69 D4
Port Glasgow PA14 69 A7
Finlaystone St ML5 121 E7
Finnart Cres PA19 44 C6
Finnart Rd PA16 45 D6
Finnart Sq G40 117 F3
Finnart St
Glasgow G40 117 F3
Glasgow G40 117 F4
Greenock PA16 45 D6
Finneston La 11 PA15 46 B3
Finneston St PA15 46 B3
Finneston Way 12 PA15 46 B3
Finnick Glen KA7 239 A3

FULLARTON
Glasgow 119 A3
Irvine 219 B1
Fullarton Ave
Dundonald KA2 225 F2
Glasgow G32 119 A2
Fullarton Cres KA10 229 F1
Fullarton Ct KA1 222 E1
Fullarton Ctyd KA10 230 B1
Fullarton Dr
Glasgow G32 119 A1
Troon KA10 229 F1
Fullarton La G32 119 A2
Fullarton Pl
Coatbridge ML5 121 E3
Stevenston KA20 217 D8
Troon KA10 230 A4
Fullarton Rd
Cambuslang G72 138 F8
Cumbernauld G68 61 E5
Glasgow G32 118 F1
Prestwick KA9 236 C6
Fullarton Rdbt KA12 219 B2
Fullarton St
Ayr KA7 238 F8
Coatbridge ML5 121 E3
Irvine KA12 219 B2
Kilmarnock KA1 222 E1
Fullers Gate G81 74 C7
Fullerton Dr KA23 190 B4
Fullerton La PA15 46 F3
Fullerton Sq KA22 205 C2
Fullerton St PA3 113 D7
Fullerton Terr PA3 113 E7
Fulmar Cres FK5 23 C5
Fulmar Ct 4 G64 97 F8
Fulmar Pk G74 159 D3
Fulmar Pl PA5 131 C6
Fulshaw Cres KA8 236 F2
Fulshaw Ct KA9 236 D5
Fulshaw Pl KA8 236 E3
Fulton Cres PA10 111 B3
Fulton Dr PA6 111 E8
Fulton Gdns PA6 111 F1
Fulton Rd
Milngavie G62 55 B1
Milngavie G62 55 B1
Fulton's La 10 KA3 222 F1
Fulton St G13 95 E7
Fulwood Ave
Glasgow G13 94 F7
Linwood PA3 112 B6
Fulwood Park Ind Est
ML3 162 B4
Fulwood Pl G13 94 F7
Furlongs The ML3 162 E5
Furnace Ct KA1 228 E6
Furnace Rd ML3 183 F3
Fyfe Park Terr PA14 47 F1
FYFE SHORE 47 E2
Fyfe Shore Rd PA14 47 F1
Fyffe Park Rd PA14 47 E1
Fyneart St ML2 165 E4
Fyne Ave ML4 141 E6
Fyne Cres ML9 184 F5
Fyne Ct ML3 162 A1
Fyne La ML4 146 E6
Fyne Way ML1 143 A5
Fynloch Pl G81 73 E7
Fyvie Ave G43 136 B5
Fyvie Cres ML6 123 F7

G

Gaaf Cl KA24 191 A6
Gaberston Ave FK10 10 C7
Gabriel St PA15 46 B2
Gadburn Sch G21 98 C5
Gadie Ave PA4 94 E2
Gadie St G33 118 D8
Gadloch Ave G66 79 D2
Gadloch Gdns G66 79 D3
Gadloch St G22 97 C6
Gadloch View G66 79 D2
Gadsburn Ct G21 98 C6
Gadshill St G21 97 F1
Gael St PA16 45 C4
Gagarin Terr KA13 207 E2
GAILES 224 F3
Gailes Pk G71 140 F2
Gailes Pl KA1 227 E4
Gailes Rd
Cumbernauld G68 61 F5
Irvine KA11 224 E5
Troon KA10 229 E7
Gailes St G40 118 B4
Gainburn Cres G67 81 F6
Gainburn Ct G67 81 F6
Gainburn Gdns G67 81 F5
Gainburn Pl G67 81 F6
Gainburn View G67 82 A6
Gainford Pl KA3 222 F4
Gain Rd
Annathill ML5 81 F1
Cumbernauld G67, ML5 82 A1
Gain & Shankburn Rd
G67 82 C2
Gainside Rd ML5 101 C6
Gairbraid Ave G20 96 D6
Gairbraid Ct G20 96 C6
Gairbraid Pl G20 96 D6
Gairbraid Terr G69 121 A5
Gair Cres
Carluke ML8 188 A3
Wishaw ML2 165 B1
Gairdoch Dr FK2 24 C3
Gairdoch St FK2 42 B8
Gairloch Gdns G66 59 B1
Gair Rd ML8 188 B6
Gair Wynd ML7 147 B3
Gaitskell Ave G83 27 D7
Gala Ave PA4 94 E2
Gala Cres ML2 165 A5
Gala St G33 98 E2
Galbraith Cres
Law ML8 187 A6
Stenhousemuir FK5 23 C4
Galbraith Dr
Glasgow G51 115 E8
Milngavie G62 75 F8
Galdenoch St G33 99 B2
Gallacher Ave PA2 113 A1
Gallacher Cres G83 19 F1
Gallacher Ct
Motherwell ML1 164 B3
Paisley PA1 113 C5
Gallacher Way G82 27 D2
Gallahill Ave PA14 69 A7
Gallamuir Dr FK7 12 D3
Gallamuir Rd FK7 12 D5
Gallan Ave 3 G23 76 E1
Gallery Gr ML5 122 A6
Gallery of Modern Art★
G1 241 A2
Gallion Wlk 14 KA1 227 F8
Galloway Ave
Ayr KA8 236 C2
Hamilton ML3 183 C7
Paisley PA3 113 E7
Wishaw ML2 165 C4
Galloway Ct
Falkirk FK1, FK2 42 B6
Irvine KA11 220 B6
Galloway Dr G73 138 B3
Galloway Pl KA21 216 E8
Galloway Rd
Airdrie ML6 122 F4
East Kilbride G74 160 C3
Galloway St
Falkirk FK1 42 B6
Glasgow G21 97 F6
Galloway Terr PA3 113 E7
GALLOWFLAT 138 C7
Gallowflat St G73 138 B8
GALLOWGATE 118 A5
Gallowgate G1, G40, G31 117 F6
GALLOWHILL 114 A7
GALLOW HILL 215 B5
Gallowhill ML9 185 A2
Gallowhill Ave G66 79 C6
Gallowhill Gr G66 79 C7
Gallowhill Prim Sch PA3 114 B7
Gallowhill Rd
Carmunnock G76 158 E8
Kirkintilloch G66 79 C6
Lanark ML11 215 A4
Paisley PA3 114 A6
Galrigside Rd KA1 227 D7
Galston Ave G77 157 A5
Galston Ct ML3 183 E7
Galston Pl KA3 223 B6
Galston Rd KA1 228 F6
Galston St G53 134 F6
Galt Ave KA12 219 D3
Galt Pl G75 180 D7
Galt St PA15 46 C3
Gambeson Cres FK7 7 D3
Gameshill View KA3 211 E8
Gamrie Dr G53 135 A7
Gamrie Gdns G53 135 A7
Gamrie Rd G53 135 A8
Gannel Hill View FK10 5 E4
Gannochy Dr G64 78 C1
Gantock Cres G33 119 B7
Ganton Ct KA13 207 B3
Gara Rd ML6 123 D5
Garden Ct 2 KA8 235 F1
Gardenhall G75 179 E8
Gardenhall Ct G75 179 E8
Garden Ho G66 58 B6
Garden Pl KA10 229 B3
GARDENSIDE 140 E5
Gardenside ML4 142 A4
Gardenside Ave
Glasgow G32 139 B8
Uddingston G71 140 F6
Gardenside Cres G32 139 B8
Gardenside Gr G32 139 B8
Gardenside Pl G32 139 B8
Gardenside Rd ML3 162 D2
Gardenside St G71 140 E6
Garden Square La KA13 207 E3
Garden Square Wlk ML6 122 D8
Garden St
Ayr KA8 235 F1
Falkirk FK1 42 C5
Kilmarnock KA3 222 F1
Gardens The KA11 220 C6
Garden Terr FK1 42 C5
Garden Veteran's Cotts
PA7 72 F5
Gardiner St KA9 236 C8
Gardner Gr G71 141 A8
Gardner St G11 96 B2
Gardrum Gdns FK1 66 D7
Gardrum Pl KA3 222 F4
Gardyne St G34 100 A1
Garelet Pl KA11 220 B2
Gareloch Ave
Airdrie ML6 102 F2
Paisley PA2 113 A2
Gareloch Cl PA15 46 A2
Gareloch La PA14 68 D8
Gareloch Rd
Greenock PA15 46 A3
Gareloch Rd *continued*
Port Glasgow PA14 68 E8
Rhu G84 15 E4
Gare Rd G84 15 B3
Garfield Ave ML4 142 C5
Garfield Dr ML4 142 C4
Garfield Pl G33 99 E6
Garfield St G31 118 A6
Garforth Rd G69 119 F4
Gargieston Prim Sch
KA2 227 C6
Gargrave Ave G69 119 F4
Garion Dr G13 95 B5
Garlieston Rd G33 119 F6
Garmouth Ct 3 G51 116 A8
Garmouth Gdns 4 G51 116 A8
Garmouth St G51 115 F8
Garnetbank Prim Sch
G3 240 B4
GARNETHILL 240 B4
Garnethill St G3 240 B4
Garnet St G3 240 B4
Garngaber Ave G66 79 D5
Garngaber Ct G66 79 E5
Garngrew Rd FK4 38 F3
Garnhall Ditch★ G68 38 E1
Garnhall Farm Rd G68 62 E8
Garnie Ave PA8 93 D8
Garnie Cres PA8 73 D1
Garnie La PA8 93 D8
Garnieland Rd PA8 73 D1
Garnie Oval PA8 73 D1
Garnie Pl PA8 73 D1
GARNKIRK 100 B6
Garnkirk La G33 99 E5
Garnock Acad KA25 149 A2
Garnock Ct
Irvine KA12 219 C2
4 Kilbirnie KA25 149 A1
Garnock Pk G74 160 B1
Garnock Rd
Kilmarnock KA1 228 A5
Stevenston KA20 217 D8
Stevenston, Stevenston Site
KA20 218 C6
Garnockside KA14 170 B6
Garnock St
Dalry KA24 191 C7
Glasgow G21 97 F2
Kilbirnie KA25 149 B2
Garnock Swimming Pool
KA25 149 A1
Garnock View
Glengarnock KA14 170 B7
Kilwinning KA13 207 E4
GARNQUEEN 101 E5
Garnqueen Cres ML5 101 D6
Garpel Way PA12 129 B2
Garrallan KA13 207 C2
Garraway Pl G84 16 F1
Garrawy Rd G84 16 F2
Garrell Ave G65 36 D1
Garrell Gr G65 36 D2
Garrell Pl G65 60 C8
Garrell Rd G65 60 C8
Garrell Way
Cumbernauld G67 61 E2
Kilsyth G65 60 C8
Garret Pl G68 61 D5
Garrick Ave G77 156 D2
Garrick Ct G77 156 D2
Garrier Ct KA11 220 F2
Garrier Pl KA1 222 D2
Garrier Rd KA11 220 F2
Garrioch Cres 1 G20 96 D5
Garrioch Dr G20 96 D5
Garrioch Gate 8 G20 96 D5
Garriochmill Rd
Glasgow G20 96 E3
Glasgow G20 96 F3
Garriochmill Way 3 G20 96 F3
Garrioch Quadrant 2
G20 96 D5
Garrioch Rd G20 96 D5
Garrion Bsns Pk ML2 186 A8
Garrion Pl ML9 185 F1
Garrion St ML2 186 C6
Garrison Pl FK1 42 B5
GARROWHILL 120 A5
Garrowhill Dr G69 119 F5
Garrowhill Prim Sch
G69 120 A5
Garrowhill Sta G69 119 F6
Garry Ave G61 76 B2
Garry Dr PA2 113 A2
Garryhorn KA9 236 D6
Garry Pl
Falkirk FK1 42 D2
Kilmarnock KA1 228 A5
Troon KA10 229 G5
Garry St G44 137 A7
Garry Way ML7 146 E6
Garscadden Prim Sch
G13 94 F7
Garscadden Rd G15 75 A2
Garscadden Road S G13 95 A8
Garscadden Sta G14 95 A6
Garscadden View 5 G81 74 D3
Garscube Mill G61 76 A2
Garscube Rd G4, G20 97 B2
Garshake Ave G82 50 C5
Garshake Rd G82 50 C5
Garshake Terr G82 50 C5
Gartartan Rd PA1 114 F5
Gartcarron Hill G68 61 C3
Gartcloss Rd ML5 101 C2
Gartclush Gdns FK7 11 E8
Gartconnell Dr G61 75 E6
Gartconnell Gdns G61 75 E6
Gartconnell Rd G61 75 E6
Gartconner Ave G66 80 B8
Gartconner Prim Sch G66 80 B8
GARTCOSH 100 F5
Gartcosh Business
Interchange G69 101 B4
Gartcosh Prim Sch G69 100 F4
Gartcosh Rd ML5 101 A1
Gartcosh Sta G69 101 A4
Gartcosh Wlk ML4 141 F5
Gartcows Ave FK1 42 A4
Gartcows Cres FK1 42 A3
Gartcows Dr FK1 42 A4
Gartcows Gdns FK1 41 F4
Gartcows Pl FK1 42 A3
Gartcows Rd FK1 42 A3
Gartcraig Pl
Glasgow G33 98 F1
Glasgow G33 99 A1
Gartcraig Rd G33 118 F8
Garten Dr ML7 147 B3
Gartferry Ave G69 80 F2
Gartferry Rd G68, G69 81 B4
Gartferry St G21 98 A4
Gartfield St ML6 123 B6
Gartgill Rd ML5 101 E2
GARTHAMLOCK 99 E2
Garthamlock Rd G33 99 E1
Garth Dr G81 94 B7
Garthill Gdns FK1 42 A4
Garthill La FK1 42 A4
Garthland Dr
Ardrossan KA22 205 C4
Glasgow G31 118 A7
Garthland La PA1 113 F5
Garth St G1 241 A2
GARTLEA 123 B6
Gartlea Ave ML6 123 B7
Gartlea Gdns 1 ML6 123 B7
Gartleahill ML6 123 B6
Gartlea Rd ML6 123 A7
Gartliston Rd ML5 101 F3
Gartliston Terr G69 121 A5
Gartloch Ct G69 100 C3
Gartloch Rd
Glasgow, Gartcosh G69 100 C3
Glasgow, Ruchazie G33 99 A1
Gartloch Way G69 100 C3
Gartly St G44 136 F4
Gartmore Gdns G71 140 E8
Gartmore La G69 81 A2
Gartmore Rd PA1 114 C4
Gartmore Terr G72 138 F3
Gartmorn Rd FK10 5 D1
Gartnavel General Hospl
G12 96 A4
Gartnavel Royal Hospl
G12 96 A4
Gartnavel Royal Hospl Sch
G12 96 A4
GARTNESS 123 E5
Gartness Dr ML6 123 E5
Gartness Rd ML6 124 A3
GARTOCHARN 20 F8
Gartocher Dr G32 119 C5
Gartocher Rd G32 119 C5
Gartocher Terr G32 119 C5
Gartons Rd G21 98 C4
GARTSHERRIE 101 E1
Gartsherrie Ave ML5 101 F5
Gartsherrie Ind Est ML5 101 F1
Gartsherrie Prim Sch
ML5 121 E8
Gartsherrie Rd ML5 121 F8
Gartshore Cres G65 59 F2
Gartshore Gdns G68 60 F1
Garturk St
Coatbridge ML5 122 B4
Glasgow G42 117 B2
Garvald Ct G40 118 B3
Garvald La FK6 21 C1
Garvald Rd FK6 39 D7
Garvald St
Glasgow G40 118 B3
Greenock PA15 46 C3
Garvally Cres FK10 10 A8
Garve Ave G44 137 A5
Garvel Cres G33 119 E6
Garvel Dr PA15 45 D3
Garvel Pl G62 54 D2
Garvel Rd
Glasgow G33 119 E6
Milngavie G62 54 E2
Garvel Specl Sch PA16 44 E5
Garven Ct KA1 228 B7
Garven Rd KA20 217 E6
Garvie Ave PA19 44 F6
Garvin Lea ML4 142 A8
Garvock Dr
Glasgow G43 136 B6
Greenock PA15 45 E3
Garwhitter Dr G62 55 B2
Gascoigne Ct 8 FK2 42 A8
Gascoyne G75 180 C7
Gaskin Path G33 99 E5
Gask Pl G13 94 F8
Gas St PA5 112 A3
Gasworks Rd ML8 187 D3
GATEHEAD 226 E5
Gatehead Cvn Pk KA2 226 E5
Gatehead Rd KA2 221 E1
Gatehouse St G32 119 C4
GATESIDE
Barrhead 133 F1
Beith 171 E7
Greenock 45 B4
Gateside KA11 219 F6
Gateside Ave
Bonnybridge FK4 40 C6
Cambuslang G72 139 D5
Greenock PA16 45 B4
Kilsyth G65 60 B8
Gateside Cres
Airdrie ML6 123 A8
Barrhead G78 134 A1
Gateside Gdns
Barrhead G78 133 F2
Greenock PA16 45 B4
Gateside Gr PA16 45 B4
Gateside Pk G65 60 B8
Gateside Pl
Kilbarchan PA10 111 A3
Kilmarnock KA1 227 F4
Gateside Prim Sch KA15 171 E8
Gateside Rd
Barrhead G78 134 A3
Stirling FK7 7 A3
Wishaw ML2 164 E4
Gateside St
Glasgow G31 118 B6
Hamilton ML3 162 E3
West Kilbride KA23 190 D6
Gates Rd PA12 129 D3
Gateway The G74 160 A4
Gaughan Quadrant ML1 163 D5
Gauldry Ave G52 115 C3
Gauze St PA1 113 F5
Gavel Gr 6 ML11 215 C3
Gavel La 4 ML11 215 C3
Gavell Rd
Kilsyth G65 60 A7
Queenzieburn G65 59 F7
Gavinburn Gdns G60 73 A7
Gavinburn Pl G60 73 A7
Gavinburn Prim Sch G60 72 F7
Gavinburn St G60 73 A7
Gavin Hamilton Ct KA7 239 C6
Gavin's Mill Rd G62 55 A1
Gavins Rd
Alloa FK10 4 F1
Clydebank G81 74 B5
Gavin St ML1 163 F5
Gavinton St G44 136 F5
Gayne Dr ML5 101 C6
Gean Ct G67 62 F4
Gean Rd FK10 9 F8
Gearholm Rd KA7 238 D3
Gear Terr G40 118 B2
Geary St 3 G23 76 D1
Geddes Hill G74 160 B4
Geddes Rd G21 98 C7
Geelong Gdns G66 33 D1
Geils Ave G82 50 C2
Geilsland Rd KA15 171 D7
Geilsland Sch KA15 171 C8
Geils Quadrant G82 50 C2
GEILSTON 48 B8
Geilston Ct G82 48 A8
Geilston House & Gdns★
G82 25 H1
Geilston Pk G82 48 A7
Geirston Rd KA25 148 F2
Gelston St G32 119 B4
Gemini Gr ML1 143 B5
Gemmell Cres KA8 236 C1
Gemmell Ct KA8 236 C1
Gemmell Way ML9 198 E2
Gemmel Pl G77 156 C4
General Roy Way ML8 202 C8
Generals Gate G71 140 E6
Gentle Row G81 73 F6
George Aitken Ct KA22 205 D3
George Ave G81 74 C3
George Cres G81 74 C3
George Ct
5 Hamilton ML3 162 A5
Irvine KA12 219 C3
Paisley PA1 113 D4
George Laing Ct FK5 23 E2
George Mann Terr G73 138 A4
George Pl
Doonfoot KA7 238 B2
Paisley PA1 113 E4
George Rd PA19 44 E6
George Reith Ave G12 95 F5
George's Ave KA8 236 B3
Georges Cl 7 ML3 162 A5
George Sq
Ayr KA8 236 A1
Glasgow G1 241 A2
Greenock PA15 45 E6
George St
Airdrie ML6 122 F7
Alexandria G83 27 F3
Alva FK12 5 A6
3 Ayr KA8 235 F1
Barrhead G78 134 B3
Chapelhall ML6 123 D3
Falkirk FK2 42 B5
Glasgow, Baillieston G69 120 B4
Glasgow G1 241 B2
Hamilton ML3 162 A5
Helensburgh G84 16 E1
Howwood PA9 130 F5
Johnstone PA5 111 F3
Laurieston FK2 42 F3
Motherwell ML1 163 F4
Motherwell, New Stevenston
ML1 143 B4
Paisley PA1 113 D4
Stenhousemuir FK5 23 C3
Stevenston KA20 217 D7

George Stewart Gdns [3]
ML3 162 A5
George Street La G83 27 F3
George Terr KA12 219 C3
George View ML2 164 F2
George Way [10] ML9 185 B4
Georgian Ct PA16 45 E6
Gerald Terr FK5 23 E3
Gerardine Ct G83 28 A8
Gerard Pl ML4 142 B7
GERMISTON 98 B2
Germiston Cres G75 180 A4
Germiston Ct G75 180 A4
Gertrude Pl G78 134 A2
Ghillies La ML1 142 C1
Gibb Ct ML9 198 E2
Gibbdun Pl FK6 39 E7
Gibbon Cres G74 160 C3
Gibbshill Pl ML7 127 D5
Gibb St
Chapelhall ML6 123 D2
Cleland ML1 144 B1
GIBSHILL 46 E2
Gibshill Rd PA15 46 E2
Gibson Ave G82 50 B4
Gibson Cres PA5 111 F2
Gibsongray St FK2 42 A7
Gibson Hts G4 241 C2
Gibson La PA13 69 D1
Gibson Quadrant ML1 142 C1
Gibson Rd PA4 94 B1
Gibson St
Denny FK6 21 E1
Dumbarton G82 50 B4
Glasgow G4 241 C1
Glasgow, Kelvingrove G12 96 E2
Greenock PA15 46 E2
Kilmarnock KA1 222 D1
Salsburgh ML7 125 B2
Giffen Rd KA21 217 A8
GIFFNOCK 136 C2
Giffnock Park Ave G46 136 C4
Giffnock Prim Sch G46 136 C2
Giffnock Sta G46 136 C3
Gifford Dr G52 115 A5
Gifford Pl ML5 121 E3
Gifford Wynd PA2 112 F2
Gigha Cres KA11 220 B2
Gigha Gdns ML8 202 A8
Gigha La KA11 220 B2
Gigha Pl KA11 220 B2
Gigha Quadrant [4] ML2 164 E1
Gigha Terr KA11 220 B2
Gigha Wynd KA11 220 B2
Gilbertfield Path G33 99 B2
Gilbertfield Pl
Glasgow G33 99 B2
Irvine KA12 219 D2
Gilbertfield Rd G72 139 E3
Gilbertfield St G33 99 B2
Gilbert Sheddon Ct KA3 195 E1
Gilbert St G3 116 C8
Gilburn Pl ML7 146 F4
Gilchrist Dr FK1 41 E6
Gilchrist St ML5 122 B8
Gilchrist Way ML2 165 B1
Gilderdale G74 159 C2
Gilfillan Ave KA21 206 A2
Gilfillan Pl
Falkirk FK2 24 C2
Overtown ML2 186 C7
Gilfillan Way PA2 132 E8
Gilhill St G20 96 D7
Gillbank Ave ML8 187 D2
Gillbank La [6] ML9 185 C2
Gillburn Gate PA13 89 D8
Gillburn Rd PA13 89 D8
Gillburn St ML2 186 C6
Gillespie Dr G84 16 D4
Gillespie Pl FK7 7 B1
Gillespie Terr FK7 12 D2
Gillie-burn Gdns ML7 146 F4
Gillies Cres G74 160 D5
Gillies Dr FK7 7 C4
Gillies Hill FK7 6 D5
Gillies La G69 120 C4
Gillies St KA10 229 E3
Gill Pk FK6 21 E2
Gill Rd ML2 186 C7
Gillsburn Gdns KA3 223 A2
Gilmartin Rd PA3 111 E6
Gilmerton St G32 119 A4
Gilmour Ave
Clydebank G81 74 B5
Thorntonhall G74 158 B2
Gilmour Cres
Eaglesham G76 178 E5
Rutherglen G73 137 F8
Gilmour Dr ML3 161 F2
Gilmour Pl
Bellshill ML4 141 F5
Coatbridge ML5 121 F8
[7] Glasgow G5 117 C4
Gilmour St
Alexandria G83 27 D5
Clydebank G81 74 C4
Eaglesham G76 178 E5
Greenock PA15 46 D2
Kilmarnock KA1 228 A7
Paisley PA1 113 E5
Stewarton KA3 195 E1
Gilmourton Cres G77 156 D3
Gilmour Wynd KA20 206 E1
Gilroy Cl ML11 215 C5
Gilsay Ct FK1 42 C2
GILSHOCHILL 96 E8
Gilshochill Sta G23 96 E7
Gimmerscroft Cres [1]
ML6 123 F6
Girdle Gate KA11 219 F5
GIRDLE TOLL 220 A6
Girdle Toll KA11 220 A5
Girdons Way G71 140 E6
Girthon St G32 119 C4
Girvan Cres ML6 123 D1
Girvan St G33 118 D8
Glade The ML9 185 B2
Gladney Ave G13 94 E8
Gladsmuir Rd G52 115 A6
Gladstone Ave
Barrhead G78 134 B2
Johnstone PA5 131 D7
Gladstone Ct [1] ML3 162 A5
Gladstone Dr G74 179 D8
Gladstone Pl FK8 7 A6
Gladstone Rd
Saltcoats KA21 217 A8
Stenhousemuir FK5 23 D3
Gladstone St
Bellshill ML4 142 B5
Clydebank G81 73 F2
[11] Glasgow G4 97 A2
Glaive Ave FK7 7 D3
Glaive Rd G13 75 D1
Glamis Ave
Carluke ML8 187 F2
Elderslie PA5 112 B1
Newton Mearns G77 156 F5
Glamis Cres [3] G72 161 D3
Glamis Ct ML1 143 C2
Glamis Dr
East Kilbride G74 159 F3
Greenock PA16 45 A5
Glamis Gait [2] G72 161 E3
Glamis Gdns G64 78 B4
Glamis La [4] G72 161 D3
Glamis Pl PA16 45 A5
Glamis Rd G31 118 D4
Glanderston Ave
Barrhead G78 134 E2
Newton Mearns G77 156 B6
Glanderston Ct G13 95 A7
Glanderston Dr G13 95 A7
Glanderston Gate G77 156 C6
Glanderston Rd G77 155 D5
GLASGOW 241 C2
Glasgow Acad The [4] G12 96 F3
Glasgow Acad The (Atholl)
G62 55 A3
Glasgow Botanic Gdns★
G12 96 D4
Glasgow Caledonian Univ
G4 241 A4
Glasgow Cath (St Mungo)★
G4 241 C3
Glasgow Central Sta G2 240 C2
Glasgow Coll of Nautical
Studies G5 117 C5
Glasgow Dental Hospl
G2 240 B3
Glasgow Dental Sch G3 240 B4
Glasgow & Edinburgh Rd
Calderbank ML1 123 A1
Coatbridge ML5 121 D3
Glasgow G69 120 D5
Motherwell, Newhouse
ML1 143 C8
Motherwell, Newhouse
ML1 143 E7
Glasgow Fort Sh Ctr G34 99 E1
Glasgow Gaelic Sch G3 116 E8
Glasgow Harbour Terr
G11 96 A1
Glasgow Homeopathic Hospl
G12 96 A4
Glasgow La KA22 205 C2
Glasgow Metropolitan Coll
(Cathedral St Campus)
G1 241 B3
Glasgow Metropolitan Coll
(Dornoch St Campus)
G40 117 F5
Glasgow Metropolitan Coll
(Florence St Campus)
G5 117 C5
Glasgow Metropolitan Coll
(North Hanover St Campus)
G1 241 A3
Glasgow Metropolitan Coll
(Rogart St Campus)
G40 117 F5
Glasgow Museum Resource
Ctr & Open Mus★ G53 134 F5
Glasgow Necropolis (cemy)★
G4 241 C2
Glasgow Prestwick Int
Airport KA9 233 E2
Glasgow Rd
Barrhead G78 134 D4
Cambuslang, Silverbank
G72 138 F6
Cambuslang, Whitlawburn G72,
G73 138 F1
Clydebank G81 94 C7
Clydebank, Hardgate G81 74 C6
Coatbridge ML5 121 D5
Cumbernauld G67 82 D8
Cumbernauld, Kildrum G67 62 B4
Denny FK6 21 E1
Dumbarton, Dennystown
G82 49 E4
Dumbarton, Dumbuck G82 50 C2
Eaglesham G76 178 E7
Glasgow Rd *continued*
Falkirk FK1 41 C6
Glasgow G71 120 A4
Hamilton G72 161 E7
Kilmarnock KA3 223 B5
Kilsyth G65 60 B8
Kirkintilloch G66 79 A8
Lanark ML11 214 E4
Longcroft FK4 39 C4
Milngavie G62 55 B1
Nerston G72 160 A8
Nerston G74 160 A7
Paisley PA1 114 C4
Port Glasgow PA14 47 E1
Renfrew PA4 94 F2
Rutherglen G73 117 F1
Stirling FK7 7 B2
Strathblane G63 31 B4
Uddingston G71 140 E7
Wishaw ML2 164 E3
Glasgow Royal Concert
Hall★ G1 241 A3
Glasgow Sch of Art The
Glasgow G3 240 B4
Glasgow G3 240 C4
Glasgow Science Ctr★
G3 116 D7
Glasgow St
Ardrossan KA22 205 C2
Glasgow G12 96 E2
Helensburgh G84 16 C2
Kilbirnie KA25 149 A2
Glasgow Steiner Sch G3 96 D1
Glasgow Vennel KA12 219 C2
Glassel Rd G34 100 D1
Glasserton Pl G43 136 F5
Glasserton Rd G43 136 F5
GLASSFORD 198 A4
Glassford Rd ML3, ML9 198 D5
Glassford St
Glasgow G1 241 A2
Milngavie G62 55 B2
Motherwell ML1 164 A4
Glassford Twr ML1 164 B3
Glasshouse Loan FK10 10 A6
Glassock Rd KA3 222 F5
Glaudhall Ave G69 100 E7
Glazertbank G66 57 C8
Glazert Mdw G66 57 E7
Glazert Park Dr G66 57 E7
Glazert Pl G66 58 B5
Glazert Rd KA3 195 C7
Glebe Ave
Bothwell G71 141 B2
Carmunnock G76 158 D7
Coatbridge ML5 121 D4
Irvine KA11 225 C8
Kilmarnock KA1 228 A8
Stirling FK8 7 A7
Glebe Cres
Airdrie ML6 123 D8
Alva FK12 5 B7
Ayr KA8 235 F2
East Kilbride G74 159 F1
Hamilton ML3 162 C2
Stirling FK8 7 A7
Glebe Ct
Beith KA15 171 B8
East Kilbride G74 160 D5
Glasgow G4 241 B3
Kilmacolm PA13 89 D8
[2] Kilmarnock KA1 228 A8
[23] Lanark ML11 215 A4
Glebe Dr [1] ML11 215 A4
Glebefield Rd G84 15 E5
Glebe Gdns
Alexandria G83 27 E4
Houston PA6 91 B2
Glebe Hollow G71 141 B2
Glebe La G77 156 D4
Glebelands Way KA15 171 B7
Glebe Pk G82 50 B5
Glebe Pl
Cambuslang G72 139 B5
Rutherglen G73 137 F8
Saltcoats KA21 216 F8
Glebe Prim Sch KA12 219 C2
Glebe Rd
Ayr KA8 235 F2
Beith KA15 171 B8
Glengarnock KA25 170 B7
Kilmacolm PA13 89 D8
Kilmarnock KA1 228 A8
Newton Mearns G77 156 D4
Glebe St
Bellshill ML4 141 F5
Denny FK6 21 E2
East Kilbride G74 159 F1
Falkirk FK1 42 B5
Glasgow G1 241 C3
Hamilton ML3 162 D2
Kilwinning KA13 207 E4
Renfrew PA4 94 D3
Saltcoats KA21 216 F8
Stevenston KA20 206 C1
Glebe Terr
Alloa FK10 10 A6
Fenwick KA3 213 A3
Glebe The
Alva FK12 5 B7
Bothwell G71 141 B2
Irvine KA11 225 C8
Lanark ML11 214 F4
Symington KA1 231 C3
Glebe Wynd G71 141 B2
GLED CRAIG 70 B3
Gleddoch Cl G52 114 E6
Gleddoch Ct G52 114 E6
Gleddoch Gate [4] G52 114 F6
Gleddoch Rd G52 114 F6
Gleddoch View G82 49 D2
Gleddoch Wynd PA14 70 D5
Gledstane Rd PA7 72 B2
Glenacre Cres G71 140 E8
Glenacre Dr
Airdrie ML6 123 D6
Glasgow G45 137 D3
Glenacre Gr G45 137 E4
Glenacre Rd G67 82 F8
Glenacre St G45 137 D3
Glenacre Terr G45 137 D3
Glenafeoch Rd ML8 188 A1
Glen Affric G74 160 B1
Glen Affric Ave G53 135 D4
Glen Affric Pl KA1 227 C6
Glen Affric Way ML6 123 D1
Glen Afton Ct KA1 227 C6
Glenafton Gr ML5 121 F5
Glenafton View ML3 183 B8
Glen Alby Pl G53 135 C4
Glenalla Cres KA7 238 D1
Glenallan Terr ML1 142 D1
Glenallan Way PA2 132 E7
Glen Almond G74 160 D2
Glenalmond Rd [3] G73 138 D3
Glenalmond St G32 119 A4
Glenalva Ct G65 36 D1
Glenan Gdns G84 16 C2
Glenapp Ave PA2 114 B1
Glenapp Ct KA13 207 C2
Glenapp Pl
Kilwinning KA13 207 C2
Moodiesburn G69 80 F3
Glenapp Quadrant KA1 228 B7
Glenapp Rd PA2 114 B1
Glenapp St G41 116 F3
Glenarklet Cres PA2 134 A8
Glenarklet Dr PA2 114 A1
Glenarn Rd G84 15 E4
Glen Arroch G74 160 B1
Glenartney PA6 91 A2
Glenartney Rd G69 80 C1
Glenashdale Way PA2 114 A1
Glen Ave
Balloch G83 28 A8
Glasgow G32 119 B6
Gourock PA19 44 F6
Larkhall ML9 184 F1
Moodiesburn G69 80 F2
Neilston G78 154 E7
Port Glasgow PA14 47 B2
Glenavon Ct
Hamilton ML3 162 B1
Larkhall ML9 199 B7
Glen Avon Dr ML6 123 D1
Glenavon Rd G20 96 D7
Glenbank FK1 42 B1
Glenbank Ave G66 79 D4
Glenbank Ct G46 135 F2
Glenbank Dr G46 135 F2
Glenbank Rd G66 79 D4
Glenbarr St G21 97 F1
Glenbervie FK5 23 A4
Glen Bervie G74 160 B2
Glenbervie Ave FK5 23 A3
Glenbervie Bsns Pk FK5 23 A4
Glenbervie Cres
Cumbernauld G68 61 F5
Larbert FK5 23 B3
Glenbervie Dr
Kilwinning KA13 207 B3
Larbert FK5 23 A3
Glenbervie Pl
[15] Glasgow G23 76 D1
Gourock PA19 44 B6
Newton Mearns G77 156 A5
Glenbervie Wynd KA11 224 F8
Glenbo Dr FK6 39 E7
GLENBOIG 101 F6
Glenboig Farm Rd ML5 101 E6
Glenboig New Rd ML5 101 F6
Glenboig Prim Sch ML5 101 F5
Glenboig Rd
Glenboig G69 101 B7
Glenboig ML5 101 C6
Glen Brae
Bridge of Weir PA11 110 D8
Falkirk FK1 42 A3
Glenbrae Ct FK1 42 B3
Glenbrae Rd
Greenock PA15 46 B2
Port Glasgow PA14 68 D7
Glenbride Rd KA23 190 C3
Glenbrittle Dr PA2 114 A1
Glenbrittle Way PA2 114 A1
Glenbuck Ave G33 98 F6
Glenbuck Dr G33 98 F6
GLENBURN 133 C8
Glenburn Ave
Cambuslang G72 138 E5
Glasgow G69 120 C5
Moodiesburn G69 80 F2
Motherwell ML1 143 C4
Glenburn Cl
Greengairs ML6 103 C8
Kilwinning KA13 207 C6
Glenburn Cres
Milton of Campsie G66 58 C5
Paisley PA2 133 D7
Uddingston G71 141 C8
Glenburn Ct
East Kilbride G74 159 A3
[3] Kirkintilloch G66 79 D8
Glenburn Dr PA13 69 D1
Glenburn Gdns
Bishopbriggs G64 77 F2
Glenburn Gdns *continued*
Glenboig ML5 101 C6
Glenburnie Pl G34 119 F7
Glenburn Ind Est KA9 236 E8
Glenburn La
Glasgow G20 96 E7
Kilmacolm PA13 69 D1
Glenburn Pl PA13 69 D1
Glenburn Prim Sch KA9 236 E8
Glenburn Rd
Bearsden G61 75 E5
East Kilbride G74 159 A3
Falkirk FK1 42 D1
Glasgow G46 136 B1
Hamilton ML3 162 B3
Kilmacolm PA13 69 D1
Paisley PA2 133 D7
Prestwick KA9 236 E8
Glenburn Sch PA16 44 E3
Glenburn St
Glasgow G20 96 E7
Port Glasgow PA14 47 A2
Glenburn Terr
Carluke ML8 201 E8
Motherwell ML1 143 C1
Glenburn Way G74 158 F3
Glenburn Wlk G69 120 C5
Glenburn Wynd [3] ML9 185 B4
Glencairn Ave ML2 164 D4
Glencairn Dr
Coatbridge ML5 121 E5
Glasgow G41 116 E2
Moodiesburn G69 80 E2
Rutherglen G73 137 F8
Glencairn Gdns
Cambuslang G72 139 D5
Glasgow G41 116 E2
Stevenston KA20 206 D1
Glencairn Ind Est KA1 227 F6
Glencairn La G41 116 F2
Glencairn Prim Sch
Motherwell ML1 163 F5
Stevenston KA20 217 D8
Glencairn Rd
Ayr KA7 239 C6
Cumbernauld G67 62 C2
Dumbarton G82 49 C4
Greenock PA16 44 E3
Kilmacolm PA13 89 E8
Langbank PA14 70 C7
Paisley PA3 114 A7
Glencairn Ret Pk KA1 227 F6
Glencairn Sq KA1 227 F7
Glencairn St
Falkirk FK1 41 B5
[5] Kirkintilloch G66 79 D7
Motherwell ML1 163 F5
Saltcoats KA21 216 F7
Stevenston KA20 206 D1
Stirling FK7 7 B3
Glencairn Terr
Kilmaurs KA3 222 B7
Stevenston KA20 206 D1
Glencairn Way [1] ML1 163 F5
Glencalder Cres ML4 142 C3
Glen Cally G74 160 B2
Glencally Ave PA2 114 B1
Glen Cannich G74 160 B1
Glen Carron G74 160 B1
Glencart Gr PA10 111 C1
Glencleland Rd ML2 164 D4
Glenclora Dr PA2 114 A1
Glen Clova G74 160 B2
Glen Clova Dr G68 61 C4
Glenclova Gdns KA2 227 C6
Glencloy St G20 96 C7
Glenclune PA14 47 E1
Glenclune Ct PA13 89 C7
Glen Clunie G74 160 D2
Glen Clunie Dr G53 135 C4
Glen Clunie Pl G53 135 C4
Glencoates Prim Sch
PA3 113 A6
Glencoats Bsns Ctr PA3 113 B5
Glencoats Dr PA3 113 A4
Glencoe Ct PA16 45 B5
Glencoe Dr ML1 143 A5
Glencoe Pl
Glasgow G13 95 F7
Hamilton ML3 183 B8
Glencoe Rd
Carluke ML8 202 A8
Rutherglen G73 138 D3
Stirling FK8 2 A1
Glencoe St G13 95 F7
Glen Cona Dr G53 135 C5
Glenconner Pl KA7 239 B6
Glenconner Rd KA7 239 B6
Glenconner Way G66 59 A1
Glencorse Rd PA2 113 C2
Glencorse St G32 118 E7
Glencraigs Dr KA3 222 F5
Glencraig St ML6 122 E7
Glencraig Terr KA3 213 B3
Glen Cren Cres G78 154 C6
Glen Cres
Falkirk FK1 42 B1
Glasgow G13 94 E7
Stevenston KA20 206 C1
Glencroft Ave G71 140 E8
Glencroft Rd G44 137 D5
Glencryan Rd G67 62 B1
Glencryan Sch G67 82 E7
Glen Ct
Coatbridge ML5 121 D5
Dalry KA24 191 A6
Motherwell ML1 164 B4
Glendale Ave ML6 123 D6

Howard St
Falkirk FK1 ... 41 F4
Glasgow G1 ... 241 A1
Kilmarnock KA1 ... 227 F8
Larkhall ML9 ... 185 C1
Paisley PA1 ... 114 A4
Howat Cres KA12 ... 219 E3
Howatshaws Rd G82 ... 50 B6
Howat St G51 ... 116 A8
Howburn Cres ML7 ... 127 E6
Howburn Rd ML7 ... 127 D6
Howden Ave
Kilwinning KA13 ... 207 E4
Motherwell ML1 ... 143 D8
Howden Dr PA3 ... 112 A5
Howden Pl ML1 ... 143 A5
Howe Gdns G71 ... 141 A7
Howe Rd G65 ... 60 D7
Howes St ML5 ... 122 B4
Howe St PA1 ... 112 F4
Howetown FK10 ... 5 D4
Howford Rd G52 ... 115 B4
Howford Specl Sch G53 ... 115 A2
Howgate KA13 ... 207 D3
Howgate Ave G15 ... 74 F3
Howgate Rd ML3 ... 183 C8
Howgate Sh Ctr [6] FK1 ... 42 B4
Howie Bldgs G76 ... 157 E8
Howie Cres G84 ... 15 A3
Howieshill Ave G72 ... 139 B5
Howieshill Rd G72 ... 139 B5
Howie's Pl FK1 ... 41 B4
Howie St ML9 ... 185 B1
Howlands Rd FK7 ... 7 A3
Howletnest Rd ML6 ... 123 D6
Howlet Pl ML3 ... 162 E1
Howson Lea ML1 ... 164 B4
Howson View ML1 ... 163 B7
Howth Dr G13 ... 95 F8
Howth Terr G13 ... 95 F8
HOWWOOD ... 130 E6
Howwood Prim Sch PA9 ... 131 A5
Howwood Sta PA9 ... 130 F5
Hoylake Pk G71 ... 140 F2
Hoylake Pl G23 ... 76 E1
Hoylake Sq KA13 ... 207 C4
Hozier Cres G71 ... 140 F8
Hozier Loan [8] ML9 ... 185 B4
Hozier Pl [9] G71 ... 141 B3
Hozier St
Carluke ML8 ... 187 F2
Coatbridge ML5 ... 122 A4
Hudson Pl KA9 ... 233 C2
Hudson Terr G75 ... 180 C8
Hudson Way G75 ... 180 C8
Hudspeth Ct G83 ... 27 D7
Hughenden Ct G12 ... 96 B4
Hughenden Dr G12 ... 96 B4
Hughenden Gdns G12 ... 96 B4
Hughenden La G12 ... 96 B4
Hughenden Rd G12 ... 96 B4
Hughenden Terr G12 ... 96 B4
Hugh Murray Gr G72 ... 139 C5
Hugh Watt Pl KA3 ... 222 A7
Hugo St G20 ... 96 F5
Hulks Rd
Greengairs ML6 ... 83 D4
Greengairs ML6 ... 84 B4
Humbie Ct G77 ... 156 F2
Humbie Gate G77 ... 156 E2
Humbie Gr G77 ... 156 E3
Humbie Lawns G77 ... 156 E2
Humbie Rd
Eaglesham G76 ... 178 C7
Newton Mearns G77 ... 156 F2
Hume Cres FK9 ... 2 A6
Hume Ct FK9 ... 2 A6
Hume Dr
Bothwell G71 ... 141 A3
Uddingston G71 ... 140 E7
Hume Pl G75 ... 180 D8
Hume Rd G67 ... 62 A3
Hume St G81 ... 74 B1
Hunter Ave KA22 ... 205 D2
Hunter Cres KA10 ... 230 A2
Hunter Dr
Irvine KA12 ... 219 B6
Newton Mearns G77 ... 156 B3
Hunterfield Dr G72 ... 138 E5
Hunter Gdns
Bonnybridge FK4 ... 40 A5
Denny FK6 ... 21 D2
HUNTERHILL ... 114 A2
Hunterhill Ave PA2 ... 113 F3
Hunterhill Rd PA2 ... 113 F3
Hunter House Mus★ G74 ... 160 C4
Hunterian Art Gall★ G12 ... 96 D2
Hunterian Mus★ G12 ... 96 D2
Hunterlees Rd ML10 ... 198 B3
Hunter Pl
Kilbarchan PA10 ... 111 A2
Kilwinning KA13 ... 208 A3
Milngavie G62 ... 54 E1
Shotts ML7 ... 146 E5
Stenhousemuir FK2 ... 24 A4
Hunter Prim Sch G74 ... 160 C2
Hunter Rd
Crosshouse KA2 ... 221 F1
Hamilton ML3 ... 162 B6
Milngavie G62 ... 54 E2
Rutherglen G73 ... 118 C1
Hunter's Ave
Ayr KA8 ... 236 B4
Dumbarton G82 ... 50 D3
Hunter's Cl [14] ML11 ... 215 A4
Hunters Cres G74 ... 160 C3
Huntersfield Rd PA5 ... 111 D1
Hunters Gr G74 ... 160 C3
Hunters Hill Ct G21 ... 97 F6
Huntershill Rd G64 ... 98 A8
Huntershill St G21 ... 97 E6
Huntershill Village G64 ... 97 F8
Huntershill Way G64 ... 97 F7
Hunters Pl
East Kilbride G74 ... 160 C3
Greenock PA15 ... 45 F5
Hunter St
Airdrie ML6 ... 103 A1
Bellshill ML4 ... 142 A5
East Kilbride G74 ... 159 F2
Glasgow G4 ... 241 C2
Paisley PA1 ... 113 E5
Prestwick KA9 ... 236 C8
Shotts ML7 ... 146 D5
Hunterston Rd KA23 ... 190 D5
Hunters Way PA12 ... 129 C2
Hunt Hill G68 ... 60 C1
Hunthill La G72 ... 161 B6
Hunthill Pl G76 ... 158 A5
Hunthill Rd G72 ... 161 B7
Hunt Hill Rdbt G68 ... 60 C1
Huntingdon Rd G21 ... 97 E2
Huntingdon Sq G21 ... 97 E2
Hunting Lodge Gdns ML3 ... 163 A2
Huntingtower Rd
Baillieston G69 ... 119 F4
Glasgow G69 ... 120 A3
Huntly Ave
Bellshill ML4 ... 142 A6
Glasgow G46 ... 136 D2
Huntly Cres FK8 ... 1 F2
Huntly Ct
Bishopbriggs G64 ... 98 A8
Kilmarnock KA3 ... 223 C3
Huntly Dr
Bearsden G61 ... 75 E7
Cambuslang G72 ... 139 B4
Coatbridge ML5 ... 121 D4
Greenock PA16 ... 44 F3
Huntly Gdns
Glasgow G12 ... 96 D3
Hamilton G72 ... 161 D3
Huntly Path G69 ... 81 A2
Huntly Pl
Kilmarnock KA3 ... 223 C2
Port Glasgow PA14 ... 47 B2
Huntly Quadrant ML2 ... 165 B5
Huntly Rd
Glasgow, Dowanhill G12 ... 96 C3
Glasgow, Hillington G52 ... 114 F8
Glasgow (Hillington Ind Est) G52 ... 94 F1
Huntly Terr
Paisley PA2 ... 114 A1
Port Glasgow PA14 ... 47 B2
Shotts ML7 ... 147 B3
Hurlawcrook Rd G75 ... 180 F2
HURLET ... 134 E7
Hurlet Cotts G53 ... 134 F6
Hurlethill Ct G53 ... 134 F7
Hurlet Rd PA2, G53 ... 134 D7
HURLFORD ... 228 F6
Hurlford Ave G13 ... 94 F7
Hurlford Prim Sch KA1 ... 228 E6
Hurlford Rd KA1 ... 228 A5
Hurly Hawkin G64 ... 98 D8
Hurworth St FK1 ... 41 F3
Hutcheson Rd G46 ... 136 A2
Hutchesons Gram Sch
Glasgow, Crossmyloof G41 ... 116 E2
Glasgow G42 ... 117 A2
Hutcheson St G1 ... 241 A2
HUTCHESONTOWN ... 117 D3
Hutchinson Pl G72 ... 139 E3
Hutchinson St ML2 ... 186 D7
Hutchinson Town Ct [8] G5 ... 117 C4
Hutchison Ct G46 ... 136 B1
Hutchison Dr G61 ... 76 A2
Hutchison Pl ML5 ... 121 F6
Hutchison St ML3 ... 162 D1
Hutton G12 ... 96 A6
Hutton Ave PA6 ... 111 C8
Hutton Dr
East Kilbride G74 ... 159 F4
Glasgow G51 ... 115 E8
Hutton Pk FK10 ... 10 C7
Huxley Pl G20 ... 96 F6
Hyacinth Way ML8 ... 201 F8
Hydepark Bsns Ctr G21 ... 97 E3
Hydepark St G3 ... 240 A2
Hyndal Ave G53 ... 115 C1
Hyndford Pl [10] ML11 ... 215 A4
Hyndford Rd ML11 ... 215 D2
HYNDLAND ... 96 A3
Hyndland Ave G11 ... 96 B2
Hyndland Ct [11] G12 ... 96 C3
Hyndland Prim Sch G11 ... 96 B2
Hyndland Rd G12 ... 96 B3
Hyndland Sec Sch G12 ... 96 B3
Hyndland St G11 ... 96 C2
Hyndland Sta G12 ... 96 A4
Hyndlee Dr G52 ... 115 C5
Hyndman Rd KA23 ... 190 C3
Hyndshaw Rd ML8 ... 187 C8
Hyndshaw View ML8 ... 187 A4
Hyslop Pl G81 ... 74 A3
Hyslop Rd KA20 ... 206 F2
Hyslop St ML6 ... 122 E8

I

Iain Dr G61 ... 75 C6
Iain Rd G61 ... 75 C6
Ian Smith Ct G81 ... 94 D8
IBM Sta PA16 ... 44 D1
IBROX ... 116 B6
Ibroxholm Ave G51 ... 116 B5
Ibroxholm Oval G51 ... 116 B5
Ibroxholm Pl G51 ... 116 B5
Ibrox Ind Est G51 ... 116 C6
Ibrox Prim Sch G51 ... 116 B5
Ibrox St G51 ... 116 C6
Ibrox Stadium (Rangers FC) G51 ... 116 B6
Ibrox Terr G51 ... 116 B6
Ibrox Underground Sta G51 ... 116 B6
Ida Quadrant ML4 ... 141 F5
Iddesleigh Ave G62 ... 55 A2
Ilay Ave
Bearsden G61 ... 95 F8
Glasgow G61 ... 96 A8
Ilay Ct G61 ... 96 A8
Ilay Rd G61 ... 96 A8
Imex Bsns Ctr ML5 ... 122 C6
Imlach Pl ML1 ... 163 D5
Imperial Dr ML6 ... 122 F6
Imperial Pl G71 ... 141 A2
Imperial Way G71 ... 141 A2
Inchbrae Rd G52 ... 115 C4
Inch Colm Ave FK5 ... 23 C4
Inchcolm Gdns G69 ... 81 A3
Inchcolm Pl G74 ... 159 C2
Inchconnachan Ave G83 ... 19 E2
Inchcruin G83 ... 27 D8
Inchcruin Pl G15 ... 74 E4
Inches Rd KA22 ... 216 B8
Inches Rdbt FK5 ... 23 C4
Inchfad Cres G15 ... 74 E3
Inchfad Dr G15 ... 74 E3
Inchfad Pl G15 ... 74 E3
Inchfad Rd G83 ... 19 E2
Inch Garve G74 ... 160 D1
Inch Garvie Terr FK5 ... 23 C4
Inchgotrick Rd KA1 ... 227 E4
Inchgower Gr G84 ... 15 D5
Inchgower Pl [2] ML1 ... 143 A2
Inchgower Rd G33 ... 99 E6
Inchgreen St PA14 ... 46 F2
Inchholm La G11 ... 95 E2
Inchholm St G11 ... 95 E2
INCHINNAN ... 93 D6
Inchinnan Bsns Pk PA4 ... 93 B4
Inchinnan Dr PA4 ... 93 C4
Inchinnan Ind Est PA4 ... 93 B5
Inchinnan Prim Sch PA4 ... 93 D7
Inchinnan Rd
Bellshill ML4 ... 141 F7
Paisley PA3 ... 113 E7
Renfrew PA4 ... 94 C4
Inch Keith G74 ... 160 D1
Inchkeith Pl
Falkirk FK1 ... 42 B2
Glasgow G32 ... 119 B7
Inchlaggan Pl G15 ... 74 E4
Inchlee St G14 ... 95 E3
Inchlonaig Dr G83 ... 19 E1
Inch Marnock G74 ... 160 D1
Inchmoan Pl G15 ... 74 E4
Inch Murrin G74 ... 160 D1
Inchmurrin Ave G66 ... 80 B8
Inchmurrin Cres G83 ... 19 E2
Inchmurrin Dr
Kilmarnock KA3 ... 223 A5
Rutherglen G73 ... 138 D2
Inchmurrin Gdns G73 ... 138 D2
Inchmurrin Pl G73 ... 138 D2
Inchna FK11 ... 4 A6
Inchneuk Path ML5 ... 101 D6
Inchneuk Rd ML5 ... 101 E6
Inchnock Ave G69 ... 101 A6
Inchoch Gr G33 ... 99 E2
Inchoch St G33 ... 99 E2
Inchrory Pl G15 ... 74 E4
Inchtavannach G83 ... 27 D8
Inchwood Ct G68 ... 82 A7
Inchwood Pl G68 ... 81 F7
Inchwood Rd G68 ... 81 F7
Incle St PA1 ... 113 F5
Indale Ave KA9 ... 236 E7
India Cotts G83 ... 27 E5
India Dr PA4 ... 93 C5
India St
Alexandria G83 ... 27 E5
Glasgow G2 ... 240 B3
Industry St G66 ... 79 D7
Inga St G20 ... 96 E7
Ingerbreck Ave G73 ... 138 D4
Ingleby Ct PA11 ... 110 D8
Ingleby Dr
Glasgow G31 ... 118 B7
Rutherglen G31 ... 118 A7
Ingleby Pl G78 ... 154 E7
Inglefield Ct ML6 ... 123 A7
Inglefield St G42 ... 117 B2
Ingleneuk Ave G33 ... 99 B5
Ingleside G66 ... 79 C6
Ingleston Ave FK6 ... 21 D4
Inglestone Ave G46 ... 136 A2
Ingleston Pk PA15 ... 46 A3
Ingleston St PA15 ... 46 A3
Inglewood Cres
East Kilbride G75 ... 180 A8
Paisley PA2 ... 112 F2
Inglewood Gdns FK10 ... 10 A8
Inglewood Ho FK10 ... 4 F1
Inglewood Rd FK10 ... 9 F8
Inglis Ct ML9 ... 198 F3
Inglis Dr FK2 ... 24 C2
Inglis Pl G75 ... 180 F7
Inglis St
Glasgow G31 ... 118 A6
Wishaw ML2 ... 164 D2
Ingliston Dr PA7 ... 71 F3
Ingram Pl KA3 ... 223 A3
Ingram St G1 ... 241 A2
Inishail Rd G33 ... 99 C1
Inkerman Ct [8] KA7 ... 235 E1
Inkerman Pl KA1 ... 222 E1
Inkerman Rd G52 ... 114 F5
Inkwood Way ML1 ... 143 B2
Innellan Cres ML7 ... 146 E6
Innellan Dr KA3 ... 222 F3
Innellan Gdns G20 ... 96 B7
Innellan Pl G20 ... 96 B7
Inner City Trad Est G4 ... 241 B4
Inner Clyde Nature Reserve★ PA7 ... 71 E7
Innerleithen Dr ML2 ... 165 D6
Innermanse Quadrant ML1 ... 143 F5
Innerpeffray Dr FK2 ... 24 A3
Innerwick Dr G52 ... 115 B5
Innerwood Rd KA13 ... 207 E5
Innes Ct
Airdrie ML6 ... 123 E8
East Kilbride G74 ... 159 E4
International Ave G72 ... 161 D4
Inverallan Ct FK9 ... 1 F8
Inverallan Dr FK9 ... 1 F7
Inverallan Rd FK9 ... 1 F7
Inveraray Gdns ML1 ... 143 C2
Inverarish PA8 ... 93 C7
Inverary Dr
Bishopbriggs G64 ... 78 B4
Gartcosh G69 ... 100 E4
Stenhousemuir FK5 ... 23 F5
Inveravon Dr ML1 ... 163 C5
Inverbervie PA8 ... 73 A2
Invercanny Dr G15 ... 75 A4
Invercanny Pl G15 ... 75 A4
Invercargill G75 ... 180 A7
Invercloy Ct G75 ... 180 B4
Invercloy Pl KA3 ... 222 E4
Inverclyde Acad PA16 ... 44 F3
Inverclyde Gdns G73 ... 138 E3
Inverclyde Royal Hospl PA16 ... 44 F4
Invercree Wlk ML5 ... 101 C6
Inveresk Pl ML5 ... 122 A8
Inveresk Quadrant G32 ... 119 A6
Inveresk St G32 ... 119 A6
Inverewe Ave G46 ... 135 D2
Inverewe Dr G46 ... 135 D2
Inverewe Gdns G46 ... 135 D2
Inverewe Pl G46 ... 135 D3
Inverewe Way G77 ... 156 B5
Invergarry Ave G46 ... 135 D1
Invergarry Ct G46 ... 135 E1
Invergarry Dr G46 ... 135 E2
Invergarry Gdns G46 ... 135 D1
Invergarry Gr G46 ... 135 D2
Invergarry Pl G46 ... 135 E2
Invergarry Quad G46 ... 135 E2
Invergarry View G46 ... 135 E2
Inverglas Ave PA4 ... 94 F1
Invergordon Ave G43 ... 136 F7
Invergordon Pl ML6 ... 123 A6
Invergyle Dr G52 ... 115 C5
Invergyle La G52 ... 115 B5
Inverkar Dr PA2 ... 113 A2
Inverkar Rd KA7 ... 239 A6
Inverkip Dr ML7 ... 146 E5
Inverkip Rd
Greenock, Cowdenknowes PA16 ... 45 C4
Greenock, Spango Valley PA16 ... 44 D2
Inverkip St PA15 ... 45 E5
Inverlair Ave G44 ... 136 F6
Inverleith St G32 ... 118 E7
Inverleven Pl KA11 ... 219 F7
Inverlochy Rd ML6 ... 122 E6
Inverlochy St G33 ... 99 D1
Inverness St G51 ... 115 D6
Inveroran Dr G61 ... 76 B4
Inver Rd G33 ... 119 E7
Invershiel Rd G23 ... 76 E1
Invershin Dr [6] G20 ... 96 D5
Inverurie St G21 ... 97 D3
Invervale Ave [3] ML6 ... 123 F6
Inzievar Terr G32 ... 119 B1
Iona ML6 ... 123 D6
Iona Ave G74 ... 160 A4
Iona Cres
Gourock PA19 ... 44 D6
Old Kilpatrick G60 ... 73 C5
Iona Ct KA11 ... 225 C8
Iona Dr PA2 ... 133 D7
Iona Gdns G60 ... 73 C5
Iona La G69 ... 81 A2
Iona Path G72 ... 161 C7
Iona Pl
Coatbridge ML5 ... 101 D1
Falkirk FK1 ... 42 B2
Irvine KA11 ... 225 C8
Kilmarnock KA3 ... 223 A5
Old Kilpatrick G60 ... 73 C5
Iona Quadrant ML2 ... 165 E5
Iona Rd
Port Glasgow PA14 ... 69 A7
Renfrew PA4 ... 94 C1
Rutherglen G73 ... 138 E3
Wishaw ML2 ... 165 F6
Iona Ridge ML3 ... 161 F1
Iona St
Glasgow G51 ... 116 B7
Greenock PA16 ... 45 C4
Motherwell ML1 ... 142 D1
Iona Way
Kirkintilloch G66 ... 80 B8
Stepps G33 ... 99 E4
Iona Wlk
Coatbridge ML5 ... 121 E4
Gourock PA19 ... 44 C6
Iona Wynd G83 ... 27 F1
Iris Ave G45 ... 138 A3
Iris Ct KA7 ... 239 C3
Irongray St G31 ... 118 C7
IRVINE ... 219 B4
Irvine Burns Mus & Club★ KA12 ... 219 C3
Irvine Cres ML5 ... 122 C7
Irvine Ct G40 ... 118 B3
Irvine Dr PA3 ... 111 F7
Irvine Gdns G66 ... 58 B5
Irvine Ind Est KA12 ... 224 D7
Irvine Mains Cres KA12 ... 219 C4
Irvine Pl
Kilsyth G65 ... 36 B1
Stirling FK8 ... 7 A8
Irvine Rd
Crosshouse KA2 ... 221 E1
Kilmarnock KA1 ... 222 C1
Kilmaurs KA3 ... 222 B7
Kilwinning KA13 ... 208 A1
Irvine Royal Acad KA12 ... 219 B5
Irvine St
Glasgow G40 ... 118 B3
Glenmavis ML6 ... 102 F4
Irvine Sta KA12 ... 219 B1
Irvine Terr ML3 ... 183 D8
Irving Ave G81 ... 74 B6
Irving Ct
Clydebank G81 ... 74 B6
Falkirk FK1 ... 41 E5
Irving Quadrant G81 ... 74 B5
Irwin St PA15 ... 46 E2
Isabella Gdns ML3 ... 163 C1
Iser La G41 ... 136 F8
Isla Ave ML2 ... 165 F6
Island Rd G67 ... 82 D8
Islands Cres FK1 ... 42 B2
Island View KA22 ... 205 B4
Islay ML6 ... 123 E6
Islay Ave
Port Glasgow PA14 ... 69 B7
Rutherglen G73 ... 138 E3
Islay Cres
Old Kilpatrick G60 ... 73 C5
Paisley PA2 ... 133 D7
Saltcoats KA21 ... 205 F2
Islay Ct
Hamilton ML3 ... 161 F2
Irvine KA11 ... 225 C8
Islay Dr
Newton Mearns G77 ... 156 B5
Old Kilpatrick G60 ... 73 C5
Islay Gdns
Carluke ML8 ... 202 A8
Larkhall ML9 ... 185 B3
Islay Pl KA3 ... 223 B5
Islay Quadrant [2] ML2 ... 164 E1
Islay Rd G66 ... 80 A8
Islay Way ML5 ... 121 D4
Isle of Pin Rd KA10 ... 230 A1
Isobel Mair Sch G76 ... 136 D1
Ivanhoe G74 ... 160 D4
Ivanhoe Cres ML2 ... 165 B3
Ivanhoe Ct ML8 ... 187 D1
Ivanhoe Dr
Kirkintilloch G66 ... 79 E8
Saltcoats KA21 ... 206 A1
Ivanhoe Pl
Motherwell ML1 ... 143 B5
Stirling FK8 ... 2 A2
Ivanhoe Rd
Cumbernauld G67 ... 82 F8
Glasgow G13 ... 95 D8
Paisley PA2 ... 112 F1
Ivanhoe Way PA2 ... 112 F1
Ivybank Ave G72 ... 139 C4
Ivybank Cres PA14 ... 47 A1
Ivybank Rd PA14 ... 47 B2
Ivy Cres PA19 ... 44 E6
Ivy Gr ML5 ... 122 B6
Ivy Pl
Ayr KA7 ... 239 D5
Hamilton G72 ... 161 C8
Motherwell ML1 ... 143 A3
Ivy Rd G71 ... 141 C8
Ivy Terr ML1 ... 143 A5
Ivy Way ML6 ... 123 E3
Izatt St FK10 ... 10 B7

J

Jackson Ct ML5 ... 122 B6
Jackson Dr G33 ... 100 A5
Jackson Pl
Bearsden G61 ... 75 E3
Carluke ML8 ... 187 E3
Renton G82 ... 27 D2
Jackson St ML5 ... 122 B7
Jack's Rd
Bothwell G71 ... 141 A5
Saltcoats KA21 ... 205 F1
Jack St
Hamilton ML3 ... 183 D8
Motherwell ML1 ... 164 B4
Jacks View KA23 ... 190 C5

JACKTON ... 179 C7
Jackton Bsns Ctr G75 ... 179 C7
Jackton Rd G75 ... 179 D5
Jacobite Pl ML4 ... 142 D4
Jacob Pl FK1 ... 42 B3
Jacobs Dr PA19 ... 44 D6
Jacob's Ladder Way
ML2 ... 186 C6
Jade Terr ML4 ... 142 A4
Jagger Gdns G69 ... 119 F4
Jamaica Dr G75 ... 159 B1
Jamaica La PA15 ... 45 E6
Jamaica St
Glasgow G1 ... 240 C1
Greenock PA15 ... 45 F6
James Aiton Prim Sch
G72 ... 139 A6
James Boyle Sq G66 ... 58 B6
James Brown Ave KA8 ... 236 E3
James Campbell Rd KA8 239 C8
James Clements Cl
KA13 ... 207 D4
James Cres KA12 ... 219 C4
James Croft Dr FK1 ... 41 F1
James Dempsey Ct ML5 . 121 F6
James Dempsey Gdns
ML5 ... 121 F6
James Dunlop Gdns G64 . 98 B7
James Gray St G41 ... 136 E8
James Hamilton Acad
KA3 ... 223 C1
James Hamilton Dr ML4 . 142 B5
James Hamilton Heritage
Pk* G74 ... 159 D4
James Healy Dr ML3 ... 183 C7
James Hemphill Ct G66 .. 57 E8
James Johnston Pl KA3 . 223 A3
James Leeson Ct G66 ... 58 C6
James Little St KA1 ... 227 F7
James MacFarlane Sch
KA22 ... 205 C3
James Miller Cres KA21 . 217 A7
James Morrison St G1 .. 241 B1
James Murdie Gdns 3
ML3 ... 162 A6
James Nisbet St G21 ... 97 F1
James Reid Sch KA21 ... 206 B2
James Shaw La 5 KA1 .. 222 F1
James Short Pk FK1 ... 42 B3
James St
3 Alexandria G83 ... 27 E5
Alva FK12 ... 5 A6
Ayr KA8 ... 236 A1
Bannockburn FK7 ... 7 C1
Bellshill ML4 ... 141 E7
Carluke ML8 ... 187 F1
Dalry KA24 ... 191 B8
Falkirk FK2 ... 42 B6
Glasgow G40 ... 117 E4
Haggs FK4 ... 39 A3
Helensburgh G84 ... 16 D2
Laurieston FK2 ... 42 F3
Motherwell ML1 ... 163 D7
Prestwick KA9 ... 236 B5
Stenhousemuir FK5 ... 23 D2
Stirling FK8 ... 2 B1
James Sym Cres KA1 ... 227 E6
JAMESTOWN ... 27 F7
Jamestown Ind Est G83 .. 27 F7
Jamestown Prim Sch G83 27 F7
James View ML1 ... 142 F3
James Watt Ave G75 ... 181 A8
James Watt Coll (Finnart
Campus) PA15 ... 45 E5
James Watt Coll (North
Ayreshire Campus)
KA13 ... 207 E4
James Watt Coll (Waterfront
Campus) PA15 ... 46 A5
James Watt Pl G74 ... 159 B3
James Watt Rd G62 ... 54 F3
James Watt St G2 ... 240 B2
James Watt Way PA15 ... 46 C4
James Wilson Pl ML8 ... 201 B2
Jamieson Ave FK5 ... 23 E3
Jamieson Ct
Clydebank G81 ... 74 B7
1 Glasgow G42 ... 117 B2
Jamieson Dr G74 ... 160 A2
Jamieson Gdns
Shotts ML7 ... 146 E5
Uddingston G71 ... 140 E6
Jamieson Pl KA3 ... 195 D1
Jamieson St
Glasgow G42 ... 117 B2
Glasgow G42 ... 117 C2
Jamieson Way KA15 ... 171 A7
Janebank Ave G72 ... 139 C4
Jane Ct ML9 ... 185 A2
Janefield Ave PA5 ... 111 E2
Janefield Pl
Beith KA15 ... 150 B1
Hamilton G72 ... 161 C6
Lennoxtown G66 ... 33 D1
Janefield St
Glasgow G31 ... 118 B5
Glasgow G31 ... 118 C4
Jane Pl G5 ... 117 C4
Jane Rae Gdns G81 ... 94 D8
Jane's Brae G67 ... 82 F8
Jane's Brae Intc G67 ... 82 F7
Janesmith St ML2 ... 164 C4
Janetta St G81 ... 74 A4
Jardine St G20 ... 96 F3
Jardine Terr
Gartcosh G69 ... 100 F5
Greenock PA16 ... 45 E7
Jarvie Ave ML6 ... 104 B2
Jarvie Cres G65 ... 60 D7
Jarvie Pl 6 FK2 ... 42 A8
Jarvie Way PA2 ... 132 E8
Jasmine Pl G67 ... 82 B6
Jasmine Rd KA1 ... 227 C7
Jasmine Way ML8 ... 201 E8
Java St ML1 ... 142 C1
Jean Armour Dr
Clydebank G81 ... 74 C3
Kilmarnock KA1 ... 227 B7
Jean Armour La PA16 ... 44 E3
Jean Armour Pl KA21 .. 206 A2
Jean Armour Terr PA16 .. 44 E3
Jeanette Ave ML3 ... 183 D7
Jeanie Deans Dr G84 ... 25 C8
Jean MacLean Pl G64 ... 78 B4
Jean St PA14 ... 47 B2
Jedburgh Ave G73 ... 138 B7
Jedburgh Ct 4 PA15 ... 46 B3
Jedburgh Dr PA2 ... 113 A1
Jedburgh Gdns 1 G20 ... 96 F3
Jedburgh Pl
Coatbridge ML5 ... 121 F3
East Kilbride G74 ... 159 F2
Jedburgh St
Hamilton G72 ... 161 D7
Wishaw ML2 ... 165 C5
Jedworth Ave G15 ... 75 B3
Jedworth Ct 3 G61 ... 75 E5
Jedworth Rd G15 ... 75 C3
Jeffrey Pl G65 ... 36 C1
Jeffrey St KA1 ... 227 F5
Jellicoe Pl G84 ... 17 A2
Jellicoe St G81 ... 73 E3
Jellyholm Rd FK10 ... 10 E8
Jennie Lee Dr ML2 ... 186 B7
JENNY LIND ... 135 D2
Jenny Lind Ct G46 ... 135 E2
Jennys Well Ct PA2 ... 114 B2
Jennys Well Rd PA2 ... 114 C2
Jermond Dr KA12 ... 219 D5
Jervis Pl G84 ... 17 A2
Jervis Terr G75 ... 180 B7
Jerviston Ct ML1 ... 143 A1
Jerviston Rd
Glasgow G33 ... 99 C2
Motherwell ML1 ... 143 A1
Jerviston St
Motherwell ML1 ... 163 F8
Motherwell, New Stevenston
ML1 ... 143 A3
New Stevenston ML1 ... 143 A4
Jerviswood ML1 ... 143 A1
Jerviswood Dr ML11 ... 215 F7
Jerviswood Rd ML11 ... 215 A4
Jessie St G42 ... 117 D1
Jessiman Sq PA4 ... 94 B1
Jimmy Sneddon Way
ML1 ... 142 D2
Joanna Terr G72 ... 161 D8
Jocelyn Sq G1 ... 241 A1
Jock Stein Ctr ML3 ... 161 E4
Jocksthorn Terr KA3 ... 222 C6
John Bassy Dr FK4 ... 38 D3
John Bowman Gdns ML4 142 B6
John Brannan Way ML4 . 141 D6
John Brogan Pl KA20 ... 217 B8
John Brown Pl G69 ... 100 C8
John Burnside Dr G81 ... 74 D7
John Burtt Pl KA3 ... 223 A3
John Campbell Ct PA19 .. 44 F7
John Campbell St PA19 .. 44 F7
John Cowane Row FK9 ... 2 A4
John Davidson Dr FK6 ... 21 C4
John Dickie St 9 KA1 ... 222 F1
John Ewing Gdns ML9 ... 185 A4
John Finnie St KA1 ... 227 F8
John Galt Prim Sch
KA12 ... 219 D4
John Gregor Pl PA12 ... 129 C2
John Hendry Rd G71 ... 141 A4
John Hillhouse Ind Est
G72 ... 138 D8
John Jarvis Sq G65 ... 36 D1
John Kennedy Pl KA3 ... 223 A3
John Knox La ML3 ... 161 D4
John Knox St
Clydebank G81 ... 94 C7
Glasgow G4 ... 241 C2
John Lang St PA5 ... 112 A3
John Logie Baird Prim Sch
G84 ... 17 A2
John McEwan Way G64 .. 78 B8
John Marshall Dr G64 ... 97 E8
John Murray Ct ML1 ... 163 E3
John Murray Dr FK9 ... 2 A8
John Neilson Ave PA1 ... 113 A4
John Ogilvie High Sch
ML3 ... 161 F4
John O'Hara Ct FK1 ... 41 D5
John Paul Acad G23 ... 76 D1
John Paul II Prim Sch
Glasgow G45 ... 137 D1
Uddingston G71 ... 141 C7
John Paul Sp Ctr G23 ... 76 D1
John Pl ML9 ... 199 B7
John Rushforth Pl FK8 ... 1 F3
Johnsburn Dr G53 ... 135 B6
Johnsburn Rd G53 ... 135 B6
Johnshaven PA8 ... 73 A2
Johnshaven St 1 G43 ... 136 C7
Johnshill PA12 ... 129 D3
John Smith Ct ML6 ... 122 F8
John Smith Gate G78 ... 134 C4
John Smith Gdns ML5 ... 122 D5
John Smith Way ML7 ... 146 D5
Johnson Ct G84 ... 16 F1
Johnson Dr G72 ... 139 B5
John St
Ayr KA8 ... 236 A1
Barrhead G78 ... 134 B3
Bellshill ML4 ... 142 A5
Carluke ML8 ... 187 F1
Falkirk FK2 ... 42 B7
Glasgow G1 ... 241 A2
Gourock PA19 ... 44 E8
Greenock PA15 ... 46 B3
Haggs FK4 ... 39 A3
Hamilton, Blantyre G72 ... 161 E8
Hamilton ML3 ... 162 E3
Helensburgh G84 ... 16 C2
Helensburgh G84 ... 16 C3
Kirkintilloch G66 ... 58 D1
Larkhall ML9 ... 185 B2
Renton G82 ... 49 D8
Wishaw ML2 ... 164 C4
Johnston Ave
Clydebank G81 ... 94 D8
Kilsyth G65 ... 60 D7
Stenhousemuir FK5 ... 23 F3
Stirling FK9 ... 2 B3
Johnston Ct 7 FK2 ... 42 A8
Johnston Dr KA10 ... 229 E6
JOHNSTONE ... 112 A4
Johnstone Ave G52 ... 115 B7
Johnstone Ct FK12 ... 5 A6
Johnstone Dr
Lochwinnoch PA12 ... 129 C2
Rutherglen G73 ... 138 A7
Johnstone High Sch
PA5 ... 131 C7
Johnstone Hospl PA5 ... 111 F4
Johnstone La ML8 ... 188 B1
Johnstone Rd ML3 ... 162 E2
Johnstone St
Alva FK12 ... 5 A6
Bellshill ML4 ... 142 C5
Menstrie FK11 ... 3 F6
Johnstone Sta PA5 ... 112 A2
Johnstone Terr G65 ... 59 F2
Johnston Pl FK6 ... 21 C1
Johnston Rd G69 ... 101 B6
Johnston St
Airdrie ML6 ... 123 B8
Bannockburn FK7 ... 7 C1
Greenock PA16 ... 45 D7
1 Paisley PA1 ... 113 E4
Johnston Terr PA16 ... 45 D7
John Street La G84 ... 16 C2
John Walker Dr KA3 ... 222 D3
John Wheatley Coll
(Easterhouse Campus)
G34 ... 120 B8
John Wheatley Coll (The
East End Campus) G31 118 C6
John Wilson Dr G65 ... 36 B1
John Wilson St PA15 ... 46 D2
John Wood St PA14 ... 47 C1
John Wright Sports Ctr
G74 ... 160 A2
Joiners La KA3 ... 195 B7
Jones Ave FK5 ... 41 C8
Jones Wynd ML1 ... 143 E1
Jonquil Way ML8 ... 201 F8
Joppa St G33 ... 118 E8
JORDANHILL ... 95 E5
Jordanhill Cres G13 ... 95 D5
Jordanhill Dr G13 ... 95 D6
Jordanhill La G13 ... 95 E5
Jordanhill Sch G13 ... 95 E5
Jordanhill Sta G11 ... 95 F4
Jordan Pl ML1 ... 144 C3
Jordan St G14 ... 95 D2
Jordanvale Ave G14 ... 95 D2
Jowitt Ave G81 ... 74 D1
Jubilee Bank G66 ... 79 C3
Jubilee Ct
Glasgow G52 ... 114 F7
Larkhall ML9 ... 185 A4
Jubilee Dr KA3 ... 195 F1
Jubilee Gdns G61 ... 75 F4
Jubilee Pl KA3 ... 195 F1
Jubilee Rd
Denny FK6 ... 21 E3
Troon KA10 ... 229 D3
Jubilee Terr PA5 ... 111 D2
Jubilee Way FK4 ... 39 F5
Julian Ave G12 ... 96 C4
Julian La G12 ... 96 C4
Junction Pl 12 FK10 ... 10 B6
Juniper Ave
East Kilbride G75 ... 180 D6
Quarriers Village PA11 ... 89 F1
Juniper Ct G66 ... 79 B5
Juniper Dr
Hamilton ML3 ... 182 F7
Milton of Campsie G66 ... 58 B4
Juniper Gn KA7 ... 239 D6
Juniper Gr ML3 ... 162 F2
Juniper Pl
Glasgow G32 ... 119 F4
Johnstone PA5 ... 132 A8
Uddingston G71 ... 141 D8
Juniper Rd G71 ... 141 D8
Juniper Terr G32 ... 119 E4
Juniper Wynd ML1 ... 143 B5
Juno La PA16 ... 44 D3
Juno St ML1 ... 142 D2
Juno Terr PA16 ... 44 D3
Jupiter La PA16 ... 44 D3
Jupiter Pl G84 ... 15 D6
Jupiter St ML1 ... 142 D1
Jupiter Terr PA16 ... 44 D3
Jura G74 ... 181 B7
Jura Ave PA4 ... 94 D1
Jura Ct
Glasgow G52 ... 115 E5
Irvine KA11 ... 225 C8
Jura Dr
Blantyre G72 ... 140 C3
Kirkintilloch G66 ... 80 A8
Newton Mearns G77 ... 156 B6
Old Kilpatrick G60 ... 73 C5
Jura Gdns
Carluke ML8 ... 202 A8
Hamilton ML3 ... 162 A2
Kilmarnock KA3 ... 222 D3
Larkhall ML9 ... 185 C3
Old Kilpatrick G60 ... 73 C5
Jura Pl
Old Kilpatrick G60 ... 73 C5
Troon KA10 ... 229 F7
Jura Quadrant 3 ML2 ... 164 E1
Jura Rd
Old Kilpatrick G60 ... 73 C5
Paisley PA2 ... 133 D7
Jura St
Glasgow G52 ... 115 F5
Greenock PA16 ... 45 C4
Jura Wynd ML5 ... 101 C6
Jutland Ct G84 ... 16 A3

K

Kaim Dr G53 ... 135 C6
Kairnhill Ct ML11 ... 214 E4
Kames Ct KA11 ... 220 B6
Kames Rd ML7 ... 146 E6
Kane Pl ML9 ... 198 D1
Kane St G82 ... 27 D2
Karadale Gdns ML9 ... 185 A2
Karries Ct FK6 ... 39 B8
Kateswell Dr ML7 ... 125 B1
Katewell Ave G15 ... 74 E4
Katewell Pl G15 ... 74 E4
Katherine St ML6 ... 123 E8
Kathleen Pk G84 ... 16 A3
Katrine Ave
Bishopbriggs G64 ... 78 B1
Uddingston ML4 ... 141 D6
Katrine Cres ML6 ... 102 F1
Katrine Ct
Alloa FK10 ... 10 C5
Kilmarnock KA1 ... 228 A5
Katrine Dr
Newton Mearns G77 ... 157 B4
Paisley PA2 ... 113 A2
Katrine Pl
Cambuslang G72 ... 139 A6
Coatbridge ML5 ... 101 D1
Denny FK6 ... 39 D6
Irvine KA12 ... 219 D6
Katrine Rd
Greenock PA15 ... 46 A3
Shotts ML7 ... 146 E6
Katrine Way 5 G71 ... 141 A3
Katrine Wynd ML1 ... 143 A5
Katriona Path 12 ML9 ... 185 C1
Kay Gdns ML1 ... 163 B6
Kay Park Cres KA3 ... 223 B1
Kay Park Gr KA3 ... 223 A1
Kay Park Terr KA3 ... 223 B1
Kay St G21 ... 97 F4
Kaystone Rd G15 ... 75 A1
Keal Ave G15 ... 95 B8
Keal Cres G15 ... 95 A8
Keal Dr G15 ... 95 A8
Keal Pl G15 ... 95 A8
Keane Path ML1 ... 164 B3
Kearn Ave G15 ... 75 B1
Kearn Pl G15 ... 75 B1
Keats Pk G71 ... 141 B3
KEILARSBRAE ... 10 D8
Keilarsbrae
Alloa FK10 ... 5 C1
Sauchie FK10 ... 10 C8
Keil Cres G82 ... 49 D3
Keil Ct G84 ... 25 B8
Keir Ave FK8 ... 2 A2
Keir Cres ML2 ... 165 B4
Keir Ct FK9 ... 2 A7
Keir Dr G64 ... 77 F2
Keirfold Ave FK10 ... 4 D3
Keir Gdns FK9 ... 2 A7
Keir Hardie Ave
Laurieston FK2 ... 42 F3
Motherwell ML1 ... 143 B5
Keir Hardie Cres KA13 ... 208 A3
Keir Hardie Ct G64 ... 78 A1
Keir Hardie Dr
Ardrossan KA22 ... 205 B4
Bellshill ML4 ... 141 F4
Kilbirnie KA25 ... 149 A1
13 Kilsyth G65 ... 60 D8
Keir Hardie Meml Prim Sch
ML1 ... 143 D3
Keir Hardie Pl
Bellshill ML4 ... 141 F4
Saltcoats KA21 ... 206 A2
Keir Hardie Rd
Alva FK12 ... 5 C7
Larkhall ML9 ... 185 C1
Stevenston KA20 ... 206 E1
Keir Hardie St PA15 ... 46 E2
Keir St
Bridge of Allan FK9 ... 2 A7
Glasgow G41 ... 116 F3
Keir's Wlk G72 ... 139 A6
Keith Ave
Glasgow G46 ... 136 D3
Stirling FK7 ... 7 C4
Keith Ct G11 ... 96 C1
Keith Pl KA3 ... 223 C2
Keith Quadrant ML2 ... 165 B5
Keith St
Bellshill ML4 ... 142 A6
Glasgow G11 ... 96 C2
Hamilton ML3 ... 162 F4
Kelbourne Cres ML4 ... 141 F5
Kelbourne Sch G20 ... 96 E4
Kelbourne St G20 ... 96 E4
KELBURN ... 47 F1
Kelburn Bsns Pk PA14 ... 48 B1
Kelburn Cres KA1 ... 227 E4
Kelburne KA13 ... 207 C2
Kelburne Dr PA1 ... 114 B5
Kelburne Gdns
Glasgow G69 ... 120 A3
Paisley PA1 ... 114 A5
Kelburne Oval PA1 ... 114 A5
Kelburn St G78 ... 134 B2
Kelburn Terr PA14 ... 48 A1
Kelhead Ave G52 ... 114 F4
Kelhead Dr G52 ... 114 F5
Kelhead Path G52 ... 114 F5
Kelhead Pl G52 ... 114 F5
Kelliebank FK10 ... 9 E6
Kellie Gr G74 ... 159 D3
Kellie Pl FK10 ... 10 A7
Kells Pl G15 ... 74 E4
Kelly Ct FK8 ... 7 A8
Kelly Dr FK6 ... 21 E3
Kelly's La ML8 ... 188 B1
Kelly St
Greenock PA16 ... 45 D5
Greenock PA16 ... 45 E6
Kelso Ave
Bridge of Weir PA11 ... 110 D7
Paisley PA2 ... 113 A1
Rutherglen G73 ... 138 B7
Kelso Cres ML6 ... 165 B6
Kelso Ct 5 PA15 ... 46 B3
Kelso Dr
Carluke ML8 ... 188 C1
East Kilbride G74 ... 160 A3
Kelso Gdns G69 ... 80 F3
Kelso Pl
Glasgow G14 ... 94 E6
Renton G82 ... 27 E2
Kelso Quadrant ML5 ... 121 F8
Kelso St G13 ... 94 F7
Kelton St G32 ... 119 B4
Kelt Rd FK4 ... 38 E4
KELVIN ... 181 B6
Kelvin Ave
Glasgow G52 ... 114 F8
Glasgow (Hillington Ind Est)
G52 ... 94 F1
Kilwinning KA13 ... 207 F1
Kelvinbridge Rdbt G64 ... 78 B8
Kelvinbridge Underground
Sta G4 ... 96 E2
Kelvin Cres
Bearsden G61 ... 75 F2
East Kilbride G75 ... 181 A7
Kelvin Ct
East Kilbride G75 ... 181 A7
Glasgow G12 ... 96 A5
1 Kirkintilloch G66 ... 58 C1
4 Troon KA10 ... 229 E5
KELVINDALE ... 96 A7
Kelvindale G64 ... 57 C1
Kelvindale Gdns G20 ... 96 D6
Kelvindale Pl 3 G20 ... 96 D6
Kelvindale Prim Sch G12 . 96 A5
Kelvindale Rd G12, G20 ... 96 C5
Kelvindale Sta G20 ... 96 B7
Kelvin Dr
Airdrie ML6 ... 103 B1
Barrhead G78 ... 134 D1
Bishopbriggs G64 ... 78 A2
East Kilbride G75 ... 180 F7
Glasgow G20 ... 96 D4
Kirkintilloch G66 ... 79 A8
Moodiesburn G69 ... 80 E2
Shotts ML7 ... 147 B4
Kelvin Gdns
Hamilton ML3 ... 161 E4
Kilsyth G65 ... 60 D7
KELVINGROVE ... 96 D2
Kelvingrove Mus & Art Gall*
G3 ... 96 D1
Kelvingrove St G3 ... 116 E8
Kelvin Hall International
Sports Arena G3 ... 96 C1
Kelvinhall Underground Sta
G11 ... 96 C2
KELVINHAUGH ... 96 C1
Kelvinhaugh Gate G3 ... 116 D8
Kelvinhaugh Pl G3 ... 116 D8
Kelvinhaugh Prim Sch
G3 ... 116 C8
Kelvinhaugh St G3 ... 116 D8
Kelvinhead G65 ... 37 F2
Kelvinhead Rd G65 ... 37 E2
Kelvin Ind Est G75 ... 181 A6
Kelvin Park S G75 ... 181 A4
Kelvin Pl G75 ... 181 A7
Kelvin Rd
Bellshill ML4 ... 142 B7
Cumbernauld G67 ... 83 A8
East Kilbride G75 ... 181 A7
Milngavie G62 ... 54 E3
Uddingston G71 ... 140 E7
Kelvin Road N G67 ... 83 A8
KELVINSIDE ... 96 A5
Kelvinside Acad G12 ... 96 D4

Kinarvie Terr G53 134 F7
Kinbuck St G22 97 D4
Kincaid Ct PA15 46 C4
Kincaid Dr G66 33 C1
Kincaid Field G66 58 C5
Kincaid Gdns G72 139 A6
Kincaid St PA16 45 B8
KINCAIDSTON 239 B3
Kincaidston Dr KA7 239 C3
Kincaidston Prim Sch
KA7 239 B3
Kincaid Way G66 58 B5
Kincardine Dr G64 98 C8
Kincardine Pl
Bishopbriggs G64 98 C7
East Kilbride G74 160 C3
Kincardine Rd FK2 24 C3
Kincardine Sq G33 99 D1
Kincath Ave G73 138 D3
Kinclaven Ave G15 75 B3
Kinclaven Gdns 2 G15 75 B3
Kinclaven Pl 1 G15 75 B3
Kincraig St G51 115 D6
Kinellan Rd G61 75 F1
Kinellar Dr G14 95 A6
Kinfauns Dr
Clydebank G15 75 B3
Newton Mearns G77 156 F5
Kingarth La G42 117 A2
Kingarth St
Glasgow G42 117 A2
Hamilton ML3 183 D8
Kingcase Ave KA9 236 B6
Kingcase Prim Sch KA9 236 B6
King Ct ML1 163 D7
King Edward Rd G13 95 F5
King Edward St G83 27 E6
Kingfisher Cres G68 81 E8
Kingfisher Dr G13 94 F7
Kingfisher Gdns G13 95 A7
King George Ct PA4 94 E1
King George Gdns PA4 94 E2
King George Park Ave
PA4 94 E2
King George Pl PA4 94 E1
King George Way PA4 94 E1
Kinghorn Dr G44 137 C7
Kinghorn La G44 137 C7
King James Dr FK10 4 C2
Kinglas Ho G82 50 B7
Kinglas Rd G61 75 C2
King O' Muirs FK10 4 F4
King O' Muirs Ave FK10 4 E4
King O' Muirs Dr FK10 4 D4
King O' Muirs Rd FK10 4 E4
King Pl G69 121 A5
King Robert Ct FK8 1 E1
Kingsacre Rd G44 137 D7
Kings Ave G72 139 B5
Kingsbarns Dr G44 137 B7
Kingsborough Gate 1
G12 96 B3
Kingsborough Gdns G12 96 B4
Kingsborough La G12 96 B3
Kingsborough Lane E G12 96 B3
Kingsbrae Ave G44 137 C7
Kingsbridge Cres G44 137 D6
Kingsbridge Dr G44 137 E6
Kingsbridge Park Gdns
G44 137 D6
Kingsburgh Dr PA1 114 B6
Kingsburn Dr G73 138 A6
Kingsburn Gr G73 138 A6
Kingscliffe Ave G44 137 D6
Kingscourt Ave G44 137 D6
Kings Cres
Cambuslang G72 139 B5
Elderslie PA5 112 D3
King's Cres
Cambuslang G72 139 B5
Carluke ML8 188 A2
Helensburgh G84 16 E1
Kingscroft Rd KA9 236 B7
Kings Ct
Alloa FK10 10 A7
Ayr KA8 236 A1
7 Falkirk FK1 42 B4
Stenhousemuir FK5 23 D2
King's Ct KA15 150 B1
Kingsdale Ave G44 137 C7
Kings Dr ML1 142 F3
King's Dr
Cumbernauld G68 61 F6
Glasgow G40 117 E4
Newton Mearns G77 157 A3
Kingsdyke Ave G44 137 D7
Kingseat Pl FK1 41 F3
KINGSFORD 196 C5
Kingsford Ave G44 136 E4
Kingsford Ct G77 156 C6
Kingsford Pl KA3 223 B5
Kingsgate Ret Pk G74 160 A6
King's Gdns G77 157 A3
Kingsheath Ave G73 137 F6
Kingshill Ave G68 60 E1
Kingshill Dr G44 137 C6
Kingshill Rd ML7 167 A8
Kingshill View ML8 187 A4
Kingshouse Ave G44 137 C6
Kingshurst Ave G44 137 C6
Kings Inch Dr G51 95 B2
Kings Inch Pl G51 95 A2
King's Inch Rd PA4, G51 94 F4
King's Knot★ FK8 6 F8
Kingsknowe Dr G73 137 E6
Kingsland Cres G52 115 B6
Kingsland Dr G52 115 C6
Kingsland La G52 115 C6
Kingslea Rd PA6 91 B2
Kingsley Ave
Glasgow G42 117 B1
Stenhousemuir FK5 23 F3
Kingsley Ct G71 141 A7
Kingslynn Dr G44 137 D6
Kingsmuir Dr
Cumbernauld G68 60 F2
Rutherglen G73 137 E6
Kings Myre ML11 215 C4
Kings Oak Prim Sch PA15 46 C3
KINGSON'S KNOWE 215 B2
KING'S PARK 137 D6
King's Park Ave G44 137 D6
King's Park Prim Sch
G44 137 D6
King's Park Rd
Glasgow G44 137 B7
Stirling FK8 7 A7
King's Park Sec Sch G44 137 C5
King's Park Sta G44 137 C6
Kings Pk G64 57 C1
King's Pl G22 97 B6
King's Rd
Beith KA15 150 B1
Elderslie PA5 112 B2
King St
Ayr KA8 235 F1
Ayr KA8 236 A1
Clydebank G81 94 D8
Coatbridge ML5 121 E6
Falkirk FK2 42 C6
Fallin FK7 8 C4
Glasgow G1 241 A1
Gourock PA19 44 E7
Greenock PA15 45 F5
Hamilton ML3 162 A4
Kilmarnock KA1 227 F8
4 Kilsyth G65 60 D8
Kilwinning KA13 207 E4
Larkhall ML9 185 A3
Paisley PA1 113 C5
Port Glasgow PA14 47 C2
Renton G82 27 D1
Rutherglen G73 138 A8
Shotts ML7 146 E4
Stenhousemuir FK5 23 D2
Stenhousemuir FK5 23 E3
Stenhousemuir FK5 23 F3
Stirling FK8 7 B7
Stonehouse ML9 198 E2
Wishaw ML2 165 B2
Wishaw, Newmains ML2 166 A6
Kingstables La 3 FK8 7 A8
KINGSTON
Bishopton 72 B3
Glasgow 116 F5
Kingston Ave
1 Airdrie ML6 123 C7
Neilston G78 154 D6
Uddingston G71 141 A8
Kingston Bus Pk PA14 47 A2
Kingston Cres 1 PA14 47 A2
Kingston Flats G65 36 D1
Kingston Gr PA7 72 B3
Kingston Ind Est G5 116 F5
Kingston Pl G81 73 D4
Kingston Rd
Bishopton PA7 72 B3
Kilsyth G65 36 D1
Neilston G78 154 D5
Kingston St G5 240 C1
King Street E G84 16 E1
King Street La
3 Kilsyth G65 60 D8
5 Rutherglen G73 138 A8
Kings View G73 137 F7
King's View G68 61 F6
Kingsway
Dalry KA24 191 A8
East Kilbride G74 160 A3
Glasgow G14 95 B5
Gourock PA19 44 D6
Kilsyth G65 36 D1
Kirkintilloch G66 59 B2
King's Way G82 49 C5
Kingsway Ct G14 95 A5
Kingswell Ave KA3 223 A5
Kingswell Pk FK10 10 C7
Kingswood Dr G44 137 C7
Kingswood Rd PA7 71 F4
Kingussie Ave KA3 195 C1
Kingussie Dr G44 137 C6
Kiniver Dr G15 75 B1
Kinkell Gdns G66 59 B1
Kinloch Ave
Cambuslang G72 139 B4
Linwood PA3 112 A5
Stewarton KA3 195 C1
Kinloch Dr ML1 142 D2
Kinloch La PA16 44 E3
Kinloch Rd
Kilmarnock KA1 228 A5
Newton Mearns G77 156 D6
Renfrew PA4 94 B1
Kinloch St G40 118 C4
Kinloch Terr PA16 44 E3
Kinloss Pl G74 159 F2
Kinmount Ave G44 137 B7
Kinmount La G44 137 C7
Kinnaird Ave
Falkirk FK2 24 B3
Newton Mearns G77 157 A5
Kinnaird Cres G61 76 B4
Kinnaird Dr
Linwood PA3 112 B6
Stenhousemuir FK5 23 E3
Kinnaird Pl G64 98 B7
Kinnaird Prim Sch FK5 23 D5
Kinnear Rd G40 118 B4
Kinneil Ho ML3 162 E5
Kinneil Pl ML3 161 F2
Kinnell Ave G52 115 D3
Kinnell Cres G52 115 C3
Kinnell Path G52 115 C3
Kinnell Pl G52 115 D3
Kinnell Sq G52 115 C3
Kinnier Rd KA21 217 A8
Kinning Park Ind Est G5 116 F5
Kinning Park Underground
Sta G41 116 D5
Kinning St G5 117 A5
Kinnis Vennel KA13 207 C4
Kinnoul Gdns G61 75 D8
Kinnoull Pl G72 161 D7
Kinnoull Rd KA1 228 A3
Kinpurnie Rd PA1 114 D5
Kinross Ave
Glasgow G52 115 B4
Port Glasgow PA14 47 C1
Kinross Pk G74 160 D3
Kinsail Dr G52 114 F6
Kinstone Ave G14 95 A5
Kintail Gdns G66 59 B1
Kintessack Pl G64 78 D2
Kintillo Dr G13 95 B5
Kintore Pk ML3 183 B7
Kintore Rd G43 136 F6
Kintore Twr G72 138 E3
Kintyre Ave PA3 112 A4
Kintyre Cres
Coatbridge ML5 121 E4
Newton Mearns G77 156 C6
Plains ML6 104 A3
Kintyre Dr ML5 121 E4
Kintyre Gdns G66 59 B1
Kintyre Pl FK1 41 C4
Kintyre Rd G72 161 C8
Kintyre St G21 98 A1
Kintyre Terr PA16 44 D3
Kintyre Wynd ML8 187 F3
Kipland Wlk ML5 122 D5
Kippen Dr G76 158 B5
Kippen St
Airdrie ML6 122 E7
Glasgow G22 97 D6
Kipperoch Rd G82 49 B7
Kippford Pl ML6 123 F1
Kippford St G32 119 C4
Kipps Ave ML6 122 E8
Kippsbyre Ct ML6 122 D7
Kirkaig Ave PA4 94 F2
Kirkandrews Pl ML6 123 F2
Kirk Ave FK5 23 E2
Kirkbean Ave G73 138 B4
Kirkbrae FK10 10 F4
Kirkbride Terr FK7 12 C3
Kirkburn FK1 86 B7
Kirkburn Ave G72 139 A4
Kirkburn Dr G63 31 C3
Kirkburn Rd G63 31 C3
Kirkcaldy Rd G41 116 D2
Kirk Cl KA24 191 C7
Kirkconnel Ave
Cumbernauld G68 60 F1
Glasgow G13 94 F6
Kirkconnel Dr G73 137 F5
Kirk Cres G60 73 A7
Kirk Ct ML9 198 F2
Kirkcudbright Pl G74 160 D3
Kirkdale Dr G52 115 E4
Kirkdene Ave G77 157 B5
Kirkdene Bank G77 157 B5
Kirkdene Cres G77 157 B5
Kirkdene Gr G77 157 B4
Kirkdene Pl G77 157 B5
KIRKFIELDBANK 214 D4
Kirkfieldbank Brae ML11 214 E4
Kirkfieldbank Prim Sch
ML11 214 D4
Kirkfieldbank Way ML3 162 A3
Kirkfield Rd
Bothwell G71 141 A3
Kirkfieldbank ML11 214 D3
Kirkfield Wynd PA9 130 E5
Kirkford KA3 211 E7
Kirkford Rd G69 80 E2
Kirkgate
Alloa FK10 10 B6
Irvine KA12 219 C2
Saltcoats KA21 216 F7
Wishaw ML2 165 F4
Kirk Glebe
Neilston G78 154 E7
Stewarton KA3 211 D8
Kirkhall Gdns KA22 205 D2
Kirkhall Pl FK6 21 E2
Kirkhall Rd ML1 143 D4
KIRKHILL 157 C4
Kirkhill
Irvine KA11 220 C6
Kilwinning KA13 207 C2
Kirkhill Ave G72 139 A3
Kirkhill Cres
Neilston G78 154 E8
Prestwick KA9 236 B6
Kirkhill Dr G20 96 D5
Kirkhill Gate G77 157 B4
Kirkhill Gdns G72 139 A3
Kirkhill Gr G72 139 A3
Kirkhill Pl
7 Glasgow G20 96 D5
Wishaw ML2 164 C2
Kirkhill Prim Sch G77 157 B6
Kirkhill Rd
Gartcosh G69 100 F5
Kirkhill Rd *continued*
Newton Mearns G77 157 B5
Uddingston G71 140 E8
Wishaw ML2 164 C1
Kirkhill St ML2 164 D1
Kirkhill Sta G72 139 A5
Kirkhill Terr G72 139 A3
Kirkholm Ave KA8 236 A4
Kirkhope Dr G15 75 B1
Kirkhope Pl ML8 187 E1
Kirkhouse Ave G63 31 C4
Kirkhouse Cres G63 31 C4
Kirkhouse Rd G63 31 C4
Kirkinner Pl PA11 110 D8
Kirkinner Rd G32 119 D3
KIRKINTILLOCH 79 E7
Kirkintilloch High Sch
G66 80 A7
Kirkintilloch Ind Est G66 58 C2
Kirkintilloch L Ctr G66 79 D7
Kirkintilloch Rd
Bishopbriggs G64 78 C5
Kirkintilloch G66 58 A2
Kirkintilloch, Waterside G66 80 C8
Lenzie G66 79 C5
Kirk La
2 Bearsden G61 75 E5
Glasgow G43 136 C7
Law ML8 187 A6
Kirkland Ave
Kilmarnock KA3 222 E3
Strathblane G63 31 C4
Kirkland Cres KA24 191 A7
Kirkland Dr FK6 21 B2
Kirkland Gdns KA3 222 C6
Kirkland Gr PA5 111 F3
Kirklandholm KA9 236 C6
Kirkland La G83 27 F3
KIRKLANDNEUK 94 B4
Kirklandneuk Cres PA4 94 A4
Kirklandneuk Prim Sch
PA4 94 B3
Kirklandneuk Rd PA4 94 B4
Kirkland Rd
Dunlop KA3 195 B8
Glengarnock KA14, KA25 170 B7
Kirklands PA4 94 B3
Kirklands Cres
Bothwell G71 141 A3
Kilsyth G65 60 D7
Kirklands Dr G77 156 D2
Kirklands Hospl G71 141 B3
Kirklandside Hospl KA1 228 C5
Kirklands Pl G77 156 D2
Kirklands Rd
Lanark ML11 215 B3
Newton Mearns G77 156 D2
Kirkland St
Glasgow G20 96 F3
Motherwell ML1 163 D7
Kirklands The FK7 6 F3
Kirkland Terr KA11 220 F2
Kirklea Gdns PA3 113 A5
Kirkle Dr G77 157 B5
Kirklee Cir G12 96 D4
Kirklee Gate G12 96 D5
Kirklee Gdns G12 96 C5
Kirklee Pl G12 96 D4
Kirklee Quadrant 1 G12 96 D4
Kirklee Rd
Glasgow G12 96 D4
Motherwell ML1, ML4 142 E2
Kirklee Terr G12 96 C4
Kirklee Terrace La G12 96 D4
Kirklee Terrace Rd 21
G12 96 C4
Kirkliston St G32 118 F6
Kirkmaiden Way 6 G72 161 D3
Kirk Mews
Alexandria G83 27 F4
Cambuslang G72 139 A5
Kirkmichael Ave 3 G11 96 A3
Kirkmichael Gdns 2 G11 96 A3
Kirkmichael Rd G84 16 F1
Kirkmuir Dr
Rutherglen G73 138 B3
Stewarton KA3 195 C1
Kirkness St ML6 123 A8
Kirknethan ML2 164 C1
Kirknewton St G32 119 B6
Kirk O' Shotts Prim Sch
ML7 125 D3
Kirkoswald G74 160 D3
Kirkoswald Dr G81 74 C3
Kirkoswald Rd
Glasgow G43 136 D6
Motherwell ML1 143 E4
Kirk Path ML7 167 A8
Kirkpatrick Cres G83 27 D7
Kirkpatrick St G40 118 A5
Kirk Pl
Bearsden G61 75 E5
Cumbernauld G67 82 A7
Uddingston G71 140 E5
Kirk Port KA7 238 F8
Kirk Rd
Bearsden G61 75 E5
Beith KA15 171 B8
Carluke ML8 187 E2
Carmunnock G76 158 D7
Dalserf ML9 186 B2
Houston PA6 91 C2
Motherwell ML1 143 D7
Shotts ML7 146 F4
Wishaw ML2 165 C3
Kirkriggs Ave G73 138 B5
Kirkriggs Gdns G73 138 B5
Kirkriggs Prim Sch G45 138 A5
Kirkriggs View G73 138 B5
Kirkriggs Way G73 138 B5
Kirkshaw Ct PA5 111 F3
KIRKSHAWS 121 E3
Kirkshaws Ave ML5 121 F3
Kirkshaws Pl ML5 121 F3
Kirkshaws Prim Sch
ML5 121 E4
Kirkshaws Rd ML5 121 E3
Kirkside Cres FK7 7 B5
Kirkslap FK6 21 E2
Kirk St
Carluke ML8 187 E2
Coatbridge ML5 121 F6
Milngavie G62 54 E2
Motherwell ML1 163 E7
Prestwick KA9 233 C1
Stonehouse ML9 198 F2
Kirkstall Gdns G64 78 B4
Kirkstone G77 157 B5
Kirkstone Cl G75 179 F6
Kirkstyle Ave ML8 187 E1
Kirkstyle Cotts ML5 121 D3
Kirkstyle Cres
Airdrie ML6 102 F2
Neilston G78 154 D7
Kirkstyle Ct KA11 220 B6
Kirkstyle La G78 154 E7
Kirkstyle Pl ML6 102 D4
Kirkstyle Prim Sch KA1 228 A6
Kirksyde Ave G66 79 E7
Kirkton
Erskine PA8 73 A3
Old Kilpatrick G60 73 A7
Kirkton Ave
Barrhead G78 134 B1
Carluke ML8 187 E1
Glasgow G13 95 A6
Hamilton G72 161 D5
West Kilbride KA23 190 D4
Kirkton Cres
Cardross G82 26 A1
Coatbridge ML5 122 D4
Glasgow G13 95 A6
Milton of Campsie G66 58 C5
Kirkton Ct
Carluke ML8 187 E1
Eaglesham G76 178 F4
Kirkton Dr G76 178 E5
Kirktonfield Cres G78 154 F7
Kirktonfield Dr G78 154 F7
Kirktonfield Pl G78 154 F7
Kirktonfield Rd G78 154 E7
Kirkton Gate G74 159 E2
KIRKTONHILL 49 D3
Kirktonholme Cres G74 159 C1
Kirktonholme Prim Sch
G74 159 D2
Kirktonholme Rd G74 159 D1
Kirktonholm Pl 1 KA1 227 F7
Kirktonholm St 13 KA1 227 F8
Kirkton Moor Rd G76 178 B4
Kirkton Pk G74 159 F2
Kirkton Pl
Coatbridge ML5 122 D4
East Kilbride G74 159 F2
Falkirk FK2 24 C3
Fenwick KA3 213 A3
Hamilton G72 161 D6
Kirkton Prim Sch ML8 187 E1
Kirkton Rd
Cambuslang G72 139 B5
Cardross G82 26 A1
Dumbarton G82 49 D3
Fenwick KA3 213 B3
Kilmarnock KA3 222 F5
Kilmaurs KA3 222 C6
Neilston G78 154 E6
Kirktonside G78 134 B1
Kirkton St ML8 187 F1
Kirkton Terr G66 32 F3
Kirkvale Cres G77 157 B5
Kirkvale Ct
Newton Mearns G77 157 B5
Wishaw ML2 165 B3
Kirkvale Dr G77 157 B5
Kirk Vennel KA12 219 C2
Kirkview G67 82 A6
Kirk View KA15 150 B1
Kirkview Ave ML7 125 C2
Kirkview Cres G77 156 E3
Kirkview Ct G67 82 A6
Kirkview Gdns G71 140 F8
Kirkville Pl G15 75 B1
Kirkwall G67 62 A5
Kirkwall Ave G72 140 C3
Kirkwall Pl KA3 223 A5
Kirkwall Rd PA16 44 F3
Kirkway FK2 14 D4
Kirkwell Rd G44 137 B5
KIRKWOOD 121 C4
Kirkwood Ave
Clydebank G81 74 E1
Stepps G33 100 A5
Kirkwood Pl ML5 121 E5
Kirkwood Quadrant G81 74 D1
Kirkwood Rd G71 140 F8
Kirkwood Sp Barn ML5 121 B4
Kirkwood St
Coatbridge ML5 121 E5
Glasgow G51 116 C5
Rutherglen G73 138 A8
Kirkwood Sta ML5 121 D5
Kirk Wynd
Eaglesham G76 178 E4

L

Lanrig Rd G69 100 C8
Lansbury Gdns PA3 113 D7
Lansbury St
- Alexandria G83 27 E7
- Greenock PA15 46 F2

Lansbury Terr ML9 185 C1
Lansdowne Cres
- Glasgow G20 96 F2
- Shotts ML7 147 B3

Lansdowne Crescent La
- G20 96 F2

Lansdowne Dr G68 61 F4
Lansdowne Rd KA8 236 A3
Lantana Gr 1 ML1 163 D8
Lanton Dr G52 115 B5
Lanton Path ML6 123 E1
Lanton Rd G43 136 E5
Lappin St G81 94 D8
Lapsley Ave PA2 113 E1
Laputa Pl KA1 227 E3
Lapwing Rd PA4 94 E4
LARBERT 23 B2
Larbert High Sch FK5 23 E1
Larbert Rd FK4 40 B6
Larbert St G4 240 C4
Larbert Sta FK5 23 C2
Larbert Village Prim Sch
- FK5 23 B1

Larch Ave
- Bishopbriggs G64 98 B8
- Kirkintilloch G66 79 C6

Larch Cl 1 G72 139 E3
Larch Cres G66 79 C6
Larch Ct
- Cambuslang G72 139 F3
- Cumbernauld G67 62 E4
- East Kilbride G75 180 B5
- Hamilton G72 161 C8

Larch Dr
- Banknock FK4 38 E2
- East Kilbride G75 180 B5

Larches The G69 81 A4
Larchfield G84 16 D2
Larchfield Ave
- Glasgow G14 95 B4
- Newton Mearns G77 156 E5
- Wishaw ML2 165 D6

Larchfield Cres ML2 165 C6
Larchfield Ct G77 156 D4
Larchfield Dr G73 138 C4
Larchfield Gdns ML2 165 D6
Larchfield Gr ML2 165 D7
Larchfield Path ML7 147 B2
Larchfield Pl
- Glasgow G14 95 B4
- Wishaw ML2 165 D6

Larchfield Rd G61 75 F1
Larch Gait G72 139 F3
Larch Gr
- Cumbernauld G67 62 E4
- Hamilton ML3 162 F2
- Milton of Campsie G66 58 B5
- Motherwell ML1 143 A5
- Stenhousemuir FK5 23 F3

Larchgrove Ave G32 119 C6
Larchgrove Pl G32 119 C7
Larchgrove Rd G32 119 C7
Larch Ho KA9 236 C6
Larch Pl
- 2 Cambuslang G72 139 E3
- Cumbernauld G67 62 D4
- East Kilbride G75 180 B5
- Johnstone PA5 132 A8
- Kilmarnock KA1 227 D8
- Uddingston G71 141 D8

Larch Rd
- Cumbernauld G67 62 E4
- Glasgow G41 116 B4

Larch Sq 3 G72 139 E3
Larch Terr KA15 171 C8
Larch Way ML3 183 F4
Larchwood Rd KA7 239 C4
Larchwood Terr G78 155 D8
Larghill La KA7 239 B5
Largie Rd G43 136 F5
Largo La G72 161 D3
Largo Pl G51 115 E7
Largs Ave KA3 223 B3
Largs Rd KA25 148 D1
LARKFIELD 44 D4
Larkfield Ct G72 161 C6
Larkfield Dr G72 161 D6
Larkfield Gr PA16 44 F4
Larkfield Ind Est PA16 44 C5
Larkfield Rd
- Gourock PA19 44 E6
- Greenock PA16, PA19 44 F4
- Kirkintilloch G66 79 E6

Larkfield St 2 G42 117 B3
LARKHALL 185 B3
Larkhall Acad ML9 184 F1
Larkhall L Ctr ML9 185 A2
Larkhall Sta
- Larkhall ML9 185 A3
- Maryhill G20 96 E5

Larkhill Ind Est ML9 199 B8
Larkin Gdns PA3 113 D7
Larkin Way ML4 141 F7
Larksfield Dr ML8 202 A8
Larkspur Dr G74 159 C4
Larkspur Way ML8 201 F8
Lark Way ML4 141 F8
Lashley Gr ML2 186 C7
Lasswade St G14 94 E6
Latherton Dr 5 G20 96 D5
Latimer Gdns G52 115 A4
Latimer Path 8 G52 115 A4
Latta Ct KA9 236 D6
Latta St G82 50 A4
Lauchlan Way KA13 207 E3
Lauchlin Pl G66 80 B7
Lauchope Rd ML6 143 D7
Lauchope St ML6 123 E2
Lauder Cres ML2 165 B6
Lauder Ct KA3 223 C3
Lauderdale Dr G77 156 C3
Lauderdale Gdns G12 96 B3
Lauderdale La G12 96 B3
Lauder Dr
- Linwood PA3 112 B5
- Rutherglen G73 138 D6

Lauder Gdns
- Blantyre G72 140 C2
- Coatbridge ML5 122 D3

Lauder Gn G74 160 B4
Lauder La ML3 161 E3
Lauder St 4 G5 117 A4
Laudervale Gdns G83 27 D8
Laughland Dr ML1 143 D3
Laughlanglen Rd KA7 239 A3
Laundry La G33 99 C5
Lauranne Pl ML4 141 E5
Laurel Ave
- Clydebank G81 73 D4
- Kirkintilloch G66 79 D6

Laurelbank ML5 122 A8
Laurel Bank
- Ayr KA7 239 C4
- Hamilton ML3 183 C8

Laurelbank Ave FK4 40 A3
Laurelbank Rd
- Glasgow G32 139 C8
- Muirhead G69 100 B7

Laurel Ct
- Cambuslang G72 139 E4
- Denny FK6 21 D3
- East Kilbride G75 180 D5
- Falkirk FK1 41 C6

Laurel Dr
- East Kilbride G75 180 D5
- Larkhall ML9 185 D2
- Wishaw ML2 164 E3

Laurel Gait G72 139 E3
Laurel Gdns
- Chapelhall ML6 123 E2
- Uddingston G71 140 F8

Laurel Gr
- Bonnybridge FK4 39 F3
- Greengairs ML6 83 F2

Laurelhill Bsns Pk FK7 6 F6
Laurelhill Bsns Pk FK8 7 A6
Laurelhill Gdns FK8 6 F5
Laurelhill Pl FK8 7 A5
Laurel La
- Cambuslang G72 139 E3
- 5 Larkhall ML9 185 C1

Laurel Park Cl G13 95 C5
Laurel Park Gdns G13 95 C5
Laurel Pl
- Bonnybridge FK4 39 F3
- East Kilbride G75 180 D5
- Glasgow G11 96 A2
- Kilmarnock KA1 227 D7

Laurel Sq FK4 38 E2
Laurel St G11 96 A2
Laurels The
- 6 Motherwell ML1 143 B2
- Newton Mearns G77 156 D5
- Tullibody FK10 4 B1

Laurel Way
- Barrhead G78 134 B3
- Quarriers Village PA11 89 F1

Laurel Wlk G73 138 C3
Laurel Wynd G72 139 F3
Laurencecroft Rd FK8 2 B2
Laurence Ct G15 74 E3
Laurence Dr
- Bearsden G61 75 D6
- Clydebank G15 74 E3

Laurence Gdns G15 74 E3
Laurenstone Terr G74 160 B3
Lauren View ML6 122 F7
Lauren Way PA2 113 A1
Laurie Ct G71 141 A7
Laurieland Ave KA2 221 E1
LAURIESTON
- Falkirk 42 F4
- Glasgow 117 B5

Laurieston Cres ML6 123 D1
Laurieston Ct KA2 225 F1
Lauriestone Pl ML5 122 D3
Laurieston Ind Est FK2 42 F3
Laurieston Rd G5 117 C5
Laurieston Way G73 138 A4
Lauriston Ct KA22 205 D1
Lauriston Gr G77 156 B5
Lauriston Way KA3 223 B6
Lavelle Dr ML5 122 C7
Lavender Ct G71 141 C7
Lavender Dr G75 180 D5
Lavender La ML8 201 E8
Laverock Ave
- Greenock PA15 45 D3
- Hamilton ML3 163 A2

Laverockhall ML11 215 B5
Laverockhall St G21 97 F3
Laverock Rd ML6 103 B3
Laverock Terr G69 80 F1
Lavery Ave FK5 23 B1
LAW 186 F5
Law Brae KA23 190 D5
Law Dr ML1 143 C4
Lawers Cres KA1 228 A4
Lawers Dr G61 75 C7
Lawers La ML1 143 C3
Lawers Pl
- Greenock PA16 45 A4
- Irvine KA11 220 A4

Lawers Rd
- Glasgow G43 136 B5
- Kilmarnock KA1 228 A4
- Renfrew PA4 94 C1

Lawfield Ave
- Newton Mearns G77 157 B5
- West Kilbride KA23 190 E4

LAW HILL 187 A4
Lawhill Ave G45 137 D4
Lawhill Rd ML8 187 B3
Lawhope Mill Rd ML6 123 F3
Lawmarnock Cres PA11 110 C7
Lawmarnock Ho PA11 110 C7
Lawmarnock Rd PA11 110 C7
Lawmoor Rd G5 117 C3
Lawmoor St G5 117 C3
Lawmuir Cres G81 74 E7
Lawmuir Pl ML4 142 A2
Lawmuir Prim Sch ML4 142 A3
Lawmuir Rd
- Bellshill ML4 142 A3
- Law ML8 186 F6

Lawn Pk G62 55 C1
Lawn St PA1 113 F5
Law Pl
- Denny FK6 21 E1
- East Kilbride G74 159 F5

Law Prim Sch ML8 187 A5
Law Rdbt G74 159 E4
Lawrence Ave
- Glasgow G46 136 D1
- Helensburgh G84 25 C7

Lawrence Ct FK5 23 B5
Lawrence Dr G83 19 F1
Lawrence St G11 96 C2
Lawrie Pl ML1 143 E1
Lawrie St
- Glasgow G11 96 B2
- Stonehouse ML9 198 E3
- Wishaw ML2 165 F5

Lawrie Way 11 ML9 185 C1
Lawson Ave ML1 163 E3
Lawson Dr KA22 205 D4
Lawson St
- Ayr KA8 236 B2
- Kilmarnock KA1 228 A7

Law St G40 118 B5
Lawswell FK10 5 E3
LAWTHORN 220 C6
Lawthorn Prim Sch
- KA11 220 A6

Lawthorn Rd KA11 220 B6
Lawthorn Rdbt KA11 220 B6
Law View ML2 186 C6
Laxdale Dr FK6 39 D7
Laxford Ave G44 137 A4
Laxford Pl ML5 122 D5
Laxford Rd PA8 72 E1
Laxford Way ML1 143 C4
Laxton Dr G66 79 E4
Laymoor Ave PA4 94 F3
Lea Ave G78 154 D7
Leabank Ave PA2 133 E8
Leadburn Rd G21 98 C4
Leadburn St G32, G33 118 E7
Leader St G33 98 D1
Leadhills Rd KA1 228 A3
Leaend Rd ML6 102 E1
Leander Cres
- Bellshill ML4 142 E5
- Renfrew PA4 94 E2

Leapark Dr FK4 39 F3
Learigg Rd ML6 104 B3
Learmonth St FK1 42 B4
Learmont Pl G62 54 F2
Leathem Pl ML2 164 C1
Leathen Pl PA8 72 E1
Lec Ct FK2 42 F4
Leckethill Ave G68 81 F7
Leckethill Ct G68 81 F7
Leckethill Pl G68 81 F7
Leckethill View G68 81 F7
Leckie Ct ML3 162 C4
Leckie Dr ML3 162 C4
Leckie Pl G83 27 E6
Leckie St G41 136 C8
Lecropt Sch (Barnardo's)
- FK1 41 C6

Ledaig Pl G31 118 C7
Ledaig St G31 118 C7
Ledard Rd G42 137 A7
Ledcameroch Cres G61 75 E4
Ledcameroch Pk G61 75 D4
Ledcameroch Rd G61 75 E4
Ledgate G66 58 D1
Ledgowan Pl G20 96 D8
Ledi Ave FK10 4 B2
Ledi Dr G61 75 B7
Ledi Path ML1 143 C3
Ledi Pl FK1 66 E7
Ledi Rd G43 136 C5
Ledi View FK9 2 B3
Ledmore Dr G15 74 F4
Ledmore Pl FK1 42 E1
Lednock Rd
- Glasgow G52 115 A5
- Stepps G33 99 C5

Ledrish Ave G83 19 F2
Ledvinka Cres ML3 162 A6
Lee Ave G33 98 E1
Leebank Dr G44 136 F2
Leeburn Ave PA6 91 C1
Leeburn Gdns PA6 91 C1
Leechford ML11 215 B5
Leechlee Rd ML3 162 E3
Lee Cres G64 98 A8
Leefield Dr G44 136 F2
Leehill Rd G21 97 E7
Lee Meadow Rd ML8 202 A4
Leemuir View ML8 202 B8
Lee Pl ML4 142 D4
Lees Burn Ct G74 160 A5
Leesburn Pl G74 159 F4
Lee's Ct ML5 122 A5
Leeside Rd G21 97 E7
Leesland G71 141 A8
Leeward Circ G75 159 A1
Leeward Pk KA7 239 A1
Leewood Dr G44 137 A2
Le Froy Gdns G75 180 C8
Le Froy La G75 180 C8
Lefroy St ML5 121 E7
Legbrannock Ave ML1 143 D7
Legbrannock Cres ML1 143 D4
Legbrannock Rd ML1 143 E5
Leggate Way ML4 142 A8
Leggatson Dr G53 135 C3
Legion Pl ML9 185 A3
Leglen Wood Cres G33 98 D6
Leglen Wood Dr G21 98 D5
Leglen Wood Gdns G21 98 D6
Leglen Wood Pl G21 98 E6
Leglen Wood Rd G21 98 D6
Leicester Ave G12 96 B5
Leighton St
- Glasgow G20 96 F6
- Wishaw ML2 165 B2

Leishman Ct EH48 107 D2
Leishman Pl ML6 103 D1
Leishman Twr FK1 42 C4
Leisuredrome G64 77 E3
Leisure Way ML9 185 A2
Leitchland Rd PA2 132 D8
Leitch St PA15 46 E3
Leith Ave ML9 198 F2
Leithland Ave 2 G53 115 B1
Leithland Rd G53 115 B1
Leith Pl FK6 39 D7
Leith St G33 118 D8
Leman Dr PA6 111 D8
Leman Gr PA6 111 D8
Lembert Dr G76 157 D8
Lemmon St PA15 45 D4
Lendale La G64 78 A4
Lendalfoot Gdns ML3 161 D2
Lendal Pl G75 179 E6
Lendel Pl G51 116 D5
Lendrick Ave FK1 41 F2
Lenihall Dr G45 137 E2
Lenihall Terr G45 137 E2
Lennox Ave
- Bishopton PA7 72 B3
- Coatbridge ML5 121 E7
- Glasgow G14 95 D3
- Milngavie G62 55 A1
- Stirling FK7 7 A4

Lennoxbank Ho 7 G83 27 E8
Lennox Cres
- Bishopbriggs G64 97 F8
- Kilmarnock KA1 222 D1

Lennox Ct 16 G65 60 D8
Lennox Dr
- Bearsden G61 75 F6
- Clydebank G81 74 C7
- Newton Mearns G77 156 E2
- Prestwick KA9 236 C5

Lennox Gdns
- Dumbarton G82 49 A4
- Glasgow G14 95 D4

Lennox Lane E G14 95 D3
Lennox Lane W
- Glasgow G14 95 C3
- Glasgow G14 95 D4

Lennoxmill La G66 57 C8
Lennox Pl G81 73 E3
Lennox Rd
- Cumbernauld G67 61 F2
- Dumbarton G82 50 B3
- Lennoxtown G66 33 C1
- Milton G82 50 F1

Lennox St
- Alexandria G83 27 E5
- Dumbarton G82 50 A3
- Glasgow G20 96 C7
- Renton G82 49 D8
- Wishaw ML2 165 E4

Lennox Terr PA3 114 A8
LENNOXTOWN 57 E8
Lennoxtown Prim Sch
- G66 57 D8

Lennox Wynd KA21 205 F2
Lentran St G34 120 D7
Lenwood Gdns G83 27 F3
Leny Cres FK1 42 A1
Leny St G20 96 F4
LENZIE 79 D5
Lenzie Acad G66 79 C6
LENZIEMILL 83 B8
Lenziemill Rd
- Cumbernauld, Greenfaulds G67 82 F7
- Cumbernauld, Lenziemill G67 83 B8

Lenzie Moss Nature Reserve* G66 79 B4
Lenzie Moss Prim Sch
- G66 79 B5

Lenzie Pl G21 97 F6
Lenzie Prim Sch G66 79 C5
Lenzie Rd
- Kirkintilloch G66 79 D7
- Stepps G33 99 D6

Lenzie St G21 97 F5
Lenzie Sta G66 79 C4
Lenzie Terr G21 97 F5
Lenzie Way G21 97 E6
Leonard Gr ML1 143 E1
Leperstone Ave
- Kilmacolm PA13 69 D2
- Port Glasgow PA14 68 E7

Leperstone Rd PA13 69 D2
Lerwick Pl KA3 223 A6
Lesley Pl KA20 206 E1
Lesley Quadrant ML4 141 F2
Leslie Ave
- Bishopton PA7 72 B3
- Newton Mearns G77 156 E7

Leslie Cres KA7 239 A6
Leslie Pl KA3 223 B2
Leslie Rd
- Glasgow G41 116 E3
- Kilmarnock KA3 223 B2

Leslie St
- Glasgow G41 116 F3
- Motherwell ML1 163 F7

Leslie Terr KA9 236 C8
Lesmahagow Rd ML11 214 A4
Lesmuir Dr G14 95 A5
Lesmuir Pl G14 94 F5
Lestrange Ave FK12 5 B7
LETHAM 24 C8
Letham Cotts FK2 24 D8
Letham Ct G43 136 E5
Letham Dr
- Bishopbriggs G64 98 D8
- Glasgow G43 136 E5

Letham Grange G68 61 F4
Lethamhill Cres G33 98 F1
Lethamhill Pl G33 98 E1
Lethamhill Rd G33 98 F1
Letham Oval G64 98 D8
Letham Terrs FK2 14 C1
Lethbridge Pl 4 G75 180 C8
Lethen View FK10 4 C3
Letherby Dr G44 137 B7
Letheron Dr ML2 165 B5
Lethington Ave G41 136 E8
Lethington Pl G41 136 F8
Lethington Rd G46 157 A7
Letterfearn Rd G23 76 E1
Letterickhills Cres G72 139 E3
LEVAN 43 E5
Levanne Gdns PA19 43 F6
Levanne Pl PA19 43 F6
Levan Point PA19 43 F5
Leven Ave
- Bishopbriggs G64 78 B1
- Helensburgh G84 25 C8
- Kilmarnock KA3 223 A3

Levenbank Gdns G83 27 F7
Levenbank Rd G83 27 F7
Levenbank Terr G83 27 F7
Levencroft Mews G83 27 E3
Leven Ct
- Alloa FK10 10 C5
- Barrhead G78 134 B5
- Dumbarton G82 49 E3
- Hurlford KA1 228 F6

Leven Dr
- Bearsden G61 75 F3
- Hamilton ML3 183 B8
- Hurlford KA1 228 F6

Levenford Terr G82 49 E3
Levengrove Ct G82 49 E3
Levengrove Terr G82 49 E3
Levenhowe Pl G83 27 E7
Levenhowe Rd G83 27 E7
Leven Path ML1 143 A5
Leven Pl
- Erskine PA8 72 E1
- Greenock PA15 46 C1
- Irvine KA12 219 D6
- Shotts ML7 146 E6

Leven Quadrant ML6 102 F2
Leven Rd
- Coatbridge ML5 101 D1
- Greenock PA15 46 C1
- Langbank PA14 70 C7
- Troon KA10 229 G5

Leven Sq PA4 94 B4
Leven St
- Alexandria G83 27 E4
- Dumbarton G82 50 A3
- Falkirk FK2 42 B8
- Glasgow G41 116 F3
- Motherwell ML1 163 E4
- Renton G82 49 D8

Leven Terr ML1 143 C2
LEVENVALE 27 D7
Levenvale Prim Sch G83 27 D7
Leven Valley Ent Ctr G82 49 D4
Leven View G81 74 B3
Leven Way
- 6 Cumbernauld G67 61 F1
- East Kilbride G75 179 F6
- Paisley PA2 112 E1

Leveret Lea KA3 228 D8
Levern Bridge Ct G53 134 F7
Levern Bridge Gr G53 134 F6
Levern Bridge Pl G53 134 F6
Levern Bridge Rd G53 134 F6
Levern Bridge Way G53 134 F6
Levern Cres G78 134 B1
Leverndale Ct G53 114 F1
Leverndale Hospl G53 114 F2
Leverndale Rd G53 114 F1
Levern Gdns G78 134 B3
Levern Grove Ct G53 134 F6

Luing Rd 1 G52 115 E5
Luma Gdns G51 115 C7
Lumloch St G21 98 A4
Lumsden La G3 96 D1
Lumsden Pl KA20 206 E1
Lumsden St G3 96 D1
Lunan Dr G64 98 C8
Lunan Pl G51 115 E7
Lunar Path ML6 123 D1
Luncarty Pl G32 119 A3
Luncarty St G32 119 A3
Lunderston Cl G53 135 B6
Lunderston Dr G53 135 A7
Lunderston Gdns G53 135 B6
Lundholm Rd KA20 217 E7
Lundie Gdns G64 98 D8
Lundie St G32 118 E3
Lurg St PA14 68 D8
Luss Ave PA15 46 B1
Luss Brae ML3 161 F2
Lusset Glen G60 73 B6
Lusset Rd G60 73 B6
Lusshill Terr G71 120 B2
Luss Pl PA15 46 B1
Luss Rd
Alexandria G83 27 D7
Glasgow G51 115 F7
Helensburgh G84 17 B5
Lybster Cres 2 G73 138 D3
Lybster Way G72 161 C3
Lychgate Rd FK10 4 B2
Lye Brae G67 62 B2
Lyell Gr G74 159 E3
Lyell Pl G74 159 E3
Lyle Cres PA7 72 A4
Lylefoot Cres PA16 45 B8
Lylefoot Pl PA16 45 B7
Lyle Gdns KA12 219 D1
Lyle Gr PA16 45 B7
Lyle Pl
Greenock PA16 45 A7
Paisley PA2 113 F2
Lyle Rd
Airdrie ML6 123 F8
Greenock PA16 45 B7
Kilmacolm PA13 89 D8
Lyle's Land PA6 91 B3
Lylesland Ct PA2 113 E2
Lyle Sq G62 54 E2
Lyle St
Greenock, Central PA15 45 F4
Greenock PA15 46 A4
Lylestone Terr KA13 208 D7
Lyman Dr ML2 165 C7
Lymburn Pl KA8 239 B8
Lymburn St G3 116 D8
Lymekilns Rd G74 159 D3
Lyndale Pl G20 96 D8
Lyndale Rd G20 96 D8
Lyndhurst Gardens La G20 96 F3
Lyndhurst Gdns G20 96 F3
Lynebank Gr G77 156 D2
Lynebank Pl G77 156 D2
Lyne Croft G64 78 A4
Lynedoch Cres G3 240 A4
Lynedoch Ct 4 PA15 46 A4
Lynedoch Ind Est PA15 46 A4
Lynedoch Pl G3 240 A4
Lynedoch St
Glasgow G3 240 A4
Greenock PA15 45 F4
Lynedoch Terr G3 240 A4
Lyne St ML2 165 A5
Lynmouth Pl PA19 44 E5
Lynn Ave KA24 191 C7
Lynnburn Ave ML4 142 A6
Lynn Ct ML9 185 A2
Lynn Dr
Eaglesham G76 178 E6
Kilbirnie KA25 149 B3
Milngavie G62 55 C2
Lynne Dr G23 76 E1
Lynnhurst G71 140 F7
Lynn Wlk
3 Balloch G83 27 E8
Bothwell G71 141 A5
Lynnwood Rd ML2 166 C6
Lynton Ave G46 136 A1
Lyon Cres FK9 2 A6
Lyoncross FK4 39 D4
Lyoncross Ave G78 134 D3
Lyoncross Cres G78 134 D3
Lyoncross Rd G53 115 B2
Lyon Rd
Erskine PA8 72 E1
Linwood PA3 112 B4
Paisley PA2 112 F1
Lyons Quadrant ML2 164 D4
Lysander Way 2 PA4 94 D1
Lysa Vale Pl ML4 141 E5
Lytham Dr G23 76 E1
Lytham Mdws G71 140 E2
Lythgow Way ML11 215 C5
Lyttleton G75 180 B7

M

Mabel St ML1 163 E5
Maberry Cl KA3 195 D1
Maberry Pl KA10 229 F6
McAdam Ct
Prestwick KA9 236 D5
Troon KA10 229 G4
MacAdam Gdns ML4 142 A6
MacAdam Pl
Ayr KA8 236 A1
East Kilbride G75 180 E8
Falkirk FK1 41 D6
Irvine KA11 219 F1
Kilmarnock KA3 223 C1
MacAdam Sq KA8 236 A1
McAlister Rd G83 27 E5
MacAllan Mews ML1 143 B2
MacAllan Pl KA11 219 F7
McAllister Ave ML6 123 D8
McAllister Ct FK7 7 D1
MacAllister Pl KA3 223 C1
MacAlpine Ct FK10 4 D3
MacAlpine Pl KA3 223 C2
McAlpine St
Glasgow G3 240 B2
Wishaw ML2 165 B2
MacAndrew Pl KA3 223 C1
Macara Dr KA12 219 E3
McArdle Ave ML1 163 B7
MacArthur Ave ML6 102 D3
MacArthur Cres G74 159 C4
MacArthur Ct G74 159 C3
MacArthur Dr G74 159 C3
MacArthur Gdns G74 159 C3
McArthur Pk G66 79 C7
McArthur St G43 136 C7
McArthur Wynd G72 139 C5
McAslin Ct G4 241 B3
McAslin St G4 241 C3
McAulay Brae FK7 12 C3
MacAulay Pl G84 16 A2
MacAuley Pl KA3 223 C1
McAuslan Pl G84 16 F2
MacBeth G74 160 B5
MacBeth Dr KA3 223 C1
MacBeth Gdns KA3 223 C1
MacBeth Pl G31 118 D4
MacBeth Rd
Greenock PA16 45 A5
Stewarton KA3 195 D1
MacBeth St G31 118 D4
MacBeth Wlk KA3 223 C1
McBride Ave G66 79 C7
McBride Path G33 99 E5
MacCabe Gdns G66 57 F7
McCall's Ave KA8 236 A2
McCallum Ave G73 138 B8
McCallum Cres PA19 44 E7
McCallum Ct G74 159 B4
MacCallum Dr G72 139 C5
McCallum Gdns ML4 141 F2
McCallum Gr G74 159 B4
McCallum Pl G74 159 B4
MacCallum Pl KA3 223 C1
McCallum Rd ML9 185 B1
McCambridge Pl FK5 23 C5
McCann Ct FK7 12 B4
McCardel Way KA3 211 E8
McCardle Way ML2 166 A6
McCarrison Rd ML2 166 A6
McCartney Rd FK5 23 C4
McCash Pl G66 79 C7
McCaull Pl KA10 229 F6
McCloy Gdns G53 134 F5
McClue Ave PA4 94 B3
McClue Rd PA4 94 C4
McClure Gdns KA12 219 C3
McClurg Ct 3 ML1 163 E5
McColgan Pl KA8 236 C3
McColl Ave G83 27 C7
McColl Pl G83 27 C6
McConnell Rd PA12 129 B2
McCormack Gdns ML1 143 E4
McCormack Pl FK5 23 D4
McCourt Gdns ML4 142 C5
McCracken Ave PA4 94 B2
McCracken Dr G71 141 C8
McCraken Ct FK1 66 F5
McCreery St G81 94 D8
MacCrimmon Pk G74 159 B4
McCrorie Pl PA10 111 A3
McCulloch Ave G71 141 D6
McCulloch La G83 27 D7
McCulloch St G41 116 F4
McCulloch Way
Neilston G78 154 D7
Stepps G33 99 F5
MacDairmid Dr ML3 183 B7
MacDonald Ave PA5 111 E1
MacDonald Ave G74 159 A4
McDonald Cres G81 94 D8
MacDonald Cres G65 60 A3
MacDonald Ct
Beith KA15 171 A7
Larbert FK5 23 B5
McDonald Dr KA12 219 D4
MacDonald Dr
Kilmarnock KA3 223 C1
Stirling FK7 7 A4
MacDonald Gdns KA3 223 C1
MacDonald Gr ML4 141 F2
McDonald Pl
Motherwell ML1 143 A5
Neilston G78 154 E7
MacDonald Pl KA3 223 C1
MacDonald St
3 Motherwell ML1 163 F5
1 Rutherglen G73 138 A7
MacDonald Wlk 5 G83 27 E8
MacDougal Dr G72 139 C5
MacDougall Dr KA3 223 C1
MacDougall Pl KA3 223 C1
MacDougall St
Glasgow G43 136 C7
Greenock PA15 46 D4
MacDougal Quadrant ML4 141 F2
McDowall Ave KA22 205 D2
McDowall Pl KA22 205 D2
MacDowall St
Johnstone PA5 111 F3
Paisley PA3 113 D6
MacDuff PA8 73 A2
MacDuff Pl G31 118 D4
MacDuff St G31 118 D4
Mace Ct FK7 7 D3
Macedonian Gr ML1 143 C4
Mace Rd G13 75 C1
McEwan Dr G84 16 F3
McEwan Gdns G74 159 A4
MacEwan Pl KA3 228 C8
McEwans Way ML9 198 D1
McEwan Wlk G83 27 E6
MacFarland Rd 5 G61 75 F3
MacFarlane Cres
Cambuslang G72 139 C5
Falkirk FK1 42 B5
MacFarlane Dr KA3 223 C1
McFarlane Rd G83 28 A8
MacFarlane Rd G61 76 A3
McFarlane St
Glasgow G4 241 C1
Paisley PA3 113 C7
MacFie Pl G74 159 B4
McGavin Ave KA13 208 A3
McGavin Way KA13 207 D4
McGhee Pl FK1 41 F2
McGhee St G81 74 B4
McGibney Dr KA12 219 D1
McGillivray Ave KA21 205 F2
MacGillvary Ave PA15 46 E3
McGoldrick Pl G33 99 F5
McGowan Pl ML3 162 A5
MacGowan Way PA15 46 E3
McGown St PA3 113 D6
McGregor Ave
Airdrie ML6 123 D8
Balloch G83 28 A8
Renfrew PA4 94 B2
Stevenston KA20 206 D1
MacGregor Ct G72 139 C5
McGregor Dr G82 50 C4
MacGregor Dr KA3 228 C8
McGregor La G82 27 D2
McGregor Path ML5 101 C6
McGregor Rd G67 61 E1
MacGregor Rd PA15 46 E3
McGregor St
Clydebank G81 94 D8
Glasgow G51 115 F6
Wishaw ML2 164 D4
McGregor Wlk G83 27 C7
McGrigor Rd
Milngavie G62 54 F3
Stirling FK7 7 A4
McGurk Way ML4 141 D6
MACHAN 185 A2
Machan Ave ML9 185 A3
Machanhill ML9 185 B2
Machanhill Prim Sch ML9 185 B3
Machanhill View ML9 185 B2
Machan Rd ML9 185 B1
McHardy Cres KA15 171 F3
Machrie Ct FK1 41 C4
Machrie Dr
Glasgow G45 137 F4
Helensburgh G84 16 F3
Newton Mearns G77 156 E6
Machrie Gn G75 180 B4
Machrie Pl KA13 207 C3
Machrie Rd
Glasgow G45 137 F4
Kilmarnock KA3 222 E4
Machrie St
Glasgow G45 137 F3
Motherwell ML1 163 B7
Mcilvanney Cres KA3 222 F2
Mcilvanney Dr KA3 223 A2
McInally Cres 1 FK2 41 F7
McInnes Ct ML2 165 B2
Macinnes Dr ML1 144 A5
McInnes Gr ML9 198 E1
MacInnes Mews ML1 143 E4
McInnes Pl ML2 186 B7
MacInnes Pl KA3 223 C1
McInnes St G83 28 A8
Mcintosh Ct 1 G31 117 F7
Macintosh Pl
East Kilbride G75 180 C7
Falkirk FK1 42 A1
Kilmarnock KA3 223 C1
McIntosh Quadrant ML4 141 F2
McIntosh St G31 117 F7
Mcintosh Way
Bellshill ML4 141 F3
Cumbernauld G67 61 F1
Motherwell ML1 163 C5
McIntyre Ave KA9 233 D2
McIntyre Pl PA2 113 E2
MacIntyre Pl KA3 223 C1
MacIntyre Rd KA9 233 C2
McIntyre St G3 240 A2
McIntyre Terr
6 Balloch G83 27 E8
Cambuslang G72 139 A6
McIsaac Rd KA21 217 A7
McIver St G72 139 E6
MacIvor Cres G74 159 A4
MacIvor Pl KA3 223 C1
McKay Cres PA5 112 B2
McKay Ct G77 156 C3
McKay Gr ML4 141 F5
McKay Pl
East Kilbride G74 159 A4
Newton Mearns G77 156 C4
MacKean St PA3 113 D6
McKechnie St G51 116 A8
McKeith St G40 117 F4
McKellar Ave KA22 205 D2
MacKellar Pl KA3 223 C2
McKell Ct FK1 42 A3
MacKendrick Pl KA3 228 C8
McKenna Dr ML6 122 E7
McKenzie Ave G81 74 B4
McKenzie Dr G83 19 F1
MacKenzie Dr
Johnstone PA10 111 B1
Kilmarnock KA3 223 B1
McKenzie Gate G72 139 E6
MacKenzie Gdns G74 159 A4
Mckenzie Pl FK1 42 A2
MacKenzie Pl FK1 41 F2
McKenzie's Cl 16 ML11 215 A4
McKenzie St PA3 113 C5
MacKenzie St PA15 46 D4
MacKenzie Terr ML4 142 A7
McKeown Gdns ML4 142 D4
McKerrell St PA1 114 A5
MacKie Ave
Greenock PA14 46 F1
Port Glasgow PA14 47 A1
Stewarton KA3 195 D2
MacKie Pl KA3 223 C1
MacKie's Mill Rd PA5 132 D8
MacKie St KA8 236 C2
McKillop Pl KA21 205 F2
McKim Wlk G82 49 D8
McKinlay Ave G83 20 A1
McKinlay Cres
Alloa FK10 10 C7
Irvine KA12 219 B1
MacKinlay Pl KA1 228 B8
MacKinley Pl G77 156 D4
MacKinnon Dr KA3 228 C8
McKinnon Pl KA21 206 A2
MacKinnon Terr KA12 219 E4
MacKintosh Ct G72 139 A3
MacKintosh Pl KA11 219 F1
McKnight Ave KA3 213 E4
Mack St ML6 123 A8
McLachlan Ave FK7 7 B2
Maclachlan Ave FK6 21 C1
Maclachlan Pl G84 16 E3
Maclachlan Rd G84 16 E3
McLachlan St FK5 23 C2
McLaren Ave PA4 94 C1
McLaren Cres G20 96 E7
McLaren Ct
Glasgow G46 136 B1
Stenhousemuir FK5 23 D2
Troon KA10 229 G4
MacLaren Ct KA10 229 G4
McLaren Dr ML4 142 D4
McLaren Gdns G20 96 E7
McLaren Gr G74 159 A4
McLaren Pl G82 27 E2
MacLaren Pl
Kilmarnock KA3 228 C8
3 Netherlee G44 136 F2
McLaren Terr FK7 7 B3
MacLaren Terr FK2 24 A2
McLauchlan View ML7 127 F6
McLaurin Cres PA5 111 D1
Maclay Ave PA10 111 A2
McLean Cres G83 19 F1
MacLean Cres FK12 5 C7
MacLean Ct
East Kilbride G74 159 B4
Stirling FK7 7 C3
McLean Dr
Bellshill ML4 141 F2
Irvine KA11 225 D8
MacLean Dr KA3 223 B1
McLean Gdns ML9 198 E2
MacLean Gr G74 159 B4
McLean Mus & Art Gall* PA16 45 E6
McLean Pl PA3 113 D7
MacLean Pl G74 159 B4
MacLean Sq G51 116 E6
McLean St KA8 236 C2
MacLean St
Clydebank G81 94 E8
Glasgow G51 116 D6
MacLean Terr EH48 107 C3
McLees La ML1 163 B7
MacLehose Ct PA16 45 E7
MacLehose Rd G67 62 C3
McLelland Dr
Kilmarnock KA1 227 E7
Plains ML6 104 B2
McLellan Galleries* G3 240 C3
MacLellan Rd G78 154 E6
MacLellan St G41 116 D5
McLennan St G42 137 B8
MacLeod Cres G84 16 B4
MacLeod Dr
Helensburgh G84 16 C4
Kilmarnock KA3 228 C8
MacLeod Pl
East Kilbride G74 160 B3
Kilmarnock KA3 228 C8
McLeod Rd G82 50 C4
McLeod St PA15 46 D3
MacLeod Way G72 139 C5
McLuckie Dr KA13 207 C4
McLuckie Pk KA13 207 C4
McMahon Dr ML2 166 A6
McMahon Gr ML4 142 B6
McMillan Cres KA15 171 A7
McMillan Ct KA10 229 F4
McMillan Dr KA22 205 A4
MacMillan Dr
Gourock PA19 44 D6
Kilmarnock KA3 223 C1
MacMillan Gdns G71 121 A1
McMillan Pl KA11 224 H6
McMillan Pl KA3 223 C1
McMillan Rd ML2 164 D2
Macmillan Sch of Music & Drama PA1 113 C4
MacMillan St ML9 184 F2
McMillan Way ML8 186 F5
McNab Gdns FK1 41 F2
MacNab Pl KA3 223 B1
McNair St G32 119 A5
MacNaughton Dr KA3 223 C1
MacNaughton Wlk KA3 223 C1
McNaught Pl
Kilmaurs KA3 222 A7
Renton G82 27 D1
McNay Cres KA21 206 A1
McNee Rd KA9 233 C3
McNeil Ave G81 74 E1
McNeil Dr ML1 143 A8
McNeil Gdns G5 117 D4
McNeill Ave KA9 233 D1
MacNeill Dr G74 159 B4
MacNeill Gdns G74 159 B4
McNeil Pl ML2 186 C7
MacNeil Pl KA3 223 B1
McNeil St G5 117 D4
MacNeil St ML9 184 F3
McNeish Way G74 159 C4
MacNichol Gdns KA3 223 C1
MacNichol Pl KA3 223 C1
MacNicol Ct G74 159 A4
MacNicol Pk G74 159 A4
MacNicol Pl G74 159 A4
McNiven Ct ML9 198 E1
McPhail Ave ML1 143 F5
Macphail Dr KA3 223 C1
McPhail St
Glasgow G40 117 E4
Greenock PA15 46 D3
McPhater St G4 240 C4
McPherson Cres ML6 123 E1
McPherson Dr
Bothwell G71 141 B3
Gourock PA19 44 D7
Macpherson Dr FK8 2 A2
Macpherson Gdns KA3 223 C1
McPherson La G83 27 D7
Macpherson Pk G74 159 C3
Macpherson Pl
Falkirk FK1 41 F2
Kilmarnock KA3 223 C1
McPherson St
Bellshill ML4 142 D5
Glasgow G1 241 B1
Macpherson Wlk KA3 223 C1
Macphie Rd G82 50 C4
Macrae Dr KA9 233 C2
Macrae Gdns G74 159 C3
Macredie Pl KA11 220 D6
Macrimmon Pl G75 180 E8
MacRobert Ave KA11 220 B1
McShane Ct ML2 166 B5
McShannon Gr ML4 142 A3
McSparran Rd G65 60 F4
McTaggart Ave FK6 21 E2
MacTaggart Rd G67 82 E8
McVean Pl FK4 39 B4
Madeira La PA16 45 D7
Madeira St PA16 45 D7
Madill Pl FK5 23 F3
Madison Ave G44 137 B5
Madison Path 9 G72 161 D7
Madras Pl
Glasgow G40 117 F3
Neilston G78 154 E7
Madras St G40 117 F3
Mafeking St
Glasgow G51 116 B6
Wishaw ML2 164 D4
Mafeking Terr G78 154 C7
Magdalen Way PA2 132 E7
Maggie Wood's Loan
Falkirk FK1 41 F4
Falkirk FK1 41 F5
Magna St ML1 163 B8
Magnolia Dr G72 139 F3
Magnolia Gdns
Ashgill ML9 185 E1
Motherwell ML1 143 C3
Magnolia Pl G71 141 C8
Magnolia St ML2 165 B5
Magnolia Terr G72 139 F3
Magnum L Ctr KA12 218 F1
Magnus Cres G44 137 B4
Magnus Rd PA6 111 D8
Mahon Ct G69 80 F1
Maidens G74 159 D3
Maidens Ave G77 157 A5
Maidland Rd G53 135 C8
Maid Morville Ave KA11 225 C8
Mailerbeg Gdns G69 80 F3
Mailie Wlk ML1 143 C3
Mailing Ave G64 78 C2
Mailings Ct G65 37 E3
Mailings Rd G65 37 E3
Mailings The G65 37 E4
Maimhor Rd KA23 190 B4
Mainhead Terr G67 62 B5
Mainhill Ave G69 120 D5
Mainhill Dr G69 120 C5
Mainhill Pl G69 120 D6
Mainhill Rd G69 120 F5

Maryfield Pl
Ayr KA8 236 B4
Falkirk FK1 41 B4
Maryfield Rd KA8 236 B4
Mary Fisher Cres G82 50 C2
Mary Glen ML2 165 D5
MARYHILL 96 C7
Maryhill Rd
Bearsden G61, G20 76 A1
Glasgow G20 97 A2
Glasgow, Maryhill G20 96 D6
Maryhill Sta G20 96 C8
Maryknowe Rd ML1 143 C2
Maryland Dr G52 115 E5
Maryland Gdns G52 115 E5
Maryland Rd G82 50 C6
Mary Love Pl KA20 206 B1
Marypark Rd PA14 70 B7
Mary Rae Rd ML4 141 E3
Mary Russell Sch The PA2 114 C2
Mary Slessor Wynd G73 138 C2
Mary Sq G69 120 F5
Mary St
Greenock PA16 45 C4
Hamilton ML3 162 D2
Johnstone PA5 112 A3
Laurieston FK2 42 F4
Paisley PA2 113 E2
Port Glasgow PA14 47 A2
Mary Stevenson Dr FK10 10 A8
Maryston St G33 98 D2
Mary Street Rdbt FK2 42 F3
MARYVILLE 140 C8
Maryville Ave G46 136 C2
Maryville Gdns G46 136 C2
Maryville La G71 140 E8
Maryville View G71 120 D1
Marywell Path G68 60 F2
Marywood Sq G41 116 F2
Mary Young Pl G76 157 F6
Mashock Path ML8 201 B1
Mason Ct ML1 163 E6
Masonfield Ave G68 61 D2
MASONHILL 239 D6
Masonhill Pl KA7 239 C5
Masonhill Rd KA7 239 D6
Mason La ML1 163 E6
Mason St
Larkhall ML9 185 C2
Motherwell ML1 163 E6
Masterton St G21 97 C3
Masterton Way G71 121 B1
Mather Terr FK2 42 F4
Matherton Ave G77 157 B5
Matheson Wlk G83 27 E7
Mathew Smith Ave KA1 227 E6
Mathie Cres PA19 44 E6
Mathieson Cres G33 99 F5
Mathieson Rd G73 118 C1
Mathieson St PA1 114 B5
Mathieson Terr 6 G5 117 D4
Mathieson Wlk G83 27 F8
Matilda Rd G41 116 E4
Matthew McWhirter Pl ML9 185 B4
Matthew Pl KA13 207 E5
Matyr's Sch★ G4 241 C3
Mauchline G74 160 E3
Mauchline Ave G66 59 A2
Mauchline Ct
Hamilton ML3 161 D2
Kilmarnock KA3 223 B6
Kirkintilloch G66 59 A2
Mauchline La PA16 44 E3
Mauchline Rd KA1 228 F6
Mauchline St G5 117 A4
Mauchline Terr PA16 44 E3
Maukinfauld Ct G32 118 D3
Maukinfauld Gdns G31 118 E4
Maukinfauld Rd G32 118 E3
Mauldslie Dr ML8 187 A6
Mauldslie Pl ML9 199 F8
Mauldslie Rd ML8 187 B2
Mauldslie St
Bellshill ML4 142 A4
Coatbridge ML5 122 A5
Glasgow G40 118 B4
Maule Dr G11 96 A2
Maunsheugh Rd KA3 213 A3
Maurice Ave FK7 7 D4
Mausoleum Dr ML3 162 F5
Mavis Bank
Bishopbriggs G64 97 F8
6 Hamilton G72 161 C7
Mavisbank Ave FK1 66 C6
Mavisbank Gdns
Bellshill ML4 142 A6
Glasgow G5 240 A1
Glasgow G51 116 E6
Mavisbank Rd G51 116 D6
Mavisbank Specl Sch ML6 122 F8
Mavisbank St
Airdrie ML6 122 E8
Wishaw ML2 166 C5
Mavisbank Terr
Johnstone PA5 111 F2
Paisley PA1 113 F3
Mavis Rd PA16 45 B4
Mavor Ave G74 160 A4
Mavor Rdbt G74 159 F4
Maxholm Rd KA1 227 E5
Maxton Ave G78 134 A3
Maxton Cres
Alva FK12 5 C7
Wishaw ML2 165 C6
Maxton Gr G78 134 A3
Maxton Terr G72 138 F3
Maxwell Ave
Bearsden G61 75 E1
Glasgow G69 120 A5
Glasgow, Pollokshields G41 116 F4
Maxwell Cres G72 161 D6
Maxwell Ct
Beith KA15 171 A7
Coatbridge ML5 122 A7
Kilmarnock KA3 223 D3
Maxwell Dr
East Kilbride G74 160 A2
Erskine PA8 72 F3
Glasgow, Garrowhill G69 120 A5
Glasgow, Pollokshields G41 116 C4
Glasgow, Pollokshields G41 116 E4
Maxwell Gdns
Glasgow G41 116 D4
Hurlford KA1 228 E6
Maxwell Gn KA11 220 A4
Maxwell Gr G41 116 D4
Maxwell La G41 116 E4
Maxwell Oval 1 G41 116 F4
Maxwell Park Sta G41 116 D2
Maxwell Path 10 ML9 185 C2
Maxwell Pl
Bridge of Weir PA11 110 D8
Coatbridge ML5 121 F5
Glasgow G41 117 A3
Kilsyth G65 36 D1
Stevenston KA20 206 E2
6 Stirling FK8 7 B8
Uddingston G71 141 A6
Maxwell Rd
Bishopton PA7 72 B3
Glasgow G41 116 F4
Maxwell St
Clydebank G81 73 F4
Glasgow G2 241 A1
Glasgow, Muirhead G69 120 B4
4 Paisley PA3 113 E5
Port Glasgow PA14 47 E1
Maxwell Terr G41 116 F4
Maxwellton Ave G74 160 B3
Maxwellton Ct PA2 113 C4
Maxwellton Pl G74 160 B3
Maxwellton Prim Sch G74 160 B3
Maxwellton Rd
East Kilbride G74 160 C4
Paisley PA1 113 B3
Port Glasgow PA14 68 F6
Maxwellton St PA1, PA2 113 C3
Maxwell Twr FK1 42 D3
Maxwelton Rd G33 98 D2
Maxwood Pl KA11 220 A5
Maybank La G42 117 A1
Maybank St G42 117 A1
Mayberry Cres G32 119 D5
Mayberry Gdns G32 119 D5
Mayberry Gr G32 119 D5
Mayberry Pl G72 161 D8
Maybole Cres G77 157 A4
Maybole Dr ML6 123 A4
Maybole Gdns ML3 161 D2
Maybole Gr G77 157 A4
Maybole Pl ML5 122 D3
Maybole Rd
Ayr KA7 239 B3
Port Glasgow PA14 68 F6
Maybole St G53 134 F6
Mayfield Ave G76 157 E7
Mayfield Cres
Howwood PA9 130 F6
Stevenston KA20 206 C1
Mayfield Ct
Howwood PA9 130 F6
Stirling FK7 7 B3
Mayfield Dr
Howwood PA9 130 F6
Longcroft FK4 39 B3
Mayfield Gdns ML8 202 A7
Mayfield Gr KA20 206 C1
Mayfield Mews FK1 41 F4
Mayfield Pl
Carluke ML8 202 A7
Coatbridge ML5 122 A3
Saltcoats KA21 217 A8
Mayfield Prim Sch KA21 206 A2
Mayfield Rd
Hamilton ML3 161 F4
Saltcoats KA21 217 A8
Stevenston KA20 206 C1
Mayfield St
Glasgow G20 96 F5
Stirling FK7 7 B4
May Gdns
Hamilton ML3 162 C5
Wishaw ML2 165 A4
Mayne Ave FK9 2 B6
May Rd PA2 133 E7
May St ML3 162 D5
May Terr
Glasgow G46 137 B8
Glasgow, Merrylee G46 136 C3
Mayville St KA20 206 C1
May Wynd ML3 162 C5
M&D's Scotland's Theme Pk★ ML1 141 E1
Meadow Ave
Hamilton G72 161 D6
Meadow Ave *continued*
Irvine KA12 219 C4
Meadowbank La
Prestwick KA9 236 B7
Uddingston G71 140 E6
Meadowbank Pl G77 156 D5
Meadowbank St G82 49 E4
Meadowburn
Bishopbriggs G64 78 A3
Bishopbriggs G64 78 A4
Meadowburn Ave
Kirkintilloch G66 79 E5
Newton Mearns G77 156 D5
Meadowburn Prim Sch G64 78 A3
Meadowburn Rd ML2 165 C3
Meadow Cl G75 180 A4
Meadow Ct
Carluke ML8 188 C1
Denny FK6 21 D4
Dumbarton G82 49 F5
Meadowfield Pl ML2 166 C6
MEADOWFOOT 190 E5
Meadowfoot Rd KA23 190 D4
Meadowforth Rd FK7 7 C7
Meadow Gn FK10 5 B1
Meadowhead Ave
Irvine KA11 224 G4
Moodiesburn G69 80 F2
Meadowhead Ind Est KA11 224 G4
Meadowhead Rd
Irvine KA11 224 H3
Plains ML6 103 F2
Wishaw ML2 164 C4
Meadowhead Rdbt KA11 224 H2
MEADOWHILL 185 B4
Meadowhill G77 156 D5
Meadowhill St ML9 185 B4
Meadow La
Bothwell G71 141 B2
Renfrew PA4 94 D5
Meadowland Rd FK9 2 A6
Meadowpark KA7 239 A5
Meadowpark Dr KA7 239 B5
Meadow Park Rd KA13 207 C5
Meadowpark St G31 118 B7
Meadow Path ML6 123 D1
Meadow Pk FK12 5 A6
Meadow Pl FK8 2 C1
Meadow Rd
Dumbarton G82 50 A4
Glasgow G11 96 A2
Motherwell ML1 163 F5
Meadow Rise G77 156 C5
Meadows Ave
Erskine PA8 73 C1
Larkhall ML9 185 B3
Meadows Dr PA8 73 C1
Meadowside
Beith KA15 171 A8
Crookedholm KA3 228 E8
Hamilton ML3 183 D6
West Kilbride KA23 190 D5
Meadowside Ave PA5 112 D2
Meadowside Gdns ML6 123 D7
Meadowside Ind Est PA4 94 D6
Meadowside Pl ML6 123 D7
Meadowside Rd G65 59 F8
Meadowside St PA4 94 D5
Meadow St
Coatbridge ML5 122 B4
Falkirk FK1 42 C4
Meadows The
Falkirk, Carronshore FK2 24 B2
Falkirk FK1 42 C4
Helensburgh G84 16 F4
Houston PA6 91 E1
Kilwinning KA13 207 D4
Stirling FK9 2 B3
Meadow View
Cumbernauld G67 62 C4
Kilwinning KA13 207 C5
Plains ML6 104 A3
Meadow Way
Kilwinning KA13 207 D5
Newton Mearns G77 156 D6
Meadowwell St G32 119 B5
Meadow Wlk ML5 122 C6
Meadside Ave PA10 111 A4
Meadside Rd PA10 111 A4
Mealkirk St G81 74 C7
Mealybrae Rd G64 56 D3
MEARNS 156 E3
Mearns Castle High Sch G77 157 A3
Mearnscroft Gdns G77 156 F3
Mearnscroft Rd G77 156 F3
Mearns Ct ML3 183 E7
Mearnskirk Rd G77 156 D2
Mearns Prim Sch G77 156 B3
Mearns Rd
Motherwell ML1 163 C8
Newton Mearns, Mearns G77 156 D1
Newton Mearns, Whitecraigs G77 157 B7
Mearns St
Greenock PA15 45 F4
Greenock PA15 45 F5
Mearns Terr PA15 45 F4
Mearns Way G64 78 D2
Medine Ave KA15 150 B1
Medine Ct KA15 150 B1
Medlar Ct G72 139 F3
Medlar Rd G67 62 D2
Medrox Gdns G67 81 F5
Medwin Ct G75 179 E7
Medwin Gdns G75 179 E7
Medwin St G72 139 E5
Medwyn Pl FK10 9 F6
Medwyn St
Glasgow G14 95 D3
Glasgow G14 95 E2
Meek Pl G72 139 B5
Meeks Rd FK2 42 B5
Meetinghouse La 5 PA1 113 E5
Megan Gate G40 117 F4
Megan St G40 117 F4
Meigle Rd ML6 122 F5
Meikelaught Pl KA21 205 F3
Meikle Ave PA4 94 C2
Meikle Bin Brae G66 57 F7
Meikle Cres
Greengairs ML6 103 D8
Hamilton ML3 183 C7
Meikle Ct KA3 195 E1
Meikle Cutstraw Farm KA3 211 F8
Meikle Drumgray Rd ML6 103 E8
MEIKLE EARNOCK 183 A7
Meikle Earnock Rd ML3 183 B7
Meiklehill Ave 4 G66 58 E1
Meiklehill Rd G66 58 E1
Meikle Pl KA11 220 B6
Meikle Rd G53 135 C8
Meiklerig Cres G53 115 C2
MEIKLERIGGS 113 B2
Meikleriggs Dr PA2 113 A1
Meiklewood Ave KA9 233 D1
Meiklewood Bsns Ctr KA3 223 D8
Meiklewood Rd
Glasgow G51 115 D6
Kilmarnock KA3 222 F5
Melbourne Ave
Clydebank G81 73 D5
East Kilbride G75 180 C8
Melbourne Ct G46 136 D3
Melbourne Gn 5 G75 180 C8
Melbourne Rd KA21 216 E7
Melbourne St G31 117 F6
Melbourne Terr KA21 216 E7
Meldon Pl G51 115 D7
Meldrum Gdns G41 116 D2
Meldrum Mains ML6 102 E4
Meldrum St G81 94 D8
Melford Ave
Glasgow G46 136 D2
Kirkintilloch G66 79 B8
Shotts ML7 147 B3
Melford Rd ML4 141 E7
Melford Way PA3 114 B7
Melfort Ave
Clydebank G81 74 C3
Glasgow G41 116 B4
Melfort Ct G81 74 C2
Melfort Dr FK7 7 C4
Melfort Est PA10 111 C1
Melfort Gdns
Clydebank G81 74 C2
Johnstone PA10 111 C1
Melfort Path ML2 165 F7
Melfort Quadrant ML1 143 D3
Melfort Rd ML3 161 E2
Mellerstain Dr G14 94 F6
Mellerstain Gr G14 94 F6
Mellock Gdns FK1 41 E2
Melness Pl 2 G51 115 D7
Melrose Ave
Chapelhall ML6 123 D2
Coatbridge G69 120 F6
Linwood PA3 112 B5
Motherwell ML1 143 B6
Paisley PA2 113 A1
Rutherglen G73 138 B7
Melrose Cres ML2 165 A5
Melrose Ct
7 Greenock PA15 46 B3
Rutherglen G73 138 B7
Melrose Gdns
Glasgow G20 96 F3
Twechar G65 59 F4
Uddingston G71 120 F1
Melrose Pl
Blantyre G72 140 C1
Coatbridge ML5 121 F7
9 Falkirk FK1 42 B4
Larkhall ML9 185 A1
Melrose Rd
Cumbernauld G67 82 E7
Port Glasgow PA14 68 F7
Melrose St
6 Glasgow G4 97 A2
Hamilton ML3 162 B5
Melrose Terr
East Kilbride G74 159 F3
Hamilton ML3 162 B6
Melvaig Pl G20 96 D5
Melvick Pl 3 G51 115 D7
Melville Cres ML1 163 F6
Melville Ct G1 241 A1
Melville Dr ML1 163 E6
Melville Gdns G64 78 A2
Melville La FK1 42 B5
Melville Pk G74 160 B3
Melville Pl
Bridge of Allan FK9 2 A7
Carluke ML8 187 E2
Melville St
Falkirk FK1 42 B5
Glasgow G41 116 F3
Kilmarnock KA3 228 B8
Melville Terr FK8 7 B6
Melvinhall Rd ML11 215 A5
Memel St G21 97 E5
Memorial Way ML1 143 C6
Memus Ave G52 115 C4
Mendip La G75 180 A4
Mennock Ct ML3 161 E2
Mennock Dr G64 78 A4
Mennock La KA10 229 G5
Mennock St ML1 144 C2
Menock Rd G44 137 D6
MENSTRIE 3 E6
Menstrie Bsns Ctr FK11 3 F6
Menstrie Castle★ FK11 3 F6
Menstrie Pl FK10 4 A6
Menstrie Prim Sch FK11 4 A6
Menstrie Rd FK10 4 C3
Menteith Ave G64 78 B1
Menteith Ct
Alloa FK10 10 C6
Motherwell ML1 163 F6
Menteith Dr G73 138 D2
Menteith Gdns G61 75 C8
Menteith Loan ML1 143 A5
Menteith Pl G73 138 D2
Menteith Rd
Motherwell ML1 163 E7
Stirling FK9 2 A3
Menzies Dr
Glasgow G21 98 B5
Stirling FK8 2 A2
Menzies Pl G21 98 B5
Menzies Rd G21 98 A5
Mercat Wynd 2 FK10 10 B6
Merchant La G1 241 A1
Merchants Cl PA10 111 A3
Merchiston Ave
Falkirk FK2 42 A7
Linwood PA3 111 F5
Merchiston Dr PA5 111 D5
Merchiston Gdns FK2 42 A6
Merchiston Ind Est FK2 42 C8
Merchiston Rd
Falkirk, Grahamston FK2 42 A6
Falkirk, Mungal FK2 42 A7
Merchiston Rdbt FK2 42 A6
Merchiston St G32 118 F7
Merchiston Terr FK2 42 A7
Mercury La PA16 44 D3
Mere Ct G68 61 D6
Meredith Dr FK5 23 F3
Merino Rd PA15 45 E3
Merkins Ave G82 50 B6
MERKLAND 58 F1
Merkland Ct
Glasgow G11 96 B1
Kirkintilloch G66 59 A1
Merkland Dr
Falkirk FK1 42 E1
Kirkintilloch G66 80 A8
Merkland Pk KA2 225 F1
Merkland Pl
Dundonald KA2 225 F1
Kirkintilloch G66 59 A1
Merkland Rd
Ayr KA7 239 A2
Coatbridge ML5 101 C2
Merkland Sch G66 58 F1
Merkland St G11 96 B2
Merkland Way G75 180 C4
Merksworth Ave KA24 191 C7
Merksworth Way PA3 113 E7
Merlewood Ave G71 141 B4
Merlewood Rd KA23 190 B4
Merlin Ave
Bellshill ML4 142 A8
Greenock PA16 45 B6
Merlinford Ave PA4 94 E3
Merlinford Cres PA4 94 E3
Merlinford Dr PA4 94 E3
Merlinford Way PA4 94 E3
Merlin La PA16 45 A6
Merlin Way PA3 114 B7
Merrick Ave
Prestwick KA9 233 D1
Troon KA10 229 G4
Merrick Ct ML6 103 A2
Merrick Gdns
Bearsden G61 75 C7
Glasgow G51 116 B5
Quarter ML3 183 E3
Merrick Path G51 116 B5
Merrick Pl
Irvine KA11 220 B2
Symington KA1 231 D4
Merrick Rd KA1 228 B4
Merrick Terr G71 141 B7
Merrick View KA3 195 E1
Merrick Way G73 138 B3
Merryburn Ave G46 136 D4
Merrycrest Ave G46 136 D4
Merrycroft Ave G46 136 D4
Merry Ct G72 161 E6
Merryflats G65 59 F4
Merrygreen Pl KA3 195 E1
Merryland Pl G51 116 C7
Merryland St
Glasgow G51 116 B7
Glasgow G51 116 C7
MERRYLEE 136 D4
Merrylee Ave PA14 68 E7
Merrylee Cres G46 136 C5
Merrylee Park Ave G46 136 D4
Merrylee Park Mews G46 136 C5
Merrylee Prim Sch G44 136 F6
Merrylee Rd G44 136 E5
Merrylees Rd G72 161 C7
Merry St ML1 163 F7
Meryston Ct ML5 121 E6

Merrystone St ML5 121 F7
Merryton Ave
Clydebank G15 75 B3
Glasgow, Merrylee G46 136 D4
Merryton Gdns 3 G15 75 B3
Merryton Rd
Larkhall ML9 184 F6
Motherwell ML1 164 C2
Merryton St ML9 184 F5
Merryton Sta ML9 184 F5
Merryton Twr ML1 164 B2
Merryvale Ave G46 136 D4
Merryvale Pl G46 136 D5
Merryvale Rd KA12 219 C1
Merryvale Rdbt KA12 219 C1
Merton Dr G52 115 A5
Merville Cres FK1 66 F5
Merville Terr FK1 66 F5
Meryon Gdns G32 119 D2
Meryon Rd G32 119 D3
Metcalfe Pl KA11 224 H6
Methil Rd PA14 68 F6
Methil St G14 95 C3
Methil Way G72 161 D2
Methlan Park Gdns G82 49 D2
Methlan Pk G82 49 E2
Methlick Ave ML6 122 E4
Methuen Rd
Paisley PA3 113 F8
Renfrew PA3 93 F1
Methven Ave
Bearsden G61 76 B5
Kilmarnock KA1 227 F4
Methven Pl
East Kilbride G74 159 C2
Kilmarnock KA1 227 F4
Methven Rd G46 157 A7
Methven St
Clydebank G81 73 F4
Glasgow G31 118 D4
Methven Terr ML5 102 B1
Metropole La G1 241 A1
Mews Ho KA7 238 E8
Mews La
Ayr KA7 238 E8
Greenock PA16 45 C8
Kilmarnock KA1 227 E7
Paisley PA3 113 F7
Mey Ct G77 156 A4
Mey Pl G77 156 A4
Mharie Pl G83 27 F2
Michael McParland Dr
G64 78 B8
Michael Terr ML6 123 D1
Micklehouse Oval 2
G69 120 B6
Micklehouse Pl 1 G69 120 B6
Micklehouse Rd G69 120 B6
Micklehouse Wynd 3
G69 120 B6
Midas Pl ML4 142 E5
MID AUCHINLECK 68 E7
Mid Ave PA14 68 F8
Mid Barrwood Rd G65 60 F8
Mid Carbarns ML2 164 D1
Midcroft G64 77 E3
Midcroft Ave G44 137 E5
MIDDLEFIELD 42 D6
Middlefield G75 180 E5
Middlefield Ind Est FK2 42 D7
Middlefield Rd FK2 42 D6
Middlefield Residential Sch
G11 96 B2
Middlehouse Ct ML8 187 D2
Middlemass Ct FK2 42 B6
Middlemass Dr KA1 228 B8
Middlemuir Ave G66 79 D5
Middlemuir Rd
Kirkintilloch G66 79 D6
Stirling FK7 7 C6
Middlepart KA20 206 C2
Middlepart Cres KA21 206 A1
Middlepenny Pl PA14 70 B7
Middlepenny Rd PA14 70 B7
Middlerigg Rd G68 61 D2
Middlesex Gdns 3 G41 116 E6
Middlesex St G41 116 E5
Middleton FK11 4 A5
Middleton Ave ML9 199 B8
Middleton Dr
Helensburgh G84 25 B8
Milngavie G62 55 C2
Middleton La G84 25 B8
Middleton Pk KA11 220 A4
Middleton Pl G68 60 F2
Middleton Rd
Irvine KA11 220 A4
Linwood PA3 112 D7
Paisley PA3 113 B6
Middleton St
Alexandria G83 27 D5
Glasgow G51 116 C6
Middle Ward St G81 74 D7
Mid Dykes Rd KA21 205 E2
Midfaulds Ave PA4 94 E2
Midland Craft Ctr KA3 213 C2
Midland St G1 240 C2
Midlem Dr G52 115 C5
Midlem Oval G52 115 C5
Mid-Loan St ML8 201 E4
Midlock St G51 116 C6
Midlothian Dr G41 116 D1
Mid Pk G75 180 E8
Mid Rd
Beith KA15 150 B1
Cumbernauld G67 82 F6
Eaglesham G76 178 E4
Mid Rig KA11 220 A4
Midthorn Cres FK2 42 E5
MIDTON 44 D6
Midton Ave KA9 236 B8
Midton Cres 10 G69 81 A3
Midton Rd
Ayr KA7 238 F6
Howwood PA9 131 B6
Kilmarnock KA1 227 F2
Prestwick KA9 236 C8
Midton St G21 97 F3
Midtown FK11 3 F7
Mid-Wharf St G4 97 C2
Migvie Pl G20 96 D5
Milford G75 180 B7
Milford Ct G33 119 A8
Milford St G33 119 A8
Milgarholm Ave KA12 219 D1
Milgarholm Rdbt KA12 219 D1
Millands Ave G72 140 C2
Millarbank St G21 97 E4
Millard Ave ML1 143 B2
Millar Gr ML3 162 B3
Millar Pl
5 Bishopbriggs G64 98 D8
Bonnybridge FK4 40 B3
Stenhousemuir FK2 24 A5
Stirling FK8 2 C1
Millar Rd KA21 217 A8
Millars Pl G66 79 D4
Millar St
Greenock PA15 46 B2
Paisley PA1 113 F5
Stonehouse ML9 198 F2
MILLARSTON 113 A3
Millarston Ave PA1 113 A4
Millarston Dr PA1 113 A4
Millarston Ind Est PA1 113 A3
Millars Wynd FK10 5 C2
Millar Terr 2 G73 118 B1
Mill Ave KA3 222 C7
Millbank Ave ML4 142 C3
Millbank Ct ML5 121 F3
Millbank Rd
Port Glasgow PA14 68 C8
Wishaw ML2 164 F1
Millbank Row KA11 220 D1
Millbarr Gr KA15 171 F4
Millbeg Cres G33 119 F5
Millbeg Pl G33 119 F5
Mill Brae
Ayr KA7 239 A7
Bridge of Weir PA11 110 D8
Millbrae Ave G69 100 D8
Millbrae Cres
Clydebank G81 94 D7
Glasgow G42 136 F7
Millbrae Ct
Ayr KA7 239 A7
Glasgow G42 136 F7
Mill Brae Ct ML5 121 D5
Millbrae Gdns G42 136 F7
Millbrae Rd G42 136 F7
Millbrix Ave G14 95 A5
Millbrook G74 159 B1
Millbrook Pl FK11 3 F6
Millburn Ave
Clydebank G81 94 E8
Renfrew PA4 94 E3
Rutherglen G73 138 A6
Millburn Cres G82 50 B3
Millburn Ct G75 179 E7
Millburn Dr
Kilmacolm PA13 89 B8
Renfrew PA4 94 E3
Millburn Gate ML9 185 F1
Millburn Gdns G75 179 E7
Millburn La ML9 185 C2
Millburn Pl ML9 199 B8
Millburn Rd
Alexandria G83 27 D3
Ashgill ML9 186 A1
Dumbarton G82 50 B3
Port Glasgow PA14 68 C8
Renfrew PA4 94 D3
Millburn St
Falkirk FK2 42 D5
Glasgow G21 98 A1
Lennoxtown G66 57 E8
Motherwell ML1 163 E7
Millburn Terr KA11 220 A6
Millburn Way
East Kilbride G75 179 E7
Renfrew PA4 94 E3
Mill Cres
Glasgow G40 117 F4
Irvine KA12 219 E3
Torrance G64 57 C1
Millcroft Rd
Cumbernauld, Carbrain
G67 62 B1
Cumbernauld G67 82 E4
Rutherglen G73 117 F2
Mill Ct
Falkirk FK2 24 B3
Hamilton ML3 162 C2
Kilbirnie KA25 149 B1
Kilmarnock KA1 228 A7
Rutherglen G73 138 A8
Milldam Rd G81 74 C7
Milldown Pl KA11 220 C2
Milledge ML8 188 A2
Millennium Ct G34 120 C8
Millennium Gdns G34 120 C7
Millennium Gr 1 G34 120 C8
Millennium Wheel Dr FK1 41 A5
Miller Cl G64 98 D8
Miller Ct G82 50 B4
Miller Dr G64 98 D8
Millerfield Pl
Glasgow G40 118 B3
Hamilton ML3 162 F3
Millerfield Rd G40 118 B3
Miller Gdns
Bishopbriggs G64 98 D8
Hamilton ML3 162 F3
Miller La G81 74 B1
Miller Pl
Airth FK2 14 E4
Ardrossan KA22 205 B4
Harthill ML7 127 F6
Miller Prim Sch G45 137 F2
Miller Rd
Ayr KA7 238 F7
Balloch G83 27 F8
Millerslea G82 50 F1
Millerslea Gdns G84 16 F1
MILLERSNEUK 79 F5
Millersneuk Ave G66 79 D5
Millersneuk Cres G33 99 B5
Millersneuk Ct G66 79 D4
Millersneuk Dr G66 79 D4
Millersneuk Prim Sch
G66 79 E4
Millersneuk Rd G66 79 D4
Miller's Pl ML6 123 B7
Miller Sq KA9 233 C2
Miller St
Carluke ML8 188 A2
Clydebank G81 74 B1
Coatbridge ML5 122 B5
Dumbarton G82 50 B4
Glasgow G1 241 A2
Glasgow, Muirhead G69 120 B4
Hamilton ML3 162 F3
Harthill ML7 127 E6
Johnstone PA5 112 B3
Larkhall ML9 185 B3
Wishaw ML2 165 A3
MILLERSTON
Busby 157 E4
Stepps 99 A4
Millerston St G31 118 B6
Miller Wlk G64 98 D8
Mill Farm KA22 205 D5
Millfield Ave
Erskine PA8 72 F1
Motherwell ML1 163 F8
Millfield Cres PA8 73 A1
Millfield Dr PA8 73 A1
Millfield Gdns PA8 73 A1
Millfield Hill PA8 72 F1
Millfield La PA8 72 F1
Millfield Mdws PA8 72 F1
Millfield Pl PA8 72 F1
Millfield View PA8 72 F1
Millfield Wlk PA8 73 A1
Millfield Wynd PA8 72 F1
Millflats St FK2 24 A1
Millford Dr PA3 112 B5
Millfore Ct KA11 220 A3
Millgate G71 140 F8
Millgate Ave G71 140 F8
Millgate Cres ML6 105 A4
Millgate Ct G71 140 F7
Millgate Rd ML3 162 C1
Millgate Terr ML3 162 C1
Millglen Cvn Pk KA22 205 C6
Millglen Pl KA22 205 D4
Millglen Rd KA22 205 D4
Mill Gr
Cambuslang G72 139 D5
Hamilton ML3 162 C2
Millhall Ct ML6 104 B3
Millhall Rd
Eaglesham G76 179 C3
Stirling FK7 7 D5
MILLHEUGH 184 F2
Millheugh ML9 184 E2
Millheugh Brae ML9 184 E2
Millheugh Pl G72 161 C6
Millheugh Rd ML3 198 E5
Mill Hill FK7 6 D6
Millhill Ave KA3 222 C7
Millhill Rd KA20 206 D1
Millhill Terr KA3 222 E4
Millholm Rd G44 137 B4
Millhouse Cres G20 96 C7
Millhouse Dr G20 96 C7
Millichen Rd G23 76 E5
Millig St G84 16 C3
Milliken Dr PA10 111 C2
MILLIKENPARK 111 C1
Milliken Park Rd PA10 111 C1
Milliken Park Sta PA5 131 C8
Milliken Rd PA10 111 C2
Mill La G84 16 A3
Mill Loan ML6 123 A8
Mill of Airthrey Ct FK9 1 F8
Mill of Gryffe Rd PA11 110 D8
MILL OF HALDANE 28 A8
Mill Pk
Dalry KA24 191 D8
Hamilton ML3 162 C2
Mill Pl
Linwood PA3 112 A6
Uddingston G71 140 F6
Millport Ave G44 137 C7
Millport Rd PA14 68 F6
Mill Rd
Airdrie ML6 103 A1
Alloa FK10 10 B6
Banton G65 37 D3
Bothwell G71 141 A1
Cambusbarron FK7 6 D6
Cambuslang G72 139 D5
Cardross G82 26 A1
Mill Rd *continued*
Carluke ML8 187 E1
Clydebank G81 94 D7
Falkirk FK2 24 B3
Hamilton ML3 162 C1
Harthill ML7 127 F5
Hartwood ML7 145 F1
Irvine KA12 219 E2
Kilbirnie KA25 149 B1
Motherwell ML1 163 F8
Queenzieburn G65 59 E7
Shotts ML7 166 F8
Wattston ML6 83 B1
Wishaw ML2 166 E5
Mill Rig G75 180 D5
Mill Rise G66 79 D4
Millroad Dr G40 241 C1
Millroad Gdns 2 G40 117 F6
Millroad St G40 117 F6
Millrock Ct KA10 229 D3
Millside Gdns KA13 207 F4
Mill St
Alloa FK10 10 B6
Ayr KA7 239 A8
Caldercruix ML6 104 F5
Glasgow G40 117 F3
Greenock PA15 45 E4
Kilmarnock KA1 227 F7
Paisley PA1 113 F4
Rutherglen G73 138 A6
Millstream Cres ML6 105 A4
Millstream Ct PA1 113 F4
Mill Street Ind Est ML6 123 A8
Mill Trail Visitor Ctr★ FK12 4 F7
Mill Vennel PA4 94 D3
Millview G78 134 D3
Millview Mdws G78 154 C7
Millview Pl G53 135 B4
Millview Terr G78 154 C7
Mill Waulk KA3 211 E8
Mill Way G66 80 A7
Mill Wlk G72 139 D5
Millwood St G41 136 E8
Mill Wynd
Ayr KA7 238 F8
Waterside KA3 213 F3
Milnbank St G31 118 A8
Milncroft Pl G33 99 A1
Milncroft Rd G33 99 A1
Milndavie Cres G63 31 C3
Milndavie Rd G63 31 C2
Milne Ct ML2 165 E4
Milne Park Rd FK7 11 E8
Milner Rd G13 95 E5
Milne Way G71 141 A6
MILNGAVIE 55 C3
Milngavie Ent Ctr G62 55 A2
Milngavie Prim Sch G62 55 A2
Milngavie Rd
Bearsden G61 76 A6
Strathblane G63 31 C2
Milngavie Sta G62 55 B1
Milnpark Gdns 1 G41 116 E5
Milnpark St G41 116 E5
Milnquarter Rd FK4 40 A3
MILNWOOD 142 D4
Milnwood Dr
Bellshill ML4 142 D4
Motherwell ML1 142 C2
Milovaig Ave G23 76 D1
Milovaig St G23 76 D1
Milrig Rd G73 137 F7
Milroy Gdns ML4 142 A8
MILTON
Dumbarton 50 F2
Glasgow 97 C7
Milton Ave
Cambuslang G72 138 E5
Kilmarnock KA3 223 C1
Miltonbank Prim Sch G22 97 C8
Milton Brae
Milton G82 50 F2
Stirling FK7 7 B2
Milton Cl FK6 21 D3
Milton Cres
Bannockburn FK7 7 C1
Carluke ML8 187 F1
Irvine KA11 220 C1
Troon KA10 229 F6
Milton Ct
Airdrie ML6 123 A8
Irvine KA11 220 D1
Milton G82 50 F2
Milton Douglas Rd G81 74 B5
Milton Dr
1 Bishopbriggs G64 97 F7
Kilmarnock KA3 223 C1
Milton Est G83 27 F6
Milton Gdns
Stirling FK7 7 B1
Uddingston G71 140 E8
Milton Gr FK7 7 C1
Milton Hill G82 50 F1
Milton Mains Rd G81 74 A5
MILTON OF CAMPSIE 58 D6
Milton Pk
Ayr KA7 239 B3
Kilbirnie KA25 149 B2
Milton Pl FK6 21 D3
Milton Quadrant KA25 149 A3
Milton Rd
Bannockburn FK7 7 C1
Carluke ML8 201 D7
East Kilbride G74 159 A2
Irvine KA11 220 C1
Kilbirnie KA25 149 A3
Kilmarnock KA3 228 C8
Kilmarnock KA3 228 D8
Milton Rd *continued*
Kirkintilloch G66 58 C1
Lennoxtown G66 57 E7
Port Glasgow PA14 68 E6
Milton Row FK6 21 E3
Milton Sch G22 97 E7
Milton St
Airdrie ML6 123 A8
Carluke ML8 187 E2
Glasgow G4 241 A4
Hamilton ML3 162 A4
Motherwell ML1 163 E8
Milton Terr
Hamilton ML3 162 A5
Stirling FK7 7 B1
Milton View KA2 226 E5
Milverton Ave G61 75 D6
Milverton Rd
Glasgow G46 136 B1
Rutherglen G46 157 A8
Mimosa Rd PA11 110 D8
Minard Rd
Glasgow G41 116 E1
Port Glasgow PA14 68 E7
Shotts ML7 146 D6
Minard Way G71 141 A7
Mincher Cres ML1 163 E4
Minch Way ML6 123 D5
Minella Gdns ML4 142 A8
Mine Rd FK9 2 A8
Minerva Ct 10 G3 116 E8
Minerva La PA16 44 D3
Minerva St G3 116 E8
Minerva Terr PA16 44 D3
Minerva Way G3 116 E8
Mingarry St G20 96 E4
Mingulay Cres G22 97 D8
Mingulay Pl G22 97 E8
Mingulay St G22 97 D8
Ministers Pk G74 158 F4
Minmoir Rd G53 134 F7
Minster Wlk G69 120 F5
Minstrel Rd G13 75 D1
Minthill Pl ML7 127 D5
Mintlaw Way G69 80 C1
Minto Ave G73 138 D4
Minto Cres G52 115 F5
Minto Ct FK12 5 B6
Minto Gdns FK12 5 B6
Minto Pk ML2 165 C6
Minto St
Glasgow G52 115 F5
Greenock PA16 45 D4
Mireton St G22 97 B5
Mirin Dr PA3 113 E7
Mirren Dr G81 73 F7
Mirren's Shore PA14 47 C2
Mirrin Wynd PA3 113 E7
Mirrlees Dr G12 96 C4
Mirrlees La G12 96 C4
Misk Knowes KA20 217 E6
Misk Rd KA20 218 C6
Mission Gdns ML2 165 C5
Mission La 8 FK1 42 B4
Mission Pl ML1 163 E8
Mitchell Arc G73 138 B8
Mitchell Ave
Cambuslang G72 139 E6
Renfrew PA4 94 B2
Mitchell Cres FK10 9 F7
Mitchell Ct
East Kilbride G74 159 C2
3 Kilmarnock KA1 228 A8
Mitchell Dr
Cardross G82 48 B6
Milngavie G62 55 C1
Rutherglen G73 138 B6
Mitchell Gr G74 159 C2
Mitchell Hill Rd G45 137 F2
Mitchell La G1 240 C2
Mitchell Liby★ G3 240 C3
Mitchell Pl
Falkirk FK1 41 E1
Saltcoats KA21 205 E1
Mitchell Rd G67 62 A3
Mitchell St
Airdrie ML6 122 F8
Beith KA15 150 B1
Coatbridge ML5 121 C5
Glasgow G1 240 C2
Greenock PA15 46 F2
Mitchell Way G83 27 E5
Mitchison Rd G67 62 A3
Mitre Ct 2 G11 95 F4
Mitre Gate 1 G11 95 F4
Mitre La G14 95 E4
Mitre Lane W G14 95 D4
Mitre Rd
Glasgow G11 95 F4
Glasgow G14 95 E4
Moat Ave G13 95 C7
Mochray Ct FK4 39 E5
Mochrum Ct KA9 236 D6
Mochrum Rd G43 136 E6
Modan Rd FK7 7 A3
Moffat Ave FK2 24 C3
Moffat Ct G75 179 E7
Moffat Gdns G75 179 E7
Moffathill ML6 123 E5
MOFFAT MILLS 123 F6
Moffat Pl
Airdrie ML6 123 F8
Blantyre G72 140 D1
Bonnybridge FK4 40 A4
Coatbridge ML5 122 E4

Moffat Pl *continued*
East Kilbride G75 . . . . 179 E7
Moffat Rd
Airdrie ML6 . . . . 123 F7
Prestwick KA9 . . . . 233 C3
Moffat St
Glasgow G5 . . . . 117 D4
Greenock PA15 . . . . 46 C3
Moffat View ML6 . . . . 104 A3
Moffat Wynd KA21 . . . . 205 F3
Mogarth Ave PA2 . . . . 132 F8
Moidart Ave PA4 . . . . 94 B4
Moidart Cres G52 . . . . 115 F5
Moidart Ct G78 . . . . 134 B4
Moidart Gdns
Kirkintilloch G66 . . . . 59 B1
Newton Mearns G77 . . . . 156 E6
Moidart Pl G52 . . . . 115 F5
Moidart Rd
Glasgow G52 . . . . 115 E5
Port Glasgow PA14 . . . . 68 E7
Moir St
Alloa FK10 . . . . 10 A8
Glasgow G1 . . . . 241 B1
Molendinar St G1 . . . . 241 B1
Molendinar Terr G78 . . . . 154 C6
Mollanbowie Rd G83 . . . . 19 F2
MOLLINSBURN 81 D4
Mollinsburn Rd
Annathill G67, ML5 . . . . 81 F2
Glenboig ML5, ML6 . . . . 101 F8
Glenmavis ML6 . . . . 102 C6
Mollinsburn St G21 . . . . 97 E3
Mollins Ct G68 . . . . 81 D5
Mollins Rd G68 . . . . 81 C7
Mollison Ave ML7 . . . . 127 E6
Monach Gdns KA11 . . . . 225 B8
Monach Rd
Glasgow G33 . . . . 119 C8
Port Glasgow PA14 . . . . 69 A7
Monaebrook Pl G84 . . . . 25 B8
Monar Dr G22 . . . . 97 B3
Monar Pl G22 . . . . 97 B3
Monar St G22 . . . . 97 B3
Monart Pl G20 . . . . 96 F4
Monar Way [5] ML2 . . . . 165 F6
Moncks Rd FK1 . . . . 42 D4
Moncrieff Gdns G66 . . . . 79 D5
Moncrieff Ave G66 . . . . 79 D5
Moncrieffe Rd ML6 . . . . 123 D4
Moncrieff St [1] PA3 . . . . 113 E5
Moncur Ct KA13 . . . . 207 C5
Moncur Rd KA13 . . . . 208 A3
Moncur St G40 . . . . 241 C1
Moness Dr G52 . . . . 115 E4
Money Gr ML1 . . . . 164 B4
Monieburgh Cres G65 . . . . 36 E1
Monieburgh Rd G65 . . . . 36 E1
Monifieth Ave G52 . . . . 115 D3
Monikie Gdns G64 . . . . 78 D1
Monkcastle Dr G72 . . . . 139 A6
Monkland Ave G66 . . . . 79 D6
Monklands KA10 . . . . 229 G7
Monklands Hospl ML6 . . . . 122 D7
Monklands Ind Est ML5 . . . . 121 F2
Monkland St ML6 . . . . 123 B7
Monkland Terr ML5 . . . . 101 D6
Monkland View
Calderbank ML6 . . . . 123 B2
Uddingston G71 . . . . 121 A1
Monkland View Cres
G69 . . . . 121 A5
Monkreddan Cres KA13 . . . . 207 C5
Monksbridge Ave G13 . . . . 75 D1
Monkscourt Ave ML6 . . . . 122 E7
Monkscroft Ave [1] G11 . . . . 96 A3
Monkscroft Ct G11 . . . . 96 A2
Monkscroft Gdns G11 . . . . 96 A2
Monks La ML8 . . . . 201 E4
Monks Rd ML6 . . . . 123 C4
MONKTON 233 D4
Monkton Brae G69 . . . . 80 C1
Monkton Cres ML5 . . . . 121 E4
Monkton Ct KA9 . . . . 233 D2
Monkton Dr G15 . . . . 75 C2
Monkton Gdns G77 . . . . 157 A4
Monktonhill Rd
Monkton KA9 . . . . 233 B7
Troon KA10 . . . . 232 F8
Monktonhill Rdbt KA9 . . . . 233 D6
Monkton Pl PA14 . . . . 68 F7
Monkton Prim Sch KA9 . . . . 233 D4
Monkton Rd KA9 . . . . 233 C1
Monkwood Pl KA7 . . . . 239 B2
Monmouth Ave G12 . . . . 96 A5
Monreith Ave G61 . . . . 75 D2
Monreith Rd G43 . . . . 136 E6
Monreith Road E G44 . . . . 137 A5
Monroe Dr G71 . . . . 120 F1
Monroe Pl G71 . . . . 120 F1
Montague La G12 . . . . 96 B4
Montague St G4 . . . . 96 F2
Montalto Ave ML1 . . . . 143 B1
Montclair Pl PA3 . . . . 112 B6
Montego Gn [2] G75 . . . . 159 A1
Monteith Dr G76 . . . . 158 A8
Monteith Gdns G76 . . . . 157 F8
Monteith Pl
[3] Glasgow G40 . . . . 117 E5
Hamilton G72 . . . . 161 E8
Monteith Row
Glasgow G1 . . . . 241 B1
Glasgow G40 . . . . 117 E5
Monteith Wlk ML7 . . . . 146 E6
Montfode Ct KA22 . . . . 205 B4
Montfode Dr KA22 . . . . 205 B4
Montford Ave G44 . . . . 137 E7
Montfort Pl FK1 . . . . 42 B3
Montgarrie St [3] G51 . . . . 115 D6
Montgomerie Cres KA21 . . . . 216 E8
Montgomerie Ct KA22 . . . . 205 C1
Montgomerie Dr KA3 . . . . 211 B7
Montgomerie Pier Rd
KA22 . . . . 205 B1
Montgomerie Rd
Prestwick KA9 . . . . 233 B1
Saltcoats KA21 . . . . 216 E8
Montgomerie St
Ardrossan KA22 . . . . 205 C1
Port Glasgow PA14 . . . . 47 D1
Montgomerieston Pl [8]
KA25 . . . . 149 A1
Montgomerieston St [9]
KA25 . . . . 149 A1
Montgomerie Terr
Ayr KA7 . . . . 235 E1
Kilwinning KA13 . . . . 208 A3
Montgomery Ave
Beith KA15 . . . . 171 C8
Coatbridge ML5 . . . . 121 F7
Paisley PA3 . . . . 114 B7
Montgomery Cres
Falkirk FK2 . . . . 24 B2
Wishaw ML2 . . . . 185 E8
Montgomery Ct
Eaglesham G76 . . . . 178 E3
Kilbirnie KA25 . . . . 149 B2
Paisley PA3 . . . . 114 B7
Montgomery Dr
Falkirk FK2 . . . . 24 B2
Glasgow G46 . . . . 136 C1
Kilbarchan PA10 . . . . 111 A4
Montgomeryfield KA11 . . . . 225 B8
Montgomery Pl
[3] East Kilbride G74 . . . . 159 F2
Falkirk FK2 . . . . 24 B2
Irvine KA12 . . . . 219 A1
[1] Kilmarnock KA3 . . . . 222 F2
Larkhall ML9 . . . . 185 B2
Montgomery Rd PA3 . . . . 114 B8
Montgomery Sq G76 . . . . 178 E4
Montgomery St
Cambuslang G72 . . . . 139 E5
Eaglesham G76 . . . . 178 E4
[4] East Kilbride G74 . . . . 159 F2
Falkirk FK2 . . . . 42 E5
Glasgow G40 . . . . 118 A4
Irvine KA12 . . . . 219 A1
Kilmarnock KA3 . . . . 222 F2
Larkhall ML9 . . . . 185 A4
Montgomery Terr G66 . . . . 58 C5
Montgomery Way FK9 . . . . 2 B3
Montgomery Well FK2 . . . . 24 B2
Montgreenan View KA13 . . . . 207 F3
Montport Gate G78 . . . . 134 E3
Montraive St G73 . . . . 118 C1
Montrave St G52 . . . . 115 D4
Montreal Ho G81 . . . . 73 D6
Montreal Pk G75 . . . . 159 C1
Montrose Ave
Glasgow, Carmyle G32 . . . . 119 C1
Glasgow G52 . . . . 114 E8
Glasgow G52 . . . . 114 F8
Glasgow (Hillington Ind Est)
G52 . . . . 94 E1
Port Glasgow PA14 . . . . 68 E6
Montrose Cres ML3 . . . . 162 D4
Montrose Ct
[7] Motherwell ML1 . . . . 143 B2
Paisley PA2 . . . . 132 F8
Montrose Dr G61 . . . . 75 E7
Montrose Gdns
Blantyre G72 . . . . 140 C2
Kilsyth G65 . . . . 36 C1
Milngavie G62 . . . . 55 A3
Montrose La ML3 . . . . 162 C4
Montrose Pl PA3 . . . . 112 A6
Montrose Rd
Paisley PA2 . . . . 132 F8
Stirling FK9 . . . . 2 C4
Montrose St
Clydebank G81 . . . . 74 C2
Glasgow G1 . . . . 241 B2
Motherwell ML1 . . . . 142 D1
Montrose Terr
Bishopbriggs G64 . . . . 98 C7
Bridge of Weir PA11 . . . . 110 D7
Montrose Way
Bonnybridge FK4 . . . . 39 D5
Paisley PA2 . . . . 132 F8
Monument Cres KA9 . . . . 233 F1
Monument Rd KA7 . . . . 238 F4
Monument View FK8 . . . . 2 B2
Monymusk Gdns G64 . . . . 78 D2
Monymusk Pl G15 . . . . 74 F5
Moodie Ct KA1 . . . . 227 F5
MOODIESBURN 80 E2
Moodiesburn St G33 . . . . 98 E2
Moonlight Pl KA22 . . . . 205 B2
Moorburn Ave G46 . . . . 136 B3
Moorburn Pl PA3 . . . . 111 F6
Moorcroft Dr ML6 . . . . 123 E7
Moorcroft Rd G77 . . . . 156 C3
Moore Dr
Bearsden G61 . . . . 75 F3
Helensburgh G84 . . . . 25 C7
Moore Gdns ML3 . . . . 183 E7
Moorend Workshops
KA11 . . . . 224 G7
Moore Pl KA20 . . . . 217 D8
Moore St
Glasgow G31, G40 . . . . 117 F6
Motherwell ML1 . . . . 143 A3
MOORFIELD 227 B8
Moorfield Ave
Kilmarnock KA1 . . . . 227 D6
Port Glasgow PA14 . . . . 68 D7
Moorfield Cres ML6 . . . . 123 F7
Moorfield Ind Est KA2 . . . . 227 A7
Moorfield La PA19 . . . . 44 C6
Moorfield Pl KA2 . . . . 226 D5
Moorfield Rd
Gourock PA19 . . . . 44 C7
Hamilton G72 . . . . 161 C6
Prestwick KA9 . . . . 236 C7
Moorfield Rdbt KA1 . . . . 227 A7
Moorfoot G64 . . . . 78 C2
Moorfoot Ave
Glasgow G46 . . . . 136 A3
Paisley PA2 . . . . 113 D1
Moorfoot Dr
Gourock PA19 . . . . 44 C6
Wishaw ML2 . . . . 164 F3
Moorfoot Gdns G75 . . . . 180 B3
Moorfoot Path PA2 . . . . 133 D8
Moorfoot Pl KA11 . . . . 220 A3
Moorfoot Prim Sch PA19 . . . . 44 C6
Moorfoot St G32 . . . . 118 E6
Moorfoot Way
Bearsden G61 . . . . 75 C8
Irvine KA11 . . . . 220 A3
Moorhill Cres G77 . . . . 156 C4
Moorhill Rd G77 . . . . 156 C3
Moorhouse Ave
Glasgow G13 . . . . 94 F6
Paisley PA2 . . . . 113 B2
Moorhouse St G78 . . . . 134 C2
Moorings The PA2 . . . . 113 C3
Moorland Dr ML6 . . . . 123 E7
Moorlands Wlk G71 . . . . 141 A5
MOORPARK 94 B2
Moorpark Ave
[3] Airdrie ML6 . . . . 123 E7
Glasgow G52 . . . . 114 F6
Muirhead G69 . . . . 100 C7
Moor Park Cres KA9 . . . . 236 C5
Moorpark Ct G51 . . . . 116 A7
Moorpark Dr G52 . . . . 115 A6
Moorpark Ind Est KA20 . . . . 217 D7
Moorpark Pl
[1] Glasgow G52 . . . . 114 F6
Kilbirnie KA25 . . . . 149 A3
Stevenston KA20 . . . . 217 D7
Moor Park Pl KA9 . . . . 236 C5
Moorpark Prim Sch
Kilbirnie KA25 . . . . 149 A3
Renfrew PA4 . . . . 94 B2
Moorpark Road E KA20 . . . . 217 D8
Moorpark Road W KA20 . . . . 217 D7
Moorpark Sq PA4 . . . . 94 B2
Moor Pk KA9 . . . . 236 C5
Moor Pl KA8 . . . . 236 C4
Moor Rd
Ayr KA8 . . . . 236 C4
Cartland ML8, ML11 . . . . 202 E2
Eaglesham G76 . . . . 178 D4
Milngavie G62 . . . . 55 B2
Strathblane G63 . . . . 31 C1
Moorside St ML8 . . . . 188 A2
Morag Ave G72 . . . . 140 C1
Moraine Ave G15 . . . . 75 B1
Moraine Cir G15 . . . . 75 B1
Moraine Dr
Clarkston G76 . . . . 157 D8
Clydebank G15 . . . . 75 B1
Moraine Pl G15 . . . . 75 B1
Morar Ave G81 . . . . 74 B4
Morar Cres
Airdrie ML6 . . . . 102 E2
Bishopbriggs G64 . . . . 77 F2
Bishopton PA7 . . . . 72 C2
Clydebank G81 . . . . 74 B4
Coatbridge ML5 . . . . 101 D1
Morar Ct
Clydebank G81 . . . . 74 B4
Cumbernauld G67 . . . . 82 B8
Hamilton ML3 . . . . 162 A1
Larkhall ML9 . . . . 184 F5
Morar Dr
Bearsden G61 . . . . 76 B3
Clydebank G81 . . . . 74 B4
Cumbernauld G67 . . . . 82 B8
Falkirk FK2 . . . . 24 C1
Linwood PA3 . . . . 112 A5
Paisley PA2 . . . . 113 A2
Rutherglen G73 . . . . 138 B3
Morar Pl
Clydebank G81 . . . . 74 B4
East Kilbride G74 . . . . 159 F3
Irvine KA12 . . . . 219 C6
Newton Mearns G77 . . . . 156 D7
Renfrew PA4 . . . . 94 B4
Morar Rd
Clydebank G81 . . . . 74 B4
Glasgow G52 . . . . 115 E5
Port Glasgow PA14 . . . . 68 E7
Morar St ML2 . . . . 165 A1
Morar Terr
Rutherglen G73 . . . . 138 D4
Uddingston G71 . . . . 141 B7
Morar Way
Motherwell ML1 . . . . 143 C3
Shotts ML7 . . . . 147 B3
Moravia Ave G71 . . . . 141 A3
Moray Ave ML6 . . . . 123 A5
Moray Ct G73 . . . . 138 A8
Moray Dr
Clarkston G76 . . . . 157 F7
Torrance G64 . . . . 57 B1
Moray Gate G71 . . . . 140 F4
Moray Gdns
Clarkston G76 . . . . 157 F8
Cumbernauld G68 . . . . 61 F5
Uddingston G71 . . . . 140 F8
Moray Pl
Bishopbriggs G64 . . . . 78 C1
Chryston G69 . . . . 100 D8
Glasgow G41 . . . . 116 F2
Hamilton G72 . . . . 161 C6
Kirkintilloch G66 . . . . 59 B1
Linwood PA3 . . . . 112 A6
Moray Quadrant ML4 . . . . 142 A5
Moray Rd PA14 . . . . 47 C1
Moray Way ML1 . . . . 143 A5
Mordaunt St G40 . . . . 118 A3
Moredun Cres G32 . . . . 119 C7
Moredun Dr PA2 . . . . 113 B1
Moredun Rd PA2 . . . . 113 B1
Moredun St G32 . . . . 119 C7
Morefield Rd [10] G51 . . . . 115 D7
Morgan Ct FK7 . . . . 7 C3
Morgan Mews [4] G42 . . . . 117 B3
Morgan St
Hamilton ML3 . . . . 162 D2
Larkhall ML9 . . . . 184 F3
Morina Gdns G53 . . . . 135 C3
Morion Rd G13 . . . . 95 D8
Moriston Ct ML2 . . . . 165 F6
Morland G74 . . . . 160 D4
Morley Cres FK7 . . . . 7 A3
Morley St G42 . . . . 137 A7
Morna La G14 . . . . 95 E2
Mornay Way ML7 . . . . 146 D5
MORNINGSIDE 166 C3
Morningside Prim Sch
ML2 . . . . 166 B4
Morningside Rd ML2 . . . . 166 C3
Morningside St G33 . . . . 118 E8
Morrin Path G21 . . . . 97 E3
Morrin St G21 . . . . 97 E4
Morris Cres
Hamilton G72 . . . . 161 D7
Hurlford KA1 . . . . 228 E6
Motherwell ML1 . . . . 143 E1
Morris Ct KA24 . . . . 191 B8
Morrishall Rd G74 . . . . 160 C3
Morrishill Dr KA15 . . . . 171 A7
Morris La KA3 . . . . 223 A1
Morris Moodie Ave KA20 . . . . 217 E7
Morrison Ave
Bonnybridge FK4 . . . . 39 F6
Stevenston KA20 . . . . 206 E1
Morrison Ct KA20 . . . . 206 E1
Morrison Dr
Bannockburn FK7 . . . . 7 C2
Lennoxtown G66 . . . . 57 F7
Morrison Gdns
Ayr KA8 . . . . 239 B8
Torrance G64 . . . . 78 C8
Morrison Ho G67 . . . . 62 A2
Morrison Pl KA3 . . . . 223 D2
Morrison Quadrant G81 . . . . 74 E1
Morrison Rd KA9 . . . . 233 C3
Morrison St
Duntocher G81 . . . . 73 F6
Glasgow G5 . . . . 240 B1
Morris Rd KA9 . . . . 233 D1
Morris St
Greenock PA15 . . . . 46 C3
Hamilton ML3 . . . . 162 D1
Larkhall ML9 . . . . 185 C1
Morris Terr FK8 . . . . 7 A8
Morriston Cres PA4 . . . . 94 F1
Morriston Park Dr G72 . . . . 139 A6
Morriston St G72 . . . . 139 A6
Morton Ave KA7 . . . . 239 A5
Morton Gdns G41 . . . . 116 C1
Morton Pl KA1 . . . . 222 F1
Morton Rd
Ayr KA7 . . . . 239 A5
Stewarton KA3 . . . . 211 C8
Morton St ML1 . . . . 163 E8
Morven Ave
Bishopbriggs G64 . . . . 78 C1
Blantyre G72 . . . . 140 C1
Kilmarnock KA3 . . . . 222 F3
Paisley PA2 . . . . 133 D8
Morven Cres KA10 . . . . 229 E2
Morven Ct FK1 . . . . 42 C2
Morven Dr
Clarkston G76 . . . . 157 D8
Linwood PA3 . . . . 112 A5
Motherwell ML1 . . . . 164 C4
Troon KA10 . . . . 229 E3
Morven Gait PA8 . . . . 93 E8
Morven Gate ML1 . . . . 164 C4
Morven Gdns G71 . . . . 140 F8
Morven La G72 . . . . 140 C1
Morven Rd
Bearsden G61 . . . . 75 E6
Cambuslang G72 . . . . 138 F3
Morven St
Coatbridge ML5 . . . . 122 A8
Glasgow G52 . . . . 115 E5
Morven Way
[1] Bothwell G71 . . . . 141 B3
Kirkintilloch G66 . . . . 80 B8
Morville Cres KA13 . . . . 207 E5
Mosesfield St G21 . . . . 97 F5
Mosque Ave G5 . . . . 117 C5
Mossacre Rd ML2 . . . . 165 C4
Moss Ave
Caldercruix ML6 . . . . 105 A5
Linwood PA3 . . . . 112 B6
Mossband La ML7 . . . . 146 E6
Mossbank
East Kilbride G75 . . . . 179 F8
Hamilton G72 . . . . 161 D6
Mossbank *continued*
Prestwick KA9 . . . . 236 E7
Mossbank Ave G33 . . . . 98 F4
Mossbank Cres ML1 . . . . 143 F4
Mossbank Dr G33 . . . . 98 F4
Mossbank Rd ML2 . . . . 165 C4
Mossbell Rd ML4 . . . . 141 E6
MOSSBLOWN 237 F7
Mossblown St ML9 . . . . 184 F3
Mossburn Ave
Balloch G83 . . . . 19 F1
Harthill ML7 . . . . 127 D5
Mossburn Ind Est ML7 . . . . 127 D5
Mossburn Rd ML2 . . . . 165 D3
Mossburn St ML2 . . . . 165 D1
Mosscastle Rd
Glasgow G33 . . . . 99 C2
Slamannan FK1 . . . . 86 A7
Moss Ct KA1 . . . . 228 F5
Mossdale G74 . . . . 159 C3
Mossdale Ct ML4 . . . . 142 D5
Mossdale Gdns ML3 . . . . 161 E2
Moss Dr
Barrhead G78 . . . . 134 A5
Erskine PA8 . . . . 93 B7
Irvine KA11 . . . . 224 H5
Mossedge Ind Est PA3 . . . . 112 C6
MOSSEND 142 D5
Mossend Ave
Helensburgh G84 . . . . 16 F1
Kilbirnie KA25 . . . . 170 A8
Mossend La G33 . . . . 119 D8
Mossend Pl G84 . . . . 16 F1
Mossend Prim Sch ML4 . . . . 142 C4
Mossend St G33 . . . . 119 D8
Mossgiel G75 . . . . 180 B7
Mossgiel Ave
Cowie FK7 . . . . 12 D7
Kilmarnock KA3 . . . . 228 C8
Rutherglen G73 . . . . 138 A5
Stirling FK8 . . . . 2 A2
Troon KA10 . . . . 229 G4
Mossgiel Cres G76 . . . . 157 F5
Mossgiel Dr
Clydebank G81 . . . . 74 C3
Irvine KA12 . . . . 219 D3
Mossgiel Gdns
Kirkintilloch G66 . . . . 58 F1
Uddingston G71 . . . . 140 E8
Mossgiel La [1] ML9 . . . . 185 C1
Mossgiel Pl
Ayr KA7 . . . . 239 A6
Rutherglen G73 . . . . 138 A5
[1] Stevenston KA20 . . . . 206 E1
Mossgiel Rd
Ardrossan KA22 . . . . 205 D4
Ayr KA7 . . . . 239 A6
Cumbernauld G67 . . . . 62 B2
Glasgow G43 . . . . 136 D6
Saltcoats KA21 . . . . 206 A3
Mossgiel St FK1 . . . . 41 B5
Mossgiel Terr G72 . . . . 140 C2
Mossgiel Way ML1 . . . . 143 C4
Mosshall Gr ML1 . . . . 143 F4
Mosshall Rd ML1 . . . . 143 D7
Mosshall St ML1 . . . . 143 F3
Mosshead Prim Sch G61 . . . . 75 E7
Mosshead Rd
Bearsden G61 . . . . 76 A7
Kilmarnock KA1 . . . . 228 A3
Moss Heights Ave G52 . . . . 115 D5
Mosshill Rd ML4 . . . . 142 B7
Mosshouse FK7 . . . . 6 F4
Mosside Pl KA3 . . . . 222 F4
Mosside Rd KA8 . . . . 236 C4
Mossknowe G67 . . . . 62 C2
Mossland Dr ML2 . . . . 165 C4
Mossland Rd
Glasgow G52 . . . . 114 E8
Glasgow (Hillington Ind Est)
G52 . . . . 94 E1
Mosslands Rd PA3 . . . . 113 E7
Mosslingal G75 . . . . 180 E5
Mossmulloch G75 . . . . 180 E5
MOSSNEUK 179 F7
Mossneuk Ave G75 . . . . 179 E8
Mossneuk Cres ML2 . . . . 165 D4
Mossneuk Dr
East Kilbride G75 . . . . 179 F7
Paisley PA2 . . . . 133 C8
Wishaw ML2 . . . . 165 C4
Mossneuk Pk ML2 . . . . 165 D5
Mossneuk Prim Sch G75 . . . . 179 F7
Mossneuk Rd G75 . . . . 180 A8
Mossneuk St ML5 . . . . 121 F3
MOSSPARK 115 E3
Mosspark Ave
Glasgow G52 . . . . 115 F3
Milngavie G62 . . . . 55 A3
Mosspark Bvd G52 . . . . 115 E4
Mosspark Dr G52 . . . . 115 E3
Mosspark La G52 . . . . 115 E3
Mosspark Oval G52 . . . . 115 E3
Mosspark Prim Sch G52 . . . . 115 E3
Mosspark Rd
Coatbridge ML5 . . . . 121 D8
Milngavie G62 . . . . 55 A3
Mosspark Sq G52 . . . . 115 E3
Mosspark Sta G52 . . . . 115 C3
Moss Path G69 . . . . 119 F3
Moss Rd
Airdrie ML6 . . . . 123 A6
Airth FK2 . . . . 13 E5
Bridge of Weir PA11 . . . . 110 E7
Cumbernauld G67 . . . . 62 F4
East Kilbride G75 . . . . 180 C4
Fallin FK7 . . . . 8 C4
Glasgow G51 . . . . 115 D8

Moss Rd *continued*
Helensburgh G82 .... 25 E4
Kilmacolm PA13 .... 89 D8
Kirkintilloch G66 .... 80 B7
Kirkintilloch, High Gallowhill G66 .... 79 B6
Linwood PA3 .... 112 C7
Muirhead G69 .... 100 C7
Port Glasgow PA14 .... 68 F7
Wishaw ML2 .... 165 E3
Moss Side Ave ML6 ...... 122 E8
Moss-Side Ave ML8 ..... 187 D2
Moss-Side Rd G41 ...... 116 E1
Moss St PA1 .... 113 E5
Mossvale Cres G33 ...... 99 C2
Mossvale La PA3 .... 113 D6
Mossvale Path G33 ...... 99 C3
Mossvale Prim Sch PA3 . 113 D7
Mossvale Rd G33 .... 99 C2
Mossvale Sq
Glasgow G33 .... 99 B2
Paisley PA3 .... 113 D7
Mossvale St PA3 .... 113 D7
Mossvale/St James Prim Sch PA3 .... 113 D7
Mossvale Terr 13 G69 .... 81 A3
Mossvale Way G33 ...... 99 C2
Mossvale Wlk G33 ...... 99 C2
Mossview Cres ML6 ..... 123 A5
Mossview La G52 .... 115 C5
Mossview Quadrant G52 115 D5
Mossview Rd G33 .... 99 E5
Mosswater Wynd G68 .... 60 F2
Mosswell Rd G62 .... 55 B3
Mossyde Ave PA14 .... 69 A7
Mossywood Ct
Airdrie ML6 .... 123 D8
Cumbernauld G68 .... 81 F7
Mossywood Pl G68 .... 81 F7
Mossywood Rd G68 ...... 81 F7
Mote Hill ML3 .... 162 E5
Mote Hill Ct ML3 .... 162 E5
Mote Hill Gr ML3 .... 162 E5
Motehill Rd PA3 .... 114 A7
Mote View KA2 .... 221 D1
MOTHERWELL 163 D8
Motherwell Bsns Ctr ML1 .... 163 F7
Motherwell Coll ML1 .... 164 B5
Motherwell Heritage Ctr★ ML1 .... 163 D7
Motherwell Rd
Bellshill ML4 .... 142 B4
Hamilton ML3 .... 163 A4
Motherwell, Carfin ML1 .. 143 C1
Motherwell ML1 .... 142 B1
Motherwell ML1 .... 144 A6
Motherwell St ML6 ...... 123 C8
Motherwell Sta ML1 .... 163 D7
Motoring Heritage Ctr★ G83 .... 27 D6
Motte Gdns KA22 .... 205 B4
Moubray Gdns FK10 .... 4 B1
Moubrey Row FK7 .... 12 D8
Moulin Cir G52 .... 115 A4
Moulin Pl G52 .... 115 A4
Moulin Rd G52 .... 115 A4
Moulin Terr G52 .... 115 A4
Mountainblue St G31 ... 118 B5
Mount Annan Dr G44 .... 137 B7
Mount Ave
Kilmarnock KA1 .... 227 D6
Symington KA1 .... 231 D4
Mount Bartholomew FK4 . 40 A5
MOUNTBLOW 73 D5
Mountblow House G81 ... 73 D5
Mountblow Rd G81 ...... 73 E5
Mount Cameron Drive N 3 G74 .... 181 A8
Mount Cameron Drive S G74 .... 181 B8
Mount Cameron Prim Sch G74 .... 181 B7
Mount Carmel Prim Sch KA3 .... 222 F5
Mountcastle Wynd KA13 207 D6
Mountcharles KA7 ...... 238 D2
Mount Charles Cres KA7 238 D2
MOUNT ELLEN 100 E6
MOUNT FLORIDA 137 C8
Mount Florida Prim Sch G42 .... 137 B7
Mount Florida Sta G42 .. 137 A8
Mountgarrie Path 8 G51 .... 115 D7
Mountgarrie Rd 9 G51 .. 115 D7
Mount Harriet Ave G33 ... 99 E6
Mount Harriet Dr G33 .... 99 E6
Mountherrick G75 ...... 180 E5
Mount Ho KA2 .... 227 B7
Mount Hope FK9 .... 2 B7
Mount Lockhart G71 .... 120 B2
Mount Lockhart Gdns G71 .... 120 B2
Mount Lockhart Pl G71 .. 120 B2
Mount Oliphant FK7 ...... 12 D7
Mount Oliphant Cres KA7 .... 239 B6
Mount Oliphant Pl KA7 .. 239 B6
Mount Pl KA1 .... 227 D6
Mount Pleasant KA20 ... 206 D1
Mount Pleasant Cres G66 58 B6
Mount Pleasant Dr G60 .. 73 B6
Mount Pleasant Pl G60 .. 73 B6
Mount Pleasant St PA15 .. 45 E4
Mount Pleasant Way KA3 .... 222 F1
Mount St G20 .... 96 F3
Mount Stewart St ML8 .. 187 E2
Mount Stuart St G41 .... 136 E8
Mount The
Ayr KA7 .... 239 B4
Motherwell ML1 .... 163 D6
MOUNT VERNON 119 D2
Mount Vernon Ave
Coatbridge ML5 .... 121 E7
Glasgow G32, G69 .... 119 E3
Mount Vernon Prim Sch G32 .... 119 D3
Mount Vernon Sta G32 .. 119 F2
Mount View KA11 .... 220 C1
Mount Village KA1 ...... 227 C7
Mount William FK10 .... 5 E1
Mournian Way ML3 ..... 162 D1
Mousa Pk G72 .... 138 F3
Mousebank La ML11 .... 214 F4
Mousebank Rd ML11 .... 214 F5
Mousemill Rd ML11 ..... 214 D5
Mowbray G74 .... 160 C4
Mowbray Ave G69 .... 100 F5
Mowbrey Ct FK7 .... 7 D4
Moyne Rd G53 .... 115 A2
Moy Path 4 ML2 .... 165 F6
Moy St G11 .... 96 C2
Muckcroft Rd G69 .... 80 C4
Mudale Ct FK1 .... 42 D1
MUGDOCK 55 C6
Mugdock Ctry Pk★ G62 .. 55 A6
Mugdock Rd
Milngavie G62 .... 55 A2
Milngavie G62 .... 55 B4
Muiralehouse Rd FK7 .... 11 E8
Muirbank Ave G73 ...... 137 F8
Muirbank Gdns G73 ..... 137 F7
Muirbrae Rd G73 .... 138 B4
Muirbrae Way G73 ...... 138 B4
Muirburn Ave G44 ...... 136 E4
Muirburn Rd
Beith KA15 .... 150 A3
Stonehouse ML10 .... 198 A2
Muir Cl KA3 .... 195 C1
Muir Cres G83 .... 27 D7
Muircroft Dr ML1 .... 144 B2
Muir Ct G44 .... 136 F2
Muir Dr
Irvine KA12 .... 219 D3
Stevenston KA20 .... 217 C8
Troon KA10 .... 229 E6
Muir Drive Cotts KA20 .. 217 C8
Muirdrum Ave G52 ...... 115 D3
Muirdyke Ave FK2 .... 24 C3
Muirdyke Rd
Coatbridge, Brackenhirst ML5, ML6 .... 102 A5
Coatbridge, Drumpellier ML5 .... 121 D8
Glenboig ML5 .... 101 F4
Muirdykes Ave
2 Glasgow G52 .... 115 A5
Port Glasgow PA14 ...... 68 D7
Muirdykes Rd
Glasgow G52 .... 115 A5
Paisley PA3 .... 113 B6
Muiredge Ct G71 .... 140 F6
Muiredge & Jersy Rd
Cleland ML1, ML7 .... 145 B6
Shotts ML7 .... 146 A8
Muiredge Prim Sch G71 141 A6
Muiredge Terr G69 ...... 120 B4
MUIREND 136 E4
Muirend Ave G44 .... 136 F5
Muirend Rd
Cardross G82 .... 48 A8
Glasgow G44 .... 136 E4
Kilmarnock KA3 .... 222 F5
Stirling FK7 .... 7 B5
Muirend St KA25 .... 149 B2
Muirend Sta G44 .... 136 F4
Muirfield Cres 6 G23 .... 76 E1
Muirfield Ct
Glasgow G44 .... 136 F4
Irvine KA11 .... 224 G7
Muirfield Mdws G71 .... 140 E2
Muirfield Pl KA13 .... 207 C4
Muirfield Rd
Cumbernauld G68 .... 62 A5
Stenhousemuir FK5 ...... 23 E2
Muir Glen 5 ML11 ...... 215 C3
Muirhall Pl
Irvine KA11 .... 220 C1
Stenhousemuir FK5 ...... 23 C3
Muirhall Rd FK5 .... 23 C3
Muirhall Terr ML7 ...... 125 B2
MUIRHEAD
Glasgow 120 C4
Stepps 100 D7
Troon 229 G4
Muirhead Ave FK2 .... 42 A8
Muirhead Cotts G66 ..... 80 B7
Muirhead Ct G69 .... 120 C4
Muirhead Dr
Law ML8 .... 187 A6
Linwood PA3 .... 112 A5
Motherwell ML1 .... 143 F4
Muirhead Gate 4 G71 ... 141 A8
Muirhead Gdns
Glasgow G69 .... 120 C4
Salsburgh ML7 .... 125 B2
Muirhead Gr G69 .... 120 C4
Muirhead Pl ML7 .... 127 D4
Muirhead Prim Sch KA10 .... 229 F4
Muirhead Rd
Glasgow G69 .... 120 B3
Stenhousemuir FK5 ...... 23 E4
Muirhead Rdbt G67 ...... 62 B3
Muirhead St
1 Kirkintilloch G66 .... 79 D7
Lochwinnoch PA12 .... 129 D2
Muirhead Terr ML1 ..... 163 E4
Muirhead Way G64 ...... 78 D1
Muirhill Ave G44 .... 136 E5
Muirhill Cres G13 .... 95 A7
Muirhill Ct ML3 .... 162 D4
MUIRHOUSE 164 B2
Muirhouse Ave
Motherwell ML1 .... 164 B3
Wishaw ML2 .... 166 B6
Muirhouse Dr ML1 ...... 164 C2
Muirhouse La 4 G75 .... 180 F8
Muirhouse Pk G61 .... 75 D8
Muirhouse Prim Sch ML1 .... 164 B2
Muirhouse Rd
Motherwell ML1 .... 164 B2
Symington KA1 .... 231 F5
Muirhouse St 1 G41 .... 117 A3
Muirhouse Twr ML1 ..... 164 B3
Muirkirk Dr
Glasgow G13 .... 95 F7
Hamilton ML3 .... 161 D2
Muirlee Rd ML8 .... 188 B1
Muirlees Cres G62 .... 54 E2
Muirmadkin Rd ML4 .... 142 B5
Muirmaillen Ave ML1 ... 144 C1
Muirpark Ave PA4 .... 94 C2
Muirpark Dr
Bishopbriggs G64 .... 98 A8
Shieldhill FK1 .... 66 D6
Muirpark Gdns FK10 .... 4 E4
Muirpark Rd KA15 ...... 150 B1
Muirpark St G11 .... 96 B2
Muirpark Terr G64 .... 98 A8
Muir Rd G82 .... 50 C6
Muirshiel Ave G53 ...... 135 C6
Muirshiel Cres G53 ..... 135 D6
Muirshiel Ct G53 .... 135 C5
Muirshiel Ctry Pk★ PA12 .... 108 A3
Muirshiel La PA14 .... 68 D8
Muirshiel Rd PA14 .... 68 D8
Muirshot Rd ML9 .... 185 B4
Muirside Ave
Glasgow G32 .... 119 E3
Kirkintilloch G66 .... 80 A8
Tullibody FK10 .... 4 C3
Muirside Ct KA13 .... 207 C2
Muirside Pl
Kilwinning KA13 .... 207 C2
21 Wishaw ML2 .... 165 F6
Muirside Rd
Glasgow G69 .... 120 B4
Kilwinning KA13 .... 207 C2
Tullibody FK10 .... 4 C3
Muirside St G69 .... 120 B4
Muirskeith Cres G44 .... 137 A6
Muirskeith Pl G43 ...... 136 F6
Muirskeith Rd G43 ...... 136 F6
Muir St
Alexandria G83 .... 27 D8
Bishopbriggs G64 .... 78 A1
Coatbridge ML5 .... 121 E7
Hamilton, High Blantyre G72 .... 161 D6
Hamilton ML3 .... 162 E4
Larkhall ML9 .... 185 A3
Law ML8 .... 186 F6
Motherwell ML1 .... 163 D7
Renfrew PA4 .... 94 D4
Stenhousemuir FK5 ...... 23 D2
Muirs The FK10 .... 4 C4
Muir Street Prim Sch 5 ML1 .... 163 D8
Muir Terr PA3 .... 114 A7
MUIRTON 7 E6
Muirton Dr G64 .... 77 F3
Muirton Rd FK7 .... 7 E6
Muirton Rdbt FK7 .... 7 F7
Muiryfauld Dr G31 ...... 118 E5
Muiryhall St
Coatbridge, Cliftonville ML5 .... 122 B7
Coatbridge ML5 .... 122 A7
Muiryhall Street E ML5 .. 122 C7
Mulben Cres G53 .... 134 F7
Mulben Pl G53 .... 134 F7
Mulben Terr G53 .... 134 F8
Mulberry Cres ML6 ..... 123 E3
Mulberry Dr G75 .... 180 C5
Mulberry Rd
Glasgow G43 .... 136 D5
Motherwell G71 .... 121 C1
Mulberry Way G75 ...... 180 C5
Mulberry Wynd G72 ..... 139 F3
Muldron Terr ML7 ...... 147 B2
Mulgrew Ave KA21 ...... 206 A2
Mull
Airdrie ML6 .... 123 D5
East Kilbride G74 .... 181 C8
Mullardoch St 12 G23 .... 76 D1
Mull Ave
Paisley PA2 .... 133 E7
Port Glasgow PA14 ...... 69 A7
Renfrew PA4 .... 94 C1
Mull Cres KA11 .... 220 A2
Mull Ct
Alloa FK10 .... 10 B5
Hamilton ML3 .... 161 F1
Irvine KA11 .... 220 A2
Mullen Ct G33 .... 99 F5
Mulloch Ave 1 FK2 ...... 42 A8
Mull Pl KA11 .... 220 A2
Mull Quadrant ML2 ..... 165 E5
Mull St G21 .... 98 B2
Mull Terr KA11 .... 220 A2
Mulvey Cres ML6 .... 122 E7
MUNGAL 42 A8
Mungalend FK2 .... 42 B7
Mungalend Rdbt FK2 ..... 42 B8
Mungalhead Rd FK2 ...... 42 A7
Mungal Mill Ct 4 FK2 .... 41 F8
Mungal Pl FK2 .... 42 B8
Mungo Pk G75 .... 180 D8
Mungo Pl G71 .... 121 A1
Munlochy Rd G51 .... 115 D7
Munnoch Cres KA22 ..... 205 B5
Munnoch Way FK7 .... 12 C4
Munro Ave
Kilmarnock KA1 .... 222 D1
Stirling FK9 .... 2 B4
Munro Ct G81 .... 73 F6
Munro Dr
Kilbirnie KA25 .... 170 B8
Milton of Campsie G66 .... 58 B5
Munro Drive E G84 .... 16 E3
Munro Drive W G84 ...... 16 D3
Munro Gate FK9 .... 2 A5
Munro Gdns FK2 .... 42 F3
Munro Pl
Alloa FK10 .... 9 F6
East Kilbride G74 .... 160 B3
Glasgow G13 .... 95 E6
Kilmarnock KA1 .... 222 E2
Saltcoats KA21 .... 206 A2
Munro Rd
Glasgow G13 .... 95 E5
Stirling FK7 .... 7 E6
Munro St
4 Alexandria G83 .... 27 E5
Greenock PA16 .... 45 A4
Stenhousemuir FK5 ...... 23 E3
Munro Wlk KA21 .... 206 A2
Murano Pl G20 .... 96 F4
Murano St G20 .... 96 F4
Murchie Dr KA9 .... 236 D5
Murchison G12 .... 96 A6
Murchison Dr G75 ...... 180 B7
Murchison Rd PA6 .... 91 C1
Murchland Ave KA3 ..... 213 A3
Murchland Way KA12 ... 219 C3
Murdieston St PA15 ...... 45 D4
Murdoch Cres KA20 ..... 217 D7
Murdoch Ct
Saltcoats KA21 .... 205 E3
1 Troon KA10 .... 229 E5
Murdoch Dr G62 .... 76 D8
Murdoch Pl
Irvine KA11 .... 224 H6
Motherwell ML1 .... 142 F3
Murdoch Rd G75 .... 180 E8
Murdoch's Lone KA7 .... 238 E1
Murdoch Sq ML4 .... 142 C7
Murdock Ct KA10 .... 229 E5
Murdostoun Cres ML7 ... 127 F6
Murdostoun Gdns ML2 .. 165 B5
Murdostoun Terr ML1 ... 144 E1
Murdostoun View ML2 .. 165 F6
Mure Ave KA3 .... 223 B5
Mure Pl G78 .... 153 B3
Muriel Blue Ct PA19 ..... 44 F7
Muriel La G78 .... 134 C3
Muriel St G78 .... 134 C3
Muriel Street Ind Est G78 .... 134 C4
Murnin Ct FK7 .... 7 C3
Murnin Rd FK4 .... 40 A4
Murnin Road Ind Est FK4 . 40 A4
Murray Ave
Kilsyth G65 .... 60 D8
Saltcoats KA21 .... 205 E2
Murray Bsns Area PA3 .. 113 D6
Murray Cres
Hamilton G72 .... 161 E6
Wishaw ML2 .... 166 A7
Murray Ct ML3 .... 162 A3
Murray Dr ML9 .... 198 F2
Murrayfield G64 .... 78 A3
Murrayfield Dr G61 ...... 75 E1
Murrayfield Pl FK7 .... 7 D1
Murrayfield St G32 ...... 118 E7
Murrayfield Terr FK7 ...... 7 D1
Murray Gdns G66 .... 58 C5
Murray Gr G61 .... 75 B8
Murrayhill G75 .... 180 D8
Murray Path G71 .... 140 E6
Murray Pl
Ayr KA8 .... 236 C3
Barrhead G78 .... 134 D4
Bellshill ML4 .... 141 E7
Cambusbarron FK7 .... 6 D5
Dumbarton G82 .... 50 C4
Gourock PA19 .... 44 E6
Kilmarnock KA3 .... 223 D2
Stirling FK8 .... 7 B7
Murray Prim Sch G75 ... 180 E8
Murray Rd
Bothwell G71 .... 141 A3
Law ML8 .... 186 F4
Murray Rdbt The G75 ... 180 F8
Murray Rd The G75 ..... 180 E7
Murray Row FK7 .... 12 E8
Murrayshall Rd FK7 .... 7 B3
Murrayside ML9 .... 198 D1
Murray Sq The 2 G75 ... 180 E7
Murray St
Ayr KA8 .... 236 C2
Greenock PA16 .... 45 C5
Paisley PA3 .... 113 D6
Renfrew PA4 .... 94 C3
Murray Terr ML1 .... 163 B7
MURRAY THE 180 E7
Murray Wlk G72 .... 161 E6
Murrin Ave G64 .... 78 D1
Murroch Ave G82 .... 50 C6
Murroch Cres G83 .... 28 B1
Murroes Rd G51 .... 115 D7
Museum Bsns Pk G53 ... 134 F5
Museum of Transport★ G3 .... 96 C1
Musgrove Pl G75 .... 180 C8
Muslin St G40 .... 117 F4
Muttonhole Rd ML3 ..... 182 E7
Mybster Pl G51 .... 115 D7
Myers Cres G71 .... 141 A5
Myers Ct ML4 .... 141 D6
Myles Ho FK8 .... 7 A8
Mylne Pl FK2 .... 24 B2
Myothill Rd FK6 .... 39 D7
Myot View FK6 .... 21 A3
Myreside Pl G32 .... 118 D6
Myreside St G32 .... 118 E6
Myres Rd G53 .... 135 D8
Myreton FK11 .... 4 A6
Myreton Ave PA13 .... 89 C7
Myreton Dr FK7 .... 11 E8
Myreton Way FK1 .... 41 F3
Myretoungate FK12 .... 4 E6
Myrie Gdns G64 .... 78 B2
Myroch Pl G34 .... 100 C1
Myrtle Ave G66 .... 79 C5
Myrtle Bank KA15 .... 171 A8
Myrtle Dr
Motherwell ML1 .... 143 B5
Wishaw ML2 .... 164 D4
Myrtle Hill La G42 ...... 137 C8
Myrtle La ML9 .... 185 C1
Myrtle Pk G42 .... 117 C1
Myrtle Pl G42 .... 137 C8
Myrtle Rd
Clydebank G81 .... 73 D4
Uddingston G71 .... 141 B8
Myrtle Sq G64 .... 98 A8
Myrtle St G72 .... 140 D1
Myrtle View Rd G42 ..... 137 C8
Myrtle Wlk G72 .... 138 F6
Myvot Ave G67 .... 82 B6
Myvot Rd
Cumbernauld, Dalshannon G67 .... 82 B6
Cumbernauld, Mollinsburn G67 .... 81 F4

N

Naburn Gate 6 G5 ...... 117 C4
Nagle Gdns ML1 .... 164 F8
Nailer Rd
Falkirk FK1 .... 41 E6
Stirling FK7 .... 7 B2
Nairn Ave
Bellshill ML4 .... 142 A6
Blantyre G72 .... 140 C2
Nairn Cl KA3 .... 195 C1
Nairn Cres ML6 .... 123 A5
Nairn Ct
Falkirk FK1 .... 42 D1
Kilwinning KA13 .... 207 B3
Nairn Dr PA16 .... 44 D5
Nairn Pl
Clydebank G81 .... 73 F3
East Kilbride G74 .... 160 C3
Nairn Quadrant ML2 .... 165 B5
Nairn Rd PA16 .... 44 D4
Nairnside Rd G21 .... 98 C7
Nairn St
Clydebank G81 .... 73 F3
Glasgow G3 .... 96 D1
Hamilton G72 .... 161 C6
Larkhall ML9 .... 184 F2
Nairn Way G68 .... 62 A5
Naismith Ct ML9 .... 198 E1
Naismith St G32 .... 139 C8
Naismith Wlk ML4 ...... 142 C7
Nansen St G20 .... 97 A3
Napier Ave G82 .... 48 B8
Napier Cres
Dumbarton G82 .... 49 D3
Falkirk FK2 .... 42 A7
Napier Ct
Cardross G82 .... 48 B8
Cumbernauld G68 .... 62 D8
Old Kilpatrick G60 .... 73 C5
Napier Dr G51 .... 116 B8
Napier Gdns PA3 .... 112 C6
Napier Hill G75 .... 180 E8
Napier La G75 .... 180 E8
Napier Pk G68 .... 62 C7
Napier Pl
Cumbernauld G68 .... 62 D8
Falkirk FK2 .... 42 A7
Glasgow G51 .... 116 B8
Old Kilpatrick G60 .... 73 C5
Napier Rd
Cumbernauld G68 .... 62 C7
Glasgow, Govan G51 ..... 116 B8
Glasgow (Hillington Ind Est) G52 .... 94 F1
Glasgow, North Cardonald G52 .... 114 F8
Napiershall La G4 .... 96 F2
Napiershall Pl 3 G20 .... 96 F2
Napiershall St G20 ...... 96 F2
Napier Sq ML4 .... 142 C7
Napier St
Clydebank G81 .... 94 D7
Glasgow G51 .... 116 B8

Napier St *continued*
Johnstone PA5 111 E3
Linwood PA3 112 C6
Napierston Rd G83 27 F5
Napier Terr G51 116 B8
Napier Way G68 62 C7
Naproch Pl G77 157 C5
Naseby Ave G11 95 F3
Naseby La G11 95 F4
Nasmyth Ave
Bearsden G61 75 B8
East Kilbride G75 181 A7
Nasmyth Pl G75 180 F7
Nasmyth Rd G52 115 A7
Nasmyth Road N G52 115 A7
Nasmyth Road S G52 115 A7
Nassau Pl [1] G75 159 A1
National Bank La G1 240 C2
National Mus of Rural Life The★ G76 158 F4
National Piping Ctr The G4 240 C4
National Wallace Monument The★ FK9 2 E4
Navar Ct ML7 147 A3
Navar Pl PA2 114 A2
Naver St G33 98 E1
Navy Way G84 15 B3
Naylor La ML6 123 B8
Naysmyth Bank G75 180 F8
Nebit The FK12 4 E6
Needle Gn ML8 187 F2
Neidpath G69 120 A3
Neidpath Ave ML5 122 B3
Neidpath Dr FK5 24 A4
Neidpath E G74 159 D2
Neidpath Pl ML5 122 A3
Neidpath Rd ML8 187 E3
Neidpath Road E G46 157 A6
Neidpath Road W G46 157 A7
Neidpath W G74 159 D1
Neil Ave KA12 219 D5
Neilsland Dr
Hamilton ML3 183 C7
Motherwell ML1 163 B6
Neilsland Oval G53 115 D1
Neilsland Prim Sch ML3 162 A1
Neilsland Rd ML3 162 B1
Neilsland Sq
Glasgow G53 115 D1
Hamilton ML3 162 C1
Neilsland St ML3 162 C1
Neilson Ct ML3 162 E2
Neilson St
Bellshill ML4 142 A5
Falkirk FK1 42 B4
Neil St
Greenock PA16 45 A4
Renfrew PA4 94 D5
NEILSTON 154 E6
Neilston Ave G53 135 C5
Neilston Ct G53 135 C5
Neilston L Ctr G78 154 E7
Neilston Pl G65 36 B1
Neilston Prim Sch G78 154 E7
Neilston Rd
Barrhead G78 134 A1
Neilston G78 154 E8
Paisley PA2 113 E2
Uplawmoor G78 153 B3
Neilston Sta G78 154 D7
Neilston Wlk G65 36 D1
Neilvaig Dr G73 138 C3
Neistpoint Dr G33 119 A7
Nellfield Ct ML8 202 A4
Nellfield Gdns ML8 202 A4
Nellfield La ML8 202 A4
Nelson Ave ML5 121 E4
Nelson Cres ML1 164 B4
Nelson Mandela Pl G1 241 A3
Nelson Pl
Ayr KA8 236 A2
Glasgow G69 120 B4
Helensburgh G84 17 A2
Stirling FK7 7 C6
Nelson Rd
Gourock PA19 44 F6
Saltcoats KA21 217 B8
Nelson St
Glasgow G5 240 B1
Glasgow, Muirhead G69 120 B4
Greenock PA15 45 E5
Kilmarnock KA1 227 F8
Nelson Terr G74 181 A8
NEMPHLAR 214 A6
Nemphlar Moor Rd
Crossford ML8 201 D1
Nemphlar ML11 214 A7
Nemphlar Rd ML11 214 A6
Nemphlar Hill ML11 214 F5
Neptune St G51 116 B7
Neptune Way ML4 142 E5
NERSTON 159 F4
Nerston Rd G74 159 E6
Nerston Residential Sch G74 160 A7
Ness Ave PA5 131 C8
Ness Dr
Blantyre G72 140 E1
East Kilbride G74 160 B1
Ness Gdns
Bishopbriggs G64 78 B1
Hulford KA1 228 F6
Larkhall ML9 199 A8
Ness Pl KA10 229 G5
Ness Rd
Greenock PA16 45 C5
Renfrew PA4 94 B4
Ness St
Glasgow G33 98 E1
Wishaw ML2 186 B8
Ness Terr ML3 162 A1
Ness Way ML1 143 A5
Nethan Ave ML2 164 C1
NETHANFOOT 201 A3
Nethanfoot Brig Rd ML8 201 B2
Nethan Gate ML3 162 C3
Nethan Glen ML8 201 A2
Nethan Path ML9 199 A8
Nethan Pl ML3 183 D6
Nethan St
Glasgow G51 116 A8
Motherwell ML1 142 C2
Nethan View ML8 201 A2
Nether Auldhouse Rd G43 136 C6
Netherbank Rd ML2 164 D2
Netherblane G63 31 A4
Netherbog Ave G82 50 B4
Netherbog Rd G82 50 B4
NETHERBURN 200 C4
Netherburn Ave
Glasgow G44 136 F2
Houston PA6 111 E8
Netherburn Gdns PA6 111 E8
Netherburn Prim Sch ML9 200 B3
Netherburn Rd ML9 200 A7
Netherby Dr G41 116 D4
Netherby Rd FK2 14 D4
Nethercairn Pl G77 157 C5
Nethercairn Rd G43 136 C4
Nethercliffe Ave G44 136 F2
Nethercommon Ind Est PA3 113 E7
Nethercraigs Dr PA2 133 C8
Nethercraigs Rd PA2 133 B7
Nethercraigs Sports Complex G52 115 D2
Nethercroy Rd G65 60 E5
Netherdale G77 157 B5
Netherdale Cres ML2 164 C2
Netherdale Dr PA1 114 F4
Netherdale Rd ML2 164 E2
Netherfaulds Dr FK6 21 D1
Netherfield St G31 118 C6
Nethergate The FK12 4 E6
Nethergreen Cres PA4 94 B3
Nethergreen Wynd PA4 94 B3
Netherhall Rd ML2 164 D2
Netherhill Ave G44 136 F1
Netherhill Cotts PA3 114 B7
Netherhill Cres PA3 114 A6
Netherhill Rd
Moodiesburn G69 80 F2
Paisley PA3 113 F6
Netherhill Way PA3 114 B7
Netherhouse Ave
Coatbridge ML5 121 F3
Kirkintilloch G66 79 E4
Netherhouse Pl G34 120 E8
Netherhouse Rd G34, G69 120 E7
NETHER KIRKTON 154 F8
Nether Kirkton Ave G78 154 E8
Nether Kirkton View G78 154 E8
Nether Kirkton Way G78 154 F8
Nether Kirkton Wynd G78 154 E8
Netherland Rd KA3 211 E8
NETHERLEE 136 F2
Netherlee Cres KA24 169 B1
Netherlee Ct G44 136 F2
Netherlee Pl G44 137 A4
Netherlee Prim Sch G44 136 F2
Netherlee Rd G44 137 A4
Nethermains Prim Sch FK6 21 D1
Nethermains Rd
Denny FK6 21 C2
Kilwinning KA13 207 E2
Milngavie G62 76 A8
Nethermiln Rd KA23 190 D4
Netherpark Ave G44 136 F1
Netherplace Cres
Glasgow G53 135 B8
Newton Mearns G77 156 C3
Netherplace Rd
Glasgow G53 135 B8
Newton Mearns G77 156 A3
Newton Mearns G77 156 C4
Nether Robertland Prim Sch KA3 195 F1
NETHERTON
Glasgow 95 E8
Strathblane 31 B4
Wishaw 164 D1
Netherton Ave
Glasgow G13 95 E8
Port Glasgow PA14 69 A7
Netherton Ct
Glasgow G45 137 F2
Newton Mearns G77 157 A7
Netherton Dr G78 134 E1
Netherton Farm La [1] G61 95 F8
Netherton Hill G66 57 B8
Netherton Ind Est ML2 164 E2
Netherton Oval G66 33 B1
Netherton Prim Sch ML2 164 E1
Netherton Rd
East Kilbride G75 180 A4
Netherton Rd *continued*
East Kilbride, The Murray G75 180 C7
Glasgow G13 95 F7
Glasgow G13 95 F8
Newton Mearns G77 156 F6
Wishaw ML2 164 E1
Netherton St
Harthill ML7 127 D5
Wishaw ML2 164 F2
Nethervale Ave G44 136 F1
Netherview Rd G44 137 A1
Netherway G44 136 F1
Netherwood Ave G68 81 F8
Netherwood Ct
Cumbernauld G68 82 A8
Motherwell ML1 164 B2
Netherwood Gr G68 82 A8
Netherwood Pl G68 81 F8
Netherwood Rd
Cumbernauld G68 81 F8
Motherwell ML1 164 B3
Netherwood Twr ML1 164 B2
Netherwood Way G68 82 A8
Nethy Way PA4 94 F1
NETTLEHIRST 171 F1
Neuk Ave
Houston PA6 91 C1
Muirhead G69 100 C7
Neuk Cres PA6 91 C2
Neukfoot La G78 153 A3
Neuk The ML2 164 E3
Neuk Way G72 139 C8
Nevan Rd KA10 229 G6
Neville G74 160 C4
Nevis Ave ML3 162 A1
Nevis Cres FK10 10 B8
Nevis Ct
Barrhead G78 134 C1
Coatbridge ML5 122 C3
Greenock PA16 45 B5
Motherwell ML1 163 E4
Nevis Dr
Motherwell ML1 164 C3
Torrance G64 57 B1
Nevison St ML9 185 B2
Nevis Pl
Falkirk FK1 42 C2
Kilmarnock KA1 228 A4
Shotts ML7 147 B3
Nevis Rd
Bearsden G61 75 B7
Glasgow G43 136 B5
Renfrew PA4 94 B1
Nevis Way
Irvine KA11 220 A4
Renfrew PA3 93 E1
New Abbey Rd G69 100 F4
New Albion Ind Est G13 94 E7
Neward Cres KA9 236 D6
Newark KA13 207 C2
Newark Ave PA16 45 C7
Newark Castle★ PA14 47 D2
Newark Cres KA7 238 B1
Newark Dr
Glasgow G41 116 E3
Paisley PA2 133 C8
Wishaw ML2 165 C6
Newark Gate ML7 166 F8
Newark Ho PA2 113 B1
Newark Pl
Port Glasgow PA14 47 D1
Wishaw ML2 165 D6
Newark Prim Sch [2] PA14 68 F8
Newark St
Greenock PA16 45 C8
Port Glasgow PA14 47 D1
Newark Terr KA9 236 D7
NEWARTHILL 143 E3
Newarthill Prim Sch ML1 143 E3
Newarthill Rd ML1 143 C2
New Ashtree St ML2 164 E3
New Ave PA9 130 F6
Newbank Ct G31 118 E4
Newbank Gdns G31 118 D4
Newbank Rd G31 118 E4
Newbarns St ML8 187 F3
Newbattle Ave ML6 123 B2
Newbattle Ct G32 119 B2
Newbattle Gdns G32 119 B2
Newbattle Pl G32 119 B2
Newbattle Rd G32 119 B2
Newbiggin Cres FK10 4 C2
New Bldgs ML11 215 A2
Newbold Ave [2] G21 97 F7
New Branziet Cotts G22 77 B8
Newbridge G66 33 A2
New Bridge St KA7 235 F1
Newburgh PA8 73 A3
Newburgh St G43 136 D7
Newcarron Ct [3] FK2 42 A8
New Carron Rd FK2, FK5 24 A3
Newcastleton Dr [9] G23 76 E1
New Century Dr ML7 146 E4
New City Rd
Glasgow G4 240 B4
Glasgow G4 240 C4
New City Row G63 31 B4
New Cordale Rd G82 27 D2
Newcraigs Dr G76 158 D7
Newcroft Dr G44 137 D5
New Cross ML3 162 E3
New Dock La PA15 46 A5
New Douglas Pk (Hamilton Academicals FC) ML3 162 C5
Newdyke Ave G66 79 E8
Newdyke Rd G66 79 E8
Newdykes Rd KA9 233 D1
New Edinburgh Rd G71, ML4 141 B6
New England Rd KA21 206 A2
NEW FARM LOCH 223 C2
New Farm Prim Sch KA3 223 C1
Newfield Cres ML3 162 B4
Newfield Dr KA2 225 F2
Newfield La [8] G71 141 B3
Newfield Pl
Dundonald KA2 225 F2
Glasgow G46 135 F2
Irvine KA11 220 B5
Rutherglen G73 137 F8
Newfield Rd ML9 198 E1
Newfield Sq G53 135 A6
Newford Gr G76 157 E5
Newgrove Gdns G72 139 A6
New Hallglen Rd FK1 42 D2
Newhall St G40 117 F3
Newhaven Rd G33 119 B8
Newhaven St G32 119 A7
New Hill Rd KA20 218 C4
Newhills Rd G33 119 E7
NEWHOUSE 144 A7
Newhouse FK8 7 A5
Newhouse Dr
Falkirk FK1 41 E2
Kilbirnie KA25 169 F8
Newhouse Ind Est ML1 143 D7
Newhouse Intc KA11 224 G5
Newhousemill Cotts G74 181 C7
Newhousemill Rd
East Kilbride G74 181 D7
Hamilton G72, ML3 161 C1
Newhouse Way KA11 220 A5
Newhut Rd ML1 142 D1
New Inchinnan Rd PA3 113 E7
Newington La FK5 22 D6
Newington St G32 118 F6
New Kirk Rd G61 75 E5
New La ML6 123 B3
New Lairdsland Rd G66 79 D8
NEW LANARK 215 A2
New Lanark Prim Sch ML11 215 A2
New Lanark Rd ML11 214 F2
New Lanark World Heritage Village★ ML11 215 A2
Newlandcraigs Ave PA5 112 D1
Newlandcraigs Dr PA5 112 D2
NEWLANDS 136 D6
Newlands Ct FK7 12 D2
Newlands Dr
Hamilton ML3 183 D8
Kilmarnock KA3 222 E5
Newlandsfield Rd G43 136 D7
Newlands Gdns PA5 112 C1
NEWLANDSMUIR 180 A6
Newlandsmuir Rd G75 180 A6
Newlands Pl
East Kilbride G74 159 E1
Kilmarnock KA3 222 E4
Tullibody FK10 4 C3
Newlands Rd
Bannockburn FK7 11 D8
East Kilbride G75 179 E5
East Kilbride, Newlandsmuir G75 180 A7
Glasgow G44 136 E6
Uddingston G71 140 F8
Newlands St
Coatbridge ML5 122 A4
Lanark ML11 215 C3
Newlands Terr
Carluke ML8 187 F2
Milton of Campsie G66 58 C6
New Line Rd FK7 11 A7
Newliston Dr G5 117 D3
New Luce Dr G32 119 D3
NEWMAINS 166 B5
Newmains Ave PA4 93 B5
Newmains Prim Sch
Renfrew PA4 94 C1
Wishaw ML2 166 A4
Newmains Rd PA4 94 C1
Newmarket FK7 7 E1
Newmarket Ctr FK1 42 B5
Newmarket St
Ayr KA7 238 F8
Falkirk FK1 42 B5
Newmill & Canthill Rd ML7 146 B6
Newmill Gdns ML7 145 F3
Newmill Rd
Dunlop KA3 195 C8
Glasgow G21 98 C5
New Mill Rd KA1 228 B7
Newmills FK10 4 B3
Newmilns Gdn KA3 223 B6
Newmilns Gdns G72 161 D2
Newmilns St G53 134 F6
NEW MONKLAND 102 E5
New Monkland Prim Sch ML6 102 E4
Newmoor Intc KA11 219 F1
Newnham Rd PA1 114 E4
Newpark Cres
Cambuslang G72 139 A7
Stirling FK7 7 A2
Newpark Rd FK7 7 B2
New Park St ML3 162 C5
New Plymouth G75 180 A7
New Rd
Ayr KA8 235 F2
Bannockburn FK7 7 D2
Cambuslang G72 139 E4
Newrose Ave ML4 142 C7
Newshot Dr PA8 73 C1
New Sneddon St PA3 113 E6
New St
Beith KA15 171 B8
Bridge of Allan FK9 1 F8
Clydebank G81 74 A6
Dalry KA24 191 C7
Hamilton G72 161 C7
Irvine KA12 219 B2
Kilbarchan PA10 111 A3
Kilmarnock KA1 227 F5
Lochwinnoch PA12 129 C2
Paisley PA1 113 E4
Slamannan FK1 86 B7
Stevenston KA20 217 D8
Stewarton KA3 195 D1
Stonehouse ML9 198 F2
Newstead Gdns G23 76 E1
NEW STEVENSTON 143 B4
New Stevenston Prim Sch ML1 142 F4
New Stevenston Rd
Motherwell ML1 143 B2
Motherwell ML1 143 C2
New Struan Sch FK10 9 F6
NEWTON 140 A6
Newton Ave
Cambuslang G72 139 D7
Elderslie PA5 112 E3
Skinflats FK2 24 F3
Newton Brae G72 139 F6
Newton Ct
Cambuslang G72 139 D6
Newton Mearns G77 156 D3
Newton Dr
Elderslie PA5 112 E3
Uddingston G71 141 A7
Wishaw ML2 166 A5
Newton Farm Rd G72 140 A6
Newton Gr G77 156 D3
Newtongrange Ave G32 119 B2
Newtongrange Gdns G32 119 B3
Newtonhead KA11 220 B5
Newtonlea Ave G77 156 F4
NEWTON MEARNS 156 B4
Newton of Barr PA12 129 B2
NEWTON ON AYR 236 B3
Newton-on-Ayr Sta KA8 236 A3
Newton Park Ct KA8 236 B2
Newton Pl
Glasgow G3 240 A4
Newton Mearns G77 156 E3
Newton Prim Sch KA8 236 A1
Newton Rd
Bishopton PA7 72 A3
Kirkintilloch G66 79 E4
Newtonshaw FK10 5 C1
Newton St
Glasgow G2, G3 240 B3
Greenock PA16 45 D6
Kilbirnie KA25 149 B1
Paisley PA1 113 C4
Newton Sta G72 139 E5
Newton Station Rd G72 139 E5
Newton Terr
Glasgow G3 240 A3
Greenock PA16 45 D6
Paisley PA1 112 F3
Newton Terrace La G3 240 A3
Newton Trad Est KA8 236 A2
Newton Way PA3 114 B7
Newton Wlk KA1 228 A7
Newtown St G65 60 D8
Newtyle Dr G53 114 F1
Newtyle Pl
Bishopbriggs G64 78 D1
Glasgow G53 114 F1
Newtyle Rd PA1 114 C4
New View Cres ML4 142 A3
New View Dr ML4 142 A3
New View Pl ML4 142 A3
New Wynd G1 241 A1
Niamh Ct PA4 93 C7
Nicholas St G1 241 B2
Nicholson Pl FK1 41 F2
Nicklaus Way ML1 143 E7
Nicol Dr PA16 45 B5
Nicolson Ct G33 99 E5
Nicolson St
Greenock PA15 45 E5
Greenock PA15 45 F5
Nicol St
Airdrie ML6 103 C1
Greenock PA16 45 B4
Niddrie Rd G42 117 A2
Niddrie Sq [1] G42 116 F2
Niddry St PA3 113 F5
Nigel Gdns G41 116 D1
Nigel St ML1 163 D6
Nigg Pl G34 120 A8
Nightingale Pl PA5 131 D6
Nikitas Ave ML9 199 B7
Nile Ct KA7 238 F8
Nile St PA15 45 F4
Nimmo Dr G51 115 F7
Nimmo Pl
Carluke ML8 187 E3
Wishaw ML2 165 C3
Nimmo Rd PA16 45 C4
Nimmo St PA16 45 C4
Nineyard St KA21 216 F7
Ninian Ave PA6 111 C8
Ninian Rd ML6 123 C5
Ninian's Rise G66 79 F7
Ninian's Terr KA13 207 F2

Nisbet Dr
Denny FK6 ... 21 D2
Prestwick KA9 ... 236 D5
Nisbet St G31 ... 118 D5
Nisbett Pl ML6 ... 123 E2
Nisbett St ML6 ... 123 E2
Nissen Pl G53 ... 114 F1
Nith Dr
Hamilton ML3 ... 183 A8
Renfrew PA4 ... 94 E2
Nith La 24 ML2 ... 165 F6
Nith Path ML1 ... 144 C2
Nith Pl KA1 ... 228 B5
Nith Quadrant ML1 ... 143 C3
Nithsdale G74 ... 160 D3
Nithsdale Cres G61 ... 75 C6
Nithsdale Cross G41 ... 116 D3
Nithsdale Dr G41 ... 116 F2
Nithsdale Pl G41 ... 116 F3
Nithsdale Rd
Ardrossan KA22 ... 205 D4
Glasgow G41 ... 116 D3
Nithsdale St G41 ... 116 F2
Nith St G33 ... 98 D1
NITSHILL ... 134 F5
Nitshill Rd G53 ... 135 C3
Nitshill Sta G53 ... 135 A5
Niven Ct KA3 ... 223 D4
Niven St G20 ... 96 C6
Noble Prim Sch ML4 ... 142 A7
Noble Rd ML4 ... 142 B5
Nobles Pl ML4 ... 141 F4
Nobleston G83 ... 28 A2
Nobles View ML4 ... 141 F4
Noldrum Ave G32 ... 139 C8
Noldrum Gdns G32 ... 139 C8
Noltmire Rd KA8 ... 236 C4
Noran Cres KA10 ... 229 G5
Norbreck Dr G46 ... 136 C4
Norby Rd G11 ... 95 F3
Nordic Cres G72 ... 161 E7
Nordic Gdns 3 G72 ... 161 E7
Nordic Gr 6 G72 ... 161 E7
Noremac Way ML4 ... 141 F7
Norfield Dr G44 ... 137 B7
Norfolk Cres G64 ... 77 E3
Norfolk Ct G5 ... 117 B5
Norfolk Rd PA16 ... 44 E4
Norfolk St G5 ... 117 B5
Norham St G41 ... 116 E1
Norman Cres KA12 ... 219 B5
Norman St G40 ... 117 F3
Norse Lane N G14 ... 95 C4
Norse Lane S 14 G14 ... 95 C4
Norse Pl G14 ... 95 C4
Norse Rd G14 ... 95 C4
Northacre KA13 ... 207 E5
Northacre Gr KA13 ... 207 D5
Northall Quadrant ML1 ... 143 B1
Northampton Dr G12 ... 96 B6
Northampton La G12 ... 96 B6
North Ave
Cambuslang G72 ... 138 F6
Carluke ML8 ... 187 D2
Clydebank G81 ... 74 A2
North Ayrshire Mus★
KA21 ... 216 F7
Northbank Ave
Cambuslang G72 ... 139 D6
Kirkintilloch G66 ... 79 C8
North Bank Pl G81 ... 94 C7
Northbank Rd G66 ... 79 C8
Northbank St 1 G72 ... 139 D6
North Bank St G81 ... 94 C8
NORTH BARR ... 73 A2
North Barr PA8 ... 73 B3
North Barr Ave PA8 ... 73 A3
NORTH BARRWOOD ... 36 F1
North Berwick Ave G68 ... 61 F5
North Berwick Cres G75 ... 180 A6
North Berwick Gdns G68 ... 61 F5
North Biggar Rd ML6 ... 123 B8
North Birbiston Rd G66 ... 57 E8
Northbrae Pl G13 ... 95 B6
North Bridge St 1 ML6 ... 122 F8
North British Rd G71 ... 140 F6
NORTH BROOMAGE ... 23 A4
North Broomage Rdbt
FK5 ... 23 A3
Northburn Ave ML6 ... 103 B1
Northburn Pl ML6 ... 103 B2
Northburn Rd ML5 ... 102 C1
Northburn St ML6 ... 104 B2
North Bute St ML5 ... 122 B4
North Caldeen Rd ML5 ... 122 C5
North Calder Dr ML6 ... 123 D6
North Calder Gr G71 ... 120 B2
North Calder Pl G71 ... 120 B2
North Calder Rd G71 ... 121 C1
North Campbell Ave G62 ... 54 F1
North Canal Bank G4 ... 97 D2
North Canal Bank St G4 ... 97 C2
North Carbrain Rd G67 ... 61 F1
NORTH CARDONALD ... 115 B7
North Castle St FK10 ... 10 A5
North Claremont La G62 ... 55 A2
North Claremont St 4
G3 ... 96 E1
North Corsebar Rd PA2 ... 113 C2
North Court La G1 ... 241 A2
Northcraig Rd KA13 ... 223 A3
North Crescent Ave
KA22 ... 205 C3
North Crescent Rd KA22 ... 205 B3
Northcroft Rd G69 ... 80 F2
North Croft St PA3 ... 113 F5
North Ct G1 ... 241 A2
North Dean Park Ave
G71 ... 141 A2
Northdoon Pl KA7 ... 238 D3
North Douglas St G81 ... 94 C8
North Dr
Glasgow G1 ... 240 C2
Kilbirnie KA25 ... 170 A8
Linwood PA3 ... 112 B6
Troon KA10 ... 229 G4
North Dryburgh Rd ML2 ... 165 B6
North Dumgoyne Ave G62 ... 54 F3
North Elgin Pl G81 ... 94 C7
North Elgin St G81 ... 94 D8
North End FK7 ... 6 D6
North Erskine Pk G61 ... 75 D5
North Faulds Rd ML11 ... 215 E5
NORTHFIELD ... 36 B1
Northfield G75 ... 179 F7
Northfield Ave
Ayr KA8 ... 236 B3
Port Glasgow PA14 ... 68 F8
Shotts ML7 ... 147 B2
Northfield Dr G83 ... 27 F5
Northfield Pl KA8 ... 236 A3
Northfield Rd
Alexandria G83 ... 28 A5
Denny FK6 ... 21 C4
Kilsyth G65 ... 36 B1
Northfield St ML1 ... 163 E8
Northflat Pl ML8 ... 202 C8
North Frederick St G1 ... 241 A3
North Gardner St 6 G11 ... 96 B3
North Gargieston Rd
KA1 ... 227 C6
Northgate Quadrant G21 ... 98 C6
Northgate Rd G21 ... 98 C7
North Glasgow Coll G21 ... 97 F3
North Gower St 1 G51 ... 116 C5
North Grange Rd G61 ... 75 E6
North Green Dr FK2 ... 14 D4
North Hamilton Pl KA1 ... 222 E1
North Hamilton St KA1 ... 222 E1
North Hanover St G1, G4 ... 241 A3
North Harbour Ind Est 10
KA8 ... 235 F1
North Harbour St KA8 ... 235 F1
Northinch Ct G14 ... 95 D2
Northinch St G14 ... 95 D2
North Iverton Park Rd
PA5 ... 112 B3
NORTH KELVIN ... 96 F4
North Kilmeny Cres ML2 ... 165 C6
North La PA3 ... 112 C6
Northland Ave G14 ... 95 C5
Northland Dr G14 ... 95 C5
Northland Gdns G14 ... 95 C5
Northland La G14 ... 95 C4
North Lodge Ave ML1 ... 163 E4
North Lodge Rd PA4 ... 94 C4
North Main St
Alexandria G83 ... 27 D6
Falkirk FK2 ... 24 C3
North Moraine La G15 ... 75 C2
NORTH MOTHERWELL ... 163 C8
NORTH MOUNT
VERNON ... 119 F3
Northmuir Dr ML2 ... 165 D4
Northmuir Rd G15 ... 75 B4
North Neuk KA10 ... 229 F7
North Newmoor Ind Est
KA11 ... 219 F2
North Orchard St ML1 ... 163 D7
Northpark Ave KA8 ... 236 B3
North Park Ave
Barrhead G78 ... 134 B3
Glasgow G46 ... 135 F4
Northpark St G20 ... 96 F4
North Portland St G1, G4 ... 241 B2
North Porton Rd PA7 ... 72 C4
North Rd
Bellshill ML4 ... 142 A7
Coatbridge ML5 ... 122 A2
Cumbernauld G68 ... 82 A8
Johnstone PA5 ... 111 F2
Port Glasgow PA14 ... 68 E8
West Kilbride KA23 ... 190 C5
North Ring Rd KA20 ... 218 B5
North Shore Rd
Troon KA10 ... 229 D4
Troon KA10 ... 229 E5
North & South Rd ML2 ... 165 E8
North Sq ML5 ... 121 E8
North St
Alexandria G83 ... 27 E5
Alloa FK10 ... 10 A7
Dalry KA24 ... 191 C8
Falkirk FK2 ... 42 B8
Glasgow G3 ... 240 A3
Greenock PA16 ... 45 C8
Houston PA6 ... 91 B3
Larkhall ML9 ... 185 A4
Motherwell ML1 ... 163 F8
Paisley PA3 ... 113 E6
Stirling FK9 ... 2 D1
North Street Ind Est G83 ... 27 E5
Northumberland St G20 ... 96 E4
North Vennel
Irvine KA11 ... 220 A3
Lanark ML11 ... 215 A4
North View G61 ... 75 D2
North View Rd PA11 ... 110 F6
North Wallace St G4 ... 241 B4
Northway G72 ... 140 C1
Northwood Dr ML2 ... 166 A6
Northwood Rd FK10 ... 4 D2
North Woodside L Ctr G4 ... 97 A2
North Woodside Rd G20 ... 96 F3
Norton St FK12 ... 5 B7
Norval St G11 ... 96 A2
Norwich Dr G12 ... 96 B5
Norwood Ave
Alloa FK10 ... 9 F7
Bonnybridge FK4 ... 40 B7
Kirkintilloch G66 ... 79 B8
Norwood Cres FK10 ... 9 F7
Norwood Ct FK4 ... 40 B7
Norwood Dr G46 ... 136 A1
Norwood Gr FK10 ... 9 F7
Norwood Pk G61 ... 75 F3
Norwood Pl FK4 ... 40 B7
Norwood Terr G71 ... 141 A7
Notre Dame High Sch
Glasgow G12 ... 96 C3
Greenock PA16 ... 45 D3
Notre Dame Prim Sch
G12 ... 96 C3
Nottingham Ave G12 ... 96 B6
Nottingham La G12 ... 96 B6
Novar Dr G12 ... 96 B4
Novar Gdns G64 ... 77 E2
Novar St ML3 ... 162 D2
Nuneaton St G40 ... 118 A4
Nuneaton Street Ind Est
G40 ... 118 A4
Nurseries Rd G69 ... 119 F6
Nursery Ave
Erskine PA7 ... 72 E4
Kilmarnock KA1 ... 228 A8
Prestwick KA9 ... 236 B6
Nursery Bldgs ML11 ... 215 A2
Nursery Ct
Carluke ML8 ... 187 E3
Lanark ML11 ... 214 E4
Nursery Dr
Ashgill ML9 ... 200 A8
Kilwinning KA13 ... 207 C5
Nursery Gdns
Kilmarnock KA1 ... 228 B7
Springside KA11 ... 221 A2
Nursery Gr
Ayr KA7 ... 239 B5
Kilmacolm PA13 ... 69 C1
Nursery Hall KA8 ... 236 D2
Nursery La
Glasgow G41 ... 116 F2
Kilmacolm PA13 ... 69 C1
Kilmarnock KA1 ... 228 B8
Nursery Pk ML8 ... 187 E2
Nursery Pl
Ardrossan KA22 ... 205 D2
Hamilton G72 ... 161 D6
Nursery Rd
Ayr KA7 ... 239 B5
Falkirk FK1 ... 41 E4
Nursery St
Glasgow G41 ... 117 A3
Helensburgh G84 ... 25 B8
Kilmarnock KA1 ... 227 F7
Nursery Wynd
Ayr KA7 ... 239 B5
Kilmarnock KA1 ... 228 A7
Kilwinning KA13 ... 207 C5
Nutberry Ct G42 ... 117 B1

O

Oak Ave
Bearsden G61 ... 75 F7
East Kilbride G75 ... 180 B6
Oakbank Ave ML2 ... 164 E1
Oakbank Dr G78 ... 155 E8
Oakbank Ind Est G20 ... 97 B3
Oakbank Rd PA14 ... 68 F8
Oakbank St ML6 ... 123 D7
Oakburn Ave G62 ... 54 F1
Oakburn Cres G62 ... 54 F2
Oakburn Gdns G83 ... 27 F5
Oakburn Wlk G83 ... 27 F6
Oak Cres
Glasgow G69 ... 120 A4
Plean FK7 ... 12 C3
Oakdene Ave
Bellshill ML4 ... 142 A7
Uddingston G71 ... 141 B7
Oakdene Cres ML1 ... 143 C3
Oak Dr
Cambuslang G72 ... 139 C4
Fallin FK7 ... 8 D4
Kirkintilloch G66 ... 79 B5
Stenhousemuir FK5 ... 23 D1
Oak Fern Dr G74 ... 159 D4
Oak Fern Gr G74 ... 159 D4
Oakfield Ave 7 G12 ... 96 E3
Oakfield Dr
Alexandria G83 ... 27 F5
2 Motherwell ML1 ... 163 E6
Oakfield La 2 G12 ... 96 E2
Oakfield Rd ML1 ... 163 E6
Oakfield Terr PA15 ... 46 C4
Oakfield Twr 1 ML1 ... 163 E5
Oak Gr ML6 ... 123 E3
Oakgrove Prim Sch 14 G4 ... 97 A2
Oakhill Ave G69 ... 119 F3
Oakland Dr KA20 ... 206 E2
Oaklands Ave KA12 ... 219 C4
Oak Lea ML3 ... 162 F2
Oaklea Cres G72 ... 161 C8
Oakleigh Dr PA16 ... 45 D8
Oakley Dr G44 ... 136 F3
Oakley Terr 4 G31 ... 117 F7
Oak Mall Sh Ctr 3 PA15 ... 45 F5
Oak Mall The 7 PA15 ... 45 F5
Oak Path ML1 ... 143 B5
Oak Pk
Bishopbriggs G64 ... 78 B1
Oak Pk continued
Motherwell ML1 ... 163 D4
Oak Pl
Coatbridge ML5 ... 122 C5
East Kilbride G75 ... 180 B6
Kilmarnock KA1 ... 227 D8
Uddingston G71 ... 141 C7
Oak Rd
Ardrossan KA22 ... 205 C4
Clydebank G81 ... 73 F5
Cumbernauld G67 ... 62 E4
Paisley PA2 ... 114 A1
Oakridge Cres PA3 ... 113 B5
Oakridge Rd G69 ... 121 B6
Oakshaw Brae PA1 ... 113 D5
Oakshawhead PA1 ... 113 D5
Oakshaw Street E PA1 ... 113 E5
Oakshaw Street W PA1 ... 113 D5
Oakside Pl ML3 ... 183 D7
Oak St
Glasgow G2 ... 240 B2
Stirling FK8 ... 1 F1
Oaks The
Glasgow G44 ... 137 B4
Johnstone PA5 ... 111 E2
Oaktree Gdns
Dumbarton G82 ... 50 C2
Glasgow G45 ... 137 F4
Oakwood Ave
Ayr KA8 ... 236 E2
Paisley PA2 ... 113 B1
Oakwood Cres G34 ... 100 D1
Oakwood Dr
Beith KA15 ... 171 A8
Coatbridge ML5 ... 121 D5
Glasgow G34 ... 100 D1
Newton Mearns G77 ... 156 F4
Oakwood Prim Sch G34 ... 120 D8
Oakwood Sch FK2 ... 42 F4
Oak Wynd G72 ... 139 F3
Oates Gdns ML1 ... 164 B4
Oatfield St G21 ... 98 B3
OATLANDS ... 117 E2
Oatlands Gate G5 ... 117 D3
Oban Ct 2 G20 ... 96 E4
Oban Dr G20 ... 96 E4
Oban La G20 ... 96 E4
Oban Pl ML6 ... 123 D6
Oban Terr PA16 ... 44 E4
Oban Way ML1 ... 143 B2
Oberon FK10 ... 9 F8
Obiston Gdns G32 ... 119 A5
Obree Ave KA9 ... 236 E5
Observatory La 10 G12 ... 96 D3
Observatory Rd G12 ... 96 C3
Ocean Field G81 ... 73 F6
Ocein Dr G74 ... 179 C8
Ochel Path ML6 ... 123 F1
Ochil Cres FK8 ... 2 B2
Ochil Ct
East Kilbride G75 ... 180 B4
Irvine KA11 ... 220 A4
Tullibody FK10 ... 4 C3
Ochil Dr
Barrhead G78 ... 134 C1
Paisley PA2 ... 133 E8
Stenhousemuir FK5 ... 23 E3
Ochil Gdns FK4 ... 39 F2
Ochil Hills Woodland Pk★
FK12 ... 5 D7
Ochilmount FK7 ... 7 F1
Ochil Pl
Glasgow G32 ... 119 A4
Kilmarnock KA1 ... 228 B3
Ochil Rd
Alva FK12 ... 5 B7
Bearsden G61 ... 75 B7
Bishopbriggs G64 ... 78 C1
Menstrie FK11 ... 4 A7
Renfrew PA4 ... 94 B1
Stirling FK9 ... 2 C4
Ochil St
Alloa FK10 ... 10 A7
Fallin FK7 ... 8 C4
Glasgow G32 ... 119 A4
Tullibody FK10 ... 4 B3
Wishaw ML2 ... 164 F4
Ochil Terr FK2 ... 24 B2
Ochiltree Ave G13 ... 95 F7
Ochiltree Cres ML5 ... 121 E5
Ochiltree Dr ML3 ... 161 E1
Ochiltree Pl KA3 ... 223 B6
Ochiltree Terr FK1 ... 41 B5
Ochilvale Terr FK10 ... 5 D3
Ochilview
Alva FK12 ... 5 A7
Cowie FK7 ... 12 E6
Ochil View
Denny FK6 ... 39 D8
Shieldhill FK1 ... 66 D7
8 Uddingston G71 ... 141 A8
Ochil View Ct FK5 ... 23 C5
Ochilview Pk
(Stenhousemuir FC & East
Stirlingshire FC) FK5 ... 23 D3
Ochre Cres FK7 ... 12 C8
O'Connor Ct KA21 ... 216 E8
Octavia Ct PA15 ... 46 D2
Octavia Terr PA16 ... 45 C8
Octavia Wlk 2 PA14 ... 47 A2
Odense Ct G75 ... 180 E6
Ogilface Cres EH48 ... 107 C2
Ogilvie Pl
Bridge of Allan FK9 ... 2 A6
Glasgow G31 ... 118 D4
Kilmarnock KA3 ... 223 C2
Ogilvie Rd FK8 ... 7 A5
Ogilvie St G31 ... 118 D4
O'Hanlon Way FK8 ... 1 F2
O'Hare G83 ... 28 A3
Oki Way G68 ... 62 C7
Old Aisle Rd G66 ... 79 F7
Old Auchans View KA2 ... 225 E2
Old Avon Rd ML3 ... 163 A2
Old Balmore Rd G64 ... 77 E7
OLD BALORNOCK ... 98 B5
Oldbarhills TP Site PA2 ... 134 D8
Old Bars Dr 6 G69 ... 81 A3
Old Bellsdyke Rd FK5 ... 23 A3
Old Biggar Rd ML6 ... 83 B1
Old Bore Rd ML6 ... 123 E8
Old Bothwell Rd
Bothwell G71 ... 141 B1
Hamilton G71 ... 162 B8
Old Brewery La FK10 ... 10 B7
Old Bridgend ML8 ... 187 F1
Old Bridge of Weir Rd
PA6 ... 91 A2
Old Bridge Rd KA8 ... 236 E3
Old Bridge St
11 Alloa FK10 ... 10 B6
Ayr KA7 ... 235 F1
Old Bridge Wynd FK9 ... 2 A4
Old Caley Rd KA12 ... 219 C4
Old Castle Gdns G44 ... 137 B6
Old Castle Rd G44 ... 137 B5
Old Church Gdns G69 ... 121 A5
Old Coach Rd G74 ... 159 F3
Old Cross
4 Airdrie ML6 ... 123 A8
Hamilton ML3 ... 162 F4
Old Dalmarnock Rd G40 ... 117 F4
Old Dalnottar Rd G60 ... 73 C5
Old Denny Rd FK5 ... 23 A3
Old Drove Rd FK7 ... 6 C5
OLD DRUMCHAPEL ... 75 A1
Old Dullatur Rd G68 ... 61 D6
Old Dumbarton Rd
Glasgow G3 ... 96 C1
Glasgow G3 ... 96 D1
Old Eastfield St ML7 ... 127 D5
Old Edinburgh Rd
Uddingston, Calderbraes
G71 ... 140 D8
Uddingston, Calderbraes
G71 ... 140 F8
Uddingston G71 ... 141 C7
Old Farm Rd
Ayr KA8 ... 236 D3
2 Bearsden G61 ... 95 F8
Old Gartloch Rd G69 ... 100 F5
Old Glasgow Rd
Cumbernauld G67 ... 62 A4
Kilwinning KA13 ... 207 F4
Stewarton KA3 ... 195 F2
Uddingston G71 ... 140 E5
Uddingston, Kylepark G71 ... 140 D7
Old Govan Rd PA4 ... 94 F3
Old Greenock Rd
Bishopton, Kingston PA7,
PA8 ... 72 D2
Bishopton PA7 ... 71 D5
Erskine, Inchinnan PA4 ... 93 D7
Erskine, West Craigend PA4 ... 93 A8
Langbank PA14 ... 70 C6
Port Glasgow PA14 ... 69 D7
OLDHALL ... 114 D5
Oldhall Dr PA13 ... 69 D1
Oldhall Rd PA1 ... 114 D5
Oldhall Rdbt KA11 ... 224 H5
Oldhall West Ind Est
KA11 ... 224 H6
Old Hillfoot Rd KA7 ... 239 B5
Old Humbie Rd G77 ... 156 E2
Old Inns Intc G67 ... 62 C5
Old Inns Rdbt G68 ... 62 B6
Old Inverkip Rd PA16 ... 45 C4
Old Irvine Rd KA1 ... 227 E8
OLD KILPATRICK ... 73 A6
Old Lanark Rd
Braidwood ML8, ML11 ... 202 B4
Carluke ML8 ... 201 F8
Cartland ML11 ... 202 E1
Old Largs Rd PA15, PA16 ... 45 E2
Old Luss Rd
Balloch G83 ... 19 B1
Helensburgh G84 ... 16 F1
Old Manse Gdns ML5 ... 122 A7
Old Manse Rd
Glasgow G32 ... 119 D5
Wishaw ML2 ... 164 E1
Old Market Rd ML11 ... 215 B3
Old Military Rd G83 ... 20 E8
Old Mill Ct G81 ... 74 A5
Old Mill Gate G73 ... 138 A6
Old Mill La G71 ... 140 F7
Old Mill Park Ind Est G66 ... 58 C1
Old Mill Rd
Bothwell G71 ... 141 B1
Cambuslang G72 ... 139 D5
Clydebank G81 ... 74 A6
East Kilbride G74 ... 159 F2
Hartwood ML7 ... 146 B1
Kilmarnock KA1 ... 228 A7
Paisley PA1, PA2 ... 113 B3
Uddingston G71 ... 140 F7
Old Mill View G65 ... 60 F3
Old Mill Way FK6 ... 21 B2
Old Mill Wlk 4 G83 ... 27 E8
OLD MONKLAND ... 121 E4
Old Monkland Prim Sch
ML5 ... 121 C4
Old Monkland Rd ML5 ... 121 E4

P

Queensberry Ave *continued*
Clarkston G76 ... 157 E7
Glasgow G52 ... 114 F7
Queensborough Gdns 4
G12 ... 96 B3
Queensby Ave 6 G69 ... 120 B6
Queensby Dr G69 ... 120 A6
Queensby Pl G69 ... 120 C6
Queensby Rd G69 ... 120 C6
Queens Cres
Bellshill ML4 ... 141 F4
Motherwell ML1 ... 142 F4
Queen's Cres
Carluke ML8 ... 188 A2
Chapelhall ML6 ... 123 D3
Cleland ML1 ... 144 B2
Coatbridge G69 ... 120 F5
Falkirk FK1 ... 41 F5
7 Glasgow G4 ... 97 A2
Glasgow G4 ... 240 B4
Queens Ct
Ayr KA7 ... 238 F8
Irvine KA12 ... 219 D2
Stenhousemuir FK5 ... 23 D3
Queen's Ct FK9 ... 1 F7
Queen's Ct G84 ... 25 A8
Queen's Ct G62 ... 76 B8
Queensdale Ave ML9 ... 199 B8
Queensdale Rd ML9 ... 199 B8
Queens Dr
Bishopton PA7 ... 72 C3
Denny FK6 ... 21 E3
Falkirk FK1 ... 41 F5
Hamilton ML3 ... 183 D6
Stenhousemuir FK5 ... 23 C3
Queen's Dr
Alexandria G83 ... 27 D4
Ardrossan KA22 ... 205 D3
California FK1 ... 66 F5
Cumbernauld G68 ... 61 F6
Glasgow G42 ... 117 A1
Kilmarnock KA1 ... 228 B6
Monkton KA9 ... 233 D5
Stenhousemuir FK5 ... 23 C2
Troon KA10 ... 229 E6
Queen's Drive La G42 ... 117 A1
Queens Drive Ret Pk
KA1 ... 228 A6
Queensferry St G5 ... 117 E2
Queen's Gate G76 ... 157 E8
Queens Gate La 9 G12 ... 96 C3
Queens Gdns FK9 ... 1 F7
Queen's Gdns G12 ... 96 C3
Queens Gr G66 ... 79 C4
Queenshaugh Dr FK8 ... 2 C1
Queenside Cres PA8 ... 72 F1
Queen's La FK9 ... 2 A7
Queensland Ct G52 ... 115 C6
Queensland Dr G52 ... 115 C6
Queensland Gdns G51 ... 115 D6
Queensland Lane E G52 115 C6
Queensland Lane W G52 115 C6
QUEENSLIE ... 119 E8
Queenslie Ind Est G33 ... 119 D8
Queenslie St G33 ... 98 D2
Queen's Park Ave G42 ... 117 B1
Queen's Park Sta G42 ... 117 A2
Queen's Pl
Glasgow G12 ... 96 C3
Kilwinning KA13 ... 208 A3
Queens Point G84 ... 15 B8
Queen Sq G41 ... 116 F2
Queen's Quadrant KA8 ... 236 A1
Queen's Rd
Elderslie PA5 ... 112 C2
Stirling FK8 ... 6 F7
Queen's St FK1 ... 66 F5
Queen St
Alexandria G83 ... 27 D4
Alloa FK10 ... 10 B7
Alva FK12 ... 5 A7
Ayr KA8 ... 236 A1
Bannockburn FK7 ... 7 C2
Falkirk FK2 ... 42 C5
Fallin FK7 ... 8 C4
Glasgow G1 ... 241 A2
Hamilton ML3 ... 162 A5
Helensburgh G84 ... 16 C3
11 Kilmarnock KA1 ... 227 F8
Kilwinning KA13 ... 208 A3
Kirkintilloch G66 ... 79 C8
Motherwell ML1 ... 163 E7
Paisley PA1 ... 113 C4
Port Glasgow PA14 ... 47 C2
Renfrew PA4 ... 94 D3
Rutherglen G73 ... 138 A8
Stirling FK8 ... 7 A8
Stonehouse ML9 ... 198 E2
Wishaw ML2 ... 165 F6
Queens Terr KA9 ... 233 B1
Queen's Terr KA7 ... 238 E8
Queen's Terr FK9 ... 2 A7
Queen's Terrace La KA7. 238 E8
Queen Street Sta G1 ... 241 A3
Queens View G64 ... 78 B8
Queensway
East Kilbride G75 ... 180 E8
Gourock PA19 ... 44 C6
Queens Way G83 ... 27 D4
Queen Victoria Ct G14 ... 95 C4
Queen Victoria Dr G14 ... 95 C4
Queen Victoria Gate G13 . 95 C5
Queen Victoria St ML6 .. 122 F7
QUEENZIEBURN ... 59 F7
Queenzieburn Ind Est
G65 ... 59 F7
Quendale Dr G32 ... 118 F3
Quentin St G41 ... 116 E1
Quinton Gdns G69 ... 120 A5

R

Raasay Cres ML6 ... 123 E6
Raasay Dr PA2 ... 133 D7
Raasay Gdns G77 ... 156 B5
Raasay Pl
Glasgow G22 ... 97 C8
Kilmarnock KA3 ... 223 A6
Raasay St G22 ... 97 C8
Racecourse Pl KA12 ... 219 A5
Racecourse Rd KA7 ... 238 E6
Racecourse View
Ayr KA7 ... 238 E5
Hamilton ML3 ... 162 E5
RADNOR PARK ... 74 A4
Radnor St
Clydebank G81 ... 74 A3
Clydebank, Kilbowie G81 ... 74 B3
Glasgow G3 ... 96 D1
Raeberry St G20 ... 96 F3
Raebog Cres ML6 ... 102 F2
Raebog Rd ML6 ... 102 F4
Raeburn Ave
East Kilbride G74 ... 160 B4
Paisley PA1 ... 114 A4
Raeburn Cres ML3 ... 161 E3
Raeburn Pl G74 ... 160 B4
Raeburn Rd FK5 ... 23 B2
Raeburn Wlk ML4 ... 142 A7
Rae Ct FK2 ... 24 C3
Raeside Ave G77 ... 156 D3
Raes Rd ML8 ... 201 B8
Rae St FK5 ... 23 D3
Raeswood Dr G53 ... 134 F8
Raeswood Gdns G53 ... 134 F8
Raeswood Pl 3 G53 ... 135 A8
Raeswood Rd G53 ... 134 F8
Raewell Cres ML4 ... 141 F3
Raggithill Ave KA6 ... 237 F6
Raglan St
Alexandria G83 ... 27 F3
Glasgow G4 ... 97 A2
Raglan Street La G83 ... 27 F3
Railway Ct G66 ... 57 D8
Railway Rd ML6 ... 122 D7
Raise St KA21 ... 216 F8
Raith Ave
Glasgow G45 ... 137 D4
Prestwick KA9 ... 236 E7
Raithburn Ave
Glasgow G45 ... 137 C3
Kilmarnock KA3 ... 222 F4
Raithburn Rd G45 ... 137 C3
Raith Dr
Bellshill ML4 ... 142 B4
Cumbernauld G68 ... 60 D1
Raithhill KA7 ... 239 B1
Raith Rd KA3 ... 213 B3
Raith Terr KA9 ... 236 E7
Raleigh Ct FK1 ... 41 E5
RALSTON ... 114 D4
Ralston Ave
Glasgow G52 ... 114 F4
Glasgow PA1 ... 114 F3
Ralston Ct G52 ... 114 F4
Ralston Dr
Crookedholm KA3 ... 228 D8
Glasgow G52 ... 114 F4
Ralston Path G52 ... 114 F4
Ralston Pl G52 ... 114 F4
Ralston Prim Sch PA1 ... 114 E5
Ralston Rd
Barrhead G78 ... 134 C2
Bearsden G61 ... 75 E5
Ralston St
Airdrie ML6 ... 122 E7
5 Paisley PA1 ... 114 A4
Ralstonyards Rd KA3 ... 228 E7
Ramage Rd ML8 ... 188 B1
Ramillies Ct
Carluke ML8 ... 188 A1
Clydebank G81 ... 74 C2
Ramoth ML11 ... 214 D4
Rampart Ave G13 ... 95 B8
Ramsay Ave
Johnstone PA5 ... 111 E1
Laurieston FK2 ... 42 F3
Ramsay Cres PA10 ... 111 B2
Ramsay Ct
Newton Mearns G77 ... 156 E3
Troon KA10 ... 229 G4
Ramsay Hill 3 G74 ... 160 A3
Ramsay Pl
Coatbridge ML5 ... 121 C5
Johnstone PA5 ... 111 E1
Stirling FK8 ... 2 A2
Ramsay St G81 ... 73 F3
Ramsey Ind Est G66 ... 58 B1
Ramsey Tullis Dr FK10 ... 4 C1
Ramsey Wynd ML4 ... 142 B7
Ram St G32 ... 118 F5
Ramstane Pl KA11 ... 220 C5
Ranald Gdns G73 ... 138 D3
Randolph Ave G76 ... 137 A1
Randolph Cres FK7 ... 7 C1
Randolph Ct FK8 ... 7 A5
Randolph Dr
Clarkston G76 ... 137 A1
Glasgow G76 ... 136 F1
Randolphfield FK8 ... 7 A5
Randolph Gate G11 ... 95 F4
Randolph Gdns
Denny FK6 ... 21 D1
Glasgow G76 ... 136 F1
Randolph La G11 ... 95 F3
Randolph Pl FK7 ... 7 C2
Randolph Rd
Glasgow G11 ... 95 F4
Stirling FK8 ... 7 B4
Randolph Terr FK7 ... 7 A4
Randyford Rd FK2 ... 42 D5
Randyford St FK2 ... 42 E5
RANFURLY ... 110 E6
Ranfurly Ct PA11 ... 110 D7
Ranfurly Dr G68 ... 61 E4
Ranfurly Pl PA11 ... 110 D7
Ranfurly Rd
Bridge of Weir PA11 ... 110 E6
Glasgow G52 ... 114 F5
Range Pl ML3 ... 162 E1
Range Rd ML1 ... 164 B4
Rangerhouse Rd G75 ... 180 F5
Range Road Ind Est ML2 164 C3
Range St ML1 ... 164 B4
Ranken Cres KA12 ... 219 D3
Ranken Dr KA12 ... 219 D4
Rankin Cres
Bonnybridge FK4 ... 39 D5
Greengairs ML6 ... 83 F2
Rankin Ct
Greenock PA16 ... 45 C4
Kilmarnock KA3 ... 223 C3
Muirhead G69 ... 100 C7
Rankin Dr G77 ... 156 C6
Rankine Ave G75 ... 181 A7
Rankine Ho G4 ... 97 C2
Rankine Pl
East Kilbride G75 ... 181 A7
Johnstone PA5 ... 111 F3
Rankine St PA5 ... 111 F3
Rankine Wynd FK10 ... 4 C2
Rankin Gate Ctr 3 ML8 . 187 F2
Rankin Rd ML2 ... 165 E4
Rankin St
Carluke ML8 ... 187 F2
Greenock PA16 ... 45 C4
Rankin Way G78 ... 134 E3
Rannoch Ave
Bishopbriggs G64 ... 78 B1
Coatbridge ML5 ... 101 D1
Hamilton ML3 ... 162 A1
Newton Mearns G77 ... 156 D7
Rannoch Cl KA3 ... 195 D1
Rannoch Ct
Alloa FK10 ... 10 C5
Cumbernauld G67 ... 82 B6
Hamilton G72 ... 161 F5
Rannoch Dr
Bearsden G61 ... 76 B3
Cumbernauld G67 ... 82 B6
Kirkintilloch G66 ... 59 B1
Renfrew PA4 ... 94 C4
Wishaw ML2 ... 165 B1
Rannoch Gdns G64 ... 78 C2
Rannoch Gn G74 ... 159 F3
Rannoch La G69 ... 81 A2
Rannoch Pl
Irvine KA12 ... 219 C6
Paisley PA2 ... 114 A3
Shieldhill FK1 ... 66 E7
Shotts ML7 ... 146 E6
Stenhousemuir FK5 ... 23 F4
Rannoch Rd
Airdrie ML6 ... 102 F1
Johnstone PA5 ... 131 F8
Kilmacolm PA13 ... 89 C7
Uddingston G71 ... 120 E1
Rannoch St G44 ... 137 A6
Rannoch Terr ML9 ... 185 C1
Rannoch Way 6 G71 ... 141 A3
Rannoch Wynd G73 ... 138 D2
RAPLOCH
Larkhall ... 184 F3
Stirling ... 1 F2
Raploch Ave G14 ... 95 B4
Raploch Com Campus FK8 .1 E2
Raploch La G14 ... 95 B4
Raploch Prim Sch FK8 ... 1 E2
Raploch Rd
Larkhall ML9 ... 184 F3
Stirling FK8 ... 1 F1
Raploch St ML9 ... 184 F3
Rashieburn PA8 ... 73 B2
Rashieglen PA8 ... 73 A2
Rashiehill PA8 ... 73 A2
Rashiehill Rd FK1 ... 86 A6
RASHIELEE ... 73 A2
Rashielee PA8 ... 73 B2
Rashielee Ave PA8 ... 73 B2
Rashielee Prim Sch PA8 .. 73 B2
Rashielee Rd PA8 ... 73 A2
Rashiewood PA8 ... 73 B2
Rashley Sq KA22 ... 205 D4
Rathlin Ave KA1 ... 227 F4
Rathlin Ho KA9 ... 236 B5
Rathlin St G51 ... 116 A8
Rathlin Terr G82 ... 49 C5
Ratho Dr
Cumbernauld G68 ... 61 E5
Glasgow G21 ... 97 E4
Ratho Pk ML3 ... 183 B7
Ratho St PA15 ... 46 C4
Rattray PA8 ... 73 A3
Rattray St G32 ... 118 E3
Ravel Row G31 ... 118 D5
Ravelston Rd G61 ... 75 E2
Ravelston St G32 ... 118 E6
Ravel Wynd G71 ... 141 B8
Raven Rd PA16 ... 45 A5
Ravenscliffe Dr G46 ... 136 B3
Ravenscourt G74 ... 158 C2
RAVENSCRAIG ... 45 A3
Ravenscraig Ave PA2 ... 113 C2
Ravenscraig Ct
Bellshill ML4 ... 142 B5
Greenock PA16 ... 45 A4
Ravenscraig Dr G53 ... 135 C6
Ravenscraig Hospl PA16 .. 45 A3
Ravenscraig Prim Sch
PA16 ... 44 E3
Ravenscraig Rd KA3 ... 211 D8
Ravenscraig Stadium & Recn
Ctr PA16 ... 44 E3
Ravenscraig Terr G53 ... 135 C5
Ravenscroft KA12 ... 219 B5
Ravens Ct 5 G64 ... 97 F8
Ravenshall ML1 ... 165 B8
Ravenshall Rd G41 ... 136 C8
Ravenshill Dr ML1 ... 144 C1
Ravenstone Dr G46 ... 136 C4
Ravenswood Ave PA2 ... 132 E7
Ravenswood Dr G41 ... 116 D1
Ravenswood Prim Sch
G67 ... 82 E8
Ravenswood Rd G69 ... 120 C5
Raven Wynd ML2 ... 165 B3
RAWYARDS ... 103 C1
Rawyards Ave ML6 ... 103 B2
Raylight Pl KA22 ... 205 B1
Raymond Pl G75 ... 159 C1
Rayne Pl G15 ... 75 B4
Ream Ave 2 ML6 ... 123 F6
Reay Ave
Cardross G82 ... 48 A8
East Kilbride G74 ... 159 B2
Reay Gdns G74 ... 159 B2
Recawr Pk KA7 ... 239 B3
Recreation Pk (Alloa Athletic
FC) FK10 ... 10 C6
Redan St 2 G40 ... 117 F5
Redbrae Pl 7 G66 ... 58 D1
Redbrae Rd
Falkirk FK1 ... 41 D6
Kirkintilloch G66 ... 79 E8
Red Bridge Ct 3 ML5 ... 122 A8
Redburn G83 ... 28 A2
Redburn Ave G46 ... 157 B8
Redburn Ct G67 ... 62 F6
Redburn Cvn Pk KA12 ... 219 A7
Redburn Gate KA12 ... 219 A7
Redburn Ind Est KA12 ... 219 C7
Redburn Pl
Cumbernauld G67 ... 62 F6
Irvine KA12 ... 219 B6
Redburn Rd
Blackridge EH48 ... 107 B2
Cumbernauld G67 ... 62 F6
Redburn Rdbt KA12 ... 219 A8
Redburn Sch G67 ... 62 C2
Redcastle Sq G33 ... 99 D1
Redcliffe Dr G75 ... 180 B8
Redclyffe Gdns G84 ... 16 D4
Reddance Terr KA24 ... 191 A8
Reddans Pk KA3 ... 195 D1
Red Deer Rd G75 ... 180 C8
Redding Ave KA3 ... 222 F4
REDDING MUIR ... 66 F6
Redding Rd FK2 ... 42 F2
Redding Road Rdbt FK2 .. 42 F2
Rederech Cres ML3 ... 161 F2
Redford St G33 ... 118 D8
Red Fox Dr G83 ... 27 E8
Red Fox Terr G83 ... 27 E8
Red Gables Sq KA22 ... 205 B3
Redgate Pl G14 ... 95 B4
Redgauntlet Rd G84 ... 25 C8
Redgrave G74 ... 160 D5
Redhall FK7 ... 8 A4
Redhaws Rd ML7 ... 147 A3
Redheugh Ave KA25 ... 149 B3
Redheugh Ct KA25 ... 149 B4
Redheugh Ho KA25 ... 149 B4
Redhill Rd G68 ... 61 D3
Redhills View G66 ... 57 F7
Redholme ML9 ... 185 B1
Redhouse La ML8 ... 187 F3
Redhurst Cres PA2 ... 133 C7
Redhurst La PA2 ... 133 C7
Redhurst Way PA2 ... 133 C7
Redlands La G12 ... 96 C4
Redlands Rd FK10 ... 4 A3
Redlands Terr 14 G12 ... 96 C4
Redlawood Pl G72 ... 140 A6
Redlawood Rd G72 ... 140 A6
Redmire Cres ML7 ... 167 B8
Redmoss Rd
Duntocher G81 ... 73 F7
Milton of Campsie G66 ... 58 B5
Redmoss St G22 ... 97 B5
Rednock St G22 ... 97 C4
Redpath Dr
Cambuslang G72 ... 139 D6
Glasgow G52 ... 115 C5
Stenhousemuir FK2 ... 24 A4
Red Rd
Glasgow G21 ... 98 B4
Helensburgh G82 ... 25 G4
Red Road Ct G21 ... 98 B3
Red Row G82 ... 27 D2
Redshank Ave PA4 ... 94 E4
Redstone Ave KA13 ... 208 A4
Redwell Pl FK10 ... 9 F7
Redwing Cres ML5 ... 122 E2
Redwing Gdns ML2 ... 165 A1
Redwood Ave G74 ... 158 E1
Redwood Cl ML3 ... 183 A7
Redwood Cres
Bishopton PA7 ... 72 C3
Cambuslang G72 ... 139 F3
East Kilbride G74 ... 158 E2
Hamilton ML3 ... 183 A7
Redwood Cres *continued*
Uddingston G71 ... 141 C8
Redwood Ct
East Kilbride G75 ... 179 E8
Greenock PA16 ... 45 E7
Redwood Dr
East Kilbride G74 ... 158 E3
Glasgow G21 ... 98 A3
Redwood Gr ML5 ... 122 B6
Redwood La ML3 ... 183 A7
Redwood Pl
East Kilbride G74 ... 158 E2
Kirkintilloch G66 ... 79 B5
Uddingston G71 ... 141 C8
Redwood Rd
Cumbernauld G67 ... 62 D2
Motherwell ML1 ... 143 B5
Redwood Way G72 ... 139 F3
Reedlands Dr FK6 ... 39 D7
Reedloch Dr KA10 ... 229 G7
Reek St KA15 ... 171 E7
Reelick Ave G13 ... 94 E8
Reelick Quadrant G13 ... 94 E8
Reema Rd ML4 ... 142 B6
Reen Pl G71 ... 141 B4
Reform St KA15 ... 150 B1
Regal Ct KA24 ... 191 C8
Regal Gr ML7 ... 146 E4
Regalia View KA12 ... 219 E6
Regency Ct ML3 ... 163 A2
Regency Way ML1 ... 142 F4
Regent Ct
Glasgow G12 ... 96 B4
1 Greenock PA15 ... 45 F4
Regent Dr G73 ... 138 A8
Regent Moray St G3 ... 96 D1
Regent Park Sq G41 ... 116 F2
Regent Pk KA9 ... 233 C1
Regent Pl G81 ... 73 E4
Regents Gate G71 ... 140 E4
Regent Sh Ctr 2 G66 ... 79 C8
Regent Sq G66 ... 79 C4
Regent St
Clydebank G81 ... 73 E4
Greenock PA15 ... 45 F4
Kirkintilloch G66 ... 79 C8
Paisley PA1 ... 114 B5
Regent Way ML3 ... 162 F3
Register Ave ML4 ... 142 A3
Register Rd G65 ... 60 E8
Regwood St G41 ... 136 D8
Reid Ave
Bearsden G61 ... 76 A6
Dalry KA24 ... 191 B6
Linwood PA3 ... 112 B5
Reid Ct
Hurlford KA3 ... 228 E7
Rutherglen G73 ... 138 B8
Reid Gr
Motherwell ML1 ... 164 B4
Stonehouse ML9 ... 198 F2
Reidhouse St G21 ... 97 F4
Reid Kerr Coll PA3 ... 113 F6
Reid Pl
Glasgow G40 ... 117 F4
Larbert FK5 ... 23 B2
Reid's Ave KA20 ... 206 D2
Reid St
Airdrie ML6 ... 103 B1
Coatbridge ML5 ... 122 B8
Glasgow G40 ... 117 F3
Hamilton ML3 ... 161 F5
Rutherglen G73 ... 138 B8
Salsburgh ML7 ... 125 B2
Reid Terr KA21 ... 217 A7
Reidvale St G31 ... 118 A6
Reilly Gdns FK4 ... 40 B3
Reilly Rd
Bonnybridge FK4 ... 40 B3
Houston PA6 ... 91 C8
Reith Dr G75 ... 180 D7
Remus Pl ML4 ... 142 E5
Renfield La G2 ... 240 C2
Renfield St
Glasgow G2 ... 240 C3
Renfrew PA4 ... 94 D4
RENFREW ... 94 E4
Renfrew Ct G2 ... 241 A3
Renfrew High Sch PA4 ... 94 D2
Renfrew La G2 ... 240 C3
Renfrew L Ctr PA4 ... 94 B2
Renfrew Mus* PA4 ... 94 D4
Renfrew Pl ML5 ... 121 C4
Renfrew Rd
Glasgow G51 ... 95 A1
Glasgow G51 ... 95 C1
Paisley PA3 ... 114 A8
Renfrew St
Coatbridge ML5 ... 121 C4
Glasgow G2 ... 240 C3
Rennie Bsns Units KA21 . 216 F7
Rennie Pl
East Kilbride G74 ... 159 A3
Saltcoats KA21 ... 216 F8
Rennie Rd G65 ... 36 B1
Rennie St
Falkirk FK1 ... 42 A3
Kilmarnock KA1 ... 228 A8
Renshaw Dr G52 ... 115 B6
Renshaw Pl ML4 ... 142 F8
Renshaw Rd
Bishopton PA7 ... 72 B3
Elderslie PA5 ... 112 C2
RENTON ... 27 C1
Renton Pk KA11 ... 220 C7

Rosslyn Ave *continued*
Rutherglen G73 . . . 138 C7
Rosslyn Ct ML3 . . . 162 A4
Rosslyn Ho 12 G12 . . . 96 C3
Rosslyn Pl KA8 . . . 236 B3
Rosslyn Rd
Ashgill ML9 . . . 199 F8
Bearsden G61 . . . 75 B6
Rosslyn Terr 18 G12 . . . 96 C4
Ross Pl
East Kilbride G74 . . . 160 C3
Rutherglen G73 . . . 138 D4
Ross Rd KA21 . . . 205 F2
Ross St
Ayr KA8 . . . 236 C2
Coatbridge ML5 . . . 122 A7
Glasgow G4 . . . 241 B1
Paisley PA1 . . . 114 A3
Ross Terr ML3 . . . 163 C1
Ross Wlk
Kilmarnock KA3 . . . 223 B2
Renton G82 . . . 27 D2
Rostan Rd G43 . . . 136 C5
Rosyth Rd G5 . . . 117 E2
Rotherwick Dr PA1 . . . 114 E4
Rotherwood Ave
Glasgow G13 . . . 75 E1
Paisley PA2 . . . 132 F8
Rotherwood La G13 . . . 75 C2
Rotherwood Pl 1 G13 . . . 95 D8
Rotherwood Way PA2 . . . 132 F8
Rothesay Cres ML5 . . . 122 B4
Rothesay Pl
Coatbridge ML5 . . . 122 B4
Kilmarnock KA3 . . . 222 F3
Rothesay Rd PA16 . . . 44 F3
Rothesay St G75 . . . 180 E8
Rothes Dr G23 . . . 96 D8
Rothes Pl G23 . . . 76 C1
Rottenrow
Glasgow G4 . . . 241 B3
Glasgow G4 . . . 241 C2
Rottenrow E G4 . . . 241 B2
Roughburn Rd FK9 . . . 2 A6
Roughcraig St ML6 . . . 103 A2
Roughlands Cres FK2 . . . 24 B3
Roughlands Dr FK2 . . . 24 A3
Roughlea Pl KA10 . . . 229 G6
ROUGHMUSSEL . . . 134 F8
ROUGHRIGG . . . 85 B2
Roughrigg Rd ML6 . . . 124 C6
Roukenburn St G46 . . . 135 F4
Rouken Glen Pk★ G46 . . . 135 F1
Rouken Glen Rd G46 . . . 136 A1
Roundel The
Falkirk FK2 . . . 42 D7
Wishaw ML2 . . . 165 C2
Roundelwood FK10 . . . 5 B1
Roundhill Dr PA5 . . . 112 E3
Roundhouse FK7 . . . 12 D8
Roundknowe Rd G71 . . . 120 C1
Round Riding Rd G82 . . . 50 B4
Rousay Wynd KA3 . . . 223 A6
Rowallan KA13 . . . 207 C2
Rowallan Cres KA9 . . . 236 D7
Rowallan Ct 6 KA7 . . . 235 E1
Rowallan Dr
Bannockburn FK7 . . . 11 F8
Kilmarnock KA3 . . . 223 A4
Rowallan Gdns G11 . . . 96 A3
Rowallan La
Clarkston G76 . . . 157 E7
Glasgow G11 . . . 96 A3
Rowallan Rd G46 . . . 135 F2
Rowallan St G84 . . . 16 B3
Rowallan Terr G33 . . . 99 B4
Rowan Ave
Beith KA15 . . . 171 C8
Milton of Campsie G66 . . . 58 C5
Renfrew PA4 . . . 94 C4
Rowanbank Pl ML6 . . . 122 D8
Rowanbank Rd KA9 . . . 236 E7
Rowan Cres
Ayr KA7 . . . 239 C5
Chapelhall ML6 . . . 123 E3
Falkirk FK1 . . . 41 A4
Kirkintilloch G66 . . . 79 C5
Menstrie FK11 . . . 3 F6
Shotts ML7 . . . 147 B4
Rowan Ct
Bannockburn FK7 . . . 7 E1
Cambuslang G72 . . . 139 F3
Wishaw ML2 . . . 164 D2
Rowandale Ave G69 . . . 120 A4
Rowand Ave G46 . . . 136 C3
Rowanden Ave ML4 . . . 142 A6
Rowan Dr
Banknock FK4 . . . 38 E2
Bearsden G61 . . . 76 A7
Clydebank G81 . . . 73 F4
Dumbarton G82 . . . 49 A4
Rowan Gdns
Glasgow G41 . . . 116 B4
Larkhall ML9 . . . 185 B2
Rowan Gr ML3 . . . 183 F3
Rowanhill Pl KA1 . . . 227 D7
Rowan Ho KA9 . . . 236 C6
Rowan La ML1 . . . 143 A2
Rowanlea ML6 . . . 103 F3
Rowanlea Ave PA2 . . . 132 E7
Rowanlea Dr G46 . . . 136 D4
Rowanpark Dr G78 . . . 134 A5
Rowan Pl
Beith KA15 . . . 171 C8
Cambuslang G72 . . . 139 C6
Coatbridge ML5 . . . 121 E4
Hamilton G72 . . . 161 D8
Kilmarnock KA1 . . . 227 D7

Rowan Pl *continued*
Troon KA10 . . . 229 E4
Rowan Rd
Cumbernauld G67 . . . 62 D3
Glasgow G41 . . . 116 B4
Linwood PA3 . . . 111 F7
Rowan Rise ML3 . . . 162 E2
Rowans Gate PA2 . . . 113 F2
Rowans Gdns G71 . . . 141 B4
Rowanside Terr KA22 . . . 205 C4
Rowan St
Greenock PA16 . . . 45 C5
Paisley PA2 . . . 113 F2
Wishaw ML2 . . . 165 B5
Rowans The
Alloa FK10 . . . 5 C2
Bishopbriggs G64 . . . 77 F2
Rowan Terr KA12 . . . 219 D4
Rowantree Ave
Motherwell ML1 . . . 143 D7
Rutherglen G73 . . . 138 B5
Uddingston G71 . . . 141 C7
Rowantree Gdns
Irvine KA11 . . . 220 A5
Rutherglen G73 . . . 138 B5
Rowantree Gr G83 . . . 27 E4
Rowantreehill Rd PA13 . . . 89 E8
Rowantree Pl
Johnstone PA5 . . . 111 F1
Larkhall ML9 . . . 185 D2
Lennoxtown G66 . . . 57 E7
Rowantree Rd PA5 . . . 112 A1
Rowantree Terr
Lennoxtown G66 . . . 57 E7
Motherwell ML1 . . . 143 B5
Rowantree Wlk FK5 . . . 23 B4
Rowan View ML11 . . . 215 B2
Rowanwood Cres ML5 . . . 121 D5
Rowchester St G40 . . . 118 A5
Rowena Ave G13 . . . 75 D1
Rowmore Quays G84 . . . 15 E4
Roxburgh Ave PA15 . . . 45 E4
Roxburgh Dr
Bearsden G61 . . . 75 E7
Coatbridge ML5 . . . 122 D4
Roxburgh Pk G74 . . . 159 F1
Roxburgh Pl
5 Hamilton G72 . . . 161 D7
Stenhousemuir FK5 . . . 23 F4
Roxburgh Rd
Hurlford KA1 . . . 228 E6
Paisley PA2 . . . 132 D7
Roxburgh Row FK7 . . . 12 E8
Roxburgh St
Glasgow G12 . . . 96 D3
Greenock PA15 . . . 45 E5
Roxburgh Way PA15 . . . 45 E4
Royal Alexandra Hospl
PA2 . . . 113 D2
Royal Bank Pl G1 . . . 241 A2
Royal Cres G3 . . . 116 E8
Royal Ct PA15 . . . 45 E5
Royal Dr ML3 . . . 163 A2
Royal Exchange Ct G1 . . . 241 A2
Royal Exchange Sq G1 . . . 241 A2
Royal Gdns
Bothwell G71 . . . 140 E2
Stirling FK8 . . . 7 A8
Royal Highland Fusiliers
Regimental Mus★ G2 . . . 240 B4
Royal Hospl for Sick Children
(Yorkhill) G3 . . . 96 C1
Royal Inch Cres PA4 . . . 94 D5
Royal Infmy Hospl G4 . . . 241 C3
Royal Scottish Acad of Music
& Drama G2 . . . 240 C3
Royal St PA19 . . . 44 E8
Royal Stuart Way FK7 . . . 7 E8
Royal Terr
Glasgow G3 . . . 96 E1
Wishaw ML2 . . . 165 C7
Royal Terrace La G3 . . . 96 E1
Royal Troon Golf Club★
KA10 . . . 232 D8
Royellen Ave ML3 . . . 161 F2
Roy St G21 . . . 97 D3
Roystonhill G21 . . . 97 F1
Roystonhill Pl G21 . . . 97 F1
Royston Prim Sch G21 . . . 97 F1
Royston Rd G21, G33 . . . 98 C3
Royston Sq G21 . . . 241 C4
Roy Young Ave G83 . . . 28 A8
ROZELLE . . . 239 A2
Rozelle Ave
Clydebank G15 . . . 75 B3
Newton Mearns G77 . . . 156 B4
Rozelle Dr G77 . . . 156 B4
Rozelle House & MacLaurin
Galleries★ KA7 . . . 238 F2
Rozelle Pl G77 . . . 156 B4
Rozelle Terr KA7 . . . 239 B1
Rubie Cres KA12 . . . 219 C1
Rubislaw Dr G61 . . . 75 E3
Ruby St G40 . . . 118 A4
Ruby Terr ML4 . . . 142 A4
RUCHAZIE . . . 99 B1
Ruchazie Pl G32, G33 . . . 118 F8
Ruchazie Rd G33 . . . 118 F7
RUCHILL . . . 97 A5
Ruchill Pl G20 . . . 96 F5
Ruchill Prim Sch G20 . . . 96 F6
Ruchill St G20 . . . 96 F5
Rue End St PA15 . . . 46 A4
Ruel St G44 . . . 137 A7
Rufflees Ave G78 . . . 134 D4
Rugby Ave G13 . . . 95 B8
Rugby Cres KA1 . . . 227 D7

Rugby Pk (Kilmarnock FC)
KA1 . . . 227 E7
Rugby Rd KA1 . . . 227 D7
Rulley View FK6 . . . 21 C4
Rullion Pl G33 . . . 118 F8
Rumford Pl KA3 . . . 223 C6
Rumford St G40 . . . 117 F3
Rumlie The FK1 . . . 86 A6
Runciman Pl G74 . . . 160 B4
Rundell Dr G66 . . . 58 C5
Rupert St G4 . . . 96 F2
Rush Hill KA7 . . . 239 C2
Rushyhill St G21 . . . 98 A4
Ruskie Rd FK9 . . . 2 B3
Ruskin La G12 . . . 96 E3
Ruskin Pl
Glasgow G12 . . . 96 E3
Kilsyth G65 . . . 60 D8
Ruskin Sq G64 . . . 78 A1
Ruskin Terr
Glasgow G12 . . . 96 E3
Rutherglen G73 . . . 118 B1
Russell Colt St ML5 . . . 122 A8
Russell Ct KA3 . . . 223 C3
Russell Dr
Alexandria G83 . . . 27 C7
Ayr KA8 . . . 236 A2
Bearsden G61 . . . 75 F6
Dalry KA24 . . . 191 D8
Russell Gdns
Newton Mearns G77 . . . 156 C4
10 Uddingston G71 . . . 141 A8
Russell Hill Ct FK5 . . . 23 B1
Russell La ML2 . . . 165 A2
Russell Pl
Bonnybridge FK4 . . . 39 D5
Clarkston G76 . . . 158 A5
East Kilbride G75 . . . 180 C7
Linwood PA3 . . . 111 F6
Russell Rd
Duntocher G81 . . . 73 E7
Lanark ML11 . . . 215 B5
Russell St
Ayr KA8 . . . 236 A1
Bellshill ML4 . . . 142 D5
Chapelhall ML6 . . . 123 E2
Hamilton ML3 . . . 161 F5
Johnstone PA5 . . . 112 A3
Paisley PA3 . . . 113 D7
6 Port Glasgow PA14 . . . 47 A2
Wishaw ML2 . . . 165 B2
Russel St FK2 . . . 42 B6
Rutherford Ave
Bearsden G61 . . . 75 B8
Kirkintilloch G66 . . . 80 B6
Rutherford Ct
Bridge of Allan FK9 . . . 2 A8
Clydebank G81 . . . 74 A2
Rutherford Grange G66 . . . 79 C6
Rutherford La G75 . . . 180 F8
Rutherford Sq G75 . . . 180 F8
RUTHERGLEN . . . 138 D8
Rutherglen High Sch
G73 . . . 138 C8
Rutherglen Ind Est G73 . . . 118 A1
Rutherglen Rd G5, G73 . . . 117 E2
Rutherglen Sh Ctr G73 . . . 138 B8
Rutherglen Sta G73 . . . 138 B8
Ruthven Ave G46 . . . 136 D1
Ruthven La
7 Glasgow G12 . . . 96 D3
Glenboig ML5 . . . 101 C6
Ruthven Pl
Bishopbriggs G64 . . . 98 C8
Troon KA10 . . . 229 F4
Ruthven St G12 . . . 96 D3
Rutland Cres G51 . . . 116 E6
Rutland Ct G51 . . . 116 E6
Rutland Pl G51 . . . 116 E6
Ryan Rd G64 . . . 78 B1
Ryan Way G73 . . . 138 C3
Ryat Dr G77 . . . 156 C6
Ryat Gn G77 . . . 156 C5
Ryatt Linn PA8 . . . 72 F1
Rydal Gr G75 . . . 179 F6
Rydal Pl G75 . . . 179 F6
Ryden Mains Rd ML6 . . . 102 D4
Ryde Rd ML2 . . . 165 C4
Ryebank Rd G21 . . . 98 C5
Rye Cres G21 . . . 98 B5
Ryecroft Dr G69 . . . 120 B5
Ryedale Pl G15 . . . 75 B4
Ryefield Ave
Coatbridge ML5 . . . 121 D7
Johnstone PA5 . . . 111 D1
Ryefield Ho KA24 . . . 169 B1
Ryefield Pl PA5 . . . 111 D1
Ryefield Rd G21 . . . 98 B5
Ryehill Pl G21 . . . 98 C5
Ryehill Rd G21 . . . 98 C4
Ryemount Rd G21 . . . 98 C5
Rye Rd G21 . . . 98 C5
Ryeside Pl KA24 . . . 169 C1
Ryeside Rd G21 . . . 98 B4
Rye Way PA2 . . . 112 E1
Ryewraes Rd PA3 . . . 112 B5
Rylands KA9 . . . 236 C6
Rylands Dr G32 . . . 119 D4
Rylands Gdns G32 . . . 119 E4
Rylees Cres G52 . . . 114 E6
Rylees Pl G52 . . . 114 E6
Rylees Rd G52 . . . 114 E6
Rysland Ave G77 . . . 156 E5
Rysland Cres G77 . . . 156 E5
Rysland Dr KA3 . . . 213 A4
Ryvra Rd G13 . . . 95 D6

S

Sachelcourt Ave PA7 . . . 72 B2
Sackville Ave G13 . . . 95 F5
Sackville La G13 . . . 95 F5
Sacred Heart Prim Sch
Bellshill ML4 . . . 142 A3
Glasgow G40 . . . 117 F4
Greenock PA16 . . . 44 E4
Saddell Rd G15 . . . 75 B4
Sadler's Wells Ct G74 . . . 160 B4
Saffron Cres ML2 . . . 164 E1
Saffronhall Cres ML3 . . . 162 D4
Saffronhall Gdns ML3 . . . 162 D4
Saffronhall La ML3 . . . 162 D4
Sainford Cres FK2 . . . 24 A1
St Abb's Dr PA2 . . . 113 A1
St Agathas Prim Sch G66 . . . 80 B8
St Agnes Prim Sch G23 . . . 96 E8
St Aidans High Sch ML2 . . . 165 B4
St Aidan's Path ML2 . . . 165 C6
St Aidans RC Prim Sch
ML2 . . . 165 C5
St Aidans Sch G32 . . . 118 D6
St Alberts Prim Sch G41 . . . 116 E4
St Aloysius Coll G3 . . . 240 B4
St Aloysius Prim Sch G22 . . . 97 E5
St Aloysius RC Prim Sch
ML6 . . . 123 E2
St Ambrose High Sch
ML5 . . . 121 E8
St Andrews Acad PA2 . . . 114 C1
St Andrews Ave G71 . . . 141 A1
St Andrew's Ave
Bishopbriggs G64 . . . 77 E2
Prestwick KA9 . . . 236 C6
St Andrew's Brae G82 . . . 50 B5
St Andrews Cl 3 G41 . . . 116 F4
St Andrews Cres G41 . . . 116 E4
St Andrew's Cres
Dumbarton G82 . . . 50 B5
Paisley PA3 . . . 113 C8
St Andrew's Cross G41 . . . 117 A3
St Andrews Ct
Bellshill ML4 . . . 142 B5
East Kilbride G75 . . . 180 C6
4 Kirkintilloch G66 . . . 79 D7
Motherwell ML1 . . . 143 A6
Saltcoats KA21 . . . 205 F3
St Andrew's Ct ML8 . . . 187 E1
St Andrew's Ct FK5 . . . 23 B3
St Andrews Dr
Bearsden G61 . . . 75 D7
Bridge of Weir PA11 . . . 110 C6
Coatbridge ML5 . . . 121 E6
Cumbernauld G68 . . . 62 B6
Gourock PA19 . . . 44 A6
Law ML8 . . . 187 A6
St Andrew's Dr
Airth FK2 . . . 14 B7
Glasgow G41 . . . 116 D3
Hamilton ML3 . . . 161 D4
Paisley PA3 . . . 113 D8
Renfrew PA3 . . . 93 E1
St Andrew's Drive W
Paisley PA3 . . . 113 D8
Renfrew PA3 . . . 93 C1
St Andrews Gate ML4 . . . 141 F5
St Andrew's Gdns
Airdrie ML6 . . . 123 B8
Dalry KA24 . . . 191 B6
St Andrews High Sch
ML5 . . . 121 F3
St Andrew's High Sch
G81 . . . 94 C8
St Andrews La
Alexandria G83 . . . 27 E4
Gourock PA19 . . . 44 A6
St Andrew's La G1 . . . 241 B1
St Andrews Path 10 ML9 . . . 185 C1
St Andrews Pl
Beith KA15 . . . 171 A7
10 Falkirk FK1 . . . 42 B4
Kilsyth G65 . . . 36 C1
St Andrew's Pl KA20 . . . 206 F2
St Andrews Prim Sch
Airdrie ML6 . . . 102 E1
Bearsden G61 . . . 75 C6
Cumbernauld G68 . . . 61 D5
Kilmarnock KA3 . . . 223 B2
St Andrew Sq PA15 . . . 46 B4
St Andrew's RC Cath★
G1 . . . 241 A1
St Andrews RC Prim Sch
FK1 . . . 42 E4
St Andrews RC Sec Sch
G32 . . . 119 A7
St Andrew's Rd
Ardrossan KA22 . . . 205 D4
Glasgow G41 . . . 116 F4
Renfrew PA4 . . . 94 C2
St Andrews & St Brides High
Sch G74 . . . 160 A1
St Andrew's Sq G1 . . . 241 B1
St Andrews St ML1 . . . 143 A5
St Andrew's St
Ayr KA7 . . . 239 A7
Glasgow G1 . . . 241 B1
St Andrew St
Greenock PA15 . . . 46 B4
Kilmarnock KA1 . . . 227 F8
St Andrews Way KA12 . . . 224 F8
St Andrew's Way ML2 . . . 165 C6
St Andrew's Wlk 2 KA1 . . . 227 F7
St Andrews Wynd G84 . . . 16 E3
St Angelas Prim Sch
G53 . . . 135 C3

St Annes Ave PA8 . . . 93 D8
St Anne's Cres FK7 . . . 7 E1
St Anne's Ct ML3 . . . 183 D8
St Annes Prim Sch
Erskine PA8 . . . 93 C8
Glasgow G40 . . . 118 A5
St Annes RC Prim Sch
ML3 . . . 183 D8
St Annes Wynd PA8 . . . 93 D8
St Ann's Dr G46 . . . 136 C2
St Anthonys Prim Sch
Johnstone PA5 . . . 131 C7
Rutherglen G73 . . . 138 D4
Saltcoats KA21 . . . 205 E2
St Athanasius' Prim Sch
ML8 . . . 187 F1
St Augustine's Prim Sch
ML5 . . . 121 F6
St Barbaras Prim Sch
G69 . . . 100 D7
St Barchan's Rd PA10 . . . 111 B2
St Bartholomews Prim Sch
ML5 . . . 101 D1
St Bartholomew's Prim Sch
G45 . . . 137 F4
St Benedicts High Sch
PA3 . . . 111 F5
St Benedict's Prim Sch
G34 . . . 100 C1
St Bernadette's Prim Sch
ML1 . . . 163 B8
St Bernadette's RC Prim Sch
FK10 . . . 4 A2
St Bernards Prim Sch
G53 . . . 135 A5
St Bernards RC Prim Sch
ML5 . . . 122 B3
St Blane's Dr G73 . . . 137 F6
St Blanes Prim Sch
Glasgow G23 . . . 76 D1
Hamilton G72 . . . 161 C8
St Boswell's Cres PA2 . . . 113 A1
St Boswells Dr ML5 . . . 122 D4
St Brendans Prim Sch
G13 . . . 94 F7
St Brendans RC Prim Sch
ML1 . . . 164 B2
St Brennans Ct KA25 . . . 170 A7
St Bride's Ave G71 . . . 141 C7
St Bride's Dr KA23 . . . 190 D5
St Bride's Pl KA12 . . . 219 C5
St Bride's Prim Sch G72 . . . 139 A5
St Brides RC Prim Sch
G71 . . . 141 A4
St Bride's Rd
Glasgow G43 . . . 136 D6
West Kilbride KA23 . . . 190 D6
St Brides Way G71 . . . 141 A4
St Bridgets Prim Sch
Glasgow G69 . . . 120 B5
Kilbirnie KA25 . . . 170 A8
St Brigid's Prim Sch
Glasgow G42 . . . 137 E8
Wishaw ML2 . . . 166 A5
St Bryde La G74 . . . 159 F2
St Bryde St 8 G74 . . . 159 F2
St Cadocs Prim Sch G77 . . . 156 C5
St Cadoc's Prim Sch
G72 . . . 139 C4
St Catherines Cres ML7 . . . 146 E6
St Catherine's Prim Sch
PA3 . . . 113 F6
St Catherines RC Prim Sch
G21 . . . 98 C5
St Catherines Rd KA8 . . . 236 F2
St Catherine's Rd G46 . . . 136 C2
St Charles Prim Sch
Cambuslang G72 . . . 139 F6
Glasgow G20 . . . 96 F4
Paisley PA2 . . . 113 F2
St Clair PA9 . . . 130 F5
St Clair Ave G46 . . . 136 C3
St Clair St G20 . . . 96 F2
St Clares Prim RC Sch
G15 . . . 75 A4
St Columba Dr G66 . . . 79 E7
St Columba Mews G84 . . . 16 D2
St Columba Pl KA20 . . . 206 F2
St Columbas High Sch
PA16 . . . 45 A6
St Columba's High Sch
G81 . . . 74 C4
St Columba's Sch (Junior)
PA13 . . . 89 C8
St Columba's Sch (Senior)
PA13 . . . 89 D8
St Columbkilles Prim Sch 1
G73 . . . 138 B7
St Constantine's Prim Sch
G51 . . . 115 E7
St Convals Prim Sch
G43 . . . 136 D8
St Crispin's Pl FK1 . . . 42 B4
St Cuthbert's Cres KA9 . . . 236 D6
St Cuthberts Ct KA21 . . . 216 E8
St Cuthberts Prim Sch
Glasgow G22 . . . 97 B4
10 Hamilton ML3 . . . 162 A5
St Cuthbert's Rd KA9 . . . 236 C6
St Cuthbert Way ML3 . . . 161 F5
St Cyrus Gdns G64 . . . 78 C1
St Cyrus Rd G64 . . . 78 C1
St David's Ct FK5 . . . 23 B1
St Davids Dr ML6 . . . 123 C4
St David's Pl ML9 . . . 185 A3

Sandwood Cres 4 G52 .. 115 A5
Sandwood Path 1 G52 .. 115 A5
Sandwood Prim Sch 6 G52 ... 115 A5
Sandwood Rd G52 ... 115 A5
Sandy Ct KA23 ... 190 C3
Sandyfaulds St 1 G5 ... 117 D4
Sandyford Ave ML1 ... 143 D7
Sandyford Pl
Glasgow G3 ... 240 A3
Motherwell ML1 ... 143 D7
Sandyford Place La G3 .. 240 A3
Sandyford Rd
Mossblown KA6 ... 237 F6
Motherwell ML1 ... 143 D7
Paisley PA3 ... 114 A8
Prestwick KA9 ... 234 B1
Sandyford St G3 ... 116 C8
Sandyford Toll Rdbt KA9 ... 237 C8
Sandyhill Ave ML7 ... 147 A3
SANDYHILLS ... 119 C5
Sandyhills Cres G32 ... 119 B3
Sandyhills Dr G32 ... 119 B3
Sandyhills Gr G32 ... 119 B2
Sandyhills Pl G32 ... 119 B3
Sandyhills Rd G32 ... 119 C3
Sandyhill Terr KA6 ... 239 E6
Sandyknowes Rd G67 ... 83 A8
Sandy La G11 ... 96 A2
Sandylands Prom KA21 .. 217 A7
Sandy Rd
Carluke ML8 ... 187 F2
Glasgow G11 ... 96 A2
Irvine KA12 ... 219 B5
Renfrew PA4 ... 94 C2
West Kilbride KA23 ... 190 C3
Sandyvale ML9 ... 198 D1
Sanford Pl 11 G3 ... 116 E8
Sannox Dr
Motherwell ML1 ... 163 B7
Saltcoats KA21 ... 206 A2
Sannox Gdns G31 ... 118 B8
Sannox Pl
Ayr KA8 ... 236 D2
East Kilbride G75 ... 180 B4
Helensburgh G84 ... 16 F3
Sannox Rd KA1 ... 222 C2
Sannox View KA8 ... 236 E2
Sanquhar Ave KA9 ... 236 D7
Sanquhar Dr G53 ... 135 A8
Sanquhar Farm Rd KA8 .. 236 D3
Sanquhar Gdns
Blantyre G72 ... 140 B2
1 Glasgow G53 ... 135 A8
Sanquhar Pl 2 G53 ... 135 A8
Sanquhar Rd G53 ... 115 A1
Sanson La ML8 ... 202 C8
Sapphire Rd ML4 ... 142 B4
Saracen Head Rd G1 ... 241 C1
Saracen Prim Sch (Keppoch Campus) G22 ... 97 C4
Saracen St
Glasgow G22 ... 97 C4
Glasgow G22 ... 97 C5
Sarazen Ct ML1 ... 164 E8
Sarazen Dr KA10 ... 232 E8
Sardinia La G12 ... 96 D3
Sark Dr KA10 ... 229 G5
Saskatoon Pl G75 ... 159 B1
Saturn Ave PA1 ... 112 E5
Saucel Cres PA1 ... 113 E4
Saucelhill Terr PA2 ... 113 F3
Saucel Pl PA1 ... 113 E3
Saucel St PA1 ... 113 F4
Sauchenford Smallholdings FK7 ... 12 A5
Sauchenhall Path 8 G69 . 81 A3
SAUCHIE ... 5 E1
Sauchie Ct FK7 ... 7 F1
Sauchiehall La
Glasgow G2 ... 240 B3
Glasgow G2 ... 240 C3
Sauchiehall St
Glasgow, Cranston Hill G3 ... 116 E8
Glasgow G2 ... 240 B3
Sauchiesmoor Rd ML8 .. 202 A8
Sauchie St FK7 ... 7 A2
Saugh Ave G78 ... 173 D8
Saughs Ave G33 ... 98 F6
Saughs Dr G33 ... 98 F6
Saughs Gate G33 ... 98 F6
Saughs Pl G33 ... 98 F6
Saughs Rd G33 ... 98 F6
Saughton St G32 ... 118 E7
Saughtree Ave KA21 ... 205 F2
Saunders Ct G78 ... 134 B3
Saunterne Rd KA9 ... 233 C1
Savoy Ct KA7 ... 238 E7
Savoy Pk KA7 ... 238 E7
Savoy Sh Ctr G2 ... 240 C3
Savoy St G40 ... 117 F4
Sawers Ave FK6 ... 21 D1
Sawmillfield St G4 ... 97 B2
Sawmill Rd G11 ... 95 F2
Saxon Rd G13 ... 95 D7
Scadlock Rd PA3 ... 113 B5
Scalloway La G72 ... 138 F3
Scalloway Rd
Cambuslang G72 ... 138 E3
Gartcosh G69 ... 100 E4
Scalpay G74 ... 160 C1
Scalpay Pass G22 ... 97 D7
Scalpay Pl
Glasgow G22 ... 97 D7
Kilmarnock KA3 ... 223 A5
Scalpay St G22 ... 97 D7
Scamadale Rd ML6 ... 84 D3
Scapa St G23 ... 96 F8
Scapa Way G33 ... 99 E6
Scapesland Terr G82 ... 50 A4
Scaraway Dr G22 ... 97 D8
Scaraway Pl G22 ... 97 D8
Scaraway St G22 ... 97 D8
Scaraway Terr G22 ... 97 D8
Scarba Dr G43 ... 136 B6
Scarba Quadrant 5 ML2 164 E1
Scarffe Ave PA3 ... 111 F5
Scargie Rd KA1 ... 227 E4
Scarhill Ave ML6 ... 122 F5
Scarhill La ML6 ... 123 A5
Scarhill St
Cleland ML1 ... 144 B2
Coatbridge ML5 ... 121 F3
Scarletmuir ML11 ... 214 F5
Scarlow St PA14 ... 47 C2
Scarrel Dr G45 ... 138 A4
Scarrel Gdns G45 ... 138 A3
Scarrel Rd G45 ... 138 A3
Scarrel Terr G45 ... 138 A4
Scaur O' Doon Rd KA7 .. 238 C3
Scavaig Cres G15 ... 74 E4
Schaw Ct
Alloa FK10 ... 5 D1
Bearsden G61 ... 75 E6
Schaw Dr
Bearsden G61 ... 75 E6
Clydebank G81 ... 74 E7
Schawpark Ave FK10 ... 5 D1
Schaw Rd PA3 ... 114 A6
Schiltron Way FK7 ... 7 D3
Scholar's Gate G75 ... 180 D6
School Ave G72 ... 139 B5
School Ho PA11 ... 89 E3
Schoolhouse La G72 ... 161 C6
School La
Bothwell G71 ... 141 B1
Cambuslang G72 ... 139 E4
Carluke ML8 ... 187 E2
Dumbarton G82 ... 49 D4
Irvine KA12 ... 219 C1
Lennoxtown G66 ... 57 D8
Menstrie FK11 ... 4 A7
Milton of Campsie G66 ... 58 C6
Shotts ML7 ... 167 B8
School Mews FK11 ... 4 A7
School Pl KA22 ... 205 C2
School Quadrant ML6 ... 102 F2
School Rd
Gartocharn G83 ... 20 F7
Kilbirnie KA25 ... 149 A2
Newton Mearns G77 ... 156 D4
Paisley PA1 ... 114 E5
Rhu G84 ... 15 D5
Salsburgh ML7 ... 125 D3
Stepps G33 ... 99 E6
Torrance G64 ... 57 C1
Tullibody FK10 ... 4 B2
Wishaw ML2 ... 166 A4
Wishaw, Morningside ML2 . 166 B4
School St
Chapelhall ML6 ... 123 D2
Coatbridge ML5 ... 122 A4
Hamilton ML3 ... 162 D1
Shotts ML7 ... 146 F4
School View ML1 ... 163 E5
Schoolwell St KA20 ... 206 D1
School Wlk FK5 ... 23 D3
School Wynd
Dundonald KA2 ... 225 F2
Kilbirnie KA25 ... 149 A2
Paisley PA1 ... 113 E5
Quarriers Village PA11 ... 89 E3
Scioncroft Ave G73 ... 138 C7
Sclandersburn Rd FK6 ... 39 C8
Scone Pl
East Kilbride G74 ... 159 D3
Newton Mearns G77 ... 157 B4
Scone St G21 ... 97 C3
Scone Wlk 3 G69 ... 120 A3
Sconser PA4 ... 93 C7
Sconser St G23 ... 76 E1
Scorton Gdns G69 ... 119 F4
Scotia Cres ML9 ... 185 A1
Scotia Gdns ML3 ... 183 C7
Scotia Pl FK2 ... 42 C5
Scotia St ML1 ... 163 C7
Scotland St G5 ... 116 F5
Scotland Street School Mus★ G5 ... 116 F5
Scotland Street W G41 ... 116 D5
Scotsblair Ave G66 ... 79 C7
Scotsburn Rd G21 ... 98 C4
SCOTSTOUN ... 95 B4
SCOTSTOUNHILL ... 95 B6
Scotstounhill Sta G13 ... 95 B5
Scotstoun L Ctr G14 ... 95 D4
Scotstoun Prim Sch G14 . 95 C4
Scotstoun Rd FK7 ... 12 E7
Scotstoun St G14 ... 95 C3
Scotstoun Way ML5 ... 122 C5
Scott Ave
Bowling G60 ... 72 D8
Johnstone PA5 ... 131 E8
Milton of Campsie G66 ... 58 C6
Scott Cres
Alloa FK10 ... 10 B5
Cumbernauld G67 ... 82 D7
Kilmarnock KA1 ... 227 E7
Troon KA10 ... 229 G4
Scott Ct
Alexandria G83 ... 27 E4
Alva FK12 ... 5 B6
Helensburgh G84 ... 16 C1
Scott Dr
Bearsden G61 ... 75 C6
Cumbernauld G67 ... 82 D7
Law ML8 ... 187 A6
Scott Gdns G82 ... 48 A8
Scott Gr ML3 ... 162 D2
Scott Hill 1 G74 ... 160 A3
Scott Ho G67 ... 62 A3
Scottish Agricultural Coll KA6 ... 237 C3
Scottish Exhibition & Conference Ctr G3 ... 116 D7
Scottish Maritime Mus★ KA12 ... 219 A1
Scottish Sch of Herbal Medicine G51 ... 95 E1
Scott Pl
Bellshill ML4 ... 142 B7
Johnstone PA5 ... 131 E8
Saltcoats KA21 ... 205 E1
Troon KA10 ... 229 E5
Scott Rd
Glasgow G52 ... 114 F8
Irvine KA12 ... 219 C1
Kilmarnock KA1 ... 227 E7
Scott's Pl ML6 ... 123 B8
Scott's Rd PA2 ... 114 D3
Scott St
Alexandria G83 ... 27 F4
Clydebank G81 ... 73 E4
Glasgow G69 ... 120 B4
Glasgow, Garnethill G3 ... 240 B4
Greenock PA15 ... 46 A4
Hamilton ML3 ... 162 D1
Larkhall ML9 ... 185 B2
Motherwell ML9 ... 163 E7
Stirling FK8 ... 2 A2
Scott Way PA14 ... 47 A3
Scotus Coll G61 ... 75 D4
Seabank Rd
Ayr KA7 ... 235 E1
Prestwick KA9 ... 233 B1
Seabank St KA21 ... 217 A7
Seabegs Cres FK4 ... 40 A4
Seabegs Pl FK4 ... 39 F4
Seabegs Rd FK4 ... 39 F4
Seabegs Wood Antonine Wall★ FK4 ... 39 E3
SEAFAR ... 61 E1
Seafar Rd G67 ... 61 F2
Seafar Rdbt G67 ... 82 E8
SEAFIELD ... 238 D5
Seafield Ave G61 ... 75 F7
Seafield Cottage La PA16. 45 D8
Seafield Cres
Ayr KA7 ... 238 E5
Cumbernauld G68 ... 60 E1
Seafield Ct
Ardrossan KA22 ... 205 B3
Falkirk FK1 ... 41 F2
Seafield Dr
Ardrossan KA22 ... 205 C3
Ayr KA7 ... 238 D5
Rutherglen G73 ... 138 D3
Seafield Ho PA16 ... 45 E7
Seafield Rd KA7 ... 238 E6
Seafield Sch KA22 ... 205 B3
Seaford St KA1 ... 227 E8
Seaforth Cres
Ayr KA8 ... 236 B4
Barrhead G78 ... 134 B4
Seaforth La G69 ... 81 A2
Seaforth Pl
Bellshill ML4 ... 141 F3
Stirling FK8 ... 7 B8
5 Stirling FK8 ... 7 B8
Seaforth Rd
Ayr KA8 ... 236 B4
Clydebank G81 ... 74 B2
Falkirk FK2 ... 24 C1
Glasgow G52 ... 115 A7
Seaforth Road N G52 ... 115 A7
Seaforth Road S G52 ... 115 A7
Seagate
Irvine KA12 ... 219 B3
Prestwick KA9 ... 233 C2
Seagrove St G32 ... 118 D6
Sea Life Loch Lomond★ G83 ... 19 D1
SEAMILL ... 190 C2
Seamill Gdns G74 ... 159 D2
Seamill Path G53 ... 134 F5
Seamill St G53 ... 134 F5
Seamill Way ML5 ... 121 F5
Seamore St 4 G20 ... 96 F2
Seath Ave
Airdrie ML6 ... 122 E7
Langbank PA14 ... 70 D6
Seath Rd G73 ... 118 A1
Seath St G42 ... 117 C2
Seaton Pl FK1 ... 42 D4
Seaton Terr
Hamilton ML3 ... 162 A4
Irvine KA12 ... 219 C5
Sea Tower Ct KA7 ... 238 E6
Seaview Rd KA21 ... 216 F7
Seaview Terr KA10 ... 230 A4
Seaward La
Glasgow G5 ... 240 A1
Glasgow G41, G5 ... 116 E6
Seaward Pl G41 ... 116 F5
Seaward St
Glasgow G5, G41 ... 116 F5
3 Glasgow G41 ... 116 E5
Second Ave
Alexandria G83 ... 27 F5
Auchinloch G66 ... 79 D1
Bearsden G61 ... 76 A3
Second Ave *continued*
Clydebank G81 ... 74 A3
Dumbarton G82 ... 50 C2
Glasgow G44 ... 137 B6
Irvine KA12 ... 224 E8
Millerston G33 ... 99 B4
Renfrew PA4 ... 94 C2
Uddingston G71 ... 120 E1
Second Avenue La G44 .. 137 B7
Second Gdns G41 ... 116 A4
Second Rd G72 ... 161 E5
Second St G71 ... 140 F8
SEEDHILL ... 114 A3
Seedhill PA1 ... 113 F4
Seedhill Rd PA1 ... 114 A4
Seggielea La G13 ... 95 D6
Seggielea Rd G13 ... 95 D6
Segton Ave KA13 ... 207 C3
Seil Dr G44 ... 137 C4
Selborne Pl 1 G13 ... 95 E5
Selborne Rd G13 ... 95 E5
Selby Gdns G32 ... 119 D5
Selby Pl ML5 ... 101 D2
Selby St ML5 ... 101 D2
Selkirk Ave
Glasgow G52 ... 115 C4
Paisley PA2 ... 133 A8
Selkirk Ct 9 PA15 ... 46 B3
Selkirk Dr G73 ... 138 C7
Selkirk Pl
East Kilbride G74 ... 160 D3
Hamilton ML3 ... 162 E2
Selkirk Rd PA14 ... 68 D8
Selkirk St
Hamilton, Blantyre G72 ... 161 D7
Hamilton, Silvertonhill ML3 162 E2
Wishaw ML2 ... 165 C5
Selkirk Way
Bellshill ML4 ... 142 B7
Coatbridge ML5 ... 122 E3
Sella Rd G64 ... 78 D2
Selvieland Farm Cotts PA3 ... 92 D3
Selvieland Rd G52 ... 114 F5
Semphill Gdns G74 ... 160 B2
Sempie St ML3 ... 161 F4
Sempill Ave PA8 ... 72 F2
Semple Ave
Bishopton PA7 ... 72 B3
Lochwinnoch PA12 ... 129 C3
Semple Pl PA3 ... 112 B7
Semple Rd KA9 ... 236 D5
Semple View PA9 ... 130 F5
Senate Pl ML1 ... 142 C1
Senga Cres ML4 ... 142 A7
Seres Rd G76 ... 157 D8
Sergeant Law Rd
Paisley G78, PA2 ... 132 E3
Uplawmoor G78 ... 153 B7
Seright Cres KA3 ... 228 D7
Seright Sq KA3 ... 228 D8
Serpentine Wlk PA15 ... 46 C3
Sersley Dr KA25 ... 148 F1
Service St G66 ... 33 C1
Seton Dr FK7 ... 7 C4
Seton La KA22 ... 205 C2
Seton St KA22 ... 205 C2
Seton Terr 3 G31 ... 117 F7
Settle Gdns G69 ... 119 F4
Seven Sisters G66 ... 79 E5
Seventh Ave G71 ... 140 F8
Seventh Rd G72 ... 161 E5
Severn Rd G75 ... 179 F7
Seymour Ave KA13 ... 207 F2
Seymour Gn G75 ... 180 B7
Seyton Ave G46 ... 136 C1
Seyton Ct G46 ... 136 C1
Seyton La G74 ... 159 E3
Shaftesbury Ct G74 ... 160 C5
Shaftesbury St
Alloa FK10 ... 10 A7
Clydebank G81 ... 73 F2
Glasgow G3 ... 240 A3
Shafton Pl G13 ... 95 E8
Shafton Rd G13 ... 95 E8
Shaftsbury Ave G81 ... 73 F2
Shaftsbury Cres ML1 ... 143 D3
Shakespeare Ave G81 ... 73 F4
Shakespeare St G20 ... 96 E5
Shalloch Pk KA7 ... 238 C2
Shalloch Pl KA11 ... 220 B2
Shamrock St
Glasgow G4 ... 240 B4
Kirkintilloch G66 ... 79 D8
Shand La ML8 ... 187 F3
Shandon Brae G83 ... 27 F8
Shandon Cres
Balloch G83 ... 27 F8
Bellshill ML4 ... 142 A8
Shandon Pl PA15 ... 46 C2
Shandon Terr ML3 ... 161 F3
Shand St ML2 ... 165 B3
Shandwick Square Sh Ctr G34 ... 120 A8
Shandwick St G34 ... 120 A8
Shankland Gr PA15 ... 46 F2
Shankland Rd PA15 ... 46 F2
Shankly Dr ML2 ... 166 C3
Shanks Ave
Barrhead G78 ... 134 C2
Denny FK6 ... 39 E8
Shanks Cres PA5 ... 111 E2
Shanks Ct KA3 ... 222 F2
Shanks Ind Pk G78 ... 134 C4
Shanks St
Airdrie ML6 ... 103 A1
Glasgow G20 ... 96 E5
Shanks Way G78 ... 134 C5
Shannon Dr FK1 ... 41 F4
Shannon St G20 ... 96 F5
Shanter Pl
Alloway KA7 ... 238 E1
Kilmarnock KA3 ... 228 C8
Shanter Way KA7 ... 238 E1
Shanter Wynd KA7 ... 238 E1
Shantron Rd G83 ... 27 E6
Shapinsay St G22 ... 97 D8
Sharlee Wynd KA23 ... 190 D6
Sharnothshield Small Holdings ML2 ... 166 E6
Sharon St KA24 ... 191 B8
Sharp Ave ML5 ... 121 C4
Sharpe Ave KA11 ... 220 D1
Sharphill Ind Est KA21 .. 206 A3
Sharphill Rd KA21 ... 216 F8
Sharp St
Gourock PA19 ... 44 F7
Motherwell ML1 ... 163 B7
Shavian Terr KA13 ... 207 E2
Shavin Brae KA7 ... 239 D6
Shaw Ave PA7 ... 72 C3
Shawbank Pl KA1 ... 228 A7
Shawbridge Arc G43 ... 136 C8
Shawbridge Ind Est G43 . 136 B7
Shawbridge St G43 ... 136 C7
Shawburn Cres ML3 ... 162 B4
Shawburn St ML3 ... 162 B4
Shaw Cres ML2 ... 164 D1
Shaw Ct
Erskine PA8 ... 72 F3
Newton Mearns G77 ... 156 F4
Shawfarm Ct KA9 ... 233 D1
Shawfarm Gdns KA9 ... 233 D2
Shaw Farm Ind Est KA9 . 233 F1
Shawfarm Pl KA9 ... 233 D1
Shawfarm Rd KA9 ... 233 E1
SHAWFIELD ... 117 F2
Shawfield Ave KA7 ... 239 A4
Shawfield Cres ML8 ... 186 F6
Shawfield Ind Est G73 ... 117 F2
Shawfield Rd G73 ... 117 F2
Shawfoot Rd ML1 ... 122 F1
Shawgill Ct ML8 ... 186 F4
SHAWHEAD ... 122 A3
Shawhead Ave ML5 ... 122 B4
Shawhead Cotts ML5 ... 122 B3
Shawhead Prim Sch ML5 ... 122 B3
Shawhill Cres G77 ... 156 E3
Shawhill Rd G43 ... 136 D8
Shawholm Cres G43 ... 136 C7
Shawholm Gdns KA12 ... 219 C3
SHAWLANDS ... 136 E8
Shawlands Acad G41 ... 116 E1
Shawlands Arcade Sh Ctr G41 ... 136 D8
Shawlands Cres ML9 ... 199 D6
Shawlands Cross 5 G41 116 E1
Shawlands Prim Sch G41 ... 136 D8
Shawlands Sta G41 ... 136 D8
Shawmoss Rd G41 ... 116 D1
Shawpark St G20 ... 96 E6
Shaw Pl
Dalry KA24 ... 191 B7
Greenock PA15 ... 45 F5
Linwood PA3 ... 112 B5
Saltcoats KA21 ... 206 A2
Shaw Rd
Milngavie G62 ... 76 A8
Newton Mearns G77 ... 156 E4
Prestwick KA9 ... 233 D1
Prestwick KA9 ... 233 E1
Shawrigg Rd ML9 ... 185 C2
SHAWSBURN ... 185 E2
Shawsgate ML9 ... 185 E1
Shaws Rd ML9 ... 199 C8
Shaw St
Glasgow G51 ... 116 A8
Larkhall ML9 ... 199 B8
SHAWSTONEFOOT ... 144 F1
Shawstonfoot Rd ML1 ... 145 A1
Shawwood Cres G77 ... 156 E3
Shearer Dr ML3 ... 183 C7
Shearer Quadrant G83 ... 28 A8
SHEDDENS ... 157 F7
Sheena Dr G83 ... 27 F2
Sheepburn Rd G71 ... 140 E7
Sheila St G33 ... 98 E4
Sheildhill 8 G75 ... 180 F7
Sheiling Hill ML3 ... 162 E4
Sheilings The FK10 ... 4 B1
Sheldrake Pl PA5 ... 131 D6
Shellbridge Way KA22 ... 205 C2
Shelley Ct G12 ... 96 A5
Shelley Dr
Bothwell G71 ... 141 B2
Clydebank G81 ... 74 A4
Shelley Rd G12 ... 96 A5
Shells Rd G66 ... 58 E1
Shepford Pl ML5 ... 121 D7
Sherbrooke Ave G41 ... 116 C3
Sherbrooke Dr G41 ... 116 C4
Sherbrooke Gdns G41 ... 116 C3
Sherbrooke Pl G75 ... 159 C1
Sherburn Gdns G69 ... 119 F3
Sherdale Ave ML6 ... 123 D2
Sheriffmuirlands FK9 ... 2 C3
Sheriffmuir Rd FK9 ... 2 D7
Sheriff Park Ave G73 ... 138 A7
Sherriff La FK5 ... 23 F3
Sherry Ave ML1 ... 143 A5
Sherry Dr ML3 ... 162 A1

South Dr *continued*
Troon KA10 229 G3
South Dumbreck Rd G65 60 B8
South Elgin Pl G81 94 C7
South Elgin St G81 94 C7
Southend Pl ML4 141 F4
Southend Rd G81 74 B5
Southern Ave G73 138 B5
Southerness Dr G68 62 A5
Southern General Hospl
G51 115 D8
South Erskine Pk G61 75 D5
Southesk Ave G64 77 F2
Southesk Gdns G64 77 F3
South Exchange Ct G1 241 A2
Southfield Ave
Paisley PA2 133 E8
Port Glasgow PA14 68 F8
Shotts ML7 147 B4
Southfield Cres
Coatbridge ML5 122 D5
Glasgow G53 135 C8
Shotts ML7 147 B4
Stirling FK8 7 A6
Southfield Dr FK1 86 A6
Southfield Pk KA7 239 A5
Southfield Rd
Cumbernauld G68 61 C1
Shotts ML7 147 B4
South Frederick St G1 241 A2
South Gargieston Dr
KA1 227 C6
Southgate G62 55 A1
South Glassford St G62 55 B1
South Green Dr FK2 14 E3
South Hamilton Ct 1
KA1 227 E8
South Hamilton Pl KA1 227 E7
South Hamilton St KA1 227 E8
South Harbour St KA7 235 E1
Southhill Ave G73 138 C5
South Hirst Rd ML7 126 D3
Southhook Rd
Kilmarnock KA1 222 D2
Knockentiber KA2 221 F3
Southinch Ave G14 94 E6
Southinch La G14 94 E6
South Isle Rd KA22 205 C5
South Kersebonny Steading
FK8 6 C7
South King St G84 16 F1
South Lanarkshire Coll
G75 181 B7
Southlea Ave G46 136 A3
South Line View ML2 164 E2
South Loan G69 100 D8
Southloch Gdns 1 G21 97 F3
Southloch St G21 97 F3
South Lodge Ct KA7 238 E6
South Mains FK7 9 B1
South Mains Rd G62 54 F1
South Medrox St ML5 101 C7
South Melville La FK1 42 B5
South Moraine La G15 75 C2
South Mound PA6 91 A2
South Muirhead Ct G67 62 A2
South Muirhead Rd G67 62 A2
Southmuir Pl G20 96 D5
South Neuk KA25 170 A7
South Newmoor Ave
KA11 219 F1
South Newmoor Ind Est
KA11 219 F2
South Nimmo St 2 ML6 123 B7
SOUTH NITSHILL 135 A4
South Rook Ave KA11 220 B5
Southpark Ave
Glasgow G12 96 E2
Prestwick KA9 236 B7
South Park Ave G78 134 C3
South Park Dr PA2 113 E2
South Park Gr ML3 162 D3
South Park Prim Sch
G75 180 C6
Southpark Rd KA7 238 E6
South Park Rd ML3 162 D2
South Park Sch KA7 239 A5
Southpark Terr G12 96 E2
South Pl ML4 141 F4
South Pleasance Ave FK1 42 B4
South Portland St 5 G5 117 B5
South Prim Sch PA2 113 E2
South Rd
Clarkston G76 158 A5
Port Glasgow PA14 68 E8
West Kilbride KA23 190 C4
South Ring Rd KA20 218 B5
South Ring Round KA20 218 A5
South Robertson Pl ML6 122 E7
South Scott St G69 120 B4
Southside Cres 2 G5 117 C4
South St
Cambus FK10 9 B8
Glasgow G14 95 C3
Greenock PA16 45 D6
Houston PA6 91 A2
Inchinnan PA4 93 B4
Stirling FK9 2 D1
South Vennel
Irvine KA11 220 A3
Lanark ML11 215 A4
South Vesalius St G32 119 A5
Southview G61 75 C5
South View
Bellshill ML4 141 E4
Blantyre G72 140 C1
Clydebank G81 73 F3
Stenhousemuir FK5 23 D1
Southview Ave G76 157 F5
Southview Cres PA11 90 D1
Southview Ct 3 G64 97 F7
Southview Dr G63 31 B3
Southview Gr G61 75 C5
Southview Pl G69 100 E6
Southview Rd G63 31 C3
Southview Terr G64 97 F7
Southward Way KA10 229 G7
South William St PA5 111 F2
Southwold Rd PA1 114 E5
Southwood Ct G77 156 D1
Southwood Dr G44 137 C6
Southwood Pl G77 156 D2
Southwood Rd KA10 232 F8
South Woodside Rd
Glasgow G4 96 E2
Glasgow G4 96 F3
Soutra Pl G33 119 B8
Spairdrum Rd ML6 82 F4
Spalehall Dr ML1 143 F3
Spallander Rd KA10 229 G6
SPANGO VALLEY 44 D2
Sparrow Gdns KA1 228 C7
Spateston Rd PA5 131 C7
Spean Ave G74 160 B1
Spean St G44 137 A6
Spectrum Ho G81 74 B2
Speedwell Sq KA7 239 B3
Speirsfield Gdns PA2 113 E3
Speirshall Cl G14 94 F5
Speirshall Terr G14 94 F6
Speirs Rd G61 76 B3
Speirs Wharf G4 97 B2
Spencer Dr PA2 132 E8
Spencerfield Gdns ML3 162 F3
Spencer St
Clydebank G81 74 A3
Glasgow G13 95 F7
Spence St
Bonnybridge FK4 40 A6
Glasgow G20 96 C8
Spey Ave
Kilmarnock KA1 228 A5
Paisley PA2 112 E1
Speyburn Pl
8 Airdrie ML6 103 A3
Irvine KA11 219 F6
Stepps G33 99 E6
Spey Ct
Airdrie ML6 123 C5
Stirling FK7 7 C5
22 Wishaw ML2 165 F6
Spey Dr
Coatbridge ML5 121 E4
Renfrew PA4 94 E2
Spey Gdns ML3 183 B8
Spey Gr G75 179 F7
Spey Pl PA5 131 C8
Spey Rd
Bearsden G61 75 C2
Troon KA10 229 G4
Spey St G33 118 F8
Spey Terr G75 179 F7
Spey Wlk
8 Cumbernauld G67 61 F1
Motherwell ML1 143 B5
Spey Wynd ML9 199 A8
Spiers Ave KA15 171 A7
Spiersbridge Ave G46 135 E2
Spiersbridge Bsns Pk
G46 135 E3
Spiersbridge La G46 135 E3
Spiersbridge Rd G46 135 F3
Spiersbridge Rdbt G46 135 F2
Spiersbridge Terr G46 135 E3
Spiers Gate ML8 187 A5
Spiers Gr G46 135 F3
Spiersland Way KA15 171 C7
Spiers Pl PA3 112 C7
Spiers Rd
Houston PA6 91 B2
Johnstone PA5 112 B3
Lochwinnoch PA12 129 B3
Spindlehowe Rd
Uddingston G71 140 F5
Uddingston, Tannochside
G71 141 A7
SPINDLESIDE 144 D1
Spindleside Rd ML1 144 D1
Spindrift Wynd KA21 205 F3
Spinkhill FK2 42 F2
Spinners Ct G81 74 B7
Spinners Gdns PA2 113 B3
Spinners La G81 74 B7
Spinningdale ML9 198 D1
Spital Rd ML9 198 F1
SPITTAL 137 F5
Spittal Hill FK9 2 C4
Spittal Prim Sch G73 137 F5
Spittal Rd G73 137 F5
Spittal St FK8 7 A8
Spoolers Rd PA1 113 C3
Spoutmouth G1 241 B1
Sprig Way ML7 127 E5
Springbank Cres
Glasgow G31 118 C4
Hamilton ML3 183 A7
Motherwell ML1 143 A2
Springbank Gdns
Falkirk FK2 42 C5
Irvine KA11 220 A7
Springbank Ind Est KA12 224 E8
Springbank Rd
Ayr KA8 236 B4
Paisley PA3 113 D7
Shotts ML7 146 D6
Stirling FK7 7 C6
Springbank St G20 97 A4
Springbank Terr
Paisley PA3 113 D7
Plains ML6 103 F3
Springbank View ML6 103 F3
SPRINGBOIG 119 D6
Springboig Ave G32 119 C6
Springboig Rd G32 119 C6
Springboig St Johns Sch
G33 119 D7
SPRINGBURN 97 F3
Springburn Acad G21 97 F5
Springburn L Ctr G21 97 F4
Springburn Pl G74 159 A3
Springburn Rd G21 97 E4
Springburn Sh Ctr 4 G21 97 F4
Springburn Sports Pk
G21 98 B4
Springburn Sta G21 97 F4
Springburn Way
3 Glasgow G21 97 E4
Glasgow G21 97 F4
Springcroft Ave G69 120 B6
Springcroft Cres G69 120 B6
Springcroft Dr G69 120 A6
Springcroft Gdns G69 120 C6
Springcroft Gr
Bonhill G83 27 F3
Glasgow G69 120 B6
Springcroft Rd G69 120 C6
Springcroft Wynd G69 120 B6
Springfield Ave
Bishopbriggs G64 98 A7
Paisley PA1 114 B4
Prestwick KA9 236 D7
Uddingston G71 140 F5
Springfield Cres
Bishopbriggs G64 98 A8
Carluke ML8 201 F8
Hamilton G72 161 C7
Uddingston G71 140 F5
Springfield Ct
Bishopbriggs G64 78 B1
Glasgow G1 241 A2
Springfield Dr
Barrhead G78 134 E1
Falkirk FK1 41 F5
Springfield Gdns
Irvine KA11 220 A7
Lanark ML11 214 F5
Uddingston G71 140 F5
Springfield Gr G78 155 D8
Springfield Park Rd G73 138 C6
Springfield Pk PA5 112 A2
Springfield Quay G5 240 A1
Springfield Quay Leisure Pk
G5 240 A1
Springfield Rd
Airdrie ML6 123 E8
Alloa FK10 10 C7
Barrhead G78 155 C8
Bishopbriggs G64 78 A1
Crosshouse KA2 221 F2
Cumbernauld G67 62 A4
Denny FK6 21 F2
Glasgow G40 118 B4
Salsburgh ML7 125 A1
Stirling FK7 7 C5
Springfield Sq G64 98 A8
Springfield Woods PA5 112 A2
Springfield Works G64 78 A1
SPRINGHALL 138 E4
Springhall Ct G73 138 D3
Springhead Rd ML7 167 A8
SPRINGHILL
Barrhead 134 C1
Shotts 147 B2
Springhill Ave
Airdrie ML6 123 B8
Coatbridge ML5 121 C4
Crosshouse KA2 226 F8
Springhill Drive S G69 120 A6
Springhill Farm Gr 3
G69 120 A6
Springhill Farm Pl 1
G69 120 A6
Springhill Farm Rd G69 120 A6
Springhill Farm Way 2
G69 120 A6
Springhill Gdns
Glasgow G41 116 E1
Kilmarnock KA1 227 E8
Springhill & Leadloch Rd ML7,
EH47 147 E2
Springhill Parkway G69 120 A7
Springhill Pl
Coatbridge ML5 121 C4
Kilmarnock KA1 227 E8
Springhill Prim Sch G78 134 B1
Springhill Rd
Barrhead G78 134 B1
Clarkston G76 157 F7
Glasgow G69 120 A5
Port Glasgow PA14 47 C1
Shotts ML7 147 B3
Springhill Terr KA11 220 F2
Springhill View ML7 147 B3
Springholm Dr ML6 102 F2
Springkell Ave G41 116 C2
Springkell Dr G41 116 B2
Springkell Gate G41 116 D2
Springkell Gdns G41 116 D2
Springkell St PA15 46 B4
Springkerse Bsns Pk FK7 7 F7
Springkerse Ind Est FK7 7 D6
Springkerse Rd FK7 7 D6
Springkerse Rdbt FK7 7 E7
Springkerse Ret Pk FK7 7 E6
Spring La ML6 104 F4
SPRINGSIDE 220 F2
Springside KA23 190 E7
Springside Gdns G15 75 A5
Springside Pl G15 75 A4
Springside Prim Sch
KA11 220 F2
Springside Terr KA11 220 F2
Springvale Ct KA21 216 F7
Springvale Dr PA2 112 F2
Springvale Pk KA7 238 F6
Springvale Pl KA21 216 F8
Springvale Rd KA7 238 F6
Springvale St KA21 216 F8
Springvale Terr 8 G21 97 E4
Springwell Cres G72 161 F7
Springwell Pl KA3 195 E1
Springwells Ave ML6 123 C8
Springwells Cres ML6 123 C8
Springwood FK7 6 F5
Springwood Ave FK8 6 F5
Springwood Dr PA13 69 D2
Spring Wynd G5 117 C4
Sprotwell Terr FK10 5 D1
Spruce Ave
Hamilton, Silvertonhill
ML3 162 F2
Hamilton, Wheatlands G72 161 C8
Johnstone PA5 112 A1
Sprucebank Ave PA14 70 C7
Spruce Ct ML3 162 E1
Spruce Dr
Cambuslang G72 139 F4
Kirkintilloch G66 79 A5
Spruce Ho KA9 236 B5
Spruce Pk KA7 239 D5
Spruce Rd
Cumbernauld G67 62 D4
Motherwell G71 121 C1
Spruce St G22 97 D5
Spruce Way
Cambuslang G72 139 F4
Motherwell ML1 143 B4
Spur Rd KA8 235 E2
Spynie Pl G64 78 D2
Spynie Way 1 ML2 165 F6
Spy's La G84 15 E4
Square of Ales 3 KA1 222 F1
Square The FK7 8 D4
Squire St G14 95 E2
Sraehouse Wynd ML8 188 B1
Stable Gr PA1 113 B4
Stable Houses KA1 231 F6
Stable Pl G62 54 F3
Stable Rd
Milngavie G62 54 F3
Shotts ML7 147 A4
Stables The
Glasgow G52 115 A3
Mugdock G62 55 B6
Paisley PA1 113 B4
Stable Wynd KA10 230 B4
Staffa G74 181 C8
Staffa Ave
Port Glasgow PA14 69 A7
Renfrew PA4 94 C1
Staffa Ct KA11 225 B8
Staffa Dr
Airdrie ML6 123 F7
Kirkintilloch G66 80 B8
Paisley PA2 133 E7
Staffa Pl FK1 42 B2
Staffa Rd G72 138 F3
Staffa St
Glasgow G31 118 B8
Gourock PA19 44 E6
Staffin Dr G23 76 D1
Staffin Path 10 G23 76 E1
Staffin Rd KA10 229 G5
Staffin St G23 76 E1
Stafflar Dr KA1 227 E4
Stafford Cres PA16 44 F4
Stafford Rd PA16 44 F4
Stafford St
Bellshill ML4 141 F4
Glasgow G4 241 B4
Helensburgh G84 16 D2
Kilmarnock KA3 222 F2
Stafford Street W G84 16 C3
Staffordway S PA16 44 F4
Stag Ct G71 141 C6
Stag St G51 116 B7
Staig Wynd ML1 164 A4
Staikhill ML11 214 F5
Staineybraes Pl ML6 102 F2
Stairlie Cres KA23 190 D5
Stalker St ML2 164 C4
Stamford Gate G31 118 B5
Stamford Pl G31 118 B5
Stamford Rd G31 118 B5
Stamford St G31 118 B5
STAMPERLAND 157 F8
Stamperland Ave G76 157 F8
Stamperland Cres G76 157 E8
Stamperland Dr G76 157 F8
Stamperland Gdns G76 157 F8
Stamperland Hill G76 136 F1
Stanalane St G46 135 F4
STAND 103 B6
Standa La KA3 222 C8
Standalane KA3 211 D8
Standburn Rd
Glasgow G21 98 D6
Glasgow G21 98 D7
Standford Hall G72 139 A6
STANE 147 A3
Staneacre Pk ML3 162 F3
Stane Brae KA3 211 E7
STANECASTLE 219 E5
Stanecastle Dr KA11 219 E5
Stanecastle Gate KA11 219 F5
Stanecastle Intc KA12 219 F4
Stanecastle Rd KA11 219 F4
Stanecastle Sch 2 KA11 220 A5
Stanecraigs Pl 20 ML2 165 F6
Stanefield Dr ML1 143 E4
Stane Gr ML7 147 A3
Stanely Ave PA2 113 B1
Stanely Cres PA2 133 B8
Stanely Dr PA2 113 D1
Stanely Gr PA2 133 B8
Stanely Grange PA2 133 B7
Stanely Rd PA2 113 C1
Stane Prim Sch ML7 147 A4
Stane Rd
Port Glasgow PA14 68 E8
Shotts ML7 147 A2
Stanford St G81 74 C1
Stanhope Dr G73 138 D5
Stanhope Pl ML2 186 A7
Stanistone Rd ML8 188 A2
Stanley Ave KA22 205 C3
Stanley Bvd G72 161 D4
Stanley Dr
Ardrossan KA22 205 C3
Bellshill ML4 142 A6
Bishopbriggs G64 78 B2
Bridge of Allan FK9 2 B7
Brookfield PA5 111 C5
Stanley La PA5 111 C5
Stanley Pk ML6 123 B8
Stanley Pl
Blantyre G72 140 D1
Saltcoats KA21 205 E1
Stanley Prim Sch KA22 205 C3
Stanley Rd
Ardrossan KA22 205 D3
Saltcoats KA21 216 E8
Stanley St
Glasgow G41 116 E5
Hamilton ML3 161 F4
Stanley Street La G41 116 E5
Stanley Terr FK12 5 A6
Stanmore Ave ML11 215 B5
Stanmore Cres ML11 215 C5
Stanmore Gdns ML11 215 D6
Stanmore House Sch
ML11 215 D6
Stanmore Rd
Glasgow G42 137 B8
Lanark ML11 215 D6
Stanners La PA15 46 B4
Stanrigg St ML6 104 A2
Stanton Ave FK10 9 F6
Stark Ave
Clydebank G81 73 E6
Falkirk FK1 41 D5
Starling Way ML4 141 E8
Starryshaw Rd ML7 146 E6
Startpoint St G33 119 A8
Station Ave
2 Greenock PA15 46 A4
Greenock PA15 46 A5
Howwood PA9 130 F5
Station Brae
Irvine KA11 220 C1
Neilston G78 154 C8
Station Brae Gdns KA11 220 C1
Station Bridge KA7 239 A7
Station Cres PA4 94 D4
Station Ct
Bellshill ML4 141 F5
Kilbirnie KA14 170 C6
Netherburn ML9 200 C4
Station Dr
Hurlford KA1 228 D6
Prestwick KA9 233 C1
Springside KA11 220 F3
Station Gate
Hamilton G72 161 E8
Netherburn ML9 200 C4
Station Pk G69 120 C4
Station Pl ML8 187 A6
Station Plaza KA13 207 D3
Station Rd
Airdrie ML6 123 E8
Ayr KA7, KA8 239 A8
Bannockburn FK7 7 E1
Bardowie G62 77 B7
Bearsden G61 75 D4
Bishopton PA7 72 B2
Blackridge EH48 107 D2
Blanefield G63 30 F4
Blantyre G72 140 E1
Bothwell G71 141 A2
Bridge of Allan FK9 1 F8
Caldercruix ML6 105 A4
Cambus FK10 4 B1
Cardross G82 48 A7
Carluke ML8 187 E1
Clarkston G46 158 A5
Cleland ML1 144 B1
Cowie FK7 12 D6
Dumbarton G82 49 F4
Dunlop KA3 195 B7
Glasgow G69 120 C4
Glasgow, Giffnock G46 136 C3
Glasgow, Maryhill G20 96 C8
Gourock PA19 44 E8
Hamilton ML3 162 E3
Helensburgh G84 25 B8
Howwood PA10 130 F6
Kilbarchan PA10 111 B2

Strone Rd *continued*
Glasgow G33 119 B7
Stronsay Ct KA11 220 A2
Stronsay Pl
Bishopbriggs G64 78 D2
Kilmarnock KA3 223 A5
Stronsay St G21 98 B2
Stronsay Way KA11 220 A2
Stronvar Dr G14 95 B4
Stroud Rd G75 180 D6
Strowan Cres G32 119 B4
Strowan's Rd G82 50 C3
Strowan St G32 119 C4
Strowan's Well Rd G82 50 C3
Struan Ave G46 136 C3
Struan Gdns G44 137 A5
Struan Rd G44 137 A5
Strude Howe FK12 5 B7
Strude Mill FK12 5 B7
Strude St FK12 5 B7
Strule St G34 120 A8
Struma Dr G76 157 C8
STRUTHERHILL 199 B8
Strutherhill ML9 199 B8
Strutherhill Ind Est ML9 199 C8
Struthers Ave KA3 228 D8
Struthers Cres G74 160 B4
Struthers Pl KA10 229 G8
Struthers Prim Sch
KA10 229 G5
Struther St ML9 199 B8
Struther & Swinhill Rd
ML9 199 D6
Stuart Ave
Old Kilpatrick G60 73 B5
Rutherglen G73 138 B5
Stuart Dr
Bishopbriggs G64 97 E8
Lanark ML11 215 B5
Larkhall ML9 185 C1
Stuart Ho G67 62 B3
Stuarton Pk G74 159 E2
Stuart Pl KA2 225 F2
Stuart Quadrant 7 ML2 164 E1
Stuart Rd
Bishopton PA7 72 B3
Carmunnock G76 158 D8
Dumbarton G82 50 C4
Stuart St
East Kilbride G74 159 F2
Old Kilpatrick G60 73 B5
Stuckleckie Rd G84 17 A1
Sturrock St KA1 227 F8
Styles Pl FK1 41 F2
Succoth St G13 95 F7
Sudbury Cres G75 159 B1
Suffolk Rd PA16 44 E4
Suffolk St
Glasgow G40 241 B1
Helensburgh G84 16 C2
Sugworth Ave G69 120 B5
Suisnish PA4 93 C7
Sumburgh St G33 119 A7
Summerfield Cotts G14 95 E2
Summerfield Rd G67 82 A6
Summerfield St G40 118 B3
SUMMERFORD 41 D4
Summerford FK1 41 D4
Summerford Gdns FK1 41 D4
Summerford Rd FK1 41 D4
Summerhill Ave ML9 185 A2
Summerhill Dr G15 75 B4
Summerhill & Garngibbock
Rd G67 82 D4
Summerhill Gdns G15 75 B4
Summerhill Pl
Clydebank G15 75 B4
Shotts ML7 166 F8
Summerhill Rd
Clarkston G76 157 F7
Clydebank G15 75 B4
Summerhill Way ML4 141 F4
Summerlea Rd
Glasgow G46 135 F4
West Kilbride KA23 190 B4
SUMMERLEE 121 F7
Summerlee Cotts ML5 121 F7
Summerlee-Mus of Scottish
Ind Life★ ML5 121 F8
Summerlee Rd
Larkhall ML9 184 F5
Wishaw ML2 164 C4
Summerlee St
Coatbridge ML5 121 F7
Glasgow G33 119 C7
Summer St G40 117 F5
SUMMERSTON 76 D1
Summerston Sta G20 96 D8
Summertown Rd G51 116 B7
Suna Path ML7 147 B3
Sunart Ave PA4 94 B4
Sunart Ct ML3 162 A1
Sunart Gdns G64 78 C1
Sunart Rd
Bishopbriggs G64 78 C1
Glasgow G52 115 F5
Sunart St ML2 165 A1
Sunbury Ave G76 157 C7
Sundale Ave G76 157 D6
Sunderland Ave G82 49 C4
Sunderland Ct KA25 170 A7
Sundrum Pl KA13 207 D2
Sunflower Gdns ML1 163 D8
Sunningdale Ave
Ayr KA7 239 A3
Newton Mearns G77 156 F6
Sunningdale Dr PA11 110 C6
Sunningdale Pl G84 25 B8
Sunningdale Rd G23 96 E8
Sunningdale Sq KA13 207 C4
Sunningdale Wynd G71 140 E3
Sunnybank ML7 146 F5
Sunnybank Dr G76 157 D7
Sunnybank Gr G76 157 D6
Sunnybank Rd FK7 7 B3
Sunnybank St G40 118 B3
Sunnydale Dr EH48 107 E3
Sunnydale Rd EH48 107 E3
Sunnyhill G65 59 F3
Sunnylaw Dr PA2 113 B2
Sunnylaw Pl
Falkirk FK1 41 F3
Glasgow G22 97 B5
Sunnylaw Rd FK9 2 A8
Sunnylaw St G22 97 B4
SUNNYSIDE 122 A8
Sunnyside
Kilmaurs KA3 222 B7
Stirling FK7 7 A4
Sunnyside Ave
Motherwell ML1 143 B5
Port Glasgow PA14 69 A8
Uddingston G71 140 F5
Sunnyside Cres ML1 143 A5
Sunnyside Ct FK10 10 B7
Sunnyside Dr
Clarkston G76 157 D8
Clydebank G15 75 A1
Coatbridge G69 121 A5
Sunnyside Gate ML1 143 A5
Sunnyside Oval PA2 113 E1
Sunnyside Pl
Barrhead G78 134 B2
Clydebank G15 75 A1
Motherwell ML1 143 A5
Stirling FK9 2 A4
Sunnyside Prim Sch
1 Alloa FK10 10 B7
Glasgow G33 99 C3
Sunnyside Rd
Alloa FK10 10 B7
Cleland ML1 165 B8
Coatbridge ML5 122 A8
Falkirk FK1 41 F5
Kilmarnock KA1 227 F2
Kirkfieldbank ML11 214 D5
Larkhall ML3, ML9 184 C3
Paisley PA2 113 D1
Sunnyside Square E KA1 227 F2
Sunnyside Square W
KA1 227 F2
Sunnyside St
Falkirk FK1 41 E6
Larkhall ML9 184 F4
Sunnyside Terr ML1 143 B5
Surcoat Loan FK7 7 E3
Surrey La 1 G5 117 B4
Surrey St 3 G5 117 B4
Susannah St 2 G83 27 E5
Sussex St G41 116 E5
Sutcliffe Ct G13 95 E7
Sutcliffe Rd G13 95 F7
Sutherland Ave
Alloa FK10 10 C7
Bearsden G61 75 E7
Glasgow G41 116 C3
Stirling FK8 2 C1
Sutherland Cres ML3 162 A4
Sutherland Ct G41 116 E4
Sutherland Dr
Airdrie ML6 122 F5
Denny FK6 39 D8
Dumbarton G82 50 C3
Glasgow G46 136 D1
Kilmarnock KA3 223 D2
Sutherland La G12 96 D2
Sutherland Pl
Bellshill ML4 141 F2
Helensburgh G84 16 B2
Sutherland Rd
Clydebank G81 74 B2
Greenock PA16 45 A4
Sutherland St
Hamilton G72 161 C5
Helensburgh G84 16 B2
Paisley PA1 113 D5
Sutherland Way G74 160 C3
Sutherness Dr G33 119 A8
Suttie Way FK9 1 F8
Sutton Ct KA13 207 B3
Sutton Park Cres FK5 23 E3
Sutton Pl FK2 42 D5
Swaledale G74 159 C3
Swallow Dr PA5 131 C7
Swallow Gdns G13 94 F7
Swallow Pl KA3 228 C7
Swallow Rd
Clydebank G81 74 D7
Wishaw ML2 165 B3
Swan Pl PA5 131 C7
Swanson Rd G83 27 D7
Swan St
Clydebank G81 73 F3
Glasgow G4 241 A4
Swanston St G40 118 A2
Swan Way ML8 186 F4
Sween Ave G44 137 A4
Sween Dr ML3 162 A1
Sween Path ML4 142 C3
Sweethill Terr ML5 122 D3
Sweethill Wlk ML4 142 C7
Sweethope Gdns G71 141 B2
Sweethope Pl G71 141 A3
Swift Bank ML3 161 E1
Swift Cl ML2 165 B3
Swift Cres G13 94 F8
Swift Pl
East Kilbride G75 179 F6
Johnstone PA5 131 D7
Swinburne Ave G72 161 B7
Swinburne Dr FK10 5 B1
Swindon St G81 73 E3
SWINHILL 199 C6
Swinhill Ave ML9 199 C6
Swinhill Rd ML9 199 C6
Swinstie Rd ML1 165 D8
Swinstie View ML1 144 C1
SWINTON 120 C6
Swinton Ave G69 120 D5
Swinton Cres
Coatbridge ML5 121 B4
Glasgow G69 120 D5
Swinton Dr G52 115 B5
Swinton Gdns G69 120 D5
Swinton Path G69 120 D5
Swinton Pl
Coatbridge ML5 121 B4
Glasgow G52 115 B5
Irvine KA11 220 B7
Swinton Prim Sch G69 120 C6
Swinton Rd G69 120 C5
Swinton View G69 120 C5
Swisscot Ave ML3 183 B8
Swisscot Wlk ML3 183 B8
Switchback Rd G61 75 F1
Swordale Pl G34 120 A8
Sword St
Airdrie ML6 122 F7
Glasgow G31 117 F6
Sword's Way FK2 24 A1
Sycamore Ave
Beith KA15 150 B2
Johnstone PA5 112 A1
Kirkintilloch G66 79 D5
Uddingston G71 141 C8
Sycamore Cres
Airdrie ML6 123 D6
Ayr KA7 239 D6
East Kilbride G75 180 D6
Sycamore Ct
Beith KA15 150 B1
East Kilbride G75 180 D6
Sycamore Dr
Airdrie ML6 123 D6
Clydebank G81 74 A4
Hamilton ML3 162 F2
Sycamore Gr G72 161 C8
Sycamore Pl
East Kilbride G75 180 D6
Gourock PA19 44 C6
Motherwell ML1 143 C3
Stirling FK8 6 F5
Sycamores The FK10 4 B1
Sycamore Way
Cambuslang G72 139 F4
Carmunnock G76 158 D7
Milton of Campsie G66 58 C5
Sydenham Ct G12 96 B4
Sydenham La G12 96 C3
Sydenham Rd G12 96 C3
Sydes Brae G72 161 B4
Sydney Dr G75 180 C8
Sydney Pl 6 G75 180 C8
Sydney St
Clydebank G81 73 D4
Glasgow G31 241 C1
Sykehead Ave ML4 142 B5
Sykeside Rd ML6 122 F4
Sykes Terr G78 154 F7
Sylvania Way G81 74 B2
Sylvania Way S G81 74 B1
SYMINGTON 231 C3
Symington Ct 6 KA10 229 E5
Symington Dr G81 74 B2
Symington Pl
Falkirk FK2 24 B3
Irvine KA11 224 H7
Symington Prim Sch
KA1 231 D4
Symington Road N KA1 231 D3
Symington Road S KA1 231 C3
Symington Sq 8 G75 180 F8
Symon Twr FK1 42 D4
Syms La KA8 236 A1
Syriam Pl 1 G21 97 F4
Syriam St G21 97 F5

T

Tabard Pl G13 95 C8
Tabard Rd G13 95 C8
Tabernacle La G72 139 A5
Tabernacle St G72 139 A5
Taggart Rd G65 60 F3
Taig Rd G66 80 B7
Tain Terr G72 161 C3
Tait Ave G78 134 D3
Tait Dr FK5 41 C8
Tait Wlk ML8 201 B1
Takmadoon Rd G65, FK6 37 A7
Tak-Ma-Doon Rd G65 36 F3
Talbot G74 160 C4
Talbot Cres ML5 121 E4
Talbot Ct G13 95 B5
Talbot Dr G13 95 B5
Talbot Pl G13 95 B5
Talbot Rd G83 28 A8
Talbot Terr
Glasgow G13 95 B5
Uddingston G71 140 E8
Talisker FK10 4 B2
Talisker Ave KA3 222 E4
Talisker Cres ML6 103 B3
Talisman G81 74 D2
Talisman Ave G82 49 C4
Talisman Cres
Helensburgh G84 25 B8
Motherwell ML1 142 D2
Talisman Rd
Glasgow G13 95 C6
Paisley PA2 132 E7
Talisman Wlk KA21 206 A2
Tallant Rd G15 75 B3
Tallant Terr G15 75 C3
Talla Rd G52 115 B5
Tall Ship The★ G3 116 C8
Tamarack Cres G71 141 C8
Tamar Dr G75 179 F6
Tambowie Ave G62 54 F2
Tambowie Cres G62 54 F2
Tambowie St G13 95 E8
TAMFOURHILL 41 C4
Tamfourhill Ave FK1 41 C4
Tamfourhill Ind Est FK1 41 C4
Tamfourhill Rd FK1 41 C4
Tammy Dale's Rd KA13 207 F3
Tam O'Shanter Dr FK7 12 D7
Tam O'Shanter Experience★
KA7 238 E1
Tam's Brig KA8 236 A3
Tamshill St G20 96 F5
Tanar Ave PA4 94 F1
Tanar Way PA4 94 E1
TANDLEHILL 111 B1
Tandlehill Rd PA10 111 B1
Tanera Ave G44 137 C4
Tanera Ct FK1 42 B2
Tanfield Pl G32 119 C7
Tanfield St G32 119 C7
Tankerland Rd G44 137 A6
Tannadice Ave G52 115 C4
Tannadice Path G52 115 C4
Tanna Dr G52 115 F3
Tannahill Cres
Johnstone PA5 111 E1
Johnstone PA5 111 F1
Tannahill Ctr The PA3 113 B6
Tannahill Dr G74 160 C3
Tannahill Rd
Glasgow G43 136 F6
Paisley PA3 113 B6
Tannahill Terr PA3 113 B6
Tanners Rd FK1 42 A4
Tannery La FK8 2 A1
Tannoch Dr
Cumbernauld G67 82 F7
Milngavie G62 55 B3
Tannoch Pl G67 82 F7
Tannoch Rd G78 153 B3
TANNOCHSIDE 141 B8
Tannochside Dr G71 121 B1
Tannochside Pk
Motherwell G71 121 B1
Uddingston G71 141 B8
Tannochside Prim Sch
G71 141 B8
Tannock St
Glasgow G22 97 B4
Kilmarnock KA1 227 F6
Tantallon Ave PA19 43 F5
Tantallon Ct ML8 187 E3
Tantallon Dr
Coatbridge ML5 101 C2
Falkirk FK2 24 A3
Paisley PA2 113 A1
Tantallon Pk G74 159 D2
Tantallon Rd
2 Bothwell G71 141 B3
Glasgow, Baillieston G69 120 A3
Glasgow, Langside G41 136 E8
Tanzieknowe Ave G72 139 B3
Tanzieknowe Dr G72 139 B3
Tanzieknowe Pl G72 139 A3
Tanzieknowe Rd G72 139 B3
Tappoch Pl FK5 23 A3
Taransay Ct G22 97 E7
Taransay St G51 116 A8
Tarbert Ave
Blantyre G72 140 C2
West Kilbride KA23 190 E5
Wishaw ML2 165 A1
Tarbert Ct ML3 162 A1
Tarbert Pl ML8 188 A1
Tarbert Way ML5 121 E4
Tarbet St PA19 44 F7
Tarbolton G74 160 D3
Tarbolton Cres ML6 123 D1
Tarbolton Dr G81 74 C3
Tarbolton Path ML9 184 F3
Tarbolton Pl KA3 223 C6
Tarbolton Rd
Cumbernauld G67 62 B2
Dundonald KA2 225 F1
Glasgow G43 136 D6
Monkton KA9 233 E4
Symington KA1 231 F5
Tarbolton Sq G81 74 C3
Tarbrax Path ML7 147 A3
Tarbrax Way ML3 162 A3
Tarduff Pl FK6 21 B2
Tarff Ave G76 178 E5
Tarfside Ave G52 115 C4
Tarfside Gdns G52 115 D4
Tarfside Oval G52 115 D4
Target Rd ML6 123 B6
Targe Wynd FK7 7 E3
Tarland St G51 115 F6
Tarn Gr G33 98 E8
Tarquin Pl 4 ML1 163 C8
Tarras Dr PA4 94 E1
Tarras Pl G72 139 D5
TARRYHOLME 224 F8
Tarryholme Dr KA12 219 D2
Tasker St PA16 45 C5
Tasman Dr G75 180 B8
Tasmania Quadrant ML2 165 E3
Tassie Pl G74 160 A2
Tassie St G41 136 D8
Tattershall Rd G33 99 C1
Tavistock Dr G43 136 D5
Tay Ave PA4 94 E3
Taybank Dr KA7 239 A3
Tay Cres
Bishopbriggs G64 78 B1
Glasgow G33 98 E1
Tay Ct
Alloa FK10 10 C6
East Kilbride G75 179 E7
Tay Gdns ML3 183 B8
Tay Gr G75 179 E7
Tayinloan Dr ML8 202 B8
Tay La ML2 166 A5
Tay Loan ML1 143 A5
Taylor Ave
Kilbarchan PA10 110 F3
Motherwell ML1 143 D2
Taylor Brown Cl KA3 211 E8
Taylor Ct
1 Ayr KA8 235 F2
Falkirk FK2 42 C7
Taylor High Sch ML1 143 A3
Taylor Pl
Glasgow G4 241 B3
Saltcoats KA21 216 F8
Taylor's Rd FK5 23 C1
Taylor St
Alexandria G83 27 C7
Ayr KA8 235 F2
Clydebank G81 94 C8
Glasgow G4 241 B3
Taymouth Dr PA19 43 F5
Taymouth St G32 119 B3
Taynish Dr G44 137 B5
Tay Pl
Dumbarton G82 50 B7
East Kilbride G75 179 E7
Johnstone PA5 131 C8
Kilmarnock KA1 228 A5
Larkhall ML9 199 A8
Shotts ML7 146 E6
Tay Rd
Bearsden G61 75 D2
Bishopbriggs G64 78 B1
Troon KA10 229 G4
Tayside ML6 102 F1
Tay St
Coatbridge ML5 101 C1
Falkirk FK2 24 C1
Greenock PA16 45 B5
Tay Terr G75 179 E7
Tay Wlk 10 G67 61 F1
Teak Pl G71 121 D1
Teal Cres G75 179 F5
Teal Ct ML4 141 E8
Teal Dr G13 95 A7
Tealing Ave G52 115 C4
Tealing Cres G52 115 C4
Teasel Ave G53 135 B3
Teawell Rd G77 156 D5
Technology Ave G72 161 C4
Teesdale G74 159 C3
Teign Gr G75 179 F6
Teith Ave PA4 94 F2
Teith Dr G61 75 D3
Teith Pl
Cambuslang G72 139 D5
Kilmarnock KA1 228 B5
Teith St G33 98 E1
Telegraph Rd ML6 105 B7
Telephone La G12 96 C2
Telford Ave ML9 199 C8
Telford Ct
Bannockburn FK7 7 D1
Clydebank G81 74 A2
3 Troon KA10 229 E5
Telford Pl
Cumbernauld G67 83 A8
Irvine KA11 219 F1
Telford Rd
Cumbernauld G67 83 A8
East Kilbride G75 180 E8
Telford Sq FK1 41 E6
Telford St ML4 142 A6
Telford Terr 7 G75 180 F8
Teme Pl G75 179 F7
Templand Cres KA24 191 C8
Templand Rd KA24 191 C8
Templar Ave G13 75 D1
TEMPLE 95 E7
Temple Cotts G67 82 B7
Temple Ct ML8 187 A6
Temple Denny Rd FK6 21 D2
Temple Gdns G13 95 F7
Templehill KA10 229 C3
Templeland Rd G53 115 C2
Temple Locks Ct 1 G13 95 F7
Temple Locks Pl 2 G13 95 F7
Temple Rd G13 96 A7
Templerigg Ct KA9 233 C1
Templerigg St KA9 233 C1
Templeton Bsns Ctr G40 117 E5
Templeton Cres KA9 236 D8
Templeton Ct G40 117 E5
Templeton St G40 117 E5
Ten Acres FK10 5 B1
Tennant Ave G74 159 A1

Tower St *continued*
Glasgow G41 116 E5
Tower Terr PA1 113 D4
Tower View FK10 5 E1
Towie Pl
[2] Glasgow G20 96 D6
Uddingston G71 140 F6
Town Burn FK7 6 F4
TOWN CENTRE 61 F2
TOWNEND 50 A4
Townend KA3 222 C7
Townend Brae KA1 231 B3
Townend La KA24 191 C7
Townend Pl KA1 231 B3
Townend Rd
Dumbarton G82 50 A5
Kilmarnock KA1 227 E3
Symington KA1 231 C4
Townend St KA24 191 C7
Townend Terr KA1 231 C4
Townfoot KA11 220 C1
TOWNHEAD
Coatbridge 101 C2
Glasgow 241 B3
Kirkintilloch 79 C8
Townhead
Beith KA15 171 B8
Irvine KA12 219 D2
Kilbirnie KA25 149 B2
Kilmaurs KA3 222 C8
Kilwinning KA13 207 D3
Kirkintilloch G66 79 D7
Kirkintilloch G66 79 D8
Townhead Apartments [9]
FK10 10 B6
Townhead Ave ML1 142 E8
Townhead Dr ML1 143 F3
Townhead Gdns KA3 223 A2
Townhead Pl G71 141 A8
Townhead Prim Sch
ML5 101 D2
Townhead Rd
Coatbridge ML5 101 C1
Helensburgh G84 17 A2
Newton Mearns G77 156 D4
Saltcoats KA21 217 A8
Townhead Rdbt G66 79 D8
Townhead St
Hamilton ML3 162 F3
Kilsyth G65 60 D8
Stevenston KA20 206 D1
Stonehouse ML10 198 E2
Townhead Terr PA1 113 D4
Townhill Prim Sch ML3 161 E2
Townhill Rd ML3 161 E3
Townhill Terr [1] ML3 161 E3
TOWNHOLM 223 A2
Townholm KA3 223 A2
Town House St FK6 21 E2
Townmill Rd G31 118 A8
Townsend St G4 97 C2
Traction Bsns Ctr ML1 163 C6
TRADESTON 117 A5
Tradeston Ind Est G5 117 A4
Tradeston St G5 117 A5
Trafalgar Ct G68 61 D6
Trafalgar St
Clydebank G81 73 F2
Glasgow G40 117 F3
Greenock PA15 45 F4
Greenock PA15 45 F5
Trainard Ave G32 118 F4
Tramore Cres KA9 236 C8
Tramway & the Hidden Gdns* G41 117 A3
Tranchard Ct [5] KA7 235 E1
Tranent Pl
Cleland ML1 144 C2
Glasgow G33 118 E8
Traquair Ave
Paisley PA2 132 E8
Wishaw ML2 165 C5
Traquair Dr G52 115 B5
Traquair Wynd [10] G72 161 C7
Treebank Cres KA7 239 C5
Treeburn Ave G46 136 B3
Treemain Rd G46 157 A8
Treesbank KA13 207 C2
Treesbank Rd KA1 227 F4
Treespark Ave G78 134 B4
Treespark Gdns G78 134 B4
Treeswoodhead Rd KA1 228 A2
Trefoil Ave G41 136 D8
Trefoil Pl KA7 239 C3
Trelawney Terr KA20 217 E6
Trent Pl G75 179 E6
Trent St ML5 101 D2
Tresta Rd G23 96 F8
Treviot Pl [1] PA15 46 B3
Triangle Sh Ctr The G64 78 A1
Tribboch St ML9 184 F3
Trident Way PA4 94 C1
Trinidad Gn [3] G75 159 A1
Trinidad Way G75 159 A1
Trinity Ave G52 115 C4
Trinity Cres KA15 150 C1
Trinity Dr
Cambuslang G72 139 C3
Dalry KA24 191 B6
Trinity High Sch
Hamilton ML3 162 E4
Renfrew PA4 94 D3
Trinity Pl G82 27 D1
Trinity Way [14] ML9 185 C1
Trinley Rd G13 75 D1
Triton Pl ML4 142 F5
Tron Ct FK10 4 B2
Trondra Gdns KA3 223 A6
Trondra Path G34 119 F8
Trondra Pl G34 119 F7
Trongate
Glasgow G1 241 A1
Stonehouse ML9 198 F2
TROON 229 C2
Troon Ave G75 180 A6
Troon Ct G75 180 B6
Troon Dr PA11 110 C7
Troon Gdns G68 61 F6
Troon Pl G77 157 A4
Troon Prim Sch KA10 229 D3
Troon Rd KA10 230 B3
Troon St G40 118 B3
Troon Sta KA10 229 E2
Trossachs Ave ML1 143 A5
Trossachs Ct G20 97 A3
Trossachs Rd G73 138 D2
Trossachs St G20 97 A3
Troubridge Ave PA10 111 B1
Troubridge Cres PA10 111 B2
Trovaig PA8 93 C7
Trows Rd ML2 186 B6
Truce Rd G13 95 B8
Truro Ave G69 80 F3
Tryfield Pl KA8 236 A2
Tryst Pk FK5 23 C5
Tryst Rd
Cumbernauld, Carbrain G67 62 A2
Cumbernauld G67 61 F1
Stenhousemuir FK5 23 D2
Stenhousemuir FK5 23 D3
Tryst Sp Ctr G67 62 A1
Tryst Wlk G67 61 F1
Tudhope Cres G83 27 D7
Tudor Lane S G14 95 E3
Tudor Rd G14 95 E3
Tudor St G69 119 F3
Tulley Wynd ML1 142 D2
Tulliallan Pl
East Kilbride G74 181 A8
Stenhousemuir FK5 24 A4
TULLIBODY 4 C3
Tullibody Rd FK10 9 F8
TULLICHEWAN 27 C7
Tullichewan Cres G83 27 D7
Tullichewan Dr G83 27 D7
Tullichewan Rd G83 27 D8
Tulligarth Pk FK10 10 A7
Tullis Ct G40 117 E4
Tullis Gdns G40 117 F4
Tullis St G40 117 F4
Tullochard Pl [1] G73 138 D3
Tulloch Gdns ML1 164 B4
Tulloch Rd ML7 147 B3
Tulloch St G44 137 A6
Tullymet Rd ML3 183 D8
Tummel Dr ML6 102 F2
Tummel Gn G74 159 E3
Tummell Way PA2 112 F1
Tummel Pl FK5 23 E3
Tummel St G33 98 E2
Tunnel St G3 116 E7
Tuphall Rd ML3 162 D2
Turnberry Ave
[2] Glasgow G11 96 B3
Gourock PA19 44 B6
Turnberry Cres
Chapelhall ML6 123 E1
Coatbridge ML5 121 E4
Turnberry Ct KA13 207 B3
Turnberry Dr
Bridge of Weir PA11 110 C6
Hamilton ML3 161 D2
Kilmarnock KA1 227 F4
Newton Mearns G77 157 A5
Rutherglen G73 137 F5
Turnberry Gdns G68 61 F5
Turnberry Pl
Dumbarton G82 49 C8
East Kilbride G75 180 B6
Rutherglen G73 137 F4
Turnberry Rd
Glasgow G11 96 A3
Glasgow G11 96 B3
Turnberry Wynd
Bothwell G71 140 E2
Irvine KA11 224 F8
Turnbull Ave G83 27 D3
Turnbull Cres G83 27 D3
Turnbull High Sch G64 77 E2
Turnbull St G1 241 B1
Turner Pl KA3 223 A3
Turner Rd PA3 113 F8
Turners Ave PA1 113 B3
Turner St ML5 121 F6
Turnhill Ave PA8 93 B7
Turnhill Cres PA8 93 B7
Turnhill Dr PA8 93 B7
Turnhill Gdns PA8 93 B7
Turningshaw Rd PA6 91 E5
Turnlaw G75 180 D5
Turnlaw Rd G72 139 A2
Turnlaw St G5 117 D4
Turnyland Mdws PA8 93 B7
Turnyland Way PA8 93 B7
Turpie Dr FK5 23 B2
Turquoise Terr ML4 142 B3
Turret Cres G13 95 D8
Turret Ct FK10 10 C6
Turret Rd G13 95 C8
Turriff St G5 117 B4
TV ML2 186 A8
Twain Ave FK5 24 A3
TWECHAR 59 F3
Twechar Prim Sch G65 60 A3
Tweed Ave PA2 112 F2
Tweed Cres
Glasgow G33 98 E1
Kilmarnock KA1 228 A5
Renfrew PA4 94 E2
Wishaw ML2 165 C5
Tweed Ct ML6 123 C5
Tweed Dr G61 75 D3
Tweed La ML1 143 B5
Tweedmuir Pl ML5 122 D3
Tweed Pl PA5 131 C8
Tweedsmuir G64 78 C2
Tweedsmuir Cres G61 75 E7
Tweedsmuir Pk ML3 183 C8
Tweedsmuir Rd G52 115 B5
Tweed St
Ayr KA8 236 B3
Coatbridge ML5 122 A3
East Kilbride G75 179 F7
Greenock PA16 45 B5
Larkhall ML9 185 A1
Tweedvale Ave G14 94 E6
Tweedvale Pl G14 94 E6
Tweed Wlk G67 61 F2
Twinlaw St G34 100 D1
Tygetshaugh Ct FK6 21 D4
Tylney Rd PA1 114 D5
Tyndrum Rd G61 76 B5
Tyndrum St G4 241 A4
Tynecastle Cres G32 119 B7
Tynecastle Path G32 119 B7
Tynecastle Pl G32 119 B7
Tynecastle St G32 119 B7
Tyne Pl G75 179 E6
Tynron Ct ML3 161 E1
Tynwald Ave G73 138 D4

U

UDDINGSTON 140 E5
Uddingston Gram Sch G71 140 E6
Uddingston Rd G71 141 A3
Uddingston Sta G71 140 E6
UDSTON 161 F4
Udston Hospl ML3 161 F4
Udston Prim Sch ML3 161 E4
Udston Rd ML3 161 F5
Udston Terr ML3 161 F5
Uig Pl G33 119 E5
Uig Way ML7 147 A3
Uist Ave PA14 69 A7
Uist Cres G33 99 E4
Uist Dr G66 80 A8
Uist La KA3 222 F6
Uist Pl ML6 123 D6
Uist St G51 115 F7
Uist Way ML2 165 E5
Ullswater G75 179 F5
Ulundi Rd PA5 111 E2
Ulva St G52 115 F5
Ulverston Terr ML3 183 D6
Umachan PA4 93 C7
Umberly Rd KA1 227 E3
Underwood KA13 207 D5
Underwood Cotts FK7 6 D5
Underwood Ct PA3 113 D5
Underwood Dr ML2 166 A7
Underwood La PA1 113 D5
Underwood Pl KA1 227 F3
Underwood Rd
Cambusbarron FK7 6 D5
Paisley PA3 113 D5
Prestwick KA9 236 D7
Rutherglen G73 138 C6
Underwood St G41 136 E8
Union Arc KA7 238 F7
Union Ave KA8 236 A3
Union Gdns FK1 41 D5
Union Pl
Glasgow G1 240 C2
Larbert FK5 23 B1
Union Rd FK1 41 D5
Union St
Alexandria G83 27 F4
[4] Alloa FK10 10 B6
Bridge of Allan FK9 2 A7
Carluke ML8 187 F1
Falkirk FK2 42 B7
Glasgow G1 240 C2
Greenock PA16 45 E6
Hamilton ML3 162 D3
Hurlford KA1 228 E6
[1] Kilmarnock KA3 222 F1
Kirkintilloch G66 79 C8
Larkhall ML9 185 A3
Motherwell ML1 143 A4
Paisley PA2 113 E2
Saltcoats KA21 216 F7
Shotts ML7 146 D5
Stenhousemuir FK5 23 E3
Stirling FK8 2 B1
Stonehouse ML9 198 F2
Troon KA10 229 C3
Union Street La G83 27 F4
Unitas Cres ML8 187 E1
Unitas Rd ML4 142 C5
Unity Pk ML7 146 D4
Unity Pl G4 97 A2
Universal Rd FK2 42 E7
University Ave G12 96 D2
University Gdns G12 96 D2
University Pl G12 96 D2
University Road W FK9 2 C6
Univ of Glasgow (Main Campus) G11, G12 96 D2
Univ of Glasgow (St Andrew's Building) G3 96 E2
Univ of Glasgow (Veterinary Medicine) G61 96 A8
Univ of Stirling FK9 2 D6
Univ of Strathclyde (John Anderson Campus) G1, G4 241 B3
Univ of Strathclyde (Jordanhill Campus) G13 95 D5
Univ of the West of Scotland (Ayr Campus) KA8 239 C7
Univ of the West of Scotland (Hamilton Campus) ML3 162 D4
Univ of the West of Scotland (Paisley Campus) PA1 113 D4
Unsted Pl [4] PA1 114 A4
Unst La G72 138 E2
Unthank Rd ML4 142 C5
Uphall Pl G33 118 E7
UP La G65 60 D8
Upland La [2] G14 95 C4
Upland Rd G14 95 C4
UPLAWMOOR 153 B3
Uplawmoor Prim Sch G78 153 B3
Uplawmoor Rd
Neilston G78 154 B6
Uplawmoor G78 153 E4
Upper Adelaide St G84 16 F1
Upper Arthur St G83 27 D4
Upper Bourtree Ct G73 138 C4
Upper Bourtree Dr G73 138 C4
Upper Bridge St
Alexandria G83 27 D4
Stirling FK8 2 A1
Upper Carman Rd G82 27 D1
Upper Cartsburn St PA15 46 A3
Upper Castlehill [2] FK8 7 A8
Upper Colquhoun St G84 16 D4
Upper Craigs FK8 7 B7
Upper Crofts KA7 238 F1
Upper Glenburn Rd G61 75 D5
Upper Glenfinlas St G84 16 E2
Upper Hall Rd G84 15 D5
Upper Loaning KA7 238 F1
Upper Mill St ML6 123 A8
Upper Mill Street Ind Est ML6 123 A8
Upper Newmarket St FK1 42 B5
Upper Smollett St G83 27 D4
Upper Stoneymollan Rd G83 27 B8
Upper Sutherland Cres G84 16 B3
Upper Sutherland St G84 16 B3
Upper Torwoodhill Rd G84 15 F4
UP Rd G65 60 D8
Ure Cres FK4 40 A6
Urquhart Cres PA4 94 C2
Urquhart Dr
East Kilbride G74 160 A3
Gourock PA19 43 F5
Urquhart Pl
Gartcosh G69 100 F4
Helensburgh G84 16 D4
Urquhart Rd KA3 223 D2
Urrdale Rd G41 116 B5
Usmore Pl G33 119 E5

V

Vaila La G72 138 F3
Vaila Pl G23 97 A7
Vaila St G23 96 F7
Vale Gr FK9 1 F5
Valence Twr G71 140 D4
Vale of Bonny View FK4 39 F5
VALE OF LEVEN 27 E4
Vale of Leven Acad G83 27 D3
Vale of Leven Hospl G83 27 C6
Vale of Leven Ind Est G82 27 E1
Vale of Leven Swim Pool G83 27 D6
Vale Pl FK6 21 E3
Valerio Ct G72 161 D8
Valetta Pl G81 73 D3
Valeview FK5 23 D2
Valeview Terr
Dumbarton G82 50 A6
Glasgow G42 137 A8
Vale Wlk G64 98 C8
Vallantine Cres G71 141 A8
Vallay St G22 97 D8
Valleybank G65 37 D3
Valley Ct ML3 162 C2
Valleyfield
East Kilbride G75 159 D1
Milton of Campsie G66 58 B6
Valleyfield Dr G68 60 E1
Valleyfield Pl FK7 7 C6
Valleyfield St [1] G21 97 E3
Valley International Pk* ML8 201 C2
Valley View ML1 164 B3
Valleyview Dr FK2 42 A8
Valleyview Pl FK2 42 A7
Vancouver Ct G75 159 B1
Vancouver Dr G75 159 B1
Vancouver La
[15] Glasgow G14 95 C4
Glasgow G14 95 D4
Vancouver Pl G81 73 D4
Vancouver Rd G14 95 D4
Vanguard St G81 74 D2
Vanguard Way PA4 94 C1
Vardar Ave G76 157 C8
Vardon Lea ML1 143 E1
Varna La G14 95 E3
Varna Rd G14 95 E4
Varnsdorf Way ML6 123 E6
Vasart Pl G20 96 F4
Vatersay Pl KA3 223 A6
Vaults La KA13 207 E3
Veir Terr G82 49 E3
Veitches Ct G81 74 A6
Veitch Pl G66 57 D8
Venachar Rd FK1 42 A1
Vennachar St ML7 146 E6
Vennacher Rd PA4 94 B4
Vennard Gdns G41 116 F2
Vennel La KA3 211 E8
Vennel (Mus) The* KA12 219 C2
Vennel St
Dalry KA24 191 B7
Stewarton KA3 211 E8
Vennel The FK6 21 E2
Vermont Ave G73 138 A7
Vermont St G41 116 E5
Vernon Bank G74 159 E3
Vernon Dr PA3 112 A6
Vernon Pl KA2 225 E2
Vernon St KA21 216 F7
Verona Ave G14 95 C4
Verona Gdns [4] G14 95 C4
Verona La G14 95 C4
Verona Pl KA22 205 D1
Vesalius St G32 119 A5
Vesuvius Dr ML1 164 B4
Viaduct Circ KA13 207 E5
Viaduct Rd G76 157 F7
Vicarfield Pl G51 116 B7
Vicarfield St G51 116 B7
Vicarland Pl G72 139 A4
Vicarland Rd G72 139 A5
Vicars Rd ML9 198 E2
Vicar St FK1 42 B5
Vicars Wlk G72 139 B5
Vickers St ML1 163 B8
Victoria Ave
Barrhead G78 134 B4
Carluke ML8 187 E1
Victoria Buildings Bsns Ctr PA1 114 A4
Victoria Cir G12 96 C3
Victoria Cottage Hospl G65 60 B8
Victoria Cres
Airdrie ML6 122 F6
Barrhead G78 134 B4
Clarkston G76 157 F7
Irvine KA12 219 B1
Kilsyth G65 60 B8
Wishaw ML2 164 D4
Victoria Crescent La G12 96 C3
Victoria Crescent Pl [4] G12 96 C3
Victoria Crescent Rd G12 96 C3
Victoria Cross G42 117 A2
Victoria Ct
Larkhall ML9 185 A4
Newton Mearns G77 156 D2
Victoria Dr
Barrhead G78 134 B4
Troon KA10 229 E2
Victoria Drive E PA4 94 C2
Victoria Drive W PA4 94 B3
Victoria East Rd KA1 228 A7
VICTORIA GARDENS 94 C1
Victoria Gdns
Airdrie ML6 122 F7
Barrhead G78 134 B4
Kilmacolm PA13 69 C1
Paisley PA2 113 C2
Victoria Glade G68 61 D6
Victoria Gr G78 134 B4
Victoria Infmy
Glasgow G42 137 A8
Helensburgh G84 16 F1
Victoria La G77 156 D2
Victoria Mans KA7 238 E6
Victoria Park* G14 95 E3
Victoria Park Cnr G14 95 D3
Victoria Park Drive N G14 95 E3
Victoria Park Drive S G14 95 D3
Victoria Park Gardens N G11 95 F3
Victoria Park Gardens S G11 95 F3
Victoria Park Lane N G14 95 D3
Victoria Park Lane S G14 95 D3
Victoria Park Sch [6] ML8 187 F2
Victoria Park St [7] G14 95 D3
Victoria Pk
Ayr KA7 238 E6
Kilsyth G65 60 B8
Victoria Pl
Airdrie ML6 122 E6
Barrhead G78 134 C4
Bellshill ML4 141 F4
Kilsyth G65 60 C8
Milngavie G62 55 B1
[4] Rutherglen G73 138 A8
Stirling FK8 7 A7
Victoria Prim Sch
Airdrie ML6 122 F7
Falkirk FK2 42 D6
[3] Glasgow G42 117 B2
Victoria Quadrant ML1 142 F5

Victoria Rd
Barrhead G78 .... 134 B4
Brookfield PA5.......... 111 D5
Dullatur G68 .... 61 D6
Falkirk FK2.......... 42 C6
Glasgow G42.......... 117 A3
Gourock PA19 .... 44 C7
Harthill ML7.......... 127 E5
Helensburgh G84.......... 16 E2
Kirkintilloch G66 .... 79 C3
Larbert FK5 .... 23 B1
Paisley PA2 .... 113 C2
Rutherglen G73.......... 138 B6
Saltcoats KA21 .... 217 A8
Stepps G33 .... 99 D5
Stirling FK8 .... 7 A8
Victoria Rdbt KA12.......... 219 B2
Victoria Sq
Newton Mearns G77 .... 156 D2
Stirling FK8 .... 7 A7
Victoria St
Alexandria G83 .... 27 E4
Alloa FK10.......... 10 A7
Ayr KA8 .... 236 A1
Dumbarton G82.......... 50 A3
Hamilton, Blantyre G72 ... 161 D7
Hamilton, Whitehill ML3 .. 162 B6
Harthill ML7.......... 127 E5
Kirkintilloch G66 .... 79 C8
Larkhall ML9 .... 185 A4
Rutherglen G73 .... 138 B8
Wishaw ML2 .... 166 A4
Victoria Terr
Dullatur G68 .... 61 D6
Kilmarnock KA1.......... 228 A7
Menstrie FK11.......... 4 B7
Victoria Way KA3 .... 195 F1
Victor St ML6.......... 104 A2
Victory Dr PA10.......... 111 A4
Victory Way G69 .... 120 B4
Viewbank G46 .... 136 A3
Viewbank Ave ML6.......... 123 B2
Viewbank St ML5 .... 101 F5
Viewfield
Airdrie ML6 .... 122 E7
Moodiesburn G69 .... 80 E4
Viewfield Ave
Bishopbriggs G64 .... 97 E8
Blantyre G72 .... 140 E1
Glasgow G69.......... 119 F5
Kirkintilloch G66 .... 79 C5
Lochwinnoch PA12.......... 129 B2
Milton of Campsie G66 .... 58 B5
Viewfield Bsns Ctr KA8.. 236 A2
Viewfield Dr
Alva FK12.......... 4 F6
Bishopbriggs G64 .... 97 E8
Glasgow G69.......... 119 F5
Viewfield La G12.......... 96 E2
Viewfield Pl
Harthill ML7.......... 127 F6
3 Stirling FK8.......... 7 B8
Viewfield Rd
Ayr KA8 .... 236 A2
Banknock FK4 .... 38 D3
Bellshill ML4 .... 141 F3
Bishopbriggs G64 .... 97 E8
Coatbridge ML5.......... 121 C4
Viewfield St
Harthill ML7.......... 127 F6
4 Stirling FK8.......... 7 B8
Viewforth FK8 .... 7 B6
Viewglen Ct G45.......... 137 D1
Viewmount Dr G20.......... 96 D7
VIEWPARK 141 C7
Viewpark
Beith KA15.......... 150 B1
Milngavie G62 .... 55 B1
Viewpark Ave G31 .... 118 B8
Viewpark Ct G73.......... 138 C6
Viewpark Dr G73.......... 138 B6
Viewpark Gdns PA4 .... 94 B2
Viewpark Pl ML1.......... 163 C6
Viewpark Rd ML1 .... 163 C6
Viewpark Sh Ctr G71,
ML4.......... 141 D6
Viewpoint Gate G21.......... 97 F6
Viewpoint Pl G21 .... 97 F6
Viewpoint Rd G21.......... 97 F6
Viking Cres PA6 .... 111 D8
Viking Rd ML6.......... 123 B5
Viking Terr G75.......... 180 E6
Viking Way
Glasgow G46 .... 135 F5
Renfrew PA4 .... 94 C1
Villabank FK6.......... 21 E2
Villafield Ave G64.......... 78 A3
Villafield Dr G64.......... 78 A3
Villafield Loan G64.......... 78 A3
Village Gdns G72 .... 140 E1
Village Rd G72.......... 139 F5
VILLAGE THE.......... 159 F2
Vincent Ct ML4 .... 142 A4
Vineburgh Ave KA12 .... 219 C4
Vineburgh Ct KA12.......... 219 B4
Vine Park Ave KA3 .... 222 B7
Vine Park Dr KA3 .... 222 B7
Vine St G11.......... 96 B2
Vines The KA12 .... 219 C4
Vinicombe La 3 G12.......... 96 D3
Vinicombe St G12.......... 96 D3
Vintner St G4.......... 97 C2
Viola Pl G64 .... 78 C8
Violet Gdns ML8 .... 201 E8
Violet Pl ML1 .... 143 B6
Violet St PA1 .... 114 A4
Virginia Ct G1 .... 241 A2
Virginia Gdns
Ayr KA8 .... 236 A2
Milngavie G62 .... 76 C8
Virginia Gr ML3.......... 182 F8
Virginia Pl G1 .... 241 A2
Virginia St
Glasgow G1.......... 241 A2
1 Greenock PA15.......... 46 A4
Virtue Well View ML6 ... 102 E3
Viscount Ave PA4.......... 94 C1
Viscount Gate G71 .... 140 E5
Vivian Ave G62 .... 54 F1
Voil Dr G44.......... 137 A4
Voil Rd FK9.......... 2 A3
Vorlich Ct G78.......... 134 C1
Vorlich Dr FK1.......... 66 E7
Vorlich Gdns G61 .... 75 C7
Vorlich Pl
Kilmarnock KA1.......... 228 A4
Stirling FK9 .... 2 A3
Vorlich Wynd ML1 .... 143 C4
Vrackie Pl KA1.......... 228 A4
Vryburg Cl G75 .... 180 A4
Vryburg Cres G75.......... 180 A4
Vulcan St
4 Glasgow G21 .... 97 E4
Motherwell ML1.......... 163 E8

W

Waddell Ave ML6 .... 102 D4
Waddell Ct
Glasgow G5.......... 117 D5
Kilmarnock KA3.......... 222 F4
Waddell St
Airdrie ML6 .... 103 A1
Falkirk FK2.......... 24 C2
Glasgow G5.......... 117 D4
Waggon Rd
Ayr KA8 .... 235 F2
Falkirk FK2.......... 42 B7
Waid Ave G77 .... 156 C6
Waldemar Rd G13 .... 95 C7
Walden Rd KA1 .... 228 E6
Waldo St 3 G13.......... 95 F7
Walker Ave
Kilmarnock KA3.......... 228 B8
Troon KA10 .... 229 E5
Walkerburn Dr ML2.......... 165 C6
Walkerburn Rd G52.......... 115 B4
Walker Ct
Glasgow G11.......... 96 B1
Hurlford KA1 .... 228 F6
Walker Dr
Bonnybridge FK4 .... 39 D5
Elderslie PA5.......... 112 C2
Walker Path 2 G71.......... 141 A8
Walker Rd KA8 .... 236 B2
Walkers Ct ML2.......... 166 A4
Walker St
Glasgow G11.......... 96 B1
Greenock PA16 .... 45 C5
5 Kilbirnie KA25.......... 149 A1
Paisley PA1 .... 113 D4
Walkinshaw Rd PA4.......... 93 C3
Walkinshaw St
Glasgow G40.......... 118 A4
Johnstone PA5.......... 112 A3
Walkinshaw Way PA3 .... 113 E7
Walkmill La G81 .... 74 B6
Walk The FK10.......... 10 A5
Wallace Ave
Bishopton PA7.......... 72 B3
Dundonald KA2 .... 225 F2
Elderslie PA5 .... 112 C2
Stevenston KA20.......... 206 D1
Troon KA10 .... 229 E6
Wallace Bldgs FK2.......... 42 B6
Wallace Cres
Denny FK6 .... 21 C2
Plean FK7 .... 12 D3
Wallace Ct
Kilmarnock KA1.......... 228 E6
2 Lanark ML11.......... 215 A4
Prestwick KA9.......... 236 D7
Stirling FK8 .... 2 B1
Wallace Dr
3 Bishopbriggs G64.......... 98 D8
Larkhall ML9 .... 185 C2
Wallacefield Rd KA10 ... 229 E3
Wallace Gate 2 G64.......... 98 D8
Wallace Gdns
Stirling FK9 .... 2 D3
Torrance G64.......... 57 B1
Wallace High Sch FK9.......... 2 C4
Wallacehill Rd KA1.......... 227 F4
Wallace Ho G67.......... 61 E2
Wallace Pl
1 Bishopbriggs G64.......... 98 D8
Blantyre G72 .... 140 E1
Cambusbarron FK7 .... 6 D5
Falkirk FK2.......... 42 C6
Fallin FK7.......... 8 C4
Greenock PA15 .... 45 F5
Hamilton ML3 .... 163 A2
Wallace Prim Sch PA5 .. 112 D2
Wallace Rd
Irvine KA12.......... 219 C4
Motherwell ML1.......... 143 B2
Renfrew PA4 .... 94 A1
Wallace St
Alloa FK10.......... 10 C7
Bannockburn FK7.......... 7 E1
Clydebank G81.......... 74 B1
Coatbridge ML5.......... 122 A5
Wallace St *continued*
Dumbarton G82.......... 50 A3
Falkirk FK2.......... 42 C6
Glasgow G5.......... 117 A5
Greenock PA16 .... 45 D4
Kilmarnock KA1.......... 227 E7
Motherwell ML1.......... 163 D7
Paisley PA3 .... 113 E6
Plains ML6.......... 104 A2
Port Glasgow PA14 .... 47 E1
Rutherglen G73 .... 138 A7
Stirling FK8 .... 2 B1
WALLACETOWN 236 B1
Wallacetown Ave KA3 ... 223 C6
Wallace View
Kilmarnock KA1.......... 227 F5
Shieldhill FK1.......... 66 D7
Tullibody FK10 .... 4 D3
Wallace Way ML11.......... 215 C4
Wallacewell Cres G21.......... 98 B5
Wallacewell Pl G21 .... 98 B5
Wallacewell Prim Sch
G21.......... 98 D6
Wallacewell Quadrant
G21 .... 98 C6
Wallacewell Rd G21.......... 98 C6
Wallace Wynd
Cambuslang G72 .... 139 A3
Law ML8 .... 187 A6
Wallbrae Rd G67.......... 82 F8
Wall Gdns FK1.......... 41 C5
Wallneuk 2 PA1.......... 113 F5
Wallneuk Rd PA3 .... 113 F5
Walls St G1.......... 241 B2
Wall St FK1.......... 41 C5
Wallstale Rd FK7.......... 7 A3
Walmer Cres G51 .... 116 C5
Walnut Cl G75 .... 180 C6
Walnut Cres
Glasgow G22.......... 97 D5
Johnstone PA5.......... 112 B1
Walnut Ct G66.......... 58 B5
Walnut Dr G66.......... 79 B6
Walnut Gate G72.......... 139 F4
Walnut Gr G75.......... 180 C6
Walnut Pl
Glasgow G22.......... 97 D5
Motherwell G71.......... 121 C1
Walnut Rd
Glasgow G22.......... 97 D5
Kilmarnock KA1.......... 227 C7
Walpole Pl PA5 .... 131 C7
Walter St
Glasgow G31.......... 118 C7
Wishaw ML2 .... 165 D3
Walton Ave G77.......... 156 C6
Walton Ct G46 .... 136 C2
Walton St
Barrhead G78 .... 134 C3
Glasgow G41.......... 136 E8
Wamba Ave G13 .... 95 E8
Wamphray Pl G75.......... 179 D7
Wandilla Ave G81.......... 74 D2
Wanlock St G51.......... 116 A8
Ward Ct KA8.......... 236 B4
Wardend Rd G64.......... 57 B1
Warden Rd G13.......... 95 D7
Wardhill Rd G21 .... 98 B5
Wardhouse Rd PA2 .... 133 C7
Wardie Pl G33 .... 119 F7
Wardie Rd G34 .... 120 A7
Wardlaw Ave G73.......... 138 B7
Wardlaw Cres
East Kilbride G75.......... 181 A7
Troon KA10 .... 230 A4
Wardlaw Dr G73 .... 138 B8
Wardlaw Gdns KA11.......... 220 B7
Wardlaw Pl FK2.......... 24 C2
Wardlaw Rd
Bearsden G61 .... 75 F1
Kilmarnock KA3.......... 223 E5
Wardneuk KA3.......... 236 C6
Wardneuk Ct KA11 .... 220 A6
Wardneuk Dr KA3.......... 223 A4
WARDPARK.......... 62 C7
Wardpark Ct G67 .... 62 D6
Wardpark East Ind Est
G68.......... 62 E8
Wardpark North Ind Est
G68.......... 62 D7
Wardpark Pl G67 .... 62 D6
Wardpark Rd G67.......... 62 D6
Wardpark Rdbt G68.......... 62 D7
Wardpark South Ind Est
G67.......... 62 D6
Ward Rd KA8 .... 236 B4
Wardrop Pl G74 .... 159 F3
Wardrop St
Beith KA15.......... 171 C8
2 Glasgow G51 .... 116 A8
Paisley PA1 .... 113 E4
Wardrop Terr KA15 .... 171 C8
Wards Cres ML5 .... 121 E5
Wards Pl KA1.......... 227 F7
Ward St FK10.......... 10 A5
Ware Rd G34 .... 120 A7
Warilda Ave G81.......... 74 C2
Warlock Dr PA11.......... 90 D1
Warlock Rd PA11 .... 90 D3
Warly Dr KA2.......... 225 F1
Warly Pl KA2 .... 225 F1
Warner St KA20.......... 217 D7
Warnock Cres ML4.......... 142 B4
Warnock Rd G77.......... 156 C7
Warnock St G31 .... 241 C3
Warren Rd ML3.......... 183 D8
Warren St G42.......... 117 B1
Warren Wlk G66 .... 57 E7
Warriston Cres G33 .... 118 D8
Warriston Ct G33 .... 118 F8
Warriston Pl G32 .... 119 B7
Warriston St G33 .... 118 E8
Warriston Way 1 G73... 138 D4
WARRIX.......... 224 G7
Warrix Ave KA12.......... 219 D2
Warrix Gdns KA10.......... 232 E8
Warrix Intc KA11.......... 219 E1
Warroch St G3.......... 240 A2
Warwick G74 .... 160 C4
Warwick Gr ML3 .... 161 E5
Warwickhill KA11 .... 220 B5
Warwickhill Pl KA1 .... 222 E2
Warwickhill Rd KA1.......... 222 D1
Warwick Rd PA16.......... 44 E4
Warwick Villas G81 .... 94 E7
Washington Rd
Kirkintilloch G66 .... 79 B8
Paisley PA3 .... 113 F8
Washington St G3 .... 240 B2
Watchmeal Cres G81.......... 74 C7
Waterbank Rd G76.......... 158 D5
Watercut Rd KA13 .... 218 F8
WATERFOOT.......... 157 D2
Waterfoot Ave G53.......... 135 C8
Waterfoot Rd
Newton Mearns, Kirkhill
G77.......... 157 B3
Newton Mearns, Mearns
G77.......... 156 F3
Waterfoot Row G76.......... 157 D3
Waterfoot Terr G53 .... 135 C8
Waterford Ct G46.......... 136 B2
Waterford Rd G46 .... 136 B3
Waterfront L Complex
PA15.......... 46 A6
Waterfront Way FK9 .... 2 A3
Waterfurs Dr FK2 .... 42 A8
Waterhaughs Gdns G33 .. 98 D7
Waterhaughs Gr G33.......... 98 D7
Water La 8 KA1 .... 227 F8
Waterlands Gdns ML8... 188 A3
Waterlands Pl ML8.......... 187 A4
Waterlands Rd ML8 .... 187 B6
WATERLOO.......... 165 D1
Waterloo Cl G66 .... 58 D1
Waterloo Dr ML11.......... 215 A5
Waterloo Gdns 6 G66 ... 58 D1
Waterloo La G2.......... 240 C2
Waterloo Rd
Lanark ML11 .... 215 A5
Prestwick KA9.......... 236 B5
Waterloo St G2 .... 240 C2
Watermill Ave G66.......... 79 D4
Water Rd G78 .... 134 C3
Water Row G51.......... 116 A8
Watersaugh Dr ML1.......... 144 B2
Watersedge Ct G84 .... 15 D4
Waters End FK2.......... 24 B2
WATERSIDE
Fenwick.......... 213 F4
Glasgow.......... 134 E5
Kirkintilloch 80 B7
Waterside
Clarkston G76 .... 157 F5
Irvine KA12 .... 219 B3
Waterside Ave G77.......... 156 C4
Waterside Ct
Carmunnock G76.......... 158 D7
Kilmarnock KA1.......... 227 F8
Waterside Dr G77.......... 156 C4
Waterside Gdns
Cambuslang G72 .... 139 E3
Carmunnock G76.......... 158 D7
Hamilton ML3 .... 162 E1
Waterside La PA10.......... 111 C2
Waterside Pl G5 .... 117 D4
Waterside Rd
Carmunnock G76.......... 158 D6
Carmunnock G76.......... 158 D8
Kilwinning KA13.......... 207 F4
Kirkintilloch G66 .... 79 E7
Waterside St
Glasgow G5.......... 117 D4
Kilmarnock KA1.......... 227 F8
Waterside Terr PA10 .... 111 C2
Waterside Way PA10.......... 111 C2
Waterslap KA3.......... 213 A2
Water St PA14 .... 47 C2
Waterston Way PA12.......... 129 C3
Wateryetts Dr PA13 .... 69 D1
Watling Ave FK1 .... 41 C5
Watling Dr FK1 .... 41 D5
Watling Gdns FK1.......... 41 D6
Watling Pl 7 G75.......... 159 A1
Watling St
Falkirk FK1.......... 41 C5
Motherwell ML1.......... 142 C1
Uddingston G71.......... 140 E8
Watson Ave
Linwood PA3 .... 112 B5
Rutherglen G73 .... 137 F7
Stonehouse ML9 .... 199 A3
Watson Cres G65 .... 60 E8
Watson Pl
Hamilton G72.......... 161 B7
Longcroft FK4 .... 39 C4
Watson St
Falkirk FK2.......... 42 B5
Glasgow G1.......... 241 B1
Hamilton G72.......... 161 C7
Kilmarnock KA3.......... 228 B8
Larkhall ML9 .... 184 F3
Motherwell ML1.......... 163 E5
4 Motherwell ML1.......... 163 E6
Uddingston G71.......... 140 F6
Watson Terr KA12.......... 219 D2
Watsonville Pk 3 ML1 .. 163 E6
Watstone Rd ML9.......... 199 A2
Watt Ave G33.......... 99 F5
Watt Cres ML4.......... 142 B7
Watt Ct
Dalry KA24.......... 191 C7
Stonehouse ML9 .... 198 E1
Wattfield Rd KA7 .... 238 F6
Watt Gdns FK1.......... 41 E6
Watt La PA11 .... 110 E7
Watt Liby & McLean Mus &
Art Gall* PA16 .... 45 E6
Watt Low Ave G73 .... 137 F6
Watt Pl
Greenock PA15 .... 46 A5
Hamilton G72.......... 161 C4
Milngavie G62 .... 54 F3
Watt Rd
Bridge of Weir PA11 .... 110 D7
Glasgow G52.......... 115 A7
Watt St
Airdrie ML6 .... 103 C1
Glasgow G5 .... 240 A1
Greenock PA16 .... 45 E6
WATTSTON.......... 103 C8
Waukglen Ave G53.......... 135 B2
Waukglen Cres G53.......... 135 C3
Waukglen Dr G53 .... 135 B3
Waukglen Gdns G53 .... 135 B2
Waukglen Path G53.......... 135 B3
Waukglen Pl G53 .... 135 B3
Waukglen Rd G53.......... 135 B3
Waulker St FK8.......... 1 F2
Waulking Mill Rd G81.... 74 C7
Waulkmill Ave G78.......... 134 D4
Waulkmill Pl KA1 .... 228 A7
Waulkmill St G46 .... 135 E4
Waulkmill Way G78 .... 134 D4
Waverley
Clydebank G81.......... 74 C2
East Kilbride G74.......... 160 D4
Waverley Ave
Helensburgh G84.......... 25 C7
Kilmarnock KA1.......... 222 C1
Waverley Cres
Bonnybridge FK4 .... 40 B3
Cumbernauld G67 .... 82 D7
Hamilton ML3 .... 161 F4
Kirkintilloch G66 .... 79 D8
Lanark ML11.......... 215 C4
Stirling FK8 .... 2 C1
Waverley Ct
Bothwell G71.......... 141 A2
Helensburgh G84.......... 16 D2
Waverley Dr
Airdrie ML6 .... 103 B1
Rutherglen G73 .... 138 C7
Wishaw ML2 .... 165 B4
Waverley Gdns
Elderslie PA5.......... 112 D2
Glasgow G41 .... 116 E1
WAVERLEY PARK.......... 116 D1
Waverley Park Rdbt G66 .. 79 E8
Waverley Pk G66.......... 79 D8
Waverley Pl KA21 .... 205 E1
Waverley Rd
Paisley PA2 .... 132 F8
Stenhousemuir FK5 .... 23 C2
Waverley St
Coatbridge ML5.......... 102 B1
Falkirk FK2.......... 42 B8
Glasgow G41.......... 116 E1
Greenock PA16 .... 45 C3
Hamilton ML3 .... 161 F4
Larkhall ML9 .... 199 A8
Waverley Terr
Dumbarton G82.......... 49 B4
Hamilton G72.......... 161 D5
Stenhousemuir FK5.......... 23 C2
Waverley Way PA2.......... 132 F7
Weardale La G33 .... 119 C8
Weardale St G33.......... 119 C8
Weaver Ave G77 .... 156 C7
Weaver Cres ML6 .... 123 A5
Weaver La PA10 .... 111 A4
Weaver Pl G75.......... 179 F7
Weaver Row FK7.......... 7 A4
Weavers Ave PA2 .... 113 B3
Weaver's Cott* PA10.... 111 A3
Weavers Ct
1 East Kilbride G74.......... 159 F2
3 Hamilton ML3.......... 162 E2
Kilbarchan PA10.......... 111 A3
Weavers Gate PA1 .... 113 B3
Weavers Rd PA2 .... 113 B3
Weaver St
Ayr KA8 .... 235 F2
Glasgow G4 .... 241 B2
Weavers Way
Saltcoats KA21 .... 205 F3
Stonehouse ML9 .... 198 E1
Weavers Wlk ML11 .... 215 A3
Weaver Terr PA2.......... 114 A3
Webster Ave FK2 .... 24 B4
Webster Groves ML2 .... 165 D5
Webster St
Clydebank G81.......... 94 E8
Glasgow G40.......... 118 A3
Wedderlea Dr G52 .... 115 B5
Wee Cl KA15.......... 171 B8
Weensmoor Rd G53.......... 134 F4
Weeple Dr PA3 .... 112 A6
Wee Row FK2 .... 42 B6
Wee Sunnyside Rd ML9 . 184 B2
Weighhouse Cl PA1 .... 113 E4
Weighhouse Rd ML8 .... 187 E3
Weir Ave
Barrhead G78 .... 134 C2

Weir Ave *continued*
Prestwick KA9 233 D1
Weir Dr FK7 8 D4
Weir Pl
Greenock PA15 46 D3
Kilbirnie KA25 149 B1
Law ML8 186 F4
Weir Rd
Ardrossan KA22 205 D4
Ayr KA8 235 F3
Weir St
Coatbridge ML5 122 A7
Falkirk FK1 42 C5
Greenock PA15 46 D2
Paisley PA1, PA3 113 F5
Stirling FK8 1 F2
Weirston Rd KA13 208 A3
Weirwood Ave G69 120 A5
Weirwood Gdns G69 119 F4
Welbeck Cres KA10 229 C2
Welbeck Ct KA10 229 C2
Welbeck Rd G53 135 B4
Welbeck St
Greenock PA16 45 C8
Kilmarnock KA1 228 A7
Weldon Pl G65 60 F3
Welfare Ave G72 139 D4
Welland Pl G75 179 E7
Wellbank Gdns KA23 190 C5
Wellbank Pl G71 140 F5
Wellbeck Ho 7 G74 159 F2
Wellbeck Mews KA10 229 C2
Wellbrae
Larkhall ML9 185 A2
Stonehouse ML9 198 E2
Wellbrae Rd ML3 162 B1
Wellbrae Terr G69 80 F2
Wellbuttslea Dr ML11 214 E3
Wellcroft Pl G5 117 B4
Wellcroft Rd ML3 161 E3
Wellcroft Terr ML3 161 E3
Welldale La ML11 214 B5
Well Dr ML11 214 E3
Wellesley Cres
Cumbernauld G68 81 E8
East Kilbride G75 179 F7
Wellesley Dr
Cumbernauld G68 60 D1
East Kilbride G75 179 F8
Wellesley Pl G68 60 D1
Wellfield Ave G46 136 B3
Wellfield St G21 97 F4
Wellgate ML11 215 A4
Wellgate Ct ML9 185 A4
Wellgate Dr FK9 2 C7
Wellgatehead ML11 215 A3
Wellgate St ML9 185 A4
Well Gn G43 136 C8
Well Green Ct G43 136 C8
Wellgreen Pl FK8 7 B6
Wellgreen Rd FK8 7 B7
Wellhall Ct ML3 162 B4
Wellhall Rd ML3 162 B3
Wellhead Ct ML11 215 B4
Wellhouse Cres G33 119 F7
Wellhouse Gdns G33 119 F7
Wellhouse Gr G33 119 F7
Wellhouse Rd G33 119 F7
Wellington G75 180 B7
Wellington Ave KA3 228 D8
Wellington Gdns KA3 228 E8
Wellington La
Ayr KA7 238 E8
Glasgow G2 240 C2
Wellington Path G69 120 B4
Wellington Pl
Clydebank G81 73 D3
Coatbridge ML5 121 C5
4 Kilmarnock KA3 222 F2
Wishaw ML2 186 D8
Wellington Rd G64 78 B4
Wellington Sch KA7 238 E7
Wellington Sq KA7 238 E8
Wellington St
Airdrie ML6 103 A1
Glasgow G2 240 C2
Greenock PA15 45 E4
Kilmarnock KA3 222 F1
Paisley PA3 113 D5
Prestwick KA9 236 B5
Wishaw ML2 164 C5
Wellington Terr ML11 214 F5
Wellington Way
Greenock PA15 45 E4
5 Renfrew PA4 94 C1
Wellknowe Ave G74 158 C2
Wellknowe Pl G74 158 C3
Wellknowe Rd G74 158 C3
Well La G66 57 D8
Wellmeadow Cl G77 156 D5
Wellmeadow Gn G77 156 D5
Wellmeadow Rd G43 136 B6
Wellmeadows Ct ML3 162 A2
Wellmeadows La ML3 162 A2
Wellmeadow St PA1 113 D4
Wellmeadow Way G77 156 D6
Wellpark KA7 238 F2
Wellpark Ave KA3 228 C8
Wellpark Bldgs 3 PA15 46 A4
Wellpark Cres FK7 6 F4
Wellpark Ct
Greenock PA15 45 F4
Kilmarnock KA3 228 C8
Wellpark Gr KA3 228 C8
Wellpark La
Neilston G78 154 D6
Saltcoats KA21 216 F8
Wellpark Pl KA3 228 C8
Wellpark Rd
Banknock FK4 38 D2
Motherwell ML1 163 C6
Saltcoats KA21 216 F8
Wellpark St G31 241 C2
Wellpark Terr
Bonnybridge FK4 40 A5
Neilston G78 154 D6
Well Rd
Bridge of Allan FK9 2 A8
Falkirk FK1 41 F3
Kilbarchan PA10 111 A3
Lanark ML11 215 B3
Wellsbourne Ho KA7 238 E7
Wellshot Dr G72 138 F5
Wellshot Prim Sch G32 118 F4
Wellshot Rd G32 118 F4
WELLSIDE 139 D4
Wellside Ave ML6 103 A1
Wellside Ct FK1 42 A5
Wellside Dr G72 139 C4
Wellside La ML6 103 B1
Wellside Pl FK1 42 A5
Wellside Quadrant ML6 103 A1
Wells Quarry Rd G76, G74 159 C5
Wells St G81 73 F3
Well St
Paisley PA1, PA3 113 C5
West Kilbride KA23 190 C5
Wellstood Ct FK4 40 C6
Wellview Dr ML1 163 D6
Wellwood KA13 207 C2
Wellwood Ave ML11 215 B5
Wellwynd ML6 122 F8
Wellwynd Gdns 2 ML6 122 F8
Wellyard La PA16 44 C3
Wellyard Way PA16 44 C2
Wellyard Wynd PA16 44 C2
Welsh Ct FK6 21 F1
Welsh Dr
Hamilton, Blantyre G72 161 D6
Hamilton, Eddlewood ML3 183 C7
Welsh Gdns FK9 2 A8
Welsh Pl KA21 205 E1
Welsh Rd KA9 233 D2
Welsh Row ML6 123 C3
Wemyss Ave G77 156 C7
Wemyss Bay St PA15 45 E3
Wemyss Cres KA10 229 F1
Wemyss Dr G68 60 E1
Wemyss Gdns G69 120 A3
Wendur Way 5 PA3 113 D8
Wenlock Rd PA2 113 F2
Wensleydale G74 159 C3
Wentworth Dr 5 G23 76 E1
Wentworth Sq KA13 207 C4
Wesley St ML6 122 F7
West Abercromby St G84 16 D3
West Academy St ML2 164 E3
West Acad St ML2 164 E3
Westacres Rd G77 156 B4
WEST ARTHURLIE 134 A2
West Ave
Carluke ML8 187 E1
Hamilton G72 161 E5
Paisley PA1 112 D4
Plains ML6 104 A3
Renfrew PA4 94 D3
Stepps G33 99 D5
Uddingston G71 141 C6
WEST BALGROCHAN 57 A1
West Balgrochan Rd G64 57 B1
Westbank Ct 7 G12 96 E2
Westbank La G12 96 E2
Westbank Quadrant G12 96 E2
West Barmoss Ave PA14 68 F7
WEST BENHAR 127 B4
West Benhar Rd ML7 127 B3
West Blackhall St
1 Greenock PA15 45 F5
Greenock PA15 45 F6
West Boreland Rd FK6 21 D2
Westborne Gdns G84 16 C2
Westbourne Ave KA9 236 D8
Westbourne Cres G61 75 C5
Westbourne Ctr G78 134 B2
Westbourne Dr G61 75 D5
Westbourne Gardens La 6 G12 96 C4
Westbourne Gardens N 7 G12 96 C4
Westbourne Gardens S G12 96 C4
Westbourne Gardens W 8 G12 96 C4
Westbourne Gdns KA9 236 D8
Westbourne Rd G12 96 B4
Westbourne Terrace Lane N 9 G12 96 C4
Westbourne Terrace Lane S 3 G12 96 B4
West Bowhouse Gdns KA11 220 A5
West Bowhouse Head KA11 220 A5
West Bowhouse Way KA11 220 A5
West Bowhouse Workshops KA11 220 A5
West Brae PA1 113 D4
Westbrae Dr G13, G14 95 E4
Westbrae Rd G77 156 F6
West Bridgend G82 49 E4
West Bridge St FK1 42 A5
West Buchanan Pl PA1 113 D4
WESTBURN 139 E6
Westburn Ave
Cambuslang G72 139 D6
Falkirk FK1 41 F4
Paisley PA3 113 B5
Westburn Bldgs 2 PA15 45 F5
Westburn Cres
Clydebank G81 74 B7
Rutherglen G73 137 F7
Westburn Dr G72 139 B6
Westburn Farm Rd G72 139 B6
Westburn Rd
Cambuslang, Newton G72 140 B5
Cambuslang, Westburn G72 139 D6
Stewarton KA3 195 E1
West Burnside St G65 60 D8
West Burn St PA15 45 F5
West Byrehill Ind Est KA13 207 B2
West Campbell St
Glasgow G2 240 C3
Paisley PA1 113 B4
West Canal St ML5 121 F7
West Carmuirs Loan FK5 40 F6
Westcastle Cres G45 137 D3
Westcastle Ct G45 137 D3
Westcastle Gdns G45 137 D3
Westcastle Gr G45 137 D3
West Chapelton Ave G61 75 F4
West Chapelton Cres G61 75 F4
West Chapelton Dr G61 75 F4
West Chapelton La G61 75 F4
Westcliff G82 49 B4
West Clyde St
Helensburgh G84 16 C1
Larkhall ML9 185 B2
Westclyffe St 3 G41 116 E1
West Coats Prim Sch G72 138 F5
West Coats Rd G72 138 F5
Westcott Pl ML11 215 C5
WEST CRAIGEND 72 F1
Westcraigs Pk EH48 107 C3
Westcraigs Rd
Blackridge EH48 107 D2
Harthill ML7 127 F6
West Cres KA10 229 G4
West Cross ML2 165 A3
Westcross Rdbt G77 156 A5
West Ct
Clydebank G81 73 E4
Irvine KA12 219 B2
West Dhuhill Dr G84 16 D4
West Doura Ave KA21 205 F1
West Doura Ct KA13 207 B3
West Doura Way KA13 207 C3
West Dr
Airdrie ML6 123 E6
Stenhousemuir FK5 23 C1
WEST DRUMOYNE 115 E7
Westend G61 76 A2
West End KA24 191 B7
Westend Ct ML8 186 F4
West End Dr ML4 141 F4
West End Gdns FK10 10 A6
Westend Park St G3 96 F2
West End Pl ML4 141 F4
Westend Ret Pk G11 96 A2
WESTER AUCHINLOCH 79 C2
Wester Boghead G66 78 F4
Westerburn St G32 118 F6
Wester Carriagehill PA2 113 E2
Wester Cleddens Prim Sch G64 78 A2
Wester Cleddens Rd G64 78 C2
Wester Cochno Holdings G81 74 A8
Wester Common Dr G22 97 A4
Westercommon Prim Sch G22 97 A4
Wester Common Rd G22 97 A4
Westercraigs G31 117 F7
Westercraigs Ct 7 G31 117 F7
Westerdale G74 159 C3
Westerfield Rd G76 158 D4
Westergate Sh Ctr G2 240 C2
Westergill Ave ML6 123 E6
Westerglen Rd FK1 42 A2
Westergreens Ave G66 79 C6
Westerhill Rd G64 78 D3
WESTER HOLYTOWN 142 E6
Westerhouse Ct ML8 187 D2
Westerhouse Rd G34 119 F8
Westerkirk Dr G23 76 E1
Westerlands G12 96 A6
Westerlands Dr
Newton Mearns G77 156 B4
Stirling FK8 7 B5
Westerlands Gdns G77 156 B4
Westerlands Gr G77 156 B4
Westerlands Pl G77 156 B5
Westerlea Ct FK9 2 A5
Westerlea Dr FK9 2 A5
Wester Leddriegreen Rd G63 31 B4
WESTERMAINS 79 B8
Westermains Ave G66 79 B7
Wester Mavisbank Ave ML6 122 F8
Wester Moffat Ave ML6 123 E7
Wester Moffat Cres 2 ML6 123 E7
Wester Moffat Hospl ML6 123 F8
Wester Myvot Rd G67 82 A4
Western Ave
Falkirk FK2 42 B6
Western Ave *continued*
Rutherglen G73 137 F8
Western Cres KA25 170 A7
Western Ind Est KA3 222 E2
Western Infmy G11 96 C2
Western Isles Rd G60 73 C5
Western Pl KA3 223 A4
Western Rd
Cambuslang G72 138 F3
Kilmarnock KA1, KA3 222 E2
Westerpark Ave G72 161 C3
Wester Rd G32 119 D3
Westerton
Cowie FK7 12 D8
Lennoxtown G66 57 F8
Westerton Ave
Clarkston G76 158 A5
Glasgow G61 95 F8
Larkhall ML9 185 A1
Westerton Ct G76 158 A5
Westerton Dr FK9 2 A7
Westerton La G76 158 A5
Westerton of Mugdock G62 55 B6
Westerton Prim Sch G61 75 E2
Westerton Rd G68 61 D6
Westerton Sta G61 75 E1
Westerton Terr FK2 24 C3
West Fairholm St ML9 184 F5
Westfarm Ave G72 139 D6
Westfarm Cres G72 139 D6
Westfarm Ct G72 139 D7
Westfarm Dr G72 139 D7
Westfarm Gr G72 139 D7
Westfarm La G72 139 D7
Westfarm Wynd G72 139 D6
West Faulds Rd ML11 215 E5
WESTFIELD
Cumbernauld 81 F7
Kilsyth 36 A1
Westfield
Dumbarton G82 49 C4
Kilbirnie KA25 170 B8
Westfield Ave G73 137 F7
Westfield Cres G61 75 E2
Westfield Ct KA21 216 E7
Westfield Dr
Bearsden G61 75 E2
Cumbernauld G68 81 F7
Glasgow G52 115 A5
Greenock PA16 45 C8
Kilmacolm PA13 89 B8
Westfield Ind Area G68 81 D6
Westfield Pl
Cumbernauld G68 81 D6
Denny FK6 21 E1
Westfield Prim Sch G68 81 F7
Westfield Rd
Ayr KA7 238 E6
Cumbernauld G68 61 A1
Cumbernauld G68 81 E7
Glasgow G46 136 A3
Kilmarnock KA3 223 C6
Kilsyth G65 36 B1
Motherwell ML1 143 C7
Port Glasgow PA14 68 F8
Westfield Rdbt FK2 42 F6
Westfields G64 77 E3
Westfield St FK2 42 E5
Westfield Trad Est FK6 21 E1
West Fullarton St KA1 222 E1
Westgarth Pl G74 159 A3
West Gate ML2 165 D3
Westgate Way ML4 141 F5
West George La G2 240 C3
West George St
Coatbridge ML5 122 A8
Glasgow G2 240 C3
7 Kilmarnock KA1 222 F1
West Glebe G76 178 F5
West Glebe Terr ML3 162 C2
West Glen Gdns PA13 69 E1
West Glen Rd PA13, PA14 69 E1
West Gr KA10 229 G4
West Graham St G3 240 B4
West Greenhill Pl G3 116 E8
West Hamilton St ML1 163 E6
Westhaugh Cvn Site FK10 5 A4
Westhaugh Rd FK9 1 F4
West High St G66 58 C1
Westhorn Dr G32 119 A1
Westhouse Ave G73 137 E7
Westhouse Gdns G73 137 E7
West James St FK12 5 A6
West Johnstone St FK12 5 A6
WEST KILBRIDE 190 D3
West Kilbride Mus* KA23 190 C5
West Kilbride Prim Sch KA23 190 C5
West Kilbride Rd KA24 191 A7
West Kilbride Sta KA23 190 D5
West King St G84 16 B2
West Kirklands Pl KA24 191 B7
West Kirk St ML6 122 F8
Westknowe Gdns G73 138 B5
West La PA1 113 B4
Westland PA13 89 C8
Westland Dr G14 95 D4
Westland Drive La 8 G14 95 D3
Westlands Gdns PA2 113 D2
West Langlands St KA1 222 E1
Westlea Pl ML6 123 B6
West Lennox Dr G84 16 D3
West Link Rd FK9 2 D5
West Lodge Gdns FK10 9 F8
West Lodge Rd PA4 94 B4
WEST MAINS 159 D1
West Mains Ind Est FK3 42 F7
West Mains Rd
East Kilbride G74 159 D2
Falkirk FK3 42 F7
West Mains Sch G74 160 A3
West Main St ML7 127 E5
Westminster Pl FK5 23 E4
Westminster Terr 3 G3 116 E8
West Montrose St G84 16 C2
Westmoor Cres KA1 227 D7
Westmoreland St G42 117 A2
Westmorland Rd PA16 44 E4
Westmuir Pl G73 137 F8
Westmuir St G31 118 D5
West Murrayfield FK7 7 D1
West Nemphlar Rd ML11 214 C6
West Netherton St KA1 227 F7
West Nile St G1 241 A3
West of Scotland Science Pk (Kelvin Campus) G20 76 B1
West of Scotland Science Pk (Todd Campus) G20 76 B1
Westonbirt Gr ML5 101 F6
Weston Pl KA9 236 D6
Weston Terr KA23 190 C5
Westpark Cres 3 FK2 41 F8
West Park Cres KA3 222 B8
Westpark Ct
8 Falkirk FK2 41 F8
Stevenston KA20 217 C7
Westpark Dr PA3 113 B5
West Park Dr KA3 222 B8
Westpark Wynd KA24 191 B8
West Pl ML2 166 A5
Westport
East Kilbride G75 159 A1
Lanark ML11 214 E3
West Port ML11 214 F4
West Portland St KA10 229 C2
WEST PORTON 72 A4
West Porton Pl PA7 71 F4
Westport St 10 G65 60 D8
West Prim Sch PA1 113 C4
West Princes St G84 16 C2
West Prince's St
6 Glasgow G4 96 E2
Glasgow G4 96 F2
West Quay PA14 47 C2
Westray Ave
Newton Mearns G77 156 C7
Port Glasgow PA14 69 B6
Westray Cir G22 97 D6
Westray Ct G67 82 E8
Westray Dr KA3 223 A6
Westray Pl
Bishopbriggs G64 78 D2
Glasgow G22 97 D7
Westray Rd G67 82 E8
Westray Sq G22 97 D7
Westray St G22 97 C7
Westray Terr FK1 42 C2
Westray Wynd 2 ML2 165 F6
West Rd
Irvine KA12 219 B3
Irvine KA12 219 B7
Kilbarchan PA10 111 A4
Port Glasgow PA14 68 E8
Stevenston KA20 218 A6
Torrance G64 57 B1
West Regent St G2 240 C3
Westreron Ho
Bridge of Allan FK9 2 A8
Stirling FK9 2 A1
WESTRIGG 107 F3
West Rossdhu Dr G84 16 D3
West Row G63 31 A4
West Sanquhar Ave KA8 236 B2
West Sanquhar Pl KA8 236 B2
West Sanquhar Rd KA8 236 B3
West Scott Terr ML3 162 D1
West Shaw St
Greenock PA15 45 E5
Kilmarnock KA1 227 F6
Westside Gdns G11 96 C2
West St
Clydebank G81 94 E8
Glasgow G5 117 A5
Paisley PA1 113 C4
West Stewart St
Greenock PA15 45 F5
Hamilton ML3 162 C4
West Stirling St FK12 4 F7
West Street Underground Sta G5 117 A5
West Thomson St G81 74 B3
West Thornlie St ML2 165 A2
West Vennel 6 FK10 10 B6
West View KA3 213 E4
Westview Cres FK10 4 C2
West View Terr KA3 195 B8
Westward Way KA10 229 F7
West Wellbrae Cres ML3 183 B8
West Whitby St G31 118 C4
WESTWOOD 180 A8
Westwood Ave
Ayr KA8 236 E2
Glasgow G46 136 B3
Westwood Cres
Ayr KA8 236 E2
Hamilton ML3 162 C2
1 Stirling FK9 2 B3
Westwood Dr ML1 144 E1
Westwood Gdns PA3 113 B5
Westwood Hill G75 180 B7
Westwood Quadrant G81 74 D1

Wishaw General Hospl
ML2 164 E3
Wishaw High Rd ML1 165 C8
Wishawhill St ML2 164 F4
Wishaw Low Rd ML1 165 A7
Wishaw Rd ML2 186 E8
Wishaw Sp Ctr ML2 164 F2
Wishaw Sta ML2 165 A2
Wisner Ct G46 135 F4
Wisteria La ML8 201 F8
Wiston St G72 139 E5
Witches Linn KA22 205 B4
Witchhill Pl KA3 222 F2
Witchhill Sch KA3 222 F2
Witchknowe Ave KA1 227 F5
Witchknowe Ct
Kilmarnock KA1 227 F4
2 Kilmarnock KA1 228 A4
Witchknowe Rd KA1 227 F4
Witch Rd KA3 222 F2
Witchwood Ct ML5 101 D2
Witcutt Way ML2 164 E1
Witherspoon St PA1 113 E4
Woddrop St G40 118 B2
Wolcott Dr G72 161 D8
Wolfe Ave G77 156 C7
Wolfe Rd FK1 42 D4
Wolseley St G5 117 D3
Wood Aven Dr G74 159 D4
Wood Avens FK10 4 B1
Woodbank Cres
Clarkston G76 157 E6
Johnstone PA5 111 F2
Woodbank Ct G83 27 C7
Woodbank Gdns G83 27 C7
Woodbank Rd KA2 221 F1
Woodburn Ave
Airdrie ML6 122 F6
Balloch G83 27 F7
Clarkston G76 157 E6
Hamilton G72 161 E8
Kilwinning KA13 207 E4
Woodburn Cres FK4 39 F3
Woodburn Ct
Lanark ML11 215 C2
Rutherglen G73 138 B6
Woodburn Dr FK10 4 F1
Woodburn Gait ML11 215 B3
Woodburn Gdns FK2 42 E5
Woodburn Gr ML3 162 E3
Woodburn Pk ML3 162 E3
Woodburn Pl PA6 111 E7
Woodburn Rd
Beith KA15 171 C8
Falkirk FK2 42 D5
Glasgow G43 136 D5
Motherwell ML1 143 D7
Woodburn St
Falkirk FK2 42 E5
Motherwell ML1 163 E8
Woodburn Terr 9 ML9 185 C2
Woodburn Way
Alva FK12 5 A6
Cumbernauld G68 61 C2
Milngavie G62 55 A1
Wood Cres
Kilwinning KA13 207 E4
Motherwell ML1 142 E1
Woodcroft Ave G11 95 F4
Wood Ct KA10 229 B2
Wooddale ML1 163 D4
Woodend G72 161 D6
Woodend Cotts KA6 239 E2
Woodend Ct G32 119 E2
Wood End Cvn Site ML7 166 F8
Woodend Dr
Airdrie ML6 103 C1
Glasgow G13 95 E5
Paisley PA1 114 D4
Woodend Gdns G32 119 D2
Woodend La 2 G13 95 E5
Woodend Oval KA6 239 E2
Woodend Pl PA5 112 B2
Woodend Rd
Alloway KA7 238 F1
Ayr KA7 239 A1
Carluke ML8 188 A2
Glasgow G32 119 E2
Rutherglen G73 138 B4
Woodend St G84 16 B2
Woodfarm Cl KA13 207 D6
Woodfarm High Sch
G46 136 A3
Wood Farm Rd G46 136 A2
WOODFIELD 236 A5
Woodfield G71 141 C6
Woodfield Ave
Ayr KA8 236 A5
Bishopbriggs G64 98 B8
Woodfield Cres KA8 236 A4
Woodfield Rd KA8 236 A4
Woodfoot Rd ML3 162 A2
Woodford Pl PA3 112 A6
Woodford St G41 136 E7
Wood Gr KA11 220 C1
Woodgreen Ave G44 137 C6
Woodgreen Ct ML2 186 A8
Woodgreen Wynd KA13 207 C5
WOODHALL 69 A8
Woodhall ML1 143 A8
Woodhall Ave
Calderbank ML6 123 B2
Coatbridge ML5 121 F3
Hamilton ML3 162 B4
Woodhall Ave *continued*
Motherwell ML1 142 F5
Woodhall Cottage Rd
ML6 123 C1
Woodhall Mill Rd ML6 123 B1
Woodhall Pl ML5 121 F3
Woodhall Rd
Braidwood ML8 201 E3
Calderbank ML6 123 B2
Wishaw ML2 165 F3
Woodhall St
Chapelhall ML6 123 D2
Glasgow G40 118 B2
Woodhall Sta PA14 48 A1
Woodhall Terr PA14 69 B8
Woodhead Ave
Bothwell G71 141 B1
Cumbernauld G68 81 F7
Kirkintilloch G66 79 D7
Woodhead Cres
Glenmavis ML6 102 E3
Hamilton ML3 183 A8
Uddingston G71 140 F7
Woodhead Ct G68 81 F7
Woodhead Gdns G71 162 B8
Woodhead Gn ML3 183 B8
Woodhead Gr G68 81 F7
WOODHEAD GREEN 183 B8
Woodhead Pl G68 81 F7
Woodhead Prim Sch
ML3 183 A8
Woodhead Rd
Cumbernauld G68 81 F7
Garnkirk G69 100 B6
Glasgow G53 135 A5
Woodhead Terr G69 100 B7
Woodhead View G68 81 F7
Woodhill Cres KA11 220 B5
Woodhill Pl KA3 222 B6
Woodhill Prim Sch G64 78 C2
Woodhill Rd
Blackridge EH48 107 B3
Glasgow G21 98 B6
Kilmarnock KA3 222 E3
Woodholm Ave G44 137 C6
Woodhouse Ct G76 158 A5
Woodhouse St G13 95 E7
Woodilee Cotts G66 79 E6
Woodilee Ind Est G66 79 E6
Woodilee Rd
Kirkintilloch G66 79 E6
Motherwell ML1 143 E4
Wood La G64 98 C8
Woodland Ave
Airdrie ML6 123 C4
Kirkintilloch G66 79 B8
Paisley PA2 133 E8
Woodland Cres
Cambuslang G72 139 C4
Eaglesham G76 178 D5
Woodland Gdns
Carmunnock G76 158 D7
Hamilton ML3 162 F2
Woodland Pl KA22 205 C3
WOODLANDS 42 B4
Woodlands
Glasgow G46 135 F3
Sauchie FK10 5 E1
Woodlands Ave
Bothwell G71 141 A3
Irvine KA12 219 D4
Lanark ML11 215 B3
Law ML8 187 A6
Mount Ellen G69 100 E6
Woodlands Cres
Ayr KA7 239 B4
Bothwell G71 141 A3
Falkirk FK1 42 A4
Glasgow G46 135 F3
Johnstone PA5 131 E8
Woodlands Ct
Alexandria G83 27 C7
8 Glasgow, Kelvingrove G3 96 E1
Glasgow, Thornliebank
G46 135 F2
Old Kilpatrick G60 73 B5
Woodlands Dr
Coatbridge ML5 121 D7
Glasgow G4 96 F2
Lanark ML11 215 B2
Motherwell ML1 142 F5
Woodlands Gate
Glasgow G3 240 A4
Glasgow, Thornliebank
G46 135 F3
Woodlands Gdns G71 141 A4
Woodlands Gr
Kilmarnock KA3 223 B4
Milngavie G62 55 A3
Woodlands Pk G46 135 F3
Woodlands Pl
Coatbridge ML5 121 D7
Kilmarnock KA3 223 B4
Woodlands Prim Sch
Cumbernauld G67 82 E7
Irvine KA12 219 D3
Linwood PA3 112 A5
Woodlands Rd
Glasgow G3 240 A4
Glasgow, Thornliebank
G46 135 F2
Motherwell, Holytown
ML1 143 D7
Motherwell ML1 163 F4
Woodlands Rd *continued*
Thornliebank G46 136 A2
Woodlands St
Milngavie G62 55 A2
Motherwell ML1 163 F4
Prestwick KA9 236 B8
Woodlands Terr G3 240 A4
Woodlands The ML4 142 D3
Woodlands View ML9 199 A3
Woodland Terr ML9 185 C1
Woodland Way
Cumbernauld G67 62 B3
Denny FK6 39 D7
Woodlea Ave ML6 123 C4
Woodlea Cres KA2 221 F2
Woodlea Ct KA2 221 F2
Woodlea Dr
Glasgow G46 136 D4
Hamilton ML3 183 D8
Woodlea Gdns
Alloa FK10 5 A1
Bonnybridge FK4 39 F5
Woodlea La PA19 45 A7
Woodlea Pk
Alloa FK10 10 B8
Sauchie FK10 5 A1
Woodlea Pl
Airdrie ML6 103 C1
Ayr KA7 239 B2
Woodlinn Ave G44 137 B5
Woodmill KA13 207 F1
Woodmill Dr G64 57 C1
Woodmill Gdns G67 81 F6
Woodneuk La G69 100 F5
Woodneuk Rd
Gartcosh G69 100 F5
Glasgow G53 135 B5
Woodneuk St ML6 123 D1
Woodneuk Terr G69 100 F5
Woodpark KA9 236 B5
Wood Pk KA7 239 B4
Wood Pl
Strathblane G63 31 A5
Troon KA10 229 B2
Wood Quadrant G81 94 E8
Wood Rd KA10 229 B2
Woodrow ML1 143 B8
Woodrow Ave
Kilmacolm PA13 69 D1
Motherwell ML1 143 B2
Woodrow Cir G41 116 D4
Woodrow Pl G41 116 C4
Woodrow Rd G41 116 D4
WOODSIDE 97 B3
Woodside
Houston PA6 91 D1
Motherwell ML1 142 E8
West Kilbride KA23 190 D3
Woodside Ave
Bridge of Weir PA11 90 D1
Glasgow G46 136 A3
5 Hamilton ML3 162 E2
Kilmarnock KA1 227 D6
Kilsyth G65 60 F8
Kirkintilloch G66 79 D5
Rutherglen G73 138 C7
Woodside Cres
Alexandria G83 28 A6
Barrhead G78 134 D2
Glasgow G3 240 A4
Paisley PA1 113 C4
Wishaw ML2 166 B6
Woodside Ct
Cambusbarron FK7 6 D5
Coatbridge ML5 121 D5
Falkirk FK1 42 B3
4 Hamilton ML3 162 E2
Woodside Dr
Calderbank ML6 123 B2
Eaglesham G76 157 D2
Woodside Gdns
Carmunnock G76 158 D7
Clarkston G76 157 D7
Coatbridge ML5 121 D4
Woodside Gr
Larbert FK5 41 D8
Rutherglen G73 138 C7
Woodside La
Brookfield PA5 111 D6
Lanark ML11 215 C2
Woodside Pl
Dunlop KA3 195 C7
Fallin FK7 8 C4
Glasgow G3 240 A4
Uddingston G71 141 C8
Woodside Place La G3 240 A4
Woodside Prim Sch ML3 162 E2
Woodside Rd
Alloa FK10 4 F1
Beith KA15 150 B1
Brookfield PA5 111 D6
Carmunnock G76 158 D7
Forrestfield ML6 106 A3
Kilwinning KA13 207 C4
Stirling FK8 2 A3
Tullibody FK10 4 A1
Woodside St
Chapelhall ML6 123 D2
Coatbridge ML5 121 D4
Motherwell ML1 164 B4
Motherwell, New Stevenston
ML1 143 A3
Woodside Terr
Clackmannan FK10 10 F4
Woodside Terr *continued*
Falkirk FK1 42 B3
Glasgow G3 240 A4
Woodside Terrace La
G3 240 A4
Woodside Twr ML1 164 B3
Woodside Wlk ML3 162 E2
Wood St
Airdrie ML6 103 C1
Coatbridge ML5 121 E7
Glasgow G31 118 B8
Greenock PA16 45 C8
Kilwinning KA13 207 E4
Motherwell ML1 163 F8
Paisley PA2 114 B3
Woodstock Ave
Glasgow G41 116 D1
Kirkintilloch G66 79 F8
Lanark ML11 215 C4
Paisley PA2 132 F8
Woodstock Dr
Lanark ML11 215 B4
Wishaw ML2 165 C4
Woodstock Pl KA1 222 E1
Woodstock Rd
Greenock PA16 45 C3
Lanark ML11 215 B4
Woodstock Specl Sch
KA1 227 E8
Woodstock St KA1 227 E8
Woodstock Way PA2 132 E8
Woodstone Ct G84 15 E4
Woodvale Ave
Airdrie ML6 123 D4
Bearsden G61 76 B2
Rutherglen G46 157 B8
Woodvale Dr PA3 113 A5
Woodview G71 141 D8
Wood View
Motherwell ML1 143 B5
Shotts ML7 166 F8
Woodview Dr
Airdrie ML6 123 A5
Bellshill ML4 142 C7
Woodview La ML6 123 A5
Woodview Rd ML9 199 A8
Woodview Terr ML3 162 B4
Woodville Park Ind Est
G51 116 B6
Woodville Pk G51 116 B6
Woodville St G51 116 B6
Woodwynd KA13 207 E4
Woodyard Rd G82 49 E3
Woodyett Pk G76 157 F5
Woodyett Rd G76 157 F5
Wooer St 4 FK1 42 B4
Woolcarders Ct FK7 6 D6
Wordle Rd FK7 6 F4
Wordsworth Way G71 141 B3
Workshop Rd KA20 218 B5
Worsley Cres G77 156 C7
Wotherspoon Dr KA15 150 B2
Wraes Ave G78 134 D4
Wraes View G78 133 F1
Wraisland Cres PA7 71 F4
Wrangholm Cres ML1 143 B3
Wrangholm Dr ML1 143 B3
Wren Ct ML4 141 E8
Wren Pl
Johnstone PA5 131 D7
Wishaw ML2 165 B3
Wren Rd PA16 45 A4
Wright Ave G78 134 A2
Wrightfield Pl KA7 238 E2
Wrightlands Cres PA8 93 E8
Wright St
Falkirk FK2 42 B6
Renfrew PA4 94 A1
Wright Way ML1 143 A3
Wyburn Pl KA8 236 A3
Wye Cres ML5 101 D1
Wykeham Pl G13 95 C6
Wykeham Rd G13 95 C6
Wyler Twr ML3 162 E3
Wylie G74 160 D5
Wylie Ave
Alexandria G83 27 D4
Newton Mearns G77 156 D7
Wylie Pl
Renton G82 27 E2
Stewarton KA3 195 E1
Wylie St ML3 162 D2
Wyllie Rd KA21 217 A8
Wyndford Dr G20 96 D5
Wyndford Pl 3 G20 96 D5
Wyndford Prim Sch
G20 96 D5
Wyndford Rd
Cumbernauld G68 62 D8
Glasgow G20 96 D5
Wyndford Terr G71 141 B7
Wyndham Ct G12 96 D4
Wyndham St G12 96 D4
Wynd The
Alva FK12 5 A7
Cumbernauld G67 62 B5
Wynyard Gn G75 180 B8
Wyper Pl G31 118 A6
Wyvil Ave G13 75 E1
Wyvis Ave
Bearsden G61 75 C7
Glasgow G13 94 F8
Wyvis Ct G77 156 D2
Wyvis Gdns KA1 228 A3
Wyvis Pl
Glasgow G13 94 F8
Irvine KA11 220 A4
Newton Mearns G77 156 C2
Shotts ML7 147 B3
Wyvis Quadrant G13 94 F8
Wyvis Rd KA1 228 A3
Wyvis Way ML1 164 D3

X

Xscape* PA4 94 F4

Y

Yair Dr G52 115 A6
Yardley Pl FK2 24 A1
Yardside Rd KA3 222 B7
Yarrow Cres
Bishopton PA7 72 C2
Wishaw ML2 165 B4
Yarrow Ct G72 139 E5
Yarrow Gardens La 2
G20 96 F3
Yarrow Gdns G20 96 F3
Yarrow Pk G74 160 A1
Yarrow Rd G64 78 A4
Yarrow Way G72 161 E8
Yate Gr G31 118 B5
Yate Rd G31 118 B5
Yate St G31 118 B5
Yementry Ct G72 138 F3
Yerton Brae KA23 190 C4
Yetholm Gdns G74 159 F4
Yetholm St G14 94 E6
Yetholm Terr ML3 161 E3
Yett Rd ML1 143 D3
Yetts Ave PA13 69 D1
Yetts Cres G66 79 F8
Yetts Hole Rd ML6 102 B5
Yetts The FK7 6 C5
Yew Dr G21 98 A3
Yew Pl PA5 111 F1
Yews Cres ML3 162 B5
YIELDSHIELDS 188 E2
Yieldshields Rd ML8 189 D3
YOKER 94 E7
Yokerburn Pl G13 94 E7
Yokerburn Terr G81 94 D7
Yoker Ferry Rd G14 94 E6
Yoker Mill Gdns G13 94 E7
Yoker Mill Rd G13 94 F8
Yoker Prim Sch G14 94 F6
Yoker Sp Ctr G14 94 F6
Yoker Sta G81 94 D7
Yonderton Pl KA23 190 D4
York Ct KA10 229 E3
York Dr
Falkirk FK2 42 D6
Rutherglen G73 138 D5
Yorke Ct KA10 229 E2
Yorke Pl KA1 222 D1
Yorke Rd KA10 229 E2
Yorkhill Par G3 96 C1
Yorkhill St G3 96 D1
York Pl
Ayr KA8 235 F2
Bellshill ML4 142 A5
1 Kirkintilloch G66 79 C8
York Rd
Greenock PA16 44 E5
Motherwell ML6 143 D8
York St
Ayr KA8 235 F2
Clydebank G81 74 D2
Falkirk FK2 42 D6
Glasgow G2 240 B2
Wishaw ML2 165 B2
York Street La KA8 235 F2
York Way PA4 94 C1
Young Ave KA10 229 E6
Younger Dr KA9 233 C3
Younger Quadrant G64 78 A1
Young Pl
East Kilbride G75 181 A5
1 Uddingston G71 141 A8
Wishaw ML2 166 B5
Young Rd ML11 215 E5
Young St
Ardrossan KA22 205 C2
Clydebank G81 74 B4
Prestwick KA8 236 B5
Wishaw ML2 165 B3
Young Terr G21 98 A4
Young Wynd ML4 142 A8
Yukon Terr G75 180 B8
Yule Way G67 62 A2
Yvetot Ave ML11 215 B4
Yvetot Ct ML8 187 E3

Z

Zambesi Dr G72 140 C1
Zena Cres G33 98 D4
Zena Pl G33 98 D4
Zena St G33 98 D4
Zetland Pl FK2 24 F3
Zetland Rd G52 114 F8

Notes

Notes